The Cambridge Handbook of Forensic Psychology

Forensic psychology has developed and extended from an original, narrow focus on presenting evidence to the courts to a wider application across the whole span of civil and criminal justice, which includes dealing with suspects, offenders, victims, witnesses, defendants, litigants and justice professionals. This handbook provides an encyclopedic-style source regarding the major concerns in forensic psychology. It is an invaluable reference text for practitioners within community, special hospital, secure unit, prison, probation and law enforcement forensic settings, as well as being appropriate for trainees and students in these areas. It will also serve as a companion text for lawyers and psychiatric and law enforcement professionals who wish to be apprised of forensic psychology coverage. Each entry provides a succinct outline of the topic, describes current thinking, identifies relevant consensual or contested aspects and alternative positions. Readers are presented with key issues and directed towards specialized sources for further reference.

Jennifer M. Brown was Professor of Forensic Psychology and Director of Crime and Justice at the University of Surrey. She is currently an honorary professor at the London School of Economics. She has been involved with the police service for over twenty years, having previously held posts as a research manager for Hampshire Police and a syndicate director on the senior command course at Bramshill.

Elizabeth A. Campbell is Senior Lecturer in Clinical Psychology in the Section of Psychological Medicine at the University of Glasgow. She is also Honorary Consultant Clinical Psychologist with NHS Greater Glasgow and Clyde and a past President of the British Psychological Society. She acts as a consultant to the Metropolitan Police and the Serious Organised Crime Agency.

The Cambridge Handbook of Forensic Psychology

Edited by

Jennifer M. Brown

and

Elizabeth A. Campbell

CAMBRIDGE UNIVERSITY PRESS
Cambridge, New York, Melbourne, Madrid, Cape Town, Singapore, São Paulo, Delhi

Cambridge University Press
The Edinburgh Building, Cambridge CB2 8RU, UK

Published in the United States of America by Cambridge University Press, New York

www.cambridge.org
Information on this title: www.cambridge.org/9780521701815

First published 2010

Printed in the United Kingdom at the University Press, Cambridge

A catalogue record for this publication is available from the British Library

Library of Congress Cataloguing in Publication data
The Cambridge handbook of forensic psychology / edited by Jennifer M. Brown and Elizabeth A. Campbell.
   p. cm. – (Cambridge handbooks in psychology)
Includes bibliographical references.
ISBN 978-0-521-87809-8 – ISBN 978-0-521-70181-5 (pbk.)
1. Forensic psychology. I. Brown, Jennifer, 1948– II. Campbell, Elizabeth A.
III. Title. IV. Series.
RA1148.C36 2010
614′.15–dc22

                                                 2010008742

ISBN 978-0521-87809-8 Hardback
ISBN 978-0521-70181-5 Paperback

To Patrick

Contents

Part IV   Psychology and criminal behaviour

Figures

Tables

Contributors

Joanne R. Adler,
Middlesex University

David A. Alexander,
Robert Gordon University

Laurence Alison,
University of Liverpool

Catherine C. Ayoub,
Massachusetts General Hospital

Peter Banister,
Manchester Metropolitan University

Anthony R. Beech,
University of Birmingham

Amanda Biggs,
Griffith University

Julian Boon,
University of Leicester

Adrian Bowers,
University of Nevada, Reno

Neil Brewer,
Flinders University

Eric Broekaert,
Ghent University

Paula Brough,
Griffith University

Jennifer M. Brown,
London School of Economics

Kevin Browne,
University of Nottingham

Elizabeth A. Campbell,
University of Glasgow

David Canter,
University of Huddersfield

Michael Carlin,
Thomas, Carlin & Pender

Shihning Chou,
University of Liverpool

Martin A. Conway,
University of Leeds

Claire Cooke,
University of Gloucestershire

David Cooke,
Glasgow Caledonian University

Ilse Derluyn,
Ghent University

Robert J. Edelmann,
Whitelands College, Roehampton
University

Vincent Egan,
University of Leicester

Tom Ellis,
University of Portsmouth

Marie Eyre,
University of Liverpool

David P. Farrington,
University of Cambridge

Seena Fazel,
University of Oxford

Daniel B. Fishman,
Rutgers University

Victoria Follette,
University of Nevada

Katarina Fritzon,
Bond University

Elizabeth Gilchrist,
Glasgow Caledonian University

Nathan D. Gillard,
University of North Texas

Renée Gobeil,
Carleton University

Agnieszka Golec de Zavala,
Middlesex University

Jane Goodman-Delahunty,
Charles Sturt University

Lynsey Gozna,
University of Lincoln

Don Grubin,
University of Newcastle

Gisli H. Gudjonsson,
King's College London

Helinä Häkkänen-Nyholm,
National Bureau of Investigation,
Finland

Guy Hall,
Murdoch University

Nathan Hall,
University of Portsmouth

Roisin Hall,
Risk Management Authority

Sean Hammond,
University College Cork

Leigh Harkins,
University of Birmingham

Grant T. Harris,
Mental Health Centre Penetanguishene

Camilla Herbert,
Brain Injury Rehabilitation Trust (BIRT)

Robert D. Hoge,
Carleton University

Todd E. Hogue,
University of Lincoln

Clive R. Hollin,
University of Leicester

Lorraine Hope
University of Portsmouth

Miranda A. H. Horvath,
University of Surrey

Kevin Howells,
University of Nottingham

Carol A. Ireland,
Merseycare NHS Trust

Jane L. Ireland,
University of Central Lancashire

Mark Kebbell,
Griffith University

Michael King,
Monash University

Bruce D. Kirkcaldy,
Psychologische Praxis

Heidi La Bash,
University of Nevada

Cara Laney,
University of Leicester

William R. Lindsay,
The State Hospital, Dundee

Elizabeth F. Loftus,
University of California

L. E. Marshall,
Rockwood Psychological Services

W. L. Marshall,
Rockwood Psychological Services

James McGuire,
University of Liverpool

Neil McKeganey,
University of Glasgow

T. M. McMillan,
University of Galsgow

Mary McMurran
University of Nottingham

Joav Merrick,
Ministry of Social Affairs, Israel

Becky Milne,
University of Portsmouth

Joanne M. Nadkarni,
West Lane Hospital

Claire Nee,
University of Portsmouth

M. D. O'Brien,
Rockwood Psychological
Services

William O'Donohue,
University of Nevada,
Reno

Darragh O'Neill,
University of Surrey

Jane Palmer,
Broadmoor Hospital

Adria Pearson,
University of Nevada

Derek Perkins,
Broadmoor Hospital

Devon L. L. Polaschek,
Victoria University of Wellington

Louise E. Porter,
Griffith University

Charlotte C. Powell,
Furnival Chambers

Graham E. Powell,
Powell Campbell Edelmann, Chartered
Psychologists

Martine Powell,
Deakin University

Christine Puckering,
University of Glasgow

Ethel Quayle,
University College Cork

Vernon L. Quinsey,
Queen's University, Kingston

Marnie E. Rice,
McMaster University

Randall Richardson-Vejlgaard,
Yale University

Richard Rogers,
University of North Texas

Louis B. Schlesinger,
City University of New York

Carolyn Semmler,
University of Adelaide

G. A. Serran,
Rockwood Psychological Services

Ralph C. Serin,
Carleton University

John L. Taylor,
Tyne and Wear NHS Trust

Max Taylor,
University of St Andrews

Brian Thomas-Peter,
University of Birmingham

Paul A. Tiffin,
Durham University

Graham Towl,
Durham University

Rosie Travers,
Interventions and Substance
Misuse Group, National Offender
Management Service

Arlene Vetere,
University of Surrey

Graham Wagstaff,
University of Liverpool

Helen Wakeling,
Interventions Group, HM
Prison Service

Fiona Warren,
University of Surrey

Brandon C. Welsh,
Northeastern University

David Wexler,
Relationship Training Institute

Margaret Wilson,
University of Surrey

Dan Yarmey,
University of Guelph

Susan Young,
Kings College London

Acknowledgements

In compiling this handbook, we placed heavy reliance on our contributors and we are very grateful to them for participating in this project.

We also had a great deal of help from Darragh O'Neill, who organized the entries and maintained our spreadsheet to keep track of them all. Nothing was ever too much trouble and we are indebted to him for his patience and organizing ability in complying with our many requests for status updates. Darren Hollet assisted in tracking down emails and affiliation details of our contributors, whilst lovely CJ and Stu helped at the copy-editing stage.

Andy Peart was our first editor at Cambridge University Press and shared our initial ambition and enthusiasm for the project; he was ably followed by Carrie Parkinson and Liz Davey, who helped with the book to completion.

We hope readers will find this book to be a reference source which is both enjoyable to read and informative.

Jennifer M. Brown
Elizabeth A. Campbell

Forensic psychology: a case of multiple identities

Jennifer M. Brown and Elizabeth A. Campbell

Introduction

This introductory essay explores the span of forensic psychology and examines the roles of forensic psychology practitioners. We adopt a broad definition for forensic psychology as witnessed by the topics included in the handbook. However, we argue that the term forensic psychologist is unhelpful and potentially misleading as no one individual can hope to have the breadth and depth of knowledge included within this volume. Rather we think that there are a family of settings within which forensic psychology is applied and that context is critical to limiting claims of expertise.

When considering the development of methods, theories and practice of an emergent forensic psychology most authorities locate its modern origins in Europe during the late nineteenth and early twentieth centuries (Gudjonsson and Haward 1998; Wrightsman and Fulero 2005; Weiner and Hess 2006). The Leipzig experimental laboratory of William Wundt is usually considered the starting point. Students influenced by this approach included Cattell, who conducted early experiments on witness testimony in the USA, as did Binet in France, Stern in Germany (Bartol and Bartol 1987) and Santamaria in Spain (Prieto *et al.* 2000). Munsterberg, a student of Wundt, was invited by William James to establish a laboratory at Harvard in 1892. Interestingly, Munsterberg attempted to apply experimental principles to many areas including work, education and the arts, as well as law.

Theoretical ideas were also being expounded by Freud, who offered models to explain psychopathological thinking as causes of criminality, and Goddard (1915), who suggested that causes of crime lay in 'mental deficiency', which was associated with intellectual and emotional incapacity.

European psychologists applied this knowledge by appearing in court to present details of experimental observations on suggestibility and errors in recall (the first American psychologist appeared in court in 1921). Other early work saw interventions in juvenile delinquency: for example, Grace Fernald worked with psychiatrist William Healy in Chicago to establish the first clinic designed to diagnose 'problem' children, with Healy publishing *Honesty: A Study of the Causes and Treatment of Dishonesty in Children* in 1915 (Bartol and Bartol 1987).

The boundaries of a discipline of forensic psychology were also being charted in the United States. Burtt produced a legal psychology text in 1931 and Toch's edited collection on the psychology of crime appeared in 1961. In the UK Haward wrote the first review paper on legal psychology in 1961, with his textbook entitled *Forensic Psychology* being published in 1981.

The 1976 volume of the *Annual Review of Psychology* saw Tapp's paper examining the forensic psychology literature, which was updated by Monahan and Loftus in 1982. Their analysis suggested that psychology's contributions to understanding and predicting legal phenomena clustered in three domains: validity of assumptions underlying substantive law (e.g. competence, deterrence); clarifying the nature of formal legal processes (e.g. roles of judges, jurors, defendants and process components such as evidence, procedures and decision rules); mapping the contours of the informal legal system in which decision makers act (criminal justice system, mental health system). They drew attention to a number of recurring themes: a divergence between theory testing and theory generating research (and they argue a place for both approaches); problems of the external validity of laboratory-based simulations and analogue research, concluding there is little value in research that has low or poor ecological validity employing unrealistic scenarios; the growing influence of psychology on the law. They were critical of the disjunction between the legal topics that psychologists study and the importance to law of these topics. For example, much research effort addresses crime and criminals yet less than 10% of law courses concern criminal law. Much effort addresses decision making in trials yet 97% of criminal convictions are negotiated guilty pleas. (A point also made by Carson (2003, p. 23) in the UK context). They suggest that one reason for the skew is the diet of crime and courtroom dramas in the media, which may operate as a heuristic bias in perception of the scope of the law. They pointed out the virtual non-existence of psychological research into tort or tax law.

Kagehiro and Laufer (1992) undertook an informal content analysis of journals publishing psycholegal research and reported that about one-third of articles dealt with either expert witnessing, jury decision making or eyewitness testimony.

During the next fifteen years a slew of textbooks and handbooks appeared, providing both general coverage such as Carson *et al.*'s (2007), which included topics such as predicting violence, identification evidence, jury decision making, contested evidence, impulsivity and offender reasoning, and more focused and specialist topics such as those appearing in the Wiley series on the psychology of crime, policing and law (Ainsworth (1995) on psychology and policing; Jackson and Bekerian (1997) on offender profiling; and Dent and Flin (1992) on child witnesses). Other texts focused more particularly on crime, e.g. Bekerian and Levey (2005) who recognize that any mainstream psychological theories and methods are relevant to the commission or investigation of crime or the assessment and treatment of offenders. Harrower (1998) proposes that our understanding of crime comes from: developmental psychology, concerned as it is with the social influences and intellectual development throughout the lifespan which may impact on offending behaviour; social psychology, which looks at attitudes, group processes and conformity as contributing to a cycle of offending; biological psychology, which draws on genetic influences that might lead to offending behaviour.

Notwithstanding this expansion, an informal survey conducted by the present authors of articles appearing in *Legal and Criminological Psychology* (1999–2008) and *Law and Human Behaviour* (1999–2005) reveal the continued absence of studies investigating non-criminal aspects of law. The bulk of papers still address legal process issues, with research into juries dominating in the American journal (a fifth of all papers) and research into witnesses and interviewing dominating the British journal.

Thus in these eclectic origins we see legacy traces of different traditions influencing the emergent and potentially divergent pathways of forensic psychology, namely: methods deriving from both experimental research and clinical assessment; early appearance as expert witnesses associated with controversy, e.g. Schrenck-Notzing's retroactive memory falsification; contribution to police stationhouse, courtroom and prison; involvement in and of embryonic developmental, social and occupational psychologies; ideas drawn from psychoanalytic and constitutional theories of criminality; practice and research roles.

With the growing expansion of topics, Carson (2003, p. 1) asks the question whether we should be considering psychology and law as a subdiscipline (i.e. of either of the respective core subjects), an interdisciplinary collaboration (between the two) or as a new integrated project (of law and psychology). Alongside the extended range of topics included within forensic psychology there has also been a functional separation. For example, Bartol and Bartol

(2008) took another approach and subdivided their textbook into areas of subspecialisms: police psychology, criminal psychology, correctional psychology, victimology and psychology of the courts. They identified up to sixteen different locations which constitute work settings for forensic psychology practitioners.

So whilst forensic psychology has emerged as an identifiable subdiscipline within psychology, this has been conflated with discussions about the writ of the psychologists who are active within this field. In this chapter we will attempt to delineate and separate these two.

Definitions: forensic psychology

In table 1 sample definitions are given from various authors differentiating attempts to delineate the subject matter, and table 2 the practical application of forensic psychology.

Brigham (1999) concluded that there are two types of definitions. The first is a broad definition such as that provided by Monahan and Loftus (1982). They suggest that all branches of the science of psychology may be considered as potentially having some application to the legal domain. In contrast, Blackburn (1993) describes forensic psychology as psychology applied to the courts. It is unclear who are entitled to call themselves forensic psychologists. Otto and Heilbrun (2002) indicate that there is a relatively small group of forensic psychology specialists, but a much larger group of psychologists who provide occasional services or do so in a circumscribed area. Some are accidental experts who provide services unexpectedly. They argue for an emergent forensic psychological assessment as a subspecialism. They base this on their estimation that literally hundreds of thousands of forensic evaluations conducted by psychologists take place in prison and mental health settings as well as non- correctional settings. Thus they suggest that a clear treatment focus is absent within the specialty area of clinical forensic psychology, whereas there has been a rapid growth in assessment methodologies. In the UK the move to integrate provision of offender mental health services within the mainstream of health provisions may further reinforce a view of forensic psychology as a clinical subspecialism. However, most forensic psychology texts now incorporate the wider remit of psychological theories as they apply to the justice system rather than exclusively to the courts, as indeed do we, as evidenced by the topics for inclusion within this handbook.

Table 1 Definitions of forensic psychology

Authors	Definition
Toch 1961	Science that studies the process whereby justice is arrived at ... examines the people who take part in the process and looks at their purposes, motives, thoughts and feelings
Monahan and Loftus 1982	All psychology is relevant to substantive law since any aspect of human behaviour may be the subject of legal regulation
Gudjonsson and Haward 1998	That branch of applied psychology which is concerned with the collection, examination and presentation of evidence for judicial purposes
Bartol and Bartol 2008	A research endeavour that examines aspects of human behaviour directly related to legal processes (e.g. eyewitness memory and testimony, jury decision making or criminal behaviour) and the professional practice of psychology within or in consultation with a legal system that encompasses both criminal and civil law and the numerous areas where they interact. Therefore FP refers broadly to the production and application of psychological knowledge to the civil and criminal justice systems
Goldstein 2003	Involves the application of psychological research theory and practice and traditional and specialized methodology to provide information relevant to a legal question
Wrightsman and Fulero 2005	Any application of psychological research methods theory and practice to a task faced by the legal system and encompasses and includes psychologists of all sorts ... is a profession as well as a field of study ... participates in the legal system ... has rich, varied and extensive sources of information
Howitt 2006	Forensic Psychology is literally psychology applied to the courts ...
Needs 2008	Forensic Psychology is the application of methods, theories and findings from a wide range of areas within psychology to the contexts and concerns of criminal and civil justice. The settings in which forensic psychologists work include the police, the courts, prisons, secure units and hospitals, probation and other community based services and academia

Table 2 Definitions of forensic psychology practice

Blackburn 1993	The provision of psychological information for the purposes of facilitating a legal decision
Heilbrun 2000	The professional practice by psychologists within the area of clinical psychology, counselling psychology, neuropsychology and school psychology when they are engaged regularly as experts and represent themselves as such, in an activity primarily intended to provide professional psychological expertise to the judicial system
APA 2008	'Forensic practitioner' refers to a psychologist when engaged in the practise of forensic psychology ... such professional conduct is considered forensic from the time the practitioner ... provides expertise on an exclusively psycho-legal issue

The psychologist as forensic practitioner

Brigham (1999, p. 280) asks why does any of this matter? His own answer is that such confusion leaves professionals in a 'definitional limbo', which is uncomfortable for them and confusing for the courts. Moreover, clarity of identity was important when the American Academy of Forensic Psychology petitioned the American Psychological Association for the discipline to be certified as a speciality because this was critical for the credentialling process. Otto and Heilbrun (2002, p. 5) argue that forensic psychology is at a cross-roads and needs to clearly distinguish practice, educate legal consumers and devote more attention to treatment issues. Carson (2003) writes that insufficient attention has been paid to the structural and thematic issues within the field and, as such, important opportunities are lost for developing relationships between researchers and practitioners, interfacing between lawyers and psychologists and growing organizational arrangements nationally and internationally.

Wrightsman and Fulero (2005) note that there is controversy as to who actually is a forensic psychologist and how to train to become one, a problem that they predict will increase as more students seek training. This is only a problem if there is a unitary and all embracing term, forensic psychologist, but is not an issue if there are agreed and recognized specialisms. Fulero and Wrightsman are of the view that forensic psychology encompasses and includes psychologists of all sorts of training and orientation (i.e. clinical, experimental, social and developmental). This suggests that psychologists who may have as one focus of their concerns examining behaviour in a forensic setting have a claim to be called forensic psychologists rather than seek an identity as a clinical or social psychologist.

Given its wider scope, Gudjonsson and Haward (1998, p. 67) propose that forensic psychology's corpus of knowledge is now too great to be claimed in its entirety by one person. Needs (2008) suggests that some commentators believe the breadth of settings and client groups is excessive and unsustainable, and attempts at integration smack of political manoeuvring, leaving practitioners vulnerable. He is of the view that no one individual could be an expert in all or even many of forensic psychology's potentially relevant areas.

Another parameter embedded in these practice definitions is the roles that may be played, with one obvious differentiation being whether the individual in question is an academic researcher or a practitioner or both. Rice (1997) discusses the scientist–practitioner split in psychology generally, but his arguments hold for forensic psychology in particular. He charts the emergence of psychology as a profession as well as a science. He discusses the 'project' of being recognized as a profession, which requires gaining control over a specialized body of knowledge providing the intellectual basis for practice and exclusive rights to control training and accreditation.

Take, for example, the psychologist as expert witness. Gudjonsson and Haward (1998, p. 67) distinguish subspecialities within the field of expert witnesses, which have specific terminology and skill sets associated with the role to be played. These are:

1. clinical assessment, in which it is the mental state of a person involved in some legal proceedings that is central and involves a personal interaction and some form of formal assessment using objective methods;
2. experimental, in which there is no direct contact with the parties involved in a case but rather a series of studies may be performed to substantiate the testimony of one of the parties;
3. actuarial, where evidence is presented on the probability or likelihood of some event, as in calculations of insurance compensation as a result of personal loss or injury;
4. advisory, when the forensic psychologist may be asked to examine evidence from another expert or provide pointers to counsel when another expert is giving evidence in court.

Professional developments, training and accreditation

In 1977, the British Psychological Society established a Division of Criminological and Legal Psychology. The majority of members of this Division were clinical psychologists with another proportion being academic psychologists. There was no training route for practitioners in forensic arenas. Most practitioners were clinical psychologists who specialized in this area.

At the time the Division was created, Lionel Haward was vehement that the founders should not use the term forensic psychology, arguing that some degree of separation should be maintained between practitioners and academics on the one hand, and on the other hand between those who provided expertise for the courts and those who worked in other settings. All could be members of the Division (Gudjonsson and Haward 1998). Farrington (1999) notes that the naming of the new Division allowed for a broad inclusion of psychologists working within a wider spectrum than just the purview of the courts, although in 1999, the name was changed to the Division of Forensic Psychology.

In the UK, there has been a major shift towards criminological psychology, with the majority of members of the Division of Forensic Psychology being prison-based psychologists, and a substantial proportion of these being trainee psychologists in the prison service. All full members of the Division are now required to have training in forensic psychology, and clinical psychologists cannot automatically become full members. This training is very much focused on prison service work.

If the curriculum of British courses in forensic psychology is examined there is an emphasis on the second of Monahan and Loftus' themes, legal processes: with one out of five areas of knowledge being devoted to the application of psychology to processes in the justice system and another looking at roles within the criminal justice service such as victims and offenders. Two areas are devoted to 'competency in communicating information' and 'undertaking research' (Needs 2008). Thus over the last ten to fifteen years the focus of British 'forensic' psychology has been narrowed to mean 'criminological' and more specifically 'penal' psychology in terms of the arenas of practice. This has also been reinforced by a rapid growth in the number of trainee forensic psychologists within the prison system who are employed to deliver or oversee the delivery of manualized, group-based programmes.

Thus during the early years, forensic practice in the UK was not seen as a distinct specialism per se with its own training pathway, but as a domain of psychological practice that was open to a range of different types of psychologists who might offer their expertise to the judicial system in any number of ways and through a diverse set of skills and expert knowledge.

However, the situation in the UK has gradually changed and a rather narrow training route now leads to the general title 'Forensic Psychologist'. This route does not require any pre-qualifications in clinical or counselling psychology and has become largely populated by trainees who are employed in the prison service. The overall membership of the Division has also shifted towards a preponderance of psychologists working in the penal system and in crime. At the time of writing, the voluntary system of regulation of psychologists by the British Psychological Society (BPS) was being relinquished for a statutory system of legally protecting certain titles, including 'Forensic Psychologist'.

In the United States, the American Psychology–Law Society (AP-LS) voted for a narrow definition as a clinical speciality in 1998. Two years later, the

American Psychological Association (APA) designated forensic psychology as a speciality (clinical, counselling and school psychology being the other specialities so designated). With the growth in applied psychology and the development of a number of domains of practice has come the desire for regulation, certification or licensing of psychologists. Some of these attempts define the required qualifications; others protect a number of titles; and others prescribe a number of years of university education either with or without a period of supervised practice. Such regulation has a primary aim of protecting the public from unqualified or unethical practitioners.

By 1977 psychologists required a licence to practise. Licensing is conducted at state level. There is an Association of State and Provincial Psychology Boards (ASPPB), which is an umbrella organization for those authorities throughout the USA and Canada who administer licensing and certification. There is now an agreed national licensing examination, the Examination for the Practice of Professional Psychology, which has been adopted across the United States and Canada (Rehm and DeMers 2006). The American Psychological Association accredits doctoral-level programmes in clinical psychology, counselling psychology and school psychology.

The American Board of Professional psychology now has a specialty certification in forensic psychology.

In Australia, psychologists working in the justice arena usually have clinical backgrounds (Priest 1994). During the 1980s Australian universities introduced courses that were entirely devoted to psychology as applied to the justice system. Forensic psychologists have to complete a minimum of six years' full-time university training plus further supervised practice.

While there is a wide range of practice across Europe in terms of regulation, there is now an agreed benchmark, the EuroPsy, which has been ratified by the psychological associations of thirty-four European countries. This requires at least five years of university education plus at least one year of supervised practice. This is a generic benchmark of the level expected for professional practice with later specialization into different areas such as psychotherapy. However, this benchmark does not have the force of a European law as such.

Given that all types of psychologists may be working in a forensic setting, it is questionable whether it makes sense to think of there being a common curriculum that could produce a generic 'forensic' psychologist. We suggest therefore that the term forensic psychologist be dropped, and if psychologists are working in a forensic setting it is their responsibility to ensure that they have the necessary competencies to practise competently and ethically. If psychologists wished to have their skills as practitioners in a forensic domain then this would be a post-registration certification as in the model adopted in the United States.

To the extent that the term forensic psychologist actually seems unhelpful, in that it does not have an agreed meaning, nor is it clear what knowledge base such a label conveys and its future is uncertain, we propose that a definitional framework might enable some conceptual differentiation between types subsumed by the term.

A definitional framework for forensic psychologists

Our definitional framework would clarify the type of activity that may be subsumed within forensic psychology and profiles different types of individuals working in the field. We employ the device of a mapping sentence to do this (see chapter 8.2, this volume). A mapping sentence lays out the critical domains of a definitional system. We have identified four such domains:

A. roles (e.g. Gudjonsson and Haward 1998);
B. disciplinary focus, i.e. having as a direct concern a forensic focus or using a forensic focus as one (of several) areas of interest (Carson 2003), discipline based, drawing from all aspects of psychology (Monahan and Loftus 1982) or subdisciplinary, meaning drawing on a narrower specified aspect (Gudjonsson and Haward 1998);
C. locations of activity (Needs 2008; Bekerian and Levey 2005; Bartol and Bartol 2008);
D. the volume of time and focus on forensic psychology (Otto and Heilbrun 2002; Bekerian and Levey 2005).

By drawing a profile across these domains we can identify, for example, a clinical practitioner offering expert services to the courts as their dominant activity (i.e. $a_2b_2c_5d_3$). This profile would give such a person a score of 12, representing the narrowest definition allowing a practitioner to provide expert testimony in court. A lawyer conducting analogue research into police decision making out of academic interest, using a sample of undergraduates, would have a score of 4 represented by a profile $a_1b_1c_1d_1$, which would be the lowest threshold for participating in the widest remit of a forensic psychology as suggested by Carson (2003). Other profiles would indicate the forensic activity by locale and specify the type of psychologist, i.e. those working in prisons or correctional institutions, police or hospital settings as an academic researcher or a professional practitioner. By considering a family of designations it can be made clearer as to what the individual's training and role qualifies them to do.

Person (x) may be defined in terms of the frequency in which s/he plays the role of

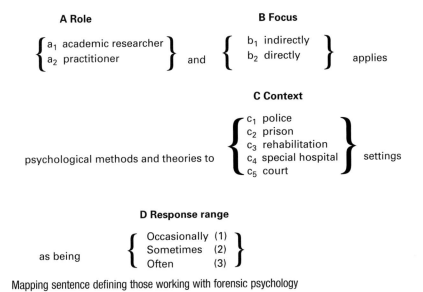

Figure 1   Mapping sentence defining those working with forensic psychology

Conclusion

What we do know about the contemporary state of forensic psychology is that there is a lack of consensus as to its definition (Howlitt 2006) and that usage of the term forensic psychology is 'chaotic' (Stanik 1992) and not universally accepted. There is a tension between the law and psychology, with forensic psychology sitting uneasily at the interstices. The parent discipline is contested, with some authorities locating forensic psychology as a specialism within clinical psychology (Otto and Heilbrun 2002), whilst Prieto *et al.*'s (2000) position is that forensic psychology sits within the broad scope of applied psychology.

Forensic psychology practitioners are often depicted in the media through fictionalized representations as offender profilers, which is but one, albeit a highly specialized, area of activity. The forensic psychologist practitioner and researcher actually work in varied settings with diverse populations; they have a variety of qualifications depending on the country in which they received their training. They play numerous roles, with perhaps the deepest divide being between practitioner and academic.

We would opt here for a definition that identifies as forensic psychology that which draws upon all relevant theories and methods on topics within the science of psychology, and psychologists whose work is focused within this legal domain are designated by the particular context.

REFERENCES

Ainsworth, P. (1995) *Psychology and Policing in a Changing World.* Chichester: Wiley.

American Psychological Association (APA) (2008) *Specialty Guidelines for Forensic Psychology.* www.ap-ls.org.

Bartol, C. and Bartol, A. (1987) History of forensic psychology. In I. Weiner and A. Hess (eds.), *Handbook of Forensic Psychology,* pp. 3–27. Chichester: Wiley.

Bartol, C. and Bartol, A. (2008) *Introduction to Forensic Psychology Research and Application,* 2nd edn. Los Angeles: Sage.

Bekerian, D. and Levey, A. B. (2005) *Applied Psychology: Putting Theory into Practice.* Oxford: Oxford University Press.

Blackburn, R. (1993) *The Psychology of Criminal Conduct: Theory, Research and Practice.* Chichester: Wiley.

Brigham, J. (1999) What is forensic psychology, anyway? *Law and Human Behaviour,* 23: 273–98.

Carson, D. (2003) Psychology and law: a subdiscipline, an interdisciplinary collaboration or a project? In D. Carson and R. Bull (eds.), *Handbook of Psychology in Legal Contexts,* pp. 1–30. Chichester: Wiley.

Carson, D., Milne, R., Pakes, F., Shalev, K. and Shawyer, A. (eds.) (2007) *Applying Psychology to Criminal Justice.* Chichester: Wiley.

Dent, H. and Flin, R. (eds.) (1992) *Children as Witnesses.* Chichester: Wiley.

Farrington, D. (1999) 21 years of the DCLP. *Forensic Update,* 56: 21–37.

Goddard, H. H. (1915) *The Criminal Imbecile: An Analysis of Three Remarkable Murder Cases.* New York: Macmillan.

Goldstein, A. (2003) Preface. In *Handbook of Psychology,* vol. 2: *Forensic Psychology.* Chichester: Wiley.

Gudjonsson, G. and Haward, L. (1998) *Forensic Psychology: A Guide to Practice.* London: Routledge.

Harrower, J. (1998) *Applying Psychology to Crime.* Oxford: Hodder and Stoughton.

Heilbrun, K. S. (2000) Petition for the recognition of a specialty in professional psychology. Submitted on behalf of the American Board of Forensic Psychology and the American Psychology–Law Society to the American Psychological Association, 20 July.

Howitt, D. (2002) *Forensic and Criminal Psychology.* Harlow: Pearson Education
    (2006) *Introduction to Forensic and Criminal Psychology,* 2nd edn. Harlow: Pearson Education.

Jackson, J. and Bekerian, D. (eds.) (1997) *Offender Profiling: Theory, Research and Practice.* Chichester: Wiley.

Kagehiro, D. K. and Laufer, W. S. (eds.) (1992) *Handbook of Psychology and Law*. New York: Springer.

Monahan, J. and Loftus, E. (1982) The psychology of law. *Annual Review of Psychology*, 33: 441–75.

Needs, A. (2008) Forensic psychology. In G. Towl, D. Farrington, D. Crighton and G. Hughes (eds.), *Dictionary of Forensic Psychology*. Cullompton: Willan.

Otto, R. and Heilbrun, K. (2002) The practice of forensic psychology: a look toward the future in light of the past. *American Psychologist*, 57: 5–19.

Priest, P. (1994) A survey of training in psychology applied to justice systems in Australia. *Australian Psychologist*, 29: 184–7.

Prieto, J., Sabourin, M., Walker, L., Aragones, J. and Amerigo, M. (2000) Applied social psychology. In K. Pawlik and M. Rosenzwieg (eds.), *International Handbook of Psychology*. London: Sage.

Rehm, L. P. and DeMers, S. T. (2006) Licensure. *Clinical Psychology: Science and Practice*, 13: 249–53.

Rice, C. E. (1997) The scientist–practitioner split and the future of psychology. *American Psychologist*, November: 1173–81.

Stanik, J. M. (1992) Psychology and law in Poland. In F. Losel, D. Bender and T. Bliesener (eds.), *Psychology and Law: International Perspectives*. Berlin: Walter de Gruyter.

Tapp, J. (1976) Psychology and the law; an overture. *Annual Review of Psychology*, 27: 359–404.

Toch, H. (ed.) (1961) *Legal and Criminological Psychology*. New York: Holt Rinehart and Winston.

Weiner, I. and Hess, A. (2006) *The Handbook of Forensic Psychology*, 3rd edn. Chichester: Wiley

Wrightsman, L. S. and Fulero, S. M. (2005) *Forensic Psychology*, 2nd edn. Belmont, CA: Thompson Wadsworth.

Part I

Psychological underpinnings

1.1 Action system applied to forensic topics

David Canter

See also chapter 1.6 Facet meta-theory, chapter 6.1 Arson, chapter 8.2 Designing research using facet theory, chapter 8.3 Drawing out the meaning in data: multidimensional scaling within forensic psychology research.

Introduction

In the search for a conceptual framework that underlies variations in criminal activity, a model derived from Parsons' (see Parsons and Shills 1951) exploration of sociopsychological systems is proving productive. This has its roots in cybernetics and the related attempts to model social and psychological processes as systems of interactions. Parsons' work was much criticized for its abstruseness and difficulties in operationalizing the central concepts, but Shye (1985) developed a robust, relatively straightforward conceptualization of behavioural actions systems that was directly open to empirical test.

Shye took Parsons' starting point that all living systems are essentially (a) 'open' in that they must interact with their surroundings in order to survive, (b) organized in that they contain distinct entities that can be distinguished from each other, but that contain a recognizable relationship to each other, i.e. are 'structured', and (c) have some stability in these components and their relationships over time. Any system containing these properties is regarded as an 'action system'.

Shye argues that the definition of an action system implies that any events in which it is engaged will have a source for its emergence and a location of the manifestation of that event. Furthermore, the source may be within the system or external to it, as may be its manifestation. This gives rise to four possible forms of event: (a) those that emerge inside the system and are actualized outside – known as the *expressive mode*, which often reflect individualistic 'personality' aspects of the system; (b) those emerging outside and manifested outside – *adaptive mode*, which typically focus on shaping physical aspects of the environment; (c)those emerging within and actualized within the system – *integrative mode*, relating to intrapersonal processes; and (d) those emerging outside and manifested inside the system – *conservative mode*, having cultural significance.

Application

Canter and his colleagues (see Fritzon, Canter and Wilton 2001) have demonstrated the utility of such an approach when applied to criminal behaviour. They have developed the action system model further by linking it to dominant theories in the explanation and differentiation of crime. They have shown its power in combining a number of different theoretical perspectives. For example, the distinction between crime as having some instrumental purpose as opposed to being of significance in its own right, often referred to as 'expressive', is apparent in the division on the one hand between conservative and adaptive actions, which are instrumental in the sense of being reactions to processes external to the individual, and on the other between integrative and expressive modes, which are both initiated within the person and thus fundamentally expressive in the sense of coming from the person to act on the environment.

Further elaboration

However, those theories of crime that distinguish between personal and social mechanisms sit on the action system in a way that is different to the expressive/instrumental division. The social theories relate more readily to integrative and conservative modes of actions, whereas the more individually oriented theories of criminality are more in accord with the expressive and adaptive modes.

The relationship to broad theories of crime therefore redefines the modes of action in a criminal context such that the *integrative* mode has strong social, but expressive components. This would relate to interactions between the target of the crime and the criminal in ways that imply personal significance or intimacy. By contrast the *adaptive* mode is a personal but instrumental activity in which the individual is seeking direct gain. The *conservative* mode within a criminal context reflects social processes that are instrumental in nature, most commonly the control of others as dominant objective. The

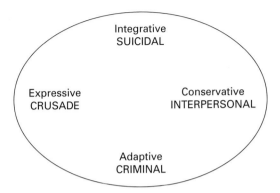

Figure 1.1.1 Definition of modes in an action sytem
The schematic representation of the relationships between the modes of an action system and themes in arson and terrorism derived from empirical study

expressive mode is personal and acting out in a way that is often referred to using the terminology of being 'expressive'. Overt hostility against others would be a typical manifestation of this mode.

The action system model goes further than just being the identification of four modes of action. The basic definitions of the modes give rise to conceptual relationships between them that can be represented as regions of a notional space (figure 1.1.1), which forms a set of hypotheses open to empirical test. Such testing is possible by identifying items that would correspond to each of the aspects of the mode and then representing their intercorrelations across an appropriate sample of occurrences by means of some form of multidimensional scaling, as illustrated in the main aspects of arson in figure 1.1.1.

This figure indicates that the integrative mode is hypothesized to contrast with the adaptive and the expressive with the conservative, so that in any study there would be higher correlations between any variables reflecting adjacent modes than modes that are opposite each other; further, expressive and conservative can be thought of as products of the adaptive and integrative modes so that the latter two would tend to be more highly correlated that the former two, which is why the model is represented as an ellipse rather than a circle.

In the context of criminal behaviour, tests of this model have been carried out, building on the approach first developed by Canter and Heritage (1990). This consists of generating content dictionaries of the actions that can occur across a sample of crimes, then measuring the proportion of times over which every action co-occurs with every other action. The patterns of co-occurrences are then represented as adjacencies in a Cartesian space such that each action is a point in the space and the more frequently any two actions occur the closer together they will tend to be in the space. In figure 1.1.1 a set of actions found in arson have been analysed and summarized. Some of these can be seen to cover attacks on buildings of significance and so have been given the label crusade. Others reflect self-destructive actions in which a suicide note has been left. A third group reflects attacks against a known individual, with the fourth being arson in which some other criminal activity, such as burglary, is present.

The strength of this model is revealed in the opportunity it provides for hypothesizing characteristics of the offender that may be inferred from the dominant mode the arson indicates. This provides a scientific basis for elaborating the 'profiling equation' central to an investigative psychology approach and to evidence-based models for deriving offender characteristics from crime scene information. So that, for example, in the case of arson it has been demonstrated that those who exhibit a strongly adaptive mode may well have a recognizable criminal background, but those whose mode is integrative are more likely to have a known history of mental illness (as demonstrated by Canter and Fritzon 1998).

Inevitably with such an ambitious and novel approach to modelling criminal behaviour there are still many aspects that require clarification, refinement and much more empirical test and development. Of particular significance is the need to integrate this model with the commonly found 'radex' of criminal actions reported in many studies since first being reported by Canter and Heritage (1990).

The 'radex' model recognizes that any action system will have a core of activities that characterize it. All the modes of which that action system can partake will share some common features. In arson, for example, this will be the act of setting fire to objects, but is also likely to include multiple points of ignition and often distinct and recognizable targets. It would be predicted that such aspects of actions would be common across many different forms of arson. It would thus also be hypothesized that such behaviours would tend to be central to any empirical representation of the co-occurrence of actions. This centrality of the conceptually core aspects of any crime type has been reported repeatedly in many empirical studies. In addition it has been shown that moving out from the central core of the actions are increasingly distinct aspects of the various modes. In the case of arson this is a movement from the general involvement in firesetting to actions that are more clearly focused on the target of the arson, as shown in figure 1.1.2. The frequency with which this structure

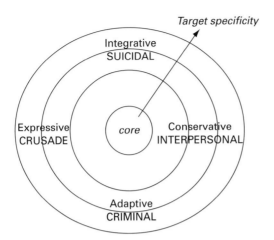

Figure 1.1.2 Radex model
The radiating structure from the generic core to specific modes that is found in most forms of crimes, here illustrated for arson

has been found has led some to mistakenly think that it is an artifact of the analysis procedure, but various studies have demonstrated this is not the case.

The combination of the radiating structure with the differentiation of the actions provides a general framework, known as a 'radex' (see Guttman 1954). The 'radex' is a structural model that is independent of content. It has been found to be applicable *inter alia* to intelligence, attitudes and quality of life, as well as crimes as varied as burglary and child abuse. Ongoing research is developing the understanding of how the four-way action system model relates to the radex structure, thereby providing a basis for considering the content of variations in criminal actions as well as the structural relationships between those contents.

Conclusion

The potential for such a combination of the radex and action system models can be seen from the consideration of the major model of sex offending demonstrated by Canter *et al.* (2003). They present four themes that distinguish sex offences, revealed from their examination of 112 rapes: hostility which involves verbal and physical violence; involvement in which some form of pseudo-intimacy occurs; control which involves threats, binding and gagging; and theft in which property is stolen from the rape victim. These can be identified quite directly as expressive, integrative, conservative and adaptive modes of action, respectively. The multidimensional analysis also demonstrates the predicted spatial relationship between each of these four modes, with control opposite hostility and involvement opposite theft. This connection between the radex and the action system models will doubtless emerge further in other datasets and types of crime as the whole approach develops.

However, the challenge, as with any system based on content analysis, is to develop definitions of the components that are clear and as objective as possible. There is always a risk that the broad headings of these systems are interpreted rather loosely to cover any mixture of variables that happen to be available. As examples accumulate there will be the necessary debates over exactly which operational procedures do indeed reflect the underlying processes that the models hypothesize.

FURTHER READING

Canter and Fritzon's paper in *Legal and Criminological Psychology* (1998) is an accessible exposition of an action systems model applied to arson, and Sean Hammond and Darragh O'Neill's chapter on multidimensional scaling (chapter 8.3, this volume) provides an account of the statistical procedures which often are used in empirical investigations using this approach.

REFERENCES

Canter, D., Bennell, C., Alison, L. J. and Reddy, S. (2003) Differentiating sex offences: a behaviourally based thematic classification of stranger rapes. *Behavioural Sciences and the Law*, 21: 157–74.

Canter, D. and Fritzon, K. (1998) Differentiating arsonists: a model of firesetting actions and characteristics. *Legal and Criminological Psychology*, 3: 73–96.

Canter, D. and Heritage, R. (1990) A multivariate model of sexual offence behaviour: developments in offender profiling. *Journal of Forensic Psychiatry*, 1: 185–212.

Fritzon, K., Canter, D. and Wilton, Z. (2001) The application of an action systems model to destructive behaviour: the examples of arson and terrorism. *Behavioural Sciences and the Law*, 19: 657–90.

Guttman, L. (1954) A new approach to factor analysis: the radex. In P. F. Lazarsfield (ed.), *Mathematical Thinking in the Social Sciences*. London: Free Press.

Parsons, T. and Shils, E. A. (1951) (eds.) *Toward a General Theory of Action*. Cambridge, MA: Harvard University Press.

Shye, S. (1985) Nonmetric multivariate models for behavioral action systems. In D. Canter (ed.), *Facet Theory: Approaches to Social Research*, pp. 97–148. New York: Springer.

Shihning Chou and Kevin Browne

See also chapter 3.5 Preventing delinquency and later criminal offending.

Definitions

The United Nations Convention on the Rights of the Child defines a child as 'every human being below the age of 18 years unless under the law applicable to the child, majority is attained earlier'. However, the statutory age limits adopted by juvenile courts, which deal with children and adolescents who have committed legal offences (i.e. offended), vary between countries. For example, in England and Wales, those under the age of 18 are commonly referred to as juveniles although a distinction is often made between children (under the age of 14) and young persons (age 14 to 16). The age of criminal responsibility also varies worldwide between the ages of 6 and 18 and is age 10 in England and Wales (i.e. a person under such age may not be found guilty of an offence) (Hazel 2008). The statutory age limit adopted by juvenile court also varies. For example, in the US, the upper age in three states is 15; 16 in another ten states and 17 in the rest of the states (Snyder and Sickmund 2006). Furthermore, in more than half of the states, legislature stipulates that in serious cases, juveniles should be prosecuted as adults. The law excludes such cases from the juvenile court and state prosecutors must file them in criminal court. In some states, it is at the prosecutors' discretion which court they file those cases in (Snyder and Sickmund 2006).

Extent of child and youth offending

It is difficult to ascertain the true extent of child and youth offending due to the limitations of each information source. Studies that rely on official records run the risk of omitting dark figures that result from unreported delinquent/

criminal behaviour, unsuccessful prosecutions and/or plea bargains, whereas self-reports from victims or the general population may be distorted due to inaccurate memory or deliberate exaggeration. Therefore, attempts have been made to combine multiple sources to increase the accuracy of estimates (Friendship, Beech and Browne 2002).

Overall, males have always been found to be significantly more likely than females to offend in all age groups, including juveniles, but the age of onset of delinquency is later in females than in males (Junger-Tas, Ribeaud and Cruyff 2004). In a cohort study following up 380 boys and 380 girls in Newcastle upon Tyne, 28% of the boys and 5.5% of the girls had appeared in court before 18.5 years of age (Kolvin et al. 1988). In a US national report on juvenile offenders (Snyder and Sickmund 2006), males were significantly more likely than females to report engaging in behaviour such as vandalism (47% and 27% respectively), theft less than $50 (48%, 38%), theft over $50 (16%, 10%), assault with intent to cause serious harm (31%, 21%), selling drugs (19%, 12%), belonging to a gang (11%, 6%) and carrying a handgun (25%, 6%) by the age of 17.

A recent survey reported the levels and trends in offending and antisocial behaviour[1] among young people aged from 10 to 25 living in the general household population in England and Wales (Wilson, Sharp and Patterson 2006). The survey showed that males were more likely to have committed an offence than females (30% and 21% respectively). This gender difference is much larger for violent offending. A Swedish study (Svensson and Ring 2007) found that in 2005, the proportion of young people who admitted a theft was 58.1% for males and 46.3% for females, whereas the proportion reporting committing a violent offence was 21.6% for males and 8.7% for females. It should be noted that although girls are less likely to offend, the most recent Youth Justice Board figures show that in the UK, there was a 25% increase in offences committed by girls, while there was a 2% decrease in offences committed by boys between 2003/4 and 2006/7 (Youth Justice Board 2008). However, this trend is not observed in Sweden (Svensson and Ring 2007). Therefore, the increase in offending by girls in the UK may reflect changes in the way agencies such as police and school respond to violent behaviour rather than the real level of increase in offending by girls.

In the UK survey (Wilson et al. 2006), 25% of young people reported committing at least an offence in the past twelve months. Nearly a third (31%) of these young offenders reported committing six or more offences

---

[1] Nuisance or unpleasant behaviour such as being noisy or rude in a public place so that people complained, involved the police or graffiti in a public place or being threatening or rude to someone because of their race or religion.

(which represented 7% of all 10- to 25-year-olds). One in two young offenders (51%) reported committing a serious offence. (This equates to 13% of all 10- to 25-year-olds.) Of those who had committed a serious offence, the majority (71%) had committed an assault resulting in injury and no other serious offence, and 1% had committed serious offences frequently. The most commonly reported offence categories in the UK were assault (16%) and other thefts (11%). Within offence types, repeat offending was particularly associated with the selling of drugs.

Among the 4% of young people who reported they had sold drugs in the past twelve months, four out of five (82%) had done so more than once, with two out of five (41%) reporting doing so six or more times. Frequent offending was also relatively common for thefts and assaults without injury (16% and 15% respectively). In the USA where youth gang culture is a more serious problem, the US national report (Snyder and Sickmund 2006) found that 8% of 17-year-olds reported belonging to a gang, 16% had sold drugs and 16% carried a gun. In addition, a quarter of juveniles who offended at ages 16 to 17 continue to offend as adults at ages 18 to 19. Even though the proportion of young people in a gang seems to be the minority, they are responsible for a disproportionately high share of violent and non-violent offences in the USA.

Characteristics and risk factors

In the recent UK survey (Wilson *et al.* 2006), the attributes that showed the strongest association with committing an offence among 10- to 25-year-olds were: antisocial behaviour, being a victim of personal crime, being drunk once a month or more, having friends/siblings in trouble with the police and taking drugs.

It was also found that those who lived with both biological parents had a lower lifetime prevalence of breaking the law than those who lived in other family types. Those who have friends or families in a gang were three times more likely to report engaging in vandalism, a major theft, a serious assault, carrying a gun, selling and using drugs and running away from home. Similar findings were also reported in the US national report on juvenile offending in response to a question about why they joined a gang (Snyder and Sickmund 2006). Over half (54%) of Rochester gang members said that they followed the lead of friends or family members who preceded them, only 19% said they joined for protection and 15% said it was for fun or excitement. Furthermore, those who were neither in school nor employment had a significantly greater risk of engaging in a wide range of problem behaviours such as using marijuana and hard drugs, running away from home, belonging to a gang, committing a major theft or a serious assault, selling drugs and carrying a gun. Respondents are more likely to report using alcohol than using using marijuana and selling drugs.

Development of delinquency and criminality

It has long been established that family environments in childhood and adolescence are associated with antisocial behaviour and delinquency (e.g. Farrington 1995; Kolvin *et al.* 1988; Loeber and Dishion 1983; Moffitt and Caspi 2001). Researchers have utilized the design of cohort follow-up to investigate the acquisition and progression of delinquent and offending behaviours. The largest cohort study on the development delinquency and criminality in the UK (Farrington 1995) found that convicted delinquents are more likely to have experienced poor parenting, characterized by harsh or erratic parental discipline, neglectful parental attitudes, parental conflicts and lax supervision in their childhood. They are also more likely to have convicted parents or delinquent older siblings. On a personal level, convicted delinquents were found to be more likely to have low intelligence, poor concentration, hyperactivity and poor educational attainment (Farrington 1995). An earlier Newcastle study also found that offenders were more likely to have been exposed to poor physical and home care and poor parenting compared to non-offenders. Those who committed their first offence before the age of 15 were more likely to have been exposed to marital instability or parental illness in their preschool years than those who committed their first offence after 15 (Kolvin *et al.* 1988). A recent Finnish study (Sourander *et al.* 2006) also found that living in a family other than the two-parent structure, low parental educational level, parent reports of conduct problems and teacher reports of hyperactivity at the age of 8 predicted a high frequency (greater than five) of all types of offences between the ages 16 and 20.

Patterson *et al.* (1989) explained the developmental progression for antisocial behaviour from the social-interactional perspective, in which children's coercive or disruptive behaviour is not effectively dealt with by parents and caregivers. There is a lack of parental supervision or positive reinforcement by caregivers with inconsistent boundary setting and erratic discipline. Children may also learn deviant and inappropriate behaviour through direct experience or observation of other family members (Bandura 1977) and perceive those behaviours as effective. Furthermore, the acquisition of deviant behaviours

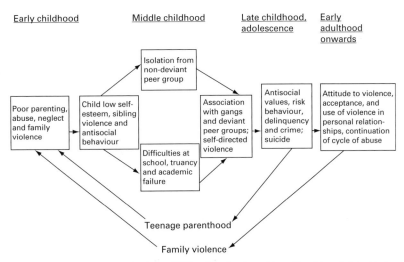

Early childhood   Middle childhood   Late childhood,   Early
                                                   adolescence   adulthood
                                                                      onwards

Figure 1.2.1 The developmental progression from childhood maltreatment to antisocial and violent behaviour (adapted from Patterson, DeBaryshe and Ramsey 1989)

may be associated with a lack of encouragement for prosocial skills as children are often ignored or responded to inappropriately (Snyder 1977). On entering school, children with coercive behaviours and poor social skills are likely to meet with peer rejection. Furthermore, growing up in a disruptive and/or disorganized family can affect concentration and compliance with educational tasks, which in turn may affect learning and increase the chances of academic under-achievement. Educational failure increases the likelihood of truancy and gang membership with other truants. In this context, deviant behaviours are learned and exhibited for social approval and increase self-esteem within the gang. This model is illustrated in figure 1.2.1.

Browne and Hamilton-Giachritsis (2005) have also reviewed the evidence showing that young offenders have a preference for violent media entertainment that supports their distorted way of thinking. This in turn may influence their attitudes and behaviour and increase the chances of them committing a violent offence. This phenomenon was observed more frequently amongst teenagers from violent family backgrounds.

From an attachment perspective, children from 'average' families usually experience sensitive and consistent parenting and learn to perceive their social environment in a positive way. As a consequence, they develop a positive sense of self and positive view of others. By contrast, children from abusive, neglectful or disorganized families are highly likely to have an insecure attachment to their primary carer (Morton and Browne 1998) as a result of harsh or inconsistent parenting. This hinders the development of a positive self-image and these children are more likely to have a negative view of self and a negative view of others, which in turn affects the development of empathy towards the others (e.g. Browne and Herbert 1997).

Furthermore, childhood victimization was also found to be highly prevalent in the background of young offenders (Falshaw and Browne 1997). A study found that four out of five young offenders (79.2%) in secure accommodation had experienced some forms of abuse and neglect in their childhood. Of the 79.2%, 8% suffered from single victimization, 15% experienced repeat victimization (by the same perpetrator), 8% experienced revictimization (abuse by different perpetrators) and 69% experienced both repeat victimization and revictimization (Hamilton, Falshaw and Browne 2002).

Although poor parenting and abuse/neglect are significant risk factors for delinquency and crime (Falshaw, Browne and Hollin 1996), only a minority of children from abusive and neglectful backgrounds go on to commit offences as juveniles (26%) and as adults (29%) (Widom 1989). Nevertheless, children without such adverse experiences are significantly less likely to have a criminal record as juveniles (17%) and as adults (21%). Therefore, most maltreated children manage to break the cycle of deprivation and crime by the experience of protective factors. For example, Farrington (1995) found that boys without convicted parents or delinquent siblings and boys who avoided contact with other boys in the neighbourhood were less likely to show delinquent and offending behaviour.

Research also found that positive interpersonal relationships outside the family (e.g. teachers), good academic achievement, positive attitudes towards authority and effective use of leisure time serve as protective factors that help prevent reoffending in delinquents and young offenders (Carr and Vandiver 2001; Hoge, Andrews and Leschied 1996). It was found that those who are able to gain positive attention and adapt more easily to social and material constraints are more likely to desist from further offending behaviour as they are perceived as being more mature, less aggressive and having greater self-control (Born, Chevalier and Humblet 1997).

McKnight and Loper (2002) investigated risk factors and resilience among adolescent girls. Analysis was carried out on 2,245 females aged between 10 and 19 years. It was found that experiencing sexual abuse and being brought up by single parents were significant risk factors for delinquency and offending. By contrast, resilience factors include perceiving teachers as being fair, and feeling trusted, loved and wanted by parents. It was also found that these resilience factors could distinguish adolescent females who reported high levels of delinquency from those who reported low delinquency with 80% accuracy.

Intervention

It is claimed that the prevention of delinquency, criminal behaviour and reoffending can be achieved by interventions that alleviate risk factors and strengthen protective factors. Projects aimed at the entire youth population are termed 'primary prevention', where universal services are provided to the entire population, for example, information leaflets or summer activities for children and young people in the community. There are also universal school interventions and curricula that take the cognitive-behavioural approach to enhance communication skills, conflict resolution, social skills and abilities to resist negative peer pressure in young people (Hahn *et al.* 2007a, 2007b; Webster-Stratton, Reid and Stoolmiller 2008; Wilson, Lipsey and Derzon 2003). Such school interventions have been found to be effective in reducing antisocial acts and behaviour problems for all age groups.

Services that target children and families with risk factors are classed as secondary prevention. At the individual level, support for academic work and cognitive-behavioural intervention are provided for children identified as being at risk. Many risk factors for antisocial behaviour and delinquency are centred on family problems and parenting. Therefore, many intervention programmes are family focused and provide parenting intervention for families with children identified as at risk. At the community level, there are after-school and community-based mentoring schemes for children and young people at risk of delinquency and offending. However, some programmes intervene with parents and teachers as well as the children. For example, Webster-Stratton and her colleagues first developed video-based behavioural parenting interventions for parents whose children displayed conduct problems in the USA (Webster-Stratton, Hollinsworth and Kolpacoff 1989). Webster-Stratton and colleagues later added concurrent sessions for the children (Webster-Stratton and Hammond 1997) and in recent years, training for teachers to improve classroom management was also added to the programme (Foster, Olchowski and Webster-Stratton 2007). Similarly, the Utrecht Coping Power Programme in the Netherlands offers cognitive-behavioural intervention for children displaying disruptive behaviours and behavioural intervention for their parents (Zonnevylle-Bender *et al.* 2007).

Another approach is to have different levels of intensity in the parenting intervention in order to suit different family needs. For example, the Triple P programme developed in Australia includes three levels of parenting programme (Sanders, Bor and Morawska 2007; Sanders *et al.* 2000). For general support, there is a self-administered (videotape) intervention with workbook. There is also the standard Triple P, which includes group sessions for parents developed by trained practitioners. For families with greater needs, an enhanced version is in place with more intensive input to address parenting issues as well as support in dealing with issues such as stress and marital relationships. So far, parenting programmes have been found effective in reducing behavioural problems in children (Brotman *et al.* 2005a; Dretzke *et al.* 2005; Woolfenden, Williams and Peat 2001) and siblings of the children also benefit from interventions (Brotman *et al.* 2005b). It was also found that programmes that offer services for both children and parents and more intensive input are found to be more effective than parent training alone (Foster *et al.* 2007; Sanders *et al.* 2007).

Primary and secondary preventions are not necessarily mutually exclusive, as some programmes incorporate multiple layers of services to meet different types of needs and different levels of problem. In England and Wales, the On Track project operates the targeted services in the universal framework to avoid labelling and stigma of the children and their families (Dinos *et al.* 2006). Under such a framework, universal services can also incorporate screening assessment for the identification of high-risk children with greater needs. However, the term 'high priority for services' is preferable to 'high risk'.

Interventions to prevent reoffending after offences have been committed are classed as tertiary prevention. Research has found evidence of effectiveness of tertiary interventions in reducing recidivism (Caldwell and Van Rybroek 2005; Schaeffer and Borduin 2005). However, institutional correctional work for serious young offenders was not found to be effective in reducing further offending in adulthood in the long run (Florsheim *et al.* 2004).

Conclusions

The UK has been criticized by the UN Committee on the Rights of the Child for incarcerating too many children in secure environments. This type of intervention, which takes away the freedom and social experiences of a child during the critical years of adolescence, has not been shown to be effective, with two-thirds of young offenders placed in secure environments reoffending within twelve months (Southall 2006). Perhaps the failure of this approach is that it does little to repair the attachment difficulties, low self-esteem and learned antisocial behaviour, which have been identified as significant precursors to offending behaviour. Recent alternative approaches such as specially trained foster carers (e.g. South Staffordshire Healthcare Intensive Fostering Programme) caring for antisocial young offenders has shown greater success with only one-third reoffending within twelve months. The foster carer provides a secure attachment figure and a positive learning environment, which may enhance self-esteem and the confidence that the young offender can break the cycle of delinquency and crime. Nevertheless, early intervention is preferable to tackling a young person's problems once they have begun. Positive parenting programmes and targeted interventions for children at risk have been shown to be more effective and less costly.

REFERENCES

Bandura, A. (1977) *Social Learning Theory*. Englewood Cliffs, NJ: Prentice Hall.

Born, M., Chevalier, V. and Humblet, I. (1997) Resilience, desistance and delinquent career of adolescent offenders. *Journal of Adolescence*, 20: 679–94.

Brotman, L. M., Gouley, K. K., Chesir-Teran, D., Dennis, T., Klein, R. G. and Shrout, P. (2005a) Prevention for preschoolers at high risk for conduct problems: immediate outcomes on parenting practices and child social competence. *Journal of Clinical Child and Adolescent Psychology*, 34: 724–34.

Brotman, L. M., Dawson-McClure, S., Gouley, K. K., McGuire, K., Burraston, B. and Bank, L. (2005b) Older siblings benefit from a family-based preventive intervention for preschoolers at risk for conduct problems. *Journal of Family Psychology*, 19: 581–91.

Browne, K. D. and Hamilton-Giachritsis, C. (2005) The influence of violent media on children and adolescents: a public-health approach. *Lancet*, 365: 702–10.

Browne, K. D. and Herbert, M. (1997) *Preventing Family Violence*. Chichester: Wiley.

Caldwell, M. F. and Van Rybroek, G. J. (2005) Reducing violence in serious juvenile offenders using intensive treatment. *International Journal of Law and Psychiatry*, 28: 622–36.

Carr, M. B. and Vandiver, T. A. (2001) Risk and protective factors among youth offenders. *Adolescence*, 36: 409–26.

Dinos, S., Tian, Y., Solanki, A.-R. and Hauari, H. (2006) *Tracking Services and Users: On Track in Practice* (Report no. 769). London: Policy Research Bureau.

Dretzke, J., Frew, E., Davenport, C., Barlow, J., Stewart-Brown, S., Sandercock, J. *et al.* (2005) The effectiveness and cost-effectiveness of parent training/education programmes for the treatment of conduct disorder, including oppositional defiant disorder, in children. *Health Technology Assessment*, 9: 1–250.

Falshaw, L. and Browne, K. (1997) Adverse childhood experiences and violent acts of young people in secure accommodation. *Journal of Mental Health*, 6: 443–55.

Falshaw, L., Browne, K. D. and Hollin, C. (1996) Victim to offender: a review. *Aggression and Violent Behavior*, 1: 389–404.

Farrington, D. P. (1995) The 12th Jack Tizard Memorial Lecture: the development of offending and antisocial behavior from childhood – key findings from the Cambridge Study in

Delinquent Development. *Journal of Child Psychology and Psychiatry and Allied Disciplines*, 36: 929–64.

Florsheim, P., Behling, S., South, M., Fowles, T. R. and DeWitt, J. (2004) Does the youth corrections system work? Tracking the effectiveness of intervention efforts with delinquent boys in state custody. *Psychological Services*, 1: 126–39.

Foster, E. M., Olchowski, A. E. and Webster-Stratton, C. H. (2007) Is stacking intervention components cost-effective? An analysis of the Incredible Years program. *Journal of the American Academy of Child and Adolescent Psychiatry*, 46: 1414–24.

Friendship, C., Beech, A. R. and Browne, K. D. (2002) Reconviction as an outcome measure in research: a methodological note. *British Journal of Criminology*, 42: 442–4.

Hahn, R., Fuqua-Whitley, D., Wethington, H., Lowy, J., Crosby, A., Fullilove, M. *et al.* (2007a) Effectiveness of universal school-based programs to prevent violent and aggressive behavior: a systematic review. *American Journal of Preventive Medicine*, 33: S114–S129.

(2007b) The effectiveness of universal school based programmes for the prevention of violent and aggressive behavior: a report on recommendations of the Task Force on Community Preventive Services. MMWR Recommendations and Reports [Online]. www.cdc.gov/mmwR/preview/mmwrhtml/rr5607a1.htm (accessed 28 May 2008).

Hamilton, C. E., Falshaw, L. and Browne, K. D. (2002) The link between recurrent maltreatment and offending behaviour. *International Journal of Offender Therapy and Comparative Criminology*, 41: 75–95.

Hazel, N. (2008) *Cross-national Comparison of Youth Justice*. London: Youth Justice Board.

Hoge, R. D., Andrews, D. A. and Leschied, A. W. (1996) An investigation of risk and protective factors in a sample of youthful offenders. *Journal of Child Psychology and Psychiatry*, 37: 419–24.

Junger-Tas, J., Ribeaud, D. and Cruyff, M. J. L. F. (2004) Juvenile delinquency and gender. *European Journal of Criminology*, 1: 333–75.

Kolvin, I., Miller, F. J., Fleeting, M. and Kolvin, P. A. (1988) Social and parenting factors affecting criminal-offence rates: findings from the Newcastle Thousand Family Study (1947–1980). *British Journal of Psychiatry*, 152: 80–90.

Loeber, R. and Dishion, T. J. (1983) Early predictors of male delinquency: a review. *Psychological Bulletin*, 94: 68–99.

McKnight, L. R. and Loper, A. B. (2002) The effects of risk and resilience factors in the prediction of delinquency in adolescent girls. *School Psychology International*, 23: 186–98.

Moffitt, T. E. and Caspi, A. (2001) Childhood predictors differentiate life-course persistent and adolescence-limited antisocial pathways among males and females. *Development and Psychopathology*, 13: 355–75.

Morton, N. and Browne, K. D. (1998) Theory and observation of attachment and its relation to child maltreatment: a review. *Child Abuse and Neglect*, 22: 1093–1104.

Patterson, G. R., DeBaryshe, B. D. and Ramsey, E. (1989) A developmental perspective on antisocial behavior. *American Psychologist*, 44: 329–35.

Sanders, M. R., Bor, W. and Morawska, A. (2007) Maintenance of treatment gains: a comparison of enhanced, standard, and self-directed triple P-positive parenting program. *Journal of Abnormal Child Psychology*, 35: 983–98.

Sanders, M. R., Markie-Dadds, C., Tully, L. A. and Bor, W. (2000) The Triple P-Positive Parenting Program: a comparison of enhanced, standard, and self-directed behavioral family intervention for parents of children with early onset conduct problems. *Journal of Consulting and Clinical Psychology*, 68: 624–40.

Schaeffer, C. M. and Borduin, C. M. (2005) Long-term follow-up to a randomized clinical trial of multisystemic therapy with serious and violent juvenile offenders. *Journal of Consulting and Clinical Psychology*, 73: 445–53.

Snyder, H. N. and Sickmund, M. (2006) *Juvenile Offenders and Victims: 2006 National Report*. Washington, DC: US Department of Justice, Office of Justice Programs, Office of Juvenile Justice and Delinquency Prevention.

Snyder, J. J. (1977) Reinforcement analysis of interaction in problem and nonproblem families. *Journal of Abnormal Psychology*, 86: 528–35.

Sourander, A., Elonheimo, H., Niemela, S., Nuutila, A. M., Helenius, H. and Sillanmaki, L. *et al.* (2006) Childhood predictors of male criminality: a prospective population-based follow-up study from age 8 to late adolescence. *Journal of the American Academy of Child and Adolescent Psychiatry*, 45: 578–86.

Southall, A. (2006) Intensive fostering – one of the first national pilot projects in the UK. Personnal communication.

Svensson, R. and Ring, J. (2007) Trends in self-reported youth crime and victimization in Sweden, 1995–2005. *Journal of Scandinavian Studies in Criminology and Crime Prevention*, 8: 185–209.

Webster-Stratton, C. and Hammond, M. (1997) Treating children with early-onset conduct problems: a comparison of child and parent training interventions. *Journal of Consulting and Clinical Psychology*, 65: 93–109.

Webster-Stratton, C., Hollinsworth, T. and Kolpacoff, M. (1989) The long-term effectiveness and clinical significance of three cost-effective training programs for families with conduct-problem children. *Journal of Consulting and Clinical Psychology*, 57: 550–3.

Webster-Stratton, C., Reid, M. J. and Stoolmiller, M. (2008) Preventing conduct problems and improving school readiness: evaluation of the Incredible Years teacher and child training programs in high-risk schools. *Journal of Child Psychology and Psychiatry*, 49: 471–88.

Widom, C. S. (1989) The cycle of violence. *Science*, 244: 160–6.

Wilson, D., Sharp, C. and Patterson, A. (2006) *Young People and Crime: Findings from the 2005 Offending, Crime and Justice Survey*. London: Home Office.

Wilson, S. J., Lipsey, M. W. and Derzon, J. H. (2003) The effects of school-based intervention programmes on aggressive behavior: a meta-analysis. *Journal of Consulting and Clinical Psychology*, 71: 136–49.

Woolfenden, S. R., Williams, K. and Peat, J. (2001) Family and parenting interventions in children and adolescents with conduct disorder and delinquency aged 10–17. *Cochrane Database of Systematic Reviews*, issue 2.

Youth Justice Board (2008) *Youth Justice Annual Workload Data 2006/07*. London: Youth Justice Board.

Zonnevylle-Bender, M. J. S., Matthys, W., Van De Wiel, N. M. H. and Lochman, J. E. (2007) Preventive effects of treatment of disruptive behavior disorder in middle childhood on substance use and delinquent behavior. *Journal of the American Academy of Child and Adolescent Psychiatry*, 46: 33–9.

1.3 Developmental perspectives on offending

Robert D. Hoge

See also chapter 1.2 Child and adolescent offending.

Introduction

This chapter will focus on contemporary theoretical and research developments in the search for developmental patterns and age-linked correlates and causes of antisocial behaviours. The advances discussed come from the emerging field of developmental criminology (see Farrington 2004; Guerra *et al.* 2008; Thornberry 2005). Research involves a search for the correlates of antisocial behaviours such as criminal acts. Males, for instance, exhibit, on average, higher levels of criminal activities than females and youth from dysfunctional home environments generally exhibit higher levels than those from more functional environments. Such information is useful in developing predictors of antisocial behaviours and in the preliminary evaluation of causal hypotheses.

Research has also explored the possibility that the factors associated with criminal activity may vary as a function of developmental level. It is clear, for example, that parental and peer-group influences play roles in the expression of criminal activities, but that their influence is very different during the early childhood and adolescent years.

However, correlational information does not provide us with direct information about causal links. Gender is not a cause of criminal activity and the dysfunctional home environment may not be contributing directly to the youth's criminal behaviour. Determining causality depends on the use of sophisticated research designs and careful construction of theoretical constructs (Rutter 2003; Rutter, Giller and Hagell 1998).

A related issue concerns the possibility of stable developmental patterns of antisocial behaviours. We will see, for example, that some adults committing serious crime exhibit a pattern whereby conduct disorders made their first appearance during the preschool years, followed by an escalation in the number and seriousness of antisocial actions during adolescence, and followed by continued criminal activity during the adult years. Other individuals show an adolescent onset of criminal activities, with no prior history of such acts.

This raises another obstacle to uncovering causes and correlates. Not only do we need to search for factors that lead to the initiation of antisocial behaviour, but if we accept the assumption of stable trajectories, we also need to explore factors associated with the persistence and desistence from those activities (Guerra *et al.* 2008).

Methodological challenges

The fundamental challenge in the search for the correlates and causation of antisocial behaviours arises from the complexity of human behaviour. Many of the early theoretical positions regarding the causes of criminality focused on a single causal variable, whether poverty, weak ego, deficient self-control, or the XXY chromosome anomaly. These approaches were clearly inadequate. We now know that a wide range of factors can influence the commission of a criminal act. Some of these are internal (e.g. aspects of temperament, social competencies, modes of perception) and some external (e.g. influences of parents and peers, features of the immediate situation in which the action occurs). Further, these factors do not operate in isolation; rather, it is complex interactions among factors that have the causal impact. Further still, the dynamics of these factors are complex. For example, individual predispositions relating, for example, to impulsivity and aggressiveness, are likely the product of complex interactions among genetic, biological and environmental influences.

While a broad range of methodological problems arise from this complexity (see Rutter 2003; Rutter *et al.* 1998), only two will be noted here. First, there are serious problems in developing reliable and valid measures of relevant constructs (Hoge 2008; Hoge and Andrews 1996). This is true for what we will refer to as the predictor or risk variables such as temperament, social skills, parental child-rearing styles and attitudes. It is also true for the outcome variables of interest, which generally refer to the incidence and nature of antisocial behaviour. Where criminal actions are the focus, official crime statistics or self-reports of antisocial behaviour are generally employed. However, both of those types of measures have limitations (Kirk 2006).

A second methodological problem concerns research design. Required are designs that permit the exploration of the causes of antisocial behaviour as they operate at different stages of the developmental process. Do, for example, parental disciplinary practices have a direct causal impact on the development of aggressive responses, and does that impact operate in the same way for a 4-year-old as a 12-year-old? To further complicate the issue, we have to consider whether the parental behaviour directly impacts the youth or whether more complex interactions between parent and youth are involved.

Cross-sectional studies collecting data on separate cohorts differing in age provide some important clues about factors associated with antisocial behaviours at different stages of the development. However, those designs provide us with no direct information about developmental processes and are of very limited value in testing causal hypotheses.

The preferred design involves prospective longitudinal designs. In this case we are following the same individuals over a period of time, tracking any changes in their behaviours, and exploring factors associated with those changes. There are several advantages associated with this design. First, we are collecting direct information about changes in the individual over time. Second, there is an opportunity to explore the factors associated with the onset and persistence of antisocial behaviour and desistence from it. Third, while there remain problems in this respect, with statistical controls, causal hypotheses can be explored. However, this type of research is very time consuming and costly. There are also conceptual and methodological problems associated with longitudinal research relating to cohort effects and attrition (Rutter 2003; Rutter *et al.* 1998). Nevertheless, important longitudinal research is underway and the quality of the work is continually improving.

The Cambridge Study in delinquent development is an example of one such study (Farrington 1997, 2003, 2004; Farrington *et al.* 2006). The study was initiated in the early 1960s with the collection of data from a group of 411 8- and 9-year-old males drawn largely from working-class districts of London. The researchers are continuing to collect measures from these participants, who are now in their late forties. A wide variety of psychological measures have been employed, including psychological tests, questionnaires completed by teachers and peers, and interviews conducted with the participants and their parents. The incidence of criminal activity on the part of the participants constitutes the primary outcome variable, and this has been measured through official records and self-reports. This research has yielded very important information about factors affecting the development of antisocial behaviours.

The search for developmental trajectories

Developmental criminology has focused on two broad and related issues: a search for stable patterns or trajectories of antisocial behaviours and a search for the causes of the initiation and persistence of, and desistence from, antisocial behaviours. Contemporary research by Arseneault *et al.* (2002), Loeber (1988), Moffitt (1997, 2003, 2006) and others has suggested two stable patterns or trajectories of antisocial behaviours. These are referred to as the life-course-persistent and adolescent-limited patterns. The former is characterized by the appearance of various forms of conduct disorder during the preschool years, an escalation of the incidence and severity of antisocial actions during early childhood and adolescence, and the persistence of the antisocial behaviours into adulthood. Individuals exhibiting this pattern are sometimes referred to as serious, violent and chronic offenders (Loeber and Farrington 1998), and a significant percentage of serious adult offenders display this pattern.

The adolescent-limited trajectory is characterized by normal development during the childhood years and the more-or-less sudden appearance of anti-social behaviours during adolescence. Youth exhibiting this pattern normally desist from further criminal actions during later adolescence and the adult years. These are youth who suddenly get into trouble during their teens, but who generally revert to a prosocial lifestyle later on.

Other patterns have been described, including cases where youth exhibit low levels of antisocial and criminal behaviours across the lifespan, and cases where criminal activities do not begin until later adolescence but persist into the adult years. However, the life-course-persistent and adolescent-limited patterns are said to describe a majority of individuals engaging in criminal activities.

Some gender differences are observed regarding these trajectories (Hoge and Robertson 2008). Youth exhibiting the life-course-persistent pattern are predominately male, while girls who do engage in antisocial actions generally reflect an adolescent-limited pattern.

While there is considerable support for these developmental patterns, two qualifications should be kept in mind. First, the patterns do not describe all individuals who engage in criminal activities. Second, and related, the evidence clearly shows that the majority of individuals who engage in antisocial activities during childhood and adolescence, whatever the pattern, desist from those actions in adulthood (Sampson and Laub 2005). Importantly, this means that the majority of youth exhibiting a life-course-persistent pattern during childhood and adolescence will not continue their criminal activities into the adult years.

Sampson and Laub (2005) have developed a somewhat broader criticism of the categorization described above by suggesting that it may not be useful to think in terms of distinct patterns defined by the age of onset of the antisocial behaviours. Their preference is to talk in terms of propensities to engage in antisocial behaviours and to conceive of these propensities as capable of expression at any point in the developmental sequence depending on environmental factors.

A developmental perspective on the causes of antisocial behaviours

A growing body of cross-sectional and longitudinal research is now available on age-related risk factors associated with antisocial behaviours (see table 1.3.1).

This information is important for purposes of assessing risk for antisocial behaviour at various developmental stages and for developing prevention and intervention programmes. However, and as we have seen above, the identification of risk factors gives an incomplete picture by not providing information about the dynamics of the risk factors (Rutter 2003; Rutter *et al.* 1998). For example, it is clear that associations with antisocial peers constitute a significant risk factor during the adolescent years. However, the way in which those associations actually impact on the youth's behaviour and the way in which the associations interact with the youth's personality dispositions and with family dynamics remains unclear. To complicate the search even further, the roles of genetic and environmental factors in the development of the constitutional factors must be addressed. Finally, much of this research has focused on risk factors and provided us with less information about important strength or protective factors.

On the other hand, longitudinal research designs and statistical procedures are enabling us to address these issues and to uncover causal chains incorporating both risk and protective factors. For example, Moffitt's (1997, 2003, 2006) longitudinal study of the life-course-persistent pattern has been able to test causal chains linking early neurological deficits to impaired learning abilities, deficient social skills acquisition, impaired relations with parents, early conduct disorders and later criminal activity. The other longitudinal studies cited above are providing similar advances. A further example is the Montreal longitudinal-experimental study in which

Table 1.3.1 Major categories of risk predictors by developmental level

Infancy/Preschool	Neurological impairments
	Cognitive impairments
	Difficult temperament
	Dysfunctional family environment
	Dysfunctional parenting
Early Childhood	Cognitive impairments
	Behaviour/personality deficits
	Poor school achievement
	Poor social skills
	Antisocial peers
	Dysfunctional family environment
	Dysfunctional parenting
Adolescence	Cognitive impairments
	Difficult temperament
	Poor school achievement
	School dropout
	Poor social skills
	Antisocial peers
	Substance abuse
	Dysfunctional family environment
	Dysfunctional parenting
	Dysfunctional neighbourhood
Adulthood	Poor employment history
	Dysfunctional neighbourhood
	Unsatisfactory marital situation
	Substance abuse

conduct-disordered boys were assigned to either an experimental group receiving a social skills training intervention or a control group with no intervention (Tremblay *et al.* 1994; Vitaro, Brendgen and Tremblay 2001). This study has yielded important results reflecting on links among early conduct disorders and later poor school achievement, antisocial attitudes and delinquent behaviours.

Work is also being advanced by theoretical efforts to tie together the empirical findings through developmental life-course-theories (see Andrews and Bonta 2007; Catalano and Hawkins 1996; Farrington 2004; Guerra *et al.* 2008; Rhee and Waldman 2002; Thornberry 2005). For example, Catalano and Hawkin's (1996) Social Development model describes causal chains leading to the development of prosocial or antisocial lifestyles as they operate at different developmental levels. The work of Rhee and Waldman (2002) is representative of efforts to elucidate the roles of heredity and environment in influencing antisocial behaviours.

Conclusions

Andrews and Bonta's (2007) Risk–Need–Responsivity model of effective treatment of antisocial behaviours emphasizes the importance of identifying the factors placing the individual at risk for criminal activity (risk factors), the risk factors amenable to change through interventions (need factors), and other characteristics of the individual or his/her situation that might affect reactions to interventions (responsivity factors). This work in developmental criminology is critical to the identification of these factors and to the evolution of meaningful prevention and treatment programmes.

FURTHER READING

The reader is referred to Farrington (1998, 2004), Guerra *et al.* (2008), Loeber and Hay (1997) and Rutter *et al.* (1998) for additional information on some of the major developments.

REFERENCES

Andrews, D. A. and Bonta, J. (2007) *The Psychology of Criminal Conduct*, 4th edn. Cincinnati, OH: Anderson.

Arseneault, L., Tremblay, R. E., Boulerice, B. and Saucier, J. F. (2002) Obstetric complications and adolescent violent behaviors: testing two developmental pathways. *Child Development*, 73: 496–508.

Catalano, R. F. and Hawkins, J. D. (1996) The social development model: a theory of antisocial behavior. In J. D. Hawkins (ed.), *Delinquency and Crime: Current Theories*, pp. 149–97. Cambridge: Cambridge University Press.

Farrington, D. P. (1997) Early prediction of violent and non-violent youth offending. *European Journal on Criminal Policy and Research*, 5: 51–66.

    (1998) Predictors, causes and correlates of male youth violence. In M. Tonry and M. H. Moore (eds.), *Youth Violence* (Crime and Justice, vol. 24), pp. 421–75. Chicago, IL: University of Chicago Press.

    (2003) Key results from the first 40 years of the Cambridge Study in Delinquent Development. In T. P. Thornberry and M. D. Krohn (eds.), *Taking Stock of Delinquency: An Overview of Findings from Contemporary Longitudinal Studies*, pp. 137–83. New York: Kluwer/Plenum.

(2004) Conduct disorder, aggression, and delinquency. In R. M. Lerner, and L. Steinberg (eds.), *Handbook of Adolescent Psychology*, 2nd edn, pp. 624–7. New York: Wiley.

Farrington, D. P., Coid, J. W., Harnett, L., Jolliffe, D., Soteriou, N., Turner, R. and West, D. J. (2006) *Criminal Careers up to Age 50 and Life Success up to Age 48: New Findings from the Cambridge Study in Delinquent Development*. London: Home Office Research.

Guerra, N. G., Williams, K. R., Tolan, P. H. and Modecki, K. L. (2008) Theoretical and research advances in understanding the causes of juvenile offending. In R. D. Hoge, N. G. Guerra and P. Boxer (eds.), *Treating the Juvenile Offender*, pp. 33–53. New York: Guilford Press.

Hoge, R. D. (2008) Assessment in juvenile justice systems. In R. D. Hoge, N. G. Guerra and P. Boxer (eds.), *Treating the Juvenile Offender*, pp. 54–75. New York: Guilford Press.

Hoge, R. D. and Andrews, D. A. (1996) *Assessing the Youthful Offender: Issues and Techniques*. New York: Plenum.

Hoge, R. D. and Robertson, L. (2008) The female juvenile offender. In R. D. Hoge, N. G. Guerra and P. Boxer (eds.), *Treating the Juvenile Offender*, pp. 258–77. New York: Guilford Press.

Kirk, D. S. (2006) Examining the divergence across self-report and official data sources on inferences about the adolescent life-course of crime. *Journal of Quantitative Criminology*, 22: 107–29.

Loeber, R. (1988) Natural histories of conduct problems, delinquency, and associated substance use: evidence for developmental progressions. In B. B. Lahey and A. E. Kazdin (eds.), *Advances in Clinical Child Psychology*, vol. 11, pp. 73–124. New York: Plenum Press.

Loeber, R. and Farrington, D. P. (eds.) (1998) *Serious and Violent Juvenile Offenders: Risk Factors and Successful Interventions*. Thousand Oaks, CA: Sage.

Loeber, R. and Hay, D. F. (1997) Key issues in the development of aggression and violence from childhood to early adulthood. *Annual Review of Psychology*, 48: 371–410.

Moffitt, T. E. (1997) Adolescence-limited and life-course-persistent offending: a complementary pair of developmental theories. In T. Thornberry (ed.), *Advances in Criminological Theory: Developmental Theories of Crime and Delinquencies*, pp. 11–54. London: Transaction Press.

(2003) Life-course-persistent and adolescence-limited antisocial behavior: a 10-year research review and research agenda. In B. B. Lahey, T. E. Moffitt and A. Caspi (eds.), *Causes of Conduct Disorder and Juvenile Delinquency*, pp. 49–75. New York: Guilford Press.

(2006) Life-course-persistent versus adolescence-limited antisocial behavior. In D. Cicchetti and D. Cohen (eds.), *Developmental Psychopathology*, 2nd edn, pp. 570–98. New York: Wiley.

Rhee, S. H. and Waldman, I. D. (2002) Genetic and environmental influences on antisocial behavior: a meta-analysis of twin and adoption studies. *Psychological Bulletin*, 128: 490–529.

Rutter, M. (2003) Crucial paths from risk indicator to causal mechanism. In B. B. Lahey, T. E. Moffitt and A. Caspi (eds.), *Causes of Conduct Disorder and Juvenile Delinquency*, pp. 3–24. New York: Guilford Press.

Rutter, M., Giller, H. and Hagell, A. (1998) *Antisocial Behavior by Young People*. Cambridge: Cambridge University Press.

Sampson, R. J. and Laub, J. H. (2005) A life-course view of the development of crime. *Annals of the American Academy of Political and Social Science*, 602: 12–45.

Thornberry, T. P. (2005) Explaining multiple patterns of offending across the life course and across generations. *Annals of the American Academy of Political and Social Science*, 602: 156–95.

Tremblay, R. E., Pihl, R. O., Vitaro, F. and Dobkin, P. L. (1994) Predicting early onset of male antisocial behavior from preschool behavior. *Archives of General Psychiatry*, 51: 737–9.

Vitaro, F., Brendgen, M. and Tremblay, R. E. (2001) Preventive intervention: assessing its effects on the trajectories of delinquency and testing for mediational processes. *Applied Developmental Science*, 5: 201–13.

The evolutionary psychology perspective

Vernon L. Quinsey

Introduction

Evolutionary psychology adopts a Darwinian approach to understanding the causes of behaviour. Traditionally, psychology has focused on the mechanisms that produce behaviour in the current environment or within the lifetime of an individual. These mechanisms explain *how* behaviour is caused and are referred to as proximal causes. Darwinian psychology, on the other hand, deals with the ultimate causes of heritable adaptations – explaining *why* behavioural or mental adaptations arose by identifying the environmental conditions in ancestral environments that selected for them by causing variations in reproductive success or 'fitness'. Every behaviour or trait has a proximal cause and each that is heritable is an adaptation or a by-product of an adaptation, thus having a direct or indirect ultimate cause (by 'by-product' is meant the characteristic in question was not selected for itself). A recent comprehensive treatment of evolutionary psychology can be found in Buss (2005).

Development

In recent years, evolutionary psychology has either become obsolete or greatly expanded its scope and explanatory power, depending on one's point of view. Stunning conceptual and technical advances in the science of development have enabled scientists to observe precisely how genes interact with the rest of the organism during its ontogenetic act of self-creation. The history of these genes and their speed of evolution can also be examined using sophisticated DNA techniques and comparative biology. Excellent and accessible non-technical accounts of the evo-devo revolution can be found in Carroll (2005) and Coen's (1999) more abstract and poetic work. One of evolutionary psychology's most important goals is to create theories of behaviour and the mind that are consilient (i.e. consistent in theory and method) with the more basic life sciences, namely evolutionary biology and the new science of development.

There have been some important applications of evolutionary psychology to forensic psychology. Aggressive and antisocial behaviours reflect conflicts of interest among individuals, traditionally labelled offenders and victims. Darwinian theory is therefore uniquely applicable to these conflicts because it is the only theory that can provide an explanation of why individuals have perceptions of self-interest at all and why there are lawful variations in these perceptions. An accessible explication of a Darwinian approach to antisocial behaviour is provided by Rowe (2002).

Application

The classic application of Darwinian principles to forensic issues is Daly and Wilson's (1988) explanation of why step-parents are much more likely to abuse and murder their children than are parents of offspring who are biologically related to them. The differential risk afforded by variations in genetic relatedness had not been studied until the prediction was derived from evolutionary theory. Variations in altruism and parental solicitude have been central to evolutionary theory since the work of Hamilton and Trivers more than thirty years ago.

Evolutionary theory has provided the only explanation to date of the fundamental data of criminology – the differences in criminal behaviour associated with age and sex. Because there has been much greater variance in reproductive success among men than among women and the number of sexual partners is the principal limiting factor on male reproductive success, men compete among each other for status and mateships. The benefits and costs of this competition vary in such a way as to explain sex and age differences in risk taking and criminal activity (Kanazawa 2003).

Sexual coercion is another area in which evolutionary psychology has made important contributions. Because the reproductive interests of men and women are correlated but not identical, there is opportunity for conflict at the behavioural and genomic levels. Men can interfere with women's reproductive strategies through sexual coercion and women with men's, through cuckoldry. Evolutionary theory has been brought to bear on sex differences in sexual coercion (for an extensive review, see Lalumière *et al.* 2005) and on individual differences among men in their propensity for sexual aggression (Harris *et al.* 2007).

Not only have our perceptions of self-interest been shaped by the past fitness consequences of variations in them but also by what we perceive to be sexually interesting. This observation leads to the application of evolutionary theory to anomalous sexual preferences, including forensically significant variations of sexual preference such as those manifested in paedophilia. Evolutionary theory is relevant to sexual behaviour directed towards children at several levels and in several different ways.

Current sexual behaviour and preferences have been shaped by ancestral variations in reproductive success, regardless of whether reproduction is currently the conscious goal. Natural selection has sculpted the male sexual preference system so that it tracks variations in female fertility. Sexually attractive features are those that have been associated with fertility and ability to produce high-quality offspring.

Male and female reproductive tactics are contingent upon circumstances. For example, male self-perceived attractiveness to women would be expected to affect the degree to which a man would compromise his mating preferences with those of a potential partner. There are a variety of other tactics that can be used by men depending on the context – sexual coercion, marrying a pre-pubescent girl (she will later become fertile) and so forth. The attractiveness of many of these options is affected by male social status. Women, of course, have their own set of preferences, tactics and counter-tactics.

Because of the asymmetry in the costs of reproduction borne by the sexes, women are much choosier than men (except where men provide long-term investment in offspring). As noted above, there is much greater variation in reproductive success among men than among women – men therefore compete more among themselves in a wide variety of ways and exhibit higher mating effort than do women (i.e. expend more effort and accept more risk in acquiring status and mating opportunities).

With that as background, we come to the first application of evolutionary theory to adult male sexual interactions with children – as a by-product of high mating effort and relative indifference to mate quality in short-term sexual interactions. This sort of an explanation does not apply to paedophilic preferences, only to behaviours. These behaviours are more likely in this instance to involve pubescent, rather than very young, girls and relatively antisocial men.

As to other applications, the male sexual preference system is an adaptation and thus ultimately an effect of genes. These genes, however, do not act at one point in time or act as a blueprint (who is there to read the blueprint?). Rather, genes participate with the rest of the organism throughout development – the organism must make itself. This is a tricky business because there are genes the effects of which are beneficial to one sex and harmful to the other, and all of these genes (save the sex-determining gene) exist in both male and female bodies.

There is thus a complex process of sexual differentiation that is driven by hormones (there are also recently discovered direct genetic effects). Perhaps the most complex part of this involves the masculinization of the brain. The brain, as the organ of behaviour, contains structures that are responsible for sex differences in reproductive behaviour and preferences. Darwinian theory and a growing body of comparative neuroscientific literature suggest that the sexual preference system involves separate structures that relate to different problems of reproduction in ancestral environments (these involve for males such things as attending to the correlates of female fertility, such as youthfulness and secondary sex characteristics). This modular organization is determined by the spatial and temporal distribution of in utero sex hormones in the brain. Because these modules are more or less distinct, they can hyperfunction or not function separately, raising the possibility that cues signalling youthfulness can become dominant over body shape cues signalling female fertility.

Although the latter possibility is simply speculation, the general outline of how the sexual preference system develops is not. A theory of the development of typical and anomalous sexual preferences in men must take into account the ultimate causes of male-typical sexual preferences and the proximal causes of their development within individuals through which these ultimate causes manifest themselves.

Talking about an evolutionary or Darwinian account of paedophilia is not to suggest that paedophilic sexual preferences have been directly selected for, but rather that any explanation of these preferences must be related to the design features of the male sexual preference system. It is necessary to understand what the system has been designed to do and what stimuli it uses. The theory makes strong predictions in this regard and even suggests something about how the system might be organized in the brain.

The term 'anomalous', when applied to sexual preferences, means that the preferences do not serve the reproductive functions for which they were designed. What are the possible explanations for anomalous preferences? It could involve pathology – the affected individual was anoxic in utero, infected with a virus, adversely affected by toxins ingested by the mother and so forth (the evidence, although scant with respect to paedophilia, generally supports the view that sexual preferences are developed very early (in utero)). Note that any explanation involving pathology must still appeal to the design features of the mechanism (for example, why an interest in children as opposed to trees?).

Another possibility is that the anomalous preferences are a by-product of some other characteristic that has been selected for. In this case, paedophilia would have at least some genetic basis (regrettably there have been no genetic studies of paedophilia to my knowledge). How could this work? One possibility is that the mother's immune system becomes sensitized to some aspect of the male fetus (e.g. the HY antigens expressed on the surface of all male cells save those in the placenta) and interferes with the hormonal process that masculinizes the brain. This sensitization would increase with each male child the mother carries. There is thus a trade-off here – the mother and her relatives benefit from sensitive immune systems at the cost of the mother's later born male children being more likely to have anomalous sexual preferences. Strong evidence for the neurohormonal theory of sexual preference development comes from the fraternal birth-order effect, in which the probability of a man preferring other men as sexual partners increases with each older brother he has borne to the same mother (e.g. Bogaert 2006).

Note that these explanations are not mutually exclusive. The final common path in the development of anomalous sexual preferences is a perturbation of brain development – this could be due to pathological causes, genetic causes, or both. For a more complete account of a Darwinian theory of paedophilia see Quinsey (2003).

Conclusion

In conclusion, this chapter offers several examples of the application of evolutionary psychology to forensic issues. There are many other examples in this growing literature. Enough, hopefully, has been said to illustrate the promise that evolutionary psychology offers of providing a consilient theory of antisocial and criminal behaviour.

REFERENCES

Bogaert, A. F. (2006) Biological versus nonbiological older brothers and men's sexual orientation. *Proceedings of the National Academy of Sciences*, 103: 10771–4.

Buss, D. M. (ed.) (2005) *The Handbook of Evolutionary Psychology*. Hoboken, NJ: Wiley.

Carroll, S. B. (2005) *Endless Forms Most Beautiful: The New Science of Evo Devo*. New York: Norton.

Coen, E. (1999) *The Art of Genes: How Organisms Make Themselves*. Oxford: Oxford University Press.

Daly, M. and Wilson, M. (1988) Evolutionary social psychology and family homicide. *Science*, 242: 519–24.

Harris, G. T., Rice, M. E., Hilton, N. Z., Lalumière, M. L. and Quinsey, V. L. (2007) Coercive and precocious sexuality as a fundamental aspect of psychopathy. *Journal of Personality Disorders*, 21: 1–27.

Kanazawa, S. (2003) Why productivity fades with age: the crime–genius connection. *Journal of Research in Personality*, 37: 257–72.

Lalumière, M. L., Harris, G. T., Quinsey, V. L. and Rice, M. E. (2005) *The Causes of Rape: Understanding Individual Differences in the Male Propensity for Sexual Aggression*. Washington, DC: American Psychological Association.

Quinsey, V. L. (2003) Etiology of anomalous sexual preferences in men. *Annals of the New York Academy of Sciences*, 989: 105–17.

Rowe, D. C. (2002) *Biology and Crime*. Los Angeles: Roxbury.

1.5 Eyewitness memory

Carolyn Semmler and Neil Brewer

See also chapter 2.6 False memory, chapter 2.9 Investigative interviewing.

Introduction

The memories of eyewitnesses play a central role in many police investigations and any subsequent legal decision making. Unfortunately, eyewitness memories are not infallible. This is readily demonstrated in the laboratory and is dramatically highlighted by the DNA exoneration cases in the United States. Over 200 innocent people, convicted and jailed for serious crimes, have thus far been exonerated by DNA evidence (Innocence Project 2007). The single biggest contributor to these false convictions has been problematic eyewitness evidence.

Since Loftus' (1979) early and influential work, eyewitness memory research has become a prominent area of psychological research. Eyewitness research has drawn upon diverse theoretical perspectives from cognitive and social psychology. Surprisingly, the latter area has been a little more prominent, perhaps reflecting a greater emphasis on understanding the impact of various practical procedures for gathering eyewitness evidence than on unravelling the intricacies of eyewitness memory and judgement processes. Encouragingly, experimental psychology has already offered practical solutions to many of the problems associated with eyewitness memory.

This is an overview, necessarily selective, of areas where programmatic research has explored factors contributing to witness unreliability and suggested ways of improving the quality of eyewitness evidence. The chapter's organization loosely parallels the sequence experienced by witnesses from the time of crime commission, through their involvement in a police investigation, to that in any subsequent trial.

The crime event

When a witness observes a crime, many factors can determine how well it is remembered. The viewing (i.e. encoding) conditions affect the amount of detail provided and its accuracy. For example, the greater the distance between the witness and the offender, the less detailed and accurate are witnesses' descriptions of the offender and the less likely they will be able to identify the offender from a group of photos (Lindsay *et al.* 2008). Similarly, the amount of time for which the witness views the offender also affects recognition accuracy (Memon, Hope and Bull 2003; Valentine, Pickering and Darling 2003).

Offender characteristics also influence witnesses' reports and judgements. The distinctiveness of an offender's appearance and behaviour can have a significant impact on witness testimony. Offenders who are more unusual in appearance are more easily identified, although this can lead witnesses to have greater confidence in their memory than is warranted by the accuracy of their testimony (Read 1995). Offenders who do or say things that are unexpected can also leave a lasting impression with the witness (Tuckey and Brewer 2003). The offender's race also affects witnesses' recognition performance. The 'cross-race' effect shows that witnesses attempting to recognize someone from another race are (a) less likely to correctly identify the offender if they are present in a group of photos and (b) more likely to incorrectly identify an innocent individual when the offender is not present (Meissner and Brigham 2001). Similar findings have been demonstrated with 'cross-age' and 'cross-gender' identification (e.g. Wright and Sladden 2003). Finally, witnesses who are confronted by an offender with a weapon have sometimes been shown to be less likely to identify the offender, leading researchers to suggest that a weapon draws the witness's focus of attention away from the face of the offender (Loftus, Loftus and Messo 1987).

There are also important witness variables that shape memory reports and eyewitness identification behaviour. The amount of stress or anxiety experienced by the witness during the event has been shown to alter witness testimony, but not simply by reducing the accuracy of the testimony. For example, stress has sometimes been shown to improve the number of accurately recalled central details of an event while memory for peripheral details is decreased (Christianson 1992). The evidence in this area of research is, however, somewhat mixed, perhaps reflecting the difficulties associated with effectively manipulating stress or anxiety in experimental settings.

The age of the witness is another important factor in determining both the quantity and quality of testimony (Dickinson, Poole and Laimon 2005). While the amount of testimony offered by very young children is likely to be small, it increases with age and, if children are given the opportunity to freely recall and report information about an event, their testimony can be highly accurate. But if children receive leading questions, or misinformation, they are very likely to be misled and report inaccuracies. They are also more likely to report inaccurate information consistent with their expectations. Finally, they have difficulty isolating the details of their memory for a specific event when they have experienced multiple similar events (such as occurs in cases of repeated sexual abuse). Children's ability to accurately identify offenders from photoarrays has also been systematically investigated. The most striking feature of this research is that children exhibit a strong tendency to make a positive identification. When the offender is not actually present in the lineup this tendency manifests itself in high rates of false identifications (Pozzulo and Lindsay 1998). Older adults (aged 60 to 80 years) also show a greater tendency than younger adults to choose from culprit-absent lineups (Memon and Gabbert 2003). In terms of older witnesses' testimonial recall, they tend to recall less and what they do recall is less likely to be accurate (Pansky, Koriat and Goldsmith 2005).

Between the event and initial contact with police

During the time between the event and the witness being interviewed by police (i.e. the retention interval), a number of factors can shape the memory reports of the witness. Both experimental and archival studies have shown that longer retention intervals are associated with a decrease in the amount of detail the witness reports about the event and the appearance of the offender. However, the accuracy of information recalled is less affected. Thus, while witnesses may recall less after longer retention intervals, much of what they do recall is likely to be accurate (assuming they are interviewed effectively) (Pansky *et al.* 2005). As far as recognition of offenders is concerned, delay tends to decrease the willingness of witnesses to choose from a lineup, reducing the rate of false identification when the culprit is absent, but also reducing correct identifications (Shepherd 1983; Valentine *et al.* 2003).

An unavoidable reality of many witnesses' experience is that they will interact with co-witnesses to the event before they are interviewed by the police. Such interactions can affect subsequent witness reports. In particular, the witness who volunteers information first is likely to change the report of a second witness

(Gabbert, Memon and Allan 2003). If the volunteered information is inaccurate this can prove problematic, especially as corroboration is likely to be viewed by the police as an indicator of testimonial reliability. Similarly, many witnesses are likely to repeatedly retrieve and retell the details of the event, particularly if it was traumatic. While repeated retrieval can help to strengthen memory for the event, it may also systematically reduce the amount of testimony by rendering related but unrehearsed information less accessible (a phenomenon known as retrieval-induced forgetting) (Shaw, Bjork and Handal 1995).

Contact with police

Contact with the police provides opportunities for a number of other variables to shape witnesses' memory reports. One of the first and most important tasks of the witness is to describe the offender. Requests for a description typically don't yield detailed accounts; witnesses provide on average 7.2 descriptors (Meissner, Sporer and Schooler 2007). The accuracy of the person descriptions provided by witnesses is affected by similar variables to those influencing recall of event details and identification evidence. As well as being asked to give a verbal description, witnesses may sometimes be asked to build a visual likeness of the offender using sophisticated software. Some evidence suggests that providing a description of the offender or constructing a composite likeness may negatively affect a witness's ability to subsequently identify the offender from a lineup (Wells, Charman and Olson 2005).

One major, and now much researched, problem identified by eyewitness memory researchers is the post-event misinformation effect. This occurs when a witness is introduced to detail or information not included in the original event and later reports this (mis)information as having been seen (Gerrie, Garry and Loftus 2005). One of the ways in which this effect can be produced is by leading interview questions, which imply characteristics of the event and/or its participants that are inaccurate. The broad issue of interviewing witnesses is the focus of chapter 2.9 (this volume).

Identifying the offender

As well as providing details about the event and offender, witnesses may also be asked to view a formal identification parade. There has been considerable research examining determinants of the identification behaviour of witnesses.

As well as the focus on variables discussed earlier in this chapter, much of this research has been motivated by the aim of developing procedures likely to decrease the rate at which witnesses wrongly identify innocent individuals (Wells 1978). Researchers have proposed different methods for presenting lineups. Under standard conditions, witnesses are shown a lineup in which all members are seen simultaneously and the witness is asked to choose among them. This type of format can create a tendency for witnesses to compare the individuals to one another and, instead of only choosing when someone closely matches their memory, choose the individual who (out of those present) looks most like the perpetrator. To overcome this problem researchers have proposed that witnesses should be shown individuals one at a time, and be required to make a decision about each individual before being shown the next person in the lineup. Once the witness has made a positive identification, the presentation ceases. This sequential lineup method typically reduces the rate of false identifications from culprit-absent lineups, but may also come at the cost of reduced accurate identifications (Steblay *et al.* 2001).

Researchers have also been interested in identifying ways of improving the composition of lineups so that the foils (individuals known to be innocent) provide enough protection against mistaken identification of an innocent suspect. Providing foils who match the description of the offender is important, rather than simply having foils who may look similar to the suspect but result in the suspect standing out in the lineup because only s/he clearly matches the witness's description (Wells, Rydell and Seelau 1993). Another method for reducing mistaken identifications has been to warn the witness that the perpetrator may not be in the lineup and to emphasize the option of responding that the perpetrator is not in the lineup. These instructions reduce the likelihood that a witness will simply assume that the perpetrator is present, thus reducing the likelihood of a mistaken identification (Steblay 1997). Researchers have also made the important recommendation that lineup administrators should not know which individual is the suspect in the lineup, thus eliminating any potential influence they may have on the witness's decision.

Assessing the accuracy of witness evidence

A major problem facing police and the courts is how to determine whether the witness has provided accurate testimony (whether it involves details of the recalled event, a description of the offender or an identification). Thus, determining the relationship between variables thought to reflect the accuracy of the witnesses' testimony and actual accuracy has been a key issue for researchers. Among the most studied independent markers of accuracy is witness confidence or certainty. Interestingly, surveys have shown that many members of the criminal justice community believe that the confidence with which testimony is given indicates its accuracy. Further, for eyewitness reports, confidence does reliably discriminate correct from incorrect answers at the within-subjects level (e.g. Perfect 2002). In other words, witnesses do seem to have a reasonable idea about which of the items they report are most likely to be accurate. Indeed, there is evidence that confidence judgements guide witnesses' decisions to volunteer or withhold information, and shape the level of detail that they are prepared to provide in answer to specific questions (Weber and Brewer 2008).

For eyewitness identification decisions, however, there are many variables which can alter confidence while leaving accuracy unaffected, thereby reducing the former's predictive value under many circumstances. For example, having witnesses repeatedly recall information about the event can increase confidence in that information, as can preparing witnesses for court. With regard to identification evidence, confidence can be greatly altered by the feedback provided to witnesses after they have made their identification decision (e.g. making comments such as 'Well done. That's the guy', indicating that they have picked the police suspect or that a co-witness has made the same decision). Similarly, disconfirming feedback can reduce witnesses' confidence in their identification decisions. Feedback can also distort estimates of the quality of viewing conditions (such as estimates of distance from the offender and time in view) and the quality of the identification (ease of the decision and time taken to make the decision) (Douglass and Steblay 2006). These effects have reinforced the need for lineup administrators to be blind to the suspect's identity, and for witnesses' confidence estimates to be recorded immediately after reporting their judgements to reduce the likelihood of social influences on confidence assessments. With these safeguards in place, research looking at the confidence–accuracy relationship indicates that confidence can provide a useful (but by no means infallible) independent marker of identification accuracy for adults (Brewer and Wells 2006), though not for children (Keast, Brewer and Wells 2007).

Another marker of accuracy used in assessing identification evidence is the length of time that the witness takes when making the identification decision. On average, accurate decisions are faster than inaccurate ones. Despite attempts to determine an optimum rule for classifying accurate versus inaccurate decisions based on decision latency, the relationship appears to be governed not only by the degree of match between the witness's memory of the offender and the lineup members but also by factors such as retention interval, lineup size and presentation method (Brewer *et al.* 2006). These complexities mean that, at present, it is difficult to conclude anything more specific than that, as the length of time taken to make a decision increases, the likelihood that the decision will be correct decreases.

Police, lawyers and jurors are also particularly swayed by the (in)consistency of witness testimony. Eyewitnesses may, for example, report an item of information on one occasion that clearly contradicts something said earlier, or report some information that had never been mentioned at previous interviews (i.e. reminiscence). Contradictions and reminiscence are likely to be viewed as indicators of unreliability by the courts. Yet the research data show two (perhaps surprising) findings. First, while contradictions are indicative of inaccuracy at the level of the individual item concerned, they are only weakly related to the overall or global level of accuracy evident in the testimony. Second, not only are reminiscent items to be expected when witnesses are provided with novel retrieval cues but they are also frequently accurate and, like contradictions, not indicative of unreliable testimony overall (Fisher, Brewer and Mitchell 2009).

Conclusion

Scientific research on eyewitness memory issues has grown steadily in the last twenty to thirty years. The ways in which a wide array of variables influence eyewitness memory are gradually becoming clearer. It is important to bear in mind that seldom do these advances in knowledge permit the exact specification of circumstances (e.g. the exposure duration to the offender at the crime or the composition of the lineup) under which some element of an eyewitness's memory will be accurate or flawed. This is because the memories, reports and behaviours of witnesses reflect a complex set of interactions between variables rather than the influence of any single factor. Indeed, it is the understanding of these interactions that will be crucial for advancing knowledge in this area. Nevertheless, as we have learned more about the characteristics of human and, particularly, eyewitness memory, there have been corresponding developments in procedures that enhance the reliability of witness reports and identification decisions. Hopefully, these trends will continue, allowing for continued improvements in the collection and evaluation of eyewitness evidence.

FURTHER READING

Brewer, N. and Williams, K. D. (eds.) (2005) *Psychology and Law: An Empirical Perspective*. New York: Guilford Press.

Cutler, B. L. and Penrod, S. D. (1995) *Mistaken Identification: The Eyewitness, Psychology, and the Law*. New York: Cambridge University Press.

Lindsay, R. C. L., Ross, D. F., Read, J. D. and Toglia, M. (eds.) (2007) *Handbook of Eyewitness Psychology*, vol. 2: *Memory for People*. Mahwah, NJ: Erlbaum.

Toglia, M., Read, J. D., Ross, D. F. and Lindsay, R. C. L. (eds.) (2006) *Handbook of Eyewitness Psychology*, vol. 1: *Memory for Events*. Mahwah, NJ: Erlbaum.

REFERENCES

Brewer, N., Caon, A., Todd, C. and Weber, N. (2006) Eyewitness identification accuracy and response latency. *Law and Human Behavior*, 30: 31–50.

Brewer, N. and Wells, G. L. (2006). The confidence–accuracy relationship in eyewitness identification: effects of lineup instructions, foil similarity and target-absent base rates. *Journal of Experimental Psychology: Applied*, 12: 11–30.

Christianson, S. (1992) Emotional stress and eyewitness memory: a critical review. *Psychological Bulletin*, 112: 284–309.

Dickinson, J. J., Poole, D. A. and Laimon, R. L. (2005) Children's recall and testimony. In N. Brewer and K. D. Williams (eds.), *Psychology and Law: An Empirical Perspective*, pp. 151–76. New York: Guilford Press.

Douglass, A. B. and Steblay, N. (2006) Memory distortion in eyewitnesses: a meta-analysis of the post-identification feedback effect. *Applied Cognitive Psychology*: 20: 859–69.

Fisher, R., Brewer, N. and Mitchell, G. (2009) The relation between consistency and accuracy of eyewitness testimony. In R. Bull, T. Valentine and T. Williamson (eds.), *Handbook of Psychology of Investigative Interviewing: Current Developments and Future Directions*, pp. 121–36. Chichester: Wiley.

Gabbert, F., Memon, A. and Allan, K. (2003). Memory conformity: can eyewitnesses influence each other's memories for an event? *Applied Cognitive Psychology*, 17: 533–43.

Gerrie, M. P., Garry, M. and Loftus, E. F. (2005) False memories. In N. Brewer and K. D. Williams (eds.), *Psychology and Law: An Empirical Perspective*. New York: Guilford Press.

Innocence Project (2007). *Innocence Project*. www.innocenceproject.org (accessed September 2007).

Keast, A., Brewer, N. and Wells, G. L. (2007) Children's metacognitive judgments in an eyewitness identification task. *Journal of Experimental Child Psychology*, 97: 286–314.

Lindsay, R. C. L., Semmler, C., Weber, N., Brewer, N. and Lindsay, M. R. (2008) Eyewitness identification accuracy from a distance: why there should not be a 15 m 'rule'. *Law and Human Behavior*, 32: 526–35.

Loftus, E. F. (1979) *Eyewitness Testimony*. Cambridge, MA: Harvard University Press.

Loftus, E. F., Loftus, G. R. and Messo, J. (1987) Some facts about 'weapon focus'. *Law and Human Behavior*, 11: 55–62.

Meissner, C. A. and Brigham, J. C. (2001) Thirty years of investigating the own-race bias in memory for faces: a meta-analytic review. *Psychology, Public Policy, and Law*, 7: 3–35.

Meissner, C. A., Sporer, S. L. and Schooler, J. W. (2007) Person descriptions as eyewitness evidence. In R. C. L. Lindsay, D. F. Ross, J. D. Read and M. P. Toglia (eds.), *Handbook of Eyewitness Psychology*, vol. 2: *Memory for People*, pp. 1–34. Mahwah, NJ: Erlbaum.

Memon, A. and Gabbert, F. (2003) Improving the identification accuracy of senior witnesses: do prelineup questions and sequential testing help? *Journal of Applied Psychology*, 88: 341–7.

Memon, A., Hope, L. and Bull, R. (2003) Exposure duration: effects on eyewitness accuracy and confidence. *British Journal of Psychology*, 94: 339–54.

Pansky, A., Koriat, A. and Goldsmith, M. (2005) Eyewitness recall and testimony. In N. Brewer and K. D. Williams (eds.), *Psychology and Law: An Empirical Perspective*, pp. 93–150. New York: Guilford.

Perfect, T. J. (2002) When does eyewitness confidence predict performance? In T. J. Perfect and B. L. Schwartz (eds.), *Applied Metacognition*, pp. 95–120. Cambridge: Cambridge University Press.

Pozzulo, J. D. and Lindsay, R. C. L. (1998) Identification accuracy of children versus adults: a meta-analysis. *Law and Human Behavior*, 22: 549–70.

Read, J. D. (1995) The availability heuristic in person identification: the sometimes misleading consequences of enhanced contextual information. *Applied Cognitive Psychology*, 9: 91–121.

Shaw, J. S., Bjork, R. A. and Handal, A. (1995) Retrieval-induced forgetting in an eyewitness memory paradigm. *Psychonomic Bulletin and Review*, 2: 249–53.

Shepherd, J. W. (1983) Identification after long delays. In S. M. A. Lloyd-Bostock and B. R. Clifford (eds.), *Evaluating Witness Evidence*, pp. 173–87. Chichester: Wiley.

Steblay, N. M. (1997) Social influence in eyewitness recall: a meta-analytic review of lineup instruction effects. *Law and Human Behavior*, 21: 283–97.

Steblay, N., Dysart, J., Fulero, S. and Lindsay, R. C. L. (2001) Eyewitness accuracy rates in sequential and simultaneous lineup presentations: a meta-analytic comparison. *Law and Human Behavior*, 25: 459–73.

Tuckey, M. R. and Brewer, N. (2003) The influence of schemas, stimulus ambiguity, and interview schedule on eyewitness memory over time. *Journal of Experimental Psychology: Applied*, 9: 101–18.

Valentine, T., Pickering, A. and Darling, S. (2003) Characteristics of eyewitness identification that predict the outcome of real lineups. *Applied Cognitive Psychology*, 17: 969–93.

Weber, N. and Brewer, N. (2008) Eyewitness recall: regulation of grain size and the role of confidence. *Journal of Experimental Psychology: Applied*, 14: 50–60.

Wells, G. L. (1978) Applied eyewitness testimony research: system variables and estimator variables. *Journal of Personality and Social Psychology*, 36: 1546–57.

Wells, G. L., Charman, S. D. and Olson, E. A. (2005) Building face composites can harm lineup identification performance. *Journal of Experimental Psychology: Applied*, 11: 147–56.

Wells, G. L., Rydell, S. M. and Seelau, E. P. (1993) The selection of distractors for eyewitness lineups. *Journal of Applied Psychology*, 78: 835–44.

Wright, D. B. and Sladden, B. (2003) An own gender bias and the importance of hair in face recognition. *Acta Psychologica*, 114: 101–14.

1.6 Facet meta-theory

Jennifer M. Brown

See also chapter 1.1 Action system applied to forensic topics, chapter 8.2 Designing research using facet theory, chapter 8.3 Drawing out the meaning in data: multidimensional scaling within forensic psychology research.

Definition

Facet theory derives from the work of Louis Guttman, whose early research was concerned with developing scales but was troubled by defining their content (Levy 2005). It was his conviction that behavioural research dealing with complex issues should proceed logically by conceptualizing and defining in substantive terms what is being studied before proceeding with data collection (Guttman and Greenbaum 1998, p. 14). Guttman's own definition of a theory is 'a hypothesis of a correspondence between a definitional system for a universe of observations and an aspect of the empirical structure of those observations, together with a rationale for such an hypothesis' (Levy 2005, p. 179).

Embedded within this are the key tenets of a facet theory approach, i.e. the design of observations (which is detailed in another entry within this volume) and the correspondence with the empirical structure of those observations. The principle of contiguity states that items which are more similar in their conceptual definition will be more similar empirically. The empirical relationship, often demonstrated as correlation coefficients, is revealed through a companion suite of multidimensional statistical analyses whereby variables are represented in an n-dimensional space, which is partitioned on the basis that conceptually similar items will be more highly correlated and found closer together in the space. The notion of a rationale is important as it is this that provides the warrant or justification for the content, but crucially enables research to proceed cumulatively to develop theory building and verification. Guttman proposed four theoretical constructs for such a project: definition, specification, rationale and hypothesis.

The metatheoretical aspect of the approach is that the design and analytic principles provide the scaffolding onto which any content theory can be built. By way of example, Hornik (2007) states that in the area of marketing, it is so complex that 'many believe that no progress could be made towards the development of theories'. Multivariate statistical analyses provide sophisticated tools for analysis, but as Hornik notes 'we still lack the tools for constructing [an] abstract framework which might help to define problem variables'. Facet meta-theory provides a means to overcome this deficiency.

A succinct statement of the approach is provided by Hackett (1993, p. 58):

Researchers may chose to adopt a facet theory design as the approach provides a definitional system for the observations which will be made and the rationale for hypotheses about relationships within the data. The definitional system is in the form of a mapping sentence, which embodies a series of multiple variables and hypotheses regarding their empirical relationships. The empirical aspect of the theory is the intercorrelations amongst observations. In adopting a facet design 3 types of sets must be defined: (1) the population whose members are to be classified (2) the variables which will be classified (3) the range of responses categories for the variables.

Principles

Facets and their constituent elements are ways of classifying variables and are formally laid out in a mapping sentence, which Hackett describes as being tailored to suit the specific investigation and enables the definitional system of observations to be in a form in which the researcher may readily see the correspondence between it and the empirical data, thus facilitating a recognition of a systematic relationship in the data. Guttman added verbal connectives in order to make a mapping sentence more readable. The mapping sentence not only provides an exhaustive definition of the universe of observations being considered, but is itself a template for the evolution and development of an area of research because such formal definitions are required for scientific progress. Subsequent studies lead to correction, deletion, extensions and insertions (adding further content facets) (Levy 2005). She further articulates the general hypothesis of facet theory, which is that the specification of formal roles for facets in a mapping sentence provides a rationale for structural theories. The concept of regionality supports this general hypothesis. 'Regional hypotheses relate to the roles that the content facets of the variables play in partitioning the [MDS]space' (Levy 2005, p. 182). Facets may play one of three roles: polar, which is an unordered or circular role whereby each element of the facet gravitates out in a different direction emanating from a common point of origin rather like the wedges of a cake; modular or ordered facets in relation to a polar facet; axial, where the order is unrelated to that of other facets. The mapping sentence gives an indication of the role that the facet is hypothesized to play, which in turn is based on the rationale. This then leads to regional hypotheses which predict the manner in which the structures can be retrieved through partitioning of a multidimensional space. The combination of roles leads to the generation of geometric shapes describing the relationships each facet plays, thereby setting out the structural model hypothesized to explain subsequent empirical observations. A single facet playing a polar role has a structure termed a circumplex, which can be graphically represented as in figure 1.6.1.

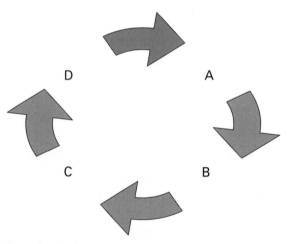

Figure 1.6.1 Circumplex structure

This is based on a correlation matrix of the following character:

Variable	A	B	C	D
A				
B	high			
C	low	high		
D	high	low	high	

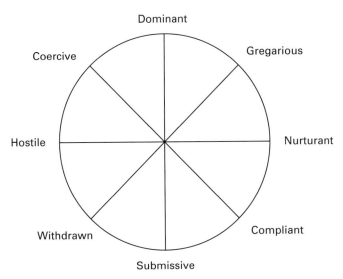

Figure 1.6.2 Blackburn's chart of interpersonal reactions in closed living environments

Blackburn's interpersonal circle is an example of a circumplex in which Blackburn and Renwick (1996) describe personality characteristics as octants, as shown in figure 1.6.2

The pattern of correlations should reflect an equidistant spacing of the scales, varying progressively from positive to scales adjacent in the circle to negative to those opposite, which indeed they do as reported by Blackburn and Renwick.

Porter and Alison (2006) found a circumplex structure in their analysis of robbery offenders' behaviours and Anderson (2002) reported a similar structure when analysing sexual offenders.

A structure frequently reported in the research literature is a radex, which comprises facets playing a modulating role combined with a polar role. Canter *et al.* (2003) presented a conceptual model of rape behaviours in which facets defined as hostility, control, theft and involvement were hypothesized as playing a polar role whilst levels of increasing violation played a modular role thereby creating a radex hypothesis. That is to say, rape is an act of violation that can be described in terms of levels (personal, physical, sexual) of violation, with sexual being the most frequent and radiating out from the centre of gravity in the same order to moderate the variety of behaviours categorized as hostility, control, theft and involvement. Canter and colleagues were thus able to derive two hypotheses:

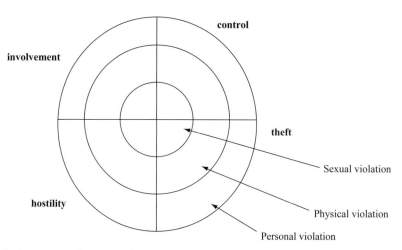

Figure 1.6.3 Radex structure of rape (after Canter *et al.* 2003)

1. The frequency pattern of actions in sexual assaults will radiate out from the centre, with the higher-frequency focal behaviours located at the centre and having a common sequence across the four content facets.
2. Behaviours will contain conceptually related items within the four content facets.

Variables derived from rape statements were categorized as belonging to a content facet and simultaneously the modulating facet, e.g. offenders forcing a victim to make sexual comments was classified as a hostile personal violation, whereas the offender offering a sexual comment was classed as an involvement sexual violation. By and large a multidimensional analysis mapped the variables in conformity to the hypothesized radex structure. Canter *et al.* conclude 'the combination of a modular facet of violation and a polarizing facet comprised of four modes of interaction results in a composite model of rape'.

An important goal of facet theory is to identify and establish recurring patterns and regularities (Guttman and Greenbaum 1998, p. 31). Through replication and confirmation, such recurring findings may lead to the ultimate goal of establishing laws of behaviour.

Santilla *et al.* (2003) demonstrated the replication aspect by using Canter and Fritzon's (1998) two-facet model of arson and applied this to juvenile firesetters. Their findings in general supported the facet model but with some important diffrences. This cumulative development of theorizing relates to the iterative nature of facet theory alluded to by Levy (2005).

Some progress towards identifying patterns and regularities has been observed by Canter (2000). He argues that forensic psychologists need to have explanatory frameworks that generate hypotheses about offender characteristics and associated offending behaviours. Facet theory offers such a framework. He proposes a facet playing a modulating role in which highly frequent or core activities typify a crime, but because they are common they are unlikely to differentiate offenders. As activities move away from this centre of gravity, actions become progressively more differentiated until at the extreme they become idiosyncratic or signature acts. Thus this facet is ordered in terms of general to specific and is also associated with frequency, the general being the more frequent. He further argues that crimes may be defined in terms of content facets, underlying which are notions that there is a transaction between the offender and victim whereby the victim is either the object or acts as a vehicle for some purpose or is a person. As such, this facet plays a polar role. The interaction of these two types of facet creates a radex that might reflect all offences to a greater or lesser extent. Canter reports such a structure with reference to serial murder, rape and arson.

Conclusion

Brown and Barnett (2000, p. 112) suggest that theoretical work can be undertaken with a facet theory approach in a 'bottom-up' way, i.e. when researchers are exploring a relatively new field or novel topic there may not be an obvious rationale to guide conceptualization of relevant variables. Thus exploratory analyses may be undertaken with a view to clarifying domains. Horvath and Brown (2005) wanted to develop a definition of drug-assisted rape and undertook some preliminary analyses to reveal a circumplex structure of consensual, contracted and coerced sex.

Brown and Barnett (2000, p. 118) précis the facet approach as being 'a metatheoretical framework into which a specific content theory is constructed and empirically verified. Facet theory comprises an input logic that defines conceptual formulations, a set of procedures for designing empirical observations and a package of multivariate statistics for analysing data. Ideally these should be used *in toto*.' Often they are not, which diminishes the cumulative aspects of the approach.

FURTHER READING

The essay by Shlomit Levy (2005) and paper by Guttman and Greenbaum (1998) provide a helpful overview of the origins and principles of facet theory. David Canter's (2000) paper on offender profiling and criminal differentiation presents a generalized model, whilst his research on rape with colleagues Bennell, Alison and Reddy (2003) provides a helpful account of the use of facet theory in practice.

REFERENCES

Anderson, D. (2002) The utility of interpersonal circumplex theory in research and treatment of sexual offenders. *Forum on Correctional Research*, 14: 28–30.

Blackburn, R. and Renwick, S. (1996) Rating scales for measuring the interpersonal circle in forensic psychiatric patients. *Psychological Assessment*, 8: 76–84.

Brown, J. and Barnett, J. (2000) Facet theory: an approach to research. In G. Breakwell, H. Hammond and C. Fife-Schaw (eds.), *Research Methods in Psychology*, 2nd edn, pp. 105–18. London: Sage.

Canter, D. (2000) Offender profiling and criminal differentiation. *Legal and Criminological Psychology*, 5: 23–46.

Canter, D. V., Bennell, C., Alison, L. J. and Reddy, S. (2003) Differentiating sex offences: a behaviorally based thematic classification of stranger rapes. *Behavioral Sciences and the Law*, 21: 157–74.

Canter, D. V. and Fritzon, K. (1998) Differentiating arsonists: a model of fire setting actions and characteristics. *Legal and Criminological Psychology*, 3: 73–96.

Guttman, R. and Greenbaum, C. (1998) Facet theory: its development and current status. *European Psychologist*, 3: 13–36.

Hackett, P. (1993) Orthodontic treatment: a facet theory approach to the study of personal reasons for the uptake of treatment for malocclusion. *Social Behavior and Personality*, 21: 55–6.

Hornik, J. (2007) The facet design approach to the construction of multivariate marketing models. *European Journal of Marketing*, 8: 146–57.

Horvath, M. and Brown, J. (2005) Drug assisted rape and sexual assault: definitional, conceptual and methodological developments. *Journal of Investigative Psychology and Offender Profiling*, 2: 203–10.

Levy, S. (2005) Guttman, Louis. *Encyclopaedia of Social Measurement*, vol. 2, pp. 175–88. Chichester: Wiley.

Porter, L. E. and Alison, L. J. (2006) Behavioural coherence in group robbery: a circumplex model of offender and victim interaction. *Aggressive Behaviour*, 32: 330–42.

Santilla, P., Häkkänen, H., Alison, L. and Whyte, C. (2003) Juvenile fire setters; crime scene actions and offender characteristics. *Legal and Criminological Psychology*, 8: 1–20.

1.7 Head injury and offending

T. M. McMillan

Introduction

Head injury is the leading cause of disability and death in young adults (Tagliaferri *et al.* 2006). Around three in 1,000 of the population in the UK are likely to suffer head injury each year. The main causes are accidents (road traffic, falls, sports) and assaults, and in a significant proportion of cases alcohol or drugs are involved (Jennett 1996). Risk of sustaining a head injury is associated with young males, drug or alcohol abuse/intoxication, lower socioeconomic status and history of previous head injury; these risk factors are similar to those associated with antisocial acts and criminal prosecution. Accidental causation can lead to civil claims for compensation for personal injury. For these reasons people with head injury are likely to be found commonly in court cases. Moreover, given that head injury can cause persisting and significant effects on cognitive function and personality (including control of emotions) in addition to physical limitations, assessment and advice regarding the legal processes (e.g. fitness to plead), appropriate placement, treatment and rehabilitation can be central to the case. With regard to the last, psychosocial factors that have the potential to be modified are related to significant changes in disability over the long term after head injury (Whitnall *et al.* 2006).

However, for a variety of reasons, the relevance of a history of head injury may be not be considered if it is not a central issue in the legal case. A sizeable proportion (e.g. 25–33%) of head injuries are not recorded in hospital (Thornhill *et al.* 2000), sometimes because the injury is not life threatening and there are other acute injuries, or alternatively when there are no other severe injuries, the severity of the head injury might be underestimated. In the latter case an individual could be discharged from hospital still suffering from post-traumatic amnesia for a time, and might legitimately not remember subsequent actions during that time (McMillan *et al.* 2009). In the former example, more persisting changes caused by the brain injury could be associated with impulsive or antisocial behaviour but the potential link with the head injury is not made.

There is some evidence to support the tenet that head injury is often not considered in forensic settings, including from work in Australia, North and South America and Europe (Schofield 2006; Slaughter *et al.* 2003; Colantonio *et al.* 2007; de Souza and Alberto 2003; Leon-Carrion and Chacartegui 2003). The often-quoted reports by Lewis *et al.* (1986, 1988) note that *all* of the 15 adult prisoners on death row and 14 juveniles condemned to death in the USA at that time had a history of head injury. On closer inspection of these studies, head injury with loss of consciousness or requiring hospital admission was evident in lower proportions (67% and 58% respectively). Nevertheless the incidence of head injury is high. More recently a similarly high incidence (75%) was reported in a qualitative study in a USA 'death row' sample (Freedman and Hemenway 2000). However, given the overlap between demographic risk factors in offending and head injury populations, it is difficult to attribute a causal relationship between head injury and offending; more sophisticated studies are required.

Neuropathology and neuropsychology

It has been long understood that head injury can have significant effects on cognition, personality and behaviour. Impairment of concentration and memory for new information is common, as is executive dysfunction – characterized by reduced information processing speed and reduced ability to plan, organize, think flexibly and solve problems. Changes in personality can often include egocentricity, tactlessness, impulsivity, poor judgement, poor insight, lack of concern, irritability and aggression, childishness and apathy. These changes can lead to offending, commonly found as violence or sexually inappropriate behaviour. Several brain areas have been associated with the production of such impulsive, disinhibited, aggressive, violent and antisocial behaviour. These include prefrontal and medial temporal cortical areas, and several subcortical structures including septum, amygdala, cingulum, hippocampus, thalamus and hypothalamus. Damage to ventromedial and orbital frontal cortices is associated with antisocial behaviour, probably via impaired decision making and planning (Damasio *et al.* 1990). A number of case studies have attested to this, including the notable case of EVR. This is the case of a 35-year-old man, described as a role model socially, until an orbitofrontal meningioma that required a bilateral frontal resection was found. Subsequently his cognitive function remained above average on tests of intellect, memory and executive function. However, he was no longer able to function as a responsible parent, or to work consistently, he was divorced (twice), became bankrupt and ultimately ended up in sheltered accommodation. It is thought that he had difficulty in appraising positive from negative actions in terms of social norms and likely contingencies, a function that is difficult to encapsulate in routine neuropsychological testing (Eslinger and Damasio 1988). Larger-scale studies support a link between ratings by self and significant others of aggression and violence and ventromedial frontal damage (Grafman *et al.* 1996).

Sudden rage has been associated with abnormality in the temporal cortex and with subcortical abnormality (van Elst *et al.* 2000). Sometimes referred to as 'episodic dyscontrol syndrome', it is commonly described as sometimes seemingly unprovoked, explosive aggression that may be unfocused in terms of target (i.e. nearest), may seem primitive (e.g. including biting) and can often be perceived as dangerous. Between outbursts the individual often seems sociable and friendly (Maletzky 1973).

Functional brain-imaging studies have associated temporal lobe abnormality with violent and/or sexual offenders, some studies implicating both frontal and temporal lobes. Few of these studies are specifically on head injury, and many use (small) samples recruited from forensic psychiatric settings (Raine *et al.* 2001).

What is clear from these studies is that damage to brain areas that have been associated with antisocial behaviour is common after head injury, especially where the brain damage is severe.

Post-traumatic amnesia and severity of injury

This refers to a period of time from recovery of consciousness until return of orientation and continuous memory for day-to-day events. In PTA there may be 'islands' of memory in a sea of amnesia (Russell and Nathan 1946). During this time some individuals appear obviously confused, while others can seem to have recovered. An example might be sports concussion, where the player returns to the match, appears unaffected, but on the following day remembers nothing of the play. The relevance in a forensic context is the potential for (i) partial or complete amnesia for events after the injury that is enduring; (ii) an association with retrograde amnesia (i.e. absence of memory prior to the injury), although there is potential for this to recover, usually with more remote events returning first; (iii) issues pertaining to responsibility for actions or fitness to plead during PTA. These are best considered on an individual basis. Although aggression is not uncommon during PTA, it is commonly associated with thwarting of goal-directed behaviour (e.g. if prevented from leaving a room) or general agitation or irritability when confused. Tools are available for assessing PTA prospectively (Ponsford *et al.* 2004) or retrospectively (McMillan *et al.* 1996).

It is relevant to consider the heterogeneity within the head injury population both in terms of severity of injury and outcome. More than 90% of head injuries are mild, with brief loss of consciousness and post-traumatic amnesia (see below) lasting for less than 24 hours. Here, a good recovery is expected in the vast majority within days, weeks or a few months. Where the head injury is more severe (loss of consciousness for more than 30 minutes and PTA lasting for more than 24 hours) some degree of persisting cognitive impairment and change in personality becomes likely. Cognitive impairment most commonly affects information processing speed, memory for new information and executive function. Change in personality can include impulsivity, impaired judgement, social disinhibition, egocentricity, apathy, indifference, tactlessness and a reduced threshold for irritability, aggression and violence. For many, even after severe head injury, persisting physical disability is relatively uncommon. In many cases, cognitive impairment and personality change are not immediately obvious, leading to head injury being described as a 'hidden epidemic' and not alerting an interviewer to this potentially significant issue (McMillan and Greenwood 2003).

The important issues here concern assessment of the validity of evidence in legal cases, responsibility for actions, ability to instruct counsel and follow legal proceedings, and implications for support, monitoring in the community and treatment.

Prevalence of head injury in an offending population

There is relatively little strong evidence here, and that which exists is often based on uncorroborated self-report of head injury in samples rather than in populations. For example, Schofield *et al.* (2006) randomly sampled 200 recently incarcerated men in Australia and found that 82% had a history of head injury, similar to a finding of 86% (of n = 118) in New Zealand (Barnfield and Leatham 1998). A cross-sectional sample in a US county jail (n = 69) reported that 87% had a history of head injury (Slaughter *et al.* 2003). In forensic mental health head injury is less commonly reported. A Canadian study reported a history of head injury in 23% of a population of 394 (Colantonio *et al.* 2007), similar to the rate found in a sample (n = 50) of forensic psychiatric patients in the US (Martell 1992).

Some studies have looked at the prevalence of head injury in specific offender groups, such as sexual offenders. In a cross-sectional study, Del Bello *et al.* (1999) looked at 25 participants in a rehabilitation programme for male sex offenders, and compared them to 15 demographically matched bipolar disorder, non-offenders. They found that whereas 36% of offenders had a history of head injury before their first sexual offence, this was the case for only 7% of the non-offenders. The proportion of offenders with both head injury and bipolar disorder was even higher (four out of eight), although the sample was clearly small.

The prevalence of head injury in the general population is difficult to determine for several reasons (for example, distinguishing between an event of head injury and recovery), but is likely to be less than 2%. Prevalence of head injury will be higher in samples where risk factors both for head injury and offending are higher, nevertheless the rates of head injury reported in offenders are high.

Relationships between head injury and offending

There are few well-controlled or prospective studies. However, a prospective study on a Finnish birth cohort (n = 12,068), checked national registers of hospitalization for ICD head injury codes up to the age of 15, and cross-referenced Ministry of Justice data on convictions up to the age of 31 (Timonen *et al.* 2002). Overall 2.7% of males had a head injury. After adjustment for demographic factors, head injury during childhood increased the risk of offending 1.6 fold. In a subgroup of males with mental health problems the risk was elevated to 4.1 fold. Figures for females were not calculated because of a low frequency of offenders. The authors point out that there could have been undetected factors increasing the risk both of head injury and offending (e.g. ADHD, poor parental control).

Others report that sexual offending and violence are significant problems after head injury, particularly in males, although they are limited by their retrospective non-blind design (Simpson *et al.* 1999). Included here are findings of a higher incidence of head injury sustained as a child in violent as opposed to non-violent offenders (Leon-Carrion and Chacartegui-Ramos 2003). Carswell *et al.* (2004) compared young offenders and a representative group of adolescents from a similar geographical area. Key factors distinguishing groups were higher incidences of substance abuse and head injury in the offender group.

Although the importance of controlling for socioeconomic factors is recognized (e.g. Turkstra *et al.* 2003), assessment of head injury severity is often by self-report without recourse to hospital admission data or validated retrospective methods of assessment, allowing a potentially significant bias in these studies.

Conclusion

It is evident that a head injury sustained around the time of an offence can be significant in assessing a case, even when the injury is not severe, if there is potential for the individual involved not to have had time to recover. The possible occurrence of a head injury should be actively considered if an individual has been involved in an assault, road traffic accident or fall, and where possible this should be corroborated by scrutiny of hospital records. Where there is a distant history of a head injury, again the occurrence and severity should be verified in medical records using primary sources when possible and evidence for other episodes of antisocial behaviour since the event investigated. Certainly the effects of head injury on behaviour have an obvious potential to lead to arrest and conviction, but given the high incidence of head injury this does not arise in most cases.

It is likely that several social and demographic factors together increase the risk of offending, and future research needs to establish the extent to which head injury alters this trajectory. What is also clear is that the forensic literature is sparse and not well linked to neurorehabilitation literature in terms of advice, education, support and treatment that might improve outcome when offenders return to the community.

FURTHER READING

Brower, M. C. and Price, B. H. (2001) Neuropsychiatry of frontal lobe dysfunction in violent and criminal behaviour: a critical review. *Journal of Neurology, Neurosurgery and Psychiatry*, 71: 720–6.

Heilbronner, R. L. (2008) *Neuropsychology in the Courtroom: Expert Analysis of Reports and Testimony*. New York: Guilford Press.

McCrea, M. A. (2008) *Mild Traumatic Brain Injury and Postconcussion Syndrome*. Oxford: Oxford University Press.

Wood, R. L. and McMillan, T. M. (2001) *Neurobehavioural Disability and Social Handicap following Traumatic Brain Injury*. Hove: Psychology Press,.

REFERENCES

Barnfield, T. V. and Leathem, J. M. (1998) Incidence and outcomes of traumatic brain injury and substance abuse in a New Zealand prison population. *Brain Injury*, 12: 455–66.

Carswell, K., Maughan, B., Davis, H., Davenport, F. and Goddard, N. (2004) The psychosocial needs of young offenders and adolescents from an inner city area. *Journal of Adolescence*, 27: 415–28.

Colantonio, A., Stamenova, V., Abramowitz, C. and Clarke, D. (2007) Brain injury in a forensic population. *Brain Injury*, 21: 1353–60.

Damasio, A. R., Tranel, D. and Damasio, H. (1990) Individuals with sociopathic behaviour caused by frontal damage fail to respond autonomically to social stimuli. *Behavioural Brain Research*, 41: 81–94.

de Souza C. A. C. (2003) Frequency of brain injury in a forensic psychiatry population. *Revista Brasileira de Psiquiatria*, 25: 206–11.

Del Bello, M. P., Soutello, C. A., Zimmerman, M. E., Sax, K. W., Williams, J. R., McElroy, S. L. and Strakowski, S. M. (1999) Traumatic brain injury in individuals convicted of sexual offenses with and without bipolar disorder. *Psychiatry Research*, 89: 281–6.

Elst, L. T. van, Woermann, F. G., Lemieux, L., Thompson, P. J. and Trimble, M. R. (2000) Affective aggression in patients with temporal lobe epilepsy: a quantitative MRI study of the amygdala. *Brain*, 123(2): 234–43.

Eslinger, P. J. and Damasio, H. (1988) Anatomical correlates of paradoxical ear extinction. In K. Hugdahl (ed.), *Handbook of Dichotomous Listening: Theory, Method and Research*, pp. 139–60. Chichester: Wiley.

Freedman, D. and Hemenway, D. (2000) Precursors of lethal violence: a death row sample. *Social Science and Medicine*, 50: 1757–70.

Grafman, J., Schwab, K., Warden, D. *et al.* (1996) Frontal lobe injuries, violence and aggression: a report of the Vietnam head injury study. *Neurology*, 46: 1231–8.

Jennett, B. (1996) Epidemiology of head injury. *Journal of Neurology, Neurosurgery and Psychiatry*, 60: 362–9.

León-Carrión, J. and Chacartegui-Ramos, F. J. (2003) Blows to the head during development can predispose to violent criminal behaviour: rehabilitation of consequences of head injury is a measure for crime prevention. *Brain Injury*, 17: 207–16.

Lewis, D. O., Pincus, J. H., Bard, B. *et al.* (1986) Psychiatric, neurological and psycho-educational characteristics of 15 death row inmates in the United States. *American Journal of Psychiatry*, 143: 838–45.

(1988) Neuropsychiatric psycho-educational and family characteristics of 14 juveniles condemned to death in the United States. *American Journal of Psychiatry*, 145: 584–9.

Maletzky, B. M. (1973) The episodic dyscontrol syndrome. *Diseases of the Nervous System*, 34: 178–85.

Martell, A. D. (1992) Estimating the prevalence of organic brain dysfunction in maximum security forensic psychiatric patients. *Journal of Forensic Sciences*, 37: 878–93.

McMillan, T. M. and Greenwood, R. J. (2003) Head injury rehabilitation. In R. J. Greenwood *et al.* (eds.), *Handbook of Neurological Rehabilitation*, pp. 465–86. Hove: Psychology Press.

McMillan, T. M., Jongen, E. L. M. M. and Greenwood, R. J. (1996) Assessment of post traumatic amnesia after closed head injury: retrospective or prospective? *Journal of Neurology, Neurosurgery and Psychiatry*, 60: 422–7.

McMillan, T. M., McKenzie, P., Swann, I. J., Weir, C. and McAviny, A. (2009) Head injury attenders at the emergency department: the impact of advice and factors associated with early symptom outcome. *Brain Injury*, 23: 509–15.

Ponsford, J. *et al.* (2004) Use of the Westmead PTA Scale to monitor recovery after mild head injury. *Brain Injury*, 18: 603–14.

Raine, A., Park, S., Lencz, T., Bihrkle, S., LaCasse, L., Widon, C., Al-Dayeh, L. and Singh, M. (2001) Reduced right hemisphere activation in severely abused violent offenders during a working memory task: an fMRI study. *Aggressive Behaviour*, 27: 111–29.

Russell, W. R. and Nathan, P. W. (1946) Traumatic amnesia. *Brain*, 69: 280–300.

Schofield, P. W., Butler, T. G., Hollis, S. J., Smith, N. E, Lee, S. J. and Kelso, W. M. (2006) Traumatic brain injury among Australian prisoners: rates, recurrence and sequelae. *Brain Injury*, 20: 499–506.

Simpson, G., Blaszczynski, A. and Hodgkinson, A. (1999) Sex offending as a psychological sequela of traumatic brain injury. *Journal of Head Trauma Rehabilitation*, 14: 567–80.

Slaughter, B., Fann, J. R. and Ehde, D. (2003) Traumatic brain injury in a county jail population: prevalence, neuropsychological functioning and psychiatric disorders. *Brain Injury*, 17: 731–41.

Tagliaferri, F., Compagnone, C., Korsic, M., Servadei, F. and Kraus, J. (2006) A systematic review of brain injury epidemiology in Europe. *Acta Neurochirurgica* (Vienna), 148: 255–68.

Thornhill, S., Teasdale, G. M., Murray, G. D., McEwen, J., Roy, C. W. and Penny, N. I. (2000) Disability in young people and adults one year after head injury: prospective cohort study. *British Medical Journal*, 320: 1631–5.

Timonen, M., Miettunen, J., Hakko, H., Zitting, P., Veijola, J., von Wendt, L. and Rasanen, P. (2002) The association of preceding traumatic brain injury with mental disorders, alcoholism and criminality: the Northern Finland 1966 Birth Cohort Study. *Psychiatry Research*, 113: 217–26.

Turkstra, L., Jones, D. and Toler, H. L. (2003) Brain injury and violent crime. *Brain Injury*, 17: 39–47.

Whitnall, L., McMillan, T. M., Murray G. and Teasdale, G. (2006) Disability in young people with head injury: a 5–7 year follow-up of a prospective cohort study. *Journal of Neurology, Neurosurgery, Psychiatry*, 77: 640–5.

1.8 Investigative decision making

Marie Eyre and Laurence Alison

See also chapter 1.9 Investigative psychology.

Definition

Investigative decision making sits largely within the academic disciplines of cognitive and social psychology though it is also allied to criminology and sociology. It has emerged from a broader set of academic disciplines that focus on generic decision making, including economics, philosophy, mathematics and, more recently, business and management studies. Investigative decision making is, therefore, an eclectic field of study based on scientific, empirical research. It focuses largely on the ways in which decision makers choose a course of action in accordance with investigative goals: how information is retrieved, the cognitive processes used to infer meaning from the information gathered and how it is used to support decision making.

As it is very much an applied field any decisions that are within the compass of police or other criminal investigations constitute a valid area of study and many factors pertinent to human decision making are explored. This means that investigative decision making covers a very wide range of dimensions. Examples are: levels of decision making, whether it is a decision to arrest (or not arrest) a child for stealing a biscuit or a decision to proactively shoot dead a suspected suicide bomber; the broad context in which decisions are made with regard to the parameters of the law or the organization whose rules, policies and procedures create the decision environment for a decision maker; the more immediate field setting with factors such as time pressure, stress, ambiguity; the dynamics of team and group decision making; personality traits of the decision maker, any or all of which may interact to potentially influence decisions. With many police forces moving towards evidence-based practice in recent times, investigative decision-making research is making a growing direct contribution to many aspects of criminal investigation.

Origins and theory

Investigative decision making draws on a lengthy body of research of general decision theory stretching back centuries. In 1670, Pascal developed a theory of economic utility and – rooted in the discipline of economics – humans were thus predicted to decide rationally to maximize benefits and minimize costs. Bernoulli (1738) agreed that humans make decisions rationally but argued that people are risk averse and introduced the idea of 'subjective' utility into decision making. Taking this view, even in an uncertain environment, decision makers may be assumed to have calculated risks and potential losses in a rational manner when making a decision. Thus the decision maker would have considered all options available, calculated the subjective expected utility (SEU) of each and chosen the option with the highest SEU. This fundamental tenet – that decision making is rational (and, hence, determinate and predictable) – prevailed until well into the twentieth century. Known now as classical or traditional decision-making theory (TDT), it remains very relevant to generic decision making today. Some features of human decision making hold across any context, so TDT findings are applicable to investigative decision making.

In 1944, von Neumann and Morgenstern introduced game theory. Game theory held with the notion that SEU had a rational decision-making aim, but it also incorporated the idea that the existence of an adversary must be considered when formulating how to maximize benefits and minimize costs. When playing a game, an opponent can anticipate what the other will decide; this simple fact will affect the other's decision making. A popular illustrative example is the rock, paper, scissors game. If a person wins £1 for playing rock or paper but £2 for playing scissors, then, rationally, in order to maximize benefits, the player will use scissors every round – and win twice as much money. However, the opponent knows this. Thus the player cannot use scissors every round, or he/she will lose every time. The player's opponent has affected the former's decision making.

As with other theories and models associated with generic decision making, game theory has a contribution to make to investigative decision making. Criminal investigative work is an arena in which adversaries must be considered when making decisions. If an officer decides to watch and gather more evidence before arrest, the surveillance might alert the suspect to flee the country; hence, his/her choices must be factored into decision making. Game theory was subsequently developed far beyond the scope for discussion here though further reading is suggested below.

From the 1970s, Kahneman and Tversky conducted seminal work, which revealed that human decision makers are far less rational than previously thought. They discovered a range of heuristics and biases that can affect decision makers. Heuristics are cognitive 'rules of thumb', built up via experience, where complex problems, interactions and so on are distilled into simple rules for use in future situations. Heuristics are likely to be employed when conditions are uncertain, when information is unavailable or time pressure is a factor. Although much expanded since Kahneman and Tversky's early work, they established three canonical heuristics known to affect decision making: (i) representativeness, wherein people assume commonality between things that are similar to a prototype; (ii) availability, which involves evaluating events according to the ease with which they can be imagined or retrieved from memory; and (iii) anchoring/adjustment, where people who have to make judgements about uncertain quantities tend to be unduly influenced by initial values. The initial values may act as an anchor for decisions thereafter and adjustments will be made with regard to the initial anchor. (Also see McGuire 1997 for details of other heuristics.)

It is well established that heuristics may cause systematic biases that can lead to errors – not least because a short cut has been deployed when a thorough consideration 'ought' (normatively or ideally) to have informed decision making. Decision makers are prone to biases such as *belief persistence* (in the face of contrary information) or *confirmation bias* (where information that does not support the hypothesis is discarded). These are generic DM biases but both may be particularly pertinent to investigative decision making. The unknown is a defining feature of the investigative environment. Investigators need, therefore, to hypothesize and are known to generate stories about what might have happened (Ormerod, Barrett and Taylor 2005), which takes considerable cognitive effort and cognitive effort is known to increase belief persistence (Marshall and Alison in press).

Alison and Crego (2008) offer an accessible summary of heuristics and biases, though the topic is not without debate. Gigerenzer has criticized Kahneman and Tversky's emphasis on cognitive biases and has focused instead on the ways in which 'fast and frugal' heuristics can prove beneficial. Heuristics work well in many circumstances – they save much cognitive processing and can, therefore, be adaptive. (See, e.g. Gigerenzer and Todd 1999; Gigernezer and Selten 2001). Gigerenzer has also argued that the cognitive processes of heuristics are vaguely defined and the intervening decades since Kahneman and Tversky's initial work during the 1970s should, by now, have fleshed out the detail. He argues that Kahneman and Tversky are overly concerned with the structure of problems whilst neglecting the content and context, both of which are seen as significant influences on decision-making reasoning. Gigerenzer may, incidentally, highlight some of the difficulties in 'hybrid' areas of study that have a multidisciplinary parentage. He argues that what is logical and sound in abstract probability theory does not transfer wholesale from mathematics to studies of human behaviour where (as just one example) semantics may be completely different (see Gigerenzer 1996, and Kahneman and Tversky 1996, for details of the debate).

Recent thinking and development

Many of the findings within the traditional decision-theory (TDT) approach were the result of laboratory-based empirical work. Other behavioural scientists have adopted a different starting point. Rather than investigate cognitive processes for the purposes of theory development, they begin with a more pragmatic focus on the world beyond the laboratory and attempt to solve everyday problems. In some arenas, this itself is termed the Pasteur heuristic (because the famous scientist preferred to focus on finding solutions to common problems). In the world of decision-making study, it is known as naturalistic decision making (NDM) and has emerged over the last two decades.

Unlike TDT, naturalistic decision-making approaches take more account of the context in which decision makers operate. In TDT studies, participants in a lab study may be asked to decide which choices are more (or less) attractive. Such studies will have been conceived with strict attention to controlling the variables to ensure that no extraneous factors contaminate the experiment. For example, if one participant sits in a quiet room, all must have the same calm environment otherwise differing results might be attributed to noise levels or stress rather than the variables under investigation. This has been criticized as unrealistic (in scientific parlance, lacking in ecological validity). Any workplace is a complex environment and features of that environment are customarily (and necessarily) uncontrolled and changing. Indeed, uncertainty and change may be said to epitomize the environment for investigative decision makers.

Essentially, the NDM approach favours investigating what people do in their everyday world – in other words, research's starting point is what *is* decided rather than what *ought* (optimally) to be decided. Thus, TDT and NDM approaches exemplify what are known in the DM literature as normative or descriptive theories (respectively). Pioneering NDM work was undertaken by Klein (1993), who investigated the decision making of forest firefighting teams. This led to novel insights and the development of new models of decision making. It transpired that, under pressure of time, expert decision makers do not (as SEU would predict) exhaustively weigh the costs and benefits of all available options. Instead, they typically come up with one option only and decide to do it. In other words, the decision making processes seem to be intuitive and implicit rather than explicitly analytical. From this initial work, Klein developed his model of Recognition Primed Decision Making (RPD) now seen as the prototypical NDM model.

In rejecting the normative emphasis of TDT approaches, NDM has, in turn, been criticized for being 'merely' descriptive. As it evolves, it is acknowledged that the goal of improving decision making must be embraced if NDM research is to have applied value. Others call for a synthesis of different theoretical and paradigmatic approaches (Eyre and Alison 2007).

Evaluation

Much of the information above refers to generic decision making theory and its applications collected from a number of disciplines rather than the arena of investigation per se. On the one hand, humans are humans wherever they make decisions and much generic DM research is transferable. However, investigative decision making is a specialist domain and some factors may pertain specifically or even exclusively to investigative decision making though, as yet, the necessary coherent body of specialized research is lacking.

It is important not to conflate issues here. A substantial body of empirical research on investigation and policing does exist (for example, studies on eyewitnesses, deception, interviewing etc.). Likewise, there is a plethora of decision-making research across many disciplines; the current entry is necessarily limited so only some approaches have been outlined above (TDT and NDM). Readers might also wish to explore, for example, a problem-solving approach (e.g. Davidson and Sternberg 2003) or the impact of expertise on decision making (e.g. Chi, Glaser and Farr 1988). However, the study of investigative decision making still needs to be developed, on a theoretical level, in terms of empirical evidence and perhaps even paradigmatically. The multidisciplinary nature of its origins perhaps makes the challenge of integration more difficult but it is necessary to define the parameters more precisely as the area grows and develops.

It may be that the complex nature of the domain is off-putting. Alternatively, it may be neglected because naturalistic settings – where work is highly confidential and may involve issues of national security – are relatively inaccessible. In an increasingly risk averse culture with greater accountability or even naming and blaming, it is uncommon to invite researchers to scrutinize such decisions being made. Specialist work does exist, for example, Brown and Horvath (2005) on investigative decision making in rape cases; Innes (2002, 2003) on homicide and work by Alison, Crego and colleagues (e.g. 2004, 2008), whose naturalistic work is helping to map the landscape of policing.

For practitioners in the UK, there has been a radical reshaping of policing in the wake of the Macpherson report (1999) into the death of Stephen Lawrence. 'Learning on the job' has receded and the police service has rolled out its Professionalising Investigations Programme (PIP), where investigators can be taught the psychology of decision making as part of their professional development. If investigative decision making is really to grow further as an applied field, it is important for researchers to continue to gather the best evidence.

Conclusion

Investigative decision making has evolved from and is still influenced by early decision theory. Generic decision-making research, for example, TDT and NDM models, has much to offer, though each has weaknesses. Although there is a good deal of valuable empirical work, investigative decision making as a specialist domain is in its early developmental stages and much remains to be explored.

FURTHER READING

Baron (2000) offers a comprehensive read on decision-making processes. Game theory may be explored in the work of John Nash (e.g. 1951, 1953), the mathematician whose life was portrayed in the film *A Beautiful Mind*, and John Maynard Smith (e.g. 1982), the evolutionary biologist who applied game theory to the potential cost/benefits for adaptive human behaviour. Glimcher (2005) offers detailed yet accessible concrete examples to illustrate game theory. Kahneman and Tversky published a fairly comprehensive book on heuristics and biases in 1982 but also see Gigerenzer and Todd (1999) or Gigerenzer and Selten (2001). Gigerenzer (1996) and Kahneman and Tversky (1996) offer a briefer version of the debate.

For further reading on NDM, see, for example, LeBeouf and Shafir (2001); Lipshitz, Klein, Orasanu and Salas (2001); Lipshitz and Strauss (1997); Zsambok and Klein (1996) or more generically, see Goldstein and Hogarth (1997). Again, although not necessarily related directly to law enforcement, Flin and Arbuthnot (2002) write on decision making in crisis environments.

For reading directly relating to policing, see Innes (2003) on homicide. Crego and Alison (2004) offer an insight into the difficulties of investigations as reported directly from senior investigating officers who led many of the most prominent investigations in the UK in the last decade, whilst Alison and Crego (2008) report on the many themes in investigative decision making that are emerging from naturalistic data.

REFERENCES

Alison, L. and Crego, J. (eds.) (2008) *Policing Critical Incidents: Leadership and Critical Incident Management*. Cullompton: Willan.

Baron, J. (2000) *Thinking and Deciding*. Cambridge: Cambridge University Press.

Bernoulli, D. (1738/1954) Exposition of a new theory of the measurement of risk. Transl. R. Sommer. *Econometrica*, 22: 23–36.

Brown, J. and Horvath, M. A. H. (2005) Police decision making and rape allegations. Paper presented at the International Association of Women Police, 43rd Annual Training Conference, Leeds.

Chi, M. T. H., Glaser, R. and Farr, M. J. (eds.) (1988) *The Nature of Expertise*. Hillsdale, NJ: Erlbaum.

Crego, J. and Alison, L. (2004) Control and legacy as functions of perceived criticality in major incidents. *Journal of Investigative Psychology and Offender Profiling*, 1: 207–25.

Davidson, J. E. and Sternberg, R. J. (eds.) (2003) *The Psychology of Problem Solving*. New York: Cambridge University Press.

Eyre, M. and Alison, L. (2007) To decide or not to decide: decision making and decision avoidance in critical incidents. In D. Carson, R. Milne, F. J. Pakes, K. Shalev and A. Shawyer (eds.), *Applying Psychology to Criminal Justice*, pp. 211–32. Chichester: Wiley.

Flin, R. and Arbuthnot, K. (2002) (eds.) *Incident Command: Tales from the Hot Seat*. Aldershot: Ashgate.

Gigerenzer, G. (1996) On narrow norms and vague heuristics: a reply to Kahneman and Tversky. *Psychological Review*, 103: 592–6.

Gigerenzer, G. and Selten, R. (2001) *Bounded Rationality: The Adaptive Toolbox*. Cambridge, MA: MIT Press.

Gigerenzer, G., Todd, P. M. and the ABC Research Group (1999) *Simple Heuristics that Make Us Smart*. New York: Oxford University Press.

Glimcher, P. W. (2005) Indeterminacy in brain and behavior. *Annual Review of Psychology*, 56: 25–56.

Goldstein, W. M. and Hogarth, R. M. (1997) (eds.) *Research on Judgment and Decision Making: Currents, Connections, and Controversies*. New York: Cambridge University Press.

Innes, M. (2002) The process structures of police homicide investigations. *British Journal of Criminology*, 42: 669–88.

(2003) *Investigating Murder: Detective Work and the Police Response to Criminal Homicide.* Oxford: Clarendon Press.

Kahneman, D. and Tversky, A. (1982) *Judgement under Uncertainty: Heuristics and Biases.* Cambridge: Cambridge University Press.

(1996) On the reality of cognitive illusions. *Psychological Review*, 103: 592–6.

Klein, G. (1993) A recognition primed decision (RPD) model of rapid decision making. In G. A. Klein, J. Orasanu, R. Calderwood and C. E. Zsambok (eds.), *Decision Making in Action: Models and Methods*, pp. 138–47. Norwood, CT: Ablex.

LeBeouf, R. A. and Shafir, E. (2001) Problems and methods in naturalistic decision making. *Journal of Behavioural Decision Making*, 14: 353–84.

Lipshitz, R., Klein, G., Orasanu, J. and Salas, E. (2001) Taking stock of naturalistic decision making. *Journal of Behavioural Decision Making*, 14: 331–52.

Lipshitz, R. and Strauss, O. (1997) Coping with uncertainty: a naturalistic decision making analysis. *Organisational Behaviour and Human Decision Processes*, 69: 149–63.

Macpherson, W. (1999) *The Stephen Lawrence Inquiry. Report of an Inquiry by Sir William Macpherson of Cluny*. London: HMSO. Available online: www.archive.official-documents. co.uk/document/cm42/4262/4262/htm (accessed May 2007).

Marshall, B. and Alison, L. (in press) Stereotyping, congruence and presentation order: interpretative biases in utilizing offender profiles. *Psychology, Crime and Law*.

Maynard Smith, J. (1982) *Evolution and the Theory of Games*. Cambridge: Cambridge University Press.

McGuire, W. J. (1997) Creative hypothesis generating in psychology: some useful heuristics. *Annual Review of Psychology*, 48: 1–30.

Nash, J. (1951) Non co-operative games. *Annals of Mathematics*, 54: 286–95.

(1953) Two-person cooperative games. *Econometrica*, 21: 128–40.

Ormerod, T. C., Barrett, E. C. and Taylor, P. J. (2005) Investigative sense-making in criminal contexts. In J. M. C. Schraagen (ed.), *Proceedings of the Seventh International NDM Conference*, pp. 1–12. Amsterdam, June 2005.

Pascal, B. (1670/1966) *Pensées*. Transl. A. J. Krailsheimer. Harmondsworth: Penguin.

Von Neumann, J. V. and Morgenstern, O. (1944) *Theory of Games and Economic Behavior*. Princeton, NJ: Princeton University Press.

Zsambok, C. E. and Klein, G. (1996). *Naturalistic Decision Making* (Expertise: Research and Applications Series). Hillsdale, NJ: Erlbaum.

Investigative psychology

David Canter

See also chapter 1.8 Investigative decision making.

Definition

The domain of *investigative psychology* covers all aspects of psychology that are relevant to the conduct of criminal or civil investigations. Its focus is on the ways in which criminal activities may be examined and understood in order for the detection of crime to be effective and legal proceedings to be appropriate. As such, investigative psychology is concerned with psychological input to the full range of issues that relate to the management, investigation and prosecution of crime.

Investigation as decision making

Its constituents can be derived from consideration of the sequence of activities that constitute the investigative process. This runs from the point at which a crime is committed through to the bringing of a case to court. This makes it apparent that detectives and others involved in investigations are decision makers. They have to identify the possibilities for action on the basis of the information they can obtain. For example, when a burglary is committed they may seek to match fingerprints found at the crime scene with known suspects. This is a relatively straightforward process of making inferences about the likely culprit from the information drawn from the fingerprint. The action of arresting and questioning the suspect follows from this inference.

However, in many cases the investigative process is not so straightforward. Detectives may not have such clear-cut information but, for example, suspect that the style of the burglary is typical of one of a number of people they have arrested in the past. Or, in an even more complex example, such as a murder, they may infer from the disorder at the crime scene that the offender was a burglar disturbed in the act. These inferences will either lead them on to seek other information or to select from a possible range of actions including the arrest and charging of a likely suspect.

Investigative decision making thus involves the identification and selection of options, such as possible suspects or possible lines of enquiry, that will lead to the eventual narrowing down of the search process. In order to generate possibilities and select from them, detectives and other investigators must draw on some understanding of the actions of the offender(s) involved in the offence they are investigating. They must have some idea of typical ways in which offenders behave that will enable them to make sense of the information obtained. Throughout this process they must amass the appropriate evidence to identify the perpetrator and prove their case in court.

Information management

It follows that three processes are always present in any investigation that can be improved by psychological study. First, the collection and evaluation of information derived from accounts of the crime. These accounts may include photographs or other recordings derived from the crime scene. There may also be records of other transactions such as bills paid or telephone calls made. Increasingly there are also records available within computer systems used by witnesses, victims or suspects. Often there will be witnesses to the crime or there will be results of the crime available for examination. There will transcripts of interviews or reports from various experts. Further, there will be information in police and other records that may be drawn upon to provide indications for action. Once suspects are elicited there is further potential information about them either directly from interviews with them, or indirectly through reports from others. In addition, there may be information from various experts that has to be understood and may lead to actions. The major task of a police investigation is, therefore, typically to collect, assess and utilize a great variety of sources of information that provide accounts of crime. This is a task that can benefit considerably from the scientific study of human memory processes and other psychological studies of the reliability and validity of reports and their assessment.

The second set of tasks is the making of decisions and the related actions that will move towards the arrest and conviction of the perpetrator. There is remarkably little study of exactly what decisions are made during an investigation, or how those decisions are made. Yet there is clearly a limited range of actions available to police officers, constrained by the legal system within which they operate. From many studies of human decision making in other contexts it is also apparent that there are likely to be many heuristic biases and other inefficiencies in the decision-making process. Awareness of these can lead to effective ways of overcoming them.

Appropriate inferences

In order for decisions to be derived from the information available inferences have to be made about the import of that information. The third set of tasks therefore derives from developing a basis for those inferences at the heart of police investigations. These inferences derive from an understanding of criminal behaviour. For appropriate conclusions to be drawn from the accounts available of the crime it is necessary to have, at least implicitly, models of how various offenders act. These models allow the accounts of crime to be processed in order to generate possibilities for action. This process of model building and testing is, in effect, a scientific, psychological development of the informal, anecdote-based process often referred to as *offender profiling*. That is only one small part of how psychology is contributing to investigations and thus a limited aspect of investigative psychology.

A simple framework for these three sets of tasks that gives rise to the field of investigative psychology is shown in figure 1.9.1.

There are many ways in which psychological knowledge and principles can be applied to criminal and civil investigations. A fruitful way of looking at the

Figure 1.9.1 Framework for investigative psychology

contributions of psychology to police investigations is how it can inform answers to ten classes of operational question that police and other investigators face in the course of their activities.

1. How can police information systems be improved and the information collected be effectively validated?
2. How can the contact with witnesses, victims and suspects be improved especially through the development of interviewing procedures?
3. How can deception be detected?
4. What aspects of a crime are important indicators of the perpetrator?
5. What searches of police records or other sources of information should be carried out to help identify the offender?
6. Where can the offender be located?
7. Which crimes are linked?
8. Where and when will the offender commit his/her next offence?
9. In what ways can investigative decision making be improved and supported?
10. What sense can be made of the offence that will help to organize the legal case?

Psychology can inform these operational issues on two levels. Most centrally, investigative psychologists are able to provide the substantive knowledge, based on empirical studies that can, increasingly, provide direct answers to these questions. Secondly, psychology can provide a framework for understanding the processes that police must go through in attempting to find the answers.

The capacity of humans to collate and organize information, so that decisions can be made on the basis of it, can be facilitated by a variety of means. One way is to provide visualizations of the material. Human beings can often see patterns between associations and within activities if they can be presented in some visual summary. Bar charts of frequencies are one common example of this, but commercially available software will chart networks of contacts and other sequences of associations or actions.

Decisions are also facilitated if extensive and disparate information can be described in some summary form. A further level of support to police decisions can be made therefore by identifying the salient characteristics of the offences and offenders and by producing summary accounts of them. This may be the production of maps that indicate the locations where there are high frequencies of crime, sometimes called criminal 'hotspots'. In these cases the salient characteristics are simply where the crimes have occurred and the description consists of some summary or averaging of the crimes over an area in order to indicate where its geographical focus might be. All description requires some selection, distillation or averaging of information and when that is done validly the description is helpful. Particularly useful to the police will be data on the relative commonness or rarity of actions in crimes they are investigating among offenders generally. This base-rate information guides the investigator towards those most salient features of an offence that will be most relevant to the process of deriving inferences about that particular offender.

FURTHER READING

An elaborated brief definition is offered in Towl *et al.* (Canter 2008). Ainsworth (2001) and Canter and Youngs (2003) provide greater details of offender profiling.

REFERENCES

Ainsworth, P. (2001) *Offender Profiling and Crime Analsyis*. Cullompton: Willan.

Canter, D. (2008) Investigative psychology. In G. Towl, D. Farrington, D. Crighton and G. Hughes (eds.), *Dictionary of Forensic Psychology*. Cullompton: Willan.

Canter, D. and Youngs, D. (2003) Beyond offender profiling. In R. Bull and D. Carson (eds.), *Handbook of Psychology in Legal Contexts*, 2nd edn, pp. 171–206.

1.10 Personality theories and offending

Vincent Egan

See also chapter 2.20 Psychopathy.

Definition

Whether the behaviour is legal or illegal, social or antisocial, patterns of conduct seem relatively consistent for most persons. This is because many actions are driven by individual differences in personality. Some traits and dispositions lead a person to behave in an objectionable and antisocial way, and may lead to the behaviour being proscribed and deemed criminal. However, what is 'criminal' is socially constructed across time and space, and influenced by local culture and history. This is why what is legal in one place, for example a particular type of sexual behaviour, may be illegal in another. The particular behaviours, traits and qualities that lead to a person to act in one way or another, and, more relevant here, to be violent or opportunistic, seem relatively constant to humanity (McCall and Shields 2008). Such qualities may have once provided additional survival value, and some contexts still do, implying an evolutionary selection pressure for what are regarded as ostensibly 'antisocial' characteristics (Rowe 2002).

Models, assessments and research strategies exploring these characteristics have involved a broad polarity whereby the clinical-descriptive tradition within psychology and psychiatry developed somewhat independently of structural psychometric models based on academic studies of general disposition. The observation of clinical cases and populations by practitioners led to the development of symptom and behavioural checklists for the diagnosis of aberrant personality; some of these are useful, some less so. Some clinical syndromes of personality seem relatively unambiguous, and can be reliably identified. DSM-IV personality disorders (see elsewhere in this volume) provide quite distinctive personality 'types', particularly in cluster B 'dramatic' personality disorders such as Borderline Personality

Disorder or Antisocial Personality Disorder, both of which are more common to offenders (Coid *et al.* 2006). Another personality model deriving from the clinical-descriptive condition is that of psychopathy (see chapter 2.20, this volume) (Blair, Mitchell and Blair 2005). Psychopathy is defined by cold, callous and manipulative behaviours, and often leads to objectionable behaviour – but, if uncoupled from impulsivity, may not necessarily lead to explicit offending; it is the conjunction of psychopathy with the behavioural disinhibition associated with Antisocial Personality Disorder (as is captured by scores on measures such as Hare's revised Psychopathy Checklist (PCL-R; Hare 1997)) that leads to the PCL-R's ability to effectively predict offending.

However, a century of academic psychology studying personality has shown that there are few genuine personality 'types' – simply dimensions of personality; moreover, these dimensions are significantly (but not completely) related to clinical observations and self-reported assessments of personality disorder (Costa and Widiger 2001). This suggests that a considerable amount – but not all – of the findings from the clinical tradition can fit into a more general typological scheme, with the strongest typological schemes in academic psychology being dimensional structural models, for example, Eysenck's dimensions of Psychoticism, Extroversion and Neuroticism (PEN; Eysenck and Eysenck 1985) and Costa and McCrae's Five-Factor Model (FFM), which comprises N, E, Openness (O), Agreeableness (A) and Conscientiousness (C) (Costa and McCrae 1992). Both DSM-IV personality disorders and psychopathy correlate with these structural models of personality (Skeem *et al.* 2005), suggesting that even clinically observed conditions are underpinned by general dispositional processes, and that personality disorders and psychopathy are probably higher-order constructs emerging from lower-level processes.

Origins and developments

Contemporary academic debate in this area focuses upon which particular traits reliably predict antisocial behaviour, the size of this relationship, whether it is confounded by other influences (for example, social class or age, which also have strong associations with offending), and whether personality is subject to situational constraints which preclude genuine prediction. Psychodynamic and humanistic personality theories of antisocial behaviour have been particularly averse to the prosaic business of operationalizing concepts into testable measures which can be revised in the light of findings, making such approaches incompatible with contemporary notions of evidence-based practice required within medical and legal settings. By contrast, empirical, trait-driven structural models of personality provide broad dimensions of personality without filling in the idiosyncratic details of the self created by experience, choice and chance, but nevertheless seem to be able to predict offending. Meta-analysis finds structural models (e.g. Eysenck's PEN or Costa and McCrae's FFM, Tellegen's three-factor model and Cloninger's seven-factor model) all have particular dimensions associated with antisocial acts (Miller and Lynam 2001).

Structural trait theories of personality are highly empirical, and thus are more testable than individually focused theories. The dimensions in such models derive typically from large-scale factor-analytic work identifying dimensions underlying the variance for a variety of self-report psychometric measures that may ostensibly examine higher-order qualities of the self. The hierarchical structural method, for example, can demonstrate that apparently disparate constructs such as 'self-esteem', 'locus of control' and 'generalized self-efficacy' are all strongly determined by N (Judge *et al.* 2002), as the more specific constructs load together to form a single factor closer to N than any specific lower-order trait. Moreover, the lower-order trait measures offer limited discriminant validity (or incremental variance) in predicting distress – once the higher-order construct of N is taken into account. Such underlying dimensions are not seen as self-validating constructs existing in a vacuum; as part of the positivist programme, researchers in this area typically seek to integrate personality findings with information from areas such as genetics, biology, primatology and experimental psychology. Such consilience of evidence buttresses scientific models so they are more than simply atheoretical quantitative notions with no genuine external bearing on reality (Wilson 1998), and ensures they remain progressive research paradigms continuing to generate fresh ideas rather than another stale replication. Deciding which structural model of personality traits is closest to the 'Goldilocks solution' (not too many, not too few) is also empirical and theoretical; contemporary model-fitting techniques can test whether data fit hypothesized underlying structures as compared to other proposed conceptions; these find that the PEN and FFM are more effective at explaining Cloninger and Tellegen's alternative models than Cloninger and Tellegen's theories themselves (Egan 2008). The debate as to which is more useful for predicting and understanding the dimensions underlying offending is therefore arguably largely between the PEN and FFM models.

Method

Personality traits are generally inferred using self-report scales. The integrity of information derived from these can be increased by the use of multiple raters, ideally these being persons who know the individual. Knowledge of the person across time and context will optimize the stability of ratings, and also their validity, but in practice this is rarely done, and self-report scales are generally regarded as sufficient for purpose, for example the NEO-PI-R and the NEO-FFI/NEO-FFI-R, all of which measure the FFM (Costa and McCrae 1992; McCrae and Costa 2004); or, for evaluating, PEN, the Eysenck Personality Questionnaire or the Eysenck Personality Profiler (Eysenck and Eysenck 1975; Bulthelier and Hicker 1997). Assessment of personality disorder can be done using self-report instruments, but these are generally only used as screening instruments before a structured clinical interview, as the screening instruments tend to generate a large number of false positive diagnoses (which is precisely what would be predicted if you assume most personality disorders are simply extremes of normal personality traits). Psychopathy is generally (but not always) assessed using screening interviews (Hare 1997). The clinical interview (but also providing a useful 77-item screening instrument) typically used to assess personality disorder is the IPDE (Loranger 1999).

Evaluation and application

Hans Eysenck's PEN model was once seen as all-encompassing. A meta-analysis of the PEN model in relation to antisocial behaviour comprising 52 studies and 97 samples found P was most strongly linked to antisocial behaviour (mean effect size = 0.39, 95% confidence interval (CI) = 0.35 to 0.42); N was also linked to antisocial activity, but less so (mean effect size = 0.19, 95% CI = 0.15 to 0.23). The effect of E on antisocial behaviour was minor (mean effect size = 0.09, 95% CI = 0.06 to 0.12) (Cale 2006). While P – a dimension claimed to capture tough-minded hostility, and involving elements of aggression, coldness, egocentricity, impulsivity and a lack of empathy – would seem to be the *sine qua non* of the more serious end of criminal personality, in fact there are a number of significant difficulties with the P dimension. P conflates the mentally ill and the behaviourally disordered, when most mentally disordered persons are not offenders; the internal reliability of P scales is low, limiting accuracy and replicability of measurement

(Caruso *et al.* 2001); and the discriminant validity of P is weak – art students score more highly on P than prisoners or the mentally ill (Woody and Claridge 1977). Under pressure to account for P's limitations, Eysenck proposed that P was a higher-order construct emerging out of lower apparent facets of P such as A and C, which suggests that P is not the underlying influence in the same way A and C may be (Eysenck 1992a, 1992b). Eysenck's robust defence did not resolve the basic issue of P being a flawed concept, however; A and C are less confused constructs, face-valid, highly reliable, correlate with P, and also correlate with P-like phenomena (McCrae and Costa 1985).

A and C are elements of the FFM, which provides a very helpful integrative structure for many psychological phenomena, and given the diversity of phenomena which correlate with traits such as N, E, O, A and C, it would seem productive to move forward with the FFM rather than other models of personality (Costa and McCrae 1995). The dramatic 'externalizing' personality disorders are particularly associated with low A, low C and high N (though not particularly high E), and are also disproportionately associated with aggression and violence (Costa and Widiger 2001). More generally, Miller, Lynam and Leukefeld (2003) examined the relationship between the FFM and a range of antisocial activities. They found N, A and C predicted the stability, variety and onset of conduct problems, aggression, and symptoms of antisocial personality disorder in 481 individuals in the community. At the domain level of these traits, lower A most consistently related to all five antisocial and aggressive outcomes, with facets from N, A and C all adding significant contributions to predicting outcome, in particular low straightforwardness, low compliance and low deliberation. Similar correlates of arrest were identified by Samuels *et al.* (2004). Other aggressive and antisocial behaviours are also predicted by aspects of the FFM, whether they be self-reported criminal activity and aggression, interests in weapons (and other violent interests), alcohol-violence expectancies, or sexual offending (Egan 2008). It is likely that the FFM could further sharpen associations with psychopathology and antisocial behaviour by adjusting scale items so they place more emphasis on maladaptive expressions of the personality traits indexed (Haigler and Widiger 2001).

Applications

There are a number of models of offending which readily integrate with the personality models advanced above. Cognitive schema are thought to maintain antisocial behaviour and maladaptive responses to challenging life events, provoking responses that may lead the individual to offend. Many of the intervention programmes in British prisons use structured cognitive-behavioural programmes to break schema down and replace them with different views and competencies. The 'What Works' principles to treat antisocial behaviour (see elsewhere in this volume) build upon such knowledge (McGuire 2002).

The Psychological Inventory of Criminal Thinking Styles (PICTS: Walters 1995) might be thought to capture such views in offenders. The PICTS's eight subscales reduce to two broad domains: thoughtlessness and callousness (Egan *et al.* 2000). Thoughtlessness can be driven by impulsivity, mental disorder or emotional upset distracting attention from what would be otherwise salient, substance misuse likewise shifting priorities or disrupting rational thought, or lower intelligence. Intervention programmes often seek to make persons more mindful and thus less inclined to offend. Callousness is more sinister, for it implies that a person knows right from wrong but chooses to take the antisocial option irrespective of how their actions may hurt another. The thoughtlessness dimension of the PICTS correlates with high N and low A, the callous dimension with low A alone.

Thoughtlessness is instantiated in impulsivity, which is core to the personality features seen in offenders (Andrews and Bonta 1994). Callousness can be formulated as either Eysenck's P, or Costa and McCrae's low A. Developmentally, personality traits drive offending over and above 'maturity gap' adolescent antisocial activity. Caspi *et al.* (1994) found greater participation in delinquent activities associated with young persons who showed greater negative emotional expression (defined by greater aggression, greater alienation and greater stress reactions) and weak constraint (i.e. low traditionalism, low harm avoidance and a lack of control, i.e. impulsivity). Lastly, nobody is suggesting that environmental influences are irrelevant in the expression of antisocial behaviour (and they never did); impulsivity is a stronger predictor of antisocial behaviour in poorer communities (Lynam *et al.* 2000). However, impulsivity and instability in adolescents are particularly associated with high N and low levels of A and C (Lynam *et al.* 2005), reiterating the importance of general personality traits to predict expressive antisocial behaviour.

Conclusions

Personality theories of offending based on a rigorous psychometric approach to measurement and conceptualization can accommodate a range of more specific processes and assessment outcomes used by clinicians and practitioners working with offenders. PEN and FFM models appear to replicably identify the same predictors of antisocial behaviour, namely high N, low A and low C (or, in an earlier typology, P). Given the various technical problems with the construct of P, it would seem expedient to focus on FFM's theory of personality, and to develop more specific theories considering the facets of these general traits, and perhaps how these and other facets of personality are protective or constructive in facilitating desistence from crime, or resilience to the possibility of offending in the first place. Given the robustness of the findings in this area, it will be most surprising if this is not found.

REFERENCES AND FURTHER READING

Andrews, D. A. and Bonta, J. (1994) *The Psychology of Criminal Conduct*. Cincinnati, OH: Anderson.

Blair, J., Mitchell, D. and Blair, K. (2005) *The Psychopath: Emotion and the Brain*. Oxford: Blackwell.

Bulthelier, S. and Hicker, H. (1997) *The Eysenck Personality Profiler – Manual*. Frankfurt/Main: SWETS Test Services.

Cale, E. M. (2006) A quantitative review of the relations between the 'Big 3' higher order personality dimensions and antisocial behaviour. *Journal of Research in Personality*, 40: 250–84.

Caruso, J. C., Witkiewitz, K., Belcourt-Dittloff, A. and Gottlieb, J. D. (2001) Reliability of scores from the Eysenck Personality Questionnaire: a reliability generalization study. *Educational and Psychological Measurement*, 61: 675–89.

Caspi, A., Moffitt, T. E., Silva, P. A., Kruger, R. F. and Schmutte, P. S. (1994) Are some people crime-prone? Replications of the personality–crime relationship across countries, genders, races and methods. *Criminology*, 32: 163–95.

Coid, J., Yang, M., Tyrer, P., Roberts, A. and Ullrich, S. (2006) Prevalence and correlates of personality disorder in Great Britain. *British Journal of Psychiatry*, 188: 423–31.

Costa, P. T. and McCrae, R. R. (1992) *Revised NEO Personality Inventory and NEO Five-Factor Inventory Professional Manual*. Odessa, FL: Psychological Assessment Resources.

(1995) Solid ground on the wetlands of personality – a reply to Block. *Psychological Bulletin*, 117: 216–20.

Costa, P. T. and Widiger, T. A. (2001) *Personality Disorders and the Five-Factor Model of Personality*, 2nd edn. Washington, DC: American Psychological Association.

Egan, V. (2008) The 'Big Five': Neuroticism, Extraversion, Openness, Agreeableness and Conscientiousness as an organisational scheme for thinking about aggression and violence. In M. McMurran and R. Howard (eds.), *Personality, Personality Disorder, and Violence: An Evidence-based Approach*, pp. 63–84. Chichester: Wiley.

Egan, V., McMurran, M., Richardson, C. and Blair, M. (2000) Criminal cognitions and personality: what does the PICTS really measure? *Criminal Behaviour and Mental Health*, 10: 170–84.

Eysenck, H. J. (1992a) Four ways five factors are not basic. *Personality and Individual Differences*, 13: 667–73.

(1992b) A reply to Costa and McCrae. P or A and C – the role of theory. *Personality and Individual Differences*, 13: 867–8.

Eysenck, H. J. and Eysenck, M. W. (1985) *Personality and Individual Differences: A Natural Science Approach*. New York: Plenum Press.

Eysenck, H. J. and Eysenck, S. B. G. (1975) *Manual of the Eysenck Personality Questionnaire*. London: Hodder & Stoughton.

Haigler, E. D. and Widiger, T. A. (2001) Experimental manipulation of NEO-PI-R items. *Journal of Personality Assessment*, 77: 339–58.

Hare, R. D. (1997) *The Hare Psychopathy Checklist – Revised*. Toronto: Multi-Health Systems.

Judge, T. A., Erez, A., Bono, J. E. and Thoresen, C. J. (2002) Are measures of self-esteem, neuroticism, locus of control, and generalised self-efficacy indicators of a common core construct? *Journal of Personality and Social Psychology*, 83: 693–710.

Loranger, A. W. (1999) *International Personality Disorder Examination*. Odessa, FL: Psychological Assessment Resources, Inc.

Lynam, D. R., Caspi, A., Moffitt, T. E., Raine, A., Loeber, R. and Stouthamer-Loeber, M. (2005) Adolescent psychopathy and the Big Five: results from two samples. *Journal of Abnormal Child Psychology*, 33: 431–43.

Lynam, D. R., Caspi, A., Moffitt, T. E., Wikström, P-O., Loeber, R. and Novak, S. (2000) The interaction between impulsivity and neighbourhood context on offending: the effects of impulsivity are stronger in poorer neighbourhoods. *Journal of Abnormal Psychology*, 109: 563–74.

McCall, G. S. and Shields, N. (2008) Examining the evidence from small-scale societies and early prehistory and implications for modern theories of aggression and violence. *Aggression and Violent Behavior*, 13: 1–9.

McCrae, R. R. and Costa, P. T. (1985) Comparison of EPI and psychoticism scales with measures of the five-factor model of personality. *Personality and Individual Differences*, 6: 587–97.

(2004) A contemplated revision of the NEO Five-Factor Inventory. *Personality and Individual Differences*, 36: 587–96.

McGuire, J. (ed.) (2002) *Offender Rehabilitation and Treatment: Effective Programmes and Policies to Reduce Re-offending* (Wiley Series in Forensic Clinical Psychology). Chichester: Wiley.

Miller, J. D. and Lynam, D. (2001) Structural models of personality and their relationship to antisocial behaviour: a meta-analytic review. *Criminology*, 4: 765–98.

Miller, J. D., Lynam, D. and Leukefeld, C. (2003) Examining antisocial behavior through the lens of the Five Factor Model of personality. *Aggressive Behavior*, 29: 497–514.

Rowe, D. C. (2002) *Biology and Crime*. Los Angeles: Roxbury.

Samuels, J., Bienvenu, J., Cullen, B., Costa, P. T., Eaton, W. W. and Nestadt, G. (2004) Personality dimensions and criminal arrest. *Comprehensive Psychiatry*, 45: 275–80.

Skeem, J. L., Miller, J. D., Mulvey, E., Tiemann, J. and Monahan, J. (2005) Using a five-factor lens to explore the relation between personality traits and violence in psychiatric patients. *Journal of Consulting and Clinical Psychology*, 73: 454–65.

Walters, G. D. (1995) The psychological inventory of criminal thinking styles. Part I: reliability and preliminary validity. *Criminal Justice and Behaviour*, 22: 307–25.

Wilson, E. O. (1998) *Consilience: The Unity of Knowledge*. New York: Alfred A. Knopf.

Woody, E. and Claridge, G. (1977) Psychoticism and thinking. *British Journal of Social and Clinical Psychology*, 16: 241–8.

1.11 Pragmatic psychology

Daniel B. Fishman and Jane Goodman-Delahunty

Definition

'Pragmatic psychology' (Fishman 1999, 2003, 2004) is a knowledge model and research method in forensic and all other areas of applied psychology. Epistemologically, pragmatic psychology is grounded within the philosophical pragmatism of William James and John Dewey, together with its postmodern reworking by thinkers like Stephen Toulmin, Richard Bernstein, Donald Polkinghorne and Richard Rorty. It integrates selective elements from the two dialectically opposed epistemological paradigms that have dominated forensic psychology: positivism and hermeneutics.

In research method, pragmatic psychology proposes the creation of peer-reviewed databases of systematic, rigorous, solution-focused case studies that draw on quantitative and qualitative data. As a result, pragmatic psychology focuses on contextualized knowledge about particular individuals, groups, organizations and communities in specific situations, sensitive to the complexities and ambiguities of the real world. By applying rigorous standards to a case study's design, method, and quantitative and qualitative data, pragmatic psychology yields a new type of scientifically legitimate empirical evidence upon which to base forensic psychology's practice and theorizing. (See Elliott, Fischer and Rennie 1999 and Patton 2002 for examples of the development of rigorous standards in qualitative research.)

The application of psychological knowledge to the legal system transcends national boundaries, but conventions regarding nomenclature vary in different communities, necessitating a cautionary note about terminology. In the USA, the application of experimental psychology to the law is commonly referred to as 'legal psychology', whereas the term 'forensic psychology' is reserved for clinical practice within the legal system (Brigham 1999) and also encompasses what in Australia is more squarely within the province of forensic psychiatry, i.e. mental illness and disorder related to the law. In the

United Kingdom, 'forensic psychology' has a broader application, and includes quantitative topics such as statistical profiling.

Until recently, most mainstream applied psychologists discounted case-based knowledge in favour of positivistically oriented, group-based knowledge. Their argument has been that since each case is unique in some ways, it is questionable to generalize to other cases based on data from a single case (as opposed to group-based data that samples a population to which generalization is statistically built in). An answer to this critique is found in the structure of judicial case law. Judicial case law operates by examining a large number of other cases to find similar ones in the past that share common and relevant characteristics with the present target case, and that can thus inform the target case. As a general rule, the more similar cases there are, the stronger the evidence is. Thus, archiving more and more cases over time increases the truth-seeking validity of this approach. The most effective way to find relevant past legal cases has been to archive them in computerized, full-text-searchable databases, such as Lexis.

Applying pragmatic psychology to the psycholegal domain leads to the 'Psycholegal Lexis Proposal', a call for developing a peer-reviewed, case archive system in forensic psychology that parallels the Lexis or similar computerized database systems so central to legal research and legal reasoning throughout much of the world. Notable here is the commonality in nature and structure between pragmatic psychology knowledge and legal knowledge. Specifically, (a) both identify the basic unit of knowledge as the case study; (b) both are organized around databases of systematic, detailed and searchable descriptions of individual cases; and (c) both use case-based reasoning (Fishman 1999, pp. 192–5) to perform cross-case analyses in the inductive search for general patterns that can serve as guidelines in understanding and deciding about new cases. This commonality is of particular value for pragmatic forensic psychologists' reports and research since it enhances the logical connection and relevance of this work to judicial knowledge, e.g. regarding the role that legal precedent plays. Moreover, this commonality enhances the accessibility and relevance of pragmatic forensic psychology knowledge to non-psychologists such as judges and lawyers, who already understand the case-based nature of legal knowledge.

Background

Forensic psychologists often distinguish applications of psychology *in* law, *and* law, and *of* law (Haney 1980). One aim of forensic psychology *in* law is to apply psychological methods and theory to help accomplish the goals of the law, which remain dominant, such as choosing fair juries, objectively assessing the reliability of eyewitness testimony, determining whether criminal acts were committed during states of insanity, and accurately assessing an offender's dangerousness. The conduct of psychology *and* law regards the two disciplines as co-equals, and applies psychological principles to examine and analyse aspects of the legal system to bring about legal change. An example is a study of psychological or extralegal factors that influence decisions to arrest, charge, prosecute and sentence a defendant. An exploration of psychology *of* law uses psychological methods to address the nature and sources of legal power, and circumstances in which it is or is not effective, for instance, to examine features that promote or diminish compliance, confidence in, and satisfaction with the law.

In working towards these diverse goals, forensic psychology has shown a split personality. On the one hand, a positivist forensic psychology identifies with the model of natural science. It strives to base every conclusion about a particular forensic issue on its 'gold standard' of evidence: experimental or quasi-experimental group studies that quantitatively test general, theoretical hypotheses through the use of sophisticated statistics. The results of such experimental studies appear to yield clear, 'objective' answers in a complex, ambiguous, troubled world – truths that seem to transcend knowledge from more subjective, qualitative and at times ideological disciplines that study human behaviour in other ways, such as history, literature and jurisprudence. Thus positivist psychologists can inform lawyers with relatively little apparent subjectivity, intuition, morality and ideology.

However, there are limitations in applying the natural-scientific/positivist psychology model to the law. For example, the quantitative, probabilistic, group-based, qualified and tentative conclusions of traditional psychological studies are typically ill-suited to the court's needs for certain knowledge that is applicable to an individual case. And the deterministic assumptions of positivist psychology frequently clash with the law's assumption that an actor has free will except under special circumstances.

The lack of complete fit between positivist psychology and the law is reflected in forensic psychology's additional practice of a clinical/hermeneutic model, as represented by the reports and testimony of clinical experts. These practitioners frequently do not base their conclusions upon group studies and statistical data. Rather, they immerse themselves in the contexts and qualitative details of individual cases. They put heavy emphasis on their intuitional and empathetic abilities, and their ability to write rich, accessible, qualitative narrative in a manner that is consistent with the clinical literature (Grove and Meehl 1996; Melton *et al.* 1997). However, this hermeneutic model lacks the quality controls to constrain the individual psychologist's subjective, personal bias in the selection and interpretation of the data included in their reports (Kahneman 2003); and this approach is not grounded in systematic comparisons of the present case with carefully documented past cases that are similar.

Pragmatic psychology proposes a third model that incorporates some of the strengths from each of the other two models (Fishman 1999, 2003, 2004, 2005). For example, in line with the hermeneutic model, a basic unit of analysis in pragmatic forensic psychology is the qualitatively described, holistic, systematic case study of a particular individual, and generalizations are inductively developed by cross-case comparisons. At the same time, in line with the positivist model and tradition, (a) quantitative, population-based measures are employed to provide a normative framework as one way of understanding the individual case; (b) there is a major investment in ensuring methodological rigour in how a case is described and interpreted, including both quantitative and qualitative data; and (c) systematic, behaviourally specific observation is emphasized.

The way in which pragmatic psychology is integrative of the positivist and hermeneutic traditions is illustrated in the prediction of dangerousness, as highlighted by Miller and Morris (1988) and later discussed by Melton *et al.* (1997). These authors differentiate two desirable approaches in assessing risk for violence, labelled 'actuarial' and 'anamnestic.'

Actuarial prediction explicitly identifies the criteria used (in gathering categories of data about each individual) and the weights assigned to each. The choice of data categories is driven by empirical research that demarcates which groups of individuals, because of specific characteristics that determine group membership, are at relatively higher risk. A rigorously actuarial approach would also involve the mathematical combination of these variables to generate the prediction.

The anamnestic approach depends on the identification of factors that have distinguished a particular subject's prior displays of aggressive behaviour. The clinician attempts to reconstruct vignettes through archival information detailing specific prior incidents of violence and through direct clinical interview of the individual and collateral sources. Analysis of these vignettes should yield insights about repetitive themes that cut across violent events, revealing person or situational factors, or person–situation interactions, that inform judgements of risk-level or risk management strategies (Melton *et al.* 1997, p. 284).

Table 1.11.1 Themes

Topic	Summary of pragmatic psychology contributions
'Scientizing' expert testimony Slobogin (2003) Dowdle (2003)	Discussion of how pragmatic psychology might accommodate the recent trend to 'scientize' expert evidence. One conclusion is that pragmatic psychology is consistent with this trend, in that it takes the traditional, clinical/hermeneutic model to a new level of rigour, defining science as 'the systematic, methodologically rigorous and scholarly collection and interpretation of empirical evidence, be it quantitative or qualitative, experimental or naturalistic, behavioral or phenomenological' (Fishman 2004, p. 184).
Adding rigour to the clinical/hermeneutic model Heilbrun, DeMatteo and Marczyk (2004)	Analysis of the forensic psychology practice literature to derive twenty-nine quality principles that apply to any individual forensic mental health report. These principles are organized around four broad stages of forensic assessment: (1) preparation; (2) data collection; (3) data interpretation; and (4) communication. These principles operationally define expert reports that have a high scientific and professional quality, based on consensual views in the scientific and professional literature in forensic psychology, thus providing guidelines for lawyers, judges and juries to evaluate the quality of expert testimony.
Integrating actuarial and anamnestic data Alison, West and Goodwill (2004)	Presentation of a specific, formal method for pragmatically integrating actuarial and anamnestic data to generate scientifically rigorous offender profiles. The model is illustrated in a detailed case report of a suspected murderer, pseudonymously named 'Jeff Myers'.
Developing therapeutic jurisprudence Birgden and Ward (2003)	In therapeutic jurisprudence (TJ), the law itself (legal rules, procedures, and the roles of legal actors) is a potential therapeutic agent. Thus, TJ brings a pragmatic, problem-solving attitude towards legal disputes, indicating a resonance between the goals of TJ and pragmatic psychology. The method of systematic case studies in pragmatic psychology captures (a) instances of a particular judicial situation that demonstrate more or less therapeutic approaches, within the legal constraints of the situation, and (b) instances of past therapeutic successes that comprise guides for present practice.
Providing systematic and detailed examples of individual case studies in pragmatic forensic psychology	Illustrations of the value of pragmatic case studies in documenting and modelling expert evidence on a forensic question about a particular individual case. The questions: whether to transfer an assaultive adolescent to adult criminal court (Witt 2003); whether an intellectually disabled individual is competent to stand trial (Schlesinger 2003); and whether the parental rights of a mother with past substance abuse problems should be terminated (Dyer 2004).
Using multiple case studies in pragmatic forensic psychology	Illustrations of the use of multiple case studies to inform a forensic policy question: how a court can more systematically and rationally determine circumstances under which 'extreme emotional disturbance' should be sustained or rejected (Kirschner, Litwack and Galperin 2004); how a court can determine appropriate accommodation for the intellectually disabled (Kinsler, Saxman and Fishman 2004); and how the court can intervene to remediate infant and child maltreatment (Lederman and Osofsky 2004).

Melton *et al.* (1997) point out that pragmatic best practice would dictate using both actuarial data, for normatively contextualizing the particular case, and anamnestic data for behaviourally individualizing the case.

Development of the pragmatic forensic psychology model

The main developments in pragmatic forensic psychology are documented in a two-part themed series of fourteen articles, titled 'Pragmatic Psychology and the Law', edited by the present authors (Fishman 2003, 2004). Specifically, the articles were created to critically explore and develop the 'Psycholegal Lexis Proposal', which, as described above, calls for enhancing forensic psychology's contribution to the law by the creation of a peer-reviewed, published archive of systemic case studies of exemplary forensic practice. To sample different disciplinary perspectives, the series includes one or more authors in the following categories: academic forensic psychologists, practising clinical forensic psychologists, academic lawyers, practising lawyers, judges and public defenders. Table 1.11.1 summarizes the themes that emerged in this series.

In sum, pragmatic psychology has been demonstrated as a relevant and appealing model for practice in forensic psychology. Finally, it should be noted that the first author (DBF) has developed and edits, and the second author (JGD) sits on the editorial board of, a peer-reviewed, open-access, fully searchable e-journal in another applied psychology area, titled *Pragmatic Case Studies in Psychotherapy* (http://pcsp.libraries.rutgers.edu). Their experience with this journal suggests that developing a parallel journal in forensic psychology is very feasible and would be an important step towards realizing the potentials of the Psycholegal Lexis Proposal.

REFERENCES

Alison, L., West, A. and Goodwill, A. (2004) The academic and the practitioner: pragmatists' views of offender profiling. *Psychology, Public Policy, and Law*, 10: 71–101.

Birgden, A. and Ward, T. (2003) Pragmatic psychology through a therapeutic jurisprudence lens: psycholegal soft spots in the criminal justice system. *Psychology, Public Policy, and Law*, 9: 334–60.

Brigham, J. C. (1999) What is forensic psychology, anyway? *Law and Human Behaviour*, 23: 273–98.

Dowdle, M. W. (2003) Deconstructing Graeme: observations on 'pragmatic psychology', forensics, and the institutional epistemology of the courts. *Psychology, Public Policy, and Law*, 9: 301–33.

Dyer, F. J. (2004) Termination of parental rights in light of attachment theory: the case of Kaylee. *Psychology, Public Policy, and Law*, 10: 5–30.

Elliott, R., Fischer, C. T. and Rennie, D. L. (1999) Evolving guidelines for publication of qualitative research studies in psychology and related fields. *British Journal of Clinical Psychology*, 38: 215–29.

Fishman, D. B. (1999) *The Case for Pragmatic Psychology*. New York: NYU Press.

(2003) Background on the 'Psycholegal Lexis Proposal': exploring the potential of a systematic case study database in forensic psychology. *Psychology, Public Policy, and Law*, 9: 267–74.

(2004) Integrative themes: Prospects for developing a 'Psycholegal Lexis'. *Psychology, Public Policy, and Law*, 10: 178–200.

(2005) Editor's introduction to PCSP – from single case to database: a new method for enhancing psychotherapy practice. *Pragmatic Case Studies in Psychotherapy*, 1: 1–50. Available: http://hdl.rutgers.edu/1782.1/pcsp_journal.

Grove, W. M. and Meehl, P. E. (1996) Comparative efficiency of informal (subjective, impressionistic) and formal (mechanical, algorithmic) prediction procedures: the clinical-statistical controversy. *Psychology, Public Policy and Law*, 2: 293–323.

Haney, C. (1980) Psychology and legal change: on the limits of factual jurisprudence. *Law and Human Behavior*, 4: 147–200.

Heilbrun, K., DeMatteo, D. and Marczyk, G. (2004) Pragmatic psychology, forensic mental health assessment, and the case of Thomas Johnson: applying principles to promote quality. *Psychology, Public Policy, and Law*, 10: 31–70.

Kahneman (2003) A perspective on judgment and choice: mapping bounded rationality. *American Psychologist*, 58: 697–720.

Kinsler, P. J., Saxman, A. and Fishman, D. B. (2004) The Vermont Defendant Accommodation Project: a case study. *Psychology, Public Policy, and Law*, 10: 134–61.

Kirschner, S. M., Litwack, T. R. and Galpern, G. J. (2004) The defense of Extreme Emotional Disturbance: a qualitative analysis of cases in New York County. *Psychology, Public Policy, and Law*, 10: 102–33.

Lederman, C. S. and Osofsky, J. D. (2004) Infant mental health interventions in juvenile court: ameliorating the effects of maltreatment and deprivation. *Psychology, Public Policy, and Law*, 10: 162–77.

Melton, G. B., Petrila, J., Poythress, N. G. and Slobogin, C. (1997) *Psychological Evaluations in the Courts: A Handbook for Mental Health Professionals and Lawyers*, 2nd edn. New York: Guilford Press.

Miller, M. and Morris, N. (1988) Predictions of dangerousness: an argument for limited use. *Violence and Victims*, 3: 263–83.

Patton, M. Q. (2002) *Qualitative Research and Evaluation Methods*, 3rd edn. Thousand Oaks, CA: Sage.

Schlesinger, L. B. (2003) A case study involving competency to stand trial: incompetent defendant, incompetent examiner, or 'malingering by proxy'? *Psychology, Public Policy, and Law*, 9: 381–99.

Slobogin, C. (2003) Pragmatic forensic psychology: a means of 'scientizing' expert testimony from mental health professionals? *Psychology, Public Policy, and Law*, 9: 275–300.

Witt, P. H. (2003) Transfer of juveniles to adult court: the case of H. H. *Psychology, Public Policy, and Law*, 9: 361–80.

1.12 Sexual offenders

Anthony R. Beech

See also chapter 3.12 Treatment of sexual offenders.

Definitions

The latest statistics, from Jansson, Povey and Kaiza (2007) for the years 2006–7, report that the police recorded 57,542 sexual offences in England and Wales (which is just under 1 per cent of all of the recorded crime for this period). Of these reported crimes, just over three-quarters (43,755) are classified as serious sexual offences, i.e. rape, sexual assault and sexual activity with children. The other (less serious) sexual offences consist of unlawful sexual activity with mostly 'consenting' adults, such as exploitation of prostitution and soliciting. Adult males are the most common perpetrators of serious sexual offending. About a third of all sexual offences are committed by juveniles (Lovell 2002). Women who sexually offend account for less than 1% of sex offenders in prison (data from National Offender Management Service, UK 2007), however, this figure can be regarded as a severe underestimate of the actual number of women who sexually abuse. For example, figures from Childline, November 2009, indicate that those children calling about being abused sexually by a female was 25%.

Most is known about the following 'types' of sexual offenders.

Exhibitionists

This type is classed as non-contact because offenders do not physically touch the victim but instead typically expose their genitals from a distance. Figures suggest that exhibitionism accounts for one-third of all identified sexual offending (Murphy and Page 2008). Exhibitionism, like most paraphilias (deviant sexual interests), is primarily a male disorder (Murphy and Page 2008), although a recent study of exhibitionistic, and voyeuristic, behaviour in a Swedish national population survey, reported by Långström and Seto (2006), found fairly high rates of self-reported exhibitionism among females. The motivation for such offences varies and influences the degree of risk of more serious contact offences presented by the offender. Rooth (1973) classified exhibitionists into: Type 1 – the 'inhibited, flaccid exposer'; and Type 2 – the 'sociopathic, erect exposer' who may well go on to commit contact sexual offences.

Internet offenders

These are a relatively new type of sexual offender who have been charged or convicted of downloading illegal sexual material (usually child pornography) from the internet. The Internet Watch Foundation (IWF 2006) reported that in 2005, 6,128 sites were reported to the IWF for investigation, with the majority being hosted in the US (40%) and Russia (28%); 211 internet newsgroups were listed as being potentially illegal, with additional notices served to internet service providers to remove 12,777 images from a further 226 newsgroups. Hence there are large numbers of individuals involved. Internet offenders can be broadly categorized into four groups (Lanning 2001; Krone 2004): those who

1. access abusive images sporadically, impulsively and/or out of curiosity;
2. access/trade abusive images to fuel their sexual interest in children;
3. use the internet as part of a pattern of offline contact offending, including
   (a) using the internet as a tool for locating and/or grooming contact victims,
   (b) using the internet to disseminate images that they have produced;
4. access abusive images for seemingly non-sexual reasons (e.g. for financial profit).

Child sexual abusers / child molesters

An NSPCC survey (Cawson *et al.* 2000) found that 16% of young adults (aged 16–24) had reported being sexually abused as a child, with 11% reporting contact sexual offences. These figures suggest that there are a huge number of individuals committing child molestation. As for report rates of this type of crime, generally speaking, the more serious the type of offence, and the more distant the relationship between victim and offender, the more likely the offence is to be reported (Myhill and Allen 2002). While, Prentky and

Burgess (2000) note that underreporting tends to be greater when offences are carried out against males rather than against females. Child molesters are often classified according to their relationship with the victim: intrafamilial/ extrafamilial; and/or gender of victim they target (i.e. male or female, or both). A more useful categorization has been provided by Beech (1998) of *High/Low* deviance offenders, related to level of psychological problems.[1] Motivations may range from men having a primary sexual interest in children (paedophiles), to individuals (hebephiles) who have offended against older age adolescents (often daughters or stepdaughters).

Rapists

In 2007 there were 13,780 reported rapes,[2] 92% (12,630) were of women and 8% (1,150) rapes of men (Jansson *et al.* 2007). Myhill and Allen (2002) suggest that women in the 16 to 24 age range are most at risk, and women were most likely to be attacked by men they knew, with current partners accounting for 45% of the rapes, with strangers only accounting for 8% of these offences. Myhill and Allen found that 74% of women raped reported the use of physical force or violence, with 37% resulting in physical injury, of these 10% reported 'severe' injury, suggesting more than a sexual motivation to these assaults. Knight and Prentky (1990) reported a typology of rapists that can be summed up as suggesting that there are three sorts of motivation (Beech *et al.* 2006): *sexual* (opportunistic; or planned sexually non-sadistic); *anger* (vindictively angry; pervasively angry); *sadistic*.

Sexual murderers

Amongst men who murder their victim, during the commission of a sexual offence, motivations may vary from those who murder their victim to prevent disclosure of the sexual offence, to anger, to those who find the murder arousing in itself. Therefore, like rapists, the motivations for this offence can be seen as *sexual, angry* or *sadistic* (Beech *et al.* 2006). Beech *et al.* estimate that approximately 6 per cent of men in prison in the UK for murder have been identified as having committed a murder with an apparent, or admitted, sexual motivation.

---

[1] Dynamic risk factors, see below.
[2] Rape is defined as 'forced sexual intercourse (vaginal or anal penetration) but does not stipulate that penetration has to be penile.

This contrasts with figures of just under 1 per cent in the USA and Canada, reported by Proulx, Cusson and Beauregard (2007).

Crossover patterns of sexual offenders

A frequent question for those involved in the field concerns the likelihood that someone who has been convicted for a particular type of sexual offence will present a risk to different types of victim. Cann, Friendship and Gozna (2007), in a sample of 1,345 male sexual offenders, report that 24.5% of the sample demonstrated 'crossover behaviour' in terms of: age (over/under 16), gender, or relationship to victim (intra/extrafamilial). Worryingly, in a study where the polygraph (lie detector) was used Heil, Ahlmeyer and Simons (2003) reported that 52% of their rapist sample reported child abuse offences, and 78% of their child molester sample reported sexually offending against adults. As for the risk of crossover in those who have committed internet offences, it has been found that a number of individuals arrested for accessing and collecting abusive images of children were also found to be abusing children (Wellard 2001; Dobson 2003).

Theories of sexual abuse

Ward and Hudson (1998) have distinguished three levels of theory in sexual offending as follows:

Level I (comprehensive) theories

The latest example of a comprehensive theory of sexual offending has been described by Ward and Beech (2006). Here they describe three sets of factors: *biological* (influenced by genetic inheritance and brain development); *ecological* niche factors,[3] i.e. social, cultural and personal circumstances; and *neuropsychological* factors. In this theory, sexual offending occurs through the ongoing confluence of *distal* and *proximal* factors that interact in a dynamic way. Genetic predispositions and social learning have a significant impact upon brain development and three interlocking neuropsychological systems: *motivational/emotional, perception and memory*, and *action selection*

---

[3] According to Steiner, 'Ecology is, by definition, the reciprocal relationship among all organisms and their biological and physical environments' (2002, p. 2). The habitat is the actual locality in which a person resides and niche is the role(s) occupied by that person in an ecological community.

and control, which underpin human behaviours. Ward and Beech suggest that genes, social learning and neuropsychological systems interact to generate the following clinical problems evident in offenders: deviant arousal; offence-related thoughts and fantasies; social difficulties; and emotional dysregulation problems.[4] While the consequences of sexually abusive behaviour function to maintain a positive feedback loop that entrenches the offender's vulnerabilities through their impact on the environment, and psychological functioning, i.e. the consequences of sexual offending will function to maintain and/or further escalate sexually deviant actions.

Level II (single factor) theories

The psychological mechanism that level II theories describe are also typically termed dynamic risk factors and have been most clearly described by Hanson and Harris (2000a) and Thornton (2002). Thornton in fact suggests that there are four dynamic risk domains (sexual interests, pro-offending attitudes, socio-affective problems, self-regulation problems (behavioural emotional)) which are described below in the risk assessment section.

Level III (process) theories

These describe the process of offending and typically describe either the process or the offence itself in terms of the build-up of behaviours during and behaviours/feelings after the offence has taken place. Ward and Hudson (1998) suggest that it is possible to classify offenders according to one of four different routes to offending. These groups are defined by the individual offender's goal towards deviant sex (i.e. avoidant or approach), and the selection of strategies designed to achieve their goal (i.e. active or passive).

Risk assessment

There are three main strategies used in the assessment of risk and treatment need in sexual offenders (see table 1.12.1)

The most commonly used actuarial risk assessment in the UK is Risk-Matrix 2000 (RM2000; Thornton *et al.* 2003). RM2000 has two scales, one for

---

[4] These problems clearly map onto dynamic risk factors (see below in the risk assessment section).

Table 1.12.1 Risk assessment techniques

Strategies	Method	Focus	Purpose
Functional analysis	Clinical tool	Investigates the antecedents, behaviours and consequences of the offence	Ascertains the type of goals and strategies a sexual offender has towards offending
Actuarial risk assessments	Checklist	Identifies presence/absence of static/historical risk factors	Provide guidance as to the general band of risk that an offender falls into (e.g. low, medium, high risk)
Dynamic risk assessment	Research/ clinical	Identifies (a) stable dynamic risk factors, (b) acute dynamic factors	Includes those areas that may be amenable to change in treatment, such as deviant sexual interest, pro-offending attitudes, socio-affective problems and self-management issues, i.e. those factors that may be related to imminent sexual offending)

measuring risk of sexual recidivism and one for measuring risk of non-sexual violent recidivism. The sexual recidivism scale, RM2000/S, uses a two-step system of risk assessment. *Step 1* contains three risk items (number of previous sexual appearances, number of criminal appearances and age), the sum of which is translated into a risk category (Low, Medium, High, Very High). *Step 2* considers four aggravating risk factors: any conviction for a sexual offence against a male; any conviction for a sexual offence against a stranger; any conviction for a non-contact sex offence; and single – never been married. The presence of two or four aggravating factors raises the risk category by one or two levels respectively.

The following systems are currently available to assess stable dynamic risk factors: (1) the Structured Assessment of Risk and Need (SARN, Thornton 2002; Webster *et al.* 2006); (2) STABLE-2007 (Hanson *et al.* 2007). SARN uses clinical ratings assessing sixteen dynamic risk factors, categorized into each of Thornton's dynamic risk domains. STABLE-2007 assesses the following dimensions: significant social influences; intimacy deficits; attitudes supportive of sexual assault; cooperation with supervision; sexual self-regulation; and general self-regulation. While ACUTE 2007 (Hanson *et al.* 2007) assesses the following acute risk factors: victim access; emotional collapse (i.e. evidence of severe emotional disturbance / emotional crisis); collapse of social supports; hostility; substance abuse; sexual preoccupations and rejection of supervision; and a 'unique factor' particular to the individual being assessed.

Any comprehensive assessment should measure all of these areas problem areas in the individual being assessed.

FURTHER READING

Richard Laws and William O'Donohue's edited book *Sexual Deviance*, 2nd edn (2008) provides useful overview of the full range of types of sexual offending. For each major type of sexual offending, a chapter on psychopathology and theory is followed by a chapter on assessment and treatment. Ward, Polaschek and Beech (2006) provide an overview of the different theories of sexual offending. For an overview of how to carry out a risk assessment of a sex offender, see Beech, Fisher and Thornton (2003). For a more in-depth description of the assessment process, see Craig *et al.* (2008). As for pulling the elements of risk together, Beech and Ward (2004) describe a 'risk-aetiology' model, where they attempt to integrate the disparate aspects of risk assessment together.

REFERENCES

Beech, A. R. (1998) A psychometric typology of child abusers. *International Journal of Offender Therapy and Comparative Criminology*, 42: 319–39.

Beech, A. R., Fisher, D. and Thornton, D. (2003) Risk assessment of sex offenders. *Professional Psychology: Research and Practice*, 34: 339–52.

Beech, A. R., Oliver, C., Fisher, D. and Beckett, R. C. (2006) *STEP 4: The Sex Offender Treatment Programme in Prison: Addressing the Needs of Rapists and Sexual Murderers*. Birmingham: University of Birmingham. Available online: www.hmprisonservice.gov.uk/assets/documents/100013DBStep_4_SOTP_report_2005.pdf

Beech, A. R. and Ward, T. (2004) The integration of etiology and risk in sexual offenders: a theoretical framework. *Aggression and Violent Behavior*, 10: 31–63.

Cann, J., Friendship, C. and Gozna, L. (2007) Assessing crossover in a sample of sexual offenders. *Legal and Criminological Psychology*, 12: 149–63.

Cawson, P., Wattam, C., Brooker, S. and Kelly, G. (2000) *Child Maltreatment in the United Kingdom: A Study of Prevalence of Child Abuse and Neglect*. London: NSPCC.

Craig, L., Browne, K. D. and Beech, A. R. (2008) *Assessing Risk in Sex Offenders: A Practitioner's Guide*. Chichester: Wiley.

Dobson, A. (2003) Caught in the net. *Care and Health*, 11: 6–9.

Hanson, R. K., Harris, A. J. R., Scott, T.-L. and Helmus, L. (2007) *Assessing the Risk of Sexual Offenders on Community Supervision: The Dynamic Supervision Project* (no. 2007–05). Ottawa: Public Safety Canada.

Heil, P., Ahlmeyer, S. and Simons, D. (2003). Crossover sexual offenses. *Sexual Abuse: A Journal of Research and Treatment*, 15: 221–36.

Internet Watch Foundation (2006) *2005 Annual and Charity Report.* www.iwf.org.uk/documents/20060306_iwf_200_annual_report_lo-res_website_final.pdf (accessed 19 October 2006).

Jansson, K., Povey, D. and Kaiza, P. (2007) Violent and sexual crime. In S. Nicholas, C. Kershaw and A. Walker (eds.), *Crime in England and Wales 2006/07*, 4th edn, pp. 49–65. London: Home Office.

Knight, R. A., and Prentky, R. A. (1990) Classifying sexual offenders: the development and corroboration of taxonomic models. In W. L. Marshall, D. R. Laws and H. E. Barbaree (eds.), *The Handbook of Sexual Assault: Issues, Theories, and Treatment of the Offender*, pp. 23–52. New York: Academic Press.

Krone, T. (2004) A typology of online child pornography offending. *Trends and Issues in Crime and Criminal Justice*, 279: 1–6.

Långström, N. and Seto, M. C. (2006) Exhibitionistic and voyeuristic behavior in a Swedish national population survey. *Archives of Sexual Behavior*, 35: 427–35.

Lanning, K. V. (2001) *Child Molesters: A Behavioral Analysis*, 4th edn. www.ncmec.org/en_US/publications/NC70.pdf (accessed 20 October 2006).

Laws, D. R. and O'Donohue, W. T. (eds.) (2008) *Sexual Deviance: Theory, Assessment and Treatment*, 2nd edn. New York: Guilford Press.

Lovell. E. (2002) *Children and Young People Who Display Sexually Harmful Behaviour.* London: NSPCC.

Murphy, W. D. and Page, J. (2008). Exhibitionism: psychopathology and theory. In D. R. Laws and W. T. O'Donohue (eds.), *Sexual Deviance: Theory, Assessment and Treatment*, 2nd edn, pp. 61–75. New York: Guilford Press.

Myhill, A. and Allen, J. (2002) Rape and sexual assault of women: the extent of the problem. Home Office Study, 237. London: Home Office. Available online: www.homeoffice.gov.uk/rds/pdfs2/hors237.pdf.

National Offender Management Service (2007) *Prison Population and Accommodation Briefing.* http://home.ps.gov.uk (accessed 20 February 2007).

Prentky, R. A. and Burgess, A. W. (2000) *Forensic Management of Sexual Offenders: Perspectives in Sexuality, Behavior, Research and Therapy.* New York: Kluwer Academic / Plenum.

Proulx, J., Cusson, M. and Beauregard, É. (2007) Sexual murder: definitions, epidemiology and theories. In J. Proulx, É. Beauregard, M. Cusson and A. Nicole (eds.), *Sexual Murderers: A Comparative Analysis and New Perspectives*, pp. 9–28. Chichester: Wiley.

Rooth, G. (1973) Exhibitionism, sexual violence and paedophilia. *British Journal of Psychiatry*, 122: 705–10.

Steiner, F (2002) *Human Ecology: Following Nature's Lead.* Washington, DC: Island Press.

Thornton, D. (2002) Construction and testing; a framework for dynamic risk assessment. *Sexual Abuse: A Journal of Research and Treatment*, 14: 137–51.

Thornton, D., Mann, R., Webster, S., Blud, L., Travers, R., Friendship, C. and Erikson, M. (2003) Distinguishing and combining risks for sexual and violent recidivism. In R. Prentky, E. Janus, M. Seto and A. W. Burgess (eds.), *Understanding and Managing Sexually Coercive Behavior* (Annals of the New York Academy of Sciences, 989), pp. 225–35. New York: Annals of the New York Academy of Sciences.

Ward, T. and Beech, A. R. (2006) An integrated theory of sex offending. *Aggression and Violent Behavior*, 11: 44–63.

Ward, T. and Hudson, S. M. (1998) A model of the relapse process in sexual offenders. *Journal of Interpersonal Violence*, 13: 700–25.

Ward, T., Polaschek, D. and Beech, A. R. (2006) *Theories of Sexual Offending*. Chichester: Wiley.

Webster, S. D., Mann, R. E., Carter, A. J., Long, J., Milner, R. J., O'Brien, M. D., Wakeling, H. C. and Ray, N. L. (2006) Inter-rater reliability of dynamic risk assessment with sexual offenders. *Psychology, Crime and Law*, 12: 439–52.

Wellard, S. (2001) Cause and effect. *Community Care*, 15–21 March, 26–7.

1.13 Social psychological theories applied to forensic psychology topics

Jennifer M. Brown

See also chapter 8.1 Criminals' personal narratives, chapter 6.5 Guns and shootings, chapter 1.12 Sexual offenders.

Definition

The aim of social psychology is 'to analyse and understand human social behaviour' (Tajfel and Fraser 1978, p. 17). At its heart is social interaction and the capacity of humans to monitor, with differing degrees of skill, the effects of one's own and others' social actions within the complexity of a social environment. Moreover, as Tajfel and Fraser expound, human beings do this within a nexus of acquired loyalties, affiliations and attitudes (about human nature, justice and injustice, social stability and change), mostly doing so according to self-interest and, as far as possible, based on value judgements. Social psychology examines social systems (groups, networks, communities) in which human behaviour is manifest and is also preoccupied with how individuals construct their social worlds (in other words, their search for meaning).

Uses

David Canter and colleagues at the Centre for Investigative Psychology at the University of Liverpool (see Canter and Alison 2000) argue that a social psychological dimension has been largely absent from consideration of criminal behaviour and also the interactions between offenders and investigators. Thus much of the research that does exist develops models of the organization of crime (leadership in criminal partnerships and gangs, development of roles with criminal networks) and styles of interactions (e.g. in hostage taking or rape). The basic premise is that criminal activity is an accessible negotiated transaction having discernible roles and rules.

Attitudes to and about specific crimes and criminals have also been the focus of interest. A related area has been prejudice and discrimination, where social psychological models have been developed examining racism, sexism and homophobia (see e.g. Borgida and Fiske (2008), who chart the theoretical basis of expert courtroom testimony in cases of race and sex discrimination).

The criminal justice practitioner and system have also been the subject of analysis using social psychological formulations. Roycroft, Brown and Inness (2007) examined why particular murder investigations seem to catch the public attention more than others, gaining media notoriety by adapting the social amplification of risk formulation. Central to the SARF framework are notions of trust, presence of a stigmatized activity and a vulnerable victim. Public concern becomes heightened especially in the presence of a leading advocate such as Mrs Lawrence in the case of the murder of her son Stephen. SARF has also been used in explaining why Megan Kanka's death in the United States in 1994 led to Megan's Law to make public the whereabouts of released sex offenders, but its counterpart in the UK, Sarah's Law after Sarah Payne's murder, did not gather the same momentum (Gowda 2003).

The concept of social identity drawing on identity process theory (Breakwell 1986) has been used to underpin exploration of policewomen's occupational identity (Brown 2007). IPT provides a model in which three key processes interact: continuity, distinctiveness and self-efficacy. Brown shows how male police officers who feel their identity is threatened seek to re-establish continuity with traditional gender roles, recreate distinctiveness between them and their women colleagues and define their self-efficacy by asserting that their superior physical proficiency is essential to good policing.

Theoretical positioning

There are a plethora of theoretical formulations and models within social psychology and no one is applicable to all behaviours. Very broadly, there are two epistemological traditions (Glassman 2000). One is based on logical empiricism effecting a neutrality of topic and framework by the researcher whereby hypotheses are formulated to test existing theory Research is designed, data generated and analysed to support or reject the theory. Social constructionism on the other hand rejects the researcher's neutrality and argues that meanings are an active process and is the product of the interaction between researcher and research participant. These approaches use different methodologies. The former tends towards quantitative approaches, the latter qualitative. Underpinning ideas of constructing meanings from research participants is Glaser and Strauss' 'Grounded Theory' (Corbin and Strauss 1990; Strauss and Corbin 1990). The basic idea of this approach is that the theory emerges from the data, which maybe an interview or field notes, and the analysis discovers or labels variables (called categories, concepts and properties). Corbin and Strauss (1990, p. 7) emphasize that categories are the 'cornerstones' of developing theory. They provide the means by which the theory can be integrated and relationships established.

Concepts

The concept of attitudes has been one of the key notions used to examine responses towards a variety of crimes and offenders. Thus community responses towards sex offenders (Church *et al.* 2008) and rape victims (Ward 1988) have been explored. More targeted groups such as young people have been the focus of inquiries in terms of their attitudes towards weapons (e.g. Branscome, Weir and Crosby 1991) and drugs (Measham, Parker and Aldridge 1998). Ajzen (2005), in discussing the concept of attitudes, declares these to be latent hypothetical characterizations inferred from observable external cues, usually behaviour and the context in which they occur. There are said to be affective, cognitive and conative components of attitude which should correlate. Thus the Ajzen and Fishbein tripartite model assumes that the presence of the object elicits an evaluative reaction and evokes a corresponding behavioural response. Attitudes are a feature of Ajzen's (1991) Theory of Planned Behaviour. Briefly stated, this predicts the relationship between attitudes and behaviour as being subject to three main influences: evaluation of the behaviour (attitudes); perception of the social pressures to engage in the behaviour (subjective norms) and perception of the controls governing performance of the behaviour (perceived behavioural control). Underlying these are specific beliefs about the consequences of engaging in behaviours (behavioural beliefs), perceived wishes of important referents (normative beliefs) and those factors which may inhibit or facilitate performance (control beliefs). Norman, Bennett and Lewis (1998) used this framework to explore the key influences on binge drinking in young people. They operationalized their measures and constructed a questionnaire distributed to 136 undergraduates. Their analyses supported the tenets of the theory and found important differences between men and women binge drinkers, with men more likely to be influenced by their own favourable attitudes and subjective norms that endorse drinking to excess.

A rather different approach was taken by Lea, Auburn and Kibblewhite (1999) when they were exploring attitudes of professionals working with sex offenders. They undertook detailed semi-structured interviews with twenty-three key workers and conducted a content analysis. What emerged from the data was a concept they term the personal professional dialectic. This was the dilemma which the workers found themselves in when their professional role encouraged engagement with these offenders in treatment interventions but their personal revulsion for the offences created a distance between them and their clients. This tension could be thought of as conflicts between subjective norms (i.e. social pressures of public disapprobation of the offence and professional pressures to be non-judgemental.) Professionals in the study responded differently, with some 'shuttling' between the personal and professional whilst others tried to separate the two. In both cases these strategies made empathizing with the offender difficult.

Critiques of models that were unable to predict differences between expressed values and performance emerged in research examining prejudicial and discriminatory attitudes, especially when psychologists began to appear in employment tribunal cases. Cosby and Bearman (2006) offered the hypocrisy explanation, whereby there appeared to be a difference between not very deeply held official ideology of workplace ethical values of equal treatment and individual self-interest. This effect was demonstrated by reactive priming, where implicit prejudicial attitudes elicited adverse responses when pairing images of black people with words having negative connotations and positive response when pairing images of white people with positively connotated words. They suggest that this may account for aversive racism (whereby a white person is distressed to discover he/she reacts negatively towards black individuals) and benevolent sexism (whereby protective attitudes towards women result in just as aggressive a stance as overtly hostile sexism). Social psychologists reconceptualized gender stereotyping as more complex than a masculinized/feminized dichotomy, but rather recast beliefs about women as being more communal (empathetic, nurturing, understanding) whilst men are seen as agentic (independent, ambitious, good leaders), i.e. women are viewed as warm but less competent whilst men are less warm but competent (Eagley 1987). Research suggested these stereotypes resulted in employment hiring and promotion decisions that judged men as suited to more high-status leadership roles. The likelihood that perceivers will gather or pay attention to stereotype disconfirming information is affected by their preference to confirm or disconfirm their stereotype. This theoretical research was drawn upon by Susan Fiske when she presented expert opinion on the adverse impact of stereotyping in the case of Ann Hopkins versus Price Waterhouse (Fiske *et al.* 1991). Ms Hopkins failed to be promoted as she was held to be too masculine, exemplifying adverse consequences when gender stereotypes are violated. The use of this research and Fiske's conclusions have been subjected to a contrary view and critical review by Barrett and Morris (1993).

Measurement

Given that both qualitative and quantitative methodologies are employed in research using social psychological formulations, some research seeks to develop and validate attitudinal assessments, e.g. community attitudes towards sex offenders' scale (Church *et al.* 2008); attitude to gun crime scale (Branscombe, Weir and Crosby 1991); attitude towards rape victims' scale (Ward 1988). These papers describe the construction of the scales, verifying their psychometric properties. Other research, such as that on implicit attitudes and priming effects, is experimental in design and resides in the social cognition domain. Such approaches are very much in the logical empiricism tradition.

More qualitative methods tend to tackle different types of research questions and examine the phenomenology of an issue or topic, e.g. the personal professional dilemmas in treating sex offenders (Lea, Auburn and Kibblewhite 1999). The social identity of women within a police occupational culture has been investigated by means of discourse analysis (Dick and Cassell 2004, ethnography (Westmarland 2001) and grounded theory (Heidensohn 1992).

Facet theory and multidimensional scaling statistical procedures have also been employed in research looking at a variety of forensic psychology topics (see Canter and Alison 2000). Brown and Barnett (2000) Facet theory offers an approach in research design, analysis and interpretation and its key essential is that a conceptual model will be confirmed if a representation of the predicted relationships can be retrieved empirically. This approach was adopted by Porter and Alison (2006) when examining emergent leadership in criminal groups.

Conclusions

Social psychological concepts, models and theories offer a rich and underused resource in understanding and explaining behaviours within the ambit of forensic psychology enquiry. Methods employed by social psychologists are diverse and lend themselves readily to research within the forensic domain.

FURTHER READING

David Canter and Laurence Alison (2007) bring together a range of studies examining roles, rules and networking within a variety of criminal activities within a social psychological perspective. Eugene Borgida and Susan Fiske (2008) provide an enlightening collection of studies showing the link between social psychological inquiry and use in the courtroom. Paul Norman and his colleagues (1998) provide an excellent summary of the Theory of Planned Behaviour and the exposition of this model in their examination of binge drinking in young people.

REFERENCES

Ajzen, I. (1991) Theory of planned behaviour. *Organisational Behaviour and Human Decision Process*, 50: 179–211.
    (2005) *Attitudes, Personality and Behaviour*, 2nd edn. Milton Keynes: Open University Press.
Barrett, G. V. and Morris, S. B. (1993) Sex stereotyping in Price Waterhouse v. Hopkins. *American Psychologist*, 48: 54–5.
Borgida, E. and Fiske, S. T. (eds.) (2008) *Beyond Commonsense: Psychological Science in the Courtroom*. Malden, MA: Blackwell.
Branscombe, N. R., Weir, J. A. and Crosby, P. (1991) A three factor theory of attitudes towards guns. *Aggressive Behaviour*, 17: 261–73.
Breakwell, G. (1986) *Threatened Identities*. London: Methuen.
Brown, J. (2007) From cult of masculinity to smart macho; gender perspectives on police occupational culture. In M. O'Neill and M. Marks (eds.), *Police Occupational Culture: New Debates and Directions* (Sociology of Crime, Law and Deviance, 8), pp. 189–210. Amsterdam: Elsevier.
Brown, J. M. and Barnett, J. (2000) Facet theory: an approach to research. In G. Breakwell, C. Fife-Schaw and S. Hammond (eds.), *Research Methods in Psychology*, 2nd edn, pp. 105–18. New York: Academic Press.
Canter, D. and Alison, L. (eds.) (2000) *The Social Psychology of Crime: Groups, Teams and Networks*. Aldershot: Ashgate.
Church, W. T., Wakeman, E. E., Miller, S. L., Clements, C. B. and Fie Sun (2008) Community attitudes towards sex offender scale: development of a psychometric assessment instrument. *Research on Social Work Practice*, 18: 251–9.
Corbin, J. and Strauss, A. (1990) Grounded theory research: procedures, canons and evaluative critera. *Qualitative Sociology*, 13: 3–31.
Crosby, F. and Bearman, S. (2006) The uses of a good theory. *Journal of Social Issues*, 62: 415–38.
Dick, P. and Cassell, C. (2004) The position of policewomen: a discourse analytic study. *Work, Employment and Society*, 18: 51–72.
Eagley, A. H. (1987) *Sex Differences in Social Behaviour: A Social Role Interpretation*. Hillsdale, NJ: Erlbaum.

Fiske, S., Bersoff, D. N., Borgida, E., Deaux, K. and Heilman, M. E. (1991) Social science research on trial: use of stereotyping research in Price Waterhouse v. Hopkins. *American Psychology*, 46: 1049–60.

Gowda, R. (2003) Integrating politics and social amplification of risk framework: insights from an exploration in the criminal justice context. In N. Pidgeon, R. Kasperson and P. Slovic (eds.), *The Social Amplification of Risk*, pp. 305–25. Cambridge: Cambridge University Press.

Glassman, W. L. (2000) *Approaches to Psychology*, 3rd edn. Milton Keynes: Open University Press.

Heidensohn, F. (1992) *Women in Control*. Oxford: Clarendon Press.

Lea, S., Auburn, T. and Kibblewhite, K. (1999) Working with sex offenders: the perceptions and experiences of professionals and para professionals. *International Journal of Offender Therapy and Comparative Criminology*, 43: 103–19.

Measham, F., Parker, H. and Aldridge, J. (1998) Teenage transition: from adolescent recreational drug use to the young adult dance culture in Britain in the mids 1990s. *Journal of Drug Issues*, 12: 18–32.

Norman, P., Bennet, P. and Lewis, H. (1998) Understanding binge drinking among young people: an application of the theory of planned behaviour. *Health Education Research*, 13: 163–9.

Porter, L. E. and Alison, L. (2006) Leadership and hierarchies in criminal groups: scaling degress of leadership behaviour in group robbery. *Legal and Criminological Psychology*, 11: 245–65.

Roycroft, M., Brown, J. and Innes, M. (2007) Reform by crisis: the murder of Stephen Lawrence and a socio-historical analysis of developments in the conduct of major crime investigations. In M. Rowe (ed.), *Policing Beyond MacPherson: Issues in Policing, Race and Society*, pp. 148–64. Cullompton: Willan.

Strauss, A. and Corbin, J. (1990) *Basics of Qualitative Research: Grounded Theory Procedures and Techniques*. London: Sage.

Tajfel, H. and Fraser, C. (eds.) (1978) *Introducing Social Psychology*. Harmondsworth: Penguin.

Ward, C. (1988) The attitude towards rape victims scale: construction validation and cross cultural applicability. *Psychology of Women Quarterly*, 12: 127–46.

Westmarland, L. (2001) *Gender and Policing: Sex, Power and Police Culture*. Cullompton: Willan.

1.14 Theories of change

Mary McMurran

See also chapter 8.4 Evaluation of systemic interventions, chapter 8.5 Evaluating offending behaviour programmes in prisons, chapter 8.8 Reliable change and clinical significance, chapter 3.11 Democratic therapeutic communities.

Definition

The theories of change addressed here relate to how offenders can be assisted to change their offending through treatment. Through an understanding of the psychology of criminal conduct, effective treatments have been developed and in many criminal justice and forensic health services the provision of programmes aimed at helping offenders stop offending is now a core activity. More recently, attention has been focused on how to motivate offenders to engage in these treatments. In a review of offender cognitive-behavioural treatment outcome studies that compared treatment completers, non-completers and those not offered treatment, McMurran and Theodosi (2007) found that treatment completers were least likely to reoffend, consistent with the evidence that treatment works. However, treatment non-completers offended at a higher rate than did those not recruited to treatment, suggesting that treatments are failing to engage high-risk offenders and non-completion of treatment may even exacerbate risk. It is important, therefore, to consider how to promote motivation to engage in treatment and change behaviour.

The Risk–Need–Responsivity (RNR) model

In the 1990s, in response to criticisms that 'nothing works' in offender treatment, researchers began to scrutinize the body of research evidence more systematically. Using the statistical procedure called meta-analysis, where the outcomes of a number of studies can be aggregated to calculate an overall treatment effect size, evidence was produced to support the effectiveness of offender treatment (e.g. Andrews *et al.* 1990; Izzo and Ross 1990). From these early meta-analyses and the many that followed over later years, Andrews and Bonta (2003; Andrews, Bonta and Wormith 2006) distilled and refined their principles of effective offender treatment into what is known as the Risk–Need–Responsivity (RNR) model.

The *Risk Principle* is that intensive treatments should be delivered to higher-risk offenders rather than those who are lower risk. Clearly, higher-risk offenders are those who are more in need of treatment. The *Need Principle* is that treatments should focus upon issues that relate to criminal behaviour, that is 'criminogenic needs'. The *Responsivity Principle* is bipartite. General responsivity refers to what is known to be effective in offender treatment, namely programmes that are based upon psychological theories and teach new skills as well as modify antisocial beliefs, expectancies and values. Specific responsivity relates to designing and delivering treatments that suit the characteristics, abilities and circumstances of the client. The kinds of issues that need to be attended to in the design and delivery of programmes include the clients' demographic profile, e.g. age, gender and culture; cognitive abilities, e.g. literacy, intelligence and learning style; personality traits; and mood states. One responsivity issue that is particularly relevant here is the client's motivation to engage in treatment and change behaviour. Theories of motivation for treatment and behaviour change may be described in three main approaches: (1) matching intervention with stage of change; (2) readiness to change; and (3) goal perspectives.

Matching intervention with stage of change

The Transtheoretical Model of Change was described first by Prochaska and DiClemente (1983) in relation to smoking cessation and was subsequently widely applied in addiction treatment. In this model, behaviour change is construed as a process rather than an event. The process was said to unfold though a series of stages: *Precontemplation*, where a person is unaware of a problem or unconcerned by his or her behaviour; *Contemplation*, where there is acknowledgement of a problem but ambivalence about change; *Action*, where change attempts are in progress; and *Maintenance*, where change is consolidated and temptations to relapse become less salient. Different interventions have been suggested as applicable at different stages of change, with education and awareness-raising for precontemplators, motivational interventions for contemplators, skills training for those in the action stage, and relapse prevention to promote maintenance. The stage model of change has been criticized as flawed in that change does not occur in genuine stages, it focuses too much on decision making and not enough on implicit processes (e.g. when stimuli trigger responses outside conscious awareness), and it may misdirect interventions (West 2005). In relation to changing offending, the model quite simply has not been empirically validated.

Of the interventions that flourished in connection with the stages of change model, motivational interviewing is probably of most relevance here. Miller (1985) observed that therapists tended to judge clients as motivated to change when clients agreed with the therapist about having a problem, acknowledged the need for treatment and did what they were told in therapy. If a client disagreed or disobeyed, then the therapist might try to persuade them to see the situation as the therapist saw it. Miller pointed out that this type of challenge simply created resistance in the client, who, being a rational human being, was put in the position of having to defend his or her behaviour. As an alternative, motivational interviewing was developed (Miller and Rollnick 2002). In this, the strategy is to elicit 'change statements' through the use of techniques such as expressing empathy, avoiding arguing for change and working on ambivalence to strengthen commitment to change. Evidence for the effectiveness of motivational interviewing is accruing in addictions treatment (Vasilaki, Hosier and Cox 2006), which is highly relevant to offenders.

Readiness to change

The principles behind motivational interviewing moved therapists towards viewing motivation to change as a product of interpersonal dynamics rather than a feature of the client alone. The construct of 'readiness to change' takes this line of thinking still further, incorporating a range of external factors along with internal states to explain treatment engagement and ability to change. Ward *et al.* (2004) described a Multifactorial Offender Readiness Model (MORM), which is depicted in figure 1.14.1 In this, the targets are treatment engagement and behaviour change. The internal conditions required for readiness to engage in treatment and change behaviour relate to *cognitions*, e.g. thoughts about oneself, the treatment on offer, the people delivering treatment and one's ability to change; *affect*, e.g. feelings of guilt or

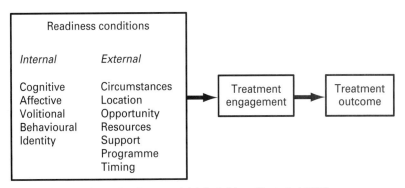

Figure 1.14.1 The Multifactor Offender Readiness model (adapted from Ward *et al.* 2004)

shame about the offence; *volitional*, i.e. choosing to pursue the goal of not offending; *behavioural*, i.e. recognizing a problem, seeking help and having the skills to enable change; and *identity*, e.g. one's overall sense of self as a non-offender and a valued contributor to society. External readiness conditions relate to what treatment programme is offered, when, where, how and by whom.

The readiness to change model has the potential to broaden the study of offender treatment engagement and behaviour change by addressing intra-personal, interpersonal and contextual factors and their interactions. The utility of this model remains to be evidenced.

Goal perspectives

The RNR model's focus on risk and criminogenic needs has attracted criticism because of the emphasis on the offender's deficits, and some scholars advocate adopting a more positive approach to offender rehabilitation. Ward and colleagues have proposed the Good Lives model (GLM) of offender rehabilitation, which focuses on helping offenders attain satisfaction in a range of life areas rather than focusing purely on reducing risk (Ward 2002; Ward and Brown 2004). The underlying principle is that offenders, as all human beings, seek satisfaction in certain life areas that are the essential ingredients of human wellbeing, but that the offender seeks satisfaction in problematic or distorted ways.

A goal perspective is one way to operationalize the GLM for practical application and empirical investigation (McMurran and Ward 2004). In evolutionary terms, goals are specific representations of what is needed for

Table 1.14.1 Types of motivation (after Deci and Ryan 2000)

Type of motivation	Characteristics
Amotivation	No intention to change. Low self-efficacy. Lack of perceived control.
Extrinsic motivation	
External regulation	Behaviour controlled by external contingencies.
Introjected regulation	Control somewhat internalized; behaviour controlled 'for appearance's sake', e.g. rewards of self-worth and self-esteem and avoidance of guilt and anxiety.
Identified regulation	Value of the behaviour accepted and done 'out of duty', i.e. rewards of doing the right thing.
Integrated regulation	Value of the behaviour accepted and congruent with one's idea of self. Consistent with self-schemas and identity, e.g. wishing to be healthy, good, or effective.
Intrinsic motivation	Self-determined behaviour that is reinforced by satisfaction of innate needs for autonomy, competence and relatedness.

survival. Maslow (1943) proposed a hierarchy of needs from basic physiological needs (e.g. oxygen, food, water), through higher-order needs for safety, belonging, esteem and self-actualization. Personal goals are what give purpose, structure and meaning to a person's life, and wellbeing is experienced when there is commitment to goal attainment, goals are achievable and goals meet the individual's explicit and implicit needs (Michalak and Grosse Holtforth 2006).

One key issue is that of intrinsic versus external motivation. Intrinsically motivated behaviours are what people do by choice, whereas externally motivated behaviours are imposed by others. Where offenders are concerned, acceptance of treatment within the criminal justice system is probably always partially externally motivated, governed by privileges, parole and release dates. Because intrinsic motivation is linked to better therapy outcomes and long-term maintenance of change, the challenge of therapy is to encourage the internalization of external motivation (Deci and Ryan 2000). In their self-determination theory, Deci and Ryan (2000) postulated a continuum from 'amotivation', through four types of extrinsic motivation, to intrinsic motivation, as described in table 1.14.1.

One way of measuring a person's goals in major life areas is the Personal Concerns Inventory (PCI: Klinger and Cox 2004). Using the PCI with offenders has revealed that offenders say they want to stop offending, and are aware that to do this they need to be self-controlled, find and keep jobs, have stable accommodation, quit drink and drugs, change support networks and find new leisure pursuits (McMurran et al. 2008). This is consistent with the targets of treatment that are identified in the RNR literature (Andrews and Bonta 2003). Consistent with the GLM, prisoners additionally express life-enhancing goals, such as wanting a better life, gaining work experience, enjoying good family relationships, acquiring skills, and getting fit and healthy. These positive aspirations are those that contribute to meaning in life (Ward and Marshall 2007), and are the goals that may sustain a person in persisting with the avoidance or risk-reduction goals that are common in the RNR model.

Empirical investigation of offenders' motivational structure by asking people first to identify their goals and then to rate them in terms of their value, attainability and imminence has revealed two factors: an adaptive motivation factor, characterized by high perceived likelihood of goal attainment, expected happiness when goals are attained and commitment to goal striving; and a maladaptive motivation factor, characterized by holding the goals low in importance, expecting no great amount of happiness at goal achievement and having low commitment to goals (Sellen *et al.* 2009). How these relate to engagement in therapy and behaviour change remains to be examined. However, offenders may respond to goal-based therapies, where attention is paid to the number, range and content of goals; their degree of conflict or coherence; whether they are externally imposed or internally driven; their clarity and specificity; whether the aims are positive gain or avoidance of something that is undesirable; their likely attainability; and whether they actually satisfy a person's fundamental needs (Michalak and Grosse Holtforth 2006).

Conclusion

Much thought has been afforded to theories and models of offenders' engagement in therapy and behaviour change, much of it drawn from the study of addictions. While there are commonalities in aspects of the theoretical approaches to understanding addictions and offending, there are also differences that require attention. It is important that theories of change are not imported from other domains of study without being subject to empirical testing. This is what is currently lacking in this area. The concepts of stages of change and treatment matching have entered the lexicon of offender treatment personnel without adequate empirical examination of their validity or utility. Training in motivational interviewing is popular for correctional treatment personnel, with little evidence that it changes practice or improves outcomes for offenders. The more recent multifactorial and teleological approaches to change hold promise but proponents need to provide evidence to support their ideas.

FURTHER READING

The books *Motivating Offenders to Change: A Guide to Enhancing Engagement in Therapy* (edited by McMurran, 2002) and *Readiness for Treatment* (edited by Sullivan and Shuker 2007) contain further information on all the topics covered.

REFERENCES

Andrews, D. A and Bonta, J. (2003) *The Psychology of Criminal Conduct*, 3rd edn. Cincinnati, OH: Anderson.

Andrews, D. A., Bonta, J. and Wormith, J. S. (2006) The recent past and near future of risk and/ or need assessment. *Crime and Delinquency*, 52: 7–27.

Andrews, D. A., Zinger, I., Hoge, R. D., Bonta, J. Gendreau, P. and Cullen, F. T. (1990) Does correctional treatment work? A clinically relevant and psychologically informed meta-analysis. *Criminology*, 28: 369–404.

Deci, E. L. and Ryan, R. M. (2000) The 'what' and the 'why' of goal pursuits: human needs and the self-determination of behaviour. *Psychological Inquiry*, 11: 227–68.

Izzo, R. L. and Ross, R. R. (1990) Meta-analysis of rehabilitation programmes for juvenile delinquents. *Criminal Justice and Behavior*, 17: 134–32.

Klinger, E. and Cox, W. M. (2004) The Motivational Structure Questionnaire and Personal Concerns Inventory: psychometric properties. In W. M. Cox and E. Klinger (eds.), *Handbook of Motivational Counseling: Concepts, Approaches, and Assessment*, pp. 177–97. Chichester: Wiley.

Maslow, A. H. (1943) A theory of human motivation. *Psychological Review*, 50: 370–96.

McMurran, M. (ed.) (2002) *Motivating Offenders to Change: A Guide to Enhancing Engagement in Therapy*. Chichester: Wiley.

McMurran, M. and Theodosi, E. (2007) Is offender treatment non-completion associated with increased reconviction over no treatment? *Psychology, Crime and Law*, 13: 333–43.

McMurran, M., Theodosi, E., Sweeney, A. and Sellen, J. (2008) What do prisoners want? Current concerns of adult male prisoners. *Psychology, Crime, and Law*, 14: 267–74.

McMurran, M. and Ward, T. (2004) Motivating offenders to change in therapy: an organising framework. *Legal and Criminological Psychology*, 9: 295–311.

Michalak, J. and Grosse Holtforth, M. (2006) Where do we go from here? The goal perspective in psychotherapy. *Clinical Psychology: Science and Practice*, 13: 346–65.

Miller, W. R. (1985) Motivation for treatment: a review with special emphasis on alcoholism. *Psychological Bulletin*, 98: 84–107.

Miller, W. R. and Rollnick, S. (2002) *Motivational Interviewing*, 2nd edn. New York: Guilford Press.

Prochaska, J. O. and DiClemente, C. C. (1983) Stages and processes of self-change of smoking: toward an integrated model of change. *Journal of Consulting and Clinical Psychology*, 51: 390–5.

Sellen, J. L., McMurran, M., Theodosi, E., Cox, W. M. and Klinger, E. (2009) Validity of the offender version of the Personal Concerns Inventory with adult male prisoners. *Psychology, Crime and Law*, 15(5): 451–68.

Sullivan, E. and Shuker, R. (2007) *Readiness for Treatment* (Issues in Forensic Psychology, 7). Leicester: British Psychological Society,

Vasilaki, E., Hosier, S. G. and Cox, W. M. (2006) The efficacy of motivational interviewing as a brief intervention for excessive drinking: a meta-analytic review. *Alcohol and Alcoholism*, 41: 328–35.

Ward, T. (2002) Good lives and the rehabilitation of offenders: promises and problems. *Aggression and Violent Behavior*, 7: 513–28.

Ward, T. and Brown, M. (2004) The Good Lives Model and conceptual issues in offender rehabilitation. *Psychology, Crime, and Law*, 10: 243–57.

Ward, T., Day, A., Howells, K. and Birgden, A. (2004) The multifactor offender readiness model. *Aggression and Violent Behavior*, 9: 645–73.

Ward, T. and Marshall, B. (2007) Narrative identity and offender rehabilitation. *International Journal of Offender Therapy and Comparative Criminology*, 51: 279–97.

West, R. (2005) Time for a change: putting the transtheoretical (stages of change) model to rest. *Addiction*, 100: 1036–9.

1.15 Therapeutic jurisprudence

Michael King and David Wexler

Definition and scope

Therapeutic jurisprudence explores the effect of law, legal processes, legal institutions and legal actors upon the wellbeing of those affected by them. It is a 'way of looking at the law in a richer way' (Wexler 2000). Just as law can be studied through the lens of economics, feminism or racial theory, so it can also be studied from the perspective of its therapeutic impact. Therapeutic jurisprudence is not a theory or philosophy but a perspective and a research agenda with law reform and the reform of practice as a principal object. It suggests that findings from the behavioural sciences can be used to reform laws, legal processes, legal institutions and the actions of legal actors to promote or minimize any negative effect upon participant wellbeing.

Some commentators have expressed concern that the concept of 'therapeutic' in therapeutic jurisprudence is too vague (e.g. Slobogin 1995; Brakel 2007). Naturally specific therapeutic jurisprudence research projects require a precise definition of 'therapeutic'. But as an approach that encourages research into diverse areas of the law and into different dimensions of human wellbeing, a general definition encourages rather than hinders research (Wexler 1995). However, in general terms, therapeutic jurisprudence explores the impact of the law upon psychological wellbeing.

Wellbeing is intimately connected with justice system goals such as offender rehabilitation, the resolution of family breakdown issues, child welfare and the resolution of conflict generally. Laws, legal processes, legal institutions and legal actors can potentially advance or hinder the attainment of these goals. The work of therapeutic jurisprudence is designed to assist in the formulation of laws and legal processes and to assist legal actors such as judicial officers, lawyers and justice system officials to ensure that therapeutic values may be maximized in such circumstances. For example, it has had a significant influence on processes used by problem-solving courts such as drug courts,

family violence courts, mental health courts and community courts in promoting offender rehabilitation. Further, it has also illustrated how some
conventional legal processes, by being coercive or paternalistic, hinder the
behavioural change the processes are intended to promote (Winick 1992).

While therapeutic values will often be congruent with other justice system
values, at times they will conflict. Therapeutic jurisprudence says that therapeutic values should not take precedence over all other justice system values,
but that they should be a factor to be considered in reaching a decision in law-
related matters (Wexler and Winick 1996). Even when a decision is to be
made that emphasizes other or even anti-therapeutic values, therapeutic
jurisprudence may be able to suggest a way of acting that minimizes anti-
therapeutic effects. For example, Judge David Fletcher of the North Liverpool
Community Justice Centre told the Third International Conference on
Therapeutic Jurisprudence that when he imposes a term of imprisonment,
he sends the offender a letter explaining the reasons for his decision and
advising that an officer from the centre will visit the offender in prison to
ensure the offender is put in touch with agencies that will support his or her
rehabilitation needs.

Offender rehabilitation is a prominent area of application of therapeutic
jurisprudence (TJ). But TJ is also concerned with a far broader range of people
and contexts, such as the impact of legal processes on victims of crime; the
effect of court processes on witnesses and jurors; the impact of judges' actions
on other judges and lawyers; the effect of legal processes in family law cases on
parents and children; the effect of civil law processes on parties to a dispute;
whether workers' compensation laws and processes promote the injured
workers' rehabilitation; and whether the processes used by mental health
tribunals and courts are therapeutic for those who come under their jurisdiction. While therapeutic jurisprudence has been mainly concerned with individual wellbeing, it has also considered group wellbeing (Des Rosiers 2000).

The development and significance of therapeutic jurisprudence

Therapeutic jurisprudence was first explicated and named in a 1987 paper
prepared by Wexler for a National Institute of Mental Health (USA) work-
shop on law and mental health (Wexler 2008a). TJ originated in mental health
law, and, in early work, Wexler and Winick (Wexler 1990; Wexler and
Winick, 1991) noted that although mental health law aimed at ensuring
those with mental health issues obtained appropriate treatment to promote

their wellbeing, mental health laws and processes and the actions of officials often had anti-therapeutic effects. A main focus of their early work was to explore how the law, its processes and actors in mental health law could better promote therapeutic outcomes (Wexler and Winick 1991).

It soon became apparent that therapeutic jurisprudence was relevant to other areas of the law – including criminal law, family law, contract law, torts, workers' compensation, child welfare law, administrative law and wills and estate planning – and, indeed, to all areas of the law (Wexler and Winick 1996). Although therapeutic values may seem remote from commercial law, complex commercial contracts and the often large and complex corporate entities involved, behind the legal fictions that are corporations, there are people at work who may be affected by corporate and legal processes (Martin 2006). Still, the application of therapeutic jurisprudence to commercial law remains largely unexplored territory. However, new areas of application of therapeutic jurisprudence continue to emerge. Recent work has explored its relevance to coronial law and practice (Freckelton 2007; King 2003, 2008b), the impact of appeal court decisions on lower court judges (King 2008a), the work of administrative law tribunals (Toohey 2006) and Indigenous issues (Auty 2006; Riley 2007).

Therapeutic jurisprudence has been described as one of the vectors of a trend towards more comprehensive, humane, therapeutic and psychologically optimal means of resolving conflict in society (Daicoff 2000). The overall trend may be referred to as the 'comprehensive law movement', a term used by Daicoff, or as 'nonadversarial justice', a term being employed in Australia (Freiberg 2007).

With its emphasis on wellbeing, there is a natural intersection between therapeutic jurisprudence and other vectors. For example, like restorative justice, mediation, collaborative law, holistic law and procedural justice, it emphasizes the therapeutic importance of values such as party participation and self-determination in processes used to resolve disputes. Thus, research has explored the relationship between therapeutic jurisprudence and other approaches, including restorative justice, preventive law, creative problem solving, mediation and problem-solving courts (Daicoff 2000; Stolle, Wexler and Winick 2000).

Therapeutic jurisprudence has also filled a gap in legal thought and the law in action. There is a history of individual judicial officers and lawyers taking what can be described as a therapeutic approach in relation to particular types of clients and circumstances. However, until the introduction of therapeutic jurisprudence there was no conceptual umbrella to describe what they were doing or a vehicle through which therapeutic principles from other disciplines could be applied to a legal problem to assist judicial officers and lawyers in taking such an approach. Therapeutic jurisprudence has therefore become a useful tool for judicial officers and lawyers who have a therapeutic approach to their work.

International trends

Although almost all of the early therapeutic jurisprudence scholarship originated in the United States, increasingly it is the subject of international development. Three international conferences on therapeutic jurisprudence have been held: in Winchester (UK), Cincinnati (USA) and Perth (Australia). The website of the International Network on Therapeutic Jurisprudence (INTJ) (www.therapeuticjurisprudence.org) contains a bibliography of therapeutic jurisprudence research and other materials and the Australasian Therapeutic Jurisprudence Clearinghouse provides resources in relation to Australasian developments (www.aija.org.au).

International research provides a useful means for the development of therapeutic jurisprudence practice. The differing constitutional, legal and social arrangements existing in each country provide a unique laboratory for the exploration of the application of therapeutic principles. What is constitutionally permissible in one country may not be permissible in another. The contributions in one country can assist in the developments in another. For example, the application of therapeutic jurisprudence principles to judging in remote areas in Western Australia has been referred to in Canada, which, like Australia, has the challenge of administering justice in remote regions as well as in metropolitan areas (Goldberg 2005). Thus, a comparative therapeutic jurisprudence is emerging whereby principles of therapeutic jurisprudence developed in one country are considered in the light of legal system practice in other countries.

Most of the work on therapeutic jurisprudence centres on Western common law jurisdictions – principally those of the US, Australia, Canada, the United Kingdom and New Zealand. Exploration of therapeutic jurisprudence in the context of continental civil law systems and Middle Eastern, Asian and African legal systems has only just begun. Cultural beliefs as to what is therapeutic in the context of particular legal systems in different societies require significant exploration. A promising development is the beginning of therapeutic jurisprudence writings in various languages. According to the INTJ website, TJ scholarship now appears in English, Spanish, French, Italian, Portuguese, Dutch, Swedish, Hebrew, Urdu and Japanese.

It was natural, with therapeutic jurisprudence's early connections with mental health law, that psychiatry and psychology would be major sources of therapeutic principles and practices for application within the legal system. Since that time, criminology and social work have also been cited as sources for therapeutic jurisprudence. Recent scholarship has suggested that public health could inform and be informed by therapeutic jurisprudence (Davidovitch and Alberstein 2007). Anthropology's relevance to therapeutic jurisprudence has been illustrated by work suggesting that the cultural dimension of Indigenous court practices facilitates their therapeutic effect (Riley 2007; Wexler 2008a). King (2008b) suggested that leadership theory – which studies leadership in various disciplines and in business, community and government contexts – can inform therapeutic jurisprudence practice, particularly in connection with legal processes that endeavour to promote positive behavioural change. A session at the Third International Conference on Therapeutic Jurisprudence in Perth, Western Australia, in 2006 explored the relationship between therapeutic jurisprudence and architecture in the context of a discussion of the connection between legal processes and the therapeutic effect of the design of places in which they take place.

This interdisciplinary aspect of therapeutic jurisprudence is likely to continue to deepen, in terms of the profundity of connections between principles from other disciplines and the law, and to broaden, in terms of incorporating other disciplines and perspectives into legal thinking and processes.

Along with the practical application of therapeutic jurisprudence to the justice system has come the necessity for both legal and behavioural science professionals to adapt to the new collaborative roles that arise from a therapeutic approach to the law. Wexler (2008a) notes that initially mental health professionals were sceptical about a collaboration with a profession that had treated them badly when they were called as witnesses at trials and who generally believed that the legal profession did not take them seriously. Similarly, some in the legal profession have thought that a therapeutic role is well beyond the judicial role of impartial arbiter or the lawyer's role as advocate (Hoffman 2000, 2002). From this perspective, the design of their processes should remain with the legal profession. Therapeutic jurisprudence suggests the role of both is problem-solver; that the legal problem is often associated with underlying problems of a lack of wellbeing; that the kind of legal processes used can affect the resolution of these underlying issues; and that a collaborative approach between legal, health and other professionals may be required to resolve the problem. Recent scholarship suggests that criminal lawyers may acquire a 'rehabilitative consciousness' and, at the same time, remain true to principles of zealous advocacy (Wexler 2008b).

Therapeutic jurisprudence is now beginning to influence the nature and content of courses offered at law schools and judicial training programmes and materials. The website of the International Network on Therapeutic Jurisprudence lists over twenty university courses on therapeutic jurisprudence. Others include the topic when teaching subjects such as administration of justice, sentencing and criminal law. In relation to judicial training, for example, the National Judicial Institute of Canada has an excellent publication on therapeutic judging (Goldberg 2005), available online in both English and French (www.nji.ca), and the National Judicial College of Australia includes therapeutic jurisprudence as a subject in its curriculum for judicial training.

Conclusion

Therapeutic jurisprudence has developed rapidly from its roots in mental health law to become an important vehicle for interdisciplinary research into the effect of the law on psychological wellbeing. Increasingly, judicial officers, lawyers and other justice system professionals see therapeutic jurisprudence as a source of techniques that they can apply to promote justice system outcomes such as the resolution of conflict, offender rehabilitation and the healing of families (see e.g. King 2009). Further work is needed in relation to its cross-cultural implications, its application to broader areas of the law such as commercial law and taxation, and its relationship to different discipline areas relating to human behaviour and behavioural change.

REFERENCES

Auty, K. (2006) We teach all hearts to break – but can we mend them? Therapeutic jurisprudence and Aboriginal sentencing courts. *ELaw, Murdoch University Electronic Journal of Law, Special Series*, 1, 101: https://elaw.murdoch.edu.au/special_series.html (accessed 11 February 2008).

Brakel, S. J. (2007) Searching for therapy in therapeutic jurisprudence. *New England Journal on Criminal and Civil Confinement*, 33: 455–99.

Daicoff, S. (2000) The role of therapeutic jurisprudence within the comprehensive law movement. In D. P. Stolle, D. B. Wexler and B. J. Winick (eds.), *Practicing Therapeutic Jurisprudence*, pp. 465–7. Durham, NC: Carolina Academic Press.

Davidovitch, N. and Alberstein M. (2007) Therapeutic jurisprudence and public health: a broad perspective on dialogue. Paper presented at the International Association of Law and Mental Health Annual Conference, Padova, Italy, June 2007 (in press in Thomas Jefferson Law Review).

Des Rosiers, N. (2000) From telling to listening: a therapeutic analysis of the role of courts in minority-majority conflicts. *Court Review*, 37(1): 54–62: http://aja.ncsc.dni.us/courtrv/cr37/cr37–1/CR9DesRosiers.pdf (accessed 14 March 2008).

Freckelton, I. (2007) Death investigation, the coroner and therapeutic jurisprudence. *Journal of Law and Medicine*, 15: 242–53.

Freiberg, A. (2007) Non-adversarial approaches to criminal justice. *Journal of Judicial Administration*, 16: 205.

Goldberg, S. (2005) *Judging for the 21st Century: A Problem-Solving Approach*. National Judicial Institute of Canada: www.nji.ca/nji/Public/Downloads.cfm (accessed 11 March 2008).

Hoffman, M. B. (2000) The drug court scandal. *North Carolina Law Review*, 78: 1437–534.

(2002) Therapeutic jurisprudence, neo-rehabilitationism, and judicial collectivism: the least dangerous court becomes the most dangerous. *Fordham Urban Law Journal*, 29: 2069–98.

King, M. S. (2003) Applying therapeutic jurisprudence in regional areas: the Western Australian experience. *ELaw, Murdoch University Electronic Journal of Law*, 10(2): www.murdoch.edu.au/elaw/issues/v10n2/king102nf.html (accessed 14 March 2008).

(2008a) Therapeutic jurisprudence, leadership and the role of appeal courts. *Australian Bar Review*, 30: 201–13.

(2008b) Problem-solving court judging, therapeutic jurisprudence and transformational leadership. *Journal of Judicial Administration*, 17: 155–77.

(2009) *Solution-Focused Judging Bench Book*. Melbourne: Australasian Institute of Judicial Administration.

Martin, W. (2006) Address to the Third International Conference on Therapeutic Jurisprudence, Perth, 8 June 2006: www.supremecourt.wa.gov.au/publications/pdf/TherapeuticJurisprudence-07062006.pdf (accessed 11 February 2008).

Riley, A. R. (2007) Good native governance. *Columbia Law Review*, 107: 1049–125.

Slobogin, C. (1995) Therapeutic jurisprudence: five dilemmas to ponder. *Psychology Public Policy and Law*, 1: 193–219.

Stolle, D. P., Wexler D. B. and B. J. Winick (2000) *Practicing Therapeutic Jurisprudence*. Durham, NC: Carolina Academic Press.

Toohey, J. (2006) Use of therapeutic jurisprudence in the work of the State Administrative Tribunal: tribunal hearings. Paper presented to the Third International Conference on Therapeutic Jurisprudence, Perth, 7–9 June 2006: www.aija.org.au/TherapJurisp06/FINALPROGRAM.pdf (accessed 11 February 2008).

Wexler, D. B. (1990) *Therapeutic Jurisprudence: The Law as a Therapeutic Agent*. Durham, NC: Carolina Academic Press.

(1995) Reflections on the scope of therapeutic jurisprudence. *Psychology, Public Policy and Law*, 1: 220.

(2000) Therapeutic jurisprudence: an overview. *Thomas M. Cooley Law Review*, 17: 125.

(2008a) Two decades of therapeutic jurisprudence. *Touro Law Review*, 24: 17.

(2008b) *Rehabilitating Lawyers: Principles of Therapeutic Jurisprudence for Criminal Law Practice*. Durham, NC: Carolina Academic Press.

Wexler, D. B. and Winick, B. J. (eds.) (1991) *Essays in Therapeutic Jurisprudence*. Durham, NC: Carolina Academic Press.

(1996) *Law in a Therapeutic Key*. Durham, NC: University of Carolina Press.

Winick, B. J. (1992) On autonomy: legal and psychological perspectives. *Villanova Law Review*, 37: 1705.

1.16 Violent offending

Kevin Howells

See also chapter 3.13 Rehabilitating violent offenders.

Definition

Defining violent offending is not straightforward. How is violent offending to be distinguished from violence, from aggression or from hostility? It is useful to think in terms of violent offending being a subset of violent behaviour which is, in turn a subset of aggression. Thus all acts of violent offending form part of the broader phenomenon of violence and, in turn, of aggression. On the other hand, it follows that not all aggressive acts are violent and not all violence involves violent offending. Aggression has been defined by Baron and Richardson (1994) as 'any form of behaviour directed toward the goal of harming or injuring another living being who is motivated to avoid such treatment'. The distinction between aggression and violence is largely based on the degree of physical harm involved. Derogating someone in an offensive and even psychologically harmful way is not usually defined as violence, whereas stabbing someone would be. There are grey areas. Emotional neglect of a child, for example, may not entail physical harm in the short term, but may do so when prolonged over many years.

Violent offending refers to acts of violence that contravene the legal code. A number of professional groups may wish to identify violent offenders and to distinguish them from non-violent offenders. A researcher may wish to test a hypothesis that violent and non-violent offenders differ in some way, for example that violent offenders have a different neuropsychological profile from non-violent offenders. Forensic clinicians may wish, in a prison setting, to separate violent offenders from the rest of the prison population to offer them a therapeutic intervention that might reduce their risk of recidivism (see discussion of anger treatment below). Politicians, government ministers and correctional administrators might all think it desirable to identify violent offenders for differential disposal and management, such as longer detention. The definition of violent offender for such purposes is, however, often problematic (Kenny and Press 2006). Is a violent offender to be identified on the basis of their total criminal history, by their index offence, by their most serious offence or by their most frequent offence type?

Current thinking, and practice

The forensic psychologist is likely to encounter the violent offender in a number of settings (court proceedings, probation and community corrections, prisons, forensic mental health services) and to be expected to have expertise in relation to the assessment, formulation, prediction and treatment of violent behaviour.

Assessment and formulation of violence

A forensic clinical formulation may be of an individual violent act, of a series or pattern of violent acts or of the broader problems of the violent person (the latter is sometimes referred to as a *case conceptualization*). In essence, a formulation attempts to clearly define the violent behaviour in question and to specify the antecedent conditions that led to the *development* of the behaviour (distal factors) and to the conditions which serve to *maintain* the behaviour in question in the present (proximal factors). Functional analysis (Daffern and Howells 2009; Sturmey 1996) is a particular type of formulation which specifies not only the antecedents for violence (triggering events, cognitions and appraisals, affective states, biological factors etc.) but also the teleological factors, that is the purposes or goals being pursued or achieved by engaging in the violent behaviour. In the forensic clinical setting, a formulation is typically a hypothesis or series of hypotheses that require testing and even attempts at refutation. It is to be expected that the factors identified in the formulation of an individual's violence will, in general, be consistent with research and findings and theoretical ideas relating to the general causation of violence (or aggression, given, see above, the fact that violence is a subcategory of aggression). It may sometimes be the case, however, that the causes of violence are idiosyncratic to the particular individual. The formulation of violent offending will involve consideration of the domains listed in table 1.16.1.

Prediction of violence

Predicting whether an individual, or a specified group of people, will engage in future violent behaviour remains an active, but contentious, area of forensic

Table 1.16.1 Assessment domains for formulation of violence*

Triggering situations and environments

Cognitive beliefs, appraisals and schema (hostile attributions, violence-supporting beliefs)

Affective states (anger, depression, mania)

Personal goals and functions of violence (instrumental, expressive and other goals)

Problem-solving and coping deficits

Personality factors (antagonism, psychopathic traits, impulsivity, provocation-sensitivity)

Self-regulatory skills (managing emotional arousal and violent impulses)

Personality disorders (antisocial, borderline etc.)

Axis 1 mental disorders (psychoses, brain damage)

Disinhibitors/inhibitors (substance use, empathy deficits, peer-group effects)

Opportunity factors (weapon availability)

Psychological strengths and 'Good Life' skills (employment, relationships, satisfactions)

* Examples in brackets.

psychological practice. The history of violence risk assessment is commonly described as having gone through three phases. In the first phase *clinical judgement* on the part of the professional was the most common method. Such judgements were often subjective, impressionistic, relatively unstructured and unreliable. In the second phase *actuarial assessments* became the preferred method, with an emphasis on determining and subsequently utilizing empirical associations between characteristics of the person (age, gender, criminal history etc.) and the probability of future violent offending. This phase has given way to a third phase in which there is an attempt to integrate actuarial data with *structured clinical judgements* to give a more rounded estimate of the probability of violence (Monahan *et al.* 2001).

Risk assessments of these sorts have become a major part of the role of many forensic psychologists. The main approach to offender rehabilitation, for example, in the past decade has been the Risk–Need–Reponsivity model (Andrews and Bonta 2003). This model leads the practitioner to organize therapeutic interventions on the basis of the Risk Principle. Groups of offenders are assessed on risk measures to ascertain which individuals have the highest risk (probability) of reoffending and high-risk groups are allocated to treatment interventions whereas low-risk offenders may be offered no treatment. Risk assessments may play a large role in the allocation of offenders to highly intensive therapeutic programmes. In England, for example, the government introduced the Dangerous and Severe Personality Disorder initiative in 2001 to provide intensive treatment for those deemed to pose a high risk of violence and to have a related severe personality disorder.

Although the targeting of high-risk individuals for therapeutic interventions has much to recommend it in terms of cost-effectiveness and likely social benefits, it is an activity that raises ethical as well as scientific questions. For a sceptical and cautionary view see Hart *et al.* (2007) who suggest that risk assessments (particularly actuarial assessments) have fundamental problems. These authors argue that the margins of error in such judgements are large indeed, particularly when judgements are made at the individual rather than group level. They conclude that actuarial risk assessment instruments 'cannot be used to estimate an individual's risk for future violence with any reasonable degree of certainty and should be used with great caution, or not at all' (2007, p. 60).

The identification in this way of individuals at high risk of violence is an example of a determination of the individual's *risk status* (focused on inter-individual variability) as opposed to *risk state* (focused on intra-individual variation in violence potential, for example variation over time or across situations). Risk status is important in deciding *whom* to treat but risk state information is the most important in the clinical management of violent people – knowing when, in what circumstances and in what mental states they are most likely to become violent assists in defining *what* to treat (Douglas and Skeem 2005). The assessment of risk states has been neglected, until recently, in violence research despite the increasing awareness that the identification of causal dynamic risk factors is critical to intervention.

Treatment of violence

Given the high frequency of violent offending in society and of violent offenders in the criminal justice system, particularly in prisons and in high-security forensic mental health services, it would be reasonable to expect that major progress would have been made and that best practice in treatment, for example, would now be clearly understood and widely implemented. Unfortunately, this is not the case. Other offender groups, particularly sex offenders, have received far more attention than have violent offenders from forensic psychologists, with the result that methods of assessment and treatment are more advanced for these other offender groups.

Internationally, many correctional systems have introduced therapeutic programmes to prevent violent offending and reoffending, with a range of treatment targets and of theoretical orientations. The rationale and evaluation of outcomes for such programmes have been reviewed by Polaschek and colleagues (Polaschek 2006; Polaschek and Collie 2004). The programmes on offer include cognitive-behavioural interventions, counselling, multisystemic therapy, anger management, feminist analysis-based interventions, aggression replacement training and others. As yet we know little about the effectiveness of such interventions in reducing aggression and violence. Again, this contrasts with the sex offending field.

Cognitive-behavioural treatments for anger are one of the most plausible and widely delivered treatments. These programmes have a convincing theoretical base and are broadly congruent with recent developments in the general psychology of emotion and with the development and success of cognitive-behavioural treatments for a wide range of mental disorders and social problems. Cognitive-behavioural treatments for anger have been shown to be effective in meta-analytic studies but the evidence in relation to violent offending outcomes is, as yet, rather thin (Howells *et al.* 2005). A number of reasons for the failure to demonstrate an effect have been proposed, including the brevity of typical programmes, the inadequacy of assessments for programme admission, the complexity of offenders' problems and their lack of readiness and motivation for such treatments (Ward *et al.* 2004). When such factors receive more attention in the research and clinical literatures, it may be possible to enhance outcomes so that they are comparable to those achieved for other populations.

Some key issues

Heterogeneity of violent acts and actors

One of the characteristics of informed psychological opinion about the causes and nature of, and remedies for, violence is that the diversity of violence is acknowledged. Typologies of violence have been proposed by many authors (Blackburn 1993), sometimes based on theories of underlying neurophysiological differences (Howard 2009). Such typologies are typically of violent people (actors) but violent acts themselves are heterogeneous. One of the most enduring distinctions has been between between *hostile* and *instrumental* violence, which have differing triggers, cognitive appraisals, affective accompaniments, goals and reinforcers. Despite a stringent critique (Bushman and Anderson 2001), the distinction survives, albeit with an unhelpful inconsistency of terminology. The hostile/instrumental distinction has major implications for treatment. The hostile aggressor is clearly suited to anger treatments (above) whereas the instrumental aggressor is not. A cautionary note, however, is that some people may engage in both hostile and instrumental acts of violence. The core difference between hostile and instrumental acts is the function of the act, that is the goal being pursued. Daffern, Howells and Ogloff (2007) have described the Assessment and Classification of Function (ACF) methodology for assessing hostile, instrumental and a range of other functions for aggressive acts in institutional settings. Different functions clearly suggest different approaches to preventative treatment.

Relevance of mental disorder

One of the longest-running, contentious and unresolved issues in forensic psychology and psychiatry has been the putative causal relationship between mental disorders and violence. The consensus as to the importance of mental disorders has shifted over time, with assertions at various points that mental disorder is a major causal antecedent, that it contributes little to violence, that it contributes in only a small proportion of the mentally disordered, that very particular disorders account for the variance in violence (for example, substance abuse and personality disorder) and that particular symptoms of disorder (for example, delusional beliefs or command hallucinations) are the critical variables. For a recent scholarly review, see Hodgins (2008). What is clear, firstly, is that the possible presence of mental disorder is one amongst many factors that needs to be assessed in conducting assessments and formulations of violence (see above). Secondly, when disorder appears to have a causal role, there is a subsequent need to describe the particular psychological and biological mechanisms that account for the association with violence (Daffern and Howells 2002; Hodgins 2008). Thirdly, there are likely to be large areas of overlap between mentally disordered and non-mentally disordered violent offenders in terms of causal antecedents such as substance abuse, impulsivity and other criminogenic needs (Bonta *et al.* 1998). Thus, treatment interventions for violence in the mentally disordered are likely to require a broader focus than simply addressing the mental disorder itself, important though this may be, and need to mirror those provided for the non-disordered.

Treatment cultures

The treatment of violent offenders is likely to occur either within the criminal justice system, where (see above) violence-reduction programmes have been developed in recent years, or within forensic mental health services. The latter may be delivered in the community but, more typically, within medium-secure and high-secure psychiatric hospitals. In the United Kingdom, very different treatment cultures, philosophies and practices appear to exist in criminal justice and forensic mental health systems (Howells *et al.* 2004), though there are indications of the beginnings of integration of cultures, particularly as a consequence of the DSPD initiative (Howells *et al.* 2007). Whereas criminal justice-based interventions have derived predominantly from offender rehabilitation principles (the 'What Works' movement) and from a substantial treatment outcome literature (Hollin and Palmer 2006; Ward and Maruna 2007), forensic mental health approaches have been less programmatic and have a relatively small empirical base, but are more individualized and able to address responsivity issues (Andrews and Bonta 2003). It has been suggested that the bringing together of the strengths of the two cultures offers a promising way forward in promoting good therapeutic outcomes (Howells *et al.* 2004).

FURTHER READING

Two journals cover the field of violent offending in a substantial way. The *Journal of Interpersonal Violence* includes empirical studies and clinical reports on a range of types of violence. *Aggression and Violent Behavior* publishes major evaluative reviews of various aspects of violence and its treatment and prevention. Several other journals have a broader focus but also include papers on violence: *Psychology, Crime and Law, Journal of Forensic Psychiatry and Psychology* and *Criminal Behaviour and Mental Health*.

Work on violent offending is often conducted within a broader framework of offender assessment and treatment. Useful texts are by Hollin and Palmer (2006) and Ward and Maruna (2007) – see below.

For an in-depth and critical review of links between schizophrenia and violent offending, see Hodgins (2008).

REFERENCES

Andrews, D. A. and Bonta, J. (2003) *Psychology of Criminal Conduct*, 3rd edn. Cincinnati, OH: Anderson.

Baron, R. A. and Richardson, D. R. (1994) *Human Aggression*. New York: Plenum.

Blackburn, R. (1993) *The Psychology of Criminal Conduct*. Chichester: Wiley.

Bonta, J., Law, M. and Hanson, K. (1998) The prediction of criminal and violent recidivism among mentally disordered offenders: a meta-analysis. *Psychological Bulletin*, 123: 123–42.

Bushman, B. J. and Anderson, C. A. (2001) Is it time to pull the plug on the hostile versus instrumental aggression dichotomy? *Psychological Review*, 108: 273–9.

Daffern, M. and Howells, K. (2002) Psychiatric inpatient aggression: a review of structural and functional assessment approaches. *Aggression and Violent Behavior*, 7: 477–97.

(2009) The function of aggression in personality disordered patients. *Journal of Interpersonal Violence*, 24: 586–600.

Daffern, M., Howells, K. and Ogloff, J. R. P. (2007) What's the point? Towards a methodology for assessing the function of psychiatric inpatient aggression. *Behavior Research and Therapy*, 45: 101–11.

Douglas, K. S. and Skeem, J. L. (2005) Violence risk assessment: getting specific about being dynamic. *Psychology, Public Policy, and Law*, 11: 347–83.

Hart, S. D., Michie, C. and Cooke, D. J. (2007) Precision of actuarial risk assessment instruments: evaluating the 'margins of error' of group v. individual predictions of violence. *British Journal of Psychiatry*, 190 (suppl. 49): s60–s69.

Hodgins, S. (2008) Criminality among persons with severe mental illness. In K. Soothill, M. Dolan and P. Rogers (eds.), *Handbook on Forensic Mental Health*, pp. 400–23. Cullompton: Willan.

Hollin, C. R. and Palmer, E. J. (eds.) (2006) *Offending Behaviour Programmes: Development, Application and Controversies*. Chichester: Wiley.

Howard, R. (2009). The neurobiology of affective dyscontrol: implications for understanding 'dangerous and severe personality disorder'. In M. McMurran and R. Howard (eds.), *Personality, Personality Disorder and Risk of Violence*, pp. 157–74. Chichester: Wiley.

Howells, K., Day, A. and Thomas-Peter, B. (2004) Treating violence: forensic mental health and criminological models compared. *Journal of Forensic Psychiatry and Psychology*, 15: 391–406.

Howells, K., Day, A., Williamson, P., Bubner, S., Jauncey, S., Parker, A. and Heseltine, K. (2005) Brief anger management programs with offenders: outcomes and predictors of change. *Journal of Forensic Psychiatry and Psychology*, 16: 296–311.

Howells, K., Krishnan, G. and Daffern, M. (2007) Challenges in the treatment of DSPD. *Advances in Psychiatric Treatment*, 13: 325–32.

Kenny, D. T and Press, A. L. (2006) Violence classifications and their impact on observed relationships with key factors in young offenders. *Psychology, Public Policy and Law*, 12: 86–105.

Monahan, J., Steadman, H. J. and Silver, E. (2001) *Rethinking risk assessment: the MacArthur study of mental disorder and violence*. New York: Oxford University Press.

Polaschek, D. L. L. (2006) Violent offender programmes: concept, theory and practice. In C. R. Hollin and E. J. Palmer (eds.), *Offending Behaviour Programmes: Development, Application and Controversies*, pp. 113–54. Chichester: Wiley.

Polaschek, D. L. L. and Collie, R. M. (2004) Rehabilitating serious violent adult offenders: an empirical and theoretical stocktake. *Psychology, Crime and Law*, 10: 321–34.

Sturmey, P. (1996) *Functional Analysis in Clinical Psychology*. Chichester: Wiley.

Ward, T., Day, A., Howells, K. and Birgden, A. (2004) The multifactor offender readiness model. *Aggression and Violent Behavior*, 9: 645–73.

Ward, T. and Maruna, S. (2007). *Rehabilitation*. London: Routledge.

Part II

Assessments

2.1　Child victims of sexual abuse

Miranda A. H. Horvath

See also chapter 5.3 Consent and capacity in civil cases, chapter 1.12 Sexual offenders, chapter 4.7 Internet sexual offending, chapter 4.12 Stalking, chapter 4.11 Sexual fantasy and sex offending, chapter 4.10 Sexual assault, chapter 2.23 Statement validity analysis.

Definition

Child sexual abuse is broadly described as 'any sexual activity involving a child where consent is not or cannot be given' (Dominguez, Nelke and Perry 2001, p. 202). Although there are a range of definitions available, it is crucial to acknowledge the different types of sexual abuse that they encompass; for example, Faller (1988) identifies seven different types of sexual abuse (e.g. non-contact, sexual penetration) and then clarifies that they can also be classified as either extrafamilial or intrafamilial. Although it is not the purpose of this chapter to review the literature on prevalence and incidence, it should be acknowledged that there is considerable variation in the estimates for childhood sexual abuse: international studies have found that for women it ranges between 3% and 29% and for men from 7% to 36% (Finkelhor 1994). The discrepancy in the figures is usually a result of sampling strategies and definitions used. Whatever the exact figures are it is widely accepted that child sexual abuse represents a significant problem in society today that can have devastating effects on the people involved (Kendall-Tackett, Williams and Finkelhor 1993; Paolucci, Genuis and Violato 2001).

Assessment for treatment purposes and for investigative purposes

Waterhouse and Carnie (1991) note that often cases lack objective evidence with the alleged perpetrator, if known, denying the allegations. They define three categories of evidence: grey (majority of cases), where there is high uncertainty, with perpetrator denial, no available corroborating medical evidence and no police involvement; black (minority of cases), where there may be an admission, corroborating medical evidence and police arrest the alleged perpetrator; white (exceptional cases), where there is reasonable confidence that the abuse did not take place.

There are two main reasons why a child suspected of being a victim of sexual abuse will be assessed: for investigative and for treatment purposes. Wolfe (2006, p. 663) highlights the fact that 'investigative interviews are often the children's entry points into the social service, mental health, and criminal justice systems'; it is often (but not always) an investigative interview that will lead to a child being assessed for treatment. The key differences between a treatment interview and an investigative one are that in the former the focus is on discovering the extent of any psychological ill effects on the child's mental state and psychological functioning, whereas in the latter it must be determined whether the abuse has occurred and, if it has, as much detail as possible must retrieved (Jones 1992). The ultimate goal of the interview also distinguishes between the two: specifically, the investigative interview should (if the abuse has occurred) lead to a criminal prosecution being brought, whereas a treatment interview is focused on devising a comprehensive treatment intervention for the child and their family. Waterhouse and Carnie (1991) note some tensions between police and social workers' interventions, with the former needing to obtain firm evidential support and the latter focusing on therapeutic interventions with the family. They found three styles of inter-agency cooperation: minimalist, collaborative and integrative, the latter deriving from the Bexley experiment which pioneered joint police/social services interviewing (Conroy, Fielding and Tunstill 1990).

Disclosure

Before exploring the available methods for assessing children suspected of being victims of child sexual abuse some consideration is needed of how the suspicions come to light and the effects of disclosing on children. Around a half to two-thirds of sexually abused children go undetected (Wolfe 2006); however, a number of studies have found that approximately one-third of children disclosed their abuse to someone during their childhood or adolescence (Arata 1998; Lamb and Edgar-Smith 1994). Of those who do disclose, approximately half disclose first to a parent, and about one in four tells a peer

(Berliner and Conte 1995; Henry 1997). Other studies have found that when the perpetrator was a stranger children are most likely to disclose, but when the perpetrator is a family member or known the likelihood of disclosure is decreased (Kogan 2004; Stroud *et al.* 2000). There are many reasons why children might avoid disclosing, the discussion of which is beyond the scope of this chapter; they include fear of being disbelieved, retaliation from the perpetrator and fear of being stigmatized. There are a growing number of people who do not disclose sexual abuse until they are adults, but they will not be addressed here and the interested reader should refer to chapter 2.19 (this volume).

There is some debate about the disclosure process which essentially concerns whether it should be considered as a series of stages, each of which can be resolved (e.g. Sorenson and Snow 1991; Summit 1983, 1992), or if the disclosure does not occur in any temporal or sequential pattern and there are just different ways a child can react having made a disclosure (e.g. Bradley and Wood 1996). Whichever side of the debate is preferred regarding the disclosure process, it is recommended that a developmental framework should be used when trying to understand why a child decides to disclose sexual abuse alongside consideration of the issues related to the abuse itself, for example, the personal characteristics of the child, whether the perpetrator still has access to them and the family set-up. In short, a good knowledge of developmental psychology is necessary to conduct effective assessments of child sexual abuse victims.

Symptoms

Physical trauma is the most obvious sign of sexual abuse but actually it is often not present in child sexual abuse (Adams *et al.* 1994; Berenson *et al.* 2000). Rieser (1991) found that often the victim's statement is the only evidence that abuse occurred in a substantial amount of validated sexual abuse cases. A wide range of emotional and behavioural characteristics can indicate child sexual abuse and symptoms have been found to tend to cluster around different developmental age bands (MacDonald *et al.* 2004; for examples of the clustering see Kendall-Tackett, Meyer-Williams and Finkelhor 1993; Trickett 1997). The most common symptoms/effects of child sexual abuse are: post-traumatic stress disorder (PTSD); sexualized behaviour (otherwise known as sexually reactive behaviour); depression and anxiety; promiscuity; general behaviour problems; poor self-esteem; disruptive behaviour disorders; sexual dysfunction;

and substance abuse (Dominguez *et al.* 2001). Furthermore, anyone embarking on an assessment should also be aware that high rates of physical and emotional abuse and exposure to domestic violence are found among victims of child sexual abuse (Bagley and Mallick 2000; Dong *et al.* 2003; Fleming *et al.* 1997).

Assessment: current thinking, research and practice

Checklists

Various checklists exist that can be used for assessing the symptoms that may arise from child sexual abuse; some measure symptoms such as depression and anxiety which are not trauma specific (e.g. the Child Behaviour Checklist, Achenbach, 1991) and others are designed to measure trauma-specific symptoms such as reactive sexual behaviour and post-traumatic stress (e.g. Trauma Symptom Checklist for Children (TSCC), Briere 1996 and Children's Impact of Traumatic Events Scale-Revised, Wolfe *et al.* 1991). In a recent article testing the validity of two such measures, Lanktree *et al.* (2008) outline some of the problems with existing measures, including variation in results depending on who completes the checklist (e.g. parent or child) and lack of standardization and validity studies. Lanktree *et al.*'s (2008) comparison of the TSCC and the Trauma Symptom Checklist for Young Children (TSCYC, Briere 2005), the former completed by the child and the latter completed by the parent, found that despite some minor issues it is recommended that both child and parent report measures should be used simultaneously to provide the most accurate picture of the child's symptomatology. Checklists provide a useful tool for the assessment of child victims of sexual abuse, but they should not be used in isolation or without the appropriate reliability and validity tests.

Interviewing

Interviewing is the main method of validating most child sexual abuse allegations and as already mentioned interviews can be required to serve dual legal and therapeutic requirements (Bannister and Print 1988). Unfortunately there are a multitude of factors that can negatively influence the outcome of interviews, some of which will now be highlighted. Perhaps the most widely acknowledged negative effects are caused by repeatedly interviewing children (Berliner and Conte 1995). However, numerous steps have been taken nationally and internationally to ensure that multiple interviews do not occur, for example in the United Kingdom, the Memorandum of Good Practice for interviewing children in criminal cases warns against interviewing a child more than once unless there is a good reason for doing so (Home Office 1992). The use of inappropriate tactics – including repeated and leading questioning, interviewer bias, bribes – have all been shown to have a deleterious effect on interview outcome. Linked to these practices are two key findings about children's memory and suggestibility:

1. Children's ability to recount information improves with age (Peterson and Bell 1996).
2. Young children (particularly preschoolers) are more suggestible than older children, adolescents and adults (Ceci and Bruck 1993).

These highlight just a few of the enormous challenges faced by interviewers of young children. It is necessary to remember that the differences outlined above between older and younger children are not relative; in other words, just because a child is very young does not mean they will be less able to remember information and be more suggestible (Eisen, Quas and Goodman 1991). There is in fact considerable variation across ages, and other factors influence memory and suggestibility such as question type and strength of memory.

Jones (1992) makes six specific recommendations about the general approach that should be taken when interviewing child victims of sexual abuse: avoid leading questions; prepare and have clear goals; do not make promises you cannot keep; be open and honest; have the flexibility to change direction at any time; and be open minded. For further details about recommendations for eliciting the most accurate information from children readers should refer to Lamb (1994). There are a number of different methods that can be employed in an interview to assist with the extraction of information from the child and to allow the child to discuss things they may not be able to verbalize; these include free and structured play (which allows behavioural observations), the use of toys and play materials, art and anatomically correct dolls (Jones 1992; anatomically correct dolls will be addressed separately in the next section). Giving children toys to play with requires the person conducting the assessment to track the number of times and in what form sexual content appears in their play (Faller 1988). Assessors can encourage the child to talk about the play they are engaging in to facilitate disclosures, but they must be careful that they do not begin to direct (and therefore unduly influence) the play (Jones 1992). Glasgow (1987, 1989) goes so far as to suggest that evidence of childhood sexual abuse can be obtained from play-based assessment even if there's no verbal disclosure from the child.

Art is very widely used and there are a number of different approaches employed, for example asking children to draw pictures of themselves, their family and sometimes even the alleged perpetrator (Goodwin 1982; Naitore 1982). If the child does not enjoy drawing they could use clay or other similar materials to make representations for the assessor. Many different themes and ideas can emerge from the pieces of art children create, which can, for example, provide insights into how the child feels in relation to their family members or their emotions or understandings of sex (e.g. Jones 1992; Stember 1980; Yates, Beutler and Crago 1985).

A couple of specific models for assessing child victims of sexual abuse in interviews exist, for example Bannister and Print (1988) and what has become known as the 'step-wise interview'. Bannister and Print (1988) propose that four key elements should be focused on before conducting the interview: planning, location, video recording and play materials. They then suggest an interview model which includes three phases, starting with introductions, engagement and reassurance. Phase two is re-enactment and the final phase is rehearsal for the future (Bannister and Print 1988). In contrast, the step-wise interview identifies two areas for consideration before the interview begins – location and participants – and then details eight steps that proceed from the general to the specific. (See Renvoize 1993 for a detailed outline and discussion of the two models.)

One final important component of interviewing is credibility assessment. A number of methods exist for assessing ratings of credibility (for example, statement validity analysis, criterion-based content analysis and observations of non-verbal behaviour during the investigative interview), which have been used with varying degrees of success, but on average a third of judgements are incorrect (Hershkowitz *et al.* 2007). In a recent study Hershkowitz *et al.* (2007) assessed the effectiveness of the National Institute of Child Health and Human Development (NICHD) investigative interview protocol and found that when it was used the child's credibility could be assessed more accurately and with higher inter-rater reliability than when it was not used. Specifically, 'experienced investigators were twice as likely to judge children's credibility accurately when the interviews were conducted using the NICHD protocol than when they were not similarly structured (59.5% vs 29.6%)' (Hershkowitz *et al.* 2007, p. 106).

Anatomically correct dolls

Anatomically correct dolls are very widely used; in fact one study in the USA found that 92% of mental health professionals who conduct child abuse investigations use them (Conte *et al.* 1991). The strengths of their use have been identified by a number of researchers: they help children provide detail about genital contacts; they can elicit sensitive information over and above the information provided by simple recall; and when used in conjunction with direct questioning they are particularly effective (Goodman *et al.* 1999; Saywitz *et al.* 1991). However, they can be misused, for example, when they are introduced to the child too early and in an undressed state, and when children are given the impression that the interviewer would rather they demonstrate what they are trying to say using the doll than give a verbal response (Everson and Boat 1994). Further, their use with very young children (aged under 4) remains the subject of much debate and controversy (Wolfe 2006). Some studies exist showing that children provide more correct information when dolls are not used, and in fact the use of dolls may actually increase the likelihood of them making errors (e.g. Bruck *et al.* 1995; Ornstein, Follmer and Gordon 1995), whereas other studies have found a significant increase in the amount of correct information recalled when dolls are used compared to a free recall task (e.g. Goodman *et al.* 1997).

Conclusion

This chapter has provided a snapshot of the vast body of research available about the assessment of child victims of sexual abuse. For almost every technique or approach there exist conflicting studies demonstrating its strengths and weaknesses. The Cleveland child abuse inquiry highlighted the dangers and difficulties of an uncoordinated protection system (Bagley and King 1990) and since then considerable work has been done making the systems more effective and child friendly. However, if children's trauma and distress is to be eradicated from the assessment process there is still a lot of progress to be made.

FURTHER READING

For a more detailed overview of many of the issues covered here Vicky Wolfe's chapter 'Child sexual abuse' in E. J. Mash's book *Treatment of Childhood Disorders* (New York: Guilford, 2006) is an excellent starting point. Jones' (1992) book *Interviewing the Sexually Abused Child* includes a concise summary of assessment issues, with particular emphasis on the investigative interview. Everson and Boat (1994) provide a useful assessment of the anatomical doll debate.

REFERENCES

Achenbach, T. M. (1991) *Manual for Child Behaviour Checklist/4–18 and 1991 Profile.* Burlington, VT: University of Vermont, Dept of Psychiatry.

Adams, J. A., Harper, K., Knudson, S. and Revilla, J. (1994) Examination findings in legally confirmed child sexual abuse: it's normal to be normal. *Pediatrics*, 94: 310–17.

Arata, C. M. (1998) To tell or not to tell: current functioning of child sexual abuse survivors who disclosed their victimisation. *Child Maltreatment*, 3: 6–71.

Bagley, C. and King, K. (1990) *Child Sexual Abuse: The Search for Healing.* London: Tavistock/ Routledge.

Bagley, C. and Mallick, K. (2000) Prediction of sexual, emotional, and physical maltreatment and mental health outcomes in a longitudinal cohort of 290 adolescent women. *Child Maltreatment*, 5: 218–26.

Bannister, A. and Print, B. (1988) *Assessment-Interviews in Suspected Cases of Child Sexual Abuse.* London: NSPCC.

Berenson, A. B., Chacko, M. R., Wiemann, C. M., Mishaw, C. O., Friedrich, W. N. and Grady, J. J. (2000) A case-control study of anatomic changes resulting from sexual abuse. *American Journal of Obstetrics and Gynecology*, 182: 820–34.

Berliner, L. and Conte, J. (1995) The process of victimisation: the victim's perspective. *Child Abuse and Neglect*, 14: 29–40.

Bradley, A. R. and Wood, J. M. (1996) How do children tell? The disclosure process in child sexual abuse. *Child Abuse and Neglect*, 20: 881–91.

Briere, J. (1996) *Trauma Symptom Checklist for Children (TSCC).* Odessa, FL: Psychological Assessment Resources.

(2005) *Trauma Symptom Checklist for Young Children (TSCYC).* Odessa, FL: Psychological Assessment Resources.

Bruck, M., Ceci, S., Francoeur, E. and Renick, A. (1995) Anatomically detailed dolls do not facilitate preschoolers' reports of a pediatric examination involving genital touching. *Journal of Experimental Psychology: Applied*, 1: 95–109.

Ceci, S. and Bruck, M. (1993) Suggestibility of the child witness: a historical review and synthesis. *Psychological Bulletin*, 113: 403–39.

Conroy, S., Fielding, N. G. and Tunstill, J. (1990) *Investigating Child Sexual Abuse: The Study of a Joint Initiative.* London: Police Foundation.

Conte, E. J., Sorenson, E., Fogarty, L. and Rosa, J. D. (1991) Evaluating children's reports of sexual abuse: results from a survey of professionals. *American Journal of Orthopsychiatry*, 61: 428–37.

Dominguez, R. Z., Nelke, C. F. and Perry, B. D. (2001) Child sexual abuse. In D. Levinson (ed.), *Encyclopaedia of Crime and Punishment*, vol. 1. Thousand Oaks, CA: Sage.

Dong, M., Anda, R. F., Dube, S. R., Giles, W. H. and Felitti, V. J. (2003) The relationship of exposure to childhood sexual abuse to other forms of abuse, neglect, and household dysfunction during childhood. *Child Abuse and Neglect*, 27: 625–39.

Eisen, M. L., Quas, J. A. and Goodman, G. S. (1991) *Memory and Suggestibility in the Forensic Interview.* Mahwah, NJ: Erlbaum.

Everson, M. and Boat, B. (1994) Putting the anatomical doll controversy in perspective: an examination of major doll uses and relative criticisms. *Child Abuse and Neglect*, 18: 113–29.

Faller, K. C. (1988) Criteria for judging the credibility of children's statements about their sexual abuse. *Child Welfare*, 67: 389–99.

Finkelhor, D. (1994) The international epidemiology of child sexual abuse: an update. *Child Abuse and Neglect*, 18: 409–17.

Fleming, J., Mullen, P. and Bamer, G. (1997) A study of potential risk factors for sexual abuse in childhood. *Child Abuse and Neglect*, 21: 49–58.

Glasgow, D. (1987) *Responding to Child Sexual Abuse*. Liverpool: Mersey Regional Health Authority.

    (1989) Play based investigative assessment of children who may have been sexually abused. In H. Blagg, J. A. Hughes and C. Wattam (eds.), *Child Sexual Abuse: Listening, Hearing and Validating the Experiences of Children*. Harlow: Longman.

Goodman, G. S., Quas, J. A., Batterman-Fraunce, J., Riddlesberger, M. and Kuhn, J. (1997) Children's reaction to and memory for a stressful event: influences of age, anatomical dolls, knowledge and parental attachment. *Applied Developmental Science*, 1: 54–75.

Goodman, G. S., Quas, J. A., Bulkley, J. and Shapiro, C. (1999) Innovations for child witnesses: a national survey. *Psychology, Public Policy and Law*, 5: 255–81.

Goodwin, J. (1982) *Sexual Abuse: Incest Victims and Their Families*. Boston, MA: Wright/PSG.

Henry, J. (1997) System intervention trauma to child sexual abuse victims following disclosure. *Journal of Interpersonal Violence*, 12: 499–512.

Hershkowitz, I., Fisher, S., Lamb, M. E. and Horowitz, D. (2007) Improving credibility assessment in child sexual abuse allegations: the role of the NICHD investigative interview protocol. *Child Abuse and Neglect*, 31: 99–110.

Home Office in conjunction with Department of Health (1992) *Memorandum of Good Practice on Video Recorded Interviews with Child Witnesses for Criminal Proceedings*. London: HMSO.

Jones, D. P. H (1992) *Interviewing the Sexually Abused Child: Investigation of Suspected Abuse*, 4th edn. London: Gaskell.

Kendall-Tackett, K. A., Meyer-Williams, L. and Finkelhor, D. (1993) Impact of sexual abuse on children: a review and synthesis of recent empirical studies. *Psychological Bulletin*, 113: 164–80.

Kogan, S. M. (2004) Disclosing unwanted sexual experiences: results from a national sample of adolescent women. *Child Abuse and Neglect*, 28: 1–19.

Lamb, M. E. (1994) The investigation of child sexual abuse: an interdisciplinary consensus statement. *Journal of Child Sexual Abuse*, 3: 93–106.

Lamb, S. and Edgar-Smith, S. (1994) Aspects of disclosure: mediators of outcome of childhood sexual abuse. *Journal of Interpersonal Violence*, 19: 307–26.

Lanktree, C. B., Gilbert, A. M., Briere, J., Taylor, N., Chen, K., Maida, C. A. and Saltzman, W. R. (2008) Multi-informant assessment of maltreated children: convergent and discriminant validity of the TSCC and TSCYC. *Child Abuse and Neglect*, 32: 621–5.

MacDonald, G., Ramchandani, P., Higgins, J. and Jones, D. P. H. (2004) Cognitive-behavioural interventions for sexually abused children (Protocol for Cochrane Review). In *The Cochrane Library*, issue 2. Chichester: Wiley.

Naitore, C. E. (1982) Art therapy with sexually abused children. In S. M. Sgroi (ed.), *Handbook of Clinical Intervention in Child Sexual Abuse*. Lexington, MA: D. C. Heath.

Ornstein, P. A., Follmer, A. and Gordon, B. N. (1995) The influence of dolls and props on young children's recall of pediatric examinations. Paper presented at the biennial meeting of the Society for Research in Child Development, Indianapolis, IN.

Paolucci, E. O., Genuis, M. L. and Violato, C. (2001) A meta-analysis of the published research on the effects of child sexual abuse. *Journal of Psychology*, 135: 17–36.

Peterson, C. and Bell, M. (1996) Children's memory for traumatic injury. *Child Development*, 6: 3045–71.

Renvoize, R. (1993) *Innocence Destroyed: A Study of Child Sexual Abuse*. London: Routledge.

Rieser, M. (1991) Recantation in child sexual abuse cases. *Child Welfare*, 70: 611–21.

Saywitz, K. J., Goodman, G. S., Nicholas, E. and Moan, S. F. (1991) Children's memories of a physical examination involving genital touch: implications for reports of child sexual abuse. *Journal of Consulting and Clinical Psychology*, 59: 682–91.

Sorenson, T. and Snow, B. (1991) How children tell: the process of disclosure in child sexual abuse. *Child Welfare*, 70: 3–15.

Stember, C. J. (1980) Art therapy: a new use in the diagnosis and treatment of sexually abused children. In *Sexual Abuse of Children: Selected Readings*. Washington, DC: US Department of Health and Human Services.

Stroud, D. D., Martens, S. L. and Barker, J. (2000) Criminal investigation of child sexual abuse: a comparison of cases referred to the prosecutor to those not referred. *Child Abuse and Neglect*, 24: 689–700.

Summit, R. C. (1983) The child sexual abuse accommodation syndrome. *Child Abuse and Neglect*, 7: 177–93.

(1992) Abuse of the child abuse accommodation syndrome. *Journal of Child Sexual Abuse*, 1: 153–63.

Trickett, P. K. (1997) Sexual and physical abuse and the development of social competence. In S. S. Luther, J. A. Burack, D. Cicchetti and J. R. Weisz (eds.), *Developmental Psychopathology: Perspectives on Adjustment, Risk and Danger*. New York: Cambridge University Press.

Waterhouse, L. and Carnie, J. (1991) Research note: social worker and police response to child sexual abuse cases in Scotland. *British Journal of Social Work*, 21: 373–9.

Wolfe, V. V. (2006) Child sexual abuse. In E. J. Mash (ed.), *Treatment of Childhood Disorders*. New York: Guilford Press.

Wolfe, V., Gentile, C., Michienzi, T., Sas, L. and Wolfe, D. (1991) The children's impact of traumatic events scale: a measure of post-sexual abuse PTSD symptoms. *Behavioural Assessment*, 13: 359–83.

Yates, A., Beutler, L. E. and Crago, M. (1985) Drawing by child victims of incest. *Child Abuse and Neglect*, 9: 183–9.

2.2 Credibility

Mark Kebbell

See also chapter 2.5 Eyewitness testimony, chapter 2.9 Investigative interviewing, chapter 2.23 Statement validity analysis, chapter 2.18 Polygraphy, chapter 4.3 Interpersonal deception detection, chapter 2.25 Vulnerable adults' capacity.

Definition

Credibility can be broadly defined as a judgement concerning the quality and veracity of evidence. In a forensic context, credibility judgements are often of critical importance because of the frequency of disputed accounts. For example, a woman might say she was raped by a man who in turn says she is lying, or a shopkeeper may accuse a person of robbery and the claim be made that it was a case of mistaken identity. In both these situations a credibility assessment needs to take into account whether an individual is being deliberately deceptive or the individual is indeed mistaken about some of the evidence he or she provides. Of course, it is possible for an individual to be both deceptive and mistaken. For example, a rape victim may try to give an honest account of the rape, which is generally accurate but has some errors, but then lie by saying she was abducted by the offender when she went with the offender voluntarily.

Origins and further developments

Where there is disagreement about what has happened, considerable attention has been paid to ways of determining how much credibility is warranted, most especially in detecting deception (see Vrij 2006 for a review). Some techniques that have been proposed include the polygraph, Statement Validity Analysis and Scientific Content Analysis. These techniques are dealt with elsewhere so will not be covered here, except to say that deception is more difficult to detect than might be expected, and people tend to overestimate their abilities to do so (again, see Vrij 2006 for a review). The focus here will be on assessing the credibility of accounts from a witness which involve judgements of the accuracy of the witness's memory.

There is a common belief that witnesses' confidence in their accuracy is reliable (e.g. Lindsay, Wells and Rumpel 1981). However, whilst witness confidence can be indicative of accuracy (e.g. Kebbell, Wagstaff and Covey 1996), particularly when witnesses are asked about items or events for which they have a strong memory, there are many situations where confidence is not a good indicator of accuracy. For instance, Luus and Wells (1994) found that feedback confirming or disconfirming witnesses' identifications had a marked impact on those witnesses' subsequent confidence in their inaccurate identifications. Hence, a more thorough assessment of credibility is likely to be necessary than simply asking the witness how sure they are of particular details.

Importantly, memory is not like a video camera. A video camera captures all of the events that are viewed in the direction in which it is pointed, records them and can replay them, but human memory cannot do this. Moreover, memory is an active, creative process that can be inaccurate for a variety of reasons. For material to be remembered it goes through three main stages: it is *encoded* into memory, *stored* there and finally *retrieved*. Problems can occur at each of these stages. Therefore, to determine witness accuracy a thorough assessment of the encoding, storage and retrieval processes, as well as the witness's capabilities more generally, is necessary.

Method

To evaluate the accuracy of an individual's account the expert should first gather as much information as possible concerning how the witness came to remember the event(s) in question. Where possible, the expert should seek documentary evidence to construct a time-line of events, and scrutinize issues that may have influenced memory production. This process might start with attempting to determine how the witness came to perceive the event, and whether they tried to deliberately encode what they were witnessing. Due to our limited capacity for attention, we can neither attend to, nor take in, all the information in our environment at any particular time and, as a consequence, information that is not attended to is unlikely to be remembered.

As people do not encode everything they observe, storage of memories often contains gaps. To make sense of these gaps, people may 'fill them in' to fit with previous attitudes, beliefs and expectations about a particular event or person. External sources may also be incorporated into memory. For example, if someone is told, incorrectly, that a person they met had a moustache, this information may be incorporated into memory and may come to be believed. In a similar fashion other people's accounts of an event may be incorporated into that of another witness. Therefore, it is important for the expert to find out what other sources of information the individual might have been exposed to, and this may be problematic as witnesses often are not aware of factors that have influenced their memories.

Successful retrieval from memory depends not only on adequate encoding and storage but on other factors as well. Retrieval strategies, such as the way a witness is interviewed, can have a profound impact. Research indicates that suggestive questioning, in particular, can have a negative impact on the accuracy of witness accounts (Loftus 1975). Therefore the expert should endeavour to find out how the memories were elicited. Finally, characteristics of the witness, for instance, if they have an intellectual disability or were intoxicated, are all likely to interact with factors at encoding, storage and retrieval to determine memory accuracy.

The fact that there may be problems with memory means that individuals may also not be able to give accurate accounts of how they came to remember events, requiring that the expert collects as much collateral information as is available. For example, the psychologist might request CCTV which gives an indication of the level of intoxication of the witness at the time of a crime, interview tapes to show how suggestive (or otherwise) the interview was, media reports that may have influenced the individual's memory over time, physical, forensic or medical evidence, the opposing side's accounts, school records, and other independent eyewitness accounts.

Evaluation

Evaluation is problematic because of the many different factors, including potential unknowns, that are likely to have an influence on the credibility of an account, such as difficulties in relying on the individual for information concerning how they came to remember the incident or person.

As a starting point, some of the critical factors that need to be considered are given in the Turnbull Ruling (R v. *Turnbull and others* 1977) and can be remembered with the mnemonic 'ADVOCATE' standing for Amount of time under observation, Distance from the eyewitness to the person/incident,

Visibility, Obstructions, Known or seen before, Any reason to remember, Time lapse since the event, Errors or material inconsistencies. In addition, factors such as stress and violence are likely to have a profound impact on memory accuracy and need to be borne in mind (see Christianson 1992).

Factors associated with the witness are also relevant; for example, research has identified a number of characteristics of the witness that may affect the accuracy of eyewitness accounts (see Kebbell and Wagstaff 1999). In general children, and indeed older adults, are poorer than adults from the general population in aspects of encoding, storage and retrieval, but their ability to give accounts is most influenced by how they are interviewed, as is discussed later. Similarly, people with intellectual disabilities also vary considerably in their ability to report details, and are sensitive to the way in which they are questioned; and while the influence of mental illness on witnessing abilities is poorly understood, it appears to have a negative impact. Alcohol and drugs can also have a negative impact as can head injuries.

Particularly important to judgements of credibility is the way in which accounts are elicited. Interviewing strategies such as hypnosis have a well-documented history of eliciting distorted accounts (for a review see Kebbell and Wagstaff 1999, and see also chapter 6.7, this volume). More appropriate interview strategies include the cognitive interview (Fisher and Geiselman 1992; see also chapter 2.9, this volume) which relies on mental reinstatement of context and open questioning. Witnesses tend to give the most accurate answers to open questions but as questions become more and more specific and closed, so accuracy rates fall. In particular, leading questions, such as 'Was his shirt red?', can decrease accuracy levels. Ideally, interviewers should have adopted a phased approach with more open questioning at the start of the interview. In these cases the initial content of the 'open' account is more accurate, potentially, than subsequent details elicited in a more closed fashion, and this is worth considering (Milne and Bull 1999).

Experts should carefully consider the above points before drawing general conclusions. There is a great deal of difficulty in generalizing from empirical evidence to particular cases, partly because of the lack of ecological validity inherent in many eyewitness studies, and partly because it is difficult to predict how multiple factors that might be both positive and negative for memory may interact. An example serves to illustrate these points. A credibility assessment was requested concerning a man who witnessed a shooting murder. He had a reason to be looking at the people involved because they were arguing loudly and it was late. The people, including the shooter, were poorly illuminated by street lights. The witness was in his sixties with reasonable eyesight and had been drinking. He gave more than ten accounts of the shooting, which gradually changed over time, and he became more confident in his accounts. It was possible to accurately determine the distance over which the witness saw the shooting and the level of illumination – both of which were quite different from what the witness reported. In this case, some factors were likely to have a positive influence on his accuracy, such as the fact that the witness paid attention to the shooting and had reasonable eyesight. However, other factors were likely to be less positive, for example, that he had been drinking and that his account, and his confidence, had changed substantially over time, the lack of light and his distance from the shooting. These various factors were taken into consideration to give an assessment of what parts of his account were more or less reliable.

Applications

Formal credibility assessments, if properly conducted, may help clarify the reliance that can be put on a witness's evidence. Recent research indicates why this might be important. Ask and Granhag (2007) found that witness evidence that was consistent with investigators' beliefs about what had happened was perceived by the investigators to be more credible than witness evidence that was not consistent. Credibility assessment can potentially reduce this effect.

Conclusion

To conclude, evaluating credibility is a complex and often ambiguous task focusing on the likely accuracy and deceptiveness of an individual. Here the focus has been on credibility in terms of memory capabilities, which is likely to be able to give a general indication of the accuracy of an account and potentially prevent over-, and under-, reliance on a witness's account.

FURTHER READING

For a general review of factors that influence eyewitness evidence the reader might wish to look at Kebbell and Wagstaff (1999). For a review of how an expert might wish to evaluate a case of delayed abuse the reader may wish to refer to L. J. Alison, M. R. Kebbell and P. Lewis (2006)

Psychological and legal problems in criminal cases of delayed reports of sexual abuse. *Psychology, Public Policy, and Law,* 12: 419–41.

REFERENCES

Ask, K. and Granhag, P. A. (2007) Motivational bias in criminal investigators' judgments of witness reliability. *Applied Social Psychology,* 37: 561–91.

Christianson, S. A. (1992) Emotional stress and eyewitness memory: a critical review. *Psychological Bulletin,* 112: 284–309.

Fisher, R. P. and Geiselman, R. E. (1992) *Memory-Enhancing Techniques for Investigative Interviewing: The Cognitive Interview.* Springfield, IL: Thomas.

Kebbell, M. R. and Wagstaff, G. F. (1999) *Face Value? Factors that Influence Eyewitness Accuracy.* London: Home Office. Available online: www.homeoffice.gov.uk/rds/prgpdfs/fprs102.pdf.

Kebbell, M. R., Wagstaff, G. F. and Covey, J. A. (1996) The influence of item difficulty on the relationship between eyewitness confidence and accuracy. *British Journal of Psychology,* 87: 653–62.

Lindsay, R. C. L., Wells, G. L. and Rumpel, C. (1981) Can people detect eyewitness identification accuracy within and across situations? *Journal of Applied Psychology,* 66: 79–89.

Loftus, E. F. (1975) Leading questions and eyewitness report. *Cognitive Psychology,* 7: 560–72.

Luus, E. C. A. and Wells, G. L. (1994) The malleability of eyewitness confidence: co-witness and perseverance effects. *Journal of Applied Psychology,* 79: 714–23.

Milne, R. and Bull, R. (1999) *Investigative Interviewing: Psychology and Practice.* Chichester: Wiley.

R. v. Turnbull and others (1977) QB 224; (1976) 3 AVE R 549 at pp. 549–50.

Vrij, A. (2006) Detecting deception. In M. R. Kebbell and G. M. Davies (eds.), *Practical Psychology for Forensic Investigations and Prosecutions,* pp. 89–102. Chichester: Wiley.

2.3 Crime pattern analysis

Jennifer M. Brown

See also chapter 6.4 Crime prevention.

Definitions

Crime pattern analysis may be thought of as the systematic approach to examining aspects of volume crime for the purposes of prevention or it may focus on a single crime, or series of a particular crime, for the purposes of detection. Analysis hopes to reveal distinctive, interpretable patterns reflecting identifiable characteristics as opposed to notions that crimes are random events. Hirschfield (2008) points out these characteristics might include identification of routine behaviours, spatial clusterings showing tendencies for incidents to occur in the same areas or to afflict the same households (repeat victimization) or to occur at certain times of the day or feature common modus operandi or indicate victims having similar demographic or social characteristics. He further suggests crime pattern analysis looks at the timing of opportunities that offenders have to commit their crimes. Crime opportunities are influenced by types and distribution of housing; accessibility; coincidence of different land use; timing; and community cohesion.

Brantingham and Brantingham (1984) define crime generators and crime attractors which arise as a consequence of the different configurations of the built environment; thus a pub might be an attractor as it occasions the bringing of people together and affords opportunities for illegal activity. Crime generators are areas of high rates of criminal activity as a by product of their accessibility to the general public, such as mainline railway stations. Crime detractors, on the other hand, are places in which there are features that discourage offenders, such as the presence of stable businesses which provide natural surveillance opportunities for mixtures of activities.

Ekblom (1998) defines crime analysis as an exploratory process whose objective is to conceive, implement and evaluate measures to prevent crime, comprising key steps that include obtaining data on a crime problem, analysis and interpretation of these data, devising preventative strategies, implementation and evaluation. Key variables include nature, location, timing, method, target, physical and social circumstances of the offence; victim characteristics; whether the crime was attempted or successful; offender characteristics; proximity of crime generators such as rowdy pubs; and location of goods or vehicles implicated in the offence.

In terms of targeted offences, 'geographic profiling is an investigative methodology that uses the locations of a connected series of crime to determine the most probable area of offender residence' (Rossmo 1999, p. 1) and has been applied to cases of serial murder, rape, arson, robbery and terrorism. Case analyses is a term given to a project set up to develop methods of looking at investigative advice rendered to ongoing police enquiries, and may be thought of as offender profiling. (See Bundeskriminalamt Kriminalistisches Institut 1998.)

Crime mapping involves the manipulation and processing of spatially referenced crime data in order for it to be displayed visually in an output that is informative to the particular user (Hirschfield and Bowers 2001, p. 1). They enumerate the potential uses as: informing police about particular problems in a territorial area; targeting resources for crime prevention; monitoring changes in the distribution of crime over time; evaluating effectiveness of crime prevention strategies; identifying hazardous spaces in which police work. Hirschfield (2008) also identifies fear of crime as another topic which may be mapped based on surveys of perceptions of neighbourhood safety or presence of antisocial behaviours. The products may be pin maps representing the location of offences, victims or offenders; chloropleth or shaded maps of different colours or density depicting frequencies of crime events; kernel-density estimates which provide contours of activity; voronoi polygrams indicating distances between offences or animations showing changes in crime distribution over time.

Small geographic areas that contain disproportionately high numbers of crime are termed hotspots and represent concentrations of criminal activity; they may be depicted as circles, ellipses, irregular polygons and street blocks (Rossmo 1999, p. 125). Hotspots can be placed in social and environmental contexts which may provide clues about risk factors associated with crime type (Filbert 2008). Other key concepts are activity or action spaces, which are those areas comprising a person's habitual geography, and anchor points, which are the most important places in a person's spatial life, such as home, work or bar.

Research on the journey to crime occupies a good deal of the available literature (summarized by Rossmo 1999), which explores the influence of demographics, prior criminal activity, and neighbour quality on type of crime committed. In summary, this research tends to find crimes often occur close to home; the number of crime occurrences decreases with increasing distance from offenders' homes; juvenile offenders tend to be less mobile and commit their crimes within their home environs; violent crime occurs closer to offenders' homes than do property crimes.

Problems

Much crime analysis involves the use of police-generated data or results of victim surveys. Williamson (2003) draws attention to the problems inherent in such sources: unreported crime, shortfalls in recording, differences in recording practices, manipulation of clear-up rates, absence of quality-assurance procedures, no weighting to seriousness of offences, accuracy of recall in witness statements, reliability of eyewitnesses, variations in interviewing techniques and quality and quantity of data yield. Ekblom (1998) also notes the validity or representativeness of police data sources as reflecting on possible biases in recording that might distort the 'true' picture; he also notes the problems of missing data, which is a further validity threat.

Rossmo (1999) notes that whilst maps are important analytic tools, displaying large amounts of information, they can also be potentially misleading because they show aggregates and may obscure individual patterns, i.e. their use may lead to the ecological fallacy of ascribing to an individual the characteristics of group data.

Hirschfield (2008) discusses the difficulties of linking offences to specific locations and identifying their function, especially in the UK, because there is a lack of consistent land use data and recording of uses of non-residential property.

Theory

Fritzon and Watts (2003) discuss the developments in crime pattern analysis deriving from environmental criminology, which starts with the premise that criminals' activities take place in time and space and that nodes represent the location of crime targets (departure and arrival points, such as bus stations), paths (the routes to and between locations) and edges (boundaries of areas where people may live, work or shop). Such approaches focus on the geographic distribution of crime and the daily routines of people's activities. Thus some crimes, such as racial attacks and shoplifting, occur at the edges of activity spaces because people from different areas not knowing each other come together at these points.

Crime pattern theory was developed by Brantingham and Brantingham (1984), who propose that offenders conduct their criminal activities at the intersection of their awareness space and target space (which is defined as places affording the minimal risk). Thus crime sites are not chosen at random but selection emerges from rational choice influenced by routine activities. They utilize the concepts of opportunity, motive, mobility and perceptions, and propose that the motivations underlying the commission of offences are many and various, with varying strength, and have both instrumental and affective components. The characteristics of motivation are linked to quantity and quality of stages in the offender's decision making; the environment emits signals about physical, spatial, cultural, legal and psychological characteristics; the offender uses these cues to locate targets; the offender learns and associates particular cues with successful criminal activities, and becomes self-reinforcing.

Harris (1999) summarizes the routine activities and criminal spatial behavioural approaches which define three components of crime: the offender, the target and the opportunity created by the absence of human or remote surveillance. From this derives an account of the cues or signals in the environment that the offender uses to assess victims or targets and the activity space which is the territory familiar to the criminal. These origins have contributed to the development of geographic profiling (Rossmo 1999). Critical to geographic profiling is the least effort principle, which states that an individual will select from a variety of possible actions the one requiring the expenditure of minimum effort.

Methods

Crime mapping certainly has its origins in the nineteenth and early twentieth centuries (Harris 1999). It began as a series of pins manually stuck onto maps representing the location of crimes, which has since given way to computerized mapping. In the UK a combination of factors encouraged the use of crime mapping: legislation which required police and local partnerships to undertake crime audits; adoption of problem-solving and intelligence-led approaches; and availability of geographic information systems (GIS) (Hirschfield and Bowers 2001). Two basic approaches are used: area-based methods, in which crime data are aggregated into specific units of territory, such as a census district or precinct; and point-based methods, which seek to identify the sites where crime occurs.

In geographic profiling, centrography employs the idea of a centroid or mean centre of gravity of crime activity located in space. This is described by a formula which attempts to locate the likely residence of an offender as a function of the crime sites, but these calculations may be distorted by outliers or by an offender operating considerable distances from home. Nearest neighbour analysis is another method employed by geographic profilers that attempts to overcome the centroid problems. Both methods are fully described by Rossmo (1999). He also details crime journeys, which are usually defined by the actual or crow flies (i.e. direct) distance between the offender's home and the crime site. Data are reported as means or mode crime trip distances (computing the arithmetic or geometric means/mode); medial circles (defining a radius containing percentages of offenders); mobility triangles (calculating distances between crime scene, offender residence and victim residence) or distance decay functions (a graphical curve showing the number of trips for different radii, say half-mile increments from the offender's home).

Costello and Wiles (2001) describe their method of analysing journey to crime by looking at offender movement from residential address to location of crime event, victim travel from home to where the offence was committed and patterns of movement of travelling offenders. Their data sources were the Police National Computer, national DNA database, victim surveys, interviews with offenders and police-recorded crime. The latter data were geocoded using GIS (i.e. a computer programme that enables data to be located usually by two coordinates), such that crime events can be spatially linked to geophysical features and/or sociodemographic features of an area. They found offenders travelled an average of less that two miles to commit their offences and were, on average, in their early twenties. They were also able to look at the lifestyle characteristics of a neighbourhood (e.g. struggling, aspiring, established) and link these to crime patterns. Thus deprived council estates were associated with high offender and offence rates compared to middle-class outer suburbs, which were associated with low offence and offender rates.

Baurmann (1998) identifies two methods of case analysis: retrospective empirical analysis of crimes in order to present a phenomenological description of crime types, such as sexually motivated crimes, whereby features of these offences are subjected to statistical cluster analysis; and pragmatic case assessment contributing to a live ongoing enquiry. In these cases the analyst will generate some hypotheses, data are reviewed and the hypotheses revised. The investigation team of detectives are then asked to evaluate the hypotheses, after which a case assessment is drawn up on the basis of these ratings. This approach is pragmatic and set against the real constraints of an ongoing enquiry.

FURTHER READING

Hirschfield and Bowers (2001) give a good overview of mapping techniques. Rossmo's (1999) book provides a detailed account of geographic profiling and its methods. The special issue of *Built Environment* (2008), 34(1) on 'Crime and the City' also provides a good range of articles covering theory and methods of crime pattern analysis in urban environments.

REFERENCES

Baurmann, M. (1998) A crime occurs and we don't know much to begin with. In Bundeskriminalamt Kriminalistisches Institut (ed.), *Methods of Case Analysis: An International Symposium*, pp. 17–53. Wiesbaden: Bundeskriminalamt Kriminalistisches Institut.

Brantingham, P. J and Brantingham, P. L. (1984) *Patterns in Crime*. New York: Macmillan.

Built Environment (2008), 34(1) special issue on 'Crime and the City'.

Bundeskriminalamt Kriminalistisches Institut (ed.) (1998) *Methods of Case Analysis: An International Symposium*. Wiesbaden: Bundeskriminalamt Kriminalistisches Institut.

Costello, A. and Wiles, P. (2001) GIS and journey to crime; an analysis of patterns in South Yorkshire. In A. Hirschfield and K. Bowers (eds.), *Mapping and Analysing Crime Data*, pp. 27–60. London: Taylor and Francis.

Ekblom, P. (1998) Getting the best out of crime analysis (Crime Prevention Unit Paper 10). London: Home Office.

Filbert, K. (2008) Targeting crime in hot spots and hot places. *Geography and Public Safety* 1: 24–7.

Fritzon, K. and Watts, A. (2003) Crime prevention. In D. Carson and R. Bull (eds.), *Handbook of Psychology in Legal Contexts*, 2nd edn, pp. 229–44. Chichester: Wiley.

Harris, K. (1999) *Mapping Crime: Principle and Practice*. Washington, DC: National Institute of Justice Crime Mapping Research Centre.

Hirschfield, A. (2008) The multi-faceted nature of crime. *Built Environment*, 34: 5–20.

Hirschfield, A. and Bowers, K. (eds.) (2001) *Mapping and Analysing Crime Data*. London: Taylor & Francis.

Rossmo, K. (1999) *Geographic Profiling*. London: CRC Press.

Williamson, T. (2003) Uses, misuses and implications for crime data. In D. Carson and R. Bull (eds.), *Handbook of Psychology in Legal Contexts*, 2nd edn, pp. 207–28. Chichester: Wiley.

Evaluating violence risk in young people

Paul A. Tiffin and Joanne M. Nadkarni

See also chapter 1.16 Violent offending.

Background

Professionals working with young people often encounter individuals who pose a risk of violence to others. The prevalence of conduct disorder amongst youth is increasing (Maughan *et al.* 2004). The 2005 Young People and Crime Survey estimated 1.8 million violent offenders aged between 10 and 25 in England and Wales. Thirty-eight per cent had committed assaults with injury (19% aged 10–17 and 19% aged 18–25) and an estimated 0.5 million were 'frequent and serious' offenders (Wilson, Sharp and Patterson 2006).

Risk evaluation in those under 18 differs in a number of respects when compared to adults. Research-based literature in the area is limited, structured tools available are fewer and risks take place against the dynamic background of developmental change (physical, cognitive, social and emotional). Particularly, it is important to take into account aspects of impulsivity, risk taking, forming identity, lack of stability of personality traits and greater peer/social influences during this period. This framework of sensitivity to change is most apparent when looking at risks over time and ways to manage this for young people.

For the purposes of this chapter, violence risk is defined as the likelihood of future physically aggressive behaviour causing harm to others.

Approach

Assessment must ultimately lead to risk management strategies. The current trend is to make structured professional judgements (Borum and Verhaagen 2006). This gives risk assessments, and their context, greater transparency. It

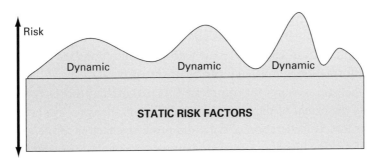

Figure 2.4.1 The static–dynamic model of risk

also brings the best aspects of clinical and actuarial approaches to risk assessment (Webster, Müller-Isberner and Fransson 2002). A clinical approach involves making human decisions about risk. In contrast, an actuarial approach considers variables that are utilized to statistically formulate the likelihood of an event occurring.

Any assessment of violence risk needs to consider the nature of the hazard; the likelihood of it occurring; its frequency; duration; potential consequences; immediacy; and relevant contextual and situational aspects (Johnstone, Cooke and Gadon 2007). These include the identification of any specific triggers, and delineating the persons, places and times that are more likely to be associated with increased risk. Static and dynamic risk factors are on a continuum and operate within this structure (see figure 2.4.1). Static 'historical' risks such as previous behaviour tend not to change and underpin reference to general levels of risk over time. Dynamic ('current') risk factors are fluid and liable to change. They may be intrinsic, as in disinhibited behaviour through acute mental illness, or extrinsic, as in environmental factors such as a conduct-disordered peer group. Violence risk assessment also needs to take into account the presence or absence of protective factors. There are also difficulties labelling risks as low, medium or high within a given time period unless a relative comparison can be given (Borum and Verhaagen 2006).

Thus, evaluation of violence risk in young people requires a formulation about the likelihood of a specific future risk and in what circumstances and time frame. It provides a structure to assist in identifying how the risk of harm through violence can be prevented, reduced, managed, monitored and evaluated. Hence, risk assessment has moved away from focusing on the individual level of 'dangerousness' towards a more specific and contextual framework.

A risk assessment process begins by obtaining relevant information from as wide a variety of sources as is practicable. A direct interview will generally be conducted with the young person. Relevant information would need to be obtained from parents/carers, education, health and Youth Offending Services (YOS). Structured instruments and psychometric assessments provide a useful framework to clinically assist with data collection (see table 2.4.1). Once the information is collated it can be used to generate a specific formulation of risk that still accounts for complexity. As part of this process it is important to assess the extent of the young person's history of aggressive behaviour, consequences, consideration of risks and protective factors. Professionals should avoid making biased or overconfident judgements. A case example is given in appendix A.

Protective factors

Factors associated with a low rate of violent offending include: female gender, high intelligence, engagement in education, well-developed social skills, good coping strategies, non-academic achievement/hobbies, a non-delinquent peer group and a stable family (Farrington and Loeber 2000; Reese *et al.* 2000; Resnick, Ireland and Borowsky 2004). Where a violent offence has occurred the probability of recidivism is reduced by a number of factors, including good engagement with services, reduction in substance misuse, motivation behavioural change, absence of psychopathic traits, victim empathy and remorse, disengagement from delinquent peers and good social support (Carr and Vandiver 2001). Some authors also emphasize protective aspects of strong attachments and resilient personality traits (Borum, Bartel and Forth 2003). The circumstances around the offence are important, including the level of provocation, any intoxication, mental illness, evidence of premeditation or use of a weapon. Protective factors are not always 'healthy'. They can involve inhibitory variables, such as 'negative symptoms' in chronic psychosis, a highly introverted personality or withdrawal during depression.

Risk factors

For both adults and adolescents the most accurate predictor of future violence is previous violence, this risk increasing with each prior episode and especially in the early months following a violent act (White *et al.* 1990). Early age of aggression is a strong predictor of violence (Borum and Verhaagen 2006). For minors, not all previous aggressive acts will appear on police records as cautions, convictions, warnings or reprimands. This is even less likely if

Table 2.4.1 A summary of some existing structured instruments which can contribute to violence risk assessment in children and adolescents

Instrument and reference	Acronym	Purpose	Structure	Published validity data
The Structured Assessment of Violence in Youth (Borum *et al.* 2003)	SAVRY	Guides violence risk assessment in males and females aged 12–18 years	24 items divided into four scales	Yes (Catchpole and Gretton 2003)
The Early Assessment Risk List for Boys (Augimeri *et al.* 2001)	EARL-20B	Guides violence risk assessment in 6–12-year-old boys	20 items cover three areas	No
The Early Assessment Risk List for Girls (Levene *et al.* 2001)	EARL-21G	Guides violence risk assessment in 6–12-year-old girls	21 items cover three areas	No
The Checklist for Risk in Childhood (Tiffin and Kaplan 2004)	CRIC	To guide and structure risk assessment in 12–18-year-olds seen by mental health services	33-item checklist covering eight areas	No
The Estimate of Risk of Adolescent Sexual Offense Recidivism (Worling and Curwen 2004)	ERASOR	Assists with estimating the short-term risk of sexual reoffending in 12–18-year-olds	25 items covering five categories	No
Juvenile Sex Offender Assessment Protocol II (Prentky and Righthand unpublished)	J-SOAP-II	Guides assessment of recidivism risk in adolescent sexual offenders	28 items divided into four scales	No
The Youth Level of Service/Case Management Inventory (Andrews and Hoge 1999)	YLS/CMI	Guide to constructing a management plan which will enhance protective factors and reduce risk in adolescents	42-item checklist covering individual, peer and family factors	Yes
The Salford Needs Assessment Schedule for Adolescents (Kroll *et al.* 1999)	SNASA	Assists with constructing a management plan addressing criminogenic and non-criminogenic needs in adolescents	A schedule that covers 21 areas of potential need	Yes
The Psychopathy Checklist – Youth Version (Forth *et al.* 2003)	PCL-YV	The quantification of emerging psychopathic traits in 12–17-year-olds	Semi-structured interview schedule, also using collateral information covering 20 domains	Yes
The Antisocial Process Screening Device (Frick and Hare 2001)	APSD	Assists with screening for emerging psychopathic traits in boys aged 6–13 years	20-item questionnaire covering three domains of behaviour	No

violence is restricted to the family home. The nature and severity of violence, along with understanding the motivation/intention of a previous violent act, is important in considering future risk. The choice of victim is also pertinent, particularly when dealing with sexual offending behaviour. Most forensic clinicians make a distinction between *proactive* or *instrumental* violence (i.e. premeditated and performed for secondary gain) and *reactive* violence, which is impulsive and a reaction to real or perceived provocation (Vitaro, Brendgen and Tremblay 2002). The former is more likely to be associated with callous-unemotional personality traits. Indeed, psychopathy is one of the main predictors of recidivist violence (Gretton, Hare and Catchpole 2004). In terms of emerging psychopathy, there is a youth version of the Psychopathy Checklist (Forth, Kossen and Hare 2003). Whilst recognizing limitations in the reliability of assessing psychopathy before adulthood, such tools can assist clinicians including aspects such as a history of cruelty to others (including animals) or during direct interview (when aloofness, superficial charm and/or fluent and plausible lying becomes evident).

There are a number of non-specific associations with violent offending. These include substance misuse, parental criminality, poor educational attendance, specific learning disorders, delinquent peer group or gang membership, family disruption, socioeconomic disadvantage and urbanicity (Farrington and Loeber 2000). In addition, self-harm, suicide attempts and history of abuse, attention deficit and hyperactivity, impulsivity/risk taking, peer rejection, stress, poor coping, lack of social support, antisocial attitude and family conflict are viewed as psychosocial risk factors (Borum and Verhaagen 2006).

The prevalence of mental health problems in young offenders is high, with often more than one disorder. As Borum and Verhaagen (2006) point out, those offending persistently through their life course tend to have more severe clinical and personality disorders, with higher rates of substance misuse than those offending more specifically during adolescence. Some studies suggest the prevalence for psychotic disorders for criminally detained juveniles is 1% (Teplin *et al.* 2002). This is similar to the general population. However, many young people in detention may experience episodes of psychosis or psychosis-like symptoms that may not fulfil the diagnostic criteria for a severe mental illness. These sometimes occur in the context of depression, personality disturbance, distress or previous trauma. Evaluating adult inpatients with mental disorder, Monahan *et al.* found 18.7% committed a violent act within twenty weeks of discharge (Monahan *et al.* 2001). In terms of symptoms of mental disorder, a diagnosis of schizophrenia was associated with a lower rate of violence than personality or adjustment disorder. Violence was associated with a comorbidity of mental disorder with substance abuse, suspicious attitude towards others and voices specifically commanding a violent act. The presence of delusions (type and content) or hallucinations (including command hallucinations) did not relate to future violence. It would be useful for future research to assess whether similar variables have a role for young people with mental disorders. One study of adolescents suggests the best predictors of violence in those with serious mental health problems may be the same as in those without (Clare, Bailey and Clark 2000).

There is little empirical evidence to suggest that young people with an autism spectrum disorder are more particularly likely to exhibit violent offending behaviour, although milder or atypical presentations of developmental disorders may be over-represented in forensic populations (Siponmaa *et al.* 2001). A model of risk assessment in such cases has been proposed (Tiffin, Shah and Couteur 2009).

Use of structured instruments

There are several structured assessment tools designed for use with young people. However, none is currently validated by widescale data relating to UK or wider European populations. Table 2.4.1 depicts some of the current tools used in connection with violence risk assessment. These include checklists and schedules such as the Structured Assessment of Violence in Youth (SAVRY) (Borum, Bartel and Forth 2003) and the Early Assessment Risk List for Boys (EARL-20B) (Augimeri *et al.* 2001) to help guide collation of risk-pertinent information. There are also tools designed to elicit and quantify emerging psychopathic personality traits with the Psychopathy Checklist – Youth Version (PCL–YV) (Forth, Kossen and Hare 2003) and Antisocial Process Screening Device (APSD) (Frick and Hare 2001). There is also the development of structured assessments to guide the evaluation of adolescent sex offenders (Worling and Curwen 2004; Prentky and Righthand unpublished). Schedules to assist in the process of developing a needs-led management plan are useful, such as the Youth Level of Service/ Case Management Inventory (YLS/CMI) (Andrews and Hoge 1999; Hoge and Andrews 2002) and the Salford Needs Assessment Schedule for Adolescents (SNASA) (Kroll *et al.* 1999). Whilst not specific to young people, the development of tools such as Promoting Risk Intervention by Situational Management (PRISM) (Johnstone, Cooke and Gadon 2007), designed for secure mental health inpatient and custodial settings, is useful in looking at preventing and managing risks across the overall system rather than risks in an individual.

Structured clinical assessments that are not 'risk-specific' may also feed into risk evaluation and formulation. The evaluation of cognitive functioning may be pertinent if specific or generalized learning disabilities are suspected. More generalized personality assessment tools such as the Millon Adolescent Clinical Inventory (MACI) may also facilitate a deeper psychological under-standing of a young person's needs (Millon, Millon and Davis 1993). In addition, if social and communication problems consistent with an autism spectrum disorder (ASD) are evident, specialized assessments can identify factors associated with violent behaviour (Tiffin, Shah and Couteur 2009).

When using risk-related structured instruments, authors often have unpub-lished/updated versions and can advise on their application and prerequisite training. Presently, structured instruments complement but do not replace structured clinical assessment. Moreover, caution needs to be exercised in using tools based on the pre-existing skills and expertise of the administrator and selecting the most appropriate instrument to use with the particular young person. If psychometric assessments are employed in medico-legal settings the limitations of the tool must be qualified.

Conclusions

Professionals involved in the care of young people are often required to evaluate, prevent and manage risk. However, there is a lack of research around understanding developmental pathways relating to assessment, prevention and interventions aimed at managing violent risk in young people. Structured instruments and psychometry complement clinical assessment. Within this, it is important to recognize mental health problems in young people exhibiting violence and to take a needs-led approach. Effective information collation, high-standard report writing and clear communication of risk are the corner-stones of good clinical practice in this area. A formulation of risk that recognizes complexity, qualifies limitations, yet is specific, enables useful management plans to be made.

FURTHER READING

Borum and Verhaagen (2006) provides an excellent resource for current thinking around assessing and managing violence risk in young people. For an overview of risk assessment in children and adolescents, see Tiffin and Kaplan (2004) in relation to mental disorder, Tiffin and

Richardson (2006) on the use of structured instruments in violence risk assessment, and Cooper and Tiffin (2006) for the evaluation and management of young people displaying psychopathic traits. Bailey and Dolan have edited a comprehensive text on mental health and offending behaviour in young people (Bailey and Dolan 2004). This book also contains a chapter on needs assessment in adolescents with offending behaviours (Kroll 2004). A more general text on violence in youth is provided by the book *Children Who Commit Acts of Serious Interpersonal Violence* (Hagell and Jeyarajah-Dent 2006). Quinsey *et al.* (1998) and Pinard and Pagani (2001) also provide useful general texts detailing the assessment/management of violence risk.

Appendix A: A case example

The example outlined below illustrates a formulation of violence risk.

Belinda

Belinda is a 17-year-old female. She has a diagnosis of attention deficit and hyperactivity disorder. She has marked obsessions and rituals. She has an extensive history of violent and non-violent offences from puberty. Her most recent and severe incident of violence involved stabbing a peer whilst intoxicated with alcohol. She is prone to volatile outbursts. She is an endearing and likeable character. She has always complied with interventions and, despite having special educational measures, has achieved seven GCSEs. She has never received a custodial sentence. She is currently in a hospital setting with plans to discharge her back home.

Assessment of risk

- Information from Belinda, her parents, professionals and case notes.
- Analysis of behaviour and functioning within the hospital setting to consider environmental and individual factors impacting Belinda's outbursts of aggression without the influence of illicit drugs/alcohol.
- Objective assessments including the Structured Assessment of Violence Risk in Youth, Millon Adolescent Clinical Inventory, State Trait Anger Inventory and Beck Youth Inventories.

Formulation of risk

Belinda is assessed as presenting with a likely risk of future violence to others including the use of a weapon based on one previous violent conviction using a knife, seven previous violent offences and numerous fights over the last five years. Injury involved superficial wounds (static risks). Her risk of being violent is influenced by her tendency to be reactive, blame others and see her violence as justified. Her risk of violence depends on how well her concentration and impulsivity related to ADHD is managed through medication plus environment and how she is coping with obsessive thoughts and rituals (intrinsic risk factors). Specific contextual factors relating to an increased risk of violence are associating with antisocial peers, access to a weapon, lack of enforcement of boundaries by parents and lack of social consequences through her peers and services making special allowances for her violent behaviour. Violence is most likely to be towards peers or acquaintances, by her or within a group. Intoxication with alcohol/illicit drugs, argument with a peer, disrespectful comment to her or a family member and rejection (particularly by a male peer) attenuates the risk of imminent violence (extrinsic and dynamic risk factors). Belinda's strengths are in her close emotional bond to parents, educational commitment/ability, peer acceptance, compliance with interventions, ability to give up smoking and endearing personality (protective factors).

Management plan

- Abstaining from illicit drugs and alcohol, with support from youth drug and alcohol team.
- Structuring time and peer relationships through college and work experience placement, avoiding 'hanging out' areas, pursuing music interest, peers at home.
- Compliance with medication related to ADHD and obsessions with psychiatric supervision. Cognitive-behavioural intervention to modify her rituals.
- Family work to support emotional separation and maintain boundaries.
- Reinforcement about negative consequences of further violence.

REFERENCES

Andrews, D. A. and Hoge, R. D. (eds.) (1999) *Youth Level of Service / Case Management Inventory.* Dinas Powys, Vale of Glamorgan: The Cognitive Centre Foundation.

Augimeri, L. K., Koegl, C. J., Webster, C. D. and Levene, K. S. (2001) *Early Assessment Risk List for Boys: Version 2.* Ontario: Earls Court Child and Family Centre.

Bailey, S. and Dolan, M. (eds.) (2004) *Adolescent Forensic Psychiatry.* London: Arnold.

Borum, R., Bartel, P. and Forth, A. E. (2003) *Manual for the Structured Assessment of Violence Risk in Youth: Version 1.1- Consultation Edition.* Florida: University of South Florida.

Borum, R. and Verhaagen, D. (2006) *Assessing and Managing Violence Risk in Juveniles.* London: Guilford Press.

Carr, M. B. and Vandiver, T. A. (2001) Risk and protective factors among youth offenders. *Adolescence,* 36: 409–26.

Catchpole, R. E. H. and Gretton, H. M. (2003) The predictive validity of risk assessment with violent young offenders at 1-year examination of criminal outcome. *Criminal Justice and Behavior,* 30: 688–708.

Clare, P., Bailey, S. and Clark, A. (2000) Relationship between psychotic disorders in adolescence and criminally violent behaviour: a retrospective examination. *British Journal of Psychiatry,* 177: 275–9.

Cooper, S. and Tiffin, P. (2006) The assessment and management of young people with psychopathic traits. *Journal of Educational and Child Psychology*, 23: 62–74.

Farrington, D. P. and Loeber, R. (2000) Epidemiology of juvenile violence. *Child and Adolescent Psychiatric Clinics of North America*, 9: 733–48.

Forth, A., Kossen, D. and Hare, R. D. (2003) *The Hare Psychopathy Checklist – Youth Version (PCL–YV)*. New York: Multi-Health Systems Inc.

Frick, P. and Hare, R. D. (2001) *Antisocial Process Screening Device: Technical Manual*. New York: Multi-Health Systems Inc.

Gretton, H., Hare, R. D. and Catchpole, R. E. H. (2004) Psychopathy and offending from adolescence to adulthood: a ten-year follow-up. *Journal of Consulting and Clinical Psychology*, 72: 636–45.

Hagell, A. and Jeyarajah-Dent, R. (eds.) (2006) *Children Who Commit Acts of Serious Interpersonal Violence – Messages for Practice*. London: Jessica Kingsley.

Hoge, R. D. and Andrews, D. A. (2002) *Youth Level of Service / Case Management Inventory: User's Manual*. Toronto: Multi Health Services.

Johnstone, L., Cooke, D. J. and Gadon, L. (2007). Promoting risk intervention by situational management. Unpublished manuscript. Glasgow University.

Kroll, L. (2004) Needs assessment in adolescent offenders. In S. Bailey and M. Dolan (eds.), *Adolescent Forensic Psychiatry*. London: Arnold.

Kroll, L., Woodham, A., Rothwell, J., Bailey, S., Tobias, C., Harrington, R. and Marshall, M. (1999) Reliability of the Salford Needs Assessment Schedule for Adolescents. *Psychological Medicine*, 29: 891–902.

Levene, K. S., Augimeri, L. K. and Pepler, D. J. (2001) *Early Assessment Risk List for Girls: Version 2*. Ontario: Earls Court Child and Family Centre.

Maughan, B., Rowe, R., Messer, R. and Goodman, H. (2004) Conduct disorder and oppositional defiant disorder in a national sample: developmental epidemiology. *Journal of Child Psychology and Psychiatry and Allied Disciplines*, 45: 609–21.

Millon, T., Millon, C. and Davis, R. (1993) *The Millon Adolescent Clinical Inventory*. Minneapolis, MN: Dicanthrien.

Monahan, J., Steadman, H. J., Silver, E., Appelbaum, P. S., Robbins, P. C., Mulvey, E. P. *et al.* (2001) *Rethinking Risk Assessment: The MacArthur Study of Mental Disorder and Violence*. New York: Oxford University Press.

Pinard, G.-F. and Pagani, L. (2001) *Clinical Assessment of Dangerousness: Empirical Contributions*. Cambridge: Cambridge University Press.

Prentky, R. and Righthand, S. (unpublished) Juvenile Sex Offender Protocol II (JSOAP-II) Manual.

Quinsey, V. L., Harris, G. T., Rice, M. E. and Cormier, C. A. (1998) *Violent Offenders: Appraising and Managing Risk*. Washington, DC: American Psychological Association.

Reese, L. E., Vera, E. M., Simon, T. R. and Ikeda, R. M. (2000) The role of families and care givers as risk and protective factors in preventing youth violence. *Clinical Child and Family Psychology Review*, 3: 61–77.

Resnick, M. D., Ireland, M. and Borowsky, I. (2004) Youth violence perpetration: what protects? What predicts? Findings from the National Longitudinal Study of Adolescent Health. *Journal of Adolescent Health*, 35: 424.e1–10.

Siponmaa, L., Kristiansson, M., Jonson, C., Nyden, A. and Gillberg, C. (2001) Juvenile and young adult mentally disordered offenders: the role of child neuropsychiatric disorders. *Journal of the American Academy of Psychiatry and the Law*, 29: 420–6.

Teplin, L. A., Abram, K. A., McClelland, G. M., Dulcan, M. K. and Mericle, A. A. (2002) Psychiatric disorders in youth in juvenile detention. *Archives of General Psychiatry*, 59: 1133–43.

Tiffin, P. and Kaplan, C. (2004) Dangerous children – assessment and management of risk. *Child and Adolescent Mental Health*, 9: 56–64.

Tiffin, P. and Richardson, G. (2006) The use of structured instruments in assessing risk of violence. In A. Hagell and R. Jeyarajah-Dent (eds.), *Children who Commit Acts of Serious Interpersonal Violence – Messages for Practice*. London: Jessica Kingsley.

Tiffin, P. A., Shah, P. and Couteur, A. (2009) Diagnosing pervasive developmental disorders in a forensic adolescent mental health setting. *British Journal of Forensic Practice*, 9: 31–40.

Vitaro, F., Brendgen, M. and Tremblay, R. E. (2002) Reactively and proactively aggressive children: antecedent and subsequent characteristics. *Journal of Child Psychology and Psychiatry*, 43: 495–505.

Webster, C., Müller-Isberner, R. and Fransson, G. (2002) Violence risk assessment: using structured clinical guides professionally. *International Journal of Forensic Mental Health*, 1: 185–93.

White, J., Moffitt, T., Earls, F., Robins, L. and Silva, P. A. (1990) How early can we tell? Predictors of childhood conduct disorder and adolescent delinquency. *Criminology*, 28: 507–33.

Wilson, D., Sharp, C. and Patterson, A. (2006) Young people and crime: findings from the 2005 Offending, Crime and Justice Survey. *Home Office Statistical Bulletin*. London: Home Office.

Worling, J. R. and Curwen, T. (2004) The estimate of risk of adolescent sexual offense recidivism (ERASOR): preliminary psychometric data. *Sexual Abuse: A Journal of Research and Treatment*, 16: 235–54.

2.5 Eyewitness testimony

Dan Yarmey

Definition

Eyewitness testimony refers to witness and victim recollections of what happened, the circumstances and description of the people involved in the incident, and the identification of the perpetrator(s). Given that most victims or bystander witnesses are truthful (see Yarmey 2009), questions arise regarding the accuracy and completeness of eyewitness testimony, and what factors influence the probability of error or bias.

Although the criminal justice system actively seeks eyewitness descriptions and identification evidence for the investigation and prosecution of crimes, such evidence is recognized as the primary cause of false convictions (Huff, Rattner and Sagarin 1986).

Warnings by psychologists of the possible limitations of eyewitness testimony based on empirical laboratory research, staged criminal incidents, field experiments, case studies, questionnaires, and archival analyses of police records and court documents (see reviews in Lindsay *et al.* 2007; Toglia *et al.* 2007), have been supported by the application of DNA technology. Over 100 convicted individuals have been exonerated by DNA tests, and of these cases more than 75% of the defendants were convicted as a function of mistaken eyewitness identification (Scheck, Neufeld and Dwyer 2000; Wells and Olson 2003).

Human memory

Sensory and perceptual experiences of an incident are not recorded in memory similar to the workings of a videotape recorder (Clifford and Bull 1978; Loftus 1979; Yarmey 1979). Instead, human memory is constructed and reconstructed from stored bits and pieces of acquired information of what actually happened and what a person intuits, discovers from others, or infers must have happened. Following the reconstructive view, memory can be divided into three stages: (1) acquisition or encoding of information; (2) retention or storage of information over time; and (3) retrieval of stored information through recall and/or recognition. Many factors such as the characteristics of the crime or situation, witness and perpetrator factors, and investigative procedures influence these stages and, consequently, the reliability of witness reports.

Characteristics of the crime or situation

Significant differences in the accuracy of reports occur as a function of differences in viewing conditions. Accuracy of recall and identification are influenced by the amount of light available during the acquisition stage; however, many witnesses remain confident in their recollections despite differences in illumination (Yarmey 1986). The greater the exposure duration of an event, the greater the opportunity to attend to more details and the greater the accuracy of recall and identification (MacLin, MacLin and Malpass 2001). However, estimations of the duration of the event are typically overestimated for relatively short-duration events (a few seconds up to two or three minutes) and underestimated for long durations (twenty minutes or more) (Loftus et al. 1986; Yarmey 2000a). Reports based on memory for distance between objects yield increasing underestimations with increasing distance (Radvansky et al. 1995). Large objects in the distance, such as a train, appear to move more slowly than smaller objects even though they are moving at exactly the same speed (Leibowitz 1985). Accuracy of facial identification is likely to be poor when observations are made at a distance of 15 metres or more, and illumination levels of less than 5 lux (Wagenaar and van der Schrier 1996). Highly emotional events typically are well retained, particularly the central or core details of the emotion-eliciting event. However, less central or more peripheral details often are given little attention and are poorly retained (Christianson 1992). The most salient details in a situation, such as a weapon, are most likely to be attended to and remembered, often at the expense of other details such as the face and other characteristics of the perpetrator (Steblay 1992).

The cross-race effect is another situational variable of importance. There is a significantly greater chance of an accurate identification from a lineup in same-race than in other-race conditions, and more mistaken identifications in other-race than in same-race conditions (Meissner and Brigham 2001).

Witness factors

The most important individual difference variable is the age of the witness. Young children (preschoolers) tend to recall fewer details of an event than do older children; however, older children are generally as accurate as adults in what they do recall. Young children, in contrast to older children, are more susceptible to suggestion; however, children are not any more suggestible than adults about information and events which are meaningful and of special interest (King and Yuille 1987). Identification research shows that both younger and older children, in contrast to adults, have a greater tendency to choose someone from a lineup rather than state the suspect is not present. Consequently, and in suspect-absent lineups in particular, there is an increased likelihood of a false identification (Pozzulo and Lindsay 1998).

Older eyewitnesses (60- to 80-year-old age range), in contrast to young adults, show more impairment in their completeness and accuracy of suspect descriptions (Yarmey 2000b). Older witnesses also show greater tendencies to choose someone from target-absent lineups, resulting in higher proportions of false identifications (Memon and Gabbert 2003).

Perpetrator factors

Changes in hairstyle and the addition and removal of perpetrators' glasses significantly influence accuracy of facial recognition (Patterson and Baddeley 1977; Read 1995). The masking of a perpetrator's hairline by the wearing of a hat can significantly decrease accuracy of identification. Faces that undergo changes in facial features and deliberate disguise between the encoding and retrieval stages are less accurately recognized than non-transformed faces (Cutler, Penrod and Martens 1987; but see also Yarmey 2004). Finally, perpetrators with more distinctive faces compared to foils are more likely to be recognized and produce fewer false recognitions (Light, Kayra-Stuart and Hollander 1979).

Investigative procedures

Retention interval

Memory does decline over time, with the greatest decrement in identification accuracy occurring after a delay of approximately one week (Shepherd 1983; Valentine, Pickering and Darling 2003). The rate of forgetting depends upon such factors as: the type and significance of the information to be remembered; the level of original learning; trace decay, the strength and similarity of previously acquired information; and the nature of events which occur during the retention interval.

Between the time that a crime was observed and the identification test memory representations can be changed, distorted or replaced by post-event misinformation. Witnesses may acquire new information about the event and the suspect through talking with other witnesses (Yarmey and Morris 1998), overhearing the statements of other witnesses, watching television reports and reading newspaper accounts, and through leading or suggestive questions by police (Loftus 1992).

Investigative interviews

The retrieval of eyewitness memories depends greatly upon the adequacy of the interview procedures utilized. Forensic hypnosis techniques have been advocated by Reiser (1989); however, critics suggest that hypnosis may contaminate memory and lead to false recall and misidentifications with high confidence for events and people that were never experienced (Orne *et al.* 1988). An improvement over hypnosis is the cognitive interview procedure. Through context reinstatement the cognitive interview involves asking victims and witnesses to recreate the crime scene and to re-experience their emotions mentally; to recall everything that may be related to the event including partial or incomplete details that may not seem to be relevant; to recall the event in different temporal orders; and to recall the event from a variety of perspectives and locations. Attention is also given to components of communication such as rapport building and interviewer social skills (Fisher

1995). Other highly regarded forensic interviewing techniques are the statement validity analysis procedure (Stellar 1989) and the Step-Wise Interview (Yuille *et al.* 1993).

Witness descriptions and the relationship between descriptions and identification accuracy

The 'fit' of a suspect to the original witness description should be accepted with caution because of general vagueness and limited descriptions (Flin and Shepherd 1986; Sporer 1996; van Koppen and Lochun 1997; Yarmey, Jacob and Porter 2002). Contrary to expectations, there is no significant relationship between the accuracy and completeness of the verbal description of the perpetrator given by the witness and the accuracy of their subsequent lineup identification (Piggott and Brigham 1985; Wells 1985).

Lineup identifications

The purpose of a lineup is to uncover information through recognition memory that was not available through recall. The goals of an identification test are to determine whether the witness can select the suspect as the perpetrator observed at the scene of the crime, and to test the validity of the witness's memory (Wagenaar and Loftus 1990). Identification tests from live lineups, photo spreads and video lineups produce similar identification rates (Cutler *et al.* 1994). Surveys of real-world estimates of foil identifications of known innocent persons in actual cases indicate that approximately 20% of cases result in foil identifications. Furthermore, in over 40% of those lineups witnesses fail to make any identification (Behrman and Davey 2001; Wright and McDaid 1996).

Properly constructed and administered lineups have two methodological components: structural properties such as the appearance characteristics of lineup members; and procedural properties such as the instructions given to eyewitnesses prior to viewing (Wells *et al.* 1998). Recommendations for good practice for lineup procedures are now available (Turtle, Lindsay and Wells 2003):

1. Witnesses' verbal descriptions of the perpetrator(s) should be gathered before the conduction of a lineup.
2. Each lineup should contain only one suspect and there should be a minimum of five foils plus the suspect present in the lineup.

3. The foils selected for the lineup should match the verbal description of the perpetrator given by the eyewitness.
4. The suspect should not stand out from the other members of the lineup because of the presence of a distinctive feature(s) that the witness failed to describe.
5. The suspect and foils should be allowed to vary in non-distinctive physical characteristics not mentioned by the eyewitness. Such a procedure would permit helpful differences in discrimination of appearance between the suspect and the foils.
6. If there are multiple witnesses a separate lineup should be constructed and administered for each witness. If this is not possible, the positions of all members of the lineup should be changed across witnesses.
7. A double-blind procedure should be followed in the administration of the lineup. The lineup administrator should not know who the suspect is among the lineup members and should inform the witness of this fact.
8. Witnesses should be told that the perpetrator may or may not be present in the lineup and to refrain from guessing.
9. Witnesses should indicate if they recognize the perpetrator and, if affirmative, indicate which person they select and where this person is remembered from (i.e. the source of their identification).
10. Witnesses should state in their own words their level of confidence in their identification decision.
11. All statements of the witness and the procedures used during the lineup administration should be recorded, preferably on videotape.
12. Sequentially administered lineups are preferred over simultaneously administered lineups because the two procedures yield similar numbers of correct identifications (hits) when the perpetrator is present, but sequential lineups produce fewer false identifications when the perpetrator is absent.

Police also may conduct one-person lineups referred to as showups. Showups are considered inherently suggestive because the witness views only one person and the identification requires only the assent of the witness. Showups may be justified when: an immediate identification would facilitate an ongoing police investigation; a quick exoneration of the innocent could be made; the identification is completed in close proximity in time and place to the scene of the crime; and the witness's memory is strongest or in its freshest state (Yarmey in press).

Meta-analytic comparison of showup and lineup presentations reveals that showups generate lower choosing rates than lineups, suggesting greater caution, but also allow more guilty persons to be undetected; the correct identification rate is very similar in both conditions (approximately 46%) when the target is present; correct rejection rates are significantly higher in showups when the target is absent; false identifications in target-absent conditions are about the same (16%), however, errors in target-absent lineups are spread across foils rather than focused on the innocent suspect in a showup; and false identifications are particularly high in showups when the innocent suspect resembles the perpetrator, such as wearing similar clothing (Steblay *et al.* 2003). It is concluded that a showup presentation is a dangerous procedure.

Conclusion

Witnesses' descriptions and lineup identifications of suspects can be accurate. They also can be error prone and lead to misidentifications of innocent persons and the exoneration of guilty individuals. Police officers and other officers of the court must be aware of the psychological processes that underlie this evidence, and the factors that lead to greater witness reliability.

REFERENCES

Behrman, B. W. and Davey, S. L. (2001) Eyewitness identification in actual criminal cases: an archival analysis. *Law and Human Behavior*, 25: 475–91.

Christianson, S.-Å. (1992) Emotional stress and eyewitness memory: a critical review. *Psychological Bulletin*, 112: 284–309.

Clifford, B. R. and Bull, R. (1978) *The Psychology of Person Identification*. London: Routledge.

Cutler, B. L., Berman, G. L., Penrod, S. and Fisher, R. P. (1994) Conceptual, practical, and empirical issues associated with eyewitness identification test media. In D. F. Ross, J. D. Read, and M. P. Toglia (eds.), *Adult Eyewitness Testimony: Current Trends and Developments*, pp. 163–81. Cambridge: Cambridge University Press.

Cutler, B. L., Penrod, S. D. and Martens, T. K. (1987) The reliability of eyewitness identifications: the role of system and estimator variables. *Law and Human Behavior*, 11: 223–58.

Fisher, R. P. (1995). Interviewing victims and witnesses of crime. *Psychology, Public Policy, and Law*, 1: 732–64.

Flin, R. H. and Shepherd, J. W. (1986) Tall stories: eyewitnesses' ability to estimate height and weight characteristics. *Human Learning*, 5: 29–38.

Huff, R., Rattner, A. and Sagarin, E. (1986) Guilty until proven innocent. *Crime and Delinquency*, 32: 518–44.

King, M. A. and Yuille, J. C. (1987) Suggestibility and the child witness. In S. J. Ceci, M. M. Toglia and D. F. Ross (eds.), *Children's Eyewitness Memory*, pp. 24–35. New York: Springer.

Leibowitz, H. W. (1985) Grade crossing accidents and human factors engineering. *American Scientist*, 73: 558–62.

Light, L. L., Kayra-Stuart, F. and Hollander, S. (1979). Recognition memory for typical and unusual faces. *Journal of Experimental Psychology: Human Learning and Memory*, 5: 212–28.

Lindsay, R. C. L., Ross, D. F., Read, J. D. and Toglia, M. (eds.) (2007) *Handbook of Eyewitness Psychology*, vol. 2: *Memory for People*. Mahwah, NJ: Erlbaum.

Loftus, E. F. (1979) *Eyewitness Testimony*. Cambridge, MA: Harvard University Press.
  (1992) When a lie becomes memory's truth: memory distortion after exposure to misinformation. *Current Directions in Psychological Science*, 1: 121–3.

Loftus, E. F., Schooler, J. W., Boone, S. M. and Kline, D. (1986) Time went by so slowly: over-estimation of event duration by males and females. *Applied Cognitive Psychology*, 1: 3–13.

MacLin, O. H., MacLin, M. and Malpass, R. S. (2001) Race, arousal, attention, exposure and delay: an examination of factors moderating face recognition. *Psychology, Public Policy, and Law*, 7: 134–52.

Meissner, C. A. and Brigham, J. C. (2001) Thirty years of investigating the own-race bias in memory for faces: a meta-analytic review. *Psychology, Public Policy, and Law*, 7: 3–35.

Memon, A. and Gabbert, F. (2003) Improving the identification accuracy of senior witnesses: Do prelineup questions and sequential testing help? *Journal of Applied Psychology*, 88: 341–7.

Orne, M. T., Whitehouse, W. G., Dinges, D. F. and Orne, E. C. (1988) Reconstructing memory through hypnosis: forensic and clinical implications. In H. M. Pettinati (ed.), *Hypnosis and Memory*, pp. 21–63. New York: Guilford Press.

Patterson, K. E. and Baddeley, A. D. (1977) When face recognition fails. *Journal of Experimental Psychology: Human Learning and Memory*, 3: 406–17.

Pigott, M. and Brigham, J. C. (1985) Relationship between accuracy and prior description and facial recognition. *Journal of Applied Psychology*, 70: 547–55.

Pozzulo, J. D. and Lindsay, R. C. L. (1998) Identification accuracy of children versus adults: a meta-analysis. *Law and Human Behavior*, 22: 549–70.

Radvansky, G. A., Carlson-Radvansky, L. A. and Irwin, D. E. (1995) Uncertainty in estimating distances from memory. *Memory and Cognition*, 23: 596–606.

Read, J. D. (1995) The availability heuristic in person identification: the sometimes misleading consequences of enhanced contextual information. *Applied Cognitive Psychology*, 9: 91–121.

Reiser, M. (1989) Investigative hypnosis. In D. Raskin (ed.), *Psychological Methods in Criminal Investigation and Evidence*, pp. 151–90. New York: Springer.

Scheck, B., Neufeld, P. and Dwyer, J. (2000) *Actual Innocence*. New York: Random House.

Shepherd, J. W. (1983) Identification after long delays. In S. M. A. Lloyd-Bostock and B. R. Clifford (eds.), *Evaluating Witness Evidence*, pp. 173–87. Chichester: Wiley.

Sporer, S. L. (1996) Psychological aspects of person descriptions. In S. L. Sporer, R. S. Malpass and G. Koehnken (eds.), *Psychological Issues in Eyewitness Identification*, pp. 53–86. Mahwah, NJ: Erlbaum.

Steblay, N. M. (1992) A meta-analytic review of the weapon focus effect. *Law and Human Behavior*, 16: 413–24.

Steblay, N., Dysart, J., Fulero, S. and Lindsay, R. C. L. (2003) Eyewitness accuracy rates in police showup and lineup presentations: a meta-analytic comparison. *Law and Human Behavior*, 27: 523–40.

Stellar, M. (1989) Recent developments in statement analysis. In J. C. Yuille (ed.), *Credibility Assessment*, pp. 135–54. Dordrecht: Kluwer.

Toglia, M. P., Read, J. D., Ross, D. F. and Lindsay, R. C. L. (eds.) (2007) *Handbook of Eyewitness Psychology*, vol. 1: *Memory for Events*. Mahwah, NJ: Erlbaum.

Turtle, J. L., Lindsay, R. C. L. and Wells, G. L. (2003) Best practice recommendations for eyewitness evidence procedures: new ideas for the oldest way to solve a case. *Canadian Journal of Police and Security Services*, 1: 5–18.

Valentine, T., Pickering, A., and Darling, S. (2003). Characteristics of eyewitness identification that predict the outcome of real lineups. *Applied Cognitive Psychology*, 17: 969–93.

van Koppen, P. J. and Lochun, S. K. (1997) Portraying perpetrators: the validity of offender descriptions by witnesses. *Law and Human Behavior*, 21: 661–85.

Wagenaar, W. A. and Loftus, E. F. (1990) Ten cases of eyewitness identification: logical and procedural problems. *Journal of Criminal Justice*, 18: 291–319.

Wagenaar, W. A. and van der Schrier, J. (1996) Face recognition as a function of distance and illumination: a practical tool for use in the courtroom. *Psychology, Crime and Law*, 2: 321–32.

Wells, G. L. (1985) Verbal descriptions of faces from memory: are they diagnostic of identification accuracy? *Journal of Applied Psychology*, 70: 619–26.

Wells, G. L. and Olson, E. A. (2003) Eyewitness testimony. *Annual Review of Psychology*, 54: 277–95.

Wells, G. L., Small, M., Penrod, S., Malpass, R. S., Fulero, S. M. and Brimacombe, C. A. E. (1998) Eyewitness identification procedures: recommendations for lineups and photospreads. *Law and Human Behavior*, 22: 603–47.

Wright, D. B. and McDaid, A. T. (1996) Comparing system and estimator variables using data from real lineups. *Applied Cognitive Psychology*, 10: 75–84.

Yarmey, A. D. (1979) *The Psychology of Eyewitness Testimony*. New York: Free Press.

(1986) Verbal, visual, and voice identification of a rape suspect under different levels of illumination. *Journal of Applied Psychology*, 71: 363–70.

(2000a) Retrospective duration estimations for variant and invariant events in field settings. *Applied Cognitive Psychology*, 14: 45–57.

(2000b) The older eyewitness. In M. B. Rothman, B. D. Dunlop and P. Entzel (eds.), *Elders, Crime, and the Criminal Justice System: Myth, Perceptions and Reality in the 21st Century*, pp. 127–48. New York: Springer.

(2004) Eyewitness recall and photo identification: a field experiment. *Psychology, Crime and Law*, 10: 53–68.

(2009) Truthfulness in witness and suspects reports. In R. Bull, T. Valentine and T. Williamson (eds.), *Handbook of Psychology of Investigative Interviewing: Current Developments and Future Directions*, pp. 285–99. Chichester: Wiley.

(in press) Showups. In B. L. Cutler (ed.), *Encyclopedia of Psychology and Law*. Thousand Oaks, CA: Sage.

Yarmey, A. D., Jacob, J. and Porter, A. (2002) Person recall in field settings. *Journal of Applied Social Psychology*, 32: 2354–67.

Yarmey, A. D. and Morris, S. (1998) The effects of discussion on eyewitness memory. *Journal of Applied Social Psychology*, 28: 1637–48.

Yuille, J. J., Hunter, R., Joffe, R. and Zaparniuk, J. (1993) Interviewing children in sexual abuse cases. In G. Goodman and B. Bottoms (eds.), *Understanding and Improving Children's Testimony: Clinical, Developmental and Legal Implications*, pp. 95–115. New York: Guilford Press.

2.6 False memory

Cara Laney and Elizabeth F. Loftus

The malleability of memory

Human memory can hold an amazing amount of information, but it is far more than a mere storage device for records of experiences. Memory is a set of dynamic processes. These processes work very well most of the time, but are also susceptible to distortion (see Schacter 2001). In particular, they are susceptible to external suggestions. These suggestions can take many forms, including post-event information like leading questions (Loftus and Palmer 1974) and conversations with co-witnesses (Wright, Self and Justice, 2000). In some cases, suggestions can even lead people to remember complete, detailed events that never happened (Loftus and Pickrell 1995).

Although appealing as a metaphor, memory does not actually function like a video recorder. There is no accurate bit of 'tape' that we can find by rewinding our minds to the right point in time. Rather, to remember something – even an event from one's own personal past – one must engage in a process of reconstruction, of putting together different traces to create a new memory. Some of these traces contain unique bits of the original event, but other traces reflect assumptions about how things are or were, or information learned since the event took place.

The 'misinformation effect' occurs when misleading information presented after an event is incorporated into an individual's memory for the event (see Davis and Loftus 2006; Loftus 2005). In studies of the misinformation effect, subjects witness an event like a mock crime or staged video, and then a subset of subjects are exposed to misleading information in the form of a narrative or conversation with a 'co-witness' (who actually saw a slightly different event). At a subsequent memory test, the misled subjects' memories are less accurate than control subjects' memories for the originally witnessed event (e.g. Loftus, Miller and Burns 1978; Loftus and Palmer 1974; Takarangi, Parker and Garry 2006; Wright et al. 2000). In these studies subjects have remembered stop signs as yield signs, the Eiffel Tower as the Leaning Tower of Pisa, unmade beds as made, and criminal accomplices or broken glass that were not there at all. These studies are particularly relevant to real-world eye-witnesses because there is substantial evidence that real eyewitnesses are likely to talk to one another (e.g. Paterson and Kemp 2006), and that police officers and lawyers do ask leading questions (e.g. Powell, Fisher and Wright 2005).

In a related line of work employing the Deese–Roediger–McDermott para-digm (after Deese 1959; Roediger and McDermott 1996), subjects learn lists of words that are all related to a critical, but not presented, word. For example, the list might include words like 'nap', 'bed', 'pillow', and 'snooze', but not the critical word 'sleep'. When subjects are subsequently tested for words from the list, they are as likely to remember the word 'sleep' as part of the list as words that were actually present. That is, they predictably, but falsely, remember the critical word.

The 'recovered memory' debate

In spite of research showing that memory can be malleable, many clinicians and some researchers seem to believe that some types of memory are com-pletely immune to distortion. They claim that some memories – particularly memories for traumatic events like child sexual abuse – can be buried in the subconscious for years or even decades and then spring to consciousness, untouched by time (e.g. Brown, Scheflin and Hammond 1998; Herman and Schatzow 1987; Terr 1991; see Poole et al. 1995 for statistics regarding the commonness of these beliefs among therapists). That is, these traumatic events can be 'repressed' when they are too painful to deal with and then 'recovered' later, when remembering will be helpful rather than harmful. Though 'repression' was a concept popularized by Freud (1896/1962) as part of his 'seduction theory' (and though Freud himself later rejected this theory), the idea is still hotly debated today (e.g. Smith and Gleaves 2006; Takarangi et al. 2008).

Proponents of memory repression and recovery argue that demonstrat-ing that memories for often trivial events can be changed says very little about the accuracy of traumatic and personally relevant memories. But as we shall show, even traumatic memories are subject to distortion. Before describing this work, we explore arguments made by some clinicians for the specialness of traumatic memories, and their use of repression as an explanation.

Terr (1991) argued that repeated traumas like recurring child sexual abuse are likely to produce repression because abused children develop skills that allow them to dissociate from their experiences of abuse. More recently, Freyd (1996) added that this dissociative response is particularly likely when the perpetrator of the abuse is someone on whom the abuse victim depends for his or her survival. Freyd called this phenomenon 'betrayal trauma', and argued that repression 'is a natural and inevitable reaction to childhood sexual abuse' (Freyd 1996, p. 4). (See McNally 2007 for a thorough refutation of these claims.)

What is the evidence for these beliefs about memory repression? Some authors have claimed that there are more than sixty studies demonstrating the validity of massive repression and recovery (see for example, Brown, Scheflin and Whitfield 1999). The majority of these studies are retrospective in nature. They ask a group of people who say that they were sexually abused as children whether there was a time in their lives when they did not remember the abuse. For example, Briere and Conte (1993) asked a group of 450 patients, all currently in treatment for child sexual abuse, whether there was a time in their childhoods that they could not remember their abuse. A majority of subjects replied affirmatively. While numerous writers have used this result as evidence for memory repression and recovery, in no way is the finding compelling proof of such cognitive mechanisms. In particular, for an affirmative response to this question to be evidence of repression and recovery, it would have to mean that the person had tried and failed to remember abuse at some point in his or her past, and could remember that past attempted remembering. But why would the person have tried to remember the abuse, unless he or she already knew that there had been abuse? And if the person knew that there had been abuse, then how can he or she be said to have fully repressed it? See McNally (2003; listed in 'Further reading') for a more thorough analysis of the misuse of these studies.

A few studies use prospective methodologies to provide evidence for repression. One classic example is that of Williams (1994). Williams found a group of 129 women that she knew had been abused (seventeen years previously) – because she had access to hospital records documenting the reported abuse. She interviewed these women and found that 49 of them (38%) failed to report the specific documented case of abuse, even when questioned specifically about sexual abuse. These results have been taken as evidence that these women – and many more like them – had successfully repressed their memories of the abuse. But there are far more parsimonious explanations for this 38% non-reporting rate. For example, some of the interviewed women had been as young as 10 months old when the specific instance of abuse occurred, so they should not be expected to remember anything from that period. In addition, 68% of the women who 'forgot' the specific case of abuse nonetheless reported other instances of abuse, which suggests that the documented instance of abuse (which was often fondling) may have simply been less memorable than other, more traumatic instances of abuse. Finally, many of these women may have failed to report the abuse because they did not want to be labelled as abused. As such, we argue that the 38% of women who failed to report abuse in Williams' study did not necessarily repress their memories for the abuse (and indeed, they did not even necessarily forget the abuse); instead, they simply failed to *report* the abuse.

Failure to disclose is not evidence of repression (see Femina, Yeager and Lewis 1990). Failure to think about an event, and even failure to remember an event do not constitute evidence of repression; rather, other mechanisms, including ordinary forgetting, provide perfectly adequate explanations (e.g. McNally 2003, 2007; Takarangi *et al.* 2008). There is also evidence that people with purported recovered memories are more susceptible to memory distortion in the Deese–Roediger–McDermott paradigm described above (e.g. Geraerts *et al.* 2005). Finally, it is worth noting that in a conceptual replication of Williams' study, Goodman *et al.* (2003) found a much lower non-disclosure rate of just 8%.

False memories for benign and traumatic events

So, if these memories for traumatic events like sexual abuse have not actually been repressed and recovered, then where have they come from? There is now more than a decade's worth of research showing that it is possible to implant wholly false memories into people's minds. The first such study used information collected from subjects' parents. Subjects were presented with three true childhood events, and one mildly traumatic false event: being lost in a shopping mall (Loftus and Pickrell 1995). Over three interviews, approximately 25% of subjects came to believe that they had indeed been lost in a mall as young children, though their parents specifically disconfirmed this. Subsequent studies using similar manipulations have convinced people that they had unlikely experiences like spilling punch on the bride's parents at a family wedding and potentially traumatic experiences like being hospitalized overnight, being attacked by a dog, or having a serious indoor or outdoor accident (Hyman, Husband and Billings 1995; Porter, Yuille and Lehman 1999). The false memories produced in these studies can be detailed, emotional, consequential and confidently held (see Loftus and Bernstein 2005).

Many researchers have explicitly sought to replicate the techniques used by therapists specializing in 'memory recovery work' when implanting false memories. For example, Scoboria and colleagues (2002) found that subjects were more susceptible to misleading information when hypnotized. Garry and colleagues (1996) used a guided imagination technique to increase subjects' confidence in a variety of childhood events. Mazzoni and colleagues (1999) used a dream interpretation paradigm to get subjects to falsely believe that they had been lost as young children.

In the last few years, researchers have developed several additional creative procedures for implanting false memories. Wade and colleagues (2002) digitally manipulated childhood photos to convince their subjects that they had been on hot air balloon rides as children. Lindsay and colleagues (2004) used genuine childhood class photos to lend credibility to a contemporaneous false event, that subjects had 'slimed' a teacher's desk and got into trouble for it. Braun and colleagues (2002) used mock advertisements to convince subjects that they had interacted with Bugs Bunny at Disneyland – an impossible event, as Bugs is a Warner Brothers character, and thus would never be encountered at a Disney theme park. Bernstein and colleagues (2005) used false computer feedback to convince subjects that they had become ill after eating dill pickles or hard-boiled eggs as children, and found that they reported less desire to eat the offending foods now. Seamon and colleagues (2006) took subjects on a walk around campus and had them perform some tasks, watch experimenters perform some tasks, and imagine performing some tasks. Two weeks later, subjects remembered performing tasks that they had only imagined performing, including, incredibly, proposing marriage to a Pepsi machine.

Conclusion

Some authors argue that false memories created in the sterility and ethical limitations of a research laboratory setting are insufficiently similar to the highly emotional circumstances reflected in recovered memories of abuse. Yet there is evidence to suggest that people can be very emotional about memories that must be false. McNally and colleagues (2004) measured the physiological responses of a group of people whose traumatic memories are almost certainly false: space alien 'abductees'. They found that these individuals were as emotional about their abduction memories as they were about genuine traumas in their lives.

At the broadest levels, false memory research tells us that even emotional, detailed, meaningful and confidently held memories may not accurately reflect reality.

FURTHER READING

Loftus, E. F. and Ketcham, K. (1996) *The Myth of Repressed Memory: False Memories and Allegations of Sexual Abuse*. New York: St Martin's Griffin.
McNally, R. J. (2003) *Remembering Trauma*. Cambridge, MA: University of Harvard Press.
Wright, D. B., Ost, J. and French, C. C. (2006) Ten years after: what we know now that we didn't know then about recovered and false memories. *Psychologist*, 19: 352–5.

REFERENCES

Bernstein, D. M., Laney, C., Morris, E. K. and Loftus, E. F. (2005) False memories about food can lead to food avoidance. *Social Cognition*, 23: 10–33.
Braun, K. A., Ellis, R. and Loftus, E. F. (2002) Make my memory: how advertising can change our memories of the past. *Psychology and Marketing*, 19: 1–23.
Briere, J. and Conte, J. (1993) Self-reported amnesia for abuse in adults molested as children. *Journal of Traumatic Stress*, 6: 21–31.
Brown, D., Scheflin, A. W. and Hammond, D. C. (1998) *Memory, Trauma Treatment, and the Law*. New York: W. W. Norton.
Brown, D., Sheflin, A. W. and Whitfield, C. L. (1999) Recovered memories: the current weight of the evidence in science and in the courts. *Journal of Psychiatry and Law*, 27: 5–156.
Davis, D. and Loftus, E. F. (2006) Internal and external sources of misinformation in adult witness memory. In M. P. Toglia, J. D. Read, D. F. Ross and R. C. L. Lindsay (eds.) *The Handbook of Eyewitness Psychology*, vol. 1: *Memory for Events*, pp. 195–237. London: Erlbaum.
Deese, J. (1959) On the prediction of occurrence of particular verbal intrusions in immediate recall. *Journal of Experimental Psychology*, 58: 17–22.
Femina, D. D., Yeager, C. A. and Lewis, D. O. (1990) Child abuse: adolescent records vs adult recall. *Child Abuse and Neglect*, 14: 227–31.
Freud, S. (1962) The aetiology of hysteria. In J. Strachey (ed., transl.), *The Standard Edition of the Complete Psychological Works of Sigmund Freud*, vol. 3, pp. 191–221. London: Hogarth Press (original work published in 1896).
Freyd, J. J. (1996) *Betrayal Trauma: The Logic of Forgetting Childhood Abuse*. Cambridge, MA: Harvard University Press.
Garry, M., Manning, C. G., Loftus, E. F. and Sherman, S. J. (1996) Imagination inflation: imagining a childhood event inflates confidence that it occurred. *Psychonomic Bulletin and Review*, 3: 208–214.

Geraerts, E., Smeets, E., Jelicic, M., van Heerden, J. and Merckelbach, H. (2005) Fantasy prone-ness, but not self-reported trauma is related to DRM performance of women reporting recovered memories of childhood sexual abuse. *Consciousness and Cognition*, 14: 602–12.

Goodman, G. S., Ghetti, S., Quas, J. A., Edelstein, R. S., Alexander, K. W., Redlich, A. D. *et al.* (2003) A prospective study of memory for child sexual abuse: new findings relevant to the repressed-memory debate. *Psychological Science*, 14: 113–18.

Herman, J. L. and Schatzow, E. (1987) Recovery and verification of memories of childhood sexual trauma. *Psychoanalytic Psychology*, 4: 1–14.

Hyman, I. E. Jr, Husband, T. H. and Billings, F. J. (1995) False memories of childhood experi-ences. *Applied Cognitive Psychology*, 9: 181–97.

Lindsay, D. S., Hagen, L., Read, J. D., Wade, K. A. and Garry, M. (2004) True photographs and false memories. *Psychological Science*, 15: 149–54.

Loftus, E. F. (2005) A 30-year investigation of the malleability of memory. *Learning and Memory*, 12: 361–6.

Loftus, E. F. and Bernstein, D. M. (2005) Rich false memories: the royal road to success. In A. Healy (ed.), *Experimental Cognitive Psychology and Its Applications: Festschrift in Honor of Lyle Bourne, Walter Kintsch, and Thomas Landauer*, pp. 101–13. Washington, DC: APA Press.

Loftus, E. F., Miller, D. G. and Burns, H. J. (1978) Semantic integration of verbal information into a visual memory. *Journal of Experimental Psychology: Human Learning and Memory*, 4: 19–31.

Loftus, E. F. and Palmer, J. C. (1974). Reconstruction of automobile destruction. *Journal of Verbal Learning and Verbal Behavior*, 13: 585–9.

Loftus, E. F. and Pickrell, J. E. (1995) The formation of false memories. *Psychiatric Annals*, 25: 720–5.

Mazzoni, G. A. L., Lombardo, P., Malvagia, S. and Loftus, E. F. (1999) Dream interpretation and false beliefs. *Professional Psychology: Research and Practice*, 30: 45–50.

McNally, R. J. (2007) Betrayal trauma theory: a critical appraisal. *Memory*, 15: 280–94.

McNally, R. J., Lasko, N. B., Clancy, S. A., Maclin, M. L., Pitman, R. K. and Orr, S. P. (2004) Psychophysiological responding during script-driven imagery in people reporting abduc-tion by space aliens. *Psychological Science*, 15: 493–7.

Paterson, H. M. and Kemp, R. I. (2006) Co-witnesses talk: a survey of eyewitness discussion. *Psychology, Crime and Law*, 12: 181–91.

Poole, D. A., Lindsay, D. S., Memon, A. and Bull, R. (1995) Psychotherapy and the recovery of memories of childhood sexual abuse: US and British practitioners' beliefs, practices, and experiences. *Journal of Consulting and Clinical Psychology*, 6: 426–37.

Porter, S., Yuille, J. C. and Lehman, D. R. (1999) The nature of real, implanted and fabricated memories for emotional childhood events: implications for the false memory debate. *Law and Human Behavior*, 23: 517–38.

Powell, M. B., Fisher, R. P. and Wright, R. (2005). Investigative interviewing. In N. Brewer and K. D. Williams (eds.), *Psychology and Law: An Empirical Perspective*. New York: Guilford Press.

Roediger, H. L. III and McDermott, K. B. (1996) Creating false memories: remembering words not presented in lists. *Journal of Experimental Psychology: Learning, Memory and Cognition*, 21: 803–14.

Schacter, D. L. (2001) *The Seven Sins of Memory: How the Mind Forgets and Remembers.* Boston, MA: Houghton Mifflin.

Scorboria, A., Mazzoni, G. A. L., Kirsch, I. and Milling, L. S. (2002) Immediate and persisting effects of misleading questions and hypnosis on memory reports. *Journal of Experimental Psychology: Applied*, 8: 26–32.

Seamon, J. G., Philbin, M. M. and Harrison, L. G. (2006) Do you remember proposing marriage to the Pepsi machine? False recollections from a campus walk. *Psychonomic Bulletin and Review*, 13: 752–6.

Smith, S. M. and Gleaves, D. H. (2006) Recovered memories. In M. P. Toglia, J. D. Read, D. F. Ross and R. C. L. Lindsay (eds.), *The Handbook of Eyewitness Psychology*, vol. 1: *Memory for Events*, pp. 299–320. London: Erlbaum.

Takarangi, M. K. T., Parker, S. and Garry, M. (2006) Modernising the misinformation effect: the development of a new stimulus set. *Applied Cognitive Psychology*, 20: 583–90.

Takarangi, M. K. T., Polaschek, D. L. L., Garry, M. and Loftus, E. F. (2008) Psychological science, victim advocates, and the problem of recovered memory. *International Review of Victimology*, 15: 147–63.

Terr, L. (1991) Childhood traumas: an outline and overview. *American Journal of Psychiatry*, 148: 10–20.

Wade, K. A., Garry, M., Read, J. D. and Lindsay, S. A. (2002) A picture is worth a thousand lies. *Psychonomic Bulletin and Review*, 9: 597–603.

Williams, L. M. (1994) Recall of childhood trauma: a prospective study. *Journal of Consulting and Clinical Psychology*, 62: 1167–76.

Wright, D. B., Self, G. and Justice, C. (2000) Memory conformity: exploring misinformation effects when presented by another person. *British Journal of Psychology*, 91: 189–202.

2.7 Intellectual disabilities and offending

John L. Taylor and William R. Lindsay

Definitions

The term *intellectual disability* (ID) now has international currency and corresponds with the term *learning disability*, commonly used in health and social care contexts in the UK. Although people with ID do not constitute a homogeneous population, the major international diagnostic classification systems, for example ICD-10 (World Health Organization 1992), include three core criteria for ID:

- significant impairment of intellectual functioning;
- significant associated impairment of adaptive or social functioning; and
- age of onset within the developmental period before adulthood.

All three criteria must be present for a diagnosis of ID to be made. Assessment of intellectual functioning, particularly in forensic contexts, should be obtained using an individually administered, reliable and valid standardized test, such as the WAIS-III (Wechsler 1999), when 'significant' impairment of intellectual functioning is conventionally understood to be a score more than two standard deviations below the population mean – that is an IQ score less than 70.

Adaptive functioning is a broad concept that is concerned with a person's ability to adapt to the demands of their environment. An assessment of adaptive functioning must, therefore, take into account an individual's age, environment and culture. There is general consensus that the 'age of onset' criterion means below the age of 18 years (e.g. British Psychological Society 2000).

Mental health legislation in England and Wales, and Scotland, has sections concerning the detention of people with ID who have offended. The Mental Health Act (MHA) 1983 for England and Wales, and MHA 1984 for Scotland, both contain categories of mental disorder termed 'mental impairment' and 'severe mental impairment'.

However, the 2007 amendment of the England and Wales Mental Health Act 1983 removes the 'mental impairment' and 'severe mental' impairment categories of mental disorder and introduces the term 'learning disability', which is defined in the revised Code of Practice for England (Department of Health, 2009) as 'a state of arrested development of the mind which includes significant impairment of intelligence and social functioning' (p. 2). The revised code also introduces a developmental criterion to the definition of learning disability under the Act, so that arrested development of mind involves 'a significant impairment of the normal process of maturation of intellectual and social development that occurs during childhood and adolescence' (p. 307).

This legal category of learning disability in the amended England and Wales Mental Health Act is not synonymous with the clinical definition of ID. While the revised 2009 Code of Practice now helpfully contains the three core clinical criteria for ID, it also includes a criterion for 'abnormally aggressive or seriously irresponsible conduct' for the purposes of detention for treatment. The revised code offers some guidance on how such behaviour might be assessed. British Psychological Society guidance recommends that for this criterion to be met, abnormally aggressive and seriously irresponsible behaviour should be observed directly, ideally by at least two reliable informants, and that there should be good-quality recordings and descriptions of this conduct in behavioural terms (Taylor *et al.* 2009).

In addition, the revised code states 'It may be appropriate to identify learning disability in someone with an IQ somewhat higher than 70 if their social functioning is severely impaired.' It also suggests that 'A person with a low IQ may be correctly diagnosed as having a learning disability even if their social functioning is relatively good' (p. 308). British Psychological Society guidance (2000), however, is that for a learning disability to be identified there is a requirement for significant impairments of both intellectual and adaptive/social functioning to coexist.

Associations between intellectual functioning and offending

Historically, ID has been viewed as a key determinant of offending behaviour. From the nineteenth century onwards a causal association between low intelligence and criminality has been suggested (Scheerenberger 1983). The evidence supporting a relationship between offending and intellectual functioning (IQ) in the general population is solid, with those with lower IQs showing greater rates of offending than those in higher-functioning groups (e.g. Goodman, Simonoff and Stevenson 1995). This relationship appears to hold when controlling for socioeconomic status (Moffit *et al.* 1991). However, where studies (e.g. McCord and McCord 1959) include participants with significantly low IQs (less than 80 IQ points), offending rates for this group have been found to be lower than those in the low average group (81 to 90 IQ points). It would seem, therefore, that if studies are extended to include participants with IQs below 80 the relationship between offending and intellectual functioning is not straightforward.

Prevalence of offending and recidivism

Studies in the UK on the prevalence of offending by people with ID yield different rates depending on the location of the study sample: community ID services, 2%–5%; police stations, 0.5%–8.6%; prisons (remand), 0%–5%; and prisons (convicted), 0.4%–0.8% (Holland, Clare and Mukhopadhyay 2002). Other sources of variation in offending rates reported across studies include the inclusion criteria used (particularly if people with borderline intellectual functioning are included or not), the method used to detect ID (e.g. IQ test vs clinical interview), and different social and criminal justice policies that are applied in the study setting. Therefore, despite the long association between IQ and criminality, and in the absence of well-designed studies comparing the prevalence of offending in populations of people with ID with that in non-ID populations, it is not clear that people with ID commit more crime than those without ID. Similarly, there is no good evidence to show that the frequency and nature of offending by people with ID differs from that committed by offenders in the general population (Lindsay and Taylor 2008).

Follow-up studies of offenders with ID have reported recidivism rates of up to 72% (Lund 1990). However, as for prevalence studies involving people with ID, reported recidivism rates vary a great deal for many of the same reasons. In a US study involving 252 offenders with ID subject to a case management community programme, Linhorst, McCutchen and Bebbett (2003) found that 25% of programme completers were rearrested within six months of finishing the programme, compared with 43% of those who dropped out of the programme. While there is a dearth of controlled studies comparing recidivism rates for offenders with ID and non-ID offenders, in another US study 43% of 79,000 general offenders on probation were rearrested (Langan and Cunnliff 1992).

Thus, based on the limited data available to date, it is not clear that recidivism rates for offenders with ID are very different to those for general offenders.

Risk assessment for offenders with ID

There has been recent research on the utility of measures designed to assess the risk of violence and sexual aggression involving offenders with ID across a range of security settings, including high, medium and low security hospitals, and community forensic ID services (Hogue *et al.* 2006). Established risk measures such as the Violence Risk Appraisal Guide, HCR-20 and Static-99 have been demonstrated to have good reliability and validity when used with ID offenders in these settings (Lindsay *et al.* 2008). Further work has shown that the severity of assessed personality disorder (including psychopathy) in offenders with ID is positively associated with measures of risk of future violence and sexual aggression (Lindsay *et al.* 2006).

Treatment interventions

The evidence for the effectiveness of interventions for offending by people with ID is quite limited but has been building steadily over recent years. Despite this, there is only very limited outcome research supporting interventions for those with ID who set fires. To date there has been one case study, two small case series and one pre-post-intervention outcome study that have provided some evidence that broadly cognitive-behavioural interventions can help with fire interest and attitudes and emotional problems associated with fire-setting behaviour in these clients (for an overview see Lindsay and Taylor 2008).

Courtney and Rose (2004) reviewed nineteen studies of treatment effectiveness for sex offenders with ID. They concluded that the outcomes for psychological interventions appear to be marginally superior to other interventions. The available evidence is based on small and methodologically weak studies that have yielded variable outcomes; however, there are indications that attitudes towards and cognitions concerning sexual offending can be improved. Lindsay and Smith (1998) found some limited evidence that mandated and longer interventions result in lower levels of sexual reoffending in this population. Unfortunately, because of ethical issues in denying potentially beneficial interventions to those presenting serious risks to others, there are no controlled trials of treatment for sex offenders with ID.

Research on three continents, using broadly similar methods, has shown aggression to be a serious issue in the ID population (Taylor 2002). It is the primary reason for the prescription of behaviour control groups in this population and the main reason for people being admitted to institutions. The evidence for the treatment of anger and aggression for offenders with ID using cognitive-behavioural therapy approaches is building. There are a number of small controlled studies showing good outcomes for treatment over waiting-list control conditions for participants treated in both community and secure hospital settings (see Taylor and Novaco 2005 for a review).

Conclusion

Historically ID has been associated with criminality and the recent policy of de-institutionalization has resulted in higher visibility of people with ID who offend. As a consequence, there have been significant developments in services for this population. Against this background, the evidence to support assessment and interventions for these clients has been building from a low baseline. There is now some limited research available to guide clinicians in providing cognitive-behavioural interventions for people with ID who are angry and violent, sexually aggressive or who set fires. There has also been some progress in the development of risk assessments to help evaluate clients' progress in treatment and rehabilitation. It is not clear whether offending is more prevalent among people with ID compared with the general population, or if people with ID are over-represented in the offender population. Also, while there are difficulties with the findings of recidivism studies involving offenders with ID, there is some evidence that, as for non-ID offenders, longer-term mandated interventions yield better outcomes than shorter voluntary treatments. Further research with this population is required to improve future practice and service developments.

FURTHER READING

See the edited collected by Lindsay, Taylor and Sturmey (2004) for an overview of developmental disabilities and Riding and Swann's *Handbook for Learning Disabilities* (2005). The chapter by Lindsay and Taylor (2008) reviews the assessment and treatment literature concerning offenders with intellectual disabilities.

REFERENCES

British Psychological Society (2000) *Learning Disability: Definitions and Contexts*. Leicester: British Psychological Society.

Courtney, J. and Rose, J. (2004) The effectiveness of treatment for male sex offenders with learning disabilities: a review of the literature. *Journal of Sexual Aggression*, 10: 215–36.

Goodman, R., Simonoff, E. and Stevenson, J. (1995) The impact of child IQ, parent IQ and sibling IQ on child and behaviour deviance scores. *Journal of Child Psychology and Psychiatry*, 36: 409–25.

Hogue, T., Steptoe, L., Taylor, J. L., Lindsay, W. R., Mooney, P., Pinkney, L., Johnston, S., Smith, A. H. W. and O'Brien, G. (2006) A comparison of offenders with intellectual disability across three levels of security. *Criminal Behaviour and Mental Health*, 16: 13–28.

Holland, T., Clare, I. C. H. and Mukhopadhyay, T. (2002) Prevalence of 'criminal offending' by men and women with intellectual disability and the characteristics of 'offenders': implications for research and service development. *Journal of Intellectual Disability Research*, 46 (suppl. 1): 6–20.

Langan, P. A. and Cunnliff, M. A. (1992) Recidivism for felons on probation. *Bureau of Statistics, Special Report* (NCJ-134177). Washington, DC: United States Department of Justice, Bureau of Justice Statistics.

Lindsay, W. R., Hogue, T., Taylor, J. L., Mooney, P., Steptoe, L., Johnston, S., O'Brien, G. and Smith, A. H. W. (2006) Two studies on the prevalence and validity of personality disorder in three forensic intellectual disability samples. *Journal of Forensic Psychiatry and Psychology*, 17: 485–506.

Lindsay, W. R., Hogue, T., Taylor, J. J., Steptoe, L., Mooney, P., O'Brien, G., Johnston, S. and Smith, A. H. W. (2008) Risk assessment in offenders with intellectual disability: a comparison across three levels of security. *International Journal of Offender Therapy and Comparative Criminology*, 52: 90–111.

Lindsay, W. R. and Smith, A. H. W. (1998). Responses to treatment for sex offenders with intellectual disability: a comparison of men with 1 and 2 year probation sentences. *Journal of Intellectual Disability Research*, 42: 346–53.

Lindsay, W. R. and Taylor, J. L. (2008) Assessment and treatment of offenders with intellectual and developmental disabilities. In K. Soothill, P. Rogers and M. Dolan (eds.), *Handbook on Forensic Mental Health*, pp. 328–50. Cullompton: Willan.

Lindsay, W. R., Taylor, J. L. and Sturmey, P. (eds.). (2004) *Offenders with Developmental Disabilities*. Chichester: Wiley.

Linhorst, D. M., McCutchen, T. A. and Bennett, L. (2003) Recidivism among offenders with developmental disabilities participating in a case management programme. *Research in Developmental Disabilities*, 24: 210–30.

Lund, J. (1990) Mentally retarded criminal offenders in Denmark. *British Journal of Psychiatry*, 156: 726–31.

McCord, W. and McCord, J. (1959) *Origins of Crime: A New Evaluation of the Cambridge–Somerville Youth Study*. New York: Columbia Press.

Moffit, T. E., Gabrielli, W. F., Mednick, S. A. and Schulsinger, F. (1991) Socio-economic status, IQ and delinquency. *Journal of Abnormal Psychology*, 90: 152–7.

Riding, T., Swann, C., Swann, B. (eds.) (2005) *The Handbook of Forensic Learning Disabilities.* Oxford: Radcliffe.

Scheerenberger, R. C. (1983) *A History of Mental Retardation.* London: Brooks.

Taylor, J. L. (2002) A review of assessment and treatment of anger and aggression in offenders with intellectual disability. *Journal of Intellectual Disability Research*, 46 (suppl. 1): 57–73.

Taylor, J. L., Hanna, J., Gilmer, B. T. and Ledwith, S. (2009) *Code of Practice Mental Health Act 1983 (as amended by the Mental Health Act 2007). Interim supplementary guidance for chartered psychologists seeking approval and acting as Approved Clinicians.* Leicester: British Psychological Society.

Taylor, J. L. and Novaco, R. W. (2005) *Anger Treatment for People with Developmental Disabilities: A Theory, Evidence and Manual Based Approach.* Chichester: Wiley.

Wechsler, D. (1999) *Wechsler Adult Intelligence Scale UK*, 3rd edn. London: Psychological Corporation.

World Health Organization (1992) *ICD-10 Classification of Mental and Behavioural Disorders: Clinical Description and Diagnostic Guidelines.* Geneva: World Health Organization.

2.8 Interrogative suggestibility and false confessions

Gisli H. Gudjonsson

Definition

Gudjonsson and Clark (1986) define interrogative suggestibility as: 'the extent to which, within a closed social interaction, people come to accept messages communicated during formal questioning, as the result of which their subsequent behavioural response is affected' (p. 84). This definition comprises five interrelated components which form an integral part of the interrogative process: (1) a social interaction (i.e. an interaction between at least two people); (2) a questioning procedure (i.e. one or more questions are asked concerned with past experiences, events and recollections); (3) a suggestive stimulus (i.e. some questions are 'leading' because they contain certain premises and expectations, which may or may not be informed and well founded); (4) acceptance of the stimulus (i.e. the suggestion must be perceived by the respondent as being plausible and credible); and (5) a behavioural response (i.e. the respondent must indicate, either verbally or non-verbally, whether or not he or she accepts the suggestion).

Broadly speaking, suggestibility refers to the tendency of the individual to respond in a particular way to suggestions. Whereas a suggestion refers to the properties contained in a stimulus (e.g. expectation, leading qualities), suggestibility refers to characteristics of the person who is being incited to respond (i.e. it is an individual difference variable). A suggestion only has the potential to elicit a reaction; whether it does or not depends on the susceptibility of the person to suggestions, the nature and characteristics of the suggestion, and the context in which the suggestion occurs.

Suggestibility needs to be distinguished from the concept of compliance. The main difference between these two concepts is that suggestibility, unlike compliance, implies personal acceptance of the information suggested. Compliance refers to the tendency of the individual to go along with propositions, requests or instructions, normally for some instrumental gain (e.g. in order to please another person or to avoid conflict and confrontation). The other main difference is that whereas suggestibility can be measured by an experimental procedure in the form of a 'mini' interrogation, compliance is difficult to measure in this way and typically relies on self-report or ratings from informants (Gudjonsson 2003a).

Kassin and Gudjonsson (2004) define false confession in the context of custodial interrogation as 'any detailed admission to a criminal act that the confessor did not commit' (p. 48). False confessions do sometimes occur and the reasons are multifaceted (Gudjonsson in press).

Origins and development of the concept and measurement of suggestibility

The concept and principles of suggestibility have a long history, dating back to the eighteenth century when Noizt pointed out that a suggestion is transformed into action by it reaching the respondent's consciousness (referred to as an 'ideo-motor' response; Coffin 1941). The concept of suggestibility was originally developed in order to explain hypnotic phenomena (Gudjonsson 2003a), and this is why the early tests of suggestibility measured the influence of suggestion upon the motor and sensory systems (i.e. movement, visual, tactile, auditory, olfactory). However, interrogative suggestibility is unrelated to the hypnotic type, and in contrast to focusing on motor and sensory experiences, it is mainly concerned with past experiences and events, recollections and remembered states of knowledge (Gudjonsson 2003a). This is why interrogative suggestibility is relevant to police questioning of suspects, victims and witnesses.

Cattell (1895) conducted one of the earliest experiments into human testimony, although the broad idea of 'interrogative suggestibility' was first introduced at the turn of the twentieth century by Binet (1900), and was subsequently used by other workers, such as Stern (1939), to demonstrate that leading questions can produce distorted responses because they are phrased in such a way as to suggest the wanted answer. Several subsequent studies have employed a similar or modified procedure to that of Stern in order to elicit this type of suggestibility (e.g. Loftus 1979; Stukat 1958). There is also another type of suggestibility, which is different to that which occurs in response to leading questions. This relates to the extent to which interviewers are able to 'shift' unwanted but perhaps accurate answers by challenge and negative feedback. This aspect of the interrogation process is implicit in some of the theories of interrogation and confessions (Gudjonsson 2003a). These two distinct types of suggestibility, referred to in the literature as 'Yield' and 'Shift', are incorporated into the Gudjonsson Suggestibility Scales (Gudjonsson 1997), which are empirical tests of interrogative suggestibility (Gudjonsson 2003a).

Gudjonsson and Clark (1986) provide a theoretical model which helps to further our understanding of interrogative suggestibility and the process and outcome of the police interview. The model integrates the 'leading questions' and 'negative feedback' aspects of suggestibility first discussed by Gudjonsson (1983). It construes suggestibility as arising out of the way the individual interacts with others within the social and physical environment. The basic premise of the model is that interrogative suggestibility is dependent upon the coping strategies that people can generate and implement when faced with two important aspects of the interrogative situation – *uncertainty* and *expectations*. When the police begin asking questions the interviewee cognitively processes this information and then employs one or more strategies of general coping. This process involves the interviewee having to deal with *uncertainty* and *interpersonal trust* on the one hand and certain *expectations* on the other. These three components are seen as essential prerequisites for the suggestibility process and can be manipulated experimentally.

Method and evaluation: the Gudjonsson Suggestibility Scales

There are two parallel forms of the Gudjonsson Suggestibility Scales (GSS), referred to as the GSS 1 and the GSS 2, which have been incorporated into a manual for researchers and practitioners, along with the Gudjonsson Compliance Scale (GCS) (Gudjonsson 1997). The GSS 1 and GSS 2 are identical in terms of administration, scoring criteria, and the nature of the free recall narratives and interrogative questions. The only difference is that the GSS 1 has a forensically relevant story, whereas the GSS 2 does not. The two Scales can be used interchangeably. They measure the extent to which the individual can be misled by leading questions ('Yield') and how he or she responds to interrogative pressure, implemented in the form of negative feedback ('Shift'). These are distinct types of suggestibility, each reflecting different kinds of vulnerabilities during questioning. Generally speaking, Yield is more related to cognitive processes (i.e. IQ, memory, confidence) and Shift to anxiety and coping. Verbal memory and confabulation, immediate and delayed, can also be measured for clinical and research purposes (confabulation is the tendency to fill gaps in one's memory by producing imagined material).

Grisso (1986) provided a review of the early work into the validity of the GSS 1 and concluded 'Construct validation research with the GSS has placed the forensic examiner in a good position to use the GSS scores when considering questions of an examinee's decreased resistance to suggestion or subtle pressure in interrogations by law enforcement officials' (p. 147). Since Grisso's review, the GSS 1 and the GSS 2 have been translated into several languages and are used internationally for research and clinical and forensic applications (Frumkin 2008). False confessors have been shown to have higher GSS and GCS scores than non-false confessors (Gudjonsson 2003a), but since these tests do not directly measure false confessions, only *susceptibility* to give misleading or false information under certain circumstances (i.e. when led and pressured), it is not appropriate to produce figures for false positive and negative error rates.

The GSS 1, GSS 2 and the GCS are favourably reviewed in the *Mental Measurement Yearbook* from the Buros Institute (Geisinger *et al.* 2007).

Application

The GSS 1, the GSS 2 and the GCS are well-researched and validated instruments that are designed to measure individual differences and vulnerabilities that are relevant to some police interviews (i.e. susceptibility to giving misleading or false information if led or pressured in interview). They were first accepted in the Court of Appeal in the UK in 1991 in the case of Engin Raghip, one of the so-called 'Tottenham Three', and are cited in many subsequent UK appeal judgements (Gudjonsson 2003a, 2006). The Scales have been also accepted in court cases in the USA and elsewhere (Gudjonsson 2003a; Frumkin 2008). The GCS often presents more problems in court than the GSS 1 and GSS 2, because it is based on self-report and a high score may be construed as self-serving. Here independent corroboration of high compliance, for example from reliable informants, or salient background information is helpful.

The GCS has a broader forensic application to disputed confession cases than suggestibility (Gudjonsson 2003a), and can also be used to identify susceptibility to being manipulated or pressured into criminal activity (Gudjonsson and Sigurdsson 2007) and taking blame (Gudjonsson, Sigurdsson and Einarsson 2007).

In spite of their legal acceptance, the GSS 1, GSS 2 and GCS are not aimed at measuring whether a confession is false; they only measure vulnerabilities that are potentially important in some cases where confessions are disputed. This is the most common misconception of the three Scales in court cases. There are no psychological instruments available for detecting whether or not a confession is false. All we are concerned with as expert witnesses are vulnerabilities that may assist the court in determining the 'reliability' and 'safety' of the self-incriminating statement that the defendant made during police questioning. Often lawyers naively ask for an assessment of suggestibility when in fact there were no leading questions or pressure in the interview and suggestibility is not relevant to the assessment.

Another common misconception in court is that a defendant could only have been truly suggestible in a police interview if he or she had agreed to all suggestions offered by police after the initial denial and resistance were broken down. This is not the case. Even innocent suspects, whose resistance is broken down during police questioning, sometimes do resist some leading questions after falsely confessing to a serious crime (Gudjonsson 2003a).

According to Gudjonsson (2003b), the outcome of a police interview involves a dynamic process that is comprised of the interaction between circumstances, custodial pressures (i.e. confinement and interrogation), physical and mental health factors, psychological vulnerabilities (e.g. suggestibility, compliance) and support factors (i.e. access to legal advice, and an 'appropriate adult' while in custody). Elevated scores on suggestibility and compliance are commonly, but not exclusively, found in cases where convictions have been overturned on appeal (Gudjonsson 2006) or in cases of proven false confessions (Gudjonsson 2003a). There are many different reasons why suspects give false confessions and each case needs to be considered on its own merits (Gudjonsson in press). Test scores, even if relevant and pertinent to the case, should not be interpreted in isolation from other information, including salient background information and the nature of the interrogation and other custodial pressures.

Conclusion

The concepts and empirical measurement of interrogative suggestibility and compliance are well established and validated in relation to identifying vulnerabilities relevant to assessing cases of disputed confession. However, the GSS 1, GSS 2 and GCS do not directly assess whether or not a confession is false; no psychological instruments are available for this purpose. Psychometric tests should only be used in conjunction with other assessment tools, including an interview and a careful consideration of other relevant material in the case.

FURTHER READING

For an overview of suggestibility and false confessions see Gudjonsson (2003a). An important review of the current issues is provided by Kassin and Gudjonsson (2004). For application in USA cases see Frumkin (2008). For an overview and critique of the GSS 1, GSS 2 and GCS see Geisinger et al. (2007).

REFERENCES

Binet, A. (1900) La suggestibilité. Paris: Doin et Fils.

Cattell, J. M. (1895) Measurements of the accuracy of recollection. Science 2: 761–6.

Coffin, T. E. (1941) Some conditions of suggestion and suggestibility: a study of certain attitudinal and situational factors influencing the process of suggestion. Psychological Monograph, 53: 1–121.

Frumkin, I. B. (2008) Psychological evaluation in Miranda waiver and confession cases. In R. Denny and J. Sullivan (eds.), Clinical Neuropsychology in the Criminal Forensic Setting, pp. 135–75. New York: Guilford Press.

Geisinger, K. F., Spies, R. A., Carlson, J. F. and Plake, B. S. (eds.) (2007) The Seventeenth Mental Measurements Yearbook. Lincoln, NE: Buros Institute of Mental Measurements.

Grisso, T. (1986) Evaluating Competencies: Forensic Assessments and Instruments. New York: Plenum Press.

Gudjonsson, G. H. (1983) Suggestibility, intelligence, memory recall and personality: an experimental study. British Journal of Psychiatry, 142: 35–7.

(1997) The Gudjonsson Suggestibility Scales Manual. Hove: Psychology Press.

(2003a) The Psychology of Interrogations and Confessions. A Handbook. Chichester: Wiley.

(2003b) Psychology brings justice: the science of forensic psychology. Criminal Behaviour and Mental Health, 13: 159–67.

(2006) Disputed confessions and miscarriages of justice in Britain: expert psychological and psychiatric evidence in the Court of Appeal. Manitoba Law Journal, 31: 489–521.

(in press) The psychology of false confessions: a review of the current evidence. In G. Daniel Lassiter and Christian A. Meissner (eds.), Police Interrogations and False Confessions: Current Research, Practice, and Policy Recommendations. New York: American Psychological Association.

Gudjonsson, G. H. and Clark, N. K. (1986) Suggestibility in police interrogation: a social psychological model. Social Behaviour, 1: 83–104.

Gudjonsson, G. H. and Sigurdsson, J. F. (2007) Motivation for offending and personality: a study among young offenders on probation. Personality and Individual Difference, 43: 1243–53.

Gudjonsson, G. H., Sigurdsson, J. F. and Einarsson, E. (2007) Taking blame for antisocial acts and its relationship with personality. Personality and Individual Differences, 43: 3–13.

Kassin, S. M. and Gudjonsson, G. H. (2004) The psychology of confessions: a review of the literature and issues. Psychological Science in the Public Interest, 5: 33–67.

Loftus, E. F. (1979) Eyewitness Testimony. Cambridge, MA: Harvard University Press.

Stern, W. (1939) The psychology of testimony. Journal of Abnormal and Social Psychology, 34: 3–20.

Stukat, K. G. (1958) Suggestibility: A Factor and Experimental Analysis. Almgvist and Wiksell: Stockholm.

2.9 Investigative interviewing

Becky Milne and Martine Powell

See also chapter 2.23 Statement validity analysis, chapter 4.3 Interpersonal deception detection.

Definition

Investigative interviewing is a method of communicating with anyone within the investigation process (be they witness, victim, suspect or the first police officer at the scene) in order to obtain the maximum quality of information. As a result, ethical investigative interviewing is at the heart of any police investigation and thus is the root of achieving justice in society (Milne, Shaw and Bull 2007). This is because there are two key aims underpinning any investigation and these are to (i) find out what happened, and if anything did happen (ii) to discover who did what (Milne and Bull 2006). In order to answer these two primary investigative questions investigators need to gather information and invariably the source of the information is a person (e.g. witness, victim, suspect, complainant, first officer at the scene of a crime, emergency services, informant, experts and so on). Thus one of the most important tools in an investigator's tool box is the ability to interview (Milne and Bull 2006). Investigative interviews conducted by police can vary greatly in purpose, scope and content (e.g. proactive and reactive investigations). Nevertheless, the common objective of all investigative interviews is to elicit the most *accurate, complete* and *detailed* account from an interviewee.

Origins and further developments

Prior to 1984 in the UK (and still existing in many countries), interviewing by police officers was considered an inherent skill that all officers possessed and which could be acquired merely by learning from more experienced colleagues. The yardstick of a good interviewer was whether a confession or damaging admission was obtained from the suspect (e.g. Plimmer 1997). Groundbreaking legislation in the UK (the Police and Criminal Evidence Act 1984 and the associated Codes of Practice), which was in part enacted to try to prevent miscarriages of justice, emerged due to the poor interviewing of suspects (e.g. the 'Guildford Four' Irish terrorist trial). This resulted in changes in working practices (e.g. the tape-recording of interviews with suspects) so that interview-room procedures previously conducted behind closed doors were now open to public scrutiny on a grand scale. In 1991 the Home Office (i.e. the relevant UK government ministry) sponsored research that assessed tape-recorded interviews with suspects. Perhaps not surprisingly, due to the lack of structure, investment and the haphazard approach to interview training, the intial evaluative findings revealed severe shortcomings in the skills demonstrated by the police officers during interviews with suspects (Milne *et al.* 2007; Baldwin 1992). The main weaknesses identified were a lack of preparation, general ineptitude, poor technique, an assumption of guilt, undue repetitiveness, a persistent or laboured questioning, a failure to establish relevant facts, and an exertion of too much psychological pressure (Baldwin 1992). It was assumed that the interviewing of adult victims and witnesses similarly was not of a consistently high standard, with the interviewers' ultimate goal being the compilation of a detailed written statement rather than allowing the person to provide their best account and best evidence in an uninterrupted and free-flowing manner (McLean 1995; Milne and Bull 2006; Milne *et al.* 2007; Shepherd and Milne 1999).

As a direct result of Baldwin's work and pressures that emanated from the widely politicized miscarriages of justice cases (e.g. another Irish terrorist case, the 'Birmingham Six'), a national review of investigative interviewing was instituted (see Gudjonsson 2003; Milne and Bull, 1999, 2003a; see also Savage and Milne 2007 for more on miscarriages of justice cases). This research evidence stimulated further development of investigative interviewing within the UK. In 1992 the seven Principles of Investigative Interviewing (the term interrogation being replaced) were formulated and promulgated through the Home Office. There have been several iterations, the most recent being the current Practical Guide to Investigative Interviewing (Centrex 2004). The seven principles are:

1. obtaining accurate and reliable information from suspects, witnesses or victims in order to discover the truth about matters under police investigation;
2. approaching with an open mind and information obtained from the person being interviewed should always be tested against what the interviewing officer already knows or what can reasonably be established;

3. when questioning anyone, a police officer must act fairly in the circumstances of each individual case;
4. not being bound to accept the first answer given. Questioning is not unfair merely because it is persistent;
5. even when the right of silence is exercised by a suspect, the police still have a right to put questions;
6. when conducting an interview, police officers are free to ask questions in order to establish the truth; except for interviews with child victims of sexual or violent abuse, which are to be used in criminal proceedings, they are not constrained by the rules applied to lawyers in court;
7. treating vulnerable people, whether victims, witnesses, or suspects, with particular consideration at all times.

Method

Having established these principles, a project team (including police officers and academics alike) devised a training programme so that officers would be provided with the skills necessary to conduct effective and ethical interviews with victims, witnesses and suspects, with integrity and in accordance with the law (Ord and Shaw 1999; Milne *et al.* 2007). This resulted in the PEACE interviewing model. PEACE is a mnemonic outlining the structure to be applied to all types of interviews: *Planning* and *Preparation* of the interview; *Engaging* the interviewee and *Explaining* the ground rules of the interview process; obtaining an *Account*, clarifying and challenging the interviewee (if necessary); and appropriate *Closure* of the interview. Finally, the interview process is to be *Evaluated*, where the key question is to ask what was achieved during the interview and how this fits into the whole investigation. Evaluation also includes the development of an interviewer's skill level, through assessment (self, peer and manager) (Centrex 2004; Milne *et al.* 2007). In addition, the initial working party, when examining what PEACE training should consist of, looked at what academia had to offer (Milne *et al.* 2007). Indeed, two models of interviewing emerged as best practice: (i) conversation management (CM; Shepherd 1993), which was deemed useful for interviewing the more resistant interviewee; and (ii) the cognitive interview (CI; Fisher and Geiselman 1992), which was more useful for interviewing the more cooperative interviewee, an interviewee who is willing to speak (however truthful). Both models were developed by psychologists (see Milne and Bull 1999 for full details).

Regardless of interview model, experts agree that one of the most critical skills of investigative interviewers (irrespective of the respondent group) is the ability to maintain the use of non-leading, open-ended questions. Non-leading questions refrain from presuming or suggesting details that were not previously mentioned by the respondent. Open-ended questions are defined as those questions that encourage elaborate (as opposed to brief or one-word) responses. In the child witness arena, open-ended questions are also defined as questions that do not dictate or suggest what information related to the event should be reported. Children are more vulnerable than adults to suggestions and social demands to provide a response (Milne and Bull 2003b). Thus it is even more critical with these interviewees that interviewers broaden the range of response options as well as encourage elaborate responses (Poole and Lamb 1998). Open-ended questions are ideal for all respondents because they maximize the accuracy of the interviewee's account of the offence and minimize the opportunity for confusion, contamination and/or misunderstandings. An open-ended questioning style is also critical to tasks such as the development of rapport and for eliciting (where appropriate) a clear and coherent disclosure or confession.

The following precepts are also seen across the experimental and experiential approaches as being critical to the success of an investigative interview: proper preparation and evaluation of the interview, keeping an open mind, being sensitive to the individual needs of the interviewee, and conducting and closing the interview in a manner that is fair and maintains (as much as possible) a positive interviewer–interviewee relationship. Obtaining a confession or disclosure of an offence should not be the primary goal of investigative interviews because these can subsequently be disputed or rejected as evidence by a court. Rather, the goal should be to obtain as much accurate information as possible to assist in establishing which hypothesis, among several alternatives, is most likely to be correct. In other words, the process of a good investigation (as with any scientific method) is not about gathering confirmatory evidence per se, but about gathering sufficient evidence to dispute alternative explanations (see Savage and Milne 2007).

Despite the presence of well-defined 'best-practice' guidelines in investigative interviewing, numerous concerns have been voiced regarding the underuse of non-leading, open-ended questions by investigative interviewers around the globe. This has led several researchers in recent years to focus on the content, structure and efficacy of investigative interviewer training courses. While research is still in its infancy, the research findings support those within the broader expertise literature: that ongoing practice of specific skills and expert feedback is critical in maintaining effective questions (see Powell, Fisher and Wright 2005 for review). In other words, poor quality of professional training is the main reason for poor interview outcome.

Evaluation

A national evaluation of the PEACE training approach, funded by the Home Office (Clarke and Milne 2001) was undertaken. This large-scale study revealed that the skills being taught on the week-long PEACE course were not being fully integrated into practice. With regard to the interviews of those suspected of crime, there was some transference of skills, with officers being seen as more confident and being able to communicate more effectively within the interview room (compared to Baldwin's research). However, the interviewers took a rather rigid approach and lacked flexibility.

The Clarke and Milne (2001) research project also examined officers' ability to interview adult witnesses to and victims of crime. Officers from across the country were asked to tape-record their interviews over a period of time. The sample included all offence types. What was revealed was a disturbing state of affairs, with interviews being mainly police led, dominated by poor questioning, and the interview being mainly focused upon the statement-taking process as opposed to trying to gain as much information from the interviewee about what had happened. Indeed, Clarke and Milne concluded that the standard of interviews of witnesses and victims of crime was far worse than the interviews of those suspected of crime.

The Clarke and Milne report concluded with a number of recommendations to improve interviewing standards, which have subsequently been taken up by the Association of Chief Police Officers (ACPO) and developed further into the ACPO Investigative Interviewing Strategy, a national initiative. As a result, a five-tiered approach to investigative interviewing, which aims to provide a developmental approach to interview training across a police officer's career dependent on their ability, was born. This strategy is underpinned by assessment and competency levels within a National Occupational Standards framework (which includes a set of statements concerning what constitutes a competent interviewer) (see Griffiths and Milne 2005 and Milne *et al.* 2007 for more on the tiers and assessment).

Applications

Any organization which interviews people as part of an investigation will recognize elements from the above outline. Although this chapter has primarily focused upon poor police interviewing practice and how attempts have been made to overcome these shortcomings, any organization whose investigators/communicators interview people about a past event need to start to evaluate their interviewing/communication training, recording process, and assessment and supervision policies to ensure the highest possible standards are met and thus the best information is gained.

Conclusion

Only when a whole organization takes stock of its interviewing and resources (human and monetary) are invested in this core skill will improvements be made. A number of countries have started to evaluate police interview training and processes (e.g. Australia, New Zealand, Norway, Sweden and the United Kingdom) in an attempt to create a more ethical investigation and interviewing framework and one which fits within the human rights philosophy.

FURTHER READING

The theoretical origins of cognitive interviewing can be found in Fisher and Geiselman's classic reference work (1992). Milne and Bull's (1999) book on investigative interviewing is a general reference work, whilst the chapter by Powell *et al.* (2005) is a more detailed exposition.

REFERENCES

Baldwin, J. (1992) *Videotaping of police interviews with suspects – an evaluation.* Police Research Series Paper no. 1. London: Home Office.

Centrex (2004) *Practical Guide to Investigative Interviewing.* London: Central Police Training and Development Authority.

Clarke, C. and Milne, R. (2001) *National Evaluation of the PEACE Investigative Interviewing Course.* Police Research Award Scheme, PRAS/149. London: Home Office.

Fisher, R. and Geiselman, R. (1992) *Memory-Enhancing Techniques for Investigative Interviewing: The Cognitive Interview*. Springfield, IL: Thomas.

Griffiths, A. and Milne, R. (2005) Will it all end in tiers: police interviews with suspects in Britain. In T. Williamson (ed.), *Investigative Interviewing: Rights, Research, Regulation*. Cullompton: Willan.

Gudjonsson, G. H. (2003) *The Psychology of Interrogations and Confessions*. Chichester: Wiley.

McLean, M. (1995) Quality investigation? Police interviewing of witnesses. *Medicine, Science and the Law*, 35: 116–22.

Milne, R. and Bull, R. (1999) *Investigative Interviewing: Psychology and Practice*. Chichester: Wiley.

(2003a) Interviewing by the police. In D. Carson and R. Bull (eds.), *Handbook of Psychology in Legal Contexts*, pp. 111–26. Chichester: Wiley.

(2003b) Does the cognitive interview help children to resist the effects of suggestive questioning? *Legal and Criminological Psychology*, 8: 21–38.

(2006) Interviewing victims of crime, including children and people with intellectual difficulties. In M. R. Kebbell and G. M. Davies (eds.), *Practical Psychology for Forensic Investigations and Prosecutions*, pp. 7–24. Chichester: Wiley.

Milne, R. and Shaw, G. (1999) Obtaining witness statements: best practice and proposals for innovation. *Medicine, Science and the Law*, 39: 127–38.

Milne, R., Shaw, G. and Bull, R. (2007) Investigative interviewing: the role of psychology. In D. Carson, R. Milne, F. Pakes, K. Shalev and A. Showyer (eds.), *Applying Psychology to Criminal Justice*, pp. 65–78. Chichester: Wiley.

Ord, B. and Shaw, G. (1999) *Investigative Interviewing Explained*. Surrey: The New Police Bookshop.

Plimmer, J. (1997) Confession rate. *Police Review*, 7 February, 16–18.

Poole, D. A. and Lamb, M. E. (1998) *Investigative Interviews of Children: A Guide for Helping Professionals*. Washington, DC: American Psychological Association.

Powell, M. B., Fisher, R. P., and Wright, R. (2005). Investigative interviewing. In N. Brewer and K. D. Williams, *Psychology and Law: An Empirical Perspective*, pp. 11–42. New York: Guilford Press.

Savage, S. and Milne, R. (2007). Miscarriages of justice – the role of the investigative process. In T. Newburn, T. Williamson and A. Wright (eds.), *Handbook of Criminal Investigation*, pp. 610–27. Cullompton: Willan.

Shepherd, E. (1993) Resistance in interviews: the contribution of police perception and behaviour. In E. Shepherd (ed.), *Aspects of Police Interviewing* (Issues in Criminological and Legal Psychology, 18). Leicester: British Psychological Society.

Shepherd, E. and Milne, R. (1999). Full and faithful: ensuring quality practice and integrity of outcome in witness interviews. In A. Heaton-Armstrong, D. Wolchover and E. Shepherd (eds.), *Analysing Witness Testimony*, pp. 124–45. London: Blackstone Press.

2.10 Mental health

Seena Fazel

See also chapter 2.4 Evaluating violence risk in young people, chapter 2.21 Risk and dangerousness in adults.

Definition

Psychiatric assessment has a number of related goals, including making a diagnosis, understanding the context of the diagnosis and establishing a therapeutic rapport. The first of these goals – that of making a diagnosis – is the primary aim as evidence-based treatments are based on this and it provides an opportunity to discuss prognosis. The main parts of an assessment are the psychiatric history and the mental state examination. The latter covers signs and symptoms elicited at interview, while the former uses information from the person assessed, and often from informants and other sources. The assessment is then completed by a physical examination and further investigations, including blood tests and occasionally brain scans.

The psychiatric history

Information about the individual's life and history is gathered as part of any psychiatric assessment. Many assessments take a chronological approach to this, with details on the family, followed by personal history leading up to the current circumstances of the individual and what led them to have a psychiatric assessment (also known as the history of the present condition or presenting complaint).

As part of the family history, information on the age and causes of death of each first-degree relative is gathered, their occupations, and any history of criminality and mental health problems. The relationships between the family members and the individual being assessed are also noted.

Table 2.10.1 Aspects of personal history

Mother's pregnancy and the birth
Early development
Childhood separations, emotional problems, illnesses, atmosphere at home,
    any emotional/physical/sexual abuse
Education including qualifications, bullying, truancy
Work history
Relationships and children
Past medical history
Alcohol and illicit drug use
Past psychiatric history including primary care contacts, admissions to
    hospital, any medications
Forensic history
Current social circumstances, including accommodation, debts

As part of the personal history, a chronological approach is commonly taken (see table 2.10.1).

This part of the assessment often benefits from speaking with an informant, especially a family member, to supplement it and confirm details. Past medical and psychiatric notes are often reviewed if an individual has a history of health problems. Even if there have been no past admissions to hospital, clarification with the general practitioner is often helpful. The forensic history should specifically ask for any history of convictions and their nature, any cautions or serious assaults (that did not lead to convictions in the past). If there is a forensic history, the age of first criminal conviction, any prison sentences, whether a weapon was used in any offending behaviour and details of any violent, sexual offences and arson should be explored. Any associations with drug and alcohol misuse and mental health problems should be enquired about.

A final part of the psychiatric history is an assessment of personality. This can be difficult in one meeting but an attempt should be made to understand hobbies and pastimes, the nature of their friendships, character traits and religious beliefs. An individual's hopes and goals can be explored, and their predominant mood and emotions (e.g. optimistic, anxious, pessimistic; and whether this is stable).

Mental state examination

The mental state examination is concerned with the signs, symptoms and behaviour during the assessment. The mental state examination is usually

Table 2.10.2 Components of mental state examination

Appearance and behaviour
Speech
Mood
Thoughts
Perceptions
Cognitive function
Insight

assessed throughout the whole interview, but it is common practice to elicit specific signs and symptoms after the history is gathered. The examination uses a standard set of headings, where the relevant signs and symptoms are recorded (see table 2.10.2).

Under the first heading, the overall appearance of the individual is usually commented on, including their emotional expression, posture and movement, and social interactions. The rate, quantity and flow of speech are considered. Mood explores the stability of the mood state, any suicidal ideation, and symptoms of depression and anxiety. The assessment of thoughts is primarily interested in the content of the thoughts and eliciting delusions, but also any obsessions and compulsions. Abnormal perceptions are assessed, in particular auditory and visual hallucinations. Cognitive function is assessed partly on the nature of the presenting problem, but tends to involve basic tests of orientation, attention and concentration, and memory. Insight is often impaired in psychiatric illnesses, and is assessed in terms of whether the individual believes that they are unwell, whether they perceive that this is a physical or mental illness, and whether they think that they require treatment.

In forensic assessments, competence to stand trial may be relevant and also be assessed. Most jurisdictions have similar criteria for this: understanding the nature of the charges and the difference between guilty and not guilty; and the ability to instruct a solicitor, challenge a juror, and follow the course of legal proceedings. The latter criterion is considered to be the most difficult to assess, and is strongly associated with psychotic symptoms (James *et al.* 2001). Research has demonstrated that a status approach to competence to stand trial is not appropriate, i.e. a specific diagnosis such as schizophrenia does not automatically render an individual incompetent to stand trial. As with other assessments of competence, a functional approach is used – does the individual being assessed meet the criteria for this competence? Diagnoses such as schizophrenia may be associated with impaired competence, but it is the assessment of whether an individual with this illness meets the criteria that determines competence or not.

Furthermore, risk assessment is integral to any psychiatric assessment, whether or not the individual has a forensic history (cf. chapter 2.21, this volume). Risk to self (suicidal risk and risk of self-neglect) and to others is routinely assessed. In inpatient settings, risk of absconding, firesetting, victimization, hostage taking, substance abuse and others may be considered.

Instruments

Two types of instruments have been developed to assist in psychiatric assessment – diagnostic ones and those for measuring specific symptoms.

There are many standardized diagnostic instruments that have been developed for use in research contexts. The best-known ones are semi-structured clinical tools. The Present State Examination (PSE) was developed from the 1950s, and retains the features of a clinical examination. It has 140 items and generates a diagnosis. The Schedules for Clinical Assessment in Neuropsychiatry, developed from the PSE, can be used to diagnose a broader range of illnesses than the PSE, and is compatible with ICD-10 and DSM-IV. The Structured Clinical Interview for Diagnosis provides DSM diagnoses, and has a separate version for personality disorders (where it provides dimensional and categorical scores for each personality disorder). The Composite International Diagnostic Interview (CIDI) leads to both DSM and ICD diagnoses, and is available in many languages.

Instruments measuring symptoms are helpful to record their severity, but also how they vary over time and in response to treatment. The best-known ones include the Brief Psychiatric Rating Scale, which has sixteen items, each scored on a seven-point scale, and is suitable for rating severe psychiatric illness. Ratings of depressive symptoms include the Beck Depression Inventory, the Hamilton Rating Scale for Depression and the Montgomery–Asberg Depression Rating Scale. Quality of life scales are less commonly used in routine clinical practice, and include the SF-36 and EuroQol. Screening instruments, such as the Mini-Mental State Examination for cognitive impairment, may also be used in specific situations.

Prisons

Systematic reviews have demonstrated high levels of psychosis, depression, substance abuse and personality disorders in prisoners. Assessments in prison should follow the basic principles outlined above but there may be difficulty in obtaining informant histories and past medical records. Prison medical records should be studied, including any reception health screen and medical assessments conducted in prison. Prison officers may provide important supplemental information on a prisoner's behaviour. An important part of any assessment in prison (or in any forensic setting) is the personal safety of the interviewer, and arrangements should be put in place for potential problems. Suicide risk requires careful assessment, particularly in high-risk groups such as those with mental illness (Fazel *et al.* 2008).

Diagnostic instruments in prison are complicated by the fact that the widely used ones have not been validated in such settings, and evidence suggests that they may overdiagnose some disorders (particularly depression and psychosis) (see Fazel and Danesh 2002). The diagnosis of drug and alcohol problems is further made difficult by the availability of such substances in prison at the particular time of the interview, and the willingness of the prisoner to divulge such information.

Physical examination

Physical examination may provide information that is useful diagnostically, such as symptoms associated with thyroid disease or drug misuse. In addition, side-effects from medication may be apparent. Furthermore, it is important to assess and record the level of physical health, including weight, nutritional status and comorbid physical health problems. More detailed neurological examination may be required in some cases, which may involve liaison with specialists, including formal neuropsychological testing of IQ and cognitive impairment, and for other more subtle neuropsychological deficits that are associated with many psychiatric disorders, particularly schizophrenia.

Blood tests are important in order to exclude some physical aetiologies for mental illnesses, including endocrine disorders, and to provide baseline information on heart and kidney function before the possible commencement of psychotropic medication. Before starting antipsychotic treatment, ECGs are now routinely conducted. Urine drug screens and other investigations (including hair tests) may be useful to assist in the diagnosis of possible drug-induced psychosis.

Integrating the information

The main topics to be addressed in any assessment include diagnosis, impact on self, and immediate risks including to self and others. Furthermore, an understanding of the predisposing, precipitating and perpetuating factors is important as they assist in planning treatment. A discussion of the individual's prognosis should start at this point. Finally, decisions about treatment are made at the end of a psychiatric assessment – is treatment indicated, and if so, what are the various options, and the implications of each in terms of efficacy, side-effects and ongoing investigations?

REFERENCES

Fazel S. and Danesh, J. (2002) Serious mental disorder in 23000 prisoners: a systematic review of 62 surveys. *Lancet*, 359: 545–50.

Fazel, S., Cartwright, J., Nott-Norman, A. and Hawton, K. (2008) Suicide in prisoners: a systematic review of risk factors. *Journal of Clinical Psychiatry*, 69: 1721–31.

James, D. D., Duffield, G., Blizard, R. and Hamilton, L. L. (2001) Fitness to plead: a prospective study of the inter-relationships between expert opinion, legal criteria and specific symptomatology. *Psychological Medicine*, 31: 139–50.

2.11 Mentally disordered offenders

Derek Perkins

See also chapter 2.17 Personality disorder classifications in forensic settings, chapter 2.20 Psychopathy.

Definitions

Definitions of mental disorder and offending behaviour vary across countries and jurisdictions and change over time. In the UK, mental disorder is defined in the Mental Health Act 1983, section 1(2), as 'mental illness, arrested or incomplete development of mind, psychopathic disorder and any other disorder or disability of mind'. The subdivisions of 'severe mental impairment', 'mental impairment', 'mental illness' and 'psychopathic disorder' are legal categories for the purpose of the Act. Although clinical diagnoses are not specified, mental illness typically includes schizophrenia, major affective disorders and some rarer, atypical and organic conditions.

A wide range of personality disorders is embraced within the Act's broad definition of Psychopathic Disorder, i.e. a 'persistent disorder or disability of mind ... which results in abnormally aggressive or seriously irresponsible conduct'. Again the Act does not require specific personality disorder diagnoses, but these are typically present as defined by the DSM (American Psychiatric Association 1994) and/or ICD (World Health Organization 1992) classification systems. Blackburn (2004) notes that about two-thirds of mentally ill offenders also meet the criteria for one or more personality disorders, further complicating understanding of the link between mental disorder and offending. Section 1(3) of the Act sets out that a person cannot be regarded as having a mental disorder only by reason of promiscuity or other immoral conduct, sexual deviancy or dependence on drugs or alcohol.

Hodgins and Müller-Isberner (2004) highlight a continuing lack of etiological and diagnostic clarity in some categories of disorder, noting in particular delusional disorders and atypical psychoses. It has been suggested that the treatment and management of mentally disordered offenders depends more on legal and procedural variations than on features of the individuals concerned (Müller-Isberner and Hodgins 2000). Bonta, Law and Hanson (1998) suggested that problems in conceptualizing mentally disordered offenders have stemmed from undue reliance on psychopathological explanations, and Andrews and Bonta (2002) argued that criminogenic needs of the offender, such as criminal peers, antisocial attitude and substance misuse, tend to be the most salient factors when considering the treatment of offending behaviour in both mentally disordered and non-disordered offenders. Treatment outcomes are shown to be more successful when interventions are designed around the characteristics of the individual offender-patients (Howells and Day 2007).

Violence

The existence of a link between mental disorder and violence continues to be debated. Whilst some have argued against a clear link (Monahan and Steadman 1983; Bonta *et al.* 1998), Hodgins (2004) draws on three types of study (birth cohort follow-ups, discharged inpatient studies and studies of convicted offenders) to argue that there is a clear and consistent association. It has been noted that factors predictive of offending behaviour in mentally disordered samples are often the same as those in non-mentally disordered offenders (Heilbrun *et al.* 1998), leading to a focus on addressing risk factors such as antisocial attitudes, poor education, impulsivity, poor reasoning and problem solving, rather than exclusively on the mental disorder (Blackburn 2004).

Offending behaviour

The relationship between mental disorder and offending behaviour varies between individuals, a fact that can be masked by group-based data. Hodgins (2007) argues that there is a need to identify subgroups of violent behaviour in order to understand the dynamic interactions between biological, psychological and social factors, and thereby develop the most effective interventions. The picture is complicated where substance use (drugs and alcohol) is involved. These are sometimes taken by the mentally ill as a form of 'self-medication' for their symptoms, but this can be counterproductive as cannabis is a known risk factor for schizophrenia and there is a similar association between cocaine use and mania (Eaves, Tien and Wilson 2000). In the case of those with personality disorder, substance use may represent another manifestation of their disorder, e.g. impulsiveness, sensation seeking or lack of concern about future consequences.

Schizophrenia

Schizophrenia is the most common mental illness, affecting about 1% of the general population (Hodgins 2004). Onset is generally between 15 and 35 years of age, and is more common in city than rural areas. Symptoms are described as 'positive symptoms' – hallucinations (such as voices), delusions (such as being plotted against), thought disorder (such as poor concentration and muddled thinking), feelings of being controlled (such as being taken over by the television) and 'negative symptoms' – lack of drive and energy, progressive loss of insight and an inability to look after oneself. Causes of schizophrenia are currently regarded as comprising genetic, biological and environmental components. Genetic research suggests that the probability of developing schizophrenia with no family member suffering from the illness is approximately 1 in 100 but with one parent suffering from schizophrenia this rises to about 1 in 10, and for an identical twin to about 1 in 2 (Bloom and Wilson 2000).

A small proportion of sufferers are involved in violence or other seriously antisocial behaviour. Detailed formulation of each case is required to establish how the two phenomena interact. For example, in a study of sexual offenders suffering from schizophrenia, Taylor and Smith (1999) discovered that whilst most of the offenders were actively mentally ill at the time of their offences, in only about 20% of subjects was there a direct functional link between symptoms of the illness (hallucinations and delusions) and enactment of the sexual offence, suggesting that criminogenic risk factors for sex offending rather than mental illness may have been primarily responsible.

Major affective disorders

Prevalence studies indicate that major depression affects about 13% of men and 21% of women (Hodgins 2004), with a mean age of onset of about 40 (Eaves *et al.* 2000). Bipolar disorder, previously known as manic-depression, has a mean onset age of about 30 and is characterized by mood swings that can range from extreme happiness (mania) to extreme sadness (depression) over periods of days or months. In the depressive phase, symptoms include feeling sad and hopeless, lack of energy, difficulty concentrating, loss of interest in everyday activities, difficulty sleeping, feelings of worthlessness and despair, and suicidal thoughts. In the manic phase, which usually comes after several periods of depression, symptoms may include feeling elated and full of energy, talking very quickly, and feeling self-important with great ideas not known to others, but also being easily distracted, irritated or agitated, not sleeping or eating, and doing things that bring negative consequences, such as over-spending and dominating others.

Delusions stemming from these disorders can lead the individuals con-cerned to become violent, for example if they believe that the lives of their families have become intolerable (depressive phase), or where they believe that no one must stand in the way of their important plans (manic phase). The mental disorder can contribute directly to serious violence, e.g. multiple homicide of loved family members. As with schizophrenia, the precise cause of bipolar disorder is unknown, although it is thought to involve physical, environmental and social factors, with about 10–15% of sufferers' nearest relatives also being affected.

Other forms of mental illness

There are a number of less common conditions that also fall within the category of mental illness and which can be associated with offending behav-iour. Some people develop organically based conditions such as tumours that can result in violent or antisocial behaviour. Some forms of epilepsy can result in, or be linked with, violence in the 'prodromal phase' (associated with irritability and mood changes), or in subsequent states of confusion or autom-atism (Nedopil 2000). So-called 'absences', during which violent and sexually disinihibited behaviours can occur, may be considered sufficient to reduce the individual's responsibility for offending behaviour (such as angry or sexual homicide), in terms of their awareness or intent, and can result in convictions for manslaughter rather than for murder. As with other forms of mental disorder, epilepsy may interact with antisocial traits in the lead-up to the offending, and treatment is therefore complicated because it involves both psychological and biological factors.

Some patients suffer from a form of mental illness in which they develop morbid (or pathological) jealousy about their partners, in which they are not dissuaded from their beliefs by normally accepted evidence. Such conditions can be very resistant to change and in extreme cases have resulted in homicides of partners who are believed to have been unfaithful. Similarly resistant to logic and evidence are some distortions of romantic attachment. 'Erotomania', or de Clerambault's syndrome, involves the person afflicted believing that someone loves them despite all evidence to the contrary. This can lead to obsessive pursuit of the desired individual through letters, phone calls and personal contact. Some people will be deterred by legal process, such as formal warnings, restriction orders etc. – applied under the Protection from Harassment Act 1997 – but others persist and may eventually be detained in prison or mental health facilities (Boon and Sheridan 2002). Both conditions can become extremely dangerous; such offenders have figured in a number high-profile homicide cases and a small number are to be found in the high-secure psychiatric services, often very resistant to treatment.

Personality disorder

Personality disorders are thought to arise through an interaction between biological and psychosocial factors during personality development (Livesley 2000). Early psychosocial adversity, such as abuse and trauma, results in beliefs and expectations ('schemata') that influence the way the person sees the world. Typically, this includes expectations that other people are untrustworthy, unreliable and unpredictable. Most theories of personality disorder recognize core features common to all manifestations of personality disorder, namely failure to form adaptive representations of the self and others, which are expressed differently within different manifestations of personality disorder (Livesley 2000). Pathology of 'the self' manifests itself in problems with interpersonal boundaries, sense of self, fragmented representations of others and problems with self-regulation. Pathology of interpersonal functioning manifests itself in maladaptive patterns of interpersonal behaviour, difficulties tolerating closeness and intimacy, and problems with collaborative and co-operative relationships.

Because of concerns that had arisen in the operation of the Mental Health Act 1959 – in which some people, who had been hospitalized under the Psychopathic Disorder category well beyond periods they would have served had they been dealt with through the criminal justice system, were, in effect, untreatable – the 1983 Act sought to address this by including a 'treatability' requirement for those detained under the category of Psychopathic Disorder.

Under the 1983 Mental Health Act, detention in hospital on the grounds of Psychopathic Disorder is only possible if the individual is, as well as being mentally disordered and dangerous, likely to benefit from treatment. Such benefit can include both amelioration of their condition and prevention of deterioration. Placement in a high-security hospital can only occur if the individual meets the above conditions and also cannot be managed in a lesser level of security, such as a medium- or low-secure unit.

Within the area of personality disorder, there are potentially confusing and overlapping sets of definitions. 'Psychopathic Disorder' in the Mental Health Act 1983 is a legal term. 'Psychopathic personality disorder' or 'psychopathy' is a clinical term with a now well-established system of diagnosis (the PCL-R) (Hare 1991). Psychopathy is characterized by three clusters of symptoms – 'interpersonal' (egocentric, manipulative, dominant, forceful and cold-hearted), affective (shallow and labile emotional expression, inability to form long-lasting bonds to people, lack of empathy, lack of anxiety and lack of genuine guilt or remorse) and 'behavioural' (impulsiveness, sensation seeking, violation of social norms including in relation to criminality, substance misuse and failure to fulfil social obligations and responsibilities). Psychopathy is associated with extreme violence and resistance to change. Other personality disorders are defined through two main diagnostic systems in use internationally, the ICD-10 and DSM-IV. Within the UK, both systems are used but most services have now moved towards adoption of the ICD-10 system. Hare's psychopathy is not included in the DSM or ICD systems but overlaps with DSM Cluster B disorders (antisocial, borderline, narcissistic and histrionic).

Personality disorders differ from normal variations in personality function by virtue of being *enduring* patterns of relating to the environment (including the self) that are exhibited in a *wide range* of social and personal contexts, in ways that are *inflexible and pervasive* across a *broad range* of personal and social situations, and in ways that cause *significant distress* or *impairment* in social or other important areas of functioning (DSM-IV). Hence, personality disorders might or might not involve personal distress to the person in question, and can stem directly from features of the disorder (e.g. impulsiveness or callousness) or exacerbate other antisocial traits (e.g. through a failure to learn from experience). It might be said that in the intersection between personality disorder and offending behaviour, 'personality disorder symptoms' and 'offending behaviour risk factors' can become one and the same. Coid (1998) demonstrated, in a high-secure psychiatric population, that different personality disorders are typically associated with different manifestations of violence. For example, schizoid disorders were associated with violence executed for excitement-seeking motives, whereas narcissistic disorders were associated with rage stemming from perceived abandonment and a sense of losing control.

Controversy continues to surround arrangements for patients classified as meeting the Psychopathic Disorder (PD) criteria in terms of variations in the operation of the treatability criterion. Some forensic psychiatric services have accepted patients only on the basis of the 'amelioration of symptoms' criterion, ignoring the 'prevention of deterioration' criterion. This issue has become the subject of intense public debate over the last ten years, with increasing concern linked to a small number of high-profile cases, e.g. following the release into the community of a paedophile gang who had been convicted for the homicide of a teenage boy; there was also the case of a man who, whilst considered to meet the PD criteria for mental disorder and dangerousness, was considered 'untreatable' and was therefore left at liberty to murder a woman and her daughter. Maden (2007) graphically describes the role of the psychiatric profession in such cases: 'The profession was seen as cynically hiding behind the "treatability" clause in the Mental Health Act 1983 to avoid responsibility for dangerous and difficult patients.'

The perceived failure to admit to hospital and treat dangerous personality-disordered individuals, together with concerns over the quality of treatment provided for those detained under the category of PD, led to the setting up of the currently trialled 'Dangerous and Severe Personality Disorder' (DSPD) services in the UK. Two facilities currently operate within the prison system (HM Prisons Frankland and Whitemoor) and two within the forensic mental health services (Broadmoor and Rampton Hospitals). Development of the DSPD services has focused attention on the links between personality disorders and violence in that the DSPD admission criteria require a functional link to be established between personality disorder symptoms and violent behaviour. Perkins (2008), in the context of assessing the links between sexual violence and mental disorder, has argued for a *dynamic formulation* approach in which information that may not be available in an initial formulation is built up as the offender-patient is closely monitored during treatment and becomes a collaborator in understanding his/her own offending.

Treatment

It is now generally accepted that treatment programmes for mentally disordered offenders should, like those for offending behaviour more generally, address the principles of 'risk', 'need' and 'responsivity' (Bonta, Law and Hanson 1988). *Risk* refers to risk of future offending, upon which most resources should be deployed. *Need* refers to the targeting of treatment at the specific (criminogenic and mental health) needs of the individual, for example poor emotional control, antisocial attitudes, or whatever else has led to offending behaviour. *Responsivity* refers to the design of treatments around the specific characteristics of the offender-patient that will impact on his/her ability to benefit from the treatment – level of intelligence or concentration, sensitivity to interpersonal threat etc. This produces practical challenges in achieving the correct balance between, on the one hand, fully individualized treatments (as exemplified in forensic mental health services' 'Care Programme Approach') and, on the other hand, providing treatment programmes that seek to maximize benefits to the largest possible group of participants within a finite budget (as has underpinned the Prison Service treatment programmes). These different approaches have come closer together with joint NHS–Prison Service initiatives such as the DSPD services. A meta-analysis found that cognitive-behavioural treatments addressing the specific needs of offenders rather than generic causes of offending demonstrated positive and promising results (McGuire 2002) and this approach is now also being adopted in the treatment of mentally disordered offenders (Duncan *et al.* 2006).

FURTHER READING

A good overview can be found in the collection edited by S. Hodgins and R. Müller-Isberner (2000) *Violent Crime and Mentally Disordered Offenders* (Chichester: Wiley).

REFERENCES

American Psychiatric Association (1994) *Diagnostic and Statistical Manual of Mental Disorders*, 4th edn (DSM-IV). Washington, DC: American Psychiatric Association.

Andrews, D. A. and Bonta, J. (2002) *The Psychology of Criminal Conduct*, 3rd edn. Cincinnati, OH: Anderson.

Blackburn, R. (2004) 'What works' with mentally disordered offenders. *Psychology, Crime and Law*, 10(3): 297–308.

Bloom, J. D. and Wilson, W. H. (2000) Offenders with schizophrenia. In S. Hodgins and R. Müller-Isberner (eds.), *Violent Crime and Mentally Disordered Offenders*, pp. 113–30. Chichester: Wiley

Bonta, J., Law, M. and Hanson, K. (1998) The prediction of criminal and violent recidivism among mentally disordered offenders: a meta-analysis. *Psychological Bulletin*, 123: 123–42.

Boon, J. C. W. and Sheridan, L. (eds.). (2002) *Stalking and Psychosexual Obsession: Prevention, Policing and Treatment*. Chichester: Wiley.

Coid, J. (1998) Axis II disorders and motivation for serious criminal behaviour. In A. E. Skodol (ed.), *Psychopathy and Violent Crime*, pp. 53–97. Washington, DC: Academic Psychiatric Press.

Duncan, E. A. S., Nicol, M. M., Ager, A. and Dalgleish, L. (2006) A systematic review of structured group interventions with mentally disordered offenders. *Criminal Behaviour and Mental Health*, 16: 217–41.

Eaves, D., Tien, G. and Wilson, D. (2000) Offenders with major affective disorders. In S. Hodgins and R. Müller-Isberner (eds.), *Violent Crime and Mentally Disordered Offenders*, pp. 131–52. Chichester: Wiley.

Hare, R. D. (1991) *The Hare Psychopathy Checklist – Revised – Manual*. Toronto: Multi-Health Systems.

Heilbrun, K., Hart, S., Hare, R., Gustafson, D., Nunez, C. and White, A. (1998) Inpatient and postdischarge aggression in mentally ill offenders. *Journal of Interpersonal Violence*, 13: 514–27.

Hodgins, S. (2004) Criminal and antisocial behaviours and schizophrenia: a neglected topic. In W. F Gattaz and H. Häfner (eds.), *Search for the Causes of Schizophrenia*, vol. 5, pp. 315–41. Darmstadt: Steinkopff Verlag.

   (2007) Persistent violent offending: what do we know? *British Journal of Psychiatry*, 190: s12–s14.

Hodgins, S. and Müller-Isberner, R. (2004) Preventing crime by people with schizophrenia: the role of psychiatric services. *British Journal of Psychiatry* 185: 245–56.

Howells, K. and Day, A. (2007) Readiness for treatment in high risk offenders with personality disorders. *Psychology, Crime and Law*, 13: 47–56.

Livesley, W. J. (ed.) (2000) *Handbook of Personality Disorders: Theory, Research and Treatment*. New York: Guilford Press.

Maden, A. (2007) Dangerous and severe personality disorder: antecedents and origins. *British Journal of Psychiatry*, 190: s8–s11.

McGuire, J. (2002) Integrating findings from research reviews. In J. McGuire (ed.), *Offender Rehabilitation and Treatment: Effective Programmes and Policies to Reduce Re-offending*, pp. 3–38. Chichester: Wiley.

Monahan, J. and Steadman, H. (1983) Crime and mental disorder: an epidemiological approach. In N. Morris and M. Tonry (eds.), *Crime and Justice: an Annual Review of Research*, pp. 145–89. Chicago: University of Chicago Press.

Müller-Isberner, R. and Hodgins, S. (2000). Evidence-based treatment for mentally disordered offenders. In S. Hodgins and R. Müller-Isberner (eds.), *Violence, Crime and Mentally Disordered Offenders: Concept and Methods for Effective Treatment and Prevention*, pp. 7–38. Chichester: Wiley.

Nedopil, N. (2000) Offenders with brain damage. In S. Hodgins and R. Müller-Isberner (eds.), *Violence, Crime and Mentally Disordered Offenders: Concepts and Methods for Effective Treatment and Prevention*, pp. 39–62. New York: Wiley.

Perkins, D. E. (2008). 'Diagnosis, assessment and identification of severe paraphilic disorders' In A. Harris & C. Page (eds.) Sexual homicide and paraphilias. (Correctional Service of Canada.

Taylor, P. J. and Smith, A. D. (1999) Serious sex offending against women by men with schizophrenia. *British Journal of Psychiatry* 174: 233–7.

World Health Organization (1992) *ICD-10: Classification of Mental and Behavioural Disorders: Clinical Descriptions and Diagnostic Guidelines*. Geneva: World Health Organization.

2.12 Memory

Martin A. Conway

See also chapter 2.2 Credibility, chapter 2.8 Interrogative suggestibility and false confessions.

Definition

The view of human memory currently emerging from scientific research is that memory is fragmentary and malleable and, most importantly, can contain errors and even wholly false memories of which the individual rememberer is completely unaware. In many countries criminal and civil actions proceed when the only available evidence, or the main evidence, is memories. This often occurs in cases of 'historic' sexual abuse in which, typically, an adult's allegations are based on memories from childhood. It can, however, occur in a wide range of other types of complaint too. For example, witness reports of war crimes, acts of genocide, physical child abuse, copyright infringements, insurance claims, asylum seeking, etc. The list is a long one and, essentially, when the only/main evidence is that of a witness or set of witnesses, then issues relating to the nature of human memory become central.

Nature of memory

Unfortunately professionals involved in such cases rarely know anything about the scientific study of human memory and instead proceedings are based on more or less explicit beliefs about human memory: more often than not these beliefs are wrong. Quite clearly, then, it would be useful for a court/tribunal to have an authoritative and accessible account of the nature of human memory – an account that they could draw upon to assist them in reaching more informed decisions. The recently published *Guidelines on Memory and the Law*, from the Research Board of the British Psychological Society (2008), aim to provide an accessible, widely agreed set of guidelines about human memory that have been

Table 2.12.1 Key guidelines

(i) *Memories are records of people's experiences of events and are not a record of the events themselves.* In this respect, they are unlike other recording media such as videos or audio recordings, to which they should not be compared.

(ii) *Memory is not only of experienced events but it is also of the knowledge of a person's life,* i.e. schools, occupations, holidays, friends, homes, achievements, failures, etc. As a general rule memory is more likely to be accurate when it is of the knowledge of a person's life than when it is of specific experienced events.

(iii) *Remembering is a constructive process.* Memories are mental constructions that bring together different types of knowledge in an act of remembering. As a consequence, memory is prone to error and is easily influenced by the recall environment, including police interviews and cross-examination in court.

(iv) *Memories for experienced events are always incomplete.* Memories are time-compressed fragmentary records of experience. Any account of a memory will feature forgotten details and gaps, and this must not be taken as any sort of indicator of accuracy. Accounts of memories that do not feature forgetting and gaps are highly unusual.

(v) *Memories typically contain only a few highly specific details.* Detailed recollection of the specific time and date of experiences is normally poor, as is highly specific information such as the precise recall of spoken conversations. As a general rule, a high degree of very specific detail in a long-term memory is unusual.

(vi) *Recall of a single or several highly specific details does not guarantee that a memory is accurate or even that it actually occurred.* In general, the only way to establish the truth of a memory is with independent corroborating evidence.

(vii) *The content of memories arises from an individual's comprehension of an experience, both conscious and non-conscious.* This content can be further modified and changed by subsequent recall.

(viii) *People can remember events that they have not in reality experienced.* This does not necessarily entail deliberate deception. For example, an event that was imagined, was a blend of a number of different events, or that makes personal sense for some other reason, can come to be genuinely experienced as a memory (these are often referred to as 'confabulations').

(ix) *Memories for traumatic experiences, childhood events, interview and identification practices, memory in younger children and older adults and other vulnerable groups all have special features.* These are features that are unlikely to be commonly known by a non-expert, but about which an appropriate memory expert will be able to advise a court.

(x) *A memory expert is a person who is recognized by the memory research community to be a memory researcher.* It is recommended that, in addition to current requirements, those acting as memory expert witnesses be required to submit their full curriculum vitae to the court as evidence of their expertise.

established through scientific research. The report lists ten key guidelines and these are reproduced in table 2.12.1.

Guidelines (i) through (v) provide more specific detail on this view of human memory, and within the report itself further sections provide reviews of the relevant legal considerations and the scientific evidence that supports each guideline. A full reference section on the scientific literature is also included for those who wish to delve further.

Consider two beliefs about human memory, currently prevalent in our courts, and which the guidelines show to be almost certainly incorrect: the first is that fragmentary, incomplete memories are unreliable; and the second is that the recall of highly vivid details indicates that a memory is being recalled accurately. In fact, memory is always time-compressed and fragmentary (guideline (iv) in table 2.12.1); it is a *representation* of experience and in no sense a literal record. Memory is not comparable to photographs, videos or other types of electronic recording media that keep an indiscriminate record of all the details they record. Thus an account of an experience that does *not* contain forgotten and poorly remembered details is the account which is unusual and which requires additional support if it is to be accepted as being of a memory. Quite the reverse of what is commonly believed.

The powerful belief that the more specific the details recalled the more likely a memory is to be correct turns out to be pervasive; consider, for example, the following study:

In an experiment that featured a mock trial of a bank robbery, mock jurors were asked to judge the credibility of the evidence of the witnesses. One set of witnesses described events simply and without any details. For example, the (mock) witness might state 'as the robber ran out of the bank I think he turned right and ran off down the street'. In another version the same witness (to a new mock jury) would state 'as the robber, who I remember was wearing a green jumper, ran out of the bank I think he turned right and ran off down the street'. This second version of events was rated as far more likely to be correct than the first version. The effect is known as 'trivial persuasion' because by inclusion of a trivial or irrelevant but highly specific detail the perceived credibility of the evidence is markedly raised.

Other evidence reviewed in the *Guidelines on Memory and the Law* shows that there is no guarantee that any detail in a memory, whether specific or otherwise, is correct. Recall of some very specific details, e.g. verbatim accounts of spoken utterances of more than a few words, etc. (see table 2.12.1 and guidelines (v) and (vi) in the report for more of these types of wholly implausible details), are very unlikely to be correct. Error and falsity seem especially characteristic of childhood memories (Cerci and Bruck 1995) but research has shown that this can occur, and indeed does occur, for memories from any age. Consider the following memory, relayed to me appropriately enough by a barrister:

A middle-aged man recalled his father distracting him when he was a young boy (about 4 years old) by asking him who was the first man on the moon. He had been intensely interested in the moon landings when he was a young boy and this incident occurred while his father was on the telephone to his mother who had just given birth to his younger brother. My informant had a vivid and fond memory of his father placating him in this way, he was highly agitated by the birth, and in his memory he could 'see' his father on the telephone and almost 'hear' his voice. It was only decades later that he realized that his brother had been born in 1968, one year before the first moon landing.

Another well-known case illustrates how memory can be simultaneously true and false. A woman was raped one evening in her apartment in New York. The police were called in and quickly developed a theory about who the attacker might be. The next day they held a lineup that included the suspect and several volunteers taken fairly randomly from the streets outside the police station. The victim singled out a man in the lineup and was strongly confident this was the man, indeed she recognized his face. But he was not the police suspect and, moreover, he had the perfect alibi: he had been on live television at the time the rape had taken place. Subsequently it seems that in fact he had been on television in the woman's apartment when the attack had taken place. The image of his face had been incorporated into her memory. Extensive research has now shown that inducing false details into memories and even creating wholly false memories is relatively easy and there is no doubt that this occurs spontaneously in everyday life.

The above example of a false detail in a memory of a rape illustrates how even a traumatic memory can be incorrect. However, it is not uncommon for memories of traumatic assaults, such as rapes, to contain relatively few details, amnesic gaps, uncertainties about temporal order, distortions and details the source of which is not known, i.e. external or internal (self-generated). But this is what memory research tells us is the nature of human memory: it is fragmentary and not a literal record of reality (Brewin 2007). It is a record of a person's *experience* of reality and that experience includes what we think and feel as well as what we sense and, additionally, it is highly selective. One very unfortunate problem that arises when people are unaware of these characteristics of human memory is an over-hasty and incautious conclusion that a witness is unreliable. The rape victim who cannot recall the face of her assailant, the torture victim who recalls just a few moments of their suffering, or the witness to violent crimes who has a fragmented and distorted set of memories, should not be classified as an unreliable witnesses. Judgements about when to prosecute are often based on appraisals of how reliable testimony is and lawyers are often keen to exploit the fragmentary nature of human memory as an indicator of reliability. Understanding the nature of human memory should help improve practice in this area.

Perhaps the main contribution of the report is to show how current scientific thinking about memory has come to fully appreciate that memories can be correct, they can be wrong (in their details), even wholly false, and, importantly, correct and wrong at the same time, with the latter combination of truth and error being more frequent than we have been able to appreciate previously. Also of note is that these memory errors can arise non-consciously and without any intent on behalf of the rememberer. The evidence reviewed in the report does not cover malingering and lying; it is, rather, solely concerned with what we might call *honest errors* or, in the case of false or confabulated memories, what have been memorably termed *honest lies*.

False memories

There are, of course, many reasons why someone might recount memories when they are false, revenge and/or financial gain being potential candidate motivations. Let us suppose that a person had a very difficult childhood, with an undermining, emotionally cold and, perhaps, physically aggressive parent or parental figure and that subsequent to childhood much else in their life had been bad. This individual remembers an incident from childhood that seems peculiar and seems to suggest some sort of abuse. They then try to image what else might have happened in this poorly remembered event, perhaps they create a visual mental image of what might have taken place. This leads to further imaging and they then begin to find it difficult to distinguish in their own mind what has been imagined versus remembered (technically this is known as a *source error*, i.e. one cannot recall the source of some information). Indeed, for them the images are now experienced *as* memories. This is the process known as *imagination inflation* and research shows that it is a power-ful way in which to create false memories (Brainerd and Reyna 2005). Now the individual has a set of abuse memories and brings a case against the hated figure from childhood. The abuse memories may serve two purposes, one being revenge on the person and the other, and this is the more interesting one, they serve to explain the various failures and disasters that have pre-dominated in the victim's life. Explaining one's life in this way is a powerful motivation to develop a set of (false) memories that one experiences as true. This analysis is speculative, nonetheless the self-defining function that memories serve in a person's life as a means of explaining who they are should not be overlooked, particularly in legal settings.

Conclusion

Finally, we should not lose sight of the fact that memory can be correct too. After all, people are abused, attacked and otherwise offended against, and their memories will usually be a mix of well-remembered details (normally just a few), a lot of forgotten details and some details that are incorrect but which they believe to be true or which they suspect might be true – that is what a typical memory looks like. Even though such memories are fragmentary and may contain (honest) errors, they can nonetheless be true, true that certain experiences took place and true about at least some details. Indeed, at more general levels memory is less prone to error (Toglia *et al.* 2007). Thus it is certainly possible that a person could remember that they had been abused, attacked or assaulted, etc. and be perfectly correct, while simultaneously having detailed memories that are wholly false. That is why additional evidence, independent of the rememberer, is virtually always required when judging the truth of memory (see guideline (vi)).

FURTHER READING

The British Psychological Society's guidelines provide a comprehensive overview.

REFERENCES

Brainerd C. J. and Reyna, V. F. (2005) *The Science of False Memory.* New York: Oxford University Press.

Brewin, C. R. (2007) Autobiographical memory for trauma: update on four controversies. *Memory*, 15: 227–48.

British Psychological Society (2008) *Guidelines on Memory and the Law: Recommendations from the Scientific Study of Human Memory.* Leicester: British Psychological Society.

Cerci, S. J. and Bruck, M. (1995) *Jeopardy in the Courtroom: A Scientific Analysis of Children's Testimony.* Washington, DC: American Psychological Association.

Toglia, M. P., Read, J. D., Ross, D. F. and Lindsay, R. C. L. (eds.) (2007) *The Handbook of Eyewitness Psychology,* vol. 1: *Memory for Events.* Mahwah, NJ: Erlbaum.

2.13 Offender profiling

David Canter

See also chapter 1.9 Investigative psychology.

Origins and definitions

Those investigating crimes have always tried to formulate some idea of the characteristics of unknown culprits as an aid to finding and convicting them. This parallels the generals of Ancient Rome building a picture of the Barbarian leaders they would face in battle. It is therefore not surprising, as discussed by Canter (1995a), that as long ago as 1888, when Jack the Ripper stalked the streets of London, some attempt was made to produce a description of the person who had committed these still unsolved crimes.

By the 1970s, as Blau (1994) makes clear, police forces throughout the USA were referring to the process of speculating about the characteristics of offenders they were looking for as 'offender profiling'. The utility of this activity was recognized by those special agents at the FBI Training Academy in Quantico, Virginia, who were tasked with improving the effectiveness of the many thousands of law enforcement agencies across America. However, it was only when Thomas Harris made the process central to his plot in his thriller *The Silence of the Lambs* (1988) that it came into public awareness. Thus accounts of 'offender profiling' have always been confused by the mixture of myth and reality that exist within Harris' and many subsequent fictional portrayals.

The device that so attracted Harris was the possibility of using an offender, in the guise of the serial killer Hannibal Lecter, as the tutor for the novice profiler, Clarice Starling. The idea for this device was derived from interviews that the FBI special agents had carried out with serial killers and rapists (Hazelwood *et al.* 1987). As many people have pointed out (Jackson and Bekerian 1997), these interviews were rather unstructured and never reported systematically in any detail so could not be recognized as valid scientific studies. As a consequence, many of the generalizations derived from them, such as the typical high intelligence of serial killers and their being nearly always white, have been shown to be invalid. It is more appropriate to see them as having followed the practice of detectives that can be traced back at least as far as François Vidocq (Edwards 1977), a nineteenth-century French detective who talked to and got to understand criminals as an aid to guiding the investigative process. However, by the 1980s, when the interviews were being conducted, a loose psychological perspective pervaded many areas of American life, and some of the FBI agents had taken courses in counselling and related subjects. Therefore, although these interviews had no theoretical basis, the FBI agents who conducted them derived from their meetings with the offenders the proposition that a careful consideration of what went on in a crime could be a fruitful basis for formulating a view of the offender.

Typologies

This approach was systematized into sets of typologies. The most widely cited of these is the suggestion that serial killers are either organized or disorganized (Ressler *et al.* 1985) and that this aspect of an offender's lifestyle is reflected in a crime scene that is either organized or disorganized. As Canter and Wentink (2004) have demonstrated, Holmes' more refined typology of serial killers is merely an elaboration of the original FBI dichotomy. Careful studies of both the original FBI dichotomy (Canter *et al.* 2004) and of Holmes' typology (Canter and Wentink 2004) have demonstrated that these classification schemes of serial killers do not withstand close empirical test.

Inferences about offender characteristics

Drawing on a background in social and environmental psychology, Canter demonstrated in *Criminal Shadows* (1995a) that the central question of offender profiling is to establish the basis for making inferences from offence actions to offender characteristics. He proposed that this may be fruitfully thought of as the need to solve what he called the A ® C equations: the formal scientific framework used to represent the relationships between a set of actions in a crime (the As) and the set of characteristics of the offender (the Cs) (Canter 1995b). As Youngs (2007) has elaborated, these equations are canonical in the statistical sense in that there may be many different sets of variables that typify the actions which may relate in a variety of ways to a mixture of the offender's characteristics. There is no expectation that there will always be a simple one-to-one relationship between any given action and any given characteristic. As a consequence, it is argued (Canter and Youngs 2002) that these A ® C equations cannot be solved by purely empirical means because there are just too many possibilities of what may relate to what under differing circumstances. Instead, some form of theoretical framework is needed that will guide the search for possible correlations between actions and characteristics.

The basis for much offender profiling has typically been clinical or other professional experience, making judgements about the personality traits or psychodynamics of the likely perpetrator of a crime under investigation. From the perspective of scientific psychology, such a process is flawed in its reliance on clinical judgement rather than actuarial assessment. These flaws have been shown in extensive studies reviewed by Meehl (1954). The clinically derived theories upon which much 'offender profiling' has relied are equally questioned by research psychologists.

The range of scientific questions inherent in offender profiling have been shown by Canter (2004) to be a subset of a broader range of issues in psychology that are relevant to police investigations. This places offender profiling within a more general field named Investigative Psychology. Interestingly, this more academically grounded approach, rather than moving away from operational concerns, is opening up the potential applications of psychological science.

The inferences that detectives make in an investigation about the perpetrator's likely characteristics will be valid to the extent that they are based on appropriate ideas about the processes by which the actions in a crime are linked to the characteristics. A number of potential processes are available within social and psychological theory. These include psychodynamic theories and personality theories, as well as frameworks drawing on interpersonal narratives and on socioeconomic factors. Any or all of these theories could provide a valid basis for investigative inferences if the differences in individuals they posit correspond to variations in criminal behaviour. One general hypothesis here is that offenders will show some consistency between the nature of their crimes and other characteristics they exhibit in other situations. This is rather different from psychodynamic models that attempt to explain criminality as a displacement or compensation activity, resulting from psychological deficiencies.

Valid inferences also depend upon an understanding of the way in which a process is operating. Conceptually there are a number of different roles that a theory can play in helping to link an offender's actions with his/her characteristics. One is to explain how it is that the offender's characteristics are the cause of the particular criminal actions. A different theoretical perspective would be to look for some common third set of intervening variables that was produced by the offender's characteristics to cause the particular offending actions. Yet a third possibility is that some other set of variables is the cause of both. The evidence so far is consonant with this general consistency model, suggesting that processes relating to both the offender's characteristic interpersonal style and his or her routine activities (Clarke and Felson 1985) may be particularly useful in helping to infer characteristics from actions.

From an applied perspective, it is also important that the variables on which the inference models draw are limited to those of utility to police investigations. This implies that the A variables are restricted to those known prior to any suspect being identified, typically crime scene information and/or victim and witness statements. The C variables are limited to those on which the police can act, such as information about where the person might be living, his/her criminal history, age or domestic circumstances.

These inference models operate at the thematic level, rather than being concerned with particular, individual clues as would be typical of detective fiction. This approach recognizes that any one criminal action may be unreliably recorded or may not happen because of situational factors. But a group of actions that together indicate some dominant aspect of the offender's style may be strongly related to some important characteristic of the offender. Davies' (1997) study showed the power of this thematic approach. She demonstrated from her analysis of 210 rapes that if the offender took precautions not to leave fingerprints, stole from the victim, forced entry and had imbibed alcohol, then there was a very high probability, above 90%, that the offender had prior convictions for burglary.

The most developed empirical examination of thematic inference hypotheses is the study of arsonists by Canter and Fritzon (1998). They drew on Shye's (1985) action systems model of behaviour to identify four styles of arson, resulting from differences in the source of the objectives for the action (Expressive or Instrumental) combined with differences in the direction of the effect of the action (Person or Object). They developed scales to measure these four Expressive Person, Expressive Object, Instrumental Person and Instrumental Object themes in the actions of arsonists. Their table relating measures on all four background scales to all four action scales showed that the strongest statistically significant correlations were, as predicted, between actions and characteristics that exhibited similar themes, and lowest between those that did not.

Studies of inference need to recognize the social or organizational context in which the criminal operates. The social processes that underlie groups, teams and networks of criminals can reveal much about the consistencies in criminal behaviour and the themes that provide their foundation. A clear example of this is a study looking at the different roles that are taken by teams of 'hit and run' burglars (Wilson and Donald 1999). They demonstrated, for example, that the offender who was given the task of driving the getaway vehicle was most often likely to have a previous conviction for a vehicle-related crime. In contrast the criminal assigned the task of keeping members of the public at bay, or controlling others who might interfere with their crime, the 'heavy', was most likely to have a previous conviction for some form of violent offence.

These results of consistency between social role and other forms of criminal endeavour are thus in keeping with the general thematic framework that is emerging through the studies of actual actions in a crime. They lend support to a general model of criminal activity that recognizes the specific role that criminality plays in the life of the offender.

FURTHER READING

The collection edited by Jackson and Bekerian (1997) provides a good rounded overview of issues. The chapter by Canter and Youngs makes the link to investigative psychology.

REFERENCES

Blau, T. H. (1994) *Psychological Services for Law Enforcement*. New York: Wiley.
Canter, D. (1995a) *Criminal Shadows*. London: HarperCollins.
    (1995b) The psychology of offender profiling. In R. Bull and D. Carson (eds.), *Handbook of Psychology in Legal Contexts*, 2nd edn, pp. 343–55. Chichester: Wiley.
    (2004) Offender profiling and investigative psychology. *Journal of Investigative Psychology and Offender Profiling*, 1: 15.
Canter, D., Alison, A. J., Alison, E. and Wentink, N. (2004) The organanized/disorganized typologies of serial murder: myth or model?. *Psychology, Public Policy and Law*, 10(3): 29.
Canter, D. and Fritzon, K. (1998) Differentiating arsonists: a model of firesetting actions and characteristics. *Legal and Criminal Psychology*, 3(7): 73.
Canter, D. and Wentink, N. (2004). An empirical test of Holmes and Holmes's serial murder typology. *Criminal Justice and Behavior*, 20(10): 26.

Canter, D. and Youngs, D. (2002) Beyond offender profiling: the need for an investigative psychology. In R. Bull and D. Carson (eds.), *Handbook of Psychology in Legal Contexts*, pp. 171–206. Chichester: Wiley.

Clarke, R. V. and Felson, M. (1985) Routine activity and rational choice. *Advances in Criminological Theory*, 5.

Davies, A. (1997) Specific profile analysis: a data-based approach to offender profiling. In J. L. Jackson and D. A. Bekerian (eds.), *Offender Profiling: Theory, Research and Practice*, pp. 191–208. Chichester: Wiley.

Edwards, S. T. (1977) *The Vidocq Dossier: The Story of the World's First Detective*. Boston, MA: Houghton Mifflin.

Hazelwood, R. R., Ressler, R. K., Depue, R. L. and Douglas, J. E. (1987) Criminal personality profiling: an overview. In R. R. Hazelwood and A. W. Burgess (eds.), *Practical Aspects of Rape Investigation: A Multidisciplinary Approach*, pp. 137–150. New York: Elsevier.

Jackson, J. L. and Bekerian, D. A. (eds.) (1997) *Offender Profiling: Theory, Research and Practice*. Chichester: Wiley.

Meehl, P. E. (1954) *Clinical versus Statistical Prediction: A Theoretical Analysis and a Review of the Evidence*. Minneapolis: University of Minnesota Press.

Ressler, R. K., Burgess, A. W., Depue, R. L., Douglas, J. E. and Hazelwood, R. R. (1985) Classifying sexual homicide crime scenes. *FBI Law Enforcement Bulletin*, 54: 6.

Shye, S. (1985) Non-metric multivariate models for behavioural action systems. In D. V. Canter (ed.), *Facet Theory: Approaches to Social Research*, pp. 97–148. New York: Springer.

Wilson, A. and Donald, I. (1999) Ram raiding: criminals working in groups. In D. V. Canter and L. J. Alison (eds.), *The Social Psychology of Crime:, Groups, Teams and Networks*, vol. 3, pp. 127–52. Aldershot: Dartmouth.

Youngs, D. (2007) Contemporary challenges in investigative psychology: revisiting the Canter offender profiling equations. In D. Canter and R. Zukauskiene (eds.), *Psychology and Law: Bridging the Gap*, pp. 23–30. Aldershot: Ashgate.

2.14 Parenting capacity and conduct

Christine Puckering

See also chapter 3.4 Parenting programmes.

Introduction

Psychologists are likely to be asked to give an opinion on the capacity of parents to provide a safe and nurturing environment in three contexts. The first is in the context of contentious interparental care arrangements; the second is when it is suspected that a child has been neglected or abused and the quality of the parenting provided by the parent(s) is under scrutiny; and the third is the related issue of the capacity of parents to provide good parenting when they themselves have mental health problems or learning difficulties which may interfere with their ability to recognize and respond to the needs of the child.

In each case the question is fundamentally the same: to what extent can this parent offer the child a safe and nurturing environment which will meet all of his or her needs, including physical, emotional, social, intellectual and cultural? Where each parent can offer good parenting but they are in conflict, compromises may need to be made. The level of conflict between them may reach such a pitch that their disagreements threaten the wellbeing of the child or children. Judy Dunn's paper on the effects of interparental conflict provide grounds for a useful warning to warring parents as to the toxic effects of their disagreement on the children (Dunn 2005).

Requests for examination of parental capacity are likely to come from members of the legal professions, such as lawyers representing parents; child protection agencies, such as social workers, guardians ad litem or safeguarders appointed by the court; and those who make decisions on child welfare, such as magistrates, judges or sheriffs. In each case the psychologist must act in the best interests of the child and make a fair and independent evaluation of parenting without regard to the agent who requested their help. The British

Psychological Society's (BPS) code of conduct makes this an obligation and it should be stated in any medico-legal report.

Assessment of parenting is a complex task and is likely to involve a major time commitment. For example, in a disputed parenting custody case it would be common to spend twelve hours or more in face-to-face contact with the child, actual and potential carers and collateral informants. To this should be added the time taken to read and review paperwork, which can be considerable if a child has been involved with social work, clinical or legal services, and time to compile a report on all aspects of the case. The task is no easy one and may require training and expertise in child development, attachment, parental and child psychopathology, measures and methods, structured and unstructured observation, questionnaires and scales.

Methods and measures

Interviews

It is almost always essential to interview all the actual and potential carers of the child. These may include the natural parents, foster parents, grandparents and other carers. There is no other arena in which feelings run so high as in the care of children, so it is necessary not only to be entirely dispassionate but also to be seen to be dispassionate. For this reason, parents should be seen in equivalent locations, either both in their homes or both in a neutral setting such as a clinic. If possible about the same amount of time should be given to each parent. It can be helpful to ask each parent about the developmental progress of the child, with lack of information or lack of consistency possibly pointing to less close involvement of one parent with the child. A useful reminder of the pitfalls of bias in decision making in child custody cases, Robb (2006) suggests ways to avoid bias both in data collection and interpretation.

If parents are partisan, the grandparents may be expected to be even more so. They will often take very trenchant positions, defending not only their own child, but that child's children and consequently scapegoating the other parent.

For these reasons, the use of other collateral informants such as teachers, who rarely have a vested personal interest in the outcome of a custody case, can provide a source of information which is both well informed by regular contact with the child(ren) and is balanced by their regular contact with many other children who give a perspective to their observations.

Observations

Detailed observation of each parent with each of the children and particularly the handover times at the beginning and end of contact can be very revealing. The use of a structured instrument with known reliability and validity offers a strong defence against accusations that observations are subjective. Depending on the age of the child, the Care Index, with known predictive power to later secure attachment, is one such instrument for young children (Crittenden 1981). Children from birth to adolescence may be observed during the administration of the HOME Inventory (Bradley and Caldwell 1988; Bradley and Corwyn 2000), a one-hour structured interview and assessment of the social, emotional and physical environment provided by the parent for the child. The inventory covers from the preschool age to teenagers. A training package for the reliable administration of this instrument is now available.

The Strange Situation protocol, devised by Ainsworth (Ainsworth *et al.* 1978) to evaluate the quality of the attachment relationship between a child and a carer is considered the 'gold standard' of attachment relationships but is time consuming to administer, and even more so to score, requiring a trained coder. For these reasons, while widely quoted in research, it is rarely used in clinical practice.

Formal tests

The use of formal tests is one area in which psychologists are in a unique position to give critical appraisal and to assist the court. Any test used should be reliable and valid and the reason for the use of the test should be laid out in the report, including the extent to which it can be used to give independent and valid information. In England, Wales and Northern Ireland, the *Framework for the Assessment of Children in Need and their Families* (Cox and Bentovim 2000a) provides a framework for understanding the needs of the child, the capacity of the parents and the environmental circumstances in which the child lives (see figure 2.14.1).

Figure 2.14.1 Framework for the assessment of children in need and their families

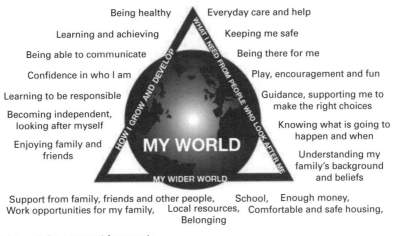

Figure 2.14.2 Integrated assessment framework

In Scotland the *Integrated Assessment Framework* (Scottish Executive 2005) serves a similar purpose (see figure 2.14.2). However, it lacks the pack of Questionnaires and Scales (Cox and Bentovim 2000b) which, with minimal training, can be used and interpreted by professionals from a variety of disciplines. The pack was produced with the aim of supplying an agreed set of measures, which could be administered for example by teachers, health visitors and social workers, as well as mental health professionals, so that the findings could be accepted across agencies and disciplines, without gaps or duplication.

Child custody

The standard legal test is that the decisions made must be in the best interests of the child, with many of the objectives in the UK framed in the Children Act 1989 and the Children (Scotland) Act 1995, which in turn reflect both the UN Convention on the Rights of the Child 1990 and the Human Rights Act 1998.

Article 9 of the UN Convention, which the UK ratified for all children in the UK except for asylum seekers, states:

1. States Parties shall ensure that a child shall not be separated from his or her parents against their will, except when competent authorities subject to judicial review determine, in accordance with applicable law and procedures, that such separation is necessary for the best interests of the child. Such determination may be necessary in a particular case such as one involving abuse or neglect of the child by the parents, or one where the parents are living separately and a decision must be made as to the child's place of residence.
2. In any proceedings pursuant to paragraph 1 of the present article, all interested parties shall be given an opportunity to participate in the proceedings and make their views known.
3. States Parties shall respect the right of the child who is separated from one or both parents to maintain personal relations and direct contact with both parents on a regular basis, except if it is contrary to the child's best interests.

The discussion then becomes why a child should not have contact with a parent, with the assumption that the ideal position is as above, with free access of the child to each parent.

Parental alienation syndrome

The concept of parental alienation (Gardner 1992), that is, the systematic denigration to the child of one parent by the other, such that the child is unable to perceive any value of the denigrated parent, is controversial. In its most extreme form, Gardner regards this as a form of 'brain washing' in which the child is 'programmed' by the custodial parent to express loathing and fear of the other parent, often with allegations of physical and sexual abuse. The child may seem to take full responsibility for their views, but these often emerge as rehearsed scripts, with simple, single incidents of less than perfect parenting given as blanket denunciation of the value of the parent. The motivation of the custodial parent (usually mother) seems to be the punishment of the other parent, with the real needs of the child lost in the search for revenge.

It is of course easier and safer for children to align themselves with the views of the parent with whom they spend the most time. However, few parents are perfect or all bad, and where the child is adamant that the other parent has no redeeming features, and seems to feel no guilt at expressing very extreme views of a parent, it should always be considered to what extent this reflects reality or an alignment of the child with a distorted view fuelled by interparental antagonism. A simple task like asking the child to write or, if too young, to describe three good things about mum and three things they don't like about mum, and the same task repeated with dad as the subject, may show whether the child can be discriminating in forming views based on his or her own experience.

The Bene Anthony Family Relations Test provides a non-threatening way for children to describe their views of family members (Bene and Anthony 1978).

Parents with mental health problems or learning difficulties

Particular difficulties can arise when a parent's capacity is compromised by learning difficulties or mental health problems. The Framework (Cox and Bentovim 2000a) and the HOME (Bradley and Caldwell 1988) between them again give evidence-based information on the adequacy of the home environment and the parent's ability to meet the needs of the child.

While, for example, postnatal depression has been repeatedly shown to be a risk factor for children's emotional wellbeing and cognitive development (Cogill *et al.* 1986; Murray, Hipwell and Hooper 1996), a prevalence of about 1 in 10 in the general population (O'Hara and Swain 1996) makes it unlikely that this would or should be grounds for assuming that a parent cannot provide adequate parenting for a child. While it might seem that more florid psychiatric disorders are of greater risk to children, interestingly, it appears that prolonged low-level parent–child interaction may be more damaging than interruptions due to brief disturbances in parental mental state, perhaps because children are more likely to be protected from contact with a parent who is psychotic while they are evidently unable to relate to the child (Perris 1966; Weissman, Paykel and Klerman 1972).

Also of concern is the involvement of the parents with drugs or alcohol, when this is to an extent that their preoccupation with their supply or lack of engagement with the child because of the effects of the drug may lead to neglect of the child's needs. This situation needs assessment over time, and in particular whether the parent is able to commit to getting help with their addiction in order to be able to offer the child a safe and loving environment. Demonstration of a capacity to change and the maintenance of change are best undertaken in a family centre or contact service which can offer therapeutic support as well as evidence-based evaluation of parenting. Such an assessment is unlikely to be carried out effectively and comprehensively in a single assessment, but psychologists can still play an important role in supporting colleagues in accessing effective, reliable and valid measures.

Report compilation

In writing a report it is helpful in providing structure if the format follows a standard pattern, although not all headings may be relevant in every case.

The following model is comprehensive.

a. Referral or instructions
b. Statement of qualifications and experience
c. Statement of independence
d. Sources of information
    i. Written or video documents
    ii. Each parent
    iii. Observation of each parent with each child
    iv. Observation of handover times
    v. Specific questionnaires or measures
    vi. Collateral informants
    vii. Child's views
e. The child's family structure and current arrangements for contact, education, healthcare, cultural and religious observances
f. The child's medical and developmental history
g. Current medical and psychological health of child
h. Current medical and psychological health of parents
i. Recommendations

In making recommendations, psychologists should be careful to stay within the remit of their task, which is to evaluate the possible options for child care and contact. Some judges can be touchy if they feel that their authority as decision makers is undermined. To avoid this it may be advisable to give a reasoned evaluation of more than one possibility. In essence, this is good practice writ large, as the examination of alternatives should form part of the decision making involved in writing the report.

RESOURCES

AACAP Official Action (1997a) 'Practice parameters for child custody evaluation'. *Journal of the American Academy Child and Adolescent Psychiatry*, 38 (supplement): 57s–58s.
    (1997b) Summary of the practice parameters for child custody evaluation. *Journal of the American Academy of Child and Adolescent Psychiatry*, 36: 1784–7.
HOME inventory: www.ualr.edu/crtldept/home4.htm
Powell, M. B. and Lancaster, S. (2003) Guidelines for interviewing children during child custody evaluations. *Australian Psychologist*, 38: 46–54.

REFERENCES

Ainsworth, M. D. S., Blehar, M. C., Waters, E. and Wall, S. (1978) *Patterns of Attachment: A Psychological Study of the Strange Situation*. Hillsdale, NJ: Erlbaum.
Bene, E. and Anthony, J. (1978) *Family Relations Test. Children's Version Manual*, 2nd edn. Oxford: NFER/Nelson.
Bradley, R. and Caldwell, B. (1988) Using the HOME Inventory to assess the family environment. *Paediatric Nursing*, 14: 97–102.
Bradley, R. H. and Corwyn, R. F. *et al.* (2000) Measuring the home environments of children and early adolescence. *Journal of Research on Adolescence*, 10: 247–88.
Cogill, S. R., Caplan, H. L., Alexandra, H., Robson, K. M. and Kumar, R. (1986) Impact of maternal postnatal depression on cognitive development of young children. *British Medical Journal*, 292: 1165–7.
Cox, A. D. and Bentovim, A. (2000a) *Framework for the Assessment of Children in Need and their Families*. London: HMSO.
    (2000b) *Questionnaires and Scales*. London: HMSO.
Crittenden, P. M. (1981) Abusing, neglecting, problematic, and adequate dyads: differentiating by patterns of interaction. *Merrill-Palmer Quarterley*, 27: 1–18.
Dunn, J. (2005) Daddy doesn't live here any more. *Psychologist*, 18: 28–31.
Gardner, R. A. (1992) *Parental Alienation Syndrome*. Cresskill, NJ: Creative Therapeutics.

Murray, L., Hipwell, A., and Hooper, R. (1996) The cognitive development of 5-year-old children of postnatally depressed mothers. *Journal of Child Psychology and Psychiatry*, 37: 927–35.

O'Hara, M. W. and Swain, A. M. (1996) Rates and risk of postpartum depression – a meta-analysis. *International Review of Psychiatry*, 8: 37–54.

Perris, C. (1966) A study of bipolar (manic-depressive) and unipolar recurrent depressive psychoses. *Acta Psychiatrica Scandinavica*, supplement, 194: 9–189.

Robb, A. (2006) Strategies to address clinical bias in the child custody evaluation process. *Journal of Child Custody*, 3: 45–69.

Scottish Executive (2005) *Integrated Assessment Framework*. Edinburgh: Scottish Executive.

Weissman, M. M., Paykel, E. S. and Klerman, G. L. (1972) The depressed woman as a mother. *Social Psychiatry*, 7: 98–108.

2.15 Parole decision making

Renée Gobeil and Ralph C. Serin

See also chapter 1.8 Investigative decision making, chapter 8.5 Evaluating offending behaviour programmes in prison.

Definition

Since most offenders are eventually released, it is important that a mechanism exists to ensure their timely and safe return to the community. To achieve this goal, most jurisdictions use parole, which allows certain offenders to serve a portion of their sentence in the community, supervised and subject to certain conditions. Two primary forms of parole exist: mandatory and discretionary. In mandatory parole, offenders are released after serving a set portion of their sentence or meeting some other codified milestone. Alternatively, offenders are released on discretionary parole when it is deemed appropriate to do so by a paroling authority, following explicit eligibility criteria regarding public safety issues and time served. Over the past decades, there have been considerable changes in the proportion of releases attributable to each type of parole. The use of discretionary release has diminished in some jurisdictions, including England and Wales (Parole Board for England and Wales, no date) and many American states (Tonry 1999). Other jurisdictions have seen the pendulum swing in the other direction. In Canada, for example, an expert panel recently recommended that mandatory conditional release be abolished in favour of exclusive use of discretionary parole (Sampson *et al.* 2007). Given that virtually all jurisdictions employ discretionary release with some offenders, often those convicted of more serious offences, discretionary parole will be the focus here.

The context for parole decisions

Typically, agencies granted the authority to reach parole decisions have a number of objectives: public safety; offender rehabilitation; consistent, fair and equitable treatment of offenders; and appropriate management of limited fiscal resources (see Collette 2007). These goals may potentially conflict. For instance, while a conservative release policy is effective in ensuring public safety, it is also very expensive in terms of incarceration costs and perhaps not fair. Further, a release strategy which changes according to operational realities (e.g. in response to institutional overcrowding) does not promote judicious treatment of offenders, nor does it consistently offer appropriate rehabilitation opportunities.

To add to the confusion, most policy documents offer parole decision makers limited specific guidance on how to reach their decisions. While numerous instruments have been developed to predict offenders' risk of reoffending, legislation and policy typically dictate that results from such instruments should not be considered in isolation in rendering release decisions. Indeed, in addition to risk, parole decision makers must consider factors outlined in their respective guiding documents, typically including such factors as psychological functioning, institutional adjustment, rehabilitation progress, release plans and victim impact statements. In one paroling authority's policy manual, the list of factors requiring consideration extends to nearly seven pages (Parole Board for England and Wales n.d.). Moreover, many jurisdictions' policy documents offer little instruction on how to weigh these differing factors. As a result, reconciling broad objectives, imprecise procedural guidelines, and case-specific factors can pose serious challenges to evidence-based practice in parole decision making.

A major obstacle in this reconciliation of competing factors is the traditional reliance on recidivism as the sole preferred indicator of quality parole decision making. This practice effectively limits investigation of effectiveness to offenders who were granted release. Given that the offenders most likely to be granted release are typically those with a lower risk profile, this process excludes from examination precisely those offenders of greater interest, as reoffending among higher-risk offenders may have particularly serious consequences. An exclusive focus on recidivism may also be problematic in instances where an offender's life circumstances change after release, such that the original release decision was appropriate, but the offender's risk status changed substantially afterwards (Douglas and Skeem 2005). In such cases, holding a parole authority accountable for subsequent reoffending presupposes an unrealistic level of foresight on the decision makers' part. For reasons such as these, it is important to widen the scope of research on parole decision making, both by viewing parole decision making as a process and by using multiple and varied indicators of quality parole decision making.

Factors influencing decision making

Though research on factors influencing parole decision making has not been voluminous, Caplan (2007) recently conducted a review in which he singled out institutional behaviour and offence history as the most important factors. Offenders with more extensive criminal histories or more serious institutional misbehaviour were less frequently granted discretionary parole, and when granted release, it was typically after having served a greater proportion of their sentence. There are a number of complications associated with reviewing this body of research. It is difficult to appraise results given the variety of research techniques and of factors used in studies. For instance, most researchers in the area have focused primarily or exclusively on offender-level factors. Some studies, however, have determined that decision-maker factors such as level of authoritarianism (Griffitt and Garcia 1979) and rehabilitative focus (Conley and Zimmerman 1982) are linked to parole decision outcome. Though an argument was made several decades ago for greater focus on decision-maker variables in parole decision making (Carroll 1978), research on this aspect has been limited. The scarcity of research in this area is disappointing, given that it precludes a full understanding of all the factors influencing parole decisions, and hence public safety.

Researchers have also investigated the processes followed in arriving at parole decisions. For instance, studies spanning more than three decades, involving paroling authorities deciding on whether to grant release in simulations of real cases, have found that parole decision makers tend not to consider all information available to them (Gobeil and Serin 2009; Wilkins *et al.* 1973). One explanation is that parole decision makers' expertise allows them to focus on the information which is most salient to parole outcome; however, researchers have also found considerable variability in parole decision makers' rank ordering of the importance of factors (Hassin 1984; Sacks 1977; Scott 1974). Porter, ten Brinke and Wilson (2009) found that some parole decision makers were more likely to grant discretionary release to those offenders who were actually at higher risk of reoffending. This interindividual variability is consistent with that found in other forensic decision-making areas (e.g. probation, Giles and Mullineux 2000; Dhami and Ayton 2001). Even if such variability is adaptive, it is nonetheless inconsistent with most jurisdictions' legislative or procedural guidelines. It is also not in line with the goals of consistency, fairness and equitable treatment held by most authorities.

In order to move towards the equity and higher benefit-to-cost ratio associated with evidence-based practice, it is necessary to attend to and expand research on parole decision making and parole outcome by developing flexible, actuarially anchored parole decision-making frameworks. Though research on parole outcome and parole decision making has grown, there is a disconnect between research and practice. In Canada, however, efforts to remedy this have begun. A structured decision-making framework (Serin 2004) has been implemented, after extensive testing, as a training tool for new parole board members. Research demonstrates that, overall, parole recommendations produced when using the framework result in lower rates of decision errors than traditional (i.e. unstructured) parole decision making (Gobeil *et al.* 2007). Moreover, by guiding parole decision makers to consider and explicitly address factors with demonstrated relevance in their decisions, the framework contributes to more equitable, transparent and defensible decision making.

Contributors to parole decision making

Given the volume of decisions made by paroling authorities, as well as the fact that in many jurisdictions, paroling authorities are distinct and separate from their corresponding correctional agency, paroling authorities typically find themselves collaborating with other agencies in order to reach quality release decisions. There are some advantages to this position, in that most correctional agencies, and some parole supervision agencies, have already begun to incorporate evidence-based practice. Paroling authorities are in the enviable position of being able to learn from their partners in this regard. This being said, collaboration with other agencies also has disadvantages. There are indications, at least in some jurisdictions, that parole decision makers do not consistently receive relevant information from their criminal justice system partners (Tidmarsh 1997). Typically, paroling agencies have access to reports from various parties having contact with offenders prior to and during their period of incarceration, including reports from judges, psychologists and frontline caseworkers. Research provides a number of suggestions for strengthening their contributions, which will be discussed with a focus on psychological reports, but which can easily be extended to reports from other sources.

Psychologists use a number of approaches in assessing risk, including unstructured clinical judgement and actuarial instruments, which make predictions of the likelihood of the offender engaging in a certain behaviour based on patterns previously found in similar groups. A considerable body of research demonstrates that actuarial assessments are more accurate than clinical judgements (Ægisdóttir *et al.* 2006; Grove and Meehl 1996). Indeed, there is evidence that some forensic clinicians are not aware which factors are predictive of risk of violence (Elgoben *et al.* 2002). Information provided by such clinicians to parole decision makers has the potential to be misleading (if factors which are not actually predictive are treated as predictors) or inadequate (if relevant factors are omitted).

Within this context, use of actuarial instruments in developing psychological reports for parole decision makers is crucial. Yet, even if such actuarial instruments are included in psychological reports, a number of cautions remain. In cases where actuarial instruments are used, clinicians' recommendations regarding risk of violence are still not consistently related to instrument results (Hilton and Simmons 2001; McKee, Harris and Rice 2007). Given that the incorporation of results from actuarial instruments generally increases accuracy, parole decision makers would be best served by psychological reports which emphasize and address actuarial results. The specific methods of presenting recommendations relating to risk should also be precise (e.g. percent likelihood statements), as general terms such as 'low risk' have been found to be very inconsistently interpreted and therefore of limited utility (Hilton *et al.* 2008). Finally, psychological reports must be free of jargon (Ackerman 2006). Reports which incorporate these points would better situate parole decision makers to be able to make accurate and high-quality decisions.

Conclusion

Campbell (2008, p. 81) recently characterized parole as the 'stepchild of the corrections system, largely ignored for many years'. She argued that not only had there been limited research in the area, but there had also been few active efforts to incorporate relevant research findings into decision-making practices and policy. Though this statement is pessimistic, at least the problem is now being noted, and a call for improvement has been made (Burke and Tonry 2006). Indeed, though research on parole decision making is scarce, this situation is changing (e.g. Caplan 2007; Huebner and Bynum 2006; Morgan and Smith 2005). There are numerous areas requiring attention. For instance, though extensive research has been conducted on the factors that predict reoffending, a second body of literature has begun to accumulate regarding the process of desistance from crime and, to date, this latter research has not been incorporated into parole decision making. Other emerging areas include the importance and impact of victim information (Morgan and Smith 2005), type of offence (Gobeil and Serin 2009; Turpin-Petrosino 1999) and re-entry initiatives (Petersilia 2001). Such research would profitably be incorporated into parole training and structured decision guidelines.

By including research findings such as these, paroling authorities can improve their ability to provide consistent, equitable and transparent release decisions. Reduction of decision errors increases public safety and enables substantial cost savings through reduced victim costs and lower rates of incarceration. In summary, given the advantages associated with this approach, it might easily be argued that a failure to move towards evidence-based parole decision making represents an ethical mis-step, neglecting the need for equitable treatment of offenders and attenuating community safety.

FURTHER READING

At a global level, persuasive arguments in support of parole are outlined in Burke and Tonry (2006), while arguments against conditional release are put forth by A. L. Solomon, V. Kachnowski and A. Bhati (2005) in *Does Parole Work? Analyzing the Impact of Postprision Supervision on Rearrest Outcomes* (Washington, DC: Urban Institute). An overview of how to incorporate evidence-based practice into parole decisionmaking is provided in Campbell (2008). Caplan's review (2007) provides more detail on factors found to be associated with parole decisions.

REFERENCES

Ackerman, M. J. (2006) Forensic report writing. *Journal of Clinical Psychology*, 62: 59–72.
Ægisdóttir, S., White, M. J., Spengler, P. M., Maugherman, A. S., Anderson, L. A., Cook, R. S. *et al.* (2006) The meta-analysis of clinical judgment project: fifty-six years of accumulated research on clinical versus statistical prediction. *The Counseling Psychologist*, 34: 341–82.
Burke, P. and Tonry, M. (2006) *Successful Transition and Re-entry for Safer Communities: A Call to Action for Parole*. Silver Spring, MD: Center for Effective Public Policy.
Campbell, N. M. (2008) *Comprehensive Framework for Paroling Authorities in an Era of Evidence-Based Practice*. Washington, DC: National Institute of Corrections.
Caplan, J. M. (2007) What factors affect parole: a review of empirical research. *Federal Probation*, 71: 16–19.

Carroll, J. S. (1978) Causal attributions in expert parole decisions. *Journal of Personality and Social Psychology*, 36: 1501–11.

Collette, R. (2007) The value of parole in a civilized society. *Journal of Community Corrections*, 17: 15–20.

Conley, J. A. and Zimmerman, S. E. (1982) Decision making by a part-time parole board: An observational and empirical study. *Criminal Justice and Behavior*, 9: 396–431.

Dhami, M. K. and Ayton, P. (2001) Bailing and jailing the fast and frugal way. *Journal of Behavioral Decision Making*, 14: 141–68.

Douglas, K. S. and Skeem, J. L (2005) Violence risk assessment: getting specific about being dynamic. *Psychology, Public Policy, and Law*, 11: 347–83.

Elgoben, E. B., Mercado, C. C., Scalora, M. J. and Tomkins, A. J. (2002) Perceived relevance of factors for violence risk assessment: a survey of clinicians. *International Journal of Forensic Mental Health*, 1: 37–47.

Giles, M. and Mullineux, J. (2000) Assessment and decision-making: probation officers' construing of factors relevant to risk. *Legal and Criminological Psychology*, 5: 165–85.

Gobeil, R., Scott, T.-L., Serin, R. C. and Griffith, L. (2007) A structured model of parole decision-making. Poster presented at the North American Corrections and Criminal Justice Psychology Conference, Ottawa, ON.

Gobeil, R. and Serin, R. C. (2009) Preliminary evidence of adaptive decision-making techniques used by parole board members. *International Journal of Forensic Mental Health*, 8: 97–104.

Griffitt, W. and Garcia, L. (1979) Reversing authoritarian punitiveness: the impact of verbal conditioning. *Social Psychology Quarterly*, 42: 55–61.

Grove, W. M. and Meehl, P. E. (1996) Comparative efficiency of formal (mechanical, algorithmic) and informal (subjective, impressionistic) prediction procedures: the clinical/statistical controversy. *Psychology, Public Policy and Law*, 2: 293–323.

Hassin, Y. (1984) Early release of Israeli prisoners – failure or success? In S. G. Chum (ed.), *Israel Studies in Criminology*, vol. 7, pp. 178–95. Chippenham: Antony Rowe Ltd.

Hilton, N. Z., Carter, A. M., Harris, G. T. and Sharpe, A. J. B. (2008) Does using nonnumerical terms to describe risk aid violence risk communication? Clinician agreement and decision making. *Journal of Interpersonal Violence*, 23: 171–88.

Hilton, N. Z. and Simmons, J. (2001) The influence of actuarial risk assessment in clinical judgments and tribunal decisions about mentally disordered offenders in maximum security. *Law and Human Behavior*, 25: 393–408.

Huebner, B. M. and Bynum, T. S. (2006) An analysis of parole decision making using a sample of sex offenders: a focal concerns perspective. *Criminology*, 44: 961–85.

McKee, S. A., Harris, G. T. and Rice, M. E. (2007) Improving forensic tribunal decisions: the role of the clinician. *Behavioral Science and the Law*, 25: 485–506.

Morgan, K. and Smith, B. L. (2005) Victims, punishment, and parole: the effect of victim participation on parole hearings. *Criminology and Public Policy*, 4: 333–60.

Parole Board for England and Wales (n.d.) *What Is the Parole Board?* Available online: www.paroleboard.gov.uk/Law1.htm (accessed 31 December 2007).

Petersilia, J. (2001) Prisoner reentry: public safety and reintegration challenges. *The Prison Journal*, 81: 360–75.

Porter, S., ten Brinke, L. and Wilson, K. (2009) Crime profiles and conditional release performance of psychopathic and non-psychopathic sexual offenders. *Legal and Criminological Psychology*, 14: 109–18.

Sacks, H. R. (1977) Promises, performance, and principles: an empirical study of parole decision making in Connecticut. *Connecticut Law Review*, 9: 347–423.

Sampson, R., Gascon, S., Glen, I., Louie, C. and Rosenfeldt, S. (2007) *Report of the Correctional Service of Canada Review Panel: A Roadmap to Strengthening Public Safety*. Ottawa, ON: Public Safety Canada.

Scott, J. P. (1974) The use of discretion in determining the severity of punishment for incarcerated offenders. *Journal of Criminal Law and Criminology*, 65: 214–24.

Serin, R. C. (2004) Release decision making manual. Unpublished manuscript submitted to Canada's National Parole Board.

Tidmarsh, D. (1997) Risk assessment among prisoners: a view from a parole board member. *International Review of Psychiatry*, 9: 273–81.

Tonry, M. (1999) *Reconsidering Indeterminate and Structured Sentencing: Issues for the 21st Century*. Washington, DC: US Department of Justice, National Institute of Justice.

Turpin-Petrosino, C. (1999) Are limiting enactments effective? An experimental test of decision making in a presumptive parole state. *Journal of Criminal Justice*, 27: 321–32.

Wilkins, L. T., Gottfredson, D. M., Robison, J. O. and Sadowsky, C. A. (1973) *Information Selection and Use in Parole Decision-Making: Parole Decision-Making Supplementary Report V*. Washington, DC: National Council on Crime and Delinquency.

2.16 Personality and crime

Sean Hammond

See also chapter 1.10 Personality theories and offending, chapter 2.20 Psychopathy.

Definitions

This chapter attempts to address the link between personality and criminal behaviour. Such a linkage inevitably implies a causal connection and this leads to strong views being exchanged, notably between those advocating a biosocial, personality-centred explanation for crime and those adopting a more sociological position (Sutherland 1949; Eysenck and Gudjonson 1989; Laub and Sampson 1991).

The fact is that some people engage in criminal behaviour and others do not. This behavioural differentiation is found within groups who share similar social conditions of economic hardship or instability. Clearly, individual differences must play a part in the choices people make that lead them towards criminality, but sociological explanations for crime should not be dismissed. Factors such as poverty and social change are indeed concomitant with increases in criminal activity, but if these are causal then they will work through psychological mechanisms. The difference between sociological and psychological explanations of crime is the level of analysis. For differential or personality psychologists the focus is upon explaining how the personal experience and character of the individual has led to the antisocial behaviour in question. The more sociological scientist uses a more general level of abstraction in which individual differentiation is implicitly viewed as error variance and the causal elements of criminal behaviour are found in the social or cultural context of the actor.

In light of the controversy surrounding the topic it is important first to be clear about the definitions we are using. For our purposes, the term 'personality' describes the character of an individual and this is based upon the observed pattern of behaviours that are typical of that person. Thus personality may be defined as a predisposition to behave consistently in a particular way. In other words, personality is a potential rather than something that may be directly observed and its nature is inferred from behaviour. In this way certain personality characteristics, particularly those termed personality disorders, may, to some extent, be inferred from pathological or criminal behaviours (Hare 1996; Lykken 1995; Millon *et al.* 1998). However, differential psychologists will typically work from the other direction and attempt to identify pre-existing and stable personality constructs that may have a causal role in criminal behaviour. These constructs are normally described as latent traits, implying their underlying influence upon all manner of behaviours. Thus we might expect someone with an elevated position on the extravert trait to be talkative or sociable in most situations. The behaviour may vary across social contexts but will be sufficiently consistent to be considered predictable. Only then does it pass muster as a personality trait.

Much of the research on personality and criminal behaviour has a descriptive focus, in which attention is drawn to the kinds of personality traits that appear most prevalent in samples of offending people. This body of work tends to identify an offending sample, measure them on some single or multitrait device and compare the obtained scores to those from a control or nonoffending sample (Fonseca and Yule 1995; Goma-i-Freixanet 2001). This kind of research is quite limited because it is predicated on the assumption that the offending sample will be homogeneous with regard to the traits in question, and this is almost never the case (Eysenck 1996).

Theories

There are few theoretical models that link personality to criminal behaviour and the most influential has been that of Hans Eysenck (1977). Building upon his biosocial model of personality, in which traits are the behavioural manifestations of neural substrates, Eysenck identifies three major personality traits that are associated with a greater probability of criminal behaviour. These are Extraversion (E), Neuroticism (N) and Psychoticism (P).

Individuals high on the extravert trait will tend to be both sociable and impulsive and this characteristic is based upon a biological predisposition towards cortical arousal. In Eysenck's theory, highly extravert individuals have low levels of cortical arousal and are thus prone to disinhibition and sensation-seeking behaviour. This low level of arousal makes such people less easily conditioned because they require higher levels of stimulation in order to learn, thus subtleties in early childhood conditioning are often missed. Eysenck (1996) further argues that the conditioning of a conscience will tend to inoculate people against antisocial behaviour. The Neurotic individual is emotionally unstable and labile and this is due, in Eysenck's model, to a highly reactive autonomic nervous system. The mixture of high E and high N will make antisocial behaviour more likely.

Psychoticism was added later to Eysenck's model of crime and personality (Eysenck and Eysenck 1976) and is less securely founded in biological theory although it is posited as a polygenetic trait. High P individuals will tend towards tough-minded attitudes, and will manifest cold and instrumental social behaviours. Originally, impulsivity was seen as an integral part of E but it was later recognized to be an important component of P (Eysenck and Eysenck 1976). It is pretty clear that while P may have greater salience to antisocial behaviour, it is theoretically less developed than E and N.

A great advantage of the Eysenckian approach is that it provides testable hypotheses with which to support or disconfirm the basic model. While there has been much research that has been broadly supportive of the theory (Eysenck and Gudjonsson 1989; Bartol and Bartol 2007; Carrascoa *et al.* 2006), there is also a body of research that is more equivocal (Farrington, Biron and LeBlanc 1982; Fonseca and Yule 1995; Van Dam, DeBruyn and Janssens 2007) and a recognition of limits to its general applicability (Palmer 2003). Two quantitative reviews of the link between personality and crime (Miller and Lynam 2001; Cale 2006) have shown that predictions around E are less well founded than for N and P. Blackburn (1993) concluded, on the basis of the equivocal findings for E, that Eysenck's theory is not well supported. One possible reason for this is the ambiguous position of impulsivity in the PEN model of personality, as this trait seems to carry a great deal of explanatory power.

It should also be recognized that the conditioning process underlying the biosocial models of crime could also predict an 'antisocialization' situation, in which the conscience of intraverts growing up in a criminal environment would be more likely to become conditioned for crime than their extravert peers (Rafter 2006).

Another theoretical model linking personality to crime is offered in Gray's Reinforcement Sensitivity Theory (Gray 1981). In this theory, which grew from a critique of Eysenck's E and N model, it is argued that there exist two motivating systems for regulating behaviour. The Behavioural Activation System (BAS) regulates responses to reward and is facilitated at the neuronal level by activation of dopaminergic neural pathways. High levels of BAS activity will lead to impulsive and sensation-seeking behaviour in situations associated with reward. The Behavioural Inhibition System (BIS), on the other hand, regulates responses to aversive stimuli. The BIS is viewed as a septo-hippocampal system, and high levels of BIS activity lead to behavioural inhibition and avoidance in situations with a perceived association with punishment.

The BIS–BAS model has clear implications for behaviour problems in children and this appears to be supported in the research literature (Quay 1986). For example, Colder and O'Connor (2004) were able to show on a sample of young children that strong BAS was associated with externalizing behaviour problems, while strong BIS predicted internalizing problems. An interesting study by Haskin (2007) showed that coping strategies can moderate the relationship between reinforcement sensitivity and antisocial behaviour. She was able to demonstrate this on a general sample of Australian adolescents and has proposed that this may serve as the basis for intervention work. This is very much in line with Eysenck's contention that treatment for antisocial individuals should be tailored to their personality.

Both Gray's and Eysenck's theories implicate impulsivity as a central element and this appears to link well with the General Theory of Crime (GTC) proposed by Gottfredson and Hirschi (1990) from a completely different, more sociological orientation. The GTC asserts that the central element of criminal behaviour is the absence of self-control. Self-control develops early in life probably due to parental example and early training, but once established is highly resistant to change. Individuals with low self-control do not consider the long-term consequences of their behaviour and their behaviour is marked by risk taking, sensation seeking and lack of thought. Pratt and Cullen (2000) carried out a quantitative review of research examining the GTC and they concluded low self-control is a very significant correlate of criminal activity. While Gottfredson and Hirschi's orientation is social rather than biosocial like Gray's and Eysenck's, it would appear clear that their central construct 'self-control' may be easily identified with impulsivity as described by Eysenck and Gray in its neuropsychological aspect.

Current position

While hugely influential, the Eysenkian model of personality is not the most widely adopted in current personality research. This honour would appear to fall upon the five-factor model (FFM) of personality traits (Costa and McRae

1992; Goldberg 1990). The FFM takes a lexical rather than a biosocial approach to defining personality and posits that there are five general personality traits with enough explanatory power to interactively account for most of the human behavioural repertoire. These factors are variously named, Extraversion (E), Neuroticism (N), Agreeableness (A), Conscientiousness (C) and Openness (O). Of course, it could be argued that A and C are components of P and that the FFM is simply a distortion of the PEN model of Eysenck, but there is ample evidence that these factors have, at least, lexical independence (John 1990; McRae 2001).

The link between the FFM and criminal behaviour has not been developed with any theoretical rigour except in relation to antisocial personality disorder (Widiger and Costa 1994). Miller and Lynam (2001), in a meta-analysis of studies linking personality traits to antisocial behaviour, concluded that low levels of A and C were consistently implicated. They also make the point that there is a clear overlap between Eysenck's P and the FFM factors A and C. However, as Wiebe (2004) points out, 13 of the 14 FFM studies they looked at used Antisocial Personality Disorder symptomatology as the dependent variable which, while informative, provides a rather indirect link to criminal behaviour.

One of the most important caveats in the study of personality and crime is the fact that criminals do not constitute a single homogeneous group. There is as much variety in style and character among people who break the law as there is among the law abiding. Most measures of personality traits demonstrate that the variance of offender samples is equivalent to that of non-offenders. The simplistic comparison of 'offender' and 'non-offender' groups by comparing aggregated personality profiles provides little insight into the role of personality in offending.

It should be obvious that different types of offence are driven by quite different motives and cognitions. Thus a child molester is likely to be quite different from a fraudster, just as a drunk driver convicted of culpable homicide is different from a serial sexual murderer. It is surely, then, naive to propose that a single underlying trait is predictive of *all* criminal activity. This point was made empirically in one of Eysenck's early studies (Eysenck, Rust and Eysenck 1977), in which 156 adult prisoners were divided into four groups on the basis of their offence (violent, theft, fraud, inadequate). The results showed a clear differentiation of the groups, with fraud offenders being low on P and N but high on E, while the 'inadequate' offenders were high on P and N but low on E.

A second issue that may serve to hinder research linking personality with crime is the fact that almost all personality measures are based upon self-report questionnaires. This requires a degree of self-knowledge of the participants and a willingness to describe their typical behavioural repertoire to the researcher through the medium of a structured set of questions. It may not be entirely surprising to find antisocial individuals to be less compliant and truthful than we might expect from a normative sample. In other words, the error associated with personality data is not likely to be insubstantial. Other strategies such as rater measures are rather more unwieldy but have been used successfully in assessing the personality of antisocial individuals (Blackburn 1995; Leahy 2007).

A study that neatly sidesteps this reliance upon self-report was conducted by Raine, Venables and Williams (1996). They concentrated on psychophysiological measures in a prospective study of adolescents, and were able to demonstrate a significant effect for conditioning and electrodermal lability in the expected direction between those participants who later went on to offend in adulthood.

Conclusion

This chapter opened with the claim that there is a schism between the sociological and psychological explanations of crime. However, the adversarial rhetoric of the two camps is perhaps unnecessary when we consider, for example, the GTC and its reliance on a characteristic very akin to Eysenck's and Gray's impulsivity. Sutherland (1949) himself stated that no crime is commited without a predisposition, although his favoured explanatory perspective was from the social and cultural level. Eysenck's and Gray's theories depend upon the socialization of individuals provided by their prevailing social context, although their favoured perspective is neuropsychological. The evidence certainly supports the contention that individual predispositions such as personality traits are important elements in criminal and antisocial behaviour. The level of analysis we choose to operate at dictates how useful we consider this fact to be.

REFERENCES

Bartol, C. and Bartol, A. (2007) *Criminal Behavior: A Psychosocial Approach*. New York: Pearson.

Blackburn, R. (1993) *The Psychology of Criminal Conduct*. Chichester: Wiley.

   (1995) Criminality and the interpersonal circle in mentally disordered offenders. *Criminal Justice and Behavior*, 25: 155–76.

Cale, E. M. (2006) A quantitative review of the relations between the 'Big 3' higher order personality dimensions and antisocial behaviour. *Journal of Research in Personality*, 40: 250–84.

Carrascoa, M., Barker, E. D., Tremblay, R. E. and Vitaro, F. (2006) Eysenck's personality dimensions as predictors of male adolescent trajectories of physical aggression, theft and vandalism. *Personality and Individual Differences*, 41: 1309–20.

Colder, C. R. and O'Connor, R. M. (2004) Gray's reinforcement sensitivity model and child psychopathology: laboratory and questionnaire assessment of the BAS and BIS. *Journal of Abnormal Child Psychology*, 32: 435–51.

Costa, P. T. and McRae, R. R. (1992) *Revised NEO Personality Inventory and NEO Five-Factor Inventory: Professional Manual*. Odessa, FL: Psychological Assessment Resources.

Eysenck, H. J. (1977) *Crime and Personality*, 3rd edn. London: Routledge & Kegan Paul.
  (1996) Personality and crime: where do we stand. *Psychology, Crime and Law*, 2: 143–52.

Eysenck, H. J. and Eysenck, S. B. G. (1976) *Psychoticism as a Dimension of Personality*. London: Hodder & Stoughton.

Eysenck, H. J. and Gudjonsson, G. (1989) *The Causes and Cures of Criminality*. New York: Plenum Press.

Eysenck, S. B. G., Rust, J. and Eysenck, H. J. (1977) Personality and the classification of adult offenders. *British Journal of Criminology*, 17: 169–79.

Farrington, D. P., Biron, L. and LeBlanc, M. (1982) Personality and delinquency in London and Montreal. In J. Gunn and D. P. Farrington (eds.), *Abnormal Offenders, Delinquency and the Criminal Justice System*, pp. 153–201. Chichester: Wiley.

Fonseca, A. C. and Yule, W. (1995) Personality and antisocial behaviour in children and adolescents: an enquiry into Eysenck's and Gray's theories. *Journal of Abnormal Child Psychology*, 23: 767–81.

Goldberg, L. R. (1990) An alternative description of personality: the big-five factor structure. *Journal of Personality and Social Psychology*, 59: 1216–29.

Goma-i-Freixanet, M. (2001) Prosocial and antisocial aspects of personality in women: a replication. *Personality and Individual Differences*, 30: 1401–11.

Gottfredson, M. and Hirschi, T. (1990) *A General Theory of Crime*. Stanford, CA: Stanford University Press.

Gray, J. A. (1981) A critique of Eysenck's theory of personality. In H. J. Eysenck (ed.), *A Model of Personality*, pp. 246–77. New York: Springer.

Hare, R. D. (1996) Psychopathy: a clinical construct whose time has come. *Criminal Justice and Behaviour*, 23: 25–54.

Haskin, P. A. (2007) Reinforcement sensitivity, coping and delinquent behaviour in adolescents. *Journal of Adolescence*, 30: 739–49.

John, O. P. (1990) The Big-Five taxonomy: dimensions of personality in the natural language and in questionnaires. In L. A. Pervin (ed.), *Handbook of Personality: Theory and Research*, pp. 66–100. New York: Guilford Press.

Laub, J. H. and Sampson, R. J. (1991) The Sutherland–Glueck debate: on the sociology of criminological knowledge. *American Journal of Sociology*, 96: 1402–40.

Lykken, D. (1995) *The Antisocial Personalities*. Mahwah, NJ: Erlbaum.

McRae, R. R. (2001) Five years of progress: a reply to Block. *Journal of Research in Personality*, 35: 108–13.

Miller J. D. and Lynam, D. R. (2001) Structural models of personality and their relation to antisocial behaviour: a meta-analytic review. *Criminology*, 39: 765–98.

Millon, T., Simonsen, E., Birket-Smith, M. and Davis, R. D. (1998) *Psychopathy: Antisocial, Criminal and Violent Behavior*. New York: Guilford Press.

Palmer, E. J. (2003) Offending behaviour: moral reasoning. *Criminal Conduct and the Rehabilitation of Offenders*. Cullompton: Willan.

Pratt, T. C. and Cullen, F. T. (2000) The empirical status of Gottfredson and Hirschi's general theory of crime: a meta-analysis. *Criminology*, 38: 931–64.

Quay, H. (1986) The behavioral reward and inhibition systems in childhood behaviour disorder. In L. M. Bloomingdale (ed.), *Attention Deficit Disorder: Research in Treatment, Psychopharmacology and Attention*, vol. 3, pp. 176–86. New York: Spectrum.

Rafter, N. H. (2006) H. J. Eysenck in Fagin's kitchen: the return to biological theory in 20th century criminology. *History of the Human Sciences*, 19: 37–56.

Sutherland, E. H. (1949) *White Collar Crime*. New York: Dryden Press.

Raine, A., Venables, P. H. and Williams, M. (1996) Better autonomic conditioning and faster electrodermal half-recovery time at age 15 years as possible protective factors against crime at 29 years. *Developmental Psychology*, 32: 624–30.

Van Dam, C., De Bruyn, E. and Janssens, J. (2007) Personality, delinquency, and criminal recidivism. *Adolescence*, 42: 763–77.

Widiger, T. A. and Costa, P. T. (1994) Personality and personality disorders. *Journal of Abnormal Psychology*, 103: 78–91.

Wiebe, R. P. (2004) Delinquent behavior and the five-factor model: hiding in the adaptive landscape? *Individual Differences Research*, 2: 38–62.

2.17 Personality disorder classification in forensic settings

Todd E. Hogue

Definition

Whether used in common parlance or in formal diagnostic terms, the concept of personality disorder is laden with an evaluative edge. Within the forensic settings, personality disorder as a DSM-IV classification (American Psychiatric Association 1994), psychopathic disorder as a Mental Health Act classification (MHA 1983) and psychopathy as a clinical concept (Hare 2003) often overlap both in common usage and clinical assessment. Although much has been written about the categorical or dimensional nature of personality disorder (see Livesley 2007), and the way in which psychopathy and personality disorder are related (see Blackburn 2007), less has been written about the practical aspects of assessing personality disorder in an applied forensic context (Moore and Hogue 2000). This chapter focuses on the practical issues to consider when making personality disorder classifications, as defined by DSM, within forensic settings.

Origins and further developments

Although there is a comprehensive literature relating to personality theory and research (see Pervin and John 1999), general personality theory does not always fit neatly with a diagnostic approach to the assessment of personality disorder. The American Psychiatric Association (APA), *Diagnostic and Statistical Manual* (DSM-IV and DSM-IV-TR: APA 1994, 2000) and the World Health Organization (WHO), *International Classification of Diseases* (ICD-10: WHO 1992) are the current dominant methods of classifying personality disorder. Widiger (2001) provides an overview of the development of current classification systems, although he warns that 'A single DSM-IV

Table 2.17.1 DSM-IV criteria for presence of Personality Disorder

Criteria A	An enduring pattern of inner experience and behaviour that deviates markedly from the expectations of the individual's culture and is manifested in at least two of the following areas: cognition, affectivity, interpersonal functioning, or impulse control
Criteria B	This enduring pattern is inflexible and pervasive across a broad range of personal and social situations
Criteria C	and leads to significant distress or impairment in social, occupational, or other important areas of functioning
Criteria D	The pattern is stable and of long duration, and its onset can be traced back at least to adolescence or early childhood
Criteria E	The pattern is not accounted for as a manifestation or consequence of another mental disorder
Criteria F	and is not due to the direct physiological effects of a substance (e.g. a drug of abuse, a medication, exposure to a toxin) or a general medical condition (e.g. head trauma)

Adapted from DSM-IV-TR, American Psychiatric Association 2000, p. 686.

personality disorder diagnosis will fail to adequately describe the complexity and individuality of any particular person's personality profile.'

Classification of personality disorder within DSM-IV-TR (APA 2000) is based on identification of a number of traits presented by the individual. It is important to remember that it is only when these traits are 'inflexible and maladaptive and cause significant functional impairment or subjective distress do they constitute Personality Disorders' (APA 2000, p. 686). To constitute personality disorder a number of diagnostic criteria must be met (see table 2.17.1).

Personality traits are defined as 'enduring patterns of perceiving, relating to, and thinking about the environment and oneself that are exhibited in a wide range of social and personal contexts'. It is only when the traits are 'inflexible and maladaptive and cause significant functional impairment or subjective distress that they constitute Personality Disorder' (DSM-IV-TR: APA 2000, p. 686).

The traits and related disorders are grouped into three clusters. Cluster A covers individuals who are often seen as odd and eccentric and includes Paranoid, Schizoid and Schizotypal Personality Disorders. Cluster B covers disorders seen as dramatic, emotional and erratic and includes Antisocial, Borderline, Histrionic and Narcissistic Personality Disorders. While Cluster C covers those appearing anxious and fearful and includes Avoidant, Dependent and Obsessive-Compulsive Personality Disorder.

Method

A number of instruments have been developed to assess and classify Personality Disorder (see Clark and Harrison 2001), with a range of new instruments being developed specifically to assist in DSM classification (Schottle 2000). Most of these instruments rely on either self-report or a structured interview and are designed to improve the otherwise poor reliability of unstandardized clinical judgement. Although short-term inter-rater and test–retest reliability can be good, long-term test–retest reliability, the convergence between different instruments and the relationship between instruments using patients vs informants as sources of information remain generally poor or insufficient (Schottle 2000). In addition, although such measures were developed to ensure good reliability and validity, their use within forensic settings and applicability with forensic populations is much less clear.

Within the United Kingdom the most frequently used tool for the classification of personality disorder is the International Personality Disorder Examination (IPDE: Loranger 1999), although a range of other tools are also used. Like most, if not all, personality disorder measures the IPDE was initially validated on a non-forensic population (Loranger *et al.* 1994), although it is now the main personality disorder assessment used within the DSPD (Dangerous and Severe Personality Disorder) Programme (DSPD Programme 2005).

Evaluation

While there is extensive information about personality disorder (e.g. Livesley 2001), much less information is available about personality disorder and its assessment in forensic populations. A number of studies have examined the use of personality disorder classifications in forensic populations (see Blackburn *et al.* 2003; Coid 2003). However, Blackburn (2000) mainly highlights critical issues related to the use of classification systems with mentally disordered offenders and the need to include a wider range of assessment information than to rely solely on a classificatory system. A range of issues are raised, including comorbidity, reliability and validity, the use of dimensional vs categorical models, and the relationship of classification systems to dimensional methods of conceptualizing personality. Much less attention has been paid to the process of undertaking an accurate, valid and reliable personality disorder classification with forensic populations. This lack of focus is in part likely due to many psychologists seeing classificatory systems as having little clinical utility (British Psychological Society 2006).

Accurate assessment is always an issue, and forensic settings and populations present additional challenges; the DSM manual warns that in forensic settings, 'there are significant risks that diagnostic information will be misused or misunderstood' (APA 2000, p. xxxii). Relatively little attention has been paid to the conditions necessary to ensure accurate assessments of personality and personality disorder in forensic settings (see Moore and Hogue 2000). There are particular motivational and situational factors which need to be considered when undertaking any kind of forensic assessment. This is particularly the case when undertaking personality disorder assessments which may have long-term implications for the individual, such as in a DSPD assessment or referral.

Applications

The following issues should be considered when undertaking assessment of personality disorder within a forensic context.

Sufficient information

To undertake an accurate assessment it is critical that sufficient information is available regarding the individual's functioning and behaviour across their life course. Often this is not the case. It is important that information regarding early life events and functioning, prior to their current institutionalization, is available to ensure that the enduring and pervasive pattern of the disorder is evidenced across multiple domains and situations. It is not sufficient to only identify traits within a single setting; adequate information must be available to assess early conduct disorder and the appearance of traits in late adolescence and early adulthood.

Observation, collateral and multiple sources of information

It is important to observe the extent to which the individual's behaviour is consistent over time and in interpersonal contexts. As such, accurate information about how an individual functions within, and outside, the forensic setting is important. Is evidence of personality traits observed when the individual interacts with a range of different people, including, for example, security, education or therapy staff? Do traits only manifest themselves when interacting with certain individuals? Does the trait/behavioural presentation occur across all settings, including ward behaviour and when in education, treatment and other settings? To what extent does an institutional context restrict or facilitate trait presentation? For example, the current presentation of traits relating to impulsive behaviours may be difficult to identify due to the controlling nature of forensic environments, where individuals may appear avoidant due to the secure setting.

A collaborative assessment process

Moore and Hogue (2000) highlighted using a range of assessment measures and strategies, including actively involving the individual in the assessment process. Working collaboratively with the client increases the likelihood that they will be more open and report both their life history and behaviour in a more accurate manner. As such, part of the assessment should be engaging the individual in the assessment and providing feedback which is likely to improve both the clarity of the classification and the therapeutic alliance with the patient (Tyre 1998).

Understanding and utilizing motivation

It is important to consider motivational factors related to the completion of the assessment. In forensic settings denial of behaviour that is likely to be criticized can be a rational response to the situation (Rogers and Dickey 1991). Individuals in forensic settings may be motivated by a range of factors such as the belief that having a mental disorder or personality disorder may be to their advantage, or disadvantage, depending on where they are within the criminal justice system. Understanding if individuals are motivated to increase or decrease the presentation of traits, depending on their motivational stance, helps the assessor to weigh the validity of the information provided. Attending to such individualized motivational factors (Jones 2002) is likely to improve the accuracy of the assessment and increase engagement with the patient, thereby providing a more accurate assessment of the full range of functioning. In addition, if the assessment is motivational in nature it will act as a positive link into developing an appropriate treatment plan increasing the overall level of therapeutic engagement.

Specific measures

In general terms, assessment measures for personality disorder classification are either self-report or interview based (Clark and Harrison 2001). Given that different assessment tools vary in their underlying assumptions and administration, it is important to adhere to the requirements of the specific measure or measures you are using. However, most assessments were not designed for forensic populations where individuals may feign or inflate trait presentation, and this needs to be considered within the assessment. For example, the IPDE (Loranger 1999) recognizes that its assessment is essentially a self-report measure and that the individual's response may differ from collateral or historical information and current presentation. An assessor override can be used to rate items differently than as clinically presented. However, it is important that the assessment does not drift into being primarily based on collateral information and the assessor's opinion, through the use of assessor override. This is of particular concern if systems are not in place to look at *all* available information, in a consistent fashion, to avoid a self-confirming negative bias in the outcome.

Multiple source classification

In undertaking an assessment a critical factor is to ask if you are undertaking a specific assessment (e.g. IPDE) or more generally a DSM classification. If you are undertaking a DSM classification, it may be appropriate to use a wider range of information. Given that the relative convergence between measures of personality disorder is low (Schottle 2000), one alternative is to use information from all available sources. Spitzer (1983) suggests a LEAD (Longitudinal, Expert, All Data) method of classification in which expert raters make consensus classifications using information from all sources, including interviews with the patient, significant others and mental health professionals. Such a model can produce a reliable personality classification (Pilkonis *et al.* 1991), and the application of such a model has been used successfully in forensic settings for the classification of personality disorder (Lindsay *et al.* 2006). In this model the assessor then weighs up the evidence, across information sources, for the presence or absence of each trait and, based on this, decides on the applicability in that case.

Diagnostic overshadowing

The assessment of forensic populations presents a number of additional difficulties. Forensic populations show high comorbidity between personality disorder diagnoses and other clinical syndromes (Coid 2003), and DSM classification is strongly related to levels of psychopathy across a number of diagnostic categories (Blackburn 2007). Similarly, there is a tendency for clinicians to diagnose in a hierarchical manner, whereby once the disorder has been identified they are less likely to assess fully for the presence of other disorders (Widiger 2001). In forensic settings it is particularly likely that the presence of high Psychopathy (Hare 2003) or Antisocial Personality Disorder will overshadow diagnostic classifications. As a result, trait presentation may be attributed to levels of psychopathy or ASPD rather than other coexisting personality disorders (e.g. Narcissistic or Paranoid Personality Disorder). It is important that individuals are assessed for the full range of traits, accepting that comorbidity between different traits and classifications of personality disorder exists.

Utility of diagnostic assessment

A DSM classification is often seen as having limited clinical utility. It is important that negative views of the assessor do not unduly influence the outcome and utility of the assessment being undertaken. If done correctly, the classification process allows the clinician to examine a wide range of trait information as presented over time. This is useful in that there is a growing research literature about the applicability of different treatment interventions for different personality disorder classifications (Duggan *et al.* 2007). The DSM structure can also be integrated with other more general aspects of personality assessment and used as a method for deciding broad treatment strategies for different patient groups. Sperry (2003) presents the use of the DSM structure in a particularly clinically useful manner which highlights the available evidence for different therapeutic approaches as well as a structure for working with personality disorder.

Conclusion

One can debate the use of different assessment systems; however, if one is to undertake a DSM-IV classification of personality disorder, then it is important that an accurate classification is made. This chapter highlights the practical issues that need to be considered in order to obtain an accurate classification with a forensic population.

FURTHER READING

Two handbooks provide full and comprehensive coverage:

Livesley, W. J. (2001) *Handbook of Personality Disorder: Theory, Research and Treatment.* New York: Guilford Press.

Sperry, L. (2003) *Handbook of Diagnosis and Treatment of DSM-IV-TR Personality Disorders,* 2nd edn. New York: Brunner-Routledge.

REFERENCES

American Psychiatric Association (APA) (1994) *Diagnostic and Statistical Manual of Mental Disorders,* 4th edn (DSM-IV). Washington, DC: American Psychiatric Association.

  (2000) *Diagnostic and Statistical Manual of Mental Disorders,* 4th edn, text revision (DSM-IV-TR). Washington, DC: American Psychiatric Association.

Blackburn, R. (2000) Classification and assessment of personality disorders in mentally disordered offenders: a psychological perspective. *Criminal Behaviour and Mental Health,* 10: s8–s32.

  (2007) Personality disorder and antisocial deviance: comments on the debate on the structure of the psychopathy checklist-revised. *Journal of Personality Disorder,* 21: 142–59.

Blackburn, R., Logan, C., Donnelly, J. and Renwick, S. (2003) Personality disorders, psychopathy and other mental disorders: co-morbidity among patients at English and Scottish high-security hospitals. *The Journal of Forensic Psychiatry and Psychology,* 14: 111–37.

British Psychological Society (2006) *Understanding Personality Disorder: A Report by the British Psychological Society.* Leicester: British Psychological Society.

Clark, L. A. and Harrison, J. A. (2001) Assessment instruments. In W. J. Livesley (ed.), *Handbook of Personality Disorder: Theory, Research and Treatment,* pp. 277–306. New York: Guilford Press.

Coid, J. W. (2003) The co-morbidity of personality disorder and lifetime clinical syndromes in dangerous offenders. *Journal of Forensic Psychiatry and Psychology,* 14: 341–66.

DSPD Programme (2005) *Dangerous and Severe Personality Disorder (DSPD) High Secure Services for Men: Planning and Delivery Guide.* London: Home Office. Available online: www.dspdprogramme.gov.uk/media/pdfs/High_Secure_Services_for_Men.pdf.

Duggan, C., Huband, N., Smailagic, N., Ferriter, M. and Adams, C. (2007) The use of psychological treatments for people with personality disorder: a systematic review of randomized control trials. *Personality and Mental Health,* 1: 95–125.

Hare, R. D. (2003) *The Hare Psychopathy Checklist – Revised.* Toronto: Multi-Health Systems.

Jones, L. (2002) An individual case formulation approach to the assessment of motivation. In M. McMurran (ed.), *Motivating Offenders to Change: A Guide to Enhancing Engagement in Therapy,* pp. 31–54. Chichester: Wiley.

Lindsay, W. D, Hogue, T. E, Taylor, J., Mooney, P., Steptoe, L., Johnston, S., O'Brien, G. and Smith, A. H. W. (2006) Two studies on the prevalence and validity of personality disorder in three forensic intellectual disability samples. *Journal of Forensic Psychology and Psychiatry,* 17: 485–506.

Livesley, W. J. (ed.) (2001) *Handbook of Personality Disorder: Theory, Research and Treatment*. New York: Guilford Press.

(2007) A framework for integrating dimensional and categorical classifications of personality disorder. *Journal of Personality Disorder*, 21: 199–224.

Loranger, A. W. (1999) *IPDE: International Personality Disorder Examination: DSM-IV and ICD-10 Interviews*. Odessa, FL: Psychological Assessment Resources, Inc.

Loranger, A. W., Sartorius, N., Andreoli, A., Berger, P., Buchheim, P., Channabasavanna, S. et al. (1994). The International Personality Disorder Examination, IPDE. The WHO/ADAMHA international pilot study of personality disorders. *Archives of General Psychiatry*, 51: 215–24.

Moore, E. and Hogue, T. E. (2000) Assessment of personality disorder for individuals with offending histories. *Criminal Behaviour and Mental Health*, 10: s34–s49.

Pervin, L. A. and John, O. P. (eds.) (1999) *Handbook of Personality: Theory and Research*. New York: Guilford Press.

Pilkonis, P. A., Heape, C. L., Ruddy, J. and Serrao, P. (1991) Validity in the diagnosis of personality disorders: the use of the LEAD standard. *Psychological Assessment*, 3: 46–54.

Rogers, R. and Dickey, R. (1991) Denial and minimization among sex offenders; a review of competing models of deception. *Annals of Sex Research*, 4: 49–63.

Schottle, C. K. W. (2000) New instruments for diagnosing personality disorder. *Current Opinion in Psychiatry*, 13: 605–9.

Sperry, L. (2003) *Handbook of Diagnosis and Treatment of DSM-IV-TR Personality Disorders*, 2nd edn. New York: Brunner-Routledge.

Spitzer, R. L. (1983) Psychiatric diagnosis: are clinicians still necessary? *Comprehensive Psychiatry*, 24: 399–411.

Tyre, P. (1998) Feedback for the personality disordered. *Journal of Forensic Psychiatry*, 9: 1–4.

Widiger, T. A. (2001 Official classification systems. In W. J. Livesley (ed.), *Handbook of Personality Disorders: Theory, Research and Treatment*, pp. 60–83. New York: Guilford Press.

World Health Organization (WHO) (1992) *The ICD-10 Classification of Mental and Behavioural Disorders: Clinical Descriptions and Diagnostic Guidelines*. Geneva: World Health Organization.

2.18 Polygraphy

Don Grubin

See also chapter 4.3 Interpersonal deception detection.

Definition

The polygraph is commonly referred to as a lie detector. It has its origins in nineteenth-century theories regarding the relationship between emotion, deception and associated physiological responses. The first attempt to record such a link in a scientific manner is usually credited to the Italian criminologist Cesare Lombroso who, in the 1890s, measured variations in pulse and blood pressure in the course of police interrogation.

The modern polygraph developed from instruments designed in the United States between 1915 and 1938 by William Marston (also known as the creator of Wonder Woman, whose magic lasso could make all who were encircled in it tell the truth), John Larson and Leonarde Keeler, mainly for use in criminal investigation. The Keeler polygraph, which was patented in 1939, made simultaneous recordings of changes in cardiovascular activity, breathing and skin conductance (caused by sweating), and is the template on which current polygraphs are based. The original instruments incorporated pens which wrote on moving paper, giving rise to the name 'polygraph' (literally, many writings), but data are now digitalized and presented on a computer screen.

Although the polygraph is closely associated with lie detection, a specific physiological 'lie response' has never been demonstrated, and is unlikely to exist. The polygraph, therefore, does not, and cannot, detect lies. Instead, it records physiological activity indicative of arousal in the autonomic nervous system, a part of the central nervous system largely outside conscious control which regulates the body's internal environment (including activity in the cardiovascular and respiratory systems, and sweating). Polygraphy is based on the notion that the act of deception causes autonomic arousal; while the responses measured by the polygraph are not unique to deception, nor are they always engendered by it, the aim of the polygraph examiner is to establish a 'psychological set' in the examinee that will increase the likelihood that any observed arousal is the result of deceptive responding.

The polygraph examination

The polygraph examination starts with a lengthy pre-test interview in which the questions to be asked during the test itself are determined, and the 'psychological set' is established. The individual is then asked a small number of questions to which 'yes' or 'no' responses are required while attached to the polygraph instrument, and data are recorded. This is followed by a post-test interview during which any significant responses are discussed. This may then develop into formal interrogation.

There are different types of polygraph test format:

The Relevant–Irrelevant Technique: This was the original test format used when polygraphy was first introduced, but it is employed less commonly now. It consists of a small number of 'relevant' questions that relate to the target issue (for example, 'Did you take the money from the safe?'), and 'irrelevant' ones not related to the issue of concern and to which the answer is known by both examiner and examinee (such as, 'Is today Monday?'). Stronger physiological responses to relevant questions are said to be indicative of deception.

The Comparison Question Technique: This, and its variants, is the most widely used test format today. Responses to relevant questions (as with the relevant–irrelevant test, related to the issue of concern) are compared with those to questions that are designed to elicit an arousal response in all subjects because of their similarity to the matter under investigation (for example, in an examination regarding theft, questions about having stolen in other situations). The theory is that the truthful innocent examinee will show a greater response to the comparison question, while the deceptive guilty one will respond more to the relevant question. These tests can either be single or multi-issue in nature.

The Concealed Information Test (also known as the Guilty Knowledge Test): In this test, the examinee is presented with multiple choice questions, the answers to which are known only to the examiner and to an individual who had knowledge about the event of concern. The basis of the test is that the examinee with relevant knowledge will respond most strongly to the correct alternative, while the examinee without such knowledge would do so only by chance; if a number of such questions can be put, then the likelihood is small that anyone other than the person with the relevant concealed information would respond consistently to the correct answers. For example, questions might relate to the object of a theft, the place from which the theft occurred, the date the theft occurred, and so on. Clearly, opportunities to administer this type of test are limited.

At the conclusion of the test the examiner reaches one of three conclusions: deception indicated, no deception indicated, or inconclusive (in some settings examiners instead use the terms 'significant response', 'no significant response' or no opinion). Some examiners base their decision on whether or not an individual has been deceptive wholly on the polygraph charts. Others also take into account the behaviour of the examinee during the polygraph interview and test.

Mode of action

The theoretical basis of polygraphy is unclear. A number of theories have been put forward to explain the relationship between deception and arousal, including:
- the fear of detection or of punishment
- a conditioned response to the act of lying, or to stimuli linked to the relevant questions
- conflict arising from lying in the face of a natural inclination to tell the truth
- orientation to threat, together with a 'defensive reaction', in this case the 'threat' inherent in the questions being asked.

None of these theories, however, adequately accounts for what takes place during a polygraph examination. For instance, strong responses are observed even in respect of questions which would not normally be associated with either fear or arousal. For example, if individuals are asked simply to pick a number and then to respond negatively when asked about which number they picked, a fairly innocuous situation, marked reactions are nevertheless typically seen. Similarly, an orienting response might be expected to a 'threat' question (for example, a relevant question in a Comparison Question exam), even when answered truthfully.

But the reality is that the theoretical basis for polygraphy is not clearly understood. It is likely, however, that the emotional salience of the question, an autobiographical memory of one's actions, and the additional cognitive work associated with lying are all involved in generating the responses observed during a polygraph test.

The accuracy and utility of polygraph testing

Although there continues to be argument about polygraph accuracy, an authoritative review of the research literature carried out by the National

Academies of Science (National Research Council 2003) concluded that accuracy is in the region of 81 to 91%, which it described as 'well above chance, though well below perfection' (–4). This compares well with studies which show that the ability of most people to differentiate truth telling from deception is little better than chance.

Polygraph accuracy, however, is dependent on test type and application. Most accurate is the concealed information test, and the comparison question technique when only a single issue is involved. Multi-issue tests, which are used in screening contexts to determine whether an individual may have engaged in one or more types of problematic behaviour (for example, in pre-employment vetting, monitoring employees for security violations, or the post-conviction testing of sex offenders on probation or parole), are believed to be less accurate, although difficulty in researching this issue means that data are limited.

Critics of polygraphy argue that because of its vulnerability to counter-measures, i.e. physical or psychological techniques that enable individuals to appear to be answering truthfully when they are in fact being deceptive, *in vivo* accuracy will be less than that found in research studies. Such methods exist, and individuals can be trained to use them; indeed, there are websites on the internet that offer advice of varying quality about them. To succeed, however, individuals must also have feedback on their responses when attached to the polygraph, something that is not readily available to most examinees.

Polygraph proponents argue that even in the absence of precise figures regarding accuracy, the polygraph has substantial utility because of its ability to elicit disclosures from examinees. There are numerous anecdotal reports to this effect in respect of criminal investigations, vetting for security breaches in intelligence agencies, and various similar applications, but data are limited. The exception relates to sex offender testing (typically referred to as Post-Conviction Sex Offender Testing, or PCSOT), where there is a growing body of evidence to demonstrate that polygraph does result in the disclosure of significant information, both quantitative and qualitative, in respect of past and current behaviour (see e.g. Grubin 2008).

It is also claimed that in addition to eliciting disclosures, polygraphy acts as a deterrent to those who might otherwise engage in problematic behaviour. Apart from sex offender testing, however, where there is a small amount of evidence demonstrating deterrence, this effect is based more in theory than empirical findings.

Controversies

Polygraph testing has been criticized because of a lack of standardization in testing procedures, variation in examiner technique, experience and skill, poor regulation of examiners, the possibility of false confessions and its susceptibility to countermeasures. Nevertheless, it is widely used in the United States as well as in many other countries, with supporters arguing that all of these problems can be overcome with proper training, supervision and testing guidelines. In the US, practically all federal (including military) and numerous local law enforcement agencies employ the polygraph in criminal investigations, in the pre-employment vetting of potential employees (although the 1988 Employee Polygraph Protection Act outlawed this latter use by private-sector employers), and in disciplinary proceedings, while PCSOT is believed to be used in the majority of sex offender treatment programmes.

A particular issue in respect of polygraph testing relates to base rates of deception. With an error rate of between 10 and 20%, there will be significant numbers of false positive results (that is, truthful individuals reported as deceptive) when the incidence of deception in a population is low. Because of this, the National Academy of Sciences review argued that for polygraphy to be viable there should be an underlying base rate of deception of at least 10% so that an acceptable balance between false positive and false negatives can be achieved, a threshold that is not reached in many screening settings in particular. Proponents of polygraph testing in this context, however, argue that so long as it forms just part of the decision-making process a relatively high false positive rate is not a major hindrance.

The use of polygraphy in court is another area that generates fierce debate. In the United States, polygraph evidence was typically disallowed under the 1923 *Frye* ruling, which required scientific evidence to be sufficiently established to have gained general acceptance in the scientific community. However, in 1993 the Supreme Court determined in *Daubert* v. *Merrell Dow Pharmaceuticals* that the *Frye* standard was too narrow, and instead the admissibility of expert evidence should be determined on a case by case basis, depending on its relevance, reliability, and the existence of a known error rate and established standards. As of 2007, polygraph evidence was accepted in nineteen states and nine of the twelve federal circuits. Its standing in the legal systems of other countries varies, but many will allow disclosures made in the course of polygraph examination, even if the exam outcome itself is not made known to the jury.

Conclusion

Supporters of polygraphy argue that when used by well-trained examiners and interpreted in conjunction with other techniques of information gathering, it can both assist in detecting deception and facilitate the disclosure of relevant information. Although others question its scientific validity, when used prudently polygraphy would seem to have a role to play in a range of applications where credibility needs to be established. It is clear, however, that the empirical and theoretical foundation to support polygraph testing is relatively thin. Until more data is available, the claims of both supporters and critics need to be viewed with caution.

FURTHER READING

A good overview of the science of polygraphy and issues associated with its use can be found in National Research Council (2003).

Accounts of the various polygraph test formats and applications are contained in M. Kleiner (2002) *Handbook of Polygraph Testing* (London: Academic Press). The chapter in this book by Honts and Amato on countermeasures provides a good critique of this issue.

Working groups of the British Psychological Society have produced two critical reports relating to polygraphy: British Psychological Society (1986) Report of the working group on the use of the polygraph in criminal investigation and personnel screening, *Bulletin of the British Psychological Society*, 39: 81–94; and British Psychological Society (2004) *A Review of the Current Scientific Status and Fields of Application of Polygraphic Deception Detection. Final Report from the Working Party* (Leicester: British Psychological Society).

For critical reviews of polygraph testing in sex offenders see T. P. Cross and L. Sax (2001) Polygraph testing and sexual abuse: the lure of the Magic Lasso, *Child Maltreatment*, 6: 195–206, and G. Ben-Shakhar (2008) The case against polygraph testing, *Legal and Criminological Psychology*, 13: 191–207. The counter-argument in support of such use is provided in D. Grubin (2008) The case for polygraph testing of sex offenders, *Legal and Criminological Psychology*, 13: 177–89.

Two interesting and imaginative studies investigating polygraph accuracy are described in A. Ginton *et al.* (1982) A method for evaluating the use of the polygraph in a real life situation, *Journal of Applied Psychology*, 67: 131–7, and F. Horvath and J. Widacki (1978) An experimental investigation of the relative validity and utility of the polygraph technique and three other common methods of criminal identification, *Journal of Forensic Science*, 23: 596–601.

Those interested in the history of polygraph testing should see D. Grubin and L. Madsen (2005) Lie detection and the polygraph: a historical review, *British Journal of Forensic Psychiatry and Psychology*, 16: 357–69, or the more detailed story told in K. Alder (2007) *The Lie Detectors: The History of an American Obsession* (New York: Free Press).

REFERENCES

Grubin, D. (2008) The case for polygraph testing of sex offenders. *Legal and Criminological Psychology*, 13: 177–89.

National Research Council (2003) *The Polygraph and Lie Detection. Committee to Review the Scientific Evidence on the Polygraph. Division of Behavioral and Social Sciences and Education.* Washington, DC: The National Academies Press.

2.19 Post-traumatic stress disorder

Adria Pearson, Heidi La Bash and Victoria Follette

See also chapter 5.1 Assessing and reporting work-related stress.

Definition

Traumatic stress and its impact on the human experience have been recognized across a very wide range of cultures and historical eras. Descriptions of this psychological phenomenon can be found in literature as broad as Ulysses' Odyssey to the Koran and the Bible (Shay 1994). Focused study of traumatic stress, in more recent history, was spurred by the large numbers of World War I combatants returning from active duty, and suffering what was then described as shell shock. Efforts to aid in the readjustment of active-duty military increased during World War II. Repatriation and the lobbying of the US Vietnam veterans resulted in the formal recognition of post-traumatic stress disorder (PTSD) in the third edition of the *Diagnostic and Statistical Manual of Mental Disorders* (DSM-III) (American Psychiatric Association 1980).

The DSM-III diagnosis of PTSD required an event, then described as 'outside the normal range of human experience', that resulted in feelings of 'intense horror and helplessness' (APA 1980). Research and clinical work since that time suggests that events experienced as traumatic (i.e. resulting in traumatic stress symptoms) were not outside statistically normative experience. For example, over the past thirty years, the incidence of rape experiences reported to mental health professionals has increased, with some studies indicating that 13 per cent of women will experience an adult rape. What was once dubbed 'rape syndrome' (Resick 2001) is now understood as a constellation of trauma-related symptoms, not unlike other traumas which are generally considered to be life threatening, with feelings of helplessness and horror. Combat exposure and sexual assault remain the primary events triggering PTSD in men and women, respectively, but a large number of events can trigger traumatic stress reactions and PTSD. These include natural disasters, motor vehicle accidents, terrorist events, homicides, violent crimes and the sudden death of a loved one (Kessler et al. 1995; Norris 1992).

It is normal to experience stress reactions after being exposed, directly or indirectly, to an event that represents a serious threat to self or others. It is when these normative reactions to life-threatening events extend beyond a month and interfere significantly in daily functioning, that an individual may meet a PTSD diagnosis, as defined in the DSM-IV-TR (APA 2000). Other criteria required to be diagnosed with PTSD include symptoms of:

a. re-experiencing (e.g. repeated dreams about the trauma, hallucinations, intense psychological reaction to thoughts or objects that are associated with the trauma, rumination);

b. avoidance and numbing (e.g. feelings of detachment, restricted range of emotions, efforts to avoid trauma-related thoughts or places);

c. increased arousal (e.g. hypervigilance, exaggerated startle response, difficulty sleeping or concentrating; APA 2000).

While outside the scope of this summary, it is important to note that exposure to a potentially traumatic event may induce a range of responses as described in the DSM, including adjustment disorder, bereavement, acute stress disorder or dissociative disorder.

Assessment

Psychological assessment may be used for diagnostic purposes, treatment planning and to evaluate the effectiveness of treatment both in clinical and research settings. The extant literature on trauma and PTSD reviews four primary assessment methods: structured diagnostic interviews; self-report questionnaires; functional analytic clinical assessment; and psychophysiological assessment. The effectiveness of any combination of these methods and the specific measures may best be determined by the assessment goals, type of trauma, administration time and method, and research design.

The process of assessing trauma, PTSD and symptom severity was addressed in a 1995 conference by the National Institutes of Mental Health and the National Center for PTSD. Ten recommendations from the conference are summarized as follows: clinical interviews should provide valuable clinical information with reliability and validity; structured diagnostic interviews that provide both dichotomous and continuous rating of PTSD symptoms are preferred; symptom frequency, intensity, distress and duration should be assessed; level of impairment and disability resulting from the symptoms is important information to gather; it is essential to evaluate components of the traumatic event and the severity of the reaction to that event; instruments which have been evaluated as to their differential impact across gender, culture and ethnic groups are preferred; self-report instruments should meet the American Psychological Association's 'Standards for Educational and Psychological Tests'; asking questions that include perceived life threat, harm, injuries, frequency, duration and age are recommended; a full assessment for other Axis I disorders with a structured clinical interview was recommended; and behaviourally anchored terminology versus specific words such as 'rape' or 'abuse' were recommended when interviewing an individual.

In consideration of these recommendations, assessment should focus both on the trauma(s) specifically as well as yielding diagnostics, and should also be comprehensive with regard to comorbid psychological problems. A comprehensive review of all trauma and PTSD assessment measures is beyond the scope of this chapter. A review of the reliability and validity of widely used structured clinical interviews and self-report questionnaires can be found in the following references: Foa, Keane and Friedman (2000), Adams and Sutker (2001) and Barlow (2001). Follette and Ruzek (2006) provide a thorough review of functional analytic clinical assessment. A review of psychophysiological measures can be found in Keane and Wilson (2004).

Structured diagnostic interviews and self-report measures

The first step in assessing the impact of a potentially traumatic event is to identify the nature and specific details of the traumatic exposure, including assessing if it meets DSM-IV-TR 'traumatic event' criterion (Fairbank, Ebert and Caddell 2000). There is disagreement on the most effective way to identify whether the trauma is significant enough to meet the description of the DSM-IV 'traumatic event' criterion (Fairbank, Ebert and Cadell 2000). However, employing both dichotomous and continuous ratings of trauma and the subsequent impact of trauma in assessment provides information on the relative impact of the trauma on life functioning, symptom severity and impairment due to current symptoms. This information may provide a more specific and thorough assessment, thereby increasing the effectiveness in diagnostics, treatment planning and treatment process and outcome evaluation. The Clinician Administered PTSD scale (CAPS) (Blake *et al.* 1990) and the Structured Interview for PTSD (SI-PTSD) (Davidson, Smith and

Kudler 1989) are two widely used clinical interviews which provide both dichotomous and continuous data. The PTSD checklist (PCL) developed by researchers at the National Center for PTSD in Boston has high reliability and validity, and has a high correlation with the CAPS (Keane, Weathers and Foa 2000) The Los Angeles Symptom Checklist (LASC) is another self-report measure that covers a range of traumas and has good psychometric properties (King *et al.* 1995).

Functional analytic clinical assessment

A functional analytic assessment may be used in conjunction with structured clinical interviews and self-report questionnaires to gain an understanding of the relationship between a behaviour, its antecedent events and consequences that maintain the behaviour in a specific context (Follette and Naugle 2006). Functional assessments can enhance the specificity of standard assessment measures by differentiating the topography of the behaviour (i.e. its form, what it looks like, client descriptions) from the function of the behaviour (i.e. the maintaining effect of the behaviour). This is important as different behaviours may serve a similar function for an individual. Functional assessment differentiates the topography of the behaviour (what it looks like, what a person reports about it) from the function of the behaviour (i.e. what the maintaining effect of the behaviour is). The process of functional assessment is to identify behaviours that have similar functions for the individual, and developing functional classes from this assessment. This process guides treatment, whereby 'target behaviours' (ones to be addressed in treatment) are identified by form and function. By its nature, functional assessment is contextually based, and therefore specifically addresses individual differences in traumatic experience and subsequent symptom constellations. In addition, functional assessment includes behaviourally specific questions, is continuous, and in conjunction with other assessment measures yields diagnostic information. Because the identification of functional classes is a comprehensive process (involving various areas of an individual's life and functioning), comorbid psychological issues may be identified.

Psychophysiological assessment

Psychophysiological assessment has been evaluated as a diagnostic tool for PTSD across several trauma populations. Over the past thirty years of research of psychophysiological assessment, studies have included combat veterans

(Keane *et al.* 1985; Blanchard *et al.* 1986; Keane *et al.* 1998; Carson *et al.* 2000; Beckham *et al.* 2002), survivors of motor vehicle accidents (Blanchard *et al.* 1996), and survivors of personal injury and/or sexual assault (McDonagh-Coyle *et al.* 2001). The prior references are only examples representing a very large existing body of literature on the topic. A meta-analysis of this research (Pole 2007) provides a thorough review of research on psychophysiological assessment tools, modes of assessment, and conclusive findings of differences between PTSD and non-PTSD populations in physiological variables. Keane and Wilson (2004) also provide a summary of the utility and methodology of psychophysiological assessment of trauma. Pole's (2007) meta-analysis shows PTSD populations as having overall heightened physiological responses when compared with adults in non-PTSD populations. Common physiological measurements assessing physiological reactivity have included heart rate, systolic and diastolic blood pressure, skin conductance and facial electromyography (Pole 2007). Common methods of psychophysiological assessment are categorized by Pole (2007). These include evaluation of resting physiology, response to trauma-related visual and audio cues (i.e. as in exposure tasks) (Elsesser, Sartory and Tackenberg 2004), measurement of physiology following a startle response, and measurement during and following imagined trauma-related scenarios. Therefore, methodology of psychophysiological assessment has a wide variety of options for clinicians or researchers depending on the assessment goal. In concordance with the NIMH/NC-PTSD guidelines, psychophysiological measurement may be a useful tool to objectively measure symptom severity and duration, and also as a conjunctive diagnostic tool. A limitation to research on the efficacy of psychophysiological measurements of PTSD is that the research has focused predominately on male combat veterans. Pole (2007) states this may limit the generalizability of the effectiveness of these measurements to other trauma populations. Another potential limitation for psychophysiological assessment may be the availability of assessment tools to clinicians either in office or assessing patients outside the office. A handbook by Fahrenberg and Myrtek (1996) provides a comprehensive review of ambulatory measurement of psychophysiological data and comparisons to laboratory measurements and methodologies.

Comorbid conditions

Substance use disorders, mood disorders and other anxiety disorders are the most commonly occurring comorbid conditions with PTSD (Pratt, Brief and

Keane 2006). Therefore, as suggested by the NIMH/NC-PTSD guidelines, a comprehensive assessment for co-occurring psychological disorders is recommended, using either a clinical interview or other psychometrically sound self-report measures. It is important to remember that individuals with a trauma history may not be forthcoming about reporting the trauma in clinical settings. This may be due to fear of a negative reaction to disclosing the trauma, including disbelief and blame, or the client's inability to recognize the experience as traumatic and understand the impact on current life functioning (Resick and Calhoun 2001). Behaviourally specific language is more useful in gaining more detailed information that will represent a continuous report of the client's experience.

When assessing PTSD, it is important to use a multi-method approach to attain accurate continuous and dichotomous measurements of the trauma exposure and its impact on the client. Attention to population characteristics and individual characteristics, such as gender, age and ethnicity, may reveal aspects of the presenting problem that may require extra attention, including potentially comorbid conditions.

Secondary trauma

In addition to becoming familiar with empirically based procedures to assess traumatic stress symptomatology in clients, it is also important to become familiar with empirically based procedures to assess those who work with traumatized populations. It is not uncommon for first responders, police officers, mental health professionals and others to experience psychological distress when working with trauma survivors. Conceptualizations of this phenomenon have been called secondary trauma, vicarious trauma and compassion fatigue (Figley 1995; McCann and Pearlman 1990).

Figley (1995) describes secondary trauma as the 'cost of caring,', with professionals experiencing characteristics associated with PTSD, including substance abuse, depression, somatic complaints and sleep disturbances. Secondary trauma may occur as a result of a professional's empathy with and internalization of the traumatic experiences of their clients (Figley 1995; McCann and Pearlman 1990). Risk factors for development of secondary traumatization include: (a) identification with the dead and survivors of a disaster; (b) working with child survivors; (c) low levels of social support; (d) number and length of exposures; (e) a prior personal history of trauma; (f) prior treatment for a psychological disorder; and (g) less experience as a helping professional with a lack of supervision (Levin and Greisberg 2003). Vicarious traumatization may impair the functioning of trained helpers in both their professional and personal lives. To remain healthy and effective, it is important to periodically monitor and assess those working with trauma survivors to circumvent any long-term problems.

FURTHER READING

The DSM provides a formal definition of PTSD and Figley's work details aspects of secondary victimization.

REFERENCES

Adams, H. E. and Sutker, P. B. (eds.) (2001) *Comprehensive Handbook of Psychopathology*, 3rd edn. New York: Springer.

American Psychiatric Association (1980) *Diagnostic and Statistical Manual of Mental Disorders*, 3rd edn (DSM-III). Washington, DC: American Psychiatric Association.

(2000) *Diagnostic and Statistical Manual of Mental Disorders*, 4th edn, text revised (DSM-IV-TR). Washington, DC: American Psychiatric Association.

Barlow, D. H. (ed.) (2001) *Clinical Handbook of Psychological Disorders,* 3rd edn. New York: Guilford Press.

Beckham, J. C., Vrana, S. R., Barefoot, J. C., Feldman, M. E., Fairbank, J., Moore, S. D. (2002) Magnitude and duration of cardiovascular responses to anger in Vietnam veterans with and without post-traumatic stress disorder. *Journal of Consulting and Clinical Psychology*, 20: 228–34.

Blake, D. D., Weathers, F. W., Nagy, L. M., Kaloupek, D. G., Klauminzer, G., Charney, D. S. and Keane, T. M. (1990) A clinical rating scale for assessing current and lifetime PTSD: the CAPS-1. *Behavior Therapist*, 18: 187–8.

Blanchard, E. B., Kolb, L. C., Gerardi, R. J., Ryan, P. and Pallmeyer, T. P. (1986) Cardiac response to relevant stimuli as an adjunctive tool for diagnosing post-traumatic stress disorder in Vietnam veterans. *Behavior Therapy*, 17: 592–606.

Blanchard, E. B., Hickling, E. J., Buckley, T. C., Taylor, E. A., Vollmer, A. and Loos, W. R. (1996) Psychophysiology of post-traumatic stress disorder related to motor vehicle accidents: replication and extension. *Journal of Consulting and Clinical Psychology*, 64: 742–51.

Carson, M. A., Paulus, L. A., Lasko, N. B., Metzger, L. J., Wolf, J., Orr, S. P. and Pittman, R. K. (2000) Psychophysiologic assessment of posttraumatic stress disorder in Vietnam nurse veterans who witnessed injury or death. *Journal of Consulting and Clinical Psychology*, 68: 890–7.

Davidson, J., Smith, R. and Kudler, H. (1989) Validity and reliability of the DSM-III criteria for posttraumatic stress disorder: Experience with a structured interview. *Journal of Nervous and Mental Disease*, 177: 336–41.

Elsesser, K., Sartory, G. and Tackenberg, A. (2004) Attention, heart rate and startle response during exposure to trauma-relevant pictures: a comparison of recent trauma victims and patients with post-traumatic stress disorder. *Journal of Abnormal Psychology*, 113: 289–301.

Fahrenberg, J. and Myrtek, M. (eds.) (1996) *Ambulatory Assessment: Computer Assisted Psychological and Psychophysiological Measures in Monitoring and Field Studies*. Seattle: Hogreff & Huber.

Fairbank, J. A., Ebert, L. and Caddell, J. M. (2000) Posttraumatic stress disorder. In H. E. Adams and P. B. Sutker (eds.), *Comprehensive Handbook of Psychopathology*, pp. 183–210. New York: Kluwer Academic/Plenum.

Figley, C. R. (1995) Compassion fatigue as secondary traumatic stress disorder: an overview. In C. R. Figley (ed.), *Compassion Fatigue*, pp. 1–20. Levittown, PA: Brunner/Mazel.

Foa, E. B., Keane, T. M. and Friedman, M. J. (2000) Guidelines for treatment of PTSD. *Journal of Traumatic Stress*, 13: 539–88.

Follette, V. M. and Ruzek, J. I. (eds.) (2006) *Cognitive-Behavioral Therapies for Trauma*, 2nd edn. New York: Guilford Press.

Follette, W. and Naugle, A. E. (2006) Functional analytic clinical assessment in trauma treatment. In V. M. Follette and J. I. Ruzek (eds.), *Cognitive Behavioral Therapies for Trauma*, 2nd edn, pp. 17–33. New York: Guilford Press.

Keane, T. M., Fairbank, J. A., Caddell, J. M., Zimering, R. T. and Bender, M. E. (1985) A behavioral approach to assessing and treating post-traumatic stress disorder in Vietnam veterans. In C. R. Figley, (ed.) *Trauma and Its Wake*, pp. 257–94. New York: Brunner/Mazel.

Keane, T. M., Kolb, L. C., Kaloupek, D. G., Orr, S. P., Blanchard, E. B., Thomas, R. G. *et al.* (1998) Utility of psychophysiology measurement in the diagnosis of posttraumatic stress disorder: results from a Department of Veterans Affairs cooperative study. *Journal of Consulting and Clinical Psychology*, 66: 914–23.

Keane, T. M., Weathers, F. W. and Foa, E. B. (2000) Diagnosis and assessment. In E. B. Foa, T. M. Keane and M. J. Friedman (eds.), *Effective Treatments for PTSD*, pp. 18–36. New York: Guilford Press.

Keane, T. M. and Wilson, J. P. (2004) *Assessing Psychological Trauma and PTSD*, 2nd edn. New York: Guilford Press.

Kessler, R. C., Sonnega, A., Bromet, E., Hughes, M. and Nelson, C. B. (1995) Posttraumatic stress disorder in the National Comorbidity Survey. *Archives of General Psychiatry*, 52: 1048–60.

King, L. A., King, D. W. Leskin, D. and Foy, D. (1995) The Los Angeles Symptom Checklist: a self-report measure of stress disorder. *Assessment*, 2: 1–17.

Levin, A. P. and Greisberg, S. (2003) Vicarious trauma in attorneys. *Pace Law Review*, 24: 245.

McCann, L. and Pearlman, L. A. (1990) Vicarious traumatization: a framework for understanding the psychological effects of working with victims. *Journal of Traumatic Stress*, 3: 131–49.

McDonagh-Coyle, A., McHugo, G. J., Friedman, M. J., Schnurr, P. P., Zayfert, C. and Descamps, M. (2001) Psychophysiological reactivity in female sexual abuse survivors. *Journal of Traumatic Stress*, 14: 667–83.

Norris, F. H. (1992) Epidemiology of trauma: frequency and impact of different potentially traumatic events on different demographic groups. *Journal of Clinical and Consulting Psychology*, 60: 409–18.

Pole, N. (2007) The psychophysiology of posttraumatic stress disorder: a meta analysis. *Psychological Bulletin*, 133: 725–46.

Pratt, E. M., Brief, D. J. and Keane, T. M. (2006) Recent advances in psychological assessment of adults with posttraumatic stress disorder. In V. M. Follette and J. I. Ruzek (eds.), *Cognitive Behavioral Therapies for Trauma*, 2nd edn, pp. 34–61. New York: Guilford Press.

Resick, P. A. (2001) *Stress and Trauma*. Philadelphia, PA: Taylor & Francis.

Resick, P. and Calhoun, K. S. (2001) Posttraumatic stress disorder. In D. Barlow (ed.), *Clinical Handbook of Psychological Disorders*, 3rd edn, pp. 60–113. New York: Guilford Press.

Shay, J. (1994) *Achilles in Vietnam: Combat Trauma and the Undoing of Character*. New York: Atheneum.

2.20 Psychopathy

David Cooke

See also chapter 2.17 Personality disorder classification in forensic settings.

Definition

Psychopathy is an important forensic construct: for example, in the context of violence risk assessment failure to assess psychopathy could constitute professional negligence (Hart 1998). Psychopathy is a personality disorder, that is, a chronic disturbance in an individual's relations with self, others and their environment resulting in distress or failure to fulfil social roles and obligations (American Psychiatric Association 2000). Personality disorders affect how individuals think, feel and behave: disturbance and dysfunction are typically long-standing in nature, starting in adolescence or early adulthood. Specifically, psychopathic personality disorder (PPD) can be regarded as having six aspects. Interpersonally, those with PPD are not only pathologically dominant, being described as antagonistic, domineering, deceitful and manipulative, but also, they may suffer from attachment difficulties, being detached, uncommitted and unempathic. In terms of emotional functioning they can be characterized as lacking anxiety, empathy and emotional depth, while cognitively they may be suspicious, intolerant and inflexible. Their sense of self is frequently distorted; they may be self-centred and have a sense of being invulnerable, unique or entitled. Behaviourally they are unreliable, reckless and aggressive (Cooke et al. 2006).

Significance in forensic contexts

PPD has broad forensic significance. Group studies indicate that PPD may be associated with future violence (Leistico et al. 2008) and is thus relevant to violence risk assessment in prisons, forensic psychiatric settings, workplace violence and child access assessments (but see below for important caveats). Those suffering from PPD are less amenable to standard forms of treatment; in general, their engagement with treatment is limited – they frequently drop out – they make poorer progress and they may interfere with the treatment of others. Critical features of the disorder include deceptiveness, impulsivity and failure to stick to rules, which can make those with PPD hard to interview, manage and monitor.

Origins of the construct

The association between psychopathic-like traits and violence has long been recognized; relevant accounts are available in the Bible and the Icelandic Sagas (Hoyersten 2001). The pattern has been recognized in many societies, including pre-industrial ones, for example, the Inuit of north west Alaska and the Yoruba tribe of Nigeria (Murphy 1976). Systematic clinical descriptions – albeit inchoate descriptions – can be indentified in the case studies of Pinel and Pritchard. The fundamental contribution of these nosologists was to argue that mental disorder may be present even where reason can be shown to be intact (Berrios 1996). Other clinicians in the nineteenth century described mental disorders characterized by disturbance of volition or emotion, variously described as *manie sans delire, monomania, moral insanity* and *folie lucide* (Millon 1981). These descriptions had a purpose that was essentially forensic. To ensure the relevance of their testimony the nineteenth-century alienists – or 'mad' doctors – had to extend their boundaries beyond 'total insanity' to include other forms of disorder. In the twentieth century a number of authors provided rich clinical descriptions of PPD (e.g. Cleckley 1976; Henderson 1939; Schneider 1958). Modern methods of evaluation have evolved from these descriptions.

Methods of evaluation

Psychopathy and cognate constructs can be assessed using a variety of procedures, including self-report (e.g. Psychopathic Personality Inventory; Lilienfeld and Andrews 1996), clinical criteria (e.g. DSM-IV or ICD-10: American Psychiatric Association 2000; World Health Organization 1992) or, most commonly in the forensic arena, the Psychopathy Checklist Revised (PCL-R: Hare 2003) and Psychopathy Checklist: Screening Version (Hart,

Cox and Hare 1995; Hart and Wilson 2008). Professional opinion warns against the use of self-report methods for assessing any personality disorder in forensic practice (British Psychological Society 2006); this concern is heightened when PPD is concerned because deceptiveness is a key diagnostic feature. A major contribution of the PCL-R has been the development of systematic ways of making judgements based on multiple sources – file review and interview – in order to combat deceptiveness and to provide a lifetime diagnostic perspective.

The PCL-R is used extensively in forensic practice; indeed, Tolman and Mullendore (2003) suggested that it is the most frequently used tool in risk assessment. Its use has increased dramatically (Walsh and Walsh 2006). Hare (2003) contended that 'Perhaps the PCL-R *saves* lives … because it helps to keep very dangerous people in prison' (p. 16, emphasis in original). Others have been less sanguine, suggesting that PCL-R scores potentially have profoundly prejudicial effects (Bersoff 2002; DeMatteo and Edens 2006; Freedman 2001; Leygraf and Elsner 2007). The key issue in forensic settings is that expert evaluators should be aware of, guard against and acknowledge limitations of the PCL-R. This is particularly important given the serious nature of decisions that take account of PCL-R scores (Edens and Petrila 2006). Just three potential limitations or concerns will be considered here; namely, problems with reliability in clinical settings, limitations of comparison groups, and the challenge of bridging the gap between group findings and the individual case.

One area of increasing concern is the level of reliability of ratings that may typically be achieved in forensic practice (Cooke and Michie 2007; Edens and Petrila 2006; Murrie *et al.* 2007). Ethical forensic practice requires practitioners to maximize their reliability and here four steps may assist. The first step is ongoing education and training, not only regarding the research base of the instrument, but also regarding advanced clinical skills. These advanced clinical skills would include techniques for interviewing these challenging individuals to ensure the collection of relevant information and would also include techniques for generating case formulations to ensure the appropriate application of the information collected (Logan and Johnstone in press). The second step is ensuring the availability of comprehensive file information; the quality of file information influences both the magnitude and reliability of scores. The third step is the use of multiple raters in high-stakes cases: average ratings should be eschewed; consensus ratings should be sought. The fourth step is the implementation of audit systems – including peer review – for the detection of rater drift.

A second area of concern is the fact that the impact of gender, age, culture, comorbid disorders – amongst other things – on scores remains unclear (e.g. Cooke and Michie 1999; Nichita and Buckley 2007; Nicholls, Odgers and Cooke 2007; Salekin 2006). (See Hare 2003, for another perspective.)

A third area of concern is not peculiar to the PCL-R but is endemic in forensic psychology: the problem of moving from group findings to inferences about an individual for the purposes of a court or other tribunal. There is an important disjunction between the perspective of science and the perspective of the law; while science seeks universal principles that apply across cases, the law seeks to apply universal principles to the individual case. Bridging these perspectives is a major challenge for psychology (Faigman 2007). Statistical predictions at the individual level are unreliable (Cooke and Michie 2007; Leygraf and Elsner 2007). Other approaches are necessary.

For psychological evidence concerning PPD to be relevant to decisions about future risk it must, in the opinion of the expert, *cause*, to some degree, the risk for future violence in *this individual* (Grisso 1986; Hart 2001; Heilbrun 2001; Morse 1978). One of the reasons that the PCL-R is associated with future violence (e.g. Leistico *et al.* 2008) – *at the aggregate level* – is because it captures a number of potential risk processes for violence (Cooke 2008). The assessor in their risk formulation must disaggregate these processes and identify those which apply to the individual they are managing. For example, the nature of the risk – and the risk management plan – of an individual who poses a violence risk because he or she is pathologically dominant, possesses a sense of entitlement, and who construes others as having malevolent intent towards him or her would be different to the management strategy for someone who is callous, reckless and impulsive. Both individuals may pose a risk as a consequence of their specific psychopathic traits; however, the psychological processes, the topography of their risk – and thereby the interventions required – would be quite different. While traditionally the PCL-R has been used as a psychometric instrument in forensic evaluations, it can, and perhaps should, be interpreted qualitatively as a form of structural professional judgement.

A final area of concern is conceptual rather than practical. The tautology inherent in defining psychopathy with reference to criminal behaviour has long been recognized. Blackburn (1988) observed that to understand the relationship between personality disorder and criminal behaviour the two constructs must be measured separately. It has been argued elsewhere that the inclusion of criminal behaviour in models and measures of psychopathy cannot be supported either empirically (Cooke, Michie and Skeem 2007) or conceptually (Skeem and Cooke in press a and b).

Conclusions

Psychopathic personality disorder has long been recognized as an important forensic construct. It has relevance for violence, treatability and manageability. It is a construct that can have a disproportionate influence on decision making, and ethical forensic practice requires practitioners to take cognizance of the limitations of our current assessments.

FURTHER READING

Comprehensive overviews of the construct of psychopathy and its forensic relevance can be found in C. J. Patrick (ed.) (2006) *Handbook of Psychopathy* (New York: Guilford Press) and Felthous and Sass (2007a, 2007b).

REFERENCES

American Psychiatric Association (2000) *Diagnostic and Statistical Manual of Mental Disorders*, 4th edn, text revision (DSM-IV-TR). Washington, DC: American Psychiatric Association.

Berrios, G. E. (1996) *The History of Mental Symptoms: Descriptive Psychopathology since the Nineteenth Century*. Cambridge: Cambridge University Press.

Bersoff, D. (2002) Some contrarian concerns about law, psychology and public policy. *Law and Human Behavior*, 26: 565–74.

Blackburn, R. (1988) On moral judgements and personality disorders: the myth of psychopathic personality revisited. *British Journal of Psychiatry*, 153: 505–12.

British Psychological Society (2006) *Understanding Personality Disorder: A Report of the British Psychological Society*. Leicester: British Psychological Society.

Cleckley, H. (1976) *The Mask of Sanity*, 5th edn. St Louis: Mosby.

Cooke, D. J. (2008) Psychopathy as an important forensic construct: past, present and future. In D. Canter and R. Zukauskiene (eds.), *Psychology and Law: Bridging the Gap*. Aldershot: Ashgate.

Cooke, D. J., Hart, S. D., Logan, C. and Michie, C. (2006) Evaluating the construct of psychopathic personality disorder: the development of a comprehensive clinical assessment. (in preparation).

Cooke, D. J. and Michie, C. (1999) Psychopathy across cultures: North America and Scotland Compared. *Journal of Abnormal Psychology*, 108: 55–68.

(2009) Limitations of diagnostic precision and predictive utility in the individual case: a challenge for forensic practice. *Law and Human Behavior*, doi: 10.1007/s10979-009-9176-x (Online article).

Cooke, D. J., Michie, C. and Skeem, J. L. (2007) Understanding the structure of the Psychopathy Checklist Revised: an exploration of methodological confusion. *British Journal of Psychiatry*, 190, special article, supplement, 49: 39–50.

DeMatteo, D. and Edens, J. F. (2006) The role and relevance of the Psychopathy Checklist – Revised in court: a case law survey of US courts 1991–2004. *Psychology, Public Policy and Law*, 12: 214–41.

Edens, J. F. and Petrila, J. (2006) Legal and ethical issues in the assessment and treatment of psychopathy. In C. J. Patrick (ed.), *Handbook of Psychopathy*, pp. 573–88. New York: Guilford Press.

Faigman, D. L. (2007) The limits of science in the courtroom. In E. Borgida and S. T. Fiske (eds.), *Beyond Common Sense: Psychological Science in the Courtroom*, pp. 303–14. Oxford: Blackwell.

Felthous, A. R. and Sass, H. (2007a) *International Handbook on Psychopathic Disorders and the Law*, vol. 1: *Diagnosis and Treatment*. Chichester: Wiley.

(2007b) *The International Handbook of Psychopathic Disorder and the Law*, vol. 2: *Laws and Policy*. Chichester: Wiley.

Freedman, D. (2001) Premature reliance on the Psychopathy Checklist – Revised in violence risk and threat assessment. *Journal of Threat Assessment*, 1: 51–64.

Grisso, T. (1986) *Evaluating Competencies: Forensic Assessments and Instruments*. New York: Plenum Press.

Hare, R. D. (2003) *The Hare Psychopathy Checklist – Revised*, 2nd edn. Toronto: Multi-Health Systems.

Hart, S. D. (1998) The role of psychopathy in assessing risk for violence: conceptual and methodological issues. *Legal and Criminological Psychology*, 3: 121–37.

(2001) Forensic issues. In W. J. Livesley (ed.), *Handbook of Personality Disorders*, pp. 555–69. New York: Guilford Press.

Hart, S. D., Cox, D. N. and Hare, R. D. (1995) *The Hare Psychopathy Checklist: Screening Version*. Toronto: Multi-Health Systems Inc.

Hart, S. D. and Wilson, C. M. (2008). Hare Psychopathy Checklist: screening version. In B. L. Cutler (ed.), *Encyclopaedia of Psychology and Law*, pp. 350–1. Thousand Oaks, CA: Sage.

Heilbrun, K. (2001) Risk assessment and risk management: toward an integration. Plenary session delivered at the International Conference, Violence Risk Assessment and Management: Bringing Science and Practice Closer Together, Sundsvall, Sweden.

Henderson, D. K. (1939) *Psychopathic States*. New York: W. W. Norton and Co.

Hoyersten, J. G. (2001) The Icelandic Sagas and the idea of personality and deviant personalities in the Middle Ages. *History of Psychiatry*, 12: 199–212.

Leistico, A. R., Salekin, R. T., DeCoster, J. and Rogers, R. (2008) A large-scale meta-analysis relating the Hare measures of psychopathy to antisocial conduct. *Law and Human Behavior*, 32: 28–45.

Leygraf, N. and Elsner, K. (2007) Risk of diagnosing psychopathic disorder. In A. R. Felthous and H. Sass (eds.), *International Handbook on Psychopathic Disorders and the Law*, vol. 1, pp. 136–46. Chichester: Wiley.

Lilienfeld, S. O. and Andrews, B. P. (1996) Development and preliminary validation of a self-report measure of psychopathic personality traits in non-criminal populations. *Journal of Personality Assessment*, 66: 488–524.

Logan, C. and Johnstone, L. (in press) Personality disorder and violence: clinical and risk formulation. *Journal of Personality Disorders*.

Millon, T. (1981) *Disorders of Personality*. New York: Wiley.

Morse, S. (1978) Law and mental health professionals: the limits of expertise. *Professional Psychology*, 9: 389–99.

Murphy, J.M. (1976) Psychiatric labelling in cross-cultural perspective: similar kinds of disturbed behavior appear to be labelled abnormal in diverse cultures. *Science*, 191: 1019–28.

Murrie, D.C., Boccaccini, M.T., Johnson, J.T. and Janke, C. (2007) Does interrater (dis)-agreement on Psychopathy Checklist scores in sexually violent predator trials suggest partisan allegiance in forensic evaluations? *Law and Human Behavior*, 32: 352–62.

Nichita, E.C. and Buckley, P.F. (2007) Comorbidities of psychopathy and antisocial personality disorder: prevalence and implications. In A.R. Felthous and H. Sass (eds.), *International Handbook on Psychopathic Disorders and the Law*, pp. 251–74. Chichester: Wiley.

Nicholls, T.L., Odgers, C.L. and Cooke, D.J. (2007) Women and girls with psychopathic characteristics. In A.R. Felthous and H. Sass (eds.), *International Handbook on Psychopathic Disorders and the Law*, pp. 347–66. Chichester: Wiley.

Patrick, C.J. (ed.) (2006) *Handbook of Psychopathy*. New York: Guilford Press.

Salekin, R.T. (2006) Psychopathy in children and adolescents: key issues in conceptualization and assessment. In C.J. Patrick (ed.), *Handbook of Psychopathy*, pp. 389–414. New York: Guilford Press.

Schneider, K. (1958) *Psychopathic Personalities*, 9th edn. London: Cassell.

Skeem, J.L. and Cooke, D.J. (in press a) Is criminal behavior a central component of psychopathy? Conceptual directions for resolving the debate. *Psychological Assessment*.

(in press b) One measure does not a construct make: directions toward reinvigorating psychopathy research. *Psychological Assessment*.

Tolman, A.O. and Mullendore, K.B. (2003) Risk evaluations of the courts: is service quality a function of specialization. *Professional Psychology: Research and Practice*, 34: 225–32.

Walsh, T. and Walsh, Z. (2006) The evidentiary introduction of the Psychopathy Checklist – Revised assessed psychopathy in US courts: extent and appropriateness. *Law and Human Behavior*, 30: 493–507.

World Health Organization (1992) *The ICD-10 Classification of Mental and Behavioural Disorders: Clinical Descriptions and Diagnostic Guidelines*. Geneva: World Health Organization.

2.21 Risk and dangerousness in adults

Grant T. Harris and Marnie E. Rice

Introduction

Many forensic psychologists appraise the risk of future violence for criminal offenders or psychiatric patients involved in the criminal justice system. Such appraisals should be used to inform decisions about sentencing and conditional release, and to apportion treatment and the intensity of post-release supervision. The available research, most of which has been conducted by psychologists, is based primarily on men who have already committed serious or violent offences. There are several systems to be relied upon for adult forensic cases, and the impetus for this work began more than fifty years ago with the recognition that formulaic, mechanical or actuarial methods are more accurate than informal clinical judgement, experience and intuition (Meehl 1954; see also Ægisdóttir *et al.* 2006; Grove and Meehl 1996), especially for violence (Hanson and Morton-Bourgon 2007; Hilton, Harris and Rice 2006). There are two kinds of formal (formulaic, mechanical) assessments for violence risk: actuarial (e.g. Hilton *et al.* 2004; Hilton, Harris, Rice *et al.* 2008; Quinsey *et al.* 2006; Rice, Harris and Hilton 2010), and non-actuarial (e.g. Boer *et al.* 1997; Kropp *et al.* 1995; Webster *et al.* 1995). Focusing on non-actuarial, a handbook of formal assessments for violence risk is available (Otto and Douglas 2010).

Actuarial systems

Actuarial systems are typically developed by selecting items (personal characteristics to attend to) using follow-up research that identifies which items, knowable beforehand, are associated with the outcome (in this case, subsequent violence). Then an optimum set is chosen based on incremental validity – selecting the most powerful predictors first and then adding items only when they improve prediction. Research in the past two decades indicates that non-clinical variables (e.g. age, violent and criminal history) as well as clinical constructs (e.g. psychopathy, conduct disorder) are central to violence risk assessment. Empirical combination of items using follow-up results typifies actuarial methods. In application, items are to be scored using the procedures of the original follow-up research. Interpretation is based on norms (proportion of cases falling above or below a particular score) plus experience tables (proportion at a particular score that met the operational definition of violent recidivism within a specified opportunity). Actuarial systems are characterized by empirical studies reporting the base rate (proportion meeting the operational definition of violent recidivism) and statistics on reliability and accuracy in development and cross-validation or replication.

The first and most thoroughly researched actuarial system for violence is the *Violence Risk Appraisal Guide* (VRAG), a twelve-item assessment for violent recidivism among men with prior criminal violence. Development, scoring and validation were described in Quinsey *et al.* (2006) and updates may be found at: www.mhcp-research.com/ragpage.htm. The VRAG was developed on violent men assessed in a secure forensic hospital (most were subsequently imprisoned). Items considered had predicted recidivism in previous research and all were scored from institutional records by researchers blind to outcomes. The outcome was a criminal charge for subsequent violence in an average of seven years' access to the community. Multiple regression selected the best item combination using techniques to maximize the likelihood predictive accuracy would replicate. Weights were based on the empirical relationship between each item and violent recidivism. Because documentary material was used in development, the recommended basis for scoring in research and individual assessment is a comprehensive psychosocial history addressing childhood conduct, family background, antisocial and criminal behaviour, psychological problems, and details of offences. Adequate psychosocial histories include more than past and present psychiatric symptoms and rely on collateral information (i.e. material gathered from family, schools, correctional facilities, police and the courts).

The VRAG predicted violent recidivism in development (base rate = 31%) with a large effect, and again when the sample was evaluated at ten years' average opportunity (base rate = 43%). In more than forty replications with new samples, average predictive effects have remained large (see Campbell, French and Gendreau 2009; Harris, Rice and Quinsey in press; Rice and Harris 2005). Under optimal conditions (high reliability; not dropping, replacing, or modifying items; fixed follow-ups; adhering to recommended scoring procedures), the VRAG has yielded even greater accuracy (Harris and Rice 2003). The VRAG has generalized across outcomes (number of violent offences, severity of recidivism, rapidity of violent failure, very serious violence, self-reported violence, institutional violence); opportunity (three months to ten years); countries (seven in North America and Europe); population (mentally disordered offenders, sexual aggressors, violent felons, developmentally delayed sex offenders, emergency psychiatric patients, wife assaulters and juvenile offenders). Obtained rates of violent recidivism have generally matched normative likelihoods for the nine categories overall, if the average score is similar, the follow-up duration the same and the outcome operationalized similarly.

Non-actuarial, structured professional schemes

After publication of the VRAG (Harris *et al.* 1993), some clinicians' resistance (Webster, personal communication) led to the promulgation of the HCR-20 using an approach intentionally not actuarial (Webster *et al.* 1995). The creators of the HCR-20, the first and most researched of several 'structured professional' schemes, surveyed the empirical and clinical literature on crime generally, not confining themselves to violence, forensic populations, predictive relationships or empirically tested risk factors. They considered each VRAG item but also gave special consideration to factors expected to be both changeable and relevant to post-release success. The result was a twenty-item checklist where each item is scored similarly. Clinical users are explicitly advised not to rely on the total score, however, and to give only a final, three-category opinion of low, moderate or high risk. The HCR-20 manual explicitly avoids a specifiable method for making this final judgement, implying that this appropriately permits each user to incorporate, with any weighting, all considerations deemed relevant. No experience tables for operationally defined violent outcomes over any duration of opportunity are available.

Superficially, the non-actuarial HCR-20 and the actuarial VRAG are similar – each comprises a list of items (some common to both) with instructions. The non-empirical methods, typical of such non-actuarial schemes, used in developing the HCR-20 contrast with actuarial techniques, however. First, because they have been based on general surveys, developers are not confined to factors included in one research programme; they may take items from the field as a whole. Second, because criteria for item selection are unspecified, empirically supported items may be omitted or changed. For example, the actuarially valid inverse association between major mental illness and violent recidivism (Bonta, Law and Hanson 1998; Harris *et al.* 1993; Monahan *et al.* 2001) was made positive in the HCR-20 because that conformed to the intuition of many forensic clinicians. Third, the HCR-20 designers could (and did) declare, without empirical evidence, that changes in items indicated altered risk (e.g. lack of insight, active symptoms of major mental illness, stress). Fourth, because the development was not empirical, the designers could recommend any process for scoring each item and overall administration; for individual decision making, they chose clinical interview, file review, and discussion with colleagues and collateral informants. Fifth, though no evidence supported it, clinical users were advised to make their own personal synthesis dispositive in individual cases. These differences can be expected to produce a scheme, popular with many clinicians, but when applied as recommended, yielding less accuracy than actuarial systems designed for the same purpose.

No empirical evidence of reliability or validity has accompanied the promulgation of structured professional schemes, but later studies have reported that the HCR-20 yields a total score with good inter-rater reliability. At the time of writing, more than thirty published follow-up studies, usually of released prisoners, forensic patients and mentally disordered offenders, in seven countries have reported that the HCR-20 ranks cases with respect to subsequent violence with moderate average effects (see also Campbell *et al.* 2009; Douglas, Guy and Weir 2006). Validation comparing observed to predicted rates is impossible. Very few studies (even those conducted by its developers) employ the recommended clinical interview plus discussion with collaterals and colleagues; data coding by file review alone predominates. Almost all studies have reported on the contra-indicated (for individual decision making) total score. Research does not permit empirical evaluation of claims for the value of incorporating unstructured clinical judgement (in moving from total score to low/moderate/high statements) – equivocal results have been reported in the very few studies that have examined the comparison. There is essentially no research on the validity of the HCR-20 when implemented as recommended for individual decision making.

Issues for future research and study

Dynamic items and personal change

Intuition leads to the expectation that, when offenders exhibit certain pre-release changes, their risk of subsequent violence changes accordingly. For example, violent men who learn non-aggressive anger management in cognitive-behavioural programmes during custody should improve on tests of such skills, and, in follow-up studies, such test score changes should improve the prediction of violent recidivism over prediction based on historical variables plus pre-treatment scores alone. Forensic clinicians are eager to nominate such 'dynamic' characteristics for risk assessment and as targets for intervention, but no empirical findings support such practice and no data indicate which pre-release changes indicate altered risk of violence (Douglas and Skeem 2005; Rice 2008).

Violence risk assessment in practice

A formal risk assessment in the hands of forensic decision makers does not guarantee effectiveness. Decisions by an independent forensic tribunal were unrelated to actuarial scores the tribunal possessed, but were associated with such invalid factors as perceived insight and physical attractiveness (Hilton and Simmons 2001; McKee, Harris and Rice 2007). This poor performance was attributable to poor advice from clinicians whose recommendations were unrelated to the actuarial scores they had for their patients – clinical opinions provided in practice were not related to recidivism in follow-up, but actuarial scores were. Clinicians evidently considered actuarial scores but deviated (based on subsequently applying clinical intuition) so that recommendations were indistinguishable from that same unaided clinical intuition. Such findings lead to the expectation that advice to interpose unstructured clinical intuition between mechanical scores and final judgements reduces accuracy.

There are few data on what strategies (in applying the empirical literature) will minimize both avoidable violent reoffending and unnecessary restriction of offenders' liberty. Some commentators (e.g. Hart, Cooke and Michie 2007; Wollert 2006) advise formal systems be avoided, urge non-specific caution, or recommend forensic clinicians abdicate decision making by shifting responsibility to others. Clearly, given available alternatives, this advice is worse than unhelpful: it is scientifically and ethically irresponsible. Other investigators (e.g. Hilton, Carter et al. 2008; Hilton et al. 2005) studied and recommended more effective ways of communicating risk information to decision makers. Another approach has been attempting to expand the formalization of all aspects (risk-related and risk-irrelevant) of the decision to minimize the deleterious effects of informal judgement (McKee, Harris and Rice 2007).

Conclusions

There is a basis for valid and ethical forensic practice in violence risk assessment. Considerable evidence supports such actuarial tools as the *Violence Risk Appraisal Guide* (VRAG) in application to adult male forensic cases. In assessing an individual case, VRAG users should rely on detailed and extensive material describing its scoring and interpretation (Quinsey *et al.* 2006). For example, because no empirical evidence supports it, instructions advise against adjusting actuarial scores based on clinical intuition. Alternatively, there is empirical support for the HCR-20. However, users could only justify attending to the total raw score. No evidence supports the HCR-20 manual's requirements to render a final three-category judgement based on idiosyncratic factors, include a clinical interview, or regard perceived changes in so-called clinical and risk-management items as indicating altered risk. More generally, however, assessing an adult forensic client's risk of violence without relying on a formal assessment designed for the purpose could not now be defended ethically or scientifically.

FURTHER READING

By dispelling invalid statistical, scientific, logical and ethical objections, several sources provide support for psychologists using formal assessments, especially actuarial violence risk assessments (see e.g. Grove and Meehl 1996). Comparative efficiency of informal (subjective, impressionistic) and formal (mechanical, algorithmic) prediction procedures can be found in the Harris and Rice article (2003). The Quinsey *et al.* (2006) volume, *Violent Offenders: Appraising and Managing Risk*, is also a good reference resource.

REFERENCES

Ægisdóttir, S., White, M. J., Spengler, P. M., Maugherman, A. S., Anderson, L. A., Cook, R. S. *et al.* (2006) The meta-analysis of clinical judgment project: fifty-six years of accumulated research on clinical versus statistical prediction. *The Counseling Psychologist*, 34: 341–82.

Boer, D. P., Hart, S., Kropp, P. R. and Webster, C. D. (1997) *Manual for the Sexual Violence Risk–20: Professional Guidelines for Assessing Risk of Sexual Violence*. Vancouver, BC: Mental Health, Law and Policy Institute, Simon Fraser University.

Bonta, J., Law, M. and Hanson, K. (1998) The prediction of criminal and violent recidivism among mentally disordered offenders: a meta-analysis. *Psychological Bulletin*, 123: 123–42.

Campbell, M., French, S. and Gendreau, P. (2009) The prediction of violence in adult offenders: a meta–Analytic comparison of instruments and methods of assessment. *Criminal Justice and Behavior*, 36: 567–90.

Douglas, K. S., Guy, L. S. and Weir, J. (2006) *HCR-20 Violence Risk Assessment Scheme: Overview and Annotated Bibliography*. Burnaby, BC: Department of Psychology, Simon Fraser University.

Douglas, K. S. and Skeem, J. L. (2005) Violence risk assessment: getting specific about being dynamic. *Psychology, Public Policy, and Law*, 11: 347–83.

Grove, W. M. and Meehl, P. E. (1996) Comparative efficiency of informal (subjective, impressionistic) and formal (mechanical, algorithmic) prediction procedures: the clinical–statistical controversy. *Psychology, Public Policy, and Law*, 2: 293–323.

Hanson, R. K. and Morton-Bourgon, K. E. (2007) *The Accuracy of Recidivism Risk Assessments for Sexual Offenders: A Meta-Analysis* (Report no. 2007–01). Ottawa, ON: Public Safety and Emergency Preparedness.

Harris, G. T. and Rice, M. E. (2003) The clinical–statistical controversy: characterizing the value of actuarial violence risk assessment. *Psychology, Public Policy and Law*, 2(2): 293–323.

Harris, G. T., Rice, M. E. and Quinsey, V. L. (1993) Violent recidivism of mentally disordered offenders: the development of a statistical prediction instrument. *Criminal Justice and Behavior*, 20: 315–35.

(in press) Allegiance or fidelity? A clarifying reply. *Clinical Psychology: Science and Practice*.

Hart, S., Michie, C. and Cooke, D. J. (2007) Precision of actuarial risk assessment instruments. *British Journal of Psychiatry*, 190 (suppl. 49): s60–s65.

Hilton, N. Z. and Simmons, J. L. (2001) Actuarial and clinical risk assessment in decisions to release mentally disordered offenders from maximum security. *Law and Human Behavior*, 25: 393–408.

Hilton, N. Z., Carter, A. M., Harris, G. T. and Sharpe, A. J. B. (2008) Does using non-numerical terms to describe risk aid violence risk communication? Clinician agreement and decision-making. *Journal of Interpersonal Violence*, 23: 171–88.

Hilton, N. Z., Harris, G. T., Rice, M. E., Houghton, R. E. and Eke, A. W. (2008) An indepth actuarial assessment for wife assault recidivism: the Domestic Violence Risk Appraisal Guide. *Law and Human Behavior*, 32: 150–63.

Hilton, N. Z., Harris, G. T., Rice, M. E, Lang, C., Cormier, C. A. and Lines, K. J. (2004) A brief actuarial assessment for the prediction of wife assault recidivism: the Ontario Domestic Assault Risk Assessment. *Psychological Assessment*, 16: 267–75.

Hilton, N. Z., Harris, G. T., Rawson, K. and Beach, C. (2005) Communication of risk information to forensic decision-makers. *Criminal Justice and Behavior*, 32: 97–116.

Hilton, N. Z., Harris, G. T. and Rice, M. E. (2006) Sixty-six years of research on the clinical versus actuarial prediction of violence. *The Counseling Psychologist*, 34: 400–9.

Kropp, P. R., Hart, S., Webster, C. D. and Eaves, D. (1995) *Manual for the Spousal Assault Risk Assessment Guide*, 2nd edn. Vancouver, BC: British Columbia Institute on Family Violence.

McKee, S. A., Harris, G. T. and Rice, M. E (2007) Improving forensic tribunal decisions: the role of the clinician. *Behavioral Sciences and the Law*, 25: 485–506.

Meehl, P. E. (1954) *Clinical vs. Statistical Prediction*. Minneapolis: University of Minnesota Press.

Monahan, J., Steadman, H., Silver, E., Appelbaum, P. S., Clark Robbins, P., Mulvey, E. P. *et al.* (2001) *Rethinking Risk Assessment: The MacArthur Study of Mental Disorder and Violence*. New York: Oxford University Press.

Otto, R. and Douglas, K. (eds.) (2010) *Handbook of Violence Risk Assessment Tools*. Oxford: Routledge / Taylor & Francis.

Quinsey, V. L., Harris, G. T., Rice, M. E., and Cormier, C. A. (2006) *Violent Offenders: Appraising and Managing Risk*, 2nd edn. Washington, DC: American Psychological Association.

Rice, M. E. (2008) Current status of violence risk assessment: is there a role for clinical judgment? In G. Bourgon, R. K. Hanson, J. D. Pozzulo, K. E. Morton-Bourgon and C. L. Tanasichuk (eds.), *Proceedings of the North American Correctional and Criminal Justice Psychology Conference*. Public Safety Canada User Report 2008-02. Ottawa: Public Safety Canada.

Rice, M. E. and Harris, G. T. (2005) Comparing effect sizes in follow-up studies: ROC, Cohen's *d* and *r*. *Law and Human Behavior*, 29: 615–20.

Rice, M. E., Harris, G. T. and Hilton, N. Z. (2010) The *Violence Risk Appraisal Guide* and *Sex Offender Risk Appraisal Guide* for violence risk assessment and the *Ontario Domestic Assault Risk Assessment* and *Domestic Violence Risk Appraisal Guide* for wife assault risk assessment. In R. Otto and K. Douglas (eds.), *Handbook of Violence Risk Assessment Tools*, pp. 99–210. Oxford: Routledge / Taylor & Francis.

Webster, C. D., Eaves, D., Douglas, K. S. and Wintrup, A. (1995) *The HCR-20 Scheme: The Assessment of Dangerousness and Risk*. Vancouver: Simon Fraser University and British Columbia Forensic Psychiatric Services Commission.

Wollert, R. (2006) Low base rates limit expert certainty when current actuarials are used to identify sexually violent predators. *Psychology, Public Policy, and Law*, 12: 56–85.

2.22 Sexual offender assessment

G. A. Serran, W. L. Marshall, L. E. Marshall and M. D. O'Brien

Introduction

Over the past several decades, clinicians and researchers have made good progress in identifying relevant issues, broadening our scope and theoretical foundation, and improving interventions for sexual offenders. One area, however, that requires more attention and fine-tuning is that of assessment. With the increased interest in theoretical issues follows the need to carefully consider the purpose and type of assessments conducted. This chapter will briefly outline and challenge the approach taken with this population.

Sexual offenders are a heterogeneous group. They differ with respect to personal and criminal histories, deviant sexual interests, relationship and skills deficits, educational and employment background, attitudes and beliefs, and offence characteristics. Assessments are therefore a key component of identifying this range of issues and translating them to risk, treatment focus and intensity, and required post-treatment supervision. Most specialized sexual offender assessments target cognitions, attitudes and beliefs, social functioning, sexual deviance, coping strategies and empathy.

With incarcerated sexual offenders, assessments may be conducted at various stages – admission, pre-treatment, during treatment, post-treatment, follow-up, pre-release and post-release – allowing for the most comprehensive analysis of issues related to risk, need and responsivity. A multimodal assessment strategy is typically utilized, considering various sources of information, including police reports and court documents, clinical interviews, physiological and psychological assessments, behavioural observation, and collateral contacts.

Assessments serve a variety of functions. Pre-treatment assessments determine treatment intensity level, provide some understanding of offence-related behaviour and background, and produce a preliminary understanding of relevant treatment targets. Over the course of treatment, ongoing assessment can provide an understanding of how the offender is responding and raise awareness of other issues that might arise. Post-treatment and follow-up assessments provide insight into how the offender is functioning in the community and whether further intervention or stricter supervision is required.

Risk assessment

Risk assessment is one of the primary areas of importance. Decision makers (e.g. sentence adjudicators, parole boards) primarily focus on risk level and whether intervention has impacted on risk. Risk assessment is seen as a critical and important part of clinical practice. As well, risk assessment plays an important role in decisions concerning dangerous offender status or confinement as a 'sexually violent predator'. Risk assessments also play a key role in community management or consideration for release (parole or detention). Due to the emphasis and weight placed upon risk assessment, it is critical that the tools employed are accurate but also informative for clinicians and others working with sexual offenders. Some researchers in the field argue that risk assessment should focus on static historical factors, as they are said to be more reliable and more accurately predictive. Instruments such as the STATIC-99 (Hanson and Thornton 1999) incorporate only these unchangeable factors. Others have argued that considering only fixed factors is of little value in planning and management strategies nor does it allow for consideration of change over time (Grubin and Wingate 1996). More recently, researchers have begun developing dynamic risk assessment tools. The STABLE-2000 (Hanson and Harris 2000) is one example of a risk assessment tool that considers stable dynamic risk factors (changeable but typically enduring features). This measure evaluates intimacy deficits, attitudes tolerant of sexual offending, problems with emotional/sexual self-regulation, and also general self-regulation as dynamic factors. Instruments such as the STABLE-2000 provide valuable information to the treatment providers. Considering both relevant static and dynamic factors allows for a comprehensive and meaningful approach to assessing risk.

Doren (2006) explores recidivism risk assessment factors and considers various controversies and issues. He notes that few instruments consider the likelihood of immediate offending, or likely frequency and severity of the offender's risk. He notes the need for assessments of risk considerations beyond simple probability, and that this requires a reliance on clinical judgement. He argues that considering certain variables above and beyond those identified in typical risk instruments can increase the overall predictive validity of the assessment. He notes, however, that that must be done as far as possible on the basis of whatever evidence is currently available. This is important because simply relying on clinical impressions does not produce reliable estimates of risk, but not allowing any consideration of clinical judgement is limiting as well. Risk assessment is constantly evolving so that we can expect accuracy to improve over time. Currently, it is important that evaluators choose demonstrably reliable and valid tools relevant to the population with whom they are working.

Deviant sexual interests

During the 1960s and early 1970s, treatment programmes for sexual offenders began to be developed consistent with the current conceptualization of the issues thought to be relevant (Laws and Marshall 2003). At that time, deviant sexual arousal was viewed as the primary motivation for committing sexual crimes, and although more comprehensive theories have since been developed, deviant arousal remains a focus of assessments and treatment. The primary technique for evaluating deviant sexual interests is phallometric assessment, which utilizes various sexual stimuli to determine age and gender preference as well as interest in sexual violence.

Hanson and Bussiere (1998) concluded that phallometric measures of sexual arousal to child stimuli are the best predictors of recidivism. Various researchers advocate the use of phallometrics, arguing that few measures match the predictive and discriminative validity of these assessments. However, a review of the research has called into question the utility of phallometric assessment (Marshall and Fernandez 2003). First, between 20 and 25% of all tested offenders display arousal that is too low to be considered meaningful. Second, clients who deny their offences typically appear normal at phallometric testing as do single-victim offenders. In fact, among non-familial child molesters only those who admit to having multiple victims respond deviantly. Among father–daughter incest offenders only 18–20% display deviant arousal to children. While some early studies found inappropriate arousal to forceful, non-consenting sexual activity among rapists, later studies failed to discriminate rapists from various other comparison groups. Most studies have also failed to detect deviant arousal among exhibitionists. Nevertheless, most sites continue to utilize phallometric assessments either for the purposes of diagnoses (e.g. paedophilia) or for the purposes of identifying treatment targets. Unfortunately, not only do phallometric assessments have psychometric problems, across sites the approach to assessment and the equipment utilized differ widely. Attempts at establishing multi-site studies aimed at developing a standardized approach to phallometric assessments have so far been unsuccessful.

Assessments and case formulation

Psychometric testing is deemed essential for most clinical problems. Generally, a series of interviews and a battery of tests are administered. Similarly, many programmes for sexual offenders employ a large battery of self-report assessment measures. The appendix describes some of the typical tests used in sexual offender assessments. We have concerns with the use of self-report tests and interviews. One of these concerns revolves around the honesty of self-reports particularly among sexual offenders who may be reluctant to reveal information for fear that this might result in them being seen as more dangerous.

It has been suggested that adding a measure evaluating impression management or including tests that have built-in measures of dissimulation (e.g. the MMPI) would address that problem. Unfortunately, the MMPI is time-consuming and its resultant data, including responses to the questions assessing faking, have not proved to be helpful with sexual offenders (Marshall and Hall 1995). In addition, the currently available measures of social desirability and impression management have unsatisfactory empirical bases. A further problem concerns the fact that most self-report measures typically used in the assessment of sexual offenders have unknown reliability and validity. To date, there are no interview strategies developed that are demonstrably reliable and valid.

Therefore, problems with the use of self-report measures for sexual offenders concern both their psychometric bases and their openness to dissimulation. Unfortunately, this has not deterred many treatment centres from developing extensive test batteries for sexual offenders that are primarily based on self-report measures. It is essential that assessors using self-report measures choose the most valid and reliable measures available, integrate them within a thorough assessment using various modalities and remain aware of the limitations inherent in the use of self-reports.

Relevance to treatment

It is often said that comprehensive assessments are necessary in order to identify appropriate treatment targets for each offender. In this view such assessments should also be repeated at post-treatment to determine treatment gains. Ward and his colleagues have argued for a formulation-based approach to individual treatment planning with sexual offenders that depends on comprehensive pre-treatment assessments. The aim of this approach is to provide a theory of the origin of each specific individual's offending behaviour and to identify all those factors that currently maintain these behaviours.

While this approach considers each offender's individual issues and strengths, it is quite a complex and time-consuming process. Whatever the outcome of this initial case formulation, we suggest that ongoing reformulations based on the client's treatment responses are essential to effective treatment. Indeed it may be argued that excessive pre-treatment assessments to develop case formulations may waste valuable time that could be better spent on treatment where the free flow of discussions will likely reveal more accurate information about treatment needs.

We suggest that a case formulation should occur throughout the client's time in treatment. Key issues such as deep-rooted schema are often only activated in the presence of strong emotion, and this requires time and the development of trust; these issues would not come to light through the use of self-report or physiological tests. Our experience with self-report measures at pre- and post-treatment has been disappointing. Some of these measures are time-consuming for the client to complete and all too often the clinical relevance of these measures is questionable. For the majority of clients who appear normal at pre-treatment testing, their revelations later in treatment contradict these early results. Furthermore, while changes from pre- to post-treatment, as revealed by various tests, may indicate statistically significant improvements, the post-treatment scores may still be well below normative functioning levels.

Our solution to these problems of psychometric assessments involves the use of a scale we developed that focuses on key treatment areas. This Therapist Rating Scale is completed halfway through treatment and again at the end of treatment. This rating scale requires therapists to estimate the client's current level of functioning on seventeen features relevant to treatment targets. For each feature, the therapist is required to rate how well the client has demonstrated his understanding of the issue (i.e. his intellectual grasp of the concept and its implications) as well as his emotional responses and practical application of the feature. These ratings are anchored against expected normative (rather than optimal) functioning for each target. Psychological tests administered at the end of treatment in most programmes may reveal how well the client has grasped the concept but not whether he is applying this understanding to his life. For example, he might be able to explain the issue of risk and identify key risk factors for himself but cannot identify when he is experiencing those risk factors. We believe the strength of the Therapist Rating Scale is that it depends on current, rich information that helps build a broad conceptualization of the offender.

We (Marshall *et al.* 2004) have generated data on the inter-rater reliability of our scale and found all seventeen items and both ratings (intellectual and emotional integration) to reach satisfactory levels. In addition, clients who reoffended in the outcome study of our programme all received overall ratings below acceptable standards.

Conclusions

Clinicians utilize a wide range of techniques and approaches when assessing sexual offenders. Although we have made considerable progress in developing theories and determining key treatment targets that serve to reduce risk to reoffend, our approach to assessment requires continued revision in order to increase its utility. Certainly, a multimodal approach has advantages, as does continued assessment at various points throughout the offender's progression through the criminal justice system. Clinicians are encouraged to consider the tools they use in their assessments and ensure that they adopt the most reliable and valid measures that are both time and cost-efficient.

Appendix: Relevant assessment instruments and procedures

Self-esteem

General self-esteem
Rosenberg's Measure (Rosenberg 1965)
Coopersmith's Measure (Coopersmith 1967)
Specific self-esteem

Body-Esteem Scale (Franzoi and Herzog 1984)
Social Self-Esteem Inventory (Lawson, Marshall and McGrath 1979)

Life history

Family Environment Scale (Moos and Moos 1981)
Childhood Attachment Questionnaire (Hazen and Shaver 1987)

Cognitive distortions

Abel's Child Molester Cognitions Scale (Abel *et al.* 1989)
Molest Scale (Bumby 1996)
Rape Scale (Bumby 1996)
Rape Myth Acceptance Scale (Burt 1980)
Hostility Toward Women Scale (Check 1984)
Justifications of Sex with Children (Mann *et al.* 2005)
Young Schema Questionnaire (Young and Brown, 2001)

Empathy

Empathy for Children (Hanson and Scott 1995)
Empathy for Women (Hanson and Scott 1995)
Child Molester Empathy Measure (Fernandez *et al.* 1999)
Rapist Empathy Measure (Fernandez and Marshall 2003)
Interpersonal Reactivity Test (Davis 1983)

Coping

Coping Inventory for Stressful Situations (Endler and Parker 1990)
Sex as a Coping Strategy (Cortoni and Marshall 2001)

Social functioning assertiveness

Social Response Inventory (Keltner, Marshall and Marshall 1981)
Rathus Assertiveness Scale (Rathus 1973)

Anger

Buss-Durkee Hostility Inventory (Buss and Durkee 1957)
State-Trait Anger Expression Inventory (Spielberger 1988a)

Anxiety

State-Trait Anxiety Inventory (Spielberger 1988b)
Fear of Negative Evaluations Scale (Watson and Friend 1969)
Social Avoidance and Distress Scale (Watson and Friend 1969)

Problem-solving

D'Zurilla and Goldfried 1971

Social supports inventory

Flannery and Weiman 1989

Relationships

UCLA Loneliness Scale (Russell, Peplau and Curtrona 1980)
Miller's Social Intimacy Scale (Miller and Lefcourt 1982)
Relationship Questionnaire (Bartholomew and Horowitz 1991)
Relationship Styles Questionnaire (Griffin and Bartholomew 1994)
Attachment History Questionnaire (Pottharst and Kessler 1990)

Sexual interests

Clarke Sexual History Questionnaire (Langevin *et al.* 1990)
Multiphasic Sex Inventory (Nichols and Molinder 1984)
Laws Card Sort (Laws 1986)
Wilson Sex Fantasy Questionnaire (Wilson 1978)
Phallometry (Murphy and Barbaree 1994)
Viewing Time (Abel 1995)

Substance use/abuse

Michigan Alcoholism Screening Test (Selzer 1971)
Drug Abuse Screening Test (Skinner 1982)

Psychopathy

Psychopathy Checklist–Revised (Hare 1991)

Relapse prevention

Self-Monitoring Procedure (McDonald and Pithers 1989)
STEP Measures of Offense Chain (Beckett, Beech, Fisher and Fordham 1994)
Situational Competency Test (Miner, Day and Nafpaktitis 1989)

Violence

Violence Risk Appraisal Guide (Harris, Rice and Quinsey 1993)

Sexual

Minnesota Sex Offender Screening Tool (Epperson, Kaul and Huot 1995)
Sex Offender Risk Appraisal Guide (Quinsey *et al.* 1998)
Rapid Risk Assessment for Sexual Offense Recidivism (Hanson 1997)
STATIC-99 (Hanson and Thornton 1999)

Social desirability / impression management

Marlow–Crowne Social Desirability Scale (Crowne and Marlowe 1960)
Paulhus Balanced Inventory of Desirable Responding (Paulhus 1991)

REFERENCES

Abel, G. G. (1995) *New Technology: The Abel Assessment for Interest in Paraphilias.* Atlanta, GA: Abel Screening Inc.

Abel, G. G., Gore, D. K., Holland, N., Camps, N., Becker, J. V. and Rathner, J. (1989) The measurement of the cognitive distortions of child molesters. *Journal of Research and Treatment,* 2: 135–52.

Bartholomew, K. and Horowitz, L. M. (1991) Attachment styles among young adults: a test of a four-category model. *Journal of Personality and Social Psychology,* 6: 226–44.

Beckett, R., Beech, A., Fisher, D. and Fordham, A. S. (1994) Community-based treatment of sex offenders: an evaluation of seven treatment programmes (Home Office occasional paper). London: Home Office.

Bumby, K. M. (1996) Assessing the cognitive distortions of child molesters and rapists: development and validation of the MOLEST and RAPE scales. *Journal of Research and Treatment,* 8: 37–54.

Burt, M. R. (1980) Cultural myths and supports for rape. *Journal of Personality and Social Psychology,* 38: 217–30.

Buss A. H. and Durkee A. (1957) An inventory for assessing different kinds of hostility. *Journal of Consulting Psychology,* 21: 343–9.

Check, J. V. P. (1984) The Hostility Toward Women Scale. Unpublished PhD dissertation, University of Manitoba, Canada.

Coopersmith, S. (1967) *The Antecedents of Self-Esteem*. San Francisco: W. H. Freeman.

Cortoni, F. and Marshall, W. L. (2001) Sex as a coping strategy and its relationship to juvenile sexual history and intimacy in sexual offenders. *Journal of Research and Treatment*, 13: 27–43.

Crowne, D. P. and Marlowe, D. (1960) A new scale of social desirability of psychopathology. *Journal of Consulting Psychology*, 24: 349–54.

Davis, M. H. (1983) Measuring individual differences in empathy: evidence for a multidimensional approach. *Journal of Personality and Social Psychology*, 44: 113–26.

Doren, D. M. (2006) Recidivism risk assessments: making sense of controversies. In W. L. Marshall, Y. M. Fernandez, L. E. Marshall and G. A Serran (eds.), *Sexual Offender Treatment: Controversial Issues*. Chichester: Wiley.

D'Zurilla, T. J. and Goldfried, M. R. (1971) Problem solving and behaviour modification. *Journal of Abnormal Psychology*, 78: 107–26.

Endler, N. S. and Parker, J. D. A. (1990) Multidimensional assessment of coping: a critical evaluation. *Journal of Personality and Social Psychology*, 58: 844–54.

Epperson, D. L., Kaul, J. D. and Huot, S. J. (1995) Predicting risk of recidivism for incarcerated sex offenders: updated development on the Sex Offender Screening Tool (SOST). Paper presented at the 14th annual conference of the Association for the Treatment of Sexual Abusers, New Orleans.

Fernandez, Y. M. and Marshall, W. L. (2003) Victim empathy, social self-esteem, and psychopathy in rapists. *Journal of Research and Treatment*, 15: 11–26.

Fernandez, Y. M., Marshall, W. L., Lightbody, S. and O'Sullivan, C. (1999) The Child Molester Empathy Measure: description and examination of its reliability and validity. *Journal of Research and Treatment*, 11: 17–31.

Flannery, R. B. and Weiman, D. (1989) Social support, life stress, and psychological distress: an empirical assessment. *Journal of Clinical Psychology*, 45: 867–72.

Franzoi, S. and Herzog, M. (1986) The Body Esteem Scale: a convergent and discriminant validity study. *Journal of Personality Assessment*, 50: 24–31.

Griffin, D. W. and Bartholomew, K. (1994). The metaphysics of measurement: the case of adult attachment. In K. Bartholomew and D. Perlman (eds.), *Advances in Personal Relationships*, vol. 5, pp. 17–52. London: Jessica Kingsley.

Grubin, D. and Wingate, S. (1996) Sexual offence recidivism: prediction versus understanding. *Criminal Behaviour and Mental Health*, 6: 349–59.

Hanson, R. K. (1997) *The Development of a Brief Actuarial Risk Scale for Sexual Offense Recidivism* (User Report 97–04). Ottawa: Department of the Solicitor General of Canada.

Hanson, R. K. and Bussiere, M. T. (1998) Predicting relapse: a meta-analysis of sexual offender recidivism studies. *Journal of Consulting and Clinical Psychology*, 66: 348–62.

Hanson, R. K. and Harris, A. J. R. (2000) Where should we intervene? Dynamic predictors of sex offender recidivism. *Criminal Justice and Behavior*, 27: 6–35.

Hanson, R. K. and Scott, H. (1995) Assessing perspective-taking among sexual offenders, nonsexual criminals, and nonoffenders. *Sexual Abuse: A Journal of Research and Treatment* 7(4): 259–77.

Hanson, R. K. and Thornton, D. (1999) *Static-99: Improving Actuarial Risk Assessments for Sex Offenders* (User Report 99–02). Ottawa: Department of the Solicitor General of Canada.

Hare, R. D. (1991) *The Hare Psychopathy Checklist – Revised*. Toronto: Multi-Health Systems.

Harris, G. T., Rice, M. E. and Quinsey, V. L. (1993) Violent recidivism of mentally disordered offenders: the development of a statistical prediction instrument. *Criminal Justice and Behavior*, 20: 315–35.

Hazan, C. and Shaver, P. R. (1987) Romantic love conceptualized as an attachment process. *Journal of Personality and Social Psychology*, 52: 511–24.

Keltner, A. A., Marshall, P. G. and Marshall, W. L. (1981) Measurement and correlation of assertiveness and social fear in a prison population. *Corrective and Social Psychiatry*, 27: 41–7.

Langevin, R., Paitich, D., Russon, A., Handy, L. and Langevin, A. (1990) *The Clarke Sex History Questionnaire Manual*. Etobicoke, ON: Juniper Press.

Laws, D. R. (1986) Sexual deviance card sort. Unpublished manuscript. Florida Mental Health Institute, Tampa.

Laws, D. R. and Marshall, W. L. (2003) A brief history of behavioral and cognitive behavioral approaches to sexual offender treatment: part 1. Early developments. *Sexual Abuse: A Journal of Research and Treatment*, 15: 75–92.

Lawson, J. S., Marshall, W. L. and McGrath, P. (1979) The social self-esteem inventory. *Educational and Psychological Measurement*, 39: 803–11.

Mann, R. E., Webster, S. D., Wakeling, H. C. and Marshall, W. L. (2005) The measurement and influence of child sexual abuse supportive beliefs. *Psychology, Crime and Law*, 13: 443–58.

Marshall, W. L. and Fernandez, Y. M. (2003) *Phallometric Testing with Sexual Offenders: Theory, Research, and Practice*. Brandon, VT: Safer Society Press.

Marshall, W. L. and Hall, G. C. N. (1995) The value of the MMPI in deciding forensic issues in accused sexual offenders. *Sexual Abuse: A Journal of Research and Treatment*, 7: 205–19.

Marshall, W. L., Webster, S., Serran, G. A., Marshall, L. E. and Fernandez, Y. M. (2004) The therapist rating scale: interrater reliability. Unpublished paper, Rockwood Psychological Services, Kingston, ON.

McDonald, R. K. and Pithers, W. D. (1989) Self-monitoring to identify high-risk situations. In D. R. Laws (ed.), *Relapse Prevention with Sexual Offenders*, pp. 96–104. New York: Guilford Press.

Miller, R. S. and Lefcourt, H. M. (1982) The assessment of social intimacy. *Journal of Personality Assessment*, 46: 514–18.

Miner, M. H., Day, D. M. and Nafpaktitis, M. K. (1989) Assessment of coping skills: development of a situational competency test. In D. R. Laws (ed.), *Relapse Prevention with Sex Offenders*, pp. 127–36. New York: Guilford Press.

Moos, R. H. and Moos, B. S. (1981) *Family Environment Scale Manual*. Palo Alto, CA: Consulting Psychologist Press.

Murphy, W. D. and Barbaree, H. E. (1994) *Assessments of Sex Offenders by Measures of Erectile Response: Psychometric Properties and Decision Making*. Brandon, VT: Safer Society Press.

Nichols, H. R. and Molinder, I. (1984). *Multiphasic Sex Inventory*. Tacoma, WA: Nichols and Molinder.

Paulhus, D. L. (1991) Measurement and control of response bias. In J. P. Robinson, P. R. Shaver and L. S. Wrightsman (eds.), *Measures of Personality and Social Psychology Attitudes*, pp. 17–59. New York: Academic Press.

Pottharst, K. and Kessler, R. (1990) The search for methods and measures. In K. Pottharst (ed.), *Research Explorations in Adult Attachment*, pp. 9–37. New York: Peter Lang.

Quinsey, V. L., Harris, G. T., Rice, M. E. and Cormier, C. A. (1998) *Violent Offenders: Appraising and Managing Risk*. Washington, DC: American Psychological Association.

Rathus, S. A. (1973). A thirty-item schedule for assessing behavior. *Behavior Therapy*, 4: 398–406.

Rosenburg, M. (1965) *Society and the Adolescent Self-Image*. Princeton, NJ: Princeton University Press.

Russell, D., Peplau, L. A. and Cutrona, C. E. (1980) The revised UCLA Loneliness Scale: concurrent and discriminant validity evidence. *Journal of Personality and Social Psychology*, 39(3): 472–80.

Selzer, M. L. (1971) The Michigan Alcohol Screening Test: the quest for a new diagnostic instrument. *American Journal of Psychiatry*, 127: 1653–8.

Skinner, H. A. (1982) The drug abuse screening test. *Addictive Behaviors*, 7(4): 363–71.

Spielberger, C. D. (1988a) *Manual for the State-Trait Anger Expression Inventory (STAXI)*. Odessa, FL: Psychological Assessment Resources.

 (1988b) *Manual for the State-Trait Anxiety Inventory: STAI (Form Y)*. Palo Alto, CA: Consulting Psychologists Press.

Watson, D. and Friend, R. (1969) Measurement of social-evaluative anxiety. *Journal of Consulting and Clinical Psychology*, 33: 448–57.

Wilson, G. (1978) *The Secrets of Sexual Fantasy*. London: J. M. Dent & Sons.

Young, J. E. and Brown, G. (2001) *Young Schema Questionnaire*, special edition. New York: Schema Therapy Institute.

2.23 Statement validity analysis

Jennifer M. Brown

See also chapter 2.9 Investigative interviewing, chapter 4.3 Interpersonal deception detection.

Definition

Statement validity analysis (SVA), also referred to as statement reality analysis, is actually a range of procedures for generating and testing hypotheses about the likely veracity of a given statement. Steller and Boychuck (1992) provide an account of the constituent elements: careful review of relevant case information; a preserved semi-structured interview; criteria-based content analysis of the transcribed interview (CBCA); validity checks on additional case information; a systematic summary of content analysis and validity checks. Köhnken (2004) offers a further elaboration of the importance of and role played by hypothesis generation when undertaking SVA and how constituent elements of SVA evaluate the assumption that the statement is true, or the alternative hypotheses that a statement is a complete or partial fabrication, consists of incorrect transference from other experiences to the event in question, is the result of instruction by others, is produced through suggestive influences or is the product of a mental illness where the witness cannot distinguish fact from fantasy. The hypotheses are set up as a result of the case file analysis. If, for example, the case file suggests that a witness was inappropriately or incompletely interviewed, or it is established that the verbal or cognitive abilities of the witness are impaired, a further investigative interview may be required (Köhnken 2004).

Origins and further developments

SVA's origins can be traced to the ramifications of a West German Supreme Court decision in 1954 which accepted expert testimony about the veracity of a juvenile's evidence and concomitant development of systematic methods by Trankell (1972) and Undeutsch (1982, 1989), and later revisions by Steller and Köhnken (1989). The theoretical basis for SVA is the 'Undeutsch hypothesis', which postulates that statements that are the product of experience will contain characteristics that are generally absent from statements that are the

Table 2.23.1 CBCA criteria

General characteristics	Details
1. Logical structure	Statement coherent and contains logical consistency
2. Unstructured production	Disorganized, unconstrained style sequence in production of description
3. Quantity of detail	Meaningful and richly subjective description of sexual events
Specific contents	
4. Contextual embedding	Existence of vocal, spatial, temporal and personal contexts of described events
5. Description of interactions	Reporting of at least three interactions, reaction of conversations with perpetrator
6. Reproduction of conversations	Details of speech reported in original form, noting unfamiliar words/ phrases
7. Unexpected complications	Unplanned changes in course of events
Peculiarities of content	
8. Unusual detail	Realistic notable, unusual or extraordinary detail
9. Superfluous detail	Contemporaneous, peripheral events outside the context of the offence
10. Accurately reported details misunderstood	Awkward, correctly described event interpreted incorrectly
11. Related external associations	Reference to related sexually toned offence but not part of allegation
12. Accounts of subjective mental state	Recalled thoughts or feelings experienced during incident
13. Attribution of perpetrator's mental state	Perception of offender's feelings, emotions or motivations or intentions
Motivation-related content	
14. Spontaneous correction	Additions or corrections spontaneously offered
15. Admitting lack of memory	Spontaneous admissions of memory lapses or knowledge of an aspect of the incident
16. Raising doubts about own testimony	Recognition of implausibility in own account, concern that parts may be unbelievable
17. Self-deprecation	Self-blame or description of own behaviour as wrong or inappropriate
18. Pardoning perpetrator	Minimize seriousness of offence, excuse or fail to blame or express ambivalence towards offender
Offence-specific elements	
19. Details characteristic of the offence	Aspects described typical of offence type but counter-intuitive or discrepant to everyday knowledge

products of imagination. Undeutsch proposed eight credibility criteria. These and other criteria were combined and integrated by Steller and Köhnken (1989) to produce nineteen criteria-based content analyses (CBCA) most often used in current analyses.

Raskin and Esplin (1991) added a further procedure; the Validity Checklist to be used in conjunction with CBCA for determining which hypothesis is the most plausible explanation for the allegation and contains four general categories of information to be evaluated. These deal with external features of the investigation and are more subjective and less formalized than CBCA. Here the presence of validity criteria detracts from credibility, whereas the presence of CBCA enhances credibility. The same problems arise as with CBCA in that there is little clarity as to which Validity Checklist criteria should be absent to indicate truthfulness or agreed

Table 2.23.2 Validity Checklist

Psychological characteristics	
1. Cognitive emotional limitations	Limited cognitive ability, unwillingness, discomfort which interfered with the interview
2. Incident specific language/ knowledge	Use of language or display of knowledge likely to have been experienced in the incident
3. Incongrous affect during interview	Behaviour during interview incongruous with emotional content of narrative
4. Susceptibility to suggestion	Suggestibility evident in account or response to questioning
Interview characteristics	
5. Interview inappropriateness	Interview deviates from good practice
6. Interview contamination	Interviewer interference in recall or production of account
Motivation	
7. Motivation to report	Evidence of revenge, malicious intention, protection or conspiracy
8. Questionable context of disclosure	Dubious origin of original report or inconsistencies in reporting
9. Pressure to report	Coercion, suggestion, coaching
Investigative questions	
10. Lack of realism	Events unrealistic or contrary to the laws of nature
11. Inconsistent statements	Major elements of statement contradicted by statement of witness /other person
12. Inconsistency in other evidence	Major elements contradicted by forensic, scene or other witness evidence
Offence-specific element	
13. Lacking offence-specific characteristics	Description lacking major elements typical of rape offences

thresholds distinguishing truth telling from fabrication. Parker and Brown (2000) propose, when using a dichotomous scoring system, that 0–3 is indicative of a credible statement, 4–5 for indeterminate and 6 or more indicates a non-credible statement.

Method

The starting point for SVA is the conducting of background research into the case in question. Köhnken (2004), in particular, stresses the criticality of gathering information on the witness, events in question, previous statements and any apparent inconsistencies which are assessed by means of a thorough analysis of case file data. This permits the generation of hypotheses and identification of a diagnostic strategy and choice of appropriate assessment techniques (which could include psychometric testing instead of / as well as application of CBCA). Such background work is not always possible or even conducted; rather, CBCA is applied to a preserved witness statement (often the product of a police interview). Colwell, Hiscock and Memon (2002) reported the superiority of the cognitive and inferential interview techniques as superior to a standard structured interview when assessing accuracy rates in detecting deception.

Usually, statements are read and coded for the presence of CBCA criteria. There is a debate in the literature about scoring methods: how many and which criteria should be present and the appropriate cut-off to determine an assessment of likely truthfulness or fabrication. Scoring may be undertaken by a simple dichotomy of presence or absence (Parker and Brown 2000) with a cut off of 8 indicating a credible statement, 6 to 7 indeterminate and 5 or less as non-credible. Horowitz (1998) suggests that such a forced choice has lower reliability than when adopting a three-point scale of absent, present, strongly present. Köhnken (2004) proposes a five-point scale, ranging from 0 not present to 4 strongly present, arguing that the wider range is more sensitive to smaller differences between truthful and fabricated statements. No suggested cut-off scores are given for the extended range coding. Tully (1998) argues for transparency in coding and provision of a rationale for the assessment rather than opting for a statistical determination. This issue remains unresolved. Kapardis (2003) has a helpful review of the various protagonists in the debate about the number and identity of criteria that should be present to indicate a probably truthful statement. The consensus suggests the presence of logical structure, unstructured production, and quality of detail, contextual embedding and description of interactions as minimal plus any two other criteria.

Relatively little research is available that reports the use of the Validity Checklist (see Lamers-Winkelman 1997 and Parker and Brown 2000 as two of the few examples). Systematic summaries of CBCA and the Validity Checklist are more likely in practice reports than research papers. Steller and Boychuk (1992) propose that this part of the procedure helps to organize facts and inferences and discloses the weights attached to the various sources of data. All the material used contributes to an estimation of the statement's credibility.

Evaluation

SVA has been said to demonstrate face validity (Steller and Boychuck 1992), and reports are readily accepted by German courts (Gudjonsson and Haward 1998); however, other opinion is more questioning. As SVA may draw evidence from a variety of sources, if the whole procedure is adopted, Howlett (2006) asks, which source of assessment leads to what conclusions? Also assessment of false negatives is under-reported. There is emerging evidence that witnesses may be coached to produce statements with CBCA-appropriate content (Köhnken 2004) and differential accuracy rates when different methods of eliciting interviews are used (Colwell, Hiscock and Memon 2002). The inter-rater reliability of coded statements is also contested. (Vrij 2005). Without appropriate training both intra- and inter-rater reliability may be compromised. Training options vary between several hours (Landry and Brigham 1992), three days (Raskin and Esplin 1991) and three weeks Köhnken (2004). All demonstrated better performance of trained coders, although Akehurst *et al.* (2004) showed that whilst before training there were no significant differences in detection accuracy between police officers (66% accuracy), social workers (72% accuracy) and students (56% accuracy), after training, the social workers were 77% accurate and significantly more accurate than the police officers (55%) and the students (61%). Thus police officers appear to deteriorate rather than improve as a consequence of training.

CBCA has been argued to have truth-detecting bias (Lucas and McKenzie 1999) and a propensity to false positive (Rassin 2001). However, in a review of 37 studies, Vrij (2005) reported that correct classification rates vary between 65 and 90%, with an average of 73% for lies and 72% for truth. There is a considerable difficulty in assessing the grounded truth of a statement in order to assess the efficacy of SVA. Whilst experimental studies can control manipulation of truthful and fabricated content, such studies often lack ecological validity. Field studies using real statements are faced with only limited certainty that their criteria for grounded truth are viable. Parker and Brown (2000) identified victim retraction, admission of fabrication, and lack of forensic corroboration as bases for establishing grounded truth, but concede these are still subject to doubt.

Applications

SVA was originally developed to assess the veracity of children's allegations of sexual abuse and has been used in over 40,000 cases in Germany, where it is undertaken by appointed expert witnesses, usually psychologists, and is beginning to be used in courts in Canada and the United States (Wrightman and Fulero 2005). The techniques have also been applied to adult rape statements (see e.g. Parker and Brown 2000).

Whilst clearly accepted in European courts, in the United States there is still discussion as to whether SVA conforms to the principles of the Kelly–Frye Rule, which requires that (1) a technique or method is sufficiently established to have gained general acceptance in its field; (2) testimony with respect to the technique and its application is offered by a properly qualified expert; and (3) correct scientific procedures have been used. In the United Kingdom there is currently no guidance as to the status or acceptability of SVA evidentially (see e.g. discussion in Home Affairs committee report: 'The conduct of investigations into past cases of abuse in children's homes', 31 October 2002).

Conclusion

SVA comprises several techniques which properly should be employed in their entirety. Whilst demonstrating face validity, reliability of the components of CBCA and the Validity Checklist remain contested. Advice from practitioners suggests that SVA requires training before use. Given the criticisms of SVA, evaluations are not accurate enough to be admitted as expert scientific evidence in criminal courts, but may be useful diagnostically for clinical interventions or police investigations and may be extended to adults' as well as children's testimony.

FURTHER READING

For a helpful overview and summary see the chapter on deception in Kapardis (2003). Köhnken (2004) is a good description of the constituent elements of SVA and provides a discussion of training. A critical overview of CBCA is provided in Ruby and Brigham (1997) and an evaluation of field and experimental studies and discussion of the limits to application can be found in Vrij (2005). Finally, a nicely worked example is presented by Stellar and Boychuck (1992).

REFERENCES

Akehurst, L., Bull, R., Vrij, A. and Köhnken, G. (2004) The effects of training professional groups and lay persons to use criteria-based content analysis to detect deception. *Applied Cognitive Psychology*, 18: 877–91.

Colewell, K., Hiscock, C. K. and Memon, A. (2002) Interviewing techniques and the assessment of statement credibility. *Applied Cognitive Psychology*, 16: 287–300.

Gudjonsson, G. H. and Haward, L. R. C. (1998) *Forensic Psychology: A Guide to Practice*. London: Routledge.

Horowitz, S. (1998) Reliability of criteria-based content analysis of child witness statements; a response to Tully. *Legal and Criminological Psychology*, 3: 189–92.

Howlett, D. (2006) *Introduction to Forensic Psychology*, 2nd edn. London: Pearson.

Kapardis, A. (2003) *Psychology and Law: A Critical Introduction*, 2nd edn. Cambridge: Cambridge University Press.

Köhnken, G. (2004) Statement Validity Analysis and the 'detection of truth'. In P. A. Granhag and L. A. Strömwall (eds.), *The Detection of Deception in Forensic Contexts*, pp. 41–63. Cambridge: Cambridge University Press.

Lammers-Winkelman, F. (1997) The second part of statement validity analysis. Paper presented at Conference on Responding to Child Maltreatment, San Diego.

Landry, K. L. and Brigham, J. (1992) The effect of training in criteria-based content analysis on the ability to detect deception in adults. *Law and Human Behaviour*, 16: 663–79.

Lucas, R. and McKenzie, I. (1999) The detection of dissimulation, lies, damn lies and SVA. *International Journal of Police Science and Management*, 1: 347–59.

Parker, A. and Brown, J. (2000) Detection of deception; statement validity analysis as a means of determining truthfulness or falsity of rape allegations. *Legal and Criminological Psychology*, 5: 237–59.

Raskin, D. and Esplin, P. (1991) Assessment of children's statement of sexual abuse. In J. Doris (ed.), *The Suggestibility of Children's Recollections*, pp. 153–64. Washington, DC: American Psychological Association.

Rassin, E. (2001) Criteria-based content analysis: the less scientific road to truth. *Expert Evidence*, 7: 265–78.

Ruby, C. L. and Brigham, C. J. (1997) The usefulness of the criteria-based content analysis technique in distinguishing between truthful and fabricated allegations; a critical review. *Psychology, Public Policy and Law*, 3: 705–37.

Steller, M. and Boychuck, T. (1992) Children as witnesses in sexual abuse cases: investigative interview and assessment techniques. In H. Dent and R. Flin (eds.), *Children as Witnesses*, pp. 47–71. Chichester: Wiley.

Steller, M. and Köhnken, G. (1989) Criteria based statement analysis. In D. C. Raskin (ed.), *Psychological Methods in Criminal Investigation and Evidence*, pp. 217–45. New York: Springer.

Trankell, A. (1972) *Reliability of Evidence*. London: Beckmans.

Tully, B. (1998) Reliability of criteria-based content analysis of child witness statements: Cohen's Kappa doesn't matter. *Legal and Criminological Psychology*, 3: 183–8.

Undeutsch, U. (1982) The development of statement reality analysis. In A. Trankell (ed.). *Reconstructing the Past: The Role of Psychologists in Criminal Trials*, pp. 27–56. Stockholm: P. A. Norstedt and Soners.

(1989) The development of statement reality analysis. In J. Yuille (ed.), *Credibility Assessment: A United Theoretical and Research Perspective. Proceedings of the NATO–Advanced Study Institute in Maratea (Italy), June 1988.* Dordrecht: Kluwer Academic Publishers.

Vrij, A. (2005) Criteria-Based Content Analysis: a qualitative review of the first 37 studies. *Psychology, Public Policy and the Law*, 11: 3–41.

Wrightsman, L. S. and Fulero, S. M. (eds.) (2005) *Forensic Psychology*, 2nd edn. Belmont, CA: Wadsworth.

2.24 Suicide risk in adolescents and adults

Bruce D. Kirkcaldy, Randall Richardson-Vejlgaard
and Joav Merrick

Rates of suicide

According to the World Health Organization (WHO), approximately one million people died from suicide worldwide in the year 2000. This number represents a 60% increase in suicide mortality over the last half-century, placing the current global mortality rate at 16 suicides per 100,000 people. This number encompasses wide variability between countries. The most recently reported data indicates that former Soviet Republics such as Lithuania, Russian Federation and Belarus have the highest yearly incidence of 75.6, 70 and 63.6 respectively, while several small developing countries such as Dominican Republic and Anguilla report incidence rates close to zero (WHO 2007). With the exception of some parts of China, in which the rate for women is slightly higher than for men, suicide rates are significantly higher among men across countries (WHO 2007).

In the United States over 30,000 people commit suicide each year. This represents the eighth leading cause of death overall, and is more than the number of homicides, which garner considerably more attention in the media. Among younger adult men, suicide ranks as high as third in causes of death. The overall rate of suicide in the US is 11.5 per 100,000 people, which is somewhat lower than international averages. The two age groups of primary concern are young adults between the ages of 19 and 25, and those over the age of 65 years.

Official reports of suicide are assumed to be lower than actual numbers. Because suicide is an emotionally charged, highly stigmatized event there may be an inherent unwillingness in the families of the deceased to acknowledge it as such. In addition, the lack of confirmatory physical evidence accompanying many suicides causes some proportion of them to be misclassified as accidents or death due to undetermined cause (Ohberg and Lonnqvist 1998). There is also wide variability in reporting practices between countries, and no international standards to ascertain intention to self-murder (Moscicki 1995). Some speculation also exists that socio-demographic factors may affect the degree to which suicide rates are under-reported in the USA, as suicides among minority groups are more likely to be misclassified (Rockett, Samora and Coben 2006).

There is considerable variability in suicide incidence across lines of age, gender, race and ethnicity, socioeconomic status, marital status and psychiatric diagnosis. In terms of race and gender, white males occupy an especially high priority in research on suicide, as they account for 72% of all suicides in the USA (AAS 2007). Rates for white men over age 85 are highest of all, ranging as high as 62.5/100,000. In general, women complete suicide with one-quarter of the frequency of men. Suicide rates for women remain consistently low (around 6 to 7/100,000) throughout early adulthood, and peak at 8.1/100,000 during ages 45–54. In older age, suicide rates among women decline, in contrast to those for men. Even among white women, who have the highest rates of suicide of any American women, rates for the highest-risk age group (45–64) peak at 8.4/100,000.

Although the incidence of completed suicide in women is relatively low, suicidal behaviour in women is a cause for public health concern due to the consequences of attempted suicide, including medical care, lost productivity and risk for future attempts. Women are significantly more likely to make attempts on their lives than men, although men are more likely to complete suicide. Non-lethal suicidal behaviour, often called parasuicidal behaviour, includes near-lethal gestures with the intention to end one's life, and deliberate self-harm with no intention to die. This is a complex set of behaviours that is difficult to quantify and organize; consequently research on prevalence and incidence rates is highly inconclusive. Current estimates suggest that yearly incidence of parasuicidal behaviour ranges from 2.6 to 1,100/100,000, while lifetime prevalence ranges from 720 to 5,930 (Welch 2001). It is generally estimated that suicide attempts outstrip completions by a ratio of 25 to 1 (Moscicki 2001). Among younger women (ages 15–24), this ratio increases to 200 to 1.

The large proportion of white male suicides does not, however, diminish the importance of studying other gender, racial and ethnic groups. Current research shows that there are distinct patterns of suicide and parasuicidal risk among members of minority groups that warrant investigation (e.g. Karch, Barker and Strine 2007; Welch 2001). The native people of North America have the highest rates of suicide of any minority group in the USA and Canada. The trend for increased mortality with older age which is seen in whites does not apply to this minority group, however. Instead, the subset with highest mortality in the USA (35.3/100,000) are those between the ages of 15 and 24 years. Currently, the suicide rate among young Native Canadians living on reservations is about five to six times higher than that of the non-native population (Merrick and Zalsman 2005). Quantz (1997) has argued that, historically, suicide was very uncommon in the ancestors of most aboriginal nations. Suicide rates increased, particularly in the twentieth century, in part as a result of cultural disintegration, including a breakdown in the religious, familial and social structures of the community.

The pattern of increased mortality among younger people, particularly males, has become more pronounced in recent decades, and also applies to blacks and Hispanics, which are the two largest minority groups in the United States (CDC 2007). With the increasing size of the Hispanic population in the USA, and the barriers to mental health treatment faced by minority groups in general, the increasing prevalence of suicidal behaviour in this group has the potential to become a major public health issue (NIMH 1999).

Since the 1960s there has been a threefold increase in the rate of suicide among older male adolescents. Age-specific mortality rates are six times higher among 15–19-year-olds compared to 10–14-year-olds, with males being four times more likely to commit suicide than females. The increase in teenage suicidal behaviour among US males has been attributed in part to the increased availability of firearms, and substance abuse.

Among females suicide rates have remained low and stable over time, but attempted suicide has been very high, with current research showing that young women attempt suicide twice as often as men (Merrick and Zalsman 2005).

Risk factors

Risk factors for suicide include those factors relating to demographics, adverse environment, socialization practices and situational determinants that create vulnerabilities in children and young people such that they may attempt to or actually intentionally kill themselves. More than 90% of people who complete suicide have a psychiatric and/or substance abuse diagnosis. This places mental illness at the top of the list of risk factors. The most common diagnoses are major depression, bipolar disorder and schizophrenia (Tanney 2000). Alcohol use disorders are the most commonly associated with suicide, occurring in as many as 56% of completed suicides (Conwell et al. 1996). As many as 40% of alcoholics attempt suicide at some time in their lives, with 7% completing (Sher 2006). Brady (2006) proposed a theoretical model which holds that alcohol misuse is depressogenic, and increases the incidence of negative life events in individuals with a genetic predisposition to such behaviour. Suicide emerges as a result of these combined factors. Research indicating that a family history of mental illness and substance abuse increases risk of suicide appears to support this model (Baca-Garcia *et al.* 2007). One of the most reliable predictors of future suicide is having made an attempt in the past (Christiansen and Jensen 2007).

Of all the situational variables associated with suicide, owning, or having access to a firearm or other lethal means of self-destruction is the most potent (Miller *et al.* 2007). Firearms are used in over half of all suicides, and are more frequently used in suicide than in homicide. In the USA firearms are used in suicide primarily by men. Whites use firearms in suicide at twice the rates of blacks or other racial/ethnic groups (Romero and Wintemute 2002).

Risk factors for suicide vary according to gender, age, culture and other factors. Some risk factors are specific to adolescents. Remschmidt and Schwab (1978) identified four important predictors of suicidal behaviour in a sample of inpatient and outpatient children and adolescents (10–18 years) in Germany. These included family conflict, romantic conflict, problems in school and developmental crises. Notably, mental disorders were not viewed as significant predictors in this sample.

Meichenbaum (1994) reported factors which identify individuals at increased risk of suicidal behaviour. These included suicidal intent (e.g. preoccupation with death and dying, availability of a weapon, expression of suicidal thoughts), psychiatric history (e.g. anxiety proneness, abuse of alcohol and drugs, marked personality changes and prior suicidal attempts), thought processes (e.g. preoccupation with the self, high self-awareness, cognitive rigidity, impulsive behaviour), depressive symptoms (e.g. change in eating and sleeping habits, sense of hopelessness, despair over personal problems), poor self-concept (e.g. guilt proneness and self-blame, shame concerning personal failure and feelings of worthlessness), psychosocial features (high frequency of critical stressful events, experience of social exclusion), and unrealistic expectations (students who perform above average suddenly displaying below average performance, teenagers unable to meet parental expectations).

Meichenbaum (1994) also pointed out an important distinction between suicidal and self-injurious behaviour. Whereas suicidal behaviour is often associated with apathy and lack of motivation and a lack of anger expression, self-injurious behaviour is often related to anger, irritability and hostility.

Agerbo, Nadescroft and Mortensen (2002) found that a dysfunctional family environment marked by mental illness or suicidality in the parent, low socioeconomic status, and poor education on the part of the parents and proband were strong predictors of completed suicide in a population case-control sample involving over 20,000 subjects in Denmark. In terms of internal factors, Groholt *et al.* (2000) found that loneliness and depression were the most important predictors of self-harm in a study of all suicide attempters between 13 and 19 years admitted to medical wards in an area of Norway. Those individuals with depression, disruptive disorders and low self-worth were significantly more likely to have attempted suicide.

Kirkcaldy, Brown and Siefen (2006) divided the determinants of self-injury and attempted suicide among adolescents into common and specific factors. For example, age, disharmony within the family and excessive parental demands were common determinants of suicidal behaviour for all adolescents. However, these factors were unrelated to self-injurious or socially disruptive behaviour. Factors specific to self-injury included parental under-involvement and feelings of hostile rejection. Their analysis also identified gender-specific predictors of self-injurious and suicidal behaviour. Among females, age was a strong predictor, whereas among males the number of siblings and disability among family members were unique predictors of self-directed aggression. In addition to risk factors, there are a number of factors that may trigger or precipitate suicidal behaviour. Several of these were enumerated by Braun-Scharm and Poustka (2004), including relationship crises; interpersonal loss; poor social support; a history of neglect or abuse, poor cognitive or social skills; excessive demands in school, family and work; and a history of suicidal behaviour. Among the personality characteristics are irritability, impulsivity, hypersensitivity to and intolerance of criticism, excessive anticipatory anxiety, and a chronic depressive mood.

Suicide is not a single behaviour, and has many determinants and complexities. Epidemiological and clinical studies have attempted to identify factors that enhance risk of suicide for use in developing theoretical models that may help minimize error in prediction. No single factor can be considered predictive. It is believed that the greater the number of risk factors present, the higher the potential for suicide (Maris 2002).

Protective factors

In general, protective factors are thought to be the opposite of risk factors, i.e. if having a mental illness increases risk of suicide, then having no mental illness should be protective. This method of determining protective factors may inaccurately assume that risk and protective factors are in a binary opposition to each other. In reality, people experience simultaneous risks and protections of varying potency. Some research has investigated cultural factors that serve a protective function for some ethnic groups with low rates of suicide. African Americans, for example have surprisingly low rates of suicide, given the number of known risk factors, such as poverty, alienation, violence and barriers to mental health care, that often co-occur in their communities. It is believed by many that religiosity (Gibbs 1997), the primacy of family networks and social support (Compton, Thompson and Kaslow 2005) play an important role in protecting African Americans from suicidal intentions. Research on cultural effects on suicide resilience has also found that African Americans report having stronger moral objections to suicide and a higher level of coping-related beliefs compared to whites (Morrison and Downey 2000).

Conclusions

The diagnosis and treatment of individuals at high risk of suicide would be greatly improved if clinicians and educators were aware of relevant risk factors that predispose and precipitate suicidal behaviour. By recognizing psychological disorders at an early age, more effective and timely interventions may be made. In the current era, much improvement is needed within educational systems to identify psychological problems among students. Effective screening in educational and primary care settings may be a valuable way to identify those at risk. Therapeutic strategies could then be implemented before a situation worsens. Jongsma and Peterson (1999) have offered a range of therapeutic interventions to deal with suicidal ideation. These include assessing and monitoring suicidal behaviour; increasing communication with significant others; facilitating feelings of being understood by providing an empathic environment; exploring sources of alienation, emotional pain and hopelessness; assisting teenagers to become aware of significant life events which may trigger suicidal ideation; encouraging normal eating and sleeping patterns; encouraging individuals to keep a record of self-defeating thoughts (cognitions related to catastrophizing and hopelessness); and getting clients to implement alternative stress-coping strategies, such as physical activity, increased emotional expression and increased social interaction.

REFERENCES

Agerbo, E., Nadescroft, M. and Mortensen, P. B. (2002) Familial, psychiatric and socio-economic risk factors for suicide in young people: nested case-control study. *British Medical Journal*, 325: 74.

Baca-Garcia, E., Perez-Rodriguez, M. M., Saiz-Gonzalez, D., Basurte-Villamor, I., Saiz-Ruiz, J., Leiva-Murillo, J. M. *et al.* (2007) Variables associated with familial suicide attempts in a sample of suicide attempters: progress in neuropsychopharmacology and biological psychiatry. un 7; [Epub ahead of print]

Brady, J. (2006) The association between alcohol misuse and suicidal behaviour. *Alcohol and Alcoholism*, 41: 473–8.

Braun-Scharm, H. and Poustka, F. (2004) *Leitlinien zu Diagnostik und Therapie von psychischen Störungen. Deutschen Gesellschaft für Kinder- und Jugendpsychiatrie und Psychotherapie, der Bundesgemeinschaft leitender Klinikärzte für Kinder- und Jugendpsychiatrie und Psychotherapie und dem Berufsverband der Ärzte für Kinder- und Jugendpsychiatrie und Psychotherapie*, 2nd edn. Cologne: Deutsche Ärzte-Verlag.

Centers for Disease Control (CDC) (2007) WISQARS website 'Fatal Injury Reports' and 'Leading Cause of Deaths Reports': www.cdc.gov/ncipc/wisqars/ (accessed 15 January 2007).

Christiansen, E. and Jensen, B. F. (2007) Risk of repetition of suicide attempt, suicide or all deaths after an episode of attempted suicide: a register-based survival analysis. *Australian and New Zealand Journal of Psychiatry*, 41: 257–65.

Compton, M. T., Thompson, N. J. and Kaslow, N. J. (2005) Social environment factors associated with suicide attempt among low-income African Americans: the protective role of family relationships and social support. *Social Psychiatry and Psychiatric Epidemiology*, 40: 175–85.

Conwell, Y., Duberstein, P. R., Cox, C., Herrmann, J. H. *et al.* (1996) Relationship of age and Axis I diagnoses in victims of completed suicide: a psychological autopsy study. *American Journal of Psychiatry*, 153: 1001–8.

Gibbs, J. T. (1997) African-American suicide: a cultural paradox. *Suicide and Life Threatening Behavior*, 27(1): 68–79.

Groholt, B., Ekeberg, O., Wichstrom, L. and Haldorsen, T. (2000) Young suicide attempters: a comparison between a clinical and an epidemiological sample. *Journal of the American Academy of Child and Adolescent Psychiatry*, 39: 868–75.

Jongsma, A. E. and Peterson, L. M. (1999) *The Complete Adult Psychotherapy Treatment Planner*. New York: Wiley.

Karch, D. L., Barker, L. and Strine, T. W. (2007) Race/ethnicity, substance abuse and mental illness among suicide victims in 13 states: 2004 data from the National Violent Death Reporting System. *Injury Prevention*, 12 (suppl. II), ii22–ii27.

Kirkcaldy, B. D., Brown, J. and Siefen, R. G. (2006) Self-injury, suicidal ideation and intent and disruptive behavioural disorders: psychological and sociological determinants among German adolescents in psychiatric care. *International Journal of Adolescent Medicine and Health*, 18: 597–614.

Maris, R. W. (2002) Suicide. *The Lancet*, 360: 319–26.

Meichenbaum, D. (1994) *Treating Post-Traumatic Stress Disorder: A Handbook and Practice Manual for Therapy*. Chichester: Wiley.

Merrick, J. and Zalsman, G. (eds.) (2005) *Suicidal Behavior in Adolescence: An International Perspective*. London/Tel Aviv: Freund.

Miller, M., Lippmann, S. J., Azrael, D. and Hemenway, D. (2007) Household firearm ownership and rates of suicide across the 50 United States. *Journal of Trauma*, 62: 1029–34.

Morrison, L. L. and Downey, D. L. (2000) Racial differences in self-disclosure of suicidal ideation and reasons for living: implications for training. *Cultural Diversity and Ethnic Minority Psychology*, 6: 374–86.

Moscicki, E. (1995) Epidemiology of suicide. *International Psychogeriatrics*, 7: 137–48.
   (2001) Epidemiology of completed and attempted suicide: toward a framework for prevention. *Clinical Neuroscience Research*, 1: 310–23.

National Institutes of Mental Health (1999) *Mental Health: A Report of the Surgeon General*. Rockville, MD: US Department of Health and Human Services, Center for Mental Health Services, National Institutes of Health, National Institute of Mental Health.

Ohberg, A. and Lonnqvist, J. (1998) Suicides hidden among undetermined deaths. *Acta Psychiatria Scandinavica*, 98: 214–18.

Quantz, D. H. (1997) Cultural and self disruption: suicide among First Nations adolescents. Paper submitted to the 8th Canadian Association for Suicide Prevention Conference, Thunder Bay, Ontario.

Remschmidt, H. and Schwab, T. (1978) Suicide behavior in children and young adults. *Acta Paedopsychiatrica*, 43: 197–208.

Rockett, R. H., Samora, J. B. and Coben, J. H. (2006) The black–white suicide paradox: possible effects of misclassification. *Social Science and Medicine*, 63: 2165–75.

Romero, M. P. and Wintemute, G. J. (2002) The epidemiology of firearm suicide in the United States. *Journal of Urban Health*, 79: 39–48.

Sher, L. (2006) Risk and protective factors for suicide in patients with alcoholism. *The Scientific World*, 6: 1405–11.

Tanney, B. L. (2000) Psychiatric diagnoses and suicide. In R. W. Maris, A. L. Berman and M. M. Silverman (eds.), *Comprehensive Textbook of Suicidology*, pp. 311–41. New York: Guilford Press.

Welch, S. S. (2001) A review of the literature on the epidemiology of parasuicide in the general population. *Psychiatric Services* 52: 368–75.

World Health Organization (WHO) (2007) Suicide rates per 100,000 by country, year and sex (table) as of December 2005. www.who.int/mental_health/prevention/suicide_rates/en/index.html (accessed 15 July 2007).

Camilla Herbert

See also chapter 2.2 Credibility.

Definition: who is a vulnerable adult?

In March 2000 the Department of Health and the Home Office published the document *No Secrets: Guidance on Developing and Implementing Multiagency Policies and Procedures to Protect Vulnerable Adults from Abuse*. This document provided a national definition of the terms 'vulnerable adult' and 'abuse'. *No Secrets* defines a vulnerable adult as *someone who is 18 or over who is or may be in need of a community care service because of mental or other disability, age or illness and who is unable to take care of him or herself, or unable to protect him or herself against significant harm or exploitation.*

The term 'community services' is used broadly to cover all social and healthcare regardless of setting or context, and 'harm' includes not only physical ill-treatment and sexual abuse but also ill-treatment that is not physical and which includes avoidable deterioration in physical or mental health.

The focus of *No Secrets* was on adult protection, and since then there has been a move towards using a broader term 'safeguarding adults'. In October 2005 the Association of Directors of Social Services (ADSS) published 'Safeguarding adults', which outlines eleven standards for all authorities to meet in terms of providing a comprehensive framework to meet the intentions set out in the *No Secrets* document. The concept of 'keeping people safe' focuses on people who may be vulnerable or in vulnerable situations. These are people who are at risk of harm or abuse because they are perceived as easy targets owing to their age or disabilities; others live with few or no social contacts or in situations where they rely on others for daily support, or they lack the mental capacity to be aware of what may be happening to them. However, there is a lack of agreement regarding the definitions of 'vulnerable' or 'vulnerable adult' within the different pieces of legislation, for example, within the Care Standards Act 2000, the Youth Justice and Criminal Evidence Act 1999 and the Safeguarding Vulnerable Groups Act 2006. Differing definitions are employed, for example, legislation in Scotland no longer uses the term 'vulnerable adult' and uses instead 'adult at risk'.

Vulnerable adults and capacity

The Mental Capacity Act 2005 applies to all adults in England and Wales and there is similar legislation in Scotland (Incapacity Act (Scotland) 2000) and in other jurisdictions. Legislation regarding capacity therefore applies to all adults and not just those who are vulnerable. Identifying that an individual lacks capacity to make a decision does not automatically mean that she or he is a vulnerable adult and, by contrast, many adults who are vulnerable may have capacity to make decisions. It is also difficult to separate intellectually and in framing legislation situations where a person lacks the mental capacity to recognize what is happening to them as abuse from those where the person does have the capacity but chooses to ignore, condone or accept the abuse.

It is beyond the scope of this chapter to consider all aspects of 'keeping people safe'; the main focus will be on the Mental Capacity Act 2005 and the Deprivation of Liberty Safeguards, i.e. on the issues that arise when a person is deemed to lack capacity to make a specific decision and the protections that are in place for those whose lack of capacity places them in a vulnerable position. Although the focus is on the implementation of the MCA 2005 and Deprivation of Liberty Safeguards, due regard should also be given to local policies on safeguarding adults.

The Mental Capacity Act (England and Wales) 2005

The Mental Capacity Act 2005 sets out a new offence of ill-treatment or neglect of a person who lacks capacity. It also clarifies the legal position in relation to the definition of capacity, and provides a legal framework to make decisions on behalf of people who lack the capacity to do so. In many cases these people will be highly vulnerable and it may be for these reasons that their capacity is being assessed or found lacking. The Scottish Parliament passed similar legislation in 2000 (Incapacity Act (Scotland) 2000).

The Mental Capacity Act (MCA 2005) includes a set of guiding principles and definitions of capacity summarized below.

The principles

1. A person must be assumed to have capacity unless it is established that s/he lacks capacity.
2. A person is not to be treated as unable to make a decision unless all practicable steps to help him/her to do so have been taken without success.
3. A person is not to be treated as unable to make a decision merely because s/he makes an unwise decision.
4. An act done, or decisions made, under this Act or on behalf of someone who lacks capacity must be done, or made in his/her best interests.
5. Before the act is done, or the decision is made, regard must be had to whether the purpose for which it is needed can be as effectively achieved in a way that is less restrictive of the person's rights and freedom of action.

How the Act defines capacity

For the purposes of this Act, a person lacks capacity in relation to a matter if at the material time s/he is unable to make a decision for him/herself in relation to the matter because of an impairment of, or a disturbance in the functioning of, the mind or brain (whether permanent or temporary) *and* if s/he is unable to do any of the following steps in decision making:

- Understand the information relevant to the decision.
- Retain that information.
- Use or weigh that information as part of the process of making the decision.
- Communicate his/her decision (whether by talking, sign language or other means).

The information relevant to a decision includes information about the reasonably foreseeable consequences of (a) deciding one way or another, or (b) failing to make the decision. The fact that a person is able to retain information relevant to a decision for a short period only does not prevent him/her from being regarded as able to make the decision.

Best interests decision making

If an individual is assessed as lacking capacity to take a specific decision then that decision can be taken on their behalf in consideration of their best interests, and the Mental Capacity Act 2005 provides a framework for that decision making. It requires the decision maker to consult widely, including with family and friends; where the individual has no family or friends and the decision is a major one (significant medical treatment and/or change of placement), the health provider or local authority is legally required to consult an independent mental capacity advocate (IMCA) to ascertain the views of the individual. It is within this context that overlap with the Safeguarding Vulnerable Adults policies may be highlighted. The Act includes a 'best interests' checklist which includes:

- One cannot consider age, appearance, condition or behaviour.
- All relevant circumstances must be considered.
- Every effort should be made to encourage and enable the person concerned to take part.
- Non-urgent decisions should be deferred if the individual could regain capacity.
- Past and present wishes, beliefs and values should be taken into account.
- Consider the views of anyone named by person to be consulted; anyone engaged in caring for the person or interested in their welfare; LPA or deputy.

A best interests meeting may be convened and would be expected to take into account the following:

- How to encourage participation in the decision-making process
- All relevant circumstances
- How to determine the person's views
- Ensuring that there is no discrimination
- Whether the person might regain capacity
- If the decision concerns life-sustaining treatment, that no assumptions are made about quality of life, and that those involved must not be motivated by death of the individual
- Consult others
- Avoid restricting the person's rights

Guidance on running a best interests meeting is set out in a booklet sponsored by the Department of Health and published by the British Psychological Society, entitled 'Best interest decision making' (2008).

Deprivation of Liberty Safeguards 2007

The Deprivation of Liberty Safeguards (2007) address the 'Bournewood Gap' arising from the case of HL. HL was an autistic man who had profound learning disabilities and who lacked capacity to consent to, or to refuse, admission to hospital for treatment. The European Court of Human Rights

(ECtHR) in October 2004 held that he was *deprived of his liberty* when he was admitted, informally, to Bournewood Hospital. The ECtHR held that the manner in which HL was deprived of liberty was not in accordance with 'a procedure prescribed by law' and breached article 5(1) of the European Convention on Human Rights (ECHR). One of the difficulties in implementing the European Court ruling has been the lack of definition of what constitutes a deprivation of liberty. The Court stated that

- To determine whether there has been a deprivation of liberty, the starting-point must be the specific situation of the individual concerned and account must be taken of a whole range of factors arising in a particular case such as the type, duration, effects and manner of implementation of the measure in question. The distinction between a deprivation of, and restriction upon, liberty is merely one of degree or intensity and not one of nature or substance. (*ECtHR HL* v. *UK* 2004)

The British government introduced legislation to ensure compliance with this ruling and from 1 April 2009 where an individual is unable to either consent or refuse a particular treatment or course of action which deprives them of (rather than restricts) their liberty, the Deprivation of Liberty Safeguards provide a procedure in law that meets the European Court's requirements and ensures compliance with the Human Rights Act. The Deprivation of Liberty Safeguards were passed by Parliament in Westminster in April 2007 and were enacted on 1 April 2009.

Where a care plan may constitute a deprivation of liberty and the individual in question lacks capacity to consent to this care plan, it may be necessary to protect the rights of that individual by applying for a Deprivation of Liberty Authorization. The Code of Practice 2008 sets out the requirements in detail. The intention of the Deprivation of Liberty Safeguards is to provide protection for those who lack the capacity to consent to their care package where that care package is such that it could constitute a deprivation of their liberty, which would not otherwise be legally justifiable. In some cases these clients may also be subject to Vulnerable Adults procedures as their ability to cope in the community may have been called into question. The Deprivation of Liberty Safeguards provide a legal framework to deprive someone of their liberty which can otherwise only be achieved using the Mental Health Act or, in criminal cases, through a prison sentence. The Deprivation of Liberty Safeguards do not provide permission to physically restrain individuals, other than as already authorized by the Mental Capacity Act (2005), i.e. as a proportionate response and in the best interests of the individual.

The Safeguards were passed by Parliament in April 2007 and came into force in 2009. They apply to all hospitals and registered care homes in England and Wales. The legislation places a requirement on the primary care trusts and local authorities managing these facilities to act as supervisory bodies to assess Deprivation of Liberty applications. The process of authorization involves six tests, to be completed within twenty-one days (seven days for an urgent authorization).

1. Age – 18 or over.
2. Eligibility – relates to the person's status or potential status under the Mental Health Act 1983, i.e. whether the person should be covered by that Act rather than the MCA (2005).
3. No refusals – to establish whether there is another authority for decision making for that person, e.g. a valid advance decision, a valid decision by an LPA or deputy appointed by the Court of Protection.
4. Mental capacity assessment, i.e. whether the person lacks capacity to consent to the arrangements proposed for their care.
5. Mental health assessment, i.e. is the person suffering from a mental disorder within the meaning of the MHA 1983 (this is not a determination of the need for mental health treatment). This must be completed by a section 12 approved doctor.
6. Best interests assessment, i.e. to determine whether a deprivation of liberty is occurring / going to occur and if so, is it in the best interests of the person and is it a proportionate response. Best interest assessors must have completed the agreed training and be accredited by the supervisory body.

In deciding whether to apply for a Deprivation of Liberty authorization the key factors to consider include whether:

- The person is allowed to leave the facility.
- The person has no or very limited choice about their life within the care home or hospital.
- The person is prevented from maintaining contact with the world outside the care home or hospital.

The responsibility for requesting an authorization for deprivation of liberty is placed upon the registered managers of care homes. Where care home managers take the view that the care plan in place restricts the liberty of an individual rather than deprives them of their liberty, they do not need to request authorization. This can be challenged and a request for authorization would then need to be made.

Other relevant legislation

There is other legislation that refers to vulnerable adults and may be relevant in relation to their capacity to make decisions.

The Fraud Act 2006 came into force on 15 January 2007. It repeals all of the deception offences in the Theft Acts of 1968 and 1978 and provides a statutory definition of the single criminal offence of fraud. Section 4 of the Act is most significant for vulnerable adults as it provides an offence of fraud by abuse of position.

The Domestic Violence, Crime and Victims Act 2004 set out a new offence of causing or allowing the death of a child or vulnerable adult through abuse/neglect.

The Sexual Offences Act 2003 came into force on 1 May 2005. This Act contains a range of new offences and provides harsher sentences for sexual offences against children and vulnerable adults. It also provides new measure to strengthen and monitor offenders. Under section 7.4 of the Act a person *consents if s/he agrees by choice and has the freedom and capacity to make that choice.* Sections 30–44 of the Act relate to sexual activity with a person with a mental disorder, which impedes their choice (sections 30–33), makes them vulnerable to threats, inducements or deceptions (sections 34–37), or in a care relationship (sections 38–41) The Act states that an individual lacks capacity to choose if they lack *sufficient understanding of nature of the act or the reasonably foreseeable consequences of what is being done or for any other reason.* This is a different definition of capacity from that included in the Mental Capacity Act 2005. It should also be noted that if an adult is deemed not to have capacity with regard to decisions about sexual relationships, no one else can make that decision on their behalf. The framework provided by the Mental Capacity Act to make decisions on behalf of those incapable of making them for themselves cannot be used to make decisions regarding sexual consent.

Summary

There is considerable overlap between legislation and guidance relating to the assessment and management of decision-making capacity and that which is designed to keep safe vulnerable adults. Identifying that an individual lacks capacity to make a decision does not automatically mean that she or he is a vulnerable adult and, by contrast, many adults who are vulnerable may have capacity to make decisions. However, people who lack capacity to make decisions for themselves can be at particular risk of harm or abuse and people who may be vulnerable or in vulnerable situations are the main focus of initiatives to 'keep people safe'. Familiarity with the relevant legislation and guidance is essential.

Relevant legislation

Care Standards Act 2000
Domestic Violence Crime and Victims Act 2004
Fraud Act 2006
Incapacity Act (Scotland) 2000
Mental Capacity Act 2005
Mental Capacity Act 2005: Deprivation of Liberty Safeguards
Safeguarding Vulnerable Groups Act 2006.
Youth Justice and Criminal Evidence Act 1999
Sexual Offences Act 2003

Guidance and codes of practice

No Secrets: Guidance on Developing and Implementing Multiagency Policies and Procedures to Protect Vulnerable Adults from Abuse (Department of Health and Home Office 2000).

Safeguarding Adults: A National Framework of Standards for Good Practice and Outcomes in Adult Protection Work (Association of Directors of Adult Social Services, 2005).

Mental Capacity Act Code of Practice (2007) Department of Constitutional Affairs, UK.

Mental Capacity Act 2005: Deprivation of Liberty Safeguards – Code of Practice to supplement the main Mental Capacity Act 2005 Code of Practice, (2008). Department of Constitutional Affairs, UK.

Part III

Interventions

3.1 Child sexual abuse

Miranda A. H. Horvath

See also chapter 1.12 Sexual offenders, chapter 2.19 Post-traumatic stress disorder, chapter 4.7 Internet sexual offending, chapter 4.10 Sexual assault, chapter 4.11 Sexual fantasy and sex offending, chapter 4.12 stalking, chapter 5.3 Consent and capacity in civil cases.

Definition of symptoms

Research has shown that sexual abuse in childhood can have both short- and long-term effects, although there is considerable individual variation as to when the symptoms manifest themselves, and their severity (Neumann *et al.* 1996; Tebbutt *et al.* 1997). For example, 20–50% of children have been found to be symptom free when they were assessed (Kendall-Tackett, Meyer-Williams and Finkelhor 1993), but within a few months of disclosure 30% of children show clinically significant problems (Wolfe, Gentile and Wolfe 1989). Between 49% and 60% of sexually abused children meet diagnostic criteria for post-traumatic stress disorder (PTSD: Dubner and Motta 1999; Wolfe and Birt 2004). Characteristic symptoms of PTSD are developed after exposure to the traumatic stressor (e.g. sexual abuse) and include disorganized or agitated behaviour, persistent re-experiencing of the traumatic event and avoidance of stimuli associated with the trauma (DSM-IV: American Psychiatric Association 1994).

Furthermore, childhood sexual abuse has been shown to be a significant risk factor for many mental health disorders and problems, and a substantial proportion of children who are victims of sexual abuse develop serious emotional and behavioural difficulties (Beitchman *et al.* 1991, 1992; Browne and Finkelhor 1986; Fergusson, Lynskey and Horwood 1996; Gomes-Schwartz, Horowitz and Cardarelli 1990; Hanson *et al.* 2001; Kendall-Tackett *et al.* 1993; Saunders *et al.* 1999). Wolfe (2006, p. 680) highlights three key findings from previous literature reviews regarding sexual abuse sequelae:

1. Sexually abused children display and report more internalizing and externalizing adjustment problems than their non-abused peers.
2. Sexually abused children display a broad range of behavioural and emotional problems, some specifically linked to their sexual abuse experience and others apparently linked to the familial and other environment circumstances often associated with sexual maltreatment (e.g. parent–child relationship problems, parental adjustment problems).
3. Two problem areas – PTSD symptoms and sexuality problems – appear to represent specific effects of sexual abuse in that they are disproportionately prevalent among sexually abused children as compared to groups of other troubled children (e.g. clinic-referred non-abused children).

Briere (1992) also draws attention to the importance of sequelae, and articulates the need for any intervention to address both the primary and secondary victimization effects. In fact, the literature on child sexual abuse has described almost every psychological problem as being experienced by victims (Berliner 1991; Briere 1992). This bleak picture highlights the critical need for effective interventions for preventing (where possible) and managing these outcomes. This chapter will provide an overview of the interventions currently available. Only child-focused interventions will be outlined as there are different needs and concerns for adult survivors (see chapter 2.19), perpetrators (see chapter 3.12) and parents (see chapter 2.14).

Interventions

There is a wide range of therapeutic treatments available that have been developed from a wide range of theoretical approaches, such as humanist, psychoanalysis, feminist and family systems (Bagley and King 1990). To complicate matters further, there are huge variations between interventions in their theoretical, clinical and empirical basis and support (Saunders, Berliner and Hanson 2004). This raises concerns about their utility, which is compounded by evidence from Berliner and Saunders (1996) that even when receiving treatments with empirical support some children's psychological wellbeing deteriorates.

Current thinking, research and practice

Issues facing those offering treatment

The treatment offered must be based on the findings of the assessment and should be explained and discussed with the child and relevant family members/carers (Saunders *et al.* 2004). Shared understanding and agreement about the need for, and plan of, treatment is a contributing factor to the likelihood of its success. The primary concern for those offering treatment is the needs of the child, but this is far from straightforward as children vary as to when they present for treatment post-disclosure, and then their needs differ widely (Wolfe 2006). There is widespread agreement in the literature that although treatment is widely recommended and treatment programmes have flourished, theory and evaluation have not kept pace (Berliner and Conte 1995; Kolko 1987).

Approaches to treatment

Wolfe (2006) proposes that sexually abused children often require treatment that has three core components: stabilization, abuse-specific treatment and social reintegration. As has already been mentioned, there are many different approaches to treatments, some of which involve the child talking about what has happened to them in the form of a narrative account, such as the 'narrative elaboration procedure' (Saywitz and Snyder 1993), or others where the child expresses what happened to them without necessarily giving a narrative account, for example play therapy.

Other interventions are multicomponent, such as 'gradual exposure' intervention (i.e. systematic desensitization and prolonged exposure) (Deblinger and Heflin 1996). Saunders *et al.*'s (2004) guidelines for treatment of child sexual abuse reviewed and evaluated a wide range of treatment approaches with the aim of establishing 'a clear, criteria-based system for classifying interventions and treatments according to their theoretical, clinical, and empirical support' (p. 20). Table 3.1.1 summarizes the child-focused interventions they reviewed and indicates the score they awarded (the lower the score the greater level of support they found for the treatment approach; the scores range from 1–6). When concluding their report, Saunders *et al.* (2004) suggest twenty-one principles of treatment that can be applied in most cases and can be used as a guide to treatment planning.

Table 3.1.1 A range of child-focused interventions. Adapted from Saunders *et al.* (2004)

Intervention	Author/Year	Target	Score
Cognitive-behavioural and dynamic play therapy for children with sexual behaviour problems and their caregivers	Bonner, Walker and Berliner (1999)	6–12-year-olds exhibiting sexual behaviour beyond normal child sexuality and that causes problems in their functioning	3
Cognitive Processing Therapy	Resick and Schnicke (1993)	Brief, structured, cognitive-behavioural treatment designed to treat PTSD and its associated features	3
Eye movement desensitization and reprocessing	Shapiro (1995)	Multicomponent therapeutic procedure for traumatic memories and PTSD	3
Resilient peer training intervention	Fantuzzo, Weiss and Coolahan (1998)	School-based intervention for young abused children based on an ecological model using competent peers and parent helpers to increase child's social competence	3
Therapeutic child development programme	Childhaven	Milieu-based intervention for maltreated preschool children that reduces risk factors and enhances protective factors	3
Trauma-focused cognitive-behavioural therapy	Deblinger and Heflin (1996)	Intervention based on learning and cognitive theories to reduce children's negative emotional and behavioural responses and correct maladaptive beliefs and attributions related to their abusive experiences	1
Trauma-focused integrative-eclectic therapy	Friedrich (1995)	Children or teenagers are treated with a psychosocial intervention based on data suggesting that persistent effects of trauma and maltreatment are best understood as a function of both the child and child's relationships and living context	3
Trauma-focused play therapy	Gil (1991)	A psychotherapeutic intervention that uses play as a mechanism for allowing abused children to use symbols (toys) to externalize their internal world, project their thoughts and feelings, and process potentially overwhelming material from a safe distance	4

Three broad groupings of treatments will now be discussed in more depth: cognitive-behavioural approaches, individual treatment and group treatment.

Cognitive-behavioural approaches

Cognitive-behavioural approaches derive from four theories of learning: respondent conditioning; operant conditioning; observational learning; and cognitive learning. They combine an integrated approach to assessment and intervention which pays careful attention to the developmental and social contexts in which learning occurs (MacDonald *et al.* 2004). Macdonald, Higgins and Ranchandani (2006) conducted a detailed review of these interventions for children who have been sexually abused; and whilst they identify many examples of effective practice, the need for a much stronger evidence base is also highlighted.

Individual treatment

Cognitive-behavioural approaches are often individual; however, they will not be discussed here as they have been covered in the previous section. Perhaps the most widely recognized form of individual treatment is individual psychotherapy, which involves the therapist and child meeting together for an hour a week. It can be either abuse focused or not. The key elements of abuse-focused psychotherapy are respect, positive regard and an assumption of growth; it takes a phenomenological perspective that focuses on the functionality of symptoms and defences. It follows a therapeutic structure where therapy is reality based and social context is considered of prime importance (Briere 1992). Sullivan *et al.* (1992) found that when used with deaf sexually abused children, individual psychotherapy was generally an effective treatment, but there were differing levels of success between boys and girls.

Another treatment that falls into this category is trauma-focused play therapy, which is usually conducted with children aged 2–12 years. It is based on integrated theories of play therapy, systems theory and child development. There are two schools of thought about play therapy, non-directive and focused; it is widely thought that non-directive is ineffective for treating child victims of sexual abuse (see Rasmussen and Cunningham 1995 for a discussion and possible solutions). Broadly, in play therapy the choice of toys is purposeful and can allow the child to use the toy as a literal symbol of the trauma. Children are encouraged to provide a narrative of their play and, if they keep getting stuck doing repetitive negative play, the therapist can intervene and guide the child through other options that can lead to more adaptive outcomes. As Saunders *et al.*'s (2004) evaluation showed (see table 3.1.1), this intervention does not have a strong theoretical basis and has not been rigorously evaluated.

Group treatment

Group treatment is considered to be the treatment of choice amongst those working with child victims of sexual abuse (Faller 1993). It is particularly useful because the children are exposed to other victims and subsequently do not feel alone. Furthermore it can be useful for helping child victims understand that people cannot simply look at them and identify them as a sexual abuse victim (Dominguez, Nelke and Perry 2001).

Group-based interventions can include group discussions, art and role play, as demonstrated in Delson and Clark's (1981) study, which found that the combination of these approaches is likely to mitigate the redevelopment of repression and denial (Gough 1993). Goal-orientated and structured group therapy can also be used (see, for example, Hall-Marley and Damon 1993). Furniss, Bingley-Miller and van Elburg (1988) outline an approach in which the goals are to help the victim find a language in which to communicate about the abuse, to improve their self-esteem and help them overcome isolation by sharing with peers. Furniss *et al.* (1988) report significant improvements post-treatment and some longer-lasting effects in follow-up, but also highlight the need for careful consideration of the sex of the therapist, how challenging behaviour by the victims is dealt with and the importance of links with the family and social worker.

Conclusion

A recurring theme in the literature is the paucity of treatment outcome studies and it has been highlighted by a number of authors that more progress has been made in the investigation than in the treatment of childhood sexual abuse (e.g. Faller 1993). Much more work is needed on prevention and therapeutic interventions for victims; however, the age-old problem remains, 'how to motivate clinicians in the field to actually use theoretically sound and empirically supported treatments?' (Saunders *et al.* 2004, p. 7). There is some evidence that abuse-specific treatment programmes are more successful than generic therapy (Gomes-Schwartz *et al.* 1990), and it is clear that effective interventions require early identification and coordinated responses from different agencies (Bagley and King 1990). Certainly considerable effort is needed to ensure that the possibility raised by Berliner and Conte (1995) does not become a reality: 'There's speculation about the possibility that intervention may be more distressing than the abuse itself, or at least that it may exacerbate the negative impact of the abuse experience' (p. 372).

FURTHER READING

Saunders, Berliner and Hanson's (2004) report is a useful up-to-date overview and critique of many of the available treatment approaches. Vicky Wolfe's chapter on child sexual abuse in Mash's (2006) book *Treatment of Childhood Disorders* is an excellent starting point for a broad overview of the area. Friedrich's 1990 and 1995 books on psychotherapy for sexually abused children will provide the interested reader with a comprehensive grounding in the issues. Any of the extensive publications by Lucy Berliner and John Briere and their numerous collaborators should be also be consulted for coverage of a range of interventions.

REFERENCES

American Psychiatric Association (1994) *Diagnostic and Statistical Manual of Mental Disorders*, 4th edn (DSM-IV). Washington, DC: American Psychiatric Association.

Bagley, C. and King, K. (1990) *Child Sexual Abuse: The Search for Healing*. London: Tavistock/Routledge.

Berliner, L. (1991) Therapy with victimized children and their families. In J. N. Briere (ed.), *Treating Victims of Child Sexual Abuse*, pp. 209–28. San Francisco: Jossey-Bass.

Berliner, L. and Conte, J. (1995) The process of victimisation: the victim's perspective. *Child Abuse and Neglect*, 14: 29–40.

Berliner, L. and Saunders, B. E. (1996) Treating fear and anxiety in sexually abused children: results of a controlled two year follow up study. *Child Maltreatment*, 1: 294–309.

Beitchman, J. H., Zucker, K. J., Hood, J. E., Dacosta, G. A. and Akman, D. (1991) A review of the short-term effects of child sexual abuse. *Child Abuse and Neglect*, 15: 537–56.

Beitchman, J., Zucker, K., Hood, J., DaCosta, G., Akman, D. and Cassavia, E. (1992) A review of the long-term effects of child sexual abuse. *Child Abuse and Neglect*, 16: 101–18.

Bonner, B., Walker, C. E. and Berliner, L. (1999) *Treatment Manual for Cognitive-Behavioural Group Therapy for Children with Sexual Behaviour Problems*. Washington, DC: National Clearinghouse on Child Abuse and Neglect.

Briere, J. N. (1992) *Child Abuse Trauma: Theory and Treatment of the Lasting Effects*. Newbury Park, CA: Sage.

Browne, A. and Finkelhor, D. (1986) Impact of child sexual abuse: a review of the research. *Psychological Bulletin*, 99: 66–77.

Childhaven, Inc. (undated) *Childhaven Therapeutic Child Development Manual*. Seattle, WA: Childhaven, Inc.

Deblinger, E. and Heflin, A. H. (1996) *Treatment for Sexually Abused Children and Their Non-Offending Parents: A Cognitive-Behavioural Approach*. Thousand Oaks, CA: Sage.

Delson, N. and Clark, M. (1981) Group therapy with sexually molested children. *Child Welfare*, 40(3): 175–82.

Dominguez, R. Z., Nelke, C. F. and Perry, B. D. (2001) Child sexual abuse. In D. Levinson (ed.), *Encyclopaedia of Crime and Punishment*, vol. 1, pp. 202–7. Thousand Oaks, CA: Sage.

Dubner, A. and Motta, R. (1999). Sexually and physically abused foster children and post-traumatic stress disorder. *Journal of Consulting and Clinical Psychology*, 67: 367–73.

Faller, K. (1993) *Child Sexual Abuse: Intervention and Treatment Issues*. US Department of Health and Human Services. Administration for Children and Families. www.childwelfare.gov/pubs/usermanuals/sexabuse/sexabuse.pdf (accessed 12 September 2008).

Fantuzzo, J., Weiss, A. and Coolahan, K. (1998) Community based partnership-directed research: actualizing community strengths to treat victims of physical abuse and neglect. In R. J. Lutzker (ed.), *Child Abuse: A Handbook of Theory, Research, and Treatment*, pp. 213–37. New York: Pergamon Press.

Fergusson, D., Lynskey, M. and Horwood, J. (1996). Childhood sexual abuse and psychiatric disorder in young adulthood: I. Prevalence of sexual abuse and factors associated with sexual abuse. *Journal of the American Academy of Child and Adolescent Psychiatry*, 34: 1355–64.

Friedrich, W. N. (1990). *Psychotherapy of Sexually Abused Children and Their Families*. New York: W.W. Norton.

  (1995) *Psychotherapy and Sexually Abused Boys*. Thousand Oaks, CA: Sage.

Furniss, T., Bingley-Miller, L. and van Elburg, A. (1988) Goal-oriented group treatment for sexually abused adolescent girls. *British Journal of Psychiatry*, 152: 97–106.

Gil, E. (1991) *The Healing Power of Play*. New York: Guilford Press.

Gomes-Schwartz, B., Horowitz, J. M. and Cardarelli, A. P. (1990) *Child Sexual Abuse: The Initial Effects*. Newbury Park, CA: Sage.

Gough D. (1993) *Child Abuse Interventions: A Review of the Research Literature*. London: HMSO.

Hall-Marley, S. E. and Damon, L. (1993) Impact of structured group therapy on young victims of sexual abuse. *Journal of Child and Adolescent Group Therapy*, 3: 41–8.

Hanson, R. F., Saunders, B. E., Kilpatrick, D. G., Resnick, H., Crouch, J. A., Duncan, R. (2001) Impact of childhood rape and aggravated assault on adult mental health. *American Journal of Orthopsychiatry*, 71: 108–19.

Kendall-Tackett, K. A., Meyer-Williams, L. and Finkelhor, D. (1993) Impact of sexual abuse on children: a review and synthesis of recent empirical studies. *Psychological Bulletin*, 113: 164–80.

Kolko, D. J. (1987) Treatment of child sexual abuse: programs, progress and prospects. *Journal of Family Violence*, 2: 303–18.

MacDonald, G., Ramchandani, P., Higgins, J. and Jones, D. P. H. (2004) Cognitive-behavioural interventions for sexually abused children (Protocol for Cochrane Review). *Cochrane Library*, issue 2. Chichester: Wiley.

MacDonald, G., Higgins, J. and Ramchandani, P. (2006) Cognitive-behavioural interventions for sexually abused children. *Cochrane Database of Systematic Reviews*, issue 4. Chichester: Wiley.

Neumann, D. A., Hauskamp, B. M., Pollock, V. E. and Briere, J. (1996) The long-term sequelae of childhood sexual abuse in women: a meta-analytic review. *Child Maltreatment*, 1: 6–16.

Rasmussen, L. A. and Cunningham, C. (1995) Focused play therapy and non-directive play therapy. *Journal of Child Sexual Abuse*, 4: 1–20.

Resick, P. A. and Schnicke, M. K. (1993) *Cognitive Processing Therapy for Rape Victims: A Treatment Manual*. Newbury Park, CA: Sage.

Saunders, B. E., Berliner, L. and Hanson, R. F. (eds.). (2004) *Child Physical and Sexual Abuse: Guidelines for Treatment (Revised Report: April 26, 2004)*. Charleston, SC: National Crime Victims Research and Treatment Center.

Saunders, B. E., Kilpatrick, D. G., Hanson, R. F., Resnick, H. S. and Walker, M. E. (1999) Prevalence, case characteristics, and long-term psychological correlates of child rape among women: a national survey. *Child Maltreatment*, 4: 187–200.

Saywitz, K. J. and Snyder, L. (1993) Narrative elaboration: test of a new procedure for interviewing children. *Journal of Consulting and Clinical Psychology*, 64: 1347–57.

Shapiro, F. (1995) *Eye Movement Desensitisation and Reprocessing: Basic Principle, Protocols, and Procedures*. New York: Guilford Press.

Sullivan, P. M., Scanlan, J. M., Brookhouser, P. E., Schulte, L. E. and Knutson, J. F. (1992) The effects of psychotherapy on behavior problems of sexually abused deaf children. *Child Abuse and Neglect*, 16: 297–307.

Tebbutt, J., Swanston, H., Oates, R. K. and O'Toole, B. I. (1997) Five years after child sexual abuse: persisting dysfunction and problems of prediction. *Journal of the American Academy of Child and Adolescent Psychiatry*, 35: 330–9.

Wolfe, V. V. (2006) Child sexual abuse. In E. J. Mash (ed.), *Treatment of Childhood Disorders*. New York: Guilford Press.

Wolfe, V. V. and Birt, J. (2004) The children's impact of traumatic events scale – revised (CITES-R): scale structure, internal consistency, discriminant validity, and PTSD diagnostic patterns. Manuscript submitted for publication.

Wolfe, V. V., Gentile, G. and Wolfe, D. A. (1989) The impact of sexual abuse on children: a PTSD formulation. *Behaviour Therapy*, 20: 215–28.

Clinical relevance of restorative justice

Guy Hall

Definition

Restorative justice is practised in many jurisdictions around the world in different formats and with significant input from indigenous communities (see, for example, Weitekamp and Kerner 2002, 2003; Walgrave 2003).

Marshall's (1999) definition of restorative justice as being 'a process whereby all the parties with a stake in a specific offence collectively resolve how to deal with the aftermath of the offence and its implications for the future' has been adopted by the United Nations (McCold 2006). The notion of restorative justice has noted common appeal, but in practice it enjoys considerable variation, and confusion (Morris 2002), and includes: conferencing; victim–offender mediation; sentencing circles; restitution programmes; and/or shuttle mediation. Any or all of these may occur pre-charge, post-charge (but prior to conviction), pre-sentence (post-conviction), post-sentence and pre-release.

Restorative justice procedures may be used with children in schools, youth in the juvenile justice system and adults in a range of conflict settings including corporate regulation (Braithwaite 2003); there is even a restorative justice prison system (Robert and Peters 2003). Mediators or facilitators of conferences can be police officers, trained mediators, volunteers, public servants or court officials.

Evaluation

Restorative justice is not without its critics (Levrant et al. 1999) and its corresponding supporters (Morris 2002). Given the above variations, the tools of the trade for psychologists, namely reliability, validity and operational definitions, become seriously problematic. Comparisons, and thus replications, are difficult because of these differences (see also McCold 2003; Shapland et al. 2007). Any demonstrated effects for restorative justice must always take into account these variations. The present focus will be primarily on conferencing, a process which includes the victim, the offender and direct stakeholders, which might include witnesses, family members or close friends of the victim and offender.

McCold (2003) notes that the there is little public opposition to restorative justice and that, rather, there is support for offender reparation and restorative justice approaches as preferable to retributive justice. This is significant since fully restorative justice processes consistently demonstrate benefits to victims, even if they do not consistently reduce offending.

Surveys of restorative justice studies consistently demonstrate higher levels of satisfaction for restorative justice (Latimer, Dowden and Muse 2005; McCold 2003; McCold and Wachtel 2002; Sherman and Strang 2007; Strang *et al.* 2006). A key observation from the McCold and Wachtel (2002) study is that for victims there is greater satisfaction with fully restorative justice practices such as conferencing over 'partly restorative' such as victim–offender mediation (which includes the victim and offender only). Levels of satisfaction reported by McCold and Wachtel (2002) were 91% for the fully restorative practices down to 82% for the mostly restorative practices. More recent studies indicate around 85% of victims were satisfied with the process (Shapland *et al.* 2007; Sherman and Strang 2007). Beven *et al.* (2005) compared the level of satisfaction for victims who went through a restorative conference with those who went through the traditional procedures and found that victims' level of satisfaction was accounted for, almost entirely, by their level of participation – the more they participated in the process the greater their level of satisfaction. Satisfaction level was lowest for those who went through traditional justice processes and highest levels were associated with high levels of participation. Interestingly, the level of satisfaction was unrelated to the level of punishment the offender received.

If restorative justice is considered to be an intervention programme then arguably principles of effective intervention should apply: risk, need, responsivity (Andrews, Bonta and Hoge 1990) and programme integrity (Hollin 1995). Bonta *et al.* specifically examined the impact of restorative justice on lower-risk compared to higher-risk offenders and found that restorative justice has a significant impact on the former but not the latter group. They note that 'the effectiveness of restorative justice programs with low-risk offenders is contrary to the rehabilitation literature where treatment provided to low risk offenders is largely ineffective' (Bonta *et al.* 2006, p. 116). They speculate that the difference might be due to either the control groups being criminalized by the justice system or because of the effect of integrative shaming on the restorative justice group. It is argued by many restorative justice practitioners that the major impact on offenders is an increase in empathy for the victim and that this then reduces reoffending. The problem with this hypothesis is that relationship between offending and empathy is weak, and once intelligence is taken into account it disappears (Jolliffe and Farrington 2004). An alternative explanation for the impact of restorative justice on recidivism is that it reduces the use of neutralizations. Sykes and Matza (1957) suggested that offenders neutralized pro-social belief systems by rationalizing their criminal behaviour. Sykes and Matza (1957) suggested that neutralizations include denial of responsivity (my criminal behaviour was beyond my control), denial of injury (harm minimization), denial of the victim (victim blaming) and condemnation of the condemners (system blaming). Offenders who meet their victim will have considerable difficulty maintaining denial of injury, denial of the victim or denial of responsibility. Finally, the reason why offender satisfaction is important is that it reduces the neutralization of condemnation of the condemner. In the Beven et al. (2005) study offenders who went through restorative justice used substantially and significantly fewer neutralizations than the control group, who went through traditional court processes without restorative justice. Another finding from Beven et al. (2005) is that offenders who went through restorative justice reported higher levels of perceived support to stay crime free and higher levels of self-efficacy (Bandura 1977). It is expected that individuals with high levels of support (more critically pro-social support) would have lower levels of reoffending as would those with higher levels of self-efficacy.

In the introduction many different forms and processes of restorative justice were noted. With respect to effective intervention, it means that the principle of programme integrity is not maintained. For restorative justice to be effective in changing offending behaviour, it needs to target criminogenic needs. Furthermore, targeting criminogenic needs the presence of both the victim and significant others. This is the practice of conferencing. Furthermore, Bonta et al. (2006) found that recent programmes (post-1995) were more effective than earlier programmes and that recent programmes 'were highly structured as evidenced by manuals or formalized routines' (p. 115).

Clinical relevance for victims

The clinical relevance of restorative justice is that it can reduce the negative impacts of the criminal justice system itself as well as aiding the psychological recovery of crime victimization. Reductions in negative impacts include:

- increase reported levels of closure (Shapland *et al.* 2007);
- reduce victim anger towards the offender (Strang *et al.* 2006);
- increase levels of sympathy to offender (Strang et al 2006);
- increase the understanding of the offender (Beven *et al.* 2005);
- reduce the desire for revenge (Sherman and Strang 2007);
- reduce fear of and from offender (Beven *et al.* 2005; Strang *et al.* 2006);
- increase forgiveness of offender by victims (Zehr 2003);
- high levels of acceptance of criminal responsibility (Beven *et al.* 2005).

For most people, their knowledge of offenders is gained from the media, as either news or entertainment. This knowledge does not help victims because it is limited in its scope (news) or is sensationalized (entertainment), and thus does not reflect the motivations and behaviours of most offenders. The offender is the only true source of information on the reason the victim was targeted. Restorative justice conferences provide victims with knowledge from the offender which allows them to cognitively appraise (or reappraise) their levels of risk and its associated fear. This process cannot be replicated by other victims, police or therapists since it is another person's view and is, in any case, abstract or divorced from the individual. Furthermore, in those cases where the victimization was random and there is no additional risk to the victim, this can be confirmed by the offender in a conference.

In those cases where there remains conflict between the parties, this can be resolved through face-to-face conflict resolution. The alternative, traditional criminal justice processes, does not resolve the conflict and the imposition of punishment may escalate it. The lack of any resolution combined with punishment will compound any fear because of the thought that the offender may feel vengeful. To cope with the fear, victims engage in avoiding the fearful stimuli (the offender) and associated stimuli (for example, the place of victimization or similar places) (Kilpatrick and Acierno 2003). This avoidance is not a long-term successful strategy because the original fearful stimulus is never desensitized. Restorative justice is effectively in-vivo desensitization since the victim meets the offender in a situation that allows the victim to learn not to fear the aversive stimulus.

Guilt, too, is a common feeling post-victimization. Victims report statements such as 'if only I had …' or 'why did I …' ruminations, with the associated belief that alternative action might not have led to victimization. These thoughts have the potential to induce depression and intrusive, ruminating thoughts. Such thoughts are difficult to shift because many of the 'if only' or 'why did I' statements cannot be disconfirmed except by the offender. When offenders accept responsibility for their actions in front of their victim, it is hypothesized that this will result in a diminution of the feelings of guilt felt by victims.

The clinical relevance for offenders

Just as the evidence for the benefits of restorative justice for victims is unambiguous, so the evidence of the benefits for offenders is unambiguous. Offenders who participate in restorative justice conferencing report:

- significantly higher levels of satisfaction compared with traditional criminal justice processing (McCold 2003; McCold and Wachtel 2002; Sherman and Strang 2007;
- being more satisfied with their sentence (Beven *et al.* 2005).

Two recent meta-analyses demonstrate that restorative justice results in a reduction of offending compared to controls who did not participate in restorative justice. Latimer *et al.* (2005) found an average effect size of +.07 with a 95% CI of +.12 to +.02, meaning that on average restorative justice produces a 7% reduction in recidivism. Bonta *et al.* (2006) report a similar result, but found that studies after 1995 produced an average phi of 0.12 (a significant improvement over earlier interventions). They suggest that later studies are better developed than earlier ones.

Conclusion

In sum, there is evidence that restorative justice produces improved psychological functioning compared to traditional processes for victims (Sherman and Strang 2007), and this can be explained by reductions of fear, guilt, anger and an increase in the ability to forgive. One important limitation of the research on the impact of restorative justice is the lack of evidence for its long-term impact on serious victimization. Maxwell, Morris and Hayes (2006) note that restorative justice has been used with serious and repeat offenders whose offences result in the most severe trauma (Kilpatrick and Acierno 2003). For offenders, it is a useful technique in reducing a range of neutralizations as well as increasing self-efficacy and promoting social support.

Restorative justice should not be seen as a stand-alone intervention. Bonta (2006) recommends that 'restorative justice programs should incorporate means to address offender problems specifically related to the criminal behaviour' (p. 2). Finally, treatment providers should incorporate restorative justice as a part of interventions to address offending behaviour as well as a part of interventions to reduce the impact of victimization.

REFERENCES

Andrews, D. A., Bonta, J. and Hoge, R. (1990) Classification for effective rehabilitation: rediscovering psychology. *Criminal Justice and Behavior*, 17: 19–52.

Bandura, A. (1977) Self-efficacy: toward a unifying theory of behavioural change. *Psychological Review*, 84: 191–215.

Beven, J. P., Hall, G., Froyland, I., Steels, B. and Goulding, D. (2005) Restoration or renovation? Evaluating restorative justice outcomes. *Psychiatry, Psychology and Law*, 12: 194–206.

Bonta, J. (2006) Restorative justice and offender treatment. *Research Summary*, 11. Ottawa, ON: Public Safety and Emergency Preparedness Canada.

Bonta, J., Jesseman, R., Rugge, T. and Cormier, R. (2006) Restorative justice and recidivism: promises made, promises kept? In D. Sullivan and T. Tofft (eds.), *Handbook of Restorative Justice: A Global Perspective*, pp. 108–20. Abingdon: Routledge.

Braithwaite, J. (2003) Corporations, crime and restorative justice. In G. M. Weitekamp and H. Kerner (eds.), *Restorative Justice in Context: International Practice and Directions*, pp. 389–412. Cullompton: Willan.

Hollin, C. (1995) The meaning and implications of 'programme integrity'. In J. McGuire (ed.), *What Works: Reducing Offending – Guidelines from Research and Practice*, pp. 195–208. Chichester: Wiley.

Jolliffe, D. and Farrington, D. P. (2004) Empathy and offending: a systematic review and meta-analysis. *Aggression and Violent Behavior*, 9: 441–76.

Kilpatrick, D. G. and Acierno, R. (2003) Mental health need of crime victims: epidemiology and outcomes. *Journal of Traumatic Stress*, 16: 119–32.

Latimer, J., Dowden, C. and Muise, D. (2005) The effectiveness of restorative justice practices: a meta-analysis. *The Prison Journal*, 85: 127–44.

Levrant, D., Cullen, F., Fulton, B. and Wozniak, J. (1999) Reconsidering restorative justice: the corruption of benevolence revisited. *Crime and Delinquency*, 45: 3–27.

Marshall, T. (1999) *Restorative Justice: An Overview*. London: Home Office Research, Development and Statistics Directorate.

Maxwell, G., Morris, A. and Hayes, H. (2006). Conferencing and restorative justice. In D. Sullivan and T. Tofft (eds.) *Handbook of Restorative Justice: A Global Perspective*, pp. 91–107. Abingdon: Routledge.

McCold, P. (2003) A survey of assessment research on mediation and conferencing. In L. Walgrave (ed.), *Repositioning Restorative Justice*, pp. 67–120. Cullompton: Willan.

(2006) The recent history of restorative justice: mediation, circles, and conferencing. In D. Sullivan and T. Tofft (eds.) *Handbook of Restorative Justice: A Global Perspective*, pp. 23–51. Abingdon: Routledge.

McCold, P. and Wachtel, T. (2002) Restorative justice theory and validation. In G. M. Weitekamp and H.-J. Kerner (eds.), *Restorative Justice: Theoretical Foundations*, pp. 110–42. Cullompton: Willan.

Morris, A. (2002) Critiquing the critics: a brief response to the critics of restorative justice. *British Journal of Criminology*, 42: 596–615.

Robert, L. and Peters, T. (2003) How restorative justice is able to transcend the prison walls: a discussion of the 'restorative detention' project. In G. M. Weitekamp and H. Kerner (eds.), *Restorative Justice in Context: International Practice and Directions*, pp. 95–11. Cullompton: Willan.

Shapland, J., Atkinson, A., Atkinson, H., Chapman, B., Dignan, J., Howes, M., Johnstone, J., Robinson, G., and Sorsby, A. (2007) *Restorative Justice: The Views of the Victims and Offenders*. Ministry of Justice Research Series 3/07. www.justice.gov.uk/docs/Restorative-Justice.pdf (accessed 2 November 2007).

Sherman, L. and Strang, H. (2007) *Restorative Justice: The Evidence*. The Smith Institute. www.sas.upenn.edu/jerrylee/RESTORATIVE JUSTICE_full_report.pdf?view=usa&ci= 0199274290 (accessed 27 October 2007).

Strang, H., Sherman, L., Angel, C. M., Woods, D. J. and Bennet, S. (2006) Victim evaluations of face-to-face restorative justice conferences: a quasi-experimental analysis. *Journal of Social Issues*, 62: 281–306.

Sykes, G. M. and Matza, D. (1957) Techniques of neutralization: a theory of delinquency. *American Sociological Review*, 22: 664–70.

Walgrave, L (ed.) (2003) *Repositioning Restorative Justice*. Cullompton: Willan.

Weitekamp, G. M. and Kerner, H. (eds.) (2002) *Restorative Justice: Theoretical Foundations*. Cullompton: Willan.

(2003) *Restorative Justice in Context: International Practice and Directions*. Cullompton: Willan.

Zedner, L. (1997). Victims. In M. Maguire, R. Morgan and R. Reiner (eds.), *The Oxford Handbook of Criminology*, 2nd edn. Oxford: Oxford University Press.

Zehr, H. (2003) Retributive justice, restorative justice. In G. Johnstone (ed.), *A Restorative Justice Reader: Texts, Sources, Context*, pp. 69–82. Cullompton: Willan.

Crisis negotiation

Carol A. Ireland

Definition

Crisis negotiation has evolved and developed over recent years. Initially referred to as hostage negotiation, crisis negotiation now represents a number of strategies that are utilized during a situation where a person or persons are in crisis, and where decision making has become irrational. Crisis negotiation is a collection of verbal strategies that allow the buying of time in order to allow strong emotions to decrease, and for rational thinking to increase (Hatcher *et al.* 1998; Dolnik 2004). Although not exclusively, crisis negotiation can be used in a range of crisis situations, including hostage situations, barricades and roof-top incidents.

The use of crisis negotiation and its accompanying techniques has proven successful in resolving a number of crisis situations, with McMains and Mullins (2006) reporting that 80% of incidents recorded by the FBI were resolved peacefully due to the use of crisis negotiation strategies. Rogan and Hammer (1995) further reported that 96% of all crisis negotiation incidents are resolved non-violently, through the use of crisis negotiation.

Origins and development of crisis negotiation

Crisis negotiation was initially introduced as hostage negotiation in the early 1970s. It was first introduced by the New York Police Department in 1973, following the 1971 Attica New York Prison Riot and the murder of the Israeli athletes in the 1972 Munich Olympics (Vecchi, Van Hasselt and Romano 2005). These incidents were dealt with in a largely disorganized, forceful and chaotic manner, leading to injury and loss of life, as well as substantial ramifications post the event for a number of individuals. For example, some twenty-six years after the Attica New York Prison Riot, some 12 million dollars in compensation was awarded to the prisoners.

This forceful and disorganized approach to a crisis situation, where there can be an unwillingness to engage in negotiations and a preference to manage such situations through force, is still utilized in some organizations and countries today. In contrast to this approach, there have also been much less forceful approaches towards crisis incidents, particularly in the 1970s and early 1980s. Such approaches were indicated by efforts to make agreements with the person in crisis in relation to any demands made, such as terrorists who have taken individuals hostage. Unfortunately, such concessions to demands demonstrated to hostage takers that hostage taking was an effective strategy, and did lead to a greater motivation to take more hostages and to issue much more substantial demands (Ireland 2007).

The difficulties in the management of such crisis incidents led to the development of more formalized and structured procedures of negotiation during crisis situations. This further persuaded the individual in crisis, such as the hostage taker, that the situation chosen is not an effective means by which to have their needs or demands met.

The evolution of crisis negotiation

Crisis negotiation is different from the more common forms of negotiation, which assume that all participants wish to bargain, are happy to do so, and happy to exchange proposals as part of the problem-solving process (Rogan and Hammer 1995). Part of the role of crisis negotiation is to make efforts to change the situation from that of crisis to a more normative problem-solving process (Rogan and Hammer 1995). Crisis negotiation attempts to do this in a number of ways, such as creating a climate where compromise and problem solving can be considered by the individual in crisis, as well as using a range of crisis negotiation strategies (Rogan and Hammer 1995). Such strategies would include communicating empathy towards the individual in crisis, subtly protecting and allowing the saving of face by the individual in crisis as part of a resolution to the situation, as well as slowing down the negotiation process and assisting in reducing the emotionality of the individual in crisis (Rogan and Hammer 1995; Taylor 2002). Understanding the emotions of the individual in crisis, as well as any attitudes or beliefs with which they present, is considered to be a key part of the negotiation process (Rogan and Hammer 1995; Taylor 2002).

Such strategies also require the development of a relationship between the negotiator and the individual who is in crisis. Early development of crisis negotiation focused predominately on the psychological traits and emotional states of the individual in crisis. This was with the aim to hopefully better predict their motivations and potential behavioural patterns (Rogan and Hammer 1995; Taylor 2002). Unfortunately, the initial focus had little theoretical or empirical grounding with which to reinforce such a notion. Whilst it can clearly be of some use to focus on the motivations of the individual in crisis, as well as the function of the situation for that individual, it is nonetheless predominantly important to focus on the appropriate building of the relationship between the crisis negotiator and individual in crisis (Vecchi *et al.* 2005). Crisis negotiation has more recently focused on this, regarding the crisis negotiation process as a dynamic interaction, where the relationship between the crisis negotiator and the individual in crisis is paramount (Rogan and Hammer 2006).

One of the most recent approaches towards developing the relationship-building process is that of the behavioural influence stairway model (Vecchi *et al.* 2005). This model of negotiation focuses on the relationship-building process between the negotiator and the perpetrator, focusing on developing a peaceful settlement of the crisis situation (Dalfonzo 2002). This model and crisis negotiation approach has been consistently used with effective outcomes in the resolution of a wide range of highly volatile crisis situations (Flood 2003). The model consists of four dynamic elements as part of the relationship-building process, with the individual in crisis moving dynamically between these stages and in alternate directions. The key stages are active listening, empathy, rapport and influence, leading to behavioural change. Active listening forms a foundation of this model (Van Hasselt, Romano and Vecchi 2008) and is something which is continued throughout the process of the negotiations. Vecchi *et al.* (2005) argue that the active listening is important when attempting to decrease high emotions, with an effort to return to more rational thinking. Once it is felt that active listening has been suitably achieved and maintained, the negotiator may then progress towards demonstrating empathy, whereby they demonstrate the ability to understand and share the feelings the individual who is in a crisis emotional state or context (Cohen and Strayer 1996). Rapport is then established where a trust is developed between the negotiator and the individual in crisis, which is derived from the empathy stage. The final stage is that of influence, where the individual in crisis is persuaded to change their behaviour in the crisis situation to a much more adaptive approach (Van Hasselt *et al.* 2008).

Whilst this model does offer a clear framework for negotiators to progress through crisis situations, there is the risk that crisis negotiators may see the crisis situation in clear blocks, and may not always recognize the dynamic nature of the situation. As a negotiator, it is important for them to recognize that an individual may not always start at the beginning of the model; likewise they may not always move effectively to the top. It is further important to note that the model is in itself theoretical, although it does have links with relational order theory (Donohue 2001) and social interaction theory (Tajfel and Turner 1986).

Crisis negotiation and its application to mental disorder

Fuselier (1988) and Strentz (1986) argued that individuals with mental disorders made up approximately 50% of all hostage takers. Despite this, there has been limited literature that has looked at the application of crisis negotiation to mental disorder, and how current models of crisis negotiation may need to be revised accordingly. Early literature has looked at the motivations behind a mentally disordered hostage taker (Fuselier 1981), yet has excluded the application of such techniques and methods outside hostage situations. There has been little literature that has focused on the importance of the relationship-building process with a mentally disordered individual who is in crisis, and indeed the challenges of doing so when engaging with such individuals. Whilst there has been some limited literature looking at mental illness and personality disorder, there has been no literature which has attempted to address the application of crisis negotiation to individuals who present with a cognitive impairment or brain injury.

When exploring mental illness and personality disorder, one of the few authors who have considered the application of crisis negotiation strategies to such individuals is Strentz (2006). For example, when negotiating with an individual in crisis who presents with paranoid schizophrenia, characterized by delusions and hallucinations with paranoid ideology, Strentz (2006) argued that there are a number guidelines to be considered. Such guidelines would include the importance of allowing the stalling of time during a hostage situation, to allow the individual in crisis to vent their frustrations onto the negotiator so that the frustration is not placed on the hostage. Strentz (2006) further emphasized the importance of negotiating with an individual who presented with antisocial personality disorder, which can be characterized as a pervasive pattern of disregard for, and violation of, the right of others that begins in childhood or early adolescence and continues into adulthood (DSM-IV-TR: American Psychiatric Association 2000). As part of the guidelines for negotiation, Strentz (2006) argued that it was important for such an individual in crisis to feel that they are very much in control of the situation, and for the negotiator to work with the traits that they may have relating to feelings of importance. Strentz (2006) further argued that attempting to gain rapport with such an individual, which is a stage in the behavioural change model, may be unlikely to succeed. Whilst such strategies have been considered, they do lack empirical grounding, a problem inherent in the field of crisis negotiation.

When examining the application of crisis negotiation to an individual who presents with a cognitive impairment or brain injury, there is very limited literature to draw inferences from. Ireland (2007) discussed the importance of applying negotiation strategies with care when engaging with an individual who presents with a cognitive impairment. A cognitive impairment would not necessarily equate to that of a learning disability, but could certainly be significant enough to impact on the day-to-day functioning of an individual. A cognitive impairment would refer to the damage to an individual's memory, affecting their ability to think, concentrate, formulate, to reason and to remember details. It is distinct from a learning disability in that it may have been acquired (although not exclusively) post-birth, possibly as a result of an accident or illness. Such changes to an individual's cognitive abilities may be minor and have little impact on the day-to-day functioning. Alternatively, they may be more obvious, ranging from mild memory problems to difficulties in effective management of emotion. Ireland (2007) argued that there were a number of factors that require consideration when negotiating with a cognitively impaired individual in crisis. For example, it is important to consider that such individuals may tire quickly, particularly after a cognitively demanding task. As a result, their judgement may decrease, stress levels may increase, and the situation may escalate as a result. It is further argued that if the individual in crisis becomes distracted, such as by noise, they may become angry or begin to focus solely on one topic of conversation and cannot be moved from this.

Summary and evaluation

One of the main challenges in the crisis negotiation literature is that of effective evaluation. A crisis situation presents with a number of factors and variables, which can be difficult to control and evaluate effectively. Nonetheless, the current method of crisis negotiation appears to be part of a process that is more likely to lead to a successful resolution of a crisis situation. What is clear in the literature is that the absence of any crisis negotiation strategy can lead to unhelpful outcomes, and can in some instances lead to substantial harm for those involved. Whilst crisis negotiation presents a number of models with regard to its effective use, it is nonetheless important to consider the individual factors for each crisis situation, and to adapt each model and technique accordingly.

FURTHER READING

For a further helpful overview and summary in relation to crisis negotiation, readers would be directed to the following key texts: Dolnik's (2004) paper; Rogan and Hammer (1995). Also Strentz's (2006) text, *Psychological Aspects of Crisis Negotiation*, provides a good overview, and Vecchi, Van Hasselt and Romano's (2005) paper provides a detailed account of current practice.

REFERENCES

American Psychiatric Association (2000) *Diagnostic and Statistical Manual of Mental Disorders*, 4th edn, text revision (DSM-IV-TR). Washington, DC: American Psychiatric Association.

Cohen, D. and Strayer, J. (1996) Empathy in conduct-disordered and comparison youth. *Developmental Psychology*, 32: 988–98.

Dalfonzo, V. (2002) National crisis negotiation course. Quantico, VA: FBI Academy.

Dolnik, A. (2004) Contrasting dynamics of crisis negotiations: barricade versus kidnapping incidents. *International Negotiation*, 8: 495–526.

Donohue, W. A. (2001) Resolving relational paradox: the language of conflict in relationships. In W. F. Eadie and P. E. Nelson (eds.), *The Language of Conflict Resolution*, pp. 21–46. Thousand Oaks, CA: Sage.

Flood, J. J. (2003) A report of findings from the Hostage Barricade Database System (HOBAS), Crisis Negotiation Unit, Critical Incident Response Group, FBI Academy, Quantico, VA.

Fuselier, G. D. (1981) A practical overview of hostage negotiations. *FBI Law Enforcement Bulletin*, 50: 10–15.

  (1988) Hostage negotiation consultant: emerging role for the clinical psychologist. *Professional Psychology: Research and Practice*, 19: 175–9.

Hatcher, C., Mohandie, K., Turner, J. and Gelles, M. G. (1998) The role of the psychologist in crisis/hostage negotiations. *Behavioural Sciences and the Law*, 16: 455–72.

Ireland, C. A. (2007) Crisis negotiation with a mentally disordered offender population: development of a training package in a high secure forensic hospital. *Forensic Update*, October 2007.

McMains, M. J. and Mullins, W. C. (2006) *Crisis Negotiations: Managing Critical Incidents and Hostage Situations in Law Enforcement and Corrections*, 2nd edn. Cincinnati, OH: Anderson.

Rogan, R. G. and Hammer, M. R. (1995) Assessing message affect in crisis negotiations: an exploratory study. *Human Communication Research*, 21: 553–74.

(2006) The emerging field of crisis/hostage negotiation: a communication-based perspective. In J. G. Oetzel and S. Ting-Toomey (eds.), *The Sage Handbook of Conflict Communication: Integrating Theory, Research, and Practice*, pp. 451–78. Thousand Oaks, CA: Sage.

Strentz, T. (1986) Negotiating with the hostage taker exhibiting paranoid schizophrenia symptoms. *Journal of Police Science and Administration*, 14: 12–16.

(2006) *Psychological Aspects of Crisis Negotiation*. Boca Raton, FL: CRC Press.

Tajfel, H. and Turner, J. (1986) An integrated theory of intergroup conflict. In S. Worschel and W. G. Austin (eds.), *Psychology of Intergroup Interactions*, 2nd edn, pp. 7–24. Chicago: Nelson-Hall.

Taylor, P. J. (2002) A cylindrical model of communication behaviour in crisis negotiations. *Human Communication Research*, 28: 7–48.

Van Hasselt, V. B., Romano, S. J. and Vecchi, G. M. (2008) Role playing: applications in hostage and crisis negotiation skills training. *Behavior Modification*, 32: 248–63.

Vecchi, G. M., Van Hasselt, V. B. and Romano, S. S. (2005) Crisis (hostage) negotiation: current strategies and issues in high-risk conflict resolution. *Aggression and Violent Behavior*, 10: 533–51.

3.4 Parenting programmes

Christine Puckering

See also chapter 2.14 Parenting capacity and conduct.

Introduction

There are three main areas in which consideration of parenting programmes are of forensic interest. These are firstly in the area of child protection, where a parent has been found to be responsible for the neglect or abuse of a child; secondly where the child has offended and failures in parenting are seen to have contributed to the child's problems; and thirdly as part of an assessment of parenting, which could include the parent's capacity to change.

Parenting is a complex task which demands that the parent nurtures, guides and educates the child so as to promote good development in physical, academic, emotional and social arenas. Underpinning this is the child's developmental agenda, so that at each stage the balance and demands of the task will change. For example, it would be considered pathological for a parent to be overly concerned with discipline of a baby who was less than a year old, but highly pertinent in the context of a rebellious teenager.

Such research as has been done on the effectiveness of parenting programmes has often been framed in a social learning framework in which the emphasis on gaining compliance of the child is seen as primary and the methods utilized based on effective management strategies, and of course with older children this is understandable. Nevertheless, there is good evidence that the roots of good social and emotional development and good behaviour lie much earlier in the child's development, even in the very early years and the development of secure attachment in the first year of life. Children who do not make secure attachment relationships, and particularly those who develop disorganized attachment patterns, thought to be closely related to parental neglect or maltreatment, are the most likely to develop antisocial attitudes and later offending. The prime cause of later violence is the failure to develop empathy, a capacity that is nurtured in the context of responsive parenting in very early childhood. In addition, the link from harsh and coercive parenting practices in childhood to the development of later aggressive behaviour is strong (Arseneault *et al.* 2000; Patterson, DeBaryshe and Ramsey 1989). Antisocial children grow up to be antisocial adults who go on to raise antisocial children (Farrington 1995).

The focus of parenting programmes, whether the underpinning of good parent–child relationships and in the extreme case the prevention of abuse or the management of child behaviour, and the age at which they are relevant, therefore play a part in defining what makes an effective parenting intervention.

Effective parenting interventions

Infant mental health

As the core tasks of parenting an infant are so different from parenting a teenager, programmes for one age are not necessarily helpful at other ages. The growing evidence of the impact of the first year of life, and indeed inter-uterine experience, on the development of the infant brain urges us to consider the need for intervention at the earliest ages, in a way that would not have been seriously contemplated in even the recent past (Chugani *et al.* 2001). There is accumulating evidence that abuse or gross lack of stimulation in the first year of life has profound effects on the structural development of the brain (Schore 1997). The rapid development of synapses, the consolidation of neural pathways that are regularly used and the atrophy of those which are not used lead to structural developments in the infant brain which are less easy to modify after this period of unprecedented rapid development with its attendant flexibility in response to environment. Within months the baby is learning that the world is benign and that people will be a resource for soothing and for stimulation or that it is a frightening, unpredictable environment where adults do not provide reliable responses and self-reliance is the only viable strategy. These attributions are so fundamental that they are likely to be relatively stable and shape the child's interaction with other people, through the child's development of self-esteem, self-efficacy, secure attachment and empathy.

Looking at intervention, the opportunities to measure outcome need long-term follow-up. Hard evidence of further abuse is relatively crude and the best available evidence may be from proxy measures such as parental sensitivity or secure attachment, which are known in the long term to be associated with good child outcomes.

Bakermans-Kranenburg and colleagues (Bakermans-Kranenburg, van Ijzendoorn and Juffer 2003) have provided a meta-analysis of the factors which are likely to be associated with effective programmes to promote parental sensitivity and secure attachment. These are:

- Focus on sensitivity
- Between five and sixteen sessions
- Between 6 and 12 months of age (no advantage in antenatal intervention)
- Programmes including fathers showed increased sensitivity in fathers but diluted effects for mothers
- The use of video feedback increased effect sizes for sensitivity.

Mellow Babies and the Sunderland Infant programme are British examples which meet these criteria but await more rigorous evaluation (Puckering 2004; Svanberg 1998).

Prevention programmes have focused either on targeting groups at high risk, for example teenage parents, or secondary prevention where abuse has already been identified. Olds *et al.* (1986) tested the effectiveness of a nurse home-visiting model for vulnerable mothers who were predominantly black, single, teenaged girls. Home visits began in pregnancy and continued through until the children were aged 2. The babies in the nurse home-visiting group had higher birth weights, and mothers spaced subsequent pregnancies more widely, the families were less likely to use welfare services and the children displayed fewer behavioural problems and better intellectual functioning. A fifteen-year follow-up showed fewer criminal convictions in the children (Olds *et al.* 2004).

Barlow and colleagues (Barlow, Coren and Stewart-Brown 2002; Barlow, Parsons and Stewart-Brown 2005), evaluated the effectiveness of group-based parenting programmes for children under 3 in improving maternal psychosocial health and reducing emotional and behavioural problems in the children. The results were consistent with some improvement in maternal mental health in the short term but longer-term follow-up is needed. The effects were less convincing for the emotional and behavioural adjustment of the children in the short term, and again the effects in the long term are less certain.

In the context of preventing further maltreatment, Zeanah *et al.* (2001) used an intensive evaluation of all children under 4 who were recorded as having experienced maltreatment in a given area (New Orleans). Their intensive examination of all the caregivers who were in contact with the child, including birth parents, foster parents and grandparents, led to more cases where parental rights were terminated but less reoccurrence of maltreatment in those families where children were returned to the care of their parents.

Middle childhood

Programmes for children aged 3–12 have tended to concentrate on the management of children's behaviour. The National Institute for Clinical Excellence (NICE) (2006) reported on the effectiveness of parenting education and training programmes for children with conduct disorders. NICE recommended that all parent-training/education programmes, whether group- or individual-based, should be:

- structured and have a curriculum informed by principles of social-learning theory
- include relationship-enhancing strategies
- offer a sufficient number of sessions, with an optimum of eight to twelve, to maximize the possible benefits for participants
- enable parents to identify their own parenting objectives
- incorporate role-play during sessions, as well as homework to be undertaken between sessions, to achieve generalization of newly rehearsed behaviours to the home situation
- delivered by appropriately trained and skilled facilitators who are supervised, have access to necessary ongoing professional development, and are able to engage in a productive therapeutic alliance with parents
- adhere to the programme developer's manual and employ all of the necessary materials to ensure consistent implementation of the programme.

Participants who did not complete the interventions were more likely to:

- be significantly younger
- come from a lower socioeconomic group
- have less social support
- have higher levels of life stress
- be significantly less educated
- be a mother with higher depression and anxiety scores on standardized scales
- have higher levels of parental dysfunction.

Parenting orders

In the last ten years courts have been able to order parents whose children are failing to attend school or are engaged in offending to engage with parenting support and education services. Youth Offending Teams were responsible for identifying suitable resources for parents mandated by the court to comply with these 'Parenting Orders' as well as for parents who had need of such help even if not under statutory obligation to attend. The pattern of services which developed, while variable in delivery, typically addressed:

- Conflict and challenging behaviour in young people
- Supervision and monitoring of children's whereabouts and behaviour
- Setting and maintaining boundaries
- Communication and negotiation
- Family conflict.

The Youth Justice Board (Ghate and Ramella 2002) published a national evaluation of the parenting interventions delivered under this scheme. The parents who attended were largely white British women, predominantly single parents, often unemployed and their children predominantly male with an average age of 13 years. Two-thirds of the 4,000 referrals were of voluntary participants, and only 16 per cent were under parenting orders. Seventy per cent of referrals started the parenting programmes, and about half of these were considered by staff to have engaged fully in the programme. Programmes were variously delivered on an individual or group basis and the majority were developed specifically for the intervention as no appropriate packages were identified. In the context of evaluation of the effectiveness of the programmes, this lack of standardization makes any extrapolation of the results of limited validity.

There were no differences between attendance figures for voluntary rather than court-ordered attendances, though of course parents would be in contempt of court if they failed to comply with the latter. Parents reported increased communication, supervision, warmth, confidence and coping in their parenting after attending the programme, and a reduction in conflict. Even where their initial reaction to the parenting order had been anger, by the end of the programme parents who agreed to be followed up tended to be positive about the content and delivery of the material. The rate of offending behaviour in the young people in the year following the programme compared with the year before intervention dropped from 89% to 62%. While this is still a substantial rate, it is demonstrably better than the pre-intervention rate, although in the absence of a control group, this change could be due simply to expected maturation as the young people pass the peak offending age of 15.

Given that the participation in the programmes was more likely to be taken up by better-functioning families, and that the return of self-report measures was also likely to be more frequent in families who had valued the programme, and given the lack of a control group, the evidence of effectiveness is slim. The authors describe the effects on the parents as substantial but the effect on the children as 'weak', but speculate that there may be unmeasured benefits for younger siblings in the family. The summary of the report (Ghate and Ramella 2002) includes recommendations for service development, staff recruitment and training, service delivery type and location and monitoring.

Treatment of delinquency

The role of parenting programmes alone in the treatment of delinquency is less clear than the implementation of programmes that work with the child or young person as well as the family, school and community systems that surround him or her. Such programmes as SNAP, Stop Now and Plan (Williams, Whiten and Singh 2004), for behaviour-disordered children and Multisystemic Therapy (Henggeler et al. 2003; Huey et al. 2000) have shown considerable effectiveness in reducing antisocial behaviour and later juvenile offences.

Parents with learning disabilities

Increasing normalization of the lives of people with learning disabilities has led to increased concern about them functioning as parents, and whether specific help is needed to enable them to meet the responsibilities of being a parent. While it is clear that strong support networks for these parents are important to their wellbeing, it is less clear that this has a direct impact on their parenting practice or that parent training increases their capacity to do the job well. Particular emphasis on practical skills, taught in settings with concrete opportunities for practising skills, and also opportunities for generalization are the most effective route. Group settings have been found to be congenial for parents, though not necessarily more effective in achieving a positive outcome for children (SCIE Research Briefing 14 2005).

FURTHER READING

See the following Cochrane reviews:

Barlow, J., Coren, E. and Stewart-Brown, S. (2007) Parent-training programmes for improving maternal psychosocial health. *Cochrane Developmental, Psychosocial and Learning Problems Group, Cochrane Database of Systematic Reviews*, 2.

Barlow, J., Johnston, I., Kendrick, D., Polnay, L. and Stewart-Brown, S. (2007) Individual and group-based parenting programmes for the treatment of physical child abuse and neglect. *Cochrane Developmental, Psychosocial and Learning Problems Group, Cochrane Database of Systematic Reviews*, 2.

Barlow, J. and Parsons, J. (2007) Group-based parent-training programmes for improving emotional and behavioural adjustment in 0–3 year old children. *Cochrane Developmental, Psychosocial and Learning Problems Group Cochrane Database of Systematic Reviews*, 2.

Coren, E. and Barlow, J. (2007) Individual and group-based parenting programmes for improving psychosocial outcomes for teenage parents and their children. *Cochrane Developmental, Psychosocial and Learning Problems Group, Cochrane Database of Systematic Reviews*, 2.

Dowling, S. and Gardner, F. (2007) Parenting programmes for improving the parenting skills and outcomes for incarcerated parents and their children. *Cochrane Developmental, Psychosocial and Learning Problems Group, Cochrane Database of Systematic Reviews*, 2.

REFERENCES

Arseneault, L., Moffitt, T. E., Caspi, A., Taylor, P. J. and Silva, P. A. (2000) Mental disorders and violence in a total birth cohort. *Archives of General Psychiatry*, 57: 979–86.

Bakermans-Kranenburg, M. J., van Ijzendoorn, M. H. and Juffer, F. (2003) Less is more: meta-analyses of sensitivity and attachment interventions in early childhood. *Psychological Bulletin*, 129: 195–215.

Barlow, J., Coren, E. and Stewart-Brown, S. (2002) Meta-analysis of the effectiveness of parenting programmes in improving maternal psychosocial health. *British Journal of General Practice*, 52: 223–33.

Barlow, J., Parsons, J. and Stewart-Brown, S. (2005) Preventing emotional and behavioural problems: the effectiveness of parenting programmes with children less than 3 years of age. *Child: Care, Health and Development*, 31: 33–42.

Chugani, H. T., Behen, M. E., Muzik, O. *et al.* (2001) Local brain functional activity following early deprivation: a study of postinstitutionalized Romanian orphans. *NeuroImage*, 1290–1301.

Farrington, D. P. (1995) The development of offending and anti-social behaviour from childhood: key findings from the Cambridge Study in Delinquent Development. *Child Psychology and Psychiatry*, 36: 929–64.

Ghate, D. and Ramella, M. (2002) *Positive Parenting: The National Evaluation of the Youth Justice Board's Parenting Programme*. London: Policy Research Bureau, Youth Justice Board.

Henggeler, S., Rowland, M., Halliday-Boykins, C. *et al.* (2003) One year follow up of multi-systemic therapy as an alternative to the hospitalization of youths in psychiatric crisis. *Journal of the American Academy of Child and Adolescent Psychiatry*, 42: 543–51.

Huey, S. J. J., Henggeler, S. W., Brondino, M. J. and Pickrel, S. G. (2000) Mechanisms of change in multisystemic therapy: reducing delinquent behavior through therapist adherence and improved family and peer functioning. *Journal of Consulting and Clinical Psychology*, 68: 451–67.

NICE (2006) *Parent-Training/Education Programmes in the Management of Children with Conduct Disorders*. TA102.

Olds, D. L., Henderson, C. R., Chamberlin, R. and Tatelbaum, R. (1986) Preventing child abuse and neglect: a randomized trial of nurse home visitation. *Pediatrics*, 78: 65–77.

Olds, D., Henderson, C. R. J., Cole, R., Eckenrode, J., Kitzman, H., Luckey, D. *et al.* (2004) Long-term effects of nurse home visitation on children's criminal and antisocial behavior: fifteen-year follow-up of a randomised control trial. In M. A. Feldman (ed.), *Early Intervention: The Essential Readings*, pp. 238–55. Malden, MA: Blackwell.

Patterson, J., DeBaryshe, B. D. and Ramsey, E. A. (1989) Developmental perspectives on antisocial behavior. *American Psychologist*, 44: 329–35.

Puckering, C. (2004) Mellow parenting: an intensive programme to change relationships. *The Signal*, 12: 1–5.

Schore, A. N. (1997) A century after Freud's project: is a rapprochement between psycho-analysis and neurobiology at hand? *Journal of the American Psychoanalytic Association*, 45: 807–40.

SCIE Research Briefing 14 (2005) Helping parents with learning disabilities in their role as parents.

Svanberg, P. O. G. (1998) Attachment, resilience and prevention. *Journal of Mental Health*, 7: 543–78.

Williams, J. H. G., Whiten, A. and Singh, T. (2004) A systematic review of action imitation in autistic spectrum disorder. *Journal of Autism and Developmental Disorders*, 34: 285–99.

Zeanah, C. H., Larrieu, J. A., Scott, H. S., Valliere, J., Hinshaw-Fuselier, S., Aoki, Y. and Drilling, M. (2001) Evaluation of a preventive intervention for maltreated infants and toddlers in foster care. *Journal of the Academy of Child and Adolescent Psychiatry*, 40: 214–21.

3.5 Preventing delinquency and later criminal offending

David P. Farrington and Brandon C. Welsh

See also chapter 1.3 Developmental perspectives on offending, chapter 8.7 Randomized control trials.

Definition

In reviewing preventative interventions, it is important to distinguish between delinquency and later criminal offending in as much as the former takes place during the juvenile years (up to age 17, usually) and the latter during the adult years. Early prevention has three defining features: interventions are implemented in the early years of the life course; they are implemented before children or young people engage in delinquency in the first place; and they are developmental or social in nature. In other words, they prevent the development of criminal potential in individuals or improve the social conditions and institutions (e.g. families, peers, social norms) that influence offending. Early childhood prevention programmes are aimed at the betterment of children's immediate learning, social and emotional competencies, as well as the improvement of children's success over the life course.

Methods

Literature reviews to assess if a particular prevention strategy (e.g. developmental, community), intervention modality (e.g. parent training, home visiting), or some other grouping of prevention programmes is effective in preventing delinquency or later criminal offending can take many different forms. The systematic review and the meta-analysis are the most rigorous methods for assessing effectiveness (Welsh and Farrington 2006). Systematic reviews use rigorous methods for locating, appraising and synthesizing evidence from prior evaluation studies, and they are reported with the same level of detail that characterizes high-quality reports of original research. A meta-analysis addresses the question: how well does the programme work? It involves the statistical or quantitative analysis of the results of prior research studies (Lipsey and Wilson 2001).

An evaluation of a crime prevention programme is considered scientifically acceptable if it possesses a high degree of internal, construct and statistical conclusion validity (Cook and Campbell 1979; Farrington 2003; Shadish, Cook and Campbell 2002). The randomized controlled trial (RCT), in which there is random assignment to experimental or control groups, is the 'gold standard' of evaluation research designs. This equates the groups before the experimental intervention on all possible extraneous variables. Therefore, any subsequent differences between the groups can be attributed to the intervention.

Randomization is the only method of assignment that controls for unknown and unmeasured confounders as well as those that are known and measured. Problems do arise with RCTs (e.g. crossover between control and experimental conditions, differential attrition, problems of maintaining random assignment) which may reduce internal validity. In addition, a sufficiently large number of units (e.g. people or areas) need to be randomly assigned to ensure that the experimental group is equivalent to the control group on all extraneous variables (within the limits of statistical fluctuation). As a rule of thumb, at least fifty units in each category are needed (Farrington 1997). This number is relatively easy to achieve with individuals, but very difficult to achieve with larger units such as communities, schools or classrooms.

A non-randomized experimental design in which experimental and control units are matched or statistically equated (e.g. using a propensity score) prior to intervention has lower internal validity than a randomized experiment. It is important to note that statistical conclusion validity and construct validity could be just as high in a non-randomized experiment as in a randomized experiment. A quasi-experimental evaluation design often involves before and after measures of crime in experimental and comparable control conditions, together with statistical control of extraneous variables.

Preventative interventions

A great deal is now known about early risk factors for delinquency and later criminal offending. These can be at the individual (low intelligence and attainment, personality and temperament, empathy, or impulsiveness), family (criminal or antisocial parents, large family size, poor parental supervision, parental conflict, or disrupted families) or environmental levels (growing up in a low socioeconomic-status household, associating with delinquent friends, attending schools with a high delinquency rate, or living in deprived areas) (Farrington and Welsh 2007).

Individual-based prevention programmes target risk factors for delinquency and later offending located within the individual. These interventions focus directly on the person and can be implemented very early in life, e.g. cognitively based preschool education (Duncan and Magnuson 2004, p. 94). Systematic and meta-analytic reviews find that two main types of individual-based programmes – preschool intellectual enrichment and child skills training – are generally effective in preventing delinquency or later criminal offending (Farrington and Welsh 2003; Lösel and Beelmann 2003, 2006). Preschool intellectual enrichment programmes are generally targeted on the risk factors of low intelligence and attainment. Improved cognitive skills, school readiness, and social and emotional development are the main goals of child skills programmes (Currie 2001).

Meta-analyses and reviews of randomized experimental evaluations by Farrington and Welsh (2003, 2006) of the effects of a wide range of early interventions on antisocial behaviour, delinquency and later offending report findings for daycare and preschool interventions. Combining the effect sizes for all programmes yielded a mean effect size of .266, which indicates that these programmes were followed by a 13% reduction in offending in the experimental group compared to the control group (e.g. from 50% to 37%).

Social skills training or social competence programmes for children are generally targeted on the risk factors of impulsivity, low empathy and self-centredness, and attempt to address social skills, effective problem solving, anger management and emotional language by teaching children social, emotional and cognitive competence (Webster-Stratton and Taylor 2001, p. 178). Lösel and Beelmann (2006) carried out a systematic review of the effects of child social skills training on antisocial behaviour (including delinquency) and reported that almost half of the comparisons produced desirable results favouring the children who received the treatment compared to those who did not, while less than one out of ten revealed undesirable results (i.e. the control group fared better than the treatment group). Control participants typically received non-intensive, basic services. The most effective social skills training programmes used a cognitive-behavioural approach with older children (13 years and over) and higher-risk groups who were already exhibiting some behavioural problems.

Family-based prevention programmes target risk factors (poor child rearing, poor parental supervision, or inconsistent or harsh discipline) for delinquency and later offending (Farrington and Welsh 2007). Parent management training, functional family therapy or family preservation are typically delivered by psychologists; these programmes attempt to change the social contingencies in the family environment so that children are rewarded in some way for appropriate or prosocial behaviours and punished in some way for inappropriate or antisocial behaviours (Wasserman and Miller 1998).

Programmes delivered by health professionals such as nurses are typically less behavioural, and provide advice and guidance to parents or general parent education. Home visits, the goals of which centre around educating parents to improve the life chances of children from a very young age, often beginning at birth and sometimes in the final trimester of pregnancy with new parents, especially mothers, are perhaps the most popular form of this type of family intervention. In the early 1990s, Hawaii became the first US state to offer free home visits for all new mothers. A small number of other states, with Colorado at the forefront, have more recently implemented more intensive but targeted versions of home-visiting programmes with the aim of eventually providing universal coverage (Calonge 2005).

A recent meta-analysis (Farrington and Welsh 2003) found that two main types of family-based programmes – general parent education (in the context of home visiting and parent education plus daycare services) and parent management training – are effective in preventing delinquency or later criminal offending. Both types of programmes also produce a wide range of other important benefits for families – improved school readiness and school performance on the part of children, greater employment and educational opportunities for parents, and greater family stability in general. There is some evidence that home-visiting programmes can pay back programme costs and produce substantial monetary benefits for the government and taxpayers. Little is known about the economic efficiency of daycare and parent management training programmes.

Many different types of parent training have been used to prevent and treat child behaviour problems and delinquency (Wasserman and Miller 1998). Parent management training refers to 'treatment procedures in which parents are trained to alter their child's behaviour at home' (Kazdin 1997, p. 1349). Patterson (1982) developed behavioural parent management training in which he attempted to train parents in effective child-rearing methods, namely noticing what a child is doing, monitoring behaviour over long periods, clearly stating house rules, making rewards and punishments contingent on behaviour, and negotiating disagreements so that conflicts and crises did not escalate. His treatment was shown to be effective in reducing child stealing and antisocial behaviour over short periods in small-scale studies (Patterson, Chamberlain and Reid 1982; Patterson, Reid and Dishion 1992).

The Farrington and Welsh (2003) meta-analysis reported that this form of early intervention was effective in preventing antisocial behaviour and delinquency. The mean effect size of these programmes was .395, corresponding to a significant 20% reduction in antisocial behaviour or delinquency (e.g. from 50% in a control group to 30% in an experimental group). Compared to the other types of early intervention that were examined in this meta-analysis, parent management training was the second most effective.

The most effective intervention in the Farrington–Welsh (2003) review was Multi-Systemic Therapy (MST), which involves individually tailored interventions targeted on the individual, the family, the peer group and the community (Henggeler et al. 1998). However, since that review two later meta-analyses have reached dramatically opposite conclusions about the effectiveness of MST; Curtis et al. (2004) concluded that it was effective, but Littell (2005) concluded that it was not. Therefore, we cannot be confident about the effectiveness of MST until this controversy is resolved by more evaluations.

School and community prevention programmes target environmental-level risk factors for delinquency and later criminal offending. There have been a number of comprehensive, evidence-based reviews of their effectiveness (Wilson, Gottfredson and Najaka 2001; see also Gottfredson, Wilson and Najaka 2006). Meta-analyses identified four types of school-based programmes that were effective in preventing delinquency: school and discipline management, classroom or instructional management, reorganization of grades or classes, and increasing self-control or social competency using cognitive-behavioural instruction methods. Reorganization of grades or classes had the largest mean effect size ($d = .34$), corresponding to a significant 17% reduction in delinquency. Three of these four effective types of school-based programmes (other than school and discipline management) were also effective in preventing alcohol and drug use, and increasing self-control or social competency using cognitive-behavioural instruction methods was effective in preventing other problem behaviours.

After-school programmes (e.g. recreation-based, drop-in clubs, dance groups and tutoring services) are based on the belief that providing prosocial opportunities for young people in the after-school hours can reduce their involvement in delinquent behaviour in the community. After-school programmes target a range of risk factors for delinquency, including alienation and association with delinquent peers. Welsh and Hoshi (2006) identified three high-quality after-school programmes with an evaluated impact on delinquency. Each programme produced desirable effects on delinquency, and one programme also reported lower rates of drug activity for participants compared to controls. Welsh and Hoshi suggested that these programmes are promising in preventing juvenile offending, but this conclusion only applies to areas immediately around recreation centres.

Community-based mentoring programmes usually involve non-professional adult volunteers spending time with young people at risk for delinquency, dropping out of school, school failure and other social problems. Mentors behave in a 'supportive, non-judgmental manner while acting as role models' (Howell 1995, p. 90). Welsh and Hoshi (2006) identified seven community-based mentoring programmes (of which six were of high quality) that evaluated the impact on delinquency and other problem behaviours. Two programmes had a direct measure of delinquency and showed mixed results: one found desirable effects on delinquency for youths with prior offences but undesirable effects on delinquency for youths with no prior offences, and the other found desirable effects on delinquency. On the basis of these two programmes and the evidence provided by the four others that measured outcomes related to offending (e.g. disruptive and aggressive behaviour), which mostly found favourable results, Welsh and Hoshi concluded that community-based mentoring represents a promising approach to preventing delinquency. Similarly, a meta-analysis by Jolliffe and Farrington (2007) concluded that mentoring was often effective in reducing reoffending.

Conclusion

Many types of early intervention programmes are effective in preventing delinquency and later criminal offending. At the individual level, preschool intellectual enrichment and child skills training programmes seem particularly effective. At the family level, parent education (in the context of home visiting and parent education plus daycare services) and parent management training programmes are effective in preventing delinquency and later offending. A number of school-based interventions are effective in preventing delinquency among youths in middle school and high school, and most also produced benefits on other fronts, such as alcohol and drug use and other problem behaviour in general. The most effective programmes in preventing delinquency and related behaviour problems (i.e. aggressive or violent behaviour) were those that targeted the highest-risk students. At the community level, after-school and mentoring programmes hold promise as effective approaches for preventing delinquency or later criminal offending, but further evaluation research is needed on them.

REFERENCES

Calonge, N. (2005) Community interventions to prevent violence: translation into public health practice. *American Journal of Preventive Medicine* 28(2S1): 4–5.

Cook, T. D. and Campbell, D. T. (1979) *Quasi-Experimentation: Design and Analysis Issues for Field Settings*. Chicago: Rand McNally.

Currie, J. (2001) Early childhood education programs. *Journal of Economic Perspectives*, 15: 213–38.

Curtis, N. M., Ronan, K. R. and Borduin, C. M. (2004) Multisystemic treatment: a meta-analysis of outcome studies. *Journal of Family Psychology*, 18: 411–19.

Duncan, G. J. and Magnuson, K. (2004) Individual and parent-based intervention strategies for promoting human capital and positive behavior. In P. L. Chase-Lansdale, K. Kiernan and R. J. Friedman (eds.), *Human Development Across Lives and Generations: The Potential for Change*, pp. 93–135. New York: Cambridge University Press.

Farrington, D. P. (1997) Evaluating a community crime prevention program. *Evaluation*, 3: 157–73.

(2003) Methodological quality standards for evaluation research. *Annals of the American Academy of Political and Social Science*, 587: 49–68.

Farrington, D. P. and Welsh, B. C. (2003) Family-based prevention of offending: a meta-analysis. *Australian and New Zealand Journal of Criminology*, 36: 127–51.

(2006) A half-century of randomized experiments on crime and justice. In M. Tonry (ed.), *Crime and Justice: A Review of Research*, vol. 34, pp. 55–132. Chicago: University of Chicago Press.

(2007) *Saving Children from a Life of Crime: Early Risk Factors and Effective Interventions*. Oxford: Oxford University Press.

Gottfredson, D. C., Wilson, D. B. and Najaka, S. S. (2006) School-based crime prevention. In L. W. Sherman, D. P. Farrington, B. C. Welsh and D. L. MacKenzie (eds.), *Evidence-Based Crime Prevention*, rev. edn, pp. 56–164. New York: Routledge.

Henggeler, S. W., Schoenwald, S. K., Borduin, C. M., Rowland, M. D. and Cunningham, P. B. (1998) *Multisystemic Treatment of Antisocial Behavior in Children and Adolescents*. New York: Guilford Press.

Howell, J. C. (ed.) (1995) *Guide for Implementing the Comprehensive Strategy for Serious, Violent, and Chronic Juvenile Offenders*. Washington, DC: US Department of Justice, Office of Juvenile Justice and Delinquency Prevention.

Jolliffe, D. and Farrington, D. P. (2007) *A Rapid Evidence Assessment of the Impact of Mentoring on Reoffending*. London: Home Office.

Kazdin, A. E. (1997) Parent management training: evidence, outcomes, and issues. *Journal of the American Academy of Child and Adolescent Psychiatry*, 36: 1349–56.

Lipsey, M. W. and Wilson, D. B. (2001) *Practical Meta-Analysis*. Thousand Oaks, CA: Sage.

Littell, J. H. (2005) Lessons from a systematic review of effects of multisystemic therapy. *Children and Youth Services Review*, 27: 445–63.

Lösel, F. and Beelmann, A. (2003) Effects of child skills training in preventing antisocial behavior: a systematic review. *Annals of the American Academy of Political and Social Science*, 587: 84–109.

(2006) Child social skills training. In B. C. Welsh and D. P. Farrington (eds.), *Preventing Crime: What Works for Children, Offenders, Victims, and Places*, pp. 33–54. New York: Springer.

Patterson, G. (1982) *Coercive Family Process*. Eugene, OR: Castalia.

Patterson, G., Chamberlain, P. and Reid, J. B. (1982) A comparative evaluation of a parent training program. *Behavior Therapy*, 13: 638–50.

Patterson, G., Reid, J. B. and Dishion, T. J. (1992) *Antisocial Boys*. Eugene, OR: Castalia.

Shadish, W. R., Cook, T. D. and Campbell, D. T. (2002) *Experimental and Quasi-Experimental Designs for Generalized Causal Inference*. Boston, MA: Houghton Mifflin.

Wasserman, G. A. and Miller, L. S. (1998) The prevention of serious and violent juvenile offending. In R. Loeber and D. P. Farrington (eds.), *Serious and Violent Juvenile Offenders: Risk Factors and Successful Interventions*, pp. 197–247. Thousand Oaks, CA: Sage.

Webster-Stratton, C. and Taylor, T. (2001) Nipping early risk factors in the bud: preventing substance abuse, delinquency, and violence in adolescence through interventions targeted at young children (0–8 years). *Prevention Science*, 2: 165–92.

Welsh, B. C. and Farrington, D. P. (eds.) (2006) *Preventing Crime: What Works for Children, Offenders, Victims, and Places*. New York: Springer.

Welsh, B. C., and Hoshi, A. (2006) Communities and crime prevention. In L. W. Sherman, D. P. Farrington, B. C. Welsh and D. L. Mackenzie (eds.), *Evidence-Based Crime Prevention*, rev. edn, pp. 165–97. New York: Routledge.

Wilson, D. B., Gottfredson, D. C. and Najaka, S. S. (2001) School-based prevention of problem behaviors: a meta-analysis. *Journal of Quantitative Criminology*, 17: 247–72.

3.6 Programmed interventions for offenders

Susan Young

See also chapter 8.5 Evaluating offender behaviour programmes in prison.

Definition

Offending behaviour programmes attempt to reduce reoffending by changing offenders' behaviour through cognitive skills training. They aim to replace thinking styles associated with offending with new cognitive skills to prevent reoffending, which is important for improvement of prosocial behaviour and for the engagement and compliance in therapeutic treatment. These have been running in HM Prison Services since the early 1990s and are based on cognitive-behavioural principles. Meta-analyses of offender treatments based on cognitive-behavioural principles have supported this approach to reducing reoffending (e.g. Andrews *et al.* 1990; Lipsey 1992; Lipton *et al.* 2002). Losel (1996, 1998) found a positive average effect size with respect to recidivism of 10–12%.

The three most widely adopted programmes are Reasoning and Rehabilitation (R&R: Ross *et al.* 1988), Enhanced Thinking Skills (Clark 2000) and Think First (McGuire 2000). These are based on a substantial research literature that indicates that many offenders either lack, or have poorly developed, cognitive skills (Ross and Hilborn 2008).

Reasoning and Rehabilitation

R&R was developed in Canada by Ross *et al.* in the 1980s. This early programme was accredited and rolled out internationally, and to date it has been translated into nine different languages. The programme is delivered in 38 two-hourly sessions which aim to replace thinking styles associated with offending with new cognitive skills that are associated with prosocial competence.

R&R was the first manualized offender rehabilitation programme. It has been highly influential in subsequent programme development in the field and various adaptations have since been developed, e.g. R&R2 (see Cognitive Centre of Canada: cogcen@canada.com), a revision for use in the English and Welsh Probation Service (Porporino and Fabiano 2000) and Straight Thinking on Probation (STOP) which was run by Mid Glamorgan Probation Service (Knott 1995; Raynor and Vanstone 1996).

Enhanced Thinking Skills

ETS was developed by the English and Welsh Prison Service (Clark 2000). It is a shortened version of the original R&R programme but its relative brevity of 20 two-hour sessions led to it becoming the programme of preference in the Prison Service of England and Wales.

Think First

Think First (McGuire 2000) was developed around the same time as ETS. It consists of 22 two-hour sessions and addresses social cognitive skills with a focus on how such skills are associated with offending.

Effectiveness of offending behaviour programmes

Despite the widespread implementation of cognitive skills programmes in forensic facilities, it is only relatively recently that attempts have been made to undertake a systematic evaluation of the impact of offending behaviour programmes in the UK. Where they have been done, published peer-reviewed studies in academic journals usually analyse outcome from attendance at an offending behaviour programme irrespective of whether the programme was R&R, ETS or Think First as they share the same theoretical basis, and none provides head-to-head comparisons.

Independent evaluations

There are no well-controlled published studies in peer-reviewed journals to date evaluating the effectiveness of ETS or Think First as stand-alone programmes. There is evidence for R&R in offender populations, including a meta-analysis of sixteen evaluations of the original 38-session R&R

programme, involving 26 different comparisons (Tong and Farrington 2006). Compared with controls, a 14% decrease in reoffending was found for R&R participants in institutional settings and a 21% decrease for participants in community settings. R&R has been shown to be effective in different countries, in community and institution settings, in smaller and larger evaluation studies, in older and newer studies and with a variety of types of offenders. Although no evaluations of recidivism rates for mentally disordered offenders in hospital settings have yet been completed, some small studies have reported programme-related improvements using R&R on psychometric measures (e.g. problem-solving and coping skills) (Clarke *et al.* 2003; Donnelly and Scott 1999; Fahy and Clarke 2003; Gretenkord 2004).

Studies evaluating R&R and ETS together

A search of the published literature revealed three studies analysing ETS and R&R alongside each other. A Home Office study compared recidivism rates in a two-year follow-up of adult male offenders serving a custodial sentence of two years or more (Friendship *et al.* 2002). The treatment group (n = 667) had voluntarily participated in either ETS or R&R. The comparison group (n = 1,801) was composed of offenders who had not participated in either of the treatment programmes but were matched to the treatment group based on a number of empirically relevant variables (current offence, sentence length, age at discharge, year of discharge, number of previous convictions and probability of reconviction). The study found a 14% reduction in recidivism for medium/low-risk offenders and 11% for medium/high-risk offenders. Extrapolating from these figures, the authors speculated that this reduction represented prevention of around 21,000 crimes.

Palmer *et al.* (2007) found that offenders who had completed one of three offending behaviour programmes (R&R, ETS and Think First) in the community had a 33% lower rate of reconviction compared to offenders who had not attended any similar programme and 68% compared to non-completers. These findings held for all three programmes separately. Only 32% completed the group programmes; however, the proportion of the 68% of non-completers that were non-starters is not reported.

The third study identified was a qualitative study conducted by the Home Office with the primary focus of examining programme processes and obtaining the experience of group participants (Clarke *et al.* 2004). The study aimed to identify not just 'what works', but 'what works for whom, in what conditions and in what type of setting', in practice, by ascertaining factors associated with successful programme delivery and impact, and identifying short-term (non-reconviction) benefits associated with programme completion. Interviews were conducted with sixty-two adult male prisoners ('programme graduates') who had recently completed either R&R or ETS, ten programme graduates who had been reconvicted since being released from prison ('reconvicted graduates'), and five ex-prisoners who had not been reconvicted ('desisting graduates'). In addition, a sample of thirty-three members of prison staff responsible for the organization and delivery of the programmes were interviewed, along with eight non-programme staff. Both prisoners and staff reported short-term benefits from participating in the groups, citing improvements in interpersonal skills (i.e. social interactions with inmates, prison staff and family), self-confidence, problem-solving skills and literacy skills. The acquisition of cognitive skills additionally helped to prepare prisoners for other offending behaviour programmes. From a delivery perspective, programme staff reported that a limitation of manualized programmes was that they did not meet the needs of all participants, especially those whose needs and abilities fell outside the 'norm'. For example, the pace of programmes suited a middle range of prisoners, in terms of learning ability, leaving the more able participants bored and frustrated and the less able participants struggling to keep up. Programme staff and participants reported the need for an adapted programme for prisoners with literacy or learning difficulties.

Limitations of offending behaviour programmes

Offending behaviour programmes are not without their limitations. These are group-based programmes, but not everyone is suitable for a cognitive skills programme and/or group work, e.g. those with learning disability or mental health problems. Sometimes these limitations are overcome by practitioners supplementing group sessions with individual treatment sessions in order to check that topics have been understood and to reinforce skills. Another limitation is that offending behaviour programmes are quite long and range between 22 and 38 sessions, which can be unsuitable for individuals with relatively short sentences. These can be completed in a shorter period by them being delivered more frequently, e.g. two or three times per week, but the relative impact of a more intensive treatment regime on outcome has not been evaluated.

Adherence problems are probably the greatest drawback to the successful implementation of all offending behaviour programmes in forensic settings, with non-start rates of almost 50% reported in probation settings, and 44% non-completers (Hollin and Palmer 2006). The reasons for 'drop-out' rates may vary depending on whether an offender is a non-starter or a non-completer. Non-starters may be individuals who are motivated to attend but are unable to start due to transfer to a new establishment. It may also reflect events that occur during time lags between referral and commencement of treatment while an adequate number of offenders are identified for the treatment (e.g. expiry of an order to attend a programme prior to allocation to a programme; the development of physical and/or mental health problems). Programme non-completion may relate more to offender characteristics (e.g. age, level of risk and previous criminal history) and motivational factors, although treatment process variables may also be influential (e.g. organizational and implementational problems that are unrelated to treatment participation such as transfer to another institution, staffing or resource problems).

An important aspect that will contribute to outcome is the extent to which an individual is motivated to engage in treatment. Usually individuals are required to attend one specific group and once this has finished there are no follow-up or 'booster sessions'. This is in contrast to individual cognitive-behavioural interventions which are often supplemented by 'booster' sessions after an intervening period; most offending behaviour programmes, however, are not easily adapted to this model because of their manualized structure. Many offenders agree to attend a programme as a 'box-ticking exercise' because they are aware that attendance will fulfil a criterion for review by parole board for early release and are only motivated to engage with the treatment at a superficial level.

It seems, however, that it is better to not attend a programme at all rather than not complete it. Indeed, not completing a programme may increase risk. Completers are least likely to reoffend, but non-completers have higher rates of reoffending than completers (McMurran and Theodosi 2007; Palmer et al. 2007). Perhaps it is only the lower-risk offenders who engage meaningfully with treatment. It may also reflect the fact that participants quickly acquire sufficient cognitive skills to improve their adaptive functioning but drop out of the treatment prior to making change related to underlying antisocial attitudes and belief systems. To address the 'completion effect' it is essential that resources promote motivation to engage in treatment, identify and address early indicators of drop-out, and target organizational and implementation problems that may interfere with programme completion in order to minimize drop-out rates. Improvement in completion rates of offending behaviour programmes have been reported with the incorporation of a mentoring role (Hollin and Palmer 2006; Jones and Hollin 2004), most likely because this combines both group and one-to-one work.

Current thinking

In the past few years we have seen a paradigm shift against the delivery of 'broadbrush' treatments towards a 'What Works' approach with its inclusion of three principles: Risk Assessment, Criminogenic Needs and Responsivity (Andrews and Bonta 2003; Langton 2007). This approach emphasizes the importance of adjusting treatment delivery to maximize learning. The effectiveness of a programme may be influenced by the level at which an offender participates and engages in programme sessions; engagement and completion rates are likely to be improved by programmes that adhere to the responsivity principle, which suggests that programmes should be tailored to match the content and pace of treatment to specific offender characteristics.

Current thinking also signals that to maximize effectiveness it is not only important to think about what treatments we should be delivering to whom, but also at what point in time they should be delivered as this may depend on the clients' 'readiness to change' (see chapter 1.14, this volume). For example, at early precontemplation/contemplation stages the goal of treatment may be the development of essential skills (to improve concentration and listening skills, to be reflective) rather than rehabilitation and the development of 'insight', which may be goals of treatment more suited to a later stage.

The effectiveness of offending behaviour programmes has most commonly been evaluated by reconviction rates. Reconviction rates are likely to underestimate 'clinical' change; they reflect more serious misdemeanours and do not account for change in cognitive skills, antisocial attitudes and behaviours more generally.

Conclusions

The future development of programmed offender interventions will respond to the 'What Works' perspective and this shift in current thinking. This has already been seen in the revision of R&R which, in response to the recent research (Ross and Hilborn 2008), has led to the development of a 'family' of R&R programmes (titled 'R&R2') tailored to meet the needs of specific groups of offenders, such as mentally disordered offenders (Young, Gudjonsson and Chick in press), offenders who evidence symptoms of Attention Deficit Hyperactivity Disorder, antisocial girls and young women, and the families and support persons of offenders (see Cognitive Centre of Canada: cogcen@canada.com for information on R&R2).

We need, however, to establish the effectiveness of offender behaviour programmes and, secondly, to understand exactly what makes them effective in reducing offender recidivism. Answers to these questions require large-scale, multi-site randomly controlled trials. However, there seems to be a gap between efficacy (i.e. whether an intervention is successful under controlled/ideal conditions) and effectiveness (i.e. whether an intervention is successful in practice). 'Real-world' evaluations of accredited cognitive-behavioural programmes in the UK prison and probation services have shown disappointingly low effect sizes, indicating that outcomes are less substantive than the research literature suggests they can be (and should be). This may be because the large-scale rolling out of offender programmes has a negative impact on the quality and/or integrity of programme implementation, and treatment delivery (Goggin and Gendreau 2006). The gap between research and practice is a challenge that needs to be addressed. If effective and constructive offender treatments are not established, the needs of the offender and of society will not be met.

FURTHER READING

Hollin, C. R. and Palmer, E. J. (eds.) (2006) *Offending Behavior Programmes: Development, application and controversies.* Chichester: Wiley.

REFERENCES

Andrews, D. and Bonta, J. (2003) *The Psychology of Criminal Conduct*, 3rd edn. Cincinnati, OH: Anderson.

Andrews, D. A., Zinger, I., Hoge, R. D., Bonta, J., Gendreau, P. and Cullen, F. T. (1990) Does correctional treatment work? A clinically relevant and psychologically informed meta-analysis. *Criminology*, 28: 369–404.

Clark, D. (2000) *Theory Manual for Enhanced Thinking Skills*. Prepared for the Joint Prison Probation Service Accreditation Panel.

Clarke, A., Simmonds, R. and Wydall, S. (2004) *Delivering Cognitive Skills Programmes in Prison: A Qualitative Study* (Home Office Research Findings 242). London: Home Office.

Clarke, A., Walwyn, R. and Fahy, T. (2003) A controlled trial of Reasoning and Rehabilitation with mentally disordered offenders. Report prepared for South London and Maudsley NHS.

Donnelly, J. P. and Scott, M. F. (1999) Evaluation of an offending behaviour programme with mentally disordered offender population. *British Journal of Forensic Practice*, 1: 25–32.

Fahy, T. and Clarke, A. (2003) *Rehabilitation and Re-offending: A Clinical Trial in Mentally Disordered Offenders.* Miami Beach, FL: International Association of Forensic Mental Health Services.

Friendship, C., Blud, L., Erikson, M. and Travers, R. (2002) *An Evaluation of Cognitive Behavioural Treatment for Prisoners.* London: Home Office.

Goggin, C. and Gendreau, P. (2006) The implementation and maintenance of quality services in offender rehabilitation programmes. In C. J. Hollin and E. J. Palmer (eds.), *Offending Behavior Programmes: Development, Application and Controversies*, pp. 209–46. Chichester: Wiley.

Gretenkord, L. (2004) R&R treatment effects Haina Pilot Study. Report prepared for the Haina Forensic Psychiatric Hospital.

Hollin, C. R. and Palmer, E. J. (2006) Offending behavior programmes: controversies and resolutions. In C. J. Hollin and E. J. Palmer (eds.), *Offending Behavior Programmes: Development, Application and Controversies*, pp. 247–78. Chichester: Wiley.

Jones, D. and Hollin, C. R. (2004) Managing problematic anger: the development of a treatment programme for personality disordered patients in high security. *International Journal of Forensic Mental Health*, 3: 197–210.

Knott, C. (1995) The STOP programme: Reasoning and Rehabilitation in a British setting. In J. McGuire (ed.), *What Works: Reducing Reoffending*, pp. 115–26. Chichester: Wiley.

Langton, C. M. (2007) Assessment implications of 'What Works' research for Dangerous and Severe Personality Disorder (DSPD) service evaluation. *Psychology, Crime and Law*, 13: 97–111.

Lipsey, M. W. (1992) Juvenile delinquency treatment: a meta-analytic inquiry into the variability of effects. In T. Cook, D. Cooper, H. Corday, H. Hartman, L. Hedges, R. Light *et al.* (eds.), *Meta-Analysis for Explanation: A Casebook*, pp. 83–127. New York: Sage.

Lipton, D. S., Pearson, F. S., Cleland, C. M. and Yee, D. (2002) The effectiveness of cognitive-behavioural treatment methods on recidivism. In J. McGuire (ed.), *Offender Rehabilitation and Treatment: Effective Programmes and Policies to Reduce Re-offending*, pp. 79–112. Chichester: Wiley

Losel, F. (1996) Working with young offenders: the impact of the meta-analyses. In C. R. Hollin and K. Howells (eds.), *Clinical Approaches to Working with Young Offenders*, pp. 57–82. Chichester: Wiley.

  (1998) Treatment and management of psychopaths. In D. J. Cooke, A. E. Forth and R. D. Hare (eds.), *Psychopathy: Theory, Research and Implications for Society*, pp. 303–54. Dordrecht: Kluwer Academic.

McGuire, J. (2000) *Theory Manual for Think First.* Prepared for the Joint Prison Probation Service Accreditation Panel.

McMurran, M. and Theodosi, E. (2007) Is offender treatment non-completion associated with increased reconviction over no treatment? *Psychology, Crime and Law*, 13: 333–43.

Palmer, E. J., McGuire, J., Hounsome, J. C., Hatcher, R. M., Bilby, C. A. L. and Hollin, C. R. (2007) Offending behaviour programmes in the community: the effects on reconviction of three programmes with adult male offenders. *Legal and Criminological Psychology*, 12: 251–64.

Porporino, F. J. and Fabiano, E. A. (2000) *Theory Manual for Reasoning and Rehabilitation (Revised)*. Ottawa: T3 Associates.

Raynor, P. and Vanstone, M. (1996) Reasoning and Rehabilitation in Britain: the results of the Straight Thinking on Probation (STOP) programme. *International Journal of Offender Therapy and Comparative Criminology*, 40: 272–84.

Ross, R. R., Fabiano, E. A. and Ewles, C. D. (1988) Reasoning and Rehabilitation. *International Journal of Offender Therapy and Comparative Criminology*, 32: 29–35.

Ross, R. R. and Hilborn, J. (2008) *Rehabilitating Rehabilitation: Neurocriminology for Treatment of Antisocial Behavior*. Ottawa: Cognitive Centre of Canada, cogcen@canada.com.

Tong, J. and Farrington, D. (2006) How effective is the 'Reasoning and Rehabilitation' programme in reducing reoffending? A meta-analysis of evaluations in four countries. *Psychology, Crime and Law*, 12: 3–24.

Young S., Gudjonsson, G. and Chick, K. (in press) A preliminary evaluation of Reasoning and Rehabilitation 2 in mentally disordered offenders (R&R2M) across two secure forensic settings in the United Kingdom. *Journal of Forensic Psychiatry and Psychology*.

3.7 Rediscovering recovery and rehabilitation in drug and alcohol services

Neil McKeganey

Introduction

In 2007 the world of substance abuse services in the UK experienced something of a bombshell when the BBC Home Affairs editor Mark Easton reported the finding that only 3% of drug users were leaving treatment drug free (BBC 2007). Given that the UK government is estimated to spend something in the region of £500 million a year on treatment and rehabilitation services for those with a substance misuse problem, it is not difficult to see why the reported 'success' rate of only 3% drug free should have been received with such evident discomfort (Hayes 2007). In the wake of the Easton report there has been considerable soul searching on the part of those providing and funding substance misuse services in the UK, with fundamental questions being asked about the nature of recovery and rehabilitation and about the contribution of substance abuse services: what are substance abuse treatment and rehabilitation services aiming to do by way of treatment and rehabilitation? Should such services be aiming to enable their clients to become drug free? Is abstinence a precondition of effective recovery and rehabilitation? How effective are substance misuse services with respect to such other aims as reducing drug users' risk behaviour, reducing drug users' mental health problems, improving their education, facilitating their employment and improving their housing conditions? In this chapter I would like to discuss some of the complexities bearing upon these fundamental questions.

Defining recovery and rehabilitation

Recently the United Kingdom Drug Policy Commission has attempted to produce a consensus statement as to the meaning of recovery within the drug dependency field. In particular, the commission has characterized recovery as a process whereby the individual exercizes:

voluntarily-sustained control over substance use which maximises health and wellbeing and participation in the rights, roles and responsibilities of society. (UKDPC 2008)

This characterization is interesting in a number of respects. First, that the commission has sought to produce a consensus definition is indicative of the divergence of views within the substance abuse field as to what recovery and rehabilitation actually means. Second, the characterization is suggesting that recovery in the case of individuals with a drug or alcohol problem is not dependent on those individuals becoming drug/alcohol free, rather their being able to exercise control over their possibly continuing substance use. Finally, the characterization is interesting because of the importance given to the individual being able to take on the rights, roles and responsibilities associated with fully participating within society. Within the UKDPC definition, recovery and rehabilitation are seen as part and parcel of the same process. An individual who is seen as having been able to overcome his or her drug/alcohol use but who remains unable to fully participate within society is still seen as in need of further help, whilst an individual who is continuing to use substances in a controlled way but who is able to participate fully in the rights, roles and responsibilities of society is seen as not in need of further help.

This characterization of recovery, although framed as a consensus statement, has become the subject of a considerably heated debate within the drug and alcohol field. It has been suggested, for example, that in drawing a parallel between those who are able to become drug free and those who are able to control their continuing drug use, the UKDPC vision of recovery effectively excludes those organizations such as Alcoholics Anonymous or Narcotics Anonymous that characterize recovery first and foremost in terms of the individual abstaining from drug and alcohol use (Boyd 2008).

If the definition of recovery is problematic within the substance misuse field so too is the notion of rehabilitation. Wrapped up in the notion of rehabilitation is the idea of returning the individual to his or her pre-drug/alcohol problem state. In the case of the individual who has developed an alcohol problem in mid life, and who has experienced various aspects of personal and social breakdown, e.g. loss of family or loss of employment as a result of his or her level of alcohol consumption, rehabilitation may be taken to mean enabling the individual to rebuild his or her life whilst remaining alcohol free or whilst continuing to drink in a controlled way. In the case of those with a substance misuse problem, who are often younger than those who have developed an alcohol problem, the individual may never have had a job or a home prior to developing his or her drug problem. In this sense rehabilitation of the person addicted to illegal drugs may mean not re-acquiring the rights and responsibilities associated with societal membership so much as gaining a job or a home for the first time.

The contribution of research

Research within the drug and alcohol field has demonstrated that with the right services in place it is possible to address individuals' substance abuse needs. For example, in the Drug Outcome Research in Scotland study, drug users who had received residential rehabilitation services were significantly more likely than their community-treated peers to have experienced an extended period of being drug free. In this study, approaching 30% of drug users receiving residential rehabilitation treatment had a ninety-day drug-free period prior to being interviewed compared to only 3% of those drug users who had received substitute prescribing services within the community (McKeganey *et al.* 2006).

Whilst the abstinence rate on the part of those receiving residential rehabilitation in the Drug Outcome Research in Scotland study may seem striking in the light of Easton's reported 3% success rate, in fact only a tiny proportion of drug users receive residential rehabilitation within the UK. In Scotland, for example, it has been estimated that there may be around 300 residential rehabilitation places. This figure compares with the estimate of some 22,000 drug users in Scotland receiving methadone prescriptions as their principal drug-dependency treatment (Scottish Government 2007).

With regard to the treatment of individuals with an alcohol problem, the UK Alcohol Treatment Trial (UKATT) has identified the effectiveness of both social behaviour / network therapy and motivational enhancement in reducing individuals' drinking (UKATT 2005). Research within the alcohol field has also shown that even relatively brief interventions can have a positive impact on reducing levels of alcohol consumption on the part of those who have developed an alcohol problem (Heather 2002).

One of the key questions in relation to research showing that services can facilitate a reduction in an individual's drug and alcohol use is the degree to which such improvements can be seen to lead to positive improvements in the individual's social circumstances, i.e. their broader rehabilitation. In the

Scottish research, McKeganey and colleagues were able to show that those drug users who had experienced a ninety-day period of being totally drug free (apart from alcohol and tobacco) were significantly more likely than their non-abstinent peers to have taken an educational course during the period of their treatment, to rate their health as better, to be less likely to have attempted suicide or self-harmed or to have committed any crime or to have been arrested. Individuals who had managed to abstain from further drug use were also less likely to have been homeless in the period since their preceding interview (McKeganey et al. 2006). These were all positive benefits associated with being drug free; however, the Scottish research confirmed the Easton report in finding that the vast majority of drug users leave treatment with a continuing drug problem.

Where research has looked in greater detail at the constituents of longer-term recovery and rehabilitation, the individual's ability to develop a new non-addict identity has been shown to be important. In qualitative research with long-term recovered heroin addicts, McIntosh and McKeganey (2001) were able to show that the process of developing a new non-addict identity could involve such elements as moving to a new area where the individual was not known as a drug user, building up a new social circle that did not include one's previous drug-using acquaintances, getting involved in work or educational activities that both absorbed the individual's time and enabled the individual to develop a sense of accomplishment in activities that were not in any way connected to their previous drug use.

Role of the family and parenting

Whilst there is no doubt that services can enable individuals to reduce their drug and alcohol use, and in that sense facilitate their longer-term rehabilitation, it is evident that where substance abuse problems have penetrated the family it is extraordinarily difficult for services to develop and sustain a broader rehabilitative function. This is nowhere more evident than in the attempt to strengthen the parenting capacity of those with a drug and alcohol problem. Whilst this is an area which has received substantial attention and funding within the UK, the global evidence suggests that even relatively intensive services are only able to have a modest impact on improving family dynamics where these have been adversely affected by parental drug and alcohol use. For example, Catalano and colleagues evaluated an intensive home-visiting and home-support project in the United States targeted on drug-using parents. In this study parents received 53 hours of parent training in small groups, including a 5-hour family retreat, thirty-two 90-minute meetings twice weekly (Catalano *et al.* 1999). Children were involved in twelve sessions and case managers supported the families over a nine-month period, with one home visit and two telephone calls per week. Despite the intensity of this programme, however, whilst it was evident that individuals were able to reduce their drug consumption and develop stronger household routines, there was very little evidence that such changes had a beneficial impact on the children. Indeed, there was some indication that where the children were older at the time the intervention began, the more likely it was that the children themselves would resent the imposition of household routines by parents whom they saw as having previously adopted a laissez faire attitude to household routines. On the basis of this study, one would have to say that rehabilitating family relationships that have been damaged by long-term drug and alcohol use is by no means as straightforward as facilitating a reduction in parental substance abuse.

Successful treatment and rehabilitation

In formulating a view of the aims and successes of substance misuse treatment and rehabilitation services, the question of the balance of responsibilities between the service provider and the client with regard to the client's progress is very often an unexplored area. It is perhaps as much for this reason as any other that the reports of the 3% success or abstinence rate on the part of drug abusers leaving treatment has most often been cast as indicative of a failure on the part of services and broader substance misuse policy. In reality, of course, any success or failure rate, however defined, in this area as in others is likely to be a composite of what any services have been able to do and what the individual has been able to do.

Rehabilitation without recovery

There is a moral dimension to the debate as to what substance misuse services can achieve that is often barely acknowledged by the field to date, but which is crucial to the issue of recovery and rehabilitation. Perhaps the clearest example of this can be seen in the suggestion that substance misuse services ought to make wider use of heroin prescribing as a way of meeting individuals' needs

(Stimson and Metrebian 2001). Within the scientific literature there is a growing evidence base that there are numerous positive benefits both for the individual and for society in the wider use of heroin prescribing (Rehm and Fischer 2008). Research has shown that those drug users prescribed heroin have reduced risk behaviour, increased social inclusion, lower levels of criminality and increased likelihood of remaining in contact with services. However, for the most part policy discussions surrounding heroin prescribing have tended only to make the case that such prescribing may be suitable for the small minority (under 5%) of drug users who fail to respond to any of the other treatments available. One could equally ask, though, whether heroin prescribing could or should be extended to a much wider range of drug users as a way of extending the reported benefits associated with such an intervention. The question here, though, is more ethical than evidential, in that treatment is generally not thought of as a process through which the individual is being provided with the substance upon which they have become dependent. However, in a situation where treatment services appear able to achieve only modest success with regard to enabling individuals to become drug free, there may be an increasing call for services to take on the provision of those substances upon which the individual has become dependent as a way of facilitating the goal of longer-term rehabilitation.

Conclusion

This chapter has sought to outline some of the complex issues underpinning rehabilitation and recovery as these terms apply within the substance misuse domain. At the present time there is considerable debate within the drugs and alcohol field as to whether services should aim to facilitate individuals' abstinence, whether abstinence is the single most important goal for services or indeed whether services should be aiming instead to facilitate individuals' rehabilitation and recovery even in the face of their continuing drug and alcohol use.

REFERENCES

BBC (2007) Drug services make slow progress. *Today Programme*, 30 October.
Boyd, D. (2008) UKDPC Non Consensus on Recovery. *Addiction Today*, 6 June.

Catalano, R., Gainey R., Flemming, C., Haggerty, K. and Johnson, N. (1999) An experimental intervention with families of substance abusers – one year follow up on the focus on families project. *Addiction*, 94: 241–54.

Hayes, P. (2007) Drug treatment in England and the BBC. www.nta.nhs.uk (accessed 4 November 2007).

Heather, N. (2002) Effectiveness of brief interventions proved beyond reasonable doubt. *Addiction*, 97: 293–4.

McIntosh, J. and McKeganey, N. (2001) *Beating the Dragon: The Recovery from Dependent Drug Use*. New York: Prentice Hall.

McKeganey, N., Bloor, M., Robertson, M., Neale, J. and MacDougall, J. (2006) Abstinence and drug abuse treatment: results from the Drug Outcome Research in Scotland study. *Drugs: Education, Prevention and Policy*, 13: 537–50.

Rehm, J. and Fischer, B. (2008) Should heroin be prescribed to heroin misusers? Yes. *British Medical Journal*, 336: 70.

Scottish Government (2007) *Reducing Harm and Promoting Recovery: A Report on Methadone Treatment for Substance Misuse in Scotland*. SACDM Methadone Project Group.

Stimson, G. and Metrebian, N. (2001) *Prescribing Heroin: What Is the Evidence?* York: Joseph Rowntree Foundation.

UKATT (2005) Effectiveness of treatment for alcohol problems: findings of the randomised UK Alcohol Treatment Trial. *British Medical Journal*, 331: 541.

United Kingdom Drug Policy Commission (2008) Consensus on recovery: developing a vision of recovery – a work in progress.

3.8 Rehabilitation of offenders

James McGuire

Definition

Within criminal justice, the word *rehabilitation* has broad and narrow meanings. The former, sometimes denoted as *resettlement, reintegration* or *re-entry*, refers to the process whereby individuals who have (frequently or seriously) broken the law – such as those being discharged from prison – are once again accepted as full members of society, and are (in principle) provided support in making that transition. The latter refers more specifically to the reduction of criminal recidivism amongst adjudicated offenders (those convicted by the courts) and is also sometimes called *tertiary prevention*. In psychological research conducted to date, the overwhelming majority of studies have employed the latter sense of the term.

In the field of *penology* (the formal study of legal punishment and how it is administered), rehabilitation is usually specified by courts of law as one of the objectives of sentencing – alongside retribution, incapacitation, deterrence and restoration (Ashworth 2005; Easton and Piper 2005; McGuire 2008). Penologists sometimes consider that the objective of rehabilitation will be indirectly achieved through other elements of sentencing; for example, via society's expression of disapproval of criminal conduct (retribution, reprobation), or the experience of being punished (deterrence). However, there is little evidence that sentencing per se either contributes to the future wellbeing of individuals, or prevents subsequent offending. An alternative view is that rehabilitative activities should be integrated within sentencing as a core aspect of it, and that it is only by this means that behaviour is likely to change.

Evidence base

The objective of most research in criminological and forensic psychology for the last thirty years has been to discover, experimentally test and apply methods of working that can reliably reduce rates of criminal recidivism. The full history of this endeavour is much longer: Gaes (1998) describes how the ideal of 'reforming the offender' has had a central place in conceptions of criminal justice since the advent of penitentiaries in the early nineteenth century. It was a dominant concept guiding the assumptions and practices of many agencies and of how their services were organized.

The long-held consensus regarding the possibility of rehabilitation was questioned during the 1970s as a result of claims that there was no evidence that any kind of intervention – education, vocational training, psychological therapy, or other initiatives – had proven effective in reducing subsequent reoffending. The much-cited paper by Martinson (1974) is widely regarded as having had a powerful influence in undermining rehabilitation as an aim of criminal justice. Martinson argued that none of the findings then available yielded any demonstrable effects in reducing rates of reoffending. His paper precipitated a lengthy and occasionally acrimonious debate in which polarized positions of 'nothing works' versus 'what works' in reducing criminal offending were expounded.

However, it soon became clear that Martinson's assertions were a misinterpretation if not an actual misrepresentation of the evidence he had surveyed. Gendreau and Ross (1980), amongst others, published rebuttals of Martinson's arguments and marshalled evidence demonstrating the positive impact of interventions. From 1985 onwards the field was reinvigorated by the introduction of meta-analysis or statistical review (Wilson 2001). Successive overviews of the research evidence showed that on balance, rehabilitative interventions were successful in reducing offender recidivism. More detailed analyses reported in later reviews (over seventy meta-analyses have now been published in this field: McGuire 2009) identified those features that contributed most dependably to better outcomes. They have included examination of:

- types of offence (general/non-specific, sexual offending, substance abuse, violence, driving while intoxicated);
- categories of offenders (young, adult, mixed age group, diagnosed with personality disorder);
- methods of intervention (cognitive-behavioural, therapeutic communities, restorative justice, education, vocational training, other skills training, relapse prevention);
- moderator individual-level variables (age, gender, ethnicity);
- aspects of delivery (staff skills and practices, treatment integrity, 'human service principles');
- settings (prison, probation, youth justice, school, family); and

- deterrent sanctions (boot camps, 'scared straight', electronic monitoring, increased surveillance, outdoor-pursuit/'wilderness-challenge' schemes, intermediate punishment/harsher penalties).

Most reviews report on more than one aspect of a delineated area.

There are undoubted difficulties in systematizing the evidence that has been generated in this field. First, offending behaviour is notoriously difficult to measure, and official records are not reliable. Second, follow-up periods have been comparatively short, with few studies employing longer periods (more than two years). Third, until recently, there were questions over the experimental rigour of some evaluations and randomized controlled trials (RCTs) were relatively uncommon. Hence some critics claim that any apparent treatment effects are likely to be a function of participant self-selection (Simon 1998). However, the use of 'practical' rather than 'demonstration' trials has been defended by Lipsey (1999) as a basis for improving the external validity of conclusions drawn. Fourth, there have been challenges to the logic of meta-analysis: Berk (2007) has propounded the view that statistical inferences are not justified on the basis of it, nor does it permit any claims regarding causality. Again Lipsey (2007) responded that such criticisms do not reflect the manner in which inferential statistics are used, and it is not necessary to base research studies on probability samples, as Berk insists.

Principal findings

Taking these caveats into account and applying appropriate interpretative caution, there is nevertheless general agreement that the overall finding from meta-analyses of offender treatment completely reverses the once pervasive and pessimistic view that 'nothing works' (Hollin 2001a; McGuire 2004). The impact of psychosocial interventions (e.g. therapeutic communities) on criminal recidivism is on average positive: that is, there is a net reduction in reoffending rates in experimental relative to comparison samples. However, within the widely endorsed conventions proposed by Cohen (1992), the average effect taken across a broad spectrum of different types of treatment or intervention is small. Expressed as a correlation coefficient, it is estimated to be approximately 0.10 (Lösel 1995). This average finding obtained from the meta-analyses corresponds to recidivism rates of 45% for experimental groups and 55% for control groups respectively. Although low, this figure is statistically significant, and it compares reasonably well with effects found in many other fields. McGuire (2002a), drawing largely on Rosenthal (1994), collated effect sizes for several healthcare interventions that are generally regarded as producing worthwhile benefits, but are commensurate with the 'grand mean' for offender treatment.

Perhaps of greater practical importance, when different subgroups of studies are compared, the variations between them show some consistent trends. These are more informative in illuminating the attributes of intervention most reliably associated with better outcomes such as:

- rehabilitation effect sizes are larger for adolescent (under 15 years) and for adult offenders (over 18 years) than for those in what is usually called the 'young adult' age range (15–18);
- community-based interventions have larger effect sizes than those delivered in institutions: the ratio of relative effect sizes obtained has ranged from approximately 1.33/1 to as high as 1.75/1;
- there are complex interaction effects between criminal justice settings, types of interventions and their quality of delivery. Even the most carefully designed interventions can have nil and possibly negative effects if the manner of delivery is poor.

There has been steadily growing recognition that the largest effect sizes are obtained by combining a number of elements in rehabilitative services (Andrews 2001; Gendreau 1996; Hollin 1999). Effective interventions are thought to possess certain common features, which Andrews and his colleagues (1990) called 'principles of human service', more recently reformulated as the Risk–Need–Responsivity (RNR) model (Andrews, Bonta and Wormith 2006). When Andrews *et al.* isolated those components that contributed separately to enhancing effect size, they found amalgamating them produced an additive effect. Interventions which possessed all components yielded an average reduction in recidivism rates of 53%. So although as noted earlier the mean effect size across all studies is small, when interventions are appropriately designed and delivered it is possible to secure much larger effects.

Adopting a different perspective, several reviews have been conducted entailing econometric analysis of rehabilitation programmes. These have revealed mainly favourable 'benefit–cost' ratios (Aos *et al.* 2001; McDougall *et al.* 2003; Prentky and Burgess 1990; Welsh and Farrington 2000).

Implications for policy and practice

Perhaps the most widely disseminated change in practice to have emerged from the above findings has been the synthesis of methods and materials into a number of prearranged formats known as *programmes*. These consist of a planned sequence of learning opportunities (McGuire 2001), usually compiled in a 'manualized' format that is reproducible (with adaptations as necessary) across different settings (McMurran and Duggan 2005). In criminal justice services in some jurisdictions, quality-control standards have been introduced governing the selection, dissemination and delivery of such programmes. This involves independent judgement by expert accreditation panels (Lipton *et al.* 2000; National Probation Service 2004), supplemented by regular monitoring of quality of delivery, of agency support and other implementation standards (Bernfeld, Farrington and Leschied 2001). To date, the majority of the devised programmes employ cognitive-behavioural intervention methods, including, for example, training in social problem solving, interpersonal skills, emotional self-regulation, anger management, moral reasoning, or allied behavioural methods such as contingency contracts (Garrido and Morales 2007; Lipsey, Landenberger and Wilson 2007; Wilson 2005).

This period of activity has led to the emergence of several empirically supported methods of working, and validated intervention programmes (see Hollin 2001b; Hollin and Palmer 2006; Marshall *et al.* 2006; McGuire 2002b; McGuire *et al.* 2008; McIvor and Raynor 2007; McMurran and McGuire 2005; Motiuk and Serin 2001). Sizeable reductions in reoffending rates have been obtained following large-scale propagation of such programmes (Hollis 2007). With reference to the United Kingdom, it has been suggested that the initial series of attempts at injecting a more methodical, 'evidence-based' approach to rehabilitation probably paid insufficient attention to organizational and contextual factors influencing the implementation process (Raynor 2004).

Nevertheless, there is a progressively increasing accord that certain features of criminal justice interventions maximize the likelihood of securing a practical, meaningful impact in terms of reduced reoffending. The major findings that arise from this include the following:

- Rehabilitative endeavours are most likely to succeed when they are based on a theory of criminal behaviour that is conceptually clear and has firm empirical support. This strengthens the rationale for the methods that are used and explicates the 'vehicle of change' thought to be at work when an individual participates in an activity designed to have a rehabilitative impact.
- It is currently regarded as essential to assess risk-of-offending levels and allocate individuals to different amounts of contact and participation accordingly. There are now several well-developed approaches to risk assessment. Applying this information, the most intensive types of programme should be reserved for those offenders assessed as posing the

highest risk of reoffending or of causing harm to others. Individuals estimated as posing a low risk should not be exposed to such interventions.

- Research on the initial onset of delinquency and continuation into adult criminality suggests that certain patterns of social interaction, low levels of interpersonal or cognitive skills, antisocial attitudes, the influence of delinquent peer groups, and other factors are associated with its onset and maintenance. Those variables are consequently set as targets of change; they are factors that need to be addressed to alter offending and have been called *criminogenic needs* or *dynamic risk factors.*

- There is virtual unanimity amongst researchers that more effective interventions are likely to comprise several ingredients, encompassing a range of the aforementioned risks and change targets. Such interventions are described as *multimodal.* Thus the most effective rehabilitation programmes are likely to incorporate several types of intervention methods.

- Certain methods or approaches, primarily those based on social learning theory, have a superior record in engaging, motivating and helping participants in criminal justice interventions to change (Andrews 2001; Gendreau and Andrews 1990; McMurran 2002).

- Rehabilitative efforts work better if they have clear, concrete objectives, their contents are structured, and there is a focus on activity and the acquisition of skills. Personnel involved in delivering them should possess high-quality relational skills and foster supportive, collaborative working within clearly defined boundaries. This aspect of interventions is called *general responsivity.* Alongside this, it is vital to adapt intervention strategies to accommodate diversity amongst participants with respect to age, gender, ethnicity, language, learning styles, and other dimensions of difference. This aspect is called *specific responsivity.*

- High-quality, evidence-based programmes are key elements in making criminal justice effective. But they are only likely to succeed in a context in which well-trained, motivated workers are provided adequate resources in agencies that have a coherent, well-managed system of service delivery, applying 'core correctional practices' (Dowden and Andrews 2004). Staff are also able to achieve an appropriate relational balance between law enforcement and engagement in change (Paparozzi and Gendreau 2005; Skeem *et al.* 2007).

- Several meta-analysts note that intervention services appear to work better when they are simultaneously being researched. Repeated collection of data on how an intervention is delivered sustains its clarity of purpose, and its adherence to the methods it was intended to utilize. This feature is called the *integrity* or *fidelity* of an intervention (Andrews and Dowden 2005;

Bernfeld 2001; Hollin 1995). In the best intervention services it is routinely monitored and where departures from it occur, remedial action is taken.

Conclusion

There are ongoing debates in relation to several aspects of this field. One concerns the relative focus or balance of interest in the welfare of individual offenders, as contrasted with society's collective interest in protecting its citizens from crime. The relationship between rehabilitation in terms of decreased recidivism and in terms of improved social integration or enhanced wellbeing of ex-offenders is under-researched and remains unclear. One argument is that the design and planning of interventions as influenced by the Risk–Need–Responsivity (RNR) model is too narrow and that the so-called Good Lives model (Ward and Maruna 2007) extends it, by locating the individual change process in a wider model of human motivation.

A second concern is the relationship between research and practice, including (a) disputes over the design of outcome evaluations; (b) the 'transfer' of innovations into routine work, where effects are typically weaker than in controlled experiments; and (c) how best to accommodate variations in culture, context and other factors.

A third problem is the extent to which psychologists challenge state policies and official responses to crime, and question the practices of criminal justice agencies. Haney (2005) has castigated fellow psychologists in the USA for their disinterest in the scale of usage of imprisonment, and psychologists are often perceived by other professional groups as adopting an illusory 'value-free' stance regarding the ethical and political aspects of crime and justice.

FURTHER READING

A wide-ranging overview of the literature on reduction of offender recidivism is given by Doris Layton MacKenzie (2006) *What Works in Corrections: Reducing the Criminal Activities of Offenders and Delinquents* (Cambridge: Cambridge University Press). Examples of methods used in several specific areas are included in McGuire (2002b). For a broader survey of research and theory, and discussion of the relationship between 'risk factors' and the design of interventions, see McGuire (2004). Several books describe programmes that address a variety of types of offending behaviour, for example Hollin and Palmer (2006). For a recent polemic concerning the relationship between the Risk–Need–Responsivity and Good Lives models, see Ward and Maruna (2007).

REFERENCES

Andrews, D. A. (2001) Principles of effective correctional programs. In L. L. Motiuk and R. C. Serin (eds.), *Compendium 2000 on Effective Correctional Programming*, pp. 9–17. Ottawa: Correctional Service Canada.

Andrews, D. A., Bonta, J. and Wormith, J. S. (2006) The recent past and near future of risk and/or need assessment. *Crime and Delinquency*, 52: 7–27.

Andrews, D. A. and Dowden, C. (2005) Managing correctional treatment for reduced recidivism: a meta-analytic review of programme integrity. *Legal and Criminological Psychology*, 10: 173–87.

Andrews, D. A., Zinger, I., Hoge, R. D., Bonta, J., Gendreau, P. and Cullen, F. T. (1990) Does correctional treatment work? A clinically relevant and psychologically informed meta-analysis. *Criminology*, 28: 369–404.

Aos, S., Phipps, P., Barnoski, R. and Lieb, R. (2001) *The Comparative Costs and Benefits of Programs to Reduce Crime*. Olympia, WA: Washington State Institute for Public Policy.

Ashworth, A. (2005) *Sentencing and Criminal Justice*, 4th edn. Cambridge: Cambridge University Press.

Berk, R. (2007) Statistical inferences and meta-analysis. *Journal of Experimental Criminology*, 3: 247–70.

Bernfeld, G. A. (2001) The struggle for treatment integrity in a 'dis-interested' service delivery system. In G. A. Bernfeld, D. P. Farrington and E. W. Leschied (eds.), *Offender Rehabilitation in Practice: Implementing and Evaluating Effective Programs*, pp. 167–88. Chichester: Wiley.

Bernfeld, G. A., Farrington, D. P. and Leschied, A. W. (eds.) (2001) *Offender Rehabilitation in Practice: Implementing and Evaluating Effective Programs*. Chichester: Wiley.

Cohen, J. (1992) A power primer. *Psychological Bulletin*, 112: 155–9.

Dowden, C. and Andrews, D. A. (2004) The importance of staff practice in delivering effective correctional treatment: a meta-analytic review of core correctional practice. *International Journal of Offender Therapy and Comparative Criminology*, 48: 203–14.

Easton, S. and Piper, C. (2005) *Sentencing and Punishment: The Quest for Justice*. Oxford: Oxford University Press.

Gaes, G. G. (1998) Correctional treatment. In M. Tonry (ed.), *The Handbook of Crime and Punishment*, pp. 712–38. Oxford: Oxford University Press.

Garrido, V. and Morales, L. A. (2007) *Serious (Violent and Chronic) Juvenile Offenders: A Systematic Review of Treatment Effectiveness in Secure Corrections*. Campbell Systematic Reviews 2007:7. DOI: 10.4073/csr.2007.7.

Gendreau, P. (1996) Offender rehabilitation: what we know and what needs to be done. *Criminal Justice and Behavior*, 23: 144–61.

Gendreau, P. and Andrews, D. A. (1990) Tertiary prevention: what the meta-analyses of the offender treatment literature tell us about 'what works'. *Canadian Journal of Criminology*, 32: 173–84.

Gendreau, P. and Ross, R. R. (1980) Effective correctional treatment: bibliotherapy for cynics. In R. R. Ross and P. Gendreau (eds.), *Effective Correctional Treatment*, pp. 3–36. Toronto: Butterworths.

Haney, C. (2005) *Reforming Punishment: Psychological Limits to the Pains of Imprisonment.* Washington, DC: American Psychological Association.

Hollin, C. R. (1995) The meaning and implications of program integrity. In J. McGuire (ed.) *What Works: Reducing Reoffending: Guidelines from Research and Practice*, pp. 195–208. Chichester: Wiley.

(1999) Treatment programmes for offenders: meta-analysis, 'what works', and beyond. *International Journal of Law and Psychiatry*, 22: 361–71.

(2001a) To treat or not to treat? An historical perspective. In C. R. Hollin (ed.), *Handbook of Offender Assessment and Treatment*, pp. 3–15. Chichester: Wiley.

(ed.) (2001b) *Handbook of Offender Assessment and Treatment.* Chichester: Wiley.

Hollin, C. R. and Palmer, E. J. (eds.) (2006) *Offending Behaviour Programmes: Development, Application, and Controversies.* Chichester: Wiley.

Hollis, V. (2007) *Reconviction Analysis of Interim Accredited Programmes Software (IAPS) Data.* London: Research Development Statistics, National Offender Management Service.

Lipsey, M. W. (1999) Can rehabilitative programs reduce the recidivism of juvenile offenders? An inquiry into the effectiveness of practical programs. *Virginia Journal of Social Policy and the Law*, 6: 611–41.

(2007) Unjustified inferences about meta-analysis. *Journal of Experimental Criminology*, 3: 271–9.

Lipsey, M. W., Landenberger, N. A. and Wilson, S. J. (2007) *Effects of Cognitive-Behavioral Programs for Criminal Offenders.* Campbell Systematic Reviews 2007:6. DOI: 10.4073/csr.2007.6.

Lipton, D. S., Thornton, D., McGuire, J., Porporino, F. J. and Hollin, C. R. (2000) Program accreditation and correctional treatment. *Substance Use and Misuse*, 35: 1705–34.

Lösel, F. (1995) The efficacy of correctional treatment: a review and synthesis of meta-evaluations. In J. McGuire (ed.), *What Works: Reducing Re-offending: Guidelines from Research and Practice*, pp. 79–111. Chichester: Wiley.

MacKenzie, D. L. (2006) *What Works in Corrections: Reducing the Criminal Activities of Offenders and Delinquents.* Cambridge: Cambridge University Press.

Marshall, W. L., Fernandez, Y. M., Marshall, L. E. and Serran, G. A. (2006) *Sexual Offender Treatment: Controversial Issues.* Chichester: Wiley.

Martinson, R. (1974) What works? – Questions and answers about prison reform. *The Public Interest*, 10: 22–54.

McDougall, C., Cohen M. A., Swaray, R. and Perry, A. (2003) The costs and benefits of sentencing: a systematic review. *Annals of the American Academy of Political and Social Science*, 587: 160–77.

McGuire, J. (ed.) (2001) Defining correctional programs. In L. L. Motiuk and R. C. Serin (eds.), *Compendium 2000 on Effective Correctional Programming*, pp. 1–8. Ottawa: Correctional Service Canada.

(2002a) Criminal sanctions versus psychologically-based methods with offenders: a comparative empirical analysis. *Psychology, Crime and Law*, 8: 183–208.

(ed.) (2002b) *Offender Rehabilitation and Treatment: Effective Practice and Policies to Reduce Re-offending.* Chichester: Wiley.

(2004) *Understanding Psychology and Crime: Perspectives on Theory and Action.* Maidenhead: Open University Press / McGraw-Hill Education.

(2008) What's the point of sentencing? Psychological aspects of crime and punishment. In G. Davies, C. R. Hollin and R. Bull (eds.), *Forensic Psychology*, pp. 265–91. Chichester: Wiley.

(2009) Reducing personal violence: risk factors and effective interventions. In S. Hodgins, E. Viding and A. Plodowski (eds.), *The Neurobiological Basis of Violence: Science and Rehabilitation*, pp. 287–327. Oxford: Oxford University Press.

McGuire, J., Bilby, C. A. L., Hatcher, R. M., Hollin, C. R., Hounsome, J. and Palmer, E. J. (2008) Evaluation of structured cognitive-behavioural programs in reducing criminal recidivism. *Journal of Experimental Criminology*, 4: 21–40.

McIvor, G. and Raynor, P. (eds.) (2007) *Developments in Social Work with Offenders*. London: Jessica Kingsley.

McMurran, M. (ed.) (2002) *Motivating Offenders to Change: A Guide to Enhancing Engagement in Therapy*. Chichester: Wiley.

McMurran, M. and Duggan, C. (2005) The manualisation of a treatment programme for personality disorder. *Criminal Behaviour and Mental Health*, 15: 17–27.

McMurran, M. and McGuire, J. (eds.) (2005) *Social Problem-Solving and Offending: Evidence, Evaluation, and Evolution*. Chichester: Wiley.

Motiuk, L. L. and Serin, R. C. (eds.) (2001) *Compendium 2000 on Effective Correctional Programming*. Ottawa: Correctional Services Canada.

National Probation Service (2004) *General Offending Behaviour / Cognitive Skills Programmes: Evaluation Manual and Scoring Supplement*. London: Home Office, National Probation Directorate.

Paparozzi, M. and Gendreau, P. (2005) An intensive supervision program that worked: service delivery, professional orientation, and organizational supportiveness. *The Prison Journal*, 85: 445–66.

Prentky, R. A. and Burgess, A. W. (1990) Rehabilitation of child molesters: a cost-benefit analysis. *American Journal of Orthopsychiatry*, 60: 108–17.

Raynor, P. (2004) The Probation Service 'Pathfinders': finding the path and losing the way? *Criminal Justice*, 4: 309–25.

Rosenthal, R. (1994) Parametric measures of effect size. In H. Cooper and L. V. Hedges (eds.), *The Handbook of Research Synthesis*, pp. 231–44. New York: Russell Sage Foundation.

Simon, L. M. J. (1998) Does criminal offender treatment work? *Applied and Preventive Psychology*, 7: 137–59.

Skeem, J., Louden, J. E., Polaschek, D. and Camp, J. (2007) Assessing relationship quality in mandated community treatment: blending care with control. *Psychological Assessment*, 19: 397–410.

Ward, T. and Maruna, S. (2007) *Rehabilitation: Beyond the Risk Paradigm*. London and New York: Routledge.

Welsh, B. C. and Farrington, D. P. (2000) Correctional intervention programs and cost benefit analysis. *Criminal Justice and Behavior*, 27: 115–33.

Wilson, D. B. (2001) Meta-analytic methods for criminology. *Annals of the American Academy of Political and Social Science*, 578: 71–89.

Wilson, D. B., Bouffard, L. A. and Mackenzie, D. L. (2005) A quantitative review of structured, group-oriented, cognitive-behavioral programs for offenders. *Criminal Justice and Behavior*, 32: 172–204.

3.9 Risk management

Roisin Hall

Definitions

The purpose of risk management in the forensic context is to minimize the likelihood and impact of offending behaviour for potential victims and all aspects of public safety. A systematic risk management approach to offending behaviour is relatively new and includes a wide range of activities which extend well beyond forensic psychology (Risk Management Authority 2007).

Effective offender risk management requires a detailed assessment and analysis of both the likelihood and the impact of further offending behaviour. This leads to a formulation of risk from which models can be drawn up of how the cluster of factors specific to the offending behaviour of the individual and his/her situation interrelate and can be managed (Hart *et al.* 2003).

Any evaluation of risk is based on both subjective and objective factors and is an inexact science. The risk posed by serious sexual or violent offending behaviour holds threats for potential victims at both the individual and the wider social and community level. It can never be wholly eliminated, just as it is not wholly predictable.

Cultural definitions of offending behaviour are based on the capacity to do harm which such acts present to individuals or society. Risk of serious harm can be defined as a risk of harmful behaviour which is life threatening and/or traumatic and from which the victim's recovery, whether physical or psychological, can be expected to be difficult or impossible (Kemshall 2003).

Current thinking and debates

The psychology of risk

Psychological approaches to risk (Breakwell 2007) have been influenced by developments over the last two decades in the social construction of harm, with the recognition that harm is not an objective entity but an evaluation of outcomes of a hazard leading to a decision as to what is acceptable. Breakwell draws from literature on the psychology of risk to integrate analysis from the individual level to the societal. She highlights how the social rejection of scientific certainties in favour of the argument that hazards are incalculable and beyond remediation has led to the use of the precautionary principle in hazard regulation and management. In criminal justice just as in public health, this has led to the use of protection and interventions against perceived, but as yet ill-defined, threats. The risk management approach is characterized by an acceptance that gains must be balanced against costs, that the principle of proportionality should be observed and that risks should be regarded as tolerable if they have been reduced to a level 'as low as reasonably practicable'. For example, the concept of the defensible decision (Kemshall 2003) is a fundamental principle in the field of public safety and offender risk management, although less accepted by the media with its powerful influence on public confidence and understanding. There is clear evidence to support the risk principle (Andrews and Bonta 2003) that interventions should be proportional to the level of risk, whilst carried out under the least restrictive conditions consistent with public safety.

The understanding of offender risk

Psychology has typically conceptualized offender risk as a problem of individual pathology. Clinical approaches to the treatment of offender abnormalities have made a significant contribution to the understanding of both assessment and treatment (Monahan *et al.* 2001; Hodgins 2007). An equally significant approach has been made by psychologists working on the psychology of criminal conduct from a social learning, social cognition position. Current risk management practice in custodial and community settings has been heavily influenced by the risk–need–responsivity (RNR) model (Andrews and Bonta 2003) and a focus on cognitive-behavioural interventions for offending behaviour (McGuire 2006).

Despite the validity of these approaches, psychologists and criminologists have argued in recent years that this focus in offender management is unnecessarily limited by the emphasis on the individual's deficits, or negative features. Reflecting the influence of cognitive and positive psychology, the approach of the good lives and desistance models stresses the importance of building on the positive goals of the individual (Ward and Maruna 2007).

At the same time, research on the effectiveness of offending behaviour interventions and risk management has repeatedly demonstrated the importance of systemic factors (Home Office 2002). Inquiry findings (Bridges 2006) also underline that systemic failings, for example problems regarding information sharing, heighten risk just as much as does individual pathology.

Offender risk assessment

The merits of different approaches and methods of offender risk assessment have been the subject of considerable debate, but there is an increasing recognition of how the specific contribution of different methods should be integrated to provide a holistic understanding which can underpin risk management (Andrews, Bonta and Wormith 2006; Beech and Craig 2007). The assessment of offender risk has evolved from unstructured clinical judgement to the introduction of actuarial assessments based on static risk factors, and more recently to more integrative approaches which analyse the interaction of both static and dynamic factors. The structured professional judgement approach uses such an analysis to formulate an understanding and to develop scenarios which can inform management planning (Hart *et al.* 2003), whilst the 'fourth generation' assessments (Andrews, Bonta and Wormith 2005; Hanson and Harris 2000) link factors relating to the management of individuals with systemic management needs.

Policy

Public safety and offender management are inevitably key issues for most governments, and public policies on risk management reflect the political context as well as academic debate. Structural organization and reorganization to facilitate effectiveness and efficiency have a direct effect on the form and resources available for risk management, whether these relate to the custodial or special hospital setting, or the community. The introduction of the Dangerous and Severe Personality Disorder (DSPD) units and the Indeterminate Public Protection (IPP) Orders have provided a different context in England to that characterized by the establishment of the Risk Management Authority (RMA) and the Order for Lifelong Restriction (OLR) in Scotland. Nevertheless, the principles of risk management are fundamental to the introduction of the Multi Agency Public Protection Arrangements (MAPPA) in both jurisdictions (Kemshall *et al.* 2005).

An outline for practice

Violent and sexual offending are complex phenomena which require individualized responses to dynamic factors. More has been published on risk assessment than on the risk management approach (O'Rourke and Bailes 2006). The RMA has published standards for risk management (RMA 2007), which include guidance in the seven key areas as outlined below, based on findings drawn from research and from offender management audit and inquiry reports:

1. *Collaborative working*
   Risk management requires plans which combine different forms of actions, presented in an integrated approach in which different agencies and disciplines collaborate.

2. *Risk assessment*
   Assessment is the foundation of risk management planning and a dynamic process that should continue throughout the lifetime of a serious offender. It should cover different types of information and should be drawn from a variety of sources. In addition to the assessment of the probability of further offending behaviour, assessment for risk management should include offence analysis and consideration of risk factors which may be static or dynamic. The dynamic group should include stable and acute factors, and early warning signs. Assessment should also include consideration of any protective factors.

3. *Risk formulation*
   Formulation provides a working model of the interaction amongst clusters of risk factors in a situation. In addition to probability, a formulation should consider the nature, severity, imminence and frequency of potential offending. This can be facilitated by scenario and contingency planning. In this way information and analysis can be translated into action and used for management planning.

4. *Risk management*
   Action plans for risk management should include details of how to address each factor and the prioritization and integration of interventions. These will depend on the nature of the factor and the current context, including external controls and victim safety planning. Plans should take

into account individual needs and protective factors and levels of readiness and engagement, whether the interventions involve cognitive-behavioural programmes or individual work.

5. *Accommodation*

Inevitably the social setting is a crucial issue in risk management and judicious attention to placement and the type of social support available can enhance the opportunity for cognitive-behavioural change to be generalized beyond the treatment setting.

6. *Responding to change*

Any action plan must allow for adaptation in the face of change and development (Prochaska and Levesque 2002). It should also provide opportunity to monitor and facilitate change (Gordon and Wong 2004). Progress should be reviewed regularly and whenever there is a change in conditions, with attention to appropriate transfer arrangements.

7. *Organizational support*

Risk management by its very nature is challenging work and its continued effectiveness requires not only staff support and resources, but also the provision of an environment which is conducive to new learning and the generalization and maintenance of new behaviours.

Conclusions

Risk management in forensic psychology provides a useful model for working with serious offenders. There are a number of ways in which this model is currently being used in offender management, albeit with a limited level of integration. Risk management is a dynamic process which requires holistic assessment and structured professional judgement as well as the engagement of the offender. The matching of the analysis of risk to different intervention strategies enables the framework and its techniques to be used to good effect by different agencies and disciplines. In this way, risk management can support the action plans which are to be used in rehabilitative or educational programmes, or in care and treatment. Practitioners find that the discipline and structure provide a support and a guide to their formulation. There are as yet no validation data and they will be challenging to assess given the manner of the approach and the individual orientation required.

REFERENCES

Andrews, D. and Bonta, J. (2003) *The Psychology of Criminal Conduct*, 3rd edn. Cincinnnati, OH: Anderson.

Andrews, D., Bonta, J. and Wormith, J. S. (2006) The recent past and near future of risk and/or need assessment. *Crime and Delinquency*, 52: 7–27.

Beech, A. and Craig, L. (2007) Risk assessment in the 21st century: towards an integrative model of risk. *Forensic Update*, 92: 46–56.

Breakwell, G. M. (2007) *The Psychology of Risk*. Cambridge: Cambridge University Press.

Bridges, A. (2006) *An Independent Review of a Serious Further Offence Case: Anthony Rice*. UK: HM Inspectorate of Probation Report.

Gordon, A. and Wong, S. (2004) *Three-Phase Delivery Model*. Violence Reduction Programme, Facilitators' Manual.

Hanson, R. K., and Harris, A. (2000) *ACUTE-2000 and STABLE-2000*. Unpublished manuscript. Department of the Solicitor General of Canada.

Hart, S. D., Kropp, R., Laws, R., Klaver, J., Logan, C. and Watt, K. (2003) *The Risk for Sexual Violence Protocol (RSVP): Structured Professional Guidelines for Assessing Risk for Sexual Violence*. Burnaby, BC: Mental Health, Law, and Policy Institute, Simon Fraser University.

Hodgins, S. (2007) Persistent violent offending: what do we know? *British Journal of Psychiatry*, 190: s12–s14.

Home Office (2002) *Probation Offending Behaviour Programmes – Effective Practice Guide* (Home Office Development and Practice Report 2). London: Home Office.

Kemshall, H. (2003) The community management of high-risk offenders: A consideration of 'best practice' – Multi-Agency Public Protection Arrangements (MAPPA). *Prison Service Journal*, 126: 2–5.

Kemshall, H., Mackenzie, G., Wood, J., Bailey, R. and Yates, J. (2005) *Strengthening Multi Agency Public Protection Arrangements (MAPPAs)* (Home Office Development and Practice Report). London: Home Office.

McGuire, J. (2006) General offending behaviour programmes: concept, theory and practice. In C. R. Hollin, and E. J. Palmer (eds.), *Offending Behaviour Programmes: Development, Applications and Controversies*, pp. 69–111. Chichester: Wiley.

Monahan, J., Steadman, H. J., Silver, E., Appelbaum, P. S., Clark Robbins, P., Mulvey, E. P. *et al.* (2001) *Rethinking Risk Assessment: The MacArthur Study of Mental Disorder and Violence*. New York: Oxford University Press.

O'Rourke, M. and Bailes, G. (2006) *Risk Assessment and Management*. British Psychological Society Faculty of Forensic Clinical Psychology: Occasional Briefing Paper.

Prochaska, J. and Levesque, D. (2002) Enhancing motivation of offenders at each stage of change and phase of therapy. In M. McMurran (ed.), *Motivating Offenders to Change: A Guide to Enhancing Engagement in Therapy*, pp. 57–74. Chichester: Wiley.

Risk Management Authority (2007) *Standards and Guidelines: Risk Management of Offenders Subject to an Order for Lifelong Restriction*. Edinburgh: R. R. Donnelley. Available on line: www.rmascotland.gov.uk.

Ward, T. and Maruna, S. (2007) *Rehabilitation*. London: Routledge.

3.10 Suicide in prisons

Graham Towl

See also chapter 2.24 Suicide risks in adolescents and adults.

Definition

In its simplest terms suicide means the act of an individual intentionally ending their own life. The term attempted suicide is often used to refer to acts intended to result in death where the person survives. A variety of terms, such as 'parasuicide' and 'deliberate self-harm', have been used to distinguish intentional self-injury behaviours not intended to result in death.

Until 1961 suicide was a criminal offence across the UK. This is still reflected in some of the language used in relation to suicide. For example, the epithet 'committed' is routinely juxtaposed with 'suicide' in much of the literature and everyday practice. Those who are feeling suicidal are sometimes referred to as 'threatening suicide' rather than 'feeling suicidal'. This is a rather pejorative way of referring to individuals who are often depressed and in need of help. In mental health practice it is unlikely to refer to individuals as 'threatening depression', a key difference perhaps being that depression has never been a criminal offence. A more compassionate approach, at least in terms of the language used, is becoming increasingly widespread with the use of the term 'completed' suicide rather than 'committed' suicide (Crighton and Towl 1997). Language is important because it can influence the shaping of policy and practice responses to suicidal prisoners. It may also impact on judgements and actions in relation to the deemed worthiness of individuals in terms of what help and support they might anticipate.

In psychiatric practice terms such as 'attention seeking' or 'manipulative' are sometimes used to describe some of the behaviours which may sometimes be evident with suicidal individuals. This may reflect the prejudices of the practitioner insofar as the use of such terms may be seen as calling into question the legitimacy of the person's 'psychological pain' or distress. Some practitioners may allow their determination not to appear to be deceived by a prisoner or patient to become too significant in their assessments and actions. Yet making misjudgements especially with suicidal prisoners can result in preventable deaths.

Suicide in prison

The term 'suicide' is defined within prisons more broadly than in the community and tends to take an inclusive rather than exclusive approach. Since the 1990s prisons in the UK have recorded all self-inflicted deaths. This includes all those deaths recorded legally as suicide and also a number that go on to be recorded under other legal verdicts, on the basis that suicide has not been proven beyond all reasonable doubt (McHugh and Snow 2002).

For the period 1988–98 the rate of suicide for men in prison in England and Wales was 94 per 100,000 (Crighton and Towl 2008). Such rates are significantly greater than those seen in the general population (McHugh and Snow 2002). Thus the recorded figures for prisoner suicide are likely, in comparison with many community studies, to represent an overestimation of rates. The broader term of Self-Inflicted Death (SID) tends to be used in some of the literature and also the term is widely used in practice in prisons This is an important ethical point to be made in reference to such deaths in prison. Prisoners are in the care of agents of the state, and there is a clear 'duty of care' to the prisoner, which extends well beyond merely keeping prisoners alive.

The most robust empirical and significant finding in the literature is the fact that prisoners are at an inflated risk of completing suicide in the earlier period of their custody. This result is sometimes misunderstood. In a study in Scotland, for example, 9% of prisoners who killed themselves did so within twenty-four hours of reception and two-thirds did so within three months of reception (Bogue and Parker 1995). This finding has been replicated a number of times (McHugh, Towl and Snow 2002). It has been misinterpreted and taken to mean that such a vulnerable time for the individual only occurs whilst they are first held on remand and/or during their initial period of imprisonment as a convicted prisoner. This is inaccurate. The relatively high levels of risk of suicide appear to occur after movement to a prison, where the pattern of deaths is similar. Thus it follows that if prisoners are moved between prisons more frequently, then the prison population level of risk of suicide increases. One popular myth about prisoner suicides is that remanded prisoners are at a greater risk of suicide than convicted prisoners. This is a question that can be empirically answered. Where deaths are calculated on the basis of average daily population, the rate of deaths was 238 per 100,000 for remand prisoners. When calculated on the basis of reception, a far more appropriate estimate of the number of remand prisoners, the rate fell to 39 per 100,000 (McHugh, Towl and Snow 2002). The notion that remand prisoners are at an inflated risk of suicide is therefore largely based on the flawed methodology of using average daily population to calculate rates of suicide for remand and sentenced prisoners. Such a snapshot of the prisoner population is inevitably limited. It is inaccurate to calculate suicide rates without reference also to overall throughput levels in a prison for both sentenced and remand prisoners. Overall the evidence is that remand status per se is not a good predictor of risk of suicide, but length of time spent in the individual prison is. In short, risk of suicide is very markedly higher in the early days of incarceration in an individual prison. The policy implication of this is clear, suggesting a need to keep the numbers of movements of prisoners to a minimum. Although it is, of course, acknowledged that in practical terms this can be extremely difficult given the pressure on prisoner places. High levels of investment in local prisons, which tend to have high levels of 'throughput', is another key policy priority, particularly in a public sector environment of limited resources in relation to levels of prisoner needs.

Particular groups: black prisoners, lifers and women

Black prisoners are under-represented in the suicide figures compared to white and Asian prisoners. This parallels international findings (Haycock 1989). One contributory explanation for this finding may be seen in terms of the institutionalized racism of the criminal justice process, whereby black prisoners are, on average, more likely to receive custodial sentences than their white counterparts. Given that the individual risk factors associated with an inflated risk of suicide, such as a history of mental health problems and/or substance abuse,correlate highly with the characteristics of criminals, it would be predicted that those less 'criminal' in this way may also show lower levels of risk factors for suicide. It is unlikely that this is a completely satisfactory explanation but it does suggest need for future research.

Those sentenced to indeterminate life sentences are not only at an increased risk of suicide but also the pattern of the timings of such suicides differs from that of the determinate sentenced population. Such prisoners have been reported to show rates of 178 per 100,000 ADP compared to a rate of 75 per 200,000 for those serving fixed sentences of five years and over (Towl and Crighton 2002). In terms of timings, whereas with the overall prisoner data, the risk of suicide for prisoners tends to decrease over time spent in an individual prison, this does not hold for lifers. Lifers appear to have peaks and troughs with their risk of suicide linked to the points at which key decisions are made at official reviews about their futures. It is uncertain whether the inflated risk of suicide is in a specific way linked to the indeterminate nature of such sentences. If it is, then it would be predicted that suicide rates in UK prisons from now onwards will start to increase more markedly than in the past. This observation is made because of the changing profile of the prisoner population. There are a growing proportion of prisoners being kept in prison on account of an Indeterminate Public Protection sentence (an indeterminate sentence imposed on the grounds of risk to the public). Another consideration when trying to understand the differences in the rates and patterns of suicide for indeterminately sentenced prisoners is that they tend to have been sentenced disproportionately for sexual and violent offences. Indeed, an index offence of a sexual or violent nature does serve to increase the risk of suicide independently of other factors.

Women tend to have lower rates of suicide than men both outside and inside prisons However, a caveat must be added in relation to the data with respect to women prisoners. Numerically there are comparatively low numbers of suicides amongst women prisoners, so it is arguably an empirically questionable practice to calculate and compare rates when the total numbers of male suicides are so much greater than the total numbers for women.

Conceptual limitations

There is a dearth of theory building in relation to understanding suicide in prisons. Indeed a problem with much of the empirical work is that it is largely descriptive. Although a great deal of data have been generated, it is uncertain how to best use such a corpus in developing knowledge of and understanding suicide in prisons further. Much of the previous work has been atheoretical, and few attempts have been made to make theoretical models explicit (Bogue and Parker 1995; HM Chief Inspector of Prisons 1999). More recently there has been growing interest in developing theoretical ideas drawing on public health models (Crighton 2002; McHugh, Towl and Snow 2002). Such models allow for multiple causal factors at a number of levels: primary, secondary and tertiary. Primary research on the function of emotions has been drawn upon by some in the field in search of a more complete psychological understanding of prisoner suicide. Such models are helpful in that they can contribute not only to helping shape future research but also current policy and practice.

Working with suicidal prisoners

Relevant interpersonal skills, including the ability to demonstrate appropriate consideration and understanding of the difficulties that the prisoner is experiencing, underpin effective work with suicidal prisoners. Often practitioners may be speaking with or in the presence of suicidal prisoners without being aware of it. This point serves to illustrate the importance of professional values. By way of illustration, the depersonalizing ritual in prisons of staff routinely referring to prisoners by second name and prison number serves as a powerful illustration of de-individualization and how at an institutional level the risk of suicide may be actively, although unnecessarily, increased. This is not about resources, but rather the attitudes and behaviour of prison staff. Switching between such a depersonalizing approach and a more individual focus can seem insincere, but it need not be.

At an individual level a number of basic counselling skills are needed; carefully and openly listening to the account given of the issues that are on the mind of the suicidal prisoner; checking understanding by way of reflecting back what the prisoner has said can also be helpful. Appropriate 'normalization' of feelings is important too, for example, by actively acknowledging that it is comparatively common for feelings of depression to result from the circumstances of prisons. Listening for and supporting a prisoner's strengths and confirming constructive coping strategies may also be valuable preventative interventions, thus exploring the ways in which the prisoner has successfully dealt with challenging circumstances previously. Knowing the relevant evidence is also critical, as is finding out about the prisoner's previous history beforehand. It is helpful to speak to staff who have had dealings with the prisoner if this is appropriate and possible. Judgements about the level of suicide risk may be made by drawing from the available empirical evidence and the evidence accumulated about an individual prisoner from interviews, discussions with staff and any other relevant documentary information.

It is important to always monitor one's own behaviour in front of prisoners and not to collude with or appear to collude with inappropriate comments at any prisoner's expense. Saying nothing or failing to rephrase or not challenging inappropriate behaviour may reasonably be viewed as collusion. Neutrality is a delusion in such circumstances, and appearing to be neutral is often to be seen to side with those in positions of power. Treating prisoners and staff with respect may well impact on how professional practitioners are assessed by prisoners and can affect their willingness to report their feelings (Bailey *et al.* 2002; Towl and Forbes 2002). Finally, it is essential to ensure that policies and procedures are informed by the evidence and are fair.

Acknowledgement

I would like to thank Professor David Crighton for his insightful and helpful comments upon an earlier version of this chapter.

FURTHER READING

The chapter on suicide in Crighton and Towl (2008) summarizes the germane research and offers some reflections on the state of the research and also possible directions for future research. The largest UK empirical study of suicide in prisons is outlined in some detail.

G. Towl, L. Snow and M. McHugh (eds.), *Suicide in Prisons* (2002; Oxford: BPS/Blackwell) is still the most comprehensive work available on prisoner suicide in England and Wales. Some fundamental methodological issues are covered on prisoner suicide research and some key studies summarized. There are also some chapters, for example, 'Risk assessment and management' and 'Working with suicidal prisoners' which are intended to give practitioners some helpful practical guidance.

REFERENCES

Bailey, J., McHugh, M., Chiswell, L. *et al.* (2002) Training staff in suicide awareness. In G. Towl, L. Snow and M. McHugh (eds.), *Suicide in Prisons*, pp. 121–34. Oxford: BPS/Blackwell.

Bogue, J. and Parker, K. (1995) Suicide in Scottish Prisons 1976–1979. *British Journal of Forensic Psychiatry*, 6: 527–40.

Crighton, D. (2002) Suicide in prisons: a critique of UK research. In G. Towl, L. Snow and M. McHugh (eds.), *Suicide in Prisons*, pp. 26–47. Oxford: BPS/Blackwell.

Crighton, D. A. and Towl, G. J. (1997) Self-inflicted deaths in England and Wales 1988–90 and 1994–95. In G. J. Towl (ed.) *Suicide and Self-Injury in Prisons: Issues in Criminological and Legal Psychology*, pp. 12–20. Leicester: BPS.

(2008) *Psychology in Prisons*, 2nd edn. Oxford: BPS/Blackwell.

Haycock, J. (1989) Race and suicide in jails and prisons. *Journal of the National Medical Association*, 81: 405–11.

HM Inspectorate of Prisons (1999) *Suicide in Prisons – Thematic Review*. London: Home Office.

McHugh, M. and Snow, L. (2002) Suicide prevention: policy and practice. In G. Towl, L. Snow and M. McHugh (eds.), *Suicide in Prisons*, pp. 1–25. Oxford: BPS/Blackwell.

McHugh, M., Towl, G. and Snow, L. (2002) Future directions. In G. Towl, L. Snow and M. McHugh (eds.), *Suicide in Prisons*, pp. 156–64. Oxford: BPS/Blackwell.

Towl, G. and Crighton, D. (2002) Risk assessment and management. In G. Towl, L. Snow and M. McHugh (eds.), *Suicide in Prisons*, pp. 66–92. Oxford: BPS/Blackwell.

Towl, G. and Forbes, D. (2002) Working with suicidal prisoners. In G. Towl, L. Snow and M. McHugh (eds.), *Suicide in Prisons*, pp. 93–101. Oxford: BPS/Blackwell.

3.11 Therapeutic communities

Fiona Warren

See also chapter 1.14 Theories of change, chapter 3.6 Programmed interventions for offenders, chapter 8.7 Randomized control trials.

Introduction

Democratic[1] therapeutic communities (DTCs) for offenders in the UK are found in both prisons and forensic psychiatric settings in high and medium security, including in the recently established services for offenders classified as having Dangerous and Severe Personality Disorder (DSPD). Therapeutic communities tend to be tailored towards offenders with personality disorders rather than offenders per se. Democratic therapeutic communities have often been positioned as outside the mainstream and are associated with social and anti-psychiatry movements. Although committed to research study of their practice from their inception, DTCs are a contested form of treatment and are vulnerable to allegations that they represent an 'expensive luxury' in our approach to offenders. Many DTCs have come and gone since the 1960s but recent years have seen the development as well as the demise of this approach.

Origins and defining features

There has been a proliferation of manualized approaches to the treatment of personality disorders such as Dialectical Behaviour Therapy (DBT) (Linehan 1993), and to rehabilitation of offenders, such as the Sex Offender Treatment

---

[1] Within the UK therapeutic communities tend to follow the democratic approach. There is a considerable literature on therapeutic communities for drug addiction in the USA but we will stick to the distinction long-maintained in the therapeutic community literature that these, often called 'concept' therapeutic communities, represent a sufficiently different type of approach as to need separate treatment. For further reading on the distinctions see Kennard (1998, chapter 1).

Programme (SOTP). Democratic therapeutic communities, however, are not so easily described prescriptively. There are many 'possible patterns' of therapeutic community (Jones 1959) and the term has been applied to a variety of institutions (Kennard 1998). However, whilst they resist simple definition, institutions can be recognized as TCs from some defining features, and recent years have seen the agreement of standards against which NHS and prison-based TCs in the UK can be peer-reviewed and accredited as TCs (Royal College of Psychiatrists 2006).

Democratic therapeutic communities represent a whole-system approach to treatment or rehabilitation. The term refers to an institution (or often a unit within an institution), including its staff, residents and all rules, processes and activities that take place within it, rather than one single treatment that is applied on a sessional basis, such as CBT or psychoanalytic psychotherapy. The DTC approach usually encompasses the whole twenty-four hours of its residents'[2] day (whether or not the TC is residential). Specific treatment programmes, such as CBT or the SOTP, may be delivered within an overall context of a therapeutic community. DTCs do not make claims to being derived from one single theoretical approach to understanding personality disorders (or offending) but elements of many approaches can be seen to be embodied in DTC practices and there have been attempts to articulate the approach within, for example, CBT theory (see below). Jones, the founder of Henderson Hospital, took a social learning perspective on the DTC, describing it as a 'living learning situation' (Jones 1966; Kennard 1998).

Democratic therapeutic communities have their roots in World War II, when in the military hospital at Northfield in Birmingham, psychiatrists Main, Bion, Foulkes, Bridger and Rickman experimented with social approaches to treating the 'social disability' of failing to reintegrate into civilian life of a large number of returning veterans with a small number of staff (Briggs 2007; Roberts 1997). Contemporaneously, another psychiatrist, Maxwell Jones, was working at Mill Hill and then the Belmont Rehabilitation Unit (which later became Henderson Hospital). A key observation Jones made at this time was that new patients accepted the medical information about their symptoms more readily from the other patients than from him or other staff (Jones 1957). The involvement of the peer group is an essential and defining feature of the DTC approach. Indeed, it is

---

[2] To refer to individuals attending DTCs for treatment or rehabilitation many different terms may be used, depending on the context and institution, such as 'residents', 'patients', 'inmates' or various other terms. In this chapter, therefore, since most individuals in TCs in a forensic context are also living in the institution, the term 'resident' will be used throughout to avoid confusion. Where the term 'community member' is used, this refers to all members of the community – both residents *and* staff.

expected that residents develop their involvement in each other's treatment, becoming 'auxiliary therapists' (Kennard 1998).

An early anthropological study attempted to summarize the operation of the DTC in four principles: democratization, permissiveness, reality confrontation and communalism (Rapoport 1960). These four tenets provide a useful introductory guide to what TCs are about and to some of the differences between TCs and other therapies.

Democratization is embodied in DTCs in the practice of staff and residents making decisions jointly, even about who is admitted and when individuals are discharged from the communities. Rapoport observed that residents were expected to take part in decision making and feel genuinely responsible for their contribution, rather than 'play-acting' a part. Offenders and people with personality disorders have problematic relationships with authority figures and rules. Their involvement in creating and applying the rules entails that the residents are part of the authority, ameliorating negative reaction and encouraging responsibility taking.

Akin to the democratic approach to running the treatment, an environment characterized by *communalism* is evident in a healthy TC. 'Tight-knit' relationships and 'extensive' and 'free' communication should be markers of this; the sharing of facilities by residents and staff; enacting the principle that everything that is said and done in the hospital is material for therapy; the disallowing of 'privileged' communications (i.e. secrets between members of the community). This spirit of 'communalism' is seen to support the development of a sense of belonging, something which offenders and those with personality disorders do not gain easily.

Within a DTC a wide range of behaviours from residents that would be likely to be considered deviant in the outside world must be tolerated. However, crucially '*permissiveness*' in a TC does not mean that 'anything goes': rules are usually set such that low-level antisocial behaviours will come to attention via rule-breaking and there are consequences to rule-breaking. What is important is that one of these consequences is the attempt to develop an understanding of the meaning of the rule-breaking and to identify other possible courses of action should a similar situation arise in the future. The therapeutic aim of permissiveness is to allow an individual to recognize his/her deviant and disordered behaviours and then to experiment with alternative ways of behaving within the safety of the treatment context (Norton 1992; Whiteley 1980).

Whilst permissiveness allows manifestation of the individual's 'true colours', residents must also be surrounded by the reflections of others' perceptions of these true colours. This *'reality confrontation'* is needed to counteract the defences of denial, distortion, withdrawal or other mechanisms that interfere with the offender or the individual with personality disorder developing self-knowledge and engaging in healthy relationships.

Democratic therapeutic communities usually have highly structured programmes of activity and clear rules, including great attention to time boundaries. Whilst some DTCs include individual therapy, the emphasis is very much on group activity. A key recognizable feature of TCs is the central place of 'community meetings', which involve all the members (residents and staff) meeting together (Kennard 1998), and which usually provide the forum for any democratic decision making. There will also be other groups in which smaller numbers of the residents meet together, for example to work together in the community garden, or for more formal 'small-group' psychotherapy. There will also be a structure of 'jobs' related to the running of the community (such as cooking, cleaning) to which residents are elected by their peers.

The *culture of enquiry* (Main 1983; Norton 1992), which is maintained in a healthy DTC, supports the process of social maturation and development (Haigh 1999) of the individual through increased self-knowledge and experimentation with responding differently to others and their environment: the reorganization of personality through the reorganization of perceptions and behaviours. The involvement of an individual in this process of living and learning is usually long term (over one year), especially in a forensic context. See table 3.11.1 for a summary of the key concepts of the DTC approach.

Table 3.11.1 Key concepts of the democratic therapeutic community approach

Democratization
Communalism
Permissiveness
Reality confrontation
Living-learning situation
Peer-group influence and responsibility-taking
Whole institution approach
Culture of enquiry
Socio-therapy
Activity-based groups
Community meetings
Groups
Jobs
Regular review meetings and supervision for staff

There may be an apparent contradiction in a treatment modality based on democracy, permissiveness and collaboration between staff and residents within custodial settings and there are particular limitations on the extent to which some features can be implemented in this context. However, this is a question of degree. Some of the aspects found in most DTCs in non-forensic settings, such as the involvement of current residents in the selection and discharge of new ones via democratic vote (for example, at the Henderson Hospital open residential TC, decisions about selection and discharge were always made with one-person-one-vote in meetings in which TC 'residents' always outnumbered staff members), have to be amended to be implemented in secure institutions. The degree of tolerance for rule-breaking is also necessarily reduced within the context of a secure setting. Nonetheless, some degree of tolerance is necessary in order for the resident to be able to fail, recognize the failure and try to do it differently next time. DTCs can be seen to be a humane framework for the rehabilitation of offenders (Jones 2005) and have been instituted successfully within the confines of high-security institutions (Kennard 2004).

HMP Grendon is credited with being the first TC in a UK prison. Opening in 1962 as an experiment, Grendon was the long-awaited realization of the recommendations of a report which in 1939 (East and de Hubert 1939, cited in Newell and Healey 2007) had recommended a new institution specially designed for the management of offenders with 'mental abnormality' that was significant but would not fall under the remit of psychiatry. Democratic therapeutic communities for offenders have seen an increase in recent years in the UK prison establishment (Newell and Healey 2007, p. 67), including the first TC for female offenders, opening forty years after DTCs had been available to male offenders (Stewart and Parker 2007).

Research evidence: outcomes and effectiveness

As with TCs in the non-forensic health system, forensic TCs have a lengthy research history and, as an intervention aimed at long-term change of offenders, the TC would seem to be a promising approach. There are some challenges to researching the effectiveness of TCs, however, some of which are intrinsic to offender research but perhaps exacerbated in the case of DTCs. These arise from the aims of TCs for offenders and the complex nature of the treatment approach. The evidence, as it stands, is suggestive rather than definitive.

Aim of therapeutic communities and choice of 'outcome measures'

There has always been, and continues to be, debate about the appropriate measure of efficacy or effectiveness for DTCs for offenders. The outcomes measured should reflect the aims of any intervention, yet the aims of DTCs for offenders are not universally agreed. Although, as an example, the first Governor and Medical Superintendent of HMP Grendon identified that the 'essence [of the TC] is to help residents mature by giving them a high degree of responsibility' (Gray 1973), breaking this down into measurable outcomes presents a challenge for the outcome researcher (see Gunn and Robertson 1982) but we might be interested in a psychological perspective: improvements in relationships, mental wellbeing, self-esteem, hostility. On the other hand, the explicit aims of Her Majesty's Prison Service are to safeguard the public and hence the interest is in lowering offending rates. The relationship between psychological improvements and reoffending is not known.

Whilst not a challenge for DTCs alone, offending rates are problematic as outcome measures: reconviction is not a wholly accurate measure of reoffending and lower rates could reflect more skilful rather than less frequent offending; for rare crimes (often also the most serious) reduction is also difficult to show. On the other hand, psychological improvements may also be difficult to assess reliably, particularly in offender groups, and the selection of key variables for study is not straightforward. Research into the effectiveness of DTCs for offenders has attempted to study change from both perspectives. Cost-effectiveness research has not yet been conducted on TCs for offenders in the UK (Warren 2005).

Reconviction studies have been conducted over various post-DTC follow-up periods from two to ten years. The findings are complex. An early study of reconviction at ten years post-DTC did not find a significant effect between men taken into Grendon for treatment and a group of matched controls, 60–70% of whom had received a custodial sentence (Gunn 1987). Later studies with larger samples have been more positive, showing lower rates of reconvictions in admissions to this prison than waiting-list controls at four years' follow-up (Marshall 1997) and again at seven years, at which point the admitted group were also less likely to be reconvicted of a violent offence (Taylor 2000). However, once differences in criminogenic variables between the admitted and comparison groups were controlled for statistically in these studies, differences in outcomes were no longer significant when the waiting-list and admitted groups were compared without reference to the length of stay in treatment for the admitted group. Looking at subgroups of offenders, after four years, offenders who had multiple convictions for sex offences had significantly lower reconviction rates for both sexual and violent sexual offences if they had received DTC treatment (18% and 31% respectively) than if they had been in the waiting-list group (43% and 72%) (Marshall 1997). After seven years the difference between the admitted and waiting-list groups only continued to be significant for reconvictions of violent sexual offences (Taylor 2000).

Within-subjects studies of changes in psychological variables show more positive effects on factors such as self-esteem, levels of hostility, depression, anxiety, attitudes towards other prisoners and staff and locus of control (Brown *et al.* 2008; Cullen 1994; Genders and Player 1995; Gunn, *et al.* 1978; Newton 1998).

One area of contention within the effectiveness literature concerns the impact of treatment on psychopaths. It has been argued strongly that TCs may increase recidivism risk in psychopathic offenders. This argument rests on a Canadian study which demonstrated an interaction effect of TC treatment and psychopathy on rates of violent recidivism over a ten-year follow-up in which just under 80% of treated versus just under 60% of untreated psychopaths recidivated (Harris, Rice and Cormier 1994; Quinsey *et al.* 2006). However, the nature of the treatment regime the offenders received is questionable (Warren 1994) as the authors also admit (Quinsey *et al.* 2006). Replication of a test of this important possibility, however, has not been attempted in UK studies. Psychopaths have been shown to have higher rates of rule-breaking within TCs in the UK, however, and to be more likely to leave early (Shine and Hobson 2000). Other authors also argue that the absence of evidence of effectiveness of interventions for psychopaths is not evidence of absence of treatability for psychopathy (Salekin 2002).

'Dose' of treatment and change

There is some evidence that suggests that change does not begin to occur immediately. This is evident in the research conducted at Grendon and also found in the more recent Dovegate study (Brown *et al.* 2008). Research seems to show with some consistency that outcomes are improved for those who stay at least twelve to eighteen months. Recidivism rates seem to reduce with length of stay in the TC with little difference between waiting-list controls and those in treatment for less than twelve months. However, those who stayed in the TC for at least eighteen months were less likely than waiting-list controls to be reconvicted in four years. This effect is more marked for sex offenders and those whose offences are both sexual and violent (Marshall

1997). There is also little change observable during treatment until one year. Not only quantitative, psychometric or reconviction data suggest eighteen months as a critical length of treatment, but also qualitative data analysed to suggest a model of therapeutic career (Genders and Player 1995).

It may be assumed that change in treatment follows a linear pattern of consistent reduction over time, a simple correlation between length of stay in (or dosage of) treatment and improvement. A longitudinal evaluation of the Dovegate TC shows a complex pattern of change over time in psychological symptomatology with exacerbation before improvement in some aspects of functioning, such as hostility (Brown et al. 2008).

Applicability and appropriateness of experimental designs to this as a complex intervention

Whilst the randomized-controlled trial (RCT) is the gold standard research design for the assessment of interventions because it allows attribution of a causal relationship between an outcome and an intervention, no experimental studies have been conducted in this area. There remains a debate about the appropriateness of this method to interventions such as DTCs. It has been argued that the complexity of the intervention, represented by the involvement of multiple therapists (including other residents), the multiplicity of interventions occurring within the programme (variety of groups), the lengthy amount of time residents usually spend in the treatment, and the dependence of the 'active treatment agent' on multiple relationships with different actors at different times, render the RCT inappropriate. One argument is that the intervention cannot meet the requirement of the RCT for the treatment to be controlled since it cannot be specified sufficiently, nor can the delivery of it be adequately monitored for an internally valid RCT to be conducted. Other concerns arise in relation to ensuring external validity when the sample recruited for study has to be agreeable to being randomized and also be highly motivated for treatment. Ethical reservations centre around the availability of a suitable alternative intervention to randomize to or the deferral of an offender's chance to reduce their risk profile and improve their relationships with family members, for example.

On the other hand, dismissing the complexity and assuming the DTC as a 'black box', feasibility studies have been conducted that suggest that RCTs could be applied and would take approximately nine years to conduct (Campbell 2003). The issue then becomes one simply of resources. Needless to say, no RCT has been undertaken in the last five years!

Conclusions

Therapeutic communities are whole-system solutions to managing people with complex interpersonal, emotional and behavioural difficulties including offenders. The evidence-base for them is suggestive but subject to some key methodological hurdles. They represent a humane approach to dealing with offenders and have been implemented successfully in forensic contexts in the UK. New DTCs both in the prison system and in forensic psychiatric settings have been developed and research from these is emerging, although the methodological hurdles have not yet been overcome.

FURTHER READING

For a theoretical discussion of why and how the therapeutic community might work for forensic personality-disordered residents with an emphasis on the psychodynamic under-standing of personality disorder see Norton (1996). Jones describes the therapeutic potential of the DTC to work with personality-disordered offenders from a cognitive-behavioural stance (Jones 1997). Many of the research studies conducted on the HMP Grendon therapeutic communities between its founding in the early 1960s and 2000 (and referenced in this chapter) have been reproduced in an edited collection (Shine 2000). Two books dedicated to the discussion of TCs for offenders in the UK are Cullen, Jones and Woodward (1997) and Parker (2007). Two other books in the Jessica Kingsley series on Therapeutic Communities/Community and Culture, edited by Rex Haigh and Jan Lees, also provide useful introductory material on the history, development and practices of TCs (Camplling and Haigh 1999; Kennard 1998).

REFERENCES

Briggs, D. (2007) Serendipity or design? Therapeutic community history and Maxwell Jones' theory. In M. Parker (ed.), *Dynamic Security: The Democratic Therapeutic Community in Prison*, pp. 83–97. London: Jessica Kingsley.

Brown, J., Miller, S., O'Neill, D. *et al.* (2008) HMP Dovegate therapeutic community: the evaluation of treatment outcome in relation to reconviction, social re-integration and psychological change. Guildford: University of Surrey.

Campbell, S. (2003) *The Feasibility of Conducting an RCT at HMP Grendon*. London: Home Office. Available online: www.homeoffice.gov.uk/rds/pdfs2/rdsolr0303.pdf.

Camplling, P. and Haigh, R. (eds.) (1999) *Therapeutic Communities: Past, Present and Future*. London: Jessica Kingsley.

Cullen, E. (1994) Grendon: the therapeutic prison that works. *Therapeutic Communities*, 14: 3–11.

Cullen, E., Jones, L. and Woodward, R. (1997) *Therapeutic Communities for Offenders.* Chichester: Wiley.

Genders, E. and Player, E. (1995) *Grendon, a Study of a Therapeutic Prison.* Oxford: Clarendon Press.

Gray, W. (1973) The therapeutic community and evaluation of results. *International Journal of Criminology and Penology*, 1: 327–34.

Gunn, J. (1987) A ten-year follow-up of men discharged from Grendon Prison. *British Journal of Psychiatry*, 151: 674–8.

Gunn, J. and Robertson, G. (1982) An evaluation of Grendon Prison. In J. Gunn and D. P. Farrington (eds.), *Abnormal Offenders, Delinquency, and the Criminal Justice System*, pp. 285–305. Chichester: Wiley.

Gunn, J., Robertson, G., Dell, S. *et al.* (1978) *Psychiatric Aspects of Imprisonment.* New York: Academic Press.

Haigh, R. (1999) The quintessence of a therapeutic environment: five universal qualities. In P. Campling and R. Haigh (eds.), *Therapeutic Communities: Past, Present and Future*, pp. 246–57. London: Jessica Kingsley.

Harris, G., Rice, M. and Cormier, C. (1994) Psychopaths: is the therapeutic community therapeutic? *Therapeutic Communities*, 15: 283–300.

Jones, D. (ed.) (2005) *Humane Prisons and How to Run Them*: Abingdon: Radcliffe.

Jones, L. (1997) Developing models for managing treatment integrity and efficacy in a prison-based TC: the Max Glatt Centre. In E. Cullen, L. Jones and R. Woodward (eds.), *Therapeutic Communities for Offenders*, pp. 121–57. Chichester: Wiley.

Jones, M. (1957) The treatment of personality disorders in a therapeutic community. *Psychiatry*, 20: 211–20.

  (1959) Towards a clarification of the 'therapeutic community' concept. *British Journal of Medical Psychology*, 32: 200–5.

  (1966) Therapeutic community practice. *American Journal of Psychiatry*, 122: 1275–9.

Kennard, D. (1998) *An Introduction to Therapeutic Communities*. London and Philadelphia: Jessica Kingsley.

  (2004) The therapeutic community as an adaptable treatment modality across different settings. *Psychiatric Quarterly*, 75: 295–307.

Linehan, M. M. (1993) *Cognitive-Behavioural Treatment of Borderline Personality Disorder.* New York: Guilford Press.

Main, T. (1983) The concept of the therapeutic community: variations and vicissitudes. In M. Pines (ed.), *The Evolution of Group Analysis*, pp. 197–217. London: Routledge & Kegan Paul.

Marshall, P. (1997) *A Reconviction Study of HMP Grendon Therapeutic Community.* London: Home Office Research and Statistics Directorate.

Newell, T. and Healey, R. (2007) The historical development of the UK democratic therapeutic community. In M. Parker (ed.), *Dynamic Security: The Democratic Therapeutic Community in Prison*, pp. 61–8. London: Jessica Kingsley.

Newton, M. (1998) Changes in measures of personality hostility and locus of control during residence in a prison therapeutic community. *Legal and Criminological Psychology*, 3: 209–23.

Norton, K. (1992) A culture of enquiry: its preservation or loss. *Therapeutic Communities: the International Journal for Therapeutic and Supportive Organizations*, 13: 3–26.

(1996) The personality-disordered forensic patient and the therapeutic community. In C. Cordess and M. Cox (eds.), *Forensic Psychotherapy: Crime, Psychodynamics and the Offender Patient*, pp. 240–56. London: Jessica Kingsley.

Parker, M. (ed.) (2007) *Dynamic Security: The Democratic Therapeutic Community in Prison*. London: Jessica Kingsley.

Quinsey, V. L., Harris, G. T., Rice, M. E. *et al.* (2006) Mentally disordered offenders. In *Violent Offenders: Appraising and Managing Risk*, 2nd edn, pp. 85–113. Washington, DC: American Psychological Association.

Rapoport, R. (1960) *The Community as Doctor*. London: Tavistock.

Roberts, J. (1997) History of the therapeutic community. In E. Cullen, L. Jones and R. Woodward (eds.), *Therapeutic Communities for Offenders*, pp. 1–22. Chichester: Wiley.

Royal College of Psychiatrists (2006) *Community of Communities: Accreditation Process Document*. London: Royal College of Psychiatrists.

Salekin, R. T. (2002) Psychopathy and therapeutic pessimism: clinical lore or clinical reality? *Clinical Psychology Review*, 22: 79–112.

Shine, J. (ed.) (2000) *A Compilation of Grendon Research*. Aylesbury: HMP Grendon.

Shine, J. and Hobson, J. (2000) Institutional behaviour and time in treatment among psychopaths admitted to a prison-based therapeutic community. *Medicine, Science and the Law*, 40: 327–35.

Stewart, C. and Parker, M. (2007) Send: The Women's Democratic Therapeutic Community in Prison. In M. Parker (ed.) *Dynamic Security: The Democratic Therapeutic Community in Prison*, pp. 69–82. London: Jessica Kingsley.

Taylor, R. (2000) *A Seven Year Reconviction Study of HMP Grendon Therapeutic Community*. London: Home Office.

Warren, F. (1994) What do we mean by a 'therapeutic community' for offenders? *Therapeutic Communities*, 15: 312–18.

(2005) Humane prisons: are they worth it? In D. Jones (ed.), *Humane Prisons and How to Run Them*, pp. 191–204. Abingdon: Radcliffe.

Whiteley, J. S. (1980) The Henderson Hospital: a community study. *International Journal of Therapeutic Communities*, 1: 38–58.

3.12 Treatment of sexual offenders

Leigh Harkins and Brian Thomas-Peter

See also chapter 1.12 Sexual offenders.

Introduction

Although there is growing support surrounding what constitutes a successful treatment approach (Andrews and Bonta 2007) and that treatment for sexual offenders can reduce recidivism for some (Hanson *et al.* 2002; Kenworthy *et al.* 2004), there is still considerable debate concerning its real effectiveness (Rice and Harris 2003). This chapter will discuss treatment approaches that have historically been used with sexual offenders. We will then discuss current treatment approaches and how these can feed into future directions in work with this population.

Historical perspective

Historically, the treatment of sexual offending has focused primarily on behavioural interventions, followed later by the addition of the cognitive component of cognitive-behavioural treatment. The behavioural interventions usually took the form of aversion therapy (i.e. pairing noxious stimuli with sexual arousal to deviant stimuli) and/or arousal reconditioning (i.e. trying to change the stimuli which the individual finds arousing to something appropriate) (Laws and Marshall 2003; Marshall and Laws 2003). More recently the behavioural component has been widened to include role-play work. In the 1970s an awareness began to develop that aspects other than sexual deviance alone contributed to sexual offending and therefore more comprehensive treatment programmes were developed (Marshall and Laws 2003). This included the examination of cognitive processes, leading to interventions targeting aspects such as victim empathy, low self-esteem and social skills, in addition to the previous focus on sexual deviance (Marshall and Laws 2003). It has been said that the most significant innovation of the 1980s was the adaptation of the relapse prevention (RP) approach from the addictions field (Marshall and Laws 2003; Pithers *et al.* 1983). RP is a self-management approach designed to teach individuals who are trying to change their behaviour how to anticipate and cope with the problem of relapse (i.e. return to sexually deviant fantasies or reoffence). It is intended to help clients maintain control of their sexual deviance over time and across various high-risk situations they may encounter in the community. Laws (1989) edited a landmark book detailing the clinical implementation of the relapse model, which was later extensively reformulated, if not rewritten, in Laws, Hudson and Ward (2000). Although the generalizability of RP as a one-size fits all approachhas been questioned, it is still a component in many current treatment programmes.

Current perspective

The current perspective that drives sexual offender treatment is that it should be offered in a manner that considers the literature surrounding 'What Works' in offender rehabilitation. The *psychology of criminal conduct* (PCC) is a theory in line with 'What Works' that can be used as a guide in providing effective treatment (Andrews and Bonta 2007). This theory takes an overall risk management approach to treatment. A key assumption of this theory is that criminal behaviour is explained by an individual's profile of risk factors, which are acquired and maintained through conditioning, observational learning and personality dispositions (Andrews and Bonta 2007; Ward, Polaschek and Beech 2006). Treatment then needs to target an individual's specific risk factors (e.g. sexual deviance and pro-offending attitudes) to reduce the likelihood of future offending (Andrews and Bonta 2007). The three principles of *Risk*, *Need* and *Responsivity* drive the manner in which effective treatment should be delivered.

- The *Risk* principle advocates that treatment should be provided at a level of intensity proportional to the (static and dynamic) risk level of the offender. For example, the highest-intensity treatment should be offered to the highest-risk offenders.
- The *Need* principle specifies that treatment should target areas of criminogenic need (e.g. those identified as dynamic risk variables for sex offenders: sexual interest, distorted thinking, socio-affective functioning and self-management; Thornton 2002) that have a demonstrated relationship with recidivism.

- The *Responsivity* principle suggests that treatment should be offered in a manner that considers those factors that have the potential to influence an individual's response to treatment (e.g. learning style, motivation: Andrews and Bonta 2007; Ogloff and Davis 2004).

It is reported that if treatment is delivered in a manner that adheres to only one of the above principles an effect size[1] (*r*) of only .02 is observed (Andrews and Bonta 2003). However, if two of the principles are adhered to the effect size (*r*) is .18, and if treatment is provided in a manner adhering to all three principles an effect size (*r*) .26 is observed (Andrews and Bonta 2003). If no treatment is offered or if none of the principles are followed, Andrews and Bonta (2003) report an effect size (*r*) of −.02, demonstrating an *increase* in criminal recidivism. Each of these principles will now be discussed in more detail in terms of how they relate to treatment.

Risk

There is a growing body of research suggesting that treatment is most effective when administered according to the *Risk* principle (Andrews and Bonta 2007; Andrews and Dowden 2006). Specifically, risk represents the individual's general level of clinical need or underlying psychological vulnerability traits (Bonta and Andrews 2007; Ward *et al.* 2007) and therefore those with the highest risk/clinical need level should receive the most treatment.

Needs

Criminogenic need variables are those such as stable dynamic risk factors, encompassed under four overarching domains proposed by Thornton (2002): (1) *sexual interests*; (2) *distorted attitudes*; (3) *socio-affective functioning*; (4) *self-management*. These have been shown to be related to recidivism (e.g. Craig *et al.* 2007; Hanson *et al.* 2007; Thornton 2002) and to change within treatment (e.g. Marques *et al.* 2005; Olver *et al.* 2007). Therefore, these are important variables to consider as treatment targets within sexual offender treatment.

Responsivity

The *Responsivity* principle states that treatment should be matched to the characteristics of an offender that may be relevant to how they respond to

---

[1] An effect size (*r*) of 0.1 represents a small difference, 0.24 a medium difference, and 0.37 a large difference (Coe 2002).

treatment (e.g. learning style, motivation, denial; Andrews and Bonta 2007). In line with the *Responsivity* principle, intra-individual characteristics have an important impact on the effectiveness of treatment. Some usefully make the distinction between internal and external responsivity factors (Looman, Dickie and Abracen 2005). Internal responsivity factors are those such as learning style, motivation and denial. Alternately, external responsivity factors are those that exist outside the individual but influence their ability to benefit from treatment, such as therapist characteristics and therapeutic climate (Looman *et al.* 2005).

Criticisms of the 'What Works' approach

There have, however, been a number of criticisms raised about the clarity and comprehensiveness of the 'What Works' approach as a theory, as described by Ward and colleagues (Ward *et al.* 2006; Ward and Stewart 2003). One issue is that treatment is approached in a rather negative way, and therapeutic work is always couched in avoidance terms, which limits the appeal it may hold for the individual offender. Another is that there is insufficient guidance on how responsivity factors should be addressed. It is also suggested that rather than just focusing on risk factors, a focus on strengths would also be useful (Ward and Stewart 2003).

Despite the criticisms, it is still acknowledged as a useful framework for treatment delivery. In fact, even treatment driven by alternative theories recognizes the utility of the principles of Risk, Need and Responsivity (e.g. Ward and Stewart 2003). It is acknowledged as the current model of choice for many working with offenders in general (Ward *et al.* 2006). In particular, Brown (2005) notes that most sexual offender programmes are offered in a manner consistent with the risk and need principles. It is also acknowledged that more attention needs to be paid to responsivity issues (Andrews and Bonta 2007; Looman *et al.* 2005; Ogloff and Davis 2004; Ward *et al.* 2006).

Future directions

Newer approaches have been suggested which address some of the criticisms of the psychology of criminal conduct. In particular, the movement towards more positively oriented (as opposed to just risk management oriented) treatment approaches are encouraging and hold great potential. This includes theories such as the Good Lives model (Ward and Stewart 2003). According to this theory, all human beings, including sex offenders, seek a set of primary 'goods' (Ward *et al.* 2006; Ward and Stewart 2003). A set of nine primary 'goods' have been identified as the following: life (including healthy living and functioning); knowledge; excellence in play and work (including mastery experiences); excellence in agency (i.e. autonomy and self-directedness); inner peace (i.e. freedom from emotional turmoil and stress); friendship (including intimate, romantic and family relationships); community; spirituality (i.e. finding meaning and purpose in life); happiness; and creativity (Ward and Stewart 2003). Sexual offending arises as a result of an attempt to obtain these goods in a manner that is inappropriate (Ward *et al.* 2006; Ward and Stewart 2003). Risk factors are viewed as distortions of internal and external conditions, which are required to achieve goods (Ward and Stewart 2003). Treatment aims to instil in the individual the knowledge, skills and competence in order to lead successful lives, incompatible with offending, in the context to which they'll be released (Ward *et al.* 2006). Such positive theories recognize the utility of offering treatment in a manner that will likely hold more appeal to the individual and thus increase their likelihood of benefiting from treatment. Further work examining treatment outcome and the therapeutic climate of treatment groups that adhere to more positive theories of sex offender treatment, such as the Good Lives model, is needed.

Conclusions

It has been suggested that the Good Lives model may converge with the principles of *Risk*, *Need* and *Responsivity* via responsivity issues (Ogloff and Davis 2004; Ward and Stewart 2003). This would mean that although the risk and need principles play a central role in treatment, individuals will derive the most benefit from it (i.e. it can best address the *Responsivity* principle) if it is offered in a manner more in line with the Good Lives model. This would allow recognition of empirically supported principles for administering treatment (i.e. *Risk, Need* and *Responsivity*), while also highlighting the benefits of recognizing the individual's inherent striving for a meaningful and fulfilling life (i.e. the Good Lives model). From this, it would seem that the most effective treatment would involve an assessment of the individual's risk level and criminogenic need areas, as well as a thorough assessment of their goals/ valued goods. Then treatment should be offered at the highest intensity to those who have the highest level of risk and need. Treatment should focus primarily on developing a Good Lives plan, with the individual's need areas used as indicators of areas where there is a problem in the way the individual is seeking their primary goods. Attention should be paid to responsivity issues in terms of how treatment should be offered, or may need to be modified, to allow for the best treatment response for the individual.

FURTHER READING

For a comprehensive review of the history of behavioural and cognitive-behavioural approaches to the treatment of sexual offenders, see the two-part article published in *Sexual Aggression: A Journal of Research and Treatment* (Laws and Marshall 2003; Marshall and Laws 2003). Andrews and Bonta (2007) provide a detailed description of the principles of Risk, Need and Responsivity in their book, *The Psychology of Criminal Conduct,* 4th edn. For a description of some of the shortcoming of the risk–needs model and information on the Good Lives model, see Ward and Stewart (2003).

REFERENCES

Andrews, D. A. and Bonta, J. (2003) *The Psychology of Criminal Conduct,* 3rd edn. Cincinnati, OH: Anderson.

(2007) *The Psychology of Criminal Conduct,* 4th edn. Cincinnati, OH: Anderson.

Andrews, D. A. and Dowden, C. (2006) Risk principle of case classification in correctional treatment. *International Journal of Offender Therapy and Comparative Criminology,* 50: 88–100.

Bonta, J. and Andrews, D. A. (2007) *Risk–Need–Responsivity Model for Offender Assessment and Rehabilitation.* Corrections Research, Public Safety and Emergency Preparedness Canada, Ottawa, Canada. Available online: www.publicsafety.gc.ca/res/cor/rep/_fl/crp2007–05-en.pdf.

Brown, S. (2005 *Treating Sex Offenders: An Introduction to Sex Offender Treatment Programmes.* Cullompton: Willan.

Coe, R. (2002) It's the effect size, stupid: what effect size is and why it is important. Paper presented at the Annual Conference of the British Educational Research Association, Exeter.

Cohen, J. (1988) *Statistical Power Analysis for the Behavioral Sciences,* 2nd edn. Hillsdale, NJ: Erlbaum.

Craig, L. A., Thornton, D., Beech, A. and Browne, K. D. (2007) The relationship between statistical and psychological risk markers to sexual recidivism. *Criminal Justice and Behavior,* 34: 314–29.

Hanson, R. K., Gordon, A., Harris, A. J. R., Marques, J. K., Murphy, W., Quinsey, V. L. and Seto, M. C. (2002) First report of the collaborative outcome data project on the effectiveness of psychological treatment for sex offenders. *Sexual Abuse: A Journal of Research and Treatment,* 14: 169–94.

440 Leigh Harkins and Brian Thomas-Peter

Hanson, R. K. Harris, A. J. R., Scott, T. and Helmus, L. (2007) *Assessing the Risk for Sexual Offenders on Community Supervision: The Dynamic Supervision Project*. Corrections Research, Public Safety and Emergency Preparedness Canada, Ottawa, Canada. Available online: www.publicsafety.gc.ca/res/cor/rep/_fl/crp2007–05–en.pdf.

Kenworthy, T., Adams, C. E., Bilby, C., Brooks-Gordon, B. and Fenton, M. (2004) Psychological interventions for those who have sexually offended or are at risk of offending. *Cochrane Database of Systematic Reviews*, issue 4.

Laws, D. R. (ed.) (1989) *Relapse Prevention with Sex Offenders*. New York: Guilford Press.

Laws, D. R., Hudson, S. M., and Ward, T. (eds.). (2000) *Remaking Relapse Prevention with Sex Offenders: A Sourcebook*. Thousand Oak, CA: Sage.

Laws, D. R. and Marshall, W. L. (2003) A brief history of behavioural and cognitive approaches to sexual offenders. Part 1 Early developments. *Sexual Abuse: A Journal of Research and Treatment*, 15: 75–92.

Looman, J., Dickie, I. and Abracen, J. (2005) Responsivity in the treatment of sexual offenders. *Trauma, Violence, and Abuse*, 6: 330–53.

Marques, J. K., Wiederanders, M., Day, D. M., Nelson, C. and van Ommeren, A. (2005) Effects of a relapse prevention program on sexual recidivism: final results from California's Sex Offender Treatment and Evaluation Program (SOTEP). *Sexual Abuse: A Journal of Research and Treatment*, 17: 79–107.

Marshall, W. L. and Laws, D. R. (2003) A brief history of behavioural and cognitive approaches to sexual offenders. Part 2 The modern era. *Sexual Abuse: A Journal of Research and Treatment*, 15: 93–120.

Ogloff, J. R. P. and Davis, M. R. (2004) Advances in offender assessment and rehabilitation: contributions of the risk-need-responsivity approach. *Psychology, Crime and Law*, 10: 229–42.

Olver, M. E., Wong, S., Nicholaichuk, T. and Gordon, A. (2007) The validity and reliability of the Violence Risk Assessment Scale – Sex Offender version: Assessing sex offender risk and evaluating therapeutic change. *Psychological Assessment*, 19: 318–29.

Pithers, W. D., Marques, J. K., Gibat, C. C. and Marlatt, G. A. (1983). Relapse prevention with sexual aggressors: a self-control model of treatment and maintenance of change. In J. G. Greer and I. R. Stuart (eds.), *The Sexual Aggressor: Current Perspectives on Treatment*, pp. 214–39. New York: Van Nostrand Reinhold.

Rice, M. E. and Harris, G. T. (2003) The size and sign of treatment effects in sex offender therapy. In R. A. Prentky, E. S. Janus and M. C. Seto (eds.), *Sexually Coercive Behavior: Understanding and Management. Annals of the New York Academy of Sciences*, 989: 428–40.

Thornton, D. (2002) Constructing and testing a framework for dynamic risk assessment. *Sexual Abuse: A Journal of Research and Treatment*, 141: 139–53.

Ward, T., Gannon, T. A. and Birgden, A. (2007) Human rights and the treatment of sex offenders. *Sex Abuse*, 19: 195–216.

Ward, T., Polaschek, D. and Beech, A. R. (2006) *Theories of Sexual Offending*. Chichester: Wiley.

Ward, T. and Stewart, C. A. (2003) The treatment of sex offenders: risk management and the good lives model. *Professional Psychology: Research and Practice*, 34: 353–60.

3.13 Rehabilitating violent offenders

Devon L. L. Polaschek

See also chapter 8.7 Randomized control trials.

Definitions

The term 'violent offender' is somewhat misleading; it implies offence specialization. A few violent offenders limit their criminal acts to assaults on family members (Holzworth-Munroe and Stuart 1994; Klein and Tobin 2008). More usually, those convicted of violent offences have diverse criminal histories comprised mainly of non-violent offending, and also tend to be the most prolific offenders (Farrington 2007; Henry *et al.* 1996). Those convicted of all types of criminal violence are predominantly male (Felson 2002).

The most important goal of interventions with violent offenders is to reduce reoffending risk. Rehabilitation resources have the most impact on people's offending, and on community safety, when dedicated to moderate to high-risk offenders (Lowenkamp, Latessa and Holsinger 2006). Combining this principle with the observations above leads to the conclusion that participants in violence rehabilitation will be mainly men, with extensive criminal histories, including convictions for violence, at high risk of further offending and at moderate to high risk of further violent acts. Throughout this chapter, the term *violent offender* thus refers to these men. Violent offences are defined here as criminal acts involving actual violence or the threat of serious violence (e.g. homicide, serious, grievous and minor assaults, robberies involving weapons, kidnapping and violent sexual assaults).

General principles of intervention for violent offenders

The 1980s saw the emergence of the 'What Works' movement: an extensive empirical enquiry into the programme, setting and offender characteristics associated with reduced recidivism. Andrews and Bonta (2007) summarized the main findings into the 'RNR model', i.e. Risk, Need and Responsivity principles.

1. The risk principle, risk and treatment intensity

Most jurisdictions that provide specialist violent offender interventions target medium- to high-risk offenders with relatively intensive programmes. At present the rule of thumb is around 150 hours for medium-risk offenders, and 300–400 hours for high-risk offenders. However, the actual risk-to-hours ratio varies quite widely; further research will be needed to establish whether this principle can be defined in absolute terms.

2. Criminogenic needs

Effective interventions target domains that are
(a) empirically linked to recidivism;
(b) relatively stable but capable of change; and
(c) if changed, change the likelihood of recidivism (e.g. a reduction in substance abuse is followed by decreased risk of conviction compared to before the reduction). These domains are known as stable dynamic risk factors (Hanson and Harris 2000), and most are feasible treatment targets, or criminogenic needs. Violent offenders are 'high-needs' offenders; assessment shows them to have a large range of offending-related needs (e.g. Hollin and Palmer 2003; Polaschek 2007; Wong and Gordon 2006).

Although a number of variables have been correlated with violent and general offending in violent offenders (e.g. antisocial and pro-violence attitudes; offending-related denial; justification and minimization; criminal peers; alcohol and drug problems; emotional misregulation; behavioural impulsivity; lack of protective intimate relationships; poor employment history; and deficient interpersonal skills, e.g. communication, negotiation, conflict resolution), their *dynamic* status has rarely been demonstrated. That is, there is a lack of evidence linking changes in the risk factors to changes in outcome (Douglas and Skeem 2005; Polaschek and Serin 2009).

3. Responsivity issues

Offender responsivity refers to those features of an individual offender (e.g. low levels of literacy, active psychosis, intellectual disability, social phobia and acquired traumatic brain injury) that should be assessed to determine the programme characteristics that may require individualized or highly specialized group interventions. Low motivation or treatment readiness can be viewed as an offender responsivity issue, but their near-invariable presence in violent offenders suggests they are better viewed as a *programme* responsivity issue. Similarly, high scores on the PCL scales also are the norm in high-risk violent offenders (Polaschek 2008); working effectively with men who commonly show egocentricity, callousness, superficiality, lack of remorse also becomes a programme responsivity issue.

Other common violent offender characteristics that programmes need to accommodate include: subtle neuropsychological difficulties present from early in life (Moffitt *et al.* 2002); low educational attainment; restlessness and attentional difficulties; and negative attitudes to classroom-style instruction. In New Zealand – as in some other jurisdictions – violent offenders are predominantly non-European, making it essential to provide intervention that will be safe for and make sense to Maori and Pacific men.

As with all offender interventions, programmes for violent offenders should adhere to the following:

- medium- to high-risk offenders should be targeted;
- programme intensity should match offender risk;
- dynamic risk factors – criminogenic needs – related to violence should be addressed by the programme;
- the programme should be responsive to common characteristics of violent offenders;
- offenders should be assessed to establish whether they are capable of responding to the programme;
- finally, programmes should be multimodal and cognitive-behavioural.

Does violent offender intervention work?

Before examining whether particular approaches to rehabilitation are effective, it is important to consider how to judge whether programme evaluation designs can adequately address this issue.

Outcome evaluation design

The first step in determining whether programmes are having their desired effects is to compare participants' rates of violent behaviour after the programme with what would have been expected if they had not attended the programme. Most evaluations use the proportion of men who are reconvicted of violence over a follow-up period, to represent actual violent behaviour.

More than one outcome variable is desirable (e.g. violent and non-violent reconviction, offences resulting in further imprisonment).

To estimate the outcomes that would have been expected for treated men had they remained untreated requires careful construction of comparison groups that are equivalent on other key variables related to outcome. Ideally, the best method is random allocation of potential participants to treatment and comparison conditions. In practice, randomized controlled trials – even when practical and ethical requirements can be met – do not necessarily result in group equivalence on important variables (see Marques *et al.* 2005), and they vary substantially on other indicators of quality. Thus they are not always the 'gold standard' for programme evaluation (Hollin 2008).

Often the most feasible rigorous design is quasi-experimental; the treatment group is compared with other people who could have participated, but did not for reasons unlikely to be related to outcome (e.g. insufficient programme places). A relatively robust design case-matches each man entering the treatment programme with an untreated man on key outcome-related variables (e.g. risk, age, gender, ethnicity, paroled for similar crimes at around the same time).[1] Both men who do and do not complete should be compared with their own untreated controls, because often non-completers have a higher estimated risk on programme entry. If men who complete a programme are compared with dropouts, any recidivism improvement in completers may be due to selective attrition of higher-risk men. Keeping completers' and non-completers' control groups separate can address the question of whether the experience of non-completion increases risk (i.e. a toxic treatment effect), by comparing non-completers with their own controls. Sometimes it is concluded erroneously that higher reconviction rates in non-completers compared to a combined comparison group indicates a toxic treatment effect.

Even with case-matching, it can be argued that a programme's success should be judged not just on its effects on those who stay to the end, but on its effects on all those who started the programme, compared to all controls. This intention-to-treat (ITT) design is a particularly demanding test of outcome if programme effect is related to dosage; programme non-completers are considered along with completers when by definition they have only experienced part of the programme. Other approaches using statistical methods

---

[1] Matching on motivation to change is usually also important, if difficult. However, the low levels of motivation in men entering violence interventions suggests its omission may not be a substantial threat in this context.

to create increased rigour are also becoming more common (e.g. propensity analysis; Cortoni, Nunes and Latendresse 2006; Jones *et al.* 2004).

Types of programmes

Low-intensity anger management programmes

Cognitive-behavioural programmes specifically for violent offenders emerged in the 1980s. Many were based on Novaco's (1975) innovative adaptation of Meichenbaum's stress inoculation approach, originally developed for anxiety problems. Leading researchers now describe anger as facilitating rather than causing violence (Howells 2004; Novaco and Welsh 1989) and as neither necessary nor sufficient for violence to occur. Novaco's view of anger and its role in violence is a nuanced one; he recognizes that both excessive anger experiences and maladaptive anger expression (e.g. in violence) are important, and further that anger can be an enjoyable, satisfying experience, and has a variety of social functions (Novaco and Welsh 1989).

In practice, low-intensity anger management programmes often are delivered by poorly trained staff who may not understand these complexities, or who may be unequal to the task of managing violent offenders with egocentric expectations about how others should behave towards them, and beliefs that violence is 'the right choice' in response to certain 'provocations'. In these circumstances the participants can readily hijack the programme, using it to excuse violence, blame victims for bringing on their own assaults, and support the use of anger expression to manipulate others (Gondolf and Russell 1986).

Low-intensity stress-inoculation-type anger management programmes will most likely be ineffective with violent offenders because they (a) are insufficiently intensive; often comprising 20 to 40 hours of programming, and (b) they do not explicitly focus on several important dynamic risk factors for violent offenders (e.g. pro-violence attitudes). Anger management programmes have benefited many people, but their ability to reduce violent offending risk in adult male violent offenders remains to be established (Polaschek 2006b; Polaschek and Collie 2004).

High-intensity multifactorial programmes

Recent programme evaluations suggest that cognitive-behavioural interventions of 150 to 300 hours' duration that address multiple criminogenic needs, and meet the other standards reviewed earlier, can reduce violent and general reconviction risk. Given the community safety concerns associated with violent offenders, most programmes are prison-based, even though offender rehabilitation has more effect in community settings (Hollin and Palmer 2006).

In addition to the New Zealand case example below, two recent positive evaluations of institutional programmes are reported by Cortoni *et al.* (2006), and Di Placido *et al.* (2006). Both showed reduced reconvictions for violence for treatment completers when compared to controls.

Three recent evaluations of institutionally hosted programmes and one of a community programme – all cognitive-behavioural – are noted below.

Cortoni *et al.* reported on the 190-hour Correctional Service of Canada's Violence Prevention Programme (VPP), and Di Placido *et al.* on a programme in a maximum-security forensic psychiatric hospital in Saskatchewan.[2,3]

New Zealand's Montgomery House Violence Prevention Programme, open since 1987, is a rare example of a community-based programme. The programme also is distinctive for its degree of embedding in a Maori cultural context. Closed groups of twelve men complete about 380 hours of programming that – in addition to targeting the dynamic risk factors above – also teaches health education, Tikanga and Te Reo Maori (Maori traditional culture and language), budgeting, physical fitness training and outdoor education (see Berry 2003; Polaschek and Dixon 2001).

Two evaluations of Montgomery House show reductions in overall violent reconviction risk for programme starters: Berry (2003) over seventeen months' follow-up and Wilson (2002), after six years. Taken together, this small body of research suggests grounds for optimism about the impact on violent behaviour of well-designed and well-delivered cognitive-behavioural programmes.

Programme design

Hypothetically, potentially effective programmes are designed by drawing on resources that include aetiological and programme theories, and empirical research into how programmes change risk. Programme theories specify how etiological theories inform *what* a programme should address, and *how* changes are to be effected: the processes of treatment (Kirsch and Becker

[2] The Aggressive Behaviour Control programme, which has been evaluated for use in DSPD treatment in the United Kingdom (Maden *et al.* 2004).

[3] A possible threat to the interpretation of this study is that the untreated sample was a mix of RPC referrals who were assessed but did not start, or started but did not complete the programme.

2006; Ward and Gannon 2006). There is a substantial gap in resources between the RNR principles and what is known theoretically or empirically about how to treat offenders.

A comprehensive programme theory for violent offenders is still to be proposed (Howells and Day 2002; Polaschek and Collie 2004), although the increasing provision of intensive programmes for violent offenders suggests a slowly evolving theoretical scaffold. Empirically, outcome evaluations can tell us if a programme is associated with reductions in risk, but are silent on the vital issue of how participants change in such programmes. The first step in addressing this question is the accurate measurement of change.

The tools most used for measuring change are offender self-report scales, on which participants often report substantial positive changes. However, the few studies that examined whether these changes correlate with recidivism outcome have found that usually they do not (Cortoni 2006; Polaschek 2006a). Other methods, such as clinician ratings, are rarely used and also often are only weakly related to outcome (Gondolf and Wernik in press). We need both more sophisticated measures of treatment change (Serin 2001) and a clearer understanding of the change process (Day et al. 2006).

Clinically, treatment can be thought of as comprising three major tasks. The first is readying offenders for change (developing therapeutic alliances, identifying how current lifestyle developed, offence triggers and processes, schemas that support violence, goals for programme). Second, the core work begins on changing stable dynamic risk factors. Traditionally – over more than two decades – this portion of intervention has been oriented towards building offenders' personal and interpersonal capacities to enable them to have more satisfying and socially competent lives (e.g. developing relationship, communication and problem-solving skills, alternative means for managing stress and distress).

However, violent offenders often 'react first, think later', so to remain in the community – and equally, in the programme – long enough to pursue better lives, they need to learn immediate self-control of affect and urges. Thus the third component of treatment has two related foci: developing strategies for the management of acute risk factors ('relapse prevention') and reintegration; planning the next steps for generalizing change into the community, or into a less structured environment.

Treatment components do not map one-to-one onto dynamic risk factors, nor should they. For example, learning and applying problem-solving skills can contribute to improved relationships, decreased behavioural impulsivity, improved work prospects, reduced substance use, reduced financial stress and so on.

Is there a place for positive psychology approaches?

Recently the potential of positive psychology has been recognized (e.g. Day *et al.* in press). Positive psychology approaches provide an important humanistic counterweight to pressure on some programmes to integrate politically driven punitive agendas into their practices.

The most extensively disseminated positive psychology proposal is Ward's Good Lives model (GLM) for child sex offenders (Ward and Stewart 2003). The need for the original GLM was partly justified with a straw man argument. It proposed that reducing offenders' risks to potential victims and increasing offenders' capabilities to lead good lives were competing supraordinate goals, and suggested that prevailing offender treatments considered only the former: '*risk management,* where the primary aim of treating offenders is to avoid harm to the community rather than to improve their quality of life' (Ward and Stewart 2003, p. 353). Yet the practice at the time in New Zealand and elsewhere saw these as two compatible subgoals: treatment was oriented towards reducing future harm to the community by both teaching offenders how to manage risk *and* improving their abilities to live healthy, lawful and meaningful lives (for example, see Hudson, Wales and Ward 1998; Polaschek and Dixon 2001).

Thus Ward and colleagues are correct that many programme designers and providers consider that ethically, the top policy-level goal for scarce correctional rehabilitative resources is increased community safety through reduced reconviction risk.[4] However, the means by which risk is reduced, and by which dynamic risk factors change, is operationalized in treatment as a series of both positive capacity-building goals and risk-management goals for clients, and the content of treatment reflects this diversity.

Ward's GLM proposals have drawn attention to the generally poor state of documented programme theory (Polaschek and Collie 2004). The GLM's explicit focus on helping offenders flourish – rather than just exist – as prosocial human beings, and the development of a human needs-based aetiological model (e.g. Ward and Gannon 2006) are also strengths of this work. The GLM is not yet developed sufficiently to provide guidance on the treatment of violent offenders as they are defined here. Its basis in child sex offenders remains evident (Ward, Mann and Gannon 2007), and it does not shed light on the core

---

[4] Of course this goal cannot ethically be achieved by any means; offenders' human rights are taken into account in determining how it is achieved.

therapeutic task of how to work with psychopathic men to pursue personally meaningful goals that also benefit those around them. Although the development of positive psychology treatment components is a laudable pursuit, as Wormith *et al.* (2007) noted, 'whether [positive psychology] is more effective than current approaches and whether it represents fundamental or semantic differences from current approaches remains unanswered (p. 886).

A case example of violent offender intervention: the Rimutaka Violence Prevention Programme

The Rimutaka Violence Prevention Unit (RVPU) is a ten-year-old thirty-bed medium-secure unit in a large prison near Wellington, New Zealand. Three cohorts of ten men enter the unit annually, complete detailed assessments and begin the closed-group seven-month modular programme led by two therapists, meeting for about 8–12 hours each week. On completion men may move on to self-care units or be paroled directly to the community. While in the programme they also begin plans for community reintegration. Up to three-quarters of men who enter the programme complete it. Programme participants are mainly Maori and Pacific men, and the programme includes some accommodation of their culture-based needs.

An evaluation of RVPU participants between 1998 and 2004 compared case-matched high-risk programme completers and non-completers with untreated controls. Over an average three and a half years post-release, 62% of programme completers were reconvicted for violence, compared to 72% of their matched controls, 71% of non-completers and 75% of non-completer controls (Polaschek in press). Four other aspects of this evaluation are noteworthy: (a) the very high-risk nature of this sample; (b) the high rates of PCL-psychopathy in the sample (mean PCL:SV score of 18); (c) that PCL scores were unrelated to outcome, suggesting that PCL-psychopathy does not preclude effective treatment (see also Skeem, Polaschek and Manchak 2009); (d) that the programme showed no treatment effect on lower-risk offenders; arguably an example of the risk principle at work.

Conclusion

To conclude, although the provision of effective offender rehabilitation has developed substantially in two decades, violent offender interventions are still more intuitively than empirically driven. Top research priorities include more investigation into the theory and measurement of change within programmes. With regard to programme development, there is substantial room for further progress. Even after completing our best programmes, most men are reconvicted of a violent offence. Clear articulation of programme theories remains an important goal. Significant changes in existing programme traditions are underway, with several jurisdictions moving away from one-size-fits-all closed-group modularized programmes. Innovations are directed towards creating a much closer fit between the programme experience and the participating offender, and extending 'treatment' outside of the therapy room and into the community.

REFERENCES

Andrews, D. A. and Bonta, J. (2007) *The Psychology of Criminal Conduct*, 4th edn. Cincinnati OH: Anderson.

Berry, S. (2003) Stopping violent offending in New Zealand: is treatment an option? *New Zealand Journal of Psychology*, 32: 92–100.

Cortoni, F. (2006) Violence and sexual offenders: program effectiveness research. Paper presented at the 11th Biennial Symposium on Violence and Aggression, Saskatoon, Saskatchewan, Canada.

Cortoni, F., Nunes, K. and Latendresse, M. (2006) *An Examination of the Effectiveness of the Violence Prevention Program* (no. R-178). Ottawa, ON: Correctional Service of Canada.

Day, A., Bryan, J., Davey, L. and Casey, S. (2006) The process of change in offender rehabilitation programmes. *Psychology, Crime and Law*, 12: 473–87.

Day, A., Gerace, A., Wilson, C. and Howells, K. (2008). Promoting forgiveness in violent offenders: a more positive approach to offender rehabilitation? *Aggression and Violent Behavior*, 13: 195–200.

Di Placido, C., Simon, T. L., Witte, T. D., Gu, D. and Wong, S. C. P. (2006) Treatment of gang members can reduce recidivism and institutional misconduct. *Law and Human Behavior*, 30: 93–114.

Douglas, K. S., and Skeem, J. L. (2005) Violence risk assessment: getting specific about being dynamic. *Psychology, Public Policy, and Law*, 11: 347–83.

Farrington, D. P. (2007) Origins of violent behavior over the life span. In D. J. Flannery, A. T. Vazsonyi and I. D. Waldman (eds.), *The Cambridge Handbook of Violent Behavior and Aggression*, pp. 19–48. Cambridge: Cambridge University Press.

Felson, R. B. (2002) *Violence and Gender Re-examined*. Washington, DC: American Psychological Association.

Gondolf, E. W. and Russell, D. (1986). The case against anger control treatment programs for batterers. *Response*, 9: 2–5.

Gondolf, E. W. and Wernik, H. (in press) Batterer treatment behaviors in predicting reassault. *Journal of Interpersonal Violence*.

Hanson, R. K. and Harris, A. J. R. (2000) Where should we intervene? Dynamic predictors of sexual offence recidivism. *Criminal Justice and Behavior*, 27: 6–35.

Henry, B., Caspi, A., Moffitt, T. E. and Silva, P. A. (1996) Temperamental and familial pre-
    dictors of violent and nonviolent criminal convictions: age 3 to age 18. *Developmental
    Psychology*, 32: 614–23.
Hollin, C. R. (2008) Evaluating offending behaviour programmes: does only randomization
    glister? *Criminology and Criminal Justice*, 8: 89–106.
Hollin, C. R. and Palmer, E. J. (2003) Level of Service Inventory – revised profiles of violent and
    nonviolent prisoners. *Journal of Interpersonal Violence*, 18: 1075–86.
    (2006) Offending behaviour programmes: history and development. In C. R. Hollin and
    E. J. Palmer (eds.), *Offending Behaviour Programmes: Development, Application, and
    Controversies*, pp. 1–32. Chichester: Wiley.
Holzworth-Munroe, A. and Stuart, G. L. (1994) Typologies of male batterers: three subtypes
    and the differences among them. *Psychological Bulletin*, 116: 476–97.
Howells, K. (2004) Anger and its link to violent offending. *Psychiatry, Psychology and Law*,
    11: 189–96.
Howells, K. and Day, A. (2002) Grasping the nettle: treating and rehabilitating the violent
    offender. *Australian Psychologist*, 37: 222–8.
Hudson, S. M., Wales, D. S. and Ward, T. (1998) Kia Marama: a treatment program for child
    molesters in New Zealand. In W. L. Marshall, Y. M. Fernandez, S. M. Hudson and T. Ward
    (eds.), *Sourcebook of Treatment Programs for Sexual Offenders*, pp. 17–28. New York:
    Plenum Press.
Jones, A. S., D'Agostino, R. B., Gondolf, E. W. and Heckert, A. (2004) Assessing the effect of
    batterer program completion on reassault using propensity scores. *Journal of Interpersonal
    Violence*, 19: 1002–20.
Kirsch, L. G. and Becker, J. V. (2006) Sexual offending: theory of problem, theory of change, and
    implications for treatment effectiveness. *Aggression and Violent Behavior*, 11: 208–24.
Klein, A. R., and Tobin, T. (2008) A longitudinal study of arrested batterers, 1995–2005: career
    criminals. *Violence Against Women*, 14: 136–57.
Lowenkamp, C. T., Latessa, E. J. and Holsinger, A. M. (2006) The risk principle in action: what
    have we learned from 13,676 offenders and 97 correctional programs? *Crime and
    Delinquency*, 52: 77–93.
Maden, A., Williams, J., Wong, S. C. P. and Leis, T. A. (2004) Treating dangerous and severe
    personality disorder in high security: lessons from the Regional Psychiatric Centre,
    Saskatoon, Canada. *Journal of Forensic Psychiatry and Psychology*, 15: 375–90.
Marques, J. K., Wiederanders, M., Day, D. M., Nelson, C. and van Ommeren, A. (2005) Effects
    of a relapse prevention program on sexual recidivism: final results from California's sex
    offender treatment and evaluation project (SOTEP). *Sexual Abuse: A Journal of Research
    and Treatment*, 17: 79–107.
Moffitt, T. E., Caspi, A., Harrington, H. and Milne, B. J. (2002) Males on the life-course-
    persistent and adolescence-limited antisocial pathways: follow-up at age 26 years.
    Development and Psychopathology 14: 179–207.
Novaco, R. W. (1975) *Anger Control: The Development and Evaluation of an Experimental
    Treatment*. Lexington, MA: Lexington Books.
Novaco, R. W. and Welsh, W. N. (1989) Anger disturbances: cognitive mediation and clinical
    prescriptions. In K. Howells and C. R. Hollin (eds.), *Clinical Approaches to Violence*,
    pp. 39–60. Chichester: Wiley.

Polaschek, D. L. L. (2006a) National Violence Prevention Unit Evaluation Report III: Psychometric and recidivism analyses for the retrospective evaluation sample. Unpublished report. Wellington, NZ: New Zealand Department of Corrections.

(2006b) Violent offender programmes: concept, theory and practice. In C. R. Hollin and M. McMurran (eds.), *Offending Behaviour Programmes: Development, Application, and Controversies*, pp. 113–54. Chichester: Wiley.

(2007) Rimutaka Violence Prevention Unit Evaluation Report IV: Interim report on prospective evaluation: intermediate measures of treatment change. Unpublished report. Wellington, NZ: New Zealand Department of Corrections.

(2008) Rimutaka Violence Prevention Unit Evaluation Report V: Interim/progress report on prospective evaluation. Unpublished report. Wellington, NZ: New Zealand Department of Corrections.

(in press) High-intensity rehabilitation for violent offenders in New Zealand: reconviction outcomes for high- and medium-risk prisoners. *Journal of Interpersonal Violence*.

Polaschek, D. L. L. and Collie, R. M. (2004) Rehabilitating serious violent adult offenders: an empirical and theoretical stocktake. *Psychology, Crime and Law*, 10: 321–34.

Polaschek, D. L. L. and Dixon, B. G. (2001) The Violence Prevention Project: the development and evaluation of a treatment programme for violent offenders. *Psychology, Crime and Law*, 7: 1–23.

Polaschek, D. L. L. and Serin, R. C. (2009). The criminogenic needs of violent offenders: theory and research. Manuscript in preparation.

Serin, R. C. (2001) Programme evaluation: intermediate measures of treatment success. In L. L. Motiuk and R. C. Serin (eds.), *Compendium 2000 on Effective Correctional Programming*. Ottawa: Ministry of Supply and Services.

Skeem, J. L., Polaschek, D. L. L. and Manchak, S. (2009) Appropriate treatment works, but how? Rehabilitating general, psychopathic, and high risk offenders. In J. L. Skeem, K. Douglas and S. Lilienfeld (eds.), *Psychological Science in the Courtroom: Consensus and Controversy*, pp. 358–86. New York: Guilford Press.

Ward, T. and Gannon, T. A. (2006) Rehabilitation, etiology, and self-regulation: the comprehensive good lives model of treatment for sexual offenders. *Aggression and Violent Behavior*, 11: 77–94.

Ward, T., Mann, R. E. and Gannon, T. A. (2007) The good lives model of offender rehabilitation: clinical implications. *Aggression and Violent Behavior*, 12: 87–107.

Ward, T. and Stewart, C. A. (2003) The treatment of sex offenders: risk management and good lives. *Professional Psychology: Research and Practice*, 34: 353–60.

Wilson, N. J. (2002) Montgomery House VPP re-imprisonment analysis. Internal memorandum, Department of Corrections Psychological Service, Wellington, New Zealand.

Wong, S. C. P. and Gordon, A. (2006) The validity and reliability of the Violence Risk Scale: a treatment-friendly violence risk assessment tool. *Psychology, Public Policy, and Law*, 12: 279–309.

Wormith, J. S., Althouse, R., Simpson, M., Reitzel, L. R., Fagan, T. J. and Morgan, R. D. (2007) The rehabilitation and reintegration of offenders: the current landscape and some future directions for correctional psychology. *Criminal Justice and Behavior*, 34: 879–92.

3.14 Victims of terrorism

Elizabeth A. Campbell

See also chapter 4.13 Terrorism research.

Specifics of terrorist attacks

Consideration needs to be given as to whether victims of terrorist attacks can be viewed as having the same kind of psychological injury as victims of other disasters or criminal assaults. A number of researchers have pointed out that there are certain specific features that are common to most terrorist attacks which make the meaning of these events different to other kinds of trauma or psychological adverse event. Some of the significant features that have been enunciated are:

- The primary objective of the terrorist is to induce communal fear.
- The individuals who are targeted are not the primary foci of the terrorist, but rather a means to the end of achieving communal disruption and anxiety.
- All of the community suffer as a result of a terrorist attack, even those who were not themselves directly injured or witnesses to an attack.
- The psychological impact of terrorist events is therefore potentially very wide since there are no geographical boundaries to the fear that can be instilled.
- Terrorist events are usually engineered to occur without any warning. This means that they are more psychologically damaging because the population is unprepared for them.
- Some terrorist events will have novel features that individuals will not have come across before; for example, in the case of biological, chemical or radiological attacks on the community.
- Terrorist events are often very difficult for the rescue and recovery first-line responders to deal with.

As summarized by Schmid (2008): 'There is something special to victims of terrorism, something that sets them apart from many other victims.

Terrorism, like genocide, is a unilateral attack of the armed on the defenceless. The victims of terrorism are threatened or destroyed in peacetime, or outside war zones, unexpectedly and without provocation. For the terrorists, the victim is only an instrument, not the ultimate target.'

Models

Given the unpredictable nature of terrorist events, there is a relatively small research evidence base from which to draw conclusions, either about the psychological impact on or the required psychosocial aid for adult or child victims. This is particularly true for systematic evaluations of psychosocial interventions. It is unlikely that it will be possible to have strictly controlled randomized controlled trials, for example, of psychosocial or psychological interventions with victims of terrorist attacks. Therefore many current guidelines rely on a combination of expert consensus and the restricted evidence base that does exist.

Some guidelines have taken a very broad approach (e.g. World Health Organization 2007), while others have focused more on the response of the health services for people with severe psychological reactions. However, from what is known of the impact on the whole community, a public health approach is required with an emphasis on the wide spectrum of psychosocial needs rather than a narrow 'mental health' approach.

Many of the guidelines refer to different time phases in responses to emergency incidents. However, the different guidelines do not have common or agreed terms to represent the different phases. Terms that are used include 'immediate, medium term and long term', others break up time into 'within the first week, within the first month, one to three months post, beyond three months'. Relatively few guidelines refer to the preparatory or pre-incident phase. Some of the current guidance only addresses issues that arise in a particular phase of response. For example, those guidelines emanating from a mental health perspective tend to focus on the medium- to long-term phases.

This parcelling up of time phases can be a somewhat artificial exercise since such time phases will be influenced by the nature of the event, whether there are ongoing threats, by location and by the ability of the authorities to respond.

Nevertheless, the use of time phases or levels to describe the range and type of psychosocial assistance following a traumatic incident does provide a schematic road map for first responders and for social care and health service providers. However, the scale of any event will also determine the feasibility of some of the recommendations in any guidelines.

Since different countries have very varied infrastructures and social/health care systems, guidelines cannot be overprescriptive about delivery of psychosocial assistance as this will vary by the organizational structures in place in each country. However, guidelines can identify the key principles and values.

The most helpful model underpinning interventions in this area is a humanitarian and public health model rather than a psychopathological model (e.g. NATO 2008). The whole community is affected by terrorism and this must be the target for psychosocial assistance. However, there does also need to be an emphasis on targeted care for those individuals who have persistent or severe psychological reactions that do not resolve in due course. The psychosocial assistance plan needs to be fully integrated into the strategic and operational plans used by government, local authorities and emergency responders.

Psychological impact of terrorist attacks

Fear and anxiety are normal, reasonable and expected reactions following terrorist attacks. Some studies have examined the level of anxiety or 'stress' in the general populations after an attack. The most recent of these were conducted after the attacks in New York in 2001, the Madrid bombings in 2004 and the London bombings in 2005 (e.g. Rubin *et al.* 2005; Schuster *et al.* 2001). Overall these studies have demonstrated a pervasive adverse impact of the events. High rates of perceived danger and fear have been reported even in those not directly exposed to the trauma. However, most people's fears diminish over a relatively short period of time and it is only a minority who have persistent levels of significantly distressing symptoms.

The concept of 'resilience' has been increasingly invoked to explain why the majority of exposed individuals do not develop enduring or severe psychological problems. Resilience is variously defined but in general it refers to features of the individual or communities that allow the withstanding of adversity or trauma and the ability to recover from any distress provoked by the trauma (Agaibi and Wilson 2005). The term has also been adopted by governments; for example, there is a UK Resilience government website which hosts news and information for emergency practitioners.

Prevalence of psychological disorder

Victims

Whalley and Brewin (2007) reviewed the literature about the impact on mental health of terrorist attacks and use of mental health services. From their review, they concluded that '30–40% of people directly affected by terrorist action are likely to develop PTSD, and at least 20% are likely still to be experiencing symptoms two years later'. Those individuals who are most likely to be at risk have been identified by Alexander (2005).

Children

Fremont (2004) reviewed the literature examining children's reactions to traumas arising from terrorist incidents. She suggests that, because of the impact on adults of such events, the ongoing threat posed by such events, and the media coverage, children can be particularly at risk of adverse psychological reactions. The type of reactions seen in children will vary by age, by degree of exposure to the event, and whether any family members were killed or seriously injured. The rates of PTSD in children ranged from 28% to 50% in the studies reviewed by Fremont (2004).

Williams (2006) and Williams et al. (2008) have produced useful reviews of the impact of severe trauma, including terrorism, on children. While cautioning against a narrow 'diagnostic' approach to the assessment of distress or behavioural problems in children exposed to various types of severe trauma, Williams et al (2008) note that the rates of PTSD in children and adolescents following exposure ranges from 39% to 100%.

Pfefferbaum et al. (2006) conducted a telephone survey of adolescents and found that 12.6% had 'probable' PTSD six to nine months after the 2001 terrorist attacks in New York.

First responders

Whalley and Brewin's (2007) review concluded that studies of emergency workers have usually shown that they have considerably lower levels of psychopathology than victims directly involved in the incident. However, the research evidence about the impact on first responders is mixed and scarce, and the NATO (2008) guidance suggests that all psychosocial plans should incorporate some provision of psychological services for emergency and healthcare staff.

Current guidelines and guidance for interventions

A number of organizations have produced guidelines for first responders and healthcare agencies for actions following mass violence or terrorist attacks.
Some of the key documents are:

- World Health Organization (2007) *IASC Guidelines on Mental Health and Psychosocial Support in Emergency Settings*
- NATO (2008) *Psychosocial Care for People Affected by Disasters and Major Incidents*
- NCTSN and NCPTSD (2006) *Psychological First Aid: Field Operations Guide*, 2nd edn
- IMPACT (2007) *Multidisciplinary Guidelines: Early Psychosocial Interventions after Disaster, Terrorism and Other Shocking Events*
- Emergency Management Australia (2003) *Guidelines for Psychological Service Practice: Mental Health Practitioners Guide*
- American Red Cross (1995) *Disaster Mental Health Services*

Different levels of intervention are required at different time points and for different groups within the population. Most guidelines have been written for dealing with adult victims, although there are a few that are specifically about children and young people. Some of these guidelines have been produced via expert consensus while others are more firmly located in the extant research. However, given that there are significant gaps in the scientific literature about reactions to terrorist events and also the research literature about the efficacy of psychological interventions, almost all of the published guidelines have a rather pragmatic approach to them.

The strategic psychosocial assistance plan should specifically identify different groups, such as vulnerable adults, who may require tailored responses. The operational plans should also have particular consideration for the needs of different groups within the community. A communication strategy which is 'age appropriate' for different groups and which can be delivered after an event needs to be drawn up in advance. Agencies, services and care providers who have responsibility for welfare, health and education should be involved in developing an integrated strategic and operational plan for psychosocial care following terrorist events.

An information strategy should be elaborated in preparation for any traumatic events which would allow the collation of data about victims and allow access to those data to key health and social agencies following any event. This is also crucial for any researchers who may be seeking to chart the psychological impact or evaluate the effectiveness of psychosocial interventions. NATO (2008) suggests a 'strategic stepped mode of care' with six levels:

1. Strategic planning
2. Preventive actions (e.g. building resilience)
3. Basic humanitarian care and support
4. Psychological first aid
5. Screening, assessment and preliminary interventions
6. Specialist mental health services.

Short term

In the immediate aftermath of a terrorist attack, the community needs to be assisted to access social support, community resources and those things necessary to foster feelings of safety and security. For example, children should be reunited with parents and family as soon as possible. Whilst it is important to normalize the immediate psychological distress that people will feel, it is important also not to assume that natural resilience means that nothing need be done. First responders and victims can be educated at this time about the normal and expected reactions to trauma and given appropriate reassurance (Alexander 2005). Hobfoll *et al.* (2007) have identified five 'essential elements' for intervening in the immediate to mid term following trauma. After a review of the pertinent research literature, they concluded that there are five 'elements' or principles arising out of the existing research base. These are: '1. Promote sense of safety. 2. Promote calming. 3. Promote sense of self and collective efficacy. 4. Promote connectedness. 5. Promote hope.' This is very similar to the psychological first aid approach, which emphasizes the reduction of immediate distress and the promotion of the individual's own coping abilities.

While some individuals may not have been direct victims of a terrorist attack, it should be remembered that they may be vicarious victims because of the impact of the event on the community as a whole. The mental health services may want to have a visible presence in the immediate aftermath and to act as strategic consultants, but it is not appropriate to offer specialist mental health services at this point.

Medium term

Screening for significant psychological distress or behavioural problems should be considered at this time, if there are services available to meet any identified needs. Outreach and proactive methods should be employed to identify victims and to provide them with information and resources for accessing support and services. Brewin (2005) reviews screening instruments and has also described the screening methods used after the London bombings (Brewin *et al.* 2008). Those individuals with known and pre-existing severe mental health problems who may be at risk of relapse or exacerbation of problems may also need to be monitored and provided with specialist psychological assessment services. There also needs to be consideration given to the needs of children (Gurwitch *et al.* 2008). First responders, volunteer workers and front-line staff can also be monitored for any adverse psychological reactions during this phase (Hyman 2004).

Long term

For those individuals with severe and distressing post-traumatic symptoms which have lasted for more than one month after the event, trauma-focused cognitive-behavioural therapy has been shown to be effective and should be offered (Gillespie *et al.* 2002; Duffy, Gillespie and Clark 2007). If other psychological symptoms are present for more than three months, then appropriate evidence-based psychological interventions should be offered after specialized assessment.

Because of the possibility of late developing symptoms, it would be good practice to monitor proactively those with ongoing and distressing symptoms who have not been offered therapy. Health and social services should make provision for continuing support and psychological specialist help for several years following the event, especially for children who may need different services as they develop. Brom, Pat-Horenczyk and Ford (2008) have produced a useful text on the treatment of traumatized children.

Training

Training programmes for first responders and mental health workers should include training about dealing with all the different groups within the community (Yule 2006). First responders should be trained in psychological first aid. (National Child Traumatic Stress Network and National Center for PTSD 2006; Everly and Flynn 2005).

Research into interventions

Early interventions

There have been relatively few systematic evaluations of the efficacy of early psychological interventions in preventing later, severe psychological disorders.

The intervention most closely examined has been 'debriefing', although this term has included a wide range of interventions at both the individual and group level. Using strict methodological criteria to screen studies of effects has led to the conclusion that debriefing is ineffective in preventing subsequent psychological symptoms, especially PTSD (Rose *et al.* 2005; Bisson *et al.* 2007). However, many of these studies used people who had one-off traumas rather than exposure to large-scale disasters or community-wide traumas.

As an initial approach in situations where there are a large number of victims, the notion of 'psychological first aid' has gained considerable currency. There is little evidence of the efficacy or acceptability of psychological first aid.

Medium- to long-term interventions

The UK National Institute for Clincial Excellence (2005) recommends that trauma-focused cognitive-behavioural therapy should be offered to all those with PTSD symptoms who present within three months post trauma. There is good scientifc evidence behind this recommendation.

Interventions with children

Fremont's (2004) review concluded that post-terrorism interventions with children required 'a systematic public health approach that provides community-based interventions, screening of children at risk, triage and referral services, community based trauma and loss programs'. However, she notes that there has been little in the way of systematic evaluation of treatments for children following exposure to terrorism.

The treatment of children with PTSD was considered by the National Institute for Clinical Excellence (2005). They concluded that, while there was evidence of the effectiveness of trauma-focused cognitive therapy for victims of sexual abuse, 'there is very little evidence from RCTs for the efficacy of any psychological interventions for … PTSD arising from other forms of trauma. This reflects not the inconclusive nature of the evidence but rather the lack of RCTs.'

Stallard's (2006) review is a helpful contribution to the literature in this area.

Conclusion

There is now considerable consensus about the best approach for psychosocial assistance following terrorist events. Humanitarian and public health approaches are favoured over an emphasis on psychopathology. The evidence base is still in development and is often patchy.

REFERENCES

Agaibi, C. E. and Wilson, J. P. (2005) Trauma, PTSD and resilience trauma. *Violence and Abuse*, 6: 195–216.

Alexander, D. A. (2005) Early mental health intervention after disasters. *Advances in Psychiatric Treatment*, 11: 12–18.

American Red Cross (1995) *Disaster Services Regulations and Procedures: Disaster Mental Health Services*. Washington, DC: American Red Cross.

Bisson, J. I., Brayne, M., Ochberg, F. M. and Everly, G. S. (2007) Early psychological intervention following traumatic events. *American Journal of Psychiatry*, 164: 1016–19.

Brewin, C. R. (2005) Systematic review of screening instruments for the detection of post-traumatic stress disorder in adults. *Journal of Traumatic Stress*, 18: 53–62.

Brewin, C. R., Scragg, P., Robertson, M., d'Ardenne, P. and Ehlers, A.(2008) Promoting mental health following the London bombings: a screen and treat approach. *Journal of Traumatic Stress*, 21: 3–8.

Brom, D., Pat-Horenczyk, R. and Ford, J. (eds.). (2008) *Treating Traumatized Children: Risk, Resilience and Recovery*. London: Routledge.

Duffy, M., Gillespie, K. and Clark, D. M. (2007) Post-traumatic stress disorder in the context of terrorism and other civil conflict in Northern Ireland: randomised controlled trial. *British Medical Journal*, 334: 1147.

Emergency Management Australia (2003) *Guidelines for Psychological Service Practice: Mental Health Practitioners Guide*.

Everly, G. S. and Flynn, B. W (2005) Principles and practice of acute psychological first aid after disasters. In G. S. Everly and C. L. Parker (eds.), *Mental Health Aspects of Disasters: Public Health Preparedness and Response*, pp. 68–76. Baltimore, MD: Johns Hopkins Center for Public Health Preparedness.

Fremont, W. P. (2004) Childhood reactions to terrorism induced trauma: a review of the past 10 years. *Journal of the American Academy of Child and Adolescent Psychiatry*, 43: 381–92.

Gillespie, K., Duffy, M., Hackman, A. and Clark, D. M. (2002) Community-based cognitive therapy in the treatment of post-traumatic stress disorder following the Omagh bomb. *Behaviour Research and Therapy*, 40: 345–57.

Gurwitch, R. H., Silovsky, J. F., Schultz, S., Kees, M. and Burlingame, S. (2008) *Reactions and Guidelines for Children Following Trauma/Disaster*. Washington, DC: American Psychiatric Association.

Hobfoll, S. E., Hall, B. J., Canetti-Nisim, D., Galea, S., Johnson, R. J. and Palmieri, P. A. (2007) Five essential elements of immediate and mid-term mass trauma intervention: empirical evidence. *Psychiatry: Interpersonal and Biological Processes*, 70: 283–315.

Hyman, O. (2004) Perceived social support and secondary traumatic stress symptoms in emergency responders. *Journal of Traumatic Stress*, 17: 149–56.

IMPACT (2007) *Multidisciplinary Guidelines: Early Psychosocial Interventions after Disaster, Terrorism and Other Shocking Events*. www.impact-kenniscentrum.nl.

National Child Traumatic Stress Network and National Center for PTSD (2006) *Psychological First Aid: Field Operations Guide*, 2nd edn. www.ncptsd.va.gov.

National Institute for Clinical Excellence (NICE) (2005) *The Management of PTSD in Adults and Children in Primary and Secondary Care*. London: Gaskell and the British Psychological Society.

NATO (2008) *Psychosocial Care for People Affected by Disasters and Major Incidents*. Geneva: NATO Joint Medical Committee.

Pfefferbaum, B., Stuber, J., Galea, S. and Fairbrother, G. (2006) Panic reactions to terrorist attacks and probable post traumatic stress disorder in adolescents. *Journal of Traumatic Stress*, 19: 217–28.

Rose, S., Bisson, J., Churchill, R. and Wessely, S. (2005) Psychological debriefing for preventing post-traumatic stress disorder (PTSD). *The Cochrane Database of Systematic Reviews*, issue 3.

Rubin G. J., Brewin, C. R., Greenberg, N., Simpson, J. and Wessely, S. (2005) Psychological and behavioural reactions to the bombings in London 7 July 2005: cross-section survey of a representative sample of Londoners. *British Medical Journal*, 331: 606.

Schmid A. P. (2008) The terrorism threat in Europe. Paper presented at University of Tilburg Conference 'Standards for victims of terrorism', March 2008.

Schuster, M. A., Stein, B. D., Jaycox, L. H., Collins, R. L., Marshall, G. N., Elliott, M. N. *et al.* (2001) A national survey of stress reactions after the September 11, 2001, terrorist attacks. *New England Journal of Medicine*, 345: 1507–12.

Stallard, P. (2006) Psychological interventions for post-traumatic reactions in children and young people: a review of randomised controlled trials. *Clinical Psychology Review*, 26: 895–911.

Whalley, M. G. and Brewin, C. R. (2007) Mental health following terrorist attacks. *British Journal of Psychiatry*, 190: 94–6.

Williams, R. (2006) The psychosocial consequences for children and young people who are exposed to terrorism, war, conflict and natural disasters. *Current Opinion in Psychiatry*, 19: 337–49.

Williams, R., Alexander, D. A. Bolsover, D. and Bakke, F. K. (2008) Children, resilience and disasters: recent evidence that should influence a model of psychosocial care. *Current Opinion in Psychiatry*, 21: 338–44.

World Health Organization (2007) *IASC Guidelines on Mental Health and Psychosocial Support in Emergency Settings*. www.who.int.

Yule, W. (2006) Theory, training and timing: psychosocial interventions in complex emergencies. *International Review of Psychiatry*, 18: 259–64.

Part IV

Psychology and criminal behaviour

4.1 Residential burglary: methodological and theoretical underpinnings

Claire Nee

Definition

Contrary to common belief, a burglary is not necessarily for theft. It can apply to any crime, such as assault or sexual harassment, whether the intended criminal act is committed or not. Originally, under English common law, burglary was limited to entry into residences at night, but it has been expanded to all criminal entries into any building, or even into a vehicle. If there is intent to commit a crime, this is burglary. If there is no such intent, the breaking and entering alone is probably at least illegal trespass, which is a misdemeanour.

Of the property crimes which make up a notable proportion of recorded offending, residential burglary has been researched the most and represents the single most-developed type of offender-based research. Over the last thirty years a small but notable strand of research on residential burglary has grown, substantially improving our understanding of who, why and how people illegally enter other people's properties. In doing so this work has created numerous important spin-offs in thinking about other types of crime and in terms of research methods, theoretical development and, importantly, crime prevention.

Historical and theoretical development

Research on specific types of offenders began to emerge in the 1970s in the USA and the early 1980s in the UK. It was driven by a desire to move away from more generic, dispositional theories of crime and a new interest in the role of environment, opportunity and choice in the decision to offend. The idea grew that a 'one size fits all' approach to understanding the development of criminality may be substantially enhanced by a more focused understanding of the motivations, behaviours and decision making behind particular crimes. The decisions and opportunities experienced by a serial predatory sex offender, for instance, may be considerably different to those of a teenage shoplifter, and it was clear that looking at different types of crimes would have substantial pay-offs in terms of crime prevention and our general understanding of crime.

Studies of convicted burglars

In the burglary field, interview studies with convicted burglars in the USA began to emerge looking at the criminal career and lifestyle of the burglar, including approaches to undertaking particular burglaries (Scarr 1973; Shover 1973; Reppetto 1974; Waller and Okihiro 1978). Maguire and Bennett (1982) in the UK looked at burglary from the perspective of the burglar, the victim and the recorded offence details. Given the growing interest in the influence of the environment on criminal decision making, these studies began to provide clues as to aspects of the scene of the crime which were important to the offender and might therefore be changed in order to prevent crime. Further, even at this exploratory stage of research, burglars were emerging as systematic decision makers in their selection of properties, not supporting the indiscriminate and opportunistic approach to target selection that had been assumed by police and policy makers. At the other end of the spectrum, neither were burglaries highly planned and organized, with perpetrators usually getting caught away from the scene of their crime due to chaotic lifestyles.

For the first time focusing directly on the scene of the crime, Bennett and Wright (1984) conducted an interview study of over 300 convicted burglars, which also involved experiments utilizing videos and photographs of a variety of properties. Their findings revealed three main things:

- the decision to offend was sequential, with the first decision usually away from the scene of the crime based on an imminent need for money, followed by a search of a vulnerable area until a suitable property was found;
- burglars were interested in cues signifying occupancy, surveillability, accessibility and security at the scene of the potential crime;
- burglars were again showing a systematic and rational approach to target selection and of the three types found (planners, searchers and opportunists) the vast majority were 'searchers'.

These findings strongly contributed to the developing theoretical perspective emerging at the time – that of Rational Choice Theory – of which the best example is Cornish and Clarke's (1986) *The Reasoning Criminal.* The basic tenets of this approach were firstly to suggest that the decision to offend may not necessarily be driven by an inexorable urge to commit crime, but may be governed by the same degree of bounded rationality that drives all decisions in everyday life, i.e. that there may be an element of choice based on previous experience. Secondly, decisions may be influenced by the vulnerability of the environment or otherwise and the degree of opportunity for criminal activity. It also assumed a broader range of offender, in which the majority of individuals would consider breaking the law if the risks are low and rewards high. Finally, rational choice theory encouraged offence-specific work such as that on burglary, suggesting that very different crime prevention lessons were to be learned by researching different types of crimes. Cornish and Clarke did not set out to explain all of criminal behaviour by their rational choice perspective, but merely saw it as a useful adjunct to the multifactorial theories of criminality which aim to describe the distal influences on such behaviour. Rational choice theory aims to explain some of the more proximal influences of the environment on cognition and as a result facilitated much useful research.

Very much in line with this theoretical perspective was Nee and Taylor's work in the late 1980s (Nee and Taylor 1988; Taylor and Nee 1988), with the final piece of the series being published later (Nee and Taylor 2000). Working in the Republic of Ireland, they sought to replicate some of the work that had been undertaken in Britain and to explore further the use of cues in decision making about properties in a more empirical way. They were also the first to involve a control group of householders, to test the burglar's supposed expertise. The first piece of research involved a survey with convicted burglars, which supported British findings in terms of lifestyle, level of skill, goods taken and cues used. The majority were 'searchers' (Bennett and Wright 1984), took middle-range goods that could be easily exchanged for money (Maguire and Bennett 1982) and used environmental cues, which Nee and Taylor identified as layout, wealth, occupancy and security cues (Taylor and Nee 1988).

Nee and Taylor then went on to simulate residential environments with groups of incarcerated burglars, using maps and slides to provide a more realistic, free-responding environment in which to gather data. They found that no type of cue was salient in decision making and that different types of cue gained in importance depending on the combination of cues available on any one property. Target selection was highly habit-driven, based on prior successful learning, and took place, as Bennett and Wright (1984) had suggested, mostly at the scene of the crime based on whatever constellation of cues and contingencies presented themselves at that particular crime scene.

The study highlighted the fact that cues change on a daily if not hourly basis, and the difficulty for crime prevention is that the law-abiding member of the public is not good at second guessing the practised decision making of the burglar. One of the most striking findings emerging from these two experiments was the notable expertise shown by burglars in relation to householders. On the one hand, when asked to put themselves in the place of the burglar searching for a target, householders were markedly haphazard and indiscriminate in relation to target selection, time taken and routes taken (Nee and Taylor 2000). On the other hand, the burglar emerged not as an opportunistic, indiscriminate, somewhat out-of-control individual, but as a systematic, expert decision maker, using the bounded rationality that Cornish and Clarke (1986) had suggested, at least at the scene of the crime.

Other work which strongly supported the idea of expertise in burglars was that of Logie, Wright and Decker (1992), which demonstrated a hierarchy of expertise in recognizing burglary cues, with young burglars as most proficient, followed by offenders with no experience of burglary, then police officers and finally householders being least proficient.

Ethnographic work

The vast majority of research on burglars up to this point had been carried out on convicted burglars in prisons. Two key pieces of research emerged in the 1990s using markedly innovative methodologies – interviewing active burglars at the scene of recent crimes (Cromwell, Olson and Avery 1991; Wright and Decker 1994). Carried out in St Louis, Missouri, and Texas respectively, these studies served to both extend our knowledge of what burglars do at the scene of the crime and support many of the prison-based findings unearthed in previous work, despite the massive cultural difference in their participants.

Cromwell et al.'s (1991) study served to educate us about drug use and decision making at the scene of the crime, and both studies supported the notion of the sequential decision chain, making final decisions based on predictable (for the burglar) combinations of cues at the scene of the crime. Like all the work before them, these burglars were looking for signs of relative wealth in their targets, easy access, preferably at the sides and back of the property, as well as good cover at the front. Security measures, unfortunately (and still to this day) were not an issue as these were either installed and unused or easily overcome (Wright and Decker 1994).

The most ground-breaking part of Wright and Decker's work was the fact that, for the first time, burglars were asked about their decision making and behaviour once *inside* the property. Interestingly, and perhaps not surprisingly, burglars described a rational, habit-driven process (which Wright and Decker (1994) called 'cognitive scripts') similar to the one they had used previously to choose the burglary targets they had now entered, in order to navigate their way around the property with minimum risk and maximum gain. Very fixed patterns were described, in which the majority went straight to the main bedroom, collecting cash, guns and drugs, and exiting within twenty minutes, with a minority stealing items from other bedrooms if they had the time. Burglars reported using these strategies to reduce anxiety and make the burglary as fast as possible with maximum gain (most were stealing from their drug dealers and were likely to be murdered if caught by the householder). The practised and methodical nature of the search inside the property described by these burglars was a compelling notion for the research community and was followed up in more recent work in the UK, as described below.

Methodological innovations

As well as the wealth of knowledge this line of research has afforded about the burglar's decision chain, the importance of cues at the scene of the crime and how to prevent burglary, it has also made a significant contribution to the development of research methodology for offence-specific work. In many ways the refining of research methods over the years in burglary studies resembles the recommended framework described by Glaser and Strauss (1967), known as 'grounded theory', which ensures that the enquiry begins and remains as relevant, valid and reliable as possible. Instead of brainstorming research ideas without any evidence base, researchers are encouraged to place the expert agent in whatever research domain is at the centre of the work, in the present case burglars. It is they who have the knowledge research investigators want and they who should, from the very start, generate the relevant research ideas and hypotheses which can be tested. The early American, British and Irish exploratory interviews with burglars could be seen as the primary stage in grounded theory in which burglars themselves define the terms of reference and the hypotheses, in this case about burglary lifestyle and decision making at the scene of the crime. Even within these early studies a progression can be seen from the more open-ended American interviews at the start to more structured interviews, informed by the previous findings in the later Irish work.

The next stage is to refine the methodology in line with research findings and new ideas that have been uncovered, always returning to the offender to verify and extend the line of enquiry. The experimental, empirical studies of Bennett and Wright (1984), Rengert and Wasilchick (1986) and Nee and Taylor (1988, 2000) are good examples of this next stage. In a further stage of refinement, the ethnographic work undertaken by Cromwell *et al.* (1991) and Wright and Decker (1994) in the United States investigated burglars' target selection and decision making in the most ecologically valid environment possible, the scene of a recent crime, verifying previous work and extending our knowledge further, particularly in relation to strategies inside the property. An added bonus of carrying out this courageous work was that it confirmed the validity of other types of research method (interviews and experiments) that had been carried out previously. With each refinement of research method we get closer to what Glaser and Strauss (1967) called 'theoretical elaboration' or the reality of the burglars' cognitions and behaviour.

Conclusion

Work on burglary continues to emerge, usually with a particular emphasis on situational crime prevention (e.g. Bernasco and Luykx 2003; Palmer, Holmes and Hollin 2002). In a truly 'grounded' sense, though, the American ethnographic work has sparked recent research more focused on the cognitions of burglars and the expertise they seem to display (Nee and Meenaghan 2006). This interview study focused on burglars' strategies inside the property for the first time in the UK, but revealed much about the cognitive mechanisms used by burglars in order to efficiently burgle the premises with least risk. Like the processes used in selecting a property to burgle, once inside, participants described using very fixed patterns of behaviour, again based on prior learning with respect to what worked most efficiently in the past, the majority starting with the main bedroom and working their way through the house within twenty minutes. Moreover, their verbalizations signified the kind of approach characterized by experts in any other domain, namely instantaneous, unconscious recognition of cues; speedy but very systematic searches; and the ability to multitask while carrying out the 'expert' behaviour.

On the crime prevention front, current findings are more pessimistic: the majority of participants had entered their most recent property through an open or unlocked window or door. Householders are 'novices' when it comes to burglary and simply do not think in the same way as the perpetrator. They install security, but fail to use it comprehensively.

The discoveries and methodological innovations that have been made with regard to research on residential burglary should not be restricted to this one crime. Work on expertise has also taken place in the field of sex offenders (Ward and Hudson 2000) and street criminals (Topalli 2005) and is beginning to reveal important insights for use in primary, secondary and tertiary crime prevention. It is highly likely that other types of crime involve a form of expertise and this needs researching. Borrowing concepts and methods from mainstream cognitive psychology, as done in recent research, is likely to yield important insights in this type of forensic psychology and is highly recommended.

FURTHER READING

For a review of expertise and how it relates to residential burglary: Nee and Meenaghan (2006). For more information on different methodologies that can be used in offender-specific work: Nee (2004). For a general review of work done in the field of burglary: Nee and Taylor (2000). For a recent description of Rational Choice Theory: G. Newman, R. V. Clarke and S. Giora Shoham (eds.) (1997) *Rational Choice and Situational Crime Prevention: Theoretical Foundations* (Aldershot: Ashgate).

REFERENCES

Bennett, T. and Wright, R. (1984) *Burglars on Burglary*. Aldershot: Gower.

Bernasco, W. and Luykx, F. (2003) Effects of attractiveness, opportunity, and accessibility to burglars on residential burglary rates of urban neighbourhoods. *Criminology*, 41: 981–1001.

Cornish, D. B. and Clarke, R. V. G. (1986) Introduction. In D. B. Cornish and R. V. G. Clarke (eds.), *The Reasoning Criminal: Rational Choice Perspectives on Offending*, pp. 1–13, New York: Springer.

Cromwell, P., Olson, J. and Avary, D. (1991) *Breaking and Entering: An Ethnographic Analysis of Burglary*. Newbury Park, CA: Sage.

Glaser, B. and Strauss, A. L. (1967) *The Discovery of Grounded Theory*. Chicago: Aldine.

Logie, R. H., Wright, R. T. and Decker, S. (1992) Recognition memory performance and residential burglary. *Applied Cognitive Psychology*, 6: 109–23.

Maguire, E. M. W. and Bennett, T. (1982) *Burglary in a Dwelling: The Offence, the Offender and the Victim*. London: Heinemann Educational Books.

Nee, C. (2004) The offender's perspective on crime: methods and principles in data collection. In A. Needs and G. Towl (eds.), *Applying Psychology to Forensic Practice*, pp. 3–17. Oxford: BPS/Blackwell.

Nee, C. and Meenaghan, A. (2006) Expert decision-making in burglars. *British Journal Of Criminology*, 46: 935–49.

Nee, C. and Taylor, M. (1988) *Residential Burglary in the Republic of Ireland*. In M. Tomlinson, T. Varley and C. McCullagh (eds.), *Whose Law and Order?*, pp. 82–103. Galway: The Sociological Association of Ireland.

(2000) Examining burglars' target selection: interview, experiment, or ethnomethodology? *Psychology, Crime and Law*, 6: 45–59.

Palmer, E. J., Holmes, A. and Hollin, C. R. (2002) Investigating burglars' decisions: factors influencing target choice, method of entry, reasons for offending, repeat victimisation of a property and victim awareness. *Security Journal*, 15: 7–18.

Rengert, G. and Wasilchick, J. (1986). *Suburban Burglary: A Time and a Place for Everything*. Chicago: Springfield.

Repetto, T. A. (1974) *Residential Crime*. Cambridge, MA: Ballinger.

Scarr, H. A. (1973) *Patterns of Burglary*. Washington, DC: Government Printing Office.

Shover, N. (1973) The social organisation of burglary. *Social Problems*, 20: 499–514.

Taylor, M. and Nee, C. (1988) The role of cues in simulated residential burglary. *British Journal of Criminology*, 28: 105–16.

Topalli, V. (2005) Criminal expertise and offender decision-making: an experimental analysis of how offenders and non-offenders differentially perceive social stimuli. *British Journal of Criminology*, 45: 269–95.

Waller, I. and Okihiro, N. (1978) *Burglary: The Victim and the Public*. Toronto: University of Toronto Press.

Ward, T. and Hudson, S. M. (2000) Sexual offenders' implicit planning: a conceptual model. *Sexual Abuse: A Journal of Research and Treatment*, 12: 189–202.

Wright, R. T. and Decker, S. (1994) *Burglars on the Job: Streetlife and Residential Break-Ins*. Boston, MA: Northeastern University Press.

David P. Farrington

Definition

A criminal career is basically a sequence of offences committed at different ages (Blumstein *et al.* 1986). It has a beginning (onset), an end (desistance) and a career length in between (duration). Only a certain proportion of each birth cohort (prevalence) commits offences and has a criminal career, and a small fraction of offenders (the chronics) commit a large fraction of all offences. During their careers, offenders commit crimes at a certain rate (frequency) while they are at risk of offending in the community (e.g. not incarcerated, abroad or incapacitated by illness). For offenders who commit several offences, it is possible to investigate to what extent they specialize in certain types of crimes. It is also important to investigate to what extent crimes are committed alone or with others.

Offending is typically measured using either official records or self-reports. The predictive and concurrent validity of self-reported delinquency in comparison with official delinquency is high (Jolliffe *et al.* 2003). Most is known about crimes committed by lower-class males living in urban areas. In order to study the development of offending and criminal careers, longitudinal (follow-up) research is needed in which persons are interviewed repeatedly from childhood to adulthood. For example, in the Cambridge Study in Delinquent Development (Farrington *et al.* 2006), about 400 south London males were followed up from age 8 to age 48. Most knowledge about criminal careers is based on arrests or convictions. This is because studies of the development of criminal careers requires exact information about the timing of offences, which is available in official records but not usually in self-reports.

Prevalence

The cumulative prevalence of arrests and convictions of males is surprisingly high. In the Cambridge Study, 41% of London males were convicted for criminal offences up to age 50, when these were restricted to offences normally recorded in the Criminal Record Office. Similarly, a longitudinal follow-up of a 1953 English birth cohort in official records by the Home Office found that 33% of males and 9% of females were convicted of 'standard list' offences up to age 45 (Prime *et al.* 2001).

Offending typically increases to a peak in the teenage years and then decreases (Farrington 1986). In the Cambridge Study, the peak age for the prevalence of convictions was 17. The median age of conviction for most types of offences (burglary, robbery, theft of and from vehicles, shoplifting) was 17, while it was 20 for violence and 21 for fraud (Farrington 1992). In national English data analysed by Tarling (1993), the peak age varied from 14 for shoplifting to 20 for fraud/forgery and drug offences.

Individual offending frequency

Much research has been concerned to estimate the individual offending frequency (the rate at which offenders commit offences) during criminal careers. In calculating this, and other criminal career features such as onset, duration and desistance, a major problem is to estimate when careers really begin and when they really end. Tarling (1993) assumed that careers began at the age of criminal responsibility (10 in England and Wales) and ended on the date of the last conviction. On this assumption, male offenders in the 1953 birth cohort had a conviction rate of 0.5 per year (one every two years), while the corresponding figure for female offenders was 0.3 per year (one every 3.3 years). However, it is important to 'scale up' from convictions to the true number of offences committed. In the Cambridge Study, convicted offenders self-reported twenty-two times as many offences as they had convictions (Farrington *et al.* 2006).

If periods of acceleration or deceleration in the individual offending fre-quency can be identified, and if the predictors of acceleration or deceleration could be established, these may well have important implications for theory and policy. There are many life events or conditions that might lead to an increase in the individual offending frequency. For example, in the Cambridge Study, London males committed offences at a higher rate during periods of unemployment than during periods of employment (Farrington *et al.* 1986). This difference was restricted to offences involving material gain, suggesting that unemployment caused a lack of money, which in turn caused an increase in offending to obtain money.

Onset

Criminal career research on onset using official records generally shows a peak age of onset between 13 and 16. In the Cambridge Study, the peak age of onset was at 14, and 5% of the males were first convicted at that age (Farrington *et al.* 2006). The main childhood risk factors for the early onset of offending before age 20 are well known: individual factors (e.g. low intelligence, low school attainment, hyperactivity, impulsiveness, risk-taking, low empathy, antisocial and aggressive behaviour), family factors (e.g. poor parental supervision, harsh discipline, child physical abuse, inconsistent discipline, a cold parental attitude and child neglect, low involvement of parents with children, parental conflict, broken families, criminal parents, delinquent siblings), socioeconomic factors (e.g. low family income, large family size, poor housing), peer factors (e.g. delinquent peers, peer rejection, low popularity), school factors (e.g. attending a high-delinquency-rate school), and neighbourhood factors (e.g. living in a deprived, high-crime neighbourhood (Farrington 2009).

In the Cambridge Study, the average age of the first conviction was 19. Males first convicted at the earliest ages (10–13) tended to become the most persistent offenders, committing an average of nine offences leading to convictions in an average criminal career lasting thirteen years up to age 50 (Farrington *et al.* 2006). While it is clear that an early age of onset foreshadows a long criminal career, aggregate results may hide different types of offenders. For example, Moffitt (1993) distinguished between 'life-course-persistent' offenders, who had an early onset and a long criminal career, and 'adolescence-limited' offenders, who started later and had a short criminal career.

There have been few studies of the characteristics of late onset offenders. However, in the Cambridge Study, Zara and Farrington (2007) found that men who were first convicted at age 21 or later tended to be rated by parents as nervous-withdrawn at age 8–10, and by teachers as anxious at age 12–14, and had high neuroticism according to the Eysenck Personality Inventory at age 16. It seemed that nervousness and having few friends was a protective factor in the teenage years against offending (Farrington *et al.* 1988), but that these protective effects wore off in adulthood.

Desistance

The true age of desistance from offending can only be determined with certainty after offenders die. In the Cambridge Study up to age 50, the average age of the last conviction was 28. Since the average age of the first conviction was 19, the average length of the recorded criminal career was nine years, with an average of 4.5 convictions per offender during this time period (Farrington *et al.* 2006).

In the Philadelphia birth cohort study, Wolfgang *et al.* (1972) showed how the probability of reoffending (persistence as opposed to desistance) increased after each successive offence. This probability was .54 after the first offence, .65 after the second, .72 after the third, and it reached an asymptote of .80 after six or more arrests. Similarly, Home Office analyses of national English data for males born in 1953 showed that the probability of persistence increased from .51 after the first conviction to .87 after the eighth. The corresponding probabilities for females were from .26 to .84 (Prime *et al.* 2001).

Several projects have explicitly investigated why offenders desist. For example, in the Cambridge Study, getting married and moving out of London both fostered desistance (Farrington and West 1995; Osborn 1980). In their follow-up of 500 Boston delinquents, Sampson and Laub (1993) identified job stability and marital attachment in adulthood as crucial factors in desistance. Some policy implications of desistance research are that ex-offenders should be helped to settle down in stable marital relationships and in stable jobs, and helped to break away from their criminal associates.

Chronic offenders

In the Philadelphia birth cohort study, Wolfgang *et al.* (1972) showed that 6% of the males (18% of the offenders) accounted for half (52%) of all the juvenile arrests, and labelled these 6% the 'chronic offenders'. The chronics accounted for even higher percentages of serious offences: 69% of all aggravated assaults, 71% of homicides, 73% of forcible rapes and 82% of robberies. Other research-ers have largely replicated these results. For example, in the Cambridge Study, about 7% of the males (and 17% of the offenders) accounted for about half of all the convictions up to age 50 (Farrington *et al.* 2006). Home Office research suggests that about 100,000 'prolific' offenders in England and Wales commit about half of all offences each year (MacLeod 2003).

The key question is to what extent the chronic offenders can be predicted in advance, and whether they differ prospectively from the non-chronic offenders in their individual offending frequency. This was investigated in the Cambridge Study using a seven-point scale based on variables measured at age 8–10, reflecting child antisocial behaviour, family economic deprivation, convicted parents, low intelligence and poor parental child-rearing behaviour (Blumstein *et al.* 1985). Of 55 boys scoring 4 or more, 15 became chronic offenders up to age 25 (out of 23 chronics altogether), 22 others were convicted and only 18 were not convicted. Hence, it was concluded that most of the chronics could have been predicted in advance on the basis of information available at age 10.

Duration

There has been less research on the duration of criminal careers. National figures for English males born in 1953 and followed up to age 45 showed that the average duration of criminal careers was twelve years (excluding one-time offenders, who had zero duration). The corresponding average duration for females was seven years (Prime *et al.* 2001).

Another important concept is the residual length of a criminal career (in years) at any given point in time. Blumstein *et al.* (1982) estimated this in the United States and found that it increased to a peak of ten years between ages 30 and 40. In the Cambridge Study, the average residual career length was eight years and it decreased steadily with the age on offending (Kazemian and Farrington 2006). One area where knowledge about residual career length is important is in estimating the incapacitative effects of imprisonment. If the average time served exceeds the residual career length, people would be imprisoned beyond the point at which they would have stopped offending anyway. Hence, valuable prison space would be wasted by incarcerating those who would in any case have desisted from offending.

Continuity

Generally, there is significant continuity between offending in one age range and offending in another. In the Cambridge Study, nearly three-quarters (73%) of those convicted as juveniles at age 10–16 were reconvicted at age 17–24, in comparison with only 16% of those not convicted as juveniles. Nearly half

(45%) of those convicted as juveniles were reconvicted at age 25–32, in comparison with only 8% of those not convicted as juveniles (Farrington 1992). Furthermore, this continuity over time did not merely reflect continuity in police reaction to crime. For ten specified offences, the significant continuity between offending in one age range and offending in a later age range held for self-reports as well as official convictions (Farrington 1989).

Specialization

In the Cambridge Study, offenders were predominantly versatile rather than specialized. About one-third of the convicted males up to age 32 (N = 50) were convicted of violence (assault, robbery or threatening behaviour). They committed a total of 85 violent offences (an average of 1.7 each), but they also committed 263 non-violent offences (an average of 5.3 each). Only seven of the fifty violent offenders had no convictions for non-violent offences. A model was tested that assumed that violent offences occurred at random in criminal careers. Since the data fitted this model, it was concluded that there was little indication that offenders specialized in violence (Farrington 1991). Furthermore, violent offenders and non-violent but persistent offenders were similar in childhood, adolescent and adult features. Hence, violent offenders are difficult to distinguish from frequent offenders.

Co-offending

In the Cambridge Study, about half of all offences were committed with (usually one or two) others, and the prevalence of co-offending was greatest for burglary and robbery (Reiss and Farrington 1991). Co-offending decreased steadily with age. This was not because lone offenders persisted while co-offenders dropped out, but because the males changed from co-offending in their teenage years to lone offending in their twenties. Generally, co-offenders were similar in age, sex and race to the males themselves, and they lived close to the males' homes and to the locations of offences. About one-third of the most persistent offenders continually committed crimes with less experienced or younger co-offenders, and hence appeared to be repeatedly recruiting others into a life of crime.

It is essential to measure co-offending in linking up offences and offenders. For example, if there are 1,000,000 burglaries in a year, each committed by two offenders on average, these could in principle lead to 2,000,000 convictions. If 20,000 persons are in fact convicted for burglary in a year, the probability of an offender getting convicted is 1 in 100 not 2 in 100. It is also essential to measure co-offending in estimating the incapacitative effects of imprisonment, since imprisoning one member of a co-offending group will not necessarily prevent the offences being committed.

Implications for practice

Criminal career research has many policy implications (Farrington and Welsh, 2007; Piquero, Farrington and Blumstein 2007). First, offending can be prevented by targeting key risk factors. Parent training and general parent education can improve parenting skills, cognitive-behavioural skills training can reduce impulsiveness and increase empathy, and preschool intellectual enrichment programmes can improve school success. Second, it is important to identify chronic offenders at an early stage and devise special programmes for them. Third, it is important to take account of residual career length in setting the length of prison sentences, because it is futile to incarcerate people after they would have stopped offending anyway. Fourth, it is important to take account of co-offending in assessing the incapacitative effects of imprisonment. Fifth, the versatility of offenders means that it does not make much sense to have specific programmes for violent offenders. Since criminal career research shows that violent offenders are essentially frequent offenders, programmes to prevent violent offending should target frequent or chronic offenders. Sixth, desistance can be fostered by programmes that help offenders to settle down with a steady job and a steady partner.

REFERENCES

Blumstein, A., Cohen, J. and Hsieh, P. (1982) *The Duration of Adult Criminal Careers.* Washington, DC: National Institute of Justice.

Blumstein, A., Cohen, J., Roth, J. A. and Visher, C. A. (1986) *Criminal Careers and 'Career Criminals'* (2 vols.). Washington, DC: National Academy Press.

Blumstein, A., Farrington, D. P. and Moitra, S. (1985) Delinquency careers: innocents, desisters and persisters. In M. Tonry and N. Morris (eds.), *Crime and Justice*, vol. 6, pp. 187–219. Chicago: University of Chicago Press.

Farrington, D. P. (1986) Age and crime. In M. Tonry and N. Morris (eds.), *Crime and Justice*, vol. 7, pp. 189–250. Chicago: University of Chicago Press.

(1989) Self-reported and official offending from adolescence to adulthood. In M. W. Klein (ed.), *Cross-National Research in Self-Reported Crime and Delinquency*, pp. 399–423. Dordrecht: Kluwer.

(1991) Childhood aggression and adult violence: early precursors and later life outcomes. In D. J. Pepler and K. H. Rubin (eds.), *The Development and Treatment of Childhood Aggression*, pp. 5–29. Hillsdale, NJ: Erlbaum.

(1992) Criminal career research in the United Kingdom. *British Journal of Criminology*, 32: 521–36.

(2009) Psychosocial causes of offending. In M. G. Gelder, J. J. Lopez-Ibor, N. C. Andreasen and J. Geddes (eds.), *New Oxford Textbook of Psychiatry*, 2nd edn, vol. 2, pp. 1908–16. Oxford: Oxford University Press.

Farrington, D. P., Coid, J. W., Harnett, L., Jolliffe, D., Soteriou, N., Turner, R. and West, D. J. (2006) *Criminal Careers up to Age 50 and Life Success up to Age 48: New Findings from the Cambridge Study in Delinquent Development*. London: Home Office (Research Study no. 299).

Farrington, D. P., Gallagher, B., Morley, L., St Ledger, R. J. and West, D. J. (1986) Unemployment, school leaving and crime. *British Journal of Criminology*, 26: 335–56.

(1988) Are there any successful men from criminogenic backgrounds? *Psychiatry*, 51: 116–30.

Farrington D. P. and Welsh, B. C. (2007) *Saving Children from a Life of Crime: Early Risk Factors and Effective Interventions*. Oxford: Oxford University Press.

Farrington, D. P. and West, D. J. (1995) Effects of marriage, separation and children on offending by adult males. In J. Hagan (ed.), *Current Perspectives on Aging and the Life Cycle*, vol. 4: *Delinquency and Disrepute in the Life Course*, pp. 249–81. Greenwich, CT: JAI Press.

Jolliffe, D., Farrington, D. P., Hawkins, J. D., Catalano, R. F., Hill, K. G. and Kosterman, R. (2003) Predictive, concurrent, prospective and retrospective validity of self-reported delinquency. *Criminal Behaviour and Mental Health*, 13: 179–97.

Kazemian, L. and Farrington, D. P. (2006) Exploring residual career length and residual number of offences for two generations of repeat offenders. *Journal of Research in Crime and Delinquency*, 43: 89–113.

MacLeod, J. (2003) A theory and model of the conviction process. In R. Morris, P. Ormerod, C. Mounfield, J. MacLeod, P. Grove, K. Hansen *et al.*, *Modelling Crime and Offending: Recent Developments in England and Wales* (Occasional Paper no. 80), pp. 2–25. London: Home Office.

Moffitt, T. E. (1993) Adolescence-limited and life-course-persistent antisocial behaviour: a developmental taxonomy. *Psychological Review*, 100: 674–701.

Osborn, S. G. (1980) Moving home, leaving London and delinquent trends. *British Journal of Criminology*, 20: 54–61.

Piquero, A. R., Farrington, D. P. and Blumstein, A. (2007) *Key Issues in Criminal Career Research: New Analyses of the Cambridge Study in Delinquent Development*. Cambridge: Cambridge University Press.

Prime, J., White, S., Liriano, S. and Patel, K. (2001) *Criminal Careers of Those Born Between 1953 and 1978* (Statistical Bulletin 4/01). London: Home Office.

Reiss, A. J. and Farrington, D. P. (1991) Advancing knowledge about co-offending: results from a prospective longitudinal survey of London males. *Journal of Criminal Law and Criminology*, 82: 360–95.

Sampson, R. J. and Laub, J. H. (1993) *Crime in the Making: Pathways and Turning Points through Life*. Cambridge, MA: Harvard University Press.

Tarling, R. (1993) *Analysing Offending: Data, Models and Interpretations*. London: HMSO.

Wolfgang, M. E., Figlio, R. M. and Sellin, T. (1972) *Delinquency in a Birth Cohort*. Chicago: University of Chicago Press.

Zara, G. and Farrington, D. P. (2007) Early predictors of late onset offenders. *International Annals of Criminology*, 45: 37–56.

4.3 Interpersonal deception detection

Lynsey Gozna and Julian Boon

There is a wide difference between speaking to deceive, and being silent to be impenetrable.

Voltaire

See also chapter 2.18 Polygraphy, chapter 2.23 Statement validity analysis, chapter 6.9 Malingering: models and methods.

Introduction

The detection of deception at an interpersonal level is a core consideration and skill for professionals working in the field of forensic psychology. The complexities of the interviewees in diverse groups require a thorough understanding of the challenges faced when determining the credibility of information that they disclose. In order to consider deception as a mechanism to assist in interpersonal interactions in the forensic domain, a definition proposed by Vrij (2000) has been presented as being: 'a successful or unsuccessful deliberate attempt, without forewarning, to create in another a belief which the communicator considers to be untrue' (p. 6). The benefit of this description is that it not only defines the deceptive act, but also emphasizes the potential for failure on behalf of the deceiver. It is realistic to expect that professionals will be the target of a number of deceptive acts when interacting with complex client groups. Accordingly, the more that professionals can understand of the prevalence and range of ways in which deceit can occur, the better they will be able to identify it and respond. From the outset it is important to acknowledge that there are different motivations for deception and that these can be variable in terms of both personal and contextually dependent factors.

Challenges

The outcome of a successful deception can unfortunately impact much more widely than the interaction between professional and suspect/offender in that the interview is but one aspect and the judicial consequences quite another. Therefore there is more at stake for professionals being unable to respond to deceit than perhaps there is for the deceiver. Whether interviewing suspects of crime, judging the credibility of defendants in court, or assessing offenders post-conviction, the task is manifestly difficult for professionals in any field. This challenge requires the acknowledgement of the influences within the dyadic interaction: i.e. the deceiver and the target(s). Furthermore, it is also crucial to consider internal personal influences, individuals on the periphery of the interaction and the context in which deception occurs.

In order to respond to this challenge, research has attempted to gauge the ways in which people lie in everyday life (DePaulo *et al.* 2003; Kashy and DePaulo 1996) and in forensic settings (Granhag *et al.* 2004; Hartwig *et al.* 2004) and notably with psychopathic prison populations (Klaver, Lee and Hart 2007; Lee, Klaver and Hart 2008; Porter and Woodworth 2007; Raskin and Hare 1978). In an area that has been largely dominated by empirically based laboratory research, understanding the intricacies of deceptive behaviour in forensic settings remains largely in its infancy – particularly in terms of the interpersonal interactions involved. A relatively sound understanding exists of the clinical factors in post-conviction settings that impede and challenge the understanding of offending behaviour. Research attention has focused, for example, on personality disorder, cognitive distortions and offence-supportive schemas; in the pre-conviction environment of the police interview, however, while these factors are present, they have not been readily identifiable.

As a result of an extensive review of the literature on detecting deception, Vrij (2004) has developed guidelines to assist in this process. The fifteen guidelines presented therein are stated with a caveat concerning the limitations of generalizing to real-life interactions. They emphasize a number of factors, including the need for no particular behavioural cue to identify deception; liars needing to experience emotions, cognitive load or control their behaviour in order to exhibit cues to deceit; that some cues will be more prevalent than others; that increased numbers of cues increase the likelihood of deceit; that attention should be given to mismatches in speech and

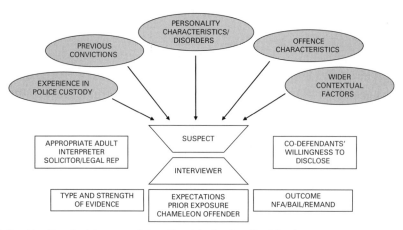

Figure 4.3.1 Considerations for interpersonal deception detection in police interviews

behaviour; that suspected liars should be encouraged to talk and repeat what they say; that lie detectors should remain suspicious; and that information provided by a suspected liar should be checked. The factors have provided a good overview of the outcome of the previous research, albeit dominated by a laboratory focus.

In the police interview setting, suspects might be identified as engaging in deception from the account they provide of the offence. This information, while potentially of operational utility, may nevertheless be irrelevant to the police investigation and the referral to the prosecuting authority for potential dispersal options. The validity of guidelines relating to such interview-derivative evidence varies and is dependent on the context of the interaction – hence the requirement to consider a holistic view of the interaction between practitioner and interviewee.

In order to illustrate the complexity of this challenge, the specific interactions occurring in police interviews will be discussed. Figure 4.3.1 presents an illustration of the specific considerations within the police interview for the detection of deceit. Here the emphasis is on the dominant dyadic interaction between the police interviewer(s) and suspect and the diversity of factors that should be considered. It is important to acknowledge here that interpersonal deception detection is potentially impeded by the internal and external influences on all parties in the interview room.

When focusing on the target of deceit, some professionals will be more vulnerable to being duped than others, that is, less able to identify when they are the subject of overt or subtle manipulation. O'Sullivan and Ekman (2004) identified what they term 'wizards' – professionals who are seen as being particularly adept at detecting deception. In their extensive research to ascertain the qualities of those who have particular skill in the detection of deceit, three main laboratory-based tasks have been explored: emotion, opinion and crime-based tasks that simulate real-life situations. The research suggested that professionals identified as especially skilled in these tasks were: (i) superior interviewers from law enforcement agencies (self-motivated); (ii) federal judges; and (iii) forensic psychologists (O'Sullivan and Ekman 2004). Interesting though these findings were, it could be argued that there may be benefit in developing more ecologically valid situations to further test their utility.

However, with awareness of the main issues, most professionals have the potential to continually learn and develop their competence and ability in honing their skills in relation to deception. Perhaps one of the most pertinent considerations for individuals who engage with complex forensic groups is the concept of the chameleon offender.

The chameleon offender

The concept of the 'chameleon offender' (Gozna and Boon 2007) has been developed in order to propose a range of considerations which create and exacerbate an already challenging interaction – be it relating to pre- or post-conviction interactions. It is acknowledged that professionals are presented with a range of interpersonally challenging and somewhat chaotic individuals. The critical aspect of interacting with individuals who can present in a 'chameleon' way is to create a method of interaction which incorporates a holistic, yet individualized, view of offenders. When attempting to detect deception, this is a crucial consideration because it ultimately impacts on professional decision making and the associated outcomes. Gozna and Boon (2007) emphasize the importance of understanding a number of factors in the consideration of the person to be interviewed. The actions of each offence for which individuals are arrested are diverse regardless of the legal definition of the offence, that is, the components of the offence(s) vary. Therefore, when a suspect is interviewed, police officers should be cognizant of the idiosyncratic nature of offenders and their actions. Whilst it is possible for generic themes to occur within legally defined offences, such as domestic violence or arson, the myriad of factors (internal and external) that resulted in the crime and subsequent arrest and conviction will vary. As a consequence, this can create a situation in which a categorical approach will increase practitioners' vulnerability to the chameleon.

Hence it is paramount that practitioners consider that each suspect/offender has the potential to: (i) be different from another; (ii) different at different times; (iii) behave differently with different professionals; (iv) behave differently across different offences committed; (v) behave differently across different interviews; and (vi) be different during each interview interaction. These considerations should be visualized as co-occurring as a composite 'chameleon' presentation and require further explanation in order that the sheer challenge of such interactions are recognized and understood.

Primarily, suspects will *be different from one another* across a multitude of demographics, life experiences, beliefs and attitudes, behaviours and views towards offending. Therefore different approaches are required for interviews and interactions in police custody settings. It is vital to acknowledge just how diverse suspects who present in an interview can be and how this can impact on the challenges for police interviewers: for example, a pre-operative transgender prostitute arrested for burglary and possession of cocaine; a female with convictions for kidnap and GBH; a male with convictions for sexual offences against boys aged 9–12 and a collection of 956,721 pornographic electronic images of children (Level 3–5); a male Polish suspect (requiring an interpreter) arrested for a series of sexual offences against prostitutes; and a female with a diagnosis of Borderline Personality Disorder, depression and PTSD whose convictions include arson, domestic violence and attempted murder. These cases highlight the complex realities with which police officers are faced. However, it is important that apparent similarities and subtle differences are considered owing to the radical implications for tailoring a bespoke approach. For example, in the case of an individual suspected of viewing child pornography, the nature and severity of the images of the children will correspondingly determine the approach that is taken. Again, the nature of deceit and the way it occurs will be as diverse as the suspect being interviewed.

Suspects will be *different at different times*, which refers to current life experiences, fluctuations in mood and the interaction with personality (characteristics/disorders). The motivation to engage with practitioners can be influenced by changes in affect and cognitions which are internal (e.g. hormones, bipolar disorder, drug dependency) or external in causation (e.g. infidelity of a partner, arguments with other professionals). Therefore the desire to be obstructive or ambivalent or to conform can be a product of diverse reasons over time – and the better these are identified and responded to, the more effective the practitioner interaction will be.

Suspects will *behave differently with different professionals* within and across disciplines (e.g. uniform/plain clothes). Depending on the environment in which the interaction is occurring, suspects will probably identify whom they should display pseudo-compliance to, and who warrants less respect. Conversely, the range of behaviours towards professional groups could be the result of such extra-interview factors as the suspect's need to portray a particular image, or mischief making, or more malign motivations of playing people off against each other. Therefore certain police officers may well be identified, either on the basis of previous reputation or the way they present, as being targets which are readily amenable to manipulation and exploitation. Moreover, particular officers might be assigned increased rapport, engendering heightened kudos, which results in suspects partitioning their disclosures, e.g. 'I only want to be interviewed by DS Barron, he's the one who dealt with me last time I was arrested.' It is therefore highly desirable for the lines of communication to remain open to keep abreast of the chameleon's unfolding manifestations, hence it is necessary for pertinent information to be identified, recorded and continually updated to all professionals who are dealing with a particular suspect.

Suspects will *behave differently across different offences committed*. Complex suspects are likely to have a number of previous convictions, engaging in offences that demonstrate similar acts and others where incredible versatility is exhibited. It is acknowledged that across offences dealt with in major crime, such as rape, arson or homicide, 'signatures' can occur. However, each offence will have potentially different antecedents, behaviours and consequences. Whilst there might be similar motivations for any given offence, the interactions during and responses to victims can be diverse. This has implications for the way in which the suspect will want to present the events within the police interview and the level of deceit they engage in.

Suspects will *behave differently across different interviews* and will *be different during each interview interaction*. These are distinct yet overlapping considerations for the interview and are therefore considered together here. Hence, whether an individual is to be interviewed extensively throughout a single day or in shorter sessions over the course of several days, it is vital to understand the potential for behaviour change within and across interactions over time. For example, it is likely that there will be differences between penetrative and non-penetrative questioning, direct and offence-focused questioning, the introduction of incontrovertible evidence and the challenge of cognitive distortions. Furthermore, fatigue can additionally lead variously to non-compliance and the move towards exercising the right to silence, or if polarized, a suspect admitting to anything in order to be released from the situation. The gradual introduction of 'no comment' responses can also be indicative of reactions to evidence as it is weighed up by the suspect. Overall there is the need to identify what the difference in mood or behaviour is and why this has occurred, whether there is a need to impression manage, a feeling of over-scrutiny or feeling threatened interpersonally or as a result of the nature of the questioning.

Ultimately the picture painted of the 'chameleon' is one of an individual who can be interpersonally challenging to interview despite any knowledge of the underlying causes of the behaviour. It is therefore paramount to focus on the constellation of behavioural characteristics, personality traits and associated decision-making inclinations in order to fully understand the likelihood of deceptive activity within the police interview.

An additional complication to the identification of deception occurs with the presence and influence of third parties on interpersonal interactions in the police interview: solicitors, appropriate adults, and interpreters. The impact of a solicitor can impede the flow of communication and also the ability to identify inconsistencies in the account being provided by a suspect. Particularly, solicitor interruptions can distract the focus of the questioning and act as a deflection of the true response that the suspect should be providing. Appropriate adults in police interviews are perhaps the least impediment to the process due to their role in assisting the 'vulnerable' suspects in understanding the procedures. Finally, the use of interpreters, which is increasing in police interviews, is an area that requires further focus for research in the future. Communicating with suspects through a third party can increase the challenge for deception detection and limits the ability of officers to identify any chameleon characteristics.

Conclusion

The identification of deception is a considerable challenge for professionals working in forensic settings. This chapter has attempted to outline the complexities of the task and to emphasize the need for a holistic approach. In the case of police suspects, it is argued that the assessment of individuals should begin at the time of arrest (or better still, beforehand, when, as suspects, they are targeted for arrest) and that assessment be ongoing and updated during the suspect's time in custody, during the police interview and any subsequent trial which may ensue. Consideration is required of the offence and the suspect and the likely motivation for engaging in deceit. The need to fully acknowledge and respond to this challenge cannot be emphasized enough.

REFERENCES

DePaulo, B. M., Lindsay, J. J., Malone, B. E., Muhlenbruck, L., Charlton, K. and Cooper, H. (2003) Cues to deception. *Psychological Bulletin*, 129: 74–118.

Gozna, L. F. and Boon, J. C. W. (2007) The chameleon offender: the synergising of psychology and psychiatry to meet the challenge. Paper presented at the Conference of Research in Forensic Psychiatry, 29–31 May.

Granhag, P. A., Andersson, L. O., Strömwall, L. A. and Hartwig, M. (2004) Imprisoned knowledge: criminals' beliefs about deception. *Legal and Criminological Psychology*, 9: 103–19.

Hartwig, M., Granhag, P. A., Strömwall, L. A. and Andersson, L. O. (2004) Suspicious minds: criminals' ability to detect deception. *Psychology, Crime and Law*, 10: 83–95.

Kashy, D. A. and DePaulo, B. M. (1996) Who lies? *Journal of Personality and Social Psychology*, 70: 1037–51.

Klaver, J., Lee, Z. and Hart, S. D. (2007) Psychopathy and nonverbal indicators of deception in offenders. *Law and Human Behavior*, 31: 337–51.

Lee, Z., Klaver, J. R. and Hart, S. (2008) Psychopathy and verbal indicators of deception in offenders. *Psychology, Crime and Law*, 14: 73–84.

O'Sullivan, M. and Ekman, P. (2004) The wizards of deception detection. In P. A. Granhag and L. A. Strömwall (eds.), *The Detection of Deception in Forensic Contexts*, pp. 269–86. Cambridge: Cambridge University Press.

Porter, S. and Woodworth, M. (2007) I'm sorry I did it … but he started it: a comparison of the official and self-reported homicide descriptions of psychopaths and non-psychopaths. *Law and Human Behavior*, 31: 91–107.

Raskin, D. C. and Hare, R. D. (1978) Psychopathy and detection of deception in a prison population. *Psychophysiology* 15: 126–36.

Vrij A. (2000) *Detecting Lies and Deceit: The Psychology of Lying and Implications for Professional Practice*. Chichester: Wiley.

(2004) Why professionals fail to catch liars and how they can improve. *Legal and Criminological Psychology*, 9: 159–81.

4.4 Domestic violence

Elizabeth Gilchrist

See also chapter 4.10 Sexual assault.

Definitions

The term domestic violence, despite its physical connotations and lack of gender specificity, has been routinely used to describe a pattern of abuse within adult intimate relationships, which is typically perpetrated by men against women, with at its core the maintenance of male power and control over women. The term 'intimate partner violence' is becoming more common in the UK as it is seen as clarifying the focus of the violence and distinguishing it from other forms of family violence such as child abuse or elder abuse. Domestic violence is seen as including more than merely physical abuse. The range has been described as being a 'constellation of abuse' incorporating 'a variety of additional intimidating, aggressive and controlling acts' (Dobash and Dobash 2004, p. 326) or being within the 'power and control wheel' developed by practitioners in Duluth, Minnesota, from victim/survivors' accounts and incorporating non-physical abuses such as psychological and emotional abuse and indirect forms of violence such as intimidation and threats against others to maintain control within a relationship (Pence and Paymar 1993). Often the abuse is seen as being purposeful, i.e. instrumental, and explanations which refer to out-of-control anger and expressive rage have generally been rejected as an explanation for most domestic violence (although the development of perpetrator typologies is challenging this). The abuse is expected to increase in severity and frequency over time with a potentially lethal outcome.

Gender symmetry

Current concerns about this approach which focus on the issue of gender symmetry are the failure to address other forms of family violence, for

Table 4.4.1 Difference between family and domestic violence

Family violence	Domestic violence
Gender neutral	Feminist
Dyadic explanations	Male to female
Conflict	Power and control
Stress	Not expressive, instrumental
Large-scale surveys	Supported by power structures
Psychology	Explanation at societal level
Explanation at level of individuals	

example, violence within same-sex relationships, and lack of explanation of common correlates of domestic violence. The issue of gender patterning has fuelled two separate approaches to researching and explaining domestic violence: the 'family violence' approach and the 'feminist approach'. These utilize very different theories of causation, based on empirical study derived from different sources (for example, general population telephone surveys vs qualitative interviews with small refuge samples) and ultimately suggest quite different approaches to tackling this phenomenon.

In brief, family violence theorists tend to claim gender symmetry in the perpetration of violence and focus on individual-level variables in the search for causation and change (Straus, Gelles and Steinmetz 1980; Dobash and Dobash 1992; Dobash *et al.* 1992). Feminist scholars tend to identify domestic violence as a male to female set of behaviours supported and facilitated by patriarchy in society, with control of women being at its core, and the focus for change at a societal level. Differences in focus are briefly summarized in table 4.4.1.

The debate as to gender symmetry in intimate partner abuse has been greatly informed by the work of Johnson (1995), who proposed that in fact there may be more than one type of intimate partner violence, one which is referred to as 'common couple violence'. Where there is gender symmetry, the violence appears to link to poor conflict resolution styles, and there is no escalation over time. The other, referred to as 'intimate terrorism', where the violence is predominantly perpetrated by men, is one behaviour within a range of abusive strategies, often increasing over time, and the abuse appears to link to ongoing dysfunctional beliefs about partners and relationships. Empirical studies have provided some support for this typology (Johnson 1999; Graham-Kevan and Archer 2003).

Methodological concerns

Methodological criticism levelled at feminist research has mostly been on
empirical grounds, as it is difficult to establish a link between societal ideology
and individual abusive or non-abusive behaviours (Sugarman and Frankel
1996). Family violence theorists have been criticized for using inappropriate
tools such as the Conflict Tactics Scale (CTS: Straus 1979), which, amongst
other problems, fails to look at injury, frequency and severity of assault and
motive for the abuse (Jacobson 1994). The feminist camp points to data from
other sources (e.g. emergency healthcare) which suggest that when men hit
women, and women hit men, women suffer more (Cascardi, Langhinrichsen
and Vivian 1992).

Key issues

In comparing domestic violence offenders to other types of violent offender,
both similar and different characteristics can be identified. Although domestic
violence crosses all social classes and groups, convicted perpetrators, in
common with other convicted groups, are likely to be unemployed, have
previous convictions for both violent and non-violent offences, and many
have witnessed domestic violence or experienced abuse within their family of
origin (Gilchrist *et al.* 2003).

In contrast to other offending groups, the level of alcohol dependence
appears higher within domestic violence perpetrators and the level of mental
health difficulties reported, including depression and anger, also seems higher.
The assaults tend to take place within the context of jealousy, separation and
childcare issues. The level of minimizing and victim blaming is higher than in
other types of offender, as are unstable attributions as to the cause of the
violence, for example blaming alcohol. The risk of collusion even by professionals is high (Gilchrist *et al.* 2003).

One final key issue to emerge from the research recently is that whilst there
are many similarities within those defined as domestic violence offenders, there
are also significant differences. It is now suggested that there may be at least
two types of domestic violence offender, whose offending follows slightly
different patterns, whose background characteristics differ, and for whom
the risk of further violence, the level at which this might be predicted and the
interventions required may differ. The differences lie in the focus of the

violence (general or only within a relationship context) and the extent to which the violence is linked to high-level emotional outbursts or to highly emotionally charged, but rather more purposive and instrumental goals. Gondolf (1988) identified three types of batterers – sociopathic, antisocial and typical. Saunders (1992) proposes three groups – family-only, emotionally volatile and generally violent. Hamberger and Hastings (1986) suggest three personality groupings – schizoidal/borderline, narcissistic/antisocial and passive/dependent/compulsive. Whilst Tweed and Dutton (1998) identified two – instrumental and impulsive. Holtzworth-Munroe and Stewart (1994) initially classified three but refined this to four groups on the basis of empirical data (Holtzworth-Munroe *et al.* 2000; Jacobson *et al.* 1994) – family only, low-level antisocial, generally violent, borderline/dysphoric; and Gilchrist *et al.* (2003), using UK data, identified a two-group typology primarily identifying an antisocial group and an emotionally volatile group. The majority of these typologies are based on aspects of personality or psychiatric diagnoses, but there are yet other typologies based on physiological difference, for example, Gottman *et al.* (1995), who suggested there may be two groups of perpetrator who vary in terms of heart-rate change, type 1 experiencing accelerated heart rate during violence and type 2 experiencing lowered heart rate during violence. Mitchell and Gilchrist (2006) suggested that two groups of perpetrator may differ in terms of the function of the violence; one group perhaps engaging in predatory attack and the other in affective defence, indicative of differences in underlying neural responses.

It is clear that there is no one accepted theoretical approach to domestic violence. Neither is there one dominant theory. Multifactor and multilevel theories are recognized as potentially providing the best approach, but as yet have not been comprehensively tested, nor even convincingly stated, and heterogeneity within this group has not been fully addressed.

Theoretical approaches

There are a number of theoretical approaches to intimate partner violence, and in seeking to explain this type of domestic violence; many of the dominant models reject any explanations at an individual level. For example, the feminist-informed sociocultural approach identifies domestic violence as being the product of a patriarchical society, proposing that society allows, and even creates, the situation of male use of violence to control women (Pence 1989; Yllo and Straus 1990). Alternative sociocultural approaches also view domestic violence as being linked to societal factors, for example, being the product of an aggressive society. It has been suggested that a particular culture can support the use of violence in general as a means of problem solving and create a 'culture of violence' where domestic violence as well as other forms of violence is able to flourish (Gelles and Straus 1979).

Further explanations focus at the interpersonal level, situating the problem within family interactions rather than focusing on the behaviour of any one individual, and identifying factors such as stress, which creates violence within the family (Lane and Russell 1989). This approach has been criticized as failing to recognize power imbalances within family interactions or acknowledge the gender bias in family violence, and even as holding victims' responsible for their abuse (Trute 1998). Despite these criticisms this approach still has some influence on 'mainstream provision' for perpetrators and victims, in both the USA and the UK.

Sociobiological theories have also been proposed, which focus on the contribution of social and biological factors to correlates of violence, for example, jealousy (Daly, Wilson and Weghorst 1982). At an individual level, psychiatric factors such as depression, alcoholism and antisocial personality disorder (Bland and Orn 1986) have been implicated in the causal path to domestic violence. Finally, specific theories which focus only on psychopathology have been suggested whereby individuals who perpetrate domestic violence are suggested to suffer from specific deficits, for example, self-esteem (Faulk 1974), jealousy (Sonkin, Martin and Walker 1985), dependency, attachment (Dutton and Browning 1988), impulse control, attitudinal variations, variations in cognitive style (Saunders *et al.* 1987) and potentially even specific personality profiles, such as the abusive personality (Dutton 1999).

One useful approach which integrates these different levels is the nested ecological approach (Dutton 1985). This proposes that a multifactor and multilevel explanation is required to explain a social phenomenon of this complexity. Within this model multiple levels are considered from the influence of broad societal structures (Macrosystem), the impact of subcultural values, e.g. influence of peers, sibling beliefs (Exosystem), the family system and the specific setting of the abuse (Microsystem) and the individual abilities and responses (Ontogenetic) must be considered. Whilst very appealing in its attempt to integrate approaches and move to a comprehensive theory, this approach has yet to be fully tested empirically and fails to be totally clear as to how these levels interact and mesh theoretically, such that the relative weighting of various factors would still be difficult to specify.

In terms of theoretical understanding as to the development of domestic violence, in line with many areas in forensic psychology, social learning theory explanations have been widely applied (Bandura 1979). Family of origin experiences, particularly witnessing or experiencing domestic violence, are proposed as influential variables in the development of abusive relationship behaviours (Ehrensaft *et al.* 2003). Mechanisms such as modelling are cited to explain the intergenerational transmission of violence, and it is suggested that the use of violence against one's partner is learned through interaction with, and modelling on, one's own family of origin, one's peers and wider society. This is reinforced through positive short-term gratification and (often) the lack of negative sanctions following the behaviour (Hamberger *et al.* 1996).

Attachment styles, again seen as deriving from early childhood experiences, are identified as being of potential use in explaining later problematic inter-action in intimate relationships. It is suggested that dysfunctional attachment schema, deriving from insecure attachment to the primary caregiver, are carried over into adulthood and then replicated in adult intimate relation-ships, resulting in conflict and abuse (Dutton 1999). Very recent work has focused on social cognition and skills deficits in perpetrators of domestic violence and suggests that poor social and conflict resolution skills, perhaps in conjunction with unhelpful interpretations of relationship interactions, contribute to abuse in intimate relationships (Eckhardt and Dye 2000; Jacobson *et al.* 1994)

Interventions and assessment

Interventions in domestic violence have been greatly informed by the 'Duluth' model of intervention (Pence and Paymar 1993), although wider cognitive-behavioural perspectives are also employed. There are debates about which intervention is most appropriate (Geffner and Rosenbaum 2001) and as to the efficacy of these programmes. Reviews have suggested that these programmes may have a small consistent effect (Babcock, Green and Robie 2004; Dobash *et al.* 1996; Gondolf 1997), however, there is little data to suggest that any one particular approach has greater impact,

In terms of assessment of domestic violence, there have been various tools developed to encourage reporting of abusive behaviours, for example, the Abusive Behaviour Inventory (Shepard and Campbell 1992), and various risk assessment tools have been developed based on assessments from both the victims' perspective, e.g. the dangerousness assessment (Campbell 1995), and from a victim-informed perpetrator perspective, e.g. the spousal assault risk assessment guide (SARA: Kropp *et al.* 1994). Whilst there is some empirical support for the utility of these tools in terms of predictions of general recidivism (Kropp and Hart 2000), the ability to predict lethal violence is limited and the applicability to the domestic violence population may be limited by lack of consideration of the identified perpetrator typologies. Recent empirical studies indicate that spousal homicide offenders do differ from non-lethal (Dobash *et al.* 2007) or non-domestic assailants (Belfrage and Rying 2004), identifying this as an area which must be addressed.

Conclusion

There is disagreement over the definition and appropriate approach to the explanation of domestic violence. These debates over gender symmetry can be addressed if there is recognition of two distinct groupings of abuser – the intimate terrorist and the common couple violent perpetrator – and there is empirical support for this split (Johnson 1995).

Whilst there have been attempts to explain domestic violence using single-factor theories at a variety of levels, current thinking across disciplines recognizes the need for multifactor integrated theories, and theories such as the 'nested ecological' approach are currently influential, at least in practice (Dutton 1985).

Further, heterogeneity is recognized within male perpetrators such that at least two if not three or more different types of perpetrator can be identified. These types are theorized to show different patterns of abuse, arising from different factors, perhaps the key distinction being the difference in pattern, motivation, escalation and potential risk seen in 'instrumental' or 'impulsive' offenders (Holtzworth-Munroe and Stuart 1994).

The assessment of domestic violence remains a developing field and heterogeneity within abusers has not been fully integrated into this area, but current indications are that this is necessary (Kropp and Hart 2000).

FURTHER READING

For a good overview of the different theories of domestic violence, see A. Cunningham, P. Jaffe, L. Baker, T. Dick, S. Malla, N. Mazaheri and S. Poisson (1998) *Theory-Derived Explanation of*

Male Violence against Female Partners: Literature Update and Related Implications for Treatment and Evaluation. (London: London Family Court Clinic). The work by Holtzworth *et al.* (various years, see below) has been very influential in identifying and researching key issues in typologies, as has the work by Dutton (see below). Gilchrist *et al.* (2003) provide a useful brief overview of characteristics of DV offenders in the UK and the work by Bowen provides good information as to the state of play in terms of intervention in the UK. Kropp and Campbell are the key writers on risk assessment and the Dobash (1992) work alongside the Babcock, Green and Robie (2004) paper will provide a good review of intervention programmes.

REFERENCES

Babcock, J.C., Green, C.E. and Robie, C. (2004) Does batterer's treatment work? A meta-analytic review of domestic violence treatment. *Clinical Psychology Review*, 23: 1023–53.

Bandura, A. (1979) *Social Learning Theory*. Englewood Cliffs, NJ: Prentice Hall.

Belfrage, H. and Rying, M. (2004) Characteristics of spousal homicide perpetrators. *Criminal Behaviour and Mental Health*, 14: 121–33.

Bland, R. and Orn, H. (1986). Family violence and psychiatric disorder. *Canadian Journal of Psychiatry*, 1: 129–37.

Bowen, E. and Gilchrist, E.A. (2004) Do court- and self-referred domestic violence offenders have the same characteristics? Comparisons of anger, locus of control and motivation to change. *Legal and Criminological Psychology*, 9: 279–94.

Bowen, E., Gilchrist, E.A. and Beech, A.R. (2005) An examination of the impact of community-based rehabilitation on the offending behaviour of male domestic violence offenders and the characteristics associated with recidivism. *Legal and Criminological Psychology*, 10: 189–209.

Campbell, J.C. (1995) Prediction of homicide of and by battered women. In J.C. Campbell (ed.), *Assessing Dangerousness: Violence by Sexual Offenders, Batterers, and Child Abusers*, pp. 96–113.Thousand Oaks, CA: Sage.

Cascardi, M., Langhinrichsen J. and Vivian, D. (1992) Marital aggression: impact, injury, and health correlates for husbands and wives: *Archives of Internal Medicine* 152: 1178–84.

Daly, M., Wilson, M.I. and Weghorst, S.J. (1982) Male sexual jealousy. *Ethology and Sociobiology*, 3: 11–27.

Dobash, R.E. and Dobash, R.P. (1992) *Women, Violence and Social Change*, London: Routledge. (2004) Women's violence to men in intimate relationships: working on a puzzle. *British Journal of Criminology*, 44: 324–49.

Dobash, R.E., Dobash, R.P., Cavanagh, K. and Lewis, J. (1996) *Research Evaluation of Programmes for Violent Men*. Edinburgh: Scottish Office.

Dobash, R.E., Dobash, R.P., Cavanagh, K. and Medina-Ariza, J.J. (2007) Lethal and nonlethal violence against an intimate partner. *Violence against Women*, 13: 329–53.

Dobash R.P., Dobash R.E., Wilson, M. and Daly, M. (1992) The myth of sexual symmetry in marital violence. *Social Problems*, 39: 71–91.

Dutton, D. G. (1985) An ecologically nested theory of male violence toward intimates. *International Journal of Women's Studies*, 8: 404–13.

(1988) *The Domestic Assault of Women: Psychological and Criminal Justice Perspectives.* Boston: Allyn & Bacon.

(1999) *The Abusive Personality: Violence and Control in Intimate Relationships.* New York: Guilford Press.

Dutton, D. G. and Browning, J. J. (1988) Power struggles and intimacy anxieties as causative factors of violence in intimate relationships. In G. Russell (ed.), *Violence in Intimate Relationships.* Great Neck, NY: PMA Publishing.

Dutton, D. G and Kropp, P. R. (2000) A review of domestic violence risk instruments. *Trauma Violence Abuse*, 1: 171–81.

Eckhardt, C. and Dye, M. (2000) The cognitive characteristics of maritally violent men: theory and evidence. *Cognitive Therapy and Research*, 24: 139–58.

Ehrensaft, M. K., Cohen, P., Brown, J., Smailes, E., Chen, H. and Johnson, J. (2003) Intergenerational transmission of partner violence: a 20-year prospective study. *Journal of Consulting and Clinical Psychology*, 71: 741–53.

Faulk, M. (1974) Men who assault their wives. *Medicine, Science and the Law*, 14: 180–3.

Geffner, R. and Rosenbaum, A. (2001) *Domestic Violence Offenders: Current Interventions, Research, and Implications for Policies and Standards.* Binghamton, NY: Haworth Press.

Gelles, R. J. and Straus, M. A. (1979) Determinants of violence in the family: towards a theoretical integration. In W. R. Burr, R. Hill, F. I. Nye and I. L. Reiss (eds.), *Contemporary Theories about the Family*, vol. 1, ch. 21. New York: Free Press.

Gilchrist, E., Johnson, R., Takriti, R., Beech, A., Kebbell, M. and Weston, S. (2003) *Domestic Violence Offenders: Characteristics and Offending Related Needs* (Research Findings no. 217). London: Home Office.

Gondolf, E. W. (1988) Who are these guys? Toward a behavioral typology of batterers. *Violence and Victims*, 3: 187–203.

(1997) Batterer programs: what we know and need to know. *Journal of Interpersonal Violence*, 12: 83–98.

Gottman, J. M., Jacobson, N. S., Rushe, R. H., Shortt, J. W., Babcock, J., La Taillade, J. J. and Waltz, J. (1995) The relationship between heart rate reactivity, emotionally aggressive behavior, and general violence in batterers. *Journal of Family Psychology*, 9: 227–48.

Graham-Kevan, N. and Archer, J. (2003) Patriarchal terrorism and common couple violence: a test of Johnson's predictions in four British samples. *Journal of Interpersonal Violence*, 18: 1247–70.

Hamberger, L. and Hastings, J. (1986) Characteristics of spouse abusers: predictors of treatment acceptance. *Journal of Interpersonal Violence*, 1: 363–73.

Hamberger, L. K., Lohr, J. M., Bonge, D. and Tolin, D. F. (1996) A large sample empirical typology of male spouse abusers and its relationship to dimensions of abuse. *Violence and Victims*, 11: 277–92.

Holtzworth-Munroe, A., Meehan, J. C., Herron, K., Rehman, U. and Stuart, G. L. (2000) Testing the Holtzworth-Munroe and Stuart (1994) batterer typology. *Journal of Consulting and Clinical Psychology*, 68: 1000–19.

Holtzworth-Munroe, A. and Saunders, D. G. (1996) Men who batter: recent history and research. *Violence and Victims*, 11: 273–6.

Holtzworth-Munroe, A. and Stuart, G. L. (1994) Typologies of male batterers: three sub-types and differences among them. *Psychological Bulletin*, 116: 476–97.

Jacobson, N. S. (1994) Rewards and dangers in researching domestic violence. *Family Process*, 33: 81–5.

Jacobson, N. S., Gottman, J. M., Waltz, J., Rushe, R., Babcock, J. and Holtzworth-Munroe, A. (1994) Affect, verbal content, and psychophysiology in the arguments of couples with a violent husband. *Journal of Consulting and Clinical Psychology*, 62: 982–8.

Johnson, M. P. (1995) Patriarchal terrorism and common couple violence: two forms of violence against women. *Journal of Marriage and the Family*, 57: 283–94.

Kropp, P. R. and Hart S. D. (2000) The Spousal Assault Risk Assessment (SARA) guide: reliability and validity in adult male offenders. *Law and Human Behavior*, 24: 101–18.

Kropp, P. R., Hart, S. D., Webster, C. W. and Eaves, D. (1994). *Manual for the Spousal Assault Risk Assessment Guide*. Vancouver, BC: British Columbia Institute on Family Violence.

Lane, G. and Russell, T. (1989) Second-order systemic work with violent couples. In P. L. Caesar and L. K. Hamberger (eds.), *Treating Men who Batter: Theory, Practice, and Programs*, pp. 134–62. New York: Springer.

Mitchell, I. and Gilchrist, E. (2006) Domestic violence and panic attacks – common neural mechanisms? *Legal and Criminological Psychology*, 11: 267–82.

Pence, E. (1989) *Domestic Assault: The Law Enforcement Response*. Duluth, MN: Minnesota Program Development, Inc.

Pence, E. and Paymar, M. (1993) *Education Groups for Men who Batter: The Duluth Model*. New York: Springer.

Saunders, D. G. (1992) Women battering. In R. T. Ammerman and M. Hersen (eds.), *Assessment of Family Violence: A Clinical and Legal Sourcebook*, pp. 208–35. New York: Wiley.

Saunders, D., Lynch, A., Grayson, M. and Linz, D. (1987) The inventory of beliefs about wife beating: the construction and initial validation of a measure of beliefs and attitudes. *Violence and Victims*, 2: 39–55.

Shepard, M. F. and Campbell, J. A. (1992) The abusive behavior inventory: a measure of psychological and physical abuse. *Journal of Interpersonal Violence*, 7: 291–305.

Sonkin, D. J., Martin, D. and Walker, L. E. (1985) *The Male Batterer: A Treatment Approach*. New York: Springer.

Straus, M. (1979) Measuring intrafamily conflict and violence: the Conflict Tactics (CT) scales. *Journal of Marriage and the Family*, 41: 75–88.

Straus, M., Gelles, R. J. and Steinmetz, S. K. (1980) *Behind Closed Doors: Violence in American Families*. New York: Doubleday.

Sugarman, D. B. and Frankel, S. L. (1996) Patriarchal ideology and wife-assault: a meta-analytic review. *Journal of Family Violence*, 11: 13–40.

Trute, B. (1998) Going beyond gender-specific treatments in wife battering: pro-feminist couple and family therapy. *Aggression and Violent Behavior*, 3: 1–15.

Tweed, R. G. and Dutton, D. G. (1998) A comparison of impulsive and instrumental subgroups of batterers. *Violence and Victims*, 4: 173–89.

Yllo, K. and Straus, M. (1990) Patriarchy and violence against wives: the impact of structural and normative factors. In M. Straus and R. Gelles (eds.), *Physical Violence in American Families: Risk Factors and Adaptations to Violence in 8,145 Families*, pp. 383–99. New Brunswick, NJ: Transaction Publishers.

4.5 Genocide

Joanna R. Adler and Agnieszka Golec de Zavala

Introduction

This chapter applies social psychological theory to the forensically challenging task of beginning to explain genocide. Forensic psychological practitioners are rarely faced with the dilemmas and realities faced by victims of extreme trauma, or survivors of ethnic cleansing, torture or genocide. We do see asylum seekers in detention centres and those of us working in the field of hate crimes may see the disturbing side-effects of factionalism and extremism. Yet the magnitude of harm committed within state-sponsored crimes is such that any discipline trying to explain and hopefully prevent criminal behaviour needs to address this issue.

Definition

Definitions of *genocide, mass killings, politicide, ethnic cleansing, pogrom* and *state-sponsored crimes* have different emphases; however, the processes that lead to them are often similar (Staub and Bar-Tal 2003). In this chapter, we will be referring to genocide, as coined by Lemkin (1944):

By 'genocide' we mean the destruction of a nation or of an ethnic group. This new word, ... is made from the ancient Greek word *genos* (race, tribe) and the Latin *cide* (killing) ... genocide does not necessarily mean the immediate destruction of a nation ... It is intended rather to signify a coordinated plan of different actions aiming at the destruction of essential foundations of the life of national groups, with the aim of annihilating the groups themselves. The objectives of such a plan would be disintegration of the political and social institutions, of culture, language, national feelings, religion, and the economic existence of national groups, and the destruction of the personal security, liberty, health, dignity, and even the lives of the individuals belonging to such groups. Genocide is directed against the national [/ethnic] group as an entity, and the actions involved are directed against individuals, not in their individual capacity, but as members of the national group.

Lemkin lost forty-nine members of his family in the Holocaust (Rosenthal 1988) but he had been developing these ideas for more than a decade, drawing on previous state-perpetrated massacres such as that now known as the Armenian genocide (Lemkin 1933). Other examples of genocide would include the events in Cambodia under the Khmer Rouge or in Rwanda during 1994.

Background to psychological explanations

After the Holocaust, at the Nuremburg International Military Tribunal, indictments were brought against twenty-two people (Conot 1983). These men could not, by themselves, have killed and enslaved millions, nor instigated a world war. To try to explain mass participation in these events, a number of scientists launched the search for a 'fascist mentality': an individual mindset of obedience and propensity for evil (e.g. Adorno *et al.* 1950). However, their numerous studies seemed to show that genocide was not perpetrated by evil people with extraordinary characteristics. It seemed to have been carried out by ordinary individuals in extraordinary social circumstances that bear certain similarities (Staub 1989; Zimbardo 2004). Genocide may be seen as a societal product (Darley 1992), the result of an interaction of various social forces. However, for any one individual, the process and experience of becoming able to commit mass killings brings a profound change. These people are more likely to commit similar acts in similar conditions in the future (Darley 1992).

Genocides are not spontaneous, sudden, unexpected events. It is not easy for people to kill great numbers systematically. A long process of societal and psychological change is needed first. It is possible to predict (for example, analysing the social structure and salient ideologies) and possibly prevent, future genocides. It is salutary to note that when writing, there were seven regions on the genocide watch of the Committee on Conscience of the US Holocaust Memorial Museum (www.ushmm.org/conscience/alert/).

Origins: conflict and hardship

Genocides most often occur in the context of intractable intergroup conflicts or long-term, often institutionalized discrimination (Staub and Bar-Tal 2003;

Coleman 2003). The sources of intergroup conflicts can lie in competition for scarce resources (material or symbolic) (Sherif 1966) or in frustrated basic human needs of one of the groups (Staub 1999; see also Burton 1987). In Rwanda, prolonged conflict over land and possessions, with tribal delineations reinforced by colonial powers, resulted in a series of massacres and wars. In 1994, a predictable genocide, which had used propaganda and made overt preparations, was propagated. As many as 800,000 people were killed in 100 days when the political elite exploited long-standing divisions to incite violence whilst the country suffered from the effects of drought, lack of trade and civil war (HRW 1999). Mass killings and deliberate attempts to wipe out competing ethnic groups in Bosnia-Herzegovina were perpetrated in the midst of the war as individual states competed for control of the former Yugoslavia in the first half of the 1990s.

Genocides are perpetrated in times of economic hardship and rapid social change. In this context, one group is stigmatized and scapegoated: designated as guilty of the bad times and experienced uncertainties (Staub 1989). In such situations, there may be no apparent, real conflict but rather, long-lasting animosity towards an out-group perceived as a threat to the wellbeing of one's own group. In Nazi Germany, pre-existing anti-Semitism was fanned and soared during the economic crisis of the 1920s and 1930s. In Turkey, Armenians were characterized as economic threats to Turks whilst the state institutions failed during 1915. Blaming another group for the causes of sacrifice and suffering endured by members of an in-group is cognitively and emotionally easier and more beneficial for the cohesiveness and mobilization of that in-group than understanding the complex social, historical and economic processes that lead to suffering.[1]

Scapegoating and out-group perception

The tangible origins of intractable conflicts or long-lasting prejudice are often unknown or lost. What matters is the division between social groups and spiralling intergroup animosity. The conflict is perceived as irreconcilable and 'zero-sum' in nature. The division between groups is central in individual

---

[1] Importantly, there have been genocides committed without pre-existing conflict or prolonged animosity. These genocides were also committed when one group of people was treated as inferior and subhuman and subsequently eliminated because of the desirable resources it possessed, e.g. the massacres of indigenous peoples as North America, South America or Australasia were colonized by the various European powers.

and public lives (Staub and Bar-Tal 2003). In this context, people rarely function as individual beings; more often they think about themselves and others as representatives of groups 'us' versus 'them' (Sumner 1906; Tajfel and Turner 1986). Differences are stressed and evil characteristics ascribed to the out-group, whose members are perceived as similar to each other in representing all the evil features. The 'other' is deeply devalued, seen as a threat to the wellbeing or even continued existence of the in-group, anything between an obstacle to achieve ideal and desirable social arrangements to a mortal enemy. One's own group is seen as innocent and superior (Gurr 2001; Pruitt, Rubin and Kim 1994; Sidanius and Pratto 1999). Individual, prejudiced, perception of a stigmatized group is strengthened by support found in the social environment, among peers and within social institutions. The prejudiced perception justifies discrimination and harm against the members of the stigmatized group and related discriminatory behaviour. Prejudice and discrimination become normative.

The societal climate in which the ideology of antagonism (Staub 1999) that justifies intergroup hostility exists, enhances individual moral disengagement from wrongdoings against that out-group (Bandura 1999). The perception of hostile action against a stigmatized group of people is altered and reinterpreted. Unlawful imprisonment of the innocent can be reconstructed as protection of the social order; killing other people, as duty. Such acts are ostensibly justified by widespread ideology and supported by the authority of social institutions (e.g. the Nuremberg laws of 1935). Negative effects for the victims are minimized and misconstrued. Euphemistic labels are used to make such consequences abstract (e.g. *causalities of war* or *final solution*). Individual responsibility is displaced (to authority figures) and dissolved between unidentified others who commit similar acts. Victims are blamed for their predicaments (see Brock and Buss 1962, regarding victim derogation) which could be reinforced by the belief in the just world (Lerner and Simmons 1966). Extreme devaluation of victims delegitimizes and dehumanizes them (Bar-Tal 1998).

Social organizations

The sheer existence of intergroup negativity and prejudice is not likely to result in genocide. Mass killing requires efficient organization of many people. The forces that help unify their actions include justifying ideology and organizations that socialize and 'train' individuals to be capable of autonomous, systematic, mass killings and of reproducing killing structures (Darley 1992). Social organizations and institutions spread ideology to justify stigmatizing and discrimination of designated social groups (e.g. Jaensch's (1938) anti-types, so central to Nazi ideology). Propaganda, 'the cognitive conditioning of hate' (Zimbardo 2004), is used on multiple levels, through multifarious social structures (schools, social institutions, families). Although we have largely concentrated on situational, societal explanations for genocide, it is important to note that dispositional explanations cannot be ignored (Walker 2002), particularly when considering political elites. The decisions and actions that are chosen may reinforce the personal dispositions of an individual and lead that individual to shift the ways in which s/he later interacts with the world. Sereny's works on Stangl (1974) and Speer (1996) give us insight into the rationalizations and interior processes of two key Nazi leaders.

Individuals are socialized to believe and act on an ideology of antagonism. They learn to commit atrocities against other human beings incrementally. They come to believe that the other can be hurt, is to be hurt and that they can do it themselves. Each step brings small changes in beliefs, attitudes and worldviews that may be mediated through cognitive dissonance reduction processes (Festinger 1957). They learn about their attitudes and preferences by observing their own behaviour (Bem 1972). Through both processes, the attitudinal changes make repeating and engaging in even more hostile actions more likely. The injustice, hostilities and atrocities become routine as individuals become habituated, desensitized and less emotionally involved in their perpetration. Discrimination against stigmatized groups is strengthened gradually, allowing collective dissonance reduction (Zimbardo 2004) and desensitizing the whole society.

Organizations that prepare people to kill others do not require everybody to realize their goals with equal zeal. There are people who internalize the hostile ideology and believe that killing others is actually moral. Others act on behalf of their group, not necessarily believing in the ideology devaluing the other, but believing that they protect the in-group. Others act through compliance, obedience and conformity. There are also inactive bystanders who contribute to the possibility of genocide and some active resistors, many of whom will be targeted by the regime.

According to some (e.g. Staub 1989), genocide is more likely in societies of strong hierarchical structure, where obedience to authority is highly valued. Blind obedience to the orders of an authority and conformity in following actions of others make genocide more likely. Obedience to orders provides an illusion that someone else takes the responsibility for the committed acts.[2] Milgram's (1974) experiments conducted in eighteen variations with more than 1,000 participants demonstrated great human potential (on average, 65%) for performing acts believed to seriously harm or kill another human being.

Performing the act: psychological processes during genocide

Triggering event

After societal and psychological preparations, genocides are triggered by mostly symbolic events, used as excuses to begin mass killings. Usually, the triggers bring disproportional reactions, e.g. the assassination of Ernst vom Rath, used as a trigger for 'Kristallnacht' in November 1938 (Gilbert 1987); or the assassination of the president, to catalyse genocide in Rwanda (HRW 1999).

Deindividuation

When an organization kills, individual responsibility is psychologically diminished (Darley 1992). Organized mass killings are usually committed in groups when individuals remain anonymous and unlikely to be recognized outside the events. People may act in crowds or execute a partial role in the process. When they feel deindividuated – deprived of their individuality and normal sense of self-control – they become more responsive to the goals and desires normative for the crowd or for the role they are performing (Zimbardo 1969, 2004). In both cases, they are more likely to perform more extreme acts than if they were acting alone. The very act of committing mass killings lessens the inhibitions and makes perpetration of further atrocities more likely.

Doubling

In an attempt to explain how people can be loving parents and staunch community members, yet actively participate in killing other men, women and children, the concept of *doubling* has arisen (Lifton 1986). Based on interviews with Nazi doctors, lawyers and judges and with concentration camp

---

[2] Under international law, the existence of illegal orders may be called in mitigation but cannot be used to excuse criminal responsibility of an individual who followed them.

survivors, Lifton's idea of a double self draws on psychoanalytic perspectives. This is an alternative explanation for processes that would result in similar effects to those we described when considering cognitive dissonance above.

The role of bystanders

Genocides happen also because of passive bystanders (individuals, groups or organizations) who do not protest when atrocities are committed. Inaction signifies support, it can silence possible protest and defence for the victims. Inaction tells perpetrators that the acts can go unpunished, are even implicitly approved. A new social norm is set: perpetrators, victims and bystanders learn that this is now an acceptable and soon normative behaviour for this social group. According to the process of informative social influence, in situations that can be seen as ambiguous and not clear (harming an individual or punishing a member of an 'evil' group), the behaviour of others is used as guidance (Sherif 1954). Milgram (1974) demonstrated that 90% of participants obeyed experimental instructions to apply apparently life-threatening electric shocks to an innocent victim after they observed a peer (confederate) complying. However, obedience dropped to 10% when participants observed a peer refusing to administer the electric shock.

Conclusion

In concluding, it is important to consider the implications of these processes. These descriptions of how people may engage in genocidal activity are not meant to imply that people act in the absence of conscious decisions. We do not seek to say that those who commit such heinous crimes, either as leaders or followers, are unaware of the consequences of their actions. Rather, as Haslam and Richer (2008) conclude, 'People do great wrong, not because they are unaware of what they are doing, but because they consider it to be right.' We have outlined some of the conditions through which genocide occurs, exploring social and psychological phenomena that partially explain how genocide can still exist. We cannot here consider the implications for prevention, intervention and supporting post-genocide survivors. Nor can we properly consider how to predict who will comply, who will stand by and who will resist future atrocities. All are important for continued psychological research and practice and all point to the enduring complexity with which we are faced when applying psychological knowledge to genocide.

REFERENCES

Adorno, T. W., Frenkel-Brunswik, E., Levinson, D. J. and Sanford, R. N. (1950) *The Authoritarian Personality*. New York: Harper.

Bandura, A. (1999) Moral disengagement in the perpetration of inhumanities. *Personality and Social Psychology Review* (special issue on Evil and Violence), 3: 193–209.

Bar-Tal, D. (1998) The rocky road toward peace: societal beliefs functional to intractable conflict in the Israel school textbooks. *Journal of Peace Research*, 35: 723–42.

Bem, D. J. (1972) Self-perception theory. In L. Berkowitz (ed.), *Advances in Experimental Social Psychology*, vol. 6, pp. 1–62. New York: Academic Press.

Brock, T. C. and Buss, A. H. (1962) Dissonance, aggression, and evaluation of pain. *Journal of Abnormal and Social Psychology*, 65: 197–202.

Burton, J. W. (1987) *Resolving Deep-Rooted Conflict: A Handbook*. Lanham, MD, and London: University Press of America.

Coleman, P. (2003) Characteristics of protracted, intractable conflict: toward the development of a metaframework – I. Peace and conflict. *Journal of Peace Psychology*, 9: 1–37.

Conot, R. E. (1983) *Justice at Nuremberg*. New York: Harper & Row.

Darley, J. (1992) Social organization for the production of evil. *Psychological Inquiry*, 3: 199–217.

Festinger, L. (1957) *A Theory of Cognitive Dissonance*. Stanford, CA: Stanford University Press.

Gilbert, M. (1987) *The Holocaust: A History of the Jews during the Second World War*. Glasgow: Fontana/Collins.

Gurr, T. R. (2001) Minorities and nationalists: managing ethnopolitical conflict in the new century. In C. Crocker, F. Hampson and P. Aall (eds.), *Turbulent Peace*, pp. 163–88. Washington, DC: USIP Press.

Haslam, S. A. and Reicher, S. D. (2008) Questioning the banality of evil. *The Psychologist*, 21: 16–19.

Human Rights Watch (HRW) (1999) *Leave None to Tell the Story. Genocide in Rwanda*. www.hrw.org/reports/1999/rwanda/ (accessed 4 October 2006).

Jaensch, E. R. (1938) Der Gegentypus. Psychologisch-anthropologische Grundlagen deutscher Kulturphilosophie, ausgehend von dem was wir überwinden wollen. *Zeitschrift für angewandte Psychologie und Charakterkunde*. Leipzig: Barth.

Lemkin, R. (1933) *Les actes constituant un danger général (interétatique) considerés comme délites des droit des gens*. Paris: A. Pedone. Translated by J. T. Fussell as *Acts Constituting a General (Transnational) Danger Considered as Offences against the Law of Nations*. www.preventgenocide.org/lemkin/madrid1933-english.htm (accessed 20 December 2007).

  (1944) Chapter IX: Genocide a new term and new conception for destruction of nations. In *Axis Rule in Occupied Europe: Laws of Occupation–Analysis of Government–Proposals for Redress* Washington, DC: Carnegie Endowment for International Peace.

Lerner, M. J. and Simmons, C. H. (1966) The observer's reaction to the 'innocent victim': compassion or rejection? *Journal of Personality and Social Psychology*, 4: 203–10.

Lifton, R. J. (1986) *The Nazi Doctors: Medical Killing and the Psychology of Genocide*. New York: Basic Books.

Milgram, S. (1974) *Obedience to Authority: An Experimental View*. New York: Harper & Row.

Pruitt D. G., Rubin, J. Z. and Kim, H. S. (1994) *Social Conflict*. New York: Random House.

Rosenthal, A. M. (1988) On my mind: a man called Lemkin. *New York Times*, 18 October.

Sereny, G. (1974) *Into that Darkness …. The Mind of a Mass Murderer*. London: Picador.

(1996) *Albert Speer: His Battle with Truth*. London: Picador.

Sherif, M. (1954) Socio-cultural influences in small group research. *Sociology and Social Research*, 39: 1–10.

(1966) *In Common Predicament: Social Psychology of Intergroup Conflict and Cooperation*. Boston: Houghton-Mifflin.

Sidanius, J. and Pratto, F. (1999) *Social Dominance*. New York: Cambridge University Press.

Staub, E. (1989) *The Roots of Evil: The Origins of Genocide and Other Group Violence*. New York: Cambridge University Press.

(1999) The roots of evil: social conditions, culture, personality, and basic human needs. *Personality and Social Psychology Review*, 3: 179–92.

Staub, E. and Bar-Tal, D. (2003) Genocide, mass killing and intractable conflict: roots, evolution, prevention and reconciliation. In D. O. Sears, L. Huddy, R. Jervis (eds.), *Oxford Handbook of Political Psychology*, pp. 710–51. New York: Oxford University Press.

Sumner, W. G. (1906) *Folkways*. New York: Ginn.

Tajfel, H. and Turner J. C. (1986) The social identity theory of intergroup behavior. In S. Worchel and W. G. Austin (eds.), *Psychology of Intergroup Relations*, pp. 7–24. Chicago: Nelson-Hall.

Walker, J. (2002) *Becoming Evil: How Ordinary People Commit Genocide and Mass Killing*. Oxford: Oxford University Press.

Zimbardo, P. (1969) The human choice: individuation, reason and order versus deindividuation, impulse and chaos. In W. J. Arnold and D. Levine (eds.), *Nebraska Symposium on Motivation*, pp. 237–309. Lincoln, NE: University of Nebraska Press.

(2004) A situationist perspective on the psychology of evil: understanding how good people are transformed into perpetrators. In A. Miller (ed.), *The Social Psychology of Good and Evil: Understanding Our Capacity for Kindness and Cruelty*, pp. 21–50. New York: Guilford Press.

4.6 Hate crime

Tom Ellis and Nathan Hall

Definitions

'Hate crime' is notoriously difficult to define accurately and effectively. As Boeckmann and Turpin-Petrosino (2002, p. 208) note:

> There is no consensus among social scientists or lawmakers on definitional elements that would constitute a global description of hate crime. Part of the reason for this lies in the fact that cultural differences, social norms, and political interests play a large role in defining crime in general, and hate crime in particular.

Hate crime is, therefore, always going to be a historically and culturally contingent social construct, such that the concept varies radically around the world (Perry 2001).

In England and Wales, the Association of Chief Police Officers defines a broader notion of hate 'incidents' as 'any incident, which may or may not constitute a criminal offence, which is perceived by the victim or any other person, as being motivated by prejudice or hate' (ACPO 2005, p. 9). Hate 'crime' is simply those incidents which also contravene the law.

The significance of these definitions is that they broaden the scope from labelling acts of 'hatred', to all acts based on prejudiced views. As such, hate crime is far more susceptible to social construction processes than other forms of crime. As Jacobs and Potter (1998) suggest, choices have to be made about the meaning of prejudice, the nature and strength of the causal link between the prejudice and the offence, as well as the types of crimes to be included. These choices ultimately determine what is, and what is not, 'hate crime', and therefore affect the size of the hate crime problem and the criminal justice response to it. As Jacobs and Potter (1998, p. 27) argue, 'how much hate crime there is and what the appropriate response should be depends upon how hate crime is conceptualized and defined'.

Inventing hate crime

Despite a long history of what we now label as 'hate crimes', it is a relatively new field of study in the UK. The murder of Stephen Lawrence in London in 1993, and the subsequent public inquiry that followed in 1999, put hate crime in the spotlight as a major social and political problem. The Stephen Lawrence Inquiry (Macpherson 1999) focused on race and racism, but the debate that followed served to draw attention to other arenas, such as homophobia.

Although the term 'hate crime' was only coined in the mid 1980s, interest in hate as a distinct motivation for crime has a somewhat longer legacy in the USA, and has been the subject of more detailed academic and policy investigation (see Petrosino 1999). This is reflected in much of the literature referred to below.

The extent of hate crime: victimization

The extent of hate crime is notoriously difficult to determine (Bowling 1999; Perry 2001). It remains significantly under-reported to the authorities for a host of reasons that include intimidation, fear of reprisals, and a lack of confidence in the criminal justice system to resolve the problem. In England and Wales, hate crime is currently not a distinct category of crime for statistical returns, but figures are collected on racially and religiously motivated offences under section 95 of the Criminal Justice Act 1991. Differences in the definitions used in these official figures further illustrate the conceptual issues outlined above. At the time of writing, 60,407 racist *incidents* were recorded (a 4% increase from 2004/5), mostly property damage or verbal harassment, but only 41,382 'racially and religiously' aggravated *crimes* (a 12% increase from 2004/5) (section 95 figures for 2005/6: Home Office 2006).

In contrast to the steadily rising number of police-recorded incidents, the annual British Crime Survey, while illustrating the inevitable under-reporting and recording in the police figures, suggests that self-reported victimization has declined from 179,000 incidents in 2004/5 to 139,000 in 2005/6 (see Jones, Singer and Magill 2007, pp. 10–15; Jannson 2006).

The 'official picture' of hate crime may or may not become clearer from 2008 onwards, as the new Ministry of Justice in England and Wales has now initiated a recording system to also capture hate *incidents* and *crimes* based on the typical target category membership, in addition to race, of the victims, i.e. faith, sexual orientation, transgender and disability issues. Again, these changes will have a profound effect on recorded levels of hate crime.

Although most official statistics and research (Clark and Moody 2002; Jarman 2002; Maynard and Read 1997) show that most hate crime is 'low-level' acts of harassment, it is the repeated and systematic nature of these acts that can have a disproportionate and cumulative impact (both psychologically and physically) on the victim *and* the wider community (Bowling 1999; Chahal and Julienne 2000; FBI 2003; Hall 2005; McDevitt *et al.* 2001).

Perpetrators of hate crime and theories of motivation

Over a decade ago Ben Bowling lamented that:

there has been almost no research on [hate crime] perpetrators. Whilst the most basic of descriptions have been formulated, they remain something of an effigy in the criminological literature … The perpetrator is unknown and, consequently, the possibility for any understanding or interpretation of his or her behaviour becomes impossible. (1999, p. 163)

Barbara Perry (2003a, p. 97) has argued similarly, and more recently, in the US that:

criminology has yet to come to terms with the phenomenon we have come to know as hate crime. Existing theory tends to neglect either or both the structural under-pinnings of hate crime, and the situated process that it entails.

Many theories from many different disciplines have been used to explain hate crime, beginning with social cognition theorists who have argued since the 1950s that we have an innate tendency to separate the world into '*us*' and '*them*' (Nelson 2002). For instance, scapegoat theory (Allport 1954; Heitmeyer 1993) suggests that during times of societal stress, there is an innate tendency to lash out against an out-group that is emotionally or cognitively linked with the source of the stress. For example, those of perceived Middle Eastern appearance suffered intense public, enforcement and media attention, plus a rise in victimization, after both the Oklahoma City bombing (which turned out to have no connection to the Middle East) and after the bombing of the World Trade Center (9/11).

On the other hand, conflict theorists see hate crimes as the product of various socioeconomic contextual stress factors (such as unemployment, economic hardship, competition for scarce resources, lack of/competition for community facilities) and the psychological characteristics of individuals who are likely to be involved in other forms of antisocial behaviour, but need someone to blame for their contextual stress (see Ezekiel 1995; Novick 1995; Sibbitt 1997; Stanton 1991). Medoff (1999), for instance, found that hate crime activity decreases with increased market earnings. However, Green, Abelson and Garnet (1999) and Green, Glaser and Rich (1998) found that hate crime perpetrators in their studies were not more likely to be economically frustrated.

Green *et al.* (1999), instead, turned to social learning theory to explain hate crime. They suggest that people's attitudes to 'out-groups' are influenced by parents and the broader social environment and found that hate crime offenders were more likely to fear diversity and immigration, while Franklin (2000) found that perpetrators of homophobic incidents were additionally motivated by their friends' ideology.

Beyond psychological theories, there are yet more competing paradigms: from the view that hate crime is used as a tool to assert and maintain perceived power structures in society (Perry 2001), to the application of the European and US traditions of anomie, which is used to explain, understand and, perhaps most importantly, provide preventive possibilities for hate crime (Hopkins Burke and Pollock 2004).

Other theories point to hate crimes being a product of boredom, retaliation, a perceived need to defend one's territory from outsiders, or in rare cases as a 'mission' to eradicate despised 'others' (McDevitt, Levin and Bennett 2002).

It is obvious that theorizing hate crime is difficult terrain to negotiate. Craig (2002) has argued that no single theory can adequately explain all types of hate crime. She suggests this is largely because contributory factors (e.g. perpetrators' motives, victims' characteristics, and cultural ideologies) differ markedly for each incident. Hate crime perpetrators can effectively be motivated by one or more of a wide range of social, psychological, political, cultural and other factors. On the basis of Craig's research, the search for a single, universal causal factor for hate crime is likely to be fruitless. Rather, it is the interplay of a number of different factors that produces perpetrators.

Perhaps the single most important exception to the lack of knowledge we have on perpetrators of hate crime is Edward Dunbar's (1999) critique of 'psycholegal defence arguments' used in hate crime trials. Dunbar concludes that there is still difficulty in establishing differences between hate crime perpetrators and those who commit other forms of violent crime. A key difference is that hate crime perpetrators *may* act in the absence of extrinsic reward. However, significant in-group differences are anticipated among these same perpetrators. The only certainty, derived from Rice's (1997) ten-year retrospective study, was that those who did not meet the criteria for psychopathy were extremely unlikely to be reconvicted of a second hate crime, while those who did meet the criteria were *more* likely to be convicted of a further hate crime *if* they had received interpersonal psychological intervention!

The future: hate crime or bias crime?

One of the most contentious areas of debate in this field concerns the enactment of legislation that seeks to establish and/or increase punishment for hate crime, such as the Crime and Disorder Act 1998 in England and Wales, or the plethora of federal and state legislation in the US (see the Anti-Defamation League, www.adl.org, for comprehensive coverage of the latter). Hate crime laws usually exhibit a fairly straightforward combination of deterrence and retribution, characteristic of most criminal law, but with little certainty of effectiveness. They represent state recognition of an apparent, emerging and increasing threat to society, and signify the importance attached to combating this threat. The potential for increased punishment of the offender signifies an appreciation of the seemingly disproportionate harm that hate crime can have on the victim and wider communities. Hate crime laws are also held to promote social cohesion by officially declaring that the victimization of 'different' groups is not acceptable in a modern democratic society, and their very existence provides strong symbolic messages concerning appropriate and inappropriate behaviour (see Levin 1999).

Many critics, however (see, for example, Jacobs and Potter 1998; Sullivan 1999), challenge the foundations upon which the case for hate crime legislation is made on moral, legal, political and practical grounds. For them, the alleged hate crime epidemic in the US is simply not 'real', but has, rather, been socially constructed. Indeed, they argue that America is freer of prejudice and hatred now that it has been for the past century. The 'hate epidemic' is, therefore, a product of: heightened public sensitivity to prejudice and discrimination; minority groups' success in moving 'identity politics' into the criminal justice arena; acceptance of broad legal definitions that encapsulate comparatively meaningless low-level offences for which the strength of the hate element is debatable; and an irresponsible media which exaggerates the latter point. Ultimately, such critics are of the opinion that there is nothing unique to hate crime that means it cannot be adequately responded to by generic criminal law. They also insist that many of the claims concerning the unique nature of hate crime are based on inconclusive evidence, and research with methodological shortcomings.

Given that hate crime per se is the subject of uncertainty, debate and a degree of confusion, critics argue that it is hard to develop an appropriate response to it. As Perry (2003b) argues, we need to be critical of the term 'hate crime' even as an adequate descriptor of 'bias-motivated behaviour'. The key gap in knowledge, for Perry, is the failure to examine the specificity of the crime experiences of the diverse victims of 'bias crime' and the impact on society as a whole. For others (Gerstenfeld 2002) the issue is that policy makers are not reading the available social psychological literature. While much of this inevitably focuses on prejudice formation, there is enough evidence, including the classic Robber's Cave Experiment (Sherif *et al.* 1961) and others (see Aronson, Bridgeman and Geffner 1978) to suggest that 'hate' or 'bias' incidents can be reduced by establishing an environment in which groups have to work together cooperatively to achieve a goal. More recent studies (e.g. Blanchard, Lilly and Vaughan 1991; Monteith, Deneen and Tooman 1996) show that those who witness others expressing antiprejudiced attitudes and actions are less likely to behave in a biased way. This said, new virtual arenas of hate are opening up, for which different approaches will have to be developed. White racist activity using internet newsgroups is now a growing phenomenon, both for recruitment and in encouraging violence against non-white people and their property (Mann, Sutton and Tuffin 2003; Sutton 2009). Certainly, Petrosino (1999) predicts a growth in hate crime as a function of greater opportunity and technological advances, and that it will become increasingly difficult to prevent.

REFERENCES

Allport, G. (1954) *The Nature of Prejudice*. Reading, MA: Addison-Wesley.

Aronson, E., Bridgeman, D. L. and Geffner, R. (1978) The effects of cooperative classroom structure on students' behavior and attitudes. In D. Bar-Tal and L. Saxe (eds.), *Social Psychology of Education: Theory and Research*. Washington, DC: Hemisphere.

Association of Chief Police Officers (2005) *Hate Crime: Delivering a Quality Service; Good Practice and Tactical Guidance.* London: ACPO.

Blanchard, F. A., Lilly, T. and Vaughan, L. A. (1991) Reducing the expression of racial prejudice. *Psychological Science*, 2: 101–5.

Boeckmann, R. J. and Turpin-Petrosino, C. (2002) Understanding the harm of hate crime. *Journal of Social Issues*, 58: 207–25.

Bowling, B. (1999) *Violent Racism: Victimisation, Policing and Social Context.* New York: Oxford University Press.

Chahal, K. and Julienne, L. (2000) *'We Can't All Be White!': Racist Victimisation in the UK.* York: York Publishing Services Ltd.

Clark, I. and Moody, S. (2002) *Racist Crime and Victimisation in Scotland.* Crime and Criminal Justice Research Findings no. 58. Edinburgh: Scottish Executive Central Research Unit. http://openscotland.gov.uk/Resource/Doc/46922/0029768.pdf.

Craig, K. M. (2002) Examining hate-motivated aggression: a review of the social psychological literature on hate crimes as a distinct form of aggression. *Aggression and Violent Behavior*, 7: 85–101.

Dunbar, E. (1999) Defending the indefensible: a critique and analysis of psycholegal defense arguments of hate crime perpetrators. *Journal of Contemporary Criminal Justice*, 15: 64–77.

Ezekiel, R. (1995) *The Racist Mind: Portraits of American Neo-Nazis and Klansmen.* New York: Viking.

Federal Bureau of Investigation (2003) *Hate Crime Statistics 2002.* Washington, DC: US Department of Justice.

Franklin, K. (2000) Antigay behaviours among young adults: prevalence, patterns and motivators in a noncriminal population. *Journal of Interpersonal Violence*, 15: 339–62.

Gerstenfeld, P. B. (2002) A time to hate: situational antecedents of intergroup bias. *Analyses of Social Issues and Public Policy*, 2: 61–7

Green, D. P., Glaser, J. and Rich, A. (1998) From lynching to gay bashing: the elusive connection between economic conditions and hate crime. *Journal of Personality and Social Psychology*, 75: 82–92.

Green, D. P., Abelson, R. P. and Garnett, M. (1999) The distinctive political views of hate-crime perpetrators and White supremacists. In D. A Prentice and D. Miller (eds.), *Cultural Divides: Understanding and Overcoming Group Conflict*, pp. 429–64. New York: Russell Sage Foundation.

Hall, N. (2005) *Hate Crime.* Cullompton: Willan.

Heitmeyer, W. (1993) Hostility and violence towards foreigners in Germany. In T. Bjorgo and R. Witte (eds.), *Racist Violence in Europe*, pp. 17–28. London: Macmillan.

Home Office (2006) *Statistics on Race and the Criminal Justice System: A Home Office Publication under Section 95 of the Criminal Justice Act 1991.* London: Home Office.

Hopkins Burke, R. and Pollock, E. (2004) A tale of two anomies: some observations on the contribution of (sociological) criminological theory to explaining hate crime motivation. *Internet Journal of Criminology.* www.internetjournalofcriminology.com/Hopkins%20Burke%20&%20Pollock%20-%20A%20Tale%20of%20Two%20Anomies.pdf.

Jacobs, J. B. and Potter, K. (1998) *Hate Crimes: Criminal Law and Identity Politics.* New York: Oxford University Press.

Jannson, K. (2006) *Ethnicity and Victimization: Findings from the 2004/05 British Crime Survey*. London: Home Office.

Jarman, N. (2002) *Overview Analysis of Racist Incidents Recorded in Northern Ireland by the RUC 1996–1999*. Belfast: The Office of the First Minister and Deputy First Minister, Research Branch. www.research.ofmdfmni.gov.uk/racistincidents/racistincidents.pdf

Jones, A., Singer, L. and Magill, C. (2007) *Statistics on Race and the Criminal Justice System: A Ministry of Justice Publication under Section 95 of the Criminal Justice Act 1991*. London: Ministry of Justice. www.justice.gov.uk/publications/statistics.htm.

Levin, B. (1999) Hate crimes: worse by definition. *Journal of Contemporary Criminal Justice*, 15: 6–21.

Macpherson, W. (1999) *The Stephen Lawrence Inquiry*. Cm 4262. London: HMSO. www.archive.official-documents.co.uk/document/cm42/4262/4262.htm.

Mann, D., Sutton, M. and Tuffin, R. (2003) The evolution of hate: social dynamics in white racist newsgroups. *Internet Journal of Criminology*. www.internetjournalofcriminology. com/Evolution%20of%20Hate%20(updated).pdf.

Maynard, W. and Read, T. (1997) *Policing Racially Motivated Incidents*. Crime Detection and Prevention Series Paper 84. London: Home Office, Police Research Group. www.home-office.gov.uk/rds/prgpdfs/fcdps84.pdf.

McDevitt, J., Balboni J., Garcia L. and Gu, J. (2001) Consequences for victims: a comparison of bias- and non-bias-motivated assaults. *American Behavioral Scientist*, 45: 697–713.

McDevitt, J., Levin, J. and Bennett, S. (2002) Hate crime offenders: an expanded typology. *Journal of Social Issues*. 58: 303–17.

Medoff, H. (1999) Allocation of time and hateful behavior: a theoretical and positive analysis of hate and hate crimes. *American Journal of Economics and Sociology*, 58: 959–73.

Monteith, M. J., Deneen, N. E. and Tooman, G. D. (1996) The effect of social norm activation on the expression of opinions concerning gay men and Blacks. *Basic and Applied Social Psychology*, 18: 267–88.

Nelson, T. D. (2002) *The Psychology of Prejudice*. Boston. Allyn & Bacon.

Novick, M. (1995) *White Lies, White Power*. Monroe, ME: Common Courage.

Perry, B. (2001) *In the Name of Hate: Understanding Hate Crimes*. New York: Routledge.
  (ed.) (2003a) *Hate and Bias Crime: A Reader*. New York, Routledge.
  (2003b) Where do we go from here? Researching hate crime. *Internet Journal of Criminology*. www.internetjournalofcriminology.com/Where%20Do%20We%20Go%20From%20Here. %20Researching%20Hate%20Crime.pdf.

Petrosino, C. (1999) Connecting the past to the future: hate crime in America. *Journal of Contemporary Criminal Justice*, 15: 22–47.

Rice, M. (1997) Violent offender research and implications for the criminal justice system. *American Psychologist*, 52: 414–23.

Sherif, M., Harvey, O. J., White, B. J., Hood, W. R. and Sherif, C. W. (1961) *Intergroup Conflict and Cooperation: The Robber's Cave Experiment*. Norman, OK: University of Oklahoma, Institute of Group Relations.

Sibbitt, R. (1997) *The Perpetrators of Racial Harassment and Racial Violence*. Home Office Research Study no. 176. London: Home Office.

Stanton, B. (1991) *Klanwatch: Bringing the Ku Klux Klan to Justice*. New York: Mentor.

Sullivan, A. (1999) What's so bad about hate? The illogic and illiberalism behind hate crime laws. *The New York Times Magazine*, 26 September.

Sutton, M. and Wright, C. (2009) Finding the far right online: an exploratory study of white supremacist websites. *Internet Journal of Criminology*, pp. 1–24. www.internetjournalof-criminology.com/Sutton_Wright_Finding_The_Far_Right_Online_Nov_09.pdf.

4.7 Internet sexual offending

Max Taylor and Ethel Quayle

See also chapter 4.11 Sexual fantasy and sex offending.

Definition

There is no agreed definition of the term internet offending and it is used to describe both a broad class of internet-facilitated crime as well as more specifically sexual crimes against children. The broader definition clearly overlaps with cybercrime, much of which might be thought of as traditional crime but committed through the use of new tools. Indeed Jewkes and Sharp (2002) have argued that there is nothing sinister in the technology itself but that computer technologies have simply provided a new means to commit old crimes. There are few crimes that can be only perpetrated within cyberspace, although intellectual property theft, identity theft and spamming may be some of these. There is a need, however, to draw a distinction between crimes in which information and communication technologies are the object or the target of offending and crimes in which technologies are the tool in the commission of an offence (Choo, Smith and McCusker 2007). The list of crimes committed through the internet is very broad and might include fraud through identity theft (Eisenstein 2008; Moore and Clayton 2008) achieved through phishing (enticing people into giving identity information) and malware (malicious software put onto computers maliciously) (Bridges 2008); intellectual property infringement, such as counterfeiting and piracy; creation and dissemination of illegal content; organized crime using denial-of-service attacks to pursue extortion (McCusker 2006); cyberstalking (Wykes 2007) and cyberterrorism (George 2007; Goodman, Kirk and Kirk 2007).

Internet offending and sexual crimes against children

A more narrow definition of internet offending, and the one most frequently used in the research literature, has as its focus sexual crimes against children. These crimes are facilitated by computer technology (Kiekegaard 2008) and include downloading illegal images from the internet (which are largely but not exclusively pornographic images of children); trading or exchanging such images with others; producing images through photographing children or modifying existing images; and engaging in the solicitation or seduction of children (sometimes referred to as online grooming) (Quayle 2008). These behaviours are not discrete but overlap and not all relate specifically to the internet (as opposed to the 'new' technologies). An example of this would be the exchange of images through the use of mobile technology where the offender has never owned a computer or had internet connectivity. Existing typologies of internet offenders involved in sexual victimization of children have tended to categorize internet offenders into four broad groups: individuals who access abusive images sporadically, impulsively and/or out of curiosity; those who access/trade abusive images of children to fuel their sexual interest in children; people who use the internet as part of a pattern of online contact offending including those who use the internet as a tool for locating and/or grooming contact victims and those who use the internet to disseminate images they have produced; and individuals who access abusive images for seemingly non-sexual reasons (such as financial profit) (Beech *et al.* 2008).

In the context of solicitation, or grooming activities, Wolak *et al.* (2008) have suggested that most internet-initiated sex crimes involve adult men who use the internet to meet and seduce underage adolescents into sexual encounters. The offenders use internet communications such as instant messages, email and chat rooms to meet and develop intimate relationships with victims who are usually teenagers. Wolak *et al.* (2008) have warned against 'moral panics' in relation to such crimes and point out that the numbers of children involved in aggressive solicitations are low and invariably do not involve deception.

Internet sex offenders

Although the population of internet sex offenders is largely described as heterogeneous, there are some striking demographic consistencies between study samples. The most notable of these relates to gender, where the majority are seen to be male (Finkelhor and Ormrod 2004; Seto and Eke 2005; Sullivan 2005; Webb *et al.* 2006; Wolak, Finkelhor and Mitchell 2005). A further characteristic is that the majority are of European descent. There is, however, less consistency in relation to age. What is much more challenging is whether internet offenders are the same as contact sex offenders. It is common practice to group together internet offenders with contact child sexual abusers for the purposes of psychological assessment and treatment. Furthermore, existing theories of child sexual abuse are assumed to be effective in explaining the behaviour of individuals who access, distribute and create child pornography (Middleton 2008). Middleton *et al.* (2006) sought to test one recent theory, Ward and Siegert's (2002) Pathways Model, in an analysis of internet sexual offenders. In the internet sample, the most common pathway was the intimacy deficits pathway. For such individuals, it might be suggested that images depicting children are less anxiety provoking and the child a more accepting partner, and they may use the internet as a maladaptive strategy to avoid their perceived likelihood of failure in adult relationships.

The second largest group in Middleton *et al.*'s internet sample belonged to the emotional dysregulation pathway. This group may use the internet to access both adult and, under certain circumstances, child pornography during times of emotional dysphoria, and to alleviate the strong negative emotions connected with this and increase feelings of wellbeing. However, it is important to note that almost half of the coded sample could not be assigned to any of the five aetiological pathways outlined by Ward and Siegert (2002). These individuals recorded no problems with intimacy or dealing with negative emotions, no distortions in their sexual scripts, and no antisocial cognitions, regarding the appropriateness of sexual contact with children, and yet had been prosecuted for using the internet to access abusive images of children. This might suggest a population of internet offenders who do not share the psychological vulnerabilities typically displayed by other sex offenders. In contrast, however, Sheldon and Howitt (2007) would argue that although there are differences between internet sex offenders and contact offenders, these are relatively insignificant compared to the similarities they share, such as cognitive distortions and sexual fantasies. A reasonable conclusion is that this is an issue that seems to be, as of now, unresolved.

The relationship between online and offline offending

One of the most contentious issues in the work on internet offending in relation to sexual offending against children is the relationship between online and offline behaviour. Specifically this has largely focused on whether viewing images of children may lead to the commission of a contact offence. However, this debate is in part complicated by differences in definitions of what constitutes internet offending across studies. For example, some authors have described internet offenders as people whose offences relate solely to downloading images (Sheldon and Howitt 2007), whereas others would define internet offenders as those where the internet is a tool used in the commission of the offence (Taylor and Quayle 2003). Marshall (2000) suggested that there is not a causal link between viewing pornography and sexual offending, but that it can accelerate psychological processes, enhancing the cognitive distortions of offenders. Seto, Maric and Barbaree (2001) also felt that the evidence for a causal link remains equivocal, and concluded that people who are already predisposed to offend are the most likely to show the effect of pornography exposure. Seto and Eke (2005) examined the criminal histories and later offending activities of child pornography offenders and found that those with prior criminal records were significantly more likely to offend again in the same way during the follow-up period. However, Wolak *et al.*'s (2005) study of child pornography possessors arrested in internet-related crimes indicated that 40% of their sample were 'dual offenders' who sexually victimized children and possessed child pornography. A further study by Seto, Cantor and Blanchard (2005) investigated whether being charged with a child pornography offence was a valid diagnostic indicator of paedophilia, as represented by a phallometrically assessed sexual arousal to children. Their results indicated that child pornography offenders had almost three times greater odds of being phallometrically identified as paedophiles than offenders against children had. However, it is likely that child pornographic images may have been used by offenders for masturbation, a factor that may complicate understanding the phallometric responses in Seto *et al.*'s results.

One of the functions of child pornography for internet offenders is that it is used in relation to sexual fantasy (Quayle and Taylor 2002) and this had led to the above assumptions that it leads to further offending behaviour (Wilson and Jones 2008). However, Sheldon and Howitt (2007) have argued that this view of sexual fantasy is both simplistic and inadequate. In their sample of offenders, internet sex offenders (those who downloaded images) had the highest levels of sexual fantasies of a paedophilic nature, which led these authors to suggest that 'internet offenders are fantasists'. They also found no clear link between sexual fantasy content and offending behaviour. However, Wilson and Jones (2008) have suggested that the transition from fantasy to reality is not a clear-cut process from the psychological to the physical and purported that a third space exists – a 'virtual space' – which is a hybrid or pseudo-realism space where elements of fantasy are blended with reality to create images, videos and sounds reflective of the other spaces and which feed into psychological or fantasy space. This pseudo-real environment is one where opportunities to offend are provoked and fantasies can be created, replicated and updated from the source materials available on the internet.

Internet offending and the law

Internet offending does not occur outside geographical and temporal boundaries. However, as Wykes (2007) has indicated, it does make us mindful of the culturally relative and constructed nature of such crime, 'because in a space unbounded by jurisdictional control or national boundaries the same activity can at once be unrecognized, a nuisance, a joke, perverted and criminal' (p. 69). This is particularly relevant to illegal content, such as abusive images of children (legally defined as child pornography). The International Centre for Missing and Exploited Children (ICMEC 2006) has conducted research into child pornography legislation currently in place in the 184 Interpol Member Countries. Their findings indicated that 95 countries have no legislation at all that specifically addresses child pornography and of the remainder that do have legislation, 54 countries do not define child pornography in national legislation; 27 countries do not provide for computer-facilitated offences; and 41 countries do not criminalize possession of child pornography, regardless of the intent to distribute. Akdeniz (2008) has strongly argued that effective implementation, enforcement and harmonization of child pornography laws could help to reduce the availability and dissemination of child pornography on the internet.

An attempt to generate 'grooming laws' has also been problematic and there is poor definition and understanding of grooming behaviour, difficulties in its identification and a failure of legislation to be truly preventative (Craven, Brown and Gilchrist 2007). It is also the case that grooming implies intent to meet the child in the offline world to commit a contact offence (Gillespie 2006). This does not adequately capture internet offences where the intent of the offender may be the engagement in 'cybersex' with a child online through text, images or web cams and where the intention was not necessarily to meet the youth in an offline context.

Conclusion

It is apparent from the above discussion that the status of internet offending, as it applies to sexual offences against children, is not clearly defined, nor is there consensus about its aetiology and its relationship with the commission of further offences. It is still a new field of enquiry, with limited empirical data and lacking any coherent theoretical models. A further complication is the rapid pace of technological changes which increasingly ease the creation of online content. Such self-generated material is a cause for concern in relation to adolescent internet users, although the potential for harm remains to be quantified.

REFERENCES

Akdeniz, Y. (2008) *Internet Child Pornography and the Law*. Aldershot: Ashgate.

Beech, A. R., Elliott, I. A., Birgden, A. and Findlater, D. (2008) The internet and child sexual offending: a criminological review. *Aggression and Violent Behavior*, 13: 216–28.

Bridges, L. (2008) The changing face of malware. *Network Security*, January, 17–20.

Choo, K-K., Smith, R. G. and McCusker, R. (2007) *Future Directions in Technology Enabled Crime: 2007–09*. Canberra: Australian Institute of Criminology. Available online: www.aic.gov.au.

Craven, S., Brown, S. and Gilchrist, E. (2007) Current responses to sexual grooming: implication for prevention. *The Howard Journal*, 46: 60–71.

Eisenstein, E. M (2008) Identity theft: an exploratory study with implications for marketers. *Journal of Business Research*, 61: 1160–72.

Finkelhor, D. and Ormrod, R. (2004) *Child Pornography: Patterns from the NIBRS*. Washington, DC: US Department of Justice Programs, Office of Juvenile Justice and Delinquency Prevention.

George, M. (2007) Cyberterrorism: hype or reality? *Computer Fraud and Security*, February, 9–12.

Gillespie, A. A. (2006). Indecent images, grooming and the law. *Criminal Law Review*, 412–21.

Goodman, S. E, Kirk, J. C. and Kirk, M. H. (2007) Cyberspace as a medium for terrorists. *Technological Forecasting and Social Change*, 74: 193–210.

ICMEC (2006). Child Pornography: Model Legislation and Global Review. Available online: www.icmec.org/en_X1/pdf/ModelLegislationFINAL.pdf.

Jewkes, Y. and Sharp, K. (2002) Crime, deviance and the disembodied self: transcending the dangers of corporeality. In Y. Jewkes (ed.), *Dot.cons: Crime, Deviance and Identity on the Internet*, pp. 1–14. Cullompton: Willan.

Kiekegaard, S. (2008) Cybering, online grooming and age play. *Computer Law and Security*, Report 24: 41–55.

Marshall, W. L. (2000) Sex offenders' use of pornography. *Journal of Sexual Aggression*, 6: 67–77.

McCusker, R. (2006) Transnational organized cybercrime: distinguishing threat from reality. *Crime, Law and Social Change*, 46: 257–73.

Middleton, D. (2008) Strengths bases approaches to risk assessment. In L. Craig, K. Brown and A. Beech (eds.), *Assessing Risk in Sex Offenders*, pp. 185–200. Chichester: Wiley.

Middleton, D., Elliott, I. A., Mandeville-Norden, R. and Beech, A. R. (2006) An investigation into the applicability of the Ward and Siegert Pathways model of child sexual abuse with internet offenders. *Psychology, Crime and Law*, 12: 589–603.

Moore, T. and Clayton, R. (2008) Evaluating the wisdom of crowds in assessing phishing websites. Paper presented at the 12th International Financial Cryptography and Data Security Conference (FC08), 28–31 January 2008, Cozumel, Mexico. Available online: www.cl.cam.ac.uk/~twm29/.

Quayle, E. (2008) Online sex offending: psychopathology and theory. In D. R. Laws and W. T. O'Donohue (eds.), *Sexual Deviance: Theory, Assessment and Treatment*, pp. 439–58. New York: Guilford Press.

Quayle, E. and Taylor, M. (2002) Child pornography and the internet: perpetuating a cycle of abuse. *Deviant Behavior*, 23: 331–61.

Seto, M. C., Cantor, J. M. and Blanchard, R. (2005) Validation of child pornography possession as a diagnostic indicator of pedophilia. Manuscript submitted for publication.

Seto, M. and Eke, A. (2005) The criminal histories and later offending of child pornography offenders. *Sexual Abuse: A Journal of Research and Treatment*, 17: 201–10.

Seto, M. C., Maric, A. and Barbaree, H. E. (2001) The role of pornography in the etiology of sexual aggression. *Aggression and Violent Behavior*, 6: 35–53.

Sheldon, K. and Howitt, D. (2007) *Sex Offenders and the Internet*. Chichester: Wiley.

Sullivan, C. (2005) *Internet Traders of Child Pornography: Profiling Research*. New Zealand: Censorship Compliance Unit.

Taylor, M. and Quayle, E. (2003) *Child Pornography: An Internet Crime*. Brighton: Routledge.

Ward, T. and Siegert, R. J. (2002) Toward a comprehensive theory of child sexual abuse: a theory knitting perspective. *Psychology, Crime and Law*, 8: 319–51.

Webb, L., Craissati, J. and Keen, S. (2006) *Characteristics of Internet Child Pornography Offenders: A Comparison with Child Molesters. Version 2: Follow-Up Study*. Bracton Centre (Oxleas NHS Trust) and London Probation Area.

Wilson, D. and Jones, T. (2008) 'In my own words': a case study of a paedophile's thinking and doing and his use of the internet. *The Howard Journal*, 47: 107–20.

Wolak, J., Finkelhor, D. and Mitchell, K. J. (2005) *Child-Pornography Possessors Arrested in Internet-Related Crimes: Findings from the National Juvenile Online Victimization Study*. Washington, DC: National Center for Missing and Exploited Children.

Wolak, J., Finkelhor, D., Mitchell, K. J. and Ybarra, M. L. (2008) Online 'predators' and their victims. *American Psychologist*, 63: 111–28.

Wykes, M. (2007) Constructing crime: culture, stalking, celebrity and cyber. *Crime, Media, Culture: An International Journal*, 3: 158–74.

4.8 Murder: legal, psychological and investigative approaches

Louis B. Schlesinger

Definitions

The legal definitions of murder vary slightly according to jurisdiction, but they all essentially involve the unlawful killing of a human being with malice aforethought, either expressed or implied. Criminal homicide constitutes murder when it is committed purposefully or knowingly, or when it is committed recklessly under circumstances manifesting extreme indifference to the value of human life (Black 1979). Recklessness and indifference are inferred mental states if the actor engaged in – or was an accomplice to – the commission of a crime such as robbery, rape, arson, burglary, kidnapping, or escape.

Most jurisdictions divide murder into various degrees depending on the level of intent. First-degree murder is committed purposefully or knowingly; second- or third-degree murder involves a lesser level of intent. In many instances, the actor's state of mind is inferred from behaviour. For example, if a human being is killed in an extremely horrific manner, malice is inferred from the act and the degree of murder is increased.

The main purpose of the various legal standards – specifically the degree of murder based on intentionality – is to assign punishment; the more intent involved, the greater the amount of punishment awarded. For instance, if someone committed a murder with a high level of planning and does so in a way that is considered heinous and that shocks the community, the penalty might be execution. If, however, a person is killed spontaneously as a result of an argument, much less intentionality is involved; the offender might be sentenced to a prison term but probably would not be eligible for capital punishment. And if an intoxicated individual causes an accident in which someone dies, a much lower level of intentionality is implied and much less punishment is imposed.

Psychological approaches

The legal classification of murder is only one approach to understanding what is a heterogeneous group of behaviours, with different aetiologies, different courses, different clinical manifestations and different prognoses. Since the mid 1950s many mental-health researchers and practitioners have developed various methods of classifying murder. For instance, Brancale (1955) offered a simple classification system encompassing two basic groups, administrative and psychiatric. Psychiatric murderers are mentally disturbed, psychotic, or mentally retarded; all other offenders – a much larger group – are placed in the administrative category. Psychiatric offenders are treated in specialized settings, whereas the others are put in prisons.

Bromberg (1961) also divided murderers into two general categories, the normal and the psychopathic. In this scheme, a man who comes upon his wife in bed with a paramour and kills one or both of them is a normal murderer. Bromberg considered this type of 'triangle murder' a reaction to extreme humiliation in a predisposed individual. Under the category of psychopathic, Bromberg included a wide range of offenders with various levels of disturbance, including sex murderers, thrill murderers, rapists who murder and substance abusers who kill. He considered psychopathic murderers to be unstable, unpredictable and without conscience; they commit homicides in an unpremeditated, impulsive manner.

Tanay (1969, 1972) offered a three-pronged classification of murder – egosyntonic, egodystonic (dissociative) and psychotic. The egosyntonic murder is essentially a goal-directed, purposeful act, while the psychotic homicide is a direct response to an overt psychosis, such as command hallucinations or delusions. The dissociative (or egodystonic) murder is carried out by an offender in an altered state, against his or her conscious wishes.

Another classification system was proposed by Halleck (1971), who divided murder into adaptive and maladaptive categories. The adaptive murder is committed for some logical, albeit socially unacceptable purpose (for example, to obtain money or to eliminate someone who interferes with plans), while the maladaptive homicide is illogical, a result of some type of psychopathology, perhaps a psychosis, intoxication, or extreme internal conflicts.

Guttmacher (1960) and Wille (1974) also proposed classification systems; both used psychiatric diagnoses as a central basis for their groupings. Simon (1977) divided murder into three groups based on diagnosis and the victim–offender relationship; his system is supported by empirical research. More recently, Salfati (2000) argued for the empirically supported grouping of murders as being either instrumental (with a logical purpose) or expressive (a result of emotional factors); her categorization is based on overt crime-scene behaviours.

In an attempt to develop a classification system of homicide that encompasses all psychological dimensions, as well as to help in prognostication, Revitch and Schlesinger (1981, 1989) and Schlesinger (2004) developed a system based on an analysis of the antisocial act itself. A small number of murders stem from primary psychiatric/neurological conditions, while the rest fall on a hypothetical spectrum of the following categories: environmental (sociogenic) offences, situational murders, murders committed by impulsive offenders, catathymic homicides, and compulsive-repetitive murders, in which the offender is driven by internal psychogenic sources.

Murder as a result of a primary psychiatric disorder.

Murders that are a result of a psychiatric/neurological condition commonly occur in the organic, toxic, or paranoid states and occasionally in psychotic depression (Malmquist 1996). Neurological conditions such as epilepsy, various encephalopathies, brain injuries and brain tumours have all been regarded as possible causes of homicide because they weaken inhibitory controls (Dinniss 1999). The most common substance associated with violence is alcohol (Fagan 1990). Other substances, such as phencyclidine, psychedelics, amphetamines, cocaine and steroids, have all precipitated sudden violence and murder (Yarvis 1990).

Paranoid schizophrenia and the various paranoid states and disorders are also frequently the cause of homicidal acts (Wilcox 1985). In fact, the classic example of an individual who carried out a murder directed by delusions of persecution is Daniel M'Naghten, and the standard legal test of insanity used in most English-speaking jurisdictions arose from the M'Naghten case.

Sociogenic, or environmentally stimulated, homicides

Many murders are a result of external, environmental or social factors. For example, contract killers, who are motivated primarily by money, have incorporated a value system (such as that found among members of organized crime) that influences their actions (Schlesinger 2001). Cult murder is another example of sociogenic homicide; it is an outgrowth of the dictates of the cult or, more often, of the cult leaders who can easily persuade their followers to kill on their behalf (Bugliosi and Gentry 1975). In addition, murders committed during times of social upheaval and war, such as the various Nazi atrocities, or gang rapes and killings, which involve group pressure, fall into this category.

Situational murders

Situational murders – which constitute about 70% of all homicides – are essentially reactions to external stress (Revitch and Schlesinger 1981). These offences cover a wide range of cases such as domestic murder and homicide in association with another felony.

Homicides committed by impulsive offenders

Impulsive offenders have a lifestyle characterized by lack of direction, randomness of actions and unpredictability (Schlesinger 2004). These individuals are passive and easily led, and their personalities are loosely integrated. Their offences are almost always poorly structured and only partially premeditated. Such offenders have frequently been raised in dysfunctional families, and sometimes they have handicaps such as attention-deficit disorder and learning disabilities. Many impulsive offenders wind up committing murder as just another in a series of antisocial acts.

Catathymic homicides

The concept of catathymia was originally introduced into the forensic field by Wertham (1937). He used this concept to explain unprovoked episodes of homicidal violence in which the offender's thinking changes as a result of emotionally charged inner conflicts. Revitch and Schlesinger (1981) and Schlesinger (2004) updated the concept of catathymia and differentiated an acute and chronic form. The acute catathymic homicide is essentially a sudden, unprovoked murder triggered by deep emotional conflict and tension that are suddenly released. Often the perpetrator of the assault cannot give a logical explanation for the murder; in many cases, the victim – in some symbolic way – ignited the underlying conflicts which overwhelmed the offender's controls.

The chronic catathymic process has three stages – incubation, violent act and relief. Future offenders develop a fixed idea: they come to believe that the only solution to their inner conflict and tension is through violence. They often ruminate for days or months about the need to commit a violent act and frequently experience a feeling of relief following the murder. The victim is usually a close acquaintance, family member, or someone with whom the offender has become obsessed. Stalking homicides are often chronic catathymic murders (Meloy 1992).

Compulsive murders

The compulsive murders are least influenced by external, environmental, or sociogenic factors and stem from internal psychogenic sources (Schlesinger 2004). The need to commit the act is compelling, and there is a high likelihood of repetition. The murder is sexually motivated in that the violent act itself is eroticized and, in essence, is part of the offender's sexual-arousal pattern. Compulsive murders are frequently committed in a ritualistic manner; the homicides may be frequent or isolated or may be repeated after long intervals. Fantasies precede the act by many years. Men are almost always the offenders while women are the victims. Compulsive murders that are planned allow the offender to elude law enforcement, and the result is often a series of homicides.

Investigative approaches

Another approach to understanding and classifying murder has been utilized by law enforcement and is based mainly on crime-scene characteristics as opposed to psychological dimensions. Douglas *et al.* (1992) differentiated forty-three different types of murder including criminal-enterprise homicide, personal-cause homicide, sexual homicide and group-cause homicide. Personal-cause homicides include domestic murders, murders triggered by arguments, or revenge killings. Included in the group-cause homicides are cult murders, murders of hostages and paramilitary homicides. For each of these categories, the authors list crime-scene and forensic findings, victim characteristics and various investigative considerations. Several other categories of murder are commonly used in the investigative approach as described next.

Sexual murder

Although there is no generally agreed-on definition of sexual murder in all its particulars, four subtypes can be identified (Schlesinger 2004): murders where there is a breakthrough of sexual conflicts, murders where there is a fusion of sex and aggression so that the aggressive act is eroticized, murders to cover up a sex crime, and sex-related homicides in which the specific motivational dynamics remain unclear. In sexual murders, the crime scene may look organized (the act itself is planned and little evidence is left), or the crime scene may be disorganized (little planning is involved and a great deal of evidence is left behind). The extent of physical evidence and the degree of planning help guide investigators in developing a profile of the unidentified offender (Douglas and 1986).

Serial murder

In serial murder one person perpetrates a string of murders. Serial killings may occur in medical settings; contract killing involving multiple victims can also be included in this category, as can murders committed by an individual in the course of committing different felonies. The serial murders that have been most studied and that are best understood are those that are sexually motivated.

Mass murder

Mass murder involves killing multiple people in the same location at the same time (Fox and Levin 1994). Dietz (1986) referred to several subtypes of mass murderers including the family annihilator (who kills the entire family), the pseudo-commando (who dresses in paramilitary garb), the disgruntled employee or student (who brings a weapon to work or school and kills a large number of people in a building or on a campus), as well as the set-and-run killer (who plants a bomb and leaves the scene). Additionally, a mentally ill person who is angry for various reasons may kill multiple random people at once.

Spree killing

A spree killing is the murder of multiple people in different locations at different times, with no significant cooling-off period between offences

(Douglas *et al.* 1992). These murders are relatively rare and are hardly studied but seem to involve anger – or the need for revenge for some supposed wrong done to the offender – as the main motivation for the killing spree.

Conclusion

Murder is a complex phenomenon that encompasses legal, psychological and investigative considerations. Each discipline approaches the topic from its own perspective and for its own purposes. The law is concerned with the degree of culpability so that punishment can be appropriately dispensed, while mental health practitioners are interested in understanding the murderer psychologically. Law enforcement, on the other hand, approaches murder from an investigative perspective with the goal being apprehension.

Developing a comprehensive approach to murder could be difficult given the divergent focus of the various disciplines; however, the different methods also have many similarities. For example, Revitch and Schlesinger's catathymic and compulsive homicides fall within the overall category of sexual murder; many mass murders are catathymic, and most other homicides – egosyntonic, adaptive, normal, administrative and spree – are situational. Although the various classification schemes are different in many respects, they have a common denominator. Most homicidal offenders have no overt psychopathology or disturbance, but a few do have psychopathological disturbances in that their acts are fuelled by various psychological factors. The latter group with psychopathological disturbances lies at the intersection of psychology and law.

A purely legal approach to the relatively small number of pathological murderers would fail not only to prevent recidivism but to protect society or help the offender. Specialized forensic centres are desperately needed to provide evaluation and treatment for those murderers with psychopathological aetiologies. These programmes should be located in correctional settings and be connected to medical schools or graduate schools in psychology and criminology so that research, teaching and evaluation can be emphasized. In the long run, this model would protect society from a group of dangerous individuals whom we need to study further. Although vast sums of money have been devoted to the apprehension, legal disposition, incarceration and punishment of murderers, much less is expended on prevention, treatment or, more important, the integrative scientific study of the problem.

REFERENCES

Black, H. C. (1979) *Black's Law Dictionary*, 5th edn. St Paul, MN: West.

Brancale, R. (1955) Problems of classification. *National Probation and Parole Association Journal*, 1: 118–25.

Bromberg, W. (1961) *The Mold of Murder: A Psychiatric Study of Homicide*. New York: Grune & Stratton.

Bugliosi, V. and Gentry, C. (1975) *Helter Skelter*. New York: Bantam Books.

Dietz, P. E. (1986) Mass, serial, and sensational homicides. *Bulletin of the New York Academy of Medicine*, 62: 477–91.

Dinniss, S. (1999) Violent crime in an elderly demented patient. *International Journal of Geriatric Psychiatry*, 14: 889–91.

Douglas, J. E., Burgess, A. W., Burgess, A. G. and Ressler, R. K. (1992) *Crime Classification Manual*. San Francisco: Jossey-Bass.

Douglas, J. E., Ressler, R. K., Burgess, A. W. and Hartman, C. R. (1986) Criminal profiling from crime scene analysis. *Behavioural Sciences and the Law*, 4: 401–21.

Fagan, J. (1990) Intoxication and aggression. In M. Tonry and J. Q. Wilson (eds.), *Crime and Justice: A Review of Research*, pp. 241–320. Chicago: University of Chicago Press.

Fox, J. A. and Levin, J. (1994) *Overkill*. New York: Dell.

Guttmacher, M. S. (1960) *The Mind of the Murderer*. New York: Farrar, Straus and Cudahy.

Halleck, S. (1971) *Psychiatry and the Dilemmas of Crime*. Los Angeles: University of California Press.

Malmquist, C. P. (1996) *Homicide: A Psychiatric Perspective*. Washington, DC: American Psychiatric Press.

Meloy, J. R. (1992) *Violent Attachments*. Northvale, NJ: Aronson.

Revitch, E. and Schlesinger, L. B. (1981) *Psychopathology of Homicide*. Springfield, IL: Thomas.
   (1989) *Sex Murder and Sex Aggression*. Springfield, IL: Thomas.

Salfati, G. C. (2000) The nature of expressiveness and instrumentality in homicide: implications for offender profiling. *Homicide Studies*, 4: 265–91.

Schlesinger, L. B. (2001) The contract murderer: patterns, characteristics, and dynamics. *Journal of Forensic Sciences*, 46: 1119–23.
   (2004) *Sexual Murder: Catathymic and Compulsive Homicides*. Boca Raton, FL: CRC Press.

Simon, R. E. (1977) Type A, AB, and B murderers. *Bulletin of the American Academy of Psychiatry and Law*, 5: 344–62.

Tanay, E. (1969) Psychiatric study of homicide. *American Journal of Psychiatry*, 125: 1252–8.
   (1972) Psychiatric aspects of homicide prevention. *American Journal of Psychiatry*, 128: 49–52.

Wertham, F. (1937) The catathymic crisis: a clinical entity. *Archives of Neurology and Psychiatry*, 37: 974–7.

Wilcox, D. E. (1985) The relationship of mental illness to homicide. *American Journal of Forensic Psychiatry*, 6: 3–15.

Wille, W. (1974) *Citizens Who Commit Murder*. St Louis: Warren Greene.

Yarvis, R. M. (1990) Axis I and axis II diagnostic parameters of homicide. *Bulletin of the American Academy of Psychiatry and Law*, 18: 249–69.

Robbery

Louise E. Porter

Definition

In England and Wales, section 8 (1) of the Theft Act 1968 states that 'a person is guilty of robbery if he[/she] steals, and immediately before or at the time of doing so, and in order to do so, he[/she] uses force on any person or puts or seeks to put any person in fear of being then and there subjected to force'. Robbery can, therefore, involve a range of threatening, forceful and/or violent behaviour, including verbal threats, physical force or weapons (armed robbery). Further, robbery can vary from stealing from organizations (banks, post offices, shops, security vehicles) to personal property, where the latter is often termed 'mugging', 'snatch theft' or 'street robbery' (so termed because of its most frequent location). Victims of robbery can range from owners of commercial establishments or their employees (commercial robbery), to individuals going about their daily routine or even in their own homes (personal robbery).

According to Smith (2003), 45% of UK personal robberies involve victims under 21 years old, with male victims of personal robberies more likely than females. In contrast, Matthews (2002) notes that commercial armed robbers most frequently target lone female employees.

Behavioural/psychological models

Many studies that explore robbery do so in terms of variations in the frequencies of offence characteristics (for example, Barker et al. 1993; Marsden 1989; Smith 2003). Further, some explore the combinations of these characteristics and propose models to explain the psychological meaning of such patterns of variation. For example, Alison et al. (2000) explored themes of robbery offence characteristics, in terms of their statistical co-occurrences, taken from interviews with armed robbers, while Porter and Alison (2006a) explored themes in group robbery offences. Both studies used Smallest Space Analysis, a multidimensional scaling technique, to explore and confirm these patterns (see chapters 8.2 and 8.3 for an explanation of these techniques).

Alison *et al.* (2000) reported three themes of robberies, termed 'Cowboys', 'Bandits' and 'Robin's men' based upon the defining features of each set of behaviours. While 'Robin's men' tended to show more evidence of planning and organization, such as controlling potential witnesses by forcing them to the floor and tying them up, 'Bandits' are described as aggressive, terrorizing victims, and using demeaning language and gratuitous violence. 'Cowboys' are described as reckless, needlessly attacking victims with violence and verbal threats, and using firearms. 'Cowboys' are also reported to be associated with more victim resistance. These themes were particularly differentiated in terms of professionalism, where 'Robin's men' were considered most 'professional', exhibiting evidence of pre-planning and control over victims, while 'Cowboys' were least professional. 'Robin's men' most clearly embody the traditional picture of robbery offenders as organized groups who target secure establishments for large amounts of money.

In contrast, Porter and Alison (2006a) specifically examined group robbery offences from the perspective of an interpersonal circumplex model (Leary 1957), seeking evidence for two dimensions of Dominance vs Submission and Cooperation vs Hostility. They found offence behaviours to co-occur in a pattern consistent with the four themes that these two dimensions represent. Offence behaviours indicative of the Dominance theme demonstrated controlling behaviours that totally disabled victims, such as binding and gagging, and similar to the methods of Alison *et al.*'s (2000) 'Robin's men'. In opposition to the Dominance theme (both in meaning and geographically in the spatial statistical output), the Submission theme showed few offender variables but a greater proportion of victim 'control', where victims refused to do as they were told, struggled and/or ran away, indicating, in contrast to the previous theme, a lack of offender control or presence of offender Submission to the victim. The theme of Cooperation incorporated behaviours designed to coerce victims into participating in the robbery, for example using verbal threats, often backed up by weapons, and demanding victims hand over goods or instructing them to open tills/safes. In opposition to this (again, both semantically and geographically) behaviour indicating Hostility showed offenders using violent means, manually restraining or searching victims and harming, sometimes killing, victims with weapons improvised from the scene of the robbery.

Further, Porter and Alison (2006a) demonstrated thematic differences between commercial and personal robberies. While commercial robberies tended to involve more co-operative behaviours than personal robberies, personal robberies tended to show more hostile features. Potential explanations for these differences may lie in the nature of the offences. For example, offenders may need to seek victims' cooperation for successful commercial robbery, given that they are likely to want access to cash registers and safes and may not have access themselves. There may also be a potentially higher number of people to control in commercial establishments (both employees and customers) than in a street robbery, and decreased physical contact (employees behind counters or screens), necessitating a more controlled approach than physical force and violence. Finally, victim cooperation may be more likely when they are not being robbed of their own personal property, meaning offenders' demands for cooperation may be more likely to be met in commercial robbery, while personal robbers may need (or expect to need) more force in order to successfully part victims and their valuables. However, Porter and Alison (2006a) also suggest that these differences in interpersonal style towards the victim could reflect differences in motivation.

Motives and processes

Ethnographic work in recent years has seen researchers conduct interviews with both active robbers 'on the street' in the US (Jacobs and Wright 1999; Wright and Decker 1997) and with convicted robbers in the UK (Wright, Brookman and Bennett 2006) to explore motivations for committing robbery. These authors concluded that while the main motivation for robbery is a need for fast cash, the 'decision' to rob is influenced by 'street culture'.

While street culture may involve transience and unemployment, leading to financial needs for subsistence, these needs are not always basic for robbery offenders, but are often for luxury items. Indeed, Jacobs and Wright (1999) argue that street culture embodies values such as a 'party' lifestyle involving excitement and hedonism, with minimal responsibilities or forward thinking. Further, such a lifestyle also involves social instability and a need for status, with pressure to display certain status symbols to indicate wealth (for example, a car, clothes, jewellery). For these individuals, legitimate work, if available, would likely be too restrictive on their lifestyle, would not pay enough to cover the lifestyle sought or offer delayed gratification (i.e. time between effort and pay). In contrast, Jacobs and Wright (1999) argue, robbery is seen as easy fast cash, unlike burglary where goods are typically stolen and then must be sold, thus delaying the cash and increasing risk through having to deal with others.

Wright, Brookman and Bennett (2006) found that UK robbers had similar motivations. However, these researchers also noted that some robbers spoke of being motivated by the 'buzz' from overpowering victims. Indeed, Wright *et al.* reported robbers whose primary goal was to fight the victim, with robbery of a passive victim seen as a failure. Further, some offenders recounted that anger at the victim, or revenge, was the chief motivation and stealing was an afterthought. This reinforces Porter and Alison's (2006a) remarks regarding personal robberies tending to be more 'hostile', with commercial robberies more 'co-operative'. As Porter and Alison note:

It is possible that personal and commercial robbers come from a different offending culture that predisposes them to behave with a particular interpersonal style. Thus, [for personal robbers] the crime in itself is a means to status, rather than just the gaining of property/money to gain status, and violence is a necessary part of the process. (Porter and Alison 2006a, pp. 340–1)

There seem, therefore, to be two perspectives regarding motivations for robbery. First, many researchers offer a rational choice perspective, describing robbers as professionals who plan their crimes and learn from their experiences as they advance through their criminal 'career' (Matthews 2002). In contrast, then, is the perspective that robbery is less rational or planned and more routed in street culture and identity.

While these perspectives seem disparate, both are offered support from the fact that robbery offences are often carried out in groups. While an instrumental perspective on co-offending may lend support to the rational choice model of robbery, theories of group influence may help to explain the more expressive forms of robbery that enhance street status.

Motivations for group robbery: instrumental

Given the complexity involved in targeting large, security-conscious commercial establishments, who often have high numbers of staff as well as customers, it may be unsurprising that a large proportion of commercial robberies involve multiple offenders. For example, studies have demonstrated that one-third of Australian bank robberies (Marsden 1989) and 59% of Canadian robberies (Gabor *et al.* 1987) involved two or more co-offenders and almost 80% of armed bank robbers in the US (Haran and Martin 1984) committed the crime with one or more accomplices.

For armed robbery (commercial), it has been suggested that co-offending has an instrumental advantage, with the number of offenders allowing role differentiation, therefore providing a division of labour that increases the ease with which the robbery is executed. Einstadter (1969) explains that a 'basic triad of roles' is necessary for successful robberies and, therefore, most armed robbers operate in groups of three: one remains outside near an automobile while two enter the establishment, armed, one as a back-up to watch customers and prevent them from leaving while one gathers the money. According to Einstadter, if the size and complexity of the robbery require, more people may take part but do not typically perform roles different to the basic triad.

Role differentiation has been identified in armed robbers through interviews by McKluskey and Wardle (2000) and also in ram-raiding teams (Donald and Wilson 2000). The latter study also found that offenders' roles within the robbery corresponded to their criminal history. For example, the 'back-up' (or 'heavy' as Donald and Wilson prefer) tended to have previous convictions for violent offences in contrast to 'drivers' who had previous convictions for non-violent offences.

With role differentiation, there can also be differences in status. McKluskey and Wardle (2000) found evidence of hierarchical structures in the roles of armed robbers, although hierarchical groups were associated with more experienced offenders. However, even in those cases where offenders claimed not to have a leader, they still detailed that one member of the group took on the role of 'planner', being consulted for advice, having ideas and helping to organize the group for the offence.

Motivations for group robbery: group influence

However, there is evidence that less 'sophisticated' street robberies also often involve multiple offenders with some form of structure. In the UK, Smith (2003) reported that 60% of personal robberies involve multiple offenders. Porter and Alison (2006b) specifically examined group robbery (both commercial and personal) for the presence of leadership. Leadership was hypothesized to involve decision making, order giving and taking action (or being the first to act, without the direct influence of another) throughout the different stages of the offence. Leaders were identified in 98% of the 105 cases, with decision making common to all but initial action being the most common form of leadership over autocratic order giving. Further, the most common group structure was a simple dichotomous leader/follower structure, where one group member (leader) displayed influence behaviour to a higher degree than all the other group members (followers) and the followers were equal to one another in the amount of influence they displayed. No discernable quantitative or qualitative differences were observed in the leadership of commercial and personal robbery groups, indicating that both have similar structures and influence processes.

Indeed, Porter and Alison (2006b) indicated that the high incidence of participative leadership of group robbers over autocratic leadership may be due to the age of the offenders. Porter and Alison (2006a) noted that group robbery is typically committed by young males in groups of two or three upon young males. Gabor *et al.* (1987) also noted that 85% of robbery offenders in their sample were under 25 years old with 18- to 21-year-olds being the highest-frequency age group for robbers. Further, within their groups, robbery offenders tend to be of a similar age to one another. Porter and Alison (2006b) suggest that more autocratic forms of leadership may be more likely where groups are organized, older or have more variation in age between members, thus suggesting that leadership style may be dependent on the legitimacy of the leader's position in the group.

Evidence suggests, however, that group robbery is typically committed by male youth peer groups. Indeed, co-offending in general has been found to be more prevalent among youth than adults (Reiss 1988). For young people, the peer group can become a significant source of reinforcement at a time when they are striving for autonomy from adults and asserting their own identity (Corsaro and Eder 1990). Unfortunately, the desire for status and acceptance among peers may encourage antisocial behaviour, particularly through the active leaders outlined above, whereby co-offending is likely to be borne out of group influence rather than any instrumental need for division of labour.

Conclusion

It is clear that different perspectives on robbery highlight different features of the crime. While some researchers draw a picture of robbery as incorporating sophisticated planning, division of labour and professionalism, others view robbery as an example of status-enhancing behaviour in juvenile peer groups.

Somewhat in response to this, Wright *et al.* (2006) argue that research into British robbery has tended to focus only on commercial robbery, thus producing a particular focus on financial motives, with many reporting robbers to spend their money on subsistence or future investment (for example, Matthews 2002). However, Matthews (2002) and Hobbs (1995) have noted a change from robbery as a professional crime to a more recent fragmentation into different forms of criminality. Barker *et al.* (1993) and Smith (2003) found that groups of young street robbers were more likely to be motivated by status and reputation and Matthews (2002) notes that even some commercial robbers spend money on frivolous, luxury items.

However, regardless of motive or target, robbery tends to be a group phenomenon, with group processes and patterns evident even in the least skilled or planned crimes. However, whether these group patterns are a product of the crime or the crime a product of the group is still a question for future research. Cause and effect with multivariate real-world phenomena will always have its challenges (and challengers), and future studies will need at the very least to consider how different motives may be mediated by the number, and characteristics, of those involved as well as the behaviour that they display and the target towards which it is directed.

FURTHER READING

Porter and Alison (2006a, b) offer more detail of the analyses present in this brief overview of types of robbers and also associated behaviours.

REFERENCES

Alison, L., Rockett, W., Deprez, S. and Watts, S. (2000) Bandits, cowboys and Robin's men: the facets of armed robbery. In D. V. Canter and L. Alison (eds.), *Profiling Property Crimes*, pp. 75–106. Aldershot: Ashgate.

Barker, M., Geraghty, J., Webb, B. and Key, T. (1993) The prevention of street robbery. Police Research Group Crime Prevention Unit Series paper no. 44. London: Home Office Police Department.

Corsaro, W. A. and Eder, D. (1990) Children's peer cultures. *Annual Review of Sociology*, 16: 197–220.

Donald, I. and Wilson, A. (2000) Ram raiding: criminals working in groups. In D. V. Canter and L. J. Alison (eds.), *The Social Psychology of Crime*, pp. 189–246. Aldershot: Ashgate.

Einstadter, W. J. (1969) The social organisation of armed robbery. *Social Problems*, 17: 64–83.

Gabor, T., Baril, M., Cusson, M., Elie, D., LeBlanc, M. and Normandeau, A. (1987) *Armed Robbery: Cops, Robbers and Victims*. Springfield, IL: Thomas.

Haran, J. F. and Martin, J. M. (1984) The armed urban bank robber: a profile. *Federal Probation*, 48: 47–73.

Hobbs, D. (1995) *Bad Business: Professional Crime in Modern Britain.* New York: Oxford University Press.

Jacobs, B. A. and Wright, R. (1999) Stick-up, street culture and offender motivation. *Criminology,* 37: 149–73.

Leary, T. (1957) *Interpersonal Diagnosis of Personality.* New York: Ronald Press.

Marsden, J. (1989) Bank robbery in Australia. In D. Challinger (ed.), *Armed Robbery,* pp. 25–36. Canberra: Australian Institute of Criminology.

Matthews, R. (2002) *Armed Robbery.* Cullompton: Willan.

McCluskey, K. and Wardle, S. (2000) The social structure of robbery. In D. V. Canter and L. J. Alison (eds.), *The Social Psychology of Crime,* pp. 247–85. Aldershot: Ashgate.

Porter, L. E. and Alison, L. J. (2006a) Behavioural coherence in group robbery: a circumplex model of offender and victim interactions. *Aggressive Behavior,* 32: 330–42.

    (2006b) Leadership and hierarchies in criminal groups: scaling degrees of leading behaviour in group robbery. *Legal and Criminological Psychology,* 11: 245–65.

Reiss, A. J. (1988) Co-offending and criminal careers. In M. Tonry and N. Morris (eds.), *Crime and Justice: A Review of Research,* vol. 10. Chicago: University of Chicago Press.

Smith, J. (2003) *The Nature of Personal Robbery.* Home Office Research Study 254. London: Home Office.

Wright, R., Brookman, F. and Bennett, T. (2006) The foreground dynamics of street robbery in Britain. *British Journal of Criminology,* 46: 1–15

Wright, R. and Decker, S. H. (1997) *Armed Robbers in Action.* Boston, MA: Northeastern University Press.

4.10 Sexual assault

Miranda A. H. Horvath

See also chapter 1.12 Sexual offenders, chapter 4.7 Internet sexual offending, chapter 4.11 Sexual fantasy and sex offending, chapter 4.12 Stalking, chapter 5.3 Consent and capacity in civil cases.

Definition

In England and Wales sexual assaults are divided into three legal categories: rape, assault by penetration and sexual assault as defined in table 4.10.1. There are many related offences such as 'abuse of a position of trust', 'sexual activity in the presence of a child', etc. (these are all covered in the Sexual Offences Act 2003) and all the above can be further elaborated by the offences of 'conspiracy to …' and 'aiding and abetting …'.

Where person B is under 13 years of age there are separate offences of rape, assault by penetration and sexual assault of a child. These differ in that the requirements regarding consent and person A not reasonably believing that B consents, do not apply, as in English law a child cannot consent to any sexual activity. Sentencing is the same for rape and assault by penetration but for sexual assault the maximum term of imprisonment is raised from ten to fourteen years.

In the research literature 'sexual assault' is frequently used interchangably with 'rape' and may refer to rape as legally defined, assault by penetration and/or sexual assault.

Current thinking, research and practice

Attrition

'Attrition' is the process by which cases are lost or dropped from various stages in the criminal justice system (CJS) (see e.g. HM Crown Prosecution Service

Table 4.10.1 Sexual Offences Act 2003: definitions of rape, assault by penetration and sexual assault

	Rape (Part 1, section 1)	Assault by penetration (Part 1, section 2)	Sexual assault (Part 1, section 3)
(1) A person (A) commits an offence if	he intentionally penetrates the vagina, anus or mouth of another person (B) with his penis,	he intentionally penetrates the vagina or anus of another person (B) with a part of his body or anything else,	he intentionally touches another person (B)
		the penetration is sexual,	the touching is sexual,
	B does not consent to the penetration, and		B does not consent to the touching, and
	A does not reasonably believe that B consents.		

(2) Whether a belief is reasonable is to be determined having regard to all the circumstances, including any steps A has taken to ascertain whether B consents.

(3) Sections 75 and 76 apply: *section 75 gives the evidential presumptions about consent and section 76 gives the conclusive presumptions about consent.*

| **(4)** A person guilty of an offence under this section is liable | on conviction on indictment, to imprisonment for life. | | (a) on summary conviction,[a] to imprisonment for a term not exceeding 6 months or a fine not exceeding the statutory maximum or both; (b) on conviction on indictment,[b] to imprisonment for a term not exceeding 10 years. |

[a] A summary conviction is a conviction in a magistrates' court.
[b] A conviction on indictment is a conviction in a crown court with a jury.

Inspectorate and HM Inspectorate of Constabulary 2002; Kelly, Lovett and Regan 2005. As a crime, rape and sexual assault are under-reported (Walby and Allen 2004), and although Home Office data show that there has been a steady increase in reporting in recent years, statistics also show a continuing decline in the conviction rate for rape over the last three decades. In 2004 it was 5.27%.

There has been a considerable amount of work (the majority of which has been policy-orientated studies) seeking to discover why it is so difficult to secure convictions.

Issues in court: consent and expert witness testimony

The question of consent is crucial in adult sexual assault cases. The Sexual Offences Act 2003, for the first time, defined consent in law with the aim of making it easier for juries to make fair and balanced decisions and to place the onus on men that it is their responsibility to obtain consent. It is too soon to assess whether this has had an impact in the conviction rate for rape and sexual assault. There have been a number of other significant measures proposed in recent years which should also have an impact on how rape and sexual assault cases are heard in court, for example: allowing adult victims of rape to give video-recorded evidence at trials; to consider further how general expert material could be presented in a controlled and consistent way with a view to dispelling myths around rape victims' behaviour; defining the law on a complainant's capacity to give consent where drink or drugs are involved (this is to assist judges and juries); and ensuring that all relevant evidence of complaints made by victims in rape cases should be admissible as evidence in a trial, irrespective of time passed since the alleged conduct.

Rape myths

Beliefs and attitudes about rape and sexual assault underpin how society perceives, understands and treats the victims and perpetrators of these crimes. The focus in forensic psychology has been on the concept of rape myths which are: 'prejudicial, stereotyped and false beliefs about rape, rape victims and rapists' (Burt 1980, p. 217). For example, if a woman is wearing a short skirt she is asking to be raped. Rape myths are still prevalent among many people working in the criminal justice system, who investigate, prosecute, defend and judge rape cases and in the general public, who make up juries in rape cases (Bohner, Siebler and Schmelcher 2006; Eyssel, Bohner and Siebler 2006; Payne, Lonsway and Fitzgerald 1999).

Rape myths are particularly problematic because they support stereotypical notions of rape, which Estrich (1987) labelled 'real rape'. Real rape is defined as committed by strangers, occurring in outdoor locations and involving weapons and injury (Kelly 2002). This in turn creates a situation in which it is perceived that only certain types of people can be victims and perpetrators and a very specific series of behaviours can be classified as a rape or sexual assault. This in turn contributes to the high levels of attrition. There is,

Table 4.10.2 Components of three rapist motivation typologies

Groth, Burgess and Holstrom (1977)	Prentky and Knight (1991)	Hazelwood (1995)
1 Anger excitation (sadistic)	Opportunistic high social competency	Selfish
2 Anger retaliation	Opportunistic low social competency	Unselfish
3 Power reassurance	Pervasively angry	
4 Power dominance	Sexual sadistic muted	
5 Opportunistic	Sexual sadistic overt	
6	Sexual non-sadistic low social competency	
7	Sexual non-sadistic high social competency	
8	Vindictive low social competency	
9	Vindictive high social competency	

however, considerable empirical evidence that the majority of rapes do not fall into the 'real rape' definition, for example, the majority of rapes are not committed by strangers but are actually committed by someone known to the victim (Walby and Allen 2004).

Typologies for understanding rape

Offender-focused classifications which focus on motivation (e.g. Groth *et al.* 1977; Hazelwood 1995; Prentky and Knight 1991) have dominated understanding and thinking about sexual assault since the 1970s. These look at characteristics of the assailant and their motivation and draw generalizations about the population of sexual deviants (see table 4.10.2).

There are a number of problems which inhibit the usefulness of this approach. Specifically, typologies of rapists do not take into account the means the offender uses to effect a rape. They also have a tendency to combine motivations, cognitions and behaviours without distinguishing between them. Furthermore, there are a number of practical and methodological problems with the taxonomies, in that they lack reliability and validity (Bishopp 2003; Grubin and Kennedy 1991). For example, whilst some (e.g. Prentky and Knight 1991) have been regularly updated and replicated on more than one sample of offenders, the majority have not, in some cases because the attempted replication has not worked and in others researchers have not attempted any replications.

Table 4.10.3 Summary of the components of rape using offence behaviours

Canter and Heritage (1990)	Heritage (1992)	Canter et al. (2003)	Salfati and Taylor (2006)
66 stranger rapes	209 stranger sexual assaults	112 stranger rapes	37 sexual homicides and 37 rapes
1 Intimacy		Involvement	
2 Violence	Aggression	Hostility	Violence
3 Impersonal		Control	Control
4 Criminality	Criminality	Theft	Exploit
5 Sexuality	Sexuality		

Further taxonomies assume that offenders will fall into one classification and do not allow for the possibility of hybrid offenders having characteristics from several classifications. Nor do typologies consider the recently established phenomenon of crossover offending, where, for example, an offender may sexually offend against both child and adult victims, across genders and also within and outside the family (Cann, Friendship and Gozna 2007; Heil, Ahlmeyer and Simons 2003). Moreover, no taxonomy has yet been able to discriminate consistently between different groups of sexual offenders, but they have helped to identify and confirm some useful psychological constructs, such as the role of anger and power.

Other approaches examine offence behaviours and the interaction between the offender and victim (e.g. Canter 1995; Canter and Heritage 1990; Heritage 1992). The assumption here is that understanding rape can be accomplished by drawing significant information about the offender from their actions during the offence. Typically data are derived from police witness statements. Using behaviours that occur during rapes and the principles of facet theory (Guttman 1954) and its associated non-metric analysis technique (Smallest Space Analysis: Lingoes 1968), Canter and Heritage (1990) identified five core components of rape behaviours which relate to different interpersonal styles of rapists (see table 4.10.3). Subsequent research utilizing the same technique has refined the components as outlined in table 4.10.3.

A major problem with focusing on the offence behaviours is the lack of predictive capacity and differentiating between consensual and coercive sex. This criticism comes from the approach which views sexual assaults as an interaction, a socially structured phenomenon (Fossi, Clarke and Lawrence 2005). Following this line of reasoning, in order to understand sexual offences fully it is necessary to analyse the behaviour of both parties involved in the offence (Fossi *et al.* 2005). The obvious problem with this is that the depth of information required to perform such analyses is not always available. However, it is argued that the general principle of considering the assault from both victim and offender perspectives and considering the interaction between the victim and offender displays the most potential for ultimately developing a comprehensive understanding of rape.

Victim-focused approaches seek to understand rape according to the offender's preference for a certain age of victim and the relationship between the victim and offender. For example, from such an approach we understand that certain offenders prefer children (paedophilia: Howitt 1995) whereas others prefer elderly people (gerontophilia: Kaul and Duffy 1991). Similarly, there is broad agreement in the literature that there are three types of rape related to the victim and offender relationship: Intimate, Acquaintance and Stranger (Harris and Grace 1999). This classification has been used to help infer the offender's motivations for rape. Other approaches have considered the way victims react to offenders in rape scenarios as a way of developing rape prevention strategies (e.g. Block and Skogan 1986; Carter, Prentky and Burgess 1995; Scully 1990).

Drugs/alcohol

The links between alcohol and sexual assault have been consistently demonstrated in international and national research (Abbey *et al.* 2001; Kelly, Lovett and Regan 2005). In recent years there has been a resurgence of interest from researchers as a result of high-profile cases and significant media coverage of 'drug-assisted/facilitated sexual assault'. The main findings of this work suggests that the term 'drug-assisted/facilitated sexual assault' is misleading as 'drug' is not commonly understood to mean alcohol yet alcohol is the drug of choice and in the majority of cases the victim has consumed the alcohol voluntarily (Horvath and Brown 2006, 2007; Scott-Ham and Burton 2005, 2006). This contradicts the media construction of the rapist slipping Rohypnol into an unsuspecting woman's drink, waiting for her to lose consciousness and then sexually assaulting her.

Another area that has received considerable research attention is perceptions of sexual assault cases where the victim was intoxicated, with the specific focus on mock jurors' perceptions (Finch and Munro 2005, 2006; Jenkins and Schuller 2007; Klippenstine, Schuller and Wall 2007). This research has shown that when a victim has consumed alcohol or drugs voluntarily, and to a lesser extent if the perpetrator has spiked her drink, the perpetrator's account of events is more likely to be believed and the victim blamed for her victimization. The relationship between alcohol use and sexual assault is complex and requires further investigation (Gidycz, Loh and Lobo 2007).

Conclusion

Sexual assault is a complex crime which forensic psychological research has only just begun to understand and explain. This chapter has given a brief overview of some of the key areas for consideration by practitioners and researchers. The complexity of sexual assault and its potential similarity to consensual encounters means that work in this area must be undertaken with sensitivity and professionalism.

FURTHER READING

Julie Alison and Lawrence Wrightsman's book (1993) *Rape: The Misunderstood Crime* (Thousand Oaks, CA: Sage) is a good introduction to rape and sexual assault as it explores the dynamics related to both rapists and rape victims. For a comprehensive explanation of attrition see Kelly, Lovett and Regan (2005; see below). For illuminating insights on researching and working with victims of rape and sexual assault see Patricia Yancey Martin's book (2005) *Rape Work: Victims, Gender, and Emotions in Organization and Community Context* (New York: Routledge). Jennifer Temkin and Barbara Krahe's book (2008) *Sexual Assault and the Justice Gap: A Question of Attitude* (Oxford: Hart) is an interdisciplinary attempt to examine the attitudinal problems which bedevil this area of law and possible strategies for addressing them. Finally, Miranda A. H. Horrath and Jennifer M. Brown (eds.) (2009) *Rape: Challenging Contemporary Thinking* (Cullompton: Willan) collates current thinking.

REFERENCES

Abbey, A., Zawacki, T., Buck, P. O., Clinton, A. M. and McAuslan, P. (2001) Alcohol and sexual assault. *Alcohol Research and Health*, 25: 43–51.

Bishopp, D. C. F. (2003) Dimensions of sexual aggression. Unpublished PhD thesis, University of Surrey.

Block, R. and Skogan, W. C. (1986) Resistance and nonfatal outcomes in stranger-to-stranger predatory crime. *Violence and Victims*, 4: 241–53.

Bohner, G., Siebler, F. and Schmelcher, J. (2006) Social norms and the likelihood of raping: perceived rape myth acceptance of others affects men's rape proclivity. *Personality and Social Psychology Bulletin*, 32: 286–97.

Burt, M. R. (1980) Cultural myths and supports of rape. *Journal of Personality and Social Psychology*, 38: 217–30.

Cann, J., Friendship, C. and Gozna, L. F. (2007) Assessing crossover in a sample of sexual offenders with multiple victims. *Legal and Criminological Psychology*, 12: 149–63.

Canter, D. V. (1995) *Criminal Shadows*. London: HarperCollins.

Canter, D. V., Benell, C., Alison, L. and Reddy, S. (2003) Differentiating sex offences: a behaviourally based thematic classification of stranger rapes. *Behavioural Sciences and the Law*, 21: 157–74.

Canter, D. V. and Heritage, R. (1990) A multivariate model of sexual offence behaviour: developments in 'offender profiling'. *Journal of Forensic Psychiatry*, 1: 185–212.

Carter, D. V., Prentky, A. and Burgess, A. W. (1988) Victims: lessons learned for responses to sexual violence. In R. K. Ressler, A. W. Burgess and J. E. Douglas (eds.), *Sexual Homicide: Patterns and Motives*, pp. 105–32. Lexington, MA: Lexington Books.

Estrich, S. (1987) *Real Rape: How the Legal System Victimizes Women Who Say No*. Cambridge, MA: Harvard University Press.

Eyssel, F., Bohner, G. and Siebler, F. (2006). Perceived rape myth acceptance of others predicts rape proclivity: social norm or judgmental anchoring? *Swiss Journal of Psychology*, 65: 93–99.

Finch, E. and Munro, V. E. (2005) Juror stereotypes and blame attribution in rape cases involving intoxicants: the findings of a pilot study. *British Journal of Criminology*, 45: 25–38.

(2006) Breaking boundaries? Sexual consent in the jury room. *Legal Studies*, 26: 303–20.

Fossi, J. J., Clarke, D. D. and Lawrence, C. (2005) Bedroom rape: sequences of sexual behaviour in stranger assaults. *Journal of Interpersonal Violence*, 20: 1444–66.

Gidycz, C. A., Loh, C. and Lobo, T. (2007) Reciprocal relationships among alcohol use, risk perception and sexual victimisation: a prospective analysis. *Journal of American College Health*, 56: 5–14.

Groth, A. N., Burgess, A. W. and Holmstrom, L. H. (1977) Rape: power, anger and sexuality. *American Journal of Psychiatry*, 134: 1239–43.

Grubin, D. H. and Kennedy, H. G. (1991) The classification of sexual offenders. *Criminal Behaviour and Mental Health*, 1: 123–29.

Guttman, L. (1954) A new approach to factor analysis: the radex. In P. F. Lazerfield (ed.), *Mathematical Thinking in Social Sciences*, pp. 258–349. Glencoe, IL: Free Press.

Harris, J. and Grace, S. (1999) *A Question of Evidence? Investigating and Prosecuting Rape in the 1990s*. London: Home Office.

Hazelwood, R. R. (1995) Analysing the rape and profiling the offender. In R. R. Hazelwood and A. W. Burgess (eds.), *Practical Aspects of Rape Investigation*, 2nd edn, pp. 169–99. Danvers, MA: CRC Press LLC.

Heil, P., Ahlymeyer, S. and Simons, D. (2003) Crossover sexual offenses. *Sexual Abuse: A Journal of Research and Treatment*, 15: 221–36.

Heritage, R. (1992) Facts of sexual assault: first steps in investigating classifications. Unpublished MPhil thesis, University of Surrey.

HM Crown Prosecution Service Inspectorate and HM Inspectorate of Constabulary (2002) *A Report on the Joint Inspection into the Investigation and Prosecution of Cases Involving Allegations of Rape*. London: HMCPSI.

Horvath, M. A. H. and Brown, J. (2006) The role of alcohol and drugs in rape. *Medicine, Science and the Law*, 46: 219–28.

    (2007) Alcohol as drug of choice: Is drug-assisted rape a misnomer? *Psychology, Crime and Law*, 13: 417–29.

Howitt, D. (1995) *Paedophiles and Sexual Offences against Children*. Chichester: Wiley.

Jenkins, G. and Schuller, R. A. (2007) The impact of negative forensic evidence on mock jurors' perceptions of a trial of drug-facilitated sexual assault, *Law and Human Behaviour*, 31: 369–80.

Kaul, A. and Duffy, S. (1991) Gerontophilia – a case report. *Medicine, Science and the Law*, 31: 110–14.

Kelly, L. (2002) *A Research Review on the Reporting, Investigation and Prosecution of Rape Cases*. London: HMCPSI.

Kelly, L., Lovett, J. and Regan, L. (2005) *A Gap or a Chasm? Attrition in Reported Rape Cases*. Home Office Research Study 293. London: Home Office.

Klippenstine, M. A., Schuller, R. A. and Wall, A.-M. (2007) Perceptions of sexual assault: the expression of gender differences and the impact of target alcohol consumption. *Journal of Applied Social Psychology*, 37: 2620–41.

Lingoes, J. C. (1968) The multivariate analysis of qualitative data. *Multivariate Behavioural Research*, 3: 61–94.

Payne, D. L., Lonsway, K. A. and Fitzgerald, L. F. (1999) Rape myth acceptance: exploration of its structure and its measurement using the Illinois Rape Myth Acceptance Scale. *Journal of Research in Personality*, 33: 27–68.

Prentky, R. A. and Knight, R. A. (1991). Identifying critical dimensions for discriminating among rapists. *Journal of Consulting and Clinical Psychology*, 59: 643–61.

Salfati, C. G. and Taylor, P. (2006) Differentiating sexual violence: a comparison of sexual homicide and rape. *Psychology, Crime and Law*, 12: 107–25.

Scott-Ham, M. and Burton, F. (2005) Toxicological findings in cases of alleged drug-facilitated sexual assault in the United Kingdom over a 3-year period. *Journal of Clinical Forensic Medicine*, 12: 175–236.

    (2006) A study of blood and urine alcohol concentrations in cases of alleged drug-facilitated sexual assault in the United Kingdom over a 3-year period. *Journal of Clinical Forensic Medicine*, 13: 107–11.

Scully, D. (1990) *Understanding Sexual Violence*. Boston, MA: Unwin Hyman.

Walby, S. and Allen, J. (2004) *Domestic Violence, Sexual Assault and Stalking: Findings from the British Crime Survey*. Home Office Research Study 276. London: Home Office.

4.11 Sexual fantasy and sex offending

Jane Palmer

See also chapter 1.12 Sexual offenders, chapter 4.10 Sexual assault.

Definition

In a very broad sense, sexual fantasies are 'almost any mental imagery that is sexually arousing or erotic to the individual' (Leitenberg and Henning, p. 471). A more detailed definition of fantasy is 'an elaborated set of cognitions (or thoughts) characterised by preoccupation (or rehearsal) anchored in emotion and originating in daydreams' (Prentky *et al.* 1989).

In this context of looking at sexual fantasies and sexual offending, work has focused on the role that deviant fantasy plays. Although 'deviance' has historically had different meanings (e.g. deviation from statistical or social/cultural norms), in this context of looking at sexual fantasies and sexual offending it may be more helpful to conceptualize deviant sexual fantasy as offence-related fantasy, or 'a sexual interest (manifested in thoughts, fantasies, urges, pornography use etc) which, if enacted, would result in illegal behaviour' (D. Perkins personal communication).

Theories linking offence-related sexual fantasy and sex offending

The observation by Abel and Blanchard (1974) that there is a 'high concordance between the presence of deviant fantasies and the occurrence of deviant behaviours' (p. 468) can be seen to exemplify the views of theorists who have put forward the notion of a functional relationship between deviant, or offence-related, sexual fantasy/arousal and sexual offending.[1]

[1] E.g. McGuire, Carlisle and Young 1965; Abel and Blanchard 1974; MacCulloch *et al.* 1983; Burgess *et al.* 1986; Laws and Marshall 1990; Hall and Hirschman 1991; MacCulloch, Gray and Watt 2000; Ward and Siegert, 2002; Ward and Beech 2006.

Abel and Blanchard (1974) hypothesized that sex offenders are aroused by more deviant offence-related stimuli than consenting sexual stimuli. Underlying this is the assumption that arousal to deviant images increases the probability of fantasizing to deviant images, and consequently, increases the possibility of acting out them out in deviant behaviour (Leitenberg and Henning 1995).

MacCulloch et al. (1983) explored the role of fantasy in personality-disordered sex offenders and found that their sample divided into two groups: sadistic, fantasy-led, and impulsive, aggression-led sex offenders. They reported that offenders with a history of sadistic fantasizing had marked deficits in social and interpersonal skills, which had led to feelings of inadequacy. From these observations, a hypothesis was put forward to explain the development of fantasy, and its link with behaviour. MacCulloch et al. (1983) postulated that difficulties in controlling 'real-life' situations, specifically sexual relationships, would lead to the person seeking to gain control through their inner world. They hypothesized that the development of deviant fantasy arises through classical conditioning (e.g. pairing arousal/masturbation with thoughts of control) and is maintained through operant conditioning (i.e. continued fantasy of control as it provides relief from feelings of inadequacy). Furthermore, MacCulloch et al. (1983) proposed that behavioural 'try-outs' of part of the fantasy are undertaken to maintain the efficacy of arousal of the fantasy. MacCulloch, Gray and Watt (2000) hypothesized that feelings of both aggression and sexual arousal elicited concurrently by childhood trauma become associated and form a stage prior to classical conditioning (sensory pre-conditioning).

Recent unpublished research[2] (Palmer 2006) which explored sadistic behaviour in sex offenders, using data from both prison and high-secure psychiatric settings in England, supported MacCulloch et al.'s (1983) theory. It found that those scoring higher on a Checklist of Sadistic Behaviour (CSB, Palmer 2006) also had more offence-related fantasies and were more likely to demonstrate deviant sexual arousal. Findings served to develop a Control Restoration Model of sadistic sexual offending (Palmer 2006), in which it is hypothesized that sadistic sexual fantasy and offending are engaged in to restore a sense of control to the offender.

Burgess et al. (1986) developed a motivational model to explain the development of deviant fantasy and cognitive structures that support sexual homicide. They observed that motivation for offending arose out of ways of thinking, either from, or influenced by, childhood experiences and a pervasive sense of social isolation coupled with repetitive antisocial cognitions, which

---

[2] Funded by the National Programme in Forensic Mental Health.

lead to fantasies for the purpose of overcoming social isolation and to provide a means by which one can experience control and mastery.

Laws and Marshall (1990) developed a theory to explain the acquisition and maintenance of deviant sexual preferences and behaviour, which is accounted for through classical and operant conditioning, but additionally included aspects of social learning theory (SLT). They proposed that once learned, deviant sexual preferences and behaviours become resilient to change and are preserved through specific autoerotic and social learning influences; they must be reinforced, either through masturbation or acting out of behaviour, to be maintained.

Offence-related sexual fantasy or arousal has also been a key feature of models of child sexual offending (e.g. Hall and Hirschman 1991; Ward and Siegert 2002). In their integrated theory of sexual offending, Ward and Beech (2006) view the development of deviant sexual fantasy as a product of deficits in managing attachment and mood problems and holding dysfunctional schema. These, coupled with deficits in sexual control and arousal driven by deviant fantasy, could lead to acting out in particular situations when an individual's vulnerabilities are activated. Ward and Beech proposed that the consequence of acting out deviant fantasy in offending behaviour 'can modify, entrench, or worsen the personal circumstances of an offender and in this way, increase or maintain the offending behaviour' (p. 57).

Research linking offence-related sexual fantasy and sex offending

Research has considered the role of fantasy in sex offending. For example, Deu and Edelmann (1997) investigated the role of criminal fantasy in 'predatory' (multiple, pre-planned offences) and 'opportunist' (single, disorganized offences) sex offenders, using a projective test known as the Criminal Fantasy Technique (Schlesinger and Kutash 1981). They found that predatory sex offenders were more organized and elaborate in their criminal fantasies than opportunists, and indicated that this strengthened the evidence towards the notion that fantasy provides a medium for prior rehearsal of premeditated and repetitive sexual offences.

In a study comparing the number of violent sexual fantasies of single and serial sexual homicide offenders, Prentky et al. (1989) found that 23% and 86% reported such fantasies, respectively. The authors suggested that the findings implied a functional relationship between serial sexual homicide offending behaviour and fantasy.

Langevin, Lang and Curnoe (1998) investigated the level of deviant fantasy in different types of sex offender and found that deviant age fantasies discriminated between paedophiles and controls, whilst sexual aggressives reported higher levels of 'deviant' act fantasies (defined in social-norm terms) than other sexual offenders.

Marshall, Barbaree and Eccles (1991) observed that over half of their sample of child molesters reported fantasizing about children, with over a fifth reporting the fantasies to have commenced prior to the commission of their first offence. However, this also implies that almost half did not report having sexual fantasies involving children, with almost four-fifths of the sample having no child sexual fantasies prior to their first offence. Other studies have demonstrated a disparity in levels of child sexual fantasy among child sexual offenders (e.g. Swaffer *et al.* 2000).

Offence-related sexual fantasy in mentally disordered sex offenders has also been considered. For example, Smith (1999) investigated the relationship between recorded aggressive sexual fantasies of psychotic sex offenders against adult women and offending behaviour. He found that almost a quarter of the sex offenders were recorded in files as engaging in aggressive sexual fantasies leading up to and/or at the time of the offence.

From this review it is apparent that findings regarding the link between sexual fantasy and sexual offending are inconsistent. Explanations for the disparity could include differing samples, populations, definitions, methodology etc., but it is clear that sex offenders are not a homogeneous group, and therefore fantasy may not be a central mechanism to offending for all sex offenders. Research suggests that for some sex offenders, such as paedophiles and those that engage in sadistic offending, serial sexual homicide, and premeditated and repetitive offending, fantasy appears to play a more central role.

The function of sexual fantasy in sex offending

A key debate is, then, what role does fantasy play in sex offending? Sexual fantasies are hypothesized to serve many functions in the development and maintenance of normal sexual behaviour (e.g. Swaffer *et al.* 2000), including providing a means of escaping from reality, releasing anger (Deu and Edelmann 1997) and maintaining and increasing arousal (Plaud and Bigwood 1997). From reviewing some of the key theories of sexual offending it can be seen that although there are multiple functions of fantasy implied (e.g. fantasy as a coping mechanism, emotion regulator, means to experience control, way to increase or maintain arousal, means to rehearse offending behaviour), there is a central assumption within all that fantasy leads to, or facilitates, sexual offending. Further research has considered the function of sexual fantasy in the commission of sexual offences. For example, Meloy (2000) reviewed research on sexual homicide offenders and suggested that fantasy provides positive reinforcement in five ways: it sustains pleasure; reduces behavioural inhibition; engenders omnipotence (control over victim) and grandiosity (fantasy as perfect); and it enables offence 'practice' prior to and in between offending. Gee, Ward and Eccleston (2003) explored the function of sexual fantasy in offending by analysing interview material using a Grounded Theory approach. They found four main themes that emerged, which formed the Sexual Fantasy Function Model;

1. Participants described fantasy as a means of affect regulation, which included alleviating dysphoric mood/affect, elevating ambivalent mood/affect and enhancing positive mood/affect.
2. The findings suggested that sexual fantasy serves to both induce and increase sexual arousal.
3. Sexual fantasy appeared to act as a coping mechanism through either providing the offender with a sense of control (through either distortion or manipulation) or as a means of escape from reality.
4. Fantasy is used to model experience, either through rehearsal of actual experiences or through creating or simulating new experiences (including planning escalating behaviours to act out).

The literature suggests that the role of sexual fantasy in offending behaviour is multifaceted. That is, it is not only that fantasy appears to play different roles for different types of offender, but that even within the same offender group there may be multiple functions of fantasy, and indeed, for the same offender there may be many functions that fantasy performs, which may change over time.

What distinguishes sexual fantasy in sexual offenders from non-sexual offenders / non-offenders?

There has been inconsistency in the outcome of research exploring the differences between fantasies of sex offenders and non-sex offenders. Some research suggests no distinction, for example Rokach, Nutbrown and Nexhipi (1988) reported no difference when comparing sex offenders and non-sex offenders on amount of aggressive sexual fantasies. There is also research to suggest similar, if not higher, levels of 'deviant' fantasy in non-offenders compared to sex offenders (e.g. Langevin *et al.* 1998).

Other research has demonstrated a distinction in the nature of deviant sexual fantasy between those who have and have not committed sexual offences. Quinsey, Chaplin and Upfold (1984) found that rapists responded significantly more to rape stimuli than non-rapists, using phallometric assessment. The authors found that the level of violence was an important differentiator of rapists from non-rapists. Rice *et al.* (1994) found rape stories which were told from the perspective of a suffering victim were the best distinguisher of rapists and non-rapists (including both non-sexual offenders and a community sample of non-offenders). Daleiden *et al.* (1998) found no difference in the level of 'deviant' fantasies between sex offenders and non-offenders, rather what distinguished the two was the dearth of 'normal' fantasies in the sex offender sample. However, findings from DiGiorgio-Miller (2007) appear to contradict this by observing a positive correlation between the level of deviant and non-deviant sexual fantasies in sex offenders. A further distinction postulated between sex offenders' and non-sex offenders' fantasies is that sex offenders have well-established deviant fantasies by adolescence, implying qualitative differences in childhood (Howitt 2004).

Regardless of whether a distinction exists, research suggests that non-offending populations do engage in deviant sexual fantasy. Leitenberg and Henning (1995) reviewed previous literature and found that the documented number of (non-offending) men reporting fantasizing about forcing someone to have sex ranged from 13% to 54%, with an average of 31%. There has also been research carried out concerning deviant fantasies regarding age of person being fantasized about. These studies have shown that non-offending populations have also reported sexual fantasies involving pre-pubescent and pubescent children (see Leitenberg and Henning 1995 for a review). For example, Briere and Runtz (1989) found in their sample of non-offending men that 21% agreed with the statement 'little children attract me sexually', with 9% admitting to sexual fantasies involving children.

In light of such findings, Howitt (2004) questioned the presence of a qualitatively different mechanism of fantasy between non-offenders (fantasy as 'harmless') and sex offenders (fantasy as driving offending). Leitenberg and Henning (1995) suggest that 'unless the boundary between fantasy and behaviour has been crossed or other risk factors for committing a sexual offence are evident, occasional experiences of fantasies such as these are not by themselves signals of significant danger' (p. 491). An implication of this may be that deviant fantasy per se is not sufficient to lead to offending, but rather interacts with other factors that increase the likelihood of offending. For example, Dean and Malamuth (1997) investigated the impact of empathy on deviant sexual fantasy in a male college student sample. They divided the sample according to whether they were 'self-centred' or 'sensitive to feelings of others'. Those in the former group sexually aggressed more than the latter group, although both groups reported high levels of fantasized sexual aggression, leading the authors to put forward the notion that empathy may act as an inhibitor to acting out deviant sexual fantasies.

How applicable are the research findings?

One question that appears relevant from the research literature is how useful is what we know currently about the role of sexual fantasy in sex offending? Howitt (2004) suggests that the link between sexual fantasy and sex offending is based on research of those offenders at the extreme end of the spectrum, therefore questioning the generalizability of findings. This may appear particularly apparent when looking at the area of sadistic fantasy and offending, where much of the research is undertaken on offenders engaging in extreme behaviours, including (sometimes serial) sexual murderers (e.g. Brittain 1970; MacCulloch et al. 1983; Dietz et al. 1990; Warren, Hazelwood and Dietz 1996; Warren and Hazelwood 2002). Warren and Hazelwood (2002) themselves described the offenders in their sample as having acted out their urges 'in the most brutal forms of violent criminality' (p. 77).

Another widely recognized issue is that although offenders may be comfortable reporting their offending behaviour, the majority of sex offenders are not forthcoming with details regarding their fantasies preceding, or at the time of, their offence (e.g. Grubin 1994; Warren and Hazelwood 2002; Marshall and Kennedy 2003). An implication of this is, does *not* reporting offence-related fantasies mean an absence of deviant fantasies? In terms of assessment, aside from disclosure during interview, fantasy information is commonly measured using self-report measures by asking respondents to indicate on a checklist of fantasies whether they have experienced them and how often, asking respondents to write a narrative of their fantasies, or to keep a fantasy diary (Leitenberg and Henning 1995), which bring with them issues of impression management, although other methods have been employed.[3]

---

[3] E.g. projective tests, penile plethysmograph as a proxy measure and using information from clinical files.

Evaluation

From this brief review of the literature on sexual fantasy and sex offending, several key points have been raised:

- Offence-related fantasy may not be a central mechanism in sexual offending for all sex offenders, but where relevant, theories have sought to account for their development and maintenance.
- There are multiple functions of offence-related sexual fantasy in sex offending.
- (Some) sex offenders have deviant fantasies, and so do (some) non-offenders.
- It is possible that the nature of deviant fantasy differs between those that sexually offend and those that do not, although it seems likely that the distinction is also related to the notion of sex offenders having deficits in areas that would normally act to inhibit acting out fantasy (e.g. empathy, coping).
- There appear to be difficulties in accessing and measuring fantasy material, and generalizing from research findings.

These key points have important implications in terms of assessment, treatment and management of sex offenders. For example, in terms of measurement and methodological issues, further work could include developing more reliable and valid measures (therefore not relying on self-report). However, self-disclosure, if it is a true reflection of the offender's internal processes, is a rich source of information, so it would be helpful for research to address how to optimize fantasy disclosure. Furthermore, future research is needed on the functions of fantasy in sex offending using different offender groups and populations, and with the same offender across their offending life, to gain a greater knowledge of the nature of fantasy as a mechanism to offending.

Conclusion

This review highlights the importance of individualized assessment of treatment and management needs. Following the 'What Works' principles of risk, need and responsivity (McGuire and Priestley 1995), the role of sexual fantasy should be considered for offenders who have committed sexual offences to assess whether it has contributed to their offending behaviour. Within this work, the function of fantasy needs to be explored on an individual basis and for this to inform treatment needs and to tailor any intervention accordingly. Fantasy does not necessarily have a linear relationship to offending, and therefore within this assessment process it will be vital to consider other factors that may interact with fantasy that make acting out fantasy more likely. It is proposed that this will facilitate identification of treatment needs and targets and shape management strategies.

REFERENCES

Abel, G. G. and Blanchard, E. E. (1974) The role of fantasy in the treatment of sexual deviation. *Archives of General Psychiatry*, 30: 467–75.

Briere, J. and Runtz, M. (1989) University males' sexual interest in children: predicting potential indices of 'pedophilia' in a non-forensic sample. *Child Abuse and Neglect*, 13: 65–75.

Brittain, R. P. (1970) The sadistic murderer. *Medicine, Science and the Law*, 10: 198–207.

Burgess, A. W., Hartman, C., Ressler, R. K., Douglas, J. E. and McCormack, A. (1986) Sexual homicide: a motivational approach. *Journal of Interpersonal Violence*, 1: 251–72.

Daleiden, E. L., Kaufman, K. L., Hilliker, D. R. and O'Neil, J. N. (1998) The sexual histories and fantasies of youthful males: a comparison of sexual offending, nonsexual offending and nonoffending groups. *Sexual Abuse: A Journal of Research and Treatment*, 10: 195–209.

Dean, K. E. and Malamuth, N. M. (1997) Characteristics of men who aggress sexually and of men who imagine aggressing: risk and moderating variables. *Journal of Personality and Social Psychology*, 72(2): 449–55.

Deu, N. and Edelmann, R. J. (1997) The role of criminal fantasy in predatory and opportunistic sex offending. *Journal of Interpersonal Violence*, 12: 18–29.

Dietz, P. E., Hazelwood, R. R. and Warren, J. (1990) The sexually sadistic criminal and his offenses. *Bulletin of the American Academy of Psychiatry and the Law*, 18: 163–78.

DiGiorgio-Miller, J. (2007) Emotional variables and deviant sexual fantasies in adolescent sex offenders. *Journal of Psychiatry and Law*, 35: 109–24.

Gee, D., Ward, T. and Eccleston, L. (2003) The function of sexual fantasies for sex offenders: a preliminary model. *Behaviour Change*, 20: 44–60.

Grubin, D. (1994) Sexual sadism. *Criminal Behaviour and Mental Health*, 4: 3–9.

Hall, G. C. Nagayama and Hirschman, R. (1991) Towards a theory of sexual aggression: a quadripartite model. *Journal of Consulting and Clinical Psychology*, 59: 662–9.

Howitt, D. (2004) What is the role of fantasy in sex offending? *Criminal Behaviour and Mental Health*, 14: 182–8.

Langevin, R., Lang, R. A. and Curnoe, S. (1998) The prevalence of sex offenders with deviant fantasies. *Journal of Interpersonal Violence*, 13: 315–27.

Laws, D. R. and Marshall, W. L. (1990) A conditioning theory of the etiology and maintenance of deviant sexual preference and behaviour. In W. L. Marshall, D. R. Laws and H. E. Barbaree (eds.), *Handbook of Sexual Assault: Issues, Theories and Treatment of the Offender*, pp. 209–27. New York: Plenum Press.

Leitenberg, H. and Henning, K. (1995) Sexual fantasy. *Psychological Bulletin*, 117: 469–96.

MacCulloch, M. J., Snowden, P. R., Wood, P. J. W. and Mills, H. E. (1983) Sadistic fantasy, sadistic behaviour and offending. *British Journal of Psychiatry*, 143: 20–29.

MacCulloch, M. J., Gray, N. and Watt, A. (2000) Brittain's sadistic murderer syndrome reconsidered: an associative account of the aetiology of sadistic sexual fantasy. *Journal of Forensic Psychiatry*, 11: 401–81.

Marshall, W. L., Barbaree, H. E. and Eccles, A. (1991) Early onset and deviant sexuality in child molesters. *Journal of Interpersonal Violence*, 6: 323–36.

Marshall, W. L. and Kennedy, P. (2003) Sexual sadism in sexual offenders: an elusive diagnosis. *Aggression and Violent Behavior*, 8: 1–22.

McGuire, R. J., Carlisle, J. M. and Young, B. G. (1965) Sexual deviation as a conditioned behaviour: a hypothesis. *Behavioral Research and Therapy*, 2: 185–90.

McGuire, J. and Priestley, P. (1995) Reviewing 'What Works': past, present and future. In J. McGuire (ed.), *What Works: Reducing Reoffending: Guidelines from Research and Practice*, pp. 3–34. Chichester: Wiley.

Meloy, J. R. (2000) The nature and dynamics of sexual homicide: an integrative review. *Aggression and Violent Behaviour*, 5: 1–22.

Palmer, J. (2006) An exploration of sadistic sex offending: phenomenology and measurement. PhD thesis, University of Surrey.

Plaud, J. J. and Bigwood, S. J. (1997) A multivariate analysis of the sexual fantasy themes of college men. *Journal of Sex and Marital Therapy*, 23(3): 221–30.

Prentky, R. A., Burgess, A. W., Rokous, F., Lee, A., Hartman, C., Ressler, R. and Douglas, J. (1989) The presumptive role of fantasy in serial sexual homicide. *American Journal of Psychiatry*, 146: 887–91.

Quinsey, V. L., Chaplin, T. C. and Upfold, D. (1984). Sexual arousal to nonsexual violence and sadomasochistic themes among rapists and non-sex-offenders. *Journal of Consulting and Clinical Psychology*, 52: 651–7.

Rice, M., Chaplin, T. C., Harris, G. T. and Coutts, J. (1994) Empathy for the victim and sexual arousal among rapists and non-rapists. *Journal of Interpersonal Violence*, 9: 435–49.

Rokach, A., Nutbrown, V. and Nexhipi, G. (1988). Content analysis of erotic imagery: sex offenders and non-sex offenders. *International Journal of Offender Therapy and Comparative Criminology*, 32: 107–22.

Schlesinger, L. B. and Kutash, I. L. (1981) The criminal fantasy technique: a comparison of sex offenders and substance abusers. *Journal of Clinical Psychology*, 37: 210–18.

Smith, A. D. (1999) Aggressive sexual fantasy in men with schizophrenia who commit contact sex offences against women. *Journal of Forensic Psychiatry*, 10: 538–52.

Swaffer, T., Hollin, C., Beech, A., Beckett, R. and Fisher, D. (2000) An exploration of child sexual abusers' sexual fantasies before and after treatment. *Sexual Abuse*, 12: 61–8.

Ward, T. and Beech, A. (2006) An integrated theory of sexual offending. *Aggression and Violent Behavior*, 11: 44–63.

Ward, T. and Siegert, R. J. (2002) Toward a comprehensive theory of child sexual abuse: a theory knitting perspective. *Psychology, Crime and Law*, 9: 319–51.

Warren, J. I. and Hazelwood, R. R. (2002) Relational patterns associated with sexual sadism: a study of 20 wives and girlfriends. *Journal of Family Violence*, 17: 75–89.

Warren, J. I., Hazelwood, R. R. and Dietz, P. (1996) The sexually sadistic serial killer. *Journal of Forensic Science*, 41: 970–4.

4.12 Stalking

Helinä Häkkänen-Nyholm

Helinä Häkkänen-Nyholm

Definition

Stalking can be defined either legally or perceptually. Legal definitions differ, but usually stalking is identified as an intentional pattern of unwanted behaviours over time towards a person or persons that result in their experiencing fear, or behaviours that a reasonable person would view as fearful or threatening (Blaauw, Sheridan and Winkel 2002; Spitzberg and Cupach 2007; University of Modena and Reggio Emilia Modena Group on Stalking 2007). The first anti-stalking law was passed in 1990 in California following a particularly highly publicized case of a celebrity stalking and murder, but was also influenced by cases of ex-partner stalking and violence and the general recognition by law enforcement, the legal establishment and the media regarding the need for making stalking illegal. Up to date all US states, the Federal government, and in total eight EU countries (e.g. United Kingdom, Belgium, the Netherlands) have specific laws against stalking (University of Modena and Reggio Emilia Modena Group on Stalking 2007).

Among researchers there has been a debate over the perceptual definition of stalking, that is to say, what elements comprise stalking. Not all researchers use the term *stalking*; alternative concepts such as *obsessional harassment* (Rosenfeld 2000), *obsessional following* (Meloy 1996; McCann 1998) and *obsessive relational intrusion* (e.g. Spitzberg and Cupach 2007) have been used. Despite a lack of a uniform concept and satisfactory definition, it is however generally agreed that researchers are referring to the same phenomenon (Sheridan Blaauw and Davies 2003). During recent years attempts have also been made to examine how lay people define stalking (e.g. Dennison and Thomson 2005; Sheridan, Davies and Boon 2001a; Tjaden, Thoennes and Allison 2000). These studies have shown that the type of relationship victims have with their stalker moderates their inclination to label the experience stalking. Thus, in common parlance, intrusive behaviour from an ex-partner in not necessarily considered stalking, even though the type of the relationship has no legal relevance.

Origins and further developments

In the case of stalking, social scientific research followed the setting of policy, beginning slowly at the end of the 1980s. However, the empirical literature on stalking has rapidly increased, and in July 2007 a search made in the Social Sciences Citation Index® (SSCI®) provided over 500 scientific articles on stalking in the world's leading scholarly social sciences journals, with approximately fifty scientific articles published annually. There is a vast amount of descriptive studies (e.g. about who stalks, who is stalked and how people stalk), of which the majority have been conducted in the US with clinical or forensic or college samples (Spitzberg and Cupach 2007).

Prevalence and nature of stalking

Prevalence rates of stalking are of course highly dependent on the definition that is employed. Therefore, lifetime prevalence estimates of stalking range from 3% to 13% for males and 8% to 32% for females. The estimated rate of false claims of stalking is about 10% (Mullen *et al.* 1999; Sheridan and Blaauw 2004). The average duration of stalking across studies is close to two years (e.g. Cupach and Spitzberg 2004; Sheridan, Blaauw and Davies 2003; Spitzberg and Cupach 2007). Furthermore, research clearly demonstrates that the majority of stalking in society emerges from previously acquainted relationships (see Cupach and Spitzberg 2004; Spitzberg 2002), usually due to multiple motives such as love, desire for a reconciliation, but also insult, revenge and intimidation (Mohandie *et al.* 2006; Spitzberg and Cupach 2007). Research with domestic violence victims further shows that the abuser's alcohol or drug problem, controlling behaviours and prior stalking predict more severe forms of stalking (Melton 2007). Overall, approximately 80% of stalkers are known to the person they pursue (Spitzberg and Cupach 2007), and from the victim's perspective, the behaviours stalkers engage in may in the beginning seem relatively indistinguishable from everyday relational activities.

In total, eight clusters of stalking behaviours have been identified: hyper-intimacy (excessive courtship activities), mediated contacts (so-called cyberstalking), interactional contacts (attempts face-to-face contacts), surveillance, invasion, harassment and intimidation, coercion and threat, and aggression (Cupach and Spitzberg 2004; Spitzberg and Cupach 2007). Recent meta-analyses show that about half of the stalking cases involve some issuance of threat, one in three involve physical violence and a little over 10% involve sexual violence (Spitzberg and Cupach 2007). Understandably, the prediction of violence in stalking cases has been said to be a quest for the Holy Grail (Meloy 2007). Several variables (e.g. presence of threats, substance abuse, a prior intimate relationship with the victim, personality disorder, a history of violent behaviour and the absence of a psychotic disorder) have been analysed, e.g. with a regression tree approach, and found to be significantly related to violence in stalking cases (e.g. Rosenfeld 2004; Rosenfeld and Lewis 2005). A study focusing specifically on serious violence (homicide and serious assaults) showed that appearing previously at the victim's home, absence of criminal record and shortened stalking duration were best predictors of serious violence (James and Farnham 2003).

A relatively large amount is known about stalkers. Approximately 75% of adult stalkers are males (Meloy 1996; Spitzberg 2002), and they are usually in their forties. The majority of stalkers in clinical and forensic settings have both Axis I mental disorders (most commonly drug abuse and mood disorder) and Axis II personality disorders (e.g. Mohandie et al. 2006; Mullen et al. 1999). Psychotic stalkers represent a minority of stalking cases, but they are significantly more prevalent when the object of pursuit is a complete stranger (Mohandie et al. 2006). In addition to having psychiatric problems, adult male stalkers frequently have a criminal history (e.g. Mullen et al. 1999; Meloy 1996).

Theoretical approach to stalking

To date, only a few studies have evaluated the possible theories that may be proffered to account for stalking. Thus, how is it that someone repeatedly pursues another who shows no interest in his or her attention and perhaps explicitly states that s/he does not want it to continue? In order to explain stalking behaviour, various stalker typologies, mainly focusing on type of underlying disorder, type of stalker–victim relationship or the primary motivation have been identified (Spitzberg and Cupach 2007). However, besides adding to the vast literature describing the phenomenon, these typologies are of limited use. Two theoretical frameworks have nevertheless emerged in stalking literature to fill our gap of knowledge with regard to explaining stalking; namely attachment theory and relational goal pursuit theory (e.g. Cupach and Spitzberg 2004; Lewis *et al.* 2001; Meloy 1996, 1998; Spitzberg and Cupach 2007). Along these frameworks stalking is viewed as originating from a relationship process and individual development and attachment pathology (Meloy 2007).

Effects of stalking and coping with it

The effects of stalking have usually been studied from the perspective of psychological trauma and disruption of victim's life. Alarming results have emerged, suggesting, for example, that one-third of stalking victims incur a psychiatric diagnosis that will persist for a long period of time (Purcell, Pathé and Mullen 2005). However, it is noteworthy that stalking is not an individual traumatic event, but a prolonged form of stress involving also anticipation of future events (Mechanic 2003). Various types of effect on victims of stalking have been identified and clustered: general disturbance, affective health, social health, resource health, cognitive health, physical health, behavioural disturbance, and resilience (for a review of the literature see Sheridan *et al.* 2003; Spitzberg and Cupach 2007).

Several studies have examined victim coping responses to stalking. In reviewing a number of studies, Cupach and Spitzberg (2004) identified a five-category functional classification of coping responses: *moving with* (e.g. efforts to negotiate with the stalker), *moving against* (e.g. threaten the stalker), *moving away, moving inward* (e.g. denial, taking drugs) and *moving outward*. According to the general opinion of experts on stalking, *moving with* tactics (e.g. 'let's just be friends') may work but are more likely to fail, especially in cases involving ex-partners hoping for more interaction (for a more thorough discussion see Sheridan *et al.* 2003; Spitzberg 2002; Spitzberg and Cupach 2007). For a number of reasons, and not least important in terms of escalating the intensity of the interaction, *moving against* tactics are usually not recommended. In contrast, *moving away* tactics (e.g. changing and unlisting phone number, changing e-mail and physical address and altering routes to daily activities) are usually considered by the experts both necessary and most effective (Boon and Sheridan 2001; Spitzberg and Cupach 2007). The question of whether *moving outward* tactics, specifically in terms of protection or restraining order (RO), are effective is still under debate, although prosecutors generally rely heavily on the use of them (Rebovich 1996). The violation rate of the RO, which has ranged from 18% to 70% (e.g. Cupach and Spitzberg 2004; Meloy *et al.* 1997), has often been considered to indicate the ineffectiveness of the ROs. Perhaps more importantly, several recent studies have shown that reoccurrence of victim-related violence and arrests are lessened in the presence of an RO (Häkkänen, Hagelstam and Santtila 2003; Logan *et al.* 2002; Nigoff, Walker and Jordan 2002; McFarlane *et al.* 2004; Meloy *et al.* 1997). Thus it is possible that the existence of the RO has in some individual cases saved the victim's life, if not by directly having an influence on the stalker's behaviour, but, for example, by affecting the behaviour and views of the authorities in an emergency situation.

Ending stalking

Despite the mass of research on stalking relatively little is still known about how to prevent or stop stalking. Studies with victims suggest that the stalking ended primarily due to *moving away* and *moving outwards* tactics: in other words, the victim moved away, the stalker entered a new relationship, or the police warned or arrested the stalker (Sheridan *et al.* 2001b; Tjaden and Thoennes 1998). Furthermore, despite universal agreement that treatment is a critical component in addressing stalking, very little exists in the research literature about the effectiveness of psychotherapy and drug therapy for stalkers. The lack of information is striking given that treatment ultimately rests upon collaboration between mental health, law enforcement, prosecutors, parole and probation officers, and victim support groups (Meloy 1997). Thus, numerous agencies have treatment-related concerns and empirical research on treatment of stalkers could provide important guidelines for practice. Furthermore, recently the societal effects of stalking (e.g. of law enforcement work, healthcare visits etc.) have been scrutinized: in 2003 the total annual societal costs due to stalking in the US were estimated at $342 million (Centers for Disease Control and Prevention 2003). One of the primary concerns in treating stalkers is, however, how to motivate them. Often the motivation of stalkers to change their behaviour is minimal to zero and they are unlikely to refer themselves for treatment (e.g. Kamphuis and Emmelkamp 2000;

Rosenfeld 2000). Unfortunately, recidivism is rather common among stalk-ers (e.g. Rosenfeld 2003).

Evaluation

Several leading experts on stalking have recently reviewed the state of current knowledge (Meloy 2007; Sheridan *et al.* 2003; Spitzberg and Cupach 2007). A general consensus suggests that sufficient research now exists to provide a basis for understanding the nature of stalking and demographics of stalkers and victims. Several ideas for future research have been outlined. For example, Meloy (2007) and Spitzberg and Cupach (2007) emphasize the need to examine the roots of 'obsessive relational intrusions' (Cupach and Spitzberg 2004), a form of stalking that appears in college students. Another line of research that may increase our understanding of stalking is the neurobiology for stalking (Meloy 2006). In the first theoretical article of this kind, Meloy and Fisher (2005) propose that certain types of neural correlates contribute to the stalker's focused attention, increased energy, following behaviours, obsessive thinking and impulsivity. Also the need to study specific victim groups (such as public figures, judicial officers etc.) has been emphasized (Meloy 2007), as well as the need to focus on specific stalker subgroups (Sheridan *et al.* 2003). Finally, as science progresses, the perspectives of stalkers themselves need to be examined.

Conclusion

The literature and research on stalking thus far has allowed practical and scientific progress to be made in recognizing, understanding and intervening in stalking cases, both at individual and state or national levels. In the future, more specific issues need to be addressed.

FURTHER READING

For more on identifying risk factors see T. McEwan, P. E. Mullen and R. Purcell (2007) Identifying risk factors in stalking: a review of current research. *International Journal of Law and Psychiatry* 30: 1–9. For managing risk factors see P. E. Mullen, R. Mackenzie, J. R. P. Ogloff, M. Pathé, T. McEwan *et al.* (2006) Assessing and managing the risks in the stalking situation.

Journal of American Academy of Psychiatry and Law 34: 439–50. For more on cyberstalking see B. H Spitzberg and G. D. Hoobler (2002) Cyberstalking and the technologies of interpersonal terrorism. *New Media and Society*, 4: 71–92. For more on psychopathology of victims see E. Blaauw, F. W. Winkel, E. Arensman, L. Sheridan and A. Freeve (2002) The toll of stalking: the relationship between features of stalking and psychopathology of victims. *Journal of Interpersonal Violence*, 17: 50–63.

REFERENCES

Blaauw, E., Sheridan, L. and Winkel, F. W. (2002) Designing anti-stalking legislation on the basis of victims' experiences and psychopathology. *Psychiatry, Psychology and Law*, 9: 136–45.

Boon, J. C. W. and Sheridan, L. (2001) Stalker typologies: a law enforcement perspective. *Journal of Threat Assessment*, 1: 75–97.

Centers for Disease Control and Prevention (2003) *Costs of Intimate Partner Violence against Women in the United States*. Atlanta, GA: Centers for Disease Control and Prevention.

Cupach, W. R. and Spitzberg, B. H. (2004) *The Dark Side of Relationship Pursuit: From Attraction to Obsession and Stalking*. Mahwah, NJ: Erlbaum.

Dennison, S. M. and Thomson, D. M. (2005) Criticisms or plaudits for stalking laws? What psycholegal research tells us about proscribing stalking. *Psychology, Public Policy and Law*, 11: 384–406.

Häkkänen, H., Hagelstam, C. and Santtila, P. (2003) Stalking actions, prior offender–victim relationships and issuing of restraining orders in a Finnish sample of stalkers. *Legal and Criminological Psychology*, 8: 189–206.

James, D. and Farnham, F. (2003) Stalking and serious violence. *Journal of the American Academy of Psychiatry and the Law*, 31: 432–9.

Kamphuis, J. H. and Emmelkamp, P. M. G. (2000) Stalking: a contemporary challenge for forensic and clinical psychiatry. *British Journal of Psychiatry*, 176: 206–9.

Lewis, S. F., Fremouw, W. J., Del Ben, K. and Farr, C. (2001) An investigation of the psychological characteristics of stalkers: empathy, problem solving, attachment and borderline personality features. *Journal of Forensic Sciences*, 46: 80–4.

Logan, T. K., Nigoff, A., Walker, R. and Jordan, C. (2002) Stalker profiles with and without protective orders: reoffending or criminal justice processing. *Violence and Victims*, 17: 541–53.

McCann, J. T. (1998) Subtypes of stalking (obsessional following) in adolescents. *Journal of Adolescence*, 21: 667–75.

McFarlane, J., Malecha, A., Gist, J., Watson, K., Batten, E., Hall, I. *et al.* (2004) Protection orders and intimate partner violence: an 18-month study of 150 black, Hispanic, and white women. *American Journal of Public Health*, 94: 613–18.

Mechanic, M. B. (2003) Responding to the psychological impact of stalking victimization. In M. P. Brewster (ed.), *Stalking: Psychology, Risk Factors, Interventions, and Law*, pp. 11.1–11.22. Kingston, NJ: Civic Research Institute.

Meloy, J. R. (1996) Stalking (obsessional following): a review of some preliminary studies. *Aggression and Violent Behavior*, 1: 147–62.

(1998) The psychology of stalking. In J. R. Meloy (ed.), *The Psychology of Stalking*, pp. 2–24. San Diego, CA: Academic Press.

(2006) *The Scientific Pursuit of Stalking*. San Diego, CA: Specialized Training Services.

(2007) Stalking: the state of the science. *Criminal Behaviour and Mental Health*, 17: 1–7.

Meloy, J. R., Cowett, P. Y., Parker, S. B., Hofland, B. and Friedland, A. (1997) Domestic protection orders and the prediction of subsequent criminality and violence toward protectees. *Psychotherapy*, 34: 447–58.

Meloy, J. R. and Fisher, H. (2005) Some thoughts on the neurobiology of stalking. *Journal of Forensic Sciences*, 50: 1472–80.

Melton, H. (2007) Predicting the occurrence of stalking in relationships characterized by domestic violence. *Journal of Interpersonal Violence*, 22: 3–25.

Mohandie, K., Meloy, R., McGowan, M. G. and Williams, J. (2006) The RECON typology of stalking: reliability and validity based upon a large sample of North American stalkers. *Journal of Forensic Sciences*, 51: 147–55.

Mullen, P. E., Pathé, M., Purcell, R. and Stuart, G. W. (1999) Study of stalkers. *American Journal of Psychiatry*, 156: 1244–9.

Pathé, M. and Mullen, P. E. (1997) The impact of stalkers on their victims. *British Journal of Psychiatry*, 170: 12–17.

Purcell, R., Pathé, M. and Mullen, P. (2005) Association between stalking victimization and psychiatric morbidity in a random community sample. *British Journal of Psychiatry*, 187: 416–20.

Rebovich, D. J. (1996) Prosecution response to domestic violence. In E. S. Buzawa and C. G. Buzawa (eds.), *Do Arrest and Restraining Orders Work?*, pp. 176–91. Thousand Oaks, CA: Sage.

Rosenfeld, B. (2000) Assessment and treatment of obsessional harassment. *Aggression and Violent Behavior*, 5: 529–49.

(2003) Recidivism in stalking and obsessional harassment. *Law and Human Behaviour*, 27: 251–65.

(2004) Violence risk factors in stalking and obsessional harassment: a review and preliminary meta-analysis. *Criminal Justice and Behavior*, 31: 9–36.

Rosenfeld, B. and Lewis, C. (2005) Assessing violence risk in stalking cases: a regression tree approach. *Law and Human Behavior*, 29: 343–57.

Sheridan, L. and Blaauw, E. (2004) Characteristics of false stalking reports. *Criminal Justice and Behavior*, 31: 55–72.

Sheridan, L., Blaauw, E. and Davies, G. M. (2003) Stalking knowns and unknowns. *Trauma, Violence and Abuse*, 4: 148–62.

Sheridan, L., Davies, G. M. and Boon, J. C. W. (2001a) Stalking. *Journal of Interpersonal Violence*, 16: 151–67.

(2001b) The course and nature of stalking: a victim perspective. *Howard Journal of Criminal Justice*, 40: 215–34.

Spitzberg, B. H. (2002) In the shadow of the stalker: the problem of policing unwanted pursuit. In H. Giles (ed.), *Law Enforcement, Communication, and the Community*, pp. 173–200. Amsterdam: John Benjamins.

Spitzberg, B. H. and W. R. Cupach (2007) Cyberstalking as (mis)matchmaking. In M. T. Whitty, A. J. Baker and J. A. Inman (eds.), *Online Matchmaking*, pp. 127–46. New York: Palgrave Macmillan.

Tjaden, P. and Thoennes, N. (1998) *Stalking in America: Findings from the National Violence against Women Survey*. Washington, DC: National Institute of Justice and Centers for Disease Control and Prevention.

Tjaden, P., Thoennes, N. and Allison, C. J. (2000) Comparing stalking victimization from legal and victim perspectives. *Violence and Victims*, 15: 7–22.

University of Modena and Reggio Emilia Modena Group on Stalking (2007) *Protecting Women from the New Crime of Stalking: A Comparison of Legislative Approaches within the European Union*. Available online: http://stalking.medlegmo.unimo.it.

4.13 Terrorism research: current issues and debates

Margaret Wilson

Introduction

Since the terrorist attacks of 11 September 2001 (9/11) there has been a dramatic increase in the number of publications on terrorism from many disciplinary perspectives, the majority of which have been characterized as 'thought pieces' (Stohl 2006). Lum, Kennedy and Sherley (2005; cited in Stohl 2006) identified 14,006 articles published between 1975 and 2002, of which 54% were published in 2001–2. A piece this short cannot hope to cover the diversity of terrorism research, and limiting the review to work conducted by psychologists would be pointless; most of the research relates to psychology in some way. So what will be outlined here are the issues and debates that appear to be central at the time of writing, with apologies in advance for the very many issues and authors inevitably omitted. However, since this piece appears in a volume on forensic psychology, it is worth pointing out that, in many areas, where there is research relating to non-terrorist crime and offenders, there is often a parallel literature on those self-same issues in relation to terrorists and terrorism. There are some notable exceptions that occur because of differences in motivation, circumstance and, of course, data access – hard enough for researchers in other areas of forensic psychology (Wilson and Lemanski in press).

Definitions

Those who write about terrorism usually start by pointing out the number of different definitions available and mention the obvious caveat that 'one man's terrorist is another man's freedom fighter'. Although there have always been issues around state-sponsored terrorism, the 'war against terrorism' has raised more debate because the West has had to ask itself some uncomfortable questions about their own actions. As Victoroff (2006) concludes, 'When we name "the war against terrorism", therefore, we are discussing the desire to restrict the privilege of civilian-killing to favored states' (p. 3). Schmid (1993), amongst others, has suggested that we label the *acts* as terrorism rather than the perpetrators, while some, following Heskin (1985), prefer to avoid judgement by using terms like 'political violence', 'combatants' and 'activists'.

Research agenda

One of the earliest questions for the psychology of terrorism was *Why do they do it?* To a certain extent this question still holds a central place in the research agenda, although the approach to answering it has changed considerably.

Research on the causes and motivations for terrorism has been conducted at a number of different levels. There are those who focus on the individual; seeking explanations for getting involved at the level of the person's characteristics or experiences. Other studies have examined the group processes that attract and sustain membership (e.g. McCauley and Moskalenko 2008), and finally societal-level causes such as perceived injustice or social and economic deprivation are considered. These levels must necessarily be linked. For example, a person who has a need for belonging may join a group that fosters their sense of identity within the context of the perceived injustice of an ongoing conflict. Nevertheless, most research can be characterized as having one principal focus.

Historically, a great deal of research was initially directed at the idea that there was a 'terrorist personality' – that something about the psychological makeup of the person might predict their desire to be involved in terrorist action. Although the idea persists today in non-academic accounts, the evidence seems to have been weighed and the notion abandoned. Although there are methodological problems with the studies reviewed, Horgan (2003) concludes – as Crenshaw did twenty years earlier – that there is no credible evidence to suggest that terrorists are not 'normal'. Perhaps Silke (2003) presents the bottom line:

In the wrong circumstances most people could either come to support a terrorist group or possibly even consider joining one. If you, your loved ones and your community were discriminated against, persecuted by the authorities, intimidated, injured or killed, then terrorism may seem an appropriate and justified response. (Silke 2003, p. 51)

Whilst the 'irrationality' theory no longer rests on mental illness or personality disorder, it has re-emerged in association with religious fundamentalism and speculation that 'new terrorists' are not negotiable in the same way that 'old terrorists' were. This remains debatable, as indeed does the idea that a 'new terrorism' exists at all. Advocates of the 'new terrorism' claim that terrorist activity has substantially changed in the last decade or so and that it is characterized by different motivations, organizational structures, and larger-scale and more destructive acts. Jenkins (1987) is often cited as stating that terrorists 'want a lot of people watching, not a lot of people dead' (p. 583). This reflects the claim that well-organized terrorist groups will avoid unnecessary casualties that reduce support for the cause. The proponents of new terrorism have suggested that this is no longer true. Alongside new terrorism is the fear of terrorists turning to weapons of mass destruction (WMDs) (Schmid 2000), and yet, as Crenshaw (2006) warns, traditional weapons can also result in large numbers of casualties – the events of 9/11 showed 'innovative use of old techniques' (p. 52). Crenshaw concludes that motivations have not changed and that it is not necessary to throw away old knowledge in favour of the new. She calls into question governmental motives for buying into the new terrorism theory. If terrorists can be portrayed as non-negotiable and non-rational then governments have no need to deal with them on political terms and this justifies their response with force.

This debate is controversial and emotive. Recent terrorist events have appeared to be aimed at inflicting indiscriminate mass casualties, but we need to remember saliency and recency effects that can make large-scale attacks with much media coverage appear more representative of terrorism than they really are. Acts of terrorism occur worldwide every day, and we should not generalize from high-profile incidents to terrorism as a whole. Ongoing empirical work on what distinguishes mass-casualty terrorism from other forms may identify whether there are any systematic differences that justify a new classification (Ackerman and Asal n.d.).

The second stream of individual-level research to court controversy has been the idea that terrorists can be 'profiled' with respect to background and social factors. In the past, commonalities in groups of activists were identified and presented as though they might contribute to their involvement. Although research has, of course, moved on considerably since the early days and the message has more or less been accepted that it is not possible to profile terrorists, there are still papers being published that tread a fine line between correlation and cause and have the potential to be misused if taken as 'terrorist profiles'.

There are a number of researchers who have based their analyses on interviews with people living in current conflict zones, and their research has provided some valuable insights into, for example, what is really going on when people choose to give their lives to take others'. Far from the 'seventy-two virgins' and the 'brainwashing' media stereotypes, there are often much sadder and more practical motivations. Suicide bombers have frequently lost loved ones (often whole families) through the conflict and feel they have nothing left to live for (see, for example, Akhmedova and Speckhart (2006) on Chechnya and Ali (2008) on Iraq). They may seek to avenge their dead and any surviving relatives may be looked after financially. In ordinary life, bereaved people kill themselves and relatives of murder victims seek retribution. To return to Silke's (2003) analysis, 'under the wrong circumstances' involvement might seem like a justified response. Whilst this research has helped understand suicide bombing, the whole terrorist profiling endeavour has a sinister side that is open to abuse, and as Victoroff concludes, 'to focus on capturing and killing terrorists is unlikely to eliminate the problem and, in many political circumstances, quite likely to be counter-productive. If a population supports terrorism, an inexhaustible supply of new terrorists will emerge' (Victoroff 2006, p. 8).

If there has to be one research area that dominates current debate, then it must be 'radicalization'. To understand this concept, it helps to visualize the model presented in the form of a 'pyramid' (McCauley and Moskalenko 2008). The basic notion is that the bottom layer is the community, only some of whom (the next layer) will support the cause. Some of these might take political action or engage in protest, and some of these may assist the activists but not engage in violence themselves. The top layer represents those who are actively engaged in violence. The problem with early interpretations of the model was that it was taken to imply a 'stage theory' – anyone at the top layer should have gone through all of the previous stages. This is the process implied in the 'ization', whether applied to an individual or used to characterize a whole community. Unfortunately, the stage theory does not seem to represent many routes into violence, and this led McCauley to transform the pyramid into a 'volcano' – the top layer has an inner core that runs down the middle of the structure (McCauley 2008).

Existing research has established that the phenomenon of sudden 'conversion' to a cause has not been a typical route into terrorist acts. More often there is a gradual process, influenced by friends and associates more than any 'cult leader' (Crenshaw 2006, p. 54.). Research by one or two authors (e.g. Alonso 2006) concludes that the motivations of status, recognition, identity and belonging are important, and suggests a more fruitful comparison would be an analogy to forensic research on the way that people join gangs. From forensic psychology there are direct comparisons with pathways into crime, and with respect to this Horgan (2005) and Silke (2003) present detailed reviews of the issues involved in becoming a terrorist.

At the societal level a whole range of potential social and economic causes have been examined. Although widely believed to be the case, terrorism is not related to poverty or lack of education (Krueger and Maleckova 2006). And yet popular stereotypes remain. Media reports on the attempted bomb attacks on London and Glasgow in 2007 consistently expressed shock at the fact that the alleged perpetrators were 'doctors', and similar surprise was expressed about the 'privileged' social and educational backgrounds of the 9/11 and 7/7 terrorists. Our image of the 'typical terrorist' does not include the wealthy or educated, but historically, there have always been such people involved in terrorist action.

It would be wrong to ignore the very large body of research that examines public attitudes and responses to terrorism as well as people's preparedness for terrorist attack. Serious issues are raised here, for example, the extent to which people will tolerate the use of torture when weighed against the likelihood of future attack, and the fear of terrorism which impacts on many people's lives. Terror management theory has emerged as a very popular direction for social psychologists interested terrorism research (e.g. Pyszczynski and Greenberg 2006). The research addresses the way that people's fear of death can influence their more general attitudes. Using a range of experimental studies, researchers have demonstrated that by heightening people's awareness of their own mortality it is possible to elicit a range of polarizing affects, including making people more prone to condoning radical political ideas that negatively target the out-group. Pyszczynski and colleagues suggest that in terror-prone regions of the world, mortality salience is high and that this may be the reason for support for terrorist action or retaliation. They offer some perspectives on reversing the trend, and work is ongoing to see if these will apply in the 'real world'.

It is also vital to identify ways to end conflicts and currently researchers are approaching this issue at a variety of levels. At the individual level, Horgan (2009) has conducted interviews with ex-terrorists in order to establish pathways out of terrorism. As many have noted, both crime and terrorism are predominantly young male activities, and it is interesting to compare them in terms of exit strategies. In terms of the efficacy of counterterrorism policy, it seems that 'tough' measures are counterproductive. 'No negotiation' policies do not act as a deterrent to hostage taking (Jenkins, Johnson and Ronfeldt 1977). Unjust and abusive treatment by the authorities increases recruitment (Hayes and Schiller 1983; Silke 2003), as do targeted assassinations, civilian casualties and military interventions (Atran 2003; Enders and Sandler 2006; Kaplan *et al.* 2005; Kruglanski 2006).

As the pyramid model suggests, terrorism thrives where the wider community are supportive if not actively involved. Once the community does not support the use of violence, terrorism should decline (Kruglanski 2006). Here, amnesties appear to work – once the community has had enough of the violence, less committed members will cooperate with the authorities (Hayes 1991). Finding routes other than terrorism through which to achieve their goals (e.g. political involvement) is also seen as potentially important in diverting people from violent action (Kruglanski 2006).

Finally, there is also still scope for studies in clinical psychology in dealing with the aftermath of terrorism, not just the PTSD left by specific incidents, but the damage still left in communities long after the fighting stops. Mullen *et al.* (2007) report on their involvement in a variety of community-based initiatives aimed at bringing communities together and healing divides.

Conclusion

Many authors have highlighted the important role psychology can play in terrorism research, and given the frequent calls for scientific research over speculation and commentary, there is plenty of room for further contribution. This brief review has only scratched the surface of what might be possible. Open this volume at the areas of forensic psychology that interest you most – the chances are that they will have applications in terrorism research.

REFERENCES

Ackerman, G. and Asal, V. (n.d.) *Understanding and Combating Mass Casualty Terrorism.* College Park, MD: National Consortium for the Study of Terrorism and Responses to Terrorism, University of Maryland.

Akhmedova, K., and Speckhart, A. (2006) A multi-causal analysis of the genesis of suicide terrorism. In J. Victoroff (ed.), *Tangled Roots: Social and Psychological Factors in the Genesis of Terrorism*, pp. 324–56. Oxford: IOS Press.

Ali, F. (2008) From mothers to martyrs. Paper presented at the 31st Annual Scientific Meeting of the International Society of Political Psychology, Paris, 9–12 July 2008.

Alonso, R. (2006) Individual motivations for joining terrorist organizations: a comparative qualitative study on members of ETA and IRA. In J. Victoroff (ed.), *Tangled Roots: Social and Psychological Factors in the Genesis of Terrorism*, pp. 187–202. Oxford: IOS Press.

Atran, S. (2003) The genesis of suicide terrorism. *Science*, 299: 1534–9.

Crenshaw, M. (2006) Have motivations for terrorism changed? In J. Victoroff (ed.), *Tangled Roots: Social and Psychological Factors in the Genesis of Terrorism*, pp. 51–61. Oxford: IOS Press.

Enders, W. and Sandler, T. (2006) *The Political Economy of Terrorism*. Cambridge: Cambridge University Press:

Hayes, R. E. (1991) Negotiations with terrorists. In V. A. Kremenyuk (ed.), *International Negotiation: Analysis, Approaches, Issues*, pp. 364–408. San Francisco, CA: Jossey-Bass.

Hayes, R. E. and Schiller, T. (1983) *The Impact of Government Activity on the Frequency, Type and Targets of Terrorist Group Activity: The Italian Experience, 1968-1982*. McLean, VA: Defense Systems, Inc.

Heskin, K. (1985) Political violence in Northern Ireland. *Journal of Psychology*, 119: 481–94.

Horgan, J. (2003) The search for the terrorist personality. In A. Silke (ed.), *Terrorists, Victims and Society: Psychological Perspectives on Terrorism and its Consequences*, pp. 3–37. London: Wiley.

(2005) *The Psychology of Terrorism*. Routledge: New York.

(2009) *Walking Away from Terrorism: Accounts of Disengagement from Radical and Extremist Movements*: London: Routledge.

Jenkins, B. M. (1987) The future course of international terrorism. In P. Wilkinson and A. M. Stewart (eds.), *Contemporary Research on Terrorism*. Aberdeen: Aberdeen University Press.

Jenkins, B. M., Johnston, J. and Ronfeldt, D. (1977) *Numbered Lives: Some Statistical Observations from 77 International Hostage Episodes*. Santa Monica: Rand Corporation.

Kaplan, E., Mintz, A., Mishal, S. and Samban, C. (2005) What happened to suicide bombings in Israel? Insights from a terror stock model. *Studies in Conflict and Terrorism*, 3: 225–35.

Krueger, A. B. and Maleckova, J. (2006) Education, poverty and terrorism: is there a causal connection? *Journal of Economic Perspectives*, 17: 119–44.

Kruglanski, A. W. (2006) The psychology of terrorism: 'syndrome' versus 'tool' perspectives. In J. Victoroff (ed.), *Tangled Roots: Social and Psychological Factors in the Genesis of Terrorism*, pp. 61–73. Oxford: IOS Press.

McCauley, C. (2008) Models and measures of political radicalization. Paper presented at the 31st Annual Scientific Meeting of the International Society of Political Psychology. Paris, 9–12 July 2008.

McCauley, C. and Moskalenko, S. (2008) Mechanisms of political radicalization: pathways toward terrorism. *Terrorism and Political Violence*, 20: 415–33.

Mullen, B., Montague, M., Corry, M., Murphy, M. and Monyneaux, Z. (2007) Societal and personal reactions to terrorism: the Ulster experience. Paper presented at Interdisciplinary Analyses of Aggression and Terrorism, 27–30 September 2007, Madrid, Spain.

Pyszczynski, T. and Greenberg, J. (2006) Crusades and jihads: an existential psychological perspective on the psychology of terrorism and political extremism. In J. Victoroff (ed.), *Tangled Roots: Social and Psychological Factors in the Genesis of Terrorism*, pp. 85–97. Oxford: IOS Press.

Schmid, A. P. (1993) Defining terrorism: the response problem as a definition problem. In A. P. Schmid and R. D. Crelinsten (eds.), *Western Responses to Terrorism*, pp. 7–13. London: Frank Cass.

(2000) Terrorism and the use of weapons of mass destruction: from where the risk? In M. Taylor and J. Horgan (eds.), *The Future of Terrorism*, pp. 106–32. London: Frank Cass.

Silke, A. (2003) Becoming a terrorist. In A. Silke (ed.), *Terrorist, Victims and Society: Psychological Perspectives on Terrorism and its Consequences*, pp. 29–53. London: Wiley.

Stohl, M. (2006) Knowledge claims and the study of terrorism. In J. Victoroff, (ed.), *Tangled Roots: Social and Psychological Factors in the Genesis of Terrorism*, pp. 23–36. Oxford: IOS Press.

Victoroff, J. (2006) Managing terror: the devilish traverse from a theory to a plan. In J. Victoroff (ed.), *Tangled Roots: Social and Psychological Factors in the Genesis of Terrorism*, pp. 1–22. Oxford: IOS Press.

Wilson, M. A. and Lemanski, L. (in press) The forensic psychology of terrorism. In J. Adler and J. Gray (eds.), *Forensic Psychology: Concepts, Debates and Practice*, 2nd edn. Cullompton: Willan.

Part V

Psychology and civil law

5.1 Assessing and reporting on work-related stress

Elizabeth A. Campbell

See also chapter 6.12 Occupational stress in police and prison staff.

Introduction

The term 'occupational stress' or 'work-related stress' has been widely used in recent years. It has become the subject of television documentaries, surveys in magazines and, increasingly, litigation in the civil courts. This chapter will focus on the issues concerning the assessment of and reporting on work-related stress for civil litigation.

There has also been a concomitant growth in the provision of occupational health services This is sometimes provided via in-house occupational health departments in large organizations or can be contracted out to private health-care providers or other agencies. In particular, there has been a growth in the provision of 'employee assistance programmes' designed to mitigate the employer's liability for any workplace stress or distress by providing telephone or face-to-face counselling services for employees.

The growth in concern for the psychological health of employees has developed out of health and safety legislation, which was originally concerned with reduction of the workplace risk of physical ill health or injury.

There are also economic considerations for employers who are concerned to counteract any adverse consequences of work-related stress, such as reduced productivity, poor staff retention, sickness absence and demoralization.

Estimates of the scale of work-related stress problems have been very variable. This is, in part, because of the lack of any consensual definition of the term and also because of the reliance on self-report measures of subjective 'stress'. The issue is further clouded by the implicit use of the term 'work-related stress' interchangeably with 'psychiatric disorder' at times.

This contrasts with the research studies which have examined the relationship between various physical illnesses and specific working conditions. In this corpus of research, there is a reliance on specific diagnostic entities that can have a reliable prevalence established through epidemiological methods.

Psychosocial hazards at work

Psychologists have attempted to develop various models that might explain work stress or adaptation (e.g. Karasek's (1979) demand control theory).

These psychological models have been explored in various ways, but there is some commonality to the kind of factors that are identified by the models as being potential stressors in the workplace. Such stressors are often referred to as 'psychosocial hazards' and can be defined as those features of the management or organization or design of the working environment, as well as the social relationships within the working environment, that can be seen as potential sources of psychological harm. The main factors that have been identified in this way are:
1. Role conflict or ambiguity
2. The organizational culture
3. The degree of decision, latitude or control that the individual has
4. The nature of interpersonal relationships
5. The design of the work tasks themselves
6. The workload or pace or schedule.

Similarly, the UK Health and Safety Executive (HSE 2000, 2002) has identified six key stressor areas: demands, control, support, relationships, role and organizational change. Although there is consensus about these broad aspects of work that may be sources of stress for the individual, there is little consensus about the concrete detail of how such stressors may operate. In a review commissioned by the UK Health and Safety Executive, Rick et al. (2001) concluded that 'it is currently not feasible to issue clear and simple directives about which stresses are most harmful, at what threshold they become harmful, how they operate or what can be done to reduce their levels'.

However, these authors then go on to further suggest that despite the fact that there are no definite conclusions that can be drawn, there are still ways of making helpful suggestions in order to ameliorate workplace stress.

Legal views on work-related stress

The driving force behind developments in occupational health provision and in psychologists' interest in occupational health has been a concern of employers to avoid the costs associated with employee absence, rehabilitation and potential litigation. Employer liability for a psychological injury arising from work-related stress was established in the UK by a case in 1995: *Walker v. Northumberland County Council* (1 All ER 737) (Brown and Porteous 2003; Tamdar and Byford 2003).

The courts in the UK have developed a set of broad principles which they expect to be addressed in any assessment of workplace stress for litigation purposes. The key things that the courts have identified are: that there should be some identifiable 'injury'; that such injury should have been foreseeable; that the employer should have complied with their duty of reasonable care; and that any psychological injury should be able to be attributed to some causal factor within the employment setting. In a UK court case, sixteen principles were enunciated with the 'threshold' principle being that of fore-seeability (*Hattan v. Sutherland* 2002 EWCA Civ 76).

It is not assumed, however, that there are some occupations that are inherently more likely to expose the individual employee to risk of psychiatric injury.

Assessment of the workplace environment

Arising out of the six categories of psychosocial hazards identified by the HSE, an 'Indicator Tool' was developed to allow organizations to assess psychosocial hazards in the workplace (Cousins *et al.* 2004). This questionnaire assesses employee perceptions of working conditions, within the six categories. As Cox *et al.* (2000) note 'questions remain about its ability to adequately assess exposure frequency and intensity'. This therefore limits the Indicator Tool's potential usefulness for assessments at the individual rather than the group level.

Other attempts to chart all the psychosocial hazards in the workplace have proved less than successful. It is very difficult for any questionnaire measure to comprehensively assess all the possible hazards within all possible occupations.

Assessment of the individual

Since mild to moderate psychological distress is relatively common in the population and almost always has some multifactorial origins, it can be very difficult to attribute particular adverse psychological responses to the work-place or its features and thus assessment of an individual is difficult under these circumstances. Smith *et al.* (2000) report for a large UK sample that almost one in five reported their work to be 'very' or 'extremely' stressful.

The other ever-present difficulty for assessing psychological injury is, of course, that most of the symptoms reported by individuals are subjective symptoms, which rely entirely on self-report. This is why it is important to also have, as well as some measure of symptoms, some assessment of the actual behavioural functioning of the individual.

Employer's reasonable care

While there is an assumption that the employer should take reasonable care, it is very difficult to establish from the scientific research literature what this care should entail. Although, as noted above, there has been a growth in the management of workplace stress through the provision of various forms of counselling, a recent review concluded that 'on the basis of current evidence …' there were 'few benefits to work places implementing many such programmes' (Kenny and Cooper 2003).

In a systematic review of interventions aimed at reducing work-related stress in healthcare workers, Marine *et al.* (2006) concluded that 'Limited evidence is available for the effectiveness of interventions.'

The provision of one-off debriefing sessions following potentially traumatic events is no longer recommended (Regel 2007). However, this does not mean that employers should not have some screening system in place that allows for the identification of individuals who may be at risk of developing significant psychological problems. This is especially a concern among those employees who might be at risk of repeated exposure to traumatic stressors, such as the emergency services. The UK National Institute for Clinical Excellence (NICE) guidelines on PTSD make recommendations for early interventions for those individuals with post-traumatic symptoms (NICE 2005).

Other groups of workers who are at greater risk of exposure to violent incidents are those where there is (a) a significant level of contact with clients and (b) if valuables or money are available at the worksite (Mayhew and Chappell 2007).

Further issues in reporting

Highlighted above is the importance of having both a functional commentary on the individual as well as a symptomatic assessment. The courts will generally require that the issue of 'injury' is established by reference to one of the standard psychiatric classificatory systems. This in practice either means DSM-IV (APA 2000) or ICD-10 (WHO 1992). There are often few sources of corroborative data available in such cases. This is especially true if the individual is attributing their condition to harassment or bullying which may not have occurred in public view. However, it is sometimes possible to have witness statements from co-workers or even to have some objective data, e.g. about sickness absence, in a particular unit of the organization.

Special groups

In some occupational settings there may be particular hazards which are relatively unique to that group. For example, employees who are at risk of violence or a life threatening physical injury may be at high risk of some kind of post-traumatic stress syndrome (Macfarlane and Bryant 2007). Those employees who are exposed to these kinds of traumatic incidents may be in particular employment areas such as the emergency services. In addition, there may be particular groups of workers who are themselves required to be directly exposed to others' extreme pain and suffering. For example, again this may be the emergency services or certain groups of health service staff. The other group whose occupational exposure carries a high risk of psychiatric injury is, of course, the military in all its different guises (Wessely 2005). Both the emergency services and the military have been developing a range of resources in order to ameliorate the effects of such exposure.

Conclusion

A summary of key issues in this area is:
- The confounding of 'work-related stress' with psychiatric disorder. Most research uses 'symptoms' as outcomes.
- Lack of reliable and valid measures of the stressors present in the workplace and a need to develop outcomes that are not entirely based on self-report (Rick et al. 2001).
- Since mild–moderate psychological problems are common in the population and usually have multi-factorial origins, attribution of psychological difficulties to work-based stressors is problematic.

- The requirement, in UK law, to establish that an individual was suffering from a recognizable psychiatric disorder may be creating a situation where genuine and severe psychological suffering is not being compensated for. This definition a rather steep hurdle for individuals to meet who may be severely functionally impaired but do not fit neatly into any diagnostic category.

FURTHER READING

Brown and Porteous (2003) provide an overview of the legal implications of stress particularly for criminal justice practitioners, whilst the HSE document (2002) is a helpful review.

REFERENCES

American Psychiatric Association (APA) (2000) *Diagnostic and Statistical Manual of Mental Disorders*, 4th edn, text revison (DSM-IV-TR) Washington, DC: American Psychiatric Association.

Brown, J. and Porteous, J. (2003) Psychological and legal implications of occupational stress for criminal justice practitioners. In D. Carson and R. Bull (eds.), *Handbook of Psychology in Legal Contexts*, pp. 559–78. Chichester: Wiley.

Cousins, R., Mackay, C. J., Clarke, S. D., Kelly, C., Kelly, P. J. and McCaig, R. H. (2004) 'Management standards' and work related stress in the UK: practical development. *Work and Stress*, 18: 113–36.

Cox, T., Griffiths, A., Barlowe, C., Randall, R., Thomson, L. and Rial-Gonzalez, E. (2000) *Organisational Interventions for Work Stress: A Risk Management Approach*. Health and Safety Executive UK, Contract Research Report 286. London: HSE Books.

Health and Safety Executive (2000) *A Critical Review of Psychosocial Hazard Measures*. London: HSE Books.
  (2002) *Review of Existing Supporting Scientific Knowledge to Underpin Standards of Good Practice for Key Work-Related Stressors – Phase 1*. London: HSE books.

Karasek, R. A. (1979) Job demands, job decision latitude and mental strain : implications for job redesign. *Administrative Science Quarterly*, 24: 285–306.

Kenny, D. T. and Cooper, C. L. (2003) Introduction to the special issue on occupational stress and its management. *International Journal of Stress Management*, 10: 275–9.

Marine, A., Ruotsalainen, J., Serva, C. and Verbeek, J. (2006) Preventing occupational stress in healthcare workers. *Cochrane Database of Systematic Reviews*.

Mayhew, C. and Chappell, D. (2007) Workplace violence: an overview of patterns of risk and the emotional/stress consequences on targets. *International Journal of Law and Psychiatry*, 30: 327–39.

McFarlane, A. C. and Bryant, R. A. (2007) Post traumatic stress disorder in occupational settings: anticipating and managing the risk. *Occupational Medicine*, 57: 404–10.

NICE (2005) *The Management of PTSD in Adults and Children in Primary and Secondary Care.* London: Gaskell and the British Psychological Society

Regel, S. (2007) Post-trauma support in the workplace: the current status and practice of critical incident stress management (CISM) and psychological debriefing (PD) within organisations in the UK. *Occupational Medicine*, 57: 411–16.

Rick, J., Briner, R. B., Daniels, K., Perryman, S. and Guppy, A. (2001) *A Critical Review of Psychosocial Hazard Measures.* London: HSE Books.

Smith, A., Johal, S., Wadsworth, E., Devey Smith, E. and Peters, T. (2000) *The Scale of Occupational Stress: The Bristol Stress and Health at Work Study.* London: HSE Books.

Tamdar, S. and Byford, J. (2003) *Workplace Stress: Law and Practice.* London: The Law Society.

Wessely, S. (2005) Risk, psychiatry and the military. *British Journal of Psychiatry*, 186: 459–66.

World Health Organization (1992) *International Statistical Classification of Diseases and Health Related Problems ICD 10.* Geneva: World Health Organization.

5.2 Asylum seekers and refugees

Elizabeth A. Campbell

See also chapter 2.2 Credibility, chapter 2.19 Post-traumatic stress disorder, chapter 4.5 Genocide.

Context

Psychologists and psychiatrists may be called upon to assess the mental state of asylum seekers and refugees with a view to their report being submitted for evidentiary purposes to an asylum adjudicator or an immigration tribunal. This is a very particular kind of report at the interface between domestic law and human rights law. In the UK, pioneering work in this area has been undertaken by the Medical Foundation for the Care of Victims of Torture. Organizations such as Physicians for Human Rights and the United Nations have been influential in developing guidelines about the assessment of victims of human rights abuses (Iacopino, Allden and Keller 2001; UNHCR 1995a).

An asylum seeker must demonstrate that they have a 'well-founded' fear of persecution by reason of race, religion, nationality or membership of a particular social group or because of their political opinion.

Prevalence of psychopathology

In a study of asylum seekers in a USA primary care setting, Asgary *et al.* (2006) found that 40% of their sample had post-traumatic stress disorder. Another US study of those seeking mental health care, found that 82% had post-traumatic stress disorder and 96% some kind of depressive disorder (Piwowarczyk 2007). Keller *et al.* (2006) described a sample of more than three hundred survivors seeking help from a torture treatment clinic in New York. More than 80% had clinically significant anxiety and 84% had clinically significant depression, while just under half of them had significant levels of post-traumatic symptoms. Symptoms of PTSD were predicted by experience of death threats, rape and torture of family. Women reported higher levels of symptoms than men.

In a meta-analysis of studies examining rates of psychopathology among refugees, Porter and Haslam (2005) reviewed fifty-six research reports. Refugees were found to be more likely than comparison groups to suffer from psychological ill-health. Mental health outcomes among refugees were influenced by post-displacement conditions such as financial insecurities, internal displacement, and living in institutional accommodation. Mental health problems were worse among refugees who were older, more educated and female.

The most important risk factors for psychopathology in Iraqi asylum seekers in the Netherlands were found to be lack of employment, family problems and asylum procedure stress (Laban *et al.* 2005).

A review by Mann and Fazil (2006) examined the relevant research literature pertaining to adults. While there was considerable variability in the prevalence rates of psychiatric disorders across studies, they concluded that high levels of anxiety, depression and post-traumatic stress disorder are common. Asylum seekers may also be at risk of suicide attempts, given the risk factors associated with this status (e.g. social isolation).

Other researchers have documented the adverse effects of detention on asylum seekers (Keller 2003; Silove, Steel and Watters 2000). Steel *et al.* (2006) found that longer detention was associated with more severe psychological problems, which had an average duration of three years following release from detention.

Lustig *et al.* (2004) reviewed the literature on child and adolescent refugee mental health and summarized the empirical findings about prevalence of psychopathology relating to different groups of refugees and also different phases of the refugee experience. Other reviews have been conducted by Fazel, Wheeler and Danesh (2005) and Ehntholt and Yule (2006).

Assessing and reporting

Psychologists, psychiatrists and other mental health professionals have been increasingly faced with complex issues relating to the assessment, treatment and legal disposal of asylum seekers and refugees. They may have to assess and report on the impact of traumatic events that are distant in time and space on individuals from diverse cultures and social backgrounds (Okawa 2008).

There is also the difficulty of trying to apply models of psychological disorder and systems of psychiatric classification that have been developed in one culture to individuals from very different cultures and backgrounds. Mental health professionals may be reluctant to impose diagnostic categories on individuals who have had an understandable and normal reaction to extreme events. However, the courts and tribunals in the UK often ask for evidence of clinically significant disorder and require or expect the application of the categories from one of the recognized psychiatric classificatory schemes.

As well as trying to assess the psychological impact of events in the applicant's country of origin, the psychologist must try to disentangle any ongoing stressors associated with the fact of being a person of uncertain status in a country which is not their home state. As well as the intrinsic stresses of being of uncertain status, there are often additional stressors faced by the refugee or asylum seeker. These might include racial harassment, lack of financial resources, or detention in a secure facility. Also there are often few or no medical records documenting the past history and therefore corroborative sources are unavailable to triangulate the person's self-report.

The importance of well-conducted assessments has implications for the likelihood of asylum being granted. Lustig *et al.* (2008), in a study conducted in the USA, found that asylum seekers who underwent medical or psychological evaluations were more likely to be granted asylum (89%) than those who did not (37.5%).

The assessment is usually requested by the solicitor or other agent of the asylum seeker. The expectations of the asylum seeker's solicitor or agent need to be made explicit in any instructions from them. It may be necessary to clarify with them exactly what they are hoping for from the assessment and report.

The expectations of the client who arrives for an assessment may also need to be drawn out and any unrealistic expectations explored. Such clients may think that the assessment will lead to some tangible benefit such as psychological therapy or improved living circumstances or the granting of asylum.

The acceptability of any interpreter who may be present should also be confirmed in advance of the interview, if possible, so that the asylum seeker can feel comfortable about the gender and ethnic identity of the interpreter. It is generally inappropriate to use family members as interpreters. The interpreter needs to be briefed as to the format and style of the interview and given an indication of the role that they are expected to play. A full discussion of the role of interpreters in mental health can be found in Tribe and Raval (2003).

Useful guidelines about interviewing are published by a number of sources including the World Health Organization (WHO 2003) and UNHCR (UNHCR 1995a and b).

Questionnaires and interviews that may be useful for the assessment of adult asylum seekers, and have been widely used in this population, include:
- The Harvard Trauma Questionnaire (Mollica *et al.* 2004)
- The Hopkins Symptoms Checklist (Mollica *et al.* 2004)
- Post-migration living problems checklist (Silove *et al.* 1997)
- Composite International Diagnostic Interview: psychiatric sections (CIDI, World Health Organization 1997)
- Modified Mini International Neuropsychiatric Interview (Durieux-Paillard *et al.* 2006).

Children and adolescents

The assessment and reporting on refugee children and adolescents also need particular expertise (Ehntholt and Yule 2006; Hodes 2000). A high proportion of young refugees may be suffering from significant levels of psychological disorder (Hodes 2000). High levels of depression, anxiety, post-traumatic stress disorder and bereavement reactions have been observed in studies of young refugees. There is considerable variation in the prevalence rates found in different samples, which can be explained by differential exposure to trauma and the type of trauma. There is also some evidence that disorders in this group are especially persistent and that children may continue to suffer adverse psychological symptoms many years after the original exposure to the trauma.

Ehntholt and Yule (2006) recommend that, initially, family members should be interviewed together, with the help of a professional interpreter, and that the child should never be asked to act as interpreter. It is also useful, if it is possible, to interview the child on their own. This is because the child may not have disclosed to other members of the family events or emotional reactions because of fear of increasing the family's distress. In addition, if a parent and child are seen together, the parent may monopolize the time by recounting their own traumas and emotional reactions. Ehntholt and Yule also point out that the interviewing style of the assessing professional is very important in establishing trust. They counsel against the use of too formal a style of interviewing since this may resonate with previous traumatic inter-rogations that the individual may have experienced.

Questionnaires identified by Ehntholt and Yule (2006) for use with young people include:
- The War Trauma Questionnaire (Macksoud 1992)
- The Revised Impact of Event Scale for children (Smith *et al.* 2003)

- The Birleson Depression Self Rating Scale (Birleson 1981)
- The revised children's manifest anxiety scale (Reynolds and Richmond 1978)
- The brief grief questionnaire (Nader *et al.* 1993)

Tufnell (2003) provides a framework for structuring the assessment of children:

1. A joint session with parents and children to explain the purpose of the assessment, to obtain a picture of the child's current functioning, and to assess the impact of the traumatic events on the parents.
2. Details of what the child has experienced as reported by the child. These are elicited via a 'trauma' interview, in which the child is asked to identify traumatic events, describe their responses at the time, and current symptoms, attributions and fears.
3. Evaluation of how any traumatic experiences have affected the child.
4. Evaluation of the likely effect on the child of being returned to their country of origin.

Credibility issues

The assessment of credibility in claims by asylum seekers and refugees is a key concern for those statutory agencies and judicial bodies who determine the immigration status of asylum seekers and refugees. The chapter on 'Credibility' in this handbook might be consulted for a fuller discussion of credibility of witnesses in general.

Byrne (2007) points to the 'technical complications' that may cause problems in the assessment of the credibility of applicants. She includes factors such as 'errors in translation, interpretation in an oral hearing, and mistakes in the transcription of serial interviews'. She also points out that the system weighs initial interviews as key documents and regards any subsequent inconsistencies in recall by applicants as evidence of lack of credibility. Byrne (2007) also notes that in international criminal tribunals there is an assumption of 'presumptive affirmation' of the experiences of victims and witnesses. However, in asylum proceedings, there is an opposite assumption of 'presumptive skepticism'.

The work of researchers in psychology is clearly very important for providing data about the likely effects on memory of the experience of past trauma and ill-treatment. Psychologists can obviously give evidence from the research literature about the effects on memory of head injuries, severe psychological distress and denial. An example of such a research study is that conducted by Herlihy and Turner (2006), who interviewed refugees on two occasions about the same events. They found that changes in accounts were more likely for memories of traumatic events and that higher levels of traumatic stress symptoms were associated with more inconsistencies when there was a greater delay between the two interviews. Chapter 2.6 in this volume addresses these issues in more depth.

Psychological interventions

There is a scarcity of randomized controlled trials of psychological treatments within this population. This is unsurprising given the variety of psychological reactions seen in asylum-seeking populations. The treatment issues for asylum seekers and refugees are addressed in an edited volume by Wilson and Drozdek (2004).

Recommendations for treatment interventions for children and adolescents include cognitive-behavioural therapy, narrative or testimonial therapies, and eye movement desensitization and reprocessing (Ehntholt and Yule 2006). There may also be a need to consider specific interventions with children who have suffered bereavements (Monroe and Kraus 2005).

FURTHER READING

Reyes, E. and Jacobs, G. A. (eds.) (2006) *Handbook of International Disaster Psychology: Refugee Mental Health*, vol 3. Westpost, CT: Prager.

Wilson, J. P. and Drozdek, B. (eds.) (2004) *Broken Spirits: The Treatment of Traumatized Asylum Seekers, Refugees, War and Torture Victims*. London: Brunner-Routledge.

Wilson, J. P. and Tang, C. S. (eds.) (2007) *Cross Cultural Assessment of Psychological Trauma and PTSD*. New York: Springer Science and Business Media.

REFERENCES

Asgary, R. G., Metalios, E. E., Smith, C. L. and Paccione, G. A. (2006) Evaluating asylum seekers/torture survivors in urban primary care: a collaborative approach at the Bronx Human Rights Clinic. *Health and Human Rights*, 9: 164–79.

Birleson, P. (1981) The validity of depressive disorder in childhood and the development of a self-rating scale: a research report. *Journal of Child Psychology and Psychiatry*, 22: 703–88.

Byrne, R. (2007) Assessing testimonial evidence in asylum proceedings: guiding standards from the International Criminal Tribunals. *International Journal of Refugee Law*, 19: 609–38.

Durieux-Paillard, S., Whitaker-Clinch, B., Bovier, P. A. and Eytan, A. (2006) Screening for major depression and posttraumatic stress disorder among asylum seekers: adapting a standardized instrument to the social and cultural context. *Canadian Journal of Psychiatry*, 51: 587–97.

Ehntholt, K. A. and Yule, W. (2006) Practitioner review: assessment and treatment of refugee children and adolescents who have experienced war related trauma. *Journal of Child Psychology and Psychiatry*, 47: 1197–210.

Fazel, M., Wheeler, J. and Danesh, J. (2005) Prevalence of serious mental disorder in 7000 refugees resettled in western countries: a systematic review. *Lancet*, 365: 1309–14.

Herlihy, J. and Turner, S. (2006) Should discrepant accounts given by asylum seekers be taken as proof of deceit? *Torture*, 16: 81–92.

Hodes, M. (2000) Psychologically distressed refugee children in the United Kingdom. *Child Psychology and Psychiatry Review*, 5: 57–68.

Iacopino, V., Allden, K. and Keller, A. (2001) *Examining Asylum Seekers: A Health Professional's Guide to Medical and Psychological Evaluations of Torture*. Cambridge, MA: Physicians for Human Rights.

Keller, A. (2003) Mental health of detained asylum seekers. *Lancet*, 362: 1721–3.

Keller, A., Lhewa, D., Rosenfeld, B., Sachs, E., Aladjem, A., Cohen, I. *et al.* (2006) Traumatic experiences and psychological distress in an urban refugee population seeking treatment services. *Journal of Nervous and Mental Disease*, 194: 188–94.

Laban, C. J., Gernaat, H. B. P. E., Komproe, I. H., Van der Tweel, I. and De Jong, J. T. V. M. (2005) Postmigration living problems and common psychiatric disorders in Iraqi asylum seekers in the Netherlands. *Journal of Nervous and Mental Disease*, 193: 825–32.

Lustig, S. L., Kia-Keating, M., Grant Knight, W., Geltman, P., Ellis, H., Kinzi, J. D. and others (2004) Review of child and adolescent refugee mental health. *Journal of the American Academy of Child and Adolescent Psychiatry*, 43: 24–36.

Lustig, S. L., Kureski, S., Delucchi, K. L., Iacopino, V. and Morse, S. C. (2008) Asylum grant rates following medical evaluations of maltreatment among political asylum applicants in the United States. *Journal of Immigrant and Minority Health*, 10: 7–15.

Macksoud, M. S. (1992) Assessing war trauma in children: a case study of Lebanese children. *Journal of Refugee Studies*, 5: 1–15.

Mann, C. M. and Fazil, Q. (2006) Mental illness in asylum seekers and refugees. *Primary Care Mental Health*, 4: 57–66.

Mollica, R. F., McDonald, L. S., Massagli, M. P. and Silove, D. M. (2004) *Measuring Trauma, Measuring Torture*. Cambridge, MA: Harvard Program in Refugee Trauma.

Monroe, B. and Kraus, F. (eds.) (2005) *Brief Interventions with Bereaved Children*. Oxford: Oxford University Press.

Nader, K., Pynoos, R. S., Fairbanks, L., Al-Ajeel, M. and Al-Asfour, A. (1993) A preliminary study of PTSD and grief among the children of Kuwait following the Gulf crisis. *British Journal of Clinical Psychology*, 32: 407–16.

Okawa, J. B. (2008) Considerations for the cross cultural evaluation of refugees and asylum seekers. In L. A. Suzuki and J. G. Ponterotto (eds.), *Handbook of Multicultural Assessment: Clinical, Psychological and Educational Applications*, pp. 165–94. San Francisco: Jossey-Bass.

Piwowarczyk, L. (2007) Asylum seekers seeking mental health services in the United States: clinical and legal implications. *Journal of Nervous and Mental Disease*, 195: 715–22.

Porter, M. and Haslam, N. (2005) Pre-displacement and post-displacement factors associated with mental health of refugees and internally displaced persons. *Journal of the American Medical Association*, 294: 602–12.

Reynolds, C. R. and Richmond, B. O. (1978) What I think and feel: a revised measure of children's manifest anxiety. *Journal of Abnormal Child Psychology*, 6: 271–80.

Silove, D., Sinnerbrink, I., Field, A., Manicavasagar, V. and Steel, Z. (1997) Anxiety, depression and PTSD in asylum seekers: associations with pre-migration trauma and post migration stressors. *British Journal of Psychiatry*, 170: 351–7.

Silove, D., Steel, Z. and Watters, C. (2000) Policies of deterrence and the mental health of asylum seekers. *Journal of the Americal Medical Association*, 284: 604–11.

Smith, P., Perrin, S., Dyregrov, A. and Yule, W. (2003) Principal components analysis of the impact of event scale with children in war. *Personality and Individual Differences*, 34: 315–22.

Steel, Z., Silove, D., Brooks, R., Momartin, S., Alzuhairi, B. and Susljik, I. (2006) Impact of immigration detention and temporary protection on the mental health of refugees. *British Journal of Psychiatry*, 188: 58–64.

Tribe, R. and Raval, H. (eds.) (2003) *Working with Interpreters in Mental Health*. London: Brunner-Routledge.

Tufnell, G. (2003) Refugee children, trauma and the law. *Clinical Child Psychology and Psychiatry*, 8: 431–43.

UNHCR (1995a) *Interviewing Applicants for Refugee Status (RLD 4)*. Geneva: UNHCR.

(1995b) *Guidelines on Evaluation and Care of Victims of Trauma and Violence*. Geneva: UNHCR.

World Health Organization (1997) *Composite International Diagnostic Interview (CIDI) (Version 2.1)*. Geneva: World Health Organization.

(2003) *Ethical and Safety Recommendations for Interviewing Trafficked Women*. Geneva: World Health Organization.

5.3 Consent and capacity in civil cases

Camilla Herbert

Definitions

Assessment of capacity has always been a relevant question in relation to people with neurological disorders but has become increasingly prominent in the United Kingdom with the legislative changes now agreed by the Parliaments for Scotland (Incapacity Act (Scotland) 2000) and for England and Wales (Mental Capacity Act 2005). Other jurisdictions, for example, in Australia, Canada and the United States, have already established legislation and codes of practice.

Capacity (or 'competence' in the United States) is a legal question and reference must therefore be made to the law and relevant codes of practice. The law uses a *functional* approach, i.e. one that is based on each individual decision at each particular point in time. This is distinguishable from an *outcome* approach, in which making an unwise decision is taken as evidence of incapacity, and from a *diagnostic* approach, in which a person is deemed to lack capacity purely because of their status or diagnosis.

Within the civil litigation process important questions arise regarding the capacity to instruct a solicitor or to litigate. Within civil compensation claims the capacity to manage financial affairs needs to be assessed, and this may include specific requests regarding capacity to accept a settlement. Where treatment or rehabilitation is part of the process, capacity to consent to the proposed treatment may also need to be assessed.

Although capacity itself is a legal concept, the assessment of capacity is often a clinical process. Without reverting to a diagnostic approach there are examples where the diagnosis itself, for example, acquired brain injury or a progressive dementia, may raise concerns about decision-making capacity. Questions may arise in relation to individuals in post-traumatic amnesia, those who lack insight, have significant cognitive difficulties, severe challenging behaviour, or clients with impulsive and disinhibited behaviours. Other dilemmas may arise around treatment approaches such as behavioural programmes, use of time out, restraint or the more general issue of 'engagement' in rehabilitation. Multidisciplinary treatment programmes often work around client's lack of awareness of their problems which may manifest itself in the form of 'refusal to participate'.

The Mental Capacity Act (England and Wales) 2005

The Mental Capacity Act 2005, implemented in full from 1 October 2007, provided a legal framework for decision making on behalf of adults who lack capacity. The Scottish Parliament passed similar legislation in 2000 (Incapacity Act (Scotland) 2000), and there are some differences in terminology and procedures. The current chapter will focus on the legislation for England and Wales, but many of the questions and issues raised will be familiar to clinicians working within the Scottish legislation, and in other jurisdictions.

The Mental Capacity Act 2005 clarified the legal position in relation to the definition of capacity, but there is ongoing discussion and case law to establish how the new legislation applies in practice. In addition, there are some areas of legal decision making not covered by the Act; for example, there is no mechanism to take decisions on behalf of an individual who is assessed as lacking capacity to make decisions themselves in the areas of family relationships, including consenting to marriage/civil partnerships, divorce, issues around adoption, or to consenting to have sexual relations (see section 27). Consent to sexual relationships is covered under the Sexual Offences Act 2003. The Mental Capacity Act also excludes treatment under the Mental Health Act (see section 28) and Voting Rights (see section 29).

The Mental Capacity Act (MCA 2005) includes a set of guiding principles and definitions of capacity summarized below.

The principles:

1. A person must be assumed to have capacity unless it is established that s/he lacks capacity.
2. A person is not to be treated as unable to make a decision unless all practicable steps to help him/her to do so have been taken without success.
3. A person is not to be treated as unable to make a decision merely because s/he makes an unwise decision.

4. An act done, or decisions made, under this Act or on behalf of someone who lacks capacity must be done, or made, in his/her best interests.
5. Before the act is done, or the decision is made, regard must be had to whether the purpose for which it is needed can be as effectively achieved in a way that is less restrictive of the person's rights and freedom of action.

How the Act defines capacity:

For the purposes of this Act, a person lacks capacity in relation to a matter if at the material time s/he is unable to make a decision for him/herself in relation to the matter because of an impairment of, or a disturbance in the functioning of, the mind or brain (whether permanent or temporary) *and* if s/he is unable to take any of the following steps in decision making:

- Understand the information relevant to the decision.
- Retain that information.
- Use or weigh that information as part of the process of making the decision.
- Communicate his/her decision (whether by talking, sign language or other means).

The information relevant to a decision includes information about the reasonably foreseeable consequences of (a) deciding one way or another, or (b) failing to make the decision. The fact that a person is able to retain information relevant to a decision for a short period only does not prevent him/her from being regarded as able to make the decision.

Training in the Act and its implementation

All NHS Trusts in England and Wales have provided training for staff in terms of the key points of the Act. There are also multiple resources available to help professionals, families, carers and individuals. The website www.publicguardian.gov.uk is a useful source of information. The Department of Health have produced training materials for use across a range of clinical settings as well as leaflets for professionals and members of the public.

Assessment of capacity

There is a two-stage test for the assessment of capacity. First, it must be demonstrated that there is an impairment of or disturbance in the functioning of the mind or brain. Second, the assessment of capacity must address the four areas listed above in relation to the specific decision in question. Formal or psychometric assessment is not necessarily required, although it may provide useful additional information. The key requirement is to consider decision making in relation to the specific topic, which will normally require a discussion with the client about that topic, their understanding of relevant information, and ability to weigh up that information as part of the decision-making process.

Before assessing a person's understanding of information relevant to the decision, efforts must be made to provide the information and explain it in a way that is most appropriate for that individual (section 3(2) of the Act). The emphasis is on information being presented in a *simple* form. Relevant information would include:

- the particular nature of the decision in question
- the purpose for which the decision is needed
- the likely effects of making or not making the decision

The onus is on the assessor to use the appropriate forms of communication (simple language, signing, visual aids, Makaton etc.).

The ability to communicate the decision is usually straightforward, but care must be taken to ensure that all reasonable steps to facilitate communication are used where communication is more problematic. Providing information in simple language, using visual aids etc. is important but does not in itself guarantee comprehension of information when other cognitive limitations are present. For more complex cases it is likely that longer interviews or several interviews focused on the key decision topic, and which explore the pros and cons in a number of different ways, will be most useful in clarifying the extent to which the individual has understood and followed the relevant information.

The ability to retain information can be a more problematic issue as the Act does not determine how long information needs to be retained for. However, given the presumption of capacity and the overall guiding principles of the Act, care should be taken not to exclude people from decision making merely on the basis of memory impairments. Efforts should be made to support retention during the discussion through written or visual material. Where there are significant memory problems and the individual fails to recall previous conversations, it may be appropriate to repeat the discussions on several occasions as this may increase confidence that the information was retained sufficiently at the time and formed part of a consistent decision-making process for the individual.

The other areas that can be particularly difficult to evaluate are the effects of executive functioning on understanding and decision making; for example, the impact of impulsivity on decision making, reduced mental flexibility reducing the choices identified, the role of limited insight into current and future behaviours, or the effect of poor social monitoring on an individual's ability to weigh up the consequences of a particular choice. The Act's focus on decision-specific and time-specific decision making may create problems and this is likely to be one of the areas where further guidance may be required as case law develops.

Assessment tools

There are some standardized assessments of capacity, which may be of assistance in some circumstances. However, the emphasis on the particular decision at a particular time means that individualized assessments will often be required. The focus of the assessment does need to be on the specifics of the topic under discussion but carried out in such a way that issues of awareness, impulsivity and other executive skills are explored and checked. This might take the form of both a detailed interview with the individual and also with other relevant people.

If standardized cognitive assessments are used it is important to consider how well they relate to everyday functioning. There are examples where individuals, particularly those with more subtle frontal deficits, can achieve a normal, and in some cases, excellent cognitive profile on tests such as the Wechsler scales but are unable to function in everyday life without high levels of support (Eslinger and Damasio 1988). The converse is also true in that individuals with significant cognitive deficits can cope well within their normal environment and be capable of making decisions relevant to their everyday functioning. The emphasis therefore does have to be on interpreting the test results and all other sources of information in terms of their relevance to the specific decision under consideration.

Lack of capacity

Where an individual is found to lack capacity to make a particular decision, the Mental Capacity Act 2005 provides the decision maker with a legal framework to follow, which allows them to take a decision on behalf of the incapacitated person. This decision must be taken in their best interests and following the best interests checklist set out in the Act and Code of Practice. Further consideration of the best interests checklist is provided in chapter 2.25 on vulnerable adults' capacity.

Conclusion

Capacity is a legal concept and criteria for the assessment of mental capacity are set out in the relevant legislation. Decisions made on behalf of an adult who lacks capacity to make the decision themselves must be taken on a best interests basis and in accordance with the Code of Practice.

ADDITIONAL READING AND REFERENCES

British Medical Association and the Law Society (2004) *Assessment of Mental Capacity: Guidance for Doctors and Lawyers*. London: BMJ Books.

British Psychological Society (2006) *Interim Guidelines on Assessment of Capacity in Adults*. Available online: www.bps.org.uk.

(2008) *Best Interest Decision Making*. Available online: www.bps.org.uk.

Eslinger, P. J. and Damasio, A. R. (1988) Severe disturbance of higher cognition after bilateral frontal ablation: patient EVR. *Neurology* 35: 1731–41.

Gerhand, S. and McKenna, P. (2007) Assessing capacity in a neuropsychology service: The Rookwood Protocol. *Clinical Psychology Forum*, September.

Grisso, T. and Appelbaum, P. S. (1998) *Assessing Competence to Consent to Treatment: A Guide for Physicians and Other Health Professionals*. New York: Oxford University Press.

Incapacity Act (Scotland) 2000. London: The Stationery Office.

Mental Capacity Act (England and Wales) 2005. London: The Stationery Office.

Murphy, G. H. and Clare, I. C. H. (2003) Adults' capacity to make legal decisions. In R. Bull and D. Carson (eds.), *Handbook of Psychology in Legal Contexts*, 2nd edn, pp. 31–66. Chichester: Wiley.

Whyte, M., Wilson, M., Hamilton, J., Primrose, W. and Summers, F. (2003) Adults with incapacity (Scotland) Act 2000: implications for clinical psychology. *Clinical Psychology*, 31: 5–8.

Wong, J. G., Clare, I. C. H., Gunn, M. J. and Holland, A. J. (1999) Capacity to make health care decisions: its importance in clinical practice. *Psychological Medicine*, 29: 437–46.

5.4 Discrimination and employment tribunals

Jennifer M. Brown

See also chapter 4.6 Hate crime, chapter 6.13 Sexual harassment, chapter 7.2 Diversity, equality and human rights, chapter 7.3 Expert witnesses in civil cases.

Definitions

Gordon Allport defined prejudice as 'an antipathy based on faulty and inflexible generalisations ... [with the effect of placing] the object of prejudice at some disadvantage' (Allport 1954, p. 9). Wrightsman and Fulero (2005) argue that there is a distinction to be made between the concept of prejudice, i.e. an attitude, and discrimination, i.e. behaviour. The former is an unjustified evaluation, often negative, attributed to a member of a particular group and usually implies the holder of the attitude is also prejudiced against the group as a whole. The latter is an overt and observable action accepting or rejecting a person on the basis of their membership of a particular group.

The law recognizes that discrimination may be unintended and it is unlikely that those discriminating will readily admit their behaviour was intentional. Since there is usually little evidence as to motive for the alleged discriminatory treatment, the onus is on the discriminator to prove the reason for different treatment was justified and was not undertaken on grounds of race, religion, sex, disability, sexual orientation or age.

Racism, sexism, heterosexism and ageism are attitudinal biases attached to specific groups promoting privileges and prompting injustices to members of these groups.

The term racism is generally taken to refer to the belief that there are clearly distinguishable human races, that these races differ not only in superficial physical characteristics, but also innately in important psychological traits, and finally that the differences are such that one race (almost always one's own) can be said to be superior to another (Schuman 1969, p. 44). McConahay and Hough (1976) coined the term modern racism to mean more abstract beliefs about black people violating cherished values and making illegitimate demands for equality. Glick and Fiske (2001) identify two forms of sexism – hostile and benevolent – with the latter being a more subtle form of prejudice, but both legitimating the maintenance of inequality between the sexes. Sexual prejudice has been defined by Herek (2000, p. 19) as 'all negative attitudes based on sexual orientation whether the target is homosexual, bisexual or heterosexual'. Homophobia has been taken to mean an irrational fear that heterosexuals might experience in regard to all things homosexual, although latterly the term heterosexism has been employed in order to focus attention on the social and cultural basis for prejudice (Hegarty 2006).

The term institutional discrimination refers to organizational structures or practices and trends observable in society that exclude minorities from accessing equal opportunities. Lord Macpherson, in his investigation into the murder of Stephen Lawrence, defined institutional racism as:

The collective failure of an organization to provide an appropriate and professional service to people because of their colour, culture, or ethnic origin. It can be seen or detected in processes, attitudes and behaviour which amount to discrimination through unwitting prejudice, ignorance, thoughtlessness and racist stereotyping which disadvantage minority ethnic people. (Macpherson 1999: para. 6.34).

Legally protected groups

Some groups are protected by law and individuals may resort to legal remedies if they believe they have been discriminated against. These groups are defined by reference to age, race, gender, sexual orientation, religion and disability. In the United States the Civil Rights Act of 1964 made the intentional discrimination or the deployment of practices which result in a disparate adverse impact on an employee through their race or gender unlawful. Title VII of this Act also made it illegal to create a hostile, intimidating or offensive working environment by the use of harassment. Table 5.4.1 provides a summary of the relevant UK laws.

Employment tribunals

Most jurisdictions enable individuals who believe they have suffered some form of discrimination to seek remedy in law. In the UK the Employment

Table 5.4.1 UK anti-discrimination laws (a more detailed account by Amanda Hart is available at www.yourrights.org. UK/yourrights/right-to-equal-treatment/index.html)

Dimension	Grounds	Legislation
Age	Anyone working under a contract, regardless of age, has the same rights in terms of employment, membership of a trade organization, professional or trade qualification or vocational training, services by employment agencies or career guidance, government-run facilities enabling obtaining of employment, further and higher education courses) and promotion	Employment Equality (Age) Regulations 2006
Gender	Sex or marriage and applies to women and men of any age, including children and transsexual people on the grounds of sex in education, provisions of goods and services, advertising and social security, pay and treatment in employment and vocational training	Equal Pay Act (EPA) 1970 Sex Discrimination Act (SDA) 1975 Sex Discrimination Act (SDA) 1975 (Amendment) Regulations 2003 Sex Discrimination (Gender Reassignment) Regulations 1999 Gender Recognition Act 2004
Race	Race, colour, nationality (including citizenship), or ethnic or national origin, in employment and training, education, housing, the provision of goods and services and advertising and the placing of a general duty on listed public authorities to promote race equality	Race Relations Act 1976 and Race Relations (Amendment) Act 2000 Race Relations Act 1976 (Amendment) Regulations 2003
Religion[a]	Religious belief or similar philosophical belief, non-belief is also covered by the regulations and covers direct or indirect discrimination, harassment or victimization	Employment Equality (Religion or Belief) Regulations 2003
Sexual orientation	Gay, lesbian, bisexual or heterosexual, discrimination on the grounds of perceived sexual orientation is also banned. The Equality Act also prohibits sexual orientation discrimination in the provision of goods, facilities and services, the disposal and management of premises, education and the exercise of public functions	Employment Equality (Sexual Orientation) Regulations 2003 Equality Act (Sexual Orientation) Regulations 2007
Disability	Discrimination against disabled people in the field of employment and applies to all those who provide goods, facilities and services to the public, education, housing and public transport, and imposes duties on authorities to address discrimination and a duty (requirement) to promote equality of opportunity for disabled people	Disability Discrimination Act (DDA) 1995 Disability Discrimination Act 2005

[a] There is an overlap between race and religion and certain religious groups such as Sikhs and Jews are covered by the Race Relations Act. The Human Rights Act can also be used to enforce rights to religious freedom.

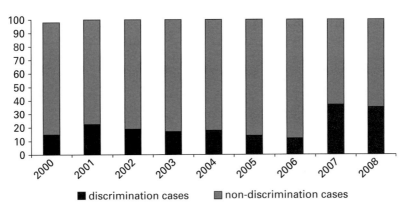

discrimination cases   non-discrimination cases

Figure 5.4.1 Percentage of discrimination and non-discrimination cases submitted between 2000 and 2008

Tribunal Service (ETS) became an agency of the Department of Constitutional Affairs in 2006. Tribunals were first created as a result of the Industrial Training Act (1964) and progressively their remit has widened to included hearings related to the claims of prescribed groups as the law has developed, and they now have powers to determine over seventy kinds of complaint. The numbers of cases submitted between 2000 and 2008 ranges from about 130,000 to 150,000 in 2007/8. It can be seen from figure 5.4.1 that discrimination claims (including equal pay) increased after 2006 as a percentage of all claims, becoming about one-third of cases.

Employment tribunals (ET) in the UK are a distinctive feature of the British legal system and were designed to provide accessible and speedy resolution of employment disputes. They are independent judicial bodies supervised by a president and supported by regional chairmen/women. The chairman/woman (recently retitled judge) is legally qualified and mostly sits with two lay members who have experience from employer and trade union backgrounds. They are expected to act impartially and apply their practical knowledge to employee relations. The decisions are binding on the disputing parties. The Advisory Conciliation and Arbitration Service (ACAS), created in 1974, plays a role in attempting to reach a conciliated settlement. An ET is initiated by the claimant (or the claimant's legal representative) by sending an ET 1 claims form (formerly called an IT 1) to their nearest regional ETS office, which determines if the application meets the judicial requirements. The ET 1 is also sent to the appropriate ACAS office. The outcome of an application includes:

- withdrawal following advice (and can include settled cases negotiated by lawyers);
- struck out as not being within the scope of legislation or having insufficient evidence;

Table 5.4.2 Percentage outcomes of employment tribunal applications 2007/8

Group	% of all applications	Withdrawn	ACAS conciliated	Struck out (not at hearing	Successful at tribunal	Dismissed at prelim hearing	Unsuccessful at hearing
Sex	10.2	42	19	30	3	1	4
Disability	2.2	31	37	8	3	6	15
Race	3.2	34	44	6	3	3	9
Religion	>1	33	38	6	2	7	14
Sexual orientation	>1	31	45	5	6	3	10
Age	1	35	45	4	3	5	8
Equal pay	6	52	16	23	7	1	1
All discrimination	**25**	**42**	**25**	**21**	**4**	**2**	**5**
All non-discrimination	**75**	**31**	**31**	**8**	**1**	**2**	**7**

- achievement of an ACAS-conciliated settlement;
- private settlement;
- full merited ET hearing in which the application is upheld (successful) or dismissed (unsuccessful).

Hayward *et al.* (2004) conducted a survey of applications made in 2002/3 to find two-thirds of all claims are made by men (although the 91% of sex discrimination claims are made by women). Most applicants are white except for race discrimination claims, where 90% are from a black or ethnic minority. Table 5.4.2 indicates the 2007/8 outcomes of discrimination and non-discrimination claims (Employment Tribunal Service annual report, 2008).

Within the discrimination claims, sex discrimination cases remain the largest group of claimants. These and equal pay cases are the largest percentages of claims that are withdrawn and are least likely to be ACAS conciliated. The overall success rate at a full merited hearing is relatively small. When comparing discrimination cases (including equal pay) with non-discrimination matters, more of the former are withdrawn or struck out and more of the latter are ACAS conciliated.

The issue of sexual harassment as a detriment suffered within the provisions of the Sex Discrimination Act 1975 was decided in the case of *Strathclyde Regional Council* v. *Porcelli* [1986] IRLR 134 CS. Mrs Porcelli was a laboratory technician at a school where two male colleagues conducted a campaign of harassment having sexual components (such as placing objects on shelving such that she needed a ladder to reach them and the men would look up her skirt). The initial tribunal dismissed Mrs Porcelli's case on the grounds that if the disliked colleague had been male the two men in question would still have treated him badly although in a different way. The case was appealed and the Court of Session held that the sexual elements were such that a woman was more vulnerable than a man, which amounted to less favourable treatment on the grounds of sex. This case established that sexual harassment was a form of sex discrimination.

Role for psychologists

Psychologists may find themselves called upon to provide expert opinion in ET cases because they are seen as having an understanding or specialized knowledge beyond that of the average person. Goodman-Delahunty and Foote (1995) explain that a psychologist can provide information that the claimant may be incapable of, or inept in, articulating as harm may develop slowly over time such that the individual lacks insight into its cause or impact. Legal counsel may retain a psychologist to provide a report and may call upon them to present their expert opinion in person. The matters which are the subject of a psychologist's expertise may include commentary on the conduct of assessment procedures in promotion or appointments, patterns of sickness absence, and psychological impacts of bullying or harassment. A psychologist may also be used to provide evidence about a claimant's mental disability in cases under the Disability Discrimination Act. Goodman-Delahunty and Foote (1995) describe factors to consider when addressing the issue of compensatory damages sufficient to meet the Daubert standards (see chapter 7.3 for a detailed explanation of this). It is the duty of the expert to present an unbiased assessment and provide well-founded and clear opinions as they are servants of the tribunal rather than of the instructing party.

Macartney-Filgate and Snow (2004) suggest that experts should conduct themselves honestly and candidly, tell the truth, be fair and independent, acknowledge limits of data and conclusions, and communicate opinion even if unfavourable to the retaining party. They may change their opinion when new facts or information comes to light. They should not allow financial considerations, allegiance to particular theories or methods influence opinion or professional judgement, or suppress information or distort findings in such a way so as to meet some preconceived opinion.

In the UK, part 35 of the Civil Procedure Rules lays out the duties of experts, as summarized in table 5.4.3.

Table 5.4.3 Requirements for expert witness

General requirements

Helps the court within area of own expertise

Independent opinion uninfluenced by pressure of litigation

Provision of objective, unbiased opinion (and should not assume an advocacy role)

Consider all material facts including those that may be detrimental

Make clear when matters fall outside their expertise or when insufficient information is available to form an opinion

Communicate any changes of view

Reports

Should be addressed to the court and not the instructing party

Give details of qualifications

Cite any literature used in the report

Provide statement of the substance of material facts and instructions

Say who carried out any examination, measurement or assessment

Summarize where there is a range of opinion and

State reason for own opinion

Summarize conclusions

Provide a qualification if a conclusion cannot be reached

Contain a statement of truth in the form:

'I confirm that insofar as the facts stated in my report are within my own knowledge I have made clear which they are and I believe them to be true, and that the opinions I have expressed represent my true and complete professional opinion.'

Full details, and also the Civil Justice Council's protocol for instructions to experts providing guidance for interpretation and compliance with these requirements, may be found at www.justice.gov.uk?civil/procrules_fin/con tents/practice_directions/pd_part35.

Damages

Rederstorff, Buchanan and Settles (2007) review some of the psychological outcomes as a consequence of suffering sexual harassment. These include increased depression and anxiety, and decreased life satisfaction. They note that in a US survey of adult women 10% met the criteria of post-traumatic stress disorder. Amongst sexual harassment plaintiffs the percentage is 68%. The study these researchers conducted found the holding of less traditional gender attitudes buffered the adverse impacts of experiences of sexual harassment for white women whereas they exacerbated effects on black women.

They suggest this may be because the black women belong to multiple marginalized groups, increasing their consciousness of oppression.

Aston, Hill and Tacey (2006) undertook a qualitative study of claimants taking race discrimination cases. They report that claimants found difficulties in differentiating between the impact of having taken the case and the impact of the discriminating workplace events. They were often distressed before lodging their case and the ET process exacerbated their distress. Most claimants said they experienced worsening physical health and emotional well-being in the aftermath of their case. Adverse health conditions seemed to persist if claimants were unhappy with the outcome of their cases.

Goodman-Delahunty and Foote (1995) give details of the nature of compensatory damages that individuals may claim as a consequence of suffering discrimination under US legislation. These include 'intangible' injuries, such as emotional pain, suffering inconvenience, mental anguish and loss of enjoyment of life, and these may be manifest by sleeplessness, anxiety, stress, depression, and loss of self-esteem or excessive fatigue. However, an award for emotional harm is 'warranted only if there is sufficient causal connection between the agency's illegal actions and the complainant's injury… a claim may be undermined if the onset of the symptoms … preceded the discriminatory conduct or if other factors in the plaintiff's life caused or contributed to the emotional harm suffered'.

Amicus curiae briefs

In the United States, the preparation of 'amicus curiae briefs', which are independent presentations of issues, have been deployed in discrimination cases. An example of such a brief can be found in the case of *Price Waterhouse* v. *Hopkins* (see Barrett and Morris 1993; Fiske *et al.* 1991; Wrightsman 1999). In this case Ann Hopkins alleged that her company, Price Waterhouse, failed to grant her a partnership because of her gender. The company claimed she was 'macho', 'overcompensated for being a woman', 'needed a course in charm school', and a colleague advised her 'to walk more femininely, talk more femininely, dress more femininely, wear make up and have her hair styled and wear jewellery'. She took her case under Title VII of the 1964 Civil Rights Act. Her attorneys instructed Professor Susan Fiske, a social psychologist, to provide testimony about sex stereotyping with particular reference to the facts in this case. The judge ruled that an employer who treated a woman with an assertive personality in a different manner than if she had been a man is guilty of sex discrimination. Moreover, the evaluative system used to assess appropriateness for admission to partnership permitted negative comments tainted by stereotyping to defeat Ann Hopkins' candidacy. Price Waterhouse appealed, arguing that the social psychological testimony was 'sheer speculation', having 'no evidentiary value'. Having lost their appeal, Price Waterhouse took the case to the Supreme Court. The American Psychological Association (APA) submitted an amicus curiae brief in order to 'disabuse the court of the notion that sex stereotyping was not an identifiable and legally cognizable source of sex discrimination... and to inform the court of the scientific validity of the methods and literature used in Fiske's testimony' (Fiske *et al.* 1991). Of particular interest was the APA's distinction between the work of research psychologists reviewing the literature and clinical psychologists interviewing and assessing an individual. The point at issue was not Ann Hopkins' mental status, but the conditions which evoked stereotyping. The court opined that they were not persuaded that the Fiske expert testimony was 'gossamer evidence' based on 'intuitive hunches'.

The APA brief was criticized by Barrett and Morris (1993), who challenged its scientific merit on the grounds that 'the presentation of the theoretical basis of discrimination was inconsistent and failed to successfully resolve the discrepancies amongst theoretical models ... the portrayal of the conditions at Price Waterhouse was biased in favour of Ms Hopkins' case and did not represent an accurate picture of the research literature on stereotyping'. They argued that the APA forfeits impartiality if briefs are slanted in favour of one side and endangers its scientific credibility by so doing.

Acknowledgement

I am grateful to Amanda Hart, barrister, who commented on an earlier draft.

FURTHER READING

The annual reports of the Employment Services Tribunal provide a helpful digest of statistics and background to UK practice. Wrightsman's (1999) chapter on the APA-organized amicus briefs provides a critical account of the *Price Waterhouse* v. *Hopkins* case. Macartney-Filgate and Snow's (2004) chapter on the practitioner as an expert witness is helpful. Liberty's website has resources written by Amanda Hart that provide details of UK legislation. Goodman-Delahunty and Foote (1995) provide a good overview of psychological injuries suffered as a consequence of discrimination and standards of evidence required to substantiate injury claims.

REFERENCES

Allport, G. W. (1954) *The Nature of Prejudice*. Reading, MA: Addison Wesley.

Aston, J., Hill, D. and Tackey, N. (2006) The experience of claimants in race discrimination employment tribunal cases. Department of Trade and Industry Employment Relations Research Series 55.

Barrett, G. V. and Morris, S. B. (1993) The American Psychological Association's amicus curiae brief in Price Waterhouse v. Hopkins. *Law and Human Behaviour*, 17: 201–11.

Employment Tribunal Service (2008) *Annual Report and Accounts*. London: The Stationery Office.

Fiske, S., Bersoff, D., Borgida, E., Deaux, K. and Heilman, M. (1991) Use of sex stereotyping research in Price Waterhouse v. Hopkins. *American Psychologist*, 46: 1049–60.

Glick, P. and Fiske, S. (2001) An ambivalent alliance: hostile and benevolent sexism as complementary justifications for gender equality. *American Psychologist*, 56: 109–18.

Goodman-Delahunty, J. and Foote, W. (1995) Compensation for pain, suffering and other psychological injuries: the impact of Daubert on employment discrimination claims. *Behavioural Sciences and the Law*, 13: 183–206.

Hayward, B., Peters, M., Rousseau, N. and Seeds, K. (2004) Findings from a survey of employment tribunal applications 2003. DTI Employment Relations Research Series 33.

Hegarty, P. (2006) Where's the sex in sexual prejudice? *Lesbian and Gay Psychology Review*, 7: 264–74.

Herek, G. M. (2000) The psychology of sexual prejudice. *Current Directions in Psychological Science*, 9: 19–22.

Macartney-Filgate, M. S. and Snow, G. (2004) The practitioner as expert witness. In D. R. Evans (ed.), *The Law, Standards and Ethics in the Practice of Psychology*, 2nd edn, pp. 287–309. Toronto: Emond Montgomery.

Macpherson, Sir W. (1999) *The Stephen Lawrence Inquiry*. Cm 4262–1. London: HMSO.

McConahay, J. B. and Hough, J. C. (1976) Symbolic racism. *Journal of Social Issues*, 32: 23–45.

Rederstorff, J. C., Buchanan, N. T. and Settles, I. H. (2007) The moderating roles of race and gender-role attitudes in the relationship between sexual harassment and psychological well being. *Psychology of Women Quarterly*, 31: 50–61.

Schuman, H. (1969) Sociological racism. *Trans-action*, 7: 44–8.

Wrightsman, L. (1999) *Judicial Decision Making: Is Psychology Relevant?* New York: Plenum Press.

Wrightsman, L. and Fulero, S. (2005) *Forensic Psychology*, 2nd edn. Belmont, CA: Wadsworth.

WEB RESOURCES

http://www.justice.gov.uk?civil/procrules_fin/contents/practice_directions/pd_part35
www.yourrights.org.UK/yourrights/right-to-equal-treatment/index.html

5.5 Personal injury

Graham E. Powell and Charlotte C. Powell

Legal definition of personal injury

Personal injuries are damages to the physical person rather than to the person's property. The Civil Procedure Rules, which apply to England and Wales, define 'personal injuries' to include not only personal injuries in the strict sense, but also any disease and any impairment of a person's physical or mental condition.

A tort is an act which causes harm to a person, whether intentionally or not. ('Tort' is simply the French word for 'wrong', which derives from the Latin *tortus*, meaning 'twisted' or 'wrung', and other terms derived from this root are the adjective 'tortious' and the adverb 'tortiously', also 'tortfeasor', the term for one who commits a tort.) A tort is a civil wrong (as opposed to a criminal wrong) and the 'law of tort' is the law of civil liability for wrongfully inflicted injury or harm (Lunney and Oliphant 2003; Oliphant 2007). Such harm could arise, for example, from the breach of an employer's duty of care to an employee, negligence during a medical or dental procedure, or from an accident rising from loss of control of a vehicle. Unlike criminal proceedings, civil actions are brought by individuals, not generally the state. Defendants are sued in the civil courts (county courts or the High Court) and it is the claimant who brings the action and who stands to benefit directly from a court judgement against the defendant.

The tortious infliction of personal injury on another person can give rise to a claim for personal injuries which is remedied by the award of damages, a sum of money, by way of compensation. Such claims will typically be founded on torts of negligence, occupiers' liability or breach of a statutory duty. More specifically, the tort of negligence, for example, requires the claimant to establish (i) the existence of a duty of care; (ii) the defendant owed the plaintiff a duty of care; (iii) the defendant breached that duty (i.e. he/she must be careless or negligent); (iv) the breach must have caused the plaintiff damage; (v) the damage is not too remote. The burden of proof is upon the claimant to prove each element, and the standard of proof is on the balance of probabilities, i.e. 51% likely or greater. How and when an action for damages for personal injury can be brought is governed by the Civil Procedure Rules.

The claimant who successfully establishes tortious liability for personal injury is entitled to recover all losses, financial or non-financial, that flow from the defendant's tort. Sometimes liability is shared between the defendant and claimant in proportions determined by the court; there may be contributory negligence on the part of the claimant, e.g. a passenger who did not use their seat belt, in which case the claimant can recover only that portion of the damages for which the defendant is liable.

Financial losses include, for example, loss of earnings or medical expenses. Non-financial losses are for the 'pain and suffering' felt by the claimant and the 'loss of amenity' caused by the personal injury. Courts do not usually distinguish between the two elements 'pain' and 'suffering'. The authorities do draw a clear distinction between damages for 'pain and suffering' and damages for loss of amenity. The former depends on the claimant's personal awareness of pain and the capacity for suffering, whereas the latter are awarded for the fact of deprivation, a substantial loss, whether the plaintiff is aware of it or not (e.g. *Lim Poh Choo* v. *Camden and Islington AHA* [1980] AC 174, 188).

Pecuniary, financial losses incurred up to the date of trial can usually be accurately calculated and are called 'special damages'. Damages for pecuniary loss that the claimant expects to incur in the future cannot be specified accurately (for example, there is always likely to be some degree of uncertainty about the claimant's promotion prospects at work had the tort not happened), and together with damages for non-pecuniary losses these are called 'general damages'.

Some portion of the damages may take the form of 'provisional damages' (section 32 of the Supreme Court Act 1981), which compensate a claimant who establishes that a chance exists that he will develop a 'serious disease' or some 'serious deterioration' in his condition after the case has settled or the trial has ended, for example, if epilepsy develops. Sometimes damages for future pecuniary loss in respect of personal injury can be ordered by the court to take the form of 'periodical payments' (section 2 of the Damages Act 1996, as amended by section 100 of the Courts Act 2003), so that a sum is paid each year that the claimant survives.

The role of the lawyer

The pre-action protocol for personal injuries (CPR (2007), vol. I, C2–001, p. 2343) is a statement of understanding between legal practitioners and others about pre-action practice. In personal injury claims worth up to £15,000 the solicitors for each party are expected to comply with it, and in larger claims the spirit of the protocol should still be applied.

Before issuing proceedings, the following matters should be dealt with in the following order:

(a) Two copies of the letter of claim should be sent to the defendant immediately sufficient information is available to substantiate a realistic claim.

(b) The defendant must reply within twenty-one days naming any insurer. Failure to comply within twenty-one days justifies the issue of proceedings without further compliance.

(c) The defendant or his insurer has up to three months to acknowledge the letter of claim and state whether liability is agreed or denied.

(d) A schedule of special damages must be sent as soon as possible thereafter.

(e) The next step is to obtain medical evidence dealing with the claimant's injuries (the protocol regards the joint selection of a single expert to be the norm). Before the claimant instructs an expert, the claimant will send the defendant a list of proposed experts. The defendant will have fourteen days to object to the use of one or more of them and, if the defendant does not object to them all, the claimant instructs one who is agreed mutually. If no agreement is reached, each party instructs its own expert. If a party acts unreasonably, there may be adverse costs consequences at the end of the proceedings. Where a medical expert is instructed, the solicitor will arrange access to medical records. Once a medical report has been written, either party may send written questions to the expert, via the claimant's solicitors. Responses by the expert should be sent directly and separately back to the asking party.

(f) The parties are encouraged to consider negotiating, and possibly alternative dispute resolution or mediation before starting proceedings.

If negotiation or mediation does not resolve the dispute, proceedings will be issued. The lawyer will be responsible for representing the claimant at every stage of the claim, the main stages of which are:

(a) Issue of proceedings

(b) Service of proceedings

(c) Service of statements of case

(d) Track allocation

(e) Directions

(f) Disclosure of documents

(g) Exchange of witnesses' statements and experts' reports

(h) Listing for trial

(i) Trial

(j) Assessment of costs

The expert witness

The behaviour of expert witnesses in England and Wales is governed by the CPR, as detailed in part 35, Experts and Assessors, and in Practice Directions 35 (see British Psychological Society 2007; Powell 2007). The duty of the expert is to the court and not to the instructing party. The report is addressed to the court, gives the expert's qualifications, lists materials and tests relied upon, states the instructions, summarizes the range of views and the reasons for the final opinion and conclusions. The report must finish with a statement of compliance of the form: *I understand my duty as an independent expert witness is to the Court. I have complied with that duty. This report includes all matters relevant to the issues on which my expert evidence is given. I have given details in this report of any matters that might affect the validity of this report. I have addressed this report to the Court.* The report must also finish with a statement of truth of the form: *I confirm that insofar as the facts stated in my report are within my own knowledge I have made clear which they are and I believe them to be true, and that the opinions I have expressed represent my true and complete professional opinion.* The expert is in contempt of court if these are found to be false statements.

The psychologist as expert witness

The role of the psychologist flows from the legal definition of injury and from the legal processes of evaluating claims arising from such injuries, as set out above. The primary areas that a psychologist's report will cover are as follows.

The nature of the injury

Psychologists will define injuries that fall within the domain of psychology. There may be a formal mental health disorder arising from the experience of the event and impairing the ability to work or function in some way (the travelling salesperson involved in a road traffic accident who develops post-traumatic stress disorder and now cannot drive to appointments and is excessively fatigued from sleepless nights due to nightmares and intrusive thoughts; or the builder who falls from faulty scaffolding who develops a specific phobia of heights and who now can only work at ground level). There may be an intellectual or cognitive loss that impairs occupational functioning (the accountant who suffers a severe head injury under collapsing shelves in a shop, with a resultant slowing of mental processing and reduced intellectual and cognitive efficiency, now not able to sustain the same rate of work output). There may also be emotional and behavioural changes which, although not neatly falling into any formal category of disorder or deficit, can nevertheless be shown to have led to pain and suffering and/or financial loss. The psychologist's formulation will need to make this chain of causality clear (e.g. the effects of a facial scar on the confidence of an actress and the resultant change in the manner of her presentation and her career trajectory).

Liability

It is rare for psychologists to be involved in liability issues with respect to physical injuries, but it is not unknown. For example, there are relevant psychological research findings regarding the protective effects of wearing motorcycle and bicycle helmets. What is more common is for the psychologist to be involved in the issue of causation. For example, a teacher might bring a claim against their employer on the basis that unreasonable pressure at work and lack of support led to depression, a failure of coping and a job change to less remunerative employment. However, a close look at the history and records might show that the teacher was already depressed from an ongoing marital breakdown, that this had already led to crippling tension headaches, and that there had already been talk with her GP about the need for a lifestyle change, such that there could have been time off work and a job change in any case regardless of what happened at work.

Non-financial loss

Pain and suffering is a subjective assessment and therefore depends on the ability of the person to perceive a loss or to experience pain. For example, a claimant may be in vegetative state and not able to have any subjective experience at all. Another claimant may have severe frontal lobe injuries and lack insight and therefore simply not appreciate the dramatic change in their roles and way of life. Loss of amenity is less subjective and the psychologist's formulation will place an injury in the appropriate person-centred context. For example, a travel phobia developed after an accident would be especially serious for a claimant nearing retirement age who had expected to lead a twin-centred life in a second home abroad.

Past financial losses

After psychological injuries it is common for the claimant to have taken time off work, and indeed they may still be off work. The key question usually put to the psychologist is whether that time off work was justifiable in psychological terms. Were they really incapable of work? If so, why? And for how long? There are often two supplementary questions. First, if their partner took time off work to look after them, was that justifiable on psychological grounds? Second, if the claimant underwent psychological treatment, was it appropriate treatment? Was the length of treatment appropriate? Was the cost reasonable?

Future financial losses

Regarding direct financial loss from reduced earnings, there are two common issues that the psychologist is asked to address from the psychological perspective. The first is what the career trajectory of the individual would have been had the injury not occurred. The second is what their earning potential is now. Can they work at all? If so, has the nature of the work they could do changed? Can they still work full time? Has the ability to do overtime been affected? Has the likely retirement age been affected? Is there the same potential for promotion?

Future financial costs

There are two main areas of cost. First, there may be future treatment needs, such as further interventions for mental health problems, or time in a rehabilitation unit regaining skills of independent living, or a formal return-to-work programme run by vocational specialists. There may also be intermittent treatment needs across the lifespan of the individual, arising from, for example, a likelihood of relapse, or a likelihood of gaps in employment when further vocational advice would be needed. Second is the issue of care. From the psychological perspective, has a care need arisen from the injuries? Is the person safe to be alone overnight? Is the person safe to be alone in the day? If so, for how long? Do they need accompanying on certain activities? Is their life so limited and restricted that they need a degree of companionship as well as care?

Capacity

In the event that the injury has given rise to a serious mental health disorder (e.g. a relapsing psychotic disorder secondary to intractable substance abuse in turn secondary to the effects of the injury) or to a significant blunting of intellectual and cognitive ability due to brain damage, then the issue of capacity may arise, i.e. the capacity to instruct a solicitor or to manage one's own financial and related affairs (British Psychological Society 2006). In England and Wales this matter is covered by the Mental Capacity Act 2005. There is a three-way test of capacity regarding any specific issue in which there is a decision to make. Is there a disability of mind? Is there evidence that the person is incapable of making decisions regarding the issue at hand? Has this incapacity arisen from the disability of mind? It is important for both parties to be clear on the matter of capacity at the time the claimant instructs the solicitor to accept an offer of settlement. For example, if at that time the person lacked the capacity to instruct a solicitor (i.e. lacked the ability to bring appropriate information to mind, to weigh and evaluate that information, to make a decision and to communicate that decision), then the acceptance of that offer is invalid and the case can be re-opened at some later date when the incapacity comes to light. As another example, if the person lacks the ability to manage their own financial affairs, then the cost of placing the person under the Court of Protection and the appointment of a receiver will have to be costed in the claim.

Conclusion

The role of the psychologist in personal injury litigation is to define from the psychological perspective the nature of the injury and to provide a formulation as to how that injury has given rise, and will give rise, to pain and suffering, loss of amenity, and to financial losses and costs. The psychologist is also expected to be skilled in working within a legal framework and in presenting oral and written evidence.

ADDITIONAL READING

The Civil Procedure Rules are accessible free, online, at www.justice.gov.uk/civil/procrules. It gives not just the rules themselves but also the most recent revisions (about fifty at the last count). Detailed analysis of the law of tort as well as damages for personal injury can be found in Oliphant (2007) and also in Lunney and Oliphant (2003). For a classic book on psychologists as expert witnesses see G. B. Melton, J. Petrila, N. G Poythress and C. Slobogin (1997) *Psychological Evaluations for the Courts: A Handbook for Mental Health Professionals and Lawyers* (New York: Guilford Press).

REFERENCES

British Psychological Society (2006) *Assessment of Capacity in Adults: Interim Guidance for Psychologists*. Leicester: British Psychological Society.

(2007) *Psychologists as Expert Witnesses: Guidelines and Procedure*. Leicester: British Psychological Society.

Civil Procedure Rules (2007) Sweet & Maxwell, London.

Lim Poh Choo v. *Camden and Islington AHA* [1980] AC 174 at 188.

Lunney, M. and Oliphant, K. (2003) *Tort Law: Text and Materials*, 2nd edn. Oxford: Oxford University Press.

Oliphant, K. (gen. ed.) (2007) *The Law of Tort*, 2nd edn. Suffolk: LexisNexis Butterworths.

Powell, G. E. (2007) The role of the expert witness and acquired brain injury. In S. Young, M. Kopelman and G. Gudjonsson (eds.), *Forensic Neuropsychology in Practice: A Guide to Assessment and Legal Processes*, pp. 247–66. Oxford: Oxford University Press.

Part VI

Special topics

6.1 Arson

Katarina Fritzon

See also chapter 1.1 Action system applied to forensic topics.

Definition and origins

Ever since Freud wrote his essay 'The acquisition of power over fire' (1932), psychologists and psychiatrists have attempted to offer explanations for perhaps one of the more puzzling of crimes: the wilful and sometimes apparently motiveless destruction of property by fire. Arson is the legal term given to describe this behaviour. Precise legal definitions vary internationally, but generally involve three elements (1) incendiary origin; (2) destruction of property; (3) intent. Because this is a behaviour which can be engaged in by even very young children, without necessarily having the same intent as an adult, we generally do not refer to children as 'arsonists'. What has become clear in contemporary research is that attempts to explain this behaviour recognize the very different psychological profiles that exist for this group of offenders, e.g. distinguishing the arson-for-profit perpetrator from the 'pyromaniac' who repeatedly sets fire to apparently random targets, for reasons that appear to be a product of complex psychopathology. In reviewing the psychological literature on arson, it is possible to identify two predominant strands of work. The first of these initially focused on identifying the main motives for firesetting, both by juveniles (Icove and Estepp 1987; Kolko 1983; Fineman 1995) and adults (Barker 1994; Geller 1992b; Puri, Baxter and Cordess 1995; Vreeland and Levin 1996) and then more recently attempted to identify the characteristics of perpetrators associated with each of these motives. The main aim of this work appeared to be to assist law enforcement investigators and has included research adopting methodology associated with the investigative psychology branch of the wider discipline of forensic psychology (e.g. Almond *et al.* 2005; Canter and Fritzon 1998; Fritzon, Canter and Wilton 2001; Santtila, Fritzon and Tamelander 2004). A second strand of research has been more clinical in focus, with the aim of developing approaches to the assessment and treatment of firesetting (e.g. Bradford 1992; Jackson, Glass and Hope 1987; Jackson 1994; Swaffer, Haggett and Oxley 2001). Within the clinical/forensic literature, arson has received sparse attention and is poorly understood compared to more direct and violent forms of interpersonal offending.

The distinction between the two is somewhat artificial in that it is only by understanding the individual pathways that lead persons with certain characteristics to commit certain forms of arson, that research can assist in both the identification and apprehension of perpetrators, as well as providing useful clinical guidance to assist in the development of treatment programmes that reduce recidivism.

What are the characteristics of arsonists?

Firesetting behaviour in adults has generally been addressed from a psychiatric perspective and has focused on the identification of clinical features commonly found for this group of individuals. Persons who commit arson attract a variety of clinical diagnoses, most commonly personality disorder, intellectual impairment, psychotic illness and substance use disorder (Enyati *et al.* 2008). Research has shown that in comparison with other offender groups, the histories of adult arsonists are more often characterized by family disturbances of some kind. Harris and Rice (1984) found that firesetters were less assertive than other patients in situations requiring the verbal expression of negative feelings, and they described themselves and were described by others as more shy and withdrawn. Furthermore, a later study by the same researchers (Rice and Harris 1991) identified variables such as social isolation (as indicated by hobbies, marital status, living arrangements, etc.), physical aggression, intelligence, age, physical attractiveness and psychiatric history as differentiating the firesetting group from other mentally disordered offenders.

What are the main motives of arsonists?

One of the interesting things about arson is that it is one of few crimes that crosses the boundary between interpersonal and property offending. There are few other crimes or acts that can be used for financial gain (insurance-fraud arson; crime concealment following a burglary) as well as being acts of interpersonal violence (burning someone's property as revenge or using fire to commit homicide or injury to a person). Other motives that have been identified include vandalism, anger, communication, psychosis, extremism (e.g. animal liberation groups) or political motives (e.g. acts of terrorism) (e.g. Faulk 1988; Geller 1992a; Inciardi 1970; Vreeland and Waller 1979; Prins 1994). Prins (1994) concludes that many of these typologies tend to confuse the motivations and the characteristics of arsonists, for example including categories such as 'arson as a product of mental illness' within a motivational typology when this is actually a description of a characteristic of the arsonist. Further, they produce overlapping categories that may be of some practical assistance but do not really help in understanding the distinct varieties of arson. More recently, Geller (1992a) also criticizes motivational classifications on the grounds that they focus on possible explanations for the firesetting behaviour, rather than describing variations in the behaviour itself.

How can we identify which individuals commit particular forms of arson?

In an attempt to overcome problems associated with descriptive motivational typologies, work by the present author and colleagues has developed a model of firesetting which is derived from systemic theories relating to behavioural action systems (Canter and Fritzon 1998; Fritzon, Canter and Wilton 2001). This model has subsequently been tested on a number of different data sets (Fritzon and Brun 2005; Miller and Fritzon 2007) and also has achieved external validity in case study applications (Santtila, Häkkänen and Fritzon 2003).

The model classifies arson according to its target and the source of the motivation to commit arson. The targets are categorized in terms of whether they are objects (e.g. business premises, schools, institutions) or specific people who were significant to the arsonist (most typically a former partner, or other known victim). The motivational distinction differentiates whether the source is external (e.g. revenge or vandalism) or internal (suicide or pathological interest in fire) to the individual. A combination of these two facets creates four distinct modes of arson, each with corresponding offender characteristics. The first, labelled *adaptive*, is best understood as an act of criminal damage directed at opportunistic objects, often in the context of another crime being committed. The offenders responsible tend to be juveniles acting in groups and engaging in a variety of other antisocial acts. The *conservative* mode refers to arson which is directed at an external source of frustration, where the goal is to restore emotional wellbeing in the perpetrator of the arson. This is often achieved through setting a multiple-seated fire, often involving accelerants and the destruction of property and endangering of lives. The perpetrator is usually an individual known to the victim, and the relationship characterized by a history of disturbed interactions, including prior threats of violence or fire. The third form, labelled *integrative*, is one where the arsonist sets fire to their own home, or occasionally, themselves, in an attempt to draw attention to emotional distress. The individual responsible is often psychiatrically disturbed, and a higher proportion of females set fires within this mode of action. Finally, the *expressive* mode combines an internal source with an external target for the arson, and can be compared to Geller's (1992c) description of communicative arson, which seeks to draw attention to an individual who may feel unable to achieve goals in a more direct manner. These cases often are serial as the individual learns that fire is an effective means of expression. The targets for this form of firesetting may be public buildings which attract significant vicarious attention through crowds and large numbers of fire appliances. The individual responsible often has personality disturbances and a history of fire-related behaviour.

How do we identify the clinical/treatment needs of arsonists?

The identification of specific treatment needs of arsonists has received little attention in the clinical/forensic literature; however, in recent years a number of private and publicly funded secure hospitals within the UK have developed and run specific treatment programmes for persons convicted of arson offences. The majority of these have focused on populations with particular characteristics, e.g. intellectual impairment, or female offenders, and outcome studies have only been published with very small amounts of data (Taylor *et al.* 2002; Taylor, Thorne and Slavkin 2004; Taylor *et al.* 2006).

A comprehensive description of a treatment package specifically designed for adult mentally disordered arsonists is described by Swaffer, Haggett and Oxley (2001). This model includes modules designed to develop inter- and intrapersonal skills with the aim of providing individuals with more socially acceptable and functional methods of problem solving. Following a general cognitive-behavioural framework, the programme includes a psycho-eduction component, victim empathy, skills development, insight and emotional regulation, and finally relapse prevention. In a recent international review of firesetting interventions, Haines, Lambie and Seymour (2006) conclude that collaboration between services providing eduction and psychological therapy appears to be the most promising model for intervention, yet very few examples are cited of this practice actually operating outside the US and Canada.

How do we know if treatment is effective?

As previously stated, outcome studies reporting on the efficacy of arson treatment are very sparse. Clinical outcome studies have reported success in terms of reductions in scores on the measures used. For example, Taylor *et al.* (2006) reported improvements in measures of self-esteem, anger and fire interest for the fourteen participants in their group. Another measure of treatment success is reduction in recidivism. Harris and Rice (1996) found that 17% of 243 mentally disordered firesetters committed further offences of arson within an eight-year follow-up period. None of the six female patients released during the two-year follow-up period of the Taylor *et al.* (2006) study committed a further act of firesetting; however, this would not necessarily have been expected even for an untreated group, given the base-rate reported by Harris and Rice.

In the absence of recidivism data, an alternative approach to measuring intervention success is offered by recent literature on 'offence paralleling behaviour' (Jones 2004). An offence paralleling behaviour is one that is functionally similar to the offence behaviour, but not necessarily topographically similar. In a study of self-harm and firesetting in female mentally disordered offenders, Miller and Fritzon (2007) found support for the idea that these two behaviours may represent different manifestations of similar psychological processes. Anecdotally, the authors noted, whilst delivering a firesetting intervention programme to a different group of female mentally disordered offenders, that a reduction in self-harming behaviour occurred whilst the group was running. Further research is clearly needed to verify whether such unintended positive consequences of firesetting intervention (a) are actually related to the intervention, and (b) are associated with a subsequent reduction in the firesetting behaviour itself.

Conclusion

This chapter has provided an overview of findings from both the investigative and clinical literature on arson. Future directions for research include the important task of conducting long-term evaluations of treatment efficacy, as well as the utilization of these research findings to further refine the treatment programmes following the principles of effective rehabilitation outlined by Andrews and Bonta (2007). The identification of behavioural variations in arson that are linked with specific offender characteristics is an important step towards better targeted intervention.

REFERENCES

Almond, L., Duggan, L., Shine, J. and Canter, D. (2005) Test of the arson action systems model in an incarcerated population. *Journal of Psychology, Crime and Law*, 11: 1–15.

Andrews, D. A. and Bonta, J. (2007) *The Psychology of Criminal Conduct*, 4th edn. Cincinnati, OH: Anderson.

Barker, A. (1994) *Arson: A Review of the Psychiatric Literature*. Maudsley Monographs no. 35. Oxford: Oxford University Press.

Bradford, J. M. W. (1982) Arson: a clinical study. *Canadian Journal of Psychiatry*, 27: 188–92.

Canter, D. and Fritzon, K. (1998) Differentiating arsonists: a model of firesetting actions and characteristics. *Legal and Criminological Psychology*, 3: 73–96.

Enyati, J., Lubbe, S., Grann, M. and Fazel, S. (2008) Psychiatric morbidity in arsonists referred for forensic psychiatric assessment in Sweden. *Journal of Forensic Psychiatry and Psychology*, 19: 139–47.

Faulk, M. (1988) *Basic Forensic Psychiatry*. Oxford: Blackwell.

Fineman, K. (1995) A model for the qualitative analysis of child and adult fire deviant behavior. *American Journal of Forensic Psychology*, 13: 31–60.

Freud, S. (1932) The acquisition of power over fire. *International Journal of Psychoanalysis*, 13: 405–10.

Fritzon, K. and Brun, A. (2005) Beyond Columbine: an action systems model of school homicide. *Psychology, Crime and Law*, 11: 53–71.

Fritzon, K., Canter, D. and Wilton, Z. (2001) The application of an action systems model to destructive behaviour: the examples of arson and terrorism. *Behavioral Sciences and the Law*, 19: 657–90.

Geller, J. L. (1992a) Arson in review: from profit to pathology. *Clinical Forensic Psychiatry*, 15: 623–45.

— (1992b) Pathological firesetting in adults. *International Journal of Law and Psychiatry*, 15: 283–302.

— (1992c) Communicative arson. *Hospital and Community Psychiatry*, 43: 76–7.

Haines, S., Lambie, I. and Seymour, F. (2006) International approaches to reducing deliberately lit fires: prevention programmes. *N. Z. F. Commission*. Auckland, NZ: Auckland UniServices: 149.

Harris, G. T. and Rice, M. E. (1984) Mentally disordered firesetters: psycho-dynamic versus empirical approaches. *International Journal of Law and Psychiatry*, 7: 19–34.

(1996) A typology of mentally disordered firesetters. *Journal of Interpersonal Violence*, 11: 351–63.

Icove, David J. and Estepp, M. H. (1987) Motive-based offender profiles of arson and fire-related crimes. *FBI Law Enforcement Bulletin*, 56: 17–23.

Inciardi, J. A. (1970) The adult firesetter – a typology. *Criminology*, 8: 145–55.

Jackson, H. (1994) Assessment of firesetters. In M. McMurran and J. Hodge (eds.), *The Assessment of Criminal Behaviours of Clients in Secure Settings*, pp. 94–126. London: Jessica Kingsley.

Jackson, H. F., Glass, C. and Hope, S. (1987) A functional analysis of recidivistic arson. *British Journal of Clinical Psychology*, 26: 175–85.

Jones, L. (2004) Offence paralleling behaviour (OPB) as a framework for assessment and intervention with offenders. In A. Needs and G. Towl (eds.) *Applying Psychology to Forensic Practice*, pp. 34–63. Malden, MA: Blackwell.

Kolko, D. J. (1983) Multicomponent parental treatment of firesetting in a developmentally-disabled boy. *Journal of Behavior Therapy and Experimental Psychiatry*, 14: 349–53.

Miller, S. and Fritzon, K. (2007) Functional consistency across two behavioural modalities: firesetting and self harm in female special hospital patients. *Criminal Behaviour and Mental Health*, 17: 31–44.

Prins, H. (1994) *Fire-Raising: Its Motivation and Management*. London: Routledge.

Puri, B., Baxter, R. and Cordess, C. (1995) Characteristics of firesetters: a study and proposed multiaxial psychiatric classification. *British Journal of Psychiatry*, 166: 393–6.

Rice, M. E. and Harris, G. T. (1991) Firesetters admitted to a maximum security psychiatric institution: offenders and offences. *Journal of Interpersonal Violence*, 6: 461–75.

(1996) Predicting the recidivism of mentally disordered firesetters. *Journal of Interpersonal Violence*, 11: 364–75.

Santtila, P., Fritzon, K. and Tamelander, A. L. (2004) Linking arson incidents on the basis of crime scene behavior. *Journal of Police and Criminal Psychology*, 19: 1–16.

Santtila, P., Häkkänen, H. and Fritzon, K. (2003) Inferring the characteristics of an arsonist from crime scene behaviour: a case study in offender profiling. *International Journal of Police Science and Management*, 5: 5–15.

Swaffer, T. M., Haggett, M. and Oxley, T. (2001) Mentally disordered firesetters: A structured intervention programme. *Clinical Psychology and Psychotherapy*, 8: 468–75.

Taylor, J., Robertson, A., Thorne, I., Belshaw, T. and Watson, A. (2006) Responses of female fire-setters with mild and borderline intellectual disabilities to a group intervention. *Journal of Applied Research in Intellectual Disabilities*, 19: 179–90.

Taylor, J., Thorne, I. and Slavkin, M. (2004) Treatment of fire setting behaviour. In W. L. Lindsey, J. L. Taylor and P. Sturmey (eds.), *Offenders with Developmental Disabilities*, pp. 221–40. Chichester: Wiley.

Taylor, J., Thorne, I., Robertson, A. and Avery, G. (2002) Evaluation of a group intervention for convicted arsonists with mild and borderline intellectual disabilities. *Criminal Behaviour and Mental Health*, 12: 282–93.

Vreeland, R. G. and Levin, B. M. (1996) Psychological aspects of firesetting. In D. Canter (ed.), *Fires and Human Behavior*, pp. 31–46. London: David Fulton.

Vreeland, R. G. and Waller, M. B. (1979) The psychology of firesetting: a review and appraisal. *National Bureau of Standards*, grant no. 7–9021. Washington, DC: US Government Printing Office.

Bullying among prisoners

Jane L. Ireland

Definition

Regardless of the target or perpetrator (i.e. children, adults, community, forensic etc.), identifying a fixed and measurable definition of bullying has proven elusive (Smith and Brain 2000; Ireland 2005a). This appears to be particularly the case when trying to define the bullying that occurs among adults and older adolescents where 'bullying' may be construed as 'childish' and the label bullying behaviour does not therefore apply. This has been cited as a reason why bullying can be under-reported in prisons, with prisoners failing to acknowledge their aggression as 'bullying' (Ireland and Ireland 2003).

Prescriptive definitions of bullying have been fraught with difficulty within prison research. Farrington's (1993) is a good example of a definition cited within early prison research, but one that has met problems when applied to prisoners. Table 6.2.1 illustrates the components of Farrington's definition and the associated difficulties with each element.

Ireland (2002) offered the following broader definition of bullying to address these difficulties as follows:

An individual is being bullied when they are the victim of direct and/or indirect aggression happening on a weekly basis, by the same perpetrator or different perpetrators. Single incidences of aggression can be viewed as bullying, particularly where they are severe and when the individual either believes or fears that they are at risk of future victimisation by the same perpetrator or others. An incident can be considered bullying if the victim believes that they have been aggressed towards, regardless of the actual intention of the bully. It can also be bullying when the imbalance of power between the bully and his/her victim is implied and not immediately evident. (p. 26)

What is absent from this definition, however, and indeed absent from this area of study as a whole, is mention of what is motivating the aggression. This is not

Table 6.2.1 Farrington's definition and associated difficulties in application

Farrington definition (1993): In order for a behaviour to be classed as bullying it must …	*Example(s)* of problems in application to prisoners
contain physical, psychological or verbal attack	No mention made of indirect aggression (e.g. subtle aggression such as gossiping, spreading rumours: Björkqvist 1994). This is known to occur at least as frequently in prisons as direct aggression (e.g. physical, verbal), if not more so (Ireland and Ireland 2008).
involve an imbalance of power	Some specific types of aggression labelled as 'bullying' by prisoners are not initially based on an explicit imbalance of power. One example would be 'baroning' where goods are lent to another prisoner by a 'baron', with a high rate of interest charged. Such behaviour is clearly exploitation yet falls outside the Farrington definition (Ireland 2002).
the victim must not have provoked the bully	The notion of a 'provocative' victim has long been acknowledged as a factor that should not influence definition (Smith and Brain 2000; Ireland 2002).
the aggression has to have occurred more than once	Prison populations can be transient, with prisoners moved around locations limiting the extent to which behaviour can be repeated (Ireland 2002). There is also an acknowledgement that it is not the frequency of the behaviour that is important but rather how *fearful* an individual is that it may reoccur (Ireland 2002), and how *severe* the incident of bullying was (Olweus 1996).
the bully must intend their actions, specifically intending to cause fear or distress	Arguing that intent has to be evident suggests an aggressor must have insight into their actions, which is clearly an oversimplification (Ireland 2002).

unique to the area of 'bullying' but is a broader criticism that can be levelled at the wider aggression literature: arguably aggression should be defined by what is motivating it (e.g. material gain, pleasure, excitement) as opposed to how it looks (e.g. physical, verbal, sexual etc.).

Thus, it could be argued that the only consensus in relation to defining bullying has been on the difficulties in determining an agreed definition that can be reliably measured. This said, there is a developing move in the literature towards removing labels, such as 'bullying', and instead describing the behaviour by referring to its discrete nature. In this instance, 'intra-group aggression' may be a more preferable term to employ (Ireland and Ireland 2008).

Origins and further developments

As an area of academic study the examination of bullying among prisoners has had a briefer history than the bullying that occurs within other settings, such as schools, where published research can be traced back to the 1970s (e.g. Olweus 1978). Within prisons, however, the first study was published in 1996, with a marked increase in research since with twenty-seven studies published between 1999 and 2007. The majority of the research has also been conducted within the UK, with only a small handful of studies conducted outside the UK, namely within Canada and the Netherlands (e.g. Connell and Farrington 1996).

Prison research has, however, covered the full ambit of the prison population, i.e. adults, young offenders, juveniles, men and women. Of these juveniles and women remain one of the least researched groups. As an area of empirical study there have perhaps been ten *core* areas of development in the last ten years as follows:

1. Increased focus on the theoretical underpinnings of prison bullying with various theoretical models proposed including the Applied Fear-Response Model (Ireland 2005b), Applied Social Processing Model (Ireland and Murray 2005), Interactional Model (Ireland 2002) and a bio-psychosocial and ecological interaction model (Gilbert 2005).
2. Refinement in the methods of measurement (Ireland 2005a). This has assisted with clarifying the nature of bullying within prisons (Ireland, Archer and Power 2007; Ireland and Ireland 2008).
3. Increased ability to predict membership to a bully, victim or bully/victim group via an analysis of behavioural characteristics (e.g. Ireland and Monaghan 2006).
4. Recognition of the mutual perpetrator-victim group, i.e. 'bully/victims' (Ireland *et al.* 2007).
5. Confirmation of an absence of sex differences in prison bullying (Ireland *et al.* 2007).
6. Enhanced approaches towards bully-group categorization, including refinement of the different groups involved (Ireland and Ireland 2008).

7. Clearer links made between prison bullying and the wider aggression literature (e.g. Ireland and Archer 2004).
8. Consideration of how 'bullying' is defined and a proposal for use of the term 'intragroup aggression' as an alternative (Ireland and Ireland 2008);
9. Recognition of the role played by the environment in understanding why bullying occurs (Ireland 2002). This has included a focus on moving attention away from psychopathology models, which focus on the 'individual' (prisoner) as opposed to how they interact with their environment (Ireland 2005a).
10. Recognition of the different types of aggression, including direct and indirect aggression (e.g. Björkqvist 1994).

Method

Although all of the ten substantive areas areas cited above provide some indication of advancements in this field, they are underpinned in part by the advances that are being made in relation to methods of measurement. Early studies into prison bullying tended to use individual interviews (e.g. Connell and Farrington 1996). Such interviews utilized the term 'bullying', asking prisoners directly 'Have you bullied/been bullied?' These methods were subsequently followed by self-report questionnaires that also used the term bullying (e.g. Ireland and Archer 1996). Such approaches tend to produce average perpetration estimates of 21% and average victimization estimates of 23% (Ireland 2002). Following these methods was the development of self-report behavioural checklists. The most utilized of these has been the Direct and Indirect Prisoner Behaviour Checklist (DIPC and also a revised version, the DIPC-R; Ireland 1999, 2005c). The DIPC/R asks prisoners to indicate a range of discrete aggressive behaviours that they have engaged in or experienced, with the use of the term 'bullying' avoided. Such checklists have produced higher overall average estimates. Using this method, average proportions for perpetration have reached 52% and for victimization 53% (Ireland 2002).

More recently there has been a focus on developing a scaled version of this behavioural checklist – the DIPC SCALED (Ireland 2005d; Ireland and Ireland 2008). This is a multiple-indicator method of assessing bullying behaviour which requires respondents to indicate the frequency at which the perpetration/victimization has occurred. The DIPC-SCALED has proven to be a reliable method comprising of identifiable aggression factors (Ireland and Ireland in press). The DIPC-SCALED has allowed for more sophisticated analyses than its predecessors, including median split analyses, intensity frequency analyses and a comparison of the overlap between different methods of group classification using contingency coefficients (Ireland and Ireland 2008).

The DIPC-SCALED also employs a different time frame than the original DIPC/R, focusing on behaviours within the last month as opposed to the last week. This therefore makes it difficult to draw any conclusions about the differences in the extent of bullying reported on the DIPC-SCALED in comparison to the DIPC/R. Nonetheless, estimates are higher on the DIPC-SCALED than with the DIPC/R (e.g. Ireland 1999; Palmer and Farmer 2002). The first study using the DIPC-SCALED indicated that 81% of prisoners reported at least one behaviour indicative of 'being bullied' in the previous month, with 67% reporting at least one behaviour indicative of 'bullying others'. One-fifth of the sample were classified into an intense bully and/or victim group, an indication that a sizeable proportion of prisoners are shown to report highly frequent perpetration and/or victimization behaviours.

Evaluation

Although conclusions can be reliably drawn in relation to the nature and extent of bullying (Ireland 2002) and the groups of prisoners involved, i.e. bully, victim, bully/victim, not-involved (Ireland 2005a), there remain areas where further work is required before definite conclusions can be drawn. This includes:

1. A need for a consensus on how bullying can best be defined with a focus on exploring how aggression motivation can be integrated into current definitions. Also relevant is the possibility that attempting to define a behaviour as fluid as bullying may be a futile task and that, rather, researchers should perhaps consider a more useful term such as 'intragroup aggression'. Such a term would undoubtedly prove of use in removing current biases in defining 'bullying'.

2. A need for the methods of measurement to become more sophisticated; a move away from presence/absence measures (e.g. DIPC/R) to frequency measures which would also allow for more sophisticated methods of analysis (e.g. the DIPC-SCALED). The latter is particularly important as

this research area moves from describing the problem of bullying towards an explicit testing of theoretical models.

3. A need to focus on theory. Although it is positive that this area of study has begun a focus on theoretical underpinnings (e.g. Ireland 2002; Ireland and Murray 2005; Gilbert 2005), a core criticism remains, namely that these theoretical models remain largely untested. A focus on the explicit testing of these models is therefore becoming more pertinent. There is a particular need to assess the environment-interaction models versus individual psychopathology approaches (Ireland 2005a).

4. More attention on the link between research findings, theory and intervention. Although interventions can be informed by empirical and theoretical evidence (Ireland 2007), there remains a need to evaluate evidence-driven intervention programmes to explore their effectiveness and, in doing so, adding further evidence to support or refute the theoretical models proposed.

Applications

There are a number of clear applications that can be drawn from the acquired knowledge on prison bullying. Some examples of how the research findings/ theoretical models can be applied in practice include:

1. A move away from considering bullying a result solely of individual psychopathology to more recognition of the role of the social and physical environment. It is the latter which requires the most attention with regard to the successful management of prison bullying.

2. An equal focus on the management of indirect methods of bullying with management strategies serving to raise awareness of this form of aggression and managing it to the same level as direct aggression.

3. Recognition of the mutual 'bully/victim' group, and moving away from considering bullying in terms of just two groups – bullies and victims. Recognizing those prisoners 'not involved' in bullying or victimization is also crucial since application should acknowledge that bullying is a product of the peer group and thus including the entire peer group in intervention becomes essential.

4. Recognition that there are no true sex differences in the nature and extent of prison bullying. Thus approaches for dealing with bullying should not be different for men and women. Instead they should account for differences in the prison environment. It is environmental differences which drive bullying behaviour, not biological sex.

Conclusion

Academic interest in bullying among prisoners is recent in comparison to other populations (e.g. children), with research into prison bullying first being published barely a decade ago. Marked advances have been made in this research field in recent years. There has been a move away from merely describing the nature and extent of bullying towards attempting to understand why it occurs. Advances are also being made with regard to the methods of assessment and analysis employed. As a research area there remains much to be done in verifying the theoretical models proposed and in determining what specific environmental factors influence prison bullying. As an area informing practice there also remains a need to evaluate evidence-based intervention programmes. What is becoming clear, however, is that interventions designed to manage prisoner bullying need to attend to the empirical literature and theory base. Ill-informed intervention approaches which fall outside the expectations of the existing literature need to be avoided, with no justification for their implementation.

FURTHER READING

There are two books which cover the research area as a whole, the first providing a summary of all literature up until 2002, and the second extending this to cover more recently published work and theoretical developments: J. L. Ireland (2002) *Bullying among Prisoners: Evidence, Research and Intervention Strategies* (Hove: Brunner Routledge) and J. L. Ireland (ed.) (2005) *Bullying among Prisoners: Innovations in Theory and Research* (Cullompton: Willan).

REFERENCES

Björkqvist, K. (1994) Sex differences in physical, verbal, and indirect aggression: a review of recent research. *Sex Roles*, 30: 177–88.

Connell, A. and Farrington, D. (1996) Bullying amongst incarcerated young prisoners: developing an interview schedule and some preliminary results. *Journal of Adolescence*, 19: 75–93.

Farrington, D. P. (1993) Understanding and preventing bullying. In M. Tonry (ed.), *Crime and Justice: A Review of Research*. Chicago: University of Chicago Press.

Gilbert, P. (2005) Bullying among prisoners: an evolutionary and biopsychosocial approach. In J. L. Ireland (ed.), *Bullying among Prisoners: Innovations in Theory and Research*, pp. 176–90. Cullompton: Willan.

Ireland, J. L. (1999) Bullying behaviors amongst male and female prisoners: a study of young offenders and adults. *Aggressive Behavior*, 25: 162–78.

    (2002) *Bullying among Prisoners: Evidence, Research and Intervention Strategies.* Hove: Brunner Routledge.

    (2005a) Bullying among prisoners: the need for innovation. In J. L. Ireland (ed.), *Bullying among Prisoners: Innovations in Theory and Research*, pp. 3–26. Cullompton: Willan.

    (2005b) Prison bullying and fear: can fear assist with explanations of victim responses? In J. L. Ireland (ed.), *Bullying among Prisoners: Innovations in Theory and Research*, pp. 129–49. Cullompton: Willan.

    (2005c) Psychological health and bullying behaviour among adolescent prisoners: a study of young and juvenile offenders. *Journal of Adolescent Health*, 36: 236–43.

    (2005d) Direct and Indirect Prisoner Behaviour Checklist – scaled version (DIPC-SCALED). University of Central Lancashire, unpublished.

    (2007) The effective management of bullying among prisoners: working towards an evidence-based approach. In G. Towl (ed.), *Psychological Research in Prisons*, pp. 95–115. Oxford: BPS/Blackwell.

Ireland, J. L. and Archer, J. (1996) Descriptive analysis of bullying in male and female adult prisoners. *Journal of Community and Applied Social Psychology*, 6: 35–47.

    (2004) The association between measures of aggression and bullying among juvenile and young offenders. *Aggressive Behavior*, 30: 29–42.

Ireland, J. L., Archer, J. and Power, C. L. (2007) Characteristics of male and female prisoners involved in bullying behavior. *Aggressive Behavior*, 33: 220–9.

Ireland, J. L. and Ireland, C. A. (2003) How do offenders define bullying? A study of adult, young and juvenile male offenders. *Legal and Criminological Psychology*, 8: 159–73.

    (2008) Intra-group aggression among prisoners: bullying intensity and exploration of victim-perpetrator mutuality. *Aggressive Behavior*, 34: 76–87.

Ireland, J. L. and Monaghan, R. (2006) Behaviors indicative of bullying among young and juvenile male offenders: a study of perpetrator and victim characteristics. *Aggressive Behavior*, 32: 172–80.

Ireland, J. L. and Murray, E. (2005) Are bullies poor problem-solvers? In J. L Ireland (ed.), *Bullying among Prisoners: Innovations in Theory and Research*, pp. 150–75. Cullompton: Willan.

Olweus, D. (1978) *Aggression in Schools: Bullies and Whipping Boys.* Washington, DC: Hemisphere.

    (1996) Bully/victim problems in school. *Prospects*, 26: 331–59.

Palmer, E. and Farmer, S. (2002) Victimising behavior among juvenile and young offenders: how different are perpetrators? *Journal of Adolescence*, 25: 469–81.

Smith, P. K. and Brain, P. (2000) Bullying in schools: lessons from two decades of research. *Aggressive Behavior*, 26: 1–9.

6.3 Child soldiers

Ilse Derluyn and Eric Broekaert

Definition

In the past decades, armed conflict has taken a deadly turn for civilians, with the vast majority of casualties of war being civilians, mostly women and children (Machel 1996, 2001; Williams 2007). Far from being incidental, the damage to children is part of a deliberate strategy of total war, in which adversaries terrorize, dominate, or destroy civilians as a means of achieving control. Children are not caught in the crossfire; they are direct targets, and even the perpetrators of violence and atrocities (Wessells 2000). Moreover, the involvement of children as soldiers has been made easier by the proliferation of inexpensive, light weapons. These guns are so light that children can use them, and so simple that they can be stripped and reassembled by a child of 10 (Machel 1996; Renner 1999).

The phenomenon of using children in armed conflict as soldiers has received increasing attention through the important study of the impact of war on children by Machel (1996). One of the most alarming trends in armed conflict, according to the report, is the participation of children as soldiers. Machel (2001, p. 6) uses the following definition:

A child soldier is a boy or girl under the age of 18 who is compulsorily or voluntarily recruited or otherwise used in hostilities by armed forces, paramilitaries, civil defence units, or other armed groups.

The Cape Town Principles and Best Practices (1997) define a child soldier as:

Any person under 18 years of age who is part of any kind of regular or irregular armed force or armed group in any capacity, including but not limited to cooks, porters, messengers, and those accompanying such groups, other than purely as family members. It includes girls recruited for sexual purposes and forced marriage. It does not, therefore, only refer to a child who is carrying or has carried arms.

Different laws and conventions have been elaborated and signed in order to prevent, combat and punish the use of child soldiers, such as the 1989 Convention on the Rights of the Child and its Optional Protocol, the Geneva Convention's Additional Protocols of 1977, the African Charter on the Rights and Welfare of the Child, the ILO Convention on the Worst Forms of Child Labour, and the regulations of the International Criminal Court (Hoiskar 2001). However, the use of children as soldiers in armed conflicts remains a worldwide phenomenon: it is estimated that about 250,000 to 300,000 children under 18 years of age are currently serving as regular soldiers, guerrilla fighters, or in support roles in more than fifty countries around the world (Ahmad 1999; Bayer, Klasen and Adam 2007). Statistics on child soldiers are nebulous for many reasons, including the constantly changing scope of many conflicts, the fact that armed groups often conceal information about children in their ranks, and the fact that children themselves may lie about their age or involvement (Pedersen and Sommerfelt 2007). However, it is generally believed that most child soldiers, especially the youngest ones, are serving in 'rebel', not government, armies (Hughes 2000). Most are adolescents, though many are 10 years of age or younger (Machel 2001). While the majority are boys, girls are also recruited.

Children are recruited into fighting forces in a variety of ways (Brett and McCallin 1998; Cohn and Goodwin-Gill 1994; HRW 1996). Many are abducted or forcibly recruited (Wessells 2005), some are coerced to join through threats made against them or their families. Others join 'voluntarily' because they believe they have no alternative, hope they will be provided with much-needed protection or food, or are drawn by promises of education, money, other material goods, or prestige (HRW 1996; Wessells 2005). Some children also join to avenge the killing of parents, other family members, or friends (Wessells 2005). Many of the children targeted for recruitment by warring factions are among the most vulnerable: often these children have been orphaned or separated from their families during the conflict, and some even are recruited from refugee camps (HRW 1996).

Once recruited as soldiers, children generally receive much the same treatment as adults – including the often brutal induction ceremonies. One of the common tasks assigned to children is to serve as porters, often carrying very heavy loads of up to 60 kilograms, including ammunition or injured soldiers. Children who are too weak to carry their loads are liable to be savagely beaten or even shot. Children are also used for household and other routine duties. Children serve in roles such as cooks, porters, spies, bodyguards, combatants and sex slaves (Wessells 2000).

The kind of experiences child soldiers have are mostly extremely horrifying; all studies on these minors' experiences report high prevalences of a diversity of traumatic events, such as having seen the killing of people, killing people themselves (their own parents or other family members), getting wounded or hurt, being seriously beaten, participating in fighting and shooting, having military training, participating in looting and abduction, setting fire to houses and people, experiencing rape, getting pregnant and delivering while being in captivity, being exposed to indoctrination activities and rites, etc. (see e.g. Bayer, Klasen and Adam 2007; Derluyn *et al.* 2004; Kanagaratnam, Raundalen and Asbjørnsen 2005; Maclure and Denov 2006).

Physical and psychological impact

Child soldiers are often both physically and psychologically abused. Not only are children forced to bear witness to and participate in atrocities, but many are beaten, tortured and deprived of food. Once demobilized or having escaped, many suffer severe injuries, malnutrition, bullet wounds, or broken limbs.

Some children are also sexually abused, and forced to abuse others (HRW 1996). The prevalence of sexual abuse in boy and girl child soldiers is only partially known: the scarce studies available report high percentages of child abuse, such as 27.8% of the population in the study of Bayer and colleagues (2007), and 35% of the interviewed girls in the study of Derluyn and colleagues (2004). But it is likely that the real incidence of sexual abuse – due to taboo factors and feelings of shame and burden – is even higher, both for girls and boys. Moreover, a widening of the parameters for sexual abuse of child soldiers might expand the extent to which boy soldiers are affected considerably: many male child soldiers are not only victim of sexual violence, but are often also coerced into becoming 'forced perpetrators' of sexual violence or have to witness sexual exploitation. Therefore, it is extremely important to recognize that, similar to the well-known trauma child soldiers face when forced to commit or witness atrocities in war, participation in sexual violence – certainly at a young age – is highly damaging and perhaps irreversibly so.

Sexual violence not only causes emotional problems, but can also cause important physical problems, such as sexually transmitted diseases and/or HIV/AIDS, becoming pregnant and giving birth at too young an age, incontinence (Hick 2001).

It will be obvious that the often horrifying experiences child soldiers have to go through can inflict severe and lasting psychological scars. The emotional problems these children and adolescents develop are diverse, and mediated by multiple factors, such as sex, age, familial characteristics and the cultural and social context. Also specific characteristics of the traumatic experience – frequency and length, exposure severity, degree of injury, exposure to death, destructiveness, loss and atrocity – might influence the kind and seriousness of problems developed. Symptoms that may occur include: symptoms of anxiety, developmental delays, feelings of guilt and shame, low self-esteem, memory loss, sleep disturbances, deep grief and mourning, nightmares, decreased appetite, withdrawn behaviour, lack of interest in play, learning difficulties, anxious or aggressive behaviour and depression (Hick 2001; Machel 1996, 2001; Mazurana and McKay 2001; Wessells 1997). Due to the traumatic nature of the experiences child soldiers have, much attention has been given to the development of symptoms of 'post-traumatic stress disorder' (nightmares, flashbacks, sleeplessness, hyperarousal, etc.). Therefore, we should not wonder that the scarce studies examining the prevalence of emotional problems in child soldier populations all focus on symptoms of post-traumatic stress. Derluyn et al. (2004) studied the level of post-traumatic stress symptoms in a group of seventy-one former child soldiers in northern Uganda, using the Impact of Events Scale – Revised: 97% of the involved participants had a clinically significant problem score, indicating that the level of PTSD in this population is very high. Kanagaratnam, Raundalen and Asjbørnsen (2005) examined a group of twenty Tamil adults who were former child soldiers in Tamil armed groups, and are now living in Norway. Also using the Impact of Events Scale – Revised, the majority of the former child soldiers reported frequent post-traumatic stress symptoms. Bayer, Klasen and Adam (2007) studied a group of 169 former child soldiers (aged 11–18 years) in rehabilitation centres in Uganda and Congo. Using the Child Post-traumatic Stress Disorder Reaction Index, this study revealed that 35% had clinically significant scores of post-traumatic stress. Moreover, children who showed more PTSD symptoms had less openness to reconciliation and more feelings of revenge.

Reintegration of former child soldiers into their community and society might be hampered significantly through public reactions of revenge, stigmatization and even rejection (Derluyn et al. 2004). Choosing between the perception of a child soldier as 'perpetrator' or 'victim' might be difficult, all the more because of the harm they brought along – many of them were even forced to kill their own family or community members. The sexual abuse many girl child soldiers experience often confronts them, once returned, with feelings of shame, and they might be rejected by their family or community due to the sexual abuse, the loss of virginity, the single parenthood or infection with HIV/AIDS. Moreover, many of them lost family members, friends, belongings and education possibilities, all factors that might hinder successful reintegration and rehabilitation even more. Finally, the long-term exposure to extreme experiences, such as killings, rape, fights, mutilation, can make it very difficult for these children and adolescents to adapt again to the 'normal' way of life in society. Children reared in a system of violence might be unable to control aggressive behaviour, due to few skills for handling conflict non-violently, and a moral development that may have been limited by early immersion in the military (Brett and McCallin 1998; Francis 2007). Building up a new life after having served as child soldier is therefore another extreme challenge for these youngsters.

Conclusion

Studies examining the wellbeing of child soldiers remain rather scarce, mainly because of the circumstances in which this topic enacted: doing research during war circumstances is rather difficult, and the phenomenon in itself is under strong taboo, to civil and army authorities, to the civil population in general, ànd also to the children involved themselves. Gathering statistics about all aspects of child soldiering worldwide therefore remains a bleak challenge.

Second, we should be careful when studying the psychological wellbeing of child soldiers. At first, attention should be paid to the limitations of a narrow interpretation of the western-oriented PTSD concept, which only highlights some of the problems these children may develop. Therefore, research should try as far as possible to link the effect of a trauma to the subjective meaning of the events and to the cultural, social and political context (Bracken, Giller and Summerfield 1995). Furthermore, considering child soldiers solely as victims of adverse circumstances is ignoring the capacity of youth (Machel 1996; Maclure and Denov 2006).

FUTHER READING

Brett, R. and McCallin, M. (1998) *Children: The Invisible Soldiers.* Stockholm: Rädda Barnen.
Cohn, I. and Goodwin-Gill, G. S. (1994) *Child Soldiers: The Role of Children in Armed Conflict: A Study for the Henry Dunant Institute Geneva.* Oxford: Clarendon Press.

Machel, G. (2001) *The Impact of War on Children*. London: Unicef–Unifem.

Wessells, M. (2007) *Child Soldiers (from Violence to Protection)*. Cambridge, MA: Harvard University Press.

WEB RESOURCES

www.child-soldiers.org

www.hrw.org

REFERENCES

Ahmad, K. (1999) UN resolves to protect children against war. *Lancet*, 354: 929.

Bayer, C. P., Klasen, F. and Adam, H. (2007) Association of trauma and PTSD symptoms with openness to reconciliation and feelings of revenge among former Ugandan and Congolese child soldiers. *Journal of the American Medical Association*, 298: 555–9.

Bracken, P. J., Giller, J. E. and Summerfield, D. (1995) Psychological responses to war and atrocity: the limitations of current concepts. *Social Science and Medicine*, 40: 1073–82.

Brett, R. and McCallin, M. (1998) *Children: The Invisible Soldiers*. Stockholm: Rädda Barnen.

Cohn, I. and Goodwin-Gill, G. S. (1994) *Child Soldiers: The Role of Children in Armed Conflict. A Study for the Henry Dunant Institute Geneva*. Oxford: Clarendon Press.

Derluyn, I., Broekaert, E., Schuyten, G. and De Temmerman, E. (2004) Atrocities of war: post-traumatic stress in former Ugandan child soldiers. *Lancet*, 363: 861–3.

Francis, D. J. (2007) 'Paper protection' mechanisms: child soldiers and the international protection of children in Africa's conflict zones. *Journal of Modern African Studies*, 45(2): 207–31.

Hick, S. (2001) The political economy of war-affected children. *Annals of the American Academy of Political and Social Science*, 575: 106–21.

Hoiskar, A. H. (2001) Underage and under fire: an enquiry into the use of child soldiers 1994–8. *Childhood: A Global Journal of Child Research*, 8: 340–60.

HRW (1996) *Children in Combat*. New York: Human Rights Watch – Children's Rights Project.

Hughes, L. (2000) Can international law protect child soldiers? *Peace Review*, 12: 399.

Kanagaratnam, P., Raundalen, M. and Asbjørnsen, A. E. (2005) Ideological commitment and posttraumatic stress in former Tamil child soldiers. *Scandinavian Journal of Psychology*, 46: 511–20.

Machel, G. (1996) *Impact of Armed Conflict on Children*. New York: United Nations.

(2001) *The Impact of War on Children*. London: Unicef–Unifem.

Maclure, R. and Denov, M. (2006) 'I didn't want to die so I joined them': structuration and the process of becoming boy soldiers in Sierra Leone. *Terrorism and Political Violence*, 18: 119–35.

Mazurana, D. and McKay, S. (2001) Child soldiers: what about the girls? *Bulletin of the Atomic Scientists*, 57: 30–5.

Murphy-Berman, V., Levesque, H. L. and Berman, J. J. (1996) UN Convention on the Rights of the Child: a cross-cultural view. *American Psychologist*, 51: 1234–8.

Pedersen, J. and Sommerfelt, T. (2007) Studying children in armed conflict: data production, social indicators and analysis. *Social Indicators Research*, 84: 251–69.

Renner, M. (1999) Arms control orphans. *Bulletin of the Atomic Scientists*, 55: 22–6.

Wessells, M. (1997) Child soldiers. *Bulletin of the Atomic Scientists*, 53: 32–9.

(2000) How we can prevent child soldiering. *Peace Review*, 12: 407–13.

(2005) Child soldiers, peace education, and postconflict reconstruction for peace. *Theory into Practice*, 44: 363–9.

Williams, R. (2007) The psychosocial consequences for children of mass violence, terrorism and disasters. *International Review of Psychiatry*, 19: 263–77.

6.4 Crime prevention

Jennifer M. Brown

See also chapter 2.3 Crime pattern analysis, chapter 3.5 Preventing delinquency and later criminal offending.

Definitions

Tilley (2005, p. 5) argues that crime prevention can be thought of as 'disarmingly simple', i.e. the everyday commonsense behaviours which people do routinely such as avoiding apparently threatening people and places. The 'complex' side relates to the 'bewildering' array of definitions, predictions, prioritization and choices of means to prevent crime.

Bottoms (1989) states that the prevention of crime has always been a primary objective of the police and gained a higher profile in the UK in the 1980s, which led to a series of government, police and voluntary-sector initiatives. Bottoms also notes that the Council of Europe and various European countries had equivalent stimulated interest in crime prevention. He makes the broad distinction between situational and social crime prevention. The former comprises measures directed at specific forms of crime, and design of the environment in which these crimes occur so as to reduce the opportunities for the commission of the targeted crime. These 'opportunity'-reducing measures include target hardening, such as more secure windows and doors; target removal, such as cash out of meters; and increasing surveillance, such as at airports, to eliminate the passage of the means, such as weapons to commit crime. Social crime prevention focuses on changing behaviour and may be thought of as interrupting the cycle of intention to commit crime and its actuality. These involve initiatives such as introducing civics into the school curriculum and involving local people in neighbourhood watch(ing) activities which engage the community in sharing responsibility for crime prevention. Toney and Farrington (1995) extend this distinction further and identify situational, community and developmental prevention.

This latter involves the organized provision of resources to families, schools and communities as well as to individuals in order to inhibit early involvement in crime in the first place.

Ekblom (2005) distinguishes between crime reduction, which seeks to decrease the frequency and seriousness of criminal events, and crime prevention, which intervenes in the causes of crime and disorder.

Two further concepts in crime prevention are the notion of displacement and diffusion. The former refers to the phenomenon where offenders adapt to some intervention that restricts crime opportunities such that the established pattern of crime changes; and the latter is the reverse, whereby crime reduction gains extend beyond the property or people targeted by a specific intervention. An example of diffusion is when a CCTV system introduced to reduce theft of and from cars at the University of Surrey resulted in a crime reduction not only in the targeted car park but also in one not having CCTV (Hamilton-Smith 2002).

Methods

Methods of crime prevention have been classified as primary (prevention of the crime event itself); secondary (prevention of criminality by those most at risk of becoming involved); and tertiary (interruption of continued criminality by those already involved) by Brantingham and Faust (1976).

Ekblom (2005) maps eleven types of preventative interventions which address immediate or proximal causes and more remote (distal) causes. These require an examination of predisposition to criminality, lack of resources such that crime represents means to achieve these, and access to resources to commit crime. Crime prevention efforts try to reduce the disposition to commit crime.

Fritzon and Watts (2003) describe an early attempt to prevent delinquency in the Cambridge–Somerville Youth Study, in which boys received personal and social counselling for up to five years (which, incidentally, was shown to have had little effect after a thirty-year follow-up). They go on to describe family-based, school-based and peer-based interventions, such as training in parenting skills and the South Baltimore Youth Centre project where young people at risk were identified and extended families were created with youth workers.

Cherney and Sutton (2007, p. 68) propose that problem solving is key to success in crime prevention. They propose a number of steps in developing effective methods of crime prevention: engaging in dialogue (i.e. between policy makers and local stakeholders, albeit within given parameters to avoid programme drift); clarity of purpose and acting strategically; localized administrative arrangements and partnerships (i.e. with schools, police, local employers, local government); identification of local key drivers (e.g. police, community support officers); and research and dissemination of good practice.

One method employed in crime prevention has been designing out crime (Armitage 2007). This concept proposes that buildings and other aspects of the physical environment can minimize the risk of crime. Thus secured-by-design (SBD) schemes involving multi-agency partnerships were said to reduce crime and disorder. Environmental features in housing scheme layouts that might occasion criminal activity are recognized and avoided by design features, e.g. the degree of surveillance permitted by positioning of houses in the scheme, and the location of footpaths allowing pedestrian movement. Armitage (p. 93) describes a risk assessment tool that produces a (Burgess) score, which is the difference between the mean rate of crime suffered generally and the rate suffered by homes with a particular characteristic. In this way the vulnerability of a property can be demonstrated and environmental factors associated with elevated crime identified.

Theories

Defensible space (Newman 1972) proposes that there is a link between the physical environment and crime. According to this theory, features in building design and layouts can increase occupants' vigilance, surveillance opportunities and sense of responsibility for their residences or places of work. As such, individuals are more likely to 'defend' these spaces. Newman argued, for example, that fences or walls are symbolic rather than physical barriers and intruders feel conspicuous and vulnerable entering defended properties (Craig 1998). However, this theoretical position suffers from definitional ambiguity and contra-evidence, such as walls or high fences, could just as equally signal wealth and therefore a desirable residence to burgle (Bennett and Wright 1984).

Tilley and Laycock (2007) discuss the theoretical underpinning of situational crime prevention, noting that this work assumed that crime could be prevented by blocking opportunities rather than addressing underlying disposition. They report a series of empirical studies to show how an intervention such as changing gas supply virtually eradicated suicide by this means, concluding that crime trends are more likely explained in terms of supply of criminal opportunities than individual criminal propensities.

Fritzon and Watts (2003) present a thumbnail description and critiques of Routine Activity Theories (RAT) and Rational Choice models, the former proposing that it is a convergence in time and space and absence of suitable 'guardians' that lead to increases in crime rates, whereas the latter focuses on the subjective states and thought processes which influence offenders' decision making. Both approaches assume a key role of situations as important determining factors in criminal activity.

France and Homel (2007) present an overview and critique of purely situational approaches, implying they are overly deterministic. They argue that social processes are critical to understanding crime and thus its prevention. Their edited collection of essays outlines 'pathways', which are lifespan influences that shape criminality, linking these to crime interruption and crime prevention initiatives, and includes analyses of moral development and socialization.

Approaches to the evaluation of crime prevention

Criticism of crime prevention interventions include the displacement problem and policy transfer issues (i.e. what might work in one place and at a particular time might not work elsewhere or, if in the same place, at another time) and failures of evaluations to support the effectiveness of interventions.

Bottoms (1989) observes that whilst situational or social interventions may have eliminated some crime (e.g. increasing the level of inspection led to a reduction in fare dodging on Dutch trains), it became evident that criminal activity 'displaced' into either other places, times or activities, i.e. spatial, temporal or offence displacement. Tilley (2005, p. 6) suggests that there is some underlying assumption that there is a 'fixed' volume of crime, and that much preventative effort not only fails to access and address the underlying causes of crime but also redistributes and may even escalate its seriousness and the citizen's fearfulness. Hamilton-Smith (2002) discusses the difficulties in attempting to measure displacement (and diffusion) impacts of an initiative such as uncertainty surrounding offenders' motivations or decision making or their versatility and mobility. Both Bottoms and Tilley, however, are rather more optimistic that evaluation research has not shown that the suffering caused by displaced crime outweighs reductions achieved by preventative efforts, with the latter arguing for a diffusion of benefit.

Jones and Newburn (2007) discuss at length the idea that not all policing interventions are transferable. They argue (p. 130) that in respect to policy transfer between the UK and USA, there are as many divergences as convergences, that context is important and that there are critical forces of resistance as well as adherents to the policy in question. The zero tolerance initiative of New York policing is a case in point. Designed to prevent more serious crime by tackling low-level disorder and incivility in an aggressive non-compromising way, both the language and methods of zero tolerance have, by and large, been rejected by British policing. Pierpoint and Gilling (1998) question the transferability of crime prevention based on urban models to rural settings, concluding 'the partnership approach to crime prevention is based on sound principles, but these principles have been formed out of an urban experience, and it may be unwise simply to transport urban solutions to rural areas'.

Methods to evaluate crime prevention interventions range from experimental methodologies, pinnacled by the randomized control trials (RCTs), through to more qualitative approaches. The experimental methods seek to exercise considerable control over the conditions in which the intervention takes place in order to eliminate possible threats to the reliability and validity of measured success, and to be able to be as certain as possible the intervention was the cause of any desistence or reduction in criminal activity. More particularly, RCTs attempt to measure and compare impacts and provide a cost–benefit analysis of a particular intervention (Cherney and Sutton 2007). Meta-analyses of various types of intervention have looked at neighbourhood watch, hotspot policing or CCTV (see e.g. Welsh and Farrington 2002). However, they critique over-reliance on such methods which exert strict experimental control and potentially compromise transferability of programmes. More qualitative approaches tend to look at process, i.e. what was it about the intervention that produced its effects. Cherney and Sutton argue that it is necessary to look at the embedded social as well as situational aspects of an intervention. Indeed, Crawford (1998, p. 5) had argued that there may be unintended consequences of an intervention which may be lost due to measurement fixation.

Bottoms (1989, p. 23) notes the neglect of effective evaluation and monitoring of crime prevention initiatives; a theme emphasized by Cherney and Sutton (2007, p. 65), who say that crime prevention innovations in south Australia became mired in controversy and argued that this experience was 'symptomatic of a broader dilemma for crime prevention', namely lack of effective leadership, inflexible top-down programme design and poor communication between policy levels and local stakeholders. Moreover, as they point out, despite considerable commitment of public expenditure in both

Australia and elsewhere, there is an absence of clear research evidence of programme cost-effectiveness.

A classic evaluative study in crime prevention is Farrell and Pease's (1993) analysis of repeat victimization, in which they examined crime prevalence (estimated percentage of the population at risk), crime incidence (average number of victimizations per head of population at risk of victimization) and crime concentration (average number of victimizations per victim), recognizing the potential confusion between prevalence and incidence, whereby it is, wrongly, assumed that incidence equates to the number of victims. They undertook a meticulous study of secondary sources (such as recorded crime figures, police incident logs, and victim survey data). They argue that such an analysis provides a rational basis for crime prevention allocation, finding that the risk of revictimization is greatest in the period immediately after the initial victimization.

FURTHER READING

Nick Tilley's edited *Handbook of Crime Prevention* (2005) is an excellent starting point, and France and Homel's (2007) collection of theoretical essays outlines new developments in conceptual thinking about processes influential in the commission and prevention of crime across the lifespan. Farrell and Pease's (1993) *Once Bitten, Twice Bitten* remains a classic methodological account evaluating revictimization. Kate Fritzon and Andrea Watt's (2003) chapter provides a good summary of, as well as presenting an integrated theoretical approach to, crime prevention.

REFERENCES

Armitage, R. (2007) Sustainability versus safety; confusion, conflict and contradiction in designing out crime. In G. Farrell, K. Bowers, S. D. Johnson and M. Townsley (eds.), *Imagination from Crime Prevention: Essays in Honour of Ken Pease*. Crime Prevention Studies 21, pp. 81–110. Monsey, NY: Criminal Justice Press.

Bennett, T. and Wright, R. (1984) *Burglars on Burglary: Prevention and the Offender*. Aldershot: Gower.

Bottoms, A. E. (1989) Crime prevention facing the 1990s. James Smart Lecture presented to Lothian and Borders Police Headquarters, Edinburgh, November.

Brantingham, P. and Faust, F. (1976) A conceptual model of crime prevention. *Crime and Delinquency*, 22: 284–96.

Cherney A. and Sutton, A. (2007) Crime prevention in Australia: beyond what works. *Australian and New Zealand Journal of Criminology*, 40: 65–81.

Craig, L. (1998) Crime by design; an exploratory investigation. *International Journal of Police Science and Management*, 1: 109–21.

Crawford, A. (1998) Community safety partnerships. *Criminal Justice Matters*, 33: 4–5.

Ekblom, P. (1997) Gearing up against crime: a dynamic framework to help designers keep up with the adaptive criminal in a changing world. *International Journal of Risk, Security and Crime Prevention*, 2: 249–65.

   (2005) How to police the future: scanning for scientific and technological innovations which generate potential threats and opportunities in crime, policing and crime reduction. In M. J. Smith and N. Tilley (eds.), *Crime Science: New Approaches to Preventing and Detecting Crime*, pp. 27–55. Cullompton: Willan.

Farrell, G. and Pease, K. (1993) Once bitten, twice bitten: repeat victimisation and its implications for crime prevention. Police Research Group Crime Prevention Unit Series paper 46. London: Home Office.

France, A. and Homel, R. (2007) *Pathways and Crime Prevention: Theory, Policy and Practice*. Cullompton: Willan.

Fritzon, K. and Watts, A. (2003) Crime prevention. In D. Carson and R. Bull (eds.), *Handbook of Psychology in Legal Contexts*, 2nd edn, pp. 229–44. Chichester: Wiley.

Hamilton-Smith, N. (2002) Anticipated consequences; developing a strategy for the targeted measurement of displacement and diffusion of benefits. In N. Tilley (ed.), *Evaluation of Crime Prevention*. Crime Prevention Studies 14, pp. 11–52. Monsey, NY: Criminal Justice Press.

Jones, T. and Newburn, T. (2007) *Policy Transfer and Criminal Justice: Exploring US Influence over British Crime Policy*. Maidenhead: Open University Press.

Newman, O. (1972) *Defensible Space*. New York: Macmillan.

Pierpoint, H. and Gilling, D. (1998) Crime prevention in rural areas. *Criminal Justice Matters*, 33: 25–6.

Tilley, N. (ed.) (2005) *Handbook of Crime Prevention and Community Safety*. Cullompton: Willan.

Tilley, N. and Laycock, G. (2007) From crime prevention to crime science. In G. Farrell, K. Bowers, S. D. Johnson and M. Townsley (eds.), *Imagination from Crime Prevention: Essays in Honour of Ken Pease. Crime Prevention Studies* 21, pp. 19–40. Monsey, NY: Criminal Justice Press.

Toney, M. and Farrington, D. (1995) *Building Safer Societies. Crime and Justice: A Review of Research*, vol. 19. Chicago: University of Chicago Press.

Welsh, B. and Farrington, D. (2002) *Crime Prevention Effects of Closed Circuit Television: A Systematic Review*. Home Office Research Study 252. London: Home Office.

Claire Cooke

Location

Shootings and firearms tragedies catch the attention of the global mass media on a periodic basis. A spree shooting is where the perpetrator embarks on a murderous assault on his/her victims over a relatively short period of time. Sadly, there are many examples of spree shootings from across the world, e.g. Virginia Tech 2007, Amish School, Pennsylvania 2006, Red Lake High, Minnesota 2005, Columbine 1999 in America; Tuusula in Finland 2007; Erfurt in Germany 2002; Zug in Switzerland 2001; Hungerford in England 1987; and the Port Arthur Massacre 1996 in Australia. However, the public and political response to such incidents varies dramatically depending upon where the shooting occurred.

In March 1996 Thomas Hamilton entered a primary school in Dunblane, Scotland, armed with two 9 mm Browning HP pistols and two Smith & Wesson .357 Magnum revolvers. He was carrying 743 cartridges, and fired 109 times. Sixteen children and their teacher were killed. Hamilton then committed suicide. This tragedy shocked UK citizens and there was an outright ban on the use or possession of handguns by private citizens. In the gun amnesty that followed, more than 162,000 handguns were handed in to local police forces (Gun Control Network 2008).

Throughout the UK guns tend to be associated with crime, and increasingly in the media with gangs and drugs, whereas in America guns for many citizens have a deeper and more meaningful significance, and are embedded in their culture. Guns are not simply a symbol of crime, but of freedom and independence (Cooke 2004; Cooke and Puddifoot 2000; Puddifoot and Cooke 2002). Many Americans proudly quote the second amendment of the US Constitution: 'A well regulated militia, being necessary to the security of a free state, the right of the people to keep and bear arms, shall not be infringed', and believe it is their 'right' to possess firearms as part of being a good, law-abiding citizen. In fact, this was recently supported by the US Supreme Court ruling that American citizens do have a constitutional right to bear arms (June 2008).

Gun ownership and protection from crime

There are currently 4.3 million members of the US National Rifle Association, a very powerful organization, of which its members are incredibly proud. Many citizens keep firearms for sporting purposes (both in the US and throughout the world). However, one of the main reasons why the ownership of firearms is so prevalent in the United States is partly because of the belief that guns can provide protection from crime. Lott and Mustard (1997) argue that law-abiding citizens should be allowed to carry concealed weapons for this reason. They suggest 1,500 murders, 4,000 rapes, 11,000 robberies and over 60,000 aggravated assaults per year in America could be prevented by allowing citizens to carry concealed weapons. Kleck and Gertz's (1995) findings support Lott and Mustard, suggesting that guns are used for self-defence approximately two and half million times a year, with 400,000 of these defenders believing that using a gun 'almost certainly saved their life'.

Currently forty-eight US states allow some form of concealed weapon carrying by law. However, it is not only carrying a weapon on the street that allows American citizens to protect themselves. Many citizens keep guns in the home for self-defence purposes. However, some studies suggest that guns are a significant risk factor for family homicide, suicide and accidental death. Azrael and Hemenway (2000) argue there is little evidence to show that guns are actually used to thwart crimes by intruders, or that weapons are used in the home for self-defence. Research suggests that this is more likely to result in a member of the family being injured or killed than an intruder (Kellerman and Reay 1986).

Azrael and Hemenway (2000) found that of the 1,906 people they contacted, 13 reported having a gun pointed at them in the home, 2 used guns in self-defence at home, and 24 reported using other weapons, such as a knife or baseball bat. This suggests that despite many American citizens' belief that guns in the home can protect them from crime, in practice other weapons are far more likely to be used. They also found that a gun in the home was more likely to be used against a member of the family than to protect the family, and also report that a gun in the home is more likely to be used against a female member of the household to frighten or intimidate her. It would appear that, rather than being used for defence, most weapons inflict injuries on the owners and their families.

The safety of children within the home where firearms are kept is of significant importance. Firearms injury is the second leading cause of non-natural death in childhood and adolescence (CDC 2008). Accidental shooting deaths are most commonly associated with one or more children playing with a gun they found in the home (Choi *et al.* 1994). In one survey, 10% of families admitted to having unlocked and loaded firearms within easy reach of children (Patterson and Smith 1987).

The relationship between gun availability and crime has been investigated by many academics. Whilst there is a vast amount of data collected in the area, particularly in the US, there is relatively little agreement concerning what these figures actually signify, especially when cross-state or cross-national comparisons are invoked. However, an exploration of national crime statistics does provide some insights.

Gun availability and crime in America

In the US for 2005 there were 30,694 deaths from firearms, distributed as follows by mode of death: suicide 17,002; homicide 12,352; accident 789; legal intervention 330; undetermined 221 (CDC 2008). This makes firearms injuries one of the top ten causes of death in America. Firearms injuries remain a leading cause of death in the US, particularly among youth. The number of non-fatal injuries is considerable, 71,417 in 2006 (CDC 2008).

In 2006, 68% of all murders, 42% of all robberies and 22% of all aggravated assaults that were reported to the police were committed with a firearm (Bureau of Justice Statistics 2008). Homicides were most often committed

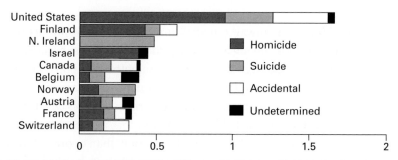

Figure 6.5.1 Firearms deaths by mode of death for children under 15 years of age, top ten countries – rate per 100,000 (adapted from Utah University 'Firearms Tutorial' website 2008)

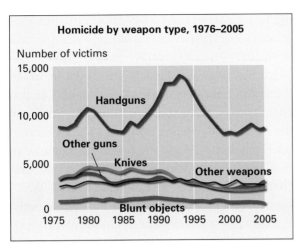

Figure 6.5.2 Homicide by weapon type 1976–2005 in US (adapted from Bureau of Justice Statistics website 2008)

with guns, especially handguns. In 2005, 55% of homicides were committed with handguns, 16% with other guns, 14% with knives, 5% with blunt objects and 11% with other weapons. Figure 6.5.2 highlights the sharp decline since the mid 1990s of the use of firearms in crime, until 2000, when figures begin to increase and fluctuate.

The data suggest that although America has many law-abiding citizens who possess and carry firearms, the use of guns in crime is a significant problem.

Guns and crime in England and Wales

Given the media attention focused upon guns, gangs and violence in the UK, to what extent do the national crime statistics for England and Wales support that view?

Crime statistics for homicides committed in England and Wales (Home Office 2008) show that the most common method of killing, at 35% of all homicide victims, involved a sharp instrument. There were 59 shooting victims in 2006/7, accounting for 8% of all homicides (10% of male homicides, 3% of female homicides).

Firearms were reported as being used in 18,489 recorded crimes in 2006/7 (9,650 excluding air weapons). Nearly half (48%) of firearms offences involved air weapons. There were 2,517 offences in which the weapon was classified as an imitation, and handguns were used in 4,175 offences. Serious or fatal injury accounted for 3% of all firearms crime. There were 566 such injuries (including fatalities) resulting from crimes that involved a firearm (including air weapons). Firearms involving any type of injury fell from 5,004 in 2005/6, to 4,065 in 2006/7.

Air weapons were nearly always fired in the crime in which they were involved (92% of crimes), but rarely caused serious injury. In contrast, other firearms were more often used as a threat or, occasionally, as a blunt instrument (imitation firearms 74%); handguns were fired in 12% of crime in which they were involved (but resulted in 33% of fatal or serious injuries), and shotguns were fired in 38% of cases (resulting in 28% of serious or fatal injuries). Of the offences not involving an air weapon, 43% involved a handgun.

Although the types of crime in which firearms are used are fairly evenly split between violence (including robbery) and non-violent property crime, the distribution varies markedly between air weapons (mostly used in criminal damage offences) and non-air weapons (where violence predominates).

The overall level of gun crime in England and Wales is very low, 0.3% of all crime recorded by the police. The number of overall offences involving firearms fell by 13% in 2006/7 compared to the previous year. Overall, firearms (including air weapons) were used in 0.3% of all recorded crimes. This number is halved when air weapons are excluded. Gun crime remains a relatively rare event.

Regulation

One way in which authorities in both Britain and America have attempted to control gun availability has been to address licensing laws. In the UK this has resulted in tightening the criteria to obtain a firearms licence, and distributing harsh punishments for any citizen possessing a firearm without a licence. The States have taken a different approach, by requiring licensed firearms dealers to observe a waiting period and initiate a background check for handgun sales. This is partly in the belief that those committing offences would do so with illegal firearms. This may be true for many offences; however, a study of Europe's most deadly mass shootings, from 1987 to 2007, shows that in nearly every case the offender used legal firearms.

This situation is not unique to Europe. A study conducted by the Violence Policy Center (Washington, DC, 2001) of 65 high-profile multiple-victim shootings in the United States over a period of forty years showed that 62% of handgun shootings and 71% of long gun shootings were committed with legally acquired firearms. Similar studies in Canada, Australia and New

Table 6.5.1 Mass shootings (eight or more dead) in Europe, 1987–2007

Date	Place	Fatalities	Legal status
7 Nov 2007	Tuusula, Finland	8 + perpetrator	Legal handgun, pistol club member
15 Oct 2002	Chieri, Italy	7 + perpetrator	Legal guns, licensed gun collector
26 Apr 2002	Erfurt, Germany	16 + perpetrator	Legal guns, pistol club member
27 Mar 2002	Nanterre, France	8	Legal guns, pistol club member
27 Sep 2001	Zug, Switzerland	14 + perpetrator	Legal guns, licensed pistol owner
9 Nov 1999	Bielefeld, Germany	7 + perpetrator	Firearm, licensing status unverified
13 Mar 1996	Dunblane, Scotland	17 + perpetrator	Legal guns, pistol club member
19 Aug 1987	Hungerford, England	16 + perpetrator	Legal guns, pistol club member

Adapted from the Gun Control Network website 2008.

Zealand confirm that most mass shootings are committed by perpetrators (98% of them male) who were lawfully entitled to possess the firearms used (Gun Control Network 2008).

Spree shootings

In terms of academic or psychological knowledge as to the motives of spree shooters, very little is known. Most perpetrators kill themselves at the scene of the crime, therefore evidence can only be gathered afterwards from eyewitnesses, or those known to the assailant. In some cases letters, diaries or videos provide information. For example, 18-year-old Pekka-Eric Auvinen posted a video announcing the massacre at the school on 'YouTube' the day before he entered his high school in Tuusula and murdered nine people. Seung-Hui Cho, perpetrator of the Virginia Tech Massacre, who killed thirty-two people and wounded many others before committing suicide, also prepared information before beginning his rampage. During the massacre Cho posted a parcel containing a DVD to NBC News containing video clips, photographs and a manifesto explaining the reasons for his actions.

Many researchers have investigated school homicides (e.g. Fritzon and Brun 2005), and attempted to understand the motives for such offences. Goldstein (1986) concluded that individuals who overcome the norms and taboos associated with certain 'sanitized' locations were more pathological than those who aggress in locations with fewer such prohibitive norms. McAdams (1988) suggested that motives deriving from the need for power were significant in the perpetrators of school homicides. Others focus on the family/home environment of children who kill, finding these children were often raised in broken homes (Hyde 1999), and describe the families of killers as violent, abusive, inconsistent and aggressive (Bush *et al.* 1990).

One of the implications of violence and homicide taking place in a school is the greater precautions needed to be taken by the school to protect staff and students. In America, risk assessments and predictions are necessary in order to identify students who pose a potential threat. In their paper 'Inherent limits of predicting school violence' Mulvey and Cauffman (2001) highlight the implications and damaging effects this can have upon the students (especially vulnerable students) and ethos of the school. Mulvey and Cauffman suggest that rather than taking a 'zero tolerance' approach, where students may feel increasingly alienated, hence placing more people at risk, schools should try to build relationships and support. 'Establishing school environments where students feel connected and trusted will build the critical link between those who often know when trouble is brewing and those who can act to prevent it' (p. 801).

Conclusion

Issues concerning firearms are very different in the UK and America. While firearms are kept under tight restriction and control of the police in England and Wales, the United States continue to allow greater freedom to law-abiding citizens to carry weapons and keep guns in the home. Unfortunately, evidence suggests that this becomes a risk factor, with large numbers of children and family members being killed, injured and intimidated. Also greater gun availability results in a greater risk of their use in suicides. Guns also play a significant role in crime in the US. While there is much concern in the UK about gun crime, the figures show that firearms are involved in 0.3% of all recorded crime in England and Wales; it is therefore relatively rare. The crime statistics suggest knife crime is more prominent, accounting for 35% of all homicides in England and Wales, and this is of great concern.

REFERENCES

Azrael, D. and Hemenway, D. (2000) In the safety of your own home: results from a national survey on gun use at home. *Social Science and Medicine*, 50: 285–91.

Bureau of Justice Statistics (2008) www.ojp.usdoj.gov/bjs (accessed June 2008).

Bush, K. G., Zagar, R., Hughes, J. R., Arbot, J. and Bussell, R. E. (1990) Adolescents who kill. *Journal of Clinical Psychology*, 46: 472–85.

Centers for Disease Control (CDC) (2008) Web-Based Injury Statistics Query and Reporting System (WISQARS), National Center for Injury Control and Prevention. www.cdc.gov/ncipc/wisqars/default.htm (accessed June 2008).

Choi, E. R., Donoghue, E. R. and Lifschultz, B. D. (1994) Deaths due to firearms injuries in children. *Journal of Forensic Sciences*, 39: 685–92.

Cooke, C. A. (2004) Young people's attitudes towards firearms in America, Britain, and Western Australia. *Aggressive Behavior*, 30: 93–104.

Cooke, C. A. and Puddifoot, J. E. (2000) Gun culture and symbolism in USA and UK females. *Journal of Social Psychology*, 140: 1–11.

Fritzon, K. and Brun. A. (2005) Beyond Columbine: a faceted model of school-associated homicide. *Psychology, Crime and Law*, 11: 53–77.

Goldstein, J. H. (1986) *Aggression and Crimes of Violence*. Oxford: Oxford University Press.

Gun Control Network (2008) www.gun-control-network.org (accessed June 2008).

Home Office (2008) *Crime in England and Wales 2006/07: Homicide, Firearms Offences and Intimate Violence 2006/07*. Available online: www. homeoffice.gov.uk/rds/pdfs07/hosb1107.pdf (accessed June 2008).

Hyde, K. M. (1999) *Young Killers: The Challenge of Juvenile Homicide*. Thousand Oaks, CA: Sage.

Kellerman, A. L. and Reay, D. T. (1986) Protection or peril? An analysis of firearm-related deaths in the home. *New England Journal of Medicine*, 314: 1557–60.

Kleck, G. and Gertz, M. (1995) Armed resistance to crime: the prevalence and nature of self defence with a gun. *Journal of Criminal Law and Criminology*, 86: 150–87.

Lott, J. R. and Mustard, D. B. (1997) Crime, deterrence, and right-to-carry concealed handguns. *Journal of Legal Studies*, 26: 1–68.

McAdams, D. P. (1988). *Power, Intimacy and the Life Story: Personological Inquiries into Identity*. New York: Guilford Press.

Mulvey, E. P. and Cauffman, E. (2001) The inherent limits of predicting school violence. *American Psychologist*, 56: 797–802.

Patterson, P. J. and Smith, L. R. (1987) Firearms in the home and child safety. *American Journal of Diseases of Children*, 141: 221–3.

Puddifoot, J. E. and Cooke, C. A. (2002) Representations of handguns by young adults in the US and UK. *Journal of Community and Applied Social Psychology*, 12: 256–70.

Utah University Firearms Tutorial (2008) http://library.med.utah.edu/WebPath/TUTORIAL/GUNS/GUNINTRO.html (accessed June 2008).

Violence Policy Centre (2001) *Where'd They Get their Guns? An Analysis of the Firearms Used in High-Profile Shootings*. Washington, DC: Violence Policy Centre.

6.6 Hostage taking: effects, coping and adjustment

David A. Alexander

See also chapter 3.3 Crisis negotiation.

Definitions

'Kidnapping' comes from 'kid' (child) and 'nap' (or 'nab') meaning to 'snatch'. It dates back to the practice of stealing children for use as servants or labourers in the North American colonies. 'Abduction', first introduced in 1768, has become a synonym, and in Scottish law the legal offences are 'abduction' or 'abduction with extortion'; 'kidnap' is the English equivalent. A 'hostage' is an individual, held against his/her will, to compel another individual, group, organization or government to act in accordance with the demands of the perpetrator.

A 'siege' is when the hostage(s) and hostage taker(s) are confined to a specific site surrounded by the authorities in a 'stand-off'. This contrasts with other kidnappings in which the victim is held in a location unknown to the authorities. Domestic incidents may develop into sieges.

Prisoners, criminals, the mentally ill, terrorists and political activists are commonly recognized as groups who use kidnapping as their modus operandi, but motives among these groups often overlap. Some are more 'instrumental', i.e. they are goal-directed such as to obtain a ransom, and others are more 'expressive', i.e. a demonstration of some deep-felt grievance or injustice – as is often the case with prison sieges (Lipsedge 2004). It should be noted that Lipsedge (2004) also identifies the 'primary victim' as the person who, or the organization which, is being coerced into fulfilling the hostage taker's demands. The hostage is the 'secondary victim'.

Hostage taking can be a highly dramatic but relatively inexpensive method of extorting money, trying to avoid capture or bargaining for some socio-political concessions. Historically, it has been used for thousands of years, but it has attained a new notoriety due to the high profile such an act achieves through the international media. In certain parts of the world, it has become a common practice, e.g. Colombia, Nigeria, Mexico and Iraq. In the last-named, the video recording of the execution of hostages has become a particularly disturbing trend.

Until about the 1960s, sieges, particularly in prisons in the USA, were mostly ended by overwhelming force (the 'Suppression Model': Needham 1977), but 'hostage negotiation' or 'crisis bargaining' is now the first-choice method of resolution. Physical force is normally a last-resource strategy, and it can be successful (e.g. the Iranian Siege in London in 1980), but it can have tragic consequences for hostages (e.g. the Munich Massacre in 1972, which resulted in the deaths of the Israeli Olympic wrestling team, and the Moscow Theatre Siege in 2002, which resulted in the deaths of 130 hostages).

The effects of being a hostage

Being taken hostage is a traumatic experience, and, as a consequence, it is likely to lead to the panoply of normal traumatic reactions as described by Alexander (2005).

Acute initial reactions include: shock, dissociation, fear and severe anxiety, disbelief, and denial. Initially, victims cannot believe what has happened to them. For example, some passengers on a hijacked plane believed it was a hoax (Jacobsen 1973), and the Moscow Theatre audience thought the initial acts of the Chechnyan terrorists were part of the musical they had gone to see (Speckard 2004). Occasionally, victims can view the event in a positive light at least in the short term. In the above-mentioned hijacking of the aircraft, a group of adolescents viewed the incident initially as an 'adventure' (Jacobsen 1973). Physical signs of hyperarousal are also not unusual: raised heart and respiratory rate (the latter can lead to Hyperventilation Syndrome), nausea, fainting and incontinence. After the acute reaction subsides, intermediate effects take over. Thus, hostages may start to blame themselves for their circumstances; ask 'why me?'; start to impose order in and control over their environment (particularly with regard to their physical needs); reflect on whether to acquiesce or seek to escape; and experience guilt at the distress their situation may cause others. Symonds (1982) has described two particular reactions of survival value: (a) 'frozen fright', whereby the victim's emotions are paralysed in a dissociative state and the individual becomes superficially co-operative; and (b) 'psychological infantilism', whereby the individual regresses to more infantile methods of coping, displaying highly dependent and clinging behaviour towards the captor(s).

Particularly in prolonged events, 'learned helplessness' (Seligman 1975) may develop. Victims display a depressed state of mind, and they believe that whatever they do will have no positive effect. This state is reflected in Bettelheim's (1960) descriptions of 'walking corpses' among concentration camp victims. Others such as Terry Waite (Waite 1993), imprisoned in the Lebanon, constantly sought out signs of hope, even through what he knew were 'illogical' means. For example, he would open his Bible at a randomly chosen page and, with eyes closed, run his finger down the text to see if it would land upon a section which would offer him some solace.

Jacobsen (1973) reported interesting group dynamics among the 149 air passengers taken hostage by the Popular Front for the Liberation of Palestine. The boundaries of groups shifted, and divisiveness sometimes occurred in response to changing circumstances, for example, when the hijackers sought out those with dual passports and when non-Kosher food was provided for Jewish passengers.

Hostages may also have to contend with physical illnesses, either those exacerbated by their circumstances or those which are a direct consequence of, for example, poor diet and a lack of exercise, sleep and daylight.

Stockholm syndrome

This was first described by a criminologist Nils Begerot, following an armed bank robbery at the Sveriges Kredit Bank in Sweden in 1973. It was noted that, despite threats to their lives, the hostages developed positive relationships with their captors and even set up a fund for the perpetrators' legal defence. This phenomenon has also been observed after high-profile kidnaps, including that of the American Patti Hearst (daughter of a wealthy businessman) by the Symbionese Liberation Army (SLA) and that of the Austrian girl Natascha Kampusch by Wolfgang Priklopil (Hall and Leidig 2006). Following an extended spell of physical, psychological and sexual abuse, and despite being offered the chance to leave the SLA, Hearst joined it (although she did not support them subsequently when she did return home). Following the suicide of her captor (who had detained her for eight years), Natascha Kampusch blamed the police for not preventing his death and grieved over his demise. A distinctive feature of the Kampusch–Priklopil relationship was that, at least episodically, Priklopil became the 'servant' and his captor became the 'mistress' in terms of their pattern of life.

It is an important phenomenon which occurs in adults and children, and it helps to protect hostages from death, injury or further abuse, and it can be developed by negotiators. (It is probably unhelpful to describe it as a 'syndrome' because this term implies some 'abnormality'.) It appears to occur mostly when the hostages and the hostage takers share common adversities (e.g. poor living conditions); when the event is prolonged; when there are opportunities for relationships to develop between hostages and their captors; when threats to life and limb are not fulfilled, and when there is a high degree of dependence on the hostage takers even for the basics of living.

It can be prevented from developing by depersonalizing and dehumanizing hostages (e.g. by taking away any personally identifying items, by not using the hostages' correct names and replacing these with numbers or pseudonyms, and by rotating the hostage guards).

The disadvantages of the Stockholm syndrome include the facts that hostages may later feel guilty about their reactions, and that the authorities cannot rely on hostages to assist in a rescue or to provide accurate forensic testimony.

How individuals cope during such an event

Most information comes from anecdotal accounts, although some research studies have generated useful information about pre-incident vulnerabilities and coping strategies. Agopian (1984) reports that younger children tend to suffer more than older ones, and Terr (1983) confirms that pre-incident family pathology is a bad prognostic indicator in kidnapped children. Markesteyn (1992) states that certain personality factors such as passive-dependent, and dogmatic and authoritarian traits, and an external locus of control may lead to more problems of adjustment.

There is general agreement about a dose–response relationship between the severity of the traumatic features of the incident and the victim's subsequent ability to cope and to adjust. Individual strategies may be helpful to combat the adverse effects. Terry Waite set himself three principles: no regrets, no false sentiment and no self pity. Also, he used mental arithmetic and reading (as did Kampusch) as ways of coping mentally in addition to regular physical exercise, and took one day at a time. He did not reflect on his family as this was too painful, but he tried to convert his solitude (four years of it) into a positive experience by preparing, in his mind, his autobiography. This is similar to Viktor Frankl's (1945) account of how he coped with the death camp,

Auschwitz, by re-enacting and analysing earlier life experiences and regarding each day as his last.

Although denial is often decried as a way of coping, Janoff-Bulman and Timko (1987) argue that, during a dreadful experience, initial denial can represent a way of moderating its impact on the victim. Navia and Ossa (2003) noted that families, whose loved ones had been kidnapped, coped better if they provided clear rules and patterns of behaviour, and retained a sense of control over at least part of their lives.

Longer-term issues of adjustment

Resilience seems to be the norm, but there is evidence that certain individuals do develop post-traumatic psychopathologies after being taken hostage. Among a sample of twenty-four kidnap victims, Favaro *et al.* (2000) reported that 46% had post-traumatic stress disorder (PTSD), and 38% had a major depression. A sample of 55 hostages and 158 family members of the hostages were followed up by Navia and Ossa (2003). After release 29% of the hostages had PTSD and almost 20% of the families also suffered from this condition. These were chronic symptoms, and less cohesive families had higher rates of PTSD.

The ICD-10 (WHO 1992) describes a particularly chronic and disabling condition known as 'Enduring personality change following catastrophic experience' (F62.0) which may follow incarceration, torture and kidnap. The typical features are:

- a hostile, distrustful attitude
- social withdrawal and estrangement
- a sense of emptiness and hopelessness
- a chronic sense of being 'on edge'.

Apart from florid psychopathology, other post-release reactions have been reported among former hostages. These include guilt, exaggerated dependence, an exaggerated sense of vulnerability (hypervigilance), avoidance of reminders of the event, and difficulty in retrieving their original identity and relationships. Adverse reactions may also be displayed at a community level. After Kampusch's escape, there was a rush by Austrian parents to buy mobile phones for their children and to insist that the police mounted patrols around the schools. One father even set fire to a neighbour in the belief that he had kidnapped his daughter (Hall and Leidig 2006).

It is widely recognized that children may be particularly vulnerable to the effects of being kidnapped. Terr (1983) followed up twenty-six children who were taken hostage in the Chowchilla (California) incident in which a school bus was hijacked and buried in a quarry until some children escaped about sixteen hours later. Every child displayed symptoms similar to PSTD four to five years later. Unfortunately, some reactions became worse over time, for example, shame, pessimism, denial, and dangerous re-enactment of the event (in play). Gill (1981) suggests that the adverse effects on children may be exacerbated by their need for medical care and loss of education.

Conclusion

Research on hostages and their families is limited for several reasons. First, the plight of such individuals is a sensitive matter, and researchers are understandably cautious about the risk of 're-traumatizing' individuals by asking them to discuss their experiences through the medium of interviews and questionnaires. Second, sample sizes (with some obvious exceptions) tend to be small and/or highly selective. Third, researchers do not always use the same standardized measures, thus it is hard to compare findings from one study to another. As Markesteyn (1992) has commented, the most serious limitation of victim research is that it is largely phenomenon-orientated, exploratory and descriptive. Little of it is theory driven. There is, therefore, an urgent need for the formulation and testing of specific hypotheses which can lead to theory generation. This is essential to bring together rather disparate findings.

There are many gaps in knowledge. These include a rigorous exploration of the 'at risk', vulnerability and protective factors relating to kidnapping. Above, some broad principles were outlined, but these have limited predictive value. Individual differences in coping strategy also require investigation. What works for whom, used when and under what circumstances is far from clear. Apart from individual coping strategies, there is the important issue of how group dynamics, when there are a number of hostages, may facilitate adjustment or, alternatively, compromise it. The Stockholm syndrome or 'Stockholm phenomenon', as it would be better named, is still insufficiently understood. There is a need to develop further understanding of the relevance of processes such as 'identification with the aggressor', in the development of this phenomenon. A better understanding of such processes would help negotiators to engineer its development in an adaptive and protective fashion.

Finally, longitudinal studies are required to identify the longer-term sequelae of kidnapping for hostages and their families.

FURTHER READING

Hearst, P. C. and Moscow, A. (1998) *Patty Hearst: Her Own Story*. New York: Avon.

Kennedy, H. G. and Dyer, D. E. (1992) Parental hostage takers. *British Journal of Psychiatry*, 160: 410–12.

Ridley, Y. (2001) *In the Hands of the Taliban: Her Extraordinary Story*. London: Robson Books.

Slater, S. and Lancaster, P. (1995) *Beyond Fear: My Will to Survive*. Oxford: ISIS Publishing.

REFERENCES

Agopian, M. W. (1984) The impact on children of abduction by parents. *Child Welfare*, 63: 511–19.

Alexander, D. A. (2005) Early mental health intervention after disaster. *Advances in Psychiatric Treatment*, 11: 12–18.

Bettelheim, B. (1960) *The Informed Heart*. New York: Free Press.

Favaro, A., Degortes, D., Colombo, G. and Santonastaso, P. (2000) The effects of trauma among kidnap victims in Sardinia, Italy. *Psychological Medicine*, 30: 975–80.

Frankl, F. I. (1945) On the problems of Chaplygin for mixed sub- and supersonic flows. *Isv. Akad. Nauk. USSR Ser. Mat.* 9: 121–43.

Gill, E. (1981) *Stolen Children: How and Why Parents Kidnap their Kids and What to Do about It*. New York: Sea View Books.

Hall, A. and Leidig, M. (2006) *Girl in the Cellar: The Natascha Kampusch Story*. London: Hodder & Stoughton.

Jacobsen, S. R. (1973) Individual and group responses to confinement in a skyjacked plane. *American Journal of Orthopsychiatry*, 43: 459–69.

Janoff-Bulman, R. and Timko, C. (1987) Coping with traumatic life events: the role of denial in light of people's assumptive worlds. In C. R. Snyder and C. E. Ford (eds.) *Coping with Negative Life Events*, pp. 135–59. New York: Plenum Press.

Lipsedge, M. (2004) Hostage-taking and domestic sieges. *Psychiatry*, 3: 24–26.

Markesteyn, T. (1992) The psychological impact of non sexual criminal offences on victims. Canada: Report no. 1992–21 prepared for the Ministry of the Solicitor General of Canada.

Navia, C. E. and Ossa, M. (2003) Family functioning, coping and psychological adjustment in victims and their families following kidnapping. *Journal of Traumatic Stress*, 16: 107–12.

Needham, J. (1977) *Neutralization of Prison Hostage Situations*. Houston, TX: Institute of Contemporary Corrections and the Behavioral Sciences.

Seligman, M. E. P. (1975) *Helplessness: On Depression, Development, and Death*. San Francisco, CA: Freeman.

Speckhard, A. (2004) Soldiers for God: a study of the suicide terrorists in the Moscow hostage taking siege. In O. McTernan (ed.), *The Roots of Terrorism: Contemporary Trends and Traditional Analysis*, pp. 1–22. Brussels: NATO Science Series.

Symonds, M. (1982) Victim responses to terror: understanding and treatment. In F. M. Ochberg and D. A. Soskis (eds.), *Victims of Terrorism*, pp. 95–104. Boulder, CO: Westview.

Terr, L. C. (1983) Chowchilla revisited: the effects of psychic trauma for years after a school bus kidnapping. *American Journal of Psychiatry*, 140: 1543–50.

Waite, T. (1993) *Taken on Trust*. London: Hodder & Stoughton.

WHO (1992) *The ICD-10 Classification of Mental and Behavioural Disorders*. Geneva: World Health Organization.

6.7 Hypnosis

Graham Wagstaff

See also chapter 2.9 Investigative interviewing.

Definition

Although hypnosis has traditionally been defined as a sleep-like altered state of consciousness or 'trance', this conception of hypnosis has long been a source of controversy (Barber 1969; British Psychological Society 2001; Kirsch and Lynn 1995; Wagstaff 1981, 2004). As a result, terms such as 'state' and 'trance' tend to be less popular in definitions of hypnosis than they used to be; for example, they do not feature in the definitions of hypnosis put forward the American Psychological Association (1994), or the British Psychological Society (2001). Instead, it has become more common to refer to hypnosis, not as a special state or condition, but as a *procedure or set of procedures*; for example, hypnosis can be described as a set of procedures in which an individual receives (more or less any) instructions or suggestions to imagine and think about certain ideas, set in a context defined or labelled as 'hypnosis'.

However, although experts still disagree as to how hypnosis should be defined, research in this area has done much to dispel the popular stereotype of the hypnotic subject as a passive automaton, possessed of transcendent powers. Thus a variety of evidence indicates that hypnotic subjects tend to be active cognizing agents; moreover, suitably instructed and motivated non-hypnotic control groups can equal and sometimes surpass hypnotic groups on a variety of performance measures (see, for example, Barber 1969; Spanos and Chaves 1989; Wagstaff 1981, 2004). These findings have obvious implications for how we view the two main points of contact between hypnosis and the law: i.e. the use of hypnosis as a coercive tool, and the use of hypnosis as a possible memory enhancement procedure.

Hypnotic coercion

Claims that people have unwittingly been hypnotized into committing criminal acts are rare and have generally been treated with scepticism (see, for example, Barber 1969; Conn 1972). Rather more common are claims that victims have been reduced by hypnosis to helpless automata and subjected to sexual assault without their consent and/or knowledge. Some of these cases appear to have received more sympathetic consideration by the courts (Wagstaff 1999a). The obvious difficulty with real-life situations, however, is that is impossible to distinguish the effects of hypnosis from other causal factors that may have influenced the behaviours in question (Barber 1969). Influential factors often include, prior to hypnosis, the existence of a close, dependent, personal relationship between hypnotist and subject. Moreover, by consenting to engage in hypnosis, the subject places him or herself in a powerful social situation in which he or she has tacitly agreed to trust the hypnotist and do what is instructed or suggested (Wagstaff 1981). Because of the difficulties involved in isolating the effects of these factors, researchers have turned to experimental methods to try to test the coercive powers of hypnosis.

A few early reports claimed that, in the laboratory, hypnotized persons can be made to perform acts that are immoral or harmful, either to themselves or others. However, a number of reviewers of these studies have concluded that the notion of a 'hypnotic state' is not necessary to explain these results; rather they occurred because, contrary to outward appearances, subjects perceived the situation to be safe, and/or they considered that someone else would take responsibility for their actions (Barber 1969; Coe, Kobayashi and Howard 1973; Orne and Evans 1965). Indeed, a variety of studies have shown that unhypnotized subjects are just as likely as (and sometimes slightly more likely than) hypnotized subjects to perform a variety of antisocial, repugnant acts and self-injurious acts that have included mutilating the Bible, cutting up the national flag, making a homosexual approach (when heterosexual), signing derogatory-slanderous statements about a superior, putting one's hand in a beaker of concentrated nitric acid and throwing acid at the experimenter, picking up a poisonous snake, and even heroin dealing (Barber 1969; Coe, Kobayashi and Howard 1973; Orne and Evans 1965; Wagstaff 1999a). These results fit in with a variety of other evidence that indicates that, regardless of whether hypnosis is used, many individuals will readily perform what appear to be dangerous and antisocial acts if the experimental context requires them to do so (see, for example, Milgram 1974).

On the basis of this and other research, there now seems to be a broad consensus amongst researchers in the field of hypnosis that hypnotized individuals do not lose consciousness or control of their behaviour. For example, the definition of hypnosis provided by the American Psychological Association states, 'Contrary to some depictions of hypnosis in books, movies or television, people who have been hypnotized do not lose control over their behaviour' (1994, p. 143). Similarly, having reviewed the scientific evidence, the independent panel appointed by the UK Home Office recommended that the public should be made explicitly aware of the fact that 'The hypnotized subject retains ultimate control over his/her actions' (1995, Annex D). (See also the British Psychological Society 2001.) It can be noted that even from the perspective of what is generally considered the most influential modern 'state' theory of hypnosis, dissociated control theory (Woody and Bowers 1994), the decision to engage or disengage with hypnotic suggestions rests ultimately with the hypnotic subject; hence the main advocate of this approach, Erik Woody, has commented, 'Common misconceptions are that hypnosis can be used to enable people to demonstrate abilities they would not otherwise possess, and make people engage in behaviour they would otherwise avoid because of ethical and moral constraints. Neither of these is true' (1998, p. 2).

Given the broad agreement that hypnotized individuals do not lose control of their behaviour, it is also perhaps not surprising that the general opinion among researchers is that subjects are capable of lying when hypnotized (Wagstaff 1999a).

Hypnosis and memory facilitation

The general reliability of testimony given under hypnosis came under particular scrutiny in the 1970s and 1980s when a number of police forces were using hypnosis as a tool to enhance eyewitness memory (e.g. Haward 1988; Hibbard and Worring 1981). However, subsequently, a variety of research evidence has indicated that, whilst hypnosis sometimes leads to an increase in the recall of correct information, it can also lead to an increase in false information, or 'pseudomemories', particularly if false or misleading information is suggested to the witness during the hypnosis session. As a result, overall accuracy (i.e. the proportion of correct to incorrect responses) is frequently not improved with hypnosis, and can even deteriorate. Moreover, there is a tendency for hypnosis to increase confidence in responses, regardless of accuracy (Erdelyi 1994; Kebbell and Wagstaff 1998; Wagstaff 1999a, 1999 b; Webert 2003). As a result of expert evidence on this subject, a number of states in the USA have enacted a per se exclusion rule, and banned victims and witnesses who have been interviewed with 'hypnosis' from giving evidence in court (Webert 2003). In the UK, the Home Office has also produced guidelines discouraging the use of hypnosis as a police interviewing tool.

The most generally accepted explanation for the hypnotic false memory effect is that, because of the expectancies associated with hypnosis (i.e. the view that hypnosis has a magical power to restore lost memories), and pressure brought to bear by the investigating hypnotist to remember more information, hypnotized witnesses sometimes adopt a more lax criterion for report (i.e. become less cautious when reporting). As a result, they tend to report details as correct that they would normally reject on the basis of uncertainty. In support of this explanation, a variety of experimental research has shown that hypnotic 'pseudomemories' can be reduced to non-hypnotic levels if subjects are given instructions that lead or invite them to adopt a more cautious criterion for reporting: such as, offering them a financial reward for correct reporting, or asking them to swear to tell the truth under oath, or telling them to use a part of their brain that knows what really happened (Wagstaff 1999a, 1999b).

Nevertheless, notwithstanding the laboratory evidence, some experts have continued to argue that hypnosis can usefully improve memory, and police in a number of countries have continued to use hypnosis for memory enhancement purposes. The main reason for this is that, despite the experimental findings, a number of anecdotal cases have allegedly shown hypnosis to be effective in this role. There are a number of possible explanations for the apparent success of hypnosis in these cases. For example, in the field, there are a number of procedures that so-called 'hypnoinvestigators' have employed in forensic investigations that might produce better results than routine police interviewing; these have included sympathetic non-authoritarian interrogators who establish trust and rapport and allow witnesses to divulge sensitive information, repeated testing, and a variety of techniques to provide memory retrieval cues, such as role-playing, picture drawing, recalling in different orders, and 'hypnotic revivification' or 'context reinstatement'; i.e. reporting everything including thoughts and feelings (Wagstaff 1982a, 1982b). In addition, hypnoinvestigators have tended to be more skilled at avoiding problems associated with standard police interviewing, such as interrupting the witness and inhibiting the elaboration of their accounts (Wagstaff 1999b).

Because of this, attempts have been made to direct the police towards non-hypnotic means of memory enhancement that share the kinds of techniques developed by hypnoinvestigators, but divorced from the troublesome context of 'hypnosis'. The most popular of these is the cognitive interview, which uses techniques such as rapport building, open 'report everything' instructions, focused attention and context reinstatement (Fisher and Geiselman 1992). Although comparable memory enhancement has been shown with the cognitive and hypnotic interviews (Geiselman et al. 1985), it is generally assumed that cognitive interviewing offers fewer practical problems; hence, in the UK and USA, the cognitive interview has generally displaced hypnosis as the preferred mode of memory facilitation in police investigations.

Nevertheless, experience in the field suggests that cognitive interviewing is still time consuming, not only in terms of time spent interviewing the witness, but in training the police interviewers; moreover, because of their complexity, officers often do not adhere to the specified procedures (Kebbell, Milne and Wagstaff 1999). Because of this, some researchers have begun to re-examine, with some success, components of hypnotic interviewing that do not require excessive time and training to administer, and when divorced from the context of 'hypnosis', do not inflate errors. These include relaxation/meditation and eye-closure, both of which appear to facilitate eyewitness memory without an increase in errors (Wagstaff et al. 2004).

Some of these considerations have obvious relevance to the rather polarized 'false memory' debate regarding the use of hypnosis to recover previously unreported childhood memories of abuse (Ofshe and Watters 1995). For example, although individuals put through hypnotic interviewing procedures may sometimes report false information about early life experiences, particularly if led to do so, it does not follow that all additional information recalled using hypnosis will necessarily be inaccurate. To some extent, factors present in hypnosis procedures such as eye-closure, meditation and context reinstatement could also help to reinstate accurate memories. Moreover, in the guise of a 'special' memory facilitation technique, set in a context that encourages trust and rapport, hypnosis may act as a face-saving device, giving witnesses 'permission' to talk about events that they might previously have been reluctant to mention. This would help to explain a sudden emergence of (independently corroborated) reports of extensive periods of abuse that people would not normally be expected to forget, without postulating the involvement of a mechanism such as repression (Wagstaff 1999b).

Conclusion

To conclude, contrary to popular public opinion, research evidence suggests that hypnosis does not make people into helpless automata; neither is it a 'truth serum' or a magical way of uncovering lost or repressed memories. On balance, in most situations, the cognitive interview is probably a better choice as an investigative tool, and if hypnosis is to be used in this role, it should be applied with considerable caution. Nevertheless, there are also indications that some of the procedures commonly used in investigative hypnosis may yet prove a valuable source of ideas for future forensic interviewing.

FURTHER READING

For an overview of the area of hypnosis generally see the British Psychological Society (2001). For a more detailed review of the specific issues raised here, see the author's chapter (Wagstaff 1999a) on forensic hypnosis. For reviews of the main issues regarding hypnosis in forensic interviewing, see Kebbell and Wagstaff (1998) and Webert (2003). The latter provides an informative legal perspective.

REFERENCES

American Psychological Association, Division of Psychological Hypnosis (1994) Definition and description of hypnosis. Reproduced in *Contemporary Hypnosis*, 11: 143.

Barber, T. X. (1969) *Hypnosis: A Scientific Approach*. New York: Van Nostrand.

British Psychological Society (2001) *The Nature of Hypnosis*. Leicester: British Psychological Society.

Coe, W. C., Kobayashi, K. and Howard, M. L. (1973) Experimental and ethical problems of evaluating the influence of hypnosis in antisocial conduct. *Journal of Abnormal Psychology*, 82: 476–82.

Conn, J. H. (1972) Is hypnosis really dangerous? *International Journal of Clinical and Experimental Hypnosis*, 20: 61–79.

Erdelyi, M. W. (1994) The empty set of hyperamnesia. *International Journal of Clinical and Experimental Hypnosis*, 42: 379–90.

Fisher, R. P. and Geiselman, R. E. (1992) *Memory Enhancing Techniques for Investigative Interviewing: The Cognitive Interview*. Springfield, IL: Thomas.

Geiselman, R. E., Fisher, R. P., MacKinnon, D. P. and Holland, H. L. (1985) Eyewitness memory enhancement in the police interview: cognitive retrieval mnemonics versus hypnosis. *Journal of Applied Psychology*, 70: 401–12.

Haward, L. R. C. (1988) Hypnosis by the police. *British Journal of Experimental and Clinical Hypnosis*, 5: 33–5.

Hibbard, W. S. and Worring, R. W. (1981) *Forensic Hypnosis: The Practical Application of Hypnosis in Criminal Investigation*. Springfield, IL: Thomas.

Home Office Review of the Hypnotism Act 1952 (1995) *Report of the Expert Panel Appointed to Consider the Effects of Participation in Performances of Stage Hypnotism*. London: Home Office, October.

Kebbell, M. R. and Wagstaff, G. F. (1998). Hypnotic interviewing: the best way to interview eyewitnesses? *Behavioral Sciences and the Law*, 16: 115–29.

Kebbell, M. R., Milne, R. and Wagstaff, G. F. (1999) The cognitive interview: a survey of its forensic effectiveness. *Psychology, Crime and Law*, 5: 101–15.

Kirsch, I. and Lynn, S. J. (1995) Altered state of hypnosis: changes in the theoretical landscape. *American Psychologist*, 50: 846–58.

Milgram, S. (1974) *Obedience to Authority*. London: Tavistock.

Ofshe, R. and Watters, E. (1995) *Making Monsters: False Memories, Psychotherapy and Sexual Hysteria*. London: André Deutsch.

Orne, M. T. and Evans, F. J. (1965) Social control in the psychological experiment: antisocial behavior and hypnosis. *Journal of Personality and Social Psychology*, 1: 189–200.

Spanos, N. and Chaves, J. F. (1989) *Hypnosis: The Cognitive-Behavioural Perspective*. Loughton: Prometheus Books.

Wagstaff, G. F. (1981) *Hypnosis, Compliance, and Belief*. Brighton: Harvester; New York: St Martin's Press.

  (1982a) Hypnosis and witness recall: a discussion paper. *Journal of the Royal Society of Medicine*, 75: 793–7.

  (1982b) Helping a witness remember – a project in forensic psychology. *Police Research Bulletin*, 38: 56–8.

  (1999a) Forensic hypnosis. In I. Kirsch, A. Capafons, E. Cardena-Buela and S. Amigo (eds.), *Clinical Hypnosis and Self-Regulation Therapy: A Cognitive-Behavioral Perspective*, pp. 277–310. Washington, DC: American Psychological Association.

  (1999b) Hypnotically elicited testimony. In A. Heaton Armstrong, E. Shepherd and D. Wolchover (eds.), *Analysing Witness Testimony*, pp. 277–310. London: Blackstone.

  (2004) High hypnotizability in a sociocognitive framework. In M. Heap, D. Oakley and R. Brown (eds.), *The Highly Hypnotizable Person*, pp. 85–114. London: Brunner-Routledge.

Wagstaff, G. F., Brunas-Wagstaff, J., Knapton, L., Winterbottom, J. Crean, V., Cole, J. and Wheatcroft, J. (2004) Facilitating memory with hypnosis, focused meditation and eye-closure. *International Journal of Clinical and Experimental Hypnosis*, 52: 434–55.

Webert, D. R. (2003) Are the courts in a trance? Approaches to the admissibility of hypnotically enhanced witness testimony in the light of empirical evidence. *American Criminal Law Review*, 40: 1301–27.

Woody, E. (1998) What is hypnosis? Introduction: Symposium on the neural basis of memory. 5th Internet World Congress for Biomedical Sciences, December, pp. 1–5.

Woody, E. Z. and Bowers, K. S. (1994) A frontal assault on dissociated control. In S. Lynn and J. Rhue (eds.), *Dissociation: Theoretical and Research Perspectives*, pp. 52–79. New York: Guilford Press.

Lorraine Hope

Definitions

In contrast with many of their European counterparts, juries in the UK are located within an adversarial, as opposed to inquisitorial, system. Under adversarial systems, a jury typically comprises a group of ordinary members of society who are required to evaluate the evidence presented at trial. After hearing the evidence in court, and receiving judge's instructions on the relevant points of law, the jury retires to deliberate over the facts and reach a verdict as to the guilt or innocence of the defendant.

Juries in England, Wales and Northern Ireland share similar characteristics (although there are some special features associated with jury trial in Northern Ireland; see Jackson, Quinn and O'Malley 1999). However, cross-border differences between jury systems in Scotland and England are considerable and both diverge from other adversarial models. For instance, neither the English nor Scottish jurisdictions enshrine any constitutional right to trial by jury and, in both Scotland and England, only a very small percentage of all trials are heard by a jury (<1–2%).

Both the Scottish and English systems differ quite radically from North America in terms of procedures to empanel the final jury for the trial. Once the random selection of jurors has been made there is very little opportunity to alter the original selection by either defence or prosecution. In both UK jurisdictions, there is no 'voir dire' procedure equivalent to that used in the US (whereby jurors may be questioned with respect to their attitudes and potential biases concerning the case).

The first significant structural difference between the English and Scottish criminal juries concerns the number of empanelled jurors. While the English jury (and the Scottish civil jury) is made up of twelve individuals, fifteen jurors are seated for a Scottish criminal jury. Verdict unanimity was a requirement for English jurors until 1967, when the Criminal Justice Act decreed a majority verdict of ten to two acceptable. Should the jury be unable to reach this majority, the jury will be declared hung and a retrial will take place. The decision rule in Scotland is markedly different and the jury can return a verdict reflecting a bare majority (i.e. an eight to seven split) for either conviction or acquittal.

The most unusual feature of the Scottish jury is the not proven verdict. Like jurors elsewhere in the UK and US, Scottish jurors can choose to convict or to acquit by means of a guilty or not guilty verdict. However, they can also choose to return a not proven verdict. The not proven verdict is actually a vote for acquittal and has the same legal effect as a not guilty verdict. In both instances, the defendant is acquitted and cannot be retried for the same crime. The difference between the verdicts is simply that a not guilty verdict reflects quite categorically that in the jury's view the defendant did not commit the crime and is innocent while the not proven verdict reflects, controversially for some, a measure of doubt that the defendant's guilt has been adequately demonstrated by the prosecution (Duff 1999; for research on use of the not proven verdict, see Hope *et al.* 2008).

With rare exceptions, jury decision making takes place behind closed doors resulting in deliberations that appear more 'puzzle' than 'process' (SunWolf in press). Consequently, there is no way of knowing how jurors reach their verdict, whether the final verdict is based on a correct or appropriate evaluation of the evidence or the extent to which particular biases or stereotypes at an individual or group level contribute to the final decision. Given that jury trials only occur for the most serious crimes, this is a legitimate concern. Further, as juries are also resource and cost intensive, there is a clear need to determine scientifically whether juries are, in fact, a just and fair system.

Psychology and jury behaviour

For social and applied psychologists, juries present the opportunity to examine small and potentially diverse groups brought together for the purpose of completing an important, complex but naturally occurring decision-making task. During the 1970s, social psychologists investigated how the physical and social characteristics of defendants could influence jury (or juror) decision making (Bartol and Bartol 1994). Psychologists also explored the role of jury size and began developing decision-making models of jury behaviour. During the 1980s and 1990s, jury decision-making research became less social and more cognitive in its emphasis, for example, the development of the story model of juror decision making (Pennington and Hastie 1986, 1992). More recently, psychologists have shifted their attention to the study of how beliefs and attitudes can influence juror decision making. There has also been an increased interest in exploring how juror performance might be improved (e.g. ForsterLee, Kent and Horowitz 2005).

Ideally, psychologists should be able to study the behaviour of real juries. However, ethical and legal restrictions make this difficult, if not impossible. For instance, under English law it is illegal to 'obtain, disclose or solicit any particular of statements made, opinions expressed, arguments advanced or votes cast by members of a jury in the course of their deliberations' (section 8 of the Contempt of Court Act 1981). Therefore, research has had to take alternative forms (such as mock juries, analyses of actual verdict statistics or interviews with other trial participants such as lawyers and judges) to explore jury decision making. Mock juries generally comprise a group of people who either hear or read about a case. They then deliberate the case, as a real jury would, with the aim of reaching a decision regarding the guilt or innocence of the defendant. This method allows the researcher to obtain both individual and group-level verdict decisions and also facilitates the observation of deliberations. In laboratory settings, researchers have used simulation methodologies involving case summaries and transcripts (Kerr and MacCoun 1985; Pennington and Hastie 1992), specially produced videotaped trials (Pritchard and Keenan 1999), post-trial interviews (Kalven and Zeisel 1966) and questionnaires (Reifman, Gusick and Ellsworth 1992). Experimental laboratory research has focused on numerous variables, including jury size and polling procedures (Kerr and MacCoun 1985); legal instruction (Smith and Kassin 1993); defendant and juror ethnicity (Perez *et al.* 1993); jury attitudes and political ideologies (Casper and Benedict 1993); individual verdict preference and leniency bias (MacCoun and Kerr 1988); and witness credibility and evidence recall (Pennington and Hastie 1992).

The mock juror (or simulation) paradigm has a number of limitations. Concerns have typically focused on the homogeneous non-community mock juror samples, unrealistic presentation format of the trial, lack of group deliberations, and absence of verdict consequences (Bornstein 1999). Furthermore, in the absence of adequate (or numerous) replications, there may also be limitations associated with case-specific (i.e. stimulus-specific) results. Happily, a review of the literature suggests that 'few differences have been found as a function of either who the mock jurors are or how the mock trial is presented' (Bornstein 1999, p. 88). Nonetheless, there is a reluctance to embrace psycholegal research (Diamond 1997; Ellsworth 1989). In the eyes of the court, research using mock juries can rarely replicate the entirety of complex and dynamic courtroom environments, while the isolated examination of a single factor necessary for theoretical development is typically too far removed from the actual jury process to be of any practical use.

Clearly, the greatest improvement that could be made to the ecological validity of jury research would be permitting research on actual juries. Limited access to the deliberations of actual juries was granted during the Arizona Jury Project in the US as part of a study of changes to Arizona's civil procedures (e.g. Diamond et al. 2003). However, the prospect of a similar concession in the UK seems somewhat unlikely at present. While the Runciman Royal Commission (1991–3) recommended that the Contempt of Court Act 1981 be amended to allow authorized research to take place in the jury room, Lord Justice Auld's review of the criminal courts (Auld 2001) and the recent consultation on jury research (Department for Constitutional Affairs 2005) were somewhat less amenable to such research.

Biases in juror decision making

Research by psychologists (and others) on how jurors process evidence during the course of a trial has followed a developmental route, whereby researchers have first of all examined the impact of particular types of evidence before progressing to examine whether jurors can differentiate good and bad evidence of that type and whether legal remedies can be devised (Greene et al. 2002). For instance, eyewitness testimony can have an important influence on juror decisions, yet research indicates that juror perceptions of eyewitness testimony are not typically influenced by factors which have been shown to generally impair eyewitness accuracy (such as event violence, presence of a weapon and perpetrator disguise). Furthermore, jurors are not usually sensitive to improper procedural factors, such as biased lineup instructions and foil selection, and can also rely too heavily on witness confidence (Brewer and Wells 2006; Cutler, Penrod and Dexter 1990). Research has also been concerned with the extent to which jurors can discriminate between valid scientific research presented by experts and unreliable or 'junk' science. To date, research suggests that potential jurors (and indeed, legal professionals) have some difficulty with this task (e.g. Kovera and McAuliffe 2000).

A large body of research evidence has also strongly suggested that jury decision making can be biased by extra-evidential influences, due to factors such as pre-trial publicity (e.g. Costantini and King 1980; Honess, Charman and Levi 2003; Hope, Memon and McGeorge 2004; Moran and Cutler 1991; Ogloff and Vidmar 1994; Ruva, McEvoy and Bryant 2007; Steblay *et al.* 1999), previous convictions (Lloyd-Bostock 2000), juror racism (Mitchell *et al.* 2005) and other prejudices. For instance, cues such as physical attractiveness (Mazella and Feingold 1994), clothing (Temple and Loewen 1993); speaking voice (Berry *et al.* 1994) and non-verbal behaviour (Baum, Fisher, and Singer 1985) have been shown to contribute to impressions formed by social perceivers and influence subsequent interpersonal behaviour (e.g. Snyder, Tank and Berscheid 1977). It seems reasonable to suggest that as jurors are not cognitively different to other individuals they may unwittingly be guided by prejudices relating to the defendant's race, gender and attractiveness (Hans and Vidmar 1986).

Models of juror decision making

A rational model of decision making based on the notion of a well-informed rational decision maker was originally applied to juror decision making. However, empirical research on juror decision making suggests that such a rational model does not constitute an accurate description of human decision making (Kahneman and Tversky 1979; Payne 1982). It is worth remembering that the juror's task is at once both well defined and complex, involving almost all higher-order cognitive processes.

The story model for juror decision making (Pennington and Hastie 1986, 1992) is the most influential cognitive model of juror decision making developed to account for the way in which verdict decisions are reached. This model proposes that jurors formulate a plausible 'story' of the crime and, subsequently, arrive at a verdict consistent with that particular narrative. Empirical tests of the Story Model have successfully established the validity of its main tenet – namely, that story structures are spontaneously generated when summarizing information from different sources and that these story structures vary with the ultimate decision outcome.

Conclusion

Although legal scholars and practitioners frequently decry the lack of research on jury decision making, psychologists have paid considerable attention to the study of juror and jury behaviour. In recent years, improved research methodologies and replications have enhanced the ecological validity of findings. Theoretical development within the context of the broader cognitive and social psychological literature has also made an important contribution to our understanding of juror behaviour. While jurors are susceptible to many forms of bias and error, research indicates that there is much the legal system could do to aid the decision-making process and lighten the heavy cognitive load faced by jurors in the unfamiliar and complicated surroundings of the courtroom.

FURTHER READING

For a useful overview of research on jury decision making, see the article by D. Devine, L. D. Clayton, B. B. Dunford, R. Seying and J. Pryce (2001) Jury decision making: 45 years of empirical research on deliberating groups, *Psychology, Public Policy, and Law*, 7: 622–727. The article by P. Darbyshire, A. Maughan and A. Stewart (2002) What can the English legal system learn from jury research published up to 2001? available at www.kingston.ac.uk/~ku00596/elsres01.pdf (accessed 30 November 2009) explores the usefulness of jury research from a legal perspective. To learn more about international jury systems from a psychological perspective, see M. F. Kaplan and A. M. Martin (2006) *Understanding World Jury Systems Through Social Psychological Research* (New York: Psychology Press). Finally, R. Hastie (1983) Social inference, *Annual Review of Psychology*, 34: 511–42, and R. Hastie (ed.) (1993) *Inside the Juror* (New York: Cambridge University Press) provide important and useful reference points for interested readers.

REFERENCES

Auld, Lord Justice (2001) *A Review of the Criminal Courts of England and Wales*. Available online: www.criminal-courts-review.org.uk (accessed 25 October 2007).

Bartol, C. R. and Bartol, A. M. (1994) *Psychology and Law: Research and Application*, pp. 173–215. Pacific Grove, CA: Brooks/Cole Publishing Company.

Baum, A., Fisher, J. D. and Singer, J. E. (1985) *Social Psychology*. New York: Random House.

Berry, D. S., Hansen, J. S., Landrypester, J. and Meier, J. A. (1994) Vocal determinants of 1st impressions of young children. *Journal of Nonverbal Behavior*, 18: 187–97.

Bornstein, B. H. (1999) The ecological validity of jury simulations: is the jury still out? *Law and Human Behavior*, 23: 75–91.

Brewer, N. and Wells, G. L. (2006) The confidence-accuracy relationship in eyewitness identification: effects of lineup instructions, foil similarity and target-absent base rates. *Journal of Experimental Psychology: Applied*, 12: 11–30.

Casper, J. D. and Benedict, K. M. (1993) The influence of case outcome information and attitudes on juror decision making in search and seizures. In R. Hastie (ed.) *Inside the Juror*, pp. 65–82. New York: Cambridge University Press.

Costantini, E. and King, J. (1980) The partial juror: correlates and causes of prejudgment. *Law and Society Review*, 15: 9–40.

Cutler, B. L., Penrod, S. D. and Dexter, H. R. (1990) Juror sensitivity to eyewitness identification evidence. *Law and Human Behavior*, 14: 185–91.

Department for Constitutional Affairs (2005) *Jury Research and Impropriety* [CP 04/05]. www.dca.gov.uk/consult/juryresearch/juryresearch_cp0405.htm (accessed 25 October 2007).

Diamond, S. S. (1997) Illuminations and shadows from jury simulations. *Law and Human Behavior*, 27: 561–71.

Diamond, S. S., Vidmar, N., Rose, M., Ellis, L. and Murphy, B. (2003) Inside the jury room: evaluating juror discussions during trial. *Judicature*, 87: 54–8.

Duff, P. (1999) The Scottish criminal jury: a very peculiar institution. *Law and Contemporary Problems*, 62: 173–201.

Ellsworth, P. (1989) Are twelve heads better than one? *Law and Contemporary Problems*, 52: 205–24.

ForsterLee, L., Kent, L. and Horowitz, I. (2005) The cognitive effects of jury aids on decision making in complex civil litigation. *Applied Cognitive Psychology*, 19: 1–18.

Greene, E., Chopra, S., Kovera, M., Penrod, S., Rose, V. G., Schuller, R. and Studebaker, C. (2002) Jurors and juries: a review of the field. In J. Ogloff (ed.), *Taking Psychology and Law into the Twenty-First Century*, pp. 225–84. New York: Kluwer/Plenum Press.

Hans, V. P. and Vidmar, N. (1986) *Judging the Jury*. New York: Plenum Press.

Honess, T. M., Charman, E. A. and Levi, M. (2003) Factual and affective/evaluative recall of pretrial publicity: their relative influence on juror reasoning and verdict in a simulated fraud trial. *Journal of Applied Social Psychology*, 33: 1404–16.

Hope, L., Greene, E., Memon, A., Gavisk, M. and Houston, K. (2008) The third verdict option: exploring the impact of the 'not proven' verdict on mock juror decision-making. *Law and Human Behavior*, 32: 241–52.

Hope, L., Memon, A. and McGeorge, P. (2004) Understanding pretrial publicity: Predecisional distortion of evidence by mock jurors. *Journal of Experimental Psychology: Applied*, 10: 111–19.

Jackson, J. D., Quinn, K. and O'Malley, T. (1999) The jury system in contemporary Ireland: in the shadow of a troubled past. *Law and Contemporary Problems*, 62: 203–32.

Kahneman, D. and Tversky, A. (1979) Prospect theory: an analysis of decision under risk. *Econometrica*, 47: 263–91.

Kalven, H. and Zeisel, H. (1966) *The American Jury*. Boston: Little, Brown.

Kerr, N. L. and MacCoun, R. J. (1985) Role expectations in social dilemmas – sex-roles and task motivation in groups. *Journal of Personality and Social Psychology*, 49: 1547–56.

Kovera, M. B. and McAuliff, B. D. (2000) The effects of peer review and evidence quality on judge evaluations of psychological science: are judges effective gatekeepers? *Journal of Applied Psychology*, 85: 574–86.

Lloyd-Bostock S. (2000) The effects on juries of hearing about the defendant's previous criminal record: a simulation study. *Criminal Law Review*, 734–55.

MacCoun, R. J. and Kerr, N. L. (1988) Asymmetric influence in mock jury deliberation: jurors' bias for leniency. *Journal of Personality and Social Psychology*, 54: 21–33.

Mazzella, R. and Feingold, A. (1994) The effects of physical attractiveness, race, socioeconomic-status, and gender of defendants and victims on judgments of mock jurors – a meta-analysis. *Journal of Applied Social Psychology*, 24: 1315–44.

Mitchell, T. L., Haw, R. M., Pfeifer, J. E. and Meissner, C. A. (2005) Racial bias in juror decision-making: a meta-analytic review of defendant treatment. *Law and Human Behavior*, 29: 621–37.

Moran, G. and Cutler, B. L. (1991) The prejudicial impact of pretrial publicity. *Journal of Applied Social Psychology*, 21: 345–67.

Ogloff, J. R. P. and Vidmar, N. (1994) The impact of pretrial publicity on jurors – a study to compare the relative effects of television and print media in a child sex abuse case. *Law and Human Behavior*, 18: 507–25.

Payne, J. W. (1982) Contingent decision behavior. *Psychological Bulletin*, 80: 439–53.

Pennington, N. and Hastie, R. (1986) Evidence evaluation in complex decision-making. *Journal of Personality and Social Psychology*, 51: 242–58.

(1992) Explaining the evidence: tests of the story model for juror decision making. *Journal of Personality and Social Psychology*, 62: 189–206.

Perez, D. A., Hosch, H. M., Ponder, B. and Chanez, G. J. (1993) Ethnicity of defendants and jurors as influences on jury decisions. *Journal of Applied Social Psychology*, 23: 1249–62.

Pritchard, M. E. and Keenan, J. M. (1999) Memory monitoring in mock jurors. *Journal of Experimental Psychology: Applied*, 5: 152–68.

Reifman, A., Gusick, S. M. and Ellsworth, P. C. (1992) Real jurors' understanding of the law in real cases. *Law and Human Behavior*, 16: 539–54.

Ruva, C., McEvoy, C. and Bryant, J. (2007) Effects of pretrial publicity and jury deliberation on juror bias and source memory errors. *Applied Cognitive Psychology*, 21: 45–67.

Smith, V. L. and Kassin, S. M. (1993) Effects of the dynamite charge on the deliberations of deadlocked mock juries. *Law and Human Behavior*, 17: 625–44.

Snyder, M., Tank, E. D. and Berscheid, E. (1977) Social perception and interpersonal behaviour: on the self-fulfilling nature of social stereotypes. *Journal of Personality and Social Psychology*, 35: 656–66.

Steblay, N. M., Besirevic, J., Fulero, S. M. and Jimenez-Lorente, B. (1999) The effects of pretrial publicity on juror verdicts: a meta-analytic review. *Law and Human Behavior*, 23: 219–35.

SunWolf (in press) Telling multicultural tales in applied contexts: unexpected journeys into healing and interconnectedness in hospitals and courtrooms. In P. J. Cooper, C. Calloway-Thomas and J. R. Hoel (eds.), *Intercultural Communication: Tellers of Tales*. Boston: Allyn & Bacon.

Temple, L. E. and Loewen, K. R. (1993) Perceptions of power – 1st impressions of a woman wearing a jacket. *Perceptual and Motor Skills*, 76: 339–48.

6.9 Malingering: models and methods

Nathan D. Gillard and Richard Rogers

Definition

The generally accepted definition of malingering, as set forth by the American Psychiatric Association (APA 2000, p. 739), is 'the intentional production of false or grossly exaggerated physical or psychological symptoms, motivated by external incentives such as avoiding military duty, avoiding work, obtaining financial compensation, evading criminal prosecution, or obtaining drugs'. As observed by Rogers (2008), the criterion is clearly the fabrication or *gross* exaggeration of multiple symptoms. Embellishments and minor exaggerations in the frequency or intensity of symptoms do not qualify. The fabrication of an isolated symptom also does not qualify.

Malingering is not a diagnosis, but is a V-code classification that should be considered in the differential diagnosis of other disorders. As such, malingering does not have formal inclusion criteria as found with DSM-IV (APA 2000) or ICD-10 (World Health Organization 1993) disorders. Clinicians sometimes commit the catastrophic error of equating DSM-IV screening items (i.e. a forensic setting, antisocial personality disorder, uncooperativeness, and results inconsistent with objective findings) with formal diagnostic criteria. The catastrophic nature of this error is clearly demonstrated in criminal forensic settings, where most referrals would be misclassified as malingerers. Rogers (1990) demonstrated empirically that applying these indicators to criminal defendants resulted in the erroneous classification of genuine patients as malingerers in four out of every five cases.

Fabricated or exaggerated symptomatology cannot be equated with malingering. Differential diagnoses must also include genuine disorders, such as Factitious Disorders, Conversion Disorders and other Somatoform Disorders that are also characterized by the *intentional* production of symptoms. In addition, traumatized patients may have extreme clinical presentations that appear grossly exaggerated but may reflect traumatogenic effects on their experience of symptoms and associated features (Rogers and Payne 2006).

An important distinction must be made between malingering and feigning. The term 'feigning' is typically used with psychological measures to designate the deliberate fabrication or gross exaggeration of psychological or physical symptoms. Feigning makes no assumptions about motivations or goals. Because no tests or measures can actually assess malingering per se (i.e. varying internal and external motivations), feigning is the preferred term for classifications based on test findings.

Prevalence of malingering and construct drift

The prevalence of malingering is an important issue, which went virtually uninvestigated for many years. Rogers and his colleagues (for a summary, see Rogers 1997) conducted two large-scale surveys of forensic experts, which indicated a prevalence rate of 15 to 17% in forensic settings and 5 to 7% in general clinical settings. Of particular note was the marked variability in prevalence rates within each category of settings. Recent research using the SIRS as a gold standard suggests slightly higher rates (e.g. 21.0%; Vitacco et al. 2007) in forensic and correctional settings. However, this higher prevalence may be due to the broadened category of feigning rather than malingering.

Construct drift, the broadening and distorting of a clinical construct, is very apparent with malingering, especially in the domain of malingered cognitive impairment. Rather than focusing on malingering, various quasi-constructs are used instead, such as 'over-reporting', 'any symptom exaggeration', 'incomplete effort', or 'suboptimal effort'. Such terms lack any precision and lead to inflated prevalence rates. For example, Mittenberg et al. (2002) conducted a widely cited survey of neuropsychologists who reported 'prevalence' rates exceeding 30%. This higher percentage is easily explainable by construct drift. Rather than estimating the prevalence of malingering per se, Mittenberg et al. chose a broader and poorly defined category that encompassed probable feigning and any symptom exaggeration.

A large-scale study of 332 consecutive referrals by Bianchini, Curtis and Greve (2006) nicely illustrates the challenges in establishing prevalence rates for malingered cognitive deficits. Using a broadened category of probable and definite malingering, they found markedly discrepant prevalence rates depending on whether the referral was state worker's compensation (16.3%) or federally based personal injury (26.7%). One limitation of the study was its inclusion of questionable detection strategies in its determination of malingered cognitive deficits; this point will be revisited in the discussion of detection strategies. Because of its broadened category and inclusion of questionable strategies, Bianchini *et al.*'s well-designed study is likely to be an overestimate of the prevalence of malingering.

Assessment of malingering

Practitioners are sometimes tempted to rely on the clinical judgement or brief screens for the evaluation of malingering. These practices are substandard, given the critical importance of malingering determinations. On the one hand, successful malingerers burden the mental health services, thwart treatment efforts and often receive unwarranted benefits (e.g. compensation or avoidance of punishment). They often burden the courts and society in general. On the other hand, genuine patients misclassified as malingerers pay a terrible price for clinician error. They are often deprived of treatment services, stigmatized, and subjected to unwarranted criminal and civil penalties.

A novice yet common error in malingering determinations is the either/or fallacy. As noted by Rogers and Bender (2003), the majority of malingerers also experience genuine disorders. Therefore, the determination of a genuine disorder does not rule out malingering. By the same token, the presence of malingering does not preclude legitimate disorders with genuine impairment.

Rogers (2008) described the major advancements in malingering evaluations, which progressed from idiosyncratic case methods and scale differences on psychological measures to systematic detection strategies. Detection strategies represent the most important development in the assessment of response styles, including determinations of malingering. Detection strategies are conceptually grounded and empirically validated methods for distinguishing a response style, such as malingering, from other response styles. They vary from scale differences in two important ways: (1) the operationalized strategy has proven effective across different measures and scales, and (2) the strategy is also effective at individual classifications of malingering rather than being simply content with group differences. The next section explores specific detection strategies.

Detection strategies

Detection strategies for feigning are designed for specific domains. For feigned mental disorders, would-be malingerers must decide on which symptoms to

Table 6.9.1 Strategies for the detection of malingering

Domain/Strategies	Description
Feigned mental disorders	
Rare symptoms	Measures reported symptoms and associated features that occur very infrequently in genuine patients. Malingerers are often unaware of this fact. This strategy represents one of the most robust strategies in the detection of feigning.
Symptom combinations	Many genuine symptoms may often occur alone, but rarely in combination with other genuine symptoms. This strategy measures unusual symptom pairs. A malingerer would need to have a sophisticated understanding of psychopathology to foil this strategy.
Indiscriminant symptom endorsement	Makes use of the fact that many malingerers endorse a high number of symptoms covering a wide array of psychopathology based on the 'more is better' stratagem. Malingerers are detected by their lack of selectivity.
Feigned cognitive impairment	
Floor effect	Uses very simple items that are answered correctly by even severely impaired patients. Malingerers can often be detected because they fail an unusual number of these simple items.
Symptom validity testing	Determines if the individual has exhibited an improbable failure rate based on statistical probability. Even a very disabled patient should not score below chance levels. This strategy is usually effective with only extreme attempts at malingering.
Performance curve	Based on the fact that genuine patients have fewer successes as the item difficulty increases. Malingerers often do not consider item difficulty; they are often detected because they do not demonstrate this diminishing pattern of successes.

portray and how to present these symptoms convincingly (Rogers and Bender 2003). For instance, what are believable responses to auditory hallucinations? For feigned cognitive impairment, the task of malingering is very different. Would-be malingerers must decide how to simulate a convincing effort while failing to perform on relevant cognitive tasks. Table 6.9.1 provides a sampling of detection strategies for feigned mental disorders and feigned cognitive impairment. For a thorough background in detection strategies, practitioners and researchers are referred to Rogers (2008) *Clinical Assessment of Malingering and Deception*.

Determinations of malingering typically rely on multiple methods and multiple detection strategies. The first step is selecting the domain of malingering (mental disorders vs cognitive impairment) to be evaluated. Otherwise, practitioners may be using detection strategies that are incompatible with the domain in question. As occurred in the Bianchini *et al.* study, a common error involves the use of the rare-symptoms strategy for malingered cognitive problems. Once the domain is selected, the next step is the choice of well-validated measures that preferably include multiple detection strategies.

In the domain of feigned mental disorders, practitioners should consider a combination of interview-based and self-report measures. As a general guideline, three measures are recommended:

1 Structured Interview of Reported Symptoms (SIRS: Rogers, Bagby and Dickens 1992) is a fully structured interview that assesses eight primary detection strategies with impressive reliability and validity. Individual classifications based on decision rules are effective at minimizing false-positives (i.e. genuine patients erroneously categorized as feigners).

2 Minnesota Multiphasic Personality Inventory (MMPI-2: Butcher *et al.* 1989) is a multiscale inventory with several highly effective detection strategies; however, only extreme scale elevations are effective for individual classifications (see Rogers *et al.* 2003). The Fp scale is particularly effective as a rare-symptom strategy.

3 Personality Assessment Inventory (PAI: Morey 2007) can be considered an alternative to the MMPI-2. The PAI has highly effective detection strategies, although they are most useful for ruling-out feigning (i.e. determining which cases are likely to be genuine).

Most practitioners use the SIRS and one multiscale inventory (MMPI-2 or PAI) in their determinations of feigning. The third and final step is the classification of malingering. Extensive clinical interviews and the use of collateral sources are likely to be necessary for concluding whether the motivation serves the sick-role (factitious disorders) or some external objective (malingering).

In the domain of feigned cognitive impairment, practitioners must also decide on the measures and detection strategies. The selection process is much more complex, given the number of specialized and embedded measures (see Rogers 2008). One recommendation is the inclusion of (1) sophisticated detection strategies, such as the performance curve (see above), and (2) symptom validity testing, the strategy that yields definitive results (i.e. significantly below-chance performance) in a minority of cases. For the third and final step (i.e. the classification of malingering), practitioners are cautioned not to make facile extrapolations. Simply because the client is involved in a disability case does not mean that he or she is motivated by unwarranted financial gain. Among other issues to be considered, the client's disabled status must be evaluated in the context of factitious disorders.

Conclusion

In closing, determinations of malingering are complex multifaceted assessments that involve (1) the selection of a malingering domain, (2) administration of well-validated measures to evaluate detection strategies systematically and (3) careful investigation of different motivations. Practitioners should resist the temptation to rely on clinical intuition and care should be used to ensure that construct drift does not occur. Given the consequential nature of malingering decisions, practitioners bear a special responsibility to ensure that these determinations meet the highest professional standards.

FURTHER READING

The book *Clinical Assessment of Malingering and Deception* (3rd edn), edited by Rogers (2008), contains chapters by leading practitioners and researchers. It provides detailed information on all topics covered in this chapter as well as other issues pertaining to malingering and its assessment. In addition, a special issue of *Behavioral Science and the Law* on malingering (Felthous 2006) contains informative articles pertaining to current scientific contributions to the assessment of malingering.

REFERENCES

American Psychiatric Association (APA) (2000) *Diagnostic and Statistical Manual of Mental Disorders*, 4th edn, text revision (DSM-IV-TR). Washington, DC: American Psychiatric Association.

Bianchini, K. J., Curtis, K. L. and Greve, K. W. (2006) Compensation and malingering in traumatic brain injury: a dose-response relationship? *Clinical Neuropsychologist*, 20: 831–47.

Butcher, J. N., Williams, C. L., Graham, J. R., Tellegen, A. and Kaemmer, B. (1989) *MMPI-2: Manual for Administration and Scoring*. Minneapolis: University of Minnesota Press.

Felthous, A. R. (ed.) (2006) *Behavioral Sciences and the Law*, 24.

Mittenburg, W., Patton, C., Canyock, E. M. and Condit, D. C. (2002) Base rates of malingering and symptom exaggeration. *Journal of Clinical and Experimental Neuropsychology*, 24: 1094–02.

Morey, L. C. (2007) *An Interpretive Guide to the Personality Assessment Inventory (PAI)*. Tampa, FL: Psychological Assessment Resources.

Rogers, R. (1990) Models of feigned mental illness. *Professional Psychology: Research and Practice*, 21: 182–8.

(ed.) (1997) *Clinical Assessment of Malingering and Deception*, 2nd edn. New York: Guilford Press.

(ed.). (2008) *Clinical Assessment of Malingering and Deception*, 3rd edn. New York: Guilford Press.

Rogers, R., Bagby, R. M. and Dickens, S. E. (1992) *Structured Interview of Reported Symptoms (SIRS) and Professional Manual*. Odessa, FL: Psychological Assessment Resources.

Rogers, R. and Bender, S. D. (2003) Evaluation of malingering and deception. In A. M. Goldstein (ed.), *Handbook of Psychology: Forensic Psychology*, vol. 11, pp. 109–29. Hoboken, NJ: Wiley.

Rogers, R. and Payne, J. W. (2006) Damages and rewards: assessment of malingered disorders in compensation cases. *Behavioral Sciences and the Law*, 24: 645–58.

Rogers, R., Sewell, K. W., Martin, M. A. and Vitacco, M. J. (2003) Detection of feigned mental disorders: a meta-analysis of the MMPI-2 and malingering. *Assessment*, 10: 160–77.

Vitacco, M. J., Rogers, R., Gabel, J. and Munizza, J. (2007) An evaluation of malingering screens with competency to stand trial patients: a known-groups comparison. *Law and Human Behavior*, 31: 249–60.

World Health Organization (1993) *The ICD-10 Classification of Mental and Behavioral Disorders: Diagnostic Criteria for Research*. Geneva: World Health Organization.

6.10 Munchausen by proxy

Catherine C. Ayoub

See also chapter 2.1 Child victims of sexual abuse, chapter 2.14 Parenting capacity and conduct, chapter 6.9 Malingering, chapter 6.15 Victimology.

Origins and definitions

In 1977, Roy Meadow, a British paediatrician, coined the term Munchausen by proxy (MBP) to describe illness-producing behaviour in a child that is exaggerated, fabricated or induced by a parent. Meadow adapted the term used by Dr Asher in 1951 for adult Munchausen syndrome to describe use of the child as a proxy. Munchausen syndrome and Munchausen by proxy were coined after the infamous eighteenth-century Baron Karl Friedrich Freiherr von Munchausen, a military mercenary who told fantastic stories of his exploits.

Experts focus on the child's victimization as well as on the parent's psychiatric disorder; the literature includes perspectives from paediatrics, psychology, social work, psychiatry, education, law and ethics. Many authors expand the discussion to include not only the interaction between the parent and the child, but also the relationships between the mother and the various healthcare providers. Munchausen by proxy is also characterized as a disorder of family and marital dysfunction, all aimed at perpetuating the child's abuse. The disorder has been widely recognized as a legitimate and quite dangerous form of child abuse in most juvenile and family courts around the USA (Kinscherff and Ayoub 2000).

Munchausen by proxy is both a paediatric and a psychiatric disorder that belongs to a group of maladies called 'disorders of deception' (Ayoub 2006). This form of victimization involves the intentional production or feigning of physical or psychological signs or symptoms in another person who is under the individual's care. Specifically, it is the exaggeration, fabrication and/or inducement of an illness, a series of symptoms or a condition in another person, most often a child. The interaction between parent and child leads to abuse of the child by a mentally ill parent/mother perpetrator. The component of the MBP disorder related to the child's victimization is a form of child abuse called *abuse by paediatric illness or condition falsification* (Ayoub *et al.* 2002). This term was coined by a multidisciplinary taskforce with the goal of providing clear and representative multidisciplinary definitions.

The second component of the disorder refers to the perpetrator's behaviours and motivations; the psychiatric diagnosis for the perpetrator is called *factitious disorder by proxy*. Factitious disorder is described in the *Diagnostic and Statistical Manual of Mental Disorders* (American Psychiatric Association 1994) as intentional behaviour in order to assume the sick role by a proxy (most often a child). Experts have described the behaviour of the perpetrator as 'imposturing' (Schreier and Libow 1993).

Prevalence

The prevalence of MBP is difficult to assess, given the convincing deception that is central to the disorder. One careful, conservative British study estimated that the combined annual incidence of MBP in the form of non-accidental poisoning and non-accidental suffocation was at least 2.8/100,000 in children aged less than a year (Kinscherff and Ayoub 2000). However, given these estimates and the wide spectrum of paediatric conditions that have been known to be feigned, the problem is far from rare. Furthermore, experts now agree that many MBP cases are likely to go undetected because of the covert nature of their presentation and the striking ability of the perpetrators to fool those around them.

Paediatric illness falsification

Children are victimized by a variety of means, limited only by the imagination of the perpetrator. They are subjected to unnecessary hospitalizations, tests, procedures and treatment for physical, psychological or educational (ADHD and learning problems) conditions. Although the majority of victims of MBP are less than 6 years of age, there are cases of serious MBP with older children and adolescents. Boys and girls are equally affected.

The number of illness presentations of the children is quite varied, again limited only by the imagination of the perpetrator. Many children have multiple symptoms and multiple organ systems involved in their physical or emotional illnesses, and many are repeatedly subjected to serious and potentially life-threatening situations in the name of their illness and its treatment. Mary Sheridan in her meta-analysis of 451 cases of MBP found that 6% of the child victims and 25% of their siblings died (Sheridan 2003). The children most likely to die are those presenting with suffocatory abuse or apnea.

Many children had multiple symptoms in at least three and as many as seven different organ systems. A typical medical history often includes many visits to physicians, often to a variety of specialists, and a number of major and minor surgical procedures to relieve symptoms that are exaggerated, fabricated and/or induced (Ayoub 2006).

The child's medical care occurs in a context of a caregiving relationship and perpetration occurs in forms difficult for a child to detect or understand as victimization, such as misadministration of medication or misrepresentation of medical history. A failure to detect or appreciate the perpetration supports continuing trauma in the child victim; these children often learn that the way to get attention is to be sick. Their mother's deception also makes it easier for them to misapprehend, deny or compartmentalize their victimization.

In the face of persistent fabrication, children risk potentially serious physical injury due to exposure to unnecessary procedures and almost universally suffer serious and long-lasting psychological trauma. The psychological impact of victimization through Munchausen by proxy is significant and chronic. Basic problems with attachment, relationship building, and social interaction as well as attention and concentration are common in these children. The presence of oppositional disorders in these victims is significant, as are patterns of reality distortion, poor self-esteem, lying, and attachment difficulties with adults and peers. Although these children can present as socially skilled and superficially well adjusted, they often struggle with the basic relationships.

Libow (1995) found that adult survivors frequently reported that abuse continued not only throughout childhood, but extended well into adulthood. Schreier and Libow (1993) note that often children are at serious physical risk even while in state custody, since some parents may attempt to increase their harm to the child or attempt abduction as they are confronted.

Factitious disorder by proxy

The second component of MBP is the psychiatric condition of the perpetrator that helps explain the motivation, wilfulness and clinical presentation of the caregiver. Caregivers intentionally falsify history, signs and/or symptoms in their children to meet their own self-serving psychological needs to maintain the caregiving role. According to the current literature, between 77% and 98% of perpetrators are women; the vast majority of them are the children's biological mothers (Sheridan 2003). It remains a fact that factitious disorder by proxy is for the most part a disorder of women and a misuse of 'mothering'. The psychological motivation for their actions is to receive status-enhancing praise and acknowledgement for their self-sacrificing, competent care of their children. Although mothers are typically extremely convincing in their roles, discovery often illustrates the deliberate and planful nature of the deception. Many mothers work to subtly manipulate people that they perceive as powerful – usually physicians, but also their child's nurses, therapists, educators or consultants. A number of mothers use their children's illness to seek notoriety for themselves by requesting special support and by contacting celebrities to publicize their children's plight. In each case the child is used as the object or vehicle to direct admiring attention to the mother's parenting. The child's needs as perceived by the mother often change as her status-seeking behaviour varies. Mothers are very knowledgeable about their children's conditions; some engage in formal careers as healthcare or educational professionals, while others are more informally schooled in their children's illness history and care. Many mothers show some evidence of fabricating, exaggerating or inducing symptoms of their own. Some women have lengthy histories of physical complaints of their own, many of which are not evident until evaluators ask about maternal medical histories. Perpetrators can show anger and resentment when faced with challenges about their child's symptoms.

Fathers and families

In two-parent families, husbands most often strongly support their wives in spite of clear evidence and legal findings of MBP abuse of their children. These fathers serve as messengers between their wives and their children and frequently encourage their children to support their mothers. Typically fathers are involved only sporadically in the life of their children and essentially enable the abuse through passivity or collusion. These fathers are most likely to continue to support their perpetrator wives after detection, making them unreliable protectors of the child.

A second group of fathers are estranged from their children at the time of the abuse. They may be separated or divorced; their wives often claim no knowledge of the father's whereabouts. With some limited detective work, these fathers are usually locatable; they often have been actively paying child support. Such fathers have been systematically shut out of their children's lives and are often willing to become re-involved with their children if they have some support and protection from their wives. Extended family, particularly paternal relatives, are also often estranged and may be positive resources for care of the children.

Fathers who are able to separate both physically and emotionally from mothers, restructure the family system to acknowledge MBP, and actively work to protect the child, have been able to safely parent following a lengthy intervention period. Safe and secure parenting is contingent upon the father's ability to function as the primary caregiver, a role for which many MBP fathers are poorly equipped; as a result, an assessment of their parenting capacity is recommended. Relative placements tend to be stressed by the intense and often unrelenting pressure placed on relative custodians by the immediate family, especially by mothers and their advocates. Active attempts to increase contact with the child and to manipulate any approved contact often escalate and make such placements quite difficult.

Careful evaluation of fathers and other family members and relatives is strongly recommended before any contact with the child victims is permitted. MBP is a family system disorder in which extended maternal family also serves as enablers, strongly supporting the mother's continued impostering.

The medical system and case management

Safety is the first and primary management issue for the MBP child victim. This frequently means removal of the child from the home with no or, at most, closely supervised contact with the perpetrating parent. Placement with another family member may be appropriate only if the relative appreciates the meaning and seriousness of the MBP diagnosis. A number of authors have proposed MBP protocols for hospitals, healthcare facilities, schools and psychiatric facilities that include:

- prompt case consultation with relevant medical specialties and a consultant knowledgeable about MBP;
- prompt notification and consultation with hospital legal staff familiar with the protocol and state child protection and criminal procedure law;
- provisions for ensuring the safety of the child, including: (1) intensive monitoring or temporary suspension of parent–child contact pending

more definitive diagnosis and/or the involvement of child protection authorities; (2) a procedure by which a preemptive court order barring removal of the child by parents might be secured prior to informing parents of the allegations of MBP; or (3) a protocol permitted under state law by which a physician might place a 'hold' upon discharge pending notification of the court;

- statements of conditions under which covert staff or electronic surveillance would be initiated as a routine element of the protocol, as well as specification of who has the authority to initiate covert staff or electronic surveillance;
- description of how the mandated reporting requirement will be accomplished, including designation of a specific person to make the mandated report and the content of the report to be made to state child protection authorities;
- indication of the steps to be followed in the event that a parent attempts to remove a child against medical advice, including the role to be played by hospital security;
- provision for designation of a single source of information to whom the family or others with an interest in the case can turn for reliable information regarding the situation and the condition of the child;
- designation of persons responsible for assessing the reactions of hospital staff, including the need for staff meetings to resolve differences regarding case management or involvement of child protection authorities.

Optimally, the MBP protocol structures a clinical management team that has access to professional consultation regarding clinical care, child protection, documentation and legal case management. Hospital child protection and/or psychiatric consultation liaison teams should be specifically trained about MBP and promptly contacted when medical or psychiatric units raise concerns about a case.

Implementing an MBP hospital protocol not only reduces the likelihood that individuals or units will make legal errors in managing suspected cases, but it also provides documentation of parental informed consent, execution of mandated legal duties, and evidence of a process of thoughtful 'professional judgement' that is the best defence in the event of formal complaints against professional licensees or a malpractice lawsuit. Use of a protocol reduces the number of false allegations and makes it more likely that genuine MBP cases are identified, and that the level of clinical risk to the child is accurately assessed.

The appropriate child protective action in MBP cases is separation of the mother and child. When children are removed from their parents' custody, hospital protocols should assure that unmonitored contact does not occur. Typically upon removal, children embrace wellness. Although a number of child victims have legitimate disorders, the severity or frequency of symptoms is reduced with separation.

Forensic assessment of Munchausen by proxy

An evaluation to address issues of parenting capacity and the best interests of the child in the light of allegations of exaggeration, fabrication and/or inducement of illness in a child by a parent is a complex process. Evaluation is strongly recommended in order to inform and expedite decision making by the court. Focus of the assessment is on the interactional patterns between the caregiver(s) and each child, with attention to:

- the child's illness experience and functioning (the child as alleged victim of child abuse by condition or illness falsification); and
- the parent's psychological functioning with attention to differentiating factitious disorder by proxy (factitious disorder NOS in the DSM-IV) and other possible psychological aetiologies of the parent's behaviour, attitudes and beliefs towards the child (Ayoub et al. 2002).

  The process of evaluation typically includes the following:
- Comprehensive record review and contacts with collaterals is a central component of any evaluation in which Munchausen by proxy is raised as an issue. Collateral contacts include both professional and lay persons, including other family members who might be able to shed light on the current situation.
- The emotional and physical functioning of each parent or primary caregiver, both in the past and in the present, is explored through a series of clinical interviews and through psychological testing. In a number of cases maternal grandparents are also interviewed either initially or as follow-up. Fathers and their family members, if they are in a position to have contact with the child, should also be evaluated, as should any other relative with interests in having contact with the child.
- A review of the child's past and present physical and emotional functioning, including but not limited to information about past and current daily routines, symptoms and behaviours, is obtained through observations, record review and interviews with past and current caregivers.

Although such an evaluation is extensive, the complexity of the MBP situation usually requires such comprehensiveness in order for juvenile and family courts to proceed with findings and dispositional issues that focus on the child's best interests. Such an evaluation, ordered by the court, provides the evaluators with the neutrality as well as the court's authority to work with all parties and to request the court's support in gaining access to individuals and records. (For more details about forensic assessment, see Sanders and Bursch 2002.)

Placement and visitation issues

Visitation should be considered very carefully in cases of alleged MBP as the child's victimization is typically significant and chronic. Victimization is likely to continue to occur with few exceptions even in the light of treatment. Children have been revictimized by their mothers even during highly structured and well-supervised visits. In addition to the physical danger, visitation can offer enormous potential for psychological harm. Child victims of MBP tend to have long-term and serious sequelae to their abuse that are impacted by contact with their perpetrators. A number of experts recommend that there be no direct or indirect contact between child and mother (or other family members who might serve as a proxy for the mother) until a forensic evaluation is complete, a treatment plan for the family is in place, and the mother has made significant progress. If visitation is to be instituted, it should always be professionally supervised. In cases where there is considerable danger of physical or emotional distress to the child, visits should be discontinued. Reduction or discontinuation of visits is strongly recommended when, over time, mothers are unable to acknowledge perpetration, unless special circumstances warrant visitation in order to meet the child's best interests.

Any potential caregiver who persists in denying the child's abuse by the parent perpetrator when confronted with a finding by the court can justifiably be denied contact with, or placement of, the child. Termination of parental rights with fathers as well as mothers is often recommended.

Continued juvenile court oversight is a central requirement for the success of any treatment process. The fragmentation of treatment goals is an ever present danger in the absence of a communication mechanism and requirement for providers. A court-based integrated treatment team is most effective when organized around the consultation and coordination of a court-appointed MBP expert and the oversight of the court.

Mental health treatment for the child typically includes developing safety and social skills, reducing self-blame, embracing wellness/releasing illness script, improving attachment relationships and reducing oppositionality, developing autonomy, reducing dissociation and compartmentalization of thinking and feeling, maintaining appropriate boundaries, understanding and managing family conflicts and loyalties, and reframing positive peer relationships. By early adolescence, most of the children were encouraged to consider and rework their understanding of MBP victimization. Young teens who are unable to work through their victimization have more difficulty negotiating adolescence than those who are able to reorganize their experiences in such a way as to reduce their sense of blame and confusion. Children who received little or no treatment directed at their victimization are more likely to struggle with acting out and oppositionality as well as depression and self-harm issues.

Conclusion

In summary, Munchausen by proxy is a disorder that includes the significant and repeated abuse of a child, most often by the child's mother, who exaggerates, fabricates, and/or induces illness in the child. The physical danger to the child is considerable and the psychological consequences to the child based on the violation of trust by the parent are tremendously powerful and enduring. Because perpetrators are so skilled at portraying 'good and caring mothers' they are often convincing, even if the underlying evidence of abuse is evident.

FURTHER READING

For more details about forensic assessment, see Sanders and Bursch (2002). For additional definitions, see Ayoub *et al.* (2002).

REFERENCES

American Psychiatric Association (1994). *Diagnostic and Statistical Manual of Mental Disorders*, 4th edn (DSM-IV). Washington, DC: American Psychiatric Association.

Ayoub, C. (2006) Munchausen by proxy. In T. G. Plante (ed.), *Mental Disorders for the New Millennium*, vol. 3: *Biology and Function*, pp. 173–93. Westport, CT: Praeger Press,

Ayoub, C., Alexander, R., Beck, D., Bursch, B., Feldman, K., Libow, J. *et al.* (2002) Position paper: definitional issues in Munchausen by proxy. *Child Maltreatment*, 7: 105–12.

Kinscherff, R. and Ayoub, C. (2000) Legal issues in Munchausen by proxy. In R. Reece (ed.), *The Treatment of Child Abuse*, pp. 242–70. Baltimore, MD: Johns Hopkins University Press.

Libow, J. (1995) Munchausen by proxy syndrome victims in adulthood: a first look. *Child Abuse and Neglect*, 19: 1131–42.

Sanders, M. and Bursch, B. (2002) Forensic assessment of illness falsification, Munchausen by proxy, and factitious disorder, NOS. *Child Maltreatment*, 7: 112–24.

Schreier, H. A. and Libow, J. A. (1993) *Hurting for Love: Munchausen by Proxy Syndrome*. New York: Guilford Press.

Sheridan, M. (2003) The deceit continues: an updated literature review of Munchausen syndrome by proxy. *Child Abuse and Neglect*, 27: 431–51.

6.11 Occupational culture

Jennifer M. Brown

Definition

The concept of culture was originally developed and employed in anthropological analyses, e.g. the classic work by Malinowski on the Trobriand Islands published in 1915. Sociologists adopted this concept to examine values, beliefs and patterns of behaviour. Occupational and organizational psychologists further adapted culture to investigate organizations to discover the basis of their effectiveness and responsivity to change. Millward (2005, p. 257) notes there are many competing definitions, most of which include elements that reflect the following: shared values, (taken for granted) assumptions, beliefs, attitudes and expectations that serve to unite a community or organization and shape behaviour and which are often expressed through rituals, myths, stories and symbols. Millward distinguishes between organizational culture and climate. The former tends to be rooted in history and held collectively and is resistant to change, whereas the latter is more subjective and affective and malleable.

Within the criminal justice system, the police occupational culture has received the most research attention. Paoline (2003, p. 200) suggests that this is often cast as the accepted practices and underlying values and attitudes that construct and transmit the norms of what it is to be a police officer and how to do policing. Two aspects of policing are identified that contribute to its distinctive culture: hazards associated with the work and use of coercive force. Robert Reiner (1986) says [male] police 'cop' culture has developed as a patterned set of understandings which help police to cope with and adjust to the pressures and tensions which confront them. His characterization includes: sense of mission, pessimism, solidarity, suspicion, action, conservatism, pragmatism, cynicism and machismo.

'Canteen' culture (Waddington 1999) often refers pejoratively to the racist, sexist and homophobic attitudes said to be pervasive amongst police officers. However there is a growing critique of the generalizations that follow from the uncritical and universal application of such attributes (see e.g. Chan 2007).

Measurement

Millward (2005) describes psychometric approaches which attempt to quantify core attributes of culture as experienced by the workforce. These include Hofstede's measure of culture and values, and Kilman's culture gap survey. They tend to be used diagnostically; they examine ideologies and behavioural styles, and are often linked to performance. As with questionnaire approaches, both measures have strengths and weaknesses in that they offer standard questions allowing comparisons to be made either over time or across organizations, but are limited by the prescribed questions and may not reveal subtler, individualistic aspects of an organization's culture.

Taxonomic approaches attempt to categorize organizations or styles within organizations according to some dimension such as structural features or prevailing work ethos, e.g. Maddock and Parkin (1993) whose classification includes the smart macho manager as being one who is driven, competitive and dismissive of employees less keen to work excessive hours or unable to cope with tight time schedules. These may be useful descriptions but often have limited explanatory power.

The cultural web (Johnson and Scholes 2002) offers a framework onto which maps a particular organization's culture and which is usually elicited qualitatively from groups within the workforce (see figure 6.11.1 and table 6.11.1).

These aspects are explored with different groups within organizations and a composite cultural web is constructed, often as a means to examine features that may be inhibiting the organization.

Mixed-method approaches are also used to construct an account of an occupational culture; for example, Hobbs *et al.* (2002) used interviews, observational fieldwork, a method of covert ethnography, and together with documentary evidence characterized the occupational culture of night-club bouncers. Fielding (1988) studied police recruits through initial training, probation and first year of service by means of essays written by recruits, tape-recorded interviews, observations and documentary analyses to examine the process whereby young probationer police officers become socialized into the police culture.

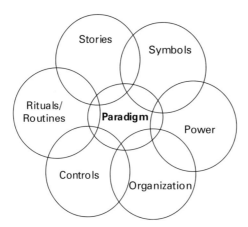

Figure 6.11.1 Cultural web (after Johnson and Scholes)
Reprinted from G. Johnson and K. Scholes, *Exploring Corporate Strategy: Text and Cases*, 6th edition (2002), with permission from Pearson Education Limited

Applications

The organization's culture has been used to provide explanations for a number of processes such as the experience of work-related stress, resistance to change, misconduct and discrimination.

Stress

Chan (2007) suggests there is a small but emergent area of research examining the relationship between stress and occupational culture in the police. She argues (2007, p. 115) that police culture can shape and be shaped by stressors, and concludes: 'whilst occupational and organizational stressors affect aspects of police culture these stressors are interpreted by officers through the assumptions and shared values embedded in the police culture'.

Brown, Cooper and Kirkcaldy (1999) demonstrated that organizational changes within the police were sources of stress as officers, promoted on the basis of their operational knowledge and skills, found themselves having to manage cultural change within the organization. Similar evidence is available for the prison service (Bryans 2000) and probation service (Audit Commission 1991).

Table 6.11.1 Aspects of the cultural web

Dimension	Details
Paradigms–taken for granted assumptions	• Real core of the culture • Difficult to identify and explain • often linked to raison d'être of the organisation
Stories	• What core beliefs do the stories reflect • How pervasive are the stories • Do stories relate to strengths and weaknesses • Success or failure • Conformity or mavericks • Who are the heroes and villains • What norms do the mavericks deviate from
Controls	• What is closely monitored/controlled • Is emphasis on reward or punishment • Are controls related to history or current strategies • Are there many/few controls
Routines and rituals	• Which routines are emphasised • Which would look odd if changed • What behaviour do routines encourage • What core beliefs do they reflect • What do training programmes emphasise • How easy are rituals/routines to change
Organizational structures	• How mechanistic/organic are the structures • How flat/hierarchical are the structures • How formal/informal are the structures • Do structures encourage collaboration/competition • What types of power structures do they support
Power structures	• What are the core beliefs of the leadership • How strongly held are those beliefs (idealistic/pragmatic) • How is power distributed • Where are the main blockages to change
Symbols	• What language and jargon are used • How internal or accessible are they • What aspects of strategy are highlighted in publicity • What status symbols are there • Are there particular symbols which denote the organization

Resistance to change

The enduring features of an organization's culture have been implicated in resistance to change (Millward 2005). She outlines how change represents a threat to the individual's self-esteem and is often experienced as a loss of familiar ways of doing things. Typically, organizations undertake some diagnostics that define the current culture and identify ways of unfreezing old attitudes and practices. Culture is considered key to an organization's performance and success, and evaluations attempt to discover performance-enhancing and inhibiting attributes; it is often driven as a top-down process. As such, individuals within the organization feel disempowered and reluctant to adopt new styles of working. On the other hand, Ocasio (1993) argues that organizations seek to protect themselves when they perceive themselves to be under threat, such as that resulting from an operational failure. Under these conditions, the dominant beliefs within the organization will dominate and senior decision makers retreat to core values and cultural assumptions, and increase their reliance on policies and practices embedded within the organization's existing cultural systems.

Misconduct

Police culture in particular has become axiomatic with a critique of police behaviour, and is often used pejoratively (Prenzler 1997). The analysis usually takes the form of a gap between formal and informal practices, and implies disregard or disdain for rules, procedures and due process (Fielding 1995). The notion of socialization into the occupational culture is suggested, in part, to contribute to the deterioration of a trainee's ideals and values and an increased tolerance of rule bending or breaking. Occupational culture has also been invoked as an explanation for the use of excessive force by police and featured in analyses undertaken by inquiries into police conduct, such as the Warren Commission in the USA and Fitzgerald and Wood inquiries in Australia. Prenzler (1997) and Waddington (1999) are more critical and suggest that the behaviour of the police is more a pragmatic reality of their street experiences rather than a process of acculturation into disregarding of rules.

Discrimination

Resistance to women and ethnic minority representation within the criminal justice system has been 'zealous' (Martin and Jurik 1996, p. 2), 'and they have not been completely incorporated into the station house, courtroom or prison'. They argue that the obstacles obstructing integration relate to the prevailing masculine (white) identity of criminal justice professionals and informal work cultures. They go on to propose (p. 123) that legal culture is a 'quintessentially' man's world from which women (and ethnic minorities) are excluded from cultural resources by virtue of their difference.

Thus the argument is made that the occupational identity as defined by the organization's culture is threatened by the presence of 'otherness', i.e. individuals who are different by virtue of their gender, race and sexual orientation. Discriminatory practices by the majority seek to maintain the status quo.

FURTHER READING

Megan O'Neill, Monique Marks and Anne-Marie Singh's edited collection (2007) *Police Occupational Culture: New Debates and Directions* (Oxford: Elsevier) is a lively collection of recent and critical thinking on police occupation culture, whilst P. A. J. Waddington's (1999) essay can be seen as the case for the defence. Susan Martin and Nancy Jurik's (1999) book looks particularly at women's experiences in criminal justice professions and extends the discussion from policing to prison working environments; it also offers a theoretical dimension underpinning explanations for the particular masculine character of criminal justice occupations. The cultural web described by Johnson and Scholes (2002) is a particularly interesting way to explore occupational cultural issues.

REFERENCES

Audit Commission (1991) *A Change of Direction: Managing Changes in Local Probation Areas.* London: Stationery Office.

Brown, J. M., and Cooper, C. L. and Kirkcaldy, B. (1999) Stressor exposure and methods of coping among senior police managers at a time of organisational change. *International Journal of Police Science and Management*, 2: 217–28.

Bryans, S. (2000) The managerialism of prison – efficiency without a purpose? *Criminal Justice Matters*, 40: 7–8.

Chan, J. (2007) Police stress and occupational culture. In M. O'Neill, M. Marks and A. Singh (eds.), *Police Occupational Culture: New Debates and Directions*, pp. 129–52. Amsterdam: Elsevier.

Fielding, N. (1988) *Joining Forces: Police Training, Socialisation and Occupational Competence.* London: Routledge.

(1995) Cop canteen culture. In T. Newburn and E. Stanko (eds.), *Just the Boys Doing Business? Men, Masculinities and Crime*, pp. 46–63. London: Routledge.

Hobbs, D., Hadfield, P., Lister, S. and Winlow, S. (2002) 'Door lore': the art and economics of intimidation. *British Journal of Criminology*, 42: 352–70.

Johnson, G. and Scholes, K. (2002) *Exploring Corporate Strategy*, 6th edn. London: Pearson Education.

Maddock, S. and Parkin, D. (1993) Gender cultures: women's choices and strategies at work. *Women in Management Review*, 8: 3–10.

Martin, S. E. and Jurik, N. (1996) *Doing Justice, Doing Gender: Women in Law and Criminal Justice Occupations*. Thousand Oaks, CA: Sage.

Millward, L. (2005) *Understanding Occupational and Organisational Psychology*. London: Sage.

Ocasio, W. (1993) The structuring of organisational attention and the enactment of economic adversity: a reconciliation of theories of failure-induced change and threat rigidity. Working Paper 3577–93. Cambridge, MA: MIT Sloan School of Management.

Paoline, E. A. (2003) Taking stock: towards a richer understanding of police culture. *Journal of Criminal Justice*, 31: 199–214.

Prenzler, T. (1997) Is there a police culture? *Australian Journal of Public Administration*, 56: 47–56.

Reiner, R. (1986) *Politics of the Police*. Brighton: Wheatsheaf.

Waddington, P. A. J. (1999) Police (canteen) culture: an appreciation. *British Journal of Criminology*, 39: 287–309.

6.12 Occupational stress in police and prison staff

Paula Brough and Amanda Biggs

Definitions and theoretical framework

Stress researchers generally agree that the term *stressor* refers to the environmental stimulus or demand (antecedent) that causes stress. *Strain* refers to the individual's physical and/or psychological response to the stressor (consequences of stress). The term *stress* usually defines the overall process and implies a relationship between stressors, strain and coping, rather than any specific component of the process itself (O'Driscoll and Brough 2003). Current conceptualizations of occupational stress are influenced by the work of Richard Lazarus and colleagues, who defined stress as a *transactional* process between the individual and his/her environment (Lazarus and Folkman 1984). The transactional stress theory emphasizes that it is the individual's *perceptions* (or appraisals) of a situation that define the core process of a strain reaction. Thus, 'stress arises when the demands of a particular encounter are appraised by the individual as about to tax or exceed the resources available, thereby threatening well-being' (Cooper, Dewe and O'Driscoll 2001, p. 12). The transactional perspective focuses upon a dynamic interplay between an individual's perceptions, resources, wellbeing and the stressful demand.

The Job–Demands–Control (JDC) model (Karasek 1979), a well-regarded theory of occupational stress, posits that while both *job demands* and *job control* independently predict occupational stress, their effects are heightened when considered in combination, or through an interaction between demands and control (Mansell and Brough 2005). An important revision of the JDC model acknowledges the beneficial effects of perceived *job support* in relieving occupational stress, and thus identifies a third construct, the Job–Demands–Control–Support (JDCS) model (Johnson and Hall 1988). The enhanced JDCS model proposes that occupational stress occurs most often for work characterized by *high job demands, low job control,* and *low support* (see van der

Doef and Maes 1999 for a review). Specific elements of job demands, control and support commonly associated with occupational stress for police and prison workers are discussed below.

Antecedents of occupational stress

Antecedents of occupational stress can be classified into eight broad categories:

1. *Work relationships*: interactions with people at work
2. *The job itself*: nature of the work performed
3. *Overload*: workload and time pressures
4. *Control*: lack of control over work processes and timing
5. *Job security*: uncertainty about the future of one's job
6. *Resources and communication*: inadequate or malfunctioning techno-logical and other resources; ineffective communication processes in the workplace
7. *Work–life balance*: interference or conflict between the job and both family and personal life
8. *Pay and benefits*: perceived or objective inadequacy of remuneration and other important tangible benefits (Johnson *et al.* 2005).

Both police and prison work commonly include all these antecedents of occupational stress, and are commonly identified as being 'high-stress' occu-pations. The type of work demands that contribute to high levels of strain in police and prison workers, and affect their health and functioning, include encountering major incidents involving death, violence, personal attacks and harassment, typically over years of exposure. These 'operational stressors' are formally recognized by the police and prison services, and are anticipated and prepared for as much as is possible via training, and managed afterwards through the provision of debriefing, support and counselling programmes (see below for details).

As well as traumatic operational stressors, the impact of frequently occur-ring minor *job stressors* or hassles also contributes to the experience of occupational stress for police and prison workers (and other workers within high-stress occupations). Thus job stressors such as interpersonal conflict with colleagues and supervisors; inadequate pay, training or career advance-ment; missing or faulty equipment; and bureaucracy, paperwork and red tape have all been associated with stress outcomes. Brough (2004), for example, demonstrated that items such as excessive paperwork and inadequate job recognition predicted psychological strain in New Zealand police, fire and ambulance officers to almost the same extent as traumatic operational stressors. Similarly, the Correctional Officer Job Demands measure, which assesses common occupational stressors such as lack of decision making, understaffing, formal complaints and management support, was associated with adverse psychological health and low job satisfaction for Australian correctional officers (Brough and Williams 2007). Liberman *et al.* (2002) also demonstrated the associations between occupational stressors and psychological strain in US police officers and concluded: 'Routine occupational stress exposure appears to be a significant risk factor for psychological distress among police officers, and a surprisingly strong predictor of post-traumatic stress symptoms' (p. 421). For a review of why research and practice are still having a limited effect on the reduction of 'chronic sources of organizationally induced stress' for police and prison workers see also Stinchcomb (2004, p. 259).

Finally, the experience of occupational stress can be exacerbated by organizational systems that are overly bureaucratic, punitive of staff and strictly managed, and during restructuring or organizational change. Police and prison services recognize the influence of occupational culture to varying extents, and have made attempts to 'soften' the culture by increasing the diversity of staff, expanding training and promotion programmes, and flattening the hierarchical structure by reducing some levels of management. Nevertheless, both police and prison work are still conducted within distinctive organizational cultures that directly influence both the antecedents and consequences of occupational stress (for a review see Chan 2007).

Consequences of occupational stress

The psychological impact of acute stressors (traumatic events) is well documented; so too are the prevention and intervention techniques employed to reduce adverse outcomes associated with acute stressors. The consequences of chronic occupational stress (daily hassles) in police and prison officers are also well established and span four categories of individual outcomes: physiological, psychological, social and behavioural. These outcomes are briefly discussed here.

Individual outcomes associated with acute stress

Vicarious or actual exposure to traumatic events at work is associated with ill health and post-traumatic stress disorder (PTSD) symptomatology, such as intrusive recollections of the event (Brown, Fielding and Grover 1999). Although pre-existing vulnerabilities do influence the development of PTSD, certain aspects of the organizational culture (e.g. the requirement to suppress emotional reactivity), and the manner in which the event is handled by the organization, may also contribute to its aetiology (Amaranto *et al.* 2003). Provisions are made by most police and prison services to support officers who experience traumatic events (e.g. debriefing and employee assistance programmes) to a greater extent than the support services provided for staff experiencing strain as a result of chronic stress (daily hassles).

Individual outcomes associated with chronic stress

Physiological processes enable the human body to cope with, and recover from, short periods of intense stressor exposure (e.g. exposure to critical incidents). Exposure to long-term *chronic* stressors, however, may prevent sufficient recovery time, and instead encourage the manifestation of psychological strain. The associations between psychological strain and physiological health outcomes, such as coronary heart disease, have been demonstrated (e.g. Bosma *et al.* 1998). Mortality data indicate that police officers experience elevated rates of mortality from malignant neoplasms, digestive diseases and arteriosclerotic heart disease (Violanti, Vena and Petralia 1998). Behavioural responses to acute traumas, chronic stress and cultural variables investigated within law enforcement populations include alcohol abuse, aggression and suicide ideation (Violanti 2004). On average, both police and prison officers experience higher rates of suicide compared to the general population. Associations between these findings and characteristics of police and prison work have been identified, such as access to firearms, social isolation and reliance on maladaptive coping strategies (Stack and Tsoudis 1997; Violanti, Vena and Marshall 1996).

Both cognitive and emotional chronic stress reactions have been extensively investigated within law enforcement occupations, including job satisfaction (Lambert, Hogan and Barton 2002) and psychological strain (Brough 2002). Due to the high level of 'emotion work' required, both police and prison officers are constantly exposed to risk factors associated with burnout, such as emotional suppression, cynicism and suspicion towards others (Amaranto *et al.* 2003). Theoretical discussions consider psychological burnout to be a syndrome of emotional exhaustion, depersonalization and reduced personal accomplishment (Maslach, Jackson and Leiter 1996) that is associated with an imbalance between demands and resources (Demerouti *et al.* 2001) and emotional incongruence (Zapf 2002; see also O'Driscoll, Brough and Kalliath (2009) for a more detailed discussion).

Research within police and prison occupations has linked psychological burnout with worker characteristics (e.g. gender), aspects of the job role (e.g. inmate contact), lack of support and role conflict (Whitehead and Lindquist 1986), organizational stress and job dissatisfaction (Manzoni and Manuel 2006), lack of reciprocity between effort expended and rewards attained (Euwema, Kop and Bakker 2004) and increased job hassles (Kohan and Mazmanian 2003). Psychological burnout has also been associated with favourable attitudes towards the use of violence in conflict situations (Burke and Mikkelsen 2005). The consequences of strain do not affect the individual in isolation but also extend to the families of police and prison workers, colleagues and the organization itself (see, for example, Hogan *et al.* 2006; Roberts and Levenson 2001).

Moderators of occupational stress

A number of variables moderate the occupational stress process and this explains why different individuals perceive the same stressor differently, and why the same individual can experience a stressor in different ways at different points in time. Common moderators of occupational stress include perceived levels of support and job control, gender, age and personality characteristics such as neuroticism. Research examining occupational stress perceived by male and female police officers has an extensive history and has resulted in practices that aim to better equalize the work environment for all officers. Berg *et al.* (2005), for example, demonstrated that female Norwegian police officers experienced fewer traumatic incidents on average at work compared to their male colleagues, but still reported the highest ratings on all aspects of occupational stress. Brough and Frame (2004) demonstrated that the experience of sexual harassment by female New Zealand police officers influenced perceptions of job satisfaction and turnover intentions, but that adequate levels of supervisor support improved these outcomes. Brown (2007) provided a comprehensive review of gender issues in policing, and suggested that British police services remain replete in masculine characteristics.

An issue of growing concern in contemporary society is the health, performance and retention of the increasing number of ageing workers. Gershon, Lin and Li (2002), for example, demonstrated that police officers aged 50 years or older are at increased risk of occupational stress compared to their younger colleagues. The associations between age, gender and occupational stress can be offset to some degree by the provision of adequate workplace support and the use of adaptive coping behaviours. These findings have particular importance for the training of supervisors and managers. The occupational stress literature repeatedly demonstrates that providing adequate levels of support, especially supervisor support, together with the use of adaptive coping behaviours, can significantly reduce occupational stress (see, for example, Anshel, Roberston and Caputi 2000; Brough and Frame 2004; Stephens and Long 2000). The provision of workplaces that actively aim to reduce occupational stress, either directly via the reduction of known stressors or indirectly via the effective management of stress symptoms, is also typically identified as an employer's obligation under occupational health and safety legislation.

Interventions for managing occupational stress

Two useful systems for categorizing occupational stress interventions are those developed by Murphy (1988) and DeFrank and Cooper (1987). Murphy's tripartite model describes *primary prevention* (elimination of stressors from the work environment to prevent stress), *secondary prevention* (detecting stress and providing stress management skills), and *tertiary prevention* (rehabilitation of stressed workers). DeFrank and Cooper's classification system focuses on the target of the interventions, and comprises interventions directed at *individuals* (equipping individuals with skills to manage stress, e.g. relaxation), the *individual/organizational interface* (interactions between individuals and their workplace, e.g. decision-making authority) and *organizations* (the organizational context, e.g. job design). Police and prison services most commonly use individual-level secondary and tertiary interventions – usually peer-support officers or trained professionals – to manage stress within the service, although failing to modify the stressful work environment tends to be ineffective at producing long-term outcomes (Bond 2004). Two of the most common stress management strategies are Critical Incident Stress Management (CISM) and Employee Assistance Programmes (EAPs).

Critical incidence stress management

CISM (e.g. Mitchell 1983) usually involves providing short-term support services to either prepare staff who are at risk of exposure to traumatic events, minimize the impact of the trauma, or promote recovery after exposure to a critical incident (Fix 2001). Critical incident stress debriefing (CISD) is a component of CISM based on the premise that retelling the event will reduce stress and the likelihood of PTSD (Bledsoe 2003). The actual value of critical incident debriefing is difficult to demonstrate empirically. In a comparison with two control groups, Carlier, Voerman and Gersons (2000) demonstrated that individual critical incident debriefing produced *no* significant differences for PTSD symptomatology within their sample of Dutch police officers. Researchers such as Matthews (1998) and Hobbs *et al.* (1996) have also demonstrated that critical incident stress debriefing alone produced no significant health improvements or actually *increased* stress-related symptoms for individuals experiencing PTSD. It is important to note that the value of critical incident stress debriefing is currently being debated, with more positive results, for example, being identified for *group* debriefing sessions rather than individual debriefing sessions (e.g. Leonard and Alison 1999). For a review of critical incident stress debriefing in law enforcement, see Malcolm *et al.* (2005).

Employee Assistance Programmes (EAPs)

EAPs are provided by most law enforcement agencies to manage occupational stress symptoms. Typically, these programmes provide referral services; offer brief counselling for a variety of personal, family and work-related issues; and are based on the premise that the provision of such services will promote organizational productivity. A pertinent criticism of these interventions is their tendency to adopt an individualistic approach and thus ignore organizational stressors (Kirk and Brown 2003). These programmes are often met with some resistance by employees in law enforcement occupations, commonly expressed as scepticism of the level of confidentiality and the actual value of these EAPs (e.g. Waters and Ussery 2007). Furthermore, there remains a pervasive stigma that officers should naturally be able to deal with stress and handle the pressure of the job. Failure to do so is therefore often regarded as an indication of personal unsuitability for the job. Research with both police and prison workers has, for example, described the social stigma associated with admissions of failing to cope with stress and the difficulties experienced by officers attempting to integrate back into the workforce after experiencing stress (Brough, Biggs and Pickering 2007).

Conclusion

Working in the police or prison services is typically a rewarding but demanding role. The dual demands of regular exposure to operational (often traumatic) stressors, and a highly regulated bureaucratic organizational system, define police and prison work as 'high-stress' occupations. Individual susceptibility to occupational stress experiences can be heightened by both organizational and individual factors, such as culture, support, gender and age. Similarly, improving individual levels of 'stress resilience' can also be approached from both an individual and an organizational level, with the most effective results emerging from a joint approach. Thus, organizational efforts to prevent or manage occupational stress necessitate effective training, education, resources and supports. Individual efforts entail stress recognition, active coping strategies and help-seeking. The nature of police and prison work ensures that occupational stress is a permanent job risk; designing and implementing practices to reduce this risk most effectively should be the focus of both service managers and researchers.

FURTHER READING

For a comprehensive review of occupational stress research including issues such as leadership, harassment, workplace safety, work–family conflict, ageing workers and organizational interventions, see J. Barling, K. Kelloway and M. Frone (eds.) (2005) *Handbook of Work Stress* (Thousand Oaks, CA: Sage). For a review of the main occupational stress issues still pertinent to police workers such as minority groups, culture, operational stressors and organizational stressors, see J. Brown and E. Campbell (1994) *Stress and Policing: Sources and Strategies* (New York: Wiley). Finally, for a more recent overview of occupational stress research within policing, prison work and similar service professions, which includes discussions of stress theories, measurement issues and occupational interventions, see M. Dollard, A. Winefield and H. Winefield (eds.) (2003) *Occupational Stress in the Service Professions* (London: Taylor & Francis).

REFERENCES

Amaranto, E., Steinberg, J., Castellano, C. and Mitchell, R. (2003) Police stress interventions. *Brief Treatment and Crisis Interventions*, 3: 47–53.
Anshel, M. H., Robertson, M. and Caputi, P. (2000) A conceptual model and implications for coping with stressful events in police work. *Criminal Justice and Behavior*, 27(3): 375–400.
Berg, A. M., Hem, E., Lau, B., Haseth, K. and Ekeberg, O. (2005) Stress in the Norwegian police service. *Occupational Medicine*, 55: 113–20.
Bledsoe, B. E. (2003) Critical incident stress management (CISM): benefit or risk for emergency services. *Prehospital Emergency Care*, 7: 272–9.

Bond, F. W. (2004) Getting the balance right: the need for a comprehensive approach to occupational health. *Work and Stress*, 18: 146–8.

Bosma, H., Peter, R., Siegrist, J. and Marmot, M. (1998) Two alternative job stress models and the risk of coronary heart disease. *American Journal of Public Health*, 88(1): 68–74.

Brough, P. (2002) Female police officers' work experiences, job satisfaction and psychological well-being. *Psychology of Women Section Review*, 4: 3–15.

(2004) Comparing the influence of traumatic and organizational stressors upon the psychological health of police, fire and ambulance officers. *International Journal of Stress Management*, 11: 227–44.

Brough, P., Biggs, A. and Pickering, S. (2007) Predictors of occupational stress: work cover claims by correctional officers. *Journal of Occupational Health and Safety – Australia and New Zealand*, 23: 43–52.

Brough, P. and Frame, R. (2004) Predicting police job satisfaction, work well-being and turn-over intentions: the role of social support and police organisational variables. *New Zealand Journal of Psychology*, 33: 8–16.

Brough, P. and Williams, J. (2007) Managing occupational stress in a high-risk industry: measuring the job demands of correctional officers. *Criminal Justice and Behavior*, 34: 555–67.

Brown, J. (2007) From cult of masculinity to smart macho: gender perspectives on police occupational culture. In M. O'Neill, M. Marks and A. M. Singh (eds.), *Police Occupational Culture: New Debates and Discussion*, pp. 189–210. Oxford: Elsevier.

Brown, J., Fielding, J. and Grover, J. (1999) Distinguishing traumatic, vicarious and routine operational stressor exposure and attendant adverse consequences in a sample of police officers. *Work and Stress*, 13: 312–25.

Burke, R. J. and Mikkelsen, A. (2005) Burnout, job stress and attitudes towards the use of force by Norwegian police officers. *Policing: An International Journal of Police Strategies and Management*, 28: 269–78.

Carlier, I. V. E., Voerman, A. E. and Gersons, B. P. R. (2000) The influence of occupational debriefing on post-traumatic stress symptomatology in traumatized police officers. *British Journal of Medical Psychology*, 73: 87–98.

Chan, J. (2007) Police stress and occupational culture. In M. O'Neill, M. Marks and A. M. Singh (eds.), *Police Occupational Culture: New Debates and Discussion*, pp. 113–35. Oxford: Elsevier.

Cooper, C. L., Dewe, P. J. and O'Driscoll, M. P. (2001) *Organizational Stress: A Review and Critique of Theory, Research and Applications*. Thousand Oaks, CA: Sage.

DeFrank, R. and Cooper, C. (1987) Worksite stress management interventions: their effectiveness and conceptualisation. *Journal of Managerial Psychology*, 2: 4–10.

Demerouti, E., Bakker, A. B., Nachreiner, F. and Schaufeli, W. B. (2001) The job demands–resources model of burnout. *Journal of Applied Psychology*, 86: 499–512.

Euwema, M. C., Kop, N. and Bakker, A. B. (2004) The behaviour of police officers in conflict situations: how burnout and reduced dominance contribute to better outcomes. *Work and Stress*, 18: 23–38.

Fix, C. (2001) Management program: responding to the needs of correctional staff in Pennsylvania. *Corrections Today*, 63: 94–6.

Gershon, R., Lin, S. and Li, X. (2002) Work stress in aging police officers. *Journal of Occupational and Environmental Medicine*, 44: 160–7.

Hobbs, M., Mayou, R., Harrison, B. and Worlock, P. (1996) A randomised controlled trial of psychological debriefing for victims of road traffic accidents. *British Medical Journal*, 313: 1438–9.

Hogan, N. L., Lambert, E. G., Jenkins, M. and Wambold, S. (2006) The impact of occupational stressors on correctional staff organizational commitment: a preliminary study. *Journal of Contemporary Criminal Justice*, 22: 44–62.

Johnson, J. and Hall, E. (1988) Job strain, work place social support and cardiovascular disease: a cross-sectional study of a random sample of the working population. *American Journal of Public Health*, 78: 1336–42.

Johnson, S., Cooper, C. L., Cartwright, S., Donald, I., Taylor, P. and Millet, C. (2005) The experience of work-related stress across occupations. *Journal of Managerial Psychology*, 20: 178–87.

Karasek, R. (1979) Job demands, job decision latitude, and mental strain: implications for job redesign. *Administrative Science Quarterly*, 24: 285–308.

Kirk, A. K. and Brown, D. F. (2003) Employee assistance programs: a review of the management of stress and wellbeing through workplace counselling and consulting. *Australian Psychologist*, 38: 138–43.

Kohan, A. and Mazmanian, D. (2003) Police work, burnout, and pro-organizational behavior: a consideration of daily work experiences. *Criminal Justice and Behavior*, 30: 559–83.

Lambert, E. G., Hogan, N. L. and Barton, S. M. (2002) Satisfied correctional staff: a review of the literature on the correlates of correctional staff job satisfaction. *Criminal Justice and Behavior*, 29: 115–43.

Lazarus, R. and Folkman, S. (1984) *Stress, Appraisal and Coping*. New York: Springer.

Leonard, R. and Alison, L. (1999) Critical incident stress debriefing and its effects on coping strategies and anger in a sample of Australian police officers involved in shooting incidents. *Work and Stress*, 13: 144–61.

Liberman, A. M., Best, S. R., Metzler, T. J., Fagan, J. A., Weiss, D. S. and Marmar, C. R. (2002) Routine occupational stress and psychological distress in police. *Policing: An International Journal of Police Strategies and Management*, 25: 421–41.

Malcolm, A. S., Seaton, J., Perara, A., Sheehan, D. C. and Van Hasselt, V. B. (2005) Critical incident stress debriefing and law enforcement: an evaluative review. *Brief Treatment and Crisis Interventions*, 5: 261–78.

Mansell, A. and Brough, P. (2005) A comprehensive test of the job demands–control interaction: comparing two measures of job characteristics. *Australian Journal of Psychology*, 57: 103–14.

Manzoni, P. and Manuel, E. (2006) Violence between the police and the public: influences of work-related stress, job satisfaction, burnout, and situational factors. *Criminal Justice and Behavior*, 33: 613–45.

Maslach, C., Jackson, S. E. and Leiter, M. P. (1996) *Maslach Burnout Inventory*, 3rd edn. Palo Alto, CA: Consulting Psychology Press.

Matthews, L. R. (1998) Effect of staff debriefing on posttraumatic stress symptoms after assaults by community housing residents. *Psychiatric Services*, 49: 207–12.

Mitchell, J. T. (1983) When disaster strikes … the critical incident stress debriefing process. *Journal of Emergency Medical Services*, 8: 36–9.

Murphy, L. R. (1988) Workplace interventions for stress reduction and prevention. In C. Cooper and R. Payne (eds.), *Causes, Coping and Consequences of Stress at Work*, pp. 310–39. Chichester: Wiley.

O'Driscoll, M. and Brough, P. (2003) Job stress and burnout. In M. O'Driscoll, P. Taylor and T. Kalliath (eds.), *Organisational Psychology in Australia and New Zealand*, pp. 188–211. Melbourne: Oxford University Press.

O'Driscoll, M. P., Brough, P. and Kalliath, T. (2009) Stress and coping. In S. Cartwright and C. L. Cooper (eds.), *The Oxford Handbook of Organizational Well-Being*, pp. 236–66. Oxford: Oxford University Press.

Roberts, N. A. and Levenson, R. W. (2001) The remains of the workday: impact of job stress and exhaustion on marital interaction in police couples. *Journal of Marriage and Family*, 63(4): 1052–67.

Stack, S. J. and Tsoudis, O. (1997) Suicide risk among correctional officers: a logistic regression analysis. *Archives of Suicide Research*, 3: 183–6.

Stephens, G. and Long, N. (2000) Communication with police supervisors and peers as a buffer of work-related traumatic stress. *Journal of Organizational Behavior*, 21: 407–24.

Stinchcomb, J. (2004) Searching for stress in all the wrong places: combating chronic organizational stressors in policing. *Police Practice and Research*, 5: 259–77.

van der Doef, M. and Maes, S. (1999) The job demand–control(–support) model and psychological well-being: a review of 20 years of empirical research. *Work and Stress*, 13: 87–114.

Violanti, J. (2004) Predictors of police suicide ideation. *Suicide and Life-Threatening Behavior*, 34: 277–83.

Violanti, J., Vena, J. E. and Marshall, J. R. (1996) Suicide, homicides, and accidental death: a comparative risk assessment of police officers and municipal workers. *American Journal of Industrial Medicine*, 30: 99–104.

Violanti, J., Vena, J. E. and Petralia, S. (1998) Mortality of a police cohort: 1950–1990. *American Journal of Industrial Medicine*, 33: 366–73.

Waters, J. A. and Ussery, W. (2007). Police stress: history, contributing factors, symptoms, and interventions. *Policing: An International Journal of Police Strategies and Management*, 30: 169–88.

Whitehead, J. T. and Lindquist, C. A. (1986) Correctional officer job burnout: a path model. *Journal of Research in Crime and Delinquency*, 23: 23–42.

Zapf, D. (2002) Emotion work and psychological well-being – a review of the literature and some conceptual considerations. *Human Resource Management Review*, 12(2): 237–68.

6.13 Sexual harassment

Adrian Bowers and William O'Donohue

See also chapter 6.11 Occupational culture, 6.12 Occupational stress in police and prison staff.

Definition

Forensic determination of sexual harassment entails a contextual understanding of the scope of sexual harassment and a determination of whether events have occurred that fall within a particular legal or institution's definition of sexual harassment. A contextual conception of sexual harassment is necessary since the boundary conditions of whether the target behaviour is or is not sexual harassment changes based on legal definitions and psychological/behavioural definitions. For example, sexually explicit jokes told by males may be sexual harassment, but might not be if first told by the claimant. All of these definitional aspects are malleable given the particular context within which the target behaviour occurs (DeSouza et al. 2003). However, in general there seem to be core aspects of sexual harassment that are seen as necessary and sufficient if present to meet legal, psychological and behavioural definitions of sexual harassment in most Western societies (Gelfand et al. 1995; Paludi and Paludi 2003).

Core aspects of sexual harassment often include: (1) hostile environment or *quid pro quo*; (2) work setting; and (3) welcomeness. Hostile environment sexual harassment refers to a work environment that is sexualized in such a way that the general experience of working there is offensive to the accuser. For example, constant sexual jokes, leering, unwanted sexual comments, fondling, sexual pictures, etc. can all contribute to a hostile sexual environment. *Quid pro quo*, or Latin 'this for that', sexual harassment refers to a work situation where a person of power either explicitly or implicitly creates a situation for a co-worker where the co-worker must engage in or endure sexualized behaviours in order to retain their job status, progress their job status, or to prevent the loss of their job status. Gender harassment is inappropriate treatment regarding gender that may not be sexual (e.g. 'All women are dumb').

Work setting refers to sexual harassment being related to the disruption of the work environment and the disruption either occurs at work or is perpetrated by a co-worker outside work (e.g. at a holiday party). Sexual misbehaviour that is not related to work generally is not thought of as sexual harassment in the legal sense of the term. For example, a woman who experiences lewd sexual comments from a passer-by on her way to work may be experiencing sexual harassment in the psychological/behavioural dimension but is not experiencing sexual harassment by the legal definition (i.e. her employer is not responsible for the harassment and cannot be prosecuted).

Welcomeness refers to whether or not the target behaviours were welcomed by the accuser. Sexualized behaviour that was welcomed is generally not considered to be sexual harassment. However, welcomeness is often very difficult to determine since it is an internal psychological state. Further complicating the determination of welcomeness is that it is an internal psychological state that must be inferred retroactively often with little corroborating evidence. For example, the accuser may have appeared to welcome sexual advances but this appearance may have been feigned 'to get along'. Conversely, an accuser may initiate sexual behaviour at work and then claim that reciprocal sexual behaviour of like kind was not welcome – a case of false allegation of sexual harassment.

Psychological/behavioural dimensions of sexual harassment by the alleged perpetrator can include leering, sexual jokes, sexual comments, sexual propositioning, sexualized posters/pictures and numerous other behaviours. See Gruber's (1996) sexual harassment typology for a more thorough listing (Gruber and O'Donohue 1997; Gruber et al. 1996).

Psychological/behavioural responses to sexual harassment can be devastating for the accuser. Findings typically report a number of psychological responses consistent with trauma reactions such as depression, PTSD, anxiety, anger, somatic symptoms and other physical problems (Palmieri and Fitzgerald 2005). Unfortunately, although symptomatology of sexual harassment may be present, symptomatology is not pathomnemonic with the occurrence of sexual harassment. Symptoms could be due to sexual harassment or they could be due to either an intentional manipulation or unintentional misunderstanding of events (i.e. false allegations of sexual harassment), or due to other causes.

Determination of sexual harassment

The scope of sexual harassment is dependent upon the particular legal precedents and laws within a society and the cultural norms of the society (DeSouza *et al.* 2003). This contextual dependence makes the forensic

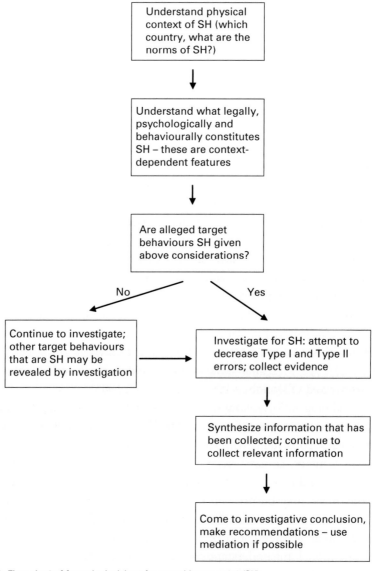

Figure 6.13.1 Flow chart of forensic decisions for sexual harassment (SH)

determination of sexual harassment especially difficult. The investigator of sexual harassment claims must have a good understanding of the boundary conditions of sexual harassment given the particular legal/cultural context within which the alleged events occurred. This understanding of contextually based boundary conditions will greatly help the investigator determine whether the alleged events may meet the necessary and sufficient legal/psychological/behavioural definitions of sexual harassment. The investigator's next task is to determine whether the alleged events actually occurred and whether the context of the events suggests sexual harassment or a false allegation of sexual harassment.

There is scarce literature related to the forensic determination of sexual harassment (Kovera 2004; Mazzeo *et al.* 2001; McQueen and O'Donohue 1997; Remick *et al.* 1990). However, a proper determination of whether or not sexual harassment took place is crucial. The investigator cannot assume that because a sexual harassment claim was made the sexual harassment took place. However, the investigator also cannot assume that the complaints are false and sensitivity must be paid to how the investigation is carried out to ensure that all parties involved are treated fairly and with respect.

In all forensic determinations of culpability the investigator hopes to achieve a result from the investigation that accurately portrays reality. For example, the investigation indicates that the harassment took place and the harassment did in fact take place. This correspondence view of forensics is a belief that through proper forensic methods the truth of what actually occurred or did not occur will be revealed to the investigator.

However, all forensic determinations have an error rate associated with them. It is hoped that this error rate is small but currently it is of unknown size. This error rate can be broken down into two parts, Type I and Type II errors. Type I errors, or *false positives*, are when an event is judged by investigators to have occurred when in reality the event did not occur. Type II errors, or *false negatives*, are when an event is judged by investigators to have not occurred when in reality the event did occur. Theoretically, both types of error are problematic because when made they paint an inaccurate corresponding view of reality. Practically, with regard to sexual harassment, determinations of both types of error are also problematic. Type II errors in sexual harassment investigations occur when investigators deem the sexual harassment to be unfounded or not to have occurred when actually the harassment took place. Type II errors harm the victim of sexual harassment because the harasser is not punished, the victim may not get the psychological and/or legal help that they need to deal with the harassment, the harassment may continue, and the victim may endure retaliation for his/her claim of sexual harassment. Further, great harm can be done to the company/organization since other members may see that legitimate sexual harassment claims are not handled correctly – further harassment may proliferate in the organization. However, Type I errors are also problematic and harmful in sexual harassment investigations. A Type I error results in harm for the alleged harasser since they in fact did not participate in sexual harassment. Further, great harm can be done to the company/organization since they may be financially responsible for sexual harassment that did not take place. Also, the organization's reputation may be damaged in such a way that good employees leave the organization and/or the organization is not able to attract good employees due to its tarnished reputation.

Reducing false positive and false negative errors in sexual harassment investigations centres on conducting a sound sexual harassment investigation. The complexities of investigating sexual harassment go beyond the scope of this chapter, but in general a sound sexual harassment investigation will (1) collect all relevant evidence; (2) synthesize all collected evidence; (3) attempt to come to a conclusion based on the evidence; (4) make appropriate recommendations for repairing damage to individuals and the organization (which may include appropriate forms of mediation) (Avina *et al.* 2004). In particular, reduction of false positive errors is a relatively new aspect to forensic determinations of sexual harassment.

However, there are similarities between false allegations of sexual harassment and other false allegation topics such as rape, child custody and other forms of false reports by alleged victims (O'Donohue and Bowers 2006). As to similarities involved in false allegations of sexual harassment, preliminary theorizing suggests that the following may be main pathways: (1) The alleged victim does not understand what sexual harassment is and is not. For example, an office worker may complain of sexual harassment because she is a women and a male supervisor is critiquing her job performance and is disappointed in aspects of it (i.e. this is not sexual harassment, it is a common workplace responsibility for a supervisor to critique a supervisee). (2) The alleged victim unintentionally distorts events and believes innocuous events to be sexual harassment. Various forms of personality disorders may exhibit this behaviour, including borderline personality disorder, histrionic personality disorder and various other forms of personality disorders (and Axis I conditions such as drug dependence) where perceptions of events are unintentionally distorted by the individual. (3) The alleged victim intentionally distorts events or creates events to appear to be sexual harassment. Again personality disorders are of primary concern to investigators, including such conditions as antisocial personality disorder and borderline personality disorder. See O'Donohue and Bowers (2006) for a further discussion of pathways to false allegations of sexual harassment. Given these personality dimensions that investigators should be wary of, it is also important to note that personality conditions themselves are not pathomnemonic with false allegations of sexual harassment.

Conclusions

Sexual harassment is complex. Its definition depends on evolving law and varies across jurisdictions. Some authors also have proposed psychological definitions, i.e. does an individual feel harassed? However, this kind of phenomenological definition also is complex as it may not be consistent with legal definitions and may be reflective of a problematic way of experiencing rather than point to an external problem. The causes of sexual harassment are unknown and this interferes not only with gaining basic understanding of sexual harassment but also with prevention programming. It is quite common for institutions to carry out some sort of sexual harassment programming, yet there is little outcome showing the efficacy of these efforts. More outcome research is needed. In addition, the error rates of sexual harassment investigations are unknown. While it is reasonable to believe that most sexual harassment claims are generally true, it is also reasonable to believe that some are false. Finally, more research is needed on treating the sexual harasser (Brunswig and O'Donohue 2002) and treating the victim.

FURTHER READING

Fitzgerald, L. F., Dragow, F., Hulin, C. L., Gelfand, J. J. and Magley, V. J. (1997) Antecedents and consequences of sexual harassment in organizations: a test of an integrated model. *Journal of Applied Psychology*, 82: 578–89.

Fitzgerald, L. F. and Swan, S. (1995) Why didn't she just report him? The psychological and legal inclinations of women's responses to sexual harassment. *Journal of Social Issues*, 51: 117–38.

O'Donohue, W. (ed.) (1997) *Sexual Harassment: Theory, Research, and Treatment.* Boston: Allyn & Bacon.

REFERENCES

Avina, C., Bowers, A. H., O'Donohue, W. T., O'Donohue, W. T. and Levensky, E. R. (2004) *Forensic Issues in Sexual Harassment.* New York: Elsevier Science.

Brunswig, K. and O'Donohue, W. T. (2002) *Relapse Prevention Therapy for Sexual Harassers.* New York: Sage.

DeSouza, E. R., Solberg, J., Paludi, M., and Paludi, C. A., Jr (2003) *Incidence and Dimensions of Sexual Harassment across Cultures.* Westport, CT: Praeger Publishers/Greenwood Publishing Group.

Gelfand, M. J., Fitzgerald, L. F. and Drasgow, F. (1995) The structure of sexual harassment: a confirmatory analysis across cultures and settings. *Journal of Vocational Behavior,* 47: 164.

Gruber, J. E. and O'Donohue, W. (1997) *An Epidemiology of Sexual Harassment: Evidence from North America and Europe.* Needham Heights, MA: Allyn & Bacon.

Gruber, J. E., Smith, M., Kauppinen-Toropainen, K. and Stockdale, M. S. (1996) *Sexual Harassment Types and Severity: Linking Research and Policy.* Thousand Oaks, CA: Sage.

Kovera, M. B. (2004) Psychology, law, and the workplace: an overview and introduction to the special issue. *Law and Human Behavior,* 28: 1.

Mazzeo, S. E., Bergman, M. E., Buchanan, N. T., Drasgow, F. and Fitzgerald, L. F. (2001) Situation-specific assessment of sexual harassment. *Journal of Vocational Behavior,* 59: 120.

McQueen, I. and O'Donohue, W. (1997) *Investigating Sexual Harassment Allegations: The Employer's Challenge.* Needham Heights, MA: Allyn & Bacon.

O'Donohue, W. and Bowers, A. H. (2006) Pathways to false allegations of sexual harassment. *Journal of Investigative Psychology and Offender Profiling,* 3: 47.

Palmieri, P. A. and Fitzgerald, L. F. (2005) Confirmatory factor analysis of posttraumatic stress symptoms in sexually harassed women. *Journal of Traumatic Stress,* 18: 657.

Paludi, M. and Paludi, C. A., Jr (2003) *Academic and Workplace Sexual Harassment: A Handbook of Cultural, Social Science, Management, and Legal Perspectives.* Westport, CT: Praeger Publishers/Greenwood Publishing Group.

Remick, H., Salisbury, J., Stringer, D., Ginorio, A. and Paludi, M. A. (1990) *Investigating Complaints of Sexual Harassment.* Albany, NY: State University of New York Press.

6.14 Undercover policing and psychological stress

Robert J. Edelmann

See also chapter 5.1 Assessing and reporting on work-related stress, chapter 6.12 Occupational stress in police and prison staff.

Definition

Covert policing, ranging from surveillance to undercover operations, is an investigative method widely used by law enforcement agencies around the world. The methods used in undercover operations are highly variable and include short-term operations, such as 'buy-bust', where the aim is to arrange a meeting with an unsuspecting target in order to purchase an illegal commodity from them, and long-term infiltrations which may last for months or even years (Band and Sheehan 1999). The extreme end-point in the latter instance is represented by 'Donnie Brasco', the alias of former FBI agent Joseph D. Pistone who worked undercover for six years infiltrating branches of the Mafia in New York City (Pistone and Woodley 1999; Pistone and Brandt 2007). Not only did this involve a significant financial and organizational commitment on the behalf of the FBI, it also required a substantial personal commitment on the part of Pistone, who still travels disguised and under assumed names more than twenty years after the infiltration ended in the successful conviction of over 100 Mafia members.

However, regardless of the type of undercover operation, there is a basic principle throughout: that is, the operative 'has to pretend to be someone else by falsifying his/her true identity and acting out a part designed to create trust and acceptance by the targeted persons' (Girodo, Deck and Morrison 2002 pp. 631–2). Because of the inevitable strain likely to be imposed by such work, many undercover programmes around the world either employ mental health professionals directly or draw on external, independent mental health practitioners to assist with selection, training, health and welfare monitoring and support and post-deployment rehabilitation (e.g. Macleod 1995).

Psychopathology and undercover policing

Psychological aspects of undercover policing remain an under-researched topic. Indeed, the psychological literature is as scant now as when Macleod (1995) examined this topic over a decade ago. This is perhaps surprising given that MacLeod observed 'that this practice of policing is dangerous and able to create psychological and psychiatric casualties is undeniable' (p. 243). However, reports of such 'casualties' within the literature are exceptionally limited. The only available research suggesting psychiatric disturbance in undercover operatives was conducted more than fifteen years ago (Girodo 1991a, 1991b, 1991c), and much has changed in the intervening years with regard to welfare support and the management of operations. In his initial study of 271 federal undercover agents, Girodo (1991a) reported a relationship between a poorly disciplined self-image and disinhibition, with misconduct and corruption. In a subsequent analysis Girodo (1991b) showed that introversion and neuroticism were associated with psychological distress and ill health. In a further study with undercover agents of another federal organization Girodo (1991c) found that 8% of preoperational, 26% of active operational and 17% of postoperational agents were at risk of psychological disturbance.

Other reports of psychiatric disturbance in undercover operatives are based on single cases or those referred to in popular publications. While this may be due to the fact that extreme cases tend to be aired in the media and only cases raising fundamental psychological issues are ever documented in the psychological literature (e.g. Alison and Canter 2005), it is also likely that careful and rigorous selection procedures, developed in the past decade and a half, mean that there are genuinely very few psychological casualties. Nevertheless, it is clear that the undercover role is psychological and emotionally demanding, with undercover programmes in most parts of the world providing independent mental health and welfare monitoring and support.

Stress of undercover policing

In evaluating the role requirements of an undercover officer the nature and degree of any potential stress will largely depend on the nature of the deployment. While all undercover operations inevitably involve potential role strain, the longer the operation the greater the likely extent of that strain. This relates both to identity maintenance as well as to the possible risk of growing sympathy towards the target. In addition, the longer the duration of any operation the greater the length of time the operative will be spending with the target(s) and away from family and friends. In summarizing possible stressors faced by undercover officers Farkas (1986), referring to declassified FBI data, details three main major sources :

(i) agent–supervisor relationship

(ii) role requirements

(iii) strain on family and social relationships.

Possible psychological reactions to such stress listed by Farkas include paranoia and hypervigilance, corruption of the officer's value system and increasing sympathy for the subject of the operation.

Similarly, Band and Sheehan (1999) refer to identification with suspects and loss of personal identity as well as personal issues as major sources of stress. These correspond with the three major sources of stress referred to by Farkas. Other stressors cited by Band and Sheehan are fear of discovery, technical concerns and the need for interagency cooperation, sufficient recovery time, good back-up and appropriate roles. In other words, as Miller (2006) notes in referring to MacLeod's (1995) study, many of the problems encountered in relation to undercover operations concern technical and strategic matters rather than psychological or health concerns. The major psychological issues concern ongoing fear of discovery, separation from family and friends, and perhaps of most significance, possible role strain.

Role strain

In any undercover operation, whatever its duration, the undercover operative is running with two parallel identities: a police/investigative identity and a false, somewhat 'shady' identity. As Miller (2006) notes, because operatives may be living a particular lifestyle for many months or even years, it would be impossible to adopt an undercover personal identity or persona completely different from one's true identity. The closer the false identity to the officer's real identity, the easier it is to maintain and the more comfortable the operative will be playing that part. The risk of course is that in very rare instances the undercover persona and the lifestyle that 'other' person leads may be more attractive than the operative's own personal lifestyle. The potential risk can increase when considered in the context of the 'friendships' the undercover operative forms in the course of a deployment.

'Undercover operations are all about forming and maintaining relation-ships' (Miller 2006, p. 206). In short, the essence of many undercover opera-tions, particularly those which are longer term and where intelligence gathering is crucial, involves befriending 'the enemy'. It is with such opera-tions that the officer may be at greatest risk of developing stress-related difficulties (Farkas 1986). Interestingly, in some countries operations with the sole objective of intelligence gathering are not formally allowed, all activities being aimed at investigating specific suspects (Klerks 2006). However, this relates more to legislative matters than arising out of concerns for the psychological welfare of undercover operatives. Undercover operations can then involve infiltration of target groups, establishing relationships with both suspects and non-criminals, while maintaining a false identity. In such instances, clearly the officer concerned has to have a degree of empathy and understanding of the beliefs and lifestyle of the target(s) in order to engage with and 'befriend' them. Problems arise if this empathy becomes sympathy. Like all segments of society, some targets will be engaging and affable and, if they were not involved in criminal activity, may even be someone the officer could imagine socializing with. While extremely rare, the danger is that the officer begins to enjoy the undercover lifestyle on any given operation, begins to question their loyalty and commitment, becomes overly sympathetic towards the target and becomes concerned about betraying the 'friendship (s)' formed. This has been referred to in the literature as the undercover Stockholm syndrome (Anderson *et al.* 1995; Marx 1988).

Separation from friends and family

It is almost inevitable in the case of longer-term infiltrations that the officer will be away from friends and family for extended periods of time. If an officer is working on their own rather than with one or more other undercover officers there is the inherent risk of loneliness, leading to the additional risk that 'friendships' with suspects assume an importance other than that required for the operation to succeed. As Band and Sheehan (1999) suggest, this can be avoided by ensuring that the operation is managed so that operatives can disappear and reappear without arousing suspicion (e.g. they are managing 'personal business' elsewhere). This enables the operative to spend time away from the undercover operation to be with their family and to take holidays as required. In addition, the provision of close supervision is essential so that the welfare as well as operational needs and concerns of the officer can be monitored and addressed. Introducing other undercover officers into the operation on an occasional basis as friends or as a visiting 'girlfriend' or 'boyfriend' can also help both to maintain an element of reality and assuage feelings of isolation and loneliness.

Fear of discovery

As Band and Sheehan (1999) note, 'whether the threat is real or imagined, when undercover officers fear discovery, they experience emotional discomfort' (p. 3). Obviously there are operational measures which can be taken to ensure the officer's identity is sound. However, at a purely psychological level, expecting to be challenged simply because the operative is 'a new face in town', treating each situation as unique and being able to judge how to react, when to front situations and when to retreat all help to keep the operative's identity intact and can help to dissipate emotional concerns.

Psychological support

Ideally, any psychological management should be at the level of monitoring welfare and preventing problems from developing rather than the traditional clinical involvement of crisis management (Miller 2006). In relation to this, Band and Sheehan (1999) suggest that 'if an effective and regimented support system regularly monitors and safeguards the operative's wellness, readiness, integrity, and personal concerns, a certified undercover employee can work undercover indefinitely' (p. 5). However, this would be an unusual scenario and time-scales of a few years are usually imposed on full-time undercover deployment. Effective psychological support in relation to undercover policing involves the establishment of a trusting relationship, the officer being able to both recognize and discuss strains inherent in undercover working and to be completely open about any issues or difficulties which arise. Concerns can then be addressed, ways of dealing with psychological stress discussed and difficulties alleviated.

Conclusion

Psychological stress associated with undercover policing remains an under-researched topic. Although it has been suggested that as many as a quarter of undercover police may be at risk of psychological disturbance, such research was conducted over a decade and a half ago; the rigorous selection procedures and welfare monitoring which have developed in the intervening time period mean that there are now likely to be very few psychological casualties. However, the undercover role is psychologically and emotionally demanding, with the strain of living with two parallel identities, frequent separation from family and friends and fear of discovery representing the most significant demands. Given such demands, undercover programmes in most parts of the world now provide independent mental health and welfare monitoring and support.

FURTHER READING

Chapter 12 in Lawrence Miller's recent book on *Police Psychology* (2006) provides a useful overview of the nature of undercover policing and the psychological issues inherent in each phase of an undercover operation.

REFERENCES

Alison, L. and Canter, D. (2005) Rhetorical shaping in an undercover operation: the investigation of Colin Stagg in the Rachel Nickell murder inquiry. In L. Alison (ed.), *The Forensic Psychologist's Casebook: Psychological Profiling and Criminal Investigation*, pp. 197–234. Cullompton: Willan.

Anderson, W., Swenson, D. and Clay, D. (1995) *Stress Management for Law Enforcement Officers*. Englewood Cliff, NJ: Prentice Hall.

Band, S. R. and Sheehan, D. C. (1999) Managing undercover stress: the supervisors role. *FBI Law Enforcement Bulletin*, February, 1–6.

Farkas, G. M. (1986) Stress in undercover policing. In J. T. Reese and H. Goldstein (eds.), *Psychological Services for Law Enforcement*, pp. 433–40. Washington, DC: US Government Printing Office.

Girodo, M. (1991a) Symptomatic reactions to undercover work. *Journal of Nervous and Mental Disease*, 179: 626–30.

(1991b) Drug corruption in undercover agents: measuring the risk. *Behavioral Sciences and the Law*, 9: 361–70.

(1991c) Personality, job stress and mental health in undercover agents: a structural equation analysis. *Journal of Social Behavior and Personality*, 6: 375–90.

Girodo, M., Deck, T. and Morrison, M. (2002) Dissociative-type identity disturbance in undercover agents: socio-cognitive factors behind false-identity appearances and re-enactments. *Social Behavior and Personality*, 30: 631–44.

Klerks, P. (2006) Covert policing in the Netherlands. Paper presented at the annual meeting of the American Society of Criminology (ASC), Los Angeles.

Marx, G. T. (1988) *Undercover: Police Surveillance in America*. Berkeley: University of California Press.

Macleod, A. D. (1995) Undercover policing: a psychiatrist's perspective. *International Journal of Law and Psychiatry*, 18: 239–47.

Miller, L. (2006). *Practical Police Psychology. Stress Management and Crisis Intervention for Law Enforcement*. Springfield, IL: Thomas.

Pistone, J. D. and Brandt, C. (2007) *Donnie Brasco: Unfinished Business*. Philadelphia, PA: Running Press.

Pistone, J. D. and Woodley, R. (1999) *Donnie Brasco: My Undercover Life in the Mafia*. London: Hodder & Stoughton.

6.15 Victimology

Jennifer M. Brown

Definition and origins

Victimology was conceived in the late 1940s somewhat independently by two lawyers (Beniamin Mendlesohn and Hans von Hentig), a criminologist (Stephen Schafer) and a psychiatrist (Frederic Wertham), whose originating disciplines may have lead Rock (1994) to suggest that the study of victims of crime is a somewhat 'amorphous' discipline. Early research attempted to identify different types of victims, but by and large Rock argues that victims were the invisible actors in the criminal justice arena and were not the feature of intellectual enquiry, nor indeed legal proceedings, until about the 1980s. He proposes that interest in the victim was stimulated first by policy makers' wish to find out about the patterns of crime, and in the UK through the introduction of the British Crime Survey. Secondly, there was the introduction of compensation schemes for victims suffering injury. Thirdly, the movement of feminist criminologists drew attention to the plight of abused, battered and sexually assaulted women. Walklate (2007) suggests victimology remains a 'contested' area, not least because of the balance of concern within the criminal justice system between the victim and offender.

Psychologists offering a definition (Bartol and Bartol 2005, p. 178) see victimology as the scientific study of the causes, circumstances, individual characteristics and social context of becoming a victim of crime.

The term victimization usually refers to understanding the nature of the victim's lifestyle and how it may have been instrumental in their targeting by an offender; it is subsumed under the broader term victimology.

Theory

Rock (2007) argues that theorizing in this area is 'thin'. Nevertheless, he identifies a number of theoretical strands. The first is victim precipitation and relates to the provocation or collusion of the victim with the offender. This position argues that there is an interaction between both, in which each influences the conduct, form and content of crime.

Bartol and Bartol (2005) discuss the related notion of victim selection by serial murderers who appear to choose people offering easy access (availability), those who are transient, and whose disappearance would not result in alarm or concern (e.g. prostitutes, runaways, itinerants). Young women on university campuses and the elderly or solitary are the next apparently preferred group. Rarely do serial murderers break in and kill middle-class strangers, although once gaining in confidence they may seek to abduct more 'challenging' victims.

Victim behaviour as a consequence of being subjected to a crime may also influence the perpetrator's behaviour. This has been conceptualized as victim resistance and victim compliance, and has been related to crimes such as robbery (Cook 1986) and sexual assault (Turvey 2002). The former suggests that resistance may result in an escalation of threats or use of force. Cook argues that some robbery victims provoke serious or even fatal attacks. Turvey (2002) on the other hand is more cautious and suggests that the degree to which a victim complies or resists is a feature of that individual's life history, experiences and personality. Compliance implies acquiescence and may even involve the victim proactively asking what the offender wants. Resistance may be verbal or physical, and Turvey notes that it is difficult to predict whether resistance may result in escalation by the offender or desistance from the attack.

However, there have been challenges to the ideas implicit in victim precipitation, which can give rise to victim blaming whereby it is they who are held to be responsible for the crime. This resonates with the notion of the 'deserving' victim. This implies there are some victims who are vulnerable and elicit our sympathy, such as children. The obverse are those victims who are said to contribute to their own victimization: the nagging wife who drives her husband to extremes or the scantily clad woman asking to be raped. Furthermore, victims, such as those suffering rape, feel as though it is they who are on trial. Rock (2007) identifies the rise of a radical feminist critique, which not only protested against the absence of women in criminal justice studies, but also drew attention to male coercion and power as a key feature of male violence and the revictimization of women proceeding through the criminal justice system. Feminist analysis drew attention to women's fear of men and the imbalance of structural resources that denies women options within domestic violence situations or physical aggression.

Crime surveys enabled new theoretical concepts to be developed such as crime hotspots in which crimes are temporally and spatially analysed, revealing that victimization is not evenly distributed through society. This work showed, for example, that one of the best predictors of victimization is previous victimization (Pease and Farrell 1993).

Lifestyle theories predict that crime occurs where there is a convergence in time and space of likely offenders, suitable targets and absence of capable guardians (Rock 2007). This is suggestive of victim risk (Hope 2007). Hope proposes four concepts: proximity and exposure to crime, attractiveness and capable guardianship. The first suggests that victimization is heightened where people likely to commit crime congregate, i.e. physical propinquity. Secondly, lifestyle choices may increase risk. Thirdly, some targets are seen as attractive or worthwhile. Finally, absence of physical security or protective services may heighten risk. Hope suggests these more environmentally focused characteristics do not take into account individual vulnerability and can lead to a form of reductionism by assuming aggregate-level analysis can permit deduction of individual action.

Methods

These can be divided into data collection for policy development and include national crime victimization surveys, methods of assessing impact on victims (including victim impact statements) and research into the experience of victimization.

The first criminal victimization surveys were conducted in the United States in 1967 (Walklate 2007). Developed so that policy makers could get a handle on the so-called 'dark figure' of crime (i.e. the unreported), they provided a wealth of information about people's experience of, and attitudes towards, crime. The first British Crime Survey was conducted in 1982 and now runs annually, allowing trends to be discerned in victimization.

Maguire (1985), in discussing the approaches to assessing victims' needs, distinguishes between assessment of psychological processes of the reactions to victimization, such as post-traumatic stress disorder, and identification of the stages through which people pass when they have been a victim of crime. Often this research has been limited to serious and high-impact crime, such as hijacking or hostage taking, although there is an accruing body of work that looks at the impacts of rape and sexual assault (e.g. Burgess and Hazelwood 1995).

The other group of studies identified by Maguire (1985) is the investigation of the impact of different kinds of crime on the financial or domestic circumstances of the victim. National victim crime surveys have produced good descriptions of levels of financial loss, physical injury and time off work following victimization. Finally, there is the evaluation of services studies which look at victims' satisfaction with services, unmet need and take-up rates (see examples in Maguire 1985). What Maguire identifies are three areas of need: information, i.e. about the progress of the case; practical help, i.e. financial, practical; and emotional support.

As a consequence of the recognition that victims are not adequately represented in the criminal justice process, victim impact statements were developed in the United States. These usually take the form of accounts from victims made available to the courts and/or prosecutor. This idea has been taken up elsewhere and statements often detail the medical, psychological, financial and emotional harm caused by the crime. An important distinction must be made in that the victim impact statements take the victim's interest into account rather than give the victim a role in the disposal of the offender. Evaluation of victim impact statements by Hoyle and colleagues found many participating victims were disappointed and expectations were raised only to be dashed. Arguments against this innovation include the potential for emotionally swaying a judge and jury to increase the severity of sentence if the offender is found guilty.

As well as the quantitative surveys described above, research into the experiences of victims is often accomplished through qualitative analysis with victims of specific crimes (e.g. rape victims: Jordan 2004). This involves the direct questioning of victims. Quantitative surveys may be cross-sectional, where a representative sample of the population in a specific locality is selected and asked if they have been a victim of crime, or purposive, in which a specific group is approached in order to examine how the person experienced the criminal justice system (Davies, Francis and Jupp 1996). Davies *et al.* also describe surveys that measure international comparisons of victimization rates.

Psychological impact

Research by Janoff-Bulman and Frieze (1983) suggests that psychological distress in victims results from the shattering of three basic assumptions: personal invulnerability; a perception that the world is meaningful and ordered (just world hypothesis); and the view of self that is positive.

Rebuilding one's life after being the victim of crime involves rebuilding one's 'assumptive world'. Emotional reactions include shock, confusion, helplessness, anxiety, fear, depression and post-traumatic stress disorder. Recovery involves re-establishing the person's conceptual systems that allow them to function effectively. This includes making sense and finding purpose in the victimization and regaining autonomy and control. Whilst research supports much of what they propose, there are some problems with this analysis. It does not take into account gender differences and the findings that women often experience an imbalance of power and control compared with men or that there are differences between different income groups.

Interventions/services for victims

There are informal networks that perform support functions for victims, and these include family, friends and neighbours. Davis (2003) observes that more than two-thirds of victims needing emotional support or practical help received this from family and friends, a far higher proportion than help received from victim assistance programmes.

Many interventions for victims were initiated by the voluntary sector. In the UK, Victim Support attempted to meet the needs of victims for support in coping with the aftermath of crime and worked with the statutory agencies. The refuge and crisis centres, in contrast, tended to be suspicious of, and criticize, the way in which the criminal justice agencies dealt with victims (Mawby 2007).

In 1964, the UK government established a non-statutory scheme which allocated public funds to victims of crime, administered by the Criminal Injuries Compensation Board. This scheme was reviewed in the 1990s, when the tariff of damages was changed to a common law basis to assess damages. There are three broad categories: personal injury or death, injuries arising from trespass on the railways and accidental injuries.

In 1990, the UK government published a Victim's Charter, which was a statement of the rights and expectations of victims of crime; it required police to respond sensitively and victims to be referred to Victim Support schemes (Morgan and Zedner 1992). This heralded the development of specialist services for especially vulnerable victims (e.g. children, young people and women), targeting particular crimes, such as rape and child sex abuse. Morgan and Zedner describe the Bexley project, which was the first UK joint management of child sex abuse cases by social services and the police. Not without its problems (because of the differing philosophies of the participating agencies, one being concerned with rehabilitation and the other with evidence gathering), such cooperation is now common practice.

Specific services such as rape crisis centres began in the voluntary sector and were progressively extended to incorporate criminal justice agencies. Thus the development of specially trained police officers, the introduction of bespoke rape examination suites and an increase in the numbers of women police surgeons were designed to give better service to rape victims (Brown and King 1998).

The Code of Practice for Victims of Crime, published in 2005, is the UK government's reformation of the services to victims. It describes the minimum level of services, introduces a complaints system (including an ombudsman dedicated to victim issues) and lists the statutory agencies responsible for victims. As a response to what was held to be services falling woefully short of expectation, the government issued a consultation document, 'Rebuilding lives' (Home Office consultation 2005), which was an attempt at rebalancing the relationship of victims (as opposed to offenders) within the criminal justice system.

Conclusion

Victimology offers, on the one hand, a picture of victims in which they may be held partially responsible for their own victimization; on the other hand, it offers analysis that helps understand the individual and environmental features that may contribute to being a victim of crime. This area of work looks at the impacts on, and services for, victims. Victimology has been used investigatively as part of the toolkit for offender profiling (trying to explore the reasoning for the offender's targeting of a particular victim in order to deduce information about the latter) and experimentally by introducing victim impact statements into court proceedings to return some power to victims within the criminal justice process.

FURTHER READING

Sandra Walklate's edited collection, *Handbook of Victims and Victimology* (2007) is an excellent compendium of key commentators in this area, and provides coverage of theoretical issues and interventions. Judith Sgarzi and Jack McDevitt's edited collection

(2003) and that of Robert Davis, Arthur Lurigio and Susan Herman (2007) discusses types of crime victims (hate crime, victimless crime, violence).The book edited by Pamela Davies and her colleagues (1996) at the University of Northumbria contains useful details of methods, including an exposition of victim crime surveys.

REFERENCES

Bartol, C. R., and Bartol, A. M. (2005) *Criminal Behaviour: A Psychological Approach*, 7th edn. Upper Saddle River, NJ: Prentice Hall.

Brown, J. M. and King, J. (1998) Gender differences in police officers attitudes towards rape; results of an exploratory study. *Psychology, Crime and Law*, 4: 265–79.

Burgess, A. W. and. Hazelwood, R. R. (eds.) (1995) *Practical Aspects of Rape Investigation: A Multi-disciplinary Approach*, pp. 37–45. New York: CRC Press.

Cook, P. J. (1986) The relationship between victim resistance and injury in non-commercial robbery. *Journal of Legal Studies*, 15: 405–16.

Davies, P., Frances, P. and Jupp, V. (1996) Understanding victimology: theory, method and practice. In P. Davies, P. Frances and V. Jupp (eds.), *Understanding Victimisation*, pp. 1–13. Gateshead: Northumbria Social Science Press.

Davis, R. (2003) The key contribution of family, friends and neighbours. In J. Sgarzi and J. McDevitt (eds.), *Victimology: A Study of Crime Victims and Their Roles*. Upper Saddle River, NJ: Prentice Hall.

Davis, R. C., Lurigio, A. J. and Herman, S. (eds.) (2007) *Victims of Crime*, 3rd edn. Los Angeles: Sage.

Hope, T. (2007) Theory and method: the social epidemiology of crime victims. In S. Walklate (ed.), *Handbook of Victims and Victimology*, pp. 62–90. Cullompton: Willan.

Jannoff-Bulman, R. and Frieze, I. (1983) A theoretical perspective for understanding reactions to victimization. *Journal of Social Issues*, 39: 1–17.

Jordan, J. (2004) *The Word of a Woman? Police, Rape and Belief.* Basingstoke: Palgrave Macmillan.

Maguire, M. (1985) Victims' needs and victims services: indications from research. *Victimology: An International Journal*, 10: 539–59.

Mawby, R. (2007) Public sector services and victims of crime. In S. Walklate (ed.), *Handbook of Victims and Victimology*, pp. 207–39. Cullompton: Willan.

Morgan, J. and Zedner, L. (1992) The Victim's Charter; a new deal for child victims. *The Howard Journal*, 31: 294–307.

Pease, K. and Farrell, G. (1993) Once bitten, twice shy: repeat victimisation and its implications for crime prevention. Home Office Crime Prevention Unit 46. London: Home Office.

Rock, P. (1994) *Victimology*. Aldershot: Dartmouth.

    (2007) Theoretical perspectives on victimization. In S. Walklate (ed.), *Handbook of Victims and Victimology*, pp. 37–61. Cullompton: Willan.

Sgarzi, J. and McDevitt, J. (eds.) (2003) *Victimology: A Study of Crime Victims and Their Roles*. Upper Saddle River, NJ: Prentice Hall.

Turvey, B. (2002) *Criminal Profiling: An Introduction to Behavioural Evidence Analysis*, 2nd edn. Amsterdam: Elsevier.

Walklate, S. (ed.) (2007) *Handbook of Victims and Victimology*. Cullompton: Willan.

6.16 Young children presenting with sudden infant death syndrome or apparent life-threatening events

Catherine C. Ayoub

Introduction

On 22 April 1995, Wanetta Hoyt, an Upstate New York mother, was convicted of murdering five of her children by suffocating them. The original cause of death listed for each of these children some twenty years earlier was 'sudden infant death syndrome' (SIDS). Her confession to police contained details about the methods she used to smother her children, including a pillow, towel and her shoulder; she stated that she did not know what to do for them when they cried.

In a hallmark article (Steinschneider 1972), two of the Hoyt children were diagnosed with prolonged apnea and were described as suffering from recurrent near-death events while at home with their mother. Yet, while being closely monitored in the hospital, their near-death events did not occur, only to return and lead to the children's deaths shortly after being discharged home. The children's repeated life-threatening events and their subsequent deaths were initially attributed to complications of prolonged apnea, when they were actually part of an 'unthinkable' crime of child abuse perpetrated by the children's mother (Grunson 1994). The Hoyt children represent an example of failure to consider or recognize fatal child abuse that presents as a recurrent apparent life-threatening event (ALTE) or sudden, unexplained death.

Definitions and identification

An apparent life-threatening event (ALTE) is defined as an event characterized by some combination of apnea, colour change, marked change in muscle tone, choking or gagging that is frightening to the observer;[1] in many cases children stop breathing and resuscitation is begun. The most common causes of ALTEs are respiratory infections, gastroesophageal reflux, seizures and metabolic disturbances (Vellody et al. 2008). Sudden infant death syndrome (SIDS) is defined as the sudden death of an infant, which is unexpected by history, and in which a thorough postmortem examination fails to demonstrate the cause of death (Beckwith 1970). Although the cause is unknown, placing infants on their backs rather than on their stomachs has significantly reduced the number of SIDS deaths worldwide. A small but important group of infants and young children presenting with ALTEs or SIDS are deliberately suffocated by an adult, usually a caregiver. As a result, suffocatory abuse should always be considered when children present with either ALTEs or SIDS.

Professionals caring for young children often find it difficult to consider the possibility that parents are capable of repeatedly smothering their children in the case of apnea and/or killing their children in the case of SIDS (Light and Sheridan 1990; Southall et al. 1997; Hall et al. 2000; Truman and Ayoub 2002). In situations of suffocatory abuse, overt physical findings of suffocation are often lacking (Reece 1993; Vellody et al. 2008). In addition, asphyxiation of the young infant – accidental or homicidal – usually produces few distinct pathological changes observable on autopsy (Kirschner 1997; Arnstad, Vege and Rognum 2002). This is especially true if the child lacks obvious or overt signs of trauma such as fractured bones, blackened eyes, retinal haemorrhages, or patterned bruising, typical of battered child syndrome.

Assessment is complicated further by the presentation of the parent as attentive and knowledgeable in management of the child's illness, a cardinal finding in Munchausen by proxy (MBP).[2] In cases of MBP, children may not be subjected to fatal suffocation, at least not at first, but their airways are restricted to the point of inducing an apparent life-threatening event (ALTE) in order for the parent to 'impostor' as the caring and competent parent of a chronically ill child (Alexander, Smith and Stevenson 1990). A second presentation of an ALTE or SIDS is in the child whose parent suffocates it in an attempt to silence its crying or activity – as in classic situations of physical child abuse. In the first group (MBP), children will typically have multiple ALTEs and eventually deteriorate physically after repeated episodes

---

[1] This definition is from the 1986 National Institutes of Health Consensus Panel on Infantile Apnea.

[2] Munchausen by proxy is a disorder in which parents, overwhelmingly mothers, abuse their children by exaggerating, fabricating and/or inducing illness (in these cases apnea) in their children. See Ayoub et al. 2002 for detailed definitions.

of anoxia. In the cases of more direct physical abuse, children may die on the first identified episode of suffocation and are labelled as SIDS deaths. This second group of children may also have evidence of trauma including head injuries, retinal haemorrhages and other evident bruises.

A number of scientific studies have described cases of infant death that have previously been attributed to SIDS and subsequently found to be infanticide or near-death episodes induced by smothering by a parent or caregiver. These reports emphasize that abuse in the form of suffocation is not an isolated occurrence. A review of studies by Truman and Ayoub (2002), spanning two decades, yielded 121 reported cases of children who presented with some form of recurrent apnea, cyanosis, bradycardia and apparent life-threatening events (ALTEs), who were subsequently discovered to be victims of repeated suffocation by caregivers (Southall et al. 1997; Makar and Squier 1990; Alexander, Smith and Stevenson 1990; Samuels et al. 1992; Boros et al. 1995; Hall et al. 2000). Although mothers were most often the perpetrators, fathers and one grandmother were also found to be responsible for suffocatory abuse. Fifty-one sibling deaths were identified among the 121 suffocatory abuse cases found in the literature. Although most of these prior sibling deaths were initially attributed to SIDS, 31% of the siblings were subsequently found to have been suffocated. Many of the reported child victims were repeatedly evaluated for apnea, seizures, cardiac abnormalities and gastroesophageal reflux. The result was long delays before reaching a diagnosis of suffocatory abuse. One of the most common reasons for the delay in diagnosing suffocatory abuse was the failure to consider repeated suffocation in the differential diagnosis. (Meadow 1990; Kravitz and Wilmott 1990). This finding was reinforced by a 1990 survey among apnea centres regarding Munchausen by proxy presenting as apnea that noted that 'retrospectively, programs could see that the pattern was clear and that they had pursued the search for physical cause long after the medical team should have recognized its futility' (Light and Sheridan 1990).

Prevalence

In several studies that have examined all of the children with ALTEs presenting to a medical facility, the rate of non-accidental trauma is between 3.0 and 3.7% (Vellody et al. 2008). However, in studies in which other overt diagnoses for the ALTE are excluded, the rate of non-accidental trauma (i.e. child abuse) is between 32% (Samuels et al. 1993) and 33% (Truman and Ayoub 2002) of the children seen.

Forensic considerations

Characteristics that assist in distinguishing SIDS or ALTEs due to natural disease states from abuse have been described in the literature since the early 1960s. The following high-risk elements, viewed in a cumulative fashion, should be considered in a child with ALTE. These characteristics together raise the possibility that non-accidental trauma is the cause of the child's difficulty or death:

- Recurrent, poorly explained ALTEs
- The same parent or caregiver (often alone) as the witness to most or all of ALTEs
- The presence of blood in the child's mouth and/or nose
- Bruising or other signs of physical injury that is inconsistent with the event/resuscitation
- The presence of siblings with other medical problems, especially apnea, ALTEs, or SIDS
- A child over 6 to 9 months of age

As suggested by a number of authors (Meadow 1990; Reece 1993, 1994), the most frequently cited suggestions of non-accidental suffocation include recurrent, poorly explained ALTEs witnessed by the same caregiver. This pattern is of particular concern if the events decrease or cease upon admission to the hospital, or if events suffered in hospital occur only in the presence of the mother. Southall and his colleagues (1997) described finding blood in the nose or mouth of children who were covertly videotaped being suffocated by caregivers. He differentiates this frank blood from the sero-sanguinous fluid described in some children with SIDS. Kirschner (1997) suggests that unexplained infant deaths presenting as possible SIDS in families with previous unexplained infant deaths should be considered suspicious for non-accidental suffocation. He describes the extremely low probability of multiple incidents of SIDS in a single family and recommends that the diagnosis of Munchausen by proxy be strongly considered.

In examining suspicious fatalities, Truman and Ayoub (2002) found children with overt evidence of physical abuse diagnosed as SIDS deaths, most of whom suffered from a small number of ALTEs before their deaths. Of these cases battered child syndrome and intentional suffocation were the most likely causes of death. In examining the living children in their sample most suspected of being abused, a pattern of numerous ALTEs witnessed by the same parent is the most typical presentation. Their high-risk group included children with as many as 135 ALTEs; children were usually toddlers, older than infants who usually present with SIDS.

Based on these findings, these researchers hypothesized that this group is likely to be a reflection of a large number of cases of Munchausen by proxy (MBP), a form of child abuse in which the parent, in the vast majority of the cases the mother, exaggerates, fabricates or induces illness (in this case apnea) in the child in order to meet her own self-serving psychological needs (Ayoub et al. 2002). These mothers do not aim to kill their children immediately, but to use them as attention-getting objects in order to enter into a relationship with physicians and healthcare professionals. Mothers present not only as good mothers, but they 'impostor' as some of the most caring and knowledgeable parents of sick children. In cases of MBP, children frequently become increasingly ill, with symptoms arising in multiple organ systems, for whom traditional and even more radical treatments do not work. Mothers are masterful in providing symptom histories that are complex and quite difficult to detect as false. It is usually the mother who is the child's 'saviour' through resuscitation. Needless to say, these situations require careful record review, accumulation of all past records and integration of all medical care for the child in order to identify patterns of deception. Interestingly, in MBP, apnea is one of the most lethal symptoms and in these groups of children serial MBP is not uncommon (Alexander et al. 1990).

Child protection teams should be consulted on all children in the high-risk group as defined by the criteria above. Careful documentation of findings that suggest concern, covert video surveillance in selected high-risk cases and careful follow-up are required in all of these situations. Because suffocatory abuse is one of the most lethal forms of child abuse, action to separate parents and the child and protect the child is often required.

In cases involving death, notification of the medical examiner with performance of autopsy, death scene investigation and careful review of the child's medical history are crucial (AAP-Committee on Child Abuse and Neglect 2001). Review of child deaths by a multidisciplinary child fatality review panel can assist in increasing the precision of ascertaining cause of death. These investigations can be supportive to both law enforcement and the family of the infant or child who suddenly dies. Reece (1994) provides a list of recommendations for better fact collection and analysis in the case of sudden unexplained deaths that reiterates these recommendations and emphasizes the need for physical examination of the child in the emergency room, as well as postmortem examinations within twenty-four hours of death. He restates the need to consider all the diagnostic elements involved in the decision about infant deaths.

Truman and Ayoub (2002) reinforce the importance of mandatory autopsy in cases of unexpected infant deaths. In their sample, 31% of the available autopsies of clinically presumed SIDS demonstrated a non-SIDS cause of death.

A careful autopsy by an experienced medical examiner should not only explore the possibility of abuse by suffocation, but will also examine alternatives, including the possibility of an 'undiscovered' metabolic disorder. Inborn errors of fatty acid oxidation may occasionally cause death following minimal symptoms and will present as an alternative to suffocation when there have been multiple SIDS deaths among siblings (Kirschner 1997). Fatty acid changes in the liver offer evidence of the presence of the disorder. Autopsy is often an important protection and information-producing process for parents. If handled with respect and concern autopsy, as well as examination of the death scene and interviews can be reassuring rather than threatening to parents whose children have not died of abuse.

Forensic assessment of suffocatory abuse

A careful medical and psychiatric evaluation to address issues of parenting capacity and the best interests of the child in the light of suffocatory abuse requires a multidisciplinary approach that often includes the child's primary physicians, emergency personnel (including the medical examiner if the child is deceased), the hospital child protection team, law enforcement representatives, and a forensic mental health professional. Careful documentation of the child's physical history and findings and the psychological presentation of the parents is recommended. Evaluation is aimed at informing and expediting decision making related to the child's ALTEs and/or SIDS death. Focus of the psychological assessment is on the interactional patterns between the caregiver(s) and each child, with attention to:

- the child's illness experience and functioning with attention to the basic evaluation for MBP (see chapter 6.10 in this volume) and for physical abuse;
- the parent's psychological functioning with attention to differentiating factitious disorder by proxy (factitious disorder NOS in the DSM-IV) and other possible psychological aetiologies of the parent's behaviour, attitudes and beliefs towards the child.

The process of evaluation typically includes the following:

- Comprehensive record review with special attention to the history of the child's prior ALTEs and the presence of the risk factors described above.
- Interviews with family and collaterals who might be able to shed light on the current situation.
- Collaboration with medical examiner and law enforcement if this is a child death. This includes gathering information from law enforcement about the crime scene, circumstances related to the incident(s) and interviews with witnesses such as relatives, ambulance personnel and emergency room staff.
- If abuse is suspected then functioning of each parent or primary caregiver, both in the past and in the present, is explored through a series of clinical interviews and through psychological testing.
- A review of the child's physical and emotional functioning including, but not limited to, information about past and current daily routines, symptoms and behaviours is obtained through observations, record review and interviews with past and current caregivers.

Ever since a letter to the editor in response to Steinschneider's 1972 prolonged apnea paper in the journal *Pediatrics*, there have been questions regarding the possibility of suffocatory abuse in cases of repeated ALTEs and multiple SIDS (Dimaio 1988). Recent attention to these concerns, both in the medical literature and the media, have led many people to question how many children with ALTEs and/or SIDS have been misdiagnosed in the past. Further improvement of our diagnostic acumen in identifying high-risk children, and an increased willingness to report such cases when reasonable suspicion is present, should be the goal for protecting children from suffocatory abuse.

FURTHER READING

See R. Firstman and J. Talan (1997) *The Death of Innocents* (New York: Bantam Books) for a history of the understanding of SIDS and a detailed account of Wanetta Hoyt's story.

REFERENCES

AAP-Committee on Child Abuse and Neglect (2001) Distinguishing sudden infant death syndrome from child abuse fatalities. *Pediatrics*, 107: 437–41.

Alexander, R., Smith, W. and Stevenson, R. (1990) Serial Munchausen syndrome by proxy. *Pediatrics*, 86: 581–5.

Arnestad, M., Vege, A. and Rognum, T. O. (2002) *Forensic Science International*, 125: 262–8.

Ayoub, C., Alexander, R., Beck, D., Bursch, B., Feldman, K., Libow, J. *et al.* (2002) Definitional issues in Munchausen by proxy. *Child Maltreatment*, 7: 105–12.

Beckwith, J. B. (1970) Discussion of terminology and definition of the sudden infant death syndrome. In A. B. Bergman, J. B. Beckwith and C. G. Ray (eds.), *Proceedings of the Second International Conference on the Causes of Sudden Death in Infants*, pp. 14–22. Seattle: University of Washington Press.

Boros, S. J., Ophoven, J. P., Andersen, R. and Brubaker, L. C. (1995) Munchausen syndrome by proxy: a profile for medical child abuse. *Australian Family Physician*, 24: 768–73.

Dimaio, V. J. (1988) SIDS or Murder? [letter to editor] *Pediatrics*, 81: 747.

Grunson L. (1994) Woman confesses in deaths of children. *New York Times*, 31 March.

Hall, D. E, Eubanks, L., Meyyazhagan, S., Kenney, R. D. and Johnson, S. C. (2000) Evaluation of covert video surveillance in the diagnosis of Munchausen syndrome by proxy: lessons from 41 cases. *Pediatrics*, 105: 1305–12.

Kirschner, R. (1997) The pathology of child abuse. In M. Helfer, R. Kempe and R. Krugman (eds.), *The Battered Child*, 5th edn, pp. 248–95. Chicago: University of Chicago Press.

Kravitz, R. M. and Wilmott R. W. (1990) Munchausen syndrome by proxy presenting as factitious apnea. *Clinical Pediatrics*, 29: 587–92.

Light, M. J. and Sheridan, M. S. (1990) Munchausen syndrome by proxy and apnea (MBPA) – a survey of apnea programs. *Clinical Pediatrics*, 29: 162–8.

Makar, A. F. and Squier, P. J. (1990) Munchausen syndrome by proxy: father as a perpetrator. *Pediatrics*, 85: 370–3.

Meadow, R. (1990) Suffocation, recurrent apnea, and sudden infant death. *Journal of Pediatrics*, 117: 351–7.

Reece, R. M. (1993) Fatal child abuse and sudden infant death syndrome: a critical diagnostic decision. *Pediatrics*, 91: 423–9.

(1994) Fatal child abuse and sudden infant death syndrome. In R. Reece (ed.), *Child Abuse: Medical Diagnosis and Management*, pp. 107–37. Philadelphia: Lea & Febiger.

Samuels, M. P., McClaughlin, W., Jacobson, R. R., Poets, C. F. and Southall, D. P. (1992) Fourteen cases of imposed upper airway obstruction. *Archives of Disease in Childhood*, 67: 162–70.

Samuels, M. P., Poets, C. F., Noyes, J. P., Hartman, H., Hewertson, J. and Southall, D. P. (1993) Diagnosis and management after life threatening events in infants and young children who received cardiopulmonary resuscitation. *British Medical Journal*, 306: 489–92.

Southall, D. P., Plunkett, M. C. B., Banks, M. W., Falkov, A. F. and Samuels, M. P. (1997) Covert video recordings of life-threatening child abuse: lessons for child protection. *Pediatrics*, 100: 735–60.

Steinschneider, A. (1972) Prolonged apnea and the sudden infant death syndrome: clinical and laboratory observations. *Pediatrics*, 50: 646–54.

Truman, T. and Ayoub, C. (2002). Considering suffocatory abuse and Munchausen by proxy in the evaluation of children experiencing recurrent life-threatening events or sudden infant death syndrome. *Child Maltreatment*, 7: 138–49.

Vellody, K., Freeto, J., Gage, S., Collins, N. and Gershan, W. (2008) Clues that aid in the diagnosis of nonaccidental trauma presenting as an apparent life-threatening event. *Clinical Pediatrics*, 20: 1–7.

Part VII

Professional practice

7.1 Ethical practice

Jennifer M. Brown

See also chapter 5.4 Discrimination and employment tribunals, chapter 7.3 Expert witnesses in civil cases.

Definitions

A key doctrine underlying ethical practice is *primum non nocere*, meaning first do no harm. This will be found in ethical codes emanating from professional societies and associations around the world. The companion doctrine is doing good both at the level of the individual and society more generally. Arising from these doctrines are notions of non-malfeasance (what not to do) and benefice (what to do), and the Canadian code, for example, advises what to do if they come into conflict. As an example of such a conflict, Blackburn (1993, p. 409), draws attention to prison settings where the punitive custodial goals of imprisonment may be required for retribution and/or public safety compared to rehabilitation goals of therapeutic support aimed at the individual whose better path may be non-custodial and the object of a forensic psychology practitioner's interventions. As Blackburn points out, ethical codes of conduct require psychologists to hold the interests of recipients of their services paramount yet psychologists are 'simultaneously the employees of a system whose primary purpose is social control' (p. 409).

The Canadian ethical code for psychologists discusses the idea of a 'social contract'. This is premised on the belief that in return for society trusting psychologists to retain autonomy over their training and development of knowledge, there is adherence to an explicit ethical standard. This code rank orders its principles with respect for dignity of person being the most important, so that if there is a clash, this principle should be invoked over all others (i.e. responsibility for caring, integrity in relationships, responsibility to society).

The British Psychological Society (2006) defines ethics as the science of morals and behaviour, and goes on to say that the philosophy underlying the BPS's code of conduct is the 'British Eclectic Tradition' (i.e. provision of guidelines for thinking about the circumstances, cultural context, prevailing law and likely consequences of a decision); the Kantian categorical imperative (i.e. treat humanity in your own person and that of others always as an end and never only as a means) is also fundamental to ethical practice. Ethics, according to the BPS, is related to the control of power, whereby the psychologist is in an advantageous position over those with whom they professionally interact (e.g. client, student, trainee, patient, prisoner or research participant).

Ethical codes by and large seek to guide rather than punish, although infractions may lead to disciplinary action against members by designated committees of the appropriate professional bodies. Pettifor and Sawchuk (2006) discuss codes of ethics from various countries and conclude that they share common objectives: to promote optimal behaviour by providing aspirational principles; and regulation of professional conduct through monitoring and disciplinary action.

The purpose of codes is to support and guide psychologists in their professional activities, reassure the public and clarify expectations about relationships and services. Gudjonsson and Haward (1998) note that formal codes offer minimum standards of conduct and cover areas such as competency, consent, confidentiality and personal conduct. Mostly codes cover the conduct of psychologists vis-à-vis recipients of services, such as clients in therapy, students in receipt of education, training or supervision, relationships with colleagues and research activity vis-à-vis participants, the broader scientific community and society at large.

Principles

The declaration of principles varies a little in detail between countries' professional bodies. Pettifor and Sawchuk (2006) state they all profess respect and dignity of persons, caring for others and concern for their welfare, and professional, scientific and personal integrity. Mostly they articulate the importance of maintaining appropriate levels of knowledge (including an undertaking to regularly update knowledge through continuing professional development) and operating within a range of competence, i.e. knowledge base. They offer advice about dual/multiple relationships, limits of confidentiality, health problems affecting practitioners and general guidance to avoid bringing the profession of psychology into disrepute. Some countries' professional bodies spell out in greater detail the duty owed to society at large to promote human welfare.

Specialty guidelines

In addition, there may be further detailed guidance by professional bodies for specific areas of practice. For example a joint statement of guidelines for work in forensic psychology was issued by the American Psychology–Law Society and Division 41 of the APA, endorsed by the American Board of Forensic Psychology and the American Academy of Forensic Psychology (Specialty Guidelines for Forensic Psychology: APA 2008). This provides discipline-specific detail under headings such as responsibility and competence, in addition to noting areas such as public and professional communication. The goal of specific guidance is to improve the quality of forensic psychology services offered to individuals, and to legal systems, ultimately to enhance forensic psychology both as a discipline and a profession.

There are also particular court rulings of relevance, e.g. the Tarasoff liability (Monahan 1993), which addresses the limits of confidentiality. This case involved the murder of Tatiana Tarasoff, who was killed by the client of a therapist who had intimated his intention to the therapist prior to the killing. The liability concerns the duty to warn third parties who may be in present danger. Monahan's guidance for dealing with this problem includes the following

(a) Be conversant with up-to-date principles and practice of risk assessment.
(b) Consult appropriate colleagues if second opinion warranted.
(c) Carefully and completely document activities related to risk assessment and management; have policies and minimum standards.
(d) Avoid tampering with documentation or publicly admitting responsibility before any inquiry has taken place.

The BPS guidance requires psychologists to take reasonable steps to maintain confidentiality but does recognize exceptions when safety of others is under threat. The guidance states that the psychologist should ensure clients are aware of the limitations of confidentiality, and restrict breaches to exceptional circumstances where there is sufficient evidence of serious concern about the safety of clients, third parties who may be endangered by clients' behaviour, and the health and welfare of children.

The Frye test (Wrightsman and Fulero 2005, p. 36) serves as a criterion in American courts for standards of expert evidence. The test states that well-recognized principles in a particular field should determine admissibility of testimony. The Parliamentary Office of Science and Technology (2008) explains that the Frye test requires techniques to have gained general acceptance in the scientific community. The Daubert test, introduced in 1992, considers whether a particular technique can be or has been tested, whether it has been subject to peer review publication, what the known or potential error rate is and whether the evidence has widespread acceptance in the scientific community. Wrightsman and Fulero capture a potential conflict between science and the law, i.e. to what extent should judges adjudicate the relevance and standing of the proffered expert testimony?

Research

Codes also provide standards for conducting research and discuss requirements to undertake risk assessment to ensure no harm or to minimize harm to participants, that they are properly informed about the study they are taking part in and that they be debriefed afterwards, that their consent is voluntary and that they may withdraw their participation without any detriment.

Forensic psychology research often involves respondents who are especially vulnerable; Gorin *et al.* (2008) describe the ethical challenges when researching hard-to-reach families, providing a helpful framework of good practice.

Teaching

Matthews (1991) looks at ethics within the educational context from two perspectives: the teaching of ethics and the ethics of teaching psychology. As well as articulating principles for the teaching of ethics, she discusses topics such as classroom participation in seminars and workshops and use of case examples which have particular resonance for forensic psychology, dealing as it does with potentially explicit and disturbing subject matter. She suggests informing students about distressing topics and extending concern for their welfare if they or people they are close to have been involved in crime as witnesses, victims or offenders.

The APA code makes explicit reference to education and teaching. Areas covered include:

- Design of programmes should provide appropriate knowledge and proper experiences to meet the requirements of licensing.
- Coverage of material should be current and up-to-date.
- Descriptions of programmes should be accurate.

Hanley (2004) discusses the particular problem of ethical dilemmas posed when students self-disclose within their written assignments and attempts to balance privacy needs against intervention.

Consultancy

Wrightsman and Fulero (2005) discuss the temptations besetting forensic psychology practitioners acting as consultants or expert witnesses:

- promising too much either by claiming successes in past case to infer likely success in a present case
- substituting advocacy for scientific objectivity, i.e. becoming sympathetic to the argument of the side that is paying
- volunteering only research evidence that supports one side of the argument
- valuing the work in the service of their employer's values rather than scientific objectivity (hired gun)
- letting own personal values override empirical findings and go beyond any legitimate basis in offering conclusions
- doing a cursory job and being less than thorough and professional.

Dilemmas

Blackburn (1993) discusses the particular dilemmas facing forensic psychology practitioners who work in prison settings. As well as the problem of being clear who your client is, Blackburn also highlights the issue of coerced participation (perhaps mandated by the courts). Here he presents the position of enforced participation as being an 'evil' of lesser gravity in that to refuse treatment is likely to involve (longer) incarceration. The other more political dilemma lies with definitions of criminal and antisocial behaviour and the primacy of the client/prisoner in deciding which of their behavioural repertoire should be added to, maintained and removed.

Another emergent issue of concern in the context of imprisonment is assessment and report writing, and the uses made of these. This can create role conflicts in terms of the therapeutic relationship and the nature of progress which may be used in parole or release decisions. Nicholson and Norwood (2000) reviewed the quality of forensic psychological assessments and, whilst reporting a general improvement, concluded that the levels of practice fall short of professional aspirations.

Lea, Auburn and Kibblewhite (1999) articulate a dilemma with respect to the psychologist's distaste for the offending behaviour, particularly sexual offences. They term this the *professional–personal dialectic*, which they formally define (p. 113) as 'the fundamental tension between the need for the professional to develop a relationship with the sex offender in the course of their professional duty whilst simultaneously negotiating the desire not to develop a relationship with the sex offender because of a personal abhorrence of his [sic] criminal activity'.

There are a number of papers that look at dilemmas in particular forensic settings e.g. clinical (McGuire 1997); prisons (Haag 2006); and secure hospital (Weinstein 2002).

Complaints

The problems and difficulties besetting forensic psychology practitioners have been identified by Gudjonsson and Haward (1998). Typical complaints include practising outside their area of competence, submitting to pressure from an employer, inadequate supervision of junior staff, using outdated techniques, use of inappropriate language in reports, personal conduct, confidentiality issues, boundary issues (conflicts of interest or role conflicts) payments, fees or insurance cover.

Preventative action

Clearly, prevention is better than breaching codes, and reflective practice, peer support, and transparency of professional activity are means to avoid contravening codes.

Gudjonsson and Haward offer the following advice to prevent or minimize the risks for forensic psychology practitioners by:

- observing professional and scientific responsibility
- respecting people's rights and dignity
- having concern for people's welfare

- substantiating findings
- knowing the relevant codes, procedures and current legislation
- engaging in continuous professional development
- proactively identifying potential problems
- consulting with knowlegable colleagues
- maintaining thorough records.

Decision making

As well as one's own conduct, codes also charge members of professional bodies to bring to notice malpractice in colleagues (Brodsky and McKinzey 2002). They note lapses of professional standards such as claiming credentials not entitled to, and failure to administer an up-to-date psychometric test or incorrectly scoring the test. Other examples they give include adversarial overzealousness when being an expert witness, or lack of proper preparation and knowledge before undertaking a task. They suggest a number of possible actions, such as a polite letter outlining the specifics of concern to the errant colleague. They also consider the opposite problem if an overzealous, overly critical colleague sends such a letter. They offer example correspondence as guidance to psychologists finding themselves in either of these situations.

Day and White (2008) provide a discussion of decision making when considering an ethical dilemma and refer to the Corey *et al.* (1998) model. This has three broad steps: problem recognition, consultation and problem solving. The BPS has similar steps: identify relevant issues and the extent of the parameters of the situation; locate relevant research evidence; seek advice of peers and legal guidance if appropriate; identify key parties involved and the ethical principles implicated; evaluate rights and responsibilities and welfare of parties concerned; generate alternative decision options; do a cost/risk analysis of both short- and long-term consequences; document process; assume responsibility; and learn from the process.

Conclusion

It behoves forensic psychology practitioners to be aware of the codes of conduct issued by their professional bodies. This not only provides guidance for professional practice but also acts as a defence if the code has been consulted when one is presented with an ethical dilemma.

Below are the web addresses of a sample of professional bodies whose sites access their respective codes.

Professional body	Web address
American	www.ap-ls.org
Canadian	www.cpa.ca
British	www.bps.org.uk
Irish	www.psihq.ie
Australian	www.psychology.org.au
New Zealand	www.psychology.org.nz

FURTHER READING

Gisli Gudjonsson and Lionel Haward's chapter on ethical and professional issues in their 1998 book is a good overview; Wrightsman and Fulero's textbook (2005) also offers a critical discussion of ethical issues facing forensic psychology; and access to codes of conduct can be made through the websites of professional societies and associations. The paper by Haag (2006) is a good overview of the dilemma facing forensic psychology practitioners working within the prison system.

REFERENCES

American Psychological Association (2008) *Specialty Guidelines for Forensic Psychology.* Available online: www.ap-ls.org.

Blackburn, R. (1993) *The Psychology of Criminal Conduct: Theory, Research and Practice.* Chichester: Wiley.

British Psychological Society (2006) *British Psychological Society Code of Ethics and Conduct.* Leicester: British Psychological Society.

Brodsky, S. L. and McKinzey, R. K. (2002) The ethical confrontation of the unethical forensic colleague. *Professional Psychology Research and Practice*, 33: 307–9.

Corey, G., Corey, M. S. and Callanan, P. (1998) *Issues and Ethics in the Helping Professions*, 5th edn. Pacific Grove, CA: Brooks/Cole.

Day, A. and White, J. (2008) Ethical practice from the perspective of the forensic psychology practitioner; commentary on the uses and value of Australian Psychological Society (2007) code of ethics. *Australian Psychologist*, 43: 186–93.

Gorin, S., Hooper, C-A., Dyson, C. and Cabral, C. (2008) Ethical challenges in conducting research with hard to reach families. *Child Abuse Review*, 17: 275–37.

Gudjonsson, G. and Haward, L. (1998) *Forensic Psychology: A Guide to Practice*. London: Routledge.

Haag, A. (2006) Ethical dilemmas faced by correctional psychologists in Canada. *Criminal Justice and Behavior*, 33: 93–109.

Hanley, M. R. (2004) Ethical dilemmas associated with self disclosures in student writing. *Teaching Psychology*, 31: 167–71.

Lea, S., Auburn, T. and Kibblewhite, K. (1999) Working with sex offenders: the perceptions and experiences of professionals and paraprofessionals. *International Journal of Offender Therapy and Comparative Criminology*, 43: 103–19.

Matthews, J. (1991) The teaching of ethics and the ethics of teaching. *Teaching Psychology*, 18: 80–5.

McGuire, J. (1997) Ethical dilemmas in forensic clinical psychology. *Legal and Criminological Psychology*, 2: 177–92.

Monahan, J. (1993) Limiting therapist exposure to Tarasoff liability: guidance for risk containment. *American Psychologist*, 48: 242–50.

Nicholson, R. A. and Norwood, S. (2000) The quality of forensic psychological assessment reports and testimony: acknowledging the gap between procedure and practice. *Law and Human Behaviour*, 24: 9–44.

Parliamentary Office of Science and Technology (2008) Science in court. No 248 1–4. Speciality guidelines for forensic psychologists. *Law and Human Behaviour*, 15: 655–65.

Pettifor, J. L. and Sawchuck, T. R. (2006) Psychological perspectives of ethically troubling incidents across international borders. *International Journal of Psychology*, 41: 216–25.

Weinstein, H. C. (2002) Ethics issues in security hospitals. *Behavioral Sciences and the Law*, 20: 442–61.

Wrightsman, L. S. and Fulero, S. M. (2005) *Forensic Psychology*, 2nd edn. Belmont, CA: Wadsworth.

7.2 Diversity, equality and human rights

Jennifer M. Brown

See also chapter 6.13 Sexual harassment, chapter 6.15 Victimology, chapter 7.1 Ethical practice.

Definitions

Diversity describes the range of both visible and non-visible differences between individuals. It is often associated with equal opportunities, but Kandola and Fullerton (1998, p. 13) elucidate the differences between the two as shown in table 7.2.1.

Equal opportunities has been considered as comprising various strands, usually those which are underpinned by law, age, religion and belief, disability, gender, race and sexual orientation. These groups have been recognized as having suffered discrimination and harassment and being excluded from resources such as housing, employment or education, or subjected to violence by virtue of their group membership. Diversity is more broadly based and takes in a wider range of differences.

The Scottish Executive (2005) offers a useful definition of both:

Equality is about creating a fairer society where everyone can participate and has the opportunity to fulfil their potential. It is mostly backed by legislation designed to address unfair discrimination based on membership of a particular group.

Diversity is about recognizing and valuing difference in its broadest sense. It is about creating a culture and practices that recognize, respect, value and harness difference for the benefit of all.

The even broader concept of human rights is discussed by Ward (2008). A summary of his position is as follows: human rights are devices that facilitate individuals' pursuit of their own goals and defend their own interest and the interests of others; that this is a claim held by individuals and not tied to any particular category of human being such as social class, racial group or gender;

Table 7.2.1 Differences between diversity and equal opportunities (adapted from Kandola and Fullerton 1998)

Diversity	Equal opportunities
Internally initiated	Externally initiated
Driven by business needs	Driven by law
Qualitative objective (i.e. improving the environment)	Quantitative objective (improving access and increasing numbers of disadvantaged groups)
Aimed at pluralism	Assumes assimilation objectives
Proactive	Reactive
Concerned with all differences between people	Focused on age race, gender, religious belief, sexual orientation

and privileges certain human and social attributes considered essential for human functioning. Ward identifies five clusters of rights:

- Personal freedom, e.g. of speech or assembly
- Material subsistence, e.g. access to resources such as food, water education
- Physical security, e.g. freedom from torture, or violence
- Elemental equality, e.g. before the law and freedom from discrimination
- Social recognition, e.g. freedom to direct the course of one's own life and be treated with dignity and respect.

Ward (2008, p. 209) argues that human rights serve important functions for forensic psychologists in that they orientate practitioners 'to the necessary conditions for a formally worthwhile life for service users'. He is particularly exercised about the lack of attention paid to the rights of offenders, although others would argue it is the victim's rights that have been neglected (see chapter 6.15, this volume).

Relevant attributes for those who can legitimately lay claim to human rights include rational agency, sentience, emotional responsiveness, having an interest in living a good life, and belonging to a human community. Ward discusses the notion of 'forfeiture', which asks the question: does violating the wellbeing of others mean the transgressor loses their own human rights? Ward argues that whilst offenders should not forfeit their rights as human beings, it is legitimate that they suffer some form of 'curtailment', meaning a restriction to some of those rights, such as freedom of movement, by virtue of their incarceration.

Another related concept relevant to practice is cultural competence. Van den Bergh and Crisp (2004) articulate this with reference to social work, but it is usefully applied to forensic psychology practice. They chart its origins in the 1970s as dual perspective practice, whereby both macro and micro forces affecting clients were taken into account. By the 1980s this had evolved into ethnic-sensitive practice, with the recognition that ethnicity intersects with social class and practitioners needed to place their clients within their wider sociocultural context. By the 1990s, with the widening base of immigration and other groups' special needs being acknowledged, multicultural, cross-cultural, and then diverse practice developed. From the late 1990s culturally competent practice came into being. Deriving from the clinical and counselling fields were professional developments thought key to the provision of effective services and interventions with clients whose beliefs and attitudes may differ from the white, heterosexual majority. This included a knowledge base about the values and norms of recognizable groups as well as being aware of barriers that might impede access to effective services together with the skills to deliver those services.

Pollack and Hafner-Burton (2000) discuss the evolution of practice in relation to gender equality: equal treatment (and pay) in the workplace; positive action which focuses on creating the conditions most likely to result in equality of outcome and includes positive discrimination whereby category membership is privileged over other considerations; and mainstreaming which involves the systematic integration of gender issues throughout government institutions and policies. They evaluated the success of mainstreaming within the European Union, but also note criticisms: that specific policies on behalf of women may be discontinued; there is an over-reliance on administrative procedures resulting in variable uptake; and a failure to challenge existing paradigms of practice.

Law

The United Nations Declaration of Human Rights was adopted in 1948 and formed the basis of the European Convention on Human Rights published in 1950. Human rights were incorporated into British law in 1998. Within the United Kingdom there was a raft of legislation that recognized and prohibited discrimination based on gender, sexual orientation, marital status, race, colour, nationality, ethnic origin, religion, beliefs, disability, pregnancy or childbirth, or because a person is (or is not) a member of a trade union.

Separate bodies existed to issue guidance, promulgate good practice and enforce adherence, but the Equality Act of 2006 amalgamated the Equal

Opportunities Commission (EOC), Commission for Racial Equality (CRE) and Disabilities Rights Commission (DRC) into the Equality and Equal Rights Commission (EERC), which came into being in October 2007.

Of particular interest is the Race Relations (Amendment) Act 2000, which arose from the recommendations of Lord Macpherson's (1999) report into the murder of a black teenager, Stephen Lawrence. The resulting legislation placed a positive duty on public bodies to promote racial harmony and develop action plans for the implementation of policies. Thus criminal justice agencies developed race equality schemes (see e.g. Home Office 2005).

This practice has generalized; for example, the BPS has an equality and diversity plan in which it seeks itself to conform to legislation and good practice requirements (British Psychological Society 2008).

Codes of practice

Guidance about appropriate professional conduct with respect to equal treatment is available within professional associations' codes of conduct. For example, the American Psychological Association (APA) code specifies that members should not engage in unfair discrimination or knowingly engage in behaviour that demeans or creates a hostile working environment based on factors associated with age, gender, gender-related identity, race, ethnicity, cultural or national origins, religion, sexual orientation, disability, socioeconomic status, or any other bases prescribed by law.

The DRC, CRE and EOC issued codes of practice containing practical guidance in relation to promoting equality of opportunity and eliminating discrimination.

Unequal treatment

Considerable research is available that suggests discriminatory treatment of offenders on grounds of race (see e.g. Britton 2000; Bowling and Phillips 2002; Newburn, Shiner and Hayman 2004), the results of which suggests a racialization of practice. Research has also highlighted the inadequacies of the prison system in handling women offenders (Fawcett Society 2003), particularly in relation to suicide and self-harm, and revictimization through bullying or sexual assault.

Research has examined the treatment of minority groups who are themselves criminal justice practitioners. Discrimination has been found within education (Bing, Heard and Gilber 1995); organizational practices (Brown 2007); and career progression (Fielding 1999). The notion of 'double jeopardy' is also explored, where there is an intersection of two potential dimensions of discrimination such as race and gender (Martin 1994; Dodge and Pogrebin 2001; Brown and Harleston 2003). This research concludes that there is a racialized form of sexism experienced by black women officers from black officers and a sexualized form of racism experienced from white officers.

Remedies

Within the United Kingdom, employment tribunals are a distinctive remedy in law which seek to adjudicate between employers and employees over matters such as unfair dismissal, unauthorized deduction of pay and discrimination claims. Tribunals are independent judicial bodies supervised by a president who is legally qualified and supported by two lay members representing the interest of the trades union and employer. Government statistics reveal that the number of applications is rising, with 86,000 cases in 2004/5 and 132,577 in 2006/7. Of these the highest percentage, 33%, were unfair dismissals, 21% were sex discrimination cases and 7% age-related discrimination. About 3% were race discrimination and less that fifteen applications were on grounds of sexual orientation or religious belief. Success rates at tribunal for sex, race, age, disability or relious belief discrimination is less than 5%. (See chapter 5.4, this volume, for more details.)

Hayward, Peters, Rousseau and Seeds (2003) undertook an analysis of cases and found there to be more male that female applicants and more white than black. Just under half were resolved through the Advisory, Conciliation and Arbitration Service. These authors found that just under half of applicants were satisfied or very satisfied with the process, and about a third reported stress and depression as a consequence. Only about 5% of applications had remained in the employment of the complained-against employer.

Training

Diversity training has mushroomed into a cottage industry (Roberson, Kulik and Pepper 2003), although its effectiveness has not been subjected to much evaluation. In some cases diversity training has been found to heighten tensions amongst groups (D'Souza 1997). Roberson, Kulik and Pepper (2003) advocate a needs assessment to design effective diversity training, not least to distinguish between awareness and skills training; narrow or broad focus, i.e. equality or diversity in terms as defined above; homogenous or heterogeneous training groups; and use of trainers from minority or majority group membership. They also discuss the use and hazards of experiential training which directly confronts prejudices of members of the majority group or seeks descriptions of negative experiences from minority group members. Their model comprises three levels of needs analysis – organizational, personal and operational – and advocates evaluative research to review the efficacy of interventions.

Lum (1999) identified four tools which allows a practitioner to work culturally competently:

- awareness both professionally and personally of differences in education and upbringing of a diverse range of clients
- acquisition of knowledge related to culturally diverse practice
- development of skills to work with multicultured clients
- continued professional development to discover new facts about multicultural clients through inductive learning.

Van Den Bergh and Crisp (2004, p. 234) add a further tool, that of obtaining supervision to deal with negative feelings that may arise about minority group membership clients.

The Scottish Executive (2005) developed a rapid impact assessment toolkit for application to proposals prior to changing organizational practice. Although with particular reference to the Health Service, this offers useful guidance to any organizational, procedural or practice changes and comprises identification of:

- affected groups
- impacts on lifestyle
- social environment
- physical environment
- relationships between groups
- equality of opportunity
- access to services.

This tool was designed to assess the potential impact of policies or functions on people who currently experience disadvantage in their dealings with the services and is intended to support recognition of the rights accorded to vulnerable groups under the existing legislative framework.

FURTHER READING

Resources to ascertain rights and guidance can be found within professional associations' websites (see chapter 7.1, this volume, for details) and at www.equalityhumanrights.com, which is the site for the UK's Equality and Human Rights Commission. Ward's (2008) article about human rights is an excellent discussion of issues relevant to forensic psychology practice.

REFERENCES

Bing, R., Heard, C. and Gilbert, E. (1995) The experiences of African Americans and whites in criminal justice education: do race and gender make a difference. *Journal of Criminal Justice Education*, 6: 123–45.

Bowling, B. and Phillips, C. (2002) *Racism, Crime and Justice*. Harlow: Longman.

British Psychological Society (2008) Our Plan for Equality and Diversity. Leicester: The British Psychological Society.

Britton, N. (2000) Race and policing. *British Journal of Criminology*, 40: 639–58.

Brown, J. M. (2007) From cult of masculinity to smart macho: gender perspectives on police occupational culture. In M. O'Neill and M. Marks (eds.), *Police Occupational Culture: New Debates and Directions*. Sociology of Crime, Law and Deviance, vol. 9, pp. 189–210. Bingley: Emerald.

Brown, J. M. and Harleston, D. (2003) Being black or Asian and a woman in the police service. *Policing Futures*, 1: 19–32.

Dodge, M. and Pogrebin, M. (2001) African-American policewomen: an exploration of professional relationships. *Policing: An International Journal of Police Strategies and Management*, 24: 550–62.

D'Souza, D. (1997) The diversity trap. *Forbes*, 159: 83.

Fawcett Society (2003) *Interim Report on Women and Offending*. London: Fawcett Society.

Fielding, N. (1999) Policing's dark secret: the career paths of ethnic minority officers. *Sociological Research Online* 4/1. www.socresonline.org.uk/socresonline/4/Lawrence/fielding.html.

Hayward, B., Peters, M., Rousseau, N. and Seeds, K. (2003) Findings of the survey of employment tribunal applications. *Employment Relations Research Series*, 33. London: Department of Trade and Industry.

Home Office (2005) *Prison Service Associate Race Equality Scheme*. London: Home Office.

Kandola, R. S. and Fullerton, J. (1998) *Diversity in Action: Managing the Mosaic*. London: CIPD Publishing.

Lum, D. (1999) *Culturally Competent Practice: A Framework for Growth and Action*. Monterey, CA: Brooks/Cole.

Macpherson, Sir W. (1999) *The Stephen Lawrence Inquiry*. Cm 4262–1. London: HMSO.

Martin, S. E. (1994) 'Outsider within' the station house: the impact of race and gender on black women police. *Social Problems* 41: 363–400.

Newburn, T., Shiner, M. and Hayman, S. (2004) Race, crime and injustice. *British Journal of Criminology*, 44: 677–94.

Pollack, M. and Hafner-Burton, E. (2000) Mainstreaming gender in the European Union. *Journal of European Public Policy*, 7: 432–56.

Roberson, L., Kulik, C. and Pepper, M. (2003) Using needs assessment to resolve controversies in diversity training designs. *Group and Organizational Management*, 28: 148–74.

Scottish Executive/NHS (2005) *Equality and Diversity Toolkit*. Edinburgh: Scottish Executive.

Van Den Bergh, N. and Crisp, C. (2004) Defining culturally competent practice with sexual minorities, implications for social work education and practice. *Journal of Social Work Education*, 40: 221–38.

Ward, T. (2008) Human rights and forensic psychology. *Legal and Criminological Psychology*, 13: 209–18.

7.3 Expert witnesses in civil cases

Elizabeth A. Campbell

See also chapter 7.1 Ethical practice, chapter 7.4 The psychologist as expert witness in criminal cases.

Definitions

The civil courts are the venue where individuals who feel that they have been wronged or injured can sue for compensation. For example, personal injury cases may constitute a claim for physical injuries, or for psychological injuries. Such cases might involve people who have had accidents at work, been victims of childhood sexual abuse, or children who have been brain injured at birth because of medical negligence. Other 'non-criminal' courts include family courts and tribunals.

There are different kinds of witnesses who may give evidence in court proceedings (Saks 1990). A witness of fact is someone who is called to give evidence about things that they have seen, heard or experienced. Such witnesses are not allowed to offer opinions which would require some expert knowledge or skill. However, sometimes mental health professionals are called as witnesses of fact to testify about, for example, whether someone was offered treatment, how often they attended the clinic and whether the treatment had any benefits.

Clinicians providing treatment need to be careful to characterize any reports they might prepare as a 'professional witness' or a 'witness of fact' in contrast to the independent reports of an 'expert witness' (Blau 1998; Greenberg and Schuman 1997).

Standards of testimony

The expert witness must, however, be able to demonstrate expertise on the specific matters that the court is considering. For example, there has been a recent miscarriage of justice in the UK court when a paediatrician gave expert evidence on the statistical likelihood of unexplained deaths. However, he did not have expertise in statistical calculations and the erroneous testimony led to a wrongful conviction (Freckelton 2007).

An expert witness is someone who the court recognizes as having specialist expertise to assist the court by explaining technical or difficult concepts and by providing opinions based on their knowledge and experience. There are no particular qualifications required, but the decision about who may be admitted as an expert for the court is at the discretion of the judge.

In the United States, the admissibility of expert scientific evidence was pronounced upon by the Supreme Court (1993) in a landmark case, *Daubert v. Merrell Dow Pharmaceuticals*. The guidelines arising from this ruling are known as the Daubert guidelines. These suggest that the trial judge should bear in mind that certain principles apply in determining whether or not expert evidence is admissible. These are that the experts should rely on peer-reviewed evidence, based on testable theories which are regarded by the scientific community as acceptable, and that the expert should choose methods which have known error rates. This guidance was also later applied to non-scientific technical or specialist knowledge.

Earlier guidance about the use of experts in the courts came from a case in 1923 (*Frye* v. *United States*). This case led to the enunciation of what has been known as the 'general acceptance rule', i.e. that for an expert's testimony to be accepted by the courts it should be based on methods that have general acceptance within the scientific community. A further elaboration of this was found in the *Federal Rules of Evidence* (1975), which also suggested that any expert opinions must be of direct relevance to the key issues in the case. Rule 702 of the *Federal Rules* was revised in 2000 as follows:

If scientific, technical or other specialized knowledge will assist the trier of fact to understand the evidence or to determine a fact in issue, a witness qualified as an expert by knowledge, skill, experience, training or education, may testify thereto in the form of an opinion or otherwise, if (1) the testimony is based upon sufficient facts or data, (2) the testimony is the product of reliable principles and methods, and (3) the witness has applied the principles and methods reliably to the facts of the case.

There are specific rules called 'Civil Procedure Rules' in England and Wales which govern the production and use of expert evidence (Civil Justice Council 2005).

It is particularly important that experts are explicit about their specific area of expertise and competency. It goes without saying that the expert needs also to be up to date with the current scientific literature pertaining to their particular area of expertise and the opinion that they are offering. As well as having the requisite technical knowledge and experience, experts must also be skilled in the presentation of both written and oral testimony. The ability to separate fact from opinion is a very important skill for experts. The courts have often taken exception to experts who might be seen to be usurping the role of the court by providing an opinion that seems to bear on the decision that lies with the court.

The skills of report writing are the core skills for expert witnesses in civil cases, as they are not often called to give oral evidence in such cases (Gudjonsson 2007). A number of authors have suggested specific formats for reports and in some jurisdictions (e.g. England and Wales) the court prescribes the elements to be included in any report.

The expert must, however, be prepared to be asked to give evidence in court and to understand the etiquette and rules of the court. There are various training courses available to provide experts with the necessary knowledge and skills for producing appropriate written and oral testimony.

Controversies

There has been considerable public controversy in the United Kingdom about the use and abuse of expert evidence.

The new civil procedure rules were designed to ensure that the expert understood their role as being to assist the court rather than to appear for one side or the other in a case. This emphasis on the need for the expert to be impartial and objective led to a specification of the content of experts' reports. Parties to any dispute were also expected, if at all possible, to instruct a single joint expert. If parties were unable to agree to a single joint expert, then the court has the power to make the selection of such an expert. A protocol for the instruction of experts in civil cases has been published (Civil Justice Council 2005).

Procedures

There are some differences in court procedures and in the requirements for expert witnesses across the UK. The implications of these for expert witnesses in Scotland and Northern Ireland are helpfully described in the British Medical Association guidance (BMA 2007).

Edmond (2008) describes the various roles that experts might play in the Australian courts, while Brodsky (1999) discusses the role of the expert in the US courts.

Experts may take a different role at different parts of the proceedings. For example, experts may advise on various aspects of the defence prior to going to trial, they may comment on other experts' reports and assist their legal colleagues in identifying pertinent factors to address. They may also be required to meet with any other experts involved in the case in order to come to some agreement about common ground.

Gudjonsson (2007) conducted a survey of UK psychologists working as expert witnesses. Most referrals came from solicitors and the majority of reports were for the civil courts (60%). Court attendance by the expert was very rare in civil cases (1.2%). Oral evidence was most commonly required for cases in family courts (22%) and tribunals (46%).

The issue of the expertise of the expert came to the fore in an English case involving a paediatrician (Freckleton 2007). In this case, the Court of Appeal in England ruled that expert witnesses did not have any 'witness immunity' if their evidence was found to be deficient or below the expected standard. This means that expert witnesses can be disciplined by their relevant professional regulatory body for any misconduct while acting as an expert witness.

Conflict of roles

It is important for an expert witness to be clear about their role in any judicial proceedings. It is not desirable for a treating clinician or therapist to be instructed as an objective expert witness in relation to their client. This is because there may well be a conflict of the roles of a clinician and an expert. In addition, the material obtained by the clinician in the course of their treatment has been collected for rather different purposes and often will not have all the elements of information that would be required for the courts' purposes. In a British case (*In re B (a minor)* 1 FLR. 871), solicitors instructed the treating clinician, a child psychiatrist, to prepare a report for the courts. When this case came to the Court of Appeal, it was noted that it was important to ensure that instructions were impartial. In addition the court noted that the child psychiatrist, by virtue of her role as treating clinician, should have realized that she was disqualified from 'making any forensic contribution'. Since the child psychiatrist had been in a therapeutic relationship with the child, she was not in a position to provide expert evidence or be a joint expert for both parties. It is worth noting that the British Medical Association guidelines (BMA 2007) state 'As an independent expert witness the doctor will not be the treating doctor who gives evidence on fact...'

Guidelines for expert witnesses

In addition to the protocols and guidance produced by legal authorities in different countries, professional associations also offer and provide guidance for their members when acting as expert witnesses. For example, the American Academy of Pediatrics (2002) have published guidelines for expert witness testimony in medical malpractice litigation. The General Medical Council in the UK published guidance entitled *Acting as an Expert Witness* in 2008.

Other professional associations provide specific guidance on elements of expert witnessing. For example, the British Psychological Society has produced a number of relevant publications including: *Statement on the Conduct of Psychologists Providing Expert Psychometric Evidence to Courts and Lawyers* (2007b), *Guidelines on Memory and the Law* (2008) and *Psychologists as Expert Witnesses: Guidelines and Procedures for England and Wales* (2007a).

The Law Society of Scotland (undated) has published a code of practice relating to solicitors engaging expert witnesses.

Expert witness associations and accreditation of expert witnesses

There are a number of registers and listings of expert witnesses available. Some of these require the expert to be endorsed by two or more solicitors. Others use the term 'accredited experts'. However, there is no unanimity about the qualifications or experience required to be an expert witness.

The British Psychological Society hosts a *Directory of Expert Witnesses*. However, this directory does not incorporate any screening for entry but accepts self-declarations of expertise from members of that Society who are Chartered Psychologists. In Gudjonsson's (2007) survey of these psychologists, the majority (77%) expressed support for professional accredited registration. Other organizations which maintain lists of expert witnesses include: the Expert Witness Directory, the Academy of Experts, and the Expert Witness Institute. In addition, lists of accredited experts are maintained by the Law Society in England and in Scotland.

Ormerod and Roberts (2006) suggest that the English courts have taken a 'liberal' stance in accepting expert evidence. They suggest that there need to be clearer rules developed to govern the admissibility of expert evidence and increased regulation of experts.

Conclusion

Redmayne (2001) draws attention to the ways in which the courts and the scientific community, represented in the courts by expert witnesses, differ in their understanding of their underlying epistemologies. In addition, they use very different methodologies to arrive at respective legal or scientific judgements. Also, whereas the world of science may regard a hypothesis as 'unproven', the courts are required to reach a decision about the facts in any given case. This can lead to difficulties if the courts instruct the expert to give an opinion as to the relative proportion of causality that can be attributed to any given outcome. Whereas a scientific expert will want to hedge any opinion with caveats and qualifications, the court may require them to quantify the proportion that can be attributed to a specific identified causal agent.

In addition, there are often contradictory scientific opinions about the nature and quality of research evidence, the validity of methodologies, and the appropriateness of various techniques of data analysis.

FURTHER READING

Useful texts are M. Costanzo, D. Krauss and K. Pezdek (eds.) (2007) *Expert Psychological Testimony for the Courts* (London: Erlbaum) and W. J. Koch *et al.* (2006) *Psychological Injuries, Forensic Assessment, Treatment and Law* (New York: Oxford University Press).

REFERENCES

American Academy of Pediatrics (2002) Guidelines for expert witness testimony in medical malpractice litigation. *Pediatrics*, 109: 974–79.

Blau, T. H. (1998). *The Psychologist as Expert Witness*, 2nd edn. New York: Wiley.

British Medical Association (2007) *Expert Witness Guidance*. www.bma.org.uk/ap.nsf/content/expertwitness.

British Psychological Society (BPS) (2007a) *Psychologists as Expert Witnesses: Guidelines and Procedure for England and Wales*. Leicester: British Psychological Society.

(2007b) *Statement on the Conduct of Psychologists Providing Expert Psychometric Evidence to Courts and Lawyers*. Leicester: British Psychological Society.

(2008) *Guidelines on Memory and the Law*. Leicester: British Psychological Society.

Brodsky, S. L. (1999) *The Expert Witness: More Maxims and Guidelines*. Washington, DC: American Psychological Association.

Civil Justice Council (2005) *Protocol for the Instruction of Experts to Give Evidence in Civil Claims*. www.civiljusticecouncil.gov.uk.

Edmond, G. (2008) Secrets of the 'hot tub': expert witnesses, concurrent evidence and judge-led reform in Australia. *Civil Justice Quarterly*, 27: 51–82.

Freckelton, I. (2007) Expert witness immunity and the regulation of experts: *General Medical Council* v. *Meadow* 2006. *Psychiatry, Psychology and Law*, 14: 183–93.

General Medical Council (GMC) (2008) *Acting as an Expert Witness*. www.gmc-uk.org.

Greenberg, S. and Schuman, D. (1997) Irreconcilable conflict between therapeutic and forensic roles. *Journal of Professional Psychology Research and Practice*, 28: 50–7.

Gudjonsson, G. H. (2007) Psychologists as expert witnesses: the 2007 BPS Survey. *Forensic Update*, 92 Winter 2007/2008. Division of Forensic Psychology, British Psychological Society.

Law Society of Scotland (undated) *Code of Practice: Expert Witnesses Engaged by Solicitors*. www.expertwitnessscotland.info/codepract.htm.

Ormerod, D. and Roberts, A. (2006) The admissibility of expert evidence. In A. Heaton Armstrong *et al.* (eds.) (2006) *Witness Testimony: Psychological, Investigative and Evidential Perspectives*, pp. 401–24. Oxford: Oxford University Press.

Redmayne, M. (2001) *Expert Evidence and Criminal Justice*. Oxford: Oxford University Press.

Rules of Evidence for the United States Courts and Magistrates (1975) Available at: www.uscourts.gov/rules/.

Saks, M. J. (1990) Expert witnesses, non expert witnesses, and non witness experts. *Law and Human Behaviour*, 14: 291–313.

The psychologist as expert witness in criminal cases

Michael Carlin

See also chapter 7.1 Ethical practice, chapter 7.3 Expert witnesses in civil cases.

Definition

An expert witness is an individual who appears before a court or tribunal. The purpose is to provide information not discernible by ordinary means, about matters not within the ken of persons other than those familiar with the science surrounding the issue about which they will speak, and concerning which they have special knowledge by reason of their learning, experience and particular skill. As such, experts are treated in a different way from other witnesses in criminal trials.

Normally witnesses in criminal trials can only give evidence about matters they have directly observed or about observable facts within their ken, e.g. a witness saw the fight which led to the injuries, or the witness heard the accused say certain things. An expert witness, on the other hand, rarely gives evidence about the factual issues relating to the criminal charges, but will give opinion evidence about peripheral matters. Only an expert witness can give evidence as to their opinion.

Types of opinion

The type of peripheral matters which may be the subject of opinion evidence could be:
(a) the level of intellectual function of an accused person, and the implications this might have for his or her ability to take part in a trial;
(b) the capacity of an individual to comprehend the police caution administered before a police interview;

(c) the vulnerability of a witness in an interrogative situation and the extent to which such vulnerability can induce coerced-compliant admissions; or

(d) the risk a person might present in terms of violent/sexual recidivism.

None of these issues leads directly to the determination of the guilt/innocence of an accused person, but might have implications as to the extent to which: normal trial procedures may need to be modified to accommodate the cognitive limitations of an accused; evidence of alleged admissions might be inadmissible; alleged admissions may be rendered unreliable; a sentence to be imposed on a convicted person may need to reflect an increased risk of recidivism.

Psychologists should be aware that a criminal trial does not have as its end the need to know all about the event which gave rise to the subject matter of the charges. It is not concerned with absolute truth, but with establishing by sufficient and relevant evidence that a particular event occurred, the behaviour involved is the subject of criminal responsibility and it was the accused who behaved as is described in the charge.

If an individual, for example, is injured after being punched about the head and body, that would not become the subject of a criminal trial if it occurred as part of an officially organized boxing match. If the injury results, however, from an unlooked-for assault, then the criminal trial will require to determine that there was punching as described, it was as a result of an intentional act, and there is evidence sufficient in law to establish that the accused was the perpetrator. The issue of 'evidence sufficient in law' is of critical importance, since there requires to be corroboration of crucial facts before a finding of guilt can be made. However, the sufficiency criterion is not applied to expert testimony as such evidence need not be corroborated.

The subject matter of expert testimony must relate to issues that cannot be discerned without expert knowledge, such as:

- evidence of psychological theory, the results of a psychometric test, or the results of experiments, e.g. compliance, the performance of an accused tested using the Wechsler Adult Intelligence Scale (WAIS) or the results of experiments carried out to test the ability of individuals to identify unfamiliar faces;
- the interpretation of psychometric data, or the prediction of risk, e.g. factors known to indicate an increased risk of recidivism, or challenging the interpretation of data produced by testing by another psychologist;
- advice as to the effectiveness of treatment programmes, e.g efficacy of sex offender treatment programmes or the fitness of an individual to be included in such programmes.

Procedure

The process which results in a psychologist being called as an expert witness starts some time before the matter ever comes to court. The psychologist, in most instances, becomes involved in the matter because they are recognized as having special knowledge about the issue of concern to the court, and their opinion is sought by either the prosecution or the defence, with a view to bolstering, in some way, the presentation of the case from the perspective of one side or another. The trial process is adversarial in nature, and each side is seeking to persuade the court as to the correctness of their position. Occasionally the psychologist may be instructed by the court itself, but this would, generally, occur after conviction when the issue might be one of risk assessment. In Scotland, for example, there is a requirement that the court obtain a report from a psychologist, in all cases where the accused person has been convicted by a jury of a sexual offence, as to the level of risk of recidivism (Criminal Procedure (Scotland) Act 1995, as amended).

No matter what the origin of the instructions, be it the prosecution, the defence or the court, the obligations on the psychologist as a person offering expertise is the same: the psychologist must provide objective opinion on matters which could not be discerned other than by someone with the appropriate expertise, based on reliable observations and/or tests. It is not for the psychologist to take sides, no matter who instructs them and no matter where their sympathy might lie.

Potential traps

The traps into which psychologists might fall include:
1. Thinking that their expertise relates to matters which are, in fact, discernible without the benefit of psychological evidence. The case of *R v. Turner* [1975] QB 834 highlights this. In *Turner*, a psychiatrist sought to give evidence, as an expert, about how people can react to stress. The court pointed out that a jury does not need to be told how stress affects normal individuals – that is within the knowledge of us all. More recently, the issue arose in a Scottish case (*HMA v. Grimmond* – www.scotcourts.gov.uk/opinions.osb1807.html). In that case, a psychologist sought to give evidence that, having read the statements of witnesses, she was of the opinion that they were reliable witnesses. The issue of reliability is not something

about which psychologists (or anyone else for that matter) have any expertise. Reliability is matter for the court to determine based upon the knowledge and skill we all have.

2. Going beyond their remit. The Scottish case of *Davie v. Edinburgh Corporation* in 1953 stated: 'The duty of the expert is to furnish the judge or jury with the necessary scientific criteria for testing the accuracy of their conclusions, so as to enable the judge or jury to form their own independent judgement by the application of these criteria to the facts proven in evidence.' Accordingly, the psychologist must provide an opinion reached as a result of scientific criteria (their knowledge of the subject and the result of applying their knowledge to the issue before the court), so that the court can answer the legal question, taking account of the evidence of the expert and the other evidence before the court. Psychological tests and instruments have been developed to assist in the assessment of psychological constructs. The courts, however, are concerned with legal concepts and these need not be equivalent to the psychological construct. Significant impairment of intellectual functioning does not equate, of itself, for instance, with lack of fitness to take part in a trial. If, the issue is 'Was the confession, alleged to have been made by the accused, fairly obtained', the psychologist must not opine that the behaviour of the police was/was not fair. What could be said by the psychologist might be that the accused presents as compliant to a significant extent and that coerced-compliant confessions may be unreliable, (or) that the accused may not be capable of comprehending the police caution, and in the course of his/her interview may not have appreciated his/her right not to answer questions, or that there are standards for ethical police interviewing and that the apparent behaviour of the police in ignoring the accused's vulnerability might have fallen below the standards of ethical interviewing. Based on such an opinion (and other evidence) the court determines if the police interview was/was not fairly conducted, and if the alleged admissions are/are not admissible in evidence.

3. Ignoring the factual aspects of the case: what the expert has to say is only one facet of a case, and the factual issues will impinge on the final decision of the court. A good example of a psychologist ignoring the factual aspects of the case occurred in the case of *HMA v. Blagojevic* 1995 SCCR 570. Mr Blagojevic had been charged with murder, and part of the evidence was the content of a police interview. The defence led the evidence of a psychologist that Mr Blagojevic was suggestible to a significant extent. The jury were instructed to ignore this evidence, as there had been no

factual evidence that Mr Blagojevic had been subjected to interrogative pressure or that he was under pressure at the time he made admissions to the police. So, no matter what evidence an expert gives, it is only part of the evidence a court requires to consider when answering the legal question.

4. Providing an inadequate scientific basis for the opinion. An expert has to provide the court with the scientific basis for the opinion they put forward. It can never be the case that the expert simply says 'I am an expert and this is what I believe to be the case.' That scientific basis may be the application of established theory to a particular set of circumstances. For example, a psychologist might base their opinion on the theory of compliant responses, where individuals who are 'outnumbered' in a social setting can behave in a compliant manner, saying things they need not believe to be true (Asch 1952, 1956). The expert can then, by the application of this theory, opine that, if the accused is correct that he/she was 'outnumbered' when interviewed by the police and just said what he/she did as a means of ending a stressful event, such behaviour can be expected in such a situation, and that compliant responses can be unreliable. Or, as the expert, Professor Brian Clifford did in the case of *Steele and Campbell* v. *Her Majesty's Advocate* (www.scotcourts.gov.uk/opinions/), set up a standard scientific experiment to test a particular hypothesis ('(1) How likely is it that all four officers were able to note the remark in such similar terms? and (2) What is the likelihood that all four officers were able to note the remark in such similar terms in the absence of any comparison or collaboration whatsoever between them?').

5. Using tests or instruments that are either out of date or inappropriate. Too often, there may be a temptation to use particular tests, simply because the psychologist is familiar with them. Heilbrun (1992) makes it clear that when using psychological tests, such tests must be relevant to the legal issues being addressed. The tests used must also be the most recent version. Many psychological tests use norms to enable the performance of an individual to be compared with the general population. If an old version of a test is used, the norms for that version may no longer apply to the current population. It is not unknown for psychologists to use an out-of-date version of the WAIS! Care must also be taken that the tests have established reliability. Just because there is a published test, does not mean that the test always produces reliable results (Cooke and Carlin 1998). This issue is acknowledged by Gudjonsson (2003, p. 372) in relation to his measure of compliance. Again, it must be remembered that the court is not so much concerned with how the subject of the assessment compares

with the general population. The concern of the court is with the function-ality of the particular individual. Saying that an individual is in the fifth percentile does not assist the court much, but saying that the implication of this is that the individual will experience difficulties in comprehending the language usually used in court might enable the court to make a determination about adapting the normal court procedures. The reliability of particular instruments may be an issue when dealing with risk assessment. Actuarial assessment instruments, for example, usually only tell you about the risk level for a particular cohort, not about the level of risk of recidivism for an individual within the cohort. The court, however, is not concerned with a cohort, but with the individual. Sometimes, there will be no test which can provide the scientific evidence needed to support an opinion, and the psychologist may have to go back to basic psychological principles and devise a test of their own (Munro and Carlin 2002).

6. Being tempted to provide an opinion outside area of expertise, e.g. in the case of Professor Sir Roy Meadow, who as an eminent paediatrician gave evidence as to the statistical likelihood of multiple cot deaths in the same family. As was discovered, after his evidence contributed to the wrongful conviction of a mother for causing the deaths of her children, he was not an expert statistician. On another occasion, the issue of 'the right expert' arose in a case where there was an allegation that a man had had sexual inter-course with a 'protected person' under mental health legislation. The prosecution proposed to lead the evidence of two psychiatrists who, with-out any evidence of testing, but simply on the basis of a brief discussion with the female concerned, would have said that the female was 'a pro-tected person'. The legislation, however, defines 'protected person' in terms of 'significant impairment of intellectual and social functioning'. Such a definition implies testing of functioning by a person qualified so to test. The prosecution changed their mind about calling the psychiatrists when there was a challenge to their expertise, and had the witness assessed by a clinical psychologist. Following such an assessment, the accused pleaded guilty (Carlin and Cooke 1997).

7. Failing to observe role boundaries: is it appropriate that the expert provides a forensic assessment for someone they have dealt with in a clinical setting, since this may give rise to conflicts of interest? If such a report is provided, the expert's objectivity will most certainly be challenged in cross-examination. Apart from that consideration, the expert has to consider the effect accepting instructions might have on the future clinical relation-ship with the subject of the report. The expert needs to be prepared to

decline instructions if such a conflict arises. Temptation to take instructions in such a case on the basis that it will help the client should be resisted – that is not the role of a forensic assessment and report. Another ethical issue relates to the matter of informed consent. Just because, for example, the expert has instructions from the defence does not relieve them of the responsibility to get the informed consent of the person to be assessed. The same is true in relation to a risk assessment instructed by the court – the expert may need to consider the issue of informed consent in such a situation too, before interviewing the subject of the report. A doctor called to a police station to take a blood sample under road traffic legislation will not take such a sample by force when the subject refuses his/her consent to provide it. The refusal to cooperate may have consequences for the subject, but the failure to obtain informed consent may have consequences for the expert. And care must be taken over the issue of confidentiality. If a subject seeks to impart something in confidence, it may only be because the expert has not spelled out, in advance, the limits to confidentiality in such a setting.

Giving evidence

The process of giving evidence is that the witness is first questioned by the side which commissioned the report about the issues on which they assert their expertise. This is referred to as 'examination-in-chief'. It is followed by further questioning by the other side in the dispute ('cross-examination'), and this may, in turn, be followed by further questioning by the original questioner ('re-examination').

The examination-in-chief should be reasonably relaxed. The person questioning the expert witness wants to present them at their best. The questioning should not be difficult. What may come as a surprise is that this may be the first time the witness meets the questioner. Lawyers tend not to speak to their expert witnesses in advance of the trial. Occasionally, they will see the witness before the trial to go over the report they have prepared, but this cannot be expected in all cases. Again, it should not come as a surprise if the questioner does not focus on what the witness thinks are the important parts of their report. The questioner selects what part of the expert evidence he/she wishes the court to have before them. In effect, it is the questioner, by selecting what the expert says, who is giving evidence.

Cross-examination is likely to be a more rigorous test of expertise. This questioner may seek to belittle the expert, challenge their expertise, suggest they are partial and not objective, and may seek to present them as unreliable. There are a variety of techniques which may be used. For example, the cross-examiner may get the expert into an acquiescent mode of responding by flattery and feeding easy questions with which it is easy to agree, and then slip in an apparently innocuous suggestion equally easy to agree with, but one which later comes back to haunt them. The questions often take the form of a monologue with the tag 'you will agree with this, will you not?' There may be much to agree with, but the expert must be sure that they agree with all of it! Later on, the questioner may be heard to tell the jury 'You heard the expert agree with me that …' and it is too late then to qualify the extent of agreement. The only way to deal with this is to listen carefully to every question, and only answer it when what is being asked is understood. If the question is not understood, the expert should say so. Again, the questioner may ignore the main aspects of the expert opinion and seek to find fault with what the expert considers secondary, unimportant parts of their report. The expert may, for example, have included a long statement on the background of the person assessed. They then go on to state that the person is poor at recalling autobiographical information. These two statements are, on the face of it, inconsistent, and this inconsistency might be embarrassing. To avoid this, the expert must ensure that they identify the sources of their information (in this case, by including the fact that medical records/ earlier reports were relied on for the background information). An exchange such as the following is then avoided:

Q. You report a detailed background, running to two pages, do you not?
A. Yes.
Q. A lot of autobiographical information?
A. Yes.
Q. But you have said he was poor at providing autobiographical information, have you not?
A. I did.
Q. Would you not agree that there is an obvious inconsistency here?
A. Yes, but the background was all taken from the case notes from X.
Q. You do not say that in your report. Are there any other significant omissions you want to tell us about before we go any further?

The re-examination, if it occurs, is usually a damage-limitation exercise.
So how can the risk of a damaging cross-examination be managed? The expert must write a report which provides no opportunity for such a form

of questioning. Too often training in report writing involves writing clinical reports. These are written for fellow professionals. The court is a different forum. Clinical assessment and forensic assessment differ in significant ways, and this will result in reporting in a different way (Melton *et al.* 1997). The expert must write a report which meets the expectations of the court – the onus to communicate effectively is on the person providing information. The communicator must design their speech/text to be comprehensible to the audience for which it is intended (Clark and Murphy 1982). The expert needs to ensure that what is put in their report is relevant, and that anything irrelevant and superfluous has been edited out. They must use language that will be understood by non-professionals (jurors and judges do not understand what is meant by 'flat affect', for example). The point is not to sound like an expert, but to be understood as an expert. It is no bad thing to have the report critically evaluated, in this regard, by a colleague who has experience of giving evidence, in advance of submitting it.

Conclusion

The psychologist who is offered instructions to act as an expert witness must ensure that
(a) they have the expertise expected in such a situation;
(b) there are no obstacles to their reporting objectively;
(c) they get informed consent from the subject of the report beforehand;
(d) their approach is scientific;
(e) their opinion is supported by evidence;
(f) they do not answer the legal question;
(g) their report is written in a manner which they can defend and which will be comprehensible to their intended audience.

By following this course of action, should the psychologist end up having to give evidence, the event will be less stressful, provided they remember to listen to the questions carefully and only answer the question which is asked, and that what they say is only one part of all of the evidence that will be used in the determination of the legal question.

In England and Wales, rules for experts in criminal cases have been drawn up and can be found in the Criminal Procedure Rules Part 33 (2008). Other useful references are Gold (2003) and Ackerman (2006).

Michael Carlin

REFERENCES

Akerman, M. J. (2006) Forensic report writing. *Journal of Clinical Psychology*, 62: 59–72.

Asch, S. E. (1952) Effects of group pressure upon modification and distortion of judgements. In G. E. Swanson, T. M. Newcomb and E. L. Hartley (eds.), *Readings in Social Psychology*, pp. 183–97. New York: Holt, Rinehart & Winston.

(1956) Studies of independence and conformity: a minority of one against a unanimous majority. *Psychological Monographs*, 70 (whole no. 416).

Carlin, M. T. and Cooke, D. J. (1997) Competence to determine 'protected person' status under the Mental Health (Scotland) Act 1984. *Expert Evidence*, 5: 58–60.

Clark, H. H. and Murphy, G. L. (1982) Audience design in meaning and reference. In J. F. Le Ny and W. Kintsch (eds.), *Language and Comprehension*, pp. 287–99. Amsterdam: North-Holland.

Cooke, D. J. and Carlin, M. T. (1998) Gudjonsson Suggestibility Scales Manual. Book review. *Expert Evidence*, 6: 62–3.

Criminal Procedure Rules, part 3 (7th update) (2008) www.justice.gov.uk.

Gold, A. D. (2003) *Expert Evidence in Criminal Law: The Scientific Approach*. Toronto: Irwin Law.

Gudjonsson, G. H. (2003) *The Psychology of Interrogations and Confessions*. Chicester: Wiley.

Heilbrun, K. (1992) The role of psychological testing in forensic assessment. *Law and Human Behavior*, 16: 257–72.

Melton, G. B., Poythress, N. G., Petrila, J. and Slobogin, C. (1997) *Psychological Evaluations for the Courts*. New York: Guilford Press.

Munro, F. M. and Carlin, M. T. (2002) Witness competence – truthfulness and reliability assessment: the role of the psychologist. *Legal and Criminological Psychology*, 7: 15–23.

7.5 Professional training and education in forensic psychology

Elizabeth A. Campbell

As indicated by the scope of this volume, the ways in which psychology can be applied to forensic issues, populations and contexts is very diverse. It would not be possible for any individual to claim to have complete expertise in such a wide range of skills and knowledge. It may therefore seem a little puzzling that some psychologists adopt the title 'forensic psychologist' since, at first glance, this would appear to be a hyperbolical claim to make if one assumes that a professional title implies professional competencies across the entire field. However, if the descriptor is taken as an indication of the general context in which an individual works then the use of such a title has some utility.

The issues identified in the introductory chapter to this volume relating to the definition of forensic psychology and forensic psychology practice are reflected in diverse training routes, systems of accreditation and licensing internationally.

The professional training and license to practice requirements in a selection of countries will be briefly reviewed.

United Kingdom

The British Psychological Society (BPS: www.bps.org.uk) is the main professional association, for practitioners, academics and students, in the United Kingdom. Until 2009, the BPS was also the voluntary regulator for psychologists as there was no system of mandatory registration for practitioner psychologists. Prior to 2009, the BPS was also the official UK body responsible for the recognition of practitioner psychologists trained in other parts of the European Community and from overseas.

Part of the BPS's role has been the accreditation of degrees in psychology in UK universities. This accreditation applied both to undergraduate degrees (three to four years duration) and to graduate degree programmes in clinical, counselling, health, education, forensic, occupational and sports and exercise psychology. The BPS provides professional examinations and certification in some areas of specialization. The BPS continues to hold a register of Chartered Psychologists which includes both academics and practitioners but this qualification is not a license to practice.

In 1977, a Division of Criminological and Legal Psychology was set up within the British Psychological Society. Membership records showed that the majority of members of this Division in the early years were clinical psychologists, with a smaller group being academic psychologists. In 1999, the Division changed its name to the Division of Forensic Psychology.

The BPS has accredited a number of one-year Master's degrees in the area of forensic psychology, many of these programmes having a primary aim of training psychologists for work in prisons. Students on some of these programmes were sponsored by the UK Home Office, the government body responsible for prisons. Over the years the increase in numbers within the Division was fuelled by psychologists working within criminal justice systems. As well as following a BPS-accredited Master's programme, students were required to undertake a minimum two-year supervised internship, the majority being completed within the prison service, and to undertake the professional examinations of the BPS in order to be certified as a Chartered Forensic Psychologist.

From mid 2009, the role of mandatory regulator of practitioner psychologists, but not academic psychologists, was given to the Health Professions Council (HPC: www.hpc-uk.org) via UK-wide legislation. The HPC is the regulator for a diverse group of health professions including paramedics, occupational therapists and physiotherapists. The HPC regulates by controlling the use of certain professional titles rather than by controlling the functions of practitioners. The title psychologist alone is not a title protected by law in the UK.

For practitioner psychologists, the HPC regulates overarching titles – registered psychologist or practitioner psychologist. In addition, the HPC also protects the following adjectival titles: clinical psychologist; counselling psychologist; health psychologist; educational psychologist; forensic psychologist; occupational psychologist; and sports and exercise psychologist. The roles of the HPC include: setting the threshold level of qualification for entry to the practitioner psychologist part of their register; describing the 'standards of proficiency' (knowledge and competencies) required for registration and used for the approval of qualifications leading to entry to the register; and disciplinary functions.

The HPC does not approve Master's level courses in forensic psychology since this is not the threshold level of qualification for the register. For entry to the forensic psychologist section of the HPC register, candidates are required to have a BPS-accredited Master's degree plus the BPS qualification in forensic psychology. Clinical, counselling and educational psychologists are required to have doctoral degrees for registration with the HPC (HPC 2009).

European Economic Area

Because of the diversity both in length and in titles of qualifications across European higher education institutions, an agreement was reached in 1999 by twenty-nine countries to harmonize degree structures into a three-year 'Batchelor's' and a two-year 'Master's' degree, the Bologna agreement (Lunt 2002). Subsequently there has also been the introduction of a Europe-wide credit system (e.g. a Batchelor's degree plus a Master's is worth 300 credits in the European Credit Transfer and Accumulation System, ECTS).

There is an umbrella organization of thirty-four European countries' psychologists' associations: the European Federation of Psychologists' Associations (EFPA). EFPA has played a very important role in attempting to raise standards for professional training in psychology and to facilitate mutual recognition and thus mobility of psychologists in Europe. The organization has facilitated agreement among its thirty-four member associations that the minimum of six years of education and training is required, of which a minimum of five years must be university based and at least one year of supervised practice (i.e. at least 360 ECTS). The EuroPsy is the name given to this benchmarking of standards (www. efpa.eu/europsy).

EFPA holds a register of practitioner psychologists who meet the EuroPsy standards on the Register of European Psychologists. The awarding of the EuroPsy recognition is made via national professional associations using the quality benchmark established by EFPA. Three broad practice contexts are recognized as education, clinical and health, and work and organizational. There is also an 'other' category but no specific forensic context. As yet, the status of a EuroPsy registered psychologist is not enshrined in legislation; however, EFPA are continuing to lobby for the European authorities to formally recognize the EuroPsy as the standard for practice as a psychologist in Europe.

United States of America

In the USA, licensing of psychologists is conducted at state level while accreditation of professional doctoral degrees is carried out by the American Psychological Association (APA 2006). There is an agreed licensing examination, the Examination for the Practice of Professional Psychology, which has been widely adopted across the USA and Canada and is administered via the Association of State and Provincial Psychology Boards (Rehm and DeMers 2006).

Within the APA, Division 41 (Psychology and Law) was established in 1980–1 and merged with the American Psychology–Law Society in 1984 (Brigham 1999). This can be found at www.ap-ls.org.

The American Board of Professional Psychology (www.abpp.org) in conjunction with the American Board of Forensic Psychology (www.abfp.com) has a specialty certification in forensic psychology. These boards embrace a broad definition of forensic psychology, and it is a requirement that candidates for the forensic diploma must already hold an APA-accredited doctoral degree as well as being state licensed. The APA (2008) has produced specialty guidelines for forensic psychology.

There are a number of joint psychology and law graduate programmes in American Universities which offer joint PhD/JD, PsyD/JD, or Master's degrees. There is a guide to Graduate Programs in Forensic and Legal Psychology 2007–8 at www.ap-ls.org/education/GraduateDirectory 2008.pdf.

Rubin et al. (2009) reviewed 231 APA-accredited clinical psychology doctoral programmes and found that more than half of them offered some specialization training stream or track during the programme. The areas of specialized training that were most common included child, health, forensic, family and neuropsychology. Packer (2008) discusses key issues around specialized forensic training.

Canada

The Criminal Justice Section of the Canadian Psychological Association (CPA: www.cpa.ca) provides an academic and practitioner forum for psychologists working in that area. However, registration as a psychologist is through the relevant Provincial and Territorial Regulatory Bodies, such as the College of Psychologists of Ontario. These bodies recognize practice at both Master's and doctoral levels. They regulate the titles psychologist and psychological associate. There is no regulation of specialist titles.

The CPA accredits university doctoral programmes and internships in professional areas of psychology on a voluntary basis.

Australia

The Australian Psychology Accreditation Council (www.apac.psychology.org. au) was formed in 2003 by both the Australian Psychological Society (APS) and the state authorities via the Council of Psychologists Registration Boards. Registration as a psychologist is through the relevant State Psychologists' Registration Board in the locality where the psychologist practises. In order to be eligible to register, the practitioner must have a four-year APAC-accredited undergraduate degree plus either an APAC-accredited postgraduate programme (APAC 2009) or two years of supervised practice as a psychologist that has been approved by the Psychologists' Registration Board. The Boards register the title psychologist but not specialist titles such as forensic psychologist.

APAC-accredited postgraduate courses include the following specialisms: clinical, community, clinical forensic, forensic, health, educational and occupational.

The APS has nine colleges covering a range of specialisms within psychology: clinical, clinical neuropsychologists, community, counselling, educational, forensic, health, organizational and sport. A minimum of six years full-time accredited university training is usually required for registration as a forensic psychologist. This is not restricted to those postgraduate programmes designated as forensic psychology training programmes.

Summary

There are various training and education routes into working in the field of forensic psychology. This seems appropriate given the wide scope of practice and expertise in this area. The best sources of information about graduate training and education can usually be found within the websites of national psychological professional bodies and the websites of national or state regulating bodies.

REFERENCES

American Psychological Association (2006) *Guidelines and Principles for Accreditation of Programs in Professional Psychology.* www.apa.org.
    (2008) *Specialty Guidelines for Forensic Psychology.* www.ap-ls.org.
Australian Psychology Accreditation Council (2009) *Rules for Accreditation and Accreditation Standards for Psychology Courses.* Melbourne: APAC.
Brigham, J. C. (1999) What is forensic psychology, anyway? *Law and Human Behavior,* 23: 273–98.
Health Professions Council (2009) *Threshold Level of Qualification for Entry to the Register.* www.hpc-uk.org/apply/psychologists/threshold/.
Lunt, I. (2002) A common framework for the training of psychologists in Europe. *European Psychologist,* 7: 180–91.
Packer, I. K. (2008) Specialized practice in forensic psychology: opportunities and obstacles. *Professional Psychology: Research and Practice,* 39: 245–9.
Rehm, L. P. and DeMers, S. T. (2006) Licensure. *Clinical Psychology: Science and Practice,* 13: 249–53.
Rubin, N. J., Bebeau, M., Leigh, I. W., Lichtenberg, J. W., Nelson, P. D., Portnoy, S., Smith, L. I. and Kaslow, N. J. (2009) Specialized training in APA-accredited clinical psychology doctoral programs: findings from a review of program websites. *Clinical Psychology: Science and Practice,* 16: 348–59.

Part VIII

Research practice

has a strong tradition in anthropology that gives importance to the

8.1 Criminals' personal narratives

David Canter

See also chapter 4.2 Criminal careers, chapter 8.3 Drawing out the meaning in data: multidimensional scaling within forensic psychology research.

Definitions

Within psychology and related social sciences there is an emerging framework for understanding a person's actions and experiences in terms of what McAdams (McAdams 1993) refers to as 'The Stories We Live By'. This reflects the approach given particular emphasis by Bruner (Bruner 1990) in his critique of the information-processing model that so dominates cognitive psychology. It is argued that people give sense to their past, current and future lives by the roles they see themselves playing in key episodes that they remember experiencing. They formulate views of their identity and self-concept through an interpretation of the unfolding storyline that they see their lives as being. Importantly, the concept of a story here is not that of a fiction but of a constructed account derived from events and interactions with others.

Growing out of personality theory, the psychological emphasis is on 'personal' narratives: the stories that people tell about themselves. This contrasts with a strong tradition in anthropology that gives importance to the dominant narratives in cultures derived from second- and third-party accounts, describing the key episodes in the lives of others. It is also distinct from the focus of many literary studies that seek to explore the nature and structure of fictional stories.

It is argued, notably by Canter (2008), that the narrative approach is particularly fruitful when considering criminality because it helps to bridge the gap between the disciplines of psychology and law. In essence, the argument is that the law deals with human beings as agents in their own actions and seeks to identify the narrative that explains how the crime came to occur.

By contrast, most of the social and behavioural sciences emphasize the processes outside the individual's control that give rise to actions; whether they be genetic, neurological, hormonal, upbringing or social pressures. Exploring how people make sense of their lives and seek to influence their destiny as active agents engaging with the people and objects around them therefore provides a social psychological framework that connects with legal explorations of *mens rea* and 'motive'. In this regard, the way in which the personal narrative approach may be considered to empower respondents, treating them as experts on their own lives (drawing on a framework emphasized by Harré 1979), accords more closely with the legal perspective on people.

Application

In one of the first explorations of this framework within the context of criminal actions it was suggested that the actions the offender carries out during a crime may be regarded as one reflection of a personal narrative (Canter 1995). This is rather different from the usual focus on verbal accounts of a person reflecting on his/her life. It was elaborated to argue that the offender's narrative was implicit in whether the victim was treated as a 'person', 'vehicle' or 'object'. One further implication of this perspective is that all crimes are in some sense interpersonal in that they imply the acting out of a relationship between the offender and explicit or implicit victims. Crimes are thus crucial episodes in an unfolding storyline the offender is living. How the criminal construes that narrative is thus of considerable psychological significance.

The challenge of this emerging framework is to operationalize the concept of a personal narrative and to develop systematic ways of studying it. There has been little substantive research on this within the criminal context, but some possibilities are looking fruitful. One such approach has been to determine if the dominant narratives identified within the realms of English literature may be relevant to real-life storylines. Both McAdams (1993) and Canter (1995) have suggested that Frye's (1957) proposal, that there are four dominant narratives that run throughout all storytelling, may be productive. Frye demonstrated that virtually all major stories could be seen as either adventures (which Frye calls 'romances'), tragedies, love stories (which he calls 'comedies') or comedy (which he calls 'irony'). Although Frye made the point that fictional stories are always likely to have a much tidier and clearer structure to them than real life. Also, by being able to draw on 2,000 years of drama and friction, Frye can identify canonical, archetypal stories that illustrate his major types (or 'mythoi' as he calls them).

In order to explore the hypothesis that criminals may see their crimes as part of one of Frye's mythoi, Canter, Kaouri and Ioannou (2003) provide one feasible, quantitative approach. They argued that one crucial aspect of a narrative was that participants are playing a role within some storyline. Therefore the nature of that role could be taken as some summary of the nature of the story it was within. For example, by asking a criminal to think of a crime he has committed and then to say how much it felt like 'being on an adventure', 'just doing a job', 'something I had to do' etc. it is possible to get quantitative answers that are open to statistical analysis. Their results, drawing on multidimensional scaling (MDS) analysis, did lend some moderate support to the hypothesis derived from Frye's work. They indicated that whilst all four types of narrative that Frye offers may not be directly applicable to criminals' views of their crimes, nonetheless there are distinctions in the roles they see themselves as playing, which broadly map onto a tragic view of themselves and their crimes, or a view of them as part of a more optimistic adventure.

A complementary approach was taken by Alison *et al.* (2000) based on published biographies and open-ended interviews with armed robbers. From the MDS analysis of the content of their interviews, they proposed that armed robbers could be seen to be playing one of three different roles, loosely related to the professionalism of the robbers. Ongoing research using a variety of structured and unstructured techniques is exploring how these roles may differ between crimes and criminals.

Conclusion

The potential value of this work runs through the whole range of forensic psychology activities. It offers the possibility of informing the formulation of *offender profiles* by enabling investigators to understand more clearly the psychological processes of which the crime is a part, and thus possible characteristics of the offender. The interviewing of offenders can also be informed by an understanding of the storyline they may consider their crimes to be key episodes within. But possibly most importantly, it provides a framework for working with offenders to help them reconstruct their understanding of their personal narratives. This connects directly with the narrative approach to therapy (White and Epston 1990) in which clients are encouraged to review their ways of thinking about key episodes in their past life as a way of finding a different future for themselves.

REFERENCES

Alison, L., Rockett, W. Deprez, S. and Watts, S. (2000) Bandits, cowboys and Robin's men: the facets of armed robbery. In D. V. Canter and L. J. Alison (eds.), *Profiling Property Crimes*. Offender Profiling Series, vol. 4, pp. 75–106. Aldershot: Ashgate.

Bruner, J. S. (1990) *Acts of Meaning*. Cambridge, MA: Harvard University Press.

Canter, D. V. (1995) *Criminal Shadows*. London: HarperCollins.

   (2008) In the kingdom of the blind. In D. Canter and P. Zukaiskiene (eds.), *Psychology and Law: Bridging the Gap*, pp. 1–22. Aldershot: Ashgate.

Canter, D., Kaouri, C. and Ioannou, M. (2003) The facet structure of criminal narratives. In S. Levy and D. Elizur (eds.), *Facet Theory: Towards Cumulative Social Science*, pp. 27–38. Ljubljana: University of Ljubljana, Faculty of Arts, Centre for Educational Development.

Frye, N. (1957) *Anatomy of Criticism*. Princeton, NJ: Princeton University Press.

Harré, R. (1979) *Social Being: A Theory for a Social Psychology*. Oxford: Blackwell.

McAdams, D. P. (1993) *The Stories We Live By*. New York: William Morrow.

White, M. and Epston, D. (1990) *Narrative Means to Therapeutic Ends*. New York: W. W. Norton.

8.2   Designing research using facet theory

Jennifer M. Brown

See also chapter 1.1 Action system applied to forensic topics, chapter 1.6 Facet meta-theory, chapter 1.9 Investigative psychology, chapter 8.3 Drawing out the meaning in data: multidimensional scaling within forensic psychology research.

Origins and definitions

Facet theory draws on principles of mathematical set theory to define variables. Dancer (1990, p. 327) states that 'the suitability of facet theory as a tool for formulating definitions of behavioural constructs comes from the clarity and precision it brings to the process of identifying basic components of a set of variables and the relation these components bring to empirical data'. Basically the method allows the testing of hypotheses concerning the correspondence between a conceptualization of the phenomenon under investigation and its empirical reality, as demonstrated through analyses of data. The architect was Louis Guttman (see Dancer 1990 for more details).

It is difficult to do justice to describing and explaining how to undertake research with a facet design in a short essay. The collection edited by Canter (1985) provides a comprehensive overview. Here a very basic outline and some examples will be provided. There are three components to the approach: facet meta-theory (see chapter 1.6 for a fuller exposition of this), facet design and facet analysis. Facet design provides the basis for conducting research through a detailed specification of the variables of interest and the establishing of hypotheses which test the correspondence between the conceptual definitions and empirical observation. The key ingredients are: facets and their constituent elements; a mapping sentence; rationale; conceptual structures (e.g. circumplex, radex) and accompanying multivariate statistical procedures for analysing data.

Facets are the conceptual categories that make up the universe of observations in an empirical investigation. There are three basic types of facets

(Donald 1995): background, which describes the population parameters such as age, sex, occupation; domain, which is the 'meat' of the conceptual thinking and in forensic psychology comprizes, e.g. threat, control, theft, hostility etc.; and range, which describes the possible responses an individual can make in terms of the domain facets (e.g. high, intermediate or low levels of threat).

Each facet is made up of elements which describe the variation within a facet, e.g. the background facet gender may be made of three elements, male, female and transgendered; the facet sexual orientation may be made of three elements, heterosexual, homosexual and bisexual. A system of notation is employed when identifying a facet and its constituent elements. Thus the capital letter A notates the facet gender and a lower-case letter and corresponding numbers represent the elements (a_1 heterosexual, a_2 homosexual and a_3 bisexual). Brown and Barnett (2000, p. 108) describe the properties of a facet as being exhaustive within its domain, whilst the elements must be mutually exclusive.

As well as identifying the facets and specifying their elements, the relationships between and within facets must be delineated. To do this there must be some underpinning rationale that firstly supports the content identification of the facet and secondly implies either a quantitative or qualitative relationship between the elements within a facet and between the facets themselves. Thus Canter and colleagues (2003), when developing a model to explain rape, identified a quantitative level (frequency) that characterized behaviours of the rapist within the facet content domains of hostility, control, theft and involvement. These facets were drawn out of a review of the relevant literature and represented a conceptual mapping of the domains of interest in constructing their model.

The next step is to specify the facets, elements and relationships with a device termed a mapping sentence (Murphy and Brown 2000). This is a verbal statement that identifies the facets and provides an account of the hypothesized relationships. Mapping sentences are extremely useful devices that permit a succinct statement of the research design which is accessible and acts as the theoretical template for the mapping of empirical observations (see figure 8.2.1).

In the hypothetical example presented in figure 8.2.1, the topic of interest is differences between adolescent and adult rapists. This then is our parameter describing our sample of rapists. The research literature tells us that behaviours of rapists are either core, i.e. very frequent, or rare signature behaviours and that the content of behaviours falls into broadly three motivational categories, anger, theft or sexual. The range for this hypothetical investigation is that the exhibited behaviours may be present or absent. The rationale would also specify that there

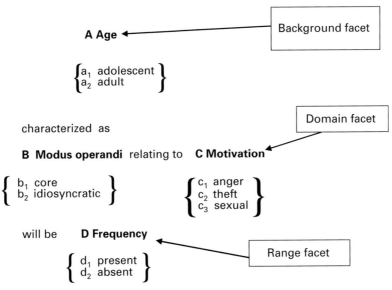

The frequency of behaviours exhibited by rapist x being an

A Age ←――――――――――― Background facet

{ a₁ adolescent
a₂ adult }

Domain facet

characterized as

B Modus operandi relating to   **C Motivation**

{ b₁ core
b₂ idiosyncratic }   { c₁ anger
c₂ theft
c₃ sexual }

will be   **D Frequency** ←―――――――――― Range facet

{ d₁ present
d₂ absent }

Figure 8.2.1 Hypothetical mapping sentence

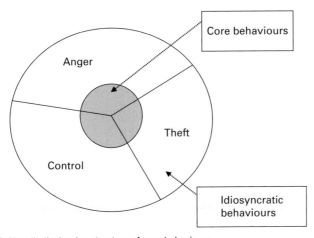

Core behaviours

Anger

Theft

Control

Idiosyncratic
behaviours

Figure 8.2.2 Hypothetical radex structure of rape behaviours

is a qualitative distinction in the motivational facets and a quantitative distinction in the modus operandi facet. These two together would then combine and describe an interacting relationship such that the modus operandi modulated the motivational aspects to form a radex structure, as presented in figure 8.2.2. When two such structures describe the offending behaviour of adolescent and adult rapists they form a stack, termed a cylindrex, as illustrated in figure 8.2.3.

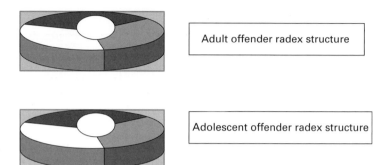

Figure 8.2.3 Hypothetical representation of adult and adolescent offending, which together combines into a cylindrex structure

The theoretical idea underpinning facet theory is that the conceptual analysis of the literature research as specified by the mapping sentence and its supportive rationale creates a model that will be recovered in the empirical observations. In other words, there will be a correspondence between the conceptual mapping and the empirical mapping. In our hypothetical example above, the analyst would precode behaviours that are demonstrations of anger, control and theft, notate each variable according to its facet specification and if there is a correspondence between this and the empirical observations, often by means of multivariate statistical analysis, then the duly notated items should fall into identified regions of a multidimensional space. Not only this, but we should also expect to find a similar representation for both adolescents and adults in the multidimensional analysis.

Canter *et al.* (2003) provide detailed workings of such an analysis and Canter (2000) offers a detailed account of the radex structure as applied to criminal activities.

Typically data employed by forensic psychology researchers using a facet design are drawn from police sources such as witness statements, crime reporting systems or other secondary sources such as law reports. Farrington and Lambert (1997) point out some inherent difficulties when employing such data which clearly are collected for other purposes rather than bespoke research projects. These sources create problems such as incomplete or inaccurate data record keeping, and missing or absent data, and represent those criminals who are caught. Such problems have to be acknowledged and taken into account. Often the analyst constructs a coding dictionary of relevant variables and many published research papers publish these in full as appendices. Primary data may be collected by questionnaire, interview or other data elicitation methods such as a sorting task.

Brown and Barnett (2000) provide a synopsis of the multivariate procedures that are particularly associated with facet design and analysis. They make the point that typically research analysts wish to examine some aspects of people (age, sex), in terms of some process (such as personality characteristics, offending behaviours) and in a context (such as time or place). Very broadly, the statistical method used to map people is multidimensional scalogram analysis (MSA); mapping processes is often done by means of smallest space analysis (SSA); and mapping contexts is done by partial order scalogram analysis (POSA). These procedures are described more fully by O'Neill and Hammond (chapter 8.3, this volume).

Some examples

Facet theory designs are increasingly being used within forensic psychological research investigations. Fritzon and Brun (2005) used the approach to examine homicides in school. Utilizing an action systems framework to identify and provide a rationale for their proposed facet structure, they hypothesized that associated behaviours could be explained by a radex structure in which frequency of actions modulated motives. They successfully recovered their conceptual model from an SSA of empirical observations coded from ninety-four cases reported in the National School Safety Centre Report on School-Associated Violent Deaths.

Porter and Alison (2006b) examined leadership behaviour in criminal gangs. They constructed a coding dictionary of variables drawn from law reports of commercial and personal robberies. Their mapping sentence specified whether or not a gang member originated the idea, selected the target, approached the victim, was involved in the criminal act, and made critical decisions about the crime. They undertook a POSA analysis to scale the presence of these features to describe the leadership propensities of individuals in robbery.

McGuickin and Brown (2001) used an MSA to investigate whether police officers, journalists and members of the public differed in their conceptualizations of different types of sex offender. This research made use of a sorting task in which a variety of different offences were represented (such as child molesters, rapists, frotteurs etc.), and respondents were asked to differentiate these by whatever constructs they could muster. Profiles of the individual respondents were then analysed in terms of their conceptualizations of the various sex offenders. Results indicated there to be clear differentiations between the three respondent groups.

Other example studies include:

- Goodwin and Canter (1997), who looked at the spatial behaviour of serial killers in the United States;
- Raveh and Landav (1993), who examined crime patterns in the USA;
- Yokota and Canter (2004), who undertook a study of the specializations of burglars;
- Santilla *et al.* (2003), who replicated findings in juvenile firesetters of a motivational model developed by Cantor and Fritzon (1998) in adult arsonists;
- Neville, Miller and Fritzon (2007), who developed a typology of behaviours exhibited by prisoners undergoing a therapeutic community regime;
- Porter and Alison (2006a), who examined behavioural coherence in a group of robbers;
- Canter, Hughes and Kirby (1998), who studied paedophilia;
- Fritzon and Garbutt (2001), who looked at intrafamilial homicides.

Conclusion

Dancer (1990) suggests that where there is a need for behavioural definitions that are devoid of vagueness and ambiguity, facet design offers precision and clarity. She also concludes that the mapping sentence offers a valuable method to permit replication and allow for a robustness in developing a line of research enquiry. Conceptual developments are possible from the model building inherent in this approach. Thus Porter and Alison (2006b) suggest that that their leadership scale developed for robbers might be applicable to rapists. Practical implications from facet analyses within the forensic field may be limited by the ex post facto interpretation of behaviours (Fritzon and Brun 2005).

FURTHER READING

Canter's edited collection (1985), chapters by Donald (1995) and by Brown and Barnett (2000), and the paper by Dancer (1990) provide readable overviews of the main principles of facet theory, whilst the Canter *et al.* (1985) is a clear exposition of how facet theory can be applied to research investigations into crime, in this case rape. The paper by Murphy and Brown (2000) provides a helpful example of using a mapping sentence to design a research investigation.

REFERENCES

Brown, J. and Barnett, J. (2000) Facet theory: an approach to research. In G. Breakwell, H. Hammond and C. Fife-Schaw (eds.), *Research Methods in Psychology*, 2nd edn, pp. 105–18. London: Sage.

Canter, D. (1985) *Facet Theory: Approaches to Social Research*. New York: Springer.

  (2000) Offender profiling and criminal differentiation. *Legal and Criminological Psychology*, 5: 23–46.

Canter, D. V., Bennell, C., Alison, L. J. and Reddy, S. (2003) Differentiating sex offences: a behaviorally based thematic classification of stranger rapes. *Behavioral Sciences and the Law*, 21: 157–74.

Canter, D. V. and Fritzon, K. (1998) Differentiating arsonists: a model of fire setting actions and characteristics. *Legal and Criminological Psychology*, 3: 73–96.

Canter, D., Hughes, D. and Kirby, S. (1998) Paedophilia: pathology, criminality or both? The development of a multivariate model of offence behaviour in child sex abuse. *Journal of Forensic Psychiatry*, 9: 532–55.

Dancer, L. S. (1990) Introduction to facet theory and its application. *Applied Psychology; An International Review*, 39: 365–77.

Donald, I. (1995) Facet theory: defining research domains. In G. Breakwell, H. Hammond and C. Fife-Schaw (eds.), *Research Methods in Psychology*, pp. 116–37. London: Sage.

Farrington, D. and Lambert, S. (1997) Predicting offender profiles from victim and witness description. In J. Jackson and D. Bekerian (eds.), *Offender Profiling: Theory, Research and Practice*, pp. 133–58. Chichester: Wiley.

Fritzon, K. and Brun, A. (2005) Beyond Columbine: a faceted model of school associated homicide. *Psychology, Crime and Law*, 11: 53–71.

Fritzon, K. and Garbutt, R. (2001) A fatal interaction: the role of the victim and function of aggression in intrafamilial homicide. *Psychology and Law*, 7: 1–23.

Goodwin, M. and Canter, D. V. (1997) Encounter and death; the spatial behavior of US serial killers. *Policing: An International Journal of Police Strategies and Management*, 20: 24–38.

McGuickin, G. and Brown, J. (2001) Managing risk from sex offenders living in communities: comparing police, press and public perception. *Risk Management: An International Journal*, 3: 47–60.

Murphy, E. and Brown, J. (2000) Exploring gender role identity, value orientation of occupation and sex of respondent in influencing attitudes towards male and female offenders. *Legal and Criminological Psychology*, 5: 285–90.

Neville, L., Miller, S. and Fritzon, K. (2007) Understanding change in a therapeutic community: an action systems approach. *Journal of Forensic Psychiatry and Psychology*, 18: 181–203.

Porter, L. and Alison, L. (2006a) Behavioural coherence in group robbery; a circumplex model of offender and victim interactions. *Aggressive Behaviour*, 32: 330–2.

  (2006b) Leadership and hierarchies in criminal groups; scaling degrees of leader behaviour in group robbery. *Legal and Criminological Psychology*, 11: 245–65.

Raveh, A. and Landav, S. F. (1993) Partial Order Scalogram Analysis with base co-ordinates (POSAC): its application to crime patterns in all the States of America. *Journal of Quantitative Criminology*, 9: 83–99.

Santilla, P., Hakkanen, H., Alison, L. and Whyte, C. (2003) Juvenile fire setters: crime scene actions and offender characteristics. *Legal and Criminological Psychology*, 8: 1–20.

Yokota, K. and Canter, D. (2004) Burglars' specialization: development of a thematic approach in investigative psychology. *Behaviormetrika*, 2: 153–67.

8.3 Drawing out the meaning in data: multidimensional scaling within forensic psychology research

Darragh O'Neill and Sean Hammond

See also chapter 1.1 Action system applied to forensic psychology, chapter 1.6 Facet meta-theory, chapter 8.2 Designing research using facet theory.

Introduction

Psychological inquiry, by its very nature, is charged with identifying the latent meaning in observable or reported phenomena. Endeavouring to achieve this, it draws upon a diverse range of analytic tools and strategies. One particular approach that has in recent years increasingly found its way into forensic psychology research is multidimensional scaling (MDS). MDS comprises a variety of methodologies in which data are represented visually based on distances between the variables or cases of interest. This representation facilitates the identification and interpretation of relationships within data and the testing of theory regarding such structural patterns. The aim of this brief discussion is to provide an introduction to the methodology and describe its use and utility within forensic psychology research.

Torgensen (1952) has been credited as one of the original proponents of MDS procedures within the field of psychology (Young 1987). He introduced a technique for the mapping of interval or ratio-level data, which is now referred to as metric MDS. Subsequent work enabled the applicability of such an approach to non-metric (or ordinal) data (Shepard 1962; Kruskal 1964, Guttman 1968). Due to the nature of the data that are generally available to psychology researchers, it is the latter approach that has proved of most utility within the forensic area.

The primary purpose of MDS analysis is to produce a spatial representation of the relationships between variables so that each is presented as a point within an n-dimensional plot. The closer two points are, the stronger their relationship. In this way a graphical representation of the pattern of intervariable relationships is provided and this enables the researcher to identify meaningful patterns or structures within the plot. The intervariable relationships can be determined in a variety of ways but most commonly by generating correlations between the variables under scrutiny.

Metric MDS is applied where the association between the observed data points is measured on an interval or ratio scale so the proximities are directly calculable. However, for ordinal data this is not as straightforward because only the order of the intervariable relationships can be relied upon. In this way, non-metric MDS can be used for a wide variety of data types, the only restriction being that the coefficients of relationship between the variables are appropriate and occupy a common range with each other. This makes MDS an extraordinarily widely applicable method for examining underlying patterns in our data.

Non-metric MDS procedures are iterative. A number of algorithms have been developed to carry out this iterative process (Borg and Groenen 2005). One of the most frequently used in forensic psychology is a variation of the one developed by Louis Guttman (1968) named 'smallest space analysis' (SSA). However, the most widely used generally are probably the packages offered by programs such as SPSS known as ALSCAL or PROSCAL.

It is axiomatic that the highest possible dimensionality is one less than the total number of variables being analysed. However, the principal aim of MDS is to represent the data in as low a dimensionality as possible. This is due to the difficulty of interpreting or even visualizing data in more than two or three dimensions. On the other hand, this reduction in dimensionality can introduce a degree of distortion from the original relationships within the data. The extent of this distortion is expressed in a stress function, with smaller stress levels indicative of a more accurate reproduction of the original data. MDS algorithms attempt to minimize this stress within the constraints that the need for low dimensionality imposes. In this way MDS procedures attempt to ensure that a succinct but accurate representation of the underlying structure of the data is found.

The plots created by MDS procedures can be interpreted in a number of ways, but most commonly regions are identified within the space whose meaning is informed by the nature of the variables occupying that space. A number of particular structures or geometric forms have been described and are sometimes termed spatial manifolds. These include the well-known circumplex of points (Lingoes 1977a, 1977b; Lingoes and Borg 1977). A particularly powerful research strategy is to combine MDS with a facet theoretic approach, as described elsewhere in this book (chapter 8.2).

Examples of use within forensic psychology

One of the earliest uses of MDS in a forensic psychology setting was carried out by Braithwaite and Law (1978), who used the technique to examine self-reported acts of delinquent behaviour. However, a more influential example of MDS's utility within forensic psychology research is the work of Canter and Heritage (1990). They explored the multivariate nature of sexual assault behaviour, with the aim of introducing greater empirical validation to the process of offender profiling. Their study began with a content analysis of police reports for sixty-six cases in which the presence or absence of offence variables as identified. These data were then subjected to an SSA. Canter and Heritage identified five regions in the space, consistent with a theoretical model the authors established on review of previous work. These regions represented different modes of interaction between the offender and victim in which particular behaviours were more likely to co-occur, ranging from *attempted intimacy* to *criminality*. Moreover, the regions were radially partitioned, demonstrating a circular order. Inferences could also be drawn regarding the co-occurrence of broader offending styles, as well as specific behaviours. Above all, the researchers note that the behaviours that group at the apparent centre of the configuration, and thus represent the primary facet underlying such offences, are neither consistent with Groth and Birnbaum's (1979) nor Marshall's (1989) typologies of sexual assault. Rather, they emphasize the centrality of the victim being seen as a sexual object.

Canter and Heritage's MDS analysis marked a shift within offender profiling away from an approach based upon clinical judgement towards a more empirically established description of offender behaviour. Its emphasis upon the need to ground theories of criminal behaviour in quantifiable and verifiable case characteristics continues to influence current modes of inquiry into a diverse range of criminal behaviours, such as arson (Häkkänen, Puolakka and Santtila 2004), serial homicide (Salfati and Bateman 2005), stalking (Canter and Iannou 2004) and terrorism (Wilson 2000). Much of this work has directly or indirectly involved Canter himself, illustrating his role as one of the primary pioneers of the MDS methodology within forensic psychology. The work has, however, broadened its scope to examine relationships between crime scene actions and offender characteristics, thus permitting a greater applicability of the research findings to investigative practice (Youngs 2004).

The use of MDS within forensic psychology has extended beyond the profiling of individual offenders. An area that has also begun to see increased application of this methodology is criminal network structures. Porter and Alison (2001, 2006) have examined leadership hierarchies within criminal groups in relation to both gang rape and group robbery, using a form of MDS known as partial order scalogram analysis with coordinates (POSAC). This approach permits exploration of multivariate data in which a latent ordering of variables is expected. The procedure operates on score profiles, accounting for qualitative differences between them as well as their quantitative order (Shye 1978). That is, the overall degree of hierarchy is identified, while variety across individual groups in the aspects used to determine this common order is also acknowledged. Porter and Alison (2001, 2006) developed a scale for the assessment of group hierarchy on review of the extant literature, and applied this to a review of secondary and tertiary data extracted from law reports and magazine articles. The POSAC analysis then allowed the researchers to establish the utility of these behaviours through an examination of relationships between variables in a spatial representation. Canter (2004), also utilizing POSAC, established that the shape of criminal networks can vary greatly, and more importantly, he identified that the strictness of hierarchy within a network is related to aspects of group communication.

An additional category of research in forensic psychology in which MDS methods have been utilized is the exploration of clinical constructs and diagnostic measures. Widiger *et al.* (1987), for example, have examined the dimensional nature of personality disorder as determined through criteria from the third edition of the *Diagnostic and Statistical Manual* (DSM-III: American Psychiatric Association 1980). The researchers identified three continuums of relevance in the interpretation of personality disorders: social involvement, assertion-dominance, and anxious rumination versus behavioural acting out. This dimensional explanation has influenced further studies into the relationship between normal personality traits and personality disorders (e.g. Watson and Sinha 1995).

MDS techniques have similarly been used to examine psychometric test structure. Bishopp and Hare (2008) have explored the latent structure of psychopathy as appraised via the Psychopathy Checklist – Revised (PCL–R), in which an underlying facet structure is observed that is consistent with theory. A further analysis of the PCL–R (O'Neill 2006) has evaluated the invariance of PCL–R structures across multiple groups and data sources using a three-way MDS procedure named common space analysis (COSPA: Schönemann, James and Carter 1979). This kind of simultaneous analysis of multiple datasets can be achieved through a number of three-way multi-dimensional scaling methods such as individual differences scaling (INDSCAL: Carroll and Chang 1970). These analyses typically provide a general plot for the variables, as well as a separate plot illustrating the degree of similarity between cases or subgroups in relation to the overall variable configuration as illustrated in the general plot. Carlier, Lamberts and Gersons' (2000) study into post-traumatic stress disorder amongst police officers is one of the few additional examples within forensic psychology in which three-way MDS is employed.

Evaluating its utility for forensic psychology

The apparent arbitrariness of the output interpretation and the lack of prob-ability statistics has been the focus of criticism of MDS analyses (e.g. Boll and Zweizig 1985; Watson and Sinha 1995). For most MDS users this is an ill-conceived criticism because it is entirely to avoid the pitfalls of forcing the data into incompatible statistical strictures that motivates the use of MDS in the first place. It is always possible to provide statistical constraints upon MDS; a maximum likelihood procedure exists that does permit inferential statistics (Young 1987). However, these forms of MDS introduce strong constraints on the types of data for which they are suitable, negating one of the primary advantages of utilizing an MDS analysis. With sufficient care and scrutiny, non-metric MDS methodologies as a whole are very capable at playing a central role in theory building and testing.

MDS, as a category of procedures, is particularly compatible with a facet theory approach to research (Guttman and Greenbaum 1998). All forms of data analysis are subject to interpretation, and accuracy of this is necessarily depen-dant on reference to a thorough understanding of prior research and theory. Moreover, this necessity extends to study design as a whole. Facet theory provides a structured method for achieving this with multivariate data, empha-sizing the need for clarity of construct definition and ensuring a more grounded and focused mode of inquiry (Guttman 1954). This culminates in the construc-tion of a mapping sentence which explicitly details the research domain in the form of a structural hypothesis (Shye, Elizur and Hoffman 1994). MDS methods are especially suited to subsequently verifying or challenging this mapping sentence through the spatial representation they produce.

As with all forms of data analysis, replication is the best guarantee of the accuracy of an interpretation, and there is evidence that this is being undertaken, ensuring the validation of previous MDS studies. For example, Häkkänen, Puolakka and Santtila (2004) have independently verified Canter and Fritzon's (1998) thematic classification of arsonists, even having employed an alternative form of MDS (PROXSCAL) to that used in the original study (SSA). On the other hand, Sturidsson and his colleagues (2006) failed to replicate the findings of Canter and Heritage (1990).

The efficacy of any analytic methodology is dependent on the quality and appropriateness of the data on which it is conducted. MDS provides the user with a set of techniques that can make sense of data that might, for researchers wedded to metric statistical modelling procedures, seem inadequate. Porter and Alison (2001), for example, relied on magazine articles which were in turn based on the secondary reporting of cases of group rape in police reports and court transcripts. However, this limitation in design was subsequently addressed in Porter and Alison (2006). Moreover, Canter and Alison (2003) note that secondary data provide a particularly informative and underused source of data for offender-profiling research.

The statistical constraints on non-metric MDS reside with the coefficients of association used to assess the intervariable relationships. If a researcher uses product–moment correlations they are implicitly assuming that Pearsonian assumptions are met in their data. Fortunately, there are a wide range of coefficients available to suit almost any form of data. Dichotomies, for example, can be analysed using a huge range of coefficients, all with slightly different advantages and limitations. It is for the researcher to be clear about the initial intervariable association coefficients that are appropriate for his/her data. For example, Canter and Heritage (1990) utilized the Jaccard coefficient which is used when joint absence of a feature is not considered a similarity criterion. It is always necessary to be aware that skewness in the data can lead to loss of common range in many coefficients and this can lead to distortions in the resulting patterns. Radex structures are particularly prone to this form of distortion so, if testing such a structure, it is advisable to opt for a coefficient that is insensitive to skew (Hammond, in press).

Unfortunately, it is not unprecedented in forensic psychology papers for the variety of the MDS method itself and/or the coefficient of intervariable association to go unspecified (e.g. Blumenthal 2007; Huss et al. 2006).

Overall, however, MDS makes notably fewer assumptions about the nature of data than do other forms of multivariate analysis such as factor analysis or cluster analysis, particularly with regard to linearity and orthogonality (Borg and Groenen 2005). It is consequently applicable to a much broader range of data. MDS interpretation, moreover, is easier than that of factor analysis, as the former is done on the interpoint distances, whilst the latter is done on the angles between vectors (Schiffman, Reynolds and Young 1981).

Conclusion

Within forensic psychology research, MDS has had its most notable impact on offender profiling. It has played a distinct role in moving it beyond clinical theorizing, to embrace and exploit empirical analysis. MDS has subsequently been used to clarify our understanding of diverse criminal behaviours and of criminality as a whole. It has shown itself to be of use in investigative and clinical settings, helping not only to identify characteristics of offenders but also to comprehend the function served by their offending behaviour (e.g. Fritzon and Garbutt 2001). Yet the relevance of MDS extends beyond this. It has been utilized in addressing a variety of research questions in forensic psychology, from establishing what coping strategies are employed by witnesses of a mass murder (North, Spitznagel and Smith 2001), to identifying the structures of criminal networks (e.g. Porter and Alison 2006), as well as exploring patterns of positive and negative behaviours amongst residents of a prison therapeutic community (Neville, Miller and Fritzon 2007). However, despite this diversity in the topics with which MDS has been used, the manner in which MDS techniques are employed remains somewhat limited.

MDS comprises a broad set of analytic procedures, yet it is only particular forms that appear to have been widely implemented by forensic psychologists. Clearly, the full utility of this approach remains underappreciated. Examples of individual differences scaling and other weighted MDS procedures within forensic psychology research are conspicuous by their general absence. Familiarity with alternative forms of MDS as well the availability of software with which to conduct them is certainly of relevance here. Despite the inclusion of selected MDS procedures in data analysis packages such as SPSS, these are generally of limited variety and in-house software remains the dominant mode of conducting MDS analysis within forensic psychology research, at least within the UK. This can hinder the propagation of the use of MDS and of general understanding of the different methodologies. Although MDS procedures have had an important role to date within this area of research, it is only when the true utility and versatility of the methods subsumed within this category are recognized that the role of MDS within the general toolkit of the forensic psychologist will become fully apparent.

For further information on this topic, the reader is directed to the work of Borg and Groenen (2005), which provides an in-depth account of MDS methods and their uses. For illustrations of its application in forensic psychology, Canter and Heritage (1990) is the seminal study. The reference section below, however, lists further examples.

REFERENCES

American Psychological Association (1980) *Diagnostic and Statistical Manual of Mental Disorders*, 3rd edn (DSM-III). Washington, DC: American Psychiatric Association.

Bishopp, D. and Hare, R. D. (2008) A multidimensional scaling analysis of the Hare PCL-R: unfolding the structure of psychopathy. *Psychology, Crime and Law*, 14: 117–32.

Blumenthal, J. A. (2007) Perceptions of crime: a multidimensional analysis with implications for law and psychology. *McGeorge Law Review*, 38: 629–51. Available online: http://ssrn.com/abstract=942311 (accessed 23 June 2007).

Boll, J. J. and Zweizig, D. (1985) Mapping a curriculum by computer. *Journal of the American Society for Information Science*, 36: 352–3.

Borg, I. and Groenen, P. J. F. (2005) *Modern Multidimensional Scaling: Theory and Applications*, 2nd edn. Mannheim: Springer.

Braithwaite, J. B. and Law, H. G. (1978) The structure of self-reported delinquency. *Applied Psychological Measurement*, 2: 221–38.

Canter, D. (2004) A partial order scalogram analysis of criminal network structures. *Behaviormetrika*, 31: 131–52.

Canter, D. and Alison, L. (2003) Converting evidence into data: the use of law enforcement archives as unobtrusive measurement. *The Qualitative Report*, 8: 151–76.

Canter, D. and Fritzon, K. (1998) Differentiating arsonists: a model of firesetting actions and characteristics. *Journal of Legal and Criminal Psychology*, 3: 73–96.

Canter, D. and Heritage, R. (1990) A multivariate model of sexual offence behaviour: developments in 'offender profiling'. *Journal of Forensic Psychiatry*, 1: 185–212.

Canter, D. and Iannou, M. (2004) A multivariate model of stalking behaviours. *Behaviormetrika*, 31: 113–30.

Carlier, I. V., Lamberts, R. D. and Gersons, B. P. (2000) The dimensionality of trauma: a multidimensional scaling comparison of police officers with and without posttraumatic stress disorder. *Psychiatry Research*, 97: 29–39.

Carroll, J. D. and Chang, J. J. (1970) Analysis of individual differences in multidimensional scaling via an n-way generalization of 'Eckart-Young' decomposition. *Psychometrika*, 35: 283–319.

Fritzon, K. and Garbutt, R. (2001) A fatal interaction: the role of the victim and function of aggression in intrafamilial homicide. *Psychology, Crime and Law*, 7: 309–31.

Groth, A. N. and Birnbaum, H. J. (1979) *Men Who Rape: The Psychology of the Offender*. New York: Plenum Press.

Guttman, L. (1954) An outline of some new methodology for social research. *Public Opinion Quarterly*, 18: 395–404.

(1968) A general nonmetric technique for finding the smallest coordinate space for a configuration of points. *Psychometrika*, 33: 469–506.

Guttman, R. and Greenbaum, C. W. (1998) Facet theory: its development and current status. *European Psychologist*, 3: 13–36.

Häkkänen, H., Puolakka, P. and Santtila, P. (2004) Crime scene actions and offender characteristics in arsons. *Legal and Criminological Psychology*, 9: 197–214.

Hammond, S. (in press) Introducing the Jaccard–Canter coefficient: a common range index of inter-variable similarity for smallest space analysis.

Huss, M. T., Tomkins, A. J., Garbin, C. P., Schopp, R. F. and Kilian, A. (2006) Battered women who kill their abusers: an examination of commonsense notions, cognitions, and judgements. *Journal of Interpersonal Violence*, 21: 1063–80.

Lingoes, J. C. (1977a) Identifying directions in the space for interpretation. In J. C. Lingoes (ed.), *Geometric Representations of Relational Data: Readings in Multidimensional Scaling*, pp. 103–13. Ann Arbor, MI: Mathesis Press.

(1977b) Identifying regions in the space for interpretation. In J. C. Lingoes (ed.), *Geometric Representations of Relational Data: Readings in Multidimensional Scaling*, pp. 115–26. Ann Arbor, MI: Mathesis Press.

Lingoes, J. C. and Borg, I. (1977) Identifying spatial manifolds for interpretation. In J. C. Lingoes (ed.), *Geometric Representations of Relational Data: Readings in Multidimensional Scaling*, pp. 127–48. Ann Arbor, MI: Mathesis Press.

Kruskal, J. B. (1964) Multidimensional scaling by optimizing goodness of fit to a nonmetric hypothesis. *Psychometrika*, 29: 1–27.

Marshall, W. L. (1989) Intimacy, loneliness and sexual offenders. *Behavioural Research in Therapy*, 27(5): 491–503.

Neville, L., Miller, S. and Fritzon, K. (2007) Understanding change in a therapeutic community: an action systems approach. *Journal of Forensic Psychiatry and Psychology*, 18: 181–203.

North, C. S., Spitznagel, E. L. and Smith, E. M. (2001) A prospective study of coping after exposure to a mass murder episode. *Annals of Clinical Psychiatry*, 13: 81–87.

O'Neill, D. (2006) A common space analysis of the PCL-R examining structural equivalence across group and method. Master's thesis in Forensic Psychology, University College, Cork.

Porter, L. E. and Alison, L. J. (2001) A partially ordered scale of influence in violent group behaviour: an example from gang rape. *Small Group Research*, 32: 475–97.

(2006) Leadership and hierarchies in criminal groups: scaling degrees of leader behaviour in group robbery. *Legal and Criminological Psychology*, 11: 245–65.

Salfati, C. G. and Bateman, A. L. (2005) Serial homicide: an investigation of behavioural consistency. *Journal of Investigative Psychology and Offender Profiling*, 2: 121–44.

Schiffman, S. S., Reynolds, M. L. and Young, F. W. (1981) *Introduction to Multidimensional Scaling: Theory, Methods and Applications*. New York: Academic Press.

Schönemann, P. H., James, W. L. and Carter, F. S. (1979) Statistical inference in multidimensional scaling: a method for fitting and testing Horan's model. In J. C. Lingoes,

E. E. Roskam, and I. Borg (eds.), *Geometric Representations of Relational Data: Readings in Multidimensional Scaling*, 2nd edn, pp. 791–826. Ann Arbor, MI: Mathesis Press.

Shepard, R. N. (1962) The analysis of proximities: multidimensional scaling with an unknown distance, Part I. *Psychometrika*, 27: 125–40.

Shye, S. (1978) Partial order scalogram analysis. In S. Shye (ed.), *Theory Construction and Data Analysis in the Behavioral Sciences*, pp. 265–79. San Francisco: Jossey-Bass.

Shye, S., Elizur, D. and Hoffman, M. (1994) *Introduction to Facet Theory: Content Design and Intrinsic Data Analysis in Behavioral Research*. Thousand Oaks, CA: Sage.

Sturidsson, K., Långström, N., Grann, M., Sjöstedt, G., Åsgård, U. and Aghede, E. (2006) Using multidimensional scaling for the analysis of sexual offence behaviour: a replication and some cautionary notes. *Psychology, Crime and Law*, 12: 221–30.

Torgensen, W. S. (1952) Multidimensional scaling: I. Theory and method. *Psychometrika*, 17: 401–19.

Watson, D. C. and Sinha, B. K. (1995) Dimensional structure of personality disorder inventories: a comparison of normal and clinical populations. *Personality and Individual Differences*, 19: 817–26.

Widiger, T. A., Trull, T. J., Hurt, S. W., Clarkin, J. and Frances, A. (1987) A multidimensional scaling of the DSM-III personality disorders. *Archives of General Psychiatry*, 44: 557–63.

Wilson, M. A. (2000) Toward a model of terrorist behavior in hostage-taking situations. *Journal of Conflict Resolution*, 44: 403–24.

Young, F. W. (1987) History. In F. W. Young and R. M. Hamer (eds.), *Multidimensional Scaling: History, Theory, and Applications*, pp. 15–40. Hillsdale, NJ: Erlbaum.

Youngs, D. (2004) Personality correlates of offence style. *Journal of Investigative Psychology and Offender Profiling*, 1: 99–119.

8.4 Evaluation of systemic interventions

Arlene Vetere

Behavioural therapy, problem-solving therapy, group therapy, and marital and family interventions have all shown some evidence of efficacy …

(DOH 2001)

Approaches to definition

Systemic psychotherapists work therapeutically with individuals, couples and families, and offer consultation and systemic interventions with teams, agencies and organizations, designed to improve communication, wellbeing and satisfaction in people's relationships. Intervention pays attention to context, connection and history, recognizing that significant relationships are both the cradle and web for human development across the lifespan (see Vetere and Dallos 2003, for a fuller description and applications).[1]

The practice of systemic psychotherapy rests on a large and growing empirical base of outcome evidence, drawn from studies of both therapeutic efficacy and effectiveness. Efficacy studies are high on internal validity but tend not to replicate the complexity and messiness of everyday therapeutic practice, with careful client screening, research therapists working to a manual, with regular process checks, and usually in a university-based setting; while the effectiveness studies are higher on external validity as they are carried out in NHS settings, with NHS therapists, and little client screening. According to Bergin and Garfield (1994), the couple and family therapy approaches have been subjected to rigorous scrutiny, with only a few other

---

[1] The outcome literature commonly reviews together studies of the efficacy of both couples therapies and the family systemic psychotherapies. Systemic psychotherapy practice encompasses a range of schools of thought, also included in the reviews that conceptualize family groups respectively as meaning-making systems; history-containing systems with entrenched meanings and patterns of behaviour; problem-solving systems; and narrative systems.

forms of psychotherapy studied as often. Studies report the use of controlled and uncontrolled group comparison designs, single case designs, and studies comparing the relative efficacy of the different family therapy approaches. The overwhelming findings from the research reviews and meta-analytic studies is that family therapy works compared to untreated control groups, with some demonstrated superiority to standard and individual treatments for certain disorders and populations (Pinsof and Wynne 1995; Carr 2000a, 2000b; Sprenkle 2002; Stratton 2005). Meta-analysis demonstrates moderate, statistically significant and often clinically significant effects (Shadish *et al.* 1995). The research literature supporting this conclusion is at least as robust as it is for other modes of psychotherapy.

The major review studies and their findings

The early studies of the outcome of the marital and family therapies, so-called, were reviewed by Gurman, Kniskern and Pinsof in 1986. Their conclusions included the following:

(a) Non-behavioural marital and family therapies produce beneficial outcomes in about two-thirds of cases, and their effects are superior to no treatment.

(b) When both spouses/partners are involved in therapy conjointly in the face of marital problems, there is a greater chance of positive outcome than when only one spouse is treated.

(c) The developmental level of the 'identified patient' (e.g. child, adolescent, adult) does not affect treatment outcomes significantly.

(d) Positive results of both non-behavioural and behavioural marital and family therapies typically occur in treatments of short duration, i.e. one to twenty sessions.

(e) Family therapy is as effective as and possibly more effective than many commonly offered (usually individual) treatments for problems attributed to family conflict.

Meta-analyses of outcome studies

The following meta-analytic reviews document a growing body of evidence that shows that the couples and family therapies work: Hazelrigg, Cooper and

Borduin (1987); Markus, Lange and Pettigrew (1990); Shadish *et al.* (1995); and Goldstein and Miklowitz (1995).

The following list of people and problems is found to benefit both clinically and significantly from the couples and family systemic psychotherapies compared to no psychotherapy:

- marital/couple distress and conflict;
- outpatient depressed women in distressed marriages;
- adults with drinking problems and drug misuse;
- adults with a diagnosis of schizophrenia;
- adolescent conduct disorder;
- anorexia nervosa, bulimia nervosa and related eating disorders in young adolescent girls;
- adolescent drug misuse;
- child conduct disorders;
- aggression and non-compliance in children with a diagnosis of ADHD;
- chronic physical illnesses in children, obesity in children and cardiovascular risk factors in children.

Roth and Fonagy (1996) further reviewed the above studies in their attempt to map the evidence for the demonstrated efficacy of the psychotherapies in controlled research conditions and clinical effectiveness in mental health and social care services as delivered. Couples and family therapy appears not to be harmful, in that no RCT study has reported poorer outcomes for treated clients than for untreated control family members (Pinsof and Wynne 1995).

Family therapy as part of multicomponent and integrative approaches

Quality of current family environment may be predictive of therapy outcome, with poorer family environment reducing effectiveness of group/individual treatments, but enhancing effectiveness of couple-based treatments. (DOH 2001)

Chamberlain and Rosicky (1995), in their review of family intervention studies for severe adolescent conduct disorder and delinquency, found that family therapy approaches appeared to decrease adolescent conduct problems and delinquent behaviour compared to individual treatment and no treatment. However, they noted that when treatment failure or 'dropout' occurred, it correlated highly with poverty and/or social isolation for the family. The Florida Network Study (Nugent, Carpenter and Parks 1993) with high-risk families found that families who received family therapy were four times as likely to stay together as families who did not, and families who received more than five treatment sessions were twice as likely to stay together as families who did not. So, for these high-risk families, family therapy may be a necessary treatment component but is not sufficient in itself. When working therapeutically with severe problems, such as schizophrenia and adolescent conduct disorder, there is increasing evidence of the value of treatment packages, of which family therapy is a part (Pinsof and Wynne 1995).

Cost-effectiveness of the family therapies

The cost effectiveness advantages of family-based interventions for some problems are beginning to emerge from a few studies. For example, there are preliminary data indicating that family therapy is more effective than alternative treatments for adult alcohol problems and adult and adolescent drug misuse. In addition, family therapy seems to be more cost-effective than standard inpatient/residential treatment for schizophrenia and severe adolescent conduct disorders and delinquency (Pinsof and Wynne 1995).

As mentioned above, the controlled, experimental clinical trials do not address adequately the complexity of modern healthcare practices. Replication in applied settings is much more difficult. Some commissioners of services do not include systemic psychotherapy in their healthcare planning since little is known about the cost of adding this service. Crane (2007) summarizes the effectiveness research on the costs of including family therapy in mental health services. Law and Crane's (2000) audit study showed that visits by family members to primary healthcare practitioners were significantly reduced following family therapy intervention, particularly for those family members described as 'high utilizers'. These data have been replicated (Crane 2007). In addition, Crane's data show that including family therapy as a treatment option does not significantly increase healthcare costs.

Methodological problems and innovations

Methodological and conceptual problems beset the conduct of outcome studies in the field. These include: (a) the need for clearer definition of the presenting problem and the level of severity; (b) tighter control for attention–placebo effects in the comparison conditions; (c) couples and family therapies need to be more empirically described and verified with more process checks made for therapist activity; (d) studies need to include larger numbers of participants; and (e) more studies need to include the evaluation of outcome at multiple levels, consistent with systemic thinking, such as behavioural change, change in meanings and beliefs, and emotional changes, at individual, interactional, contextual and time-related levels (Pinsof and Wynne 1995; Vetere and Dallos 2003). Change needs to be demonstrated at both first-order level, i.e. change in the defined problem, and second-order level, i.e. reorganization of what the problem means and the dynamics around it.

The third generation of outcome researchers have turned their attention to these knotty problems, whose solutions will benefit the field of psychotherapy outcome research in general. For example, the London Intervention Depression Trial (Leff et al. 2000), an RCT study of antidepressants versus systemic couples therapy in the treatment and maintenance of depressed people with a regular partner, used a manual for the couples therapy and specified the treatment length within circumscribed goals of the study, and was situated in a real-life therapy setting. The study demonstrated the effectiveness of systemic couples therapy for moderate to severe depression. As another example, outcome researchers are advocating 'progress' research which links process research to outcome research, by treating each client/therapist identified process moment in therapy as an outcome in its own right, worthy of study, and with the potential to illuminate moment-by-moment change (Pinsof and Wynne 1995).

These innovations and methodological issues set the challenge for the future. And the political context is changing too. The National Institute for Clinical Excellence (NICE) in the UK recommends treatment choices for mental health problems, modelled on the 'evidence-based medicine' approach used in physical healthcare settings. Current NICE guidelines recommend couples/family-based treatments for adolescent eating disorders, adults with a diagnosis of schizophrenia, children with a diagnosis of depression, and adults living with a regular partner who have a diagnosis of depression. In an increasingly resource-limited NHS, opportunities for clinician-involved research are shrinking. Modern evidence-based psychotherapies need to rise to this challenge, but also to retain their roots in the recursive link between clinical practice, clinical experience, and the research that both develops and tests hypotheses.

REFERENCES

Bergin, A. and Garfield, S. (eds.) (1994) *Handbook of Psychotherapy and Behavior Change*, 4th edn. New York: Wiley.

Carr, A. (2000a) Evidence-based practice in family therapy and systemic consultation I. *Journal of Family Therapy*, 22: 29–60.

(2000b) Evidence-based practice in family therapy and systemic consultation II. *Journal of Family Therapy*, 22: 273–95.

Chamberlain, P. and Rosicky, J. (1995) The effectiveness of family therapy in the treatment of adolescents with conduct disorders and delinquency. *Journal of Marital and Family Therapy*, 21: 441–59.

Crane, R. D. (2007) Effectiveness research on the cost of family therapy. *Psychotherapeuten-journal*, 23: 20–4.

DOH (2001) *Treatment Choice in Psychological Therapies and Counselling*. London: HMSO.

Goldstein, M. and Miklowitz, D. (1995) The effectiveness of psychoeducational family therapy in the treatment of schizophrenic disorders. *Journal of Marital and Family Therapy*, 21: 361–76.

Gurman, A., Kniskern, D. and Pinsof, W. (1986) Research on the process and outcome of marital and family therapy. In S. Garfield and A. Bergin (eds.), *Handbook of Psychotherapy and Behavior Change*, 3rd edn, pp. 565–624. New York: Wiley.

Hazelrigg, M., Cooper, H. and Borduin, C. (1987) Evaluating the effectiveness of family therapies: an integrative review and analysis. *Psychological Bulletin*, 101: 428–42.

Law, D. and Crane, R. (2000) The influence of marital and family therapy on health care utilization in a health maintenance organization. *Journal of Marital and Family Therapy*, 26: 281–92.

Leff, J., Vearnals, S., Brewin, C. R., Wolff, G., Alexander, B., Asen, E. *et al.* (2000) The London depression intervention trial. Randomised controlled trial of antidepressants v. couple therapy in the treatment and maintenance of people with depression living with a partner: clinical outcome and costs. *British Journal of Psychiatry*, 174: 95–100.

Markus, E., Lange, A. and Pettigrew, T. (1990) Effectiveness of family therapy: a meta-analysis. *Journal of Family Therapy*, 12: 205–21.

Nugent, W., Carpenter, D. and Parks, J. (1993) A statewide evaluation of family preservation and family reunification services. *Research on Social Work Practice*, 3: 40–65.

Pinsof, W. and Wynne, L. (1995) The efficacy of marital and family therapy: an empirical overview, conclusions and recommendations. *Journal of Marital and Family Therapy*, 21: 585–613.

Roth, A. and Fonagy, P. (1996) *What Works For Whom? A Critical Review of Psychotherapy Research*. New York: Guilford Press.

Shadish, W., Ragsdale, K., Glaser, R. and Montgomery, L. (1995) The efficacy and effectiveness of marital and family therapy: a perspective from meta-analysis. *Journal of Marital and Family Therapy*, 21: 345–60.

Sprenkle, D. (ed.) (2002) *Effectiveness Research in Marital and Family Therapy*. Alexandria, VA: American Association for Marriage and Family Therapy.

Stratton, P. (2005) *Report on the Evidence Base of Systemic Family Therapy*. Warrington: UK Association for Family Therapy.

Vetere, A. and Dallos, R. (2003) *Working Systemically with Families; Formulation, Intervention and Evaluation*. London: Karnac.

8.5 Evaluating offending behaviour programmes in prison

Helen Wakeling and Rosie Travers

See also chapter 8.7 Randomized control trials.

Introduction

Offenders in prisons in England and Wales have access to a suite of accredited interventions designed to reduce reoffending. The programmes offered are generally cognitive-behavioural in nature, and address a range of offending behaviours and maladaptive thinking styles (e.g. Clarke 2000; Mann and Thornton 1998). The programmes are designed from an evidence base to meet the identified criminogenic needs of the offender population and are continually developed and refined from research and evaluative findings. These offending behaviour programmes are accredited according to ten evidenced-based standards of best practice by a panel of international experts (the Correctional Services Accreditation Panel), which was established in 1996 to ensure that programmes meet the 'What Works' criteria of offender rehabilitation (Andrews and Bonta 2003). This system of programme accreditation persists to this day. Evaluation is central to this process; to achieve accreditation, programmes must have in place a short- and longterm evaluation strategy, and demonstrate that robust systems are in place to monitor implementation and effectiveness.

Rationale

It is critically important to demonstrate the effectiveness of prison programmes: to ensure that the intervention provided is having the desired effect in reducing recidivism, and that it represents value for money with regard to the investments made and savings incurred. Evaluation is central to the initial accreditation process, to the ongoing refinement of a programme's implementation, and to the allocation of limited resources (within the context of an overstretched prison system with many competing demands). The National Offender Management Service (NOMS), which brings together the prison and probation services, is committed to the reduction of reoffending by working positively and proactively with those in their care. Accredited offending behaviour programmes are a key element in the Reducing Reoffending plan, and therefore evaluating the effectiveness of these programmes is a central focus for NOMS.

This chapter will focus on how programmes are evaluated in a prison setting across England and Wales. The What Works debate has dominated the literature on correctional research for many years now (McGuire 1995). This addressed questions such as: can interventions with offenders really impact on reoffending? what are the characteristics of those interventions that do seem to make a difference? Importantly, this body of work has led to the emergence of clearly significant principles associated with effective interventions: the principles of Risk, Need and Responsivity (Andrews and Bonta 2003).

Meta-analyses findings

The meta-analytic method has been a useful tool in the What Works area (Lipsey and Wilson 2001). Meta-analysis is a statistical technique for amalgamating, summarizing and reviewing previous quantitative research, which allows the combination of the findings from many individual studies into a single large study with many participants. Although many individual outcome studies have demonstrated a positive effect of programmes on future reoffending, there have been many others unable to find evidence of such an effect. Meta-analyses can bring these varying and conflicting results into a meaningful summary of the evidence. Pearson *et al.,* in their 2002 review of studies of correctional interventions, found strong evidence that cognitive-behavioural programmes generally, and cognitive skills training specifically, can significantly reduce reoffending. Landenberger and Lipsey's (2005) meta-analysis of cognitive skills (CS) interventions with offenders summarized the outcomes of fourteen methodologically sound evaluations. They described an average reduction in reoffending of 25% in those treated compared to a control group. Higher-risk participants and higher-quality interventions were associated with greater effect sizes. Tong and Farrington (2006) reviewed the effectiveness of the 'Reasoning and Rehabilitation' cognitive skills programme. Of the sixteen reviewed studies, they found a 14% decrease in recidivism for programme participants in comparison to controls.

Lösel and Schmucker (2005) compared the recidivism rates of 9,000 treated sexual offenders with over 12,000 controls. They reported a positive treatment effect; the treated group reoffended significantly less than the control group. Further, they concluded that cognitive-behavioural programmes were generally more effective than other psychosocial treatment techniques. Jolliffe and Farrington (2007) examined interventions for adult male violent offenders, and found that programmes reduced general reoffending by 8–11% and violent reoffending by up to 8%. In 2006, the Washington State Institute for Public Policy conducted a comprehensive review of evidence-based programmes for adult offenders, and concluded that programmes designed for the general offender population, for drug-involved offenders and for sexual offenders, are, on average, effective at reducing recidivism. The consensus must be that the right programmes delivered in the right way to the right individuals can be effective in reducing crime.

Problems with evaluation studies

The evaluation challenge for individual programmes is still, however, a considerable one. Once the research question has been set there are many issues to address to optimize the success of an evaluation. These include the choice of methodology, of outcome, of outcome measurement, of comparison group and analysis. The Association for the Treatment of Sexual Abusers' Collaborative Outcome Data Committee (2007) has produced useful guidelines for evaluating programmes for sexual offenders. The criteria they describe include the importance of having control of the independent variable, considering experimenter expectancies, sample size, attrition, the equivalency of groups, defining and selecting outcome variables and conducting a correct comparison.

There continues to be much debate on the appropriate methodology to apply in researching programme effectiveness. Harper and Chitty (2005) and others (e.g. Colledge, Collier and Brand 1999; Marques et al. 2005; Rice and Harris 2003) argue that randomized control trials (RCTs) are the gold standard in research design for outcome evaluations and should be used whenever possible. Others (e.g. Gondolf 2004; Harkins and Beech 2007; Hollin 2006, 2008; Marshall and Marshall 2007; Pawson and Tilley 1994) argue that the limitations, including the ethical and practical difficulties of RCTs, mean that quasi-experimental designs will often be more appropriate. Essentially, studies of programme outcome need to balance the internal and external validity of their research design to ensure that the outcomes observed are useful and can be generalized.

It is UK policy to populate the evaluation strategies for each programme with a range of research designs that will best answer specific research questions. Thus the focus extends from looking at the feasibility of RCTs and quasi-experimental outcome studies, through to descriptive process studies, risk band designs, quasi-experimental designs, within-treatment change studies, and qualitative investigations. All relevant and necessary offenders' demographic and assessment data need to be collected and collated in a standardized and routine manner. Without this thorough information gathering, any evaluation is unlikely to yield useful or replicable findings.

Aside from collecting the right information, evaluating programmes necessitates consideration of a whole host of other factors. Offenders must give informed consent for their personal data to be used for research, and research plans must adhere to strict ethical and diversity principles. In recent years, research staff have also striven to improve the quality of data collected, and significant improvements have been made. As the quality of our data improves, so too will the quality of our research findings.

The UK evaluation approach

The NOMS Interventions Group (IG) routinely collects both demographic and criminal variables on every offender undergoing treatment. This dataset has recently been augmented by the Offender Assessment System (OASys) risk and needs assessment system, now operational in both the prison and probation services. The OASys system yields important, standardized data on an individual's criminal history, risk of harm, risk of reconviction and criminogenic needs. OASys assessments also generate indicators of individuals' strengths and protective factors, which will be of real value in examining programme impact.

Her Majesty's Prison Service (HMPS) uses a system of annual audits in which programme sites are assessed on criteria derived from the What Works literature reflecting institutional support, treatment management and integrity, continuity and resettlement, and quality of delivery. A quality rating resulting from the audit is applied to the number of programme completions at each site determining whether that prison has met its reducing reoffending key performance indicator. This score then acts as an incentive to maintain programme integrity and implementation best practice. The audit process monitors the quality of treatment provided within the establishments (by methods such as video monitoring and interviews), and adherence to the manual and treatment methods. This annual audit allows for corrective action to reinforce integrity of programme implementation which is, of course, an essential ingredient for the evaluation of outcomes.

Further to the audit, all programmes are now subject to an annual process and targeting review examining the demographic and criminal history data on participants as well as other elements of delivery. This is a useful process for ensuring the integrity of data collection methods and for recommending actions to improve practice in programme teams. More importantly, the annual reviews allow for an examination of whether participants have been appropriately targeted for programmes along the dimensions of risk and need.

The relevance of appropriate targeting is highlighted in a recent study by Palmer et al. (2007), who, in comparing predicted and actual reconviction rates of cognitive skills participants in the community setting, found no programme effect among those with a low risk of reconviction (below the recommended risk score band for the programmes), but observed a significant treatment effect for both medium- and high-risk offenders. Together, the audit procedures and process studies provide a yearly record of intervention delivery, which will be invaluable for future outcome studies.

The evaluation strategy for each programme also includes a long-term outcome study. For many of the smaller programmes, e.g. the Healthy Relationships programme (for domestic violence offenders) and CALM (anger management), it will take years to accrue a sample big enough for a recidivism study, but plans need to be put in place at an early stage. These plans include ensuring the correct information is being collected on each programme participant, identifying an appropriate comparison group, and ensuring procedures are in place to follow up the individuals following release. In parallel to long-term outcome studies, there are a number of additional research projects which are invaluable in evaluating programmes, and which form part of the HMPS programme evaluation strategy. Large-scale recidivism outcome studies cannot tell us how or why programmes are effective nor for whom they work best. For these questions other research designs are required. Qualitative techniques, for example, have been used to examine offenders' experiences of treatment, and to help us understand how programmes are working for individuals (e.g. Wakeling, Webster and Mann

2005). Other research priorities include examining the effectiveness of risk assessment tools, examining the short-term impact of programmes with the use of psychometrics, and behavioural monitoring strategies.

All HMPS-accredited offending behaviour programmes utilize a set of psychometric assessments aligned to treatment targets which are administered before and after the course to measure short-term treatment impact. For some programmes (e.g. the Sex Offender Treatment Programme) these psychometric scores are fed into treatment progress reports and risk assessment documents (e.g. Thornton 2002). For other programmes (e.g. Enhanced Thinking Skills) the psychometrics are an evaluative tool used to more broadly determine programme effectiveness. It is essential that the use of psychometrics in programme evaluation is based on evidence that they are valid and reliable indicators of the constructs they aim to capture. Over the past few years there has been a process of validating a number of the psychometric tools in use to ensure they are both reliable and valid with the population they are being used for, and sensitive to short-term treatment change (e.g. Mann *et al.* 2007; Wakeling 2007; Webster *et al.* 2006; Williams *et al.* 2007). In order to further the use of psychometrics, one current research study is examining the predictive value of the psychometric tools in terms of future reoffending. Knowing more about this relationship will enable better targeted programmes, to refine the programmes or psychometric tools, and to better identify those for whom the course appears to have had the most impact.

UK outcome studies

It is also important to briefly examine the outcome studies pertaining specifically to HMPS programmes. The only large-scale outcome evaluation of programmes for sexual offenders was conducted by Friendship, Mann and Beech (2003). They found that the Core Sex Offender Treatment Programme, as delivered between 1992 and 1996, had a significant impact on sexual and violent reconviction for medium-risk sexual offenders (high-risk sexual offenders appeared to need more extensive treatment, in line with the Risk Principle of offender rehabilitation). Three outcome studies of Enhanced Thinking Skills and Reasoning and Rehabilitation cognitive skills programmes in prisons in England and Wales, however, produced equivocal results. Friendship *et al.* (2002) found a substantial effect on reconviction for participants compared to a matched comparison group. Subsequently,

Falshaw *et al.* (2003) and Cann *et al.* (2003), using the same methodology, found no substantial effect of programme participation on reconviction rates (although the latter found a small but significant reduction in one-year reconviction rates once non-completers were excluded from the sample).

The HMPS response to the mixed results of the reconviction studies of cognitive skills programmes was to commission two further studies. The first of these was a qualitative inquiry into the experiences of those who facilitate and participate in the programme (Clarke, Simmonds and Wydall 2004). The second was a randomized waiting list study of ETS participants to explore the impact of the programme on the psychometric test battery and other short-term outcomes, and to identify those for whom the intervention was having the most impact (McDougall *et al.* 2009). Both of these studies have yielded useful information on the correlates of successful implementation and the characteristics of those that seem to benefit most from programme participation. Clarke *et al.*'s study, for example, described the limited responsivity of the programme at some sites to the needs and learning styles of individual offenders (a limitation addressed in the new Thinking Skills Programme currently under development).

Conclusion

There is still much scope for examining other ways of capturing programme impact on offender behaviour in the immediate prison environment (e.g. adjudications for rule breaking, self-harm, relationships with significant others, the take-up of support services, educational opportunities and further interventions), and on release (e.g. indices of resettlement success concerning employment, accommodation, substance misuse, family relationships etc). For example, there is a current research project planned which aims to capture good-quality information about adjustment in the post-release period for offenders attending Focus on Resettlement (FOR), an accredited resettlement programme for prisoners. If successful, the mechanisms for capturing this post-release behaviour will be of real value in our future effectiveness research. It is acknowledged that much will happen to the offender between the end of a programme in prison and the point two years after release when reoffending data is collected; the more that is known of the post-custody experience of that offender, the better will be any account of programme impact.

The field of intervention research is exciting and challenging; there are constant developments and an associated need to constantly review and refine procedures. Evaluation and programme development go hand in hand; evaluation is the key to maximizing programme effectiveness. One immediate priority for the future is to look further at whether the needs of particular groups such as women and ethnic minority prisoners are met by the current interventions available. A further challenge is to establish the contribution of any single intervention to individuals who are likely to have myriad needs and will receive varying support and interventions during a period in custody and then under licence in the community. The purpose of providing programmes within the prison setting is to reduce reoffending and protect future victims. Research into what, how, why and for whom these interventions work is critical, and is clearly the only ethical way to ensure that we are providing the best programmes with the best possible outcomes.

REFERENCES

Andrews, D. A. and Bonta, J. (2003) *The Psychology of Criminal Conduct.* Cincinnati, OH: Anderson.

Association for the Treatment of Sexual Abusers' Collaborative Outcome Data Committee (2007) *Sexual Offender Treatment Outcome Research: CODC Guidelines for Evaluation. Part 1: Introduction and Overview.*

Cann, J., Falshaw, L., Nugent, F. and Friendship, C. (2003) *Understanding What Works: Accredited Cognitive Skills Programmes for Adult Men and Young Offenders.* Home Office Research Findings 226. London: Home Office.

Clarke, A. (2000) *Theory Manual for Enhanced Thinking Skills Programme. Prepared for Joint Prison/Probation Accreditation Panel.* London: Home Office.

Clarke, A., Simmonds, R. and Wydall, S. (2004) *Delivering Cognitive Skills Programmes in Prison: A Qualitative Study.* Home Office Research Findings 242. London: Home Office.

Colledge, M., Collier, P., and Brand, S. (1999) *Crime Reduction Programme – Guidance Note 2. Programmes for Offenders: Guidance for Evaluators.* London: Home Office.

Falshaw, L., Friendship, C., Travers, R. and Nugent, F. (2003) *Searching for 'What Works': An Evaluation of Cognitive Skills Programmes.* Home Office Research Findings 206. London: Home Office.

Friendship, C., Blud, L., Erikson, M. and Travers, R. (2002) *An Evaluation of Cognitive Behavioural Treatment for Prisoners.* Home Office Research Findings 161. London: Home Office.

Friendship, C., Mann, R. E. and Beech, A. (2003) Evaluation of a national prison-based treatment programme for sexual offenders in England and Wales. *Journal of Interpersonal Violence,* 18: 744–59.

Gondolf, E. W. (2004) Evaluating batterer counselling programs: a difficult task showing some effects and implications. *Aggression and Violent Behavior,* 9: 605–31.

Harkins, L. and Beech, A. R. (2007) Measurement of the effectiveness of sex offender treatment. *Aggression and Violent Behavior*, 1: 36–44.

Harper, G. and Chitty, C. (2005) *The Impact of Corrections on Re-offending: A Review of 'What Works'*. Home Office Research Study 291, 2nd edn. London: Home Office.

Hollin, C. R. (2006) Offending behaviour programmes and contention: evidence-based practice, manuals and programme evaluation. In C. R. Hollin and E. J. Palmer (eds.), *Offending Behaviour Programmes: Development, Application and Controversies*, pp. 33–67. Chichester: Wiley.

   (2008) Evaluating offending behaviour programmes: does only randomization glister? *Criminology and Criminal Justice*, 8: 89–106.

Jolliffe, D. and Farrington, D. (2007) A systematic review of the evidence on the effectiveness of violence reduction programmes and other interventions for violent offenders. Unpublished paper.

Landenberger, N. A. and Lipsey, M. W. (2005) The positive effects of cognitive-behavioural programs for offenders: a meta-analysis of factors associated with effective treatment. *Journal of Experimental Criminology*, 1: 451–77.

Lipsey, M. W. and Wilson, D. B. (2001) *Practical Meta Analysis*. Thousand Oaks, CA: Sage.

Lösel, F. and Schmucker, M. (2005) The effectiveness of treatment for sexual offenders: a comprehensive meta-analysis. *Journal of Experimental Criminology*, 1: 117–46.

Mann, R. E. and Thornton, D. (1998) The evolution of a multi-site sex offender treatment programme. In W. L. Marshall, Y. M. Fernandez, S. H. Hudson and T. Ward (eds.), *Sourcebook of Treatment Programs for Sexual Offenders*, pp. 47–58. New York: Plenum Press.

Mann, R. E., Webster, S. D., Wakeling, H. C. and Marshall, W. L. (2007) The measurement and influence of child sexual abuse supportive beliefs. *Psychology, Crime and Law*, 13: 443–58.

Marques, J. K., Wiederanders, M., Day, D. M., Nelson, C. and von Ommeren, A. (2005) Effects of a relapse prevention program on sexual recidivism: final results from California's Sex Offender Treatment and Evaluation Project (SOTEP). *Sexual Abuse: A Journal of Research and Treatment*, 17: 79–107.

Marshall, W. L. and Marshall, L. E. (2007) The utility of the random controlled trial for evaluating sexual offender treatment: the gold standard or an inappropriate strategy? *Sex Abuse*, 19: 175–91.

McDougall, C., Clarbour, J., Perry, A. E. and Bowers, R. (2009) *Evaluation of HM Prison Service Enhanced Thinking Skills Programme: Report of the Implementation of a Randomised Trial* (Ministry of Justice Research Series 4/09). London: Ministry of Justice.

McGuire, J. (1995) *What Works: Reducing Reoffending*. Chichester: Wiley.

Palmer, E. J., McGuire, J., Hounsome, J. C., Hatcher, R. M., Bilby, C. A. L. and Hollin, C. R. (2007). The importance of appropriate allocation to offending behaviour programs. *International Journal of Offender Therapy and Comparative Criminology*, 52: 206–21.

Pawson, R. and Tilley, N. (1994) What works in evaluation research? *British Journal of Criminology*, 34: 291–306.

Pearson, F. S., Lipton, D. S., Cleland, C. M. and Yee, D. (2002) The effects of behavioral/cognitive-behavioral programs on recidivism. *Crime and Delinquency*, 48: 476–97.

Rice, M. E. and Harris, G. T. (2003) The size and sign of treatment effects in sex offender therapy. In R. A. Prentky, E. S. Janus and M. C. Seto (eds.), *Sexually Coercive Behaviour: Understanding and Management*, pp. 428–40. New York: New York Academy of Sciences.

Thornton, D. (2002) Constructing and testing a framework for dynamic risk assessment. *Sexual Abuse: A Journal of Research and Treatment*, 14: 139–53.

Tong, L. S. and Farrington, D. P. (2006) How effective is the 'Reasoning and Rehabilitation' programme in reducing reoffending? A meta-analysis of evaluations in four countries. *Psychology, Crime and Law*, 12: 3–24.

Wakeling, H. C. (2007) The psychometric validation of the Social Problem Solving Inventory – Revised with UK incarcerated sexual offenders. *Sexual Abuse: A Journal of Research and Treatment*, 19: 217–36.

Wakeling, H., Webster, S. D. and Mann, R. E. (2005). Sexual offenders' experiences of HM Prison Service sex offender treatment. *Journal of Sexual Aggression*, 11, 171–186.

Washington State Institute for Public Policy (2006). *Evidence-Based Adult Corrections Programs: What Works and What Does Not.* Available online: www.wsipp.wa.gov.

Webster, S. D., Mann, R. E., Wakeling, H. C. and Thornton, D. (2006). Further validation of the short self-esteem scale with sexual offenders. *Legal and Criminological Psychology*, 12: 207–16.

Williams, F., Wakeling, H. and Webster, S. (2007) A psychometric study of six self-report measures for use with sexual offenders with cognitive and social functioning deficits. *Psychology, Crime and Law*, 13: 505–22.

8.6 Qualitative approaches in relation to forensic research practice

Peter Banister

Definition

A starting point is to see qualitative methods as being concerned with words, meanings, understandings and interpretation versus quantification. The aim is to be realistic, naturalistic, holistic, to understand behaviour in a natural setting from the perspective of the research participant and to understand the meanings people give to their actual lived experience. Richness reflecting the world rather than reductionism is the goal. There is also an emphasis on attempting to rectify perceived power imbalances between the researched and the researcher. What is presented in this contribution is inevitably a brief summary and it is not attempting to produce a detailed account of qualitative methods (see e.g. Banister *et al.* 1994), but to talk about their actual and potential contribution to forensic psychology. There are a number of qualitative approaches, including open-ended, semi-structured and unstructured interviews, focus groups, observation, participant observation, ethnography, action research, feminist research, discourse analysis, phenomenological analysis, protocol and conversational analysis, personal construct theory, case studies, grounded theory, and diaries.

Textbooks often do not devote much space to methodology, but take it as being axiomatic that quantitative methods are the best way to establish arguments which will stand the scrutiny of trained advocates in a courtroom situation, or to produce 'evidence-based practice'. However, qualitative methods increasingly have a place in forensic psychology.

The problem with quantitative approaches

These have been well rehearsed elsewhere (see e.g. Banister *et al.* 1994), and cover many problems including the suitability of the natural science model for researching humans and social problems. The demand for measurement, for instance, assumes that important variables (e.g. attitudes) 'exist', are reliably and validly quantifiable. This essentially reductionist approach has been criticized in that it may lead to producing results which conceal rather than reveal important differences; for instance criminal statistics normally miss repeat victimization.

Moreover, there is the worry that experimental results may not be generalizable, as the experiment becomes a social occasion, with implicit assumptions by the participants as to what they are expected to do, which may in extreme cases lead them (seeing psychology in a mental health light) to provide the results that they think are being looked for. Even if this does not occur, there are still pressures to 'do as you're told … don't question … trust the experimenter'; such inherent power imbalances may ultimately render the results useless. In forensic contexts there is the realization that people (in e.g. prisons) taking part in studies are likely to be constantly thinking about the need to present themselves in the best possible light in order to persuade others of their reform and readiness for release.

In addition to this, other possible biasing effects might be who takes part in experiments (see Sears 1986 for an interesting critique of this area), the characteristics of the experimenter and the usually intractable effect of the presence of the experimenter him or herself. The tendency of much forensic research is to use incarcerated offenders, who may not be a random sample of criminals.

There is also the recognition that the tradition of the looking in from outside approach favoured by quantitative approaches may not answer important questions concerning criminal behaviour, motives and experiences. Often there is a need to involve participants directly in the research process, which thus involves the necessity of attempting to gain more by way of an insider perspective.

Many of these problems are well known, and a number of attempts have been made to reduce them, e.g. trying to tell the participant as little as possible, in cases misinforming and in extremis deceiving them as to the true purposes of the study. This may lead to the unfortunate common perception that lay people should never trust psychologists as they never tell the truth about what they are doing. Such procedures inevitably raise ethical difficulties. Another solution is to move the research from the artificial environment of the laboratory to more natural settings (e.g. field experiments). This solves some problems, but creates further ethical dilemmas.

There is uncertainty as to whether it is useful to think there is a fixed 'out there' which can be quantified and treated in a reductionist fashion, or favour a more relativist approach, suggesting that a lot of what people do may be socially constructed, and not necessarily amenable to investigation by natural science approaches (e.g. reactions to being 'tagged' or being given an Antisocial Behaviour Order (ASBO)). Rather than utilizing measurement that is attempting to screen out interpretation, the qualitative emphasis is very much on interpretation, the 'making sense' of the results, with the recognition that the researcher may be central to the sense that is being made. There is a realization that findings may not be readily generalizable across time, people or locations, are always 'in the making' and never finished (always developing and changing, sometimes reactive).

As with quantitative research methods, there are problems with qualitative approaches, which can similarly be overcome to some extent. These include dangers of idiosyncratic interpretations, of participant selection, of the social psychology of the research situation, assumptions that language is transparent, that inner experience is there to be accessed (people may be inconsistent, ambiguous, change over time, 'mindless'), difficulties in the researcher separating themselves out from the situation, and the intractable position of the presence of the researcher. In addition, there are possible ethical problems (which include the position of unobtrusive observation or the revelations about criminal activity in a research interview setting).

In an attempt to get round some of these problems, qualitative researchers have replaced the notions of 'reliability' and 'validity' with somewhat different conceptualizations. Lincoln and Guba (in Robson 2002) suggest there is a need to ask whether findings are 'true', are applicable to other settings or participants, are consistent over time and are determined by the participants and the situation, not the researcher. They are emphasizing whether the findings are credible, generalizable, dependable and potentially confirmable. Do the findings make sense, are they confirmed by other researchers ('triangulation', where evidence from different sources using different methods and different researchers hopefully produces similar results)? In a similar vein, Sapsford (1984; in Banister et al. 1994) suggests using criteria such as whether participants agree with the accounts of life we as researchers provide them with ('agreement'), whether there is general agreement ('consensus'), and whether the research makes sense of all of the evidence ('plausibility').

Qualitative approaches within forensic psychology

Although the contrasts above seem to be 'either/or', in actuality qualitative and quantitative approaches may be viewed as being complementary rather than being in fundamental opposition. Some would see qualitative methods as being of use in the initial stages of research (e.g. Robson (2002) recommends that pilot studies can be useful in the development of a questionnaire), whilst others (for instance Breakwell *et al.* 2006) would see them as useful in carrying out pioneering work in a previously unlooked at area, a starting point in what essentially may be an exploratory study, ensuring that what is being investigated comes from the participant, and is not just a reflection of the researcher's preconceptions. The approach can also be seen as an adjunct, providing complementary and illustrative material; 'bringing life' to data, emphasizing and supporting points via the telling quotation or case study.

The contribution of qualitative methods is far more widespread within forensic psychology than the casual perusal of recent journals would indicate. Often work is unacknowledged but is an important part of the research process. An example of this is that published research may involve working directly with criminal populations, many of whom may have literacy problems. At times test and questionnaire administration can only be carried out verbally. Inevitably this will produce richer data than simple written questionnaire completion, and will demonstrate problems with what is being asked. Sometimes serendipitous findings occur; often the most illuminating comments come after the recorder is switched off. This is a well-known phenomenon, which Robson (2002) calls the 'hand on the door'.

As well as often unacknowledged contributions to studies, qualitative material may be used in an overt fashion to illuminate findings. An example of this is in Wright and Holliday (2005), who carried out a study of the perceptions held by police officers of older eyewitnesses. Although the data gathered were subjected to content analysis, the article additionally included qualitative material. Thus when discussing cognitive interviews the illustrative comment is made that with older witnesses 'it is a very good idea to explain [the interview] to the witness first, and subject to circumstances, inject some humour, for example when looking at the scenario from an alternative view' (p. 218). This adds to the findings of the research, opening up potential avenues for future research, and it might have been usefully discourse analysed.

Cognitive distortions as an example

Qualitative approaches are extensively used in forensic psychology (see e.g. Banister 2008); one area which is of particular relevance is that of cognitive distortions.

These are important given the emphasis on using cognitive-behavioural methods to tackle criminal behaviour, if only for the realization that participants can gain additional distortions as a result of programme participation.

Various studies that have been done on violence, for instance, which have contributed to the development of theory and have also helped to suggest ways in which techniques can be developed to help minimize aggression. Novaco and Welsh (1989) looked at the cognitive distortions of violent males, and found that they see the world as being an aggressive place, and perceive others to have hostile intentions. They are likely to think that victims will react violently, and they interpret victims' behaviour as being challenging and a potential threat. A consequence of this is that they feel that the other is likely to hurt them if they do not strike first, and thus they attack to prevent being attacked themselves. Such offenders have difficulties in seeing situations from the viewpoints of others, see a violent response as being the only possible behaviour and overbelieve in the importance of their first impressions of the other and the situation.

Related to the above, an interesting qualitative approach is personal construct theory. From such research Winter (2003) suggests that violent offenders construe too tightly, tend to be cognitively simple and unable to communicate well with others, deficient in the ability to anticipate both the construing and the behaviour of others, and lacking in the ability to integrate conflicting information about others. These findings emphasize a need for some form of cognitive restructuring in an endeavour to make violence less likely to occur.

A similar approach is that of Houston (1998), who says that 'historically researchers have long been interested in the ways in which offenders make sense of their own behaviour' (p. 3). She suggests that criminals may justify or neutralize their behaviour by denying their responsibility, denying the amount of harm done, saying the victim deserves it, condemning the condemners and appealing to other factors such as the need for peer approval.

The above examples demonstrate some of the potential of the approach. There is a wealth of other studies, such as observational studies of shoplifting behaviour or jury behaviour in the courtroom, or interview studies examining criminals' modus operandi and reasoning, in areas such as burglary, robbery, arson and joyriding. Studies can take place in settings not otherwise easy to research (e.g. Bloor's (1997) observational and interview-based study looking at the risk-taking behaviour of male prostitutes in Glasgow).

Conclusions

The thesis developed here is that there is no 'best' approach to carrying out forensic research, as a lot will depend on the nature of the question being asked and the problem being examined. Considerations include access, time constraints, feasibility, practicability and the skills of the researcher. All research should involve an element of reflexivity, where the researcher thinks about their part in the whole process; standing back, looking at the study, analysing how effective the chosen methods were for answering the research question, what it felt like to be the researcher/co-researcher. The philosophy should be of valuing and respecting the other as a person, engaging in a mutual voyage of discovery. Flaws in the design should be looked at, as should possibilities for future research and improvements, and considering the implications of the research.

Qualitative approaches undoubtedly have a place within forensic psychology, and the British Psychological Society emphasizes them as an essential part of the undergraduate curriculum. All research approaches have advantages and disadvantages; both need to be part of the research 'toolkit' of a forensic psychologist, and it is becoming increasingly obvious that boundaries are becoming blurred. In particular, all research needs to involve the 'qualitative eye/ear'; a good researcher needs to be constantly aware of how the researched is viewing the research, and should be always open to the unexpected input.

FURTHER READING

For a good general introduction to qualitative methods in psychology see Banister *et al.* (1994). For a detailed review of qualitative methods in forensic psychology see the chapter by Banister (2008). Other general methodological handbooks include Breakwell *et al.* (2006), V. Jupp, P. Davies and P. Francis (2000) *Doing Criminological Research* (London: Sage) and Robson (2002).

REFERENCES

Banister, P. (2008) Forensic psychology. In C. Willig and W. Stainton Rogers (eds.), *The Sage Handbook of Qualitative Research in Psychology*, pp. 505–23. London: Sage.

Banister, P., Burman, E., Parker, I., Taylor, M. and Tindall, C. (1994) *Qualitative Methods in Psychology: A Research Guide*. Buckingham: Open University Press.

Bloor, M. (1997) Addressing social problems through qualitative research. In D. Silverman (ed.), *Qualitative Research: Theory, Method and Practice*, pp. 221–38. Thousand Oaks, CA: Sage.

Breakwell, G., Hammond, S. M., Fife-Schaw, C. and Smith, J. (2006) *Research Methods in Psychology*. London: Sage.

Houston, J. (1998) *Making Sense with Offenders: Personal Constructs, Therapy and Change*. Chichester: Wiley.

Novaco, R. W. and Welsh, W. N. (1989) Anger disturbances: cognitive mediation and clinical prescriptions. In K. Howells and C. Hollin (eds.), *Clinical Approaches to Violence*, pp. 39–60. Chichester: Wiley.

Robson, C. (2002) *Real World Research*. Oxford: Blackwell.

Sears, D. O. (1986) College sophomores in the laboratory: influences of a narrow data base on social psychology's view of human nature. *Journal of Personality and Social Psychology*, 51: 515–30.

Winter, D. A. (2003) A credulous approach to violence and homicide. In J. Horley (ed.), *Personal Construct Perspectives on Forensic Psychology*, pp. 15–54. Hove: Brunner Routledge.

Wright, A. M. and Holliday, R. E. (2005) Police officers' perceptions of older eyewitnesses. *Legal and Criminological Psychology*, 10: 211–23.

8.7 Randomized control trials

Clive R. Hollin

Why randomize?

A great deal of research aims to demonstrate causality, seeking to show if manipulation of an *independent variable* has a direct effect on a *dependent variable*. In order to achieve this aim research must be *valid* and utilize designs that impart high levels of validity. Cook and Campbell (1979) describe four types of validity. *Construct validity* is the theoretical cogency of the research and its potential to advance theory. *External validity* is the degree of generalizability of the findings to other settings or groups. *Internal validity* is the level of confidence the research design allows in attributing changes in the dependent variable to manipulation of the independent variable. *Statistical conclusion validity* refers to adherence to the rules of measurement and statistical analysis.

The four types of validity may not be independent or even necessarily in sympathy. For example, very strict participant sampling criteria will maximize internal validity but may reduce external validity by restricting generalizability. All four types of validity are important, but internal validity is critical for research concerned with causality. Attribution of causality demands confidence that it was manipulation of the independent variable that directly caused changes in the dependent variable. Systematic differences between experimental and control groups pose an obvious threat to internal validity: randomization of participants to condition increases the likelihood that the groups are equivalent from the onset.

The distinction may be made between *experimental* designs that employ randomization, and *quasi-experimental* designs that use methods other than randomization to achieve internal validity. Randomized designs are the researcher's 'gold standard' and are commonly found in medical research as *randomized control trials* (RCTs: Everitt and Wessely 2004). There is a range of RCT designs and randomization techniques of varying methodological quality (Jadad *et al.* 2001; Juni, Altman and Egger 2001; Lewis and Warlow 2004).

Randomized control trials in forensic psychology

In field (as opposed to laboratory) research, randomized studies are relatively uncommon in criminological research (Farrington and Welsh 2005) as they encompass a range of ethical, legal and practical difficulties (Asscher *et al.* 2007; Gondolf 2001; Lum and Yang 2005). First developed for evaluating drug-based treatments, RCTs are the optimum choice when the integrity of the intervention can be precisely controlled. However, some aspects of psychological practice, such as the therapeutic alliance, cannot be randomized (Munro 2005), and it may be difficult maintaining treatment integrity so that all participants are treated identically (Hollin 1995). While RCTs provide important evidence, the complexities of evaluating psychological treatment may best be achieved using a range of research designs (Gilbody and Whitty 2002; Victora, Habicht and Bryce 2004).

In laboratory-based experimental forensic psychology randomized studies are desirable. Is the same true of RCTs? In forensic psychology RCTs are most likely to be used in the evaluation of attempts to change offenders' behaviour. For example, Van Voorhis *et al.* (2004) randomly assigned parolees to experimental and control conditions. In the experimental condition offenders participated in the Reasoning and Rehabilitation (R & R) treatment programme (Tong and Farrington 2006).

Van Voorhis *et al.* directly compared outcomes for the experimental and control groups and failed to find a treatment effect. Analysis based on initial allocation to condition within an RCT, regardless of whether the treatment was actually delivered, is called *Intention to Treat* (ITT). ITT analysis was originally devised for biomedical trials, hence its use in the evaluation of complex psychological interventions has been referred to as a 'drug metaphor' (Shapiro *et al.* 1994).

Alternatively, analysis based on *Treatment Received* (TR), considers outcomes when treatment is completed. Van Voorhis *et al.* noted that 60 per cent of offenders starting the programme failed to complete. Van Voorhis *et al.* compared the outcomes for the three naturally formed groups – completer, dropout and comparison – and found a significant reduction in reoffending for the completers.

The dilemma is that forming subgroups within conditions violates randomization, negating the integrity of the RCT. However, the precision of an ITT analysis is compromised by high levels of attrition. Further, if large numbers of the experimental group do not comply with the intervention a poor outcome for non-compliers may nullify a positive outcome for those who participate fully.

In reality ITT and TR analyses give answers to different questions. Sherman (2003) suggests that ITT analysis tests a policy of offering something; TR analysis shows what happens when that offer is accepted.

Quasi-experimental designs

Quasi-experimental designs offer an alternative to an experimental design by maintaining internal validity through methodological or statistical control of differences between experimental and control conditions. A quasi-experimental design may form a control group by matching individuals on a case-for-case basis according to key variables related to outcome. A large number of matching variables may cause difficulties in finding exactly matching pairs (see Friendship *et al.* 2003). Alternatively, control over key variables may be achieved statistically (see Palmer *et al.* 2007). Nonetheless, the absence of randomization may allow systematic variation between groups, threatening internal validity in that a group difference in outcome could be caused by the (unidentified) variation, not the intervention. Given this potential threat, how cautious must we be about findings from quasi-experimental designs compared to RCTs?

Heinsman and Shadish (1996) statistically compared the findings from randomized and non-randomized experiments, concluding that when equally well designed they produced similar findings. Heinsman and Shadish note several features of quasi-experimental studies that increase the probability of a reliable effect size: control over the extent to which participants self-select into and out of conditions; group matching or statistical control of pre-treatment differences between groups; and minimizing attrition (see Des Jarlais, Lyles and Crepaz 2004).

Weisburd, Lum and Petrosino (2001) compared outcomes from fully randomized studies and other experimental designs in crime prevention studies. In contrast to Heinsman and Shadish, Weisburd *et al.* noted an inverse relationship between research design and outcome, suggesting that non-randomized designs may introduce a bias in favour of treatment. The criminological literature contains a mixture of findings regarding the outcomes from experimental and non-experimental studies (Lum and Yang 2005).

In a meta-analysis of offender treatment studies, Lipsey (1992) commented 'More surprising was the finding that the nature of the subject assignment to groups (random versus nonrandom), often viewed as synonymous with design quality, had little relationship to effect size. What mattered far more was the presence or absence of specific areas of non-equivalence – for example sex differences – whether they occurred in a design or not' (p. 120).

Lipsey, Chapman and Landenberger (2001) conducted a systematic review of fourteen studies, eight experimental and six quasi-experimental, of interventions with offenders. The non-randomized studies gave a slightly larger treatment effect, but there was no statistical difference in outcome according to design. Babcock, Green and Robie (2004) included quasi-experimental and experimental studies in a meta-analysis of treatment outcome for men who had committed domestic violence. Babcock *et al.* reported that both designs showed a significant treatment effect of similar magnitude. Wilson, Bouffard and Mackenzie (2005) compared findings of offender treatment programmes and reported that high-quality studies, using either random allocation or statistical control, produced broadly similar findings. Lösel and Schmucker's (2005) meta-analysis of treatment effectiveness for sex offenders found no difference in outcome between experimental and quasi-experimental designs.

Conclusion

The issues associated with the use of RCTs to evaluate complex interventions have led researchers to produce guidelines for conducting high-quality quasi-experimental studies (Des Jarlais *et al.* 2004). Slade and Priebe's (2001) comment, in the context of mental health research, is apposite: 'RCTs can give better evidence about some contentious research questions, but it is an illusion that the development of increasingly rigorous and sophisticated RCTs will ultimately provide a complete evidence base' (p. 287). This view is one that is increasingly finding sympathy in some quarters of forensic psychology (Hollin 2008; Marshall and Marshall 2007).

REFERENCES

Asscher, J.J., Deković, M., van der Laan, P., Prins, P.J.M. and van Arum, S. (2007) Implementing experiments in criminal justice settings: an evaluation of multi-systemic therapy in the Netherlands. *Journal of Experimental Criminology*, 3: 113–29.
Babcock, J.C., Green, C.E. and Robie, C. (2004) Does batterers' treatment work? A meta-analytic review of domestic violence treatment. *Clinical Psychology Review*, 23: 1023–53.

Cook, T. D. and Campbell, D. T. (1979) *Quasi-Experimentation: Design and Analysis Issues for Field Settings*. Boston, MA: Houghton Mifflin.

Des Jarlais, D. C., Lyles, C. and Crepaz, N. (2004) Improving the quality of nonrandomized evaluations of behavioral and public health interventions: the TREND statement. *American Journal of Public Health*, 94: 361–6.

Everitt, B. S. and Wessely, S. (2004) *Clinical Trials in Psychiatry*. Oxford: Oxford University Press.

Farrington, D. P. and Welsh, B. C. (2005) Randomized experiments in criminology: what have we learned in the last two decades? *Journal of Experimental Criminology*, 1: 9–38.

Friendship, C., Blud, L., Erikson, M., Travers, L. and Thornton, D. M. (2003) Cognitive-behavioural treatment for imprisoned offenders: an evaluation of HM Prison Service's cognitive skills programmes. *Legal and Criminological Psychology*, 8: 103–14.

Gilbody, S. and Whitty, P. (2002) Improving the delivery and organisation of mental health services: beyond the conventional randomised controlled trial. *British Journal of Psychiatry*, 180: 13–18.

Gondolf, E. W. (2001) Limitations of experimental evaluation of batterer programs. *Trauma, Violence, and Abuse*, 2: 79–88.

Heinsman, D. T. and Shadish, W. R. (1996) Assignment methods in experimentation: when do nonrandomized experiments approximate answers from randomized experiments? *Psychological Methods*, 1: 154–69.

Hollin, C. R. (1995) The meaning and implications of 'programme integrity'. In J. McGuire (ed.), *What Works: Reducing Reoffending*, pp. 195–208. Chichester: Wiley.

— (2008) Evaluating offending behaviour programmes: does only randomisation glister? *Criminology and Criminal Justice*, 8: 89–106.

Jadad, A. R., Moore, R. A., Carroll, D., Jenkinson, C., Reynolds, J. M., Gavaghon, D. J. and McQuay, D. M. (2001) Assessing the quality of reports of clinical trials: is blinding necessary? *Controlled Clinical Trials*, 17: 1–12.

Juni, P., Altman, D. G. and Egger, M. (2001) Assessing the quality of controlled clinical trials. *British Medical Journal*, 323: 42–6.

Lewis, S. C. and Warlow, C. P. (2004) How to spot bias and other potential problems in randomised controlled trials. *Journal of Neurology, Neurosurgery and Psychiatry*, 75: 181–7.

Lipsey, M. W. (1992) Juvenile delinquency treatment: a meta-analytic inquiry into the variability of effects. In T. D. Cook, H. Cooper, D. S. Cordray, H. Hartmann, L. V. Hedges, R. J. Light *et al.* (eds.), *Meta-Analysis for Explanation: A Casebook*, pp. 83–127. New York: Russell Sage Foundation.

Lipsey, M. W., Chapman, G. L. and Landenberger, N. A. (2001) Cognitive-behavioral programs for offenders. *Annals of the American Academy of Political and Social Science*, 578: 144–57.

Lösel, F. and Schmucker, M. (2005) The effectiveness of treatment for sexual offenders: a comprehensive meta-analysis. *Journal of Experimental Criminology*, 1: 117–46.

Lum, C. and Yang, S.-M. (2005) Why do evaluation researchers in crime and justice choose non-experimental methods? *Journal of Experimental Criminology*, 1: 191–213.

Marshall, W. L. and Marshall L. E. (2007) The utility of the random controlled trial for evaluating sexual offender treatment: the gold standard or an inappropriate strategy? *Sexual Abuse: A Journal of Research and Treatment*, 19: 175–91.

Munro, A. J. (2005) The conventional wisdom and activities of the middle range. *British Journal of Radiology*, 78: 381–3.

Palmer, E. J., McGuire, J., Hounsome, J. C., Hatcher, R. M., Bilby, C. A. and Hollin, C. R. (2007) Offending behaviour programmes in the community: the effects on reconviction of three programmes with adult male offenders. *Legal and Criminological Psychology*, 12: 251–64.

Shapiro, D. A., Harper, H., Startup, M., Reynolds, S., Bird, D. and Suokas, A. (1994). The high water mark of the drug metaphor: a meta-analytic critique of process-outcome research. In R. L. Russell (ed.), *Reassessing Psychotherapy Research*, pp. 1–35. New York: Guilford Press.

Sherman, L. W. (2003) Misleading evidence and evidence-led policy: making social science more experimental. *Annals of the American Academy of Political and Social Science*, 589: 6–19.

Slade, M. and Priebe, S. (2001) Are randomised controlled trials the only gold that glitters? *British Journal of Psychiatry*, 179: 286–7.

Tong, L. S. J. and Farrington, D. P. (2006). How effective is the 'Reasoning and Rehabilitation' programme in reducing re-offending? A meta-analysis of evaluations in four countries. *Psychology, Crime and Law*, 12: 3–24.

Van Voorhis, P., Spruance, L. M., Ritchey, P. N., Listwan, S. J. and Seabrook, R. (2004) The Georgia cognitive skills experiment: a replication of Reasoning and Rehabilitation. *Criminal Justice and Behavior*, 31: 282–305.

Victora, C. G., Habicht, J.-P. and Bryce, J. (2004) Evidence-based public health: moving beyond trials. *American Journal of Public Health*, 94: 400–5.

Weisburd, D., Lum, C. M. and Petrosino, A. (2001) Does research design affect study outcomes in criminal justice? *Annals of the American Academy of Political and Social Science*, 578: 50–70.

Wilson, D. B., Bouffard, L. A. and Mackenzie, D. L. (2005) A quantitative review of structured, group-orientated, cognitive-behavioural programs for offenders. *Criminal Justice and Behavior*, 32: 172–204.

Reliable change and clinical significance

Darragh O'Neill

See also chapter 8.7 Randomized control trials.

Introduction

Traditionally, efforts to establish the efficacy of clinical interventions have adopted a nomothetic, or aggregating, approach, relying on mean score analysis and focusing on statistically significant overall change at a group level. Such statistical comparisons, however, are limited in terms of identifying variability in outcome within these groups. Moreover, the administration of such interventions in practice is predominantly individual-oriented. Thus, in contrast to the majority of research approaches, real-world clinical assessments most commonly occur at an idiographic, or single-case, level. There subsequently exists a distinct divide in the methodologies utilized in research and in practice, i.e. actual therapy provision, the former focusing on statistical meaningfulness, the latter on the clinical significance of change. The importance of alternative approaches that bridge this division is therefore quite apparent.

Reliable change index

Hammond and O'Rourke (2007) provide an informative overview of methodologies for individual-level analysis within forensic settings, with a specific focus on multiple card-sorting procedures. This chapter explores another example: the reliable change index (RCI) as proposed by Jacobson and his colleagues (Jacobson, Follette and Revenstorf 1984; Jacobson and Truax 1991). This technique was developed as part of efforts to establish more empirically the efficacy of psychotherapeutic interventions and to address the need for objective measurement of therapy participants' progress (Ogles, Lunnen and Bonesteel 2001). The RCI approach achieves this by calculating whether change in an individual's test score on a psychometric assessment is greater than that which could be attributed to variance due to measurement error. The formula for the method is written as follows:

$$RCI = \frac{x_2 - x_1}{SE_{diff}}$$

where x_1 = participant's pre-treatment score, x_2 = participant's post-treatment score, and SE_{diff} = standard error of difference between the two scores.

Through the standard error of difference, the RCI takes into account the reliability of the psychometric scale. This would most appropriately be in the form of a test–retest correlation from parallel forms of the test, but due to the difficulty in obtaining such statistics, standard test–retest reliability is advocated by Jacobson and his colleagues. Practice effects and variability in correlation coefficients used to establish test–retest stability have been underlined by some critics as reason for employing indices of internal consistency instead (Bauer, Lambert and Nielsen 2004; Evans, Margison and Barkham 1998; Martinovich, Saunders and Howard 1996; Tingey *et al.* 1996a). However, the appropriateness of this substitution has been questioned, as temporal stability and internal consistency are not synonymous (Hammond and O'Rourke 2007), and accordingly test–retest reliability remains the most commonly adopted statistic.

In addition to reliability, the standard error of difference also incorporates the standard deviation as observed in either the control group, the normal population, or the pre-treatment group (Jacobson and Truax 1991). Thus the formula for the standard error of difference is:

$$SE_{diff} = \sqrt{2 \times (sd\sqrt{1 - r})^2}$$

where sd = the group standard deviation and
$\quad\quad\quad r$ = the measure's test–retest reliability.

The outputted RCI value can be interpreted as a z score: where it is greater than 1.96 or less than −1.96, the change is deemed significant at $p<0.05$. A cutoff of either 1.65 or −1.65, depending on expected direction of the change, has been suggested for one-tailed hypotheses (Beech, Fisher and Beckett 1998; Hinton-Bayre *et al.* 1999).

Clinical significance

Although the RCI calculation establishes the statistical significance of the change that has occurred between assessments, it does not per se detail the nature of the change. It may, for example, represent an improvement or deterioration. Therefore, it is also necessary to explore the clinical meaningfulness of the change. This is most commonly done through methods founded on the concept of social validity (Kazdin 1977; Wolf 1978), which deem clinical change to have occurred where test scores indicate a shift in an individual's functioning towards that expected or observed in the normal population (Hansen and Lambert 1996; Ogles *et al.* 2001).

When introducing the RCI, Jacobson, Follette and Revenstorf (1984) additionally proposed a set of methods for determining whether this shift has occurred, adopting the view that a clinically meaningful threshold can be established between the dysfunctional and functional populations. The first method, referred to as *cutoff point a*, defines clinical change as movement from the dysfunctional population and calculates the threshold as two standard deviations from the dysfunctional mean. The second method, *cutoff point b*, utilizes the functional mean and labels a shift to within two standard deviations of this value as clinically significant. Finally, *cutoff point c* labels as clinically significant movement across the midway point between the dysfunctional and functional means. The latter cutoff point is considered most appropriate as it utilizes both distributions and is a less arbitrary metric as a consequence (Jacobson and Revenstorf 1988; Jacobson and Truax 1991). It is computed using the following equation:

$$c = \frac{(sd_1 \times \bar{x}_2) + (sd_2 \times \bar{x}_1)}{sd_1 + sd_2}$$

where $\bar{x}_1$, $\bar{x}_2$ = the means, and sd_2, sd_2 = the standard deviations of the functional and dysfunctional normative samples respectively

Tingey *et al.* (1996b) noted that these formulae are inappropriate for constructs where it is improbable that individuals in the treatment will return to functional levels of scoring (e.g. schizophrenia). Jacobson has acknowledged that in such circumstances the cutoff criteria may be too stringent (Jacobson *et al.* 1999). However, decisions on precisely what population distribution represents a sufficiently functional alternative to that of the pre-treatment client group can be made in light of the aims and expectations of the intervention (Evans *et al.* 1998). Moreover, multiple thresholds may be calculated to represent varying levels of improvement in functioning.

The proposals by Jacobson and his colleagues have been the subject of criticism, modification and replacement by some researchers (e.g. Hsu 1989; Speer 1992), who have focused on such limitations as the failure to account for regression to the mean. Nonetheless, research that has compared alternative RCI techniques has failed to demonstrate that newer procedures are superior to that of Jacobson and Truax's (Atkins *et al.* 2005; Bauer *et al.* 2004; Maassen 2000; McGlinchey, Atkins and Jacobson 2002; McGlinchey and Jacobson 1999). Hence, Jacobson and Truax's approach to evaluating reliable change and determining clinical significance continues to be the most widely employed method (Ogles *et al.* 2001).

Utilizing Jacobson and Truax's criteria, there are four possible categories into which individuals can be assigned (Bauer *et al.* 2004):

i. *Recovered* – showing both reliable (RCI) and clinical change (cutoff)
ii. *Improved* – showing reliable change, but not passing the cutoff
iii. *Unchanged* – not passing either criteria
iv. *Deteriorated* – showing reliable change but in an undesired direction.

While it is not explicitly stated, it is implied that the improved label is applied only to those individuals who show reliable change in a desired direction. Although in clinical practice this approach can be, and is, applied in the examination of progress achieved by individual clients, a broader perspective on the movement of client groups can be obtained through an examination of sample proportions that show different types and degrees of change. It is in this percentage form that RCI findings are typically reported in published forensic psychology research.

Sample applications within forensic psychology

The reliable change index and the corresponding clinical change aspect have been employed with a variety of topics within forensic psychology research and related areas. One example is a recent investigation by North American researchers into the developmental paths of psychopathic traits (Blonigen *et al.* 2006). Using the RCI method, they analysed the continuity and change in two factors underpinning the construct as manifested within a sample of paired twins aged between 17 and 24. Blonigen *et al.* reported proportions of their sample, as a whole and split according to gender, which showed either statistically significant increases or decreases in these factors. They failed, however, to elaborate on whether these changes represented movements between clinically meaningful groupings, possibly because this was a general population sample.

The full approach to establishing reliable and clinical change, however, was used by Newton (1998). She employed it to ascertain the proportion of residents within a prison therapeutic community who demonstrated a statistically significant shift to within normal functioning levels on the Eysenck Personality Questionnaire (EPQ; Eysenck and Eysenck 1975). It was found that 31% of the TC residents showed 'recovery' in self-reported neuroticism, while between 20 and 24% showed such positive progress on the other scales (namely extraversion, psychoticism and criminality); 27% also showed 'recovery' in feelings and expressions of hostility. Like Blonigen et al., Newton reported the frequency of change occurring in an undesired direction. No deterioration was evident in the sample's hostility or criminality levels, while at most 4% showed such undesired change on the other EPQ scales. Given that Newton makes use of multiple outcome measures, it is impossible to obtain an integrated overview of change for each participant, as in a unitary indicator of the extent of progress achieved. Solutions to this issue have been outlined by Jacobson and Revenstorf (1988), such as establishing a weighted composite of the various measures through either factor analysis or standardized true score estimates.

The RCI and clinical change cutoff methods were used in a related context by Dolan, Warren and Norton (1997). They employed the techniques in their exploration of the utility of a hospital-based therapeutic community intervention for treating borderline symptoms experienced by severely personality disordered residents. Additional examples of the application of the reliable and clinical change formulae are available with regard to other treatment programmes within more specifically forensic contexts. The differential impact of two treatments for spousal abusers were examined by O'Leary, Heyman and Neidig (1999) using both the RCI and clinical cutoff procedures. In a similar fashion, interventions with potential familial child abusers were explored by Dawe and Harnett (2007) using both the RCI and clinical cutoff procedures. Beech and his colleagues utilized the methodology in analysis of sex offender therapies (Beech, Fisher and Beckett 1998; Bowen, Gilchrist and Beech 2008; Keeling, Rose and Beech 2006; Keeling, Rose and Beech 2007). It has likewise been employed in victimology research, particularly the evaluation of treatment programmes for adults who had been sexually abused as children (Möller and Steel 2002; Price et al. 2004; Stalker et al. 2005). Individual-level response to such sexual abuse survivor interventions has also been examined at an earlier developmental stage with adolescent clients (Jaberghaderi *et al.* 2004). With the exception of Möller and Steel's study, these examples report reliable and clinical change results alongside results from more traditional, mean-based statistics, thus providing a comprehensive insight into the efficacy of the therapies under inquiry.

Although therapy evaluation represents the most common context in which the RCI and clinical meaningfulness analyses have been implemented within forensic psychology research, it has also been used with experimental designs. Unsworth, Devilly and Ward (2007) provide an illustration of such usage. They looked at anger induced in adolescents by means of a violent video game paradigm and found that less than 2% of their sample demonstrated a reliable and clinically meaningful increase in anger as a result of playing the game.

Issues regarding its application to date

An important limitation of the RCI approach is its assumption of normally distributed constructs (Tingey *et al.* 1996b). Unsworth *et al.* (2007), like the other examples cited above, failed to identify whether their anger measures implied that the latent construct is normally distributed. However, the failure of researchers to address this is reflective of a wider issue within psychology research, namely the overassumption of normality and of test robustness (Micceri 1989).

An additional omission evident in many of the above studies is an account of how functional and dysfunctional groupings were established. One of the necessary prerequisites of the clinical significance approach, as set out by Jacobson and his colleagues, is that the subjects of the analysis initially belong to a distinguishable dysfunctional grouping, and that pre-existing differences do in fact exist between what is deemed normative functional and dysfunctional distributions. The forensic psychology studies here described, however, regularly fail to report that appropriate distinctions existed between the normative sets. Moreover, they commonly lack any detail regarding the source of the normative data employed, which would have enabled subsequent researchers or clinicians to replicate their work or utilize their findings. This is particularly important given that research that employs this methodology can help guide clinical practice by providing normative change criteria for particular psychometric tools which can then be used in the analysis of an individual client's progress in therapy. A noteworthy example where such detail is provided is Keeling *et al.* (2006); here comprehensive information regarding adopted clinical cutoffs is reported.

Most of the above sample studies employed only two distributions in establishing clinical significance. Although in the original descriptions of the technique this approach is recommended, bimodal conceptualizations of constructs could alter the rate of false negatives, and result in unrealistic expectations of the intervention to effect test score change. Subsequent work has highlighted the increased accuracy achievable through the use of a range of intermediate normative score distributions (Hansen and Lambert 1996; Tingey *et al.* 1996b).

Conclusions

The brief introduction offered here has illustrated both the strengths and limitations of one method for exploring individual-level change in test score responding. The reliable change index, combined with the clinical significance cutoffs, permits a unique insight into the nature of test score shift over time and thus provides an important method for establishing the efficacy of therapeutic interventions, as well as for within-group analyses more generally. It identifies those individuals who demonstrate meaningful change, be it in a positive or negative direction, as well as those who fail to show any change. It is subsequently of particular assistance in establishing admission criteria for therapy programmes, or for modifying the interventions themselves. It is equally important for examining individual clients' progress in clinical practice.

Within forensic psychology, it has been used in exploring a diverse range of topics, from the change evidenced by members of a prison therapeutic community to the treatment of adult survivors of childhood sexual abuse. However, although the set of examples listed here is not exhaustive, the use of this approach within forensic psychology research has been markedly rare. This may be attributable to a number of factors, such as its absence from major statistical packages or a lack of awareness regarding its utility. In cases where it has been employed, a number of shortcomings have been evident.

The RCI and clinical significance analyses provide an important perspective on test score change, but they will never be exploited to their full potential unless they are utilized appropriately. Consequently, it is essential that future usage is founded on clear and articulated justification and attempts to address the oversights evident in some previous applications. This will ensure the benefits and insight achievable through this methodology are fully realized.

The procedure provides an important bridging point between forensic psychology research and clinical practice, both in terms of analytic approach and the shaping of how outcome data is conceptualized. It is evidently a methodological tool of unique utility and accordingly deserves wider recognition and appropriate application.

FURTHER READING

A detailed outline of the RCI and the clinical meaningfulness calculation is available in Jacobson and Truax (1991). For a broader introduction to individual-level analyses and their use in forensic psychology, the reader is guided to Hammond and O'Rourke (2007).

REFERENCES

Atkins, D. C., Bedics, J. D., McGlinchey, J. B. and Beauchaine, T. P. (2005) Assessing clinical significance: does it matter which method we use? *Journal of Consulting and Clinical Psychology*, 73: 982–9.

Bauer, S., Lambert, M. J. and Nielsen, S. L. (2004) Clinical significance methods: a comparison of statistical techniques. *Journal of Personality Assessment*, 82: 60–70.

Beech, A. R., Fisher, D. and Beckett, R. (1998) *STEP 3: An Evaluation of the Prison Sex Offender Treatment Programme*. London: Home Office.

Blonigen, D. M., Hicks, B. M., Krueger, R. F., Patrick, C. J. and Iacono, W. G. (2006) Continuity and change in psychopathic traits as measured via normal-range personality: a longitudinal-biometric study. *Journal of Abnormal Psychology*, 115: 85–95.

Bowen, E., Gilchrist, E. and Beech, A. R. (2008) Change in treatment has no relationship with subsequent re-offending in UK domestic violence sample: a preliminary study. *International Journal of Offender Therapy and Comparative Criminology*, 52: 598–614.

Dawe, S. and Harnett, P. (2007) Reducing potential for child abuse among methadone-maintained parents: results from a randomized controlled trial. *Journal of Substance Abuse Treatment*, 32: 381–90.

Dolan, B., Warren, F. and Norton, K. (1997) Change in borderline symptoms one year after therapeutic community treatment for severe personality disorder. *British Journal of Psychiatry*, 171: 274–9.

Evans, C., Margison, F., and Barkham, M. (1998) The contribution of reliable and clinically significant change methods to evidence-based mental health. *Evidence Based Mental Health*, 1: 70–2.

Eysenck, H. J., and Eysenck, S. B. G. (1975) *Manual of the Eysenck Personality Questionnaire*. London: Hodder and Stoughton.

Hammond, S. and O'Rourke, M. (2007) The measurement of individual change: a didactic account of an idiographic approach. *Psychology, Crime and Law*, 13: 81–95.

Hansen, N. B. and Lambert, M. J. (1996) Clinical significance: an overview of methods. *Journal of Mental Health*, 5: 17–24.

Hinton-Bayre, A. D., Geffen, G. M., Geffen, L. B., McFarland, K. A. and Frijs, P. (1999) Concussion in contact sports: reliable change indices of impairment and recovery. *Journal of Clinical and Experimental Neuropsychology*, 21: 70–86.

Hsu, L. M. (1989) Reliable changes in psychotherapy: taking into account regression toward the mean. *Behavioral Assessment*, 11: 459–67.

Jaberghaderi, N., Greenwald, R., Rubin, A., Zand, S. O. and Dolatabadi, S. (2004) A comparison of CBT and EMDR for sexually-abused Iranian girls. *Clinical Psychology and Psychotherapy*, 11: 358–68.

Jacobson, N. S., Follette, W. C. and Revenstorf, D. (1984) Psychotherapy outcome research: methods for reporting variability and evaluating clinical significance. *Behavior Therapy*, 15: 336–52.

Jacobson, N. S. and Revenstorf, D. (1988) Statistics for assessing the clinical significance of psychotherapy techniques: issues, problems, and new developments. *Behavioral Assessment*, 10: 133–45.

Jacobson, N. S., Roberts, L. J., Berns, S. B. and McGlinchey, J. B. (1999) Methods for defining and determining the clinical significance of treatment effects: description, application, and alternatives. *Journal of Consulting and Clinical Psychology*, 67: 300–7.

Jacobson, N. S. and Truax, P. (1991) Clinical significance: a statistical approach to defining meaningful change in psychotherapy research. *Journal of Consulting and Clinical Psychology*, 1: 12–19.

Kazdin, A. E. (1977) Assessing the clinical or applied importance of behavior change through social validation. *Behavior Modification*, 1: 427–52.

Keeling, J. A., Rose, J. L. and Beech, A. R. (2006) An investigation into the effectiveness of a custody-based cognitive-behavioural treatment for special needs sexual offenders. *Journal of Forensic Psychiatry and Psychology*, 17: 372–92.

(2007) Comparing sexual offender treatment efficacy: mainstream sexual offenders and sexual offenders with special needs. *Journal of Intellectual and Developmental Disability*, 32: 117–24.

Maassen, G. H. (2000) Principles of defining reliable change indices. *Journal of Clinical and Experimental Neuropsychology*, 22: 622–32.

Martinovich, Z., Saunders, S. and Howard, K. (1996) Some comments on 'assessing clinical significance'. *Psychotherapy Research*, 2: 124–32.

McGlinchey, J. B., Atkins, D. C. and Jacobson, N. S. (2002) Clinical significance methods: which one to use and how useful are they? *Behavior Therapy*, 33: 529–50.

McGlinchey, J. B. and Jacobson, N. S. (1999) Clinically significant but impractical? A response to Hageman and Arrindell. *Behavior Research and Therapy*, 37: 1211–17.

Micceri, T. (1989) The unicorn, the normal curve, and other improbable creatures. *Psychological Bulletin*, 105: 156–66.

Möller, A. T. and Steel, H. R. (2002) Clinically significant change after cognitive restructuring for adult survivors of childhood sexual abuse. *Journal of Rational-Emotive and Cognitive-Behavior Therapy*, 20: 49–64.

Newton, M. (1998) Changes in measures of personality, hostility and locus of control during residence in a prison therapeutic community. *Legal and Criminological Psychology*, 3: 209–23.

Ogles, B. M., Lunnen, K. M. and Bonesteel, K. (2001) Clinical significance: history, application, and current practice. *Clinical Psychology Review*, 21: 421–46.

O'Leary, K. D., Heyman, R. E. and Neidig, P. H. (1999) Treatment of wife abuse: a comparison of gender-specific and conjoint approaches. *Behavior Therapy*, 30: 475–505.

Price, J. L., Hilsenroth, M. J., Callahan, K. L., Petretic-Jackson, P. A. and Bonge, D. (2004) A pilot study of psychodynamic psychotherapy for adult survivors of childhood sexual abuse. *Clinical Psychology and Psychotherapy*, 11: 378–91.

Speer, D. C. (1992) Clinically significant change: Jacobson and Truax (1991) revisited. *Journal of Consulting and Clinical Psychology*, 60: 402–8.

Stalker, C. A., Palmer, S. E., Wright, D. C. and Gebotys, R. (2005) Specialized inpatient trauma treatment for adults abused as children: a follow-up study. *American Journal of Psychiatry*, 162: 552–9.

Tingey, R., Lambert, M. J., Burlingame, G. and Hansen, N. B. (1996a) Assessing clinical significance: proposed extensions to method. *Psychotherapy Research*, 6: 109–23.

 (1996b) Clinically significant change: practical indicators for evaluating psychotherapy outcome. *Psychotherapy Research*, 6: 144–53.

Unsworth, G., Devilly, G. J. and Ward, T. (2007) The effect of playing violent video games on adolescents: should parents be quaking in their boots? *Psychology, Crime and Law*, 13: 383–94.

Wolf, M. M. (1978) Social validity: the case for subjective measurement or how applied behavior analysis is finding its heart. *Journal of Applied Behavior Analysis*, 11: 203–14.

Author index

Subject index

psychiatric 528, 529, 533
rehabilitation 400–6
restorative justice and 358
rights 759
risk assessment 412
risk management 410–14
see also sexual offenders
Oklahoma City bombing 513
older adults as witnesses 156, 179
On the Track project 30
open questions, witness accuracy 156
Order for Lifelong Restrictions (OLR) 412
organizational culture *see* occupational culture
out-group perception 504–5

Pack of Questionnaires and Scales 245–6
paedophiles, sexual fantasies 555
paedophilia 45–7, 523, 548
paranoid schizophrenia 357
    and homicidal acts 529
parent management training 379–80
parental alienation syndrome 246–7
parenting
    intervention programmes 29–30, 368–73, 379–80
    and juvenile delinquency 26–8, 379–80
    orders 372–3
parenting capacity
    assessment of 242–9
    learning difficulties and 247–8, 373
    and substance abuse 248, 396–7
Parliamentary Office of Science and Technology 752
parole decision making 251–6
partial order scalogram analysis (POSA) 799
partial order scalogram analysis with coordinates
    (POSAC) 806
Pathways Model 522
Payne, Sarah 112
PCL-R diagnostic system 226
PEACE interviewing model 210–12
PEN model of personality 87, 88, 92, 260–1, 263
Personal Concerns Inventory (PCI) 122–3
personal construct theory 834
personal injury
    legal definition 612–13
    role of lawyer 614–15
    role of psychologist 618, 619
personal narratives 791–2
    criminals' 792–4
personality 259–60
    assessment 215–16
    change 664
    and criminal behaviour 259–64
    presentation of 271
    theories 86–92

Personality Assessment Inventory (PAI) 677
personality disorders 221, 225–7
    assessment of 273
    Borderline 86
    classification (forensic settings) 267–73
    crisis negotiation and 364–5
    dimensional nature of 806
    and false allegations of sexual harassment 722–3
    instruments to assess 269
    treatment 423–7, 431
    treatment research 847
    see also Antisocial Personality Disorder;
        Dangerous and Severe Personality Disorder
        (DSPD); psychopathy
phallometric assessment 309–10
Philadelphia birth cohort study 478
phishing 512
Physicians for Human Rights and the United
    Nations 588
Pistone, Joseph, D. (Donnie Brasco) 725
play therapy 347, 349–50
police
    occupational culture 700–1, 702, 704
    occupational stress 708–14
    undercover 725–30
Police and Criminal Evidence Act (PACE) (1984) 209
polygraph 153, 276–81
    accuracy 278–9
    comparison question technique 277, 279
    concealed information test (guilty knowledge
        test) 277, 278, 279
    evidence 280
    relevant–irrelevant technique 277
    test formats 277–8
Popular Front for the Liberation of Palestine 662
pornography, child 522–4
Port Arthur Massacre, Australia (1996) 652
positivist psychology 97–100
Post-Conviction Sex Offender Testing (PCSOT)
    279, 280
post-event misinformation 52
post-migration living problems checklist 591
post-traumatic amnesia 67–8
post-traumatic stress disorder 283–9
    after being taken hostage 664, 665
    assessment 284–8
    in asylum seekers 588–9, 591
    causes 283–4, 345
    in child soldiers 641
    comorbid conditions 287–8
    following terrorist attacks 456, 459–61
    functional analytic 286
    NICE guidelines 584
    and occupational stress 709–10